Bud Hardcastle: The Truth Tracker

Hot on the trail of Jesse

Bud Hardcastle: The Truth Tracker
Hot on the trail of Jesse
By Rosanne Wilcoxson Priddy

Copyright 2025 by Rosanne Wilcoxson Priddy
Cover copyright 2025 by Creative Texts Publishers, LLC
"Creative Texts" and "Creative Texts Publishers LLC" are registered trademarks of Creative Texts Publishers, LLC
All Rights Reserved

This book or parts thereof may not be reproduced in any form, stored in a retrieval system, or transmitted in any form by any means—electronic, mechanical, photocopy, recording, or otherwise—without prior written permission of the publisher, except as provided by United States of America copyright law.

The opinions expressed in our published works are those of the author(s) and do not reflect the opinions of the Publisher or its Editors.

Published by Creative Texts Publishers, LLC
PO Box 50
Barto, PA 19504
www.creativetexts.com
All rights reserved

ISBN: 978-1-64738-139-4

Special Dedication

Charles C. (Charlie) Holman
1949-2009

Bud desires to dedicate this book to Charlie. He was Bud's right-hand man. Charlie came to Bud in an effort to team up in the hunt for Jesse. When Charlie came knocking on Bud's door for the first time, Bud looked down from his tall stature of 6 foot to a little bearded plump fellow. Bud said, "If you had come with a top hat on, I'd think you were a leprechaun." From that moment on, Bud called him "Little Leprechaun" and they hit it off.

Charlie was instrumental in helping Bud in more ways than one. He introduced Bud to one of Jesse James' grandsons, Burleigh Dale James. As a team, Bud and Charlie put their heads and muscles together to decipher maps and clues, leading them to Jesse's buried treasure. Charlie took it upon himself to dive into tight snake infested holes, cold water wells, deep ravines, and rugged mountains. It never got too tough for Charlie.

Did Bud and Little Leprechaun Charlie find gold?

They found so much more. The ultimate treasure they uncovered was an everlasting friendship more priceless than **GOLD**!

Bud Hardcastle: The Truth Tracker

Hot on the trail of Jesse

by Rosanne Wilcoxson Priddy

Table of Contents

Special Acknowledgements i
Preface iii
Introduction v
Chapter One: Deep in the Heart of History 1
Chapter Two: Alive and Well 17
Chapter Three: What's in a Name? 26
Chapter Four: For the Love of Family 39
Chapter Five: The War Between the States 54
Chapter Six: The Secret War Within 68
Secret #1: The Root of All Evil 68
Secret #2: The Powers that Be 75
Chapter Seven: Trading Fallacies for Truth 98
Chapter Eight: The Fast Progression of Freemasonry, leading to the American Civil War 133
Chapter Nine: The Spy System and the Knights of the Golden Circle 148
Chapter Ten: Was JJ an Outlaw or Vindicator for his Beloved Southland 165
Chapter Eleven: The Starr that outshined them all 180
Chapter Twelve: The Sioux who captured his heart 197
Chapter Thirteen: The Man Behind the Silver Star 231
Chapter Fourteen: The significance of Brownwood, Tx. and Roswell, N.M. 253
Chapter Fifteen: Billy 286
Chapter Sixteen: Dead or Alive – 1881-1882 311
Chapter Seventeen: In and Out of the Red 337
Chapter Eighteen: Taming the Territory 355
Chapter Nineteen: Wranglin' the Range 381
Chapter Twenty: The Art of Horsemanship/Marksmanship/Showmanship 411
Chapter Twenty-One: A Brother from Another Father or Mother? 427
Chapter Twenty-Two: Word of Mouth/Word of Honor 450
Chapter Twenty-Three: Black Gold, Texas Tea 462
Chapter Twenty-Four: Buddies in Texas 468
Chapter Twenty-Five: A New Woman in His Life 484
Chapter Twenty-Six: The Coming Out Party 491
Chapter Twenty-Seven: Back to His Old Hideout 506
Chapter Twenty-Eight: Taking the Stand 523
Chapter Twenty-Nine: Trust 533
Chapter Thirty: "I am Jesse James" 541
Chapter Thirty-One: The Hidden Sons Who Kept Their Mouths Shut 557
Chapter Thirty-Two: Exhumation 572
Chapter Thirty-Three: There's Gold in them thar hills 591
Chapter Thirty-Four: Dropping Nuggets of Gold 609
Conclusion 653
Epilogue 663
Final Thoughts 670
Appendices 675
Bibliography 712
Notes 764

Special Acknowledgements

(Barbara and Bud)

(Curtis and Rosie)

Many, many thanks go to our spouses, **Barbara Hardcastle and Curtis Priddy**. They were the most supportive factor in our venture. They had to put up with numerous phone calls, visits, and occasions of hearing the same stories time and time again in order to get this book completed. My husband, Curtis, told Bud, "I won't have to buy the book, I've already heard all the stories." Bud just loved that! Bud and Curtis were two of a kind. They loved each other and joked with one another all the time. Likewise, I love Barbara! She is the perfect wife for Bud and allows him his freedom to do what he loves best, being with family and hunting Jesse and his treasures. Barbara and Curtis were troopers and no negativity entered the scenario regarding the time we had to spend on the project. Barbara and Curtis, thank you so much for your love for us, for your patience, and warm hospitality that you extended to us both. May everyone be so blessed to have spouses as we do! May God bless you always!

Love, Bud and Rosie

Special Thanks

To our Friends and Researchers who contributed immensely:

Charlie Holman, Lou Kilgore, Grace Hopkins, John & Jo Ella Tatum, Joyce Morgan, Burleigh Dale James, Jesse Quanah James, Charles A. James, Joe Wood, Eddie James, Wells Blevins, Rex and "Grandma" Ruby Leath, Ola & Aubrey Everhard, Dr. William Tunstill, Mitch Graves, Eddie Schneberger, Kenny Brown, Ralph Epperson, Jay Longley, Johnny Means, Jarret Bowers and Gary Bowen, Kenneth and Karen Ford.

For Literary support:

Amber Slade

For help and understanding of the Old West Law/ Legends/ Lingo/ Guns/ Territory:

Curtis Priddy

Preface

As of the completion of this book, I look back at the past seven years that I was truly blessed to get to know my buddy, Bud. Little did I know that four months ago, he would be heading down the trail to his Heavenly Home. Oh, my heart breaks, that he was not able to see the final product of his extensive labor in hunting for the truth, but now I know he knows, and he is at peace. He found the truth and now that he is amongst the angels, he clearly sees the truth in its entirety. What is so amazing is that the last few months we were able to speak to one another, 555 miles apart, we were able to complete all the gathering of information, complete the interviews, the research, and even fit in a special trip to Buzzard's Roost. What a journey it's been. We both felt it was complete and was what God had in mind when he put us together as a team. His timing was perfect.

I was so blessed and honored to be chosen to fulfill this task. Bud could have had any professional he desired to write this book for him, but he chose me. I gave him plenty of chances to back out, but no, he wanted me. He had the patience of Job. His encouragement kept me going. He had confidence that I would finish and do a good job. Bud, I hope you are well pleased. I miss you so! Its not the same without you!

I loved Bud so much! He was like a father to me. His integrity and character were next to none. His passion for truth resonated with me and we began our mission in the early part of 2017 with a prayer. Bud loaded me up with all his personal papers, documents, photos, letters, video tapes, audio tapes in massive amounts and with all this, many, many personal visits, and numerous phone calls. Slowly, but surely, the project began to take shape.

I am leaving the manuscript as written. It was written while Bud was alive on earth, not written as if he had already passed.

He's still alive, for his spirit remains with us.

Bud, nor I, can take full credit of the outcome of this book. It was God's hand in all of this, and I pray that this will enhance your own search for the truth.

For we trust the next chapter because we know the Author.

> "The World Deserves the Truth. History has been wrong for so long…"
>
> -Bud Hardcastle

Introduction

Jesse James was not only a historical figure of the Civil War and the Wild West, but he also was a man who became a legend, producing and directing one of the top five unsolved mysteries of America.

The "Wild West" was full of colorful desperadoes, but Jesse James rose above them all. People around the world are fixated upon this character in American History, more so than any other figure who walked/rode upon the western trails. Surprisingly, more and more people are trying to connect to Jesse through blood and kinship as well as an association to his past. Where does the need for this intimacy with Jesse come from? What pulls people into this mesmerizing force of brotherhood with Jesse?

Ironically, the sentiment is the same for Billy the Kid. Is it deep down inside us all; a desire to have the courage and bravery to take the reins in our own hands and become rebels, righting wrongs, and fighting for what we believe? Maybe it is the mystery, the controversy, the conspiracy that drives the soul to want to discover the truth, the whole truth and nothing but….and solve this thing once and for all.

No matter what the reader's opinion is before or after they read this entire book, the majority of the population only desires one thing: the truth.

For over 150 years, Jesse James has become the subject of many books, movies, stories, whether it be fact or fiction. Many have used the same old information, maybe dressed up a bit, to tell his story. Were these stories true or were they created to be intentionally misleading to direct the public, and most especially the children, to believe a delusion of the man on the silver screen? What is Jesse's story, his true story? Has anyone ever really dug deep into the truth? Many, many have tried.

What makes this book any different? It is the man behind the truth of Jesse. His name is **Bud Hardcastle**, the "Truth Tracker." He has dedicated his life, his time, his finances, and his passion to an incredible journey uncovering the well-guarded secrets of Jesse. Rolling up his sleeves and taking on this task, he has dug deep for the cold hard facts. His quest for the truth and his crackerjack skills, successfully gained Bud the title of being the most renowned expert on the life of Jesse Woodson James.

I met Bud while researching Jessie for a book I was writing on my family regarding my 2nd great granduncle who supposedly rode with Jesse in North Texas and Indian Territory. This whole subject was foreign to me.

At first, I was in denial that our family had any connection with outlaws. I came from a family of heroic peace officers with a deep faith in God. I was hesitant to pursue this branch of the family which had been kept hidden. Those who know me, especially those who I worked with, know that when something is presented to me or a responsibility or a task is assigned to me, I take it seriously. I put all my effort in understanding the whole picture. I seek out multiple sources to weigh against each other. I'm a stickler for detail, rule of law, validity, character, integrity, and truth. It was how I was raised.

Do I successfully achieve these actions, qualities, and characteristics in every situation I'm involved in? No way, I'm human like the rest of us, but I try my darnedest and with the Lord's help, "I can do all things through Christ who strengthens me."

My intention, my aim is to follow what my grandmother always told me; "Trust in the Lord, say your prayers, and do what's right."

The "right thing" in this matter, began to come into view when I compiled large amounts of information, documents, and statements made by family members that awakened my curiosity and investigative spirit. It brought on a new obligation for me. Did I want the stories of my family to fade into history, even though it included a dark side, or should I preserve it for future generations? I chose the latter.

After 12 years of research and learning the outlaws were within a 100-mile radius from my home in North Texas and in the Texas Panhandle where I grew up, my hunger for the truth developed into a passion.

In my findings, the outlaws didn't fit the "Jesse profile" that the world had been taught. Who were these men that rode with Jesse? What were they made of? Who was Jesse himself? Was he truly the man depicted on the black and white screen of the television set or on the big screen at the Saturday matinees that all of us "baby boomers" grew up with? We all had our impression of Jesse. We all have our embedded opinions, also.

Sadly, our children are no longer being taught in school about Jesse James, nor are they really taught about the Civil War. For that matter, they are no longer being taught the very fundamentals and values of our great American History. Was our generation taught the truth? Remember, the history books written after the Civil War, were written by the victors to glorify their own cause and those who had a deeper cause to move America in a different direction.

Most of us had family on both sides of the war. The war was not civil. Both sides believed they were right. Both sides believed strongly in God and His principles and felt that He was on their side. It split the country in half, as well as families; and remains a scar in America's history that remains deep today.

So, what is the truth about Jesse? I went searching. My investigation involved many researchers and experts who helped me put the pieces together. I wanted to learn everything I could, being careful of the falsehoods that are still being spread throughout Jesse's legacy.

I followed my 2nd great granduncle's path to learn how in the world he met up with Jesse. In numerous newspaper articles it revealed the story. John Wesley Haskew, my 2nd great granduncle was elected as the 2nd City Marshal of the newly found town, Bowie, Texas in Montague County in 1883. He was fiercely respected as the law of the land and treated the citizens equally, no matter the social status. The citizens were pleased with his duties and abilities. He was a giant of a man. Haskew was reelected in 1884.

Trouble came when he was accused of being involved in a robbery. It's a long story, but he was thrown in jail with the Ex-City Marshal who had preceded him, along with several others, one being a "Dolton". Fifty masked men broke them out and they fled across the Red River and eventually wound up in Johnsonville, Indian Territory where a shootout occurred with Deputy U.S. Marshal James Guy in January 1885. The deputy was also a sergeant in the Indian Police force. He was a Chickasaw.

Haskew had several connections to the Nail and Folsom families in the Choctaw and Chickasaw Nations and several friends in the territory but was shot by Guy, without one shot being fired from his side, which was the outlaw side. Haskew lay bleeding with a "gut shot" in a cabin near the Canadian River at Johnsonville. Guy left him to die with a black man. Guy would later be charged with manslaughter for the killing of Haskew, but the family story states that Haskew lived and rode off with Jesse James and they settled outside of Texhoma in "No Man's Land" in the Texas and Oklahoma Panhandle.

This was an incredible story and I was very skeptical. I had never heard this story from my family and knew that Jesse James was supposed to have been killed in 1882. John Wesley Haskew didn't break out of jail until the Fall of 1884 and the shootout didn't occur until January 1885, so how could my relative ride off with Jesse James?

I traveled to Johnsonville, Oklahoma to do some research on the subject. I had never been in that part of Oklahoma before. There was not much left of Johnsonville, just a few houses, an old cemetery, and a very old one lane bridge that crossed the Canadian River. I traveled back to Byars, Oklahoma and stopped into a little store in a very old building and learned of a woman's name that I could talk to that knew the history of that area. I called and spoke to her and asked her if they ever heard of the shoot out involving J.W. Haskew or if Jesse James had ever been in those parts. She told me that it is believed Jesse was in the area and also that he had interest in a gold mine there, on her property in fact. She told me that if I wanted to know anything about Jesse James, I needed to contact **Bud Hardcastle** in the City of Purcell just 25 miles west of there. This was the first time I had heard about Bud. She gave me the phone number for his used car business, Kar Korner. I called and the phone had been disconnected. The business was closed.

(Bud's business card)

    I had wanted to go to Purcell anyway because of the story that my 2nd great grandfather, Dr. William Decatur Stout's first wife, Elvira Nail, died there at the age of 17 during the height of the Civil War in 1863. Of course, Purcell hadn't yet been established at that time, and the area was harsh and untamed. The nearest sign of civilization were remnants of the old Camp Arbuckle established in 1850. There were small farms that decorated the landscape consisting of Chickasaws, Blacks, and some whites. This was Chickasaw Country.

    Dr. Stout and Elvira were married in October 1862 at Roberson's Crossroads in Bledsoe County, Tennessee. Why would they be in Indian Territory in the heat of the Civil War? Elvira's father, Abraham Nail and her grandfather, William Nail who was a Methodist circuit rider preacher and missionary, had a passion for the Indians and desired to minister to them. The Nails were part Choctaw and Cherokee. They also married into the Folsom family.

    Dr. William D. Stout watched and worked with his father, John Stout to build a two-story school building in their small community of Sequatchie Valley in East Tennessee before the Civil War started. The desire for teaching and doctoring was a natural instinct to help those who were in the midst of severe conflict in Indian Territory.

    Dr. Stout had an uncle, Jesse Rector who was helping him establish connections with his cousin, Major Elias Rector who had been U.S. Marshal of the Western District of Arkansas and Indian Territory for sixteen years, appointed by President Andrew Jackson and carried by President Polk as well as other presidents. He was appointed Superintendent of Southwestern Indian affairs and held that position until 1861 when the war forced change amongst the new inhabitants of Indian Territory. The Indians had only lived there for a little over twenty-years. Rector was connected with the Choctaw agency at Skullyville, Indian Territory.

    In 1861, the Confederacy controlled Indian Territory as well as its resources because the Union troops abandoned their stations to go fight in the Eastern theater of the war. The majority of the Indians did not want to get involved in the Civil War of this ever-growing country called the United States of America, but they had no choice; they were caught in the middle. Because of the influx of the CSA in their territory and mutual sentiment against the U.S. government, the Choctaw and Chickasha Nations joined with the Confederates.

    In September 1862, Union General J.M. Schofield directed his field commanders to ignite a new tactic to drive the Confederates out of Arkansas and Indian Territory. General James Blunt made his move toward Fort Wayne in late October.

The Fall of 1862 was a critical time as the Union forces took control. They invaded Fort Wayne in the Eastern portion of Indian Territory, overtaking it from the Confederates in October of 1862, the same month William and Elvira got married. Union Troops had also succeeded in gaining control of Fort Gibson and Tahlequah. The Union forces began their strategy to move in and take control of all the forts where the Confederate heads were based.

During this time, those living within the Indian Nation were moved or banished, completely broken by the cruelty of soldiers and losing their very sustenance to stay alive. Some escaped to Kansas, some across the Red River to Texas. Many were imprisoned, and some were forced onto reservations near forts, now being overseen by the Union. Thousands of Indian men, women, and children huddled in tents or other makeshift shelters outside of the forts, suffering beyond belief from the harsh reality of war. There was nowhere to call home. The cold, the hunger, and the disease set in during the winters of 1861-1862. As resources dwindled, many were buried daily.

President Lincoln heard the cry of the Five Tribes in Indian Territory and he sympathized with the need of his fellow citizens. He desired to send "public service" to the people, but again, his generals were slow in action.

Dr. William D. Stout's uncle, Brigadier General James Gallant Spears, who fought on the Union side, must have encouraged Dr. Stout to provide "public service" to the Indians, knowing that he had extreme compassion for those in need, along with his new wife, Elvira who both grew up in great families who promoted servitude. They carried with them skills of doctoring, teaching, and missionary work. There is no other reason why they would leave their home in East Tennessee and go into the pit of Hell during the war.

In the mid 1840's, after the Indian removal from the southeast to Indian Territory, many educational buildings were built in the new Indian Territory which would later become Oklahoma. The schools were called Manual Labour Schools. The Indian Nations partnered in this endeavor with Protestant denominations in which the missionary board had control of the school's operations. The first one built in the Chickasaw Nation was in 1844, with more being added in 1852 when the Wapanucka Academy for girls was established near Bromide, Oklahoma.

They taught men different trades as well as how to grow crops, moving them into more of the white man's way of living. The women were taught "social graces," including housekeeping, sewing, cooking, and fundamental skills in maintaining a home. They added art, music, theater, speech, and dancing.

Surprisingly, the schools appeared to be identical to the schools that were being built in Tennessee before the war, one being Sequatchie College that the Stouts and Haskews helped build.

The schools were overtaken by the Confederate soldiers during the war, used for hospitals and the imprisonment of Union soldiers. Later, the Union took them over and there was not much left of them after it was all said and done.

When it appeared that the Union was taking control of East Tennessee, William and Elvira gained permission to travel to the West. They started their journey after their harvest of corn in the Fall of 1862.

Dr. Stout and Elvira started out going to Fort Smith, Arkansas and from there, would travel the California Road along the Canadian River established by Randolph Marcy to escort settlers and miners to California. Marcy built Camp Arbuckle along the southside of the Canadian near the areas which would later be known as Johnsonville in 1850. They built a 200 x 25 feet log building to house the soldiers and the gold seekers on the trail. It was abandoned in 1851 due to many men getting ill with Malaria. The Delaware Indians moved in and moved out just before the Civil War started.

Prior to the Civil war, about 10 miles northeast of present-day Purcell and 2 miles northeast of present-day Washington, we find Montford Johnson and his family living in the area. Johnson's mother was a Chickasaw and she died very young. Montford and his sister ended up living with their Chickasaw grandmother while their father went East. Montford had horrific trials during the Civil War, but later he became very wise in expanding his territory with cattle. He had a ranch in the area where Camp Arbuckle was established. That area would soon become Johnsonville, named after Montford. He made a good living. Montford gained more land and more cattle, developing a great cattle empire. His blessings would be extended towards creating great business opportunities for the Indians and Blacks. He had an incredible story.

An excellent book on the Johnson family is "The Chickasaw Rancher," by Neil R. Johnson, 1960. An excellent documentary called, "Montford Johnson: An Original Brand," came out in 2022 and it is a movie that is well worth your time, "Montford, The Chickasaw Rancher" are both on Netflix and Prime Video. They depict what a treacherous time that the Indians had to endure during the Civil War and the fight thereafter for freedom for all cultures. I believe this was also the ultimate goal of William and Elvira (Nail) Stout.

So, it appears that William and Elvira settled not too far from the settlers and Indians near Johnsonville and in around the area where the future Purcell would be located. The winter of 1862-1863 was a severe one in Indian Territory. It stayed fairly mild at the beginning but, by the middle of January 1863, the cold weather had set in hard. Sleet, snow, and a constantly descending thermometer made the skirmishes within that region die down as well as the movement of people. Smallpox also began to show its ugly head in February and March. It spread quickly through the camps. Its victims included both the young and the old. I can only imagine that Dr. Stout and his new bride helped as much as possible to heal the sick and mend the wounded.

The life of Elvira was stolen from her in this wilderness far from home. She died March 28, 1863 at the age of 17. This was documented by Dr. William Decatur Stout's testimony in the Southern Claim Commission papers. Whether her death was caused by childbirth, disease, the elements, a tragic accident, or something even more devastating than that, we will never know. William and Elvira were up against everything. This left Dr. Stout broken. This was trying on his faith, as a doctor, but most especially as a protective husband.

William had to bury Elvira in a strange land. Many relatives document that she was buried in Purcell, or at least in that general area. Dr. Stout returned to Bledsoe County, Tennessee alone no later than May of 1863. He is noted as living on the farm of his father-in-law, Abraham Nail, just east of his father, John Stout. William helped plant the 30-35 acres of corn that June with Abraham. The guilt he carried by losing Abraham's daughter to the wilds and ravages of the West, leading to her death, must have been heavy on his heart. Since the war had started 2 years before, he had lost his mother, sister, and now his wife.

After the war, Dr. Stout helped rebuild the Sequatchie College, allowing both ex-Union and ex-Confederates to study there. He remarried Nancy Elizabeth Haskew, sister of John Wesley Haskew and they both lived and worked in the Sequatchie College, later moving to Haskew Flats east of Woodward, Oklahoma. They were the writer's 2nd great grandparents.

Elvira's father, Abraham Hamilton Nail (1818-1907) was the grandson of Jonathan Nail and Rhoda Fulsom, a full-blooded Choctaw. Abraham's mother was Delliah Hamilton, born in the Cherokee Nation. Her maternal grandfather was a full-blooded Cherokee.

Abraham had previously obtained land in the Choctaw and the Chickasaw Nation and was able to return to it in 1874 to resume farming. He became one of the largest landowners, maintaining cattle and horses, along with farming. Ironically, he died and is buried in the Hillside Cemetery in Purcell, Oklahoma, close to where his daughter Elvira was placed to rest. All roads lead to Purcell.

For all of these reasons I had to go. The museum in Purcell was closed and I had no idea where to find a man named **Bud Hardcastle**. I was not familiar with that part of the country. Little did I know that God had all this planned out already, perfectly.

I was told by many credible sources, that **Bud Hardcastle** was the expert on Jesse James. After several attempts to contact Bud, I finally was honored to talk with him on the phone and I finally met the man. Purcell, Oklahoma was where he had lived all of his life. Not only did he help me with my story, but oh my, he had a story to tell himself.

Bud was as genuine as they come, a patriot of truth. Stories of his loyalty, fairness, generosity, kindness, sacrifices for his family, and integrity were shared by his friends and employees at his wife's popular restaurant, "Ruby's." There Bud meets daily with a host of friends for breakfast, including Steve, Jim, Cheryl, Paul, Kenny, and "Two Cup" (a nickname given to a man that always drinks two cups of coffee, no more, no less).

Bud's reputation speaks volumes of his character. He is admired by many and serves his community well. He takes much pride in his hometown and they in return take pride in him.

This hometown boy lost his parents involving a horrific truck accident when Bud was 11 years old, just a young boy. He was not injured, but two of his brothers were. There were so many tragedies that followed. He grew up in the home of relatives, but he never let the adversities of life overtake his undaunting spirit.

(Bud's father, Arthur Hayward "Buck" Hardcastle (1906-1950))

(Bud's mother, Lola Hazel Hays (1913-1950))

As a young boy Bud knew what hard work was like. In high school, Bud was taken in by a friend of his father's, A. B. Green. Bud learned a lot from Mr. Green and one of the many things he taught Bud was the importance of character in a man. Green told Bud, "Bud, show me a man who don't like a dog and don't like kids and I'll show you a no good S.O.B." Mr. Green took him under his wing and Bud worked for Mr. Green at his service station during his high school years, 36 hours a week. "He was the next thing to a Dad I had." Green Avenue in front of Ruby's was named after him.

Bud's experiences as a youth built his character indeed. He knew what it was like to have no parental guidance nor love from his own mother and dad, but yet he received love from many family and friends that deeply cared for him. He would later use these experiences to reach out to those who were walking in the same shoes as he did. What a remarkable man.

Young Bud became a football hero in high school, playing right tackle in the late 50's. Bud was honored as a member of the "All 50's Decade Football Team" in Purcell. He was offered various football scholarships to go to any choice college he desired, but he went directly into the army and served in active duty for six months in the years, 1959-60 in communications and seven and a half years in the reserves. It knocked him out of going to college on a football scholarship.

("Bud escorting the High School Homecoming Queen for Purcell High")

His love for football continued. At the age of 31, he tried out for semi-pro football with the Oklahoma City Plainsmen. He gained a place on the team, and all the young teammates called him "Pops." His reply, "Just come around my way and I'll introduce you to "Pops"! Bud wasn't just anybody you needed to mess with. At one time, he was bouncer at the 62 Club in Chickasha. Bouncer Bud kept them settled down pretty good.

Bud said the first football game they played was against the McAlester Prison inmates. It was a pretty rough game. The inmates had nothing to lose and this venue was an outlet for their anger and aggression. Bud stated that they were not very good sports. He came away with some major bruises, but it certainly didn't bruise his ego or pride. Bud gained the confidence and satisfaction that he could still play with the big boys and the pigskin.

Bud's interest in sports and youth stand out today, through leadership as head of the Booster Club which supports the town's athletes. His encouragement to young people is inspiring and has been shown in the way he raised three of his nephews, Mike Carmack, Tim and Tom Hardcastle, as well as giving his other two nephews, Zach Harp and Casey Paul Hardcastle, great life lessons. Bud is extremely involved in the Tourism Committee, Cemetery Board, Veteran's parade, and the Patriot Guard. He owned a used car business for forty years. His word was always good, as well as the vehicles he sold.

Bud married a beautiful and smart businesswoman, Barbara whose family had owned and operated "Ruby's Inn and Restaurant" for over 60 years. Both Bud and Barbara work hard every day, keeping things running smoothly. The fruit of their labor is evident by the patrons that fill their rooms and their tables.

Hardcastle started out as a great historian of Oklahoma's rich Western history. He became interested in Jesse and the probability of him roaming the prairies, hills, and mountains found throughout the great state of Oklahoma, known earlier as Indian Territory. The more he learned, the question rose again and again whether Jesse James had been killed in 1882. Many contradictory stories came out of the woodwork, spurring Bud to seek the truth.

Bud said that at the beginning, he never intended to get so heavily involved in this hunt for Jessie and the truth but once he got a taste of it, he couldn't stop and he continues his hunt today at the age of 85, with the full support of his loving wife. He has spent half of his life in this pursuit.

It was in 1979 that Bud became very passionate about the subject. Little did he know at the time, that this passion was deeply rooted in his own DNA. During the course of writing this book, Bud learned that he was related to Jesse through the Woodsons. Little did we know, the writer was also. Was that the driving force that propelled them both to find the truth? I believe it was.

Bud expressed many times how doors would open for him, people would connect, leading to others who would open another path, another clue in solving this mystery. Things did not happen by chance. Bud was chosen for this very complicated task.

Anna Ralston once said, "the truth about the James boys will never be known." Anna was believed to be the wife of Frank James. The story of the James brothers is indeed the most twisted tale in history and has never been completely solved, even Bud will admit to that. There was a lot to hide and a lot to uncover.

Bud traveled many miles, discovering people who had met Jesse, those who cared for him, those who were descendants of family members who had ties with Jesse, and Jesse's own grandchildren from various mothers. Once people learned of Bud's pursuit for the truth, people came to Bud via letters, phone calls, or showing up at his door. He followed up on their stories, seeking documents, historical records, eye-witness accounts, and maps and locations of treasure that Jesse buried. Bud was one of the first to uncover the connection and existence of the Knights of the Golden Circle and their secret code system. The media, at that time, made fun of Bud and said there was no such thing. Now, they are eating their words.

Bud had to work through ridicule and resistance, but he also had to do things the hard way. With no internet like we have today or a quick look at our phones to have information on a subject, maps, compasses, and immediate latitude and longitude coordinates, Bud had to depend on one page at a time on microfilm or documents, one person at time, and one clue at a time. He had to depend on his natural intuition and his "horse sense."

People have used Bud's knowledge, extensive valuable work, and evidence accumulated on Jesse, to write books and documentaries. Bud has helped many in treasure hunting with the code system Jesse used and with maps leading them straight to the treasure. Not only did Bud climb rugged mountains with rattlesnake dens at every turn but shimmied through tight caves and dark caverns in search of Jesse's treasure. He left no stone unturned. His discoveries added more pieces to the puzzle, only further validating the life of Jesse. Along with the treasure, greed had a way of creeping in and just like Jesse, Bud has been burned many times.

Nothing seemed to ever dampen Bud's passionate spirit. His hunger for the truth multiplied. Bud meticulously set out to prove a DNA connection to a man who late in his life claimed that he was Jesse in 1948, J. Frank Dalton. All evidence seemed to point in this man's direction.

For five years, Bud pressed hard through court battles, affidavits, retrieving permission from actual family members, and forking over $10,000 of his own money to exhume the body of Dalton who was buried in Granbury, Texas in 1951.

Bud's mission and passion in life is to prove the truth about Jesse. This was a promise Bud made to a man who held in his hands, a manuscript, carefully written by his wife, Ola Everhard who wrote down every word from the man who said he was J. Frank Dalton. Ola knew very well who this man was without him telling her. He was Jesse, a distant cousin. His words were concise, never contradictory, and full of wit and wisdom. Bud was given this manuscript by Ola's husband, Aubrey Everhard, with the understanding that Bud would prove the truth and declare who Jesse James really was. Everything Mr. Dalton/Jesse told this woman, Bud has proven and verified beyond a doubt.

Bud's book, "The Hoax That Let Jesse James Live" produces the entire document of Ola's manuscript. This book is a "must have" to completely understand the clues in which Jesse left for Bud to follow. Excerpts of this book, along with information gathered from Bud's visit with Aubrey Everhard and William Tunstill who had a long extensive visit with Ola and Aubrey, all videoed, will be used throughout this book.

Was Jesse the ruthless and cold-hearted killer that has always been depicted? Did he die in 1882 from the gun of Robert Ford? Many have their own theories and opinions, but Bud has the evidence to prove that the history books were wrong. While Bud searched for the facts of Jesse's death, the cause and effect that the Civil War had upon Jesse, and Jesse's outlawry days, Bud encountered another side of Jesse that the general public didn't know. Bud's search for the true inner soul of Jesse would become a priority. It was the" right thing" to do. All Bud asks is that we keep an open mind.

In no way does the writer, nor Mr. Hardcastle want to give outlaws any glory or notoriety. The outlaws, gangsters, terrorists, and those living against the law of the land, and most especially those living against the law of God who vandalize, murder, and rob innocent people, by no means deserve to be idolized. Their acts were vicious and were despicably evil. *"Woe to those who call evil good and good evil."* (Isaiah 5:20)

Why did a man or a woman in those days get swept up into this line of work? It is hard to say, and it is hard to understand. We were not there, nor did we walk in their boots. Hardcastle says, "some good folks were just changed by the times."

Some were coerced, in the wrong place at the wrong time, and some, like Jesse, were caught in a brutal, uncivilized synchronized effort to divide America. He watched his family being tortured and murdered, stripped of everything, and felt the excruciating pain on his own body when trying to defend his own. What would you have done? Bud says, "If you were any kind of man and witnessed your family going through this horror, you would have done the same thing."

This book will reveal Bud's lifelong search for Jesse; the information he gathered, received, and verified. Bud will also enlighten the readers on the treasure hunts, maps, the secret codes, the identifying landmarks, and the techniques used by the outlaws to bury their prized Confederate gold.

This journey and hunt for Jesse has been down a long, dusty 'ole trail, covered up by time and tales. Those who were close to Jesse are long gone and their stories are fading. They were told to keep their mouths shut. Thankfully, Bud tracked down the remnants of these folks before they and their stories were taken to the grave.

Bud had many good people helping him along the way. We will acknowledge them, giving them credit where it is due. This is what Bud desired, not taking full glory for himself. Sadly, his contributions and trust given freely to others, have been breached by those who seek the glory.

*"When **pride** comes, then comes disgrace, but with **humility** comes **wisdom**."*

Proverbs 11:2

Bud's character outshines them all and I believe therefore he has been successful. I am extremely blessed and honored to be a part of this project and to be called a friend of Bud Hardcastle's. At our first meeting in Altus, Oklahoma, it didn't take long for both Bud and I to see how important the truth was to each of us. When Bud started handing me items to take home and make copies, requesting for me to later return them, I said, "Bud, you have great faith in me and you don't even know me. If you need to talk with people from our hometown and do a background check….." Bud interrupted and said, "I don't have to, I'm forming my own opinion." He asked, "Are you a truthful person?" I answered, "Yes Sir, I always try to be." I told him my grandmother always said to do the right thing and Bud's reply, "Well, mine said if you're word is not any good, you're not either. And I kind of live by that."

The search continues as many new researchers and investigators are following Bud in this pursuit. They each have a story, they each have a theory, and they each have the evidence scattered across the continent that Jesse left behind in bits and pieces. While Bud leads the way with cold hard facts the old-fashioned way, others will follow with new technology, DNA, and scientific evidence. The completion of the puzzle has a way to go, but with Bud's accumulated knowledge and facts, the pieces are falling in place. Bud hopes to help the future researchers and treasure hunters who have an appetite for this sort of stuff. Bud himself leaves us many clues in the following pages.

We have Bud to thank for this progression of knowledge into the life of Jesse James. For if it wasn't for his passion and desire for the truth, we would not be this far in tracking Jesse. It took a man of great character, perseverance, and his focus on the "all-seeing eye" to accumulate what Bud did. The evidence is overwhelming and he's willing to share what he's unearthed, the TRUTH.

Rosanne (Wilcoxson) Priddy

(Bud and I, meeting for the first time at a BBQ joint in Altus, Oklahoma, 2017)

"History better get ready to open up their mind and start taking in the truth rather than what's been written in the history books that's incorrect."

-Bud Hardcastle

Chapter One: Deep in the Heart of History

Bud's experience in historical investigation was not only in books, records, traveling, interviewing old timers, and the great outdoors where the clues were hidden, but also in the history of his own family. Deep in his search for the truth about Jesse, Bud pierced into the very heart of his own family, and the truth began to pour out.

Bud did not have the luxury of having his parents tell him of his ancestors, so he went searching for himself. As he was exploring his past, he found pure gold within his own ancestry, along with tragedies. Tragedy and heartache; it is in every family, in every closet tucked away in time. Even though pain of the past is hurtful, it is sobering, bringing us into reality of what our ancestors suffered and endured.

We cannot fully understand the mindset of those who lived before us, nor the choices they made. We never lived in the era that they did, nor face the incredible obstacles they were up against daily. The environment, the setting, and the attitudes were totally different from what it is today. Could we, as people living in the 21st century, survive what they went through? The patriots of our past were tough as nails.

History is valuable, and its preservation is critical. It deserves respect and honor, not desecration. History, the good and bad, is our foundation in which we learn and build upon. It binds us as a country, as families, as one, experiencing defeat and victory in the midst of pain. If we allow it, the truth of our history can be a healing balm and not a curse.

This book is all about truth and honesty. Bud wanted it this way. He is willing to share a portion of his family stories to reveal the harshness of life during the birth of America and the Wild West. Bud's family traveled the same trails as Jesse did in Indian Territory and Texas. It was a very crude and brutal place to be before, during, and after the Civil War. Like Jesse, Bud's family met life and death at the end of a gun.

The gun during the Wild West days was on every man's hip. It was the law of the land. This phrase sums up its value in the West; "God made man and Sam Colt made them equal." It was protection for the lawful and deadly for the lawless.

The Hardcastles

Bud's paternal family, the Hardcastles, came from Yorkshire, England. At the age of 20, Matthew Hardcastle was noted as coming over on the ship *Jacob* in 1624, landing in Jamestown, Virginia. He was listed as a servant to Farrar Flinton, settling in Elizabeth City. Matthew's descendants would spread out of Virginia into North Carolina, Tennessee, and eventually into Arkansas.

Bud's 2nd great grandfather, Richard F. Hardcastle was a Confederate soldier in the Civil War; Hardy's 24th Regiment of the Arkansas Infantry, Company C and F. He was temporarily attached to the 19th Arkansas Infantry commanded by Col. C. L. Dawson. Richard's service was for a period of three years, enlisting June 17, 1863.

Bud's grandfather, Albert Hardcastle was the first to settle in Oklahoma. He married Mary Jane Whatley in 1901. Their son, Arthur Hayward "Buck" Hardcastle was Bud's father. When Buck was 14, there was trouble brewing at home. Buck's father left the home and remained gone for several weeks without telling anyone where he was. Mary took her children and stayed with her parents, Burrell Whatley and Samurilla Black, 5 miles away from her home.

Albert came home to an empty house and became furious. He saw one of his boys working in the field and asked where his mother was. He screamed at his son and told him to go to his mother and tell her that if she is not home in 30 minutes to sign the divorce degree, he would kill her. The boy made haste and reached the Whatleys to warn them. Another son rode to Fort Towson and requested a warrant to be issued for him.

In the meantime, Albert took a sledgehammer to their home, destroying everything in his path, including furnishings, bed clothing, clothes, and all the food they had in storage. His rage continued and he picked up his Winchester and headed towards the Whatley home. Seeing Mary in the yard of her parent's, he aimed his gun, fully cocked and before he could pull the trigger, he was stopped by a double-barreled shotgun. Mary's brother came to her rescue, stopping Albert cold in his tracks. The buckshot went directly into Albert's heart, killing him instantly.

The Whatleys

Bud's paternal grandmother, Mary Jane (Whatley) Hardcastle never remarried, but lived a long life. Her brother had a son who would be a celebrity in the Cowboy arena. Todd Whatley was a second cousin to Bud, both endowed with superhuman strength and stamina. Bud could bench press 425 pounds.

(Mary Jane (Whatley) Hardcastle (1883-1973))

(Todd Whatley (1920-1966))

    Todd became a bull rider in local rodeos of Oklahoma at the age of 17. He advanced in the rodeo circuit, winning several bull riding titles in Houston and Cheyenne, two of the largest rodeo venues in the country in 1945. Whatley won the first Rodeo Cowboy Association title of World Champion All-around Cowboy in 1947. The RCA, which was previously known as "The Turtles', would later form the PRCA, the Professional Rodeo Cowboy Association. Todd also won the World Champion Steer Wrestler that year, and in 1953, Todd won the World Champion Bull Rider title. You have to compete in two events to be eligible for the All-Around Cowboy Champion. He was inducted into the National Cowboy and Western Heritage Museum in 1955. Tragically, his life was cut short at the age of 45 when jealousy overtook an intoxicated man with a gun.

    The Whatleys were good people and Bud continued to stay in touch with them throughout the years. Bud and his good friend, John Tatum, were traveling through Oklahoma and came to the town Wright City, where his Whatley kinfolk lived. Bud made a special effort to stop at the Whatleys to introduce this incredibly unique man, Tatum, who was related to Jesse. The Whatleys were very aware of Bud's intriguing investigation of Jesse James and were thrilled to have him visit.

    Bud introduced his friend to the Whatleys, stating that John Tatum, as a young boy, shared his bedroom with an old man who played the fiddle and harmonica. This old man had come to visit John's parents in California and later they would travel to see the old man in Oregon performing at a shooting exhibition. Years later, John's parents revealed that the old man was none other than Jesse James. After Bud's elaborate introduction of John, referring to him as kin to Jesse, the Whatleys said, "So what Bud, you're kin to Jesse too." Bud was taken back by this statement and was in total shock. Laughingly, John Tatum said, "I knew that was going to happen."

    Bud put this revelation on the back burner, as he continued to pursue Jesse. When this writer was revealing to Bud of her kinship with Jesse, he admitted he thought that he was too. In 2018, the writer found out exactly how Bud was related to Jesse. It was indeed true. Surprisingly, in my own research months before, I had discovered my mysterious family's past, revealing that I was related to Jesse in his paternal and maternal heritage, on both my maternal and paternal side in four different branches.

    In this research, I found multiple blood connections to Jesse's family with my own family, including the Woodson, James, Dalton, Younger, Anderson, Tucker, Estes, Thomason, Simpson, Ferris, Harris, Crittenden, Cocke, Lewis, Hughes, Hackley, Warren, Goode, Bennett, Yancey,

Dever, Amos, Meador, Mimms, Martin, Webb, Daniel, Owen, Key, Tarleton, Pryor, Rountree, and the Porter families.

Like Bud, I too was quite shocked, but the revelation allowed a clear path to find Bud's connections. What brought Bud and the writer together in this pursuit of Jesse? Was this coincidence, fate, kinship, or divine intervention? The answer is all the above. The proof is in the pudding, DNA.

With some of the top experts in DNA and genetics, the writer has learned throughout the years that DNA plays a vital part in our past as well as our future. There is a connection which lies deep in our blood, connected with the blood of our ancestors. There is a passion and an attraction for the land where our ancestors lived, the history, and the people who share this blood and kindred spirit. It is a beautiful mystery of God's design.

I question why it has never been revealed to us. Many of these families Bud and I connect to produced the most revered men and women dedicated with leadership abilities in making a difference in our country, including Jesse James. Their own history in Europe planted a fervor inside their spirits to establish a country based on freedom, liberty, Godly principles and justice for all. Justice seems to be the backbone of these families.

Why has their story been hidden from Bud and I? Were our families unaware of our past, ashamed of it, or were we being protected?

The revelation of our family's amazing story is now unfolding; all within God's perfect timing. Throughout our research, things have fallen into place, indicating God's hand was certainly upon us, led by His spirit to reveal the truth about our families and Jesse, even though he was noted as a cold-blooded killer. Hard times can harden a young, impressionable soul. But again, we cannot judge the man and the history written about him. Its easy to dig up dirt on the dead and buried, but its harder and more rewarding to find the gold.

The history that Bud and I share connects to Jesse in our English and Scots-Irish heritage. We share the same DNA with the Napier, Drummond, Lindsay, Campbell, Fitzpatrick, Fleming, Booth, Warburton, Tucker, Pleasants, Woodson, Ferris, Winston, Dabney, Tate, Wright, Johnson, Davenport, Jouett, Perrin, and Royall families.

Bud's 7th great grandparents, John Woodson III (1655) and Mary Tucker descend from my Ferris and Tucker ancestors.

The Tuckers

Mary Tucker's grandfather was the famous Captain William Tucker, the captain of the *Mary and James* arriving in America in 1610. Tucker was one of the first subscribers to the Virginia Company. He was from Cornwall, England and made extensive voyages across the sea.

Tucker is described as a shrewd and hard businessman. He was assigned by the Company to be over Kecoughtan (Elizabeth City). Tucker was a strong military leader commanding forces against the Indians.

At the very beginning, it appeared that the Indians and new colonists were only curious about one another. The interactions did not appear threatening. In the Jamestown vicinity, there was a type of "confederate" clan which consisted of Chief Powhatan, Wahunsunacawh who was their King. He had under him eight different tribes and approximately 200 villages. For the most part, he and his followers wanted to welcome the new guests and treat them kindly with gifts. The chief also wanted to acquire their help to fight off hostile tribes. They were a clannish race though, and if one of their own was injured or humiliated in any way, they would turn in an instant to defend, stopping at nothing.

Colonies were spreading and growing beyond Jamestown. More settlers were allowed to come from England in the fall of 1621 with breeding stock to start the cattle industry as well as to grow tobacco. However, there was a problem brewing. The plantations were widely spread apart, and the white men and women became more and more congenial with the Indians. Men were teaching the

Indians how to use their weapons and allowed them to freely come and go into their homes. They finally could exist with those who long claimed this land as theirs.

This all changed in 1622. Chief Powhatan had died and left his brother, Opechancanough, in charge. His demeanor was not the same as Powhatan. His plan was to annihilate the "whites" with a massive attack.

On a spring day the Indians filtered in from everywhere, coming into the settlements as tradesmen, dining and socializing with the colonists, staying overnight. It was March 22, 1622 when their masks of friendliness turned into vicious hatred. They murdered, mutilated, and hacked to death women, children, and unarmed men. The former friendships that they had established proved to be unsubstantial during this time. The hatred for the pale faces was very vivid that day. The Indians used whatever they could find to mutilate the settlers. The horror was unimaginable. Out of 1240 inhabitants of Virginia, 347 perished and 19 women were captured.

By December 1623, Captain William Tucker was appointed to meet with Opechancanough and other prominent Powhatans. Tucker would seek for a peace negotiation, securing the exchange of prisoners taken in the 1622 massacre. During the peace talks, Captain Tucker proposed a toast with a drink, laced with poison, prepared by Dr. John Potts. Sadly, 200 Powhatans die instantly, a violent death, and another 50 are slaughtered, along with 150 Powhatans injured, including their chief, Opechancanough.

Both parties gave in to their desire for justice; neither one was innocent of their own deeds. The ironic story here, is that Captain William Tucker was the ancestor of Bud and I, and Opechancanough was my ancestor as well as Jefferson Davis, the President of the Confederacy.

The Woodsons

John Woodson III was the grandson of the immigrant, Dr. John Alexander Woodson. Dr. Woodson and his wife, Sarah Winston came to America in 1619 on the ship *George*. John was a surgeon under the leadership of the new governor, Sir George Yeardley who was also aboard the ship. John was sent to attend to the English militia, as well as the settlers. His home before America was Devonshire, England.

The Woodson family settled in Flowerdeau Hundred and survived the 1622 massacre, but 6 of the 30 occupants died. Sarah gave John two sons; John II, from whom Bud descends and Robert, who married Elizabeth Ferris, a sister of the writer's 7th great grandfather, Richard Ferris. Robert and Elizabeth Ferris Woodson were the direct ancestors of Jesse James. These families would be the cornerstone of many famous leaders of our country, including the Taylors (Zachary Taylor), the Lees (General Robert Edward Lee) who married into the Youngers and the Youngers who married into the Daltons, the Henrys (Patrick Henry), the Crittendens (Governor Thomas Theodore Crittenden), and the President of the Confederacy, Jefferson Davis.

Dr. Woodson would not survive another massacre. He was killed in the Indian Massacre of 1644. Over 400 settlers were killed in a single April morning in and around Jamestown. Opechancanough was 99 years of age at the time and still had disdain for the white settlers who were completely devouring their Mother Earth. He had to be carried into battle, having his men take turns holding his eyelids open for him to see.

Sarah Winston Woodson was home at the time, scrambling to protect her children and her homestead. A man was there at the home by the name of Colonel Thomas Ligon, my 10th great grandfather. Thomas married into the Harris family who were all connected to the Ferris' and Woodsons. He helped Sarah defend her family from the invaders. Sarah retrieved an old long-barreled (eight foot) muzzle-loading rifle which had been in the family prior to 1625.

Sarah gave Col. Ligon her husband's gun, while at the same time searched for a place to hide the children, John Jr., Robert, and Deborah. There is no account regarding where she hid Deborah, but where she hid the boys would be branded into their names for centuries. The oldest son, John, was hidden under a large washtub and Robert was placed in the potato pit where potatoes were stored underground. Thus, the boys are known as John "Washtub" Woodson and Robert "Tator Hole" Woodson. (Keep this nickname in mind as we stumble upon it again in Jesse's life).

Col. Ligon was able to kill at least seven of the Indians who were approaching the house by using the long-barreled gun while Sarah acted fast when two Indians tried to come down the chimney into their home and were met with a douse of boiling water and a heavy iron roasting spit. She was a tough lady and with all her might and God's help, she was able to keep her family intact. Later, she would learn that her husband was killed.

The eight-foot gun was given to the Virginia Historical Society and is on display at the Museum of the Virginia Historical Society in Richmond, Virginia.

The Eppersons and the Blacks

Not only were the Woodsons an incredibly famous part of the Whatley tree, but there were other members with notoriety. Bud's great grandmother, Samurilla Houston Black (1859) made a name for herself. Her name alone tells a story. Her father was Dr. Reeves Karr Black and mother, Susan Malinda Epperson. Susan's parents were Mark Epperson (1795) and Margaret Hill. The Eppersons played a big part in Texas History and its unique path to liberty.

During the very first session of the First Congress of the Republic of Texas, it was established that a half league of land, approximately 2,214.2 acres were offered to any settler who would operate a ferry across the Sulphur River along Trammel Trace. This trail was blazed by the East Texas Caddo Indians, followed by the remnants of the Spanish De Soto's expedition. Over 600 Spanish explorers started out on the Florida coast in 1539, traveling west into the southeastern portion of the United States. Their mission was set to retrieve and confiscate gold and other riches from the natives and discover the fountain of youth. The leader, Hernando De Soto died in what would become Arkansas and the man who took over the expedition was Luis de Moscoso Alvarado. At this point, the plan and mission were changed, and the crew was given a new name; the Moscoso Expedition.

Their primary goal was to head south, establishing a colony and a byway into New Spain (Mexico). The latest interpretation of the route suggests that the Spaniards came into the area where Fulton, Arkansas is and crossed the Red River, into Texas, traveling along what would later be called Trammel's Trace.

Trammel's Trace was the first passage into Texas from the north. During the 1800's, it was an avenue for those who wished to settle in the land that would eventually become the Republic of Texas. Upon its path, were great men such as Stephen F. Austin, Sam Houston, Davy Crockett, James Bowie, and men who helped defend the Alamo. A difficult and treacherous portion of the trail was at the Red River and the Sulphur River which is south of where Maud, Texas sits.

By April 1837, a year after the Battle of the Alamo and Sam Houston along with 800 Texans defeated the mighty force of Santa Anna's Mexican Army at the Battle of San Jacinto, Mark Epperson took up the challenge to establish a ferry across the Sulphur River where Trammel's Trace dipped into its deep waters. Epperson accepted the half league of land in exchange for this venture. He built a sturdy ferry, the Epperson's Ferry. The area nearby would incorporate a small community. Congress designated the Postmaster General to run a major mail route from Nacogdoches to Epperson's Ferry and on to the county seat of Red River County.

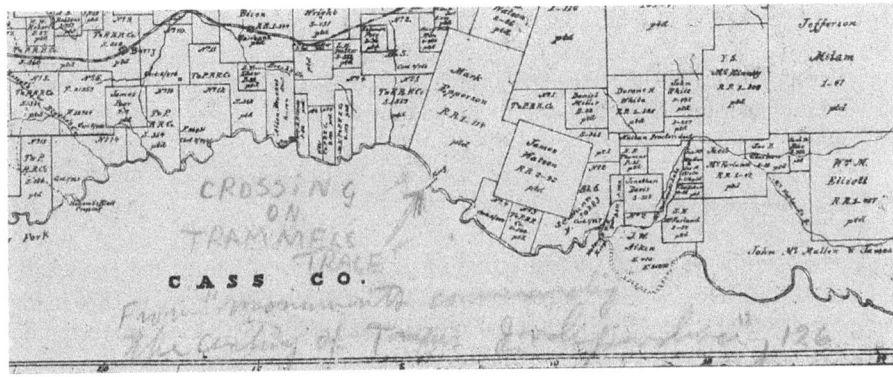

(Epperson's Ferry Crossing on the Sulphur River along Trammel's Trace (map originally by CW Pressler, 1899 found in the 1936 book, "Monuments Commemorating the Centenary of Texas Independence." – source – "Epperson's Ferry in Bowie County, Texas;" by Robin Cole-Jett; www.redriverhistorian.com))

Mark and Margaret Hill Epperson, his second wife, had several children, one being Susan Malinda Epperson born in 1839. She married Reeves Karr Black in 1856. They apparently lived close by her parents in the same community of Epperson's Ferry. The Sulphur River was the border of Bowie County and Cass County, Texas. We find Mark's property in Bowie County and the Black's in Cass County. Common sense tells you that Susan and her husband must have been running the southside of the ferry while her father ran the northside. This explains the encounter they had.

Sam Houston, a strong and influential leader in the military and political fields, became well known in Tennessee. Houston served as the state's 6th governor. Coming to Texas with his own personal fervor, he led the new Texian army, made up of men from other states, including Tennessee, who came to fight alongside men who were seeking a new life as settlers in a very raw piece of land. Houston's victory over Santa Anna's Mexican Army in the Texas Revolution made him a hero in the eyes of Texas.

Houston served as the first and third president of the Republic of Texas and later became a senator in 1846. During the early months of 1859, Sam Houston was traveling on Trammel's Trace and crossed the Sulphur River on Epperson's Ferry. He decided to stay a few days with the Eppersons and Blacks. It is more than likely that Houston had come that way before many times and had become friends with the Eppersons. Houston and Epperson had a lot in common; both came from the state of Tennessee, served in the War of 1812, and put their heart and soul into Texas.

Sam Houston likely could have been on the campaign trail while traveling Trammel's Trace. The gubernatorial race was in full swing that year and Sam was in the heart of it. Sam was never shy but bold and boisterous. He noticed Susan Epperson Black was expecting a little one. As he was leaving, Sam said, "When that boy's born, name it after me." Well, when the baby was born, it was not no boy, but a girl. As a term of endearment for good ole' Sam Houston, Reeves and Susan Black named the girl, Samurilla Houston Black.

Samurilla was born in July 1859 and just a few short weeks later, Sam Houston won the election for governor of Texas on August 1, 1859. This was during the time of unrest between the states. Houston strongly opposed secession and did everything in his power to keep Texas out of the Confederacy. Even though he strongly agreed with State's Rights, he knew that this fight would end in defeat. Sam refused to take an oath of allegiance to the Confederate States of America and was forced out of office in 1861. He died two years later.

The Eppersons and Blacks withstood the ravages of the Civil War and remained by their ferry. Troops from the 6th Texas Infantry Regiment, serving in the Confederate States Army, marched to the Sulphur River from south Texas and crossed on the Epperson Ferry. They were headed to

Arkansas. The regiment was ordered to help construct a Confederate fort to defend the Arkansas River. They were engaged in the Battle of Arkansas Post in January 1863 and Missionary Ridge later that year.

After the war, Samurilla Houston Black (1859-1930) married Burrell Hawkins Whatley (1856-1936) in 1877 and later moved from Cass County, Texas to Pushmataha County, Oklahoma. They were Bud's great grandparents.

The Hays and the Ryans

Perhaps the family who Bud is most proud of, is his mother's family, the Hays and Ryans. William Grant Hays (1846-1929) and Malinda Ryan (1848-1943) were married in 1870 in Malinda's parent's home, Thomas Ryan (1808) and Charlotte (Lottie) Rice (1812) in a small community of Pine Knot, Kentucky.

(Bud's maternal 2nd great grandparents, Thomas Ryan and Charlotte Rice)

The Hays, Ryans, and Rices were of Irish decent; strong-willed, courageous, and bold. Their ancestors had traveled to America within the century of its birth. In the late 1700's they migrated to Kentucky. William Grant and Malinda (Ryan Hays) settled in Pine Knot, Whitley County, Kentucky.

(Bud's maternal great grandfather, William Grant Hays)

William and Malinda's oldest son, John William Hays (1870-1945) carried a strong and fervent spirit of the Irish. When he was 16 or 17, John encountered a man by the name of T J Bruce, who for some unknown reason had issues with John's father. Bruce came to the house and was going to kill William Grant Hays, but before he could accomplish this deadly act, John stepped in and shot the man who had come to murder his father. T J Bruce did not live past the first bullet that hit him and the other man who was with Bruce, Gid Strunk, said in his testimony, that when he witnessed the deadly aim of Hays's gun, he went "running and running fast."

John Hays and his father knew that there would be a price to pay, even though it was self-defense. John gathered a few belongings and headed west on a train to Indian Territory, a haven to lose one's past. This was 1887 when Indian Territory was where most outlaws were absorbed. It was a rough place and was left to the U.S. Marshals assigned by Judge Isaac Parker headquartered in Fort Smith, Arkansas to serve justice over the broad span of 74,000 square miles in the Western District of Arkansas which included Indian Territory.

John maintained his freedom in the Chickasaw Nation, which later formed McClain County resting along the Canadian River. Possibly the reason John chose this area was the formation of a town, Purcell where the Gulf, Colorado and Santa Fe Railway was being laid. John very well could have been one of the men who picked up work on the railroads. The railroad was completed in 1887.

One of John's greatest adventures would be when he turned 18. He had heard of the unassigned land in Indian Territory that would be opening for anyone who was willing to make the Run of '89. Land would be for the taking at 160 acres per registered contestant who would plant the first stake in the selected acreage, bearing his/her name.

The land where John resided, near Purcell, was the southern border of the mapped-out territory of the run which stretched through the heart of Indian Territory to Guthrie, the northern boundary.

John's excitement must have increased when he began witnessing thousands of people streaming into town to join the event. He anxiously purchased a ticket of his own and hopped on the "boomer" train for Guthrie a few days ahead of time. Why he did not stay in Purcell and make the run on the southern end, is unknown. It would have been more convenient, but not challenging enough.

On April 22, 1889, at high noon, the gun was fired, igniting the race to begin. John Hays hit the trail hard and gained a piece of choice farmland, between Guthrie and Crescent, planting his stake firmly in the raw piece of land. It was near the Cimarron River. He was required to maintain it and improve upon it for five years. After that period, he would have been given a free title to the land.

John Hays never acquired a fondness for the area, so he moved back to McClain County, where he had started. He settled on a piece of property that later would become the town of Rosedale, between Johnsonville and Purcell. It was parallel to the Canadian River. He took a bride, Eva True, and they had many children; one of them was Lola Hazel Hays (1913-1950), Bud's mother.

We learn from an old photograph that Bud had in his possession, John's brothers, Charley, Big Ed, Tom, and Bates Hays joined him in settling this portion of the West, as well as their parents from Kentucky. In 1890, the Hays, William Grant and Malinda, their children, and Malinda's brother and his family traveled in a covered wagon to McClain County through Kansas. Malinda and brother, Thomas Granville Ryan had lost their father who lived in McCracken, Kansas the year before, and it is thought that they stopped to see their mother, Lottie in Kansas before proceeding into Indian Territory.

It is noted that John, his brothers, and friends built the first log cabin in McClain County. The cabin was fashioned after the Old Kentuckian style, squared hand-hewn logs with dove tailed corners. There was a strong community spirit within this neck of the woods, and all came together to help a neighbor.

The sturdy pioneers who made the Run of '89 were blessed with a strong community spirit and often helped each other when things needed to be done. Such was the case with this log cabin. At the top is John Hays, who made the Run. At the left, on the horse is Charley Hays, and standing are Big Ed Hays, Tom Hays, and Bates Hays. None of the others are identified. The home was being built for Harve Cobb who is in the upper right. John Hays sent for his family and parents after the Run and they settled in the Rosedale area. John was the father of Luther Hays and Alice Mack of Purcell, and the grandfather of Willard Carmack, Al Hays, Paul, Bud, Pat, Bill and Carmen of Purcell. Photo courtesy of Bud Hardcastle.

(First cabin built in McClain County, Indian Territory by John Hays and brothers)

William Grant Hays settled in Purcell, while Malinda Ryan Hays' brother, Thomas Granville Ryan settled in a small town, Fred, west of Purcell, near the town that would become Chickasha. This area was the main crossroads of the Chisholm Trail and the Fort Cobb Stage Road. Bud said that there is a marker where Fred was, indicating that Frank James brought a horse there to bred. Jesse did also. This was in 1889 when Jesse was supposed to be dead. That was their territory.

In the old dry-goods store's notebook, kept by Mr. Fletcher, who lives near Old Fred, I.T., there is a record of Frank James coming to the home of Mr. Fletcher to bring his horse to stud on March 22, 1889. The next entry indicates that Jesse James was there and brought his horse for the same service in April 8, 1889.

Charlotte Susan Ryan (1873-1965), Thomas Granville Ryan and Martha Davis' daughter, just three years younger than her cousin John Hays, was fascinated by this uncivilized country. She was only 17 when her father moved the family to the Chickasaw Nation. She was affectionately called "Susie" and became a schoolteacher in Purcell.

Susie had received a watch on her way to Indian Territory, in Kansas, possibly a gift from her grandmother, Lottie. It was a beautiful old watch. Within the cover, there was a place for a photograph. Susie cut out a photo of herself, placed in the frame, and carried the watch at all times. It stopped ticking, so she gave the watch to a neighbor to take it to town to have it repaired in Fred.

There are several stories that surfaced about this watch that would find its way into an outlaw's hands and eventually be recovered by one of the fiercest Deputy U.S. Marshals in the territory. The newspaper account in the Fort Worth Gazette, April 27, 1891, titled "Cupid's Arrow in the Shape of a Watch," shared the tale of a young lady whose dream of romance would come true in the Wild West, but at a cost.

The watch was in the coat pocket of a young boy named Hiatt, supposedly the neighbor who took the watch to J. H. Carey's General Store in Fred, I. T. The year was 1890, the same year that Susie and her family settled in Fred. Of course, being in the crossroads where drovers, gangs, and outlaws traveled, made the area dangerous for a beautiful young woman.

General stores were one of the most vulnerable entities in which outlaws seized upon to gather cash, goods, and supplies for their on-the-run ventures. A gang of vicious outlaws burst into Carey's store, demanding money. They grabbed $68 in cash and forced all those in the store to hand over what they had in their pockets, including Susie's watch that Hiatt was safely keeping. When one of the patrons, William "Bill" Carey, did not oblige, he was shot dead. The outlaws slipped away to the Little Washita River.

Deputy U.S. Marshals working for Judge Parker out of Purcell were hot on the trail in pursuit of the outlaw leader, Bill Hudgins. Marshals Selden Lindsey and John Swain caught up to Hudgins and severely wounded him. Hudgins had the watch in his possession. While lying in a pool of blood, Hudgins stated that he was infatuated with the lady whose photo was in the watch. He knew she lived in Fred. He wanted to go back for her. When Swain saw the photo, he too became entranced. He made it his mission to seek the lady that delighted so many eyes of men.

Hudgins, facing death, revealed his hideout, 22 miles north of Tishomingo. There, officers found one kidnapped person, a skeleton of another, and loot valued up to $5,000. The outlaws had been bad to the bone.

Deputy U.S. Marshal Swain searched for this sweetheart in the photo and found her, Miss Susie Ryan. Swain returned the watch and Susie was so overtaken by the hero; their mutual love was instantaneous. Susie married Swain, April 1891, after two months from the time the marshal returned her watch. This was only the beginning of their exciting lives together.

Swain had served as a posse man as far back as 1886 under the famous U.S. Deputy Marshal Heck Thomas. John Swain was sworn in as a Deputy U.S. Marshal under "Hanging Judge" Isaac Parker when Deputy U.S. Marshal John A. McAllister was shot and killed in February 1889 by Charles Stein in Purcell. McAllister had less than a year of service. Swain immediately tracked down Stein, killing him after a struggle to arrest the man. Swain would go on to hold dual commissions from Ft. Smith, Arkansas and the Eastern District of Texas in Paris, Texas.

In the Purcell Register newspaper of McClain County, January 4, 1895, Swain was noted as "participating in many dangerous conflicts, bearing himself at all times with courage and proving himself a man of indomitable nerve".[1] This was a statement made by Deputy U.S. Marshal Heck Thomas. In his book, Deputy U.S. Marshal Selden Lindsey, who killed Bill Dalton, stated that John Swain, on his own, was the equivalent to four men. Swain could get the job done. He was highly thought of throughout the marshal service; those who rode with him and those who he stuck his neck out for.

In June 1892, Marshal Swain organized a posse to track down some vicious outlaws who pulled off a train robbery. The Santa Fe Express at Red Rock, Oklahoma Territory was ambushed and robbed. The suspected culprits were believed to be the Daltons.

In the Austin Weekly Statesmen, June 9, 1892, the story describes the scene. The Santa Fe Express passenger train was loaded with passengers and was pulling a Wells Fargo express car, guarded by various "messengers" who protected the car and its contents. On board the express car, contained the valuables of the train, such as mail, money, gold, important documents, and precious cargo. The messenger was always putting himself on the line, susceptible to all kinds of bandits and desperadoes who would do anything to get their hands on the cargo.

"The robbery was the most unique one in the history of Indian Territory outlawry,"[2] the newspaper stated. It occurred on June 1st, around one o'clock in the afternoon. There were men aboard the train who were said to have been well dressed and acted as gentlemen. After the train pulled into the Red Rock station, which is northeast of the town of Perry in the north central part of Oklahoma, things began to get a little out of hand. Red Rock was a popular cattle shipping point in the Cherokee Strip. It sat on the Otoe and Missouri reservations. Much of this land was leased by the famous 101 ranch and was used for grazing. The ranch was located north of Red Rock.

When the train stopped, two masked men leaped over the tender and into the engineer's galley. Armed, the men demanded for the engineer to take the train down to the stockyards. The engineer complied and five more masked men met the train. The outlaws grabbed the engineer and fireman and headed to the Wells Fargo express car. The messengers inside the car refused any kind of entry for these masked men and held their ground. The bandits began shooting at every angle of the car, even underneath, to force their way through, while the messengers inside were shooting toward the door. Bullets were ricocheting off the steel walls and rails in every direction. At least 200 bullets were fired, and miraculously, no one was injured.

After one of the outlaws broke through the door with an ax, they gained access at gunpoint to all the valuables inside. They took it all and jumped onto their horses and fled to the southwest. The robbers were believed at the time to be the notorious Dalton Gang. It has been proven since that it was. The gang reorganized in the spring of 1892 and this was their first appearance that year and they came out with a bang.

An incredible clue and validation of this event surfaced. In the book, "*Billy the Kid: An Autobiography,*" by Daniel A. Edwards, word for word statements from Brushy Bill Roberts to William V. Morrison outlines Brushy's life in full color. Another "must have" book. At the end of Brushy's life, he finally let go of the secret he held for decades; he was Billy the Kid. It took some prodding, but he finally confessed this to Morrison.

Brushy/Billy claims he did not die in 1881, but another man paid the price. His story was incredible, relaying how he escaped and what he did with his life after his "supposedly" death. Brushy told the story of going to Indian Territory and joining the Deputy U.S. Marshal service under Judge Isaac Parker in 1892. He saw 6 train holdups. This is an excerpt from the book on Billy's statement. "The Daltons held up a train in the spring of '92. I think it was the spring. They killed a deputy who failed to put them up fast enough. One of them looked at me and said, 'We know who you are. Put 'em up or I'll kill you. I put 'em up, too, I did."

Brushy continued, "When this judge asked why we let them get away, I told him I knew the Daltons and I didn't want to fight them alone, either. We all put up our hands except one man, and he is buried out there."[3]

Brushy and the other deputies must have arrived during the robbery and tried to overtake them. It's clear that they would have had plenty of time to get to the scene with all the gunfire and all the noise made as the outlaws were hacking away at the door of the train car. The deputies just didn't have enough to stop them.

Judge Parker was frustrated. He called for the very best of men, quality and quantity to take care of this issue. Deputy U.S. Marshal Swain was notified of the event and organized a posse to track the desperate characters. They packed their horses into a freight car and traveled on train from Purcell to the end of the track at Englewood, Kansas. They scoured "no man's land" in the Oklahoma Panhandle to no avail. They learned that the men got fresh mounts and was way ahead of the law. Swain and his men abandoned their search. Justice eventually caught up with the Daltons in Coffeyville four months later. The Dalton Gang was no more.

(Deputy U.S. Marshal John Swain with the posse of eight men to hunt down the Daltons after the Red Rock robbery. From Bud Hardcastle's personal collection. Given to Bud by Mike Towler, writer and historian; Elmore City, Oklahoma. (John Swain is the 7th man from the left))

Many instances of Swain's law and order is described in books, newspaper articles, and court records. He was pretty tough and took care of business. Swain fought for justice under the law and above the law. A lawman in those days had to in order to stay alive. Stories of his last serving of justice come from January 1895, his last shootout.

The event that would change the lives of Swain and Susie was in all the papers. Most stories in books and newspapers reflect the view of the other party, the Vincents who had an ongoing rivalry and disdain for Deputy U.S. Marshal John Swain. Even back then, there was fake news. Bud's great grandfather, William Grant Hays, cringed after reading stories and hearing Vincent's testimony. "That's not the way it happened!" cried William Grant Hays. Let's hear the side of Bud's family and the court records that Bud discovered.

It all began over a land dispute between Swain and William Garland "Garl" Vincent and his son, Charley Vincent. John Swain was first married to Anna Morse, niece of Chief Cyrus Harris, first Governor of the Chickasaw Nation who served five non-consecutive two-year terms. The land was deemed as Anna's property per rights of her Chickasaw heritage and Swain was considered an intermarried citizen of the Chickasaw Nation. Anna died at an early age.

Several stories suggest that Garl Vincent and his son, Charley Vincent were also Deputy U.S. Marshals, but are not listed in any of Judge Parker's rosters. Some state that Garl served under Deputy U.S. Marshal Heck Thomas. The Vincents may have been considered posse men at one time. One of the newspaper articles state that Garl was a deputy in the Ardmore Court.

Garl Vincent came from Missouri and was known to be part of Shelby's Missouri Cavalry, the Iron Brigade in the Civil War. One story indicates that he was in a band of Quantrill Raiders. He is noted as killing at least 20 men and endowed with fierce courage and might. Some of his victims were Union soldiers who had strung up his brother, Grant. He gained respect after the war in Texas as a stockman and eventually moved to Indian Territory.

The dispute between Vincent and Swain was over the property claimed by Swain and Garl's son, Charley Vincent who stated that he had leased it. Charley was considered a citizen of the Chickasaw Nation because of intermarriage, same as Swain and they were both claiming this particular piece of property which bordered Swain's land. One newspaper from the "Minco Minstrel," January 11, 1895, stated that Swain and Vincent were fighting over Mr. Poor Lo's land. It is unknown who this was or the story behind it.

Many stories which surfaced, indicate that Swain was kind to the less fortunate, especially the Indians and the Black families who came to settle in Indian Territory after the Civil War. Vincent appeared to be the opposite and began mistreating the Blacks who Swain was allowing to live on the property. Apparently, Charley Vincent moved his belongings into the family's' home and caused havoc and chaos. The family threw out Vincent's possessions and forced Vincent off the land. The Vincents took the Black families to court and Swain took the side of the Blacks, going on bond for them. Bitterness grew intensely and the feud festered.

On January 9, 1895, Swain was riding his horse alongside a wagon hauling his father-in-law, Thomas Ryan and Thomas' brother-in-law, William Grant Hays, Bud's great grandfather. They were southeast of Purcell, near Rosedale.

On the road, they met Garl Vincent and his son, Charley in a wagon. Words were exchanged. Some accounts state that Swain rode up next to Garl with his hand near his pistol and Garl grabbed his Winchester and shot John Swain in the gut. Swain's horse reared and pitched, throwing him to the ground with his foot caught in the stirrup. He was dragged for several feet, while the horse kicked Swain in the head and face.

Garl jumped from his wagon and lunged towards Swain to finish him off with the butt of the rifle, but that was a big mistake. Swain somehow gathered his strength and willpower, got loose from the stirrup, and while profusely bleeding, wrestled with Garl and his weapon, yanking Garl towards him. Face to face with the man who just tried to kill him, Swain took his six shooter and ended Garl's life.

Vincent's son, Charley was hiding behind the wagon and shots were exchanged between him and the gravely injured Swain. The second bullet hit Swain, which ended the life of the bravest lawmen in the territory. Charley was indicted for the murder of Swain but was found innocent due to self-defense four years later in a court of law in Paris, Texas. Ironically, Grant Vincent, a brother to Garl later became a sheriff of McClain County from 1911-1914.

Susie was of course devastated but wanted to honor and preserve John's memory and his service in which he gave it all to the citizens of Indian Territory. Susie sent a photo to a sculptor in Italy to chisel out a replica of the man she loved and admired.

(Deputy U.S. Marshal John Swain on the left and Deputy U.S. Marshal Matt Clark)

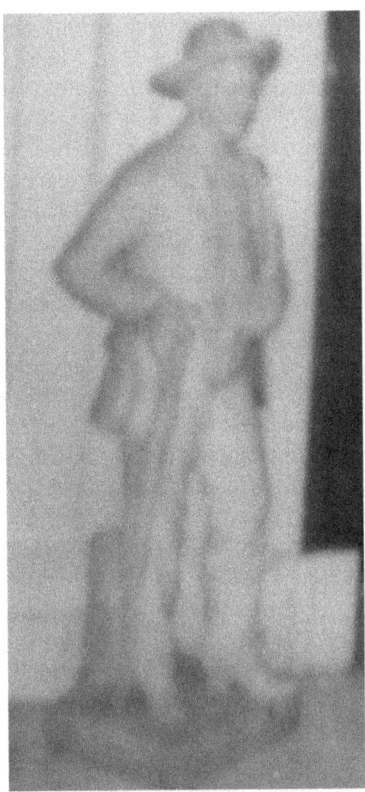

(Statue of Deputy U.S. Marshal John Swain)

In a newspaper out of Muskogee, Oklahoma, February 21, 1895 – "This will be the finest piece of work erected in the Territory. The statue is to be the exact height of the deceased, with hat on, belt and revolver on and Winchester standing by his side. The work when complete will stand nine feet six inches in height. The deceased was a United States marshal and his heart-broken wife forfeits the handsome sum of $600 to erect a monument manufactured after the way she saw him most in this life."[4]

The money Mrs. Swain used to honor her husband, was given to her from the "Woodmen" in which Swain was a member, receiving $3,000 in insurance money. After the crate arrived from Italy, the marble statue of Deputy U.S. Marshal John Swain was placed in the Purcell Cemetery upon his grave. Susie later donated the statue to the Oklahoma Historical Society which was on display for years in Oklahoma City.

Susie Ryan Swain remarried to James Willard Peters in 1901. Eerily, her life began to replay the tragedies that she had once encountered. She was married to John Swain only four years when his life was ended in a gunfight and she would be left a widow once more after four years of marriage with Peters. His life was ended in a gunfight in 1905. On June 29, 1911, she married Oscar L. Shaffer in Oklahoma City, but he was also murdered.

After three major tragedies in Susie's life, her attention was turned towards others. Susie put all her energy in helping the Indians who were adjusting to the white man's way of life. She was following in the path of her first love, John Swain.

In 1916, she was appointed by the Bureau of Indian Affairs as Field Matron to help in the transitioning of the Indians and his ways to become a more civilized race, but Susie saw a different purpose in her very being. It was not to change the Indian or their precious heritage, but to celebrate it and preserve it.

Bud was able to visit Sally Stonum who wrote an article, honoring Susan Ryan Peters in the book, "Kiowa Voices – Myths, Legends, and Folktales" by Maurice Boyd; 1983. Ms. Stonum knew Susie well and did not know at the time, that she was dealing with history. In her writings, Ms. Stonum honored Susie as a heroine of the Kiowa Nation. She stated that Susie was the most influential person in reviving and bringing awareness of the beauty of Indian art. Ms. Stonum gave Bud a personal copy of the article she wrote for the Susan Peters Gallery in Anadarko, Oklahoma.

In this article, Sally writes, "With fear and trembling," (Susie's own words), she set out toward the southeastern part of Indian Territory to teach the Choctaws. It was no easy task and many dangers were met with courage that she had never used before.

A year later, she was transferred to the Kiowa Nation. As a teacher, she began to use her skills in teaching the Indian women basic household skills, but they in turn began to teach Susie the beauty of bead and leather work.

"She saw the men's artistic abilities, and contrary to U.S. policies to discourage all their old customs, she secretly helped them to use these God-given talents which produced dancers, beautiful artifacts and paintings. She impressed upon them the fact that they would not only be preserving the customs of their ancestors, but they could become professional and make a living in the new world. This they did, with Susan's help."[5]

Susie saw an enormous talent in young artists and supplied various teachers, supplies, and avenues to encourage, advance, and promote their work. These artists, the Kiowa Five became world famous; Steve Mopope, Spencer Asah, Jack Hokeah, James Auchiah, Monroe Tsatoke and Lois Smokey.

Even after retirement, she continued to promote, support, buying and selling artwork, sharing her meager income, helping the sick, and bailing out young boys who were aiming towards the wrong side of the law.

Her friendship and love for the Kiowa people grew and she was made a "blood sister" during the Kiowa ceremonies in 1954. She was given the name Gome-tah-gya (Good Friend). Susie received the merit of honor in the National Hall of Fame of Famous American Indians when the Susan Peters Gallery was established in Anadarko. In 1982, out of 92 nominees., Susie was selected as one of the first eight inductees into the Oklahoma Woman's Hall of Fame.

When Susie died in 1965, she was 91 years old. She died in Anadarko, Oklahoma, but she had requested to be buried by her first love, the Deputy U.S. Marshal, John Swain in Purcell. Every year, on Memorial Day, Bud places fresh flowers on the graves of Susie and John Swain as well as the rest of his family in the Purcell Cemetery. He has been doing this for years out of honor and respect.

Bud's family has experienced it all, mostly in the heart of Indian Territory. After 137 years since John Hays came to the territory, the spirit, the fervor, the toughness, the generosity, and the sacrifices for the good of men continues to flow within Bud's veins as it did in his ancestors.

One last note: Bud was very proud that his grandfather, John Hays made the Run of '89. Hardcastle was geared up for the celebration of the 100th anniversary of the run in 1989. A wagon train traveling through Oklahoma which honored those who made the run, came to Purcell. The organizer asked Bud if he knew anyone who could feed these folks. Bud said, "Me." Bud took it upon himself to feed all the people on the wagon train (up to 120), using his own funds and cooking skills to muster up some grub. It was a feast. Bud did this for two years and then others began to volunteer to help, serving at the Expo Center for 25 years or more.

Hardcastle has certainly proven to be worthy and credible in his knowledge of the history in Indian Territory. Bud's involvement and research into the run led him to another clue, another link. Jesse was in the Run of '89. How can that be? Jesse was killed in '82. Remember, he was not too far from Purcell in 1889 at Fred.

Keep your eyes and ears open, and you too will see the puzzle pieces form the most intricate tale of the Wild West.

"History is not history unless it is the truth"

-Abe Lincoln

Chapter Two: Alive and Well

Bud set out to find the pure gold in Jesse's history. Not just the physical gold that Jesse left behind, but the treasures within Jesse, in which he rarely showed.

How did Bud discover the real Jessie? He looked to those who knew him; those who fought alongside him, rode the trails with, shared in kinship/friendship/brotherhood, those he lived with, interviewed with, was acquainted with, had a brief encounter with, those who followed his treasure maps, and those hard-working researchers that have studied him.

Jesse James's story is a sad story. What a life; surrounded by a multitude of loyal friends on one hand and a vast array of traitors on the other. It was a lonely life, especially toward the end. When was the end? Was it 1882 at the age of 34 or 1951 at the age of 103?

The picture on the cover is one of Bud's favorites. He received this picture from a man, Raymond Edward "Eddie" Schneberger. Eddie called Bud after seeing him on the news and reading articles of Bud's pursuit of Jesse.

Bud was getting his name out there. He made a dedication speech for the opening of the Cement Historical Museum and Jesse James Visitor Center in Cement, Oklahoma. This small town in the southwest part of the state, is approximately 18 miles from Chickasha, between Oklahoma City and Lawton. Bud donated documents and information to the museum, enhancing its content and attraction to Wild West history buffs. The news of the upcoming event caught Eddie Schneberger's eye, and you better believe he wasn't going to miss the event in Cement.

Eddie lived between Cyril and Apache, Oklahoma, on the northside of the road, within a 10-mile radius from Cement. This was right in the middle of a hotbed of loot buried by Jesse James himself. In their phone conversation, Eddie told Bud he had an amazing story to tell about his younger days growing up in this country of the Keechi Hills.

Bud agreed to meet with Eddie, honored that he was contacted by him. Bud was familiar with the Keechi Hills and was already in the area, exploring Buzzard's Roost. This huge mound-like formation juts out of the small hills and prairies of Oklahoma, used by the Indians and outlaws as an identifying landmark. In 1934, Joe Hunter found a tea kettle that Jesse and a few of his gang members hid inside the cavities of Buzzard Roost. This was a regular hangout of Frank and Jesse's.

(Buzzard's Roost)

Notice the slanted white rocks on the side of the old buzzard. It was here, underneath those rocks, a small cave where the kettle was found. Not far from that location was where Frank James dug up $6,000 worth of gold. Bud found the hole where the money was buried.

At Eddie's home, Bud began to hear the story that Eddie was so eager to tell. Eddie was just a young boy of 12-14 years of age when he encountered an old man knocking on his door in the early 1940's. After the tea kettle was found on Buzzard's Roost, many treasure hunters began scouring the area, but this man was different. The old man asked Eddie's parents if he could look around on the family's farm and they allowed him to do so. Eddie described him as being very distinguished, wore nice clothes, and reflected a nice, gentleman-like quality.

(Raymond Edward "Eddie" Schneberger at 12 years old, 1940. (courtesy of granddaughter, Mandy Moore))

The old man ventured north on the property, towards the creek without hesitation. It was evident that he had been there before. He did not give his name but came back several times to travel the same trail behind their farmhouse, looking for something.

When the man left, Eddie tried to trace the man's trail and found nearby, a drawing of a turtle carved into a tree. Eddie had no idea what this meant. What was the old man looking for? Was he looking for Jesse's gold, deposits left decades ago? The young boy was intrigued by the man. They developed a mutual fondness for one another.

Eddie knew that the old man's visits were coming to an end. Before he left for the last time, the old man gave Eddie a photograph of himself. The man told him, "This won't mean a thing to you now, but someday it will."

The young boy's curiosity kept growing stronger. Who was this man? He appeared to be a cowboy, wearing a nicely fitted wide, brimmed cowboy hat and slick-looking boots made of the finest leather.

In those days, war was knocking at America's door in the early 40's. To keep the young minds occupied and not troubled, movies and comic books depicting the Wild West, took them on adventures with characters such as Hopalong Cassidy, Gene Autry, Deadwood Dick, Billy the Kid, the Dalton Gang, and of course, the most notorious outlaw of them all, Jesse James. It was a young boy's dream to become like their heroes, dressed in full attire, a felt cowboy hat, holsters loaded with guns made of metal, boots, bandana, and of course their stick horse. Eddie grew up in this era, loving the tales of the Old West. Little did he know…he had something of great value, a part of the real Wild West in his back pocket.

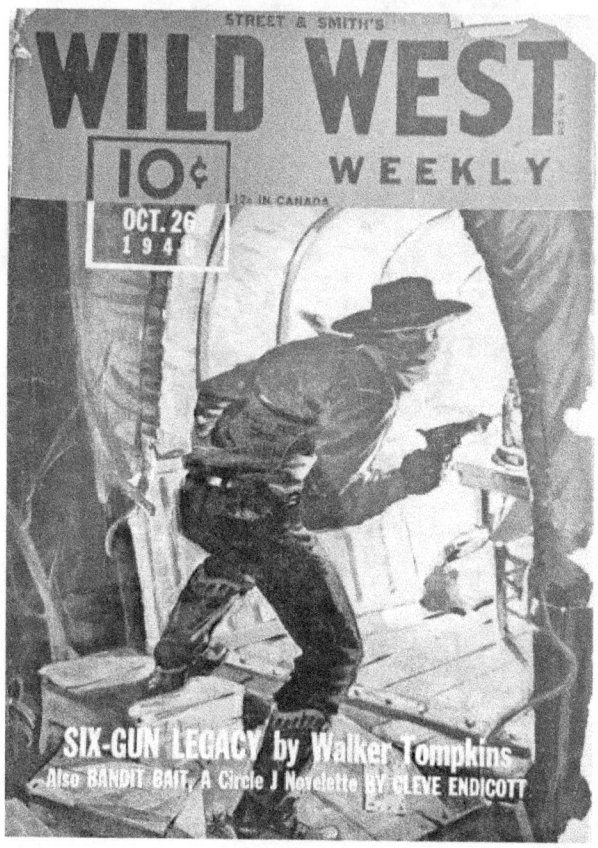

(Comic Book back in 1940)

    The photo that the old man gave to this young whippersnapper, was taken out of its hiding place and viewed by Eddie many times; it was well worn. He may have even taken it to school for "show and tell." He pulled the photo out once again in the month Eddie was graduating from high school, in 1948.

    Eddie had heard about a man who stirred up many questions in Lawton, Oklahoma. Eddie got a hold of a newspaper from the Lawton Constitution, dated May 19, 1948, and on the front page, the headlines read, "Jesse James is Alive! In Lawton." Eddie's jaw dropped when he saw a picture of the man claiming to be Jesse. "I had been talking to Jesse James!" said Eddie. The man in the paper was the same old man who came to his house numerous times. Eddie's family said, "my goodness, Jesse James, that's the man who went looking around our place."

    This man, who went by the name of J. Frank Dalton, drew a crowd of 30,000 or more people in Lawton on May 22, 1948. He had two speaking engagements, claiming he was the real Jesse James and that he had faked his death in 1882. He told the story that Charles Bigelow bit the dust that day in his place in St. Joseph, Missouri. There is a short video of Dalton in the convertible transporting him around Lawton on Youtube.com. You will notice all the young people around him, fascinated.

    The photo given to Eddie by Dalton, was the one used to design a photo card or business card you might say, with the inscription:

*"Frank Dalton
Last of Quantrill's Raiders
Born March 8, 1848
Author Lecturer Soldier
Outlaw and Peace Officer"*

Dalton distributed these cards to people he encountered, and for a bonus, they could hear the amazing tales of the days he rode with Quantrill. This was prior to the big reveal in 1948.

Aubrey Everhard, a man whose wife, Ola was kin to Jesse and had nursed him back to health many times in their home, gave Bud a letter that he had of Dalton writing to a man named "Howk", thanking him for the photos. It suggests that Dalton was referring to these pictures that were on the cards and the actual photo given to Eddie. The letter states, "Say Howk, them pictures were simply swell, and I'm proud of them. I show them to all my visitors, and they all admire them."[6] The letter was dated September 12, 1942.

A picture of the card was on the cover of the book, "Chasing Rivers, Trains, and Jesse James," by author, Reggie Anne Walker-Wyatt. She received this card from an old gentleman by the name of Virgil "Cowboy" "Slim" Williams who had received it from J. Frank Dalton himself. Bud was contacted by Reggie to help her with some information on Jesse and Frank when writing her book.

Bud went down to Louisiana to help Reggie and indeed he did. She called the television station and their meeting was filmed. The book is filled with information and photos that Bud supplied and the main attraction of Reggie's book was firsthand stories from "Cowboy." He had met J. Frank Dalton in 1946 at an old country café in Longview, Texas. Cowboy became Dalton's friend and lived in the same motel as he. Dalton was afoot, so Cowboy offered him transportation on a daily basis. Their adventures were quite amusing to say the least.[7]

Bud Hardcastle, Reggie, and Cowboy were able to meet in San Antonio at the Folk Fest and Hog Hunter Convention in June 2001.

(Bud and Cowboy Williams at Folk Fest)

(Larry Jones interviewing Cowboy (off of Bud's video))

Bud captured an interview with Cowboy on camera conducted by Larry Jones and learned more about Cowboy's history with Dalton. Many of the stories that Cowboy heard from Dalton, coincide with the stories told to Ola Everhard by J. Frank Dalton. Inside Reggie's book, is a typewritten letter from Ola to Cowboy. They kept in touch.

Another one of these cards, was given to Mrs. Ethel Chennault on October 15, 1942. The Chennault family gave this to Bud. The writing on the card matches perfectly with the handwriting in the letter and on the "calling card" Cowboy received from Dalton.

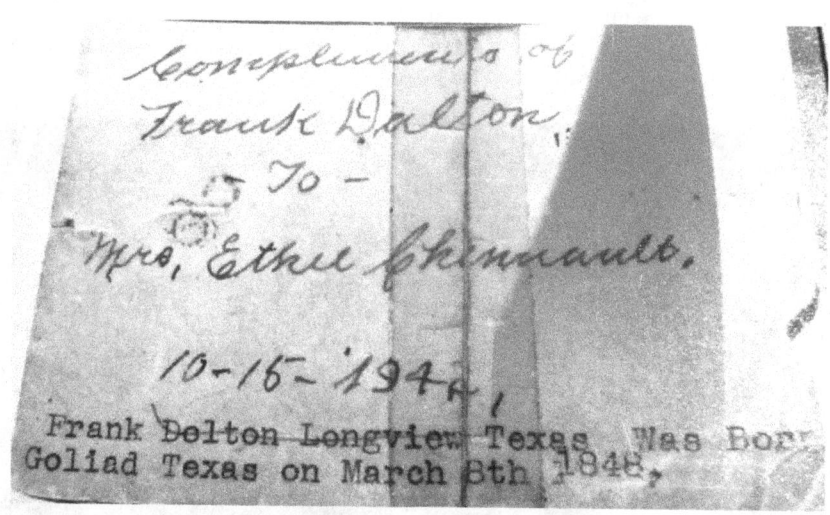

(In back of Dalton's calling card)

The Chennaults were one of the many families Bud contacted when hunting Jesse. They had a homestead in southwestern Oklahoma, near Hollis. Dalton made several trips to their home, just as he did to Eddie's, searching for something.

Like many who Bud met along the way, friendships developed including the one with Eddie Schneberger. Bud and Eddie would visit often when Eddie would come to Purcell where his son, Don Schneberger was a football coach and principal.

Eddie called Bud one day, said he had something for Bud. It was the photo that Jesse gave Eddie. What a gift. It meant a lot to Bud. It was supposed to happen.

Eddie has passed on in this life; the same holds true to many who have helped Bud in the clues leading to Jesse. Bud has an extreme respect for Eddie and is grateful that he shared his story and his priceless photo of the man in question. The photo belongs on the front cover of this book. It tells a story in of itself. It reveals a very distinguished older gentleman, firm in his stance, radiating authority, and demanding respect.

Who really was the old man, known as J. Frank Dalton, who claimed he was the authentic Jesse Woodson James, living past the century mark?

Was Jesse James, alias J. Frank Dalton, his real name or did he just carry it during the Civil War and his outlaw days? Were there several Jesse James? Who was the authentic "Jesse James" whether he be associated by blood and kinship of the James' family or who took on an incredible persona, developing the character of Jesse James? There was a lot to explore and a lot to prove.

This was Bud Hardcastle's focus. Bud was the right man to solve this mystery. All roads and evidence were stacking up to convince him that Dalton was the real deal. Nothing that Hardcastle came across ever came close to nullify Dalton's claim.

One of the many fascinating and well documented stories Bud discovered through first-hand knowledge and letters is the story from Mitchell Clark Graves, another man who knew J. Frank Dalton well and who was another key player in the saga of Jesse James.

By the turn of the 21st century, Bud had already substantiated enough evidence to finally put the story of J. Frank Dalton and Jesse James to rest, but the big finale would be the exhumation of the body of J. Frank Dalton, comparing the DNA with known James' descendants on May 30, 2000. This event didn't bring this mystery to a final conclusion as hoped, but it brought great publicity around the world, drawing out more and more first-hand experiences with this old codger.

Mitch Graves would become the source that would put the nail in the coffin, allowing Jesse Woodson James to finally have eternal rest he deserved. Mitch's story only enhanced the probability that J. Frank Dalton was no doubt the real Jesse Woodson James.

Bud received a phone call from Mitch Graves shortly after the exhumation, one of many who contacted Hardcastle after the televised event in Granbury, Texas. Mitch had been intensely following the story as the story of Dalton and Jesse was very personal to Mitch.

On the call, Mitch introduced himself to Bud. He was calling all the way from Iron River, Alberta, Canada. Bud said, "Well Mitch, I know who you are, but I didn't think you would still be alive. "Bud knew Mitch's story from the Everhards and from letters provided to Bud that Mitch had wrote to Ola.

Mitch had a story alright and had a picture of that old man who called himself, Frank Dalton in Canada. It was the same man who claimed he was Jesse James in Lawton, Oklahoma in 1948 and whose picture was publicized near his time of death in Granbury in 1951.

Mitch told Bud the story of his life with Dalton. Mitch said, "Bud, you was more near right than anybody else regarding the truth about Jesse and Dalton. They were one in the same."

Mitch sent Bud a photo claiming it was Dalton by the cabin he had built in Canada. It was taken in 1924 in the area noted as Lea Park in Vermilion River County, Alberta Canada. The old cowboy standing with his horses and dog was a hard-working old man, who rarely stopped to rest from his daily chores. He had built this cabin in 1919 at the age of 72.

Mitch was born in 1913 in Ontario, Canada. He traveled with his parents to Alberta when he was only 3 months old. At the age of 20, in **1933**, he had moved from his old home and into another in the general vicinity of Lea Park. Before Christmas of that year, Mitch went back to his past home to pick up something, expecting to travel back to his new home for Christmas. It was 6 below, with blowing snow, making it difficult to travel. He stopped at one home to seek shelter, but they wouldn't let him in.

Mitch came upon another cabin with a soft amber glow coming from the window. He knocked on the door and an older man came to the door. Mitch asked if he could come in and get warm. The jolly old man replied, "Hell yes, come to the fire while I put your horse in the stable and put a blanket on 'em."

(Dalton by the cabin he built in Alberta, Canada, 1924)

The old man went by the name of Frank Dalton and he and Mitch became great friends. The old man told him, "If you ever gets to needing a job, well, come back and I'll put you to work." Within two months, Mitch began working for the man who went by the name of Frank Dalton. Mitch said he was a good man, good heart, and good soul.

Mitch witnessed Dalton treat horses extremely well. Dalton, at the time was raising and selling work horses for a living, as well as raising thoroughbred racehorses on another ranch nearby.

Many men came to visit Dalton and it seemed as though Dalton was well known and well loved. Dalton's charisma, sense of humor, uncanny wit, and laughter were contagious.

Mitch told Bud that Dalton and his buddies were excellent horsemen and marksmen. They would often have a shooting match. Dalton would have Mitch throw a tin can into the air, only to be shot all to pieces in a matter of seconds with two long-barreled pistols he carried in holsters underneath his long coat. Using the cross-arm draw technique, Dalton would fire his Frontier Model Smith and Wesson revolver and his Colt .45 continuously keeping the can in the air until all the bullets were dispensed.

Mitch told Bud that Dalton would enter Turkey Shoots. One time, he shot three turkeys. On the way home, Dalton would stop by three different houses and provide the family a turkey for supper, while he settled for pheasant for his own meal.

Mitch would catch phrases here and there from Dalton and his friends, leading to many questions. Mitch overheard one of the men call Dalton, "Jesse." Mitch thought that was odd, but clues began to add up.

When the subject of Jesse James came up one time at the breakfast table, Mitch started singing the "Ballad of Jesse James" by an unknown author which was first recorded by Bentley Ball in 1919 and Vernon Dalhart in 1925. The song portrayed Jesse as an American Robin Hood. The catchy phrase, "The dirty little coward, that shot Mr. Howard, has laid poor Jesse in his grave" was the most popular part of the song. As Mitch was singing the song, Dalton looked sternly at Mitch and said, "You young whipper-snapper, you don't know what you are singing about."

In 1935, Frank Dalton was summoned by Henry Huston Crittenden, son of former Governor Thomas Theodore Crittenden, to write an excerpt in the book that Henry was editing for his father, "The Crittenden Memoirs" published in 1936. It was a book relaying the story of Governor Crittenden's life and the events that occurred during his governorship of Missouri. His son, Henry wanted a special section of the book to touch upon the governor's effort to rid the state of the James Gang.

H.H. Crittenden knew the man who could relive and relay the fascinating stories on outlawry in Missouri. A man who experienced life with the James Gang. The man was Frank Dalton; the man Mitch was working for. How did Crittenden know this man, much less know where to find him? He knew right where he was. Crittenden sent money directly to Dalton in Canada to come to the States to write his story.

Dalton at the time was around 88 years of age. When Dalton learned of the request, he had his "most trusted" friend, Dewitt Travis travel from Gladewater, Texas all the way to Lea Park, Alberta, Canada to stay and manage Dalton's horses while he was away. Travis is mentioned in one of Dalton's letters to Crittenden as "Dr. Travis." Dalton and Travis had a mutual friend who also lived in Gladewater, Texas, in the 30's and 40's, Brushy Bill Roberts, none other than Billy the Kid.

Mitch remembers when Travis came to take over the management of Dalton's place while Dalton traveled to the States. Dalton introduced Mitch to Dewitt Travis as Bill Dalton, supposedly kin. The real Bill Dalton was killed in 1894 by U. S. Deputy Marshal Selden T. Lindsey after the Longview, Texas bank robbery.

Mitch was puzzled when he learned of the request from Crittenden. He didn't quite understand why Mr. Crittenden wanted the old man to write a story about Jesse James and his gang; the man who took him in during a blizzard one night, fed him, put him to work, treated him like a son, and studied the Bible with him nightly by a dimly-lit lantern. What did the kind, gentle old man know about Jesse James? Bill Dalton (Dewitt Travis) answered that young man's question with, "He should know about Jesse, cause that's who he is."

"A man has three names: the name he inherits, the name his parents give him, and the name he makes for himself."

-Abraham Lincoln

Chapter Three: What's in a Name?

"**Jesse Woodson James** (1847-1882) - was an American outlaw, bank and train robber, guerrilla, and leader of the James–Younger Gang. Raised in the "Little Dixie" area of western Missouri, James and his family maintained strong Southern sympathies. He and his brother Frank James joined pro-Confederate guerrillas known as "bushwhackers" operating in Missouri and Kansas during the American Civil War. As followers of William Quantrill and "Bloody Bill" Anderson, they were accused of committing atrocities against Union soldiers and civilian abolitionists, including the Centralia Massacre in 1864.
After the war, as members of various gangs of outlaws, Jesse and Frank robbed banks, stagecoaches, and trains across the Midwest, gaining national fame and often popular sympathy despite the brutality of their crimes. The James brothers were most active as members of their own gang from about 1866 until 1876, when as a result of their attempted robbery of a bank in Northfield, Minnesota, several members of the gang were captured or killed. They continued in crime for several years afterward, recruiting new members, but came under increasing pressure from law enforcement seeking to bring them to justice. On April 3, 1882, Jesse James was shot and killed by Robert Ford, a new recruit to the gang who hoped to collect a reward on James's head and a promised amnesty for his previous crimes. Already a celebrity in life, James became a legendary figure of the Wild West after his death". ("Jesse Woodson James" – Wikipedia)

The majority of this article is true, but not in its entirety. It is not the end of the story. Bud has proven to the writer beyond a shadow of a doubt, that Jesse lived beyond 1882. Many people who have seen the truth and thoroughly did their research, believe this side of the story. It's plain as day to this writer. We ask that you do your own research and keep an open mind, Bud reminds us.
Many say, "Why look into the past when the future is more important? Most of the younger generation do not even know who Jesse James was." Well, its certainly important to the last two generations alive today. We grew up with the tales and legends of Jesse James depicted as a cold-blooded killer on one hand and on the other hand, a modern day Robinhood. If you don't do your own research, and question things that do not make sense or gel together, then your beliefs are subject to what you are fed. We have all been duped and its time we all open our eyes and use the common sense God has given us. It's a lesson for us all, even for today, even for the future.
Does it make sense that Jesse, who was the most famous outlaw in American History, was shot down in his own home in St. Joseph, Missouri, with both of his guns laid down, when he was known to always have his side arms around his waist at all times, even when swimming in swimming holes? Does it make sense, that he was straightening a picture that was at arm's length above him, but he chose to stand up in a chair with his back to men with guns in their holsters? Does it make sense that his own mother claimed the dead man was not her son? Does it make sense that the coroner refused to sign a death certificate for Jesse? Does it make sense that the Ford Brothers were pardoned by Governor Crittenden shortly after they were sentenced to hang? Does it make sense that Frank James, or any of Jesse's closest friends did not seek to avenge his death as Ola would say? Does it make sense that when Frank James turned himself in, he had a quick trial and was acquitted after only 5 minutes of deliberation?
Anyone can find the story of Jesse's death in 1882. The story varies somewhat in books and movies, but the outcome is still the same; dead by the hand of Robert Ford in 1882, end of story.

What really happened? Ola and Aubrey Everhard, as well as many others who interviewed J. Frank Dalton, received a different story, but one that remained the same every time it was told; Jesse lived on.

Who really was Jesse? He went by many names and disguises to conceal his identity and self-preservation. This protection of one's self was his number one goal in life, at any cost. He told Ola and Aubrey Everhard that if he had told people who he was, before 1948, he would have been hung for treason. Many times, Jesse would dye his hair, wear a protruding instrument in his mouth to project a larger lower jaw, wear false beards or mustaches, and would wear false gold teeth.

The Everhards figured that Jesse had at least 38 aliases. The famous historian and author, Ralph Epperson, who had researched Jesse for over 45 years, states that Jesse had close to 73 aliases. The Lawton Constitution stated that Dalton lived under 72 aliases. The most noted name he used was J. Frank Dalton, J for Jesse, Frank for his brother, and Dalton for his mother's real maiden name. Sometimes Jesse would use the name of Frank Dalton in his writings and also John F. Dalton when he was applying for a Confederate pension. Bud has uncovered where he used the name of Tom Vaughn, John D. Howard, Jesse Howard, David Howard, and R.H. Howard.

Many men back in the West hid their past in new names that they adopted, even the famous Texas Ranger, George Washington Arrington. His real name was John Cromwell Orrick, Jr. The author and Orrick share the same ancestor in our Slade family. Orrick uncannily followed the same trail as J. Frank Dalton and I'm sure they were well acquainted.

Starting in this chapter, notice the **names** emphasized in the text with *italics*. They are clues Jesse has left us. If you "tune-in," you will see a pattern of localities, activities, numbers, and names that form an intricate network designed by hyperintelligent men, Jesse James included.

Orrick was a *spy* in an *elite guerrilla unit* for Colonel John Singleton Mosby, the "Gray Ghost" of *the Confederacy*. After the war, John went back to his home in Alabama, but after two years, became restless and joined up with seven men who rode down to *Mexico* to join the cause with *Emperor Maximilian*.

After Orrick returned home, he got into a squabble with a black businessman who had called Orrick a liar. Orrick wasn't about to take the insult, so he fired 3 shots into the man, killing him instantly. Orrick was on the run and ended up in *Central America*.

Orrick later returned to the States and took on the name of Arrington. He worked for the Houston and Texas Central *Railroad* in *Houston*. He was hired as a *drover* to take a herd of *cattle* up to *Brown County, Texas*. This was a hotspot for many *outlaws*, sympathizers of the *Confederacy*, and the *Masonic brotherhood*.

Arrington stayed *in Brown County* and enlisted in *Company E for the newly organized Frontier Battalion of the Texas Rangers*.

Early in 1874, the Texas legislature appropriated $300,000 for frontier defense. This authorized the Texas Rangers to develop a battalion of 450 volunteers. These were formed into 6 companies of 75 men each. These units were commanded by a captain and a first and second lieutenant. The companies were designated A, B, C, D, E, and F and received the official name of the Frontier Battalion of Texas Rangers. John B. Jones of Corsicana, Texas was commissioned major of the command. Jones was a *Mason* and achieved the position of Grand Master of the Grand Lodge of Austin by 1879.

The frontier would now be patrolled by men who were mostly ex-Confederates who were familiar with battle maneuvers, marksmanship, and highly skilled in the saddle. They would be fighting a different enemy who were led by leaders who knew savage warfare, the territory, and who were one with their pony. It would be a point in history that would turn the plains of Texas from a vast spread of wild grassland which sustained the buffalo and Indian, into a tamed populated sea of plowed earth.

In an article published in the Texas Ranger Dispatch Magazine, titled, "George W. Arrington," it is noted that there was confusion on when Arrington enlisted in the Frontier Battalion. Several of the records are missing as many of us researchers are familiar with, but a letter from Adjutant

General Henry Hutchins, dated June 4, 1917, pinpoints the date. Hutchins was writing to the commissioner of pensions in Washington D.C. and informed the commissioner that Arrington was on the muster rolls from August 31, 1874, to August 31, 1876, in Company E. Jesse James was in the same unit from June 6, 1874, to May 31, 1875 under the name of Benjamin Franklin Johnson. This B.F. Johnson was a freight driver for the Rangers. This has been verified by Bud and the writer at the Texas Ranger Research Center in Waco, Texas.

By 1877, Arrington's bravery during missions against the "hostiles' was impressive. He was assigned captain of Company C, stationed at *Coleman, Texas.*

Arrington was later assigned to handle vigilantes in Fort Griffin, Texas, outside of Albany. A vigilante group had been formed called "The Tin Hat-Brand Brigade, which gave the criminals "no slack' from the rope of justice. One of the members of this group, John Selman, who was crooked in his dealings with the leader of the vigilante committee, Sheriff John Larn, had both been cattle rustling themselves and were making a huge profit on inspections and selling meat to the government for the soldiers and Indians at Fort Griffin. Selman was caught in 1880, but escaped to *Chihuahua, Mexico* until 1888. The charges were dropped. He moved to El Paso and became a city constable. Selman was the man who killed the famous gunman John Wesley Hardin in a saloon in El Paso.

George W. Arrington later moved into the Texas Panhandle and continued his *law enforcement* career in several communities. He reached a *high degree in the Mason Organization*. He gained a nice size *ranch* outside of Canadian, Texas and this is where he retired.

An interesting note: the last scene in Tom Hank's movie, "Cast Away" was filmed at the Arrington Ranch on the flat plains of the *Texas Panhandle.*

There are many signs of Jesse in the Texas Panhandle, as well as Jesse's brother, Frank, Billy the Kid, and Pat Garrett during those wild days of the west where a name was not always disclosed. They left their boot print in Tascosa and possibly treasure under Saddle Mountain just south of the Canadian River just a short distance from there. Tascosa was where we find the frontier doc, Henry F. Hoyt who had met Billy the Kid there in 1878.

As we explore further into Jesse's life, remember Arrington's story and the similarities between the two. We hear stories of Confederate soldiers who fled to Texas as well as Indian Territory and Mexico during the Reconstruction period after the Civil War. There was indeed a comradery amongst them which spread and infiltrated into the wide-open prairies. The bond between these men could not be broken as well as the men themselves. Jesse was the glue that held these men together. Their duty was not to serve themselves, but others in their brotherhood. They would protect and defend one another until their death.

Focusing back on Jesse during and after the Civil War, he too took on many names and many looks. In the book, "Jesse James was One of His Names," by Del Schrader, the author gathered many stories from Orvus Lee Howk, who claimed to be Jesse James' grandson. Howk was a man who took care of Jesse during his last few years on earth and clung to Jesse, his stories, and his possessions. Howk revealed that J. Frank Dalton was the real Jesse James and had used 72 aliases. Howk changed his own name after Jesse died in 1951 to Jesse "Lee" James III. The book was published in 1975.[8]

In another book that Howk wrote himself, written in 1961, "Jesse James and the Lost Cause", by Jesse Lee James (Howk), said Jesse was quoted as saying, "In those days there wasn't one cowboy in one thousand that used his own name."[9]

In "Jesse James and the Lost Cause," Howk stated that he tried to use Jesse's statements word for word, but he said he used his diaries also. All the scrapbooks, photos, diaries, guns, and mementos fell into Howk's lap after Jesse died. Some of the stories told by Howk do not make any sense. Some are completely changed from the stories and the people who were directly involved with Jesse. Bud has the proof.

Bud Hardcastle has thoroughly examined these books, and states there are many truths in which he validated and appear legitimate though. He believes that Del Schrader did an excellent job on his book with the material he had, and it took great effort to compile the stories of Jesse in one book. He must have had a tremendous amount of valid and verified resources to write a book on Jesse Woodson James, placing his own name on the line.

Bud said toward the end of the book project, Howk and Schrader had a falling-out because of Howk wanting more money, but Bud stated that Schrader finished the book on what he had learned and had enough evidence to support what was written.

The first-hand stories Bud said, from Howk's own words, may have complicated some very simple nuggets of truth. Some of the stories told by Howk were extravagant fallacies and exaggerations. It may have all been a part of Howk's plan to fit his own narrative or Jesse's grand scheme to lead people away from the truth, especially when it comes to his family.

Caution needs to be used. Researchers have relied upon Howk's books for information on Jesse, believing it to be the gospel truth. So, let's not be so quick on the trigger to believe everything Howk wanted us to believe. It is quite easy to be passive and depend on others to do the work and research for us, but when you put forth an effort, do your own research, seeing for yourself the truth of the matter, it becomes quite clear. Bud had to sift through the information and go down many rabbit holes to find the answers. He wanted the truth. So, do we, but we have to work for it.

Bud believed in hard work. I just can't imagine what Bud has gone through to decipher what is truth and what is fiction in Howk's books. I know it frustrated him, because some of the stories are so outlandish and confusing, setting you on a wrong path and even with myself as a writer and researcher with today's technology, it frustrates the fool out of me. Here Howk had a perfect opportunity to tell the true story in its entirety, but he has skewed and twisted the truth so that we may never know for positive what the truth really is. We will just go with what Bud has investigated and found to be true. He was up for the task. The rest, our answer will have to be, "We don't know," and the reader can make their own conclusion.

In Bud's investigations, he became great friends with Betty Lou Kilgore, Aubrey Everhard, and Mrs. Rudy Turilli (Francena), those who knew Howk personally.

Lou Kilgore – A sweetheart of a lady who has firsthand knowledge of Jesse and Frank in Arkansas. All her life she had heard the story that her grandfather had told her around the old wood stove. It was a story about his neighbor in Newton County, Arkansas. The neighbor was Joe Vaughn who later claimed to be Frank James on his death bed. Lou's sister-in-law was Joe Vaughn's 3rd great granddaughter.

Lou met Howk through her boyfriend, Jake Wilson who were engaged, living in Rye, Texas. Jake owned and operated Trinity River Sand and Gravel Company. Both Howk and Jake took care of Dalton in the 40's and 50's. Lou has researched high and low, not only in documental proof of Jesse and Frank, but also in the very trails and hideouts where Jesse stashed his cache. She had numerous letters and maps from Howk and corresponded frequently with him.

Howk came to Lou's home in Jasper, Arkansas. She said, "He seemed alright, but he was supposed to be in prison when he was out "running around."

Lou stated that, "Little of Howk's info is right and there is very much wrong. A lot of the things Howk wrote about Jesse's family was not right, with the intention of throwing readers off the track.

Lou didn't think Howk took care of Dalton. Howk was financially in trouble. Dalton had his own money and that is why Howk took care of him. No doubt that Howk was using Dalton. "Oh, he was, no doubt," Lou said. Lou was very adamant that Howk had no family connection to Jesse.

Lou delved into Howk's ancestry with the help of LDS and many other sources. Her findings show clearly Howk's true ancestry: Orvus Lee Howk was born April 27, 1905, in St. Louis, Missouri to Arthur Lee Howk and Charlotte A. "Lottie" Baxter.

Howk's mother had complications in childbirth and died 17 days after the birth of her son. His father died when he was 10 years old and was then raised by his grandfather, David Baxter.

Bud received a newspaper article, written sometime in 1948, published in the area of Meramec Caverns near Stanton and Sullivan, Missouri, relaying the news from the Lawton Constitution on Jesse coming out in Oklahoma. It states, "Lately, Dalton has been living at *Centerville*, Texas with

Lee Howk, who claims to be a **grandson** of a James' "henchman" named **Baxter."**[10] The definition in the Merriam-Webster Dictionary is "a trusted follower; a right-hand man; a political follower whose support is chiefly for personal advantage." Another definition describes, "a trusted follower or supporter who performs unpleasant, wrong, or illegal tasks for a powerful person (such as a politician or criminal)."[11]

Per David Baxter's death certificate, he came from England and was a cabinet maker in St. Louis, Missouri, born in 1834.[12] Earlier records indicate that Baxter lived in Michigan. He was drafted into the Union forces in Camden, Michigan in the 15th Infantry, 1864 during the Civil War. He later moved to Illinois before moving to Missouri around 1885. He, nor Orvus Lee Howk have no blood connection to Jesse.

Could David Baxter be the man whose name was carved on the brass bucket along with Jesse James? The name inscribed was Roy Baxter. We will discuss this further in another chapter.

Lou has proven to Bud and the writer that her knowledge is extensive and accurate. Lou has gone deeply into the whole picture of Jesse's life, the Knights of the Golden Circle, and many hidden facts that would change history forever. She has been a tremendous help to Bud and his search. The writer has been extremely fortunate to get to speak with her.

Howk became acquainted with Dalton/Jesse possibly in the late 30's, early 40's. One article in a journal, "The American Barbed Wire" written June 1975, Howk told the reporter that "he cared for the old man during the last 18 years of his life."[13] From other evidence that Bud has gathered from letters Howk wrote, it appears that they possibly met in the oil business in Texas.

Before that in 1932, Howk was living in Jacksonville, Illinois and working for American Bankers Insurance Company. (The Jacksonville Daily Journal, May 1, 1932).[14] In **1933**, Jesse began selling oil leases in Gladewater and Howk was involved he said as "working and curing titles before drilling" per a letter written by Howk in Bud's personal collection. In the 1940 census in Tyler, Texas, Howk is listed as a life insurance agent. On his draft card for World War II, he was an agent for Illinois Bankers Life Insurance in Tyler, Texas. By 1950, he was shown living in Great Falls, Montana as a Land Oil Line Dealer with his wife, Nadine and daughter, Sidney.[15]

Jesse referred to him as "Old Hawk" in his letters. Howk saw an opportunity to gain knowledge about Jesse, his treasure, and many hidden secrets that Jesse kept buried deep within himself. Howk thought he had gained trust from Jesse by providing him shelter, food, medical care, transportation, photos for Jesse's calling card, and an avenue and encouragement to tell his story. But Jesse was no fool. He knew what Howk's intentions were and he played along, using Howk for his own benefit and transportation. Jesse was cunning. Nothing could get passed Jesse.

Howk was asked by Jesse to take him to treasure sights. There were places that Jesse did not allow Howk to go. Jesse was not digging up any treasure at that time, but just like at Eddie's homestead, Jesse was checking to ensure the treasure was undisturbed. It wasn't about money for Jesse. His true passion, his mission in life, was to further the cause for the South. The money, the gold was for the South to rise again. He never let go of that effort.

Jesse did appease Howk with clues and many stories; some true, some fabricated. Jesse was extremely intelligent and was very guarded on much of the information that he was still preserving for the KGC and the South, even after 80 years since the war. Jesse, in very detailed form, gave Howk instructions to draw out some of the treasure maps indicating the value of the treasure, the booby traps, and various clues to reach it. Jesse never did give specific details of the exact location. Bud has obtained many of these maps and he has successfully located several treasure troves which match the maps exactly. The maps appear authentic.

But we do have one thing to thank Howk for. He is the one who opened the pages of the deep, dark, mysterious book of The Knights of the Golden Circle, the KGC to the public. Many who read Howk/Schrader's book could not completely comprehend the complex intricate system of the underworld that Jesse was involved in. The unknown was a bit scary and people were just not ready to hear about it. The KGC stories died off with not much interest to pursue. Bud used the bits and pieces of the information and put life back into the subject of the KGC. "I revived it," Bud said. He gave it credibility with evidence, structure, and reasoning, all for the South to rise again.

At the end, Jesse wanted the truth to be told. This is what Ola and Aubrey Everhard heard directly from Jesse's mouth.

Ola and Aubrey Everhard- The first time Ola and Aubrey met J. Frank Dalton (Jesse) and Howk was in *Centerville,* Texas in 1948, before Dalton told the world who he was. Ola had read in the Austin newspaper where they were living, that Frank Dalton was in the Dallas hospital and had turned 100 years old. Ola was following some of Dalton's articles in the newspaper as early as 1939 and became very interested in the old man. She was curious to know if this is the same man her mother, Bertha knew and claimed kinship with.

Dalton's newspaper articles were stories of being the last of the Quantrill Raiders. Another interesting article popped up in 1947 stating the 100-year-old man was finally awarded a Confederate pension. Ola and Bertha had been keeping up with him. Bertha was living with Ola and Aubrey at the time. They felt very sure this was the kinfolk that her Dad always talked about and who always came to their farmhouse in Indian Territory. Bertha knew his true identity.

Ola's mother was Bertha Underwood (1883-1973), daughter of James Anderson Underwood (1855-1931) and Savannah Elizabeth O'Daniel. On the ancestry website, it shows and clarifies that James' middle name was actually "Alexander," but Ola signed her mother's death certificate, showing her father's name as James <u>Anderson</u> Underwood. In the videos, Ola was very adamant that this was his name.

As a young girl, Bertha had seen Jesse when her family lived in Indian Territory. Jesse would come by often and visit. Underwood told his daughter, Bertha that this man was kinfolk, but to keep her mouth shut on what she sees and hears. Growing up in the "wilds" of Indian Territory, Bertha's memories of the handsome, well dressed Deputy U.S. Marshal never left her mind or her curiosity.

Yes, as Dalton's calling card suggests, he was a peace officer both in the Texas Rangers and as a Deputy U.S. Marshal. He had many roles. This man was very impressionable to young Bertha. He wore a large five-point star badge on his hat and roamed the countryside, protecting the innocent and controlling the crime, one way or another. His hat resembled Bloody Bill Anderson's hat worn during the Civil War. He was a Deputy U.S. Marshal in and around Ardmore, Oklahoma from 1894 – 1896, assigned to what was then, the Chickasaw Nation, White Bead, *Woodford*, Fort Arbuckle and the surrounding area. He was using the name, Frank Dalton.

After the Everhards found out Dalton was moved out of the hospital and into the Sullivan Hotel in *Centerville,* they went there to see him. *Centerville* is a very small community, southeast of Waco. Howk was caring for him at that time and said Jesse had lived there in Centerville since 1944. When Ola and Aubrey entered the room, Ola explained to Dalton whose daughter/granddaughter she was. He lightened up and said, "Is that a fact, I knew them all, I knew them well."

In Jesse's final years on this earth, he chose to stay with the Everhards multiple times, especially when he became quite ill and unable to care for himself. Jesse's hip had been broken and wouldn't mend. He was paralyzed in his right arm, and also going blind due to a continuous and persistent eye condition known as conjunctivitis.

Howk became very jealous of Ola's and JJ's relationship and the care given to him. He despised Ola and threatened to kill her several times. Ola, even though crippled at birth gave her entire life, energy, and passion in trying to preserve Jesse's life and his story. Howk would continuously speak ill against Ola, using her handicaps against her and spoke of her as, "Crooked body, crooked mind."

There were times Howk showed up out of nowhere and took the old man away from their home or from the hospital straight out of bed with guns drawn.

When Bud asked Aubrey what he thought of Howk, Aubrey stated, "Well, I wouldn't want to say publicly, it wouldn't be very nice in church what I'd say about him. He was a con man, crook, scoundrel, and a deadbeat. He always married nurses. He married four nurses that I know of, to make a living for him, to take care of him. He was no good. Jesse said the same thing. Jesse got so mad at Howk one time while he was in the hospital and wanted Ola to slip him a gun to kill Howk." Needless to say, Ola wouldn't have any part of that.

Both Ola and Aubrey stated that Howk used a nickname of "Hawk.," given to him by Jesse. The Everhards said, "He's no hawk, he's a buzzard feeding on the James legend." In a newspaper article from the Granbury Tablet, April 26, 1984, Ola Everhard was quoted as saying "My cousin Jesse told me he was so old and hard up that he had to let it happen."[16] This phrase meant that he had to allow Howk to exploit him in a way so that Jesse could even some scores or in other words, use him to achieve Jesse's own goals. This was quite confusing and there is a mention of Jesse and Howk having a contract together. Jesse was always good at his word and apparently fulfilled his portion of the contract to the man that required so much from Jesse.

Ola specifically asked Jesse if Howk was any kin and he said very sternly, "Hell no, never was and never will be!"

As we continue looking for the true character of Jesse, the writer feels that Ola and Aubrey knew him best, the real Jesse. This is why Bud has leaned so heavily upon following Ola and Aubrey's course. The thing that made the writer feel more confident in the Everhard's story is what they had to back up with what they were saying, but most especially what Bud has found to give it all credibility.

What really impressed me as a writer is in the video that Bud's cousin, Kenny Brown filmed in 1990 at Aubrey Everhard's house. There are many questions posed here on the life of the true Jesse James and J. Frank Dalton, but just like Aubrey Everhard told Bud Hardcastle, we want the truth to be told. Aubrey said, "If I don't know, I'll say I don't know. If you don't know it, don't put it down. That way, you don't have to coverup or stammer around and make excuses." Aubrey with such fondness in his eyes, said, "That's what Ola Mae did," pointing to her very well-worn typewriter. "If she didn't know it, she would say she didn't' know it. She was very strong to get the truth out, you know."

Bud's response, "I wasn't going to say a thing in here unless I can prove it. Nobody can argue with the documented truth."

The truth was important to the Everhards, but they firmly believed everything Jesse and Ola's mother had told them. They too researched on their own to verify the things Jesse was saying and Ola would not have written it down, had it not been true.

The Everhards were not the only ones that got to know Jesse well and there are many stories and versions to tell. He was widely known all across America and into Europe, maybe not always known by his real name. We must continue to examine and filter out the fiction that has been used for multiple purposes. This is the reasoning behind the people introduced in this chapter.

Three others have documented their dealings with Howk, not to be crude, but to shed some light on who Howk was, straining the truth from the impurities, so that the information on Jesse can be accurate, as accurate as can be.

Francena Turilli – This fine lady was the wife of Rudi Turilli, who owned and operated Merrimac Caverns. Jesse stayed there a good part of 1949-1950. Bud went to meet with Francena and on tape she stated that "Howk was a fraud." He took $1,500-$12,000 from several people to contribute in his effort to find Jesse's gold. Howk claimed that he knew where the treasure was, but he needed money for expenses to find it. Howk left them cold. He didn't follow through with his promises. Howk took the money and went to another state to continue his money schemes. The Turilli's had to ask Howk to leave Merrimac Caverns on the day of Jesse's 102nd birthday party. (See Appendix A-19)

Elsie Nadine Thompson (Nadine Mueller) – Nadine married Orvus Lee Howk in 1945 when she was 25 years old in Huntsville, Texas. She was a nurse from Bozeman, Montana. Howk had been married numerous times, with the last one in 1942, Mildred Talbot in Townsend, Montana. Nadine was with Howk when they took Jesse to Lawton in 1948 to reveal who he was. She wrote a letter to Bud to clarify that Orvus never stated he was Jesse James' son. (See Appendix A-20)

In the Great Falls Tribune, June 9, 1950, the paper speaks that Nadine was granted a divorce from Howk and had alleged "extreme cruelty and said her husband insulted her, falsely accused her of unseemly conduct, once struck her and failed and refused to take regular employment and provide for his family."[17]

Al Jennings – Famous outlaw in Indian Territory. He wrote to Ola Everhard, "Old Howk was worse than any damn pickpocket I ever knew while I was in the pen."[18]

William V. Morrison – This man was a descendant of Lucien Bonaparte Maxwell's family, a famous figure in New Mexico's history, which involved the Maxwell Land Grant. Morrison is well known by his extensive research into a man named William H. "Brushy Bill" Roberts. He followed a lead from a court case involving an old outlaw by the name of Jesse Evans who stated Brushy Bill was Billy the Kid.

After extensive research and locating Brushy, Morrison still had to break down the barriers that Brushy refused to move. Brushy did not at first want to admit he was Billy the Kid, for fear of retaliation. Brushy finally opened up to Morrison when he was promised that Morrison would do everything in his power to secure a pardon that was promised many decades ago from the governor of New Mexico.

Morrison and Brushy Bill had encountered Howk through Dalton, who had also declared Brushy Bill as Billy the Kid. In Daniel A. Edwards' Book, "Billy the Kid: An Autobiography," he reveals that Morrison and Brushy believed that Howk was a "charlatan and fraud."[19] Howk tried his best to have Brushy leave Morrison behind so that Howk could be the one to write Brushy's story. Howk could see only dollar signs; Morrison and Billy could see the deceit and greed. This in turn damaged the reputation and credibility of J. Frank Dalton because of his association with Howk.

Sadly, toward the end of Jesse's final days on earth, Howk again exploited the man. He put up posters and signs around the place where Jesse lay in bed dying. "Come and see Jesse James," Howk was charging a fee for those who wanted to enter and see Jesse for themselves. Howk was able to manipulate the dire situation to his advantage, taking every last breath and every ounce of dignity from Jesse.

After Jesse's death, Howk continued using Jesse to his benefit in money making schemes and taking on his name. Bud had a letter that Howk wrote to Mrs. Clovis Herring on August 24, 1982. Howk wrote, "It was real amusing, at the antics of experts, the controversy raged over Grandpa (Jesse), but when properly understood a controversy is good, a controversy brings forth greater interest and therefore makes money for us."[20]

The newspapers claimed that Howk died in 1984, but Bud says he can prove Howk faked his death. He was on the run. The law was after him. One of Howk's sons, who wholeheartedly believed Howk's story of kinship with Jesse, told Bud himself in Granbury in 2000, "I have yet to be at my father's funeral."

Lou Kilgore herself stated that she had taken Howk to the Houston airport. He was on the run, guilty of mail fraud. He pulled a "Jesse." Never was seen again, until...

Bud had a picture of Howk at a Waco dig in 1992. Lou, who knew Howk personally identified Howk in that picture, as well as John Tatum who could identify him. Bud, Lou, Charlie Holman, John Tatum, and Jake Wilson went down to Waco during the dig, but it looked like they had abandoned the dig. The place was near Black Cemetery. Keep this in mind. A pattern that Bud found is that Jesse hid a lot of his caches near or in a cemetery.

In the cemetery, there were Masonic symbols and evidence of clues pointing to the Knights of the Golden Circle. There were women's tombstones with Masonic symbols and some tombstones turned the wrong way, not toward the east, but to the west.

Strangely, there were three railroad tank cars sunk in the spot where they were digging. Per Lou, the sons of Howk and foreign officials, not sure why they were involved, were digging up a 12-ton safe that contained gold and valuable documents that Jesse threw off the bridge over into the

Brazos River, now swallowed up by mud. It was too costly to continue the search and as far as we know, nothing had been found.

Again, Jesse left another gold digger empty handed.

Name-Dropping:

Names are what reputations are hung on. "Walk with the wise and become wise, for a companion of fools suffers harm." Proverbs 13:20

With Ola and Aubrey at the top of the list, Bud also hit the research hard on others who were in direct contact with J. Frank Dalton and Jesse James. These are the men and women who will be introduced throughout this book who were associated with this remarkable man. Their story sheds light on Jesse's untold story. They each had an important part in his life's long journey.

His War Buddies:

Frank James – Older brother of Jesse James.
William Clarke Quantrill- the man who led the Confederate Guerillas – Quantrill Raiders during the Civil War. Note: Most of Jesse's writings referred to the spelling, "Quantrill," but there are some instances he wrote, or the writer for him wrote it out as "Quantrell." Either way, we definitely know who he is talking about.
"J. H. "Wild Henry" Roberts -Brushy Bill Roberts' father who was in Quantrill Raiders.
William T. "Bloody Bill" Anderson – A fierce and deadly leader in the Confederate Guerillas. Young Jesse James was placed under his command at age 15.
Jim Anderson – Bloody Bill's brother.
Cole Younger – Was part of Quantrill's Raiders and involved in the James/Younger Gang.
John Younger- Cole Younger's youngest brother who was supposedly killed by the Pinkerton's Detective Agency. He was in the James/Younger Gang.
General Joseph O. "Jo" Shelby – Was a Brigadier General in the Confederate Army.
General Sterling Price – He was involved the Mexican-American War, served as governor of Missouri, and became a general in the Confederate Army.
Sol "Red Fox" Strickland – He was a scout for Quantrill Raiders.
Colonel James R Davis – He was a Civil War Veteran, rode with Quantrill and in Jesse's gang.
John Trammel – cook for Jesse James and his gang.
Elbert Dewitt Travis – In the Confederate 3rd Battalion, Mississippi Cavalry Reserves. He was Dewitt Travis' father.
John (Henry) Underwood – Ola Everhard's great grandfather who fought with Quantrill Raiders.
Allen Parmer – Was in Quantrill's Raiders, husband of Susan James, sister of Jesse and Frank.
Sheriff Lee McMurtry – Rode with Quantrill's Raiders, Sheriff in Wichita County, Texas.
John Bud Shirley – Belle Starr's (Myra Marybelle Shirley) twin brother who was killed in the Civil War.
Jim Reed – Myra Marybelle Shirley's first husband – part of James' Gang.
Isaac Markham – Private in the Confederate 8th Infantry in Louisiana – Great grandfather of John Thomas Tatum.
William Mayfield James – Enlisted in the Confederacy in 1861 and served as captain in Henderson's Company C, 3rd Arkansas cavalry. He fought in Missouri, Arkansas and Mississippi, then served under General Bedford Forrest at Columbia, Tennessee. Fought in Dalton, Georgia where they fought Sherman on his march to the sea. He was the great grandfather of John Thomas Tatum.
Jacob Colston James (1852-1916) –His daughter, Rachel James who married Emmett Tatum, were parents of John Thomas Tatum. Rachel's father, Jacob ran away from home to be with his father during the war. He was only 12-13. He was too young, so he was put in charge of feeding and

watering the horses. When Jacob grew into manhood, he was always gone for weeks at a time and no one knew where he was. He was suspected of being involved with Jesse James.
Sam Collins – A man that supposedly was the double for Frank James.
Albert Pike – One of the top leaders of Freemasonry and the Knights of the Golden Circle.
Major John Edwards – He was a part of Shelby's Iron Brigade in the Civil War – A newspaperman who placed Jesse in the spotlight as a Robinhood-type character.
Sheriff Jim Timberlake – He served in the Confederate Army of Missouri in the cavalry division. He became 2nd lieutenant under Shelby. He traveled to Mexico after the war with General Shelby to support Maximilian. He married Bloody Bill Anderson's 2nd cousin, Katie Thomason, granddaughter of Wild Bill Thomason. He became a lawman in Missouri and was credited by Governor Thomas T. Crittenden as being responsible for the breakup of Jesse's gang.
Ben Davis – Probably an alias but was one of Jesse's closest friends in Canada per Mitch Graves. Bud believes he was another one of Quantrill's men.

Gang members

Arthur McCoy – Man who went west to California during the gold rush with Jesse's father and later rode with the James Gang.
Lucky Johnson – Black man who took care of the horses and a horse trainer. He was with Jesse in Guthrie, Ok.
Charlie Ford and Bob Ford – In 1882, the two brothers joined Jesse's gang and were in the house in St. Joseph, Missouri when Jesse was supposedly shot by Bob.

Relatives:

Bertha Maddox – 2nd cousin to Jesse.
Ola Everhard – 3rd cousin to Jesse.
Joseph Jesse "Tazmawaste" Chase – Son of Jesse James with a Santee Sioux Indian woman, Margaret "Maggie" Hanyatusnawin Wabashaw.
Grace Hopkins – Joseph Jesse Chase's great granddaughter,
William M. "Wild Bill" Thomason - who was a step uncle of Jesse and Frank James. Wild Bill is documented as teaching Frank and Jesse James to shoot and ride like an Indian. He was the grandfather of Bloody Bill Anderson.
Dr. Frank James – A cousin of Jesse who was at Jesse's beckon call when the need of doctoring came up. Supposedly rode with Jesse and his gang.
Eddie James –Son of Dr. Frank James who actually saw Jesse and became good friends with Bud,
Jesse Cole James – Son of Jesse, rode in his gang.
Burleigh Dale James (1934-2005) – **Jesse Quanah "Tubby" James (1923-2005)**- **Charles A. "Shorty" James** (1939-2022) – grandsons of Jesse. Descends from **Jesse Cole James** (1882-1964), son of Jesse and Emma Anders who was 20 years younger than Jesse.
Vincel Simmons – Vincel believes his grandfather was J. Frank Dalton who was Jesse James. Vincel reached out to Bud and was interested in meeting Joe Wood who had spent 18 months with Dalton. Bud arranged the meeting in Missouri and later Vincel met with Bud at his home in Purcell.
Mary Plina Norris, husband Charles Norris, and son, Henry Norris. Mary is believed to be the only daughter of Frank James. Ola Everhard and Jesse's grandsons, Dale, Charles, and Jesse Quanah James believed this and had letters from her while Jesse was staying with Ola. Mary was at Jesse's 102nd birthday party.
Belle Starr – married to Jesse for 3 weeks and the marriage ended because of infidelity. There may be another story here.
Joe Vaughn – On his death bed and in a book that he had written, claimed he was the real Frank James. Both Dalton and John Trammell visited at Joe's house often.

Friends who knew Jesse:

Dewitt Travis – One of the closest friends Jesse had whom he could trust. Lived in Gladewater and Longview, Texas.

Arlo Norman – He was the nephew of Dewit Travis. He was at Dalton's funeral in Granbury and said the casket was open and it was indeed Jesse.

Buffalo Bill Cody – a longtime friend of Jesse James. He was a rider for the Pony Express, served in the Union Army, a civilian scout for the U.S. Army during the Indian Wars, and an entertainer, performing shows depicting the Wild West. Jesse was supposedly in Buffalo Bill's shows periodically as a horseman and sharpshooter.

Robert E. Lee – A bodyguard for Buffalo Bill Cody. He was there when Jesse came to see Buffalo Bill at the Chicago's World's Fair in 1893.

Ozark Jack Berlin – Born in 1867, and as a young boy of 14, met Frank and Jesse James in the Ozark Mountains of Missouri. He became a close friend of Jesse James. Jesse would refer to him as Pres. Webb. (Preston Webb)

Orvus Lee Howk – A man who teamed up with Jesse in the last decade or two of his life, promoting and encouraging Jesse to come out with his real identity. After Jesse died, Howk claimed to be Jesse's grandson, Jesse "Lee" James III.

Jake Wilson – he was a man who took Jesse into his home and cared for him with Howk.

Mitch Graves – he was a young boy who encountered Jesse at his cabin in Canada. Mitch ended up working for him, without knowing his true identity. Later he learned who he was. Ola Everhard corresponded with him and he reached out to Bud in his final year of life.

Garland Farmer – Publisher of the Henderson Times in Henderson, Texas. He published several stories that Jesse wrote, or stories told to Farmer.

Calamity Jane (Martha Jane Canary) – Good Friend of Jesse's. She was a frontierswoman, sharpshooter, and close to Wild Bill Hickok. She appeared in Buffalo Bill's Wild West shows. She knew Jesse before 1882, and after, when he went by the name of Dalton.

Joe Wood – He was an exceptional writer, investigator, photographer for the St. Louis Globe-Democrat newspaper. He met J. Frank Dalton at Meramec Caverns and did not think he was the real Jesse James. Joe investigated every inch of Dalton and gathered all the facts, including meeting those who knew him. He changed his mind about the old man. He truly believed Dalton was the authentic Jesse James. He became a great friend of Jesse's and Bud Hardcastle's.

Lester Dill - He was the owner and operator of Meramec caverns near Stanton, Missouri and invited J. Frank Dalton to stay at the caverns.

Rudy Turilli – He was the son-in-law of Lester Dill. He became great friends of Dalton and poured out his time and money to prove who Dalton really was.

Francena Turilli – Wife of Rudy Turilli and daughter of Lester Dill. She at first did not believe Dalton was Jesse, but later changed her mind. Bud was able to interview her.

Frank Hall & Lindsay Whitten – Newspaper reporters and Investigators who broke the story, "Jesse James is Alive" in the Lawton Constitution Newspaper in 1948.

Cowboy Williams – A man who met Dalton in Longview and was able to spend time with him before he came out with who he really was. Bud was able to interview him.

Al Jennings - was an attorney in Indian Territory and after his brother Ed was killed and his brother John was wounded by Temple Houston, he turned to outlawry, robbing banks, and trains. He knew Jesse well.

Emmett Tatum Sr. – John Tatum's father who helped Jesse rebury treasure.

John Tatum – A man who became a good friend to Bud. They hit it off quickly, both wanting to seek the truth. Claimed he was related to Jesse who stayed in his home when he was 14 years old.

Joseph "Joe" Wilson – John Tatum's father-in-law who helped Jesse rebury treasure. Joseph's grandfather, John McHenry Wilson was a Confederate Patriot; was a 1st Sgt. In Company D of the Neshoba Rifles, 11th Mississippi Infantry, Captain of the Neshoba Ranger, 1st Sgt. Of Company D, 26th Mississippi Infantry, and 2nd Lt. Company G, 40th Mississippi Infantry.

Charles Coleman Ford (1883-1950)– Man who owned the "Last Chance" Grocery Store in Longview, Texas. Became good friends with Jesse and allowed him to live in his trailer. His grandfather, Norman M. Ford was in Company C, 21st Georgia CSA.

George Kenneth Ford (1921-1998) – Son of Charles Coleman Ford who had wondered who the old man was who stayed around his father's store and lived in the trailer beside the store. It was Jesse in the 40's.

Red Lucas – He was a Deputy U.S. Marshal in Indian Territory and took a gun off of Jesse in 1902 at Fort Gibson. Lucas also remembered Jesse back in 1870 in Madrid, Missouri, robbing a train. He knew both the outlaw Jesse James and J. Frank Dalton, one in the same and identified him as such.

Dr. James Sanford Preston -He treated Jesse James for eye issues which was a constant problem all his life.

Acquaintances:

John Shevlin – Was chief detective in Hot Springs, Arkansas and became an attorney. He brushed the shoulders of Frank and Jesse James and identified J. Frank Dalton as Jesse James in 1948 at Lawton, Oklahoma.

Pilot Ralph Swaby – He flew J. Frank Dalton from Lawton to Pueblo, Colorado in 1948 after the big reveal. He reached out to Bud.

Eddie Schneberger – Jesse came to his house in the 40's to look around on his property. Eddie reached out to Bud.

Researchers/Historians:

Lou Kilgore- An avid researcher of Jesse and Frank James, knew two of the men who took care of Jesse; Howk and Jake Wilson. Lou's grandfather was a neighbor to Joe Vaughn who claimed to be the real Frank James. Bud and Lou became good friends and traveled often together to investigate new leads on Jesse.

Dr. William Tunstill – He was a teacher and an administrator for the Fort Worth School District. He was a great historian and researcher. His passion was to find the truth regarding Billy the Kid. He spent 6 years with Ola Everhard to gather enough information and documents to prove that Brushy Bill Roberts was Billy the Kid and his connection to Jesse James, alias J. Frank Dalton. He was the author of "Billy the Kid and Me Were the Same." William and Bud became great friends.

Dr. Jannay Parkins Valdez – He had a PhD in education, was a teacher, coach, and principal and author of many books, including "Billy The Kid "Killed" in New Mexico – Died in Texas." He was a member of the Sons of Confederate Veterans.

Judge Bob Hefner – Newspaperman, Justice of the Peace of Hico, Texas. He co-wrote the book on Billy the Kid with Dr. Valdez. He has authored other books. Hefner founded the Billy The Kid museum in Hico. Both Hefner and Valdez were big supporters of Bud and his pursuit of Jesse.

Ralph Epperson – A famous historian, researcher, author and lecturer who also supported Bud.

Daniel A. Edwards – Author of *Billy the Kid: An Autobiography*. He has done extensive research on Brushy Bill Roberts who claimed to be Billy the Kid. He has been featured on nationally syndicated radio programs, podcasts, and tv programs.

Steve Wilson – Steve was born and raised in southwestern Oklahoma near the Wichita Mountains. His interest and thirst for the history and the mining ruins in Oklahoma and Texas has never been fully quenched. He has written many articles and books, such as *Oklahoma Treasures & Tales* in 1976 which blew open the doors to not only the hidden history of the plains, but the secrets of Jesse James. Bud knows him well and believes very deeply that Steve is an expert on the subject. They knew a lot of the same stories, history, but most of all the same people who helped in their search for the truth.

Treasure Hunters:

Tommy Hays, Terry Hickman, Glenn Magill – Were treasure hunters whose interest was in the Superstition Mountains.

Charlie (Leprechaun) Holman – He was Bud's right-hand man. Charlie was the man who introduced Bud to Jesse's grandsons and helped him in numerous treasure hunting expeditions.

Wells Blevins – He lived at Medicine Park near Lawton, Oklahoma. He came from North Carolina and inherited some of the maps of Jesse's. The source is not known. Bud contacted Wells and had the maps in hand. Bud met often with Wells and went on numerous treasure hunts together. Wells knew Joe Hunter.

Joe Hunter – Was a police officer in Rush Springs, Oklahoma when an old stranger came to visit and had maps to give him to locate buried treasure of Jesse's. In 1937, Joe found a tea kettle at Buzzard's Roost that contained a small fortune and went on to find the brass bucket, signed by several men of the James/Younger gang.

Archie Penick – Archie and his father, Herbert were with Joe Hunter when they found the tea kettle at Buzzard's Roost that Jesse buried. Bud was able to visit with Archie when he was 72 years old. Archie took Bud to the place near Tarbone Mountain where they found the brass bucket of Jesse's.

Jay Longley – He is an historian, treasure hunter, and researcher, delving in mostly the history and stories of Bloody Bill Anderson, Jesse James, and the KGC. He lives in Brownwood, Texas, considered a hotspot for Jesse, his buddies, and his gold.

Bob Brewer and **Warren Getler** - These men learned alot from Bud and have gone on to become some of the most prolific treasure hunters in the country. Their book, "Rebel Gold" opened many doors for other treasure hunters to follow.

We will learn who these people were and the role they played in JJ's life. Each character in this fantastic story, weaves in and out of one another. The fibers all connect and form a great lasso that gets stronger and tighter as we go further into this story, drawing the reader closer to the truth.

"No one could have listened to him relate in minute detail the events of his life without knowing he was telling the truth. The trouble is he was not telling the WHOLE truth in order to protect the family name. It is my firm belief had he really wanted to, he could have proved to the world beyond any doubt his true identity."

-Joe Wood

Chapter Four: For the Love of Family

Joe Wood said the only thing that made him extremely mad when questioning Jesse, was when Jesse evaded questions about his family. He was protecting them. That included his parents, his siblings, wives, children, his cousins, and Belle Starr.

While Jesse was hiding behind many names and places, he was hiding the faces of his family. His family to this day is a great mystery, but his whole life, his survival depended upon his family.

It was all about family. So many people who were involved with Jesse were either of a blood kinship or a part of the pledged brotherhood of the Knights of the Golden Circle. He could trust no one else out of this circle.

Both Bud and the Everhards believed Jesse's mother was Zerelda and his father, Robert Sallee James, but the true bloodline may not be what we have always thought.

This has become a very complicated subject to research, to analyze, to assimilate, and to be able to feel confident that we have uncovered the truth of the matter. We will present our findings, but still, it is not clear, nor verifiable to accurately pinpoint the real Jesse Woodson James' family tree per J. Frank Dalton or Bertha's family tree per Ola Everhard. The records are sketchy and misleading in several areas found in genealogy, census, and burial records. They have been manipulated, changed, and destroyed. Then you have to contend with stories from other sources, family Bibles that suddenly appear with different dates, different family members, and those amateur genealogists that try their darndest to build their family trees that may contain unintentional errors.

Howk had his own version of Jesse's family tree that he said came from Jesse's own mouth. There was also a man, claiming to be Frank James who came out with another surprise branch in the family tree. We also have those who extensively, in great detail, researched the James family tree that has been used as the solid family history, but is that even correct? This is the part of Jesse's story that is so frustrating! This is why Joe Wood was frustrated! Jesse just didn't want the American public to know the true story of his family. I think, the closest story to understanding Jesse's family is through Ola, whom Jesse trusted his secrets with.

We will present what has been shared on the unconventional lines and what has been found to support this. Caution and research are advised when using this information.

Zerelda and her family:

Bertha Underwood Maddox, Ola Everhard's mother remembers very well that her father, James Anderson Underwood told her that his mother, Sally was a sister to Zerelda, Jesse James' mother. It was believed that Zerelda and Sally's mother was Sarah "Sally" Lindsay and their father was a Dalton, not a Cole that has always been placed behind Zerelda's name.

Indeed, Zerelda's grandmother was a "Cole," everyone agrees on that. Zerelda's mother supposedly married her cousin, James Cole in **1822**. Family Search shows they married in **1824**. James Cole had always been noted as Zerelda's father, but Zerelda and Sally's father, according to J. Frank Dalton and Bertha was a Dalton and the girls were sisters to James Lewis Dalton, father of the Dalton brothers. This would make their father be, Benjamin Lewis Dalton who was married to Nancy Rabourn at the time. Ola said that when their father died, their mother married James Cole and they became the "Cole girls." The father died in 1834 when Zerelda was 9 years old.

I believe this is correct, and the 1850 census showing Robert James and "Sarelda" in the Platte Township in Clay County, Missouri shows "Sarelda" 28 years old making her date of birth in 1822, not the 1825 everyone has documented. So this could prove that she was not James Cole's child since her mother had married Cole in either 1822 or 1824.

Howk had stated that Jesse told him that his mother was a Dalton, but Howk claimed that Jesse's mother was "Mollie" Dalton and Zerelda was Jesse's aunt.[21]

Bud believes Zerelda was Jesse's mother, but possibly was a different woman than who portrayed her in later years. Same goes for other members of the family. We believe Zerelda and Sally were Daltons through their paternal side, and they were Lindsays and Coles through their maternal side. The Cole name was very important in Jesse's family, the Dalton family, as well as the Younger family. We will dish this out to the reader, bite by bite and allow you to digest what has been suggested along with evidence in records, whether they have been manipulated or not. Its up to the reader to form their own opinion.

Jesse thoroughly explained to Ola about their kinship they shared through the Daltons when they were together in the hospital and in her home. They also shared in the Scots-Irish blood, carrying down the auburn hair and steel blue eyes. Several times in Ola's manuscript, she mentions the family tree that Jesse laid out time and time again. The truth was extremely important to Ola and I have no reason to believe that her story is not true.

Bertha was the oldest of all the Underwood children. Bertha would always be the one helping her father. One day, while working, her father slowly eased into a conversation about his folks. He allowed her to see the Family Bible, which was tightly locked away in a small trunk. There were five generations listed in the family record and Bertha remembers seeing some of the names. One of the names that jumped out at her, was "Dalton." This was the name of her father's mother. Bertha knew about the infamous Dalton Brothers whose desperado days were between 1890-1892. Her father also showed her a picture of her paternal grandfather, Henry Underwood who rode with Quantrill.

Henry Underwood and Sally Dalton were supposedly married and lived in the vicinity of Henry County, Tennessee which is the northwestern portion of Tennessee and near the Kentucky border. This was not far from Humphreys County, where Jesse had lived in later years. Ola said that her grandfather James Anderson Underwood was the oldest of the three children. There was James, Eliza Ann, and William.

When the war was looming on the horizon in 1860 and 1861, "military units, including the Fifth Tennessee Infantry Regiment, organized on the courthouse lawn. Henry County sent more than 2,500 volunteers to the Confederacy and earned the title "Volunteer County of the Volunteer State.""[22] This must have been the time that Henry joined.

Looking up James A. Underwood's family genealogy records, it shows that his father was David Underwood and his mother was Amanda Alexander. Many people claim that James middle name was "Alexander," but Bertha and Ola adamantly claimed that it was "Anderson." There are no records of Amanda Alexander or her family, except for a marriage record between her and David in 1850 in Henry County.

In the 1850 census in Henry County, District 9, it lists David Underwood, age 24 and Amanda, age 17, living with a one month old baby, Eliza and an elderly lady, Nancy Singleton, age 72 (Head of the household). David and Amanda may have been boarders with Ms. Singleton.

This is where the mix up lies. The Eliza shown here, born in 1850 went by the official name of Elizabeth Jane or Eliza Jane. She would stay in Henry County and marry William Thomas Scott. Many people believe she was James' sister, but it is not so. His sister was Eliza Ann, also known as Anna Liza or Anna Louisa. She was born Sept 17, 1858 and married James Casius Alexander in Henry County in 1872. They would eventually travel to Oklahoma, to Carter county where her brother James lived.

I believe David Underwood and Amanda Alexander were part of the family and maybe helped in raising the children, but they were not James and Eliza's parents. Their parents both died when the children were young. It's quite an amazing story. Everything that Ola has stated matches up with what is revealed here. We will be basing the information from Ola's stories and from her Great Aunt Eliza Ann Underwood's family stories.

Eliza Ann tells her family that her father was John Underwood. That may have been his real name and used "Henry" during the war, reflecting the county he lived in. Also, the name "Henry" was the Younger's father's name whose half-sister, Adaline married James Lewis Dalton, the parents of the Dalton brothers. James Lewis Dalton would be the brother-in-law of John "Henry" Underwood.

Bertha explains the deep hurt that her father, James A. Underwood, born in 1855 went through during the Civil War. When Henry went off to war, Sally had tremendous struggles to keep the house and family afloat.

We learn that Union troops began to occupy Henry County and the courthouse in 1862. As Ola describes the story from her mother, James was 8 and Eliza was 5 when horrific events occurred in the family. This would put the year at 1863.

Sally (Dalton) Underwood was warned that the Yankees were heading her way. She took the children and hid in bushes. The Yankees ransacked their home, took what they wanted, and burned it to the ground. Due to extreme exposure and grief, Sally died. James and his sister, Eliza Ann, and William, the baby were taken in by family and then they were placed with Dr. Rainey in Cottage Grove, Tennessee to raise. Baby William did not survive this tremendous chain of events.

There was a Dr. Josiah Lawson Rainey (1832-1905), living in Cottage Grove. In the book, "Some Turn of the Century Henry County, Tennessee Obituaries (1898-1913)" he is described as a "gallant Confederate soldier and served four years in the Civil War. He was a prominent mason."[23] He was a prisoner of war and was held at Camp Morton until 1864. He then moved to Henry County and started his medical practice.

Some believe their father, Henry never came back after the war, so basically the children were orphaned, but they were blessed to be raised by the best. "Ola's grandpa always said, "A better man than Doctor Rainey never lived."[24]

Eliza married in 1872 to James C. Alexander and James Underwood married Savannah Elizabeth O'Daniel (1865-1927) on December 21, 1882 in Henry County, Tennessee. Savannah's parents were Henry Jackson O'Daniel and Susan Helen Alexander. So here we see two "Alexanders" in the mix. I believe they were related somehow and possibly related to Amanda Alexander who died of bronchitis in 1860 before the war.

James and Savannah's first born was Bertha in 1883, born in Henry County, Tennessee. By 1888, Bertha had a brother, Waco Jackson Underwood. By the Fall of 1888, James took his family to Indian Territory to the community of Butcher Knife. Bertha was only 5 years old, so this was where she was raised. We will learn later what the family went through in those harsh Wild West days in the raw and untamed Indian Territory. James' sister, Eliza and her family moved to the same area.

James and Savannah Underwood later settled in the small community of *Woodford*, northwest of Ardmore, Oklahoma and Eliza and her family settled in Wilson, just west of Ardmore.

The families were quite happy living in those communities in which were growing in leaps and bounds. One Sunday morning in 1899, tragedy hit again. Bertha told Ola that the family was attending church and when headed for home, they could see smoke in the direction of their home. Sadly, their house had burned to the ground and all its contents were burnt to a crisp, including the trunk that held the Family Bible and the pictures of the Underwood and Dalton families. They were devastated. At age 16, Bertha was extremely distraught at the treasures that were lost and documents of their family history.

Thankfully, Bertha's Aunt Eliza maintained a photo album of her Dalton family. Aunt Eliza Ann showed Bertha a picture of the Dalton boys in her family album. In Ola's manuscript, she wrote, referring to what Aunt Eliza said, "Now honey, they was mighty good boys. They were only trying to get justice. Aunt Sis and grandpa loved their folks."[25]

Bertha also had met Jesse when he was a Deputy U.S. Marshal in Indian Territory as a little girl and he was responsible for helping the family move to a safer area northwest of Ardmore, Oklahoma.

Bertha and Jesse had numerous talks about the family and had much to share and confirm the Dalton connection.

I have searched high and low to find if any member of the Dalton family fought against this claim that J. Frank Dalton, using their name, was a fake. Nothing from the Dalton family has been found after he came out as Jesse Woodson James to debunk his claim.

Civil War was devastating to so many families, so many losses, but there was so much involved beyond what you could imagine; especially when it involved Jesse James and his family. Everything was about family; both in blood and brotherhood with the Knights of the Golden Circle. Jesse had numerous sources in various locations who ensured that records were destroyed, removed, or altered which involved the families and those connected to Jesse, the Quantrill Raiders, and the KGC. Courthouses, homes, businesses, and publishing companies were very often burned to the ground by some of these operatives. Bud has extensive knowledge about this practice, and I have run into these shenanigans with my family also.

Howk would refer to Zerelda as Jesse's aunt which also coincides with a letter that J. Frank Dalton wrote during the time he was with Howk. Also, J. Frank Dalton who wrote the Crittenden Memoirs refers to Zerelda as his aunt. That doesn't necessarily mean that this was "gospel", as it may have been written to keep the story flowing on what he told Howk and for family protection and preservation, especially from Howk.

Dalton never told Ola the lineage Howk wrote out in his books, never even hinted it.

There definitely are two women appearing to be Zerelda. One is in the photo at Jesses' funeral in 1882, the mother who first denied that the corpse was her son, and then later stated that he was. She had a milder, gentler appearance than the Zerelda who is portrayed in all the pictures history has given us. Her bone structure was different. The Zerelda we have known was big boned, had a very prominent wide nose, and tall. Her face was longer compared to the round face shown on the woman in the funeral picture and another photo of Zerelda during that time period. She was more of a petite version of Zerelda and she had her right arm showing. The picture of Zerelda by the tombstone at the Samuels farm shows that her right arm is missing or not shown.

(Zerelda at the funeral of Jesse's, 1882)

(Zerelda at the tombstone of Jesse on the Farm)

(Version of Zerelda who appears to match the one at the funeral and in the threesome photo that will follow)

Another interesting picture found was of Zerelda, without a right arm, much older woman with a notation that she may have been the mother of the "brown-eyed" Frank or Alex Frank? Bud has found documented evidence and information from family members that the real Frank James had blue eyes. The brown-eyed, sometimes referred to as "black-eyed Frank," was the Frank James who stood trial, was pardoned, and lived on the farm in Fletcher, Oklahoma. The big-boned Zerelda and this Frank have the same nose. Neither one look like the Jesse James we know. We will learn more in later chapters.

(Zerelda, mother of brown eyed Frank James)

Stories throughout Howk and Schrader's book indicate how cruel Jesse was towards Zerelda and treated her very harshly, especially during the time of Jesse's fake death in 1882. But the words coming directly from Jesse's mouth to Ola and Aubrey, indicated a great fondness, respect, and love for his mother, whom Jesse always stated was Zerelda.

Bud Hardcastle believes wholeheartedly that Jesse's mother was Zerelda and he protected her with his life. I believe that also. We as the public, have been led to believe that she was the hardnosed woman who lived on the Samuel's Farm. Just think about it, Jesse wouldn't put his mother in harm's way during their outlawry days, nor put her out in the limelight, like the lady who portrayed her, who allowed strangers to come visit Jesse's grave on her property. We don't have concrete proof, but we do know how much Jesse's family was being protected and the real Zerelda was carefully hidden, especially after Jesse's funeral in 1882.

Jesse gave Ola the picture of his mother and her two sons, Jesse and Frank. Bud was able to verify these photos when he visited Aubrey back in 1990. These were prized possessions to Jesse and to Ola. One photo has Jesse holding the picture of his mother, himself, and brother, Frank with great affection. Ola stated that the photo below, of the three were taken separately and then someone went to a lot of trouble to group the three together. Ola showed this photo to William Tunstill in his video, which Bud has, and she described the photo, saying Jesse gave it to her while Jesse was going under the name, J. Frank Dalton. Jesse wrote on the picture and gave it to Ola.[26] Bud captured this photo on Ola's wall in her home in Lovington, New Mexico and it is shown on Bud's video that Kenny Brown filmed. Bud has no doubt that the three shown in the picture are the true Jesse, Zerelda, and Frank James.[27]

(Jesse holding the famous threesome picture)

(Zerelda's photo with her sons)

Lou was given this threesome picture by Howk. We will explore it later as we go along. Also, a pilot who transported Dalton after the big reveal in Lawton in 1948, Pilot Ralph Swaby told Bud that the picture was in the room with Dalton in Lawton. The man in the picture on the left of the mother was the man he saw and flew out of there to Pueblo. That was the true Jesse.

In the photo taken at Jesse's fake funeral in 1882, all three of the subjects are shown. Zerelda was identified as his mother during this event and very clearly, she is the same woman as in the treasured photo above. The man standing by Zerelda looks like the Frank in the threesome photo. Jesse told Ola herself that he was at his own funeral and was at the head of the casket. Was he the man with the protruding lower lip? Jesse said one of his disguises was a lower jaw mouthpiece to change the look of his mouth. Was he the gruff-looking character by the head of the corpse? We are not sure.

(JJ's funeral in 1882)

Five of the men who were pallbearers at Jesse's funeral in 1882 were identified, including J.D. *Ford*, Deputy Marshal *J.T. Reed*, Charles *Scott*, James Henderson, and William Bond, who was most likely Dr. Ruben Samuel's family, Zerelda's second husband. His mother was a Bond. There was one man whose true identity remained unknown. He was a very stout man. In the article of "The Funeral of Jesse James," by Rebecca Beatrice Brooks, the 6th man was going by the name of James *Vaughn*.[28] We will later learn how significant the name "Vaughn" was.

The Ford brothers, who were involved in the so-called killing of Jesse, had a father named J.T. Ford. Was he the J.D. Ford listed as one of the pallbearers? Jesse clarified with Ola, that the Ford brother's mother was a Dalton, sister of Bertha Underwood's grandmother, sister of Zerelda, and a sister to Lewis Dalton, father of the Dalton boys. The story gets even crazier.

The Daltons

History does not identify Zerelda as a "Dalton." Ola states in a letter to a "Mr. Eugene T. Huff" in which Hardcastle has in his possession, provided by Marsha Swope that Zerelda was born in Scott County, Kentucky on January 29, 1825. Her father was Louis Dalton, Sr. Ola stated that sometime after his death, her mother married a "Cole". Ola states in her manuscript that her great grandmother, Sarah "Sally" Dalton was another daughter of Louis Dalton. Jesse added that there were 6 Dalton girls, one whom married a Mr. J. T. Ford (parents of Bob, who supposedly shot Jesse in 1882 and Charles Ford), and one son, James Lewis Dalton, the father of the boys of the Dalton gang. Ola had a photo book and she had photos of Uncle and Aunt Dalton. This goes along with census records found in 1820 and 1830 on Benjamin Lewis Dalton (1794-1835), the suspected father.

(Uncle and Aunt Dalton)

The Daltons were of Irish blood, with their name originating from "O'Dalton." They had a mix of Cherokee.

We look to James Lewis Dalton for more information on this family. The parentage has been hard to uncover or explain. Benjamin Lewis Dalton and his brother James Lewis Dalton were born and raised in Virginia, but came to Estill and Montgomery County, Kentucky in 1812. I believe they both entered into service during the War of 1812. Benjamin served in Captain Silvanus Massie's Company, 2nd regiment, Kentucky Militia.

After the war, the brothers married sisters, Benjamin married Nancy Raybourn in 1815 and James Lewis married Matilda Raybourn in 1821. Benjamin and Nancy would end up in Indiana, north of Kentucky, and James Lewis and Matilda would end up in Missouri.

By 1820, Benjamin and Nancy had 4 girls per the census records in Lawrence County, Indiana. By 1830, they were in Owen County, Indiana and listed were 5 girls and 1 boy, James Lewis Dalton, born in 1826. His son Charles believed James was born in Montgomery County, Kentucky. This goes along with what Jesse said, but there should be one more girl, 6 girls altogether and 1 boy. In all the genealogy records, the names of only 4 girls are listed. Could Sally and Zerelda be the other two girls? Zerelda was born in 1822 or 1825 and it is unknown when Sally was born. The only possible way that this could be a probability would be that they were illegitimate children between Sarah Lindsay Cole and Benjamin Dalton who would be 9 years her senior. The other thought is that Zerelda's mother was not Sarah Lindsay as we have been told, but could it have been Nancy Rabourn? I don't know the answer.

Benjamin named his son after his brother, James Lewis Dalton. We find in an article regarding an interview with Charles Benjamin Dalton, first born son of James Lewis Dalton, that the boy was named after his two grandfathers, Charles Younger and Benjamin Dalton.

We learn from this interview, "Our family, he continues, "was from Kentucky near Mount Sterling. (This was in Montgomery County). Father (James Lewis Dalton -1826) was raised here and went through the Mexican war as a member of Col. Cleary's regiment. He was the fifer. At the battle of Buena Vista, he blew the long roll which ordered the American soldiers when the Mexicans were trying to surprise them. I hear him tell the story. The sergeant came to the place where my father was sleeping, grabbed him by the foot and pulled him out. "The Mexican are coming," he said, "blow the long roll." Without waiting a moment my father began to fife, the Americans fell into line and the surprise the Mexicans had planned fell through."[29]

James Lewis Dalton (1826-1890) had served for a solid year under Zachary Taylor as a fifer for Company I, 2nd Regiment of Kentucky Foot Volunteers during the Mexican American War as a member of Col. Cleary's regiment.

Charles was asked about the kinship between the James and the Daltons. He said there was no kinship at all.

James Lewis Dalton married Sarah Adeline Lee Younger in 1851. Adeline was the sister of Bruce Younger (the man whom Jesse used his name when marrying Belle Starr) and half-sister of Henry Washington Younger, father of Cole and all the Youngers. Several old books and newspaper articles refer to Jesse Woodson James being cousins to the Youngers and the Daltons. One book, *Fifty Years on the Owl Hoot Trail, Jim Herron* who knew the Daltons and James personally, said that they were cousins.[30]

In an article Bud had from the Police Gazette, by McGrath, Jesse was telling his story on his death bed. "So, we were driven into the life we lived – my brother, Frank, and **our cousins**, the **Youngers**, and the rest of our gang."[31]

James Lewis Dalton came from Kentucky, in the same area as Zerelda. Some people indicate that the county he lived in was *Montgomery County*, two counties over from Scott County, Kentucky. Dalton moved to Cass County, Missouri and then later to West Point in Bates County, Missouri where he was a neighbor to David Pugh Thomason shown on the census. The Thomasons and Timberlakes (David's paternal family) were heavily involved through marriage and relationships with Jesse's family in the same area in Kentucky and Missouri as well with the Daltons. The author has gone into great depth in genealogical research on these families, which includes her maternal and paternal bloodline trickling down into both Jesse's maternal and paternal families through, the Thomasons, McGehees, Owens, Simpsons, Daltons, Keys, Thornton, Mynns (Means) Lindsays, Drummonds, Devers, Andersons, Mimms, Woodsons, Porters, Amos', and Ferris'.

Dalton began trading horses and running a saloon. A very interesting article written by Melinda E. Cohenour, 2009, who is an author and genealogist connected to the Daltons through her paternal lineage stated that Dalton was a man of mystery. "He lived a life filled with frequent moves, indebtedness, and extreme rancor from the father and benefactor of his wife, Adeline." She was speaking of Adeline's father, Charles Lee Younger who revised his will to exclude Dalton.

"James closed his saloon business in Cass County, Missouri in 1882, and began to take his family to Indian Territory." This was the year of Jesse's fake death. "He (Dalton) died in 1890 while enroute to Indian Territory to stake a claim on a plot of land the family wished to inhabit, 6 miles north of Kingfisher. He contracted pneumonia (by one story) or suffered a fatal attack of cholera morbis (by another) and died in the horse-drawn wagon before arriving at the intended destination."[32]

A newspaper article, in from *The Coffeyville Weekly Journal*, Coffeyville, Kansas, July 18, 1890 states he died at Mr. Taylor's in Fawn Creek. "He was taken with "cramp" which terminated fatally. He was the father of the famous "Dalton Boys" of the Indian Territory, and **by marriage was related** to the notorious **James family**. Dalton served the Confederate government on his own account in Missouri and Arkansas." He died in Coffeyville, *Montgomery County*, Kansas; eerily the same place where Grat and Bob Dalton, his sons died during the famous bank robbery. *Montgomery County* in Kentucky is where James Lewis Dalton was born and raised per his son, Charles. Adeline was left with 15 children to raise.

Interesting items out of that article was that he served the Confederate government and "by marriage" he was related to the James. This would have been through the Younger side.

The Lindsay and Cole Family

To create less confusion, if that's even possible, I will refer to Sarah Lindsay (1803-1851) the designated mother of Zerelda as Sarah and Zerelda's sister as Sally (Ola's great grandmother) who is also designated as being the daughter of Sarah Lindsay. There is no one or any documentation to support that Sarah was the mother of James Lewis Dalton, born a year after Zerelda in 1826. They could have been half siblings, but who really knows.

Sarah Lindsay's grandfather, Anthony Lindsay, Jr. was a great patriot, fighting two wars including the Revolutionary War. Anthony became one of the earliest explorers of Kentucky, fighting long and hard against the Shawnee. He established a fort/station for the protection of his neighbors called Lindsay's Station. It is located a few miles north of Stamping Ground, Kentucky. The site is marked by the Kentucky Historical Society with a plaque telling the Lindsay story. Many believe that during Jesse's outlaw days, he went back to this same area and buried gold.

By 1788, the area that Lindsay owned, fell in *Woodford* County. A name we will find quite frequently in Jesse's life. By 1792 when Kentucky became a state, *Scott* County was formed from Woodford County. *Scott* is another word used often. This is where we find Sarah's father and mother living when Sarah was growing up. The historical plaque indicates that all the children of Anthony Lindsay Jr., including Sarah "Sallie" Lindsay's father, Anthony III, lived close to Lindsay's station. This was where Sarah was born in 1803.

Sarah Lindsay's mother was Alice "Aisley" Cole. Sarah was raised at Lindsay's Station and both of her parents died and were buried there. Per Ola (told by Jesse), Zerelda was born in Scott County.

Many writers indicate that Zerelda was born in the Black Horse Tavern which was considered to be in Woodford County. It was an old tavern owned by Richard James Cole, Jr., brother of Alice "Aisley" Cole, Sarah Lindsay's mother. The father of Zerelda is dubbed as Richard's son, James R. Cole, Sarah Lindsay's first cousin. The U.S. and International Marriage Records show a marriage date of 1822 between the two, but Family Search shows it to be in 1824. In 1822, James Cole would have been 17 and Sarah Lindsay, 19.

In a newspaper article, The Choctaw Herald, February 16, 1911, was announcing Zerelda's death and had stated that "Mrs. Samuels was born in Kentucky in 1824 and was educated at a convent in Lexington, Kentucky. Her father was a soldier in the revolutionary war and her mother was the daughter of a prominent Kentucky family."[33] This statement would disqualify James Cole and Benajmin Dalton as the father. Maybe the newspaper writer was referring to a grandfather. As you can see, the census records and news articles are not always dependable in stating the facts.

In Family Search (ancestors.familysearch.com) it lists that Sarah Lindsay and James Cole had two girls and 1 boy. The other daughter listed was Mary Adeline Cole born 1823, died 1910. No other record indicates that Sarah had two girls, nor can I find any record of Mary Adeline Cole. Quite a mystery.

There is one clue Jesse left us. The name "Mollie" is derived from the name Mary. Could Mary really be Mollie, the mother of Jesse Woodson James? This would make Zerelda his aunt. Also, not publicly known, Jesse told Ola that after his brother, Alexander was born, he had a sister, the first daughter, "Mary" who died during the start of the Civil War, and Jesse himself named his own daughter with Zee Mimms, "Mary".

Maybe what Howk was saying about Molly Dalton being Jesse's mother was true.

James Cole ran the Black Horse Tavern in *Woodford* County, Kentucky. The tavern was previously owned by Zachary Taylor and later, Taylor's nephew, Major John Hancock Lee. Take note how all these people relate to one another. The Taylors and Lees are in my family and I have been studying them for years. Major Lee and his wife, Elizabeth Bell (granddaughter of Zachary Taylor) had a daughter, Sarah Lee (1787) who married Governor John Jordan Crittenden, also a member of my family throughout several branches, including Crittenden's mother, Judith Harris. Governor John J. Crittenden, governor of Kentucky was the uncle of Governor Thomas Theodore Crittenden (1832-1909), governor of Missouri. He was governor at the time of Jesse James' heyday.

Governor John Jordan Crittenden also was the father of Thomas Leonidas Crittenden, who served as an aide to Zachary Taylor in the Mexican War. He would later serve as a Union officer, Major General, leading the 5th Division in the Army of the Ohio in the Battle of Shiloh. His son, John Jordan Crittenden III served in the U.S. Army and died alongside Lt. Col. George Armstrong Custer at the Battle of Little Bighorn in 1876.

All these clues are like breadcrumbs leading to the truth. The relationship of all these families, tying to the elite is one of the keys in understanding this entire saga of Jesse James, the Civil War, and beyond. There was such an intricate web of people involved. The Lees and Taylors lead to General Robert E. Lee and the President of the Confederacy, Jefferson Davis. Even the Youngers descend from the Lees, Hancocks, and the Corbins who all tie into the Taylors.

The Cole name was used frequently in the family. Jesse himself named one of his sons, Jesse Cole James. Also, Henry Washington Younger named his son, Coleman "Cole" Younger and James Lewis Dalton named one of his sons, Henry Cole Dalton. There is definitely something behind the Cole name in all these families.

James Cole was on the rough side and got into several brawls with a knife at the tavern. He died at the age of 22 when he broke his neck in a horse accident in 1827, so Zerelda would have been 2 or 5 years old. Between 1827 and 1838, Sarah Lindsay must have had several beaus. She later married Robert Thomason in 1838. The girls were sent to a convent, St. Catherine's Academy, Sisters of Charity of Nazareth, at Lexington, Kentucky and became known as "The Cole Girls." (per Ola's letter to Mr. Huff, June 24, 1981).

The Lindsays connect to the Flemings and Drummonds who are in both mine and Bud's ancestral line. Robert Thomason, a member of my Thomason family who married Sarah Lindsay Cole, was the brother of William M. "Wild Bill" Thomason. He has been documented as being a mountain man character who lived with the Indians. Per Jim Cummins who was in Jesse James' gang stated that "Wild Bill was a powerful man, more than a match for any two frontiersmen. He had muscles like steel. His hair was black as the raven's wing, thick and heavy as the mane of a mustang, and hung below his belt. He was a lover of this country. He enlisted in the Mexican War, becoming a lieutenant. In one battle, becoming separated from the main force, went over the breastworks into a battery of Mexican artillery and captured the whole company single handed and along." "Wild Bill could stop a cannon ball just by looking at it."[34]

Jim Cummins stated that "Wild Bill" taught Frank James, who would have been a step great uncle to Frank and Jesse, how to ride and shoot like the Comanches. Wild Bill Thomason's daughter, Martha Jane Thomason would be the mother of Bloody Bill Anderson.

A granddaughter of "Wild Bill" Thomason, Anna Thomason, daughter of Grafton Thomason, married Sheriff Jim Timberlake of Clay County who played a big role in Jesse's life and death.

William Thomason Anderson (Bloody Bill Anderson) was born in 1839 to William C. Anderson (1820-1862) and Martha Jane Thomasson, daughter of William M. "Wild Bill" Thomason and Susanna McQuiddy who lived in the Agnes City Township of Breckenridge County, Kansas. On Bloody Bill's paternal side, his family is related to the Woodsons and Mimms' families of Jesse and the Wests, Napiers and Ferris' family of Bud and I. Bloody Bill's maternal side is descending from the Thomasons, McGehee's, Paynes, Flemings, Tarletons, and Woodsons.

Sarah (Lindsay) Thomason and her husband Robert moved to Clay County, Missouri and had several children together.

The James Family

Howk claimed that Jesse's father was George James, the man who ordered the first shot to be fired in the Civil War. He was supposedly the brother of Robert Sallee James. I cannot find the relationship between this George and Robert Sallee James.

Jesse's father was Reverend Robert Sallee James born in 1818 in Lickskillett, *Logan* County, Kentucky to Rev. John Martin James and Mary Poore. The name *Logan* is also an important name to remember. The Poore and Mimms family descend from the Woodsons, Pryors, Porters, and Ferris.'

In Bud's collection of documents, photos, and various newspaper and magazine articles, Bud had an article that spoke of a very hard life for Robert also. His parents both died in 1827 when he was only nine years old and his older sister, *Mary*, married to John Mimms, took Robert and four of his brothers and sisters in to raise. Robert's mother's name was *Mary* as well as his oldest sister, who at 18 at the time took over as "Mother". As we will see later, the name "Mary" was very special to Robert and would be very important to both Frank and Jesse. Frank named his only daughter, "*Mary*."

Robert James graduated from Georgetown College, with a degree in Bachelor of Arts. He became an ordained Baptist preacher in 1839. His future wife, Zerelda Cole was at a revival and met Robert. In December 1841, he and Zerelda Cole, at the age of 16, were married in Stamping Ground, Scott County, Kentucky where Lindsay Station was located.

Ola stated that Robert and Zerelda moved to Adairsville, Kentucky and there had a son Alexander Franklin James in 1843 which coincides with the date this article listed. Many say Alexander was born in 1844, but Bud has found a different date that throws a kink in what we thought we knew.

Robert was a circuit riding preacher and rarely stayed at home. Later they decided to settle on a farm near what would be known as *Centerville*, Missouri. They had a son, Robert Reuben James in 1845 who did not live, then Jesse Woodson James in 1847, and another daughter, Susan Lavenia in 1849.

Centerville, Missouri was not officially a town until the spring of 1856. Another settlement began developing around the nearby newly established Kansas City and Cameron Railroad after the Civil War. This settlement became Kearney and the two settlements of Kearney and Centerville merged, officially incorporated as Kearney in 1869. Centerville was in the southeastern portion of Kearney.

Zerelda was known as a strong, domineering, outspoken, and fiercely protective of her children. She was 5'8" and over 200 lbs. She had to do most of the raising of their children.

("Robert Sallee James")

The same year that Jesse was born, 1847, Robert left his wife with her mother in Clay County, Missouri, while he went back to school. Robert James returned to school to get his master's degree. He was constantly gone from the home. He poured his life into the ministry. Robert was one of the founding members of William Jewell College, a private liberal arts college in Liberty, Missouri. It was founded in 1849 by the Missouri Baptist Convention.

Robert founded two churches, the Providence Baptist Church in Clay County, Missouri and the Pisgah Baptist Church near Excelsior Springs, Missouri. He was very well educated, gifted as an orator, and a successful farmer. He became a pastor of a New Hope Baptist Church in Clay County.

In 1849, Jesse's father had left the family when Jesse was only 2 years old, traveling to California during the gold rush with his brother, Drury Woodson James and William Sallee. As a minister, he felt that someone needed to preach the gospel to the gold diggers, but others believe he desired to seek his own fortune. Others believed that he desired to distance himself from his domineering wife.

Zerelda received a letter stating that Robert died of Cholera at Hangtown Gold Camp near Placerville in *El Dorado* County, California on August 18, 1850.

One month later, in the 1850 census, dated September 28, 1850, Robert and his family are listed in the Platt Township in Clay County, Missouri. This was in the northwestern part of Clay County. Listed are Robert (a B.P. preacher – age 31); Sarelda (age 28, born in 1822?), Franklin (age 10, born 1840?), Jesse R. (4 years old, born 1846?), and Susan (9 months old). Where is Mary? As we learn later, Jesse stated that his oldest sister was Mary, so she had to of been born before Susan. This census would indicate who all was in the household as of June 1, 1850. Either this census has been manipulated or the truth lies within it. I don't know. We will address this later.

History states that Robert died in California, but Bud believes this was all a coverup to be able to be free from Zerelda's overbearing personality, but there may be more to it. Bud believes Robert James lived, remarried, served in the Civil War, and met up with his boys after the war. Another version to consider is that he died in a Civil War skirmish.

Zerelda married Benjamin Sims in 1852, who was the great uncle of Johnny Ringo. He was also a great uncle of the wife of Thomas Coleman Younger, uncle of Cole Younger. Sims was married in 1823 in Woodford County, Kentucky where Zerelda was from. The Sims possibly migrated with Zerelda's family to Missouri. Mr. Sims was documented as being very harsh on Zerelda's sons and she was ready to divorce him when he had a horse accident and died in 1854. She married again in 1855 to Dr. Reuben Samuel whom Jesse and the rest of the family thought very highly of.

Zerelda and Dr. Samuel had several children together. Bud said that Zerelda had a black son. In Ancestry.com it said the child, Perry Bremans Samuel (1868-1938) was a mixed-race child of Dr. Samuel and his slave housekeeper, Charlotte. This has not been proven. On Perry's death certificate, his parents were listed as unknown.

Perry was shown in 1870 as age 3 and lived with his mother, Charlotte and other siblings close to the Samuels, but a few doors away in a different household than the Samuels. In 1880, Perry is in the home of Samuels, age 11 listed as a servant. No mention of his mother, Charlotte thereafter. Ancestry shows that Charlotte was born in 1830 in Woodford, Kentucky where the James, Coles, and Daltons originated.

Perry was treated as a son. He was adopted into the family. The James' boys thought of Perry as a brother. Perry proudly claimed that he helped Frank and Jesse by being the lookout for them.

This family history is quite a complicated story and it is very hard to follow or to even rely on the mounds of information out there. Jesse didn't want it all to be known and we can respect that. But as you can see, all these characters are within the same family. There was a lot of nobility attached, as well as a very intricate and mysterious persona. Jesse had family in various places and in various degrees of relationships and social status. His family had many branches, reaching into families that were strongly connected to one another. There was so much more about Jesse and his family than meets the all-seeing eye, but one thing for sure, family was everything to him and it was within their family circle that he put his trust.

> "Let us tell our simple story,
> How we fought to shield our homes
> From the thugs and border ruffians,
> Tho' we had to fight alone."

*Excerpt from the poem, "The Men of Quantrell" By Frank Dalton
(The Crittenden Memoirs, compiled by H.H. Crittenden, 1936)*

Chapter Five: The War Between the States

We find that Jesse wanted people to know about himself. He did not just want to be known as an outlaw, which he did not regret, but wanted to also be known as an Author, Lecturer, Soldier, and Peace Officer as shown on his "calling card".

In this chapter, we will explore **Jesse's stories** told to Ola Everhard and Cowboy Slim Williams regarding his role as a soldier in the Civil War, backed up by Crittenden Memoirs, written by Frank Dalton (Jesse), and other articles Bud Hardcastle has secured in which Jesse described the war, a simple story.

Jesse James was a soldier, a darn good one at that. It was in this role that he found his purpose in life; a duty and an honor to fight for his family and his homeland, the South.

The Civil War was known as the War of the Rebellion, the Slaveholders' Rebellion, the War of Northern Aggression, the Freedom War, the War of Secession, and Jesse's term he used the most, the War Between the States. It was one of the most horrific times in America (1861-1865). Families who lived through the Civil War had to overcome the loss they suffered before they could even muster up the courage to talk about it and share the memories with their descendants. Some never did. The ugliness of the uncivilized war would rarely be discussed until the turn of the century when the two sides came together as one.

It was a very confusing time in American history, very bloody, and it forever changed the lives of every family that survived it. We Americans are remnants of the Civil War, from the more than 620,000 men who died as well as those who were left permanently scarred and disfigured within and without.

The only story I heard regarding my family in the war in which was recorded in "Knox E. Greer in History of Rhea County, Tennessee", compiled by Bettye J. Broyles, *Rhea County Historical and Genealogical Society,* 1991 went like this: My 4th great grandfather, John Stout who lived in Broylesville, Washington County, Tennessee, was hung by soldiers because of gold he had hidden on his property. John was nearing the age of 90 and had $50,000 in gold buried around his home. Soldiers, unknown if they wore blue or grey, heard of Stout's gold. Stout was a Union man and had known Andrew Jackson, James Polk, and Andrew Johnson well. They passed by his Stage Stop often near the Little Limestone Creek.

Stout refused to tell the soldiers where his gold was, so they strung him up. When his wife could stand it no more, she told the soldiers where a part of it was buried. The soldiers seized what they could dig up and left the scene swiftly. Stout survived, but only lived a few years after the war. Years later, a cache of gold was found on the Stout's place near a tree by timbermen, thought to have been a part of Stout's hidden gold.

The Civil War was not just in the battlefields, but in the homes and churches. Families and brethren began to split. This is what occurred in the home of John Stout. His sons swore allegiance to different sides.

This story increased my passion to seek out the truth about the war and my family's involvement. I dove deeply into history for 14 years, researching the war and my kin who lived in the midst of a divided state, Tennessee. Even in the eastern portion of the state where they lived, the sentiment was divided, and the land became the battleground of the largest civilian uprising which occurred during the war and thereafter. It truly was the darkest days in America's history.

I was careful in not only reading books, historical military papers, newspapers, and family stories that were one-sided, mostly written by the Union supporters, but also, I sought out the stories that were harder to find from soldiers and families from the Confederacy, which proved way more devastating. The stories were brutal as well as the photos taken by Matthew Brady, Alexander Gardner, and Timothy O'Sullivan. No words, no photos can describe the emotion, pain, and suffering that these men experienced, as well as their families.

The war first and foremost changed the lives of the soldiers. Going to war was an adventure to these young men who had never faced it before. They dreamed of becoming heroes for the cause. Those who left their safe havens were hit hard with the reality of war. They were either maimed for life (physically and emotionally), severely deprived of their health, or their young life was taken from them and their families.

It hit the home the hardest. The civilians were slapped with this war, whether they believed in it or not. Many wanted to remain neutral. Their families decreased in number and women were left to fill the void. Women suffered severely. Not only did they have to step up and be the protector of their homes and children while the men folk went to war, they also had to manage and work the farms left behind. The women had to continue with their duties as a homemaker and mother. They were commissioned to help feed, nurse, act as spies against their fellow neighbor, and protect what they had left; no matter what side they were on. The worst part of it, many were violated, "insulted" and abused, forced to meet the soldier's needs.

Jesse's mother and her family faced the same hardships on a daily basis. They lived in one of the most divided states during the Civil War also, the great state of Missouri.

Trouble came early to the family with the Jayhawkers and Red Legs, prior to the Civil War. Kansas and Missouri borders were one of the roughest and most dangerous places in the United States before and after the Civil War. This area had a civil war within its own borders. The term "Bleeding Kansas" described a period of time between the years 1854 to 1858 when Kansas was in conflict with itself, whether to become a free state or a slave state. Kansas was considered prior to that as an undeveloped territory under the Missouri Compromise. Upon the eve of creating a government and forming a state, many anti-slavery organizations from the north began settling in this area to establish Free-State settlements.

An example of this was found in the newspaper out of Atchison, Kansas, *Squatter Sovereign*, August 7, 1855.

"Watch the Abolitionists"

"Circumstances have transpired within a few weeks past in this neighborhood, which place beyond a doubt the existence of an organized band of abolitionists in our midst. We counsel our friends who have money in slave property, to keep a sharp look out lest their valuable slaves may be induced to commit acts which might jeopardize their lives."

"Mr. **Grafton Thomason** of this place, lost a valuable negro about a week ago, and we have not the least doubt but that she was persuaded by one of this lawless band to destroy herself, rather than remain in slavery. In fact, one of this gang was heard to remark, "that she did perfectly right in drowning herself," and just as he would have done, or what every negro who is held in bondage should do. We ask, shall a man expressing such sentiments be permitted to reside in our very midst, be permitted to run at large among our slaves, sowing the seeds of discord and discontent, jeopardizing our lives and our property. We may justly be branded as "ruffians" and cowards did we permit it."

The response- "An Abolitionist Badly Whipped"

"The most interesting ceremony ever witnessed in this town, was the whipping of a "live Abolitionist" with the euphonious name of J.W.B. Kelly, who hails all the way from Cincinnati, Ohio; by Mr. **Grafton Thomason**, late of Clay County, Missouri. Mr. Thomason, a short time ago, lost a valuable negro woman, who it was thought was induced to drown herself by the thieving scoundrel who is the subject of this article. Kelly who was heard to express himself in the matter, severely reproached Mr. Thomason for being a slave holder. Mr. Thomason on hearing of the matter, called on the said Kelly, who gave him to understand that he did not speak to men who owned negroes. Mr. Thomason did not wait for a further expression from him but seized the independent individual and nearly wore him out against the ground. A friend attempting to interfere was, by one blow from the powerful fist of Mr. Thomason, landed backwards, "on the other side of Jordan."

Grafton Thomason was the nephew of Robert Thomason who was the stepfather of Zerelda James and the uncle of Bloody Bill Anderson. Grafton's father, "Wild Bill" is the one who taught Frank James how to ride and shoot. Grafton founded the town of Liberty, Missouri.

The pro-slavery men were labeled the "Border Ruffians." The anti-slavery or "free-state" groups were known as the Jayhawkers, Red Legs, and Abolitionists. In one of Jesse's poems, he refers to the men who attacked his home and family as "border ruffians", but I believe he was generally speaking of the definition of a ruffian; "a scoundrel, rascal, or unprincipled, deceitful, brutal and unreliable person" identified in the 1913 Webster's dictionary. In Ola's writings, she wrote that Jesse also called the attackers, the Red Legs and the Jayhawkers.

The "Border Ruffians," mostly from Missouri, flooded across the border into Kansas to answer the issues that were rising and to set their agenda as well. An election was held, and the majority of the voters were not legal residents. The proslavery vote won, but after one week, the anti-slavery group met and drafted the Topeka Constitution, forming a shadow government; creating another revolution against the voted-in laws of the land.

This created a total nightmare. The "Border Ruffians" took on the "Jayhawkers" (pro-union) and Kansas/Missouri border became a battlefield. It was vicious on both sides. Homes, businesses, and families were destroyed. Men were hacked to death, hung, and burned. They each formed armies of men, banding together. A total of 56 people died. When the Civil War broke out, this continued and an additional guerrilla-type violence commenced by the hand of these independent groups, bringing havoc on the border between Kansas and Missouri.

William Clark Quantrill, per the Reeves Museum in Dover, Ohio was born in Dover, 1837 – Thomas and Caroline Quantrill were his parents. His father was 2nd superintendent of the Dover schools. He was accused of embezzlement and assault. William left home and went to various places and at times he taught school. Went to Kansas with former classmates of the Dover and was said to have gotten involved in gambling and lost a lot of money. He was going by the name of Charles Hart, per the Reeves Museum.[35] Apparently, he went back to teaching in Kansas.

The Watonga Republican newspaper out of Watonga, Blaine County, Oklahoma, April 28, 1920, prints an article, "Barbara Fritchie and Quantrell". In the story, it speaks of Charles Hart who was related to the Quantrell family. A man by the name of Abe Ellis who lived in the southeastern part of Kansas was superintendent of public instruction of Douglas County, Kansas. The young man, Charles Hart, bringing documentation and letters of recommendations from where he had lived prior to coming to Kansas, requested of Ellis a permit to teach in that county. The permit was granted, and young Charles Hart began teaching. Ellis came to watch Charles Hart in action and learned that Hart was barely scraping by and needed an advance to pay his room and board. Ellis helped him out and they became good friends. Charles Hart became very well liked in Lawrence, Kansas and it seemed to be a place he could call home, but then the border war and politics became an issue.

(Young Quantrill)

By 1861, when the Civil War had begun, Kansas was legally a free state; entered into the Union. A young mild-mannered teacher, Charles Hart who said he was from Kentucky and raised as a Unionist, desired to remain neutral and continue to teach in Lawrence, Kansas. Union soldiers came to his home one night and forced Hart to declare what side he was on. After many replies of neutrality, the soldiers finally got Hart's final answer. "My brother is in the Confederate Army and naturally my allegiance is to the South." This infuriated the soldiers.

Jesse wrote later under the alias of Frank Dalton in the Crittenden Memoirs, "Lawrence was a hotbed of abolition and all who did not openly and vigorously espouse the Northern cause were looked on with suspicion. Indeed, so rabid was the stand taken by Jim Lane and other leaders that men suspected of being Southern sympathizers were often either taken out and shot or hung, or horse-whipped and told to get out of the country."

"Hart was put in jail that night, and the next day he was taken out and tied to a tree in the center of the town's business street, where he was publicly whipped, after which he was told to leave the country."

This enraged Hart. It set him on a new path. He changed his name to William Clarke Quantrill, and became a leader of an independent guerrilla band of men against pro-Union towns, pro-Union businesses, and pro-Union families. Jesse wrote: "His military training came in handy now, as it made it possible for him to take a bunch of boys and build up the most perfect fighting organization that the Civil War produced on either side and the "black flag" of Quantrell was more feared and dreaded by the "Yankees" along the Missouri and Kansas border than any other organization. He secured a Confederate commission as a captain of partisan rangers."[36]

Jim Cummins who was a part of Jesse's gang stated that Quantrill was a "handsome man; looked much more like a minister of the gospel than one bearing the reputation that he did. He was refined in his manner, but a man of few words, quick and determined in his actions." ("The Last Chapter Written For a Fighting Frontiersman", *The Kansas City Star,* July 10, 1929.)

Jesse's brother, Frank James was attending the Masonic College in Lexington, Missouri when the war broke out. ("A Sensitive Set, Contributions of Reminiscences by F. A. Mitchel of Chicago, History of Frank," The Kansas City Times, April 6, 1882). The Federalists took over the college campus. He joined the Missouri State Guard and then Quantrill's group in 1861 when he was 18 because he had seen what harsh tactics were being forced upon the Southerners by not only the Redlegs and Jayhawkers but also the Union soldiers. They were burning homes, barns, stealing cattle and horses, and raping the women. They had tried to hang Dr. Samuels and had placed Zerelda and her other children in jail.

Scanning over Jesse's writings and Ola's writings on what Jesse said, you could easily miss something very vital in explaining the sentiment of hatred towards these groups that were causing the chaos. Jesse told Ola that he had a sister, an older sister, Mary who was a "beautiful girl in the bloom of young womanhood when she died at the beginning of the War Between the States."[37] He said no more about her and did not explain what happened, nor is she listed in the family. He named his daughter, Mary Susan, after his two sisters.

The persecution and destruction were horrendous, and Frank had had a belly full. He hooked up with Quantrill. Jesse fervently wanted to join, but he was only 14 at the time and was not allowed.

Frank's enlistment pleased Quantrill, for it is said that he recruited and targeted young men between 16-18 that personally hated the Yankees for all the deprivations that they caused in the South. Quantrill fueled his recruit's emotions with fire and hate.

When Bud interviewed Slim Williams who had lived with Jesse and taxied him around Longview, Texas in 1946, Bud learned that Jesse told Slim that before he became a member of the Quantrill Militia, he was a horse boy for generals of the Confederacy; mentioning General James Ewell Brown "Jeb" Stuart and General Nathan Bedford Forrest. Williams said that Jesse knew his grandfather, Verge Williams who was a horseshoer for General Nathan Bedford Forrest.

Jesse had to take over the farm work as Dr. Samuels suffered injuries from the excessive force during his hanging used by the Union forces. Jesse was small in stature, but large in guts and determination. From Jesse's own words, he told Ola Everhard, "One day some Yankees came out to our place, mistreated my mother and stepfather so bad, then came out in the field where I was plowing and wanted to know where Quantrills' men were camped. I told them I didn't know, I didn't, but I wouldn't have told them if I had. They got mad as hell and one of them damn near beat me to death. Cut the blood out of my back with a whip. I went running to the house with blood running down my back. That picture you've got of me when I was 14 years old was taken in Liberty, Missouri, that's how I looked and how old I was when that damn Yankee damn near beat me to death. That was in 1862 before I was 15 years old in September."[38]

You can see the deep hurt and anger in his eyes.

(Young Jesse after joining the raiders)

What has always concerned me was Jesse's burned feet. When did this occur? In the Lawton Constitution, May 19, 1948, Jesse said; "He recounts how his home was overrun by the Yankees when he was only 14. With steel in his eyes, he remembers how they attempted to exploit information from him by torture. They burned his feet. As proof of the atrocity, he points to the scars on his feet which were burned unmercifully."[39]

Continuing with what Jesse told Ola:

"They came back to the farm one morning a while later. I was out in the field plowing. They asked me again where Quantrill's camp was and about Cole Younger in particular. It was Cole's birthday and my mother was fixing him a nice birthday dinner because she knew if he could, he'd be coming by and could eat. When I told them that I didn't know where Quantrill's camp was, one of the Yankee's threw a rope around my neck and pulling me half-running behind his horse out to the barn, threw the rope up over the hay lift and pulled me up, then they rode off. My mother was watching and as soon as they rode off, she ran out to the barn, cut the rope with a butcher knife, and helped me into the house."

"That happened like this morning, and it was late tomorrow evening before I realized just how close to death I came. As soon as I was able, I got on my horse and went and found Quantrill's camp. On March 8, 1863, Quantrill took me into his outfit. I was placed under command of Captain Bloody Bill Anderson. We went through a lot, but I can say this: Quantrill's men were the toughest group of men and boys that the Civil War produced."[40]

Bloody Bill always wore a short-brim pliable woolen hat, turned up in the front and pinned with a five-point star. This star would be with him throughout his life. It would also be an important symbol for Jesse.

(Bloody Bill Anderson and his famous woolen hat)

In Crittenden Memoirs, Frank Dalton (Jesse) wrote that Cole Younger, who was later called "Bud", had joined Quantrill in 1862 and Cole's brother, John Younger, age 15, joined in March 1863, same time as Jesse. John Younger was born in 1851, and it is written (Younger Family Genealogy on the official website for Frank and Jesse James Ancestry) that John Younger and his brother, Bob were too young to join the guerillas, but they later joined the James/Younger Outlaw gang. If he joined the guerillas the same time Jesse did, John would have only been 12 at the most. Was Jesse really mirroring John as himself? Frank Dalton describes in the memoirs that John Younger did not die by the hands of the Pinkertons as described but lived on to a normal life.?????

Dalton mentions John quite frequently and his fondness for him was revealed in the words describing his character. Through several stories told by Dalton and Cole Younger, comparing them to stories told by the men closest to Dalton, it appears that John Younger did live on and would take on another identity. I, the writer believe he took on the name of Colonel James Russell Davis. Howk wrote in his book that John Younger became Judge Isaac Parker in Fort Smith. Both Bud and I do not believe that.

Howk also wrote that Dewitt Travis' father, Elbert Dewitt Travis was Quantrill. We also do not believe that.

Several false stories are also shared about Bloody Bill Anderson. It is very hard to decipher the truth, but the story that seems the most legit is from Paul R. Petersen, author of "Quantrill of Missouri." Bill was only 21 years old when his mother was struck by lightning and killed. He was 23 when his father's life was taken at the age of 42.

"After William Quantrill's raid on Aubry, Kansas on March 7, 1862, a Federal company from Olathe, Kansas sent a patrol from Company D, Eighth Kansas Jayhawker Regiment to investigate. Southern sympathizers living nearby were sought out and accused of aiding the raiders. Willian Anderson's father and uncle were named as such. When the Jayhawker company arrived at the Anderson farm on March 11th, William and his younger brother Jim (James Monroe Anderson) were delivering 15 head of cattle to the U.S. commissary agent at Fort Leavenworth. When the brothers returned to their farm, they found their father and uncle hanged in retaliation, their home burned to the ground, and all their possessions were stolen."[41]

Within a day or two, young William and his brother Jim joined up with Quantrill. Later we find in documents that Bloody Bill's brother Jim rode with Jesse and Arthur McCoy in their outlaw days. Jim was later killed in 1871 by having his throat slit in Austin by William Poole. This has been confirmed on *Find a Grave.com* but on *Legendsofamerica.com*, it claims George W. Shepherd, another Quantrill guerrilla and member of the James/Younger gang killed Jim Anderson.

When Bloody Bill was asked why he joined Quantrill, Anderson replied, "I have chosen guerilla warfare to revenge myself for wrongs that I could not honorable revenge otherwise. I lived in Kansas when this war commenced. Because I would not fight the people of Missouri, my native state, the Yankees sought my life but failed to get me. They revenged themselves by murdering my father and destroying all my property, and since that time murdered one of my sisters and kept the other two in jail for twelve months."[42]

As a very young man, Jesse grew up hard and fast. He had blood in his eyes when he joined Quantrill. Could you blame him? The bitter hatred for the Union grew deeper and deeper throughout the war. When the Union commanders ordered all captured guerillas to be shot, then Quantrill ceased taking prisoners and began killing. He was known as a feared Rebel raider, but for his supporters, he was a dashing, free-spirited hero. He must have put on an air of legality to what he was doing, drenched in his neighbor's blood.

In 1863, a horrendous accident involving female prisoners, who were related to the guerrilla army, turned the fierce Quantrill guerillas into temporary psychotic madmen. The women, including three sisters of Bloody Bill Anderson, Molly (17), Josephine (age 14), and Martha (age 11) were captured and imprisoned on the suspicion of aiding and abetting the Confederate cause. The Anderson farm was near Gallatin and two of the sisters would walk the road to town and sell vegetables and dairy products. They were being carefully watched by the federals who with their spies, concluded that the girls were divulging the Union plans to the Confederates.

The Federal soldiers captured the girls as they were heading back home. They were taken to Gallatin and thrown in a makeshift prison which was an old three-story brick building. The building was in such ill repair and the lady prisoners were told often by the prison guards that the building was unstable, and it would eventually fall. The guards stayed clear of the building.

For some odd reason, brick pillars in the basement were removed that were supporting the first floor, but gravely weakened the entire building. Dr. Joshua Thorne, after visiting the prison to ensure health and safety of the women, knew the building was unsafe and notified the military authorities of the fact, suggesting the removal of the women prisoners, but his suggestion was not heeded. The building collapsed and Josephine Anderson, Susan Womack, and two others were killed and others critically injured. Molly Anderson suffered serious back injuries and facial lacerations and Martha Anderson's legs were horribly crushed and crippled for life.

What a horrible tragedy! The ladies were only young girls. I can't even start to imagine the intense sorrow and rage that these families were swallowed up in. Bloody Bill, Quantrill, and their men, including Frank and Jesse became bloodthirsty vigilantes. Within a week, they rode into Lawrence, Kansas in the early morning hours where the stronghold of the anti-slavery forces in

Kansas were stationed at. Harrison Crow was amongst them. They stayed the entire day. They dragged out every man and every boy that they could find and murdered them in front of their families. The ages of the murdered victims were from 14 to 90 years of age; 169 dead. They looted every building, every house, and burned them to the ground. Only two businesses were spared. They never touched the women, but all but two men were killed. One hid out in a well and the other dressed up in a woman's Mother Hubbard dress and sun bonnet and escaped. The two were believed to be Jim Lane, a leader of the Jayhawkers and Charles Jennison who would later take vengeance against Jesse's family. Jesse called Lane a "rank abolitionist." "We almost had him," Jesse said on the audio tape on his 102nd birthday.

A story posted in the Watonga Republican spoken of earlier, regarding Charles Hart/Quantrill's friend, Abe Ellis, tells a different side of Quantrill. When Quantrill was raiding Lawrence, Ellis was on the 2nd floor of a hotel and was shot by one of his raiders. Luckily, the bullet just creased his scalp and didn't penetrate his skull. Ellis describes Quantrill coming upstairs and recognizing him and telling Ellis how much he regretted that this had happened and would not have allowed it had he known. At that moment, Ellis had seen a glimpse of the old Charles Hart who was kindhearted and had shown mercy to others, but the war changed him.

Ellis' encounter with the mild-mannered Charles Hart and the heartless Quantrill was a story he told many times at the reunions of G.A.R. (Grand Army of the Republic), a Union veterans organization formed after the war.

To clear up a popular belief written about Bloody Bill Anderson describing him as a savage blood-thirsty villain, I must notate again what author, Paul R. Petersen found. It was a statement made by Anderson himself to a Federalist, to his face. "Bill Anderson and his men are often labeled as being known to scalp Union soldiers and having their scalps hanging from their saddle bows. This myth is shattered by the statement made by Anderson himself to a Union soldier he took off the train as a prisoner at Centralia, Missouri on September 27, 1864. "You are Federals, and Federals scalped my men, and carry their scalps at their saddle bows. I have never allowed my men to do such things."

"How the story came about in the Yankee Press, occurred after October 11, 1864 when Captain John Pringle, a large redheaded guerilla leader and his one group of guerrillas from the area of Boonville, Missouri rode into town next to Anderson's men to meet with General Sterling Price concerning the guerrillas aiding him on his recent raid into Missouri. Pringle and some of his men reportedly had Federal scalps hanging from their horses' bridle bits. This inevitably led to the erroneous story being attributed to Anderson and his men."[43]

War was indeed hell, as Jesse described it. It grieved him so to talk about the war which changed his family's way of life. He would always refer to it as "The War Between the States". He said, "It is the only war ever fought that never ended. Never will. Some folks call it the Civil War, but there wasn't a damn thing civil about it. It was the War Between the States and war is hell."[44]

Jesse always brought out in his writings and his oral commentaries between the years 1936-1951, that "Our women and girls were always the ones to suffer worst in these raids for the fighting was nearly all won on southern soil and often our women folks were subjected to outrage and unspeakable abuse. On one occasion a company of Jennison's Jayhawkers took my mother and sisters, and the mother and sisters of Frank and Jesse James, stripped them to their waist, and tied them to trees, and whipped them with a blacksnake mule whip. They whipped them until they got tired and rode away leaving them tied. Our slaves cut them down and washed and bandaged their bleeding backs and bodies and nursed them until they were well, although **Aunt Zerelda** and my **oldest sister** hovered between life and death for several days. This they claimed, when we finally overtook them, was in retaliation for their defeat by us at the Battle of Bowers Mill. And so it went, one outrage following on the heels of another, made the war a personal matter with us, and not just sides. We had to fight to keep our families from being destroyed and after the war was over and the men of Quantrill were outlawed and being hunted by reward hungry brutes, how loyal were the people among whom we had fought. They were always ready and willing to give us sanctuary until what few, what very few, that was left alive of us were finally granted amnesty." ("Battle of Centrailia," Short Stories, by Frank Dalton, pg.7)

In a James' family story, it is told that Zerelda while she was pregnant and Susan, her daughter, age 14, were imprisoned because they refused to cooperate with the Federal authorities in hunting Frank James and Quantrill in 1863. This was the same time they hung Dr. Samuels three times that day, causing serious brain injuries and never recovered fully. They beat Jesse to a pulp. When the ladies were released after being forced to sign an oath of allegiance, Zerelda had her baby and named her Fannie "Quantrill" Samuels in defiance.

Slim Williams, when talking with Bud, emphasized over and over again that Jesse during the Civil War and outlaw days, was trying to get back what was taken from the southerners and get a hold of the Yankees who were doing all the destruction in the south.

Jesse told Slim about the time that he was taken prisoner. The Union soldiers lined them up and placed each of them on a horse to take them through a procession march to the compound facility where they would be imprisoned. Jesse could sense something was up and remembered that the Union had declared that they would take no prisoners.

Jesse was very smart, so he eased up on an old mule and moved toward the back of the line. When the procession started, the Yankees came out of bushes and behind trees and ambushed these men, killing as many as they could as though they were in a turkey shoot. Jesse turned his mule and headed for Quantrill's camp. A Yankee's bullet must have grazed his forehead, strong enough to knock Jesse out, but not powerful enough to do any more damage than making a deep dent in his head near his hairline. He was a very lucky man. The next thing he remembers, was him still sitting on the mule at the edge of Quantrill's camp. The dent remained as a reminder throughout his life. On the postmortem document for J. Frank Dalton in 1951, the dent was found.

Jesse left Quantrill's outfit 4 days earlier than when the war was declared over, and General Lee had surrendered. Jesse, first lieutenant of Anderson's unit at 17 years old, led 14 of the men into Lexington, Missouri, carrying the white flag of surrender. They were stopped short by a Yankee soldier firing upon them. Jesse was hit in his right lung. It took several months to recover and continued to give him problems throughout his life.

Daily, Jesse, going by the name of Frank Dalton, made the statement to Slim that when he turned 100, he would shock the nation. In one vulnerable moment when the two had drank up the night with the money Jesse got for selling his "calling card" for 35 cents apiece, Jesse had to be helped to bed by Slim. As Slim began helping Jesse remove his shirt and pants, Slim clearly could see the deep red rope burn marks around his neck that was usually covered up by his high collar and neck tie he always wore. Slim saw bullet holes in his chest and the dent deep in his forehead. What was most disturbing was when Slim removed Jesse's socks and saw his blackened burnt soles of his feet. Slim could not believe his eyes. Jesse was out of it but must have known by morning what Slim had discovered. Jesse was gone by early morning, with the help of a waitress friend, leaving nothing behind, but memories for Slim to treasure for the rest of his life. That's the last time Slim ever saw him.

Prior to Slim's encounter with the old man, 67 years older than he, Jesse began writing under the name of Frank Dalton, known only as the "last of Quantrills Raiders." His words, "The Civil War and its aftermath has blighted and ruined my life, of course, is a fact as you can realize, but at this day, I try to hold grudges against no one although my mother and sisters as well as other women and girls of our Southland were cruelly wronged and abused by a ruthless and arrogantly raiding force. Our Southland has not recovered, nor will it ever recover, from the terrible four years of blood and carnage of over seventy-five years ago." (Apparently, he had written this near the year 1940) "When the war was over, our Confederate money had no value of course, so we of the South were penniless. These days of our prosperity and happiness are over, nor will they ever return. They are but a memory, a memory that is fondly cherished by a very few of us that lived through them and are still alive to tell of them. God grant that we never have another war. How cruel, how useless it all is." Yours truly, Frank Dalton.

Cole Younger's story is pretty much the same. He writes in his book, "Story of Cole Younger", "The conflicts and troubles centered on our home planted a bitterness in my young heart which cried out for revenge and this feeling was only accentuated by the cruelties of war which followed. I refer in particular to the shameful and cowardly murder of my father for money which he was known to have in his possession, and the cruel treatment of my mother at the hands of the Missouri Militia. Father was in the employ of the United States government and had the mail contract for five hundred miles. While in Washington attending to some business, regarding this matter, a raid was made by the Kansas Jayhawkers upon the livery stable and stage line for several miles out into the country. The robbers also looting his store and destroying his property generally. When my father returned from Washington and learned of these outrages, he went to Kansas City, Missouri, headquarters of the State Militia, to see if anything could be done. He had started back to Harrisonville in a buggy, but was waylaid one mile south of Westport, a suburb of Kansas City, and brutally murdered, falling out of his buggy into the road with three mortal bullet wounds."[45]

On the History Channel documentary, "In Search of History – Quantrill's Raiders," narrated by David Ackroyd, they stated that Cole Younger was disgusted after the Lawrence Raid and even more so after Baxter Springs; more drinking, robbing civilians, and death of innocent people. William Gregg and Cole Younger leave the raiders with disgust.[46]

After the war, they could not go back to their farms. The Quantrill Militia was considered outlaws and were to be shown no mercy but shot or hung when and where they were captured. "The country was overrun by the riff-raff and trash of both armies, and major crimes were of almost daily occurrence, especially in the South and middle West, and bank and train robberies were common, and as we of Quantrill's men were refused amnesty and were declared outlaws for fighting to protect our home against northern invaders, all the bank and train robberies that were committed were laid to us whether we were guilty or not." (Jesse James)

What was the main cause of the war? Jesse, noted as Frank Dalton, stated in one of his writings in "The Crittenden Memoirs", published in 1936, that "the war was to bankrupt and demonstrate the South, where we were fast building up the **grandest system of aristocracy** the world has ever known, an aristocracy based alone on honor and integrity. The war was over states' rights. The South wanted each state to pass its own laws, to legislate for its self, while the North wanted **to centralize** all legislations, for instance, if we of Texas wished to create a local law pertaining to cotton, the union wanted a man from up North who had never seen a stalk of cotton and knew nothing about it to share an equal right to make laws pertaining to it as a man who was raised in the South and therefore could legislate intelligently. That is what brought on the Civil War; the slavery question was not brought into it 'till 1863."

Slavery is the answer always given, mostly those who supported the North. If you do your research, Jesse was indeed correct when he said the slavery question was not brought up until 1863, two years after the war started. Slavery was a horrible practice and needed to have ended many years before, but the war was so, so much more than slavery.

From a Confederate soldier's interview by General Julius Franklin Howell, Company "K," 24th Virginia Cavalry; "The south did not fight for the preservation or extension of slavery. As a boy, I didn''t think about abolitionist nor slavery, my mind wasn't developed enough to take in what the **politicians** had in mind. I couldn't understand it. The war was fought for states' rights."

Many believe that at the very beginning, the division was created by Congress seated in the North. The North was known as the industrial giant and producer of food crops for the United States and was favored by the political system. The South was known for its production of cotton and other raw commodities. The North depended upon machinery and the south depended on slave labor and their own sweat. Congress began creating hardships for the southerners by implementing strict taxes on their Northern goods, making it extremely difficult for southerners to purchase. Very few southerners were large plantation owners with slave laborers. The majority of the southerners were families of small farms working their own crops, with maybe a few slaves to work alongside them.

Congress forbid the south to sell their goods to other countries, but strictly sell to the factories in the North. This whole scenario developed into an economic issue and a road towards control and power of the government. The needs and provisions of each southern state were different from the North and were not being met. This is where "States Rights" come into play.

The Confederate Song, "Bonnie Blue Flag," by Harry McCarthy

"We are a bank of brothers and native to the soil.
Fighting for our liberty, with treasure, blood and toil.
And when our rights were threatened, the cry rose near and far,
Hurrah, Hurrah! For Southern rights, Hurrah!
Hurrah for the Bonnie Blue Flag that bears a single star.
As long as the Union was faithful to her trust,
Like friends and like brethren, kind we were, and just.
But now, when Northern treachery attempts our rights to mar,
We hoist on high the Bonnie Blue Flag that bears a single star.
Hurrah, Hurrah! For Southern rights, Hurrah.
Hurrah for the Bonnie Blue Flag that bears a single star.
Then here's to our Confederacy, strong we are and brave.
Like patriots of old we'll fight, our heritage to save.
And rather than submit to shame, to die we would prefer.
So cheer, cheer for the Bonnie Blue Flag that bears a single star."

(Cover sheet music for "The Bonnie Blue Flag" words by Harry McCarthy, New Orleans: A.E. Blackmar & Bro., 1861 (color cover image from the Library of Congress) – The Project Gutenberg EBook of The Good Old Songs We Used to Sing, '61 to '65, by Osbourne H. Oldroyd -

http://www.gutenberg.org/etext/21566. Notice on the top, "To Albert G. Pike, Esq., The Poet Lawyer of Arkansas.)

Songs that were written during this era, ring out the message of liberty from a powerful government and economics. Take the time to listen to the words of these songs which inspired the soldiers to continue. Many common farmers, plantation owners, industrial manufacturers, transportation entities, grocers, cattlemen, and financial institutions had no desire to cut off relationships between producers of all goods in this country, but the threat became evident with all the arguments that were being presented on both sides.

When President Lincoln called to raise Northern troops against the South due to the insurrection and secession, it placed a wedge between North and South that brought fear of "Big Brother" and control of their way of doing things. The southerners saw it as their freedom being taken away, their property removed, and their way of life.

Young men who had studied and who had heard stories of the Revolutionary War had their doubts about big government and the road the United States was on. They did not want to contend with those in rule such as the British who imposed their forces, their taxes, and their way of life. This thought brought out the rebel in many a young man.

Below is an excerpt written by a man who was there amongst them; by Randolph H. McKim, D.D.; First Lt. and A.D. Third Brigade, Army of Northern Virginia. He said the war was not about slavery.

"Such were the private soldiers of the Confederacy as I knew them. Not for fame or for glory, not lured by ambition or goaded by necessity, but, in simple obedience to duty as they understood it, these men suffered all, sacrificed all, dared all, and died! I would like to add a statement which doubtless will appear paradoxical, but which my knowledge of those men, through many campaigns, and on many fields, and in many camps, gives me, I think, the right to make with confidence, viz: the dissolution of the Union was not what the Southern soldier had chiefly at heart. The establishment of the Southern Confederacy was not, in his mind, the supreme issue of the conflict. Both the one and the other were secondary to the preservation of the sacred right of self-government. They were means to the end, not the end itself."[47]

These words are very sobering and cuts the heart in two, just as the war did our sovereign nation. It left many scars upon Jesse and all who had to participate, willingly or unwillingly. We truly can hear it in Jesse's words that lingered in his thoughts daily, staying with him forever. I believe the war was the thing that he regretted the most.

Towards the end of his life, Jesse reflected on all that had occurred and what he had learned. He had learned the secrets of war, which would forever be the downfall of mankind.

The Men of Quantrill
By Frank Dalton

*When the Civil war was over,
And the South had laid down their arms
And came back to wives and sweethearts,
To their villages or farms.*

*Quantrill's men were classed as criminals,
We had not been mustered in
To the regular Southern armies,
We were a band of outlawed men.*

*Hunted down and shot like wild things.
Like a coyote, wolf, or bear;
Chased from one state to another,*

Bud Hardcastle: The Truth Tracker

Hunted, hounded everywhere.

Not a crime so dark or fiendish,
Nor an act so mean or low,
But twas charged to the men of Quantrill,
"Yes, it must be them, you know."

And when the war was over
And we'd scattered o'er the land,
Here and there arose a rumor,
"Yes he's one of Quantrill's band.

Some were chased and killed or captured,
Others ran or hid away,
But it's time the Truth was spoken,
We are feeble, old and gray.

Let us tell our simple story
How we fought to shield our homes
From the thugs and border ruffians,
Tho we had to fight alone.

Some made good while others didn't,
Some gained wealth and honor too,
Others took the "Owl Hoot" trail,
That there was nothing else to do.

But no matter what their station,
Or how well we became known,
The cloud of "65" was present
And our names were not our own.

But our secret well was guarded
By the men who knew us well,
"Quantrill's oath" took care of that,
"What you know don't ever tell."[48]

Chapter Six: The Secret War Within

Secret #1: The Root of All Evil

War was Hell. The aftermath was 10 times worse for those who supported the Confederacy and was far worse than the Civil War itself.

Finally, liberty was given to the slaves. They began to taste freedom, but also at a cost. It was all new to them. Some left the plantations to seek a new life, some stayed where they had worked because of the security that they had felt with their masters and could continue to work for pay. Some were at a loss on where to go. Free at last, but they too had a hard road ahead. Would their freedom continue?

Would Jesse ever gain freedom? As the poem suggests, Jesse and his men were in hiding and couldn't go back to their homes. Because they were guerillas and not a part of the Confederate Army, they did not receive amnesty. They became homeless and on the run. Jesse was 17 at the end of the war and the only ones he could depend on was his family, the Southerners who supported him, and most of all his brothers within the Quantrill Militia. Their relationship and brotherhood expanded, growing quite strong, but more importantly, growing in knowledge and secrecy.

Secrets and the art of keeping secrets were learned by Jesse during the war, empowering him to become a master at it. This practice would be gradually built upon throughout his life, gaining knowledge, wisdom, wealth, power, control, and self-preservation.

The next two chapters delve into the deep dark secrets that Jesse obtained, but only gave us a glimpse of. He was extremely careful with his secrets. He never divulged them to Ola or Aubrey; he was protecting them.

These were the hardest chapters to write in this book, but it must be told. It was a part of Jesse's story, even though he never spoke of it. There were two aspects of the war that have rarely appeared in history books: money and secret societies. The next four chapters will expose some of the clandestine operations that were in full force during the Civil War. In fact, most of these operations had their birth as early as the Revolutionary War.

I am in no way an expert on the subjects we are about to discuss, nor have I had firsthand experience, but I do my research in all directions. I depend highly on facts from both sides of the spectrum. I focus on historical documents (Confederate and Union), firsthand knowledge, family stories, autobiographies, common sense, and most of all spiritual discernment that we are all gifted with. My trust is in God's guidance, directing me in the path He wants me to pursue.

Bud always told me that so many things opened up for him to discover the truth about Jesse. Well indeed, I have experienced it also. In these next few chapters, the only explanation on the material gathered here, is through Divine guidance. It was amazing how God directed me to so many places, people, books, websites, and new territory that opened many doors for this writer. I am so grateful and honored that God was so faithful to us in this search for the truth. All glory goes to God.

I began to see the strong political aspect of the Civil War that was fueling this massive, divisive ideology. It was not until I met Bud Hardcastle, that my research was directed into a deep dark realm of reality which has been hidden beneath the surface.

Just a note: I take full responsibility of this chapter and the next three that follow. Bud has led me in this direction but has not fully discussed this issue with me in detail. He knows more than he will tell. When I was going over questions about the cause of the war and what Jesse was involved in, I asked Bud what he wanted me to write on that subject. His answer was, "let me think about it." I believe he was protecting me in a chivalrous way, such as Jesse was trying to protect Ola. *

It is within these chapters that I disclose what I have found in my own research. In no way do I want the readers to pin these issues or opinions onto Bud, but they certainly coincide with the direction he was taking me. I respectfully received full permission from Bud to include these chapters in his book, enabling the reader to see the full picture of how our country was formed within its foundation and framework, as Jesse James stepped into manhood at the very young age of 15. Everything relates to Jesse and what he became involved in.

I lay the facts out for the reader to research and form their own opinion. Research with your own eyes and your vision will become clearer. As Bud and his good friend, Joe Wood always said, "Research, research, and then research some more."

The war was over, but war was still brewing. It was a political and economic war, lingering in the smoky haze of past artillery fire. Had it been there all along, creating its own haze to hide the true cause of the war? We see evidence in the last chapter that it truly was there years before the war. There were smoke screens that were implemented to blind the innocent victims of this senseless war. If you carefully read Jesse's words, you'll find the answer. His words of wisdom in later years speak volumes to those who will tune in.

Even though many of the men who fought this uncivilized war had a purpose, a cause, and an explanation for the reasoning of it, which all truly mattered and was definitely part of the whole picture, the majority had no clue what was behind it all; money, greed, power, and control. It was a dark, sinister, and evil plot to keep control of the American population, its money, economics, and commerce.

Researching the war, I was able to find articles in newspapers during those critical years, before, during, and after the war. The newspapers in those days, as well as the news outlets today, were filled with propaganda. The propaganda war moved into position like those non-residents moved into areas such as Kansas and Missouri to stir up controversy and set the scene for war. They were "professional agitators."

Just one droplet of news on a daily basis was designed to coerce the most intelligent into believing an idea, a philosophy, and to manipulate the minds of the people, drip by drip. Newspapers were bought up by the wealthy elite who had an agenda to divide our country. Editorials were written in such harsh ways, criticizing President Lincoln. Southern newspapers placed horrendous words in print, calling the Unionists, "Lincolnpoops" or "Black Republicans."

Northern newspapers printed, "Rebels dehumanized Unionists, characterizing them as the roughest and lowest forms of life and advocating that they be driven out of the valley."[49]

By 1864, the Union newspapers began to have the upper hand and began drawing out strong supporters of the Union to use speech and propaganda to draw more blood. The most outspoken Unionists of course was William Brownlow of the "Knoxville Whig." He was a special *treasury* agent for East Tennessee, and he used this power to devour the secessionists and help his friends. Brownlow referred the secessionists as "Imps from Hell." His hate poured from his lips, stating that the Union men who had suffered during the Confederate occupations would be "justified in shooting them down on sight."[50]

It is truly an eye opener to read what the printing press laid out on newsprint during those years. Everyone needs to research the old newspapers and see what actually was going on. It was appalling and disgusting! We certainly could not get away with that today, or are we?

America? Seems as though we are falling back into the same trap! There was and now is so much hype, so much propaganda in our world today that has been going on for centuries. Let's stop and think for ourselves, not allowing others to dictate our thoughts or shape our country into something it was never intended to be.

The divisive monologue was spread throughout the newspapers, signs, songs, organizations, and even churches. From the inside of this nation's heart and soul, a big gulf was widening as the pulpits poured out their fiery sermons against the enemy. Both sides had their own enemy. Both sides condemned the other to Hell.

The war, as with all wars, was designed to divide and conquer. There was a lot of money to be made at a very high cost. The meticulous design set forth to weaken America through its people and the economic system was working, just as it had done in the 18th century.

The thought and design of this evil entity to globalize the world's economic system became strong and apparent during and after the Revolutionary War, but it must have always been in the world arena for centuries.

America's Forefathers, not at all perfect, were indeed ordained by God to serve out a particular purpose. They were fervent in their beliefs and were determined to create a nation based on faith and freedom. They had their faults just like us, but had it not been for these men who took the lead role in establishing our country, creating our founding documents such as the Declaration of Independence, the Constitution, and the Bill of Rights, and leading the colonists to fight against a tyrannical government, we would not be free.

Our Founding Fathers wanted a free world, a God-given right. They pursued justice and liberty for all and fought long and hard for our country's foundation to be based on Godly principals. This idea did not set well with the British Monarchy.

After the surrender of the British in the Revolutionary War in 1781, a meeting between Charles Cornwallis or his servant and General George Washington was planned to discuss the articles of surrender. There are various renditions of this meeting, so it is not clear if it was Cornwallis himself or a representative which carried the words of Cornwallis. A book written that very year by Jonathan Williams in "Legions of Satan" addressed the conversation. Cornwallis told Washington, "A holy war will now begin on America, and when it is ended, America will be supposedly the citadel of freedom, but her millions will unknowingly be loyal subjects to the Crown. Your churches will be used to teach the Jew's religion and in less than two hundred years the whole nation will be working for divine world government. That government that they believe to be divine will be the British Empire. All religions will be permeated with Judaism without even being noticed by the masses, and they will all be under the invisible all seeing eye of the Grand Architect of Freemasonry."[51] (This book was removed from the Library of Congress in the 80's or 90's)

Was America the one who was actually surrendering after the Revolutionary War?

British Prime Minister William Pitt was overwhelmed with Britain's excessive debt during the American Revolution and said, "Let the American people go into their debt-funding schemes and banking systems, and from that hour their boasted independence will be a mere phantom."[52]

Nine years later, in 1790, Mayer Amschel Rothschild, a Ashkenazi Jewish banker and founder of the Rothschild banking dynasty stated: "Let me issue and control a nations' money and I care not who writes the laws."[53]

By 1791, the Rothschilds were in control of the money flowing in and out of America. The nation's first *"centralized* bank" was created by Rothschild and founded by Alexander Hamilton, their agent in the Washington cabinet. Stockholders of the bank consisted of foreigners across the ocean. It was affiliated with the European Central Banks. They began to dominate the financial policies of every country in the world.

The first bank in America was called the First Bank of the United States. It was allowed a 20-year charter. During the 20 years, President Thomas Jefferson, the author of the Declaration of Independence, saw firsthand how unconstitutional this central banking institution was and would be in the time of a national crisis. In a letter to Albert Gallatin in December 13, 1803, Jefferson wrote: "I deem no government safe which is under the vassalage of any self-constituted authorities, or any other authority than that of the nation or its regular functionaries. What an obstruction could not this bank of the United States, with all its branch banks, be in time of war? It might dictate to us the peace we should accept or withdraw its aids. Ought we then to give further growth to an institution so powerful, so hostile?"[54]

The charter was not renewed in 1811, under the watch of President James Madison, who led in designing and creating the Bill of Rights which he introduced in 1789. This document spelled out American's rights in relation to their government. It was passed and ratified in 1791, the same year Rothschilds took over the money of America.

British financiers who owned two-thirds of the Bank's stock was extremely upset that the charter would not be renewed in 1811. By the wealth and financial power of the Rothschilds, the British declared war in 1812 against the United States. There are many opinions on why the war was started, just as those opinions about the Civil War, occurring 49 years later. I believe the reason is obvious.

The War of 1812 crippled America's economic system. Many believe the Rothschilds plan was to cause the United States to build up such a debt in fighting this war that they would have to surrender to the Rothschilds and give in to their money, allowing the charter to be renewed.

American and British intelligence have documented evidence that the house of Rothschild, and other international bankers, have financed both sides of every war, since the American Revolution. It is even noted that they helped finance the British armies against Napoleon in Spain and France.

President Jefferson was on to their scheme. Ten years prior to his death, he wrote a letter to John Taylor on May 28, 1816. "And I sincerely believe, with you, that banking establishments are more dangerous than standing armies; and that the principle of spending money to be paid by posterity, under the name of funding, is but swindling futurity on a large scale."[55]

At the very end of President James Madison's term as president, in 1816, the American Congress passed a bill permitting another 20-year charter for a Rothschild dominated central bank. It would be known as the Second Bank of the USA, giving the Rothschild's control of the American money supply again. The action was taken to restore the United States economy devastated by the War of 1812.

The bank was run by Nicholas Biddle who claimed he had more personal power than the president. He had a strong influence in the political arena, using his money to promote candidates who had the same philosophy as he or one who could be persuaded to his. The politicians sought after his money to rev up their campaign and have a voice in Biddle's editorial page of the numerous newspaper institutions he owned.

The next year, 1817, we had a new president, James Monroe. As president, Monroe signed the Missouri Compromise we spoke of earlier which admitted Missouri as a slave state and banned slavery from territories north of the parallel 36 degrees 30' North.

In 1832, President Andrew Jackson runs for his 2nd term in office with a slogan; "Jackson and no bank".[56] Having served as general in the War of 1812 and as president in his first term, he saw the corruption and understood how tyrannic the banking system had become. He wanted to take control of the American money system, which would benefit the American people and not the Rothschilds and their European stockholders who definitely had control of this Nation, enslaving its citizens.

President Andrew Jackson's quotes:

"Some of powers and privileges possessed by the existing Bank are unauthorized by the Constitution, subversive to the rights of the States, and dangerous to the liberties of the people."

"Controlling our currency, receiving our public moneys, and holding thousands of our citizens in dependence, it would be more formidable and dangerous than the naval and military power of the enemy."[57]

In 1833, President Jackson started removing the government's money from the Rothschild controlled Second Bank. He is persuaded by Democratic bankers to deposit the money into local and state banks directed by them. This action caused the Rothschilds to panic and so Biddle began stockpiling the Bank's reserves and contracting credit, causing the interest rates to soar and bring on a depression.

Jackson knew exactly what they were doing, "You are a den of vipers. I intend to rout you out, and by the Eternal God, I will rout you out. If the people only understood the rank injustice of our money and banking system, there would be a revolution before morning."[58]

"The Bank is thus converted into a vast electioneering engine, with means to embroil the country in deadly feuds, and extend its corruption through all the ramifications of society."

"The men who profit by the abuses and desire to perpetuate them will continue to besiege the halls of legislation in the General Government and will seek by every artifice to mislead and deceive the public servants."[59]

The country began to change under the leadership of Jackson, reverting back to what was intended by our founding fathers. The national economy was booming. The federal government, through duty revenues and sale of public lands was able to pay off the entire national debt by January 1, 1835. Twenty-nine days later, January 30, 1835, there was an attempt to kill the sitting president of the United States outside the Capitol. By God's divine protection, the assassin's two pistols misfired. Jackson was spared. Jackson claimed Rothschilds were to blame.

By 1836, Jackson finally succeeds in removing the Rothschilds Central Bank out of America. The bank's charter was not renewed.

In Andrew Jackson's farewell address in 1837, his words were powerful. "Providence has showered on this favored land, blessings without number, and has chosen you as the guardians of freedom, to preserve it for the benefit of the human race." [60]

In 1841, President John Tyler, who after just one month of becoming vice president to President William Henry Harrison, became president overnight when Harrison died just one month after taking the office. Tyler was an advocate of states' rights and citizen's rights. He vetoed the act to renew the charter for the Bank of the United States. He receives hundreds of letters on threats of assassination.

When the Civil War started in 1861, the economy was unstable. The Central Bank did not have a charter in the U.S., but their hand was involved in state-chartered banks. President Lincoln contacted the large banks in New York, who were under the influence of the Rothschilds, to try to obtain loans to support the ongoing American Civil War. The banks were more than happy to offer Lincoln a deal. The loans offered had an attached interest rate of 24-36 percent. Lincoln declined the offer.

"I have two great enemies, the Southern Army in front of me, and the bankers in the rear. Of the two, the one at my rear is my greatest foe."[61]   Abraham Lincoln

In a very valuable piece of newsprint in Bud's collection from Janesville Daily Gazette out of Janesville, Wisconsin, August 26, 1958, an article was printed titled, "Voice of the People" written by W.D. Chesney. We will learn more about him in a later chapter. It describes a letter from President Abraham Lincoln to Ezra Erasmus Chesney, the writer's father and describes some prophetic words. "It was written in 1863 and states that he deplores the tendency to neglect to heed G. Washington's advice, given in his farewell address to his officers, at Fraunces Tavern, New York, that this country stay out of Europe's never-ending intrigues and wars. The letter continues: "Due to wars corruptions have been enthroned and an era of corruption in high places will follow. The people's wealth is being aggregated into a few hands, and the nation will be destroyed."

The Civil War was creating tremendous debt. The international bankers were eager to step in. Otto von Bismark, chancellor of Germany, 1876 was quoted as saying, "The division of the United States into federations of equal force was decided long before the Civil War by the high financial powers of Europe. These bankers were afraid that the US, if they remained as one block, and as one nation, would attain economic and financial independence, which would upset their financial domination over the world."[62]

"It is practically certain that war between the North and the South was fomented by the money interest of Britain, the purpose being to divide the states, that the "old mother country" might profit thereby." [63]

Lincoln knew of Edmund "Dick" Taylor, a politician in Illinois and had heard from General Grant's headquarters that Taylor had an idea to secure finance for the war. Lincoln and Taylor met, and the suggestion of Taylor's was the issuance of treasury notes, bearing no interest, printed on quality paper.

In Article One, Section Eight of the United States Constitution, it reads: "The Congress shall have power...to coin money, regulate the value thereof, and of foreign coin, and fix the standard of weights and measures."[64]

The Greenback dollar was born. Lincoln had 450 million dollars in Greenbacks printed, new bills using green ink on the back to identify them versus other notes. It was legal tender, representing a dollar's worth of obligation on the part of the government. It was not backed by the gold standard.

Greenbacks could be used to pay the soldiers, suppliers, and government contractors. Best of all, it was full legal tender, debt free money used for both public and private debts.

The Confederacy printed their own money, called the Greyback and was placed into circulation in April 1861.

Lincoln's plans were working, and it infuriated those who had been in charge of the world's wealth. In the London Times, 1865, the newspaper was describing what was occurring in America during the war; a little behind in its news, but you can read through the lines on what the British elite's sentiment was and the panic it caused. "If this mischievous financial policy, which has its origin in North America, shall become indurated down to a fixture, then that Government will furnish its own money without cost. It will pay off debts and be without debt. It will have all the money necessary to carry on its commerce. It will become prosperous without precedent in the history of the world. The brains, and wealth of all countries will go to North America. That country must be destroyed, or it will destroy every monarchy on the globe."[65]

By 1863, Lincoln was in the heart of the war and more money was needed. He could not ask Congress to print any more money, but the elite bankers proposed an idea, "the National Bank Act."

A man by the name of John Sherman introduced the bill to reform the nations' financial system in 1863. The National Bank Act passed, "was designed to create a national banking system, float federal war loans, and establish a national currency." [66]

Sherman was a politician from Ohio who was a Master of Finance and an anti-slavery activist. Prior to the Civil War, as a congressman, he traveled to Kansas to investigate the unrest between pro and anti-slavery partisans there. The main goal was to prevent the expansion of slavery to Kansas. After two months, he filed an 1,188-page report on the conditions in 1856. His report concluded that the Missourians, who were not living in the Kansas territory, used violence to coerce the Kansans to elect pro-slavery members to the territorial legislature.

During the Civil War, Sherman was on the Senate Finance Committee. He did not believe the greenbacks would solve the revenue problem. They did not have gold or silver to redeem the notes if presented for payment. Congress authorized issuance of $150 million in bonds to solve this problem, along with the Revenue Act of 1861; the first federal income tax in America's history. The banks began refusing to redeem the notes for gold. The precious gold began to disappear in circulation.

A change needed to be made. Sherman supported the reform of the financial system with the National Banking Act of 1863. Sherman introduced the bill, hoping that state banking would be eliminated and shift to a national bank system. Sherman contacted the Rothschilds.

A letter written by the Rothschild brothers on June 25th, 1863 to bankers of London, and Ikleheimer, Morton, and Vandergould of Wall Street relating to the National Banking Act of 1863.

"Dear Sirs,

A Mr. John Sherman has written us from a town in Ohio, U.S.A. as to the profits that may be made in the National Banking business under a recent act of your Congress, a copy of which act accompanied his letter. Apparently, this act has been drawn upon the plan formulated here last summer by the British Banker's Association and by that Association recommended to our American friends as one that if enacted into law, would prove highly profitable to the banking fraternity throughout the world.

Mr. Sherman declares that there has never before been such an opportunity for capitalists to accumulate money, as that presented by this act and that the old plan, of State Banks is so unpopular, that the new scheme will by mere contrast, be most favorably regarded, notwithstanding the fact that it gives the National Banks an almost absolute control of the National finances. The few who can understand the system, will either be so interested in its profits, or so dependent on its favors, that there will be no opposition from that class, while on the other hand, the great body of the people, mentally incapable of comprehending the tremendous advantages that capital drives from the system, will bear its burdens without complaint, and perhaps without even suspecting that the system is inimical to their interests.

Please advise us fully as to this matter and also, state whether or not you will be of assistance to us, if we conclude to establish a National Bank in the City of New York. If you are acquainted with Mr. Sherman, he appears to have introduced the National Banking Act, we will be glad to know something of him. If we avail ourselves of the information he furnished, we will of course make due compensation.

Awaiting your reply, we are,
Your Respectful Servants,
Rothschild Brothers"[67]

The National Bank Act remained the law until 1913, when the Federal Reserve, the central banking system came into place. It was set up during the presidency of Woodrow Wilson. Today, the Treasury still coins and prints our money under the authority of Congress, but neither regulates the value or issuance of it. That's done exclusively by the Federal Reserve. The Federal Reserve Bank is a private corporation that lends the money they print to the U.S. Government which includes interest on dollars issued and circulated.

Sherman after the war voted for the Confiscation Act of 1861, allowing the government to confiscate any property being used to support the Confederate war effort, including slaves, and for the act abolishing slavery in DC.

"Sherman became known as a "friend of England" in Washington DC. He frequently made reference to British history in his speeches. Sherman believed there was alot America could learn from England as an example with respects to economic systems, railroads and governance, and he was fond of highlighting the English origins of American political thought." [68]

Sherman often met with William Ewart Gladstone, Prime Minister of the UK. As senator, he met John Bright and Benjamin Disraeli. Sherman, returning from England on numerous trips was extremely convinced, "it was in America's interests to pursue a close and amiable relationship with Great Britain." [69]

The saga of the power of money and its loyal subjects continue. Are we the loyal subjects? Are we being held as collateral for the debts of those who orchestrated these wars? There is a huge debate going on currently that asks these questions. Are we a republic or a corporation? Decide for yourself as you look into the District of Columbia Organic Act of 1871 under the administration of Ulysses S. Grant which was put into place when the country was weakened and financially depleted after the Civil War.

James Garfield became president in March of 1881. His words of wisdom speak loudly to us all. "Whoever controls the volume of money in our country is absolute master of all industry and commerce. And when you realize that the entire system is very easily controlled, one way or another, by a few powerful men at the top, you will not have to be told how periods of inflation and depression originate." [70] Within weeks of making this statement, he was assassinated.

June 4, 1963, President John F. Kennedy signed the Executive Order 11110. This order would return to the U.S. government, the power to issue currency, without loans from the Federal Reserve with high interest. It would give the Treasury the power to issue silver certificates against any silver bullion in the Treasury. The silver backed currency of nearly 4.3 billion dollars in U.S. notes went into circulation. If enough of the silver certificates were to come into circulation, they would have eliminated the demand for Federal Reserve notes which is not backed by anything. Debt would have been paid off rather quickly. President Kennedy knew this was the right thing to do because he knew that the most successful vehicles used to drive up debt was war and the creation of money by a privately owned central bank.

Five months from the time President Kennedy signed this executive order, he was assassinated. The circulation of the U.S. silver backed notes was stopped.

"I do conscientiously and sincerely believe that the Order of Freemasonry, if not the greatest, is one of the greatest moral and political evils under which the Union is now laboring… a conspiracy of the few against the equal rights of the many… Masonry ought forever to be abolished. It is wrong-essentially wrong – a seed of evil, which can never produce any good."

-John Quincy Adams

Secret #2: The Powers that Be

Cornwallis' prophecy was coming true, the British Empire engaged in all aspects of America's birth, wars, religion, education, and money. That's only half of it; the last statement, "and they will all be under the invisible all-seeing eye of the Grand Architect of Freemasonry."[71]

This is chilling. There are signs everywhere in our Nation's capital, around the country, and on our money, signifying Freemasonry is alive and well in America. What exactly does it all mean? How does all this tie together? What effect did Freemasonry have on our country, the Civil War, and upon Jesse Woodson James? He made a blood oath with the brotherhood and became a knight in its high court.

The deep, dark secrets of the Civil War were embedded in the money, fueled and funded for both the Union and Confederacy. The vessel or driving force used to distribute the money, while at the same time stripping away the wealth of the citizens of the United States, was in the secret societies. These organizations were utilized to further the cause to divide and conquer and take over the power of the world. Their biggest prize was the United States. The ultimate summation of it all; evil at its worst.

There is so much more about the war than our eyes and ears can fathom. No man on earth can ever truly capture all the components that comprised this war. There are a lot of "I don't knows", but there are many clues, symbols, and deep, dark archives of courthouses, newspaper offices, and libraries that were spared during this conflict that tell a portion of the story. The men Jesse looked up to the most was his brother, cousins, and a whole slew of Quantrill Raiders. He was neck deep into protecting his clan and would follow their lead into a deeper and darker cause for the South, the Knights of the Golden Circle which had its beginnings in Freemasonry.

Freemasonry & The Framing of America

To truly understand the background and history of the men Jesse became involved with, we had to go back into the deep past. What was their goal? Who were their associates? What were they involved in? Hold on for a major history lesson and watch for the clues and symbols. It all comes together in history.

Freemasonry, defined by the Grand Lodge of Ohio, "Freemasonry is the leading fraternal organization in the world, its origins are lost in the unrecorded history of medieval time, but it formally organized in London, England in 1717. As a fraternal organization, Freemasonry unites men of good character who, though of different religious, ethnic or social backgrounds, share a belief in the fatherhood of God and the brotherhood of mankind."[72]

In the Britannica definition: "Spread by the advance of the British Empire, Freemasonry remains most popular in the British Isles and in other *countries originally* within the empire. Estimates of the worldwide membership of Freemasonry in the early 21st century range from about two million to more than six million." [73]

It sounds all well and good. Many of us have or had Freemasons in our family and circle of friends; wonderful upstanding citizens who stood on Christian principles and have contributed immensely to our nation, our communities, and our churches. Many a great man such as George Washington, Benjamin Franklin, James Monroe, and Andrew Jackson were Freemasons. The list goes on and on, including a massive amount of men in high places today within our country. They were a big part of the growth and prosperity of this country.

Freemasonry was founded in the early 1700's in England by the Venetian Party. They were involved in the East India Company and the Royal African Company of Slavers.

The Freemasons began to grow in the 1730's in America. They extended their hand of friendship to the young men who would later become leaders in this New World. They knew how to encourage, organize, delegate, rationalize/reason, build, function as a body in an orderly fashion, unify, and conduct business. Freemasons were brilliant in the design of America, in words, in laws, in governing bodies, and in liberty. They expressed charity, good will, community service, and brotherhood. Their goal for America was to build a nation of good character, a belief in a higher deity, where there was no monarchy, nor a controlled religion such as the Vatican. They believed in balance of power, three branches of government, ensuring checks and balances in a self-governing society.

Washington

George Washington, the "Father of Our Country" was indeed a Freemason. He became a surveyor in his younger years, was a leader and aid for General Braddock in the French and Indian War, chosen commander and chief of the Continental Army, leading the Patriot forces to victory in the American Revolutionary War and was the United States' first elected president.

The true test of Washington's courage and strength during the heart of the Revolutionary War was at Valley Forge where he took his troops to camp over the winter of 1777-1778. General Washington had to face some tough issues. There were 10,000-12,000 men who were marching to Valley Forge with a quarter of the troops barefoot, in need of shoes/boots. There were very few blankets; many had none nor warm clothing. The one pair of pants and one shirt that were either issued to the soldiers or those who had to wear their own clothing, could not hold up to the treacherous elements of wartime. Their threads were literally unraveling off their backs.

General Washington cared about his troops and even offered a reward of $10 to anyone who could supply raw hides for shoes for these men. Morale was so low, with desertion on the minds of many. Washington even offered a pardon on October 24th, 1777 to all deserters who would return by January 1st. He knew this war was very costly to both his men's physical and mental health.

The men began building log shelters to sustain them in the harsh winds of winter that was upon them. The shelters were not sufficient enough to keep out the drafts or the melting snow. Sickness and disease began to spread, along with malnourishment. The air within the huts was thick with smoke, which created respiratory problems.

There were only small supplies of meat and bread. The majority of the men could only eat the "fire cakes" made of flour and water. There were 2,500 men who met their death at the encampment. Nearly 4,000 men became unfit for duty. Several thousand deserted and approximately 2,000 joined the British Army due to the desperation for basic necessities to keep themselves alive. Even horses starved to death or died of exhaustion. Not only was their health and clothes deteriorating, but their spirits were as well.

Washington was always with the troops, not in his warm headquarters. He assured them that he would also share in their hardship and inconveniences. He rallied his troops, speaking of unity and perseverance which could only manifest strength; with one heart and one mind. He encouraged them to profess fortitude and patience for the "sacred cause" for which they were engaged. On the outside, Washington appeared strong, but in the inside, his compassion for these men was tearing him apart.

Valley Forge was a turning point in the war. A Prussian military soldier arrived from Europe, Baron Von Steuben, a mason, who was unable to speak English, but he was able to change the habits, discipline, and drilling patterns/techniques within the units. It made a difference, it made the American Army a more coordinated, unified, and disciplined mighty machine. The spirit returned.

Washington displayed humbleness and gratitude to the great "Author" of all, for sustaining his troops through this time of trial. A beautiful portrait of Washington kneeling in prayer at Valley

Forge was painted in 1866. Some believe there was not enough proof that Washington actually did this, but there is great evidence that he did. He sought divine guidance, direction, and comfort from God, but not for all to see. He was a very private man, especially when it came to his faith.

It is documented that when George Washington was 21 years of age, he was commissioned by Governor Dinwiddie of Virginia; he was to lead dispatches to the French Commander St. Pierre in November 1753. Before leaving, he went to his mother. Words of wisdom to her son as she was bidding him goodbye was "Remember that God only is our sure trust. To Him I commend you." Out the door, Mrs. Washington said to her son, "My son, neglect not the duty of secret prayer." George never did forget his mother's words.

General George Washington was seen by his troops to frequently visit a secluded grove. On one occasion, Isaac Potts who quartered with Washington at Valley Forge, passed through the woods nearby, and heard a voice speaking in earnest. He explored further and found our wonderful Commander-in-Chief of the American forces on his knees in prayer.

Potts left the area and went to where his wife was and exclaimed, "I have this day seen what I never expected. Thee knows that I always thought that the sword and the gospel were utterly inconsistent; and that no man could be a soldier and a Christian at the same time. But George Washington has this day convinced me of my mistake…If George Washington be not a man of God, I am greatly deceived, and still more shall I be deceived, if God do not, through him, work out a great salvation for America."[74]

When spring came, food became more plentiful, with more provisions provided. Congress recommended to the United States of America to set apart April 12, 1778 to observe a day of Fasting, Humiliation, and Prayer. An order was issued from the Headquarters at Valley Forge, "that at one time, and with one voice, the righteous dispensations of Providence may be acknowledged, and His goodness and mercy towards our arms supplicated and implore: the General directs that the day shall be most religiously observed in the Army; that no work shall be done thereon, and that the several chaplains do prepare discourses suitable to the occasion." [75]

On May 2, 1778, another order was issued at Valley Forge, "The Commander-in-Chief directs that Divine service be performed every Sunday at 11 o'clock, in each Brigade which has a Chaplain. Those Brigades which have none will attend the places of worship nearest to them. It is expected that officers of all rank will, by their attendance, set an example for their men. While we are zealously performing the duties of good Citizens and soldiers, we certainly ought not to be inattentive to the higher duties of religion. To the distinguished character of a Patriot it should be our highest glory to add the more distinguished character of a Christian. The signal instances of Providential goodness which we have experienced, and which have now almost crowned our labours with complete success, demand from us, in a peculiar manner, the warmest returns of gratitude and piety to the Supreme Author of all Good." [76]

There was also an order issued for a Day of Thanksgiving on May 5, 1778; "for gratefully acknowledging the Divine Goodness and celebrating the event, which we owe to His benign interposition." [77]

All of this acknowledgement of God's mighty power and favor for America can only describe why this ragtag group of men, under the leadership of a great man of God, won the American Revolution over such a mighty British Army.

It amazes me when I read about George Washington. He was indeed protected by the Almighty. Indians thought he was a god, because arrows that were flung toward him did not puncture him in anyway. Bullets never penetrated his flesh during the war. He had several bullet holes in his clothing, but none in the skin. He had several horses that were shot underneath him, but yet he walked away. Truly, he was a man of God under divine protection. Truly, he was God's servant to guide our country to victory.

An Indian Chief, in his dying days, along with a company of Indians came up upon Washington and his friend, Dr. James Craik, who were traveling together for the purpose of exploring land near the great Kanawha and Ohio Rivers. It was close to the year of 1770. A council fire was started, and the old Indian Chief began to speak. He had been traveling long and hard to meet Washington, "the young warrior of the battle."

The chief described a time of battle, the French and Indian War. He had observed how the daring warrior, George Washington, had the wisdom of an Indian and fought as an Indian warrior. Their rifles were aimed at Washington, but it was as if he was shielded. He was never touched.

As the Indian Chief continued speaking, Washington had a mission, a prompting, that he had to fulfill before he left this earth. He said, "I am old, and soon shall be gathered to the great council fire of my father's in the land of shades, but ere I go, there is something bids me speak in the voice of prophecy. Listen! The Great Spirit protects that man and guides his destinies. He will become the chief of nations, and a people yet unborn will hail him as the founder of a mighty empire." [78]

A very touching story needs to be also shared here. After the war and Washington was selected to be president or so-called magistrate of the newly formed United States, he went to visit his mother in Fredericksburg before he departed for New York. She had breast cancer that was ravaging her aging body. This is the conversation: Washington said, "The people, Madam, have been pleased, with the most flattering unanimity, to elect me to the chief magistracy of these United States; but before I can assume the functions of my office, I have come to bid you an affectionate Farwell. So soon as the public business, which must necessarily be encountered in arranging a new government, can be disposed of, I shall hasten to Virginia and ..." His mother stopped him from continuing. She said, "And you will see me no more. My great age, and the disease, which is fast, approaching my vitals, warn me that I shall not be long in this world. I trust in God that I may be somewhat prepared for a better. But go George, fulfill the high destinies which Heaven appears to have intended you for; go, my son, and may that Heaven's and mother's blessing be with you always." [79]

George Washington was a Master Mason and was divinely placed upon the earth for a divine reason. "He privately prayed and read the Bible daily, and he publicly encouraged people and the nation to pray." "Washington believed in a "wise, inscrutable, and irresistible" Creator God who was active in the Universe, contrary to deistic thought. He referred to God by the Enlightenment terms Providence, the Creator, or the Almighty, and also as the Divine Author or the Supreme Being." [80] His Freemasonry oath nor his allegiance to the brotherhood was not the most important thing in his life, but it was his God, country and countrymen.

In some of Washington's letters, they suggest that he believed in God as the Great Architect of the Universe, which is a belief in Freemasonry. My thoughts are that he had a lot of influence in Freemasonry, but it was, as said earlier, not the upmost importance. In a letter near the end of his life, he states that he hasn't been to a Lodge meeting in 30 years, meaning his last meeting was sometime in the 1760's. He was way too busy to do much of anything except save this country from English rule.

George Washington was the most beloved Founding Father in America. He displayed integrity, steadfastness, humility, honor, duty, and maintained a sterling reputation. He never desired glory or rewards but set his mind to fulfill his mission here on earth as a soldier for liberty and justice. Although many wanted him to continue in power, Washington declined knowing that if he stayed for a 3rd term, the nation was in danger of another monarchy. He did not want to be a King. He set the country on the right path to follow with sound judgement, morals, good character, self-control, and self-sacrifice for the common good.

Hamilton, Jefferson, Madison

The forming of a new government was not just the idea of Freemasons. There were noted Non-Masons, who are at least not documented as Freemasons, who contributed immensely to America's foundation. They were Alexander Hamilton, Thomas Jefferson, and James Madison.

Alexander Hamilton was the first Secretary of Treasury of this country and his brilliant idea of capitalism served this country well, bringing in innovation, invention, trade, and enterprise.

Thomas Jefferson was a delegate for Virginia in the Continental Congress in 1775-1776. He recognized rights for all men. He stated once, "The God who gave us life gave us liberty at the same time." [81]

Thomas Jefferson was given the momentous task to write the Declaration of Independence, the document which identified our true birth of liberty. He was the principal author along with a small committee of four other men who wrote revisions to the original document. The words were elegant, carefully chosen and the message was clear; defining what America hoped for and would become. The authors were careful not to appear overbearing in religious beliefs, as the Mother Country was, but to be a separate nation who puts liberty and equal rights for all men at the forefront of all matters. They framed this idea of a country, not with "religiousology," but of faith, linking God as the divine source of creation and the source of all liberty for all men.

Jefferson said, "God watches over our country's freedom and welfare. We are not a world ungoverned by the laws and the power of a superior agent. Our efforts are in His hand and directed by it; and He will give them their effect in his own time." [82]

Jefferson became the first United States Secretary of State under Washington. After the Revolutionary War, the nation began to have a monetary crisis. Alexander Hamilton and his Federalists believed in a strong national government requiring a national bank and foreign loans to function, creating a more industrial and progressive nation. Jefferson on the other hand believed in the people to govern their way of life by states, building farms, with the priority for the yeoman farmer and planters; "those who labour in the earth, are the chosen people of God, if ever he had a chosen people, whose breasts he has made his peculiar deposit for substantial and genuine virtue." [83]

Jefferson had no desire to cozy up with Britain and their banks just to stay afloat. We had just cut our ties with the British and he wanted our country to stand on its own. The British were still considered our enemy.

Jefferson was opposed to aristocracy, corruption, bankers, the industrial revolution, and most of all slavery. Surprised? Yes, slavery. Prior to the Revolutionary War, he led men in the Commonwealth of Virginia to apply to Britain to allow them to abolish slavery. The Crown denied the request. Jefferson stated that the British monarchy is the source for initiating, allowing, and requiring slavery in America.

By the Spring of 1776, the Pennsylvania Assembly was hanging on to their patriotism and patriotic duty to Britain. They were not ready to stand with the radicals for independence. This slowed progress for the Continental Congress, who was striving towards the creation of a new form of government giving authority to the people.

In May of 1776, leaders from Pennsylvania counties presented a new form of government to the people, rejecting all authority of the Pennsylvania Assembly. They called for a new constitutional convention including delegates elected by the people and for the people. The new radical leaders began rallying for support in Northampton County. The proclamation included, "To rid yourselves forever of tyrannical government is now in your power. If you embrace it, your descendants will glory in their ancestors; if you neglect it, you will entail slavery on your posterity, and they will justly execrate your memory as unworthy of a parent's name." [84]

The sentiment against the British monarchy was growing. Thomas Jefferson was given the task to write the first draft of the Declaration of Independence. In it, he wrote a scathing rebuke against the inhumane trade of slavery created by the British. "He (King George) has waged cruel war against human nature itself, violating its most sacred rights of life and liberty in the persons of a distant people who never offended him, captivating and carrying them into slavery in another hemisphere or to incur miserable death in their transportation thither. This piratical warfare, the opprobrium of infidel powers, is the warfare of the Christian King of Great Britain. Determined to keep open a market where Men should be bought and sold, he has prostituted his negative for suppressing every legislative attempt to prohibit or restrain this execrable commerce." [85]

This was the beginning of opposition towards Jefferson. The delegates in Philadelphia who were to approve the Declaration of Independence created the most intense debate in the summer of

1776. The majority of the delegates wanted this section removed from the declaration, replacing it with a passage about King George's incitement of "domestic insurrections among us."

The Philadelphia delegates got their wish and the anti-slavery section was removed. Later, Jefferson blamed the removal on delegates who represented merchants actively involved in the Trans-Atlantic slave trade.

All the original 13 colonies utilized slavery; the south used them to produce tobacco, cotton, and other cash crops to export back to Britain. The North, via shipping merchants, trafficked enslaved Africans. Who was the winner above all? The British.

Jefferson believed that in order to not violate "the consent of the people", he could only hold the "wolf" by the ear until he could safely let him go. Jefferson did everything he could to construct the framework based on antislavery principles, to lead this country into freedom for all, but he knew it might take a Civil War to see the fruition of his efforts.

Yes, Thomas Jefferson had a lot of slaves. Some of the stories are hidden about his treatment of slaves. One constitutionalist has discovered in the archives that Jefferson bought slaves out of empathy and the desire to keep all the families of the slaves together. He treated them like family. Stories are found where his slaves loved him. When Jefferson returned home from a trip, his slaves ran out to greet him and hoisted him up on their shoulders, bringing him to his house.

In the late 1790's we see a series of issues that rise against Thomas Jefferson. It was a political war. Jefferson's feud and conflicts between him and the staunch Federalist Hamilton, created two different political parties, the Federalists and the Republicans. Jefferson's frustration led to his resignation from Washington's cabinet in 1793. In 1797, Thomas Jefferson became vice president under John Adams. It was during this period that the air was changing in Washington and became heavy with divisiveness over political power and philosophies.

A Philadelphia newspaper was ticked off by something Jefferson did, so they ran a story in their paper stating that a lot of Jefferson's slaves looked like him. The year 1798, all sorts of false accusations were raised against Jefferson. Exactly two centuries later in 1998, the stories were brought up again, defaming our Founding Father. It was during the time that President Clinton was being impeached for the Monica Lewinsky affair. The news media stated, "Clinton's apologists made part of their defense the notion that every President – even Jefferson- has his 'sexual indiscretions.'" (Independent Scholars Commission) This was when the newspapers everywhere were frantically milking this story to ease the guilt off of Clinton.

DNA tests were done on descendants of Sally Heming's son, Eston who was born in 1808. Many claimed that Thomas Jefferson was the father. They claimed that Thomas Jefferson had a long affair with his slave Sally after his wife's death. Truth is, Thomas Jefferson's wife, Martha was a half-sister to Sally Hemings. Thomas took her in and cared for her and gave her a special room in his home.

The DNA study in Sally's descendants revealed that there was indeed evidence of ancestral DNA strands from the Jefferson family and cited Thomas Jefferson as the father of Eston. Two-hundred twenty-one newspapers plastered it at every newsstand in 1998 but did not address the findings 8 weeks later from the same people who performed the study. The DNA test did not prove that Thomas Jefferson fathered any children of Sally Hemmings at all. Results were twisted. The DNA used was not from any of Thomas Jefferson's descendants, he had no male descendants. The DNA used was from an uncle. Thomas Jefferson was 1 out of 26 male Jeffersons who lived in the area. The most likely Jefferson to be the father was Randolph Jefferson, Thomas' younger brother. He was single, would come often to visit Thomas, and would rather stay around the slaves, singing, playing his fiddle, and dancing all night long than staying in the main house with Thomas. Randolph lived there for a period of time when the child was conceived. The child that Sally bore was named Eston, which was a Randolph family name.

The Independent Scholars Commission studied the DNA and evidence for over a year and came to the same conclusion as the original company who performed the DNA testing and analysis in 1998. "The circumstantial case that Eston Hemings was fathered by the President's younger brother is many times stronger than the case against the President himself." (Independent Scholars Commission). [86] This has never been corrected by the news media.

The attacks continued for Jefferson in the year of 1798 when his political career was soaring. Jefferson's political opponents were scheming throughout that year and the next. Jefferson and James Madison anonymously wrote the Kentucky and Virginia Resolution in 1798 and 1799 which strengthened states' rights, nullifying the federal Alien and Sedition Acts. The resolutions promoted the idea that the states had the right and the duty to declare unconstitutional, the acts of Congress that the Constitution did not authorize. This went against the Federalists' ideas. This promoted the idea that citizens of the United States are made up of the Union of the States. The resolution expressing Jefferson's doctrine of states' rights resonated into ideas leading to the Civil War.

The resolutions changed everything. It was during this time that Thomas Jefferson became a target. Stories were spread during the time of great bitterness between Jefferson and other members of the political arena. An accusation suggested that Thomas Jefferson was in the Hell Fire Club with Benjamin Franklin and Thomas Paine. Others suggested he was in the esoteric Rosicrucian Society and even worse, the Illuminati.

Nine years earlier, in 1789, John Robinson, a professor of rural philosophy at Edinburgh University in Scotland, a Freemason, said he was asked to join the Illuminati. After researching and studying the group he concluded his findings in the book, "Proofs of A Conspiracy" in 1798. "I have found that the covert of a Mason Lodge had been employed in every country for venting and propagating sentiments in religion and politics, that could not have circulated in public without exposing the author to great danger. I found, that this impunity had gradually encouraged men of licentious principles to become more bold, and to teach doctrines subversive of all our notions of morality – of all our confidence in the moral government of the universe – of all our hopes of improvement in a future state of existence and of all satisfaction and contentment with our present life, so long as we live in a state of civil subordination. I have been able to trace these attempts, made through a course of fifty years, under the specious pretext of enlightening the world by the torch of philosophy, and of dispelling the clouds of civil and religious superstition which keep the nations of Europe in darkness and slavery. I have observed these doctrines gradually diffusing the mixing with all the different systems of Free Masonry; till , at last, an association has been formed for the express purpose of rooting out all the religious establishments and overturning all the existing governments of Europe."

"And when we see that the methods which were practiced by this Association for the express purpose of breaking all the bands of society, were employed solely in order that the Leaders might rule the world with uncontrollable power, while all the rest, even of the associated, should be degraded in their own estimation, corrupted in their principles, and employed as mere tools of the ambition of their unknown superiors." [87]

A warning was sent out to religious groups and leaders of the Masonic Lodges to be aware of the evils of the Illuminati and the possible infiltration of them into your organizations. Some believe the warnings were put out by the President of Harvard and another one states that it was declared by the President from Yale. They bring in the name of President John Quincy Adams who they say organized the New England Masonic Lodges, and who wrote three letters to Colonel William L. Stone, a top Mason, exposing how Jefferson was using Masonic lodges for subversive Illuminist purposes. This story is not documented accurately and appears to have inconsistencies. John Quincy Adams was one of the most profound anti-masonic presidents there ever was. There is no evidence that he was ever a Freemason. They say the proof of Jefferson's involvement is in a library in Philadelphia, and another story states that the papers are missing.

In a letter to Reverend G. W. Snyder on September 25, 1798, George Washington writes; "I have heard much of the nefarious, and dangerous plan, and doctrines of the Illuminati, but never saw the Book until you were pleased to send it to me. The same causes which have prevented my acknowledging the receipt of your letter have prevented my reading the Book, hitherto; namely the multiplicity of matters which pressed upon me before, and the debilitated state, in which I was left after, a severe fever had been removed. And which allows me to add little more now, than thanks for your kind wishes and favorable sentiments, except to correct an error you have run into, of my Presiding over the English Lodges (Masonic) in the Country. The fact is, I preside over none, nor have I been in one more than once or twice, within the last thirty years. I believe notwithstanding that none of the Lodges in the Country are contaminated with the principles ascribed to the Society of the Illuminati." [88]

This appears to be a plan of Jefferson's enemies to smear him. There is no other proof or story that supports that Jefferson was a Freemason or in the Illuminati. He is though, documented attending Masonic events and being closely involved with members of Freemasonry. Some of his architect designs promote the idea.

Elections for the next president was on the horizon and it was during the early 1800's of the Anti-Masonry movement led by John Quincy Adams, son of President John Adams who Jefferson was running against in the presidential election.

Jefferson went on to become the third president of the United States; 1801-1809 and his vice president was Aaron Burr. In 1808, Jefferson led the way to outlaw the Atlantic Slave Trade which was found to be illegal. This created more enemies for Jefferson.

Our Founding Fathers had previously been living in the era of British control, religious control under strict Catholicism, and financial control. They were influenced by the desire of freedom in all aspects of life, which included the value of human happiness, pursuit of knowledge obtained by means of reason and evidence of the senses, liberty, progress, toleration, fraternity, constitutional government, and separation of church and state. This was the philosophy that started the Age of Enlightenment, beginning in Europe and transplanted into America. It consisted of a Philosophy of Reason which attracted powerful aristocrats, politicians, intellectuals, artists, political activists, and Freemasonry.

The Philosophy of Reason was the idea of applying logic to existing evidence and information with the aim of seeking the truth. This was the philosophy that Thomas Jefferson adopted, which resonated in the Declaration of Independence; "We hold these truths to be self-evident, that all men are created equal, that they are endowed by their Creator with certain unalienable Rights, that among these are Life, Liberty, and the pursuit of Happiness. That to secure these rights, Governments are instituted among Men, deriving their just powers from the consent of the governed, That whenever any Form of Government become destructive of these ends, it is the Right of the People to alter or to abolish it, and to institute new Government, laying its foundation on such principles and organizing its powers in such form, as to them shall seem most likely to affect their Safety and Happiness." [89]

In Jefferson's letters, there is a lot of evidence of his love and devotion to the Creator, Infinite Power, Nature's God, and Providence, words that were spoken of God in those days, but he never could accept, as a believer in the Philosophy of Reason, that Jesus Christ was deity in the flesh. Although Jefferson called himself a Christian, he rejected the Trinity, Biblical miracles, the Book of Revelation ("merely the ravings of a maniac"), the virgin birth, Jesus' atonement of men's sin, the resurrection, and ascension. Jefferson believed Jesus was a religious teacher who projected moral and ethical philosophies. He believed that the Bible contained useful lessons, in spite of its corruptions, ("corrupted by inferior minds") but Jefferson took it upon himself to dissect the Bible, cutting out the supernatural references (beyond reason) with a razor to reveal Jesus as only a moral teacher, not the son of God. He published his own, "Jefferson Bible" and wrote, "The Life and Morals of Jesus of Nazareth" in 1820.

Jefferson was "a firm believer in man's free will, he thought that good works were the way to salvation and that rewards and punishments for actions on earth were "an important incentive" for people to act ethically." [90] There was no need for a Savior. This philosophy is similar to the train of thought in Freemasonry. Whereas Freemasonry requires a belief in a "Deity" and good works, Christians believe that there is one God, that God loved the world so much that He sent His only son to earth, God in the flesh, not to condemn, but to redeem men from their sins and give everlasting life through Jesus Christ, our Savior.

"For it is by grace you have been saved, through faith, and this is not from yourselves, it is the gift of God, not by works, so that no one can boast." Ephesians 2:8-9

Jefferson's belief in Jesus and his death was final, the end, but in the Christian faith, Jesus' death was just the beginning.

*"Jesus answered, "I am the way and the **truth** and the life. No one comes to the Father except through me."* John 14:6

The Philosophy of Reason and Freedom of Religion also had ties to Freemasonry and other esoteric secret societies.

The mysterious Guidestones found in Elbert County, Georgia is a structure built in 1980 funded by a group of mysterious fellows. It eerily mirrors a display of the Ten Commandments, but it was not from the hand of God. The stones are engraved with a set of ten guidelines written in eight modern day languages. The structure includes four standing slabs of granite, which surrounds one single pillar in the middle, with a topping of a capstone, all astronomically aligned. The guidelines suggest population control, improvement of human genetics, excluding the inferior, and Internationalism, such as a One World Order. A few feet west of the structure is a piece of granite embedded in the ground with a message. The middle portion is written in English, while the border of the stone contains the message written in Babylonian, Classical Greek, Sanskrit, and Ancient Egyptian. "Let these be guidestones to an age of Reason." [91]

James Madison was a delegate to the Congress of the Confederation in 1786-1787 and the author of the first draft of the Constitution creating a framework for the limited government of the United States. He joined Alexander Hamilton and John Jay in writing The Federalist Papers to promote the ratification of the United States Constitution. There were 13 Freemasons who signed the final draft of the Constitution, making it the supreme law of the United States of America. Even Frederick Douglass stated that he had studied the Constitution and did not find it to be pro-slavery. It was a masterpiece and solid as a rock, but amendments to the Constitution were needed to be added to meet the needs of its citizens.

Madison was the main force behind the first ten amendments called "The Bill of Rights" – Freedom of speech, Freedom of the press, Freedom to exercise religion, the right of the people to peaceably assemble, to petition the Government for a redress of grievances, the right to have a well-regulated Militia necessary for the security of a free State, the right of the people to keep and bear arms, and restriction for soldiers to be quartered in private homes. The last few amendments dealt with individuals accused of crime; the right of every person to secure houses, papers, and effects, against unreasonable searches and seizures, no warrants, but upon probable cause, and the protection against double jeopardy and self-incrimination, guaranteeing the rights to due process, rights for a speedy and public trial with an impartial jury and to have a counsel of defense, to not allow excessive bail, nor excessive fines, nor cruel and unusual punishments, and allowing the authority and preservation of the rights of the States in which the Federal Government has not been granted authority over; and separation of powers.

These amendments would secure a protection against an overreach of government. In a republic, the people are the government.

In 1790, Madison opposed the economic and centralization of power favored by Alexander Hamilton. Madison served as Secretary of State under Thomas Jefferson, forming the Democratic-Republican Party. He was Jefferson's right hand man in overseeing the Louisiana Purchase. Madison became 4th president of the United States from 1809-1817.

Madison wrote, "I never was a mason, and no one perhaps could be more a stranger to the principles, rites, and fruits of the institution." [92] Madison wasn't playing with the "Big Boys," but there is a sense he wasn't at all naive of the plans and goals of secret societies.

During Madison's presidency, in 1810, Senator Philip Reed proposed the "Title of Nobility" Amendment which goes along with the philosophy of Madison, described within the language of the Constitution.

The amendment (Title of Nobility) states, *"If any citizen of the United States shall accept, claim, receive, or retain any title of nobility or honour, or shall without the consent of Congress, accept and retain any present, pension, office, or emolument (payment or stipend) of any kind whatever, from any emperor, king, prince, or foreign power, such person shall cease to be a citizen of the United States, and shall be incapable of holding any office of trust or profit under them, or either of them."* [93]

The Title of Nobility was prohibited in the Constitution, but the addition of an amendment increased the message of concern that the Founding Fathers had. This suggested new amendment, the 13th amendment "would amplify both Article I, Section 9, which prohibits the federal government from issuing titles of nobility or honor, and section 10, which prohibits the states from issuing them." [94]

During the early periods of America, in the 1600's/1700's, they had seen corruption within the land, governed by British rule, part of the elite and aristocracy. There were men from England who came specifically to control the politics and religion of the New World. The law of the land was controlled by the Burgesses and Governors. Men were given titles of various sorts including Earls, Lords, Knights, and Esquires. The Esquires were barristers (lawyers/attorneys) under the Four Inns of Court in London, one being the Inner Temple. The Inns were a professional body of barristers who provided legal training, selection, and regulation. It was a requirement to join if a man desired to become a barrister. The Inns were ruled by the governing council, Parliament, made up of Masters of the Bench, led by a one term treasurer. The Temple's name is derived from the Knights Templar, who originally leased the land to the Temple until the knights were abolished in 1312.

The American colonists suffered through excessive abusive power by the privileged, the so-called Noble men with these titles. Not all of them, but the majority appear to have set themselves apart as superior, gaining favor, luxuries and immunities, not available to all citizens. There were tendencies of bribes or pensions, and under the table deals with the Mother Country and other foreign entities.

The Title of Nobility Amendment was planned out to protect the country from foreign invasion, corruption, leading to treasonous acts. During the early 1800's, the United States began seeing this activity corrupt their army and their political fields. This is what Jefferson and Madison warned about.

Both the Senate and the House overwhelmingly passed the new 13th amendment and then sent to the States for ratification. Records show that 12 states out of 18 ratified the amendment. Thirteen states were needed, but before the other states could put in their votes, the War of 1812 started by the British, broke out.

James Madison led the United States in the War of 1812 and afterwards, the 13th amendment was still hanging. Virginia was one state that did not complete its ratification process. A Revisal Committee was formed in 1817 to revise Virginia's State's Laws. By March 1819, it was complete and written up in book form, "Revised Codes of the Laws of Virginia" which included the Constitution, the amendments, including the 13th amendment, concerning the Title of Nobility.

The Virginia General Assembly acknowledged and accepted the ratification of the 13th amendment. It would be the Law of the land. The official copy was given as a formal notification to the State Department and was placed in the Library of Congress in 1819. A copy was delivered to President Monroe, Secretary of State, Thomas Jefferson, James Madison, and both houses of Congress.

(The 13th Amendment pamphlet)

The 13th amendment was placed as one of the amendments to the Constitution in law books, pamphlets of the Constitution, history books, presidential addresses, newspapers, "The American Citizen's Manual of Reference: Being a Comprehensive Historical, Statistical, Topographical, and Political View of the United States of North America and of the Several States and Territories"; published by W. Hobart Hadley in 1840, and various literature throughout the United States of America. Strangely though, as the years went by, it had faded, and by 1860, it fell through the cracks never to be found again. How could this happen? Who allowed this to disappear? Who would it effect the most; judges, lawyers, esquires, political figures, those who were connected to England or other countries?

To this day, men are chosen in honor of their service to humanity with titles of "honorary knighthood," given by rulers of the British Monarchy. There have been men in high official positions in the United States government, as well as presidents that have been given this title. Many others have been given titles of nobility from other foreign countries. Doesn't this go against the original 13th amendment? Where did it go? If it was enforced, the participants would lose their citizenship. We will see as we progress through this history lesson.

The high ideals of the Founding Fathers, put to pen, portrayed and established a well-balanced Constitutional republic. The United States of America; a more perfect union; united we stand, divided we fall. Even though these men were not perfect or had different philosophies, I believe every one of these men were ordained by God to serve out a particular purpose.
"For it is God who works in you to will and to act in order to fulfill his good purpose." Philippians 2:13
"For we are God's handiwork, created in Christ Jesus to do good works, which God prepared in advance for us to do." Ephesians 2:10
The founders were fervent in their beliefs and were determined to create a nation based on faith and freedom. Had it not been for these men who took the lead role in establishing our country, we would be under a tyrannical government. Our Founding Fathers gave us a country that has fought for others, protected our liberty, who has spread the gospel to all nations, and one of the first to come to the aid of people who are suffering. These men wanted a free world, a God-given right.

Even though there were men who had evil schemes in their heart for this nation, God took what was intended for evil and used it for good.

The Grand Architect of Freemasonry

"By faith Abraham, when called to go to a place he would later receive as his inheritance, obeyed and went, even though he did not know where he was going. By faith he made his home in the promised land like a stranger in a foreign country; he lived in tents, as did Isaac and Jacob, who were heirs with him of the same promise. For he was looking forward to the city with foundations, whose architect and builder is God." Hebrews 11: 8-10

The United States was built upon many great men who firmly believed in the Divine Providence and Godly principles, but was it built upon Freemasonry? The Freemason author, Robert W. Sullivan IV of the book, "The Royal Arch of Enoch, The Impact of Masonic Ritual, Philosophy, and Symbolism," 2012 states, "the United States was a Grand Masonic Experiment, a Grand Masonic Republic."

Some believe it was, and the push for freedom, freed up the ability for the secret societies to rise in America. They believe that the freedom actually legalized all types of religions and cultures to infiltrate this New World, including Paganism, Witchcraft, and Luciferianism. Was this intentional?

In 1791, President Washington commissioned a French-born architect and city planner, Pierre Charles L'Enfant to design the new capital of the United States, Washington D.C. Pierre was a Freemason. He sought the help of a Scottish surveyor, Alexander Ralston to lay out the city. Scotland and Ireland were two of the top countries who perfected the art of surveyorship. The practice was learned and fine-tuned by apprenticeship/mentorship, such as George Washington with Lord Fairfax, or by a family dynasty. It involved education in mathematics and geometry, as well as engineering. It was a very noble thing to procure a surveyor's title.

To complete a survey, there had to be at least two chainmen to measure distance. The chain consisted of a steel or brass chain that had to be carefully rolled up and laid out precisely to measure the area. The chain was sixty-six feet long and was one of the most important survey instruments besides the magnetic compass and the sextant.

Another part of the survey team were highly educated mathematicians who could correctly transpose and calculate all the findings into field notes and accurately create a map of the area. Freemasons frequently added astronomers in the survey team, especially in the layout of Washington D.C. and other important areas such as ports where lighthouses were placed. All members of the survey team, especially the surveyor and the chainmen had to take an oath, proclaiming they would be faithful, accurate, and would record their results without favor to anyone.

By 1792, conflicts arose between three commissioners who were appointed to supervise the capital's construction. Apparently, they were not agreeing with the design. Washington dismissed L'Enfant from the project and hired Andrew Ellicott to complete the design with changes applied. Ellicott would later become Meriwether Lewis' mentor and survey guide in the Lewis and Clark Expedition.

Many brilliant men came together to establish a strong foundation for the United States, but there is more than meets the Eye. We will later explore the layout of Washington D.C. and America to reveal a unique and precise technique utilizing the ley of the land. The work ahead was massive, and the surveyors would become the most valued members of Freemasonry.

The Eye Upon Land and Trade

While the framework of the Nation's Capital was being built, men were set out to explore this great country, which involved Freemasons and Albert Pike. As a researcher, I wanted to know the who's, the why's, the where's, and the how's to try to put the pieces of this complicated puzzle together. I'm very detailed as you can see, but I do not feel that I'm doing any justice or service to Bud or the reader if I don't understand myself of the background of these men I'm studying. I want to present it to the reader as complete as I can, to be able to visualize the country during these critical years of our growth and to understand the motives and plans of very powerful people, such as Albert Pike who greatly changed America and the life of Jesse James.

My human frailty limits my understanding of the complete story and details, but I will do my best to paint the picture of what has been documented and the things we do know. Going deeper into history, the reader will be able to visualize the architecture and design from the foundation to the top, of a society built by the hands of the most powerful men on earth. Their **Eye** was on **land** and its priceless **resources**.

Meriwether Lewis

America was experiencing extreme growing pains during the period from 1800-1850. While President Thomas Jefferson was in office in 1803, the president began to plan for an expedition across the newly acquired land called the Louisiana Purchase; territory purchased from Napoleonic France. Jefferson believed the United States needed to expand its territory to ensure its survival and prosperity. The massive land mass extended from New Orleans to two Canadian provinces. It included 15 present day U.S. states; *Arkansas, Missouri,* Iowa, *Oklahoma, Kansas,* and *Nebraska*; parts of North and *South Dakota,* Montana, *Wyoming, Colorado, Minnesota,* the northeastern section of *New Mexico,* northern portions of *Texas, Louisiana,* and *Alberta* and *Saskatchewan, Canada.* These states are significant in the life of Jesse James.

There was a tremendous amount of territory to cover and explore. Jefferson selected Meriwether Lewis to lead the expedition to map out the northern area, catalog new plants and species, and locate a direct water route to the Pacific. Jefferson appropriated $2500 for the mission even before the land was purchased.

Some believe this was actually a secret mission, to explore the possibilities of a previous claim on the entire United States by Britain and/or the Welsh. There were several tribes of Indians in the West that spoke Welsh and had features similar to the Welsh people. The whole legitimacy of the United States weighed upon Jefferson, but this story has not been proven.

Meriwether Lewis (1774-1809) became a Freemason in 1796. In 1801, he was in the Virginia Militia putting down the Whiskey Rebellion and then joined the U.S. Army. Lewis was personally selected to be the private secretary to President Thomas Jefferson. They maintained a very close and trusting relationship.

Lewis chose William Clark, a Freemason, as his partner and their famous venture would be known as the Lewis and Clark Expedition. Clark was a lieutenant under General Anthony Wayne and was Lewis' commanding officer in the U.S. Army. Lewis was captain under Clark and the roles of leadership would switch in this expedition.

Lewis chose Andrew Ellicott, a surveyor, mathematician, and astronomer to join his crew on the expedition. He became a mentor for Lewis studying survey techniques and equipment. Ellicott was instrumental in surveying a large portion of the United States as well as taking over the design of Washington D.C.

The official launch would begin at Camp Wood, outside of St. Louis in the summer of 1804. The two-year trip was filled with unbelievable tales of things they saw and witnessed in the pristine wilderness of the West. Their tenacious bravery and perseverance through encounters with wildlife not seen before, and Indians, who never had seen white men, proved to sustain their drive to complete one of the greatest achievements of mankind.

Lewis and Clark and the men who were by their side were considered national heroes, putting their lives at risk, forging a path for Western expansion in America and establishing diplomatic relationships with the Native Americans. It was all part of "Manifest Destiny" which was the idea that the United States was destined by God to become a great nation of freedom and that the freedom should be expanded from sea to shining sea.

They reached the Pacific Ocean by 1805. Their mission was a success, but their resources, pocketbook, and bodies were stressed to the max. They headed back, but not with empty hands. They had gained a world of knowledge and wonder of this great country.

Captain Zebulon Montgomery Pike - Opens the Door for Trade with Mexico

During this period of time, another man was set out to explore other areas of the new property. They would look to a man named Captain Zebulon Montgomery Pike who was from the same family tree as Albert Pike. Zebulon was stationed at various frontier posts to work on logistics and payroll for the military. His main base was at Fort Belle Fontaine near St. Louis. While Meriwether Lewis was arriving at the Pacific Ocean, Zebulon Pike was sent to explore where the headwaters of the Mississippi River originated. Zebulon was to confer with the traders and Indians, informing them that they were now in the boundaries of the United States and to abide by its laws. He encouraged trade to continue; legally. He traveled into Minnesota, spending a winter among the Sioux. Zebulon Pike became close friends to Chief "Wahpehda" Wapasha II (1779-1835). Pike arranged a treaty with the Sioux who were very important people to Jesse James. In fact, Jesse, in his outlaw days would meet up with the Chief's granddaughter and take her for his bride.

Trade was a huge part of America at this time and became the main source of income for its inhabitants. Jefferson and men underneath his authority was getting very interested in the southern portion of the Louisiana Territory, but also began to set their eye further into forbidden territory, the Spanish Empire.

In the south, Native trade began years before with Coronado and DeSoto. Members of the Francisco Vasquez de Coronado expedition in the 1550s edged into New Mexico's pueblos in search of the rumored Seven Cities of Gold or known as the Seven Cities of Cibola. They would bring gold, silver, and many valuable treasures to trade with the Indians, in hopes that the Indians would provide them with gold, priceless items, and the trails to these golden cities.

Coronado traveled all the way through New Mexico and up to Kansas, but never found the cities of gold, only poor pueblo people and their adobe dwellings. Sadly, Coronado and his men, being frustrated, were labeled as being violent towards the Pueblo people.

Convinced there was still gold to be found, other expeditions followed. Spaniards were encouraged by the Crown to colonize the area of northern Mexico and New Mexico in the late 1590s. Gold seekers and those interested in colonization traveled back into the area of the Pueblos. Stories of mines in the Sandia Mountains spread, but the Pueblo Indians quickly snuffed out the rumor and directed them to the east.

Trade began to pick up between the Pueblo people and the Spaniards. Sometimes the Indians would trade back things that Coronado used for trade such as wooden crosses, books, and artifacts. There still was a strong sense of distrust towards the newcomers. They had every right to be.

By 1598, Juan de Onate, a Spanish Conquistador and the colonial governor of the province of Santa Fe de Nuevo Mexico in the viceroyalty of New Spain, decreed that inhabitants of the vaguely defined region of New Mexico were now subject to the Spanish Crown and under the jurisdiction of the Catholic Church. The people of New Mexico were promised protection, peace, and everlasting bliss through conversion; Catholicism. The Spaniards, seeing that the Pueblo Indians were very vulnerable, changed their focus from gold to mass conversion and conformity into a brand-new religion and culture. They would take more from these people than they were willing to give.

History repeats itself. The Spaniards felt that they were superior and wanted control of this new population. They began to present plays or reenactments in front of the Pueblo Indians to program them into a new way of thinking, psychological warfare and propaganda. It was a scare tactic, using Spanish warriors portraying their might in battles and conquest of the Aztecs. It was dramatically displayed as a warning; any act of resistance to Spanish rule would be quashed with military might.

Most of the Pueblo Indians were peaceful and were focused on agriculture. The Spaniards, mostly the Franciscans and Jesuits took advantage of these people. They began to implement slavery to work the fields and then take most of the Indian's produce away from them, leaving them with minimal amount to feed their own people.

The Spaniards forced Catholicism into their way of life, requiring them to build many churches and missions in their community. Men who did not become involved with the mission work or any work for that matter, forced upon them, were abused. Many lost one of their feet or hands to an axe if they rebelled. The Spanish conquistadors were known for their cruelty, striking fear in the hearts of the indigenous people who didn't fully understand what was happening. The psychology of fear was used to control the masses.

The Pueblo Indians were suffering. They were poorly fed, forced to conform to a new religion they were unfamiliar with, and were restricted to use any of their old customs, religion, education, dress, cultivation of crops and medicine. The Friars concentrated on educating the young. The old customs began to mingle in with the new, creating friction between the two races who were steadily intertwining.

Slave Trade became prominent in the 1600s, not with African slaves, but with the capturing of native Pueblo Indian children, Apache, Ute, and Navajo. In 1630, the governor, Francisco de la Mora y Ceballos issued permits authorizing this, treating the children as cattle. Franciscans themselves took captive children for the purpose of Christianizing them. Others kidnapped the orphan children and turned them into slaves for the Spanish colonists. Spanish utilized attacks on the different Indian tribes to take the children captive. Franciscans gave their blessings.

Forty-seven medicine men were arrested from several different Pueblos for practicing wizardry on Fray Andres Duran. They were flogged and four of them were hanged. A united force of Tewa Indians showed up at the governor's palace in Santa Fe and demanded the medicine men to be released. Due to a fear of uprising, they were set free.

A Franciscan, Fray Salvador de Guerra viciously whipped a Hopi man until "he was bathed in blood" because it was reported that he was idol worshipping. Guerra not only did it once, but twice the same day with the final punishment of pouring turpentine over his open wounds; causing the man's excruciating death.

Famine, smallpox, and drought appeared during the years 1640-1676 and each side, Franciscans, governors and the indigenous people were blaming the other for the problems. Priests accused secular Spanish colonists of introducing the Pueblo people to hard drink, smoke, swearing, and prostitution. The extensive restriction on use of their old ways and customs led to the confiscation and destroying of the Indian's altars, kivas, masks, and prayer sticks.

The Indians finally had enough. The Pueblo people in New Mexico and bands of other Indian tribes, including a portion from Arizona rose up and started a revolt against the Spaniards in 1680. They were led by Po'pay, a Tewa Indian religious leader from Ohkay Owingeh. Po'pay went to Taos Pueblo and began planning a rebellion. All they wanted was to destroy the Spanish and their influence to give them peace, prosperity, and independence. Po'pay murdered his own son-in-law, Nicolas Bua, because of fear he would betray the plot to the Spanish. The Spaniards living within the missions were slaughtered. There were 400 Spaniards, men, women, and children killed and 21 of 32 priests killed. The churches were all burned to the ground. The Spanish colonists fled south.

The Pueblos were trying to regain what they had lost within the last 80 years. It was extremely hard. They were not used to war as the Europeans or the practice of manipulation of people, land, and its resources. Some wanted to go back to all the old ways and customs and others wanted to maintain what they had learned from the Spaniards and further the growth of new crops which had been introduced. Division settled in and gave the Spaniards an avenue to move back in, twelve years later. The Franciscans reduced their strategy of force and control and allowed the Pueblos to merge their customs into Christianity.

Storyteller Emmett "Shkeme" Garcia from the Santa Ana Pueblo of New Mexico put it best to describe how the Pueblos survived after this atrocity. "It took all we had to war", "we didn't know that life, we didn't know killing in mass numbers, or to defeat people for land resources, so it took a whole lot for our people to be actually driven to that point of the Pueblo Revolt." [95]

Garcia points out that it was **"Passive Resistance"** for their survival, going along with colonization, trying to figure out a way to coexist with the many men coming into their land. His ancestors at that time used their ingenuity to put on a front of compliancy, taking their culture underground. Practicing in secret was the new way of life for the Pueblo Indians. It was a safe way to maintain their existence on their ancient land and not be displaced into a reservation like most tribes of Indians were in the 1800's. They outsmarted the Spanish Empire, using their wisdom and ingenuity.

Anthropologist Edward P. Dozier emphasized, "Pueblos compartmentalized their spiritual, social, economic and political lives in order to both adapt to Spanish rule and simultaneously preserved their cultural heritage." [96]

In the U.S. Capitol building, there is the National Statuary Hall Collection, in which each of the 50 states could contribute two statues to honor persons notable in their histories. The 100th and last statue for the collection was that of Po'pay from New Mexico. It was placed in the Emancipation Hall in 2005.

After the rebellion in the 1700's, Spanish was controlling New Mexico and the population increased with a mixture of races called Mestizos, a person claiming both Spanish and Native American ancestry.

Annual trade fairs began in Taos, some involved slave trade and others involved commodities. Comanches were growing in number in Texas. The colonists who were moving in the area in present day Texas carried an attitude of defiance with the Comanches and refused trade relationships with them. Raids on the settlements in Texas increased and the goods and livestock that the Comanches brought for trade in Taos were goods that were stolen from the Texas settlers. Trade in Taos included the Comanches, Utes, and Navajos. Competition between tribes invited bloody skirmishes between 1750-1770.

By 1786, a new government in Spain implemented new reforms that created conditions unifying peaceful agreements between all parties within the Spanish Empire, including the Pueblos, Comanches, Utes, and Navajos. There was a period of peace.

In 1806, as soon as Captain Zebulon Pike returned from his first expedition, he was ordered by General James Wilkinson, to begin a 2nd expedition. Some researchers believe that President Jefferson did not know about this, but later after his return, Jefferson deemed it worthy and an important move for trade. But again, there was a suspicion that Wilkinson sent Zebulon to spy on the Spanish Empire and its properties.

Zebulon Pike's expedition would travel to the southern portion of the Louisiana Purchase. The southern borders of the Louisiana Purchase met with borders of Mexico, which was still under the reign of Spain. The Spanish Empire extended to California and north to the Arkansas River and along the Red River.

Captain Zebulon Pike was ordered to explore, map and find the headwaters of the Arkansas and Red Rivers. Zebulon led a small party of men, including Dr. John H. Robinson, who was affiliated with Western Star Masonic Lodge No. 107 in Kaskaskia, Illinois, near St. Louis. They traveled to the edge of the Spanish colonial settlements near present day Colorado, New Mexico, and Texas. He explored the area of a great peak in Colorado, later named "Pikes Peak" after Zebulon. He was ordered to become friendly with the Natives and secure a tribal allegiance with the United States.

The next part is not well known. In an old book, it describes that "there is a strong reason to suspect that he had other instructions, not in writing, that required him to push his explorations much nearer the Spanish capital of Santa Fe than his published orders or his skillful disclaimer in his journal would indicate." [97]

Zebulon Pike built a camp, a so-called fort "on the west bank of the Rio Grande and hoisted the American flag in the very faces of the Spaniards." Albert Pike even described that Zebulon was on the Del Norte, which was the earlier name for the Rio Grande, "but every circumstance of the expedition indicates that it was all a scheme to get into Santa Fe and learn what he could of the country without having his purpose suspected." [98]

Zebulon Pike and his men wound up inside the boundaries of Mexico whether by accident or not, and was captured by a Mexican army, still under control of Spain who were patrolling the area. Pike and his men were taken to their commanding officer, Facundo Melgares in Santa Fe.

Melgares was positioned in the northern portion of Mexico to maintain and restrain any Americans who would enter its portals. He was also on a mission to intercept any American explorers moving beyond the American borders. He was pleased in capturing Pike.

Zebulon Pike was transported to Chihuahua in present day Mexico for interrogation. Pike and Melgares became great friends and their friendship would become a vital part of trade between the two countries. The Spanish government escorted Pike throughout New Mexico, portions of Mexico and then through Texas to reach Louisiana on his return trip back to the United States.

After his return to the States, he was dispatched to the Secretary of War to answer questions about his relationship with General James Wilkinson. Pike was suspicioned to be a part of Wilkinson and Aaron Burr's plot *to illegally seize the Southwest from Spain*. He was cleared of any wrongdoing.

In 1810, Zebulon Pike published his account of his trip into the forbidden land, painting a picture of the people, the land, the culture, and the resources they had to offer. He saw a huge trade opportunity with Mexico, as they were in need of textiles, cloth, and most of all cotton. Mexico in turn could trade with silver and gold coins, but Pike must have seen something a whole lot more valuable while there.

Pike kept a journal while captured, where he spoke of the "Lost City of Palanor" or "Zebulon's Gift." It is deemed a myth by some and truth by others. His original journals were confiscated, and pages were removed, only to turn up 100 years later. Two stories linger in mystery within the missing pages; (1) Pike had acquired great treasure, and (2) he hid the treasure in the lost city of Palanor, built by pre-Columbian European settlers.

Captain Zebulon Pike would become a leader in blazing the trail for others to follow in establishing the Santa Fe Trail from Missouri into New Mexico Territory creating an enormous trade thoroughfare. Three years after Zebulon published his book, he died during the War of 1812 in a munition explosion set off by the British.

Meriwether Lewis goes Eye to Eye and Toe to Toe with General James Wilkinson

Once back in St. Louis from the successful Lewis and Clark Expedition, Meriwether Lewis was rewarded with 1,600 acres of land by President Jefferson and was appointed governor of the Louisiana Purchase Territory in 1807. He settled in St. Louis and helped organized the Freemasonry Lodge the following year. William Clark, a Freemason would become the territorial agent of Indian Affairs.

St. Louis held one of the earliest Freemasonry Lodges in the West, Lodge No. 111, organized in 1808, the year before Albert Pike was born. The St. Louis Lodge was considered a Territorial Freemason Lodge and had to rely on a Grand Lodge that was incorporated in another state. St. Louis' Lodge 111 received its charter from the Grand Lodge of Pennsylvania. Meriwether Lewis was nominated to serve as the first Master of the St. Louis' Lodge.

Shortly after a hero's welcome, Lewis began seeing men by their true colors and the color that showed up the most was green (envy). Men viciously attacked Lewis in his political and private affairs, one being Frederick Bates. Bates became a political rival against Meriwether Lewis. Bates was selected by Thomas Jefferson to become Secretary of the Louisiana Territory and began building a political base in St. Louis before Meriwether Lewis could set up his office. It was said that Bates was constantly battling Lewis over various issues. Bates contacted Lewis' superiors in D.C. complaining about the way Lewis had been managing things.

Another rival was James Wilkinson. He served in the Continental Army during the Revolutionary War and became Senior Officer of the U.S. Army. Wilkinson was appointed as the first Governor of the Louisiana Territory in 1805 by President Jefferson while Meriwether Lewis was seeing the Pacific Ocean for the first time.

Wilkinson married Ann Biddle who was from the prominent Biddle family of Philadelphia; the same family of Nicholas Biddle who ran the Second Bank in America we spoke of earlier.

James Wilkinson was known for his jealousy over matters of the military and positions that were won by others that he felt he deserved. General George Washington even noticed Wilkinson's fragile ego and promoted him to brigadier general in consolation of selecting Anthony Wayne to be the commanding general in charge of the extended continental forces after the Revolutionary War.

Wilkinson was involved in many controversial issues. His gossiping and bragging indicated that he was a participant in the Conway Cabal, which was a conspiracy to replace George Washington with Horatio Gates as commander-in-chief of the Continental Army. Gates compelled Wilkinson to resign his position and instead of his superiors reprimanding Wilkinson, he was given the position of clothier-general in the Army.

Suspicions grew regarding Wilkinson and his role as a very highly paid spy for the Spanish in the years after the Revolutionary War. He moved to Kentucky and in 1787 he made a trip to New Orleans to meet with Spanish Governor Esteban Rodriguez Miro. Wilkinson encouraged and convinced the governor to allow Kentucky to have a trading monopoly on the Mississippi River in return of a promise to promote Spanish interest in the west. Wilkinson signed an expatriation declaration and swore allegiance to the King of Spain in 1787. He was known as Secret Agent Number 13.

Kentucky was just starting to be explored and opened its doors to settlers after the Revolutionary War. A political club was formed in Danville in 1786, earlier than the Masonic Lodge. Twelve of the thirty-five men of the group were Freemasons. It was considered as a "training ground" for the State's future leadership. Little is documented about the group, but one of the topics that they discussed was to secure Spain as an ally of Kentucky, leading a secession from the United States.

Lexington was the very center of Kentucky and was the best choice to secure a Freemasonry Lodge. Lexington Lodge No. 25, chartered by the Virginia Grand Lodge was established in 1788. It later became Lexington Lodge No.1 when Kentucky received its charter. It is very hard to find evidence, but there is one book that suggests that General James Wilkinson was a Freemason who was an active participant in two Danville conventions where he called for Kentucky's statehood and maintained closer ties to Spain. The book, "How & Why Freemasonry Came to Kentucky: The Backstory," by John W. Bizzack, Ph.D. 2015.

James Wilkinson was a very powerful man and it appeared that he was getting away with a lot of treasonous acts that had gone undetected. In 1798, he was accused by Andrew Ellicott, surveyor for Washington and Meriwether Lewis, of receiving pensions from Spain, raising a suspicion of treason. This accusation was not pursued. He continued as a senior officer of the U.S. Army under President Jefferson. Wilkinson used his position to advise the Spanish on any advances that the United States was making towards the expansion of the states, including the Lewis and Clark Expedition. He would also give them information on how to contain the Americans within their boundaries in exchange for a renewal of his Spanish pension. The pension started out to be $2,000 per year and increased to $4,000 per year.

Still in the dark about this man, President Jefferson appointed Wilkinson to be the first Governor of Louisiana Territory. His secretary was Dr. Joseph Brown, brother-in-law of Aaron Burr. They were headquartered in St. Louis. Aaron Burr was the vice president to President Thomas Jefferson. Burr's legacy is defined by his extreme opposition towards Alexander Hamilton, the first secretary of the treasury under President George Washington and founder of the nation's financial system. Aaron Burr was slandered by Hamilton when running for president and was noted as saying he was "unprincipled and unworthy." Taking offense, Aaron Burr challenged Hamilton to a duel in 1804. Burr got the first shot off and wounded Hamilton, in which Hamilton died the following day.

Aaron Burr was later suspicioned to be involved in treason and President Jefferson removed him from his cabinet. Aaron Burr was a Mason.

James Wilkinson met up with Aaron Burr and became involved in an alleged plot with Burr to use their international connections to separate the western states and territories from the United States and establish an independent nation. It is noted that Wilkinson invited Meriwether to go in with them, but Lewis wanted no part of it. There were also some suspicions that Zebulon Pike was a spy for Wilkinson and Burr, and possibly the Spanish government as suggested earlier.

To save himself from these suspicions, Wilkinson sent a letter to Jefferson advising him of Burr's plans, while maintaining his own innocence, but it became clearer and clearer of Wilkinson's guilt and coverup. He was removed from the Louisiana Territory governor's office after being publicly criticized for a heavy-handed administration and abuse of power. He was replaced by Meriwether Lewis as the new governor of the Louisiana Territory. It would not surprise me if Meriwether Lewis passed on information to Jefferson in which he received from Ellicott on their expedition regarding the treasonous acts of Wilkinson, confirming his suspicions.

Tragically, this story leads us back to Lewis, the hero of all time. He was being slandered and ridiculed, especially by Bates and Wilkinson. After Wilkinson lost his position of governorship, he was extremely envious of Lewis.

As a spy, Wilkinson used schemes and trickeries to obtain one of the most important weapons that Lewis had helped President Jefferson create, one of the very first secret code of communications used by the White House. It was a layout of letters and numbers used as a method of transforming a text in which the meaning was concealed, in other words a cipher. A keyword would be used, only known between the author of the message and receiver, to decipher the text that was concealed. Jefferson and Lewis' key word was "Artichokes".

It was a brilliant way to correspond in secret when sending messages containing government secrets. The basis of this system was from a 200-year-old French system called the Trithemius. This technique was used by the Freemasons, the KGC, and John Wilkes Booth who was a member. A diagram of this practice was found in Booth's trunk in the hotel he was staying at just shortly before he shot President Abraham Lincoln. The document is found in the "International Spy Museum" in Washington D.C.

The system would be utilized by the U.S. Army and one of the army's officers, James Wilkinson knew this practice quite well and perfected it while carefully watching Lewis and Jefferson. It is documented Wilkinson used this technique between him and the Spanish during his treasonous acts.

Jefferson knew the Lewis' expedition would be of the upmost secretive and sensitive mission ever in the United States, therefore they designed a cipher to be used before, during, and after the expedition. It was considered unbreakable.

For three years after the Lewis and Clark Expedition, Meriwether Lewis worked on his journal that he kept while on his journeys. A publishing company would be putting it into a book, but there was something in that journal that someone wanted along with papers that never left Lewis' side.

In 1809, Meriwether Lewis was on his way to Washington D.C. to deliver his manuscript and take papers to Ex-President Thomas Jefferson. He also needed to clarify and clear up the matters with the current president, James Madison regarding matters that Bates was using to slander him with, as well as to resolve issues of denied payments of drafts he had drawn against the War Department while serving as governor.

A fascinating program; Brad Meltzer's Decoded: "Jefferson's Secret Presidential Codes," breaks down this story piece by piece and has found evidence of foul play on the way to Washington.

Lewis did not plan to go alone. He had a military escort suspiciously ordered by General James Wilkinson who placed Major James Neely as Lewis' protector. Two servants went on the trip. On their journey, they would take a route directly to the gulf and board a ship to take him to Washington. During the trip, the course was changed unexpectedly near Memphis. They started heading north through dense wooded areas meeting up with the Natchez Trace, an old military road, in present day Hohenwald, Tennessee. The trail was known for lurking vicious highwaymen.

Sadly, his journey came to an end before he reached Washington. Lewis stopped on the trail of the Natchez Trace and sought lodging at Grinder's Stand, 70 miles southwest of Nashville. Strangely he was alone. His escorts were trying to round up some of their horses who got away mysteriously, so they advised him to go on ahead to seek lodging at this inn.

Lewis arrived at the Grinder's cabin which had a one room cabin for him to lodge in. Mrs. Grinder was the only one there at the time, along with her children and servants. She told Lewis that her husband was gone hunting, but some believe Mr. Grinder was actually attending to his still, supplying the Indians in that area with corn liquor. Mrs. Grinder allowed Lewis to stay and prepared a meal for him. After supper, Lewis went to his cabin and there after midnight he was either murdered or committed suicide; shot twice, once in the gut and once in the head. Lewis always carried two flintlock pistols and if it was self-inflicted, the pistols would have caused immense damage at close range. Would he have had enough stamina to reload his pistol or pick up the second one to finish himself off?

Mrs. Grinder was the only witness, she said, but had three different accounts. The main account was that he committed suicide after having been out of his mind that night, but he lived for a short while after the shots and spoke as if he committed suicide. Other accounts involve Mrs. Grinder seeing Lewis wondering outside crying for help, and the third account, three men who got into an argument with him and they challenged him to a duel. Something ain't right.

The Nashville Democratic Clarion published that his throat was slit. Another paper suggests that there was also razor marks on his arm and hand. (The Vermont Journal, Nov. 20,1809 states, "Meriwether Lewis, Esq. Governor of Upper Louisiana, is stated, in the Baltimore papers, to have destroyed himself in a fit in insanity." All the newspapers were claiming it was suicide. Strangely, very few articles have been preserved except the ones claiming suicide, same word for word article. Strangely, there is not much evidence of Lewis' great friends, Thomas Jefferson's or William Clark's reaction; only that they accepted it as suicide.

The Lewis' family believed he was murdered. There has been recent evidence after over 200 years that indicate he was indeed murdered.

Shortly, after this incident, we find James Wilkinson and Burr wrapped up in court battles regarding their scheme of creating another nation. Wilkinson faced a military court in 1811, resulting in a court martial that exonerated Wilkinson. Again, he received freedom from punishment. Burr was tried for treason but was acquitted.

James Wilkinson got back into military service during the War of 1812. Ironically, he was posted as a diplomat in Mexico City where he died in 1825. During an extensive archival research in the Spanish archive in Madrid in 1854, an historian, Charles Gayarre exposed Wilkinson as having been a spy in the service of the Spanish Empire. He had proof, but a little too late.

Also, between the years of 1811-1819, the 13th Amendment, "Title of Nobility" was ratified and placed in the Constitution to protect the country from espionage and treason.

During this critical time in history, the Freemasons were being exposed. In 1826, William Morgan, some believe was a Freemason, disappeared after threatening to expose the Freemasonry's secrets and publish their rituals. He was thought to have been kidnapped and murdered, following the guidelines of his oath, if he ever divulged the secrets. As we stated earlier, those who are initiated into this society are required to take a blood oath, vowing to never reveal the secrets of masonry or his throat will be cut from ear to ear and his bowels will be cut out and given to the beast of the field.

John Quincy Adams, who was president during this time, was not a Freemason and despised this secret organization. "Masonry ought forever to be abolished. It is wrong – essentially wrong- a seed of evil which can never produce any good."

I believe during this time, Freemasonry and other secret societies went underground.

A little over 20 years later, in 1848, a Tennessee committee was commissioned to have the body of Meriwether Lewis removed from the shallow grave near the Grinder's cabin and placed in a grave in Pioneer Cemetery in Hohenwald. The committee was also required to identify the body of Meriwether Lewis. This was forty years after his death. In their report, their findings indicated that Meriwether Lewis died at the hands of an assassin. His skull revealed a huge hole in the back of the head.

Other evidence includes the only statement made by a witness prior to Lewis' death from Major Gilbert Russell. Lewis supposedly stopped by Pickering Fort on his way to D.C. where Major Russell was stationed. Russell wrote a letter to the president stating that he had to put Meriwether Lewis under house arrest because he was acting deranged and suicidal. He stated that Lewis tried committing suicide two times between St. Louis and Fort Pickering. The letter is included in the Jefferson Papers. During an inquest in 1996, the handwriting of the letter was analyzed with Major Russell's other documents and were found to be forged.

Another letter a few weeks later, arrived to Thomas Jefferson from Major Russell, indicating that Meriwether Lewis had drank heavily and later vowed never to drink any Spirits again. Russell also wrote that the agent of the Chickasaws, James Neely who rode with him, encouraged Lewis to drink. "From everything I can learn, gave the man every chance to seek an opportunity to destroy himself. And from the statement of Grinders wife where he killed himself. I cannot help believing that Purney was rather aiding and abetting in the murder than otherwise." Now he's referring to murder.

It is believed that Neely was the first one to report Lewis' suicide in a formal report to Jefferson. Neely reported that he arrived the following morning and found Lewis dead at Grinder's cabin and it appeared to be suicide. Just recently, evidence found by Tony Turnbow, Chairman of the Lewis County Museum, supports Neely was 60 miles away in Franklin, Tennessee in court regarding a law suit against him on the very day Neely said he was there at Grinder's cabin and writing his report. A handwriting expert concluded that the signature of Neely's report to Jefferson and his signature on court documents were the same.

Neely ended up with Meriwether's guns and other valuable items such as his priceless papers. There is a suggestion that Meriwether Lewis was carrying a cipher to Jefferson of the utmost sensitive nature, regarding Wilkinson. Remember Wilkinson had conspired with Aaron Burr, vice president of Jefferson's, to overthrow the government and form a new country.

Neely brought the journals and important papers to Washington D.C., but they appeared to be ruffled up by the time they arrived, possibly due to the long trip or being thoroughly examined by someone. Several pages were missing in Lewis' journals. Many believe James Neely was hired by General James Wilkinson to murder Lewis.

One author who has studied this case for years, Kira Gale suggests that Mr. Robert Grinder, the owner of the inn, murdered Lewis in exchange for money. Grinder suddenly came into a large sum of money and moved. Lewis supposedly had $200 on him, approximately $1500 in today's money, but was never recovered. Robert Grinder was questioned when two unmarked graves were found on his property, he was charged with murder, but released for lack of evidence. Was one of the men in the grave, Meriwether Lewis who was later buried under the heavy concreted, concealed monument in 1848? There indeed was a coverup.

It appears that Neely was in on it and the only man capable of organizing it could be General Wilkinson. He was known to be an assassin himself and also hired people to kill those who got in his way. The Grinders were paid off to promote the death as being a suicide. A theory raises its ugly head with the idea that Meriwether Lewis had some damaging information about Wilkinson, possibly treason, and Lewis was on the way to expose him.

What is really fascinating is the Masonic Apron of Meriwether Lewis', which is described as the badge of a Freemason. It is given to a mason, reaching the third level and who is deemed a Master Mason. It would be worn to identify one's self as a Freemason and worn outside of the lodge when traveling in dangerous situations, possibly to alert other Freemasons for help. Meriwether Lewis was carrying his apron in his breast pocket, carefully folded. Blood stains were splattered on the apron. The apron was given to the family of Meriwether and in 1924, the Masons of Missouri purchased it from the widow of a distant Lewis relative. In 1960, Montana's retiring Grand Master, Joseph Hopper bought the apron for $500 and gave it to the Grand Masonic Lodge in Helena, Montana. This was a perfect resting place for the apron because Meriwether Lewis traveled through Montana on his Northwest Expedition.

With today's techniques in DNA analysis, we get a few answers. In the 1970's at the University of Oregon, the blood on the apron was tested and came to conclusion that some of the stains were from a deer and the other was human blood. Another test was done in Canada very recently and the blood samples collected by the History Channel, featured in "America Unearthed," hosted by Scott Wolter, was compared to blood samples of known Lewis' family members. The findings indicate that there were two different male DNAs on that apron and neither of them were of Meriwether Lewis. Quite shocking news. This can only mean several things; it was not the apron of Lewis, the Lewis family tested were not true descendants, or the blood spilled were two other men in Lewis' room.

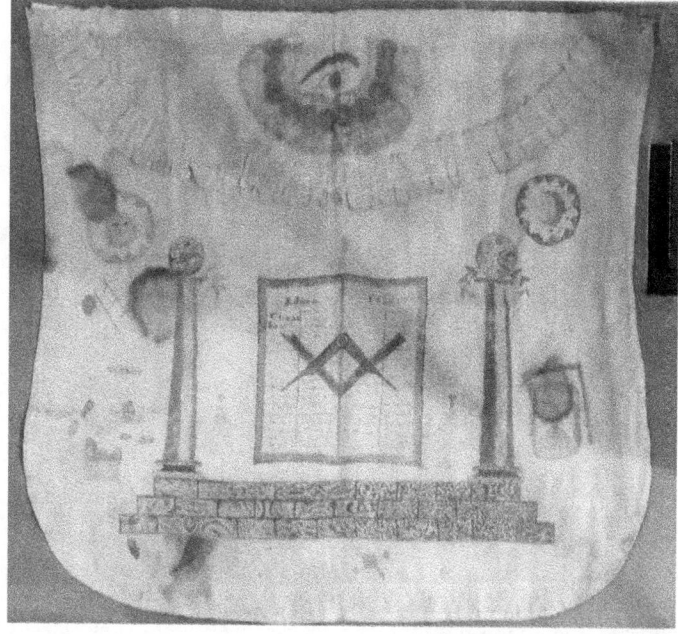

(Meriwether Lewis' Masonic apron (Courtesy of Grand Lodge Ancient Free and Accepted Masons of Montana, Helena - https://ellenbaumler.blogspot.com/2013/10/Meriwether-lewis-and-forensic-mystery.html))

If Meriwether was shot at close range, the apron would have been drenched with blood. Who was the skeleton that they dug up to rebury? Remember there were two unmarked graves on the Grinder's property. An exhumation would end this conspiracy and put the nail on the coffin, but the park where Lewis is assumed buried with a towering monument on his grave will not allow it. Cover up? You bet.

An interesting note: John Pernier (Pearny) was with Meriwether Lewis on the fateful trip. He was Lewis' personal servant. Pernier was a free mulatto, who worked for President Thomas Jefferson at the presidential mansion from 1804-1807 when he became a servant to Lewis. Many scoffers suggested that on that trip, Pernier was negligent and others accused him of murdering Lewis. Six months from the death of his employer, Pernier died of an opium overdose.

In the 1990's, the descendants of Meriwether Lewis petitioned the government to exhume his body. The Department of Interior granted approval which would allow the grave to be opened in 2008. But when the Obama Administration took office in 2009, the feds ruled against any future disruption of Lewis' remains.

What's even more mysterious, James E. Starrs, coauthored Kira Gale's book, "The Death of Meriwether Lewis: A Historic Crime Scene Investigation; 2009. Starrs was also the leader in the Jesse James' exhumation in Kearney, Missouri in 1995.

"Men occasionally stumble over the truth, but most of them pick themselves up and hurry off as if nothing ever happened."

-Sir Winston Churchill

Chapter Seven: Trading Fallacies for Truth

Just like in all organizations, such as political parties, government, media, entertainment, religious bodies, military, law enforcement, businesses, and the general population; there are always the good and the bad, even in secret institutions. It's not the people themselves, but the evil that infiltrates the human soul or the institution. Keep that in mind as we discuss the players of the game of strategy within the secret societies and travel deep into Freemasonry.

We go straight to the top of the most powerful secret society, Freemasonry; Albert Pike, the "Pope" of the American Freemasons. Pike would become known as head of the Washington D.C. Masonic Order, Head of the American Masonic Order, and Head of the World Masonic Order. Pike was indeed the "head" man as Jesse was climbing his way to the top in Freemasonry and the Knights of the Golden Circle.

To be honest with you, Albert Pike is a man and a subject that I would like to skip over, but I can't. His history is one that affected the progression of America and Secret Societies that would have a huge effect on Jesse James. Pike's story will give the reader a better understanding of the underworld, not seen on the surface, in which Pike developed and perfected.

There is extreme controversy over Pike and Freemasonry. It stirs up intense anxiety, nauseousness, and spiritual apprehension in me; especially when it comes to the secrets of whom they serve. Many masons place Pike on a pedestal and claim his true faith is in the one living God, while others believe that his god is Lucifer, the bearer of light.

"No man can serve two masters for either he will hate the one and love the other; or else he will hold to the one and despise the other. Ye cannot serve God and mammon." Matthew 6:24.

In this particular section of the book, there was a need to put on the whole armor of God during research and when writing about this subject. My spirit yearned for the **truth**, and at the same time, my heart was pulling me in the direction of the sensitivity of the subject and the desire to not offend anyone. Both Bud and I have or had members of our family in Freemasonry. I had two very well-known famous 33rd degree Freemasons during the 20th century in my family. I saw very good Christian men involved in these societies, some came through it alright, but some were used as pawns and were later destroyed as well as their reputation.

But this book is about **truth**. I can't be shy on this subject, nor can I ignore it. This chapter is a book within itself, but it is extremely important. Bear with me and your perception will be broadened on the whole scope of things, hidden in plain sight.

I have and will continue to douse this chapter with prayer and use the sword of the Spirit, which is the Word of God to help us all get through this portion of the book. If any reader is a member of these societies, please take time to do your own research, especially into the degrees above you and into the inner circle of these groups.

*"Finally, be strong in the Lord, and in the strength of his might. Put on the whole armor of God, that ye may be able to stand against the wiles of the devil. For our wrestling is not against flesh and blood, but against the principalities, against the powers, against the world-rulers of this darkness, against the spiritual hosts of wickedness in the heavenly places. Wherefore take up the whole armor of God, that ye may be able to withstand in the evil day, and, having done all, to stand. Stand therefore, having girded your loins with **truth**, and having put on the breastplate of righteousness; And having shod your feet with the preparation of the gospel of peace; withal taking up the shield of faith, wherewith ye shall be able to quench all the fiery darts of the evil one. And take the helmet of salvation, and the sword of the Spirit, which is the **Word** of God: with all prayer and supplication*

*praying at all seasons in the Spirit, and watching thereunto in all perseverance and supplication for all the saints; and on my behalf, that utterance may be given unto me, in opening my mouth, to make known with **boldness** the mystery of the gospel, for which I am an ambassador in chains; that in it I may speak **boldly**, as I ought to speak."* Ephesians 6: 10-20

The Trail to Taos

Albert Pike, born in 1809 when men were exploring the west, was self-educated, becoming a teacher in Massachusetts. He grew up in a home with an alcoholic father who died young and a mother who pushed hard for Albert to become a minister. In March 1831, at the age of 22, he moved, travelling to Cincinnati by stage, to Nashville on a steamer, back North to Paducah, Kentucky on foot, by keel-boat down the Ohio River, and up the Mississippi to St. Louis, Missouri. Quite a zigzag of a route on land and waterways. It was shortly after his arrival in Missouri, in 1831, when Pike joined a party of 30 men, led by Captain Charles Bent, in route to Taos, New Mexico from St. Louis. It was documented that the party of men were on a hunting and trading expedition. Traders began traveling into the area of New Mexico from Missouri beginning in 1821 when New Mexico won their independence from Spain, opening trade with the United States.

Why did Albert Pike leave his teaching job in Massachusetts and travel to Cincinnati, all the way to Nashville and then to Paducah, and directly on to St. Louis, immediately teaming up with a hunting and trade expedition? It appears that it was all in the plan.

Cincinnati, Nashville and St. Louis were in the heart of KGC (Knights of the Golden Circle) country, not yet thoroughly developed in those days, but Freemasonry was thriving. Cincinnati chartered their first Masonic Lodge in 1791 and was known as the birthplace of the KGC. Nashville organized their first Masonic Lodge, Saint Tammany Lodge No. 1 in 1789 under the provision of the Grand Lodge of North Carolina. Later, Nashville would become the Supreme Headquarters for the Knights of the Golden Circle. The St. Louis Lodge was already established by Meriwether Lewis. It appears that St. Louis was the hub at that time for trade, where Zebulon Pike and Meriwether Lewis claimed as their headquarters.

Prior to 1821, Mexico was part of the Spanish Empire of New Spain for three centuries and after a decade of conflict between the royal army and Mexican insurgents, Mexico gained their independence. The conflict though destroyed the silver-mining districts of Zacatecas and *Guanajuato, Mexico*. *Guanajuato was a future target for the Knights of the Golden Circle.

The many wars and conflicts left Mexico very weak financially and physically, so they looked to trade.

Melgares had been serving as the Spanish Governor of New Mexico and with Mexico's independence, he became the first Mexican Governor of New Mexico. With the friendship he had with Zebulon Pike, he began welcoming other Americans. William Becknell plowed a path from Missouri, through the Cimarron Desert to Santa Fe that would enable wagon trains and draft teams enough room to travel. It would become known as the Santa Fe Trail, a gateway to the West, and a stream of commerce.

Soon, traders were taking woven cloth, manufactured goods, cotton, guns, steel, knives, and other useful items down the trail in which they could trade. The people of Santa Fe were willing to pay high prices for cotton cloth and calico which sold at $3 a yard, extremely high for that time. Becknell claimed on his first trade in Santa Fe, his investment of $300 in trading goods had a return of $6,000 in gold and silver coins. The second trip began with a load of goods valued at $3,000, giving him a profit of $91,000. People were becoming wealthy overnight.

Instead of a one-way track for the Missouri merchants to trade in Mexico, the release from Spanish control allowed Mexican merchants to travel north to the States, trading mules, wool, silver, gold, jewels, and artifacts. It became a very profitable highway for both sides.

It is documented that many Masons traveled down the path of enrichment to New Mexico, even though Mexico had made the practice of Freemasonry illegal in Mexican territory. One man was noted as the first Mason to settle in New Mexico. He was a mountain man, a trapper/fur trader, by the name of Charles Bent. In 1828, Mr. Bent and his brother, William from their headquarters in St. Louis, took a wagon train of goods down the Santa Fe Trail. They established mercantile contacts and began a series of trading trips back and forth from St. Louis to Santa Fe. This is when Albert Pike jumped on the wagon.

Whether it was Captain Zebulon Pike's book on lost treasure or the excitement of an expedition into the wilds of New Mexico, Albert Pike made his way to St. Louis to join the caravan of men led by Charles Bent on one of these hunting and trading expeditions down the Santa Fe Trail. Albert Pike writes very little of his trip except of his return trip through Texas and Oklahoma with a "bigger-than-life" man he met in Taos, Aaron B. Lewis. Pike writes more about the stranger's (Lewis) venture into the mountains on the Santa Fe trail who had taken a separate path, not with Bent or Pike, but eventually followed the same trail into the freezing mountain ranges.

We see glimpses of Pike's trip through a serial-type article he placed in his newspaper, "The Arkansas Advocate," titled "Narrative of a Journey in the Prairie" written three years after his return in 1835.

In the article, he describes Aaron B. Lewis, whom he had never met before, as a man whom he teamed up with to return back to civilization in the United States in 1832 after the caravan reached Taos, New Mexico. Even though Pike spoke more of Lewis than himself, it appears that their stories are parallel. Pike started out in August 1831 from St. Louis and Lewis started out a month later from Fort Towson, in present day Choctaw County, Oklahoma near the confluence of the Kiamichi River and the Red River.

Fort Towson was established to become an outpost to guard the southern border between the United States and Mexico which at that time was the Red River. The commander of Fort Towson was Col. Matthew Arbuckle. By 1831, the year of Pike and Lewis' journey, it would become a permanent fort and was assigned to be an establishment that would be involved in the removal of the Choctaw from Mississippi into Indian Territory, under the Indian Removal Act. This Act was signed into law in 1830 by President Andrew Jackson which authorized the president to negotiate with Native American tribes living in their ancestral land east of the Mississippi to transfer themselves into new Federal land in "Indian Territory", (Oklahoma) in exchange for the white settlers to move south into their homeland. The government felt the need to remove them to a land they could practice their own way of life, not be interfered with, and would preserve their culture, protecting them from the culture of the European Americans.

Fair trade? No, it was truly one-sided. The resources that lay in the land of the south that the Native Americans thrived upon was more valuable than the land in the north, and land that lay in Oklahoma. Greed prompted the need for this takeover, not the security and wellbeing of the Native Americans. Many tragedies occurred for the Native Americans who lost so much, including their dignity.

Was the removal of the Indians in the mind of those Anglo-American men who ventured into New Mexico in 1831? Could have been, as well as riches. We are enlightened to some of the reasoning Lewis had on traveling to New Mexico from Fort Towson, and possibly the motive for Albert Pike himself.

Pike writes "allured by the **supposed immense riches** in that country and the opportunity which he imagined there was in making a fortune there. He looked upon **New Mexico** as a sort of Utopia, a country where **gold and silver** were abundant and easily obtained. In short, his ideas of it were precisely such as the word **Mexico** generally suggest to the mind. **Neither has he been alone in his delusion**. With a blindness unaccountable, men still continue rushing to Santa Fe, as if fortunes were to be had there for the asking. Men who by hard and incessant labor have amassed a little money, laying that out to the last farthing, and in addition, mortgaging perhaps their farms to obtain farther credit, convey the goods thus obtained to Santa Fe, hoping thus and there to gain a fortune, notwithstanding they have seen numbers returning poor and impoverished, after starting, as they are doing, with high hopes and full wagons. Here and there an individual, by buying beaver or trading to Sonora and California for mules, returns home a gainer, **but generally the case is far otherwise**."

With these words, Pike seems to also be referring to himself as being lured into the promise of instant wealth on this journey.

But the thought comes to mind that since Pike was traveling with Charles Bent, the first Mason who settled in New Mexico, that there was a possibility that either Albert Pike was a Mason at that time or was on the trail of influence to become one. I don't know, but it seems as though he was involved in the grand scheme of things that was just beginning in New Mexico and Mexico. It is noted that Freemasons were sent out to different territories, even other countries to establish Lodges of Freemasonry, as well as the Knights of the Golden Circle who were sent to establish "Castles".

The move of the newcomers into New Mexico brought on more racial issues and ethnicity problems. The Missouri traders, in 1831 when Albert Pike was a part of the group, brought in a profit of $250,000. The Mexican government was doing well in the trade also. The only ones not making a profit were the Nuevomexicanos, who were the Spanish and Mexican settlers in New Mexico, with a mix of Mestizo, who were a mixed group of European and Indigenous people.

It is recorded that Charles Bent set out of St. Louis on the Santa Fe Trail in August 1831. Albert Pike was amongst the 30 men in the party with ten wagons. This was the first time they pulled the wagons with oxen instead of mules or horses. The mindset of Bent to change the mode of power was to deflect Indian raids. Indians were only interested in horses and mules, not the big, bulky, and sluggish animal, the oxen. Bent also had incurred times of desperate measures when the supply of food was down to nothing. The oxen could supply meat if it came down to that. There were about 8 or 10 oxen to a wagon. Not only did the men in the caravan have to take care of themselves, but also had to take care of livestock on the open prairie and rugged mountain trails. It was no task for the weak.

What's really interesting is a book, "Prairie Traveler" written by Randolph Barnes Marcy in 1859, who was an officer in the U. S. Army. He wrote this handbook for thousands of Americans wanting to head west. He had been all over and had developed skills to survive a long overland trip. He was a captain in the Mexican War. Marcy had escorted many people through Texas and Oklahoma and describes that if you are on a very long trip, the oxen is preferred, less liable to stampede, less likely driven off by Indians, used for beef, and can be used to ride with a saddle. His book is quite interesting, explaining the type of clothing needed, camp gear, how to deal with quick sand, how to decipher Indian smoke signals, treatment of snake bites, treatment of animals, wagon repair, tracking and pursuing Indians, method of making war, and methods of attack.

The journey from St. Louis, Missouri to Taos, New Mexico, nearly 1,000 miles was described as being a very slow progress. On your best day, you could make 15 miles. There were threats to your survival based on water resources, safe places to camp overnight, Indian raids, those who followed in the shadows to steal your goods, wild animals, and wild weather.

In Albert Pike's own words in "Narrative of a Journey in the Prairie," they came to the Cimarron River on October 25, 1831. They followed the river along the original trail through Kansas and Oklahoma.

They set camp along the river. It was already getting cold and snowing. Pike had the watch that night, with no fire. The air was bitter cold, and a horse froze to death overnight. It is not clear if this was Pike's horse, but other renditions of his journey relay that his horse got away from him along the Cimarron River and he was on foot the rest of the way; 500 miles to go; more likely 400 miles, but still it was a treacherous trek on foot.

The part of the trip that was gutsy was the stretch through the flat, Cimarron desert facing them after crossing a branch of the Canadian River at McNees Crossing, close to the border of Oklahoma and New Mexico. They could see the landmark of Rabbit Ear Mountains and knew that the true test of manhood was just beyond.

Streams, water, vegetation, and wood would become scarce along the vast prairie they were stepping foot upon. Many stream beds were dry. It was also an area where the most casualties occurred. Today, if you travel down the old trail along this route, which by now is private property, you will find many, many tombstones of the past that are still standing, where families, wagon masters, and friends of the trail said their last goodbye.

On November 18th, they were at the Point of Rocks, between the current day Clayton and Springer, New Mexico. Point of Rocks was like an oasis in the desert. It was a perfect place to set up camp. The rock formation jutted out of the flat landscape forming a horseshoe, allowing shelter for the caravan and their livestock. From the very midpoint of the rocks, a natural spring flowed giving a source of water for the exhausted travelers; a much-needed commodity after doing without.

The Indians watched this area and commenced to attack those who stopped for rest. The camp is noted as being a place of violence. There are eleven known graves at the site. Again, the men took turns to be on watch.

While they were setting up their tents, they could tell a storm was brewing. Snow began to fall. Pike's words, "Two or three hours before daylight, the storm commenced with terrific violence, and I never saw a wilder or more terrible sight than was presented to us when day came. The wind swept fiercely out of the canon, driving the snow horizontally against the wagons, and sweeping onward into the wide prairie, in which a sea of snow seemed raging." [100]

They moved out the next day into the vast plains of white. If you have ever gotten caught out in a major snowstorm with the wind blowing on U.S. Hwy 56, which is parallel to the trail, you will understand what state of mind they were in. There are times you can't see in front of you and become snow blind. You feel as though you are in a deep sea of billowy white waves rippling through the tall prairie grass. There are moments you feel like you're in a dream, lost, not knowing if you will ever see the light of day or blue sky again. It's a frightening experience.

While digging out of the snow from their tents, they weren't making much progress as the wind whipped in circles laying the snow right back across their cleared area. The men began to see the effects of the storm. Six or eight oxen had froze to death in the snow. The caravan had lost a portion of their mode of power to pull at least one of their wagons. They may have had to leave one wagon behind. There were only one or two horses left. With the resources they had, they again headed out into the thick sea of white. Pike describes running back and forth in the tracks of the wagons in which the ice-cold snow penetrated his leather shoes.

They continue the trail west, meeting the Canadian River where there is only one safe crossing to cross upon a natural flat stone floor. This crossing is to the southeast of the present town, Springer. The Canadian River crossing was also being watched carefully by Indian tribes and was a dangerous site for traders and settlers to be ambushed. Little did Albert Pike know that this crossing in which he and the others were running their wagons across would become a death zone for one of their own a year later.

While Pike was crossing the Canadian River, Aaron Lewis and his two men from Fort Towson were coming in from the east, following the Canadian River to the branch of the Mora River (Demora), approximately 30 miles directly south where Pike was.

Heading southwest, the Bent caravan followed a tributary of the Canadian which was more than likely the Ocate Creek or Ocate River which directed the travelers to the Ocate Trail. This path was known as the shortcut to Taos over two mountain ranges and had been officially surveyed and outlined by Joseph Brown, the surveyor for the Santa Fe Trail in 1825-27.

The crossing at Ocate Creek was a common camping spot for those on the Santa Fe Trail who were coming into New Mexico from the North through Raton, into the town of Cimarron, and through Rayado on their way to Santa Fe. It was also where those coming from the Cimarron desert route would rest, veering off the main trail, who were taking the shortcut to Taos through the rugged mountains which was advised by the survey, noted as the safest, but hardest. Other parts of the Santa Fe Trail followed further south into Wagon Mound, Watrous, San Miguel and on to Santa Fe.

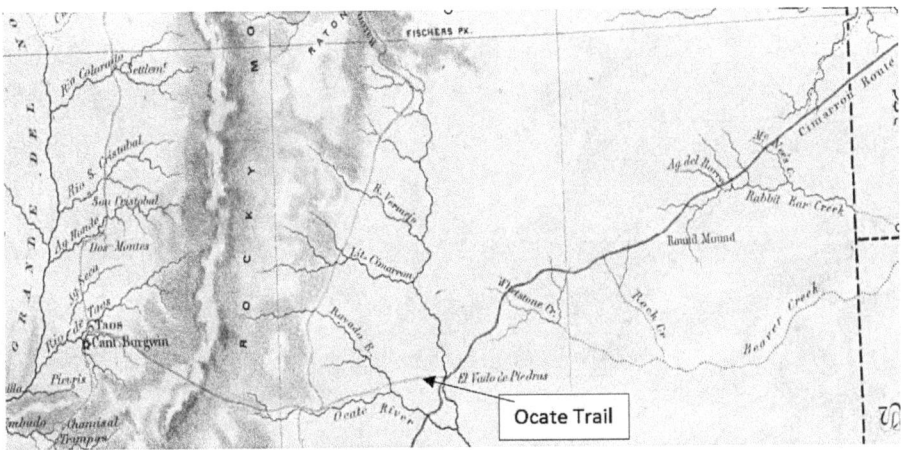

(The Octate Trail shown on Territory and military department of New Mexico 1859 map.[101])

Ocate Creek meandered along in a beautiful, lush valley. It was a very welcoming site after the long exhausting trek through the Cimarron desert. It was flowing with fresh sparkling water, good timber, and pure mountain air. The small community of Ocate, which is 5-6 miles to the west of the crossing was the exchange point for merchandise and goods to be transferred to wagons going through the mountains to Taos on the Ocate Trail and the rest would be taken south to Santa Fe on the main Santa Fe Trail.

The Ocate Trail followed the Ocate Creek which flowed into a narrow canyon, called Manueles Canyon surrounded by tall rock cliffs to the north and gentle mountain terrain to the south. Tall healthy timber lined the narrow path which ran parallel with the creek. It was the first time that the travelers had access to timber for over 200 miles on the trail.

(Ocate Trail with tall cliffs rock looming overhead)

(Strange rock formation on the Ocate Trail)

    The trail was fairly new to the Anglo-American trappers and traders, but it was a trail initially made by the Ute Indians who traveled through the mountain passes with no problem. Some parts of the canyon were barely wide enough for a wagon to pass and curved throughout the landscape on a rocky and rough trail. Parts of it were heavily wooded, while other portions dipped down into open valleys.

    A portion of the Ocate Trail is currently New Mexico State Road 120. It's a beautiful drive, very narrow and unpaved, but left in its primitive state as it was nearly 200 years ago.

    Heavy snow had fallen during the last storm and was knee deep along the mountain pass. In places, they would be swallowed up to their belly in snow. This was extremely hard to move the wagons through; the wagons bogged down, and the oxen could not be manipulated to pull the extra weight. They had to leave the wagons and pack as much merchandise on the animals and mules they had. It appears that some of the men had gone ahead with pack mules, while others such as Pike stayed behind to secure the goods. Luckily, Pike was able to follow their tracks. He was 17 miles from the foot of the first high mountain to cross, just a few miles into the Manueles Canyon.

    Pike stated that all of his party, except one or two froze their feet. The trail eventually began descending into a beautiful valley called "Black Lake." This is one of the areas where the movie "Lonesome Dove" was filmed.

(Traveling on the Ocate Trail down into the Black Lake area from the East. (courtesy photo by Johnese Turri))

(Looking from the other side (West) of the valley towards the trail Pike would be climbing down the mountain to reach the bottom of the valley called Black Lake. He would then have to follow Coyote Creek from the lake, north, reaching Osha Pass. Imagine what it would be like in Winter.)

When Pike came to Black Lake, he traveled Northwest. The Moache Utes had first settled here. It was a wide-open valley, with a large pond and creeks flowing through it. The land produced some of the best grassland for grazing in the period between April and September. The Taos Pueblo Indians would bring their livestock from Taos each summer to graze and fatten them up for the winter. The valley was also used for the growing of their summer crops.

The Indians would travel from their Pueblos, driving their livestock even up into the 1930's-1940's through Taos Canyon, witnessed by my father at the age of 8 where he was helping his grandparents build a log cabin in the area of Shady Brook. The Indians traveled up the mountain pass where Valle Escondito lies. They would follow the old paths to Osha Pass over the mountain and descend close to where the Osha Pass Road is currently; Forest Road 76 off of Hwy 434. They followed Coyote Creek to the lush beautiful valley of Black Lake, once called "Osha."

It would take Pike 4 full days to travel from where they left the wagons, traveling into Black Lake, up the trail on Osha Pass, through Valle Escondito, through Taos Canyon and to the still-house. Pike states, "This day, (November 28, 1831) about ten in the evening, our party reached the still house in the valley, within three miles of Taos." [102]

Pike's own personal story of his trip through the Ocate Trail and Osha Pass is swallowed up into the deep dark abyss, very vague, leaving just bits and pieces of crumbs here and there to tell the story. A little help from authors of old, history experts, and personal knowledge enabled the writer to make sense of his clues along his journey. Pike only mentions "our wagons' or "a party of us" made it through to Taos, and "all of his party," except one or two froze their feet. He never speaks about himself in the first person. Was he alone on this path or with the party of men? What kind of condition was he in?

He may have very well suffered frostbite and hyperthermia. In one book, "Lure, Lore, and Legends of the Moreno Valley," by Members of the Moreno Valley Writers Guild, 1997, an excellent book describes Albert Pike traveling over Osha Pass and suffering severe frostbite. He was taken in by a Taoseno family. They treated his wounds with boiled onions and a variety of herbs. It is definitely one of the legends in these here parts.

Pike's custom way of writing was confusing at times and hard to follow. Even the poem he wrote about Taos is hard to understand, but exudes the idea of beauty all around him, shadowed by extreme trauma, the contemplation of death, drumming up courage, and the want for home. Here are the last three stanzas.

Taos

"What is there left, that I should cling to life?
High hopes that storms smote down when scarce expanded.
A broken censer with faint odor rife,
a waning sun, a vessel half-ensanded,
Life's prospects on sharp rocks and shallows stranded.
A star just setting in a midnight ocean,
A smoking altar, broken and unbanded,
Lit with the flame of hopeless love's devotion.
A bosom shattered with its own intense emotion.
Unmanly Heart! Repine not but be calm! Take courage, Heart!
Let us not madly mar the effect of the sweet scene. Hope holds her palm, Like an old friend to me,
and sets her star once more upon the waves of life afar.
It shall not sink again; but ever lift Cheerily its eye above the stormy bar
I thank thee, Hope, for thy most princely gift! No longer, eyeless, on life's clashing waves I drift.
Farewell to thee, New England once again!
The echo of thy name has reached my soul,
And it has vibrated; oh, not in vain, If thou and thine shall hear. Now for the goal!
Dash through the waves, bold Heart, that madly roll Across thy path!
Much waiteth to be done. Before Time's billows o'er my dead brain roll:
Behold the last complaining words of one,
Who has been, is, will ever be, New England's son."
(https://allpoetry.com/poem/8588561-Taos-by-Albert-Pike)

Many people said Albert Pike was a genius, way above my head, but it seems as though he was hiding something in plain sight. In Pike's narrative, very little is said about his trip from this point on. The only thing we learn from his first impression of Taos was one of disgust by the sight of the locals at the Fandangos and of Santa Fe's mud huts instead of grand staircases and beautiful architecture. It was indeed a disappointment.

What is there missing during his trip over the mountain and what did he experience in Taos and Santa Fe during the next 9-10 months he was there? The poem is very revealing.

Did Pike get left behind because he was on foot with frost bitten feet and had to find his own way? Why did he not elaborate on his story? Was it embarrassment, a disagreement between him and Bent for leaving the wagons and they parted their ways, or was he covering up something? **I don't know.** I can only tell his story and stories written by other authors. Pike never mentions Bent's name throughout his story. Pike was known for having arguments and sometimes duels with those he didn't agree with; especially those in command over him.

Maybe we can learn what happened to Pike through the story he tells of Aaron B. Lewis. In Pike's own words in the narrative, he states, "The readers need not expect much delineation of character. Trappers are like sailors – when you describe one the portrait answers for the whole genus." [103]

Pike switches back to the trail and begins telling Lewis' story in the "first person." It's as if Pike had possession of Lewis' detailed journal, laying out dates and day by day events, but there was none. Pike states that Lewis told his story in his own words, that he was an unlettered man, and Pike writes this all by memory. Pike would have to be a genius or have a photographic memory to have retained all these dates and detailed events of Aaron B. Lewis' travels.

The trip gets horrifically treacherous for Lewis, a well-seasoned explorer/trapper which is related to the lines in Pike's poem. Was Pike actually writing about his own story and not Lewis'? The portion of the poem above seems to indicate this very idea; the sense of loneliness, despair, pain, and death, but yet mustering up the hope to carry on.

On December 1st, while Albert Pike was recovering, Aaron Lewis and his men neared the junction of the Mora River and Sapello River which is slightly northeast of Watrous, New Mexico. Back in those days I believe the community was called La Junta. This area was approximately 20 miles directly South of Ocate.

Even though one of Lewis' men knew his way to Taos with a wife waiting on him there, they decided not to go the familiar route of the guide's, which was through Mora (the old village) and up a broken trail, most likely what is now the high road to Taos (NM 518). The guide feared that the snow would be very deep in that area and that it would be safer going directly North to the shortcut on the Ocate Trail. They started toward that direction and was a few days behind the Bent Caravan.

It would take two days for Aaron B. Lewis to travel through the valley towards the Ocate Trail. Nature was at its worst. It had turned bitter cold and the ground was covered with a heavy layer of snow, some places up to his waist. It was December 3rd when he reached Manueles Canyon on the Ocate Trail. Lewis and his two companions, Andrews and Chambers were extremely weak and had a hard time carrying their guns and supplies. They were on foot and very scantily clad. Lewis only had a pair of linen pantaloons, a shirt, and a partial piece of deer hide thrown across his back and breast, used as a poncho. His feet were only covered by a thin layer of deerskin fashioned into a moccasin.

They had lost their ride somewhere in the Cross Timbers between the Canadian River and the Red. Frustrated by the lethargic effect that the weather conditions were having on his crew, Lewis set out alone.

He reached what he had determined as Black Lake. Pike describes it as "a hollow prairie where water is sometimes and about six miles across." [104] He believed it was the coldest place that he ever had been to. Snow was coming down violently and he began to weep and pray inwardly. Lewis became increasingly aware of the loneliness, despair, the chill to the bone, and swelling feet. Lewis believed he would not make it out of the big valley and wanted heartily to die, but he hated to kill himself, so he kept moving. The only companion he kept by his side was a smoldering chunk of wood to start the next fire when he reached another place to rest on the journey. He was not quite sure if he was going in the right direction, but he knew that Taos was directly Northwest. He finally came to another canyon that ascended from the Black Lake valley; in the direction he knew he had to travel. He began to follow a trail alongside Coyote Creek and ran in to mule tracks that were probably the remnants of Bent's party. Even though his feet were cut all to pieces and blood was gathering in the soles of his shoes, he knew he could not quit now.

This canyon has to be the road to Osha Pass, or near there, present day Forest Road 76, which is south of Angel Fire. The miles they traveled described by Pike appears that this is so. This was the shortcut to Taos. Directly from the bottom of the Black Lake Valley, Taos is due Northwest from this spot.

On top of Osha Pass, one can see that they made it over the second mountain range and then the descension begins, down into a deep dark valley below. "The thought of turning coward would raise me again, and I kept on until I reached the top of the mountain. You know what a dark, black-looking place it is on the other side, away down, down in the depths of the valley. When I looked off from the summit of the mountain, and saw it, the thought flashed into my mind that this must be the Black Lake. No man in the world can express the feeling which came over me then."[105]

(Top of Osha Pass. Pretty Hefty climb to the top and this is in front of you, covered in snow.)

Lewis was halfway down the other side when he gave up his chunk of fire and was ready to die, but something inside did not allow him to do so. He could not move his hands, but with all that he had left in him, he forced his legs to move. Once he reached Taos Canyon where Valle Escondito is, he noticed the path where the mules had trodden.

He followed the canyon alongside the Rio Fernando de Taos River for another twelve miles. He could hear what was sweet music to him, the moo of a cow and the clucking sound of a chicken. In a distance, he saw the adobe mud house called the "still" house. "Taos Lightening" was popular in that day, made of wheat and the "still house" was a place where it flowed as swift as the river.

Quite a frightful sight Lewis was, a big man, his face blackened by the pine smoke from the campfires, hair jet black, barely clothed, and staggering sluggishly towards the house where two men were cautiously sizing him up. They believed he was an Indian. When Lewis began speaking English, they recognized him as an American.

Several people in the community began taking care of Lewis, providing whiskey, feeding him and treating his frostbitten limbs with great care. When Lewis had to cut and peel off his moccasins from his swollen feet, all were taken back at the sight. They were the size of a "bull's head." One man roasted onions in ashes and made a poultice for his feet to draw out the fluid and infection. The caring man stayed up all night to change the bandages and added more of the poultice in intervals to the damaged feet. I'm sure Lewis' exposed legs and hands had to be treated as well.

Lewis stayed at the still house for 6 weeks to heal. His blackened skin began to fall off, exposing some of his bones and tenons. He developed pleurisy and was transferred to Rio Hondo where the gracious community continued diligently in supplying his every need. He had completely healed by April. He was tough as a boot. He was trapping again when May rolled around.

Pike describes in cinematic color of Lewis' trapping adventures. According to Pike, Lewis was an extraordinary mountain man who knew all the techniques in trapping. I'm sure Pike learned a tremendous amount of knowledge from Lewis and was a man to be idolized and looked up to.

Lewis and his team caught 40 beavers in the mountains. They also killed several mountain sheep and white bear. Pike also described the wicked Del Norte River, which is the Rio Grande River. "It is a terrible place, and once in it, there is no egress except at the lower end of it. Some Spaniards unwittingly entered it once in a canoe and were carried violently down it about forty miles." [106] It has a mind of its own and the force of it can overtake you in the rapids or the whirlpools which can take you under.

These mountains are familiar ground to this writer. They have a spirit of their own; mesmerizing and sacred. They sense your purpose and intentions while passing through. They demand respect. There are those who come and feel a strong connection to the peaks, the pine, the rivers, the wildlife, and there are those who feel smothered, distressed, and leave with an unpleasant experience. It's hard to explain until you experience it for yourself. The Indians believe that these mountains are indeed sacred. The Taos Pueblo Indian's beautiful Blue Lake, that rests high up in the tallest peaks, is where they believe was the very beginning of their existence.

Maybe Lewis' story explains what really happened to Pike. Furthermore, I cannot find an Aaron B. Lewis, except when this particular story of his journey is told, and the trip that Pike and Lewis took together back through Texas and Oklahoma. Could Pike be using the name of Aaron Burr plus Meriwether Lewis to create the character of Aaron B. Lewis or hide the true identity of this individual? I don't know, but what sways the thinking of concealment or a name change of a character whose name Pike wished to remain anonymous was found in Pike's manuscript, "Among the Americans with whom I became acquainted, shortly after my arrival in Santa Fe, there was one in particular who excite my interest and won my esteem. And here I beg leave to remark, that in what I am about relating, I shall, for reasons which will doubtless be obvious to all who follow my brief tale to the conclusion, **conceal** the actual names of the person's interested in it. Most of the circumstances are facts, although the time at which they actually occurred was a little anterior to the date of the tale. Most of them are facts, and the actors yet alive." [107] He speaks of "Refugio" who fancies riches of ancient and modern lore.

It's odd that in Pike's narrative he mentions Aaron Burr and Zebulon Pike. Albert Pike stated, "It was on the heads of the Del Norte (Rio Grande River) that General Pike (Zebulon), then a lieutenant was taken by the Mexicans. Has it ever been satisfactorily known why he was there? I think not. He could not have been mistaken in the river. He knew it not to be the Arkansas, and he knew himself to be in the Mexican territory. Was he not seeking a place for the army of Aaron Burr to enter and subdue Mexico? He was no traitor, I know; and neither, in my opinion, was Burr. Neither ever aimed to raise a hand against our own country. I find some proof of Pike's (Zebulon) intentions in his book." [108]

This piece of political information placed into the narrative, seemed out of place except for the location. There are numerous hints that suggest that Albert Pike possibly had the same motives. Was he exploring the area, such as Zebulon Pike was, who happened to share the same family tree as

Albert Pike? The relationship is clarified in the book, "The Life Story of Albert Pike," by Fred William Allsopp, 1920. Were they both looking at starting a new country? Were they both interested in the vast riches that this land held, hidden in plain sight?

Unlocking the Llano Estacado

It is quite odd that Zebulon Pike wrote extensively about his trip from Missouri into New Mexico, charting the area, including the Dona Ana Mountains, but he did not expand on his trip back through Texas. Albert Pike on the other hand didn't expand on his trip going to New Mexico but did as he traveled back through Texas and present-day Oklahoma. Was there something to hide or was there a plant of clues for the brotherhood within the manuscript to follow. They will lead to Jesse.

Pike wrote about who he chose to travel back to Missouri with from New Mexico. He had heard that John Harris of Missouri was gathering men in Taos "for the purpose of entering and trapping in the Comanche country, upon the heads of Red River and the Fore Washita; and I was induced, by the prospect of gain, and by other motives, to go up from Santa Fe to Taos, and join him." ("Narrative of a Second Journey in the Prairie" in *Prose sketches and poems: written in the western country*, by Albert Pike, 1834).

Several parties joined forces. Traveling with them were between 70 to 80 men in the caravan, including Aaron B. Lewis. Many caravans had Mexican dragoons or military personnel to escort them on the trails, mostly due to the Comanches or Apaches. Some went along to protect their cargo. They possibly were carrying with them something of value such as gold or silver. This was the case in many stories of the traders who began using these trails through dangerous and isolated territories. Their intentions may have also included uncovering valuables along the way.

It appears that Albert Pike learned a lot from these men on this trip, changing his path into a different direction, a new purpose in life. Pike described Aaron B. Lewis as a man he met up with in Taos, New Mexico. His description of Lewis was that he was a large and very tall man, red faced, of undaunted bravery, coolness, composed under stress, an excellent hunter, and of constant good humor.

Pike, in his masterful way, may have combined his literary skills, his survival skills, and his egotistical demeanor to form the character of Aaron B. Lewis or maybe it was just plain and simple, Lewis was the real deal and Pike was a great admirer of the man. There's no doubt, Pike was totally enthralled with Lewis and his story.

On their return trip to the United States, they traveled back along the Pecos River, the town of Mora, down the Gallinas Creek, Ft. Sumner, on to the Llano Estacado in Texas or what was known as the Staked Plains, which was considered the Great American Desert. Pike described the "Spaniards" as terrified of this boundless ocean of "scorched by fire" earth where the Comanche would not allow the traveler to escape alive. They had been engrained with stories of terror and prophecies foreseeing their death. The Spaniards did not want to continue, and they were not going to defend the Americanos. The group split, leaving the Spaniards behind.

This was a new route for all of them. Of course, there were paths made by the Indians, Spaniards, and buffalo who had long before treaded upon this dry, dusty soil. The land was harsh, leading them to a dramatic drop in elevation off the caprock into a rough and tumbling terrain known as the Rolling Plains, Cowboy Alley, the Big Empty, and for the most part, the "Breaks." Southeast of the current town of Post, Texas in Garza County, they crossed over to the Double Mountain Fork of the Brazos River near Justiceburg and camped at the junction of the forks in western Kent County. The article written by David Donoghue, "Explorations of Albert Pike in Texas," describes their detailed trek.

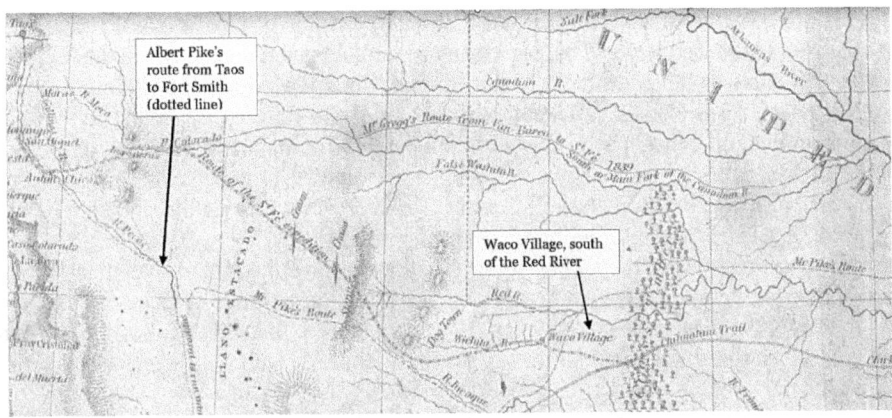

(Pike's journey through Texas [109])

It was fascinating to read Pike's rendition of what he saw and experienced in his book, "Prose Sketches and Poems: Written in the Western Country;" 1834. Remember this was when Texas was rough and raw, not many people except for a population of Comanches and other Indian tribes, Spaniards along with what Pike called "mesquito" (mesquite) bushes. He described the area as the "mesquito prairie."

Pike learned what it was to be tough, to be dirty and greasy, longing for civilized comforts, such as a fork and a bed. He encountered barren badlands, flat prairies that went for miles and miles, having to eat what they could find, sometimes buffalo or horse meat and drink what was available from mud holes, blood of an animal, and salty water. He engaged with Indians who were friendly, but their women folk were none too pretty.

His eyes were fascinated by the wild horses and the dominating stallion which would lead and prod the others to push on for survival. His writings seemed to emphasize a strong connection to the stallion and its leadership abilities. He saw bear, elk, deer, and prairie dogs living in the breaks surrounded by red rugged terrain which only allowed the salty water to flow through its hellish veins and gullies. There was strong evidence of a vast prehistoric body of water that once took over the landscape.

The area where Pike traveled is one of the most fascinating areas in Texas to explore for Paleontologists, especially those from the Houston Museum of Natural Science who have been studying this part of Texas for several years. They focus their study near the Wichita River in Baylor County. They believe that the area northwest of Seymour was a vast sea full of prehistoric animals, a world before the dinosaurs, over 290 million years ago. It is in an area known as the Texas Red Beds from the Early Permian. It extends through Wichita Falls and into south-central Oklahoma. The scientists have uncovered remnants of a variety of mammals, reptiles, fish, and other species that roamed the area in which has never been discovered before or was just overlooked.

They traveled down the Double Mountain Fork to the northwest corner of Fisher County. Pike left the Double Mountain Fork and went northeast, crossing the Salt Fork of the Brazos into eastern Kent County, through western Stonewall County, north of current day Aspermont, and crossing the Brazos River where it widens with the confluence of the two forks; the Double Mountain Fork and the Salt Fork.

Rivers and sources of water were extremely important to trappers and explorers. The waterways were the highways back then. Landmarks such as rivers, tributaries, forks, Indian mounds, unusual formations in the landscape, etc. were often used to map out trails with distinguishable drawings of the terrain. You will also see this on treasure maps.

It was written that Lewis, Pike, and the other men were exploring new land and new waterways. It was noted that on this trip, that Pike named the Salt Fork of the Brazos River.

Pike claimed that from the Del Resgate (Rescata) branch of the Brazos River, that it was another 140 miles to the Red River. There are many researchers who debate where this location was. I believe the Rescata was the confluence of the Double Mountain Fork and Salt Fork of the Brazos River. At this point, the Brazos River becomes rather large and flows north, east, and then south all the way down to the gulf coast. The junction of the Double Mountain and Salt Fork of the Brazos is just inside the eastern border of Stonewall County. It is southwest of the small town of Rochester, Texas and north of Rule, Texas in Haskell County. This very spot was significant, being mentioned in Pike's book. Put an "X" at this spot on your treasure map.

They knew exactly where they were going. They must have heard and read many a great tale of treasures just waiting to be found in Texas; possibly from the writings of Zebulon Pike, Refugio, or stories told by the old Mestizos or Navajos they encountered. Instead of following the path near the Canadian River that they were familiar with, they chose a path following the waters of the Brazos.

Naturally their route piqued my interest because of living in this area for most of my life along the Brazos River and on the famous Western Trail. The Salt Fork of the Brazos River was not a place to drink from or to freshen up. The water is salty, and the clay and mineral deposits stain your clothes a nice Texas Longhorn burnt orange. My husband grew up right on the Brazos River and his mother always knew where he had been when she found in the laundry pile, rusty red underwear.

I ran across an article on the Texas State Historical Association Handbook of Texas website. According to author Kenneth E. Hendrickson, Jr. in his article titled, "Brazos River," a very interesting story appeared. Pike was told in 1831, presumably while in Taos or Santa Fe on his expedition trip, of the story of Spanish miners who were working on the San Saba River in Texas. The drought was extremely harsh, so they gathered their *precious bullion* and buried it, whether at the mine or as they journeyed toward a stream they believed would never run dry. They named the river of salvation, the "Los Brazos de Dios" (The Arms of God).

This particular story by Hendrickson directs the reader to San Saba River that begins near Menard, way south of where Pike's trail was. If the miners were on the San Saba, they would have first run into the mighty Colorado River that has always been plentiful. The headwaters of the Colorado actually form further southwest of the Brazos, near the present Texas town of Lamesa.

The confusion of which river they were on may have been a diversion. It doesn't appear that Pike ever made it to the San Saba River or the Colorado, at least not on this trip. The map indicates they stayed in North Texas, but in stories found later in history, the San Saba River was a hotspot for silver.

The story told to Pike was that the Spaniards traveled north toward the Waco Indian Village. I believe this is where the confusion gets tangled. Many believe they were referring to the town of Waco which was founded upon the site of a Waco Village on the Brazos River, which was another 100 miles to the northeast from the Colorado River. I don't believe they would have continued another 100 miles after reaching the Colorado River to get to the Waco Village on the Brazos for their salvation.

When studying the old maps, it all came together. Following Pike's path, we see he was following the Brazos River at its headwaters in the north and then along the Wichita River. There was another Waco Village shown north of the Salt Fork of the Brazos River in Wichita County. It was near the sight of the present-day city of Wichita Falls which was established near the Wichita River, running parallel to Pike's trek. This must be the Waco Village the story was referring to and Pike was following the Spanish tale's trail.

Again, we see treasure in the story, but what is quite interesting is that the route Pike took through North Texas takes us directly through an area that has been pinpointed as where Spanish treasure has been located.

In an article written by Bob Brewer on "the hootowltree.com" describing the book "The Spider's Web" by George Mitchell, he states the book was to be written about a true story of the hunt for the Spider Rocks Spanish Treasure Mystery in and around Stonewall and Kent counties in

Texas. He described that the Spanish miners were working at the junction of the Salt Fork and Double Mountain Fork of the Brazos River.

This location is most likely the Del Resgate or Rescata Pike spoke of in his book. The miles that Pike indicated between the Resgate/Rescata and the Red River fit perfectly in the general area of the fork's confluence, 140 miles to the Red.

Other stories suggest that it wasn't just the drought that pushed the Spaniards to flee from their mining area, but that they were overtaken by hostile Indians. They began hiding their gold and silver, along with church artifacts in an underground vault or mine.

The story gets more intriguing and the treasure hunt becomes more aggressive after the Civil War and into the early 1900's. There were several newspaper articles that support what Pike may have come across on this trail in 1832 and the possibilities of treasure.

We hear of the old Confederate soldier, Dave Arnold, living in Texas after the war who had a map drawn out on sheepskin or tablet, which depicted the exact location of the Spanish treasure which was supposedly drawn out by those who had worked in the mines. It would reveal a complex map directing them to key signs, codes, symbols, and hieroglyphics, eventually leading them to the treasure. Arnold began looking for the treasure as early as 1902. He believed it was the Aztecs who buried the treasure. He acquired this map from an old native of Mexico upon his death, against the will of his sister who was in her 90's. The old man begged Arnold to swear that he would keep it and protect it. Whatever it led to was of great importance.

While staying in the home of the old man and sister, Arnold secretly hid the treasure map and later was awoken by the crackling sound of a fire. The sister had set fire to the old adobe home and yelled, "I told ye no white man would ever profit by the great secret or take out the silver bars" as she died in the flames.

The Spaniards were searching for silver mines throughout Texas, basically on the same trail in which Pike traveled on, even on into Santa Fe. It is believed the Spaniards had brought with them massive quantities of gold from Mexico and was planning to stash it with other treasures found along the way for safe keeping. Could this gold be part of Montezuma's gold?

An article written in the Fort Worth Star Telegram in November 17, 1907, relays the story of the old lady whom described herself as being from a tribe of Indians who were "enslaved and driven in gangs into the pits beneath the tingling lash of the Montezumas." [110] She apparently was speaking of the Aztec Empire that collapsed after the Spanish Conquest in the early 16th century in 1521. Montezuma was in power of the Aztec's who was considered a god, a manifestation and perpetuator of the *sun*. Montezuma was interested in the arts, astrology, philosophy and human sacrifice. The carvings of the Aztecs made in those days, were very similar to the items found on the map leading Dave Arnold to Texas.

Montezuma had met the Spanish Conquistadors, led by Cortes, and gave them gifts of gold. It wasn't long before the Spanish were taken over by gold fever and they began to devise a plan to conquer Montezuma, the land, and of course all the stash of his gold underneath his palace. Before the Spanish overtook the power, Montezuma had thousands of his people, warriors and slaves to travel north with his empire's gold. When Cortes arrived at Montezuma's palace, all the gold and treasure was gone. Cortes ordered that Montezuma would be killed. Where did the gold and artifacts go? Many believe that Montezuma advised the Aztecs to take it back to the land of their ancestors, Aztlan, which is supposedly in *Utah*.

The old man who had given Dave Arnold the sheepskin map was a descendant of those who had worked for Montezuma in his underground fortress where he had hidden his great wealth and treasures of the Aztecs. The History Channel, "New Evidence of Montezuma's Golden Treasure, Cities of the Underworld" reveals that the people who took out the gold and treasures were possibly an ancient Indian tribe who had their beginnings on an island in the middle of the Great Salt Lake in Utah in the 600's. Supposedly, due to the changes in climate, they traveled south and could have been dispersed into the Pueblo Indians of New Mexico and Arizona. It is assumed that many traveled further south or was captured and taken to the land of Montezuma to work for his empire. What's really fascinating is that it fits perfectly into the story of Pike and later we will see how it fits in with Salt Lake City. Who settled there?

The Aztec descendants spoke Uto-Aztecans which is a combination of the native Ute language with the dialect of the Aztecs. The Utes were very numerous in Utah and Northern New Mexico, especially where Albert Pike traveled. They had their summer campgrounds in the Moreno Valley, near Black Lake, Angel Fire, and Cimarron Canyon in Northeastern New Mexico. Most of the trails made throughout the mountain terrain were forged by the Utes.

The Utes were hunter/gatherers. They believed they were created by Sinawav (the Creator) and were placed in the mountains as strong warriors and protector of the lands. They were extremely attached to the land in Utah. When the Mormons began moving in and utilizing the Utes's resources, there rose a great rebellion. It became a hostile situation when the Ute's began defending their land and raiding the newcomers. Brigham Young ordered extermination and/or the expulsion of the hostile Indian tribes in the area.

Another strange bit of information from "America Unearthed: Montezuma's Gold Stashed Away in Utah" by the History Channel, reveals that Montezuma's treasure was hidden in various parts of the United States, one being near the four corner area of Utah, Arizona, New Mexico and Colorado near Kanab, Utah. As far as we know, the treasure in Utah has not been found, but it is suspected to be hidden in underground caves that have been flooded. There are also strategic areas within the limestone rock caves, carved out by humans, that contain booby traps indicating that the treasure may have at one time been placed there. The caves were later filled in and sealed up. There are also signs in the rocks nearby that appears to be a symbol of gold; a circle and a line drawn from the outside of the circle to the center of the circle, pointing in a certain direction.

When Montezuma's treasures were hidden, many of the slaves were killed as human sacrifices and left near the treasure so that their ghosts would guard the treasures. Some believe that the area where the treasures are hidden is cursed. This was the case in Kanab, Utah and at the area in Stonewall and Haskell County, Texas. Stories of murder and near-death experiences have occurred on these sites. Booby traps and strange unexplainable occurrences encourage one not to pursue the treasure. The trap technique was used throughout Montezuma's treasure troves, as well as the Spaniards, and later we find evidence that Jesse James used these same methods.

We also hear about a man named Stewart, an Oklahoma treasure hunter who began searching in the forks of the Double Mountain and Salt Fork of the Brazos River and found rock carvings in Stonewall County. There was also another "stranger" that entered the picture named, Forrest. The story gets a little construed by several accounts, but one of these men, maybe even a Mexican sheep herder with the group of Arnold's, found the "Spider Rock". It was found on *a lone hill*, southwest of the junction of the Double Mountain and Salt Forks of the Brazos River. It had intricate spider web carvings on them which appear very similar to Aztec carvings. It was a map of treasure. Lone Hill was another important site in Oklahoma.

The Spider Rock map held key points and directions towards treasure. The etchings on the rock was filled in with copper with inscriptions of roman numerals such as XXI, I8XII, 8LXXI, and LXVII. There were letters, such as F's, H, and CX. There were pictures of an arrow, a cross, a diamond, squares with circles inside, and circles within a circle. The men who uncovered the rock found copper artifacts and other objects that would lead them to more treasure.

Spider Rock was concealing a large flat base rock, and underneath that rock they discovered after 15 feet down, decayed bodies and relics. They also found prehistoric animal bones.

A quarter mile east of the *Spider Rock* Hill are the remains of a crude Spanish smelter. To the northwest, 3 miles, the ruins of the Spanish mission was found. Two miles northeast of the hill on the west rim of the Salt Fork is another Spanish smelter.

"Many of the clues the map laid out have been discovered and some of the reputed treasure even found," stated Steve Wilson in Oct.13, 1963, "Wichita Falls Times." [111] In the 40's, 50's, and 60's, treasure hunting fever was in full swing. The hunt for lost treasure of the Aztecs, Spanish gold, and Jesse James exploded in Oklahoma, Texas, and New Mexico. This was about the same time

Victorio Peak's treasure was being extensively explored near Dona Ana, New Mexico. They all connect.

George Mitchell took up the investigation of the Spider Rock Treasure, and had compiled many maps, letters, photos, and typed an enthralling and intriguing manuscript. He was unable to complete his investigation, but his daughter took what was left of his documents and with author Bill Townsley's help, they published Mitchell's book, "The Spider's Web."

There supposedly is a Spider Rock found in Callahan (Clyde), Stonewall (Aspermont), and Fisher (Rotan) Counties all relating to treasure in that area. The three locations form a near perfect isosceles triangle. The northern portion of the triangle is in the 33rd degree parallel.

The area of the far northwest corner of Haskell County and far northeast corner of Stonewall County that meet, indicates deep mining shafts where numerous human bones and copper deposits were. Many believe these were native slaves who were used to work the mines during the Spanish conquistador era, but again, it could have been the slaves from Montezuma's palace who were left to guard the treasure.

Another scenario indicates that the Montezuma treasure was uncovered by the Spaniards in the early days of their reign and continued to collect and store many treasures at that sight, along with mining the area. The Spanish mission shows that it was a very important sight for the Spanish and possibly a trade station. When Mexico regained their country back in 1821, the Spaniards may have created these maps to hide the treasure from the Mexicans who would be populating Texas once again as well as the newcomers from the United States who were settling there prior to the Texas Revolution.

A newspaper article in the Times Record News of Wichita Falls on December 6, 1956, "Lost Diamond Mine Object of Intense Treasure Hunt," describes the last remaining treasure hunter, J. Kelly Johnson from Munday, Texas who first explored this area in the early 1900's with Dave Arnold. He claimed they were actually looking for a diamond mine, but never found it. Johnson at that time, still believed there was one in the hills of Stonewall County. Johnson stated that they had a map which led them to many relics, but most of them were found in the grave of a Spanish priest which contained relics, parts of a pack saddle, a pearl necklace, diamond necklace, a pipe, bridle bits, gold buckles, gold rings, gold earrings, a silver cross, a clay lamb, and walking cane.

Johnson stated that the items were taken to a bank and then later displayed at Terrell's Drug Store, the store of Dave Arnold's partner who was the head of the exploration of the site. Johnson claims that the fire that supposedly burned Terrell's Drug Store and the priceless relics, did not consume the relics, but the items were removed before or shortly after the fire. He had no idea who had them, but claimed they were stolen.

The group went back and dug up copper plates, knives, etc. and Mr. Johnson stated there was still a lot of money in them thar hills to find. Later, evidence and treasure found in the area by Dave Arnold and his helpers indicate a series of copper mines with some gold, silver, and lead in the mix as well as crumbled adobe walls of the old mission.

With numerous newspaper articles, such as in the Wichita Falls Times written in July 28, 1963, by Steve Wilson, "Four Decades of Searching Yields Clues, Little Treasure," collaborates stories told in other literature of those who recall the local lore. The Spanish mission was built and dated 1812, twenty years earlier than when Pike passed through the area. Could it have been inhabited when Pike traveled through there? Possibly. The remnants would have definitely still been there and many clues that would lead them to something spectacular.

In a news article, "Two Maps May Hold Key to "Spider Rock" Gold", written by Steve Wilson in the Wichita Falls Times in October 13, 1963 describes the mystery further and he would later write the book, "The Spider Rock Treasure, A Texas Mystery of Lost Spanish Gold". Wilson was able to support the tales of Spaniards spreading out into the North Texas area around the time Zebulon Pike was exploring the edges of the Mexican border in 1806-1808.

These stories, these trails and points of interest were right in line of Albert Pike's interest. This exact point on the Brazos River was definitely a hot spot. Why else would Albert Pike and the men take this route? They knew. This may have been the location where Pike learned the tricks and techniques of these ancient empires regarding hidden treasures. It was amazing to read about all the different treasure sites in Texas and Oklahoma that reveals ancient civilizations who lived in the southwest prior to 500 B.C. Many sites indicate a possibility of Ancient Egyptians and Irish Celts who once inhabited this continent, as well as unidentified people. There is plenty of evidence to support their existence.

This raises questions regarding the mounds that were placed within these two states. Treasures have been dug out of them, but they appear to be for ceremonies, sacrifices, and landmarks. There is so much we do not know of our history and the civilization that once lived on this land. Maybe it is something that has been hidden from us, but we do know that Pike's interest in ancient civilizations and their cultures, peaked during this time and is indicated in his books regarding this trip, as well as others.

Did Pike and the men have something to do with mapping and marking these places for further exploration? Did they hide their own treasures there, such as treasure they found in New Mexico?

Pike and the men continued into Knox County, Texas where they were succumbed by more aggressive rugged badlands. I believe they traveled near present day Benjamin where the famous official photographer for the Lone Star State, Wyman Meinzer thrives amongst the wildlife in the rough untamed terrain.

Pike and his men followed the South Fork and North Fork of the Wichita River into Foard County passing through the area that would become the famous Waggoner Ranch, established in 1852, twenty years later from the time Pike walked the roads, and is considered to be the largest ranch in the United States under one fence. Pike and his men traveled along the Wichita River through the area where Lake Kemp lies today. The Wichita River then flows into Lake Diversion and meanders through Wichita Falls which was established near the Waco Village we spoke of earlier. This Native American tribe was a division of the Tawakoni people, a band of the Wichita tribe. Pike describes several abandoned Indian villages along the trail.

The Wichita River took the party to the Red River. The main Wichita River and the Little Wichita River running parallel with each other would become another place to mark an "X" on your treasure map. Pike's trail as well as the old Dona Ana Trail established in 1852, same year as the Waggoner Ranch was established, appears to cross over the Red River at the same area. Another trail forged by Randolph Marcy's Indian guide also crosses at that spot.

Pike continued to write about the Mexicans who came into New Mexico and Texas, who built fortifications, possibly referring to caves, tunnels, and mounds and leaving their hieroglyphics to lead them to their treasures and their home. He suggests it could have been Phoenicians (Albert Pike believed in this particular theory) who were of the Canaanite religion. He also suggested that Egyptians or Aboriginals were here in America, long before the Native Americans. There is a Mystery Rock in New Mexico that is written in the Phoenician and Hebrew language.

Pike speaks of the "Nabajos," which I believe he was referring to the Navajos who had a Welsh Bible. This coincides with the story about Jefferson and Meriwether Lewis and the story told of the Welsh who were the first explorers to arrive in America many years before Columbus.

Is our history hidden in plain sight? I believe Pike knew the answer and wanted it kept from the common man. All of this information is not just coincidence.

The entire trek that Pike traveled upon in Texas was within the 33rd degree parallel all the way to the Red River. They cross the Red River into Indian Territory, to the Washita River in Garvin County, following the Washita through the Arbuckle Mountains, hooking up to the Blue River, down to the Red River, across the Boggy to the Kiamichi and traveling to Fort Smith, arriving December 10, 1832. We will explore further into the treasures that lay in Oklahoma in these areas in which Bud Hardcastle has uncovered.

Pike returned home to Missouri and learned of the fate of one of his traveling companions on the Bent Caravan to Taos. While Pike was traveling back through Texas, twelve men of Bent's original caravan were returning home to Missouri through the same route they had taken coming in, through the Cimarron desert. It was in the dead of winter in December 1832. One of the men was Mr. Schenck who had shared the same tent with Pike at Point of Rocks. As the twelve approached the Canadian River rock crossing, they were viciously ambushed by Comanches.

The Comanches killed all the caravan's animals, confiscated the men's property, and as the men were fleeing on foot down the river, ten were able to escape, leaving two men who were wounded to face the enemy alone. Those who survived made it back to Missouri to tell the story and told of Mr. Schenck being wounded in the leg. Neither of the men they left were never heard of again. Albert Pike's poetic words were formed in a poem titled "Lines" written about Schenck's experience after he was wounded and the loneliness he felt, left alone to die. In the lines of this poem, Pike places himself inside the mind of Schenck to relate his side of the story, just as he did for Lewis.

If you were not a man when you left civilization in St. Louis, you would be after the rendezvous and entanglement of the wild frontier.

"These unsettled conditions bred a class of men whose "double" will never again be seen on American soil, if anywhere on the globe. For brain and brawn, for courage and generalship, their leaders stand unrivaled. Their battlefields were scattered over the interior of America from the Missouri to the Columbia, and beyond, to the headwaters of the great Oregon River, even to the Umpqua, near the California boundary.

"Unfortunately, the wars were not always with Indians, but quite as often between rival trading companies. Commerce has always been a relentless pioneer, as it is the most successful civilizer. Except for trade there would be "open doors" nowhere on the earth. It has always required blood to make fertile the soil of its most productive regions, the more productive-the more blood." [112]

This subject was fascinating to the writer and we all need to pay tribute to the Mountain Men who forged this nation with their blood and determination between 1800-1840 and for those who keep their legacy alive.

(Painting of Gary Bowen, Mountain Man of Modern Day (courtesy of Gary Bowen, artist unknown))

One of the most interesting fellows in our neck of the woods is Gary Bowen. He is a true Mountain Man, living the life he was destined for and as he put it, "he was chosen to live here." He came from the city of Wichita Falls, Texas and was drawn to the northeastern mountains of New Mexico in the Sangre de Cristos in the late 1990's.

As a young boy, he was swallowed up into history and the natural way of living and surviving. He started out in the Boy Scouts and soaked up education on how to live off the land. The scouts were all about falling back into the old traditions and initiations of the Native Americans and of the Mountain Men between the years 1800-1840.

Gary's first lesson learned was how to start a fire with flint and steel and to keep the fire going all night long. His love for the wilderness life expanded by the age of 10 when he began bow hunting. By the time he was 13, his friend Johnny and his Dad helped Gary make a primitive Osage bow with arrows. Their technique and skills came naturally as they were full-blooded Cherokee. Gary was then able to kill his first deer with the bow in northeastern Oklahoma. The boys would continue to hunt and fish with their bow and arrows and became quite good at it along the Verdigris River.

Their experiences were heightened when they built a raft and canoe, taking them down the Arkansas River. Their interest spread into Flintlock Rifles.

In an Outdoor Magazine, Gary read an article in 1968 about 7 men, who were Vietnam Veterans, who were starting an organization of American Mountain Men. Gary just knew he desperately wanted to be a part of this, but he was only 17 years old and too young at the time to join. He bought his own Flintlock rifle and began his journey towards the goal of being a true mountain man by 1969.

Gary continued to do his own research in the Mountain Men era and historical techniques that they used. He learned a lot on his own. By 1996, Gary applied and was invited into the American Mountain Men Association. He attended two nationals and two territorials produced by the American Mountain Men in Wyoming, Colorado, and Montana.

When he moved to northeastern New Mexico and became an interpreter State Park Ranger, his knowledge increased. He learned the land, the wildlife, and the way of raw mountain living. This allowed Gary to continue working towards the 20 requirements to become a full-fledged member of the American Mountain Men Association.

Gary shared some of the 20 requirements to become a member, after the acceptance of the application and invite into the American Mountain Men. You are required to go on a five day trek, making as many miles as you can on horseback, foot, or bullboat, which is a boat made out of a willow structured frame covered in buffalo hide made on your own.

You need to go on a three-day, two-night stay, in the wilderness, with nothing but your own hands to forage for food by fishing out of streams, eating roots and cattails, surviving off the land. You are required to demonstrate your ability to trap, snare, or catch wild game in the primitive way. You are required to demonstrate the art of field dressing hides through brain tanning to make the hides into clothing. You are required to hand sew all your clothing, cloth or buckskin, that was available during the time period of 1800-1840.

The journey and mission of the American Mountain Men is to preserve the Mountain Men traditions and way of life, but most specially to teach and demonstrate how they survived, living off the land. They promote conservation of the natural wilderness and the wildlife that calls it home.

During the course of his life, Gary had to stop pursuing this Mountain Man venture, but at the age of 72, he is starting all over. In 2023, he was a huge part of hosting and organizing the first annual Mountain Man Encampment in the original area that was considered the hub of the southwest fur trade in Taos, New Mexico from 1800-1840 that was comparable to Montreal, Canada and St. Louis, Missouri. Taos had a huge role in the expansion of the southwest.

The men from the American Mountain Men association camped out on the grounds of the historic Hacienda de Los Martinez, built during the Spanish colonial era in 1804, as a fortress for protection. The setting is beautiful, along the banks of the Rio Pueblo de Taos.

As a Mountain Man, when you join in any encampment of the American Mountain Men, you are required to wear the period clothing and only carry items that were available during those days such as period guns, knives, and period cooking containers and drinking vessels.

The first Taos encampment, with much hard work put forth by Gary, was a success. There were an estimate of 30 Mountain Men from all over the country. The 2nd annual encampment drew triple the number of participants than the first. It is free to the public to go and observe the many demonstrations that are performed. Gary said that they had demonstrations of period fishing, how they would use horse hair for lines and netting such as snoods, the use of plants for medicinal and edible purposes, how to make bow and arrows, trapping, skinning beaver and fur animals, tanning and preparing hides, cloth making, cooking with clay pots, and a lesson on how the men took care of the hygiene aspect. It will always be held on the grounds of the Martinez Hacienda in Taos, occurring in June of each year.

Gary's love of history for the country, for the states, and especially for New Mexico has spurred him on to be able to teach that part of American history to people, especially children, which perpetuates where we came from and how we got where we are. He advocates support for the

Martinez Hacienda museum, as well as other museums in the state of New Mexico. He strives to teach that many nationalities came to New Mexico during the 1700's -1800's and gelled together to make civilization work in New Mexico, which included the Native Americans, the Hispanics from Mexico and Spain, and the Anglos. "We're still one people," said Gary.

(Shelter made out of canvas and branches)

(Carreta)

(Rio Pueblo de Taos)

(Martinez Hacienda)

The Road to Chihuahua

Once Albert Pike returned home in 1832, it was as if he had opened the flood gates to Texas. Sam Houston came to Texas who was also a Freemason and good friend of Pike. Houston had some work to do in Texas.

Pike settled in Little Rock, Arkansas. He began focusing on writing and teaching. In 1834, he bought the Little Rock Arkansas Advocate from the people he had worked for. This was a very important part of Freemasonry, the control of the newspapers and the filtering of news. While Albert Pike was writing "Narrative of a Journey in the Prairie" in 1835, tensions began building in the land that he was writing about; the entire area of Mexico, including Texas before it was annexed and New Mexico which were under the control of the Mexican government and Santa Anna.

When Santa Anna began transitioning the Mexican government into a *centralized* government, it caused extreme hardships and rebellion amongst many citizens of the Mexican Empire. In 1835, Santa Anna ordered 500 soldiers to Texas to quell a rebellion against the government. Texians (settlers who lived in the Mexican ruled Texas) stood together and began to defend their settlements and rights. Many volunteers came from all parts of the United States to join in the fight.

After extensive battles with Mexico and the help of Sam Houston, Texas gained its independence in 1836. They became the Republic of Texas which included the eastern part of New Mexico. General Santa Anna of the Mexican Army was exiled to Cuba.

During this time, settlers, trade, and businesses exploded within the boundaries of the new republic. Trade invited all kinds of traders into New Mexico. The markets were flooded with goods. This caused the traders to move further south into Chihuahua, Mexico. The main trail that the traders would follow from Santa Fe is close to I-25 and the Rio Grande river to Albuquerque, Socorro, Truth or Consequences, Dona Ana, Las Cruces, Mesilla, El Paso, and into the northern Mexico state of Chihuahua. This trail was later named the El Camino Real or the King's Road.

This was a very dangerous trail. The area was very vulnerable to attacks by Comanche, Mescalero Apache, and Navajo Native Americans. The Comanches were noted as raiding ranches and stealing livestock for their own sustenance.

The Apaches claimed this land and were the best of all warriors. They were indeed blood thirsty. In Albert Pike's writings, he describes how fatal a blow they would have on the settlers. They extended from Taos all the way to Mexico City and from the Texas Panhandle, Llano Estacado, and the Big Bend area. Their arrow was to be avoided.

The Apaches gathered rattlesnakes, centipedes, and scorpions and placed them in a confined area. They continuously aggravated the venomous creatures until they would become insanely violent. The Apaches then would kill a sheep and take its beating heart out and placed it into the midst of the outraged and tormented vermin. Naturally they struck the heart with their fangs and stingers continuously until the heart was filled with the most powerful and murderous poison. The Apaches remove the heart and place it in a vessel to sit for several days. The heart became a sickly mass, a green putrid color. They dipped the points of their arrows in the chunk of death and in battle, the recipient of this poisonous arrow dies an agonizing death.

The path to Chihuahua was not only dangerous but had become a necessity to gamble the trip for trade. It would also be an area where the movement of priceless items was very prevalent. This occurred from the time of Zebulon Pike, during Spanish reign, and when Mexico gained their independence. There was a lot of transferring of wealth, of gold, silver, and priceless treasures. This road was a very hot spot, especially near Dona Ana.

Henry Connelly must have seen the value of Chihuahua. He was from Kentucky who became a merchant and doctor in Missouri. He joined the trade caravan to Chihuahua. He moved to Chihuahua and later attempted to establish a shorter route to Missouri through Texas instead of the El Camino Real and the Santa Fe Trail. In 1839, he set out to blaze a trail through the driest part of Mexico and Texas with 100 men, escorted by 50 Mexican dragoons, carrying $200,000-$300,000 worth of gold and silver.

Connelly's party traveled from Chihuahua through Fort Leaton, to present day Presidio, north of Alpine, to Big Spring, up across the Colorado River, to Snyder, and near the junction of the Double Mountain Fork of the Brazos River, very close to the point where Pike had traveled. It appears on the map that they crossed the Salt Fork of the Brazos south of present-day Seymour, just north of Miller Creek. After getting lost, they reached the Red River and crossed at the mouth of the Little Wichita River into Indian Territory. Again, this was the same crossover as Pike's route into Indian Territory. Delaware Indians had to escort Connelly and his men to Fort Towson, after much trouble.

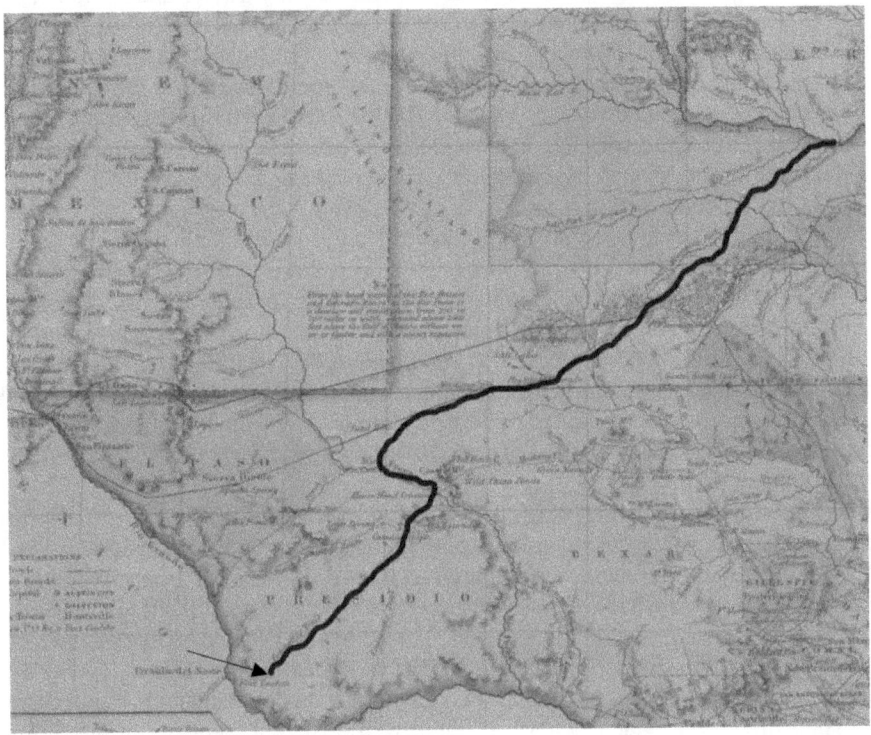

*(State of Texas in 1855, showing **Connelly's** route from Chihuahua to Indian Territory.* [113] *)*

Connelly reached Fort Smith, Arkansas and took a steamboat down to New Orleans to exchange his gold and silver for merchandise for trade. On their return route, they inherited another party who were part of a circus act wishing to perform in Mexico.

They started in Fulton, Arkansas, crossing over the Red River and entered into Lamar, Fannin, Grayson (south of Sherman), Cooke (north of Gainesville), Montague (St. Jo and between Montague and Nocona, north of Brushy Mound, and northwest of Bowie), Clay, and Archer counties. Once in Archer County, they located their incoming trail, crossing over the Brazos south of Seymour and within a few miles west, they turned south and continued to follow the trail they had started out on.

Once they arrived in Mexico, the government ramped up the tariffs on all trade goods and it turned out that it was not feasible to continue this venture. Connelly moved to New Mexico and would continue his trading business in Chihuahua, Missouri, and New Orleans, but never again on the original trail he blazed. During the Civil War, President Lincoln appointed Connelly to become governor of New Mexico.

Conflict on the Border

It would take years for Mexico to agree and recognize Texas as a republic on its own, but the annexation of Texas into the United States as the 28th state to join in 1845, caused severe animosity between the two countries.

President James Polk, who was a Master Mason in Freemasonry, and the leaders of Mexico began to see on the horizon, that there would be conflict over boundary lines between the newly annexed state of Texas and Mexico.

In July 1845, President Polk sent Brigadier General Zachary Taylor and 3,500 Americans to stand ready at the Nueces River. Taylor was ordered to take his troops to the south, not to provoke war, but to prepare for a fight if Mexico became aggressive. The troops' presence was designed to show force that could possibly lead to negotiations for the border issues and the expansion of land in New Mexico and California owned by Mexico. Many also believed that the show of force was to lure Mexico into starting the conflict. The Mexicans struck first, and President James Polk and Congress declared war on Mexico. Another heavy cost in lives and in money.

Later, Ulysses S. Grant who was one of Taylor's army lieutenants wrote that "A better army, man for man, probably never faced an enemy than the one commanded by General Taylor in the earliest two engagements of the Mexican war."

Many famous men fought in the Mexican-American War; Zachary Taylor, Ulysses S. Grant, Robert E. Lee, Jefferson Davis, Sterling Price, Albert Pike (who had become a captain under Archibald Yell's Cavalry – while under a new commander, Pike challenged the man to a duel that ended with no bloodshed), Captain Randolph Marcy under Zachary Taylor, William "Wild Bill" Thomason, and James Lewis Dalton, father of the Dalton boys and uncle to Jesse Woodson James. Dalton served an even 365 days under Zachary Taylor as a fifer for company I, 2nd Regiment of Kentucky Foot Volunteers.

At the same time this was happening, another fight was brewing between the Northern and Southern States of the U.S.; the desire for the expansion of territory for the United States that Mexico held. The demand for cotton and other textiles was expanding and the land that the cotton was growing in was weakened by its heavy use. There was a need to expand their cotton fields to meet the demands and the answer would be an expansion into northern Mexico, in the state of Chihuahua. The Democrats were all for it and they had the lead of their Democratic president, James K. Polk.

It all appears to be the same battle that was fought over and over again, for land, treasure, and the progression of slavery. Many believe all three were essential elements in the origin of the Mexican American War in 1846-1848. The South wanted the territory, the gold and silver mines, and turn it into slave states, balancing the states. The North was growing fast. John Quincy Adams opposed the Mexican War as well as Illinois Representative Abraham Lincoln and Frederick Douglass.

The United States persisted in the pursuit of complete control of the land. By August of 1846, while Polk opposed to a national bank and signed the Independent Treasury Act into law, allowing public revenues to be retained in the Treasury building and in sub-treasuries in various cities, separate from private state banks, U.S. General Stephen Kearny came down into New Mexico from Fort Leavenworth, Kansas and without a fight, declared New Mexico Territory for the United States. Kearny declared himself as military governor of New Mexico in Santa Fe. He appointed Charles Bent as New Mexico's first territorial governor who would be stationed in Taos where his wife and children were, as well as his stores and trading businesses.

Charles Bent, the man who was head of the trading and hunting expedition that Albert Pike was on in 1831, was now in charge of New Mexico. Kit Carson, also from Missouri, came into the area of Taos in 1828. Carson became a very famous frontiersman, trapper, wilderness guide, Indian agent, and U.S. Army officer who led the Navajo off their land on the long walk from Arizona to Eastern New Mexico in 1864, described as an ethnic cleansing to isolate and Americanize them.

Under the leadership of General James Carleton, Kit Carson was ordered in 1862 to kill every Mescalero Apache man in New Mexico territory and remove the women and children to a reservation known as Bosque Redondo on the Pecos River. This was located near Fort Sumner. General Carleton's motives were to irradicate all the hostiles in the southwest territory ending their abuse upon the inhabitants from various cultures. It was a motive that opened a door for every rat who wanted a piece of the political pie, land, and its valuable resources.

Carleton then turned towards the removal of the Navajo and ordered Kit Carson to travel to Arizona to the Navajo's sacred mother, the land called Canyon de Chelly. What was in this vast land that the Navajo held sacred? Some believed gold, but it was what the land brought forth for their sustenance in the bosom of their loving and caring Mother Earth. They existed for centuries upon their expert care of the land thriving on their crops of corn and wheat, as well as their beautiful herds of sheep who were part of their family.

A military strategy used upon the removal of Indians, throughout the history of America, was once again used for the removal of the Navajo. The known "scorched earth" policy, aimed to destroy anything that might be useful to the enemy was implemented upon the Navajo stripping them of their crops, their livestock, their culture, and their homeland.

Deep in the canyons of the Navajo's intriguing ancient land, a towering sandstone spire of over 800 feet was revered as their mother/grandmother of their tribe, known as *Spider Rock*. The rock formation reached over 800 feet from the floor of the canyon. It is named for Spider Woman, a figure in Navajo lore, who is known to live on the top of Spider Rock.

The story of the Navajo is another tragic story in the southwest. They had no choice, but to go with the soldiers who enticed them with food and empty promises. The long walk to Bosque Redondo was over 350 miles which was in the months of February and March, the coldest time of the year. Many women and young girls were molested along the way and those who were pregnant and could not keep up, were shot like lame horses as well as the elderly.

Kit Carson, compelled to follow the orders of his commanders "for the good of the country," followed through, but his conscience caught up with him and he wrote a letter of resignation. His commanders did not accept his letter.

Kit Carson joined the Masonic *Montezuma* Lodge No. 109 in Santa Fe. He as well as Bent, General Sterling Price, Ferdinand Maxwell (brother of Lucien Maxwell and uncle to Pete Maxwell and Paulita Maxwell who were good friends with Billy the Kid), and Pike were all Freemasons. Ferdinand Maxwell was a 2nd great grandfather to William V. Morrison who stirred up the subject that Brushy Bill Roberts was Billy the Kid.

*Just a Note - Billy the Kid was known to have a love relationship with Pete's sister, Paulita and some believe she had Billy's baby. Paulita was born in 1864 in Mora, New Mexico. She claims in 1925 that the love relationship between her and Billy was not true. In research, I learned that Paulita's daughter with her later husband, Jose Jaramillo, Luz Jaramillo Flanner (1891-1974) lived in Dalhart, Texas, my hometown and her husband was a jeweler in Dalhart, Charles Flanner. They began living in Dalhart in 1924.

The further we get, the tighter the rope surrounds all these families who were connected.

Charles Bent and Carson were extremely good friends and connected in the brotherhood. Charles Bent married a woman from Taos, Maria Ignacia Jaramillo and her sister married Kit Carson. They all claimed Taos as their home.

By 1832, Bent would form a partnership with Ceran St. Vrain who was also a Mason. They established the Bent and St. Vrain Company. They had stores in Taos and Santa Fe and began to establish fortified trading posts along the Santa Fe Trail. One of the most important posts, trading with the Plains Indians was Bent's Fort, outside of La Junta, Colorado. William Bent, Charles' brother built the trading post at Adobe Walls in the Texas Panhandle under the company in 1843. The post was used for trading with buffalo hunters and the Comanche, Kiowa, and Prairie Apaches along the Canadian River. It would become the site of the greatest battle of Kit Carson's in 1864 and a 2nd battle involving the Comanche and Cheyenne Indians led by Chief Quanah Parker.

Another interesting tidbit was found in (San Angelo Evening Standard, March 2, 1924. The original Adobe Walls area *"was seized by Major Bent, having been occupied by people from Spanish settlements in Old Mexico."* Lots of buried treasure was said to have been removed from a pack train and hidden there during an Indian attack. This is another sight that Howk suggests that treasure is buried, "Col. Kit Carson's Battle Against Texans Treasure." [114]

The Bents and Ceran St. Vrain had a monopoly of trade in and out of New Mexico, Colorado, and Texas. In order to gain a greater ability in trade, St. Vrain became a naturalized Mexican citizen. The trade business that they had built drew many types of men and businesses into the territory, some good, some bad.

Charles Bent and St. Vrain developed grist mills in Taos and Mora. The famous flour mill, St. Vrain's Mill in Mora still stands strong in the small and historic community. They also added lumber mills and distilleries. At least twelve distilleries were active in the Taos Valley; a perfect place to make the raw whiskey without restrictions from the United States or the Mexican government.

Charles Beaubien, another fur trader who was licensed by William Clark to enter Indian Territory in New Mexico and Guadalupe Miranda had submitted a petition for a land grant to Governor Manuel Armijo in 1841. He had married into a prominent and wealthy Spanish family who were natives of New Mexico. This marriage gave leverage to become a future landholder and an inheritance of wealth and notoriety.

Before the intense time of the Mexican American War, Beaubien's desire was to develop resources on the eastern slopes of the Sangre de Cristo Mountains. Land extending 1,700,000 acres was granted and Beaubien and Miranda became self-enriched landowners in Northern New Mexico. A quarter of that property went to Charles Bent to help establish ranches along the Ponil, Vermejo, Cimarron, and Rayado Rivers. Beaubien applied for another grant of one million acres, east of the Rio Grande into the Sangre de Cristo Mountains into southern Colorado.

About the time when Albert Pike and Arron B. Lewis was in Taos, a massive new business was thriving about 10 miles north. It was Turley's Mill, established by Simeon Turley. It sat in the Arroyo Hondo Valley along the Rio Hondo River. It was approximately two stories high; walls were one yard thick and the adobe building was the size of a football field. Turley's Mill became a popular stop for trappers and traders who were coming in on the Santa Fe Trail through the mountain route. This was the same place where Aaron B. Lewis was taken to recover from his frostbite at Turley's hostel. The mill was believed to have been a distillery also; loads of grain and loads of whiskey tainted with chili powder, gunpowder, and tobacco.

Turley built a dam on the Rio Hondo to power the mill, but it also caused issues for the locals in the narrow little valley as well as the influx of patrons that overtook the landscape. The amount of wood it would take to run the distillery would project heavy smoke along the valley floor, that could linger throughout the day. The mill/distillery caused great air pollution, noise pollution, and some suggest an air of promiscuity.

Turley was described as hiring plenty of locals to work, both Mexicans and Indians who were paid and fed well. He became rich overnight, but yet his generosity and kindness was noted. He came from Boone's Lick, Missouri; same place that Kit Carson came from and they were the best of buds. William Becknell also was from their Missouri community, who blazed the Santa Fe Trail.

Turley continued his profitable business by expanding his enterprise into Colorado and into the Missouri trade, utilizing traveling salesmen and setting up stores and warehouses. His success came to an abrupt end during the Mexican American War.

After the Americans took over control of New Mexico the locals were again leery of any kind of takeover. Their past, their history, had been tossed "to and fro" from one empire to another. They were completely content on their way of life, their simplicity, their culture, their hospitality, their passiveness, but it was time to stand up.

New Mexicans and Pueblo Indians were planning a revolt around Christmas time shortly after Bent was elected as their governor in 1846 to take back their territory and defend its culture, starting in Santa Fe. The plan was discovered, so it was changed to another location, another time. It was Taos, January 19, 1847. Two main targets were Governor Charles Bent and Turley's Mill.

In the very early hours of the morning, the Taos Revolt of 1847 began, led by Pablo Montoya, a New Mexican and Tomas Romero, a Taos Pueblo Indian. Romero and his force broke down the door of Bent's and sprayed him with a string of arrows, scalping him alive while his family watched. Bent was later killed while trying to help his family escape. Other American government officials in Taos and 7-8 traders were killed as they were passing through Mora.

The next day, the rebels took on Turley's Mill. It was approximately 500 of them who flooded the narrow valley demanding Turley to surrender the mill. Turley would not budge. The rebels slaughtered the animals and commenced to burn down the two-story mill. After all the destruction and fire power that flew that day and night, several of the Americans defending the mill died, but some escaped, including Turley, only to be killed later after a "so-called" Mexican friend turned him over to the enemy.

The hatred for these men showed up in the violence that occurred in this small community. It was horrible, but it didn't stop there. Colonel Sterling Price who was in command of the U.S. forces in New Mexico gathered a troop of Missouri Volunteers who joined with 65 men who volunteered under Ceran St. Vrain's command to take down the rebels.

Their march from Santa Fe to Taos forced many rebels hiding within the canyon of the Rio Grande to flee to Taos and take refuge in the thick-walled adobe church in the Taos Pueblo. There was estimated around 1500 Mexican and Indian rebels that retreated.

The Missouri Volunteers and St. Vrain's volunteers surrounded the church and kept them from fleeing into the mountains. The brutal American forces contained the men inside, and after numerous attempts, was able to penetrate one of the walls of the church, firing their canon with all the fire power and might they had. They set the church ablaze out of pure revenge. Approximately 150 men died and over 400 men were captured.

Punishment was swift the next day and 28 were convicted of treason and murder by Judge Charles Beaubien and a foreman of the jury. They both had lost family members in the revolt. The men were hung/executed in Taos Plaza, the main center of town. Beaubien was looked down upon amongst the locals. Father Martinez accused him "of endeavoring to kill all the people of Taos." ("Charles H. Beaubien" – Wikipedia)

*Note -The Taos Plaza is very unique and has always been the main hub of Taos. So much history surrounds it. The center of the plaza is where many events are held and where the men were hung after the Taos Revolt. It is said there are many tunnels underneath that area, spread throughout the main part of town. Currently, the center of the Taos Plaza is being totally renovated. "The sudden project came about because Taos County, which is restoring its historic courthouse on the plaza, needed to dig beneath the plaza brickwork to connect a new sewer line, which it did in a matter of days. But the excavation gave the town an opportunity to pursue two long-held objectives: Improve the plaza's drainage system, which is old and inadequate, and beautify the park area." [115]

After the revolt, Ceran St. Vrain settled in Mora, New Mexico and supplied flour to the U.S. Army garrison at nearby Fort Union and Fort Garland in southwestern Colorado. He also started the first English language newspaper in Northern New Mexico, the Santa Fe Gazette. He died in 1870 and was buried in Mora. The locals state that over 2,000 people came to the funeral in this small community of 1,084. It was assumed a lot of the attendees were Freemasons.

Of course, we only hear from the side of the Americans, the victors, but what really happened. Albert Gonzales, PhD suggests that the revolt, especially against Turley's Mill was due to the severe and drastic change in society, bringing in the *Industrial Revolution*, the use and abuse of the environment and natural resources, pollution, and the general sense of infectious discontent.

I have exhausted all my efforts to understand the New Mexican and Pueblo Indian's side of the story. Sadly, we fully don't understand what all they went through that caused their peaceful villages to rise up with extreme passion to fight. Was it personal against these men, such as hints suggesting that the American forces and Bent mistreated the local people or was it a rebellion against the entire American Empire that wanted their land and resources?

A sobering reminder lies within the Taos Pueblo. Out of the ruins of the adobe church, stands the remnants of a lone bell tower as a reminder of the undying spirit, courage, and endurance of these proud people of the Taos Pueblo who have lived and survived on this land for many thousands of years. The Pueblo Elders keep an oral history that is shared only to their people regarding their culture and history to be passed on to their future generations. My respect and empathy for the Taos Pueblo Indians and their privacy will always be honored and they will forever remain in my heart.

(Ruins of the Church in the Taos Pueblos (courtesy of Patricia Henschen))

Charles Beaubien had lost his son, Narcisco who was killed along with his son-in-law, Sheriff Stephen Lee in the Taos Revolt. Since he had no male heir to pass down the huge land grant of 1,700,000 acres, it just so happened that his next choice would fall into the hands of Lucien Maxwell, who would become Beaubien's son-in-law, marrying Beaubien's 13-year-old daughter. Maxwell became one of the largest private landowners in the United States.

Lucien Maxwell established the Rayado settlement with Kit Carson, who had been long time friends as fur trappers/hunters/guides and traveled with John C. Fremont on his expedition to Oregon in 1842. Maxwell was with Fremont on the controversial expedition in 1845-46 when the U.S. seized California from Mexico.

Again, land became important. Maxwell gained a herd of livestock and hired Buffalo Bill Cody as the manager of Maxwell's goat ranch. Maxwell moved near the Cimarron River and established the town of Cimarron. There in that town, Buffalo Bill organized his first Wild West Show. Maxwell secured a contract with the U.S. Army, furnishing supplies to the troops including beef and grain. Maxwell also joined up with Captain William Moore, the founder of Elizabethtown, forming the Copper Mining Company in 1861. Maxwell eventually got involved in the Railway Company.

Maxwell became very wealthy through mining, timber, and those who wanted to settle on the land grant and raise crops in which Maxwell received a percentage of the profits off the land. This caused severe friction between Maxwell and those who worked the land. Ownership and rights became an issue.

The legal issues and the fighting amongst the inhabitants and workers of the land grant became more than any one man could manage. Maxwell received an offer from a Syndicate from England to take the Land Grant off Maxwell's hand. He sold it to the Syndicate in 1870. The Syndicate planted their headquarters at the three story adobe Clifton House, a famous overnight stage stop on the Mountain Branch of the Santa Fe Trail, located 6 miles south of Raton. Maxwell moved to Fort

Sumner, which lay in the bed of cattle trails. In Fort Sumner, he turned over his business affairs to his son, Peter.

*Another interesting note, Howk lists a treasure sight of Jesses's at Maxwell Trading Post and Cimarron Creek Crossing.

The Maxwell Land Grants were later divided and placed within private organizations and private owners; the Philmont Scout Ranch, Ted Turner's Vermejo Park Ranch, Chase Ranch, CS Ranch, Express UU Bar Ranch, and the National Rifle Association's Whittington Center.

After the New Mexico takeover during the Mexican and American War, the U.S. became more aggressive and went into the heartland of Mexico and conquered Mexico City. They were considering annexing Mexico into the United States, but Senator John C. Calhoun, said it would threaten the U.S. institutions and character of this country.; incorporating Mexicans and Indians. Calhoun and his racial argument would become a big player in the secret societies. Jefferson Davis pushed for an amendment to only annex most of northeastern Mexico, which was Chihuahua, but it was rejected. His desire for Chihuahua did not die.

The U.S. ceased part of the Mexican territory that consisted of California, Nevada, Utah, Arizona, New Mexico, Colorado, and Wyoming. The Treaty of Guadalupe Hidalgo was signed in 1848 with Mexico ceding this territory over to the United States. The U.S. Senate approved this treaty and ended the war. Polk was pleased with the expansion of the United States.

The U.S. paid Mexico 15 million dollars for the damage incurred and assumed 3.25 million in debt to the U.S. citizens. Mexico lost the most. They lost 54 percent of their original territory.

The desire to have control of more land in Latin America was still on their minds. They certainly did not want the British to have their hands on it, The Mallarino-Bidlack Treaty would allow construction of the Panama Railway and helped to establish a stronger American influence in *Central America*. The U.S. would be justified for its military interventions. Polk also desired Cuba, but Spain wouldn't negotiate, and it could only be had by means of another war. Polk laid off. The conquest would be for another day.

Forging more trails into Texas

The trails from this new territory into Texas merge with each point of destination which has an incredible attachment to treasure. We have Pike's route in 1832, Josiah Gregg's route in 1839, Henry Connelly forging a new trail along the Chihuahua Trail in 1839/1840, and Randolph Marcy's trail in 1849, in which I believe was part of the old Dona Ana trail, D.A.T. following the alternate route along the Wichita River, across the Red River into Indian Territory.

An old map was created after the expedition of Captain Randolph Marcy, the same man who wrote the trail guide for western travelers. Marcy had established a trail from Fort Smith, Arkansas to Santa Fe to allow immigrants to travel safely over the plains in 1849, seventeen years later from Pike's and Lewis' trip. The trail basically followed the Canadian River which a portion of the trail followed the same trek as Aaron B. Lewis' trip from Fort Towson to Taos.

Marcy was ordered by Colonel J.J. Abert, head of the Corps of U.S. Topographical Engineers to explore the area for a possible railroad line that could follow a route close to the Canadian River and the route Josiah Gregg had forged which appeared to be the same route of Aaron B. Lewis' eight years earlier.

When Marcy was preparing for his trip to Santa Fe in 1849, hundreds of gold seekers began to appear from steamboats and other various ways of transportation at Fort Smith, those interested in Santa Fe and California. Marcy was ordered to guide and protect the parties of treasure hunters. He and his soldiers with 479 adventurers, 75 wagons, 500 oxen, 500 mules, and hundreds of pack and saddle horses and mules crossed the plains to Santa Fe.

Once Marcy reached Santa Fe safely, his traveling companions continued west to California to get caught up in gold fever that was getting hot out west. One of Albert Pike's closest friends, Elias Rector was also a man who loved exploration and the search for treasure. Rector led an expedition of local men near Fort Smith, Arkansas to search for gold in California in 1850, possibly the same route as Marcy.

It was either Marcy or Rector that led Jesse James' father to California in April 1850, along with his brother Drury James. Another man traveled on the journey about that time, Arthur Charles McCoy who tried his luck in the gold fields. He later became a great soldier in the Confederacy and his wife and brother-in-law did their share as spies and deliverers of goods and letters to the Gray. Arthur McCoy would team up with Jesse James and his gang after the war to continue serving the South.

Marcy traveled south from Santa Fe to Dona Ana, along the Rio Grande just north of Las Cruces. Dona Ana was a small settlement but had a heart of GOLD. This was another place to mark an "X."

Marcy's trail from Dona Ana to Fort Smith is shown on the map below and crosses the Guadalupe Mountains and the Pecos River. The trail appears to coincide with the Chihuahua Trail in the central part of Texas which was forged in 1839-1840. The Chihuahua Trail begins in Chihuahua, Mexico and runs parallel with Pike's Route along the Brazos River and ends in Fulton, Arkansas. The Chihuahua Trail also was used by a man named Connelly to forge an easier trading trail to Missouri.

The map below shows two routes taken from Fort Smith, along the Canadian River, across West Texas to Santa Fe, New Mexico and the other from Dona Anna, New Mexico to Fort Smith. More details of the map on a zoomed-in image can be found on the *Portal to Texas History*, website.

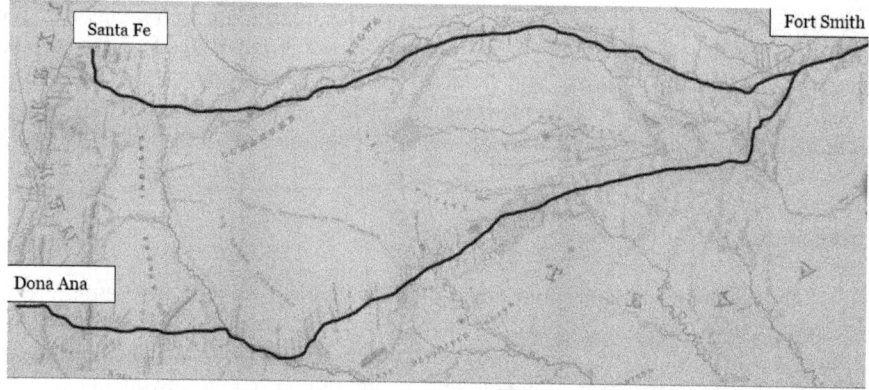

(Marcy's trail – (1850))[116]

From Marcy's trail, there is an alternate route, called ""Route proposed by Beaver" shown along the dotted line to the north of Marcy's trail. That trail was very close to the trail that Pike had made years before beginning at the Double Mountain Fork of the Brazos. This alternate route crosses the Red at the same area where Pike crossed. Pike's trail took him east after the crossing and then north on up to Fort Smith. The Beaver trail goes directly Northeast after the Red River Crossing and connects with Marcy's trail established along the Canadian River on to Fort Smith. What's important to focus on is the Red River crossing near the *Little Wichita River* and just off of that trail to the northwest is *Cache Creek*. These were extremely important areas for Jesse James.

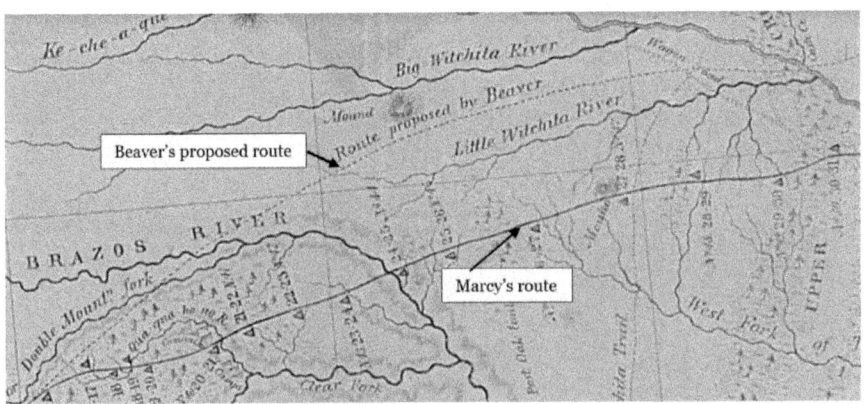

(Marcy's trail with route proposed by Beaver.)

An interesting article found on www.redriverhistorian.com, expands the story to explain who "Beaver" was. Black Beaver, Chief of the Delawares was Randolph Marcy's guide and interpreter.[117]

Another interesting note is that Pike's Trail and the Beaver trail are very close in being the same. Along the trail, a creek was named "Beaver Creek" which runs through the Waggoner Ranch and ran right through the Allen Parmer's Ranch in Wichita County, Texas. Allen Parmer was Jesse James' brother-in-law. After crossing the Red River at the point shown, by the Little Wichita River, you could either go northwest to the Wichita Mountains or due north to Buzzard's Roost, the two most popular hideouts and treasure troves of Jesse James.

In 1852, Marcy was again crossing the Oklahoma and Texas territory and discovering numerous valuable mineral deposits. Marcy was sent this same year to lead an official expedition to discover the head waters of the Red River into the Wichita Mountains. The mountains were known for Spanish exploration and mining of precious metals. He predicted that the area would become a productive mining district. This would later be near the sight of Fort Sill.

Oddly, in 1854 when Freemasonry was picking up speed, Marcy was sent to survey Indian reservations in North Texas and a map showing this expedition, pinpoints a spot shown as Marcy's Observation Point which, would you believe, was near the junction of the Double Mountain Fork and the Salt Fork of the Brazos River in Stonewall County.

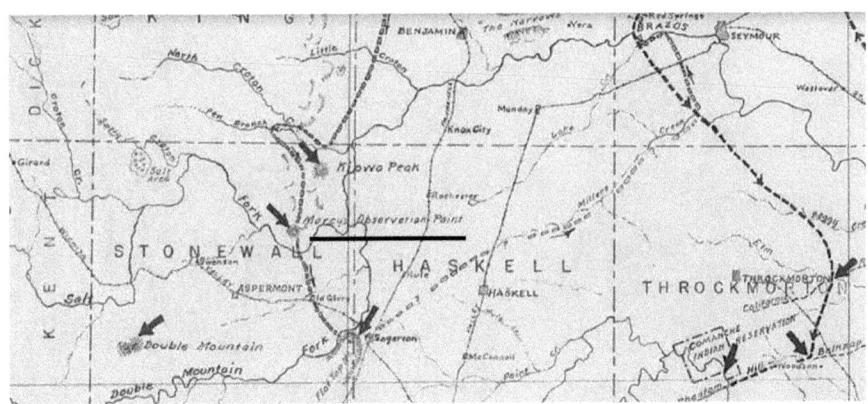

(Marcy's observation point, 1854.[118])

In 1856, Marcy explored the headwaters of the Big Wichita and Brazos Rivers. Just like Albert Pike, Marcy was also from Massachusetts. Marcy's trail from Fort Smith to Dona Ana would serve the famous Butterfield's Overland Express in 1858.

"The very word 'secrecy' is repugnant in a free and open society; and we are as a people inherently and historically opposed to secret societies, to secret oaths, and to secret proceedings."

-*John F. Kennedy*

Chapter Eight: The Fast Progression of Freemasonry, leading to the American Civil War

In President Ulysses S. Grant's memoirs, published in 1885, he spoke of Texas and the Mexican-American War, "Generally, the officers of the army were indifferent whether the annexation of Texas was consummated or not; but not so all of them. For myself, I was bitterly opposed to the measure, and to this day regard the war, which resulted, as one of the most unjust ever waged by a stronger against a weaker nation. It was an instance of a republic following the bad example of *European monarchies*, in not considering justice in their desire to acquire additional territory." He also expressed the view that the war against Mexico had brought punishment on the United States in the form of the American Civil War. "The Southern rebellion was largely the outgrowth of the Mexican war. Nations, like individuals, are punished for their transgressions. We got our punishment in the most sanguinary and expensive war of modern times." [119]

Strong words, but oh so true.

History teaches us how important land became power to the powerful. In this pursuit, the outcome was deadly. The conquest for land was important to the Freemasons which filtered into the Knights of the Golden Circle. Not just any piece of property, but land that lined up with their philosophy, wealth and power. Truly, the Mexican American War and Freemasonry led up to the Civil War in their hunger for more.

Through hefty research, this portion of the book will travel in the depths of what is revealed and known, and documented about Albert Pike and Freemasonry that has been pulled from various creditable sources to form the foundational aspect of Freemasonry and Albert Pike's philosophy. There is still so much that is guarded and secretly hidden. It is overwhelming and can never be completely explained or exposed.

This chapter is not to be judgmental of Freemasonry or other powerful organizations, but only to reveal the truth and how America was developed by the minds and deeds of some very powerful and hyperintelligent men. Keep in mind that the British empire established Freemasonry in 1717.

During the 1800's, the southwest was its target. We see a lot of influx of Freemasons settle into Utah, New Mexico, Missouri, Indian Territory (Oklahoma), and Texas.

Albert Pike was involved with many Freemasons in Arkansas, Missouri, New Mexico, Indian Territory, and Texas. He was said to have joined the Odd Fellows in 1840 before the Mexican American War, but his interest was craving for something much more; something deeper that would challenge his intellect.

Arthur McArthur, Judge of the Supreme Court of the District of Columbia wrote about Albert Pike. He stated that after the Mexican American War, Pike returned in a train as a mule driver from **Chihuahua** to Fort Smith.

Pike became an editor, owner of the Arkansas Advocate, Lawyer, and Chief of the Whig party. He studied ancient history back to medieval Jewish and Sanskrit Masonry. He was admitted to the bar of the Supreme Court of the United States in 1849. He specialized in cases on behalf of Native Americans, such as the Creeks, Choctaw, and Chickasaw.

There are key issues that continue to appear throughout Albert Pike's life and his comrades that we will uncover; Secrets, Power, Money, Treasure, Expansion of Land, Conquest, Slavery, Mining, Mexico, New Mexico, Louisiana Territory, St. Louis, Little Rock, New Orleans, Indian land and affairs, Cotton, Trade, and ancient history of the Phoenician and Egyptian Empires.

Pike was involved with several well-known gentlemen, Robert Crittenden, 1st Secretary and acting governor of the Arkansas Territory-born in *Woodford County*, Kentucky and was uncle to Governor Thomas T. Crittenden, 24th Governor of Missouri), Sam Houston, General Zachary Taylor, Elias Rector, and General Matthew Arbuckle.

Pike and Rector had similar interests, especially when it came to the management of Native Americans. As a major, headquartered at Fort Smith, Rector was appointed by President Andrew Jackson and carried by President Polk to become a U.S. Marshal of the Western District of Arkansas and Indian Territory in 1831 for 16 years. Rector became superintendent of the Five Tribes agency and in 1855 led a survey of the Washita Valley adjacent to the 98th Meridian to establish a reservation in Indian Territory. Remember the 98th Meridian, a very important spot.

Rector put an end to the Seminole War in Florida when he was put in full charge of removing the Seminole Indians from Florida to Indian Territory. Captain Randolph Marcy served alongside Elias Rector in the Seminole War. He became Superintendent of Southwestern Indian Affairs in 1857. Rector's first cousin, Henry Massie Rector had a huge political career and served as U.S. Surveyor-General of Arkansas in 1853-1857. He would become Governor of Arkansas in 1860 prior to the Civil War.

The earliest record that is recorded for public view of Albert Pike's Freemasonry status was the year of 1850. He was a member of the Western Star Lodge #1 and became a Worshipful Master the same year. He had numerous titles and positions in Freemasonry in Little Rock, but he desired to expand his own territory.

His friend, Major Elias Rector owned a cotton plantation and began chartering a boat to take his Arkansas cotton crop down river to New Orleans. This sparked interest in Pike towards New Orleans and new modes of transportation. Pike became involved with persuasive speeches, newspaper essays, and the promotion of the Southern Pacific Railroad. Pike spoke to the legislature in Baton Rouge and persuaded the members to connect a Pacific railroad traveling from New Orleans to the Pacific. His wheels were turning.

I believe this is when Pike began to eye that fair city as being very profitable. Pike moved to New Orleans in 1853. He joined the "Know Nothing Society," a secret political society who opposed Catholicism and Irish immigration. Later, when he learned that the group was not going to adopt a pro-slavery policy, he walked out.

That same year, Pike received 28 degrees in the Scottish Rite Freemasonry up to the 32nd degree. Between the years 1854-1855, he revised the Scottish Rites rituals and degrees. By 1857, he returned to Arkansas and he received a 33rd degree in the Scottish Rite Freemasonry. There were not that many 33rd degree Freemasons at that time who had climbed the pyramid of Freemasonry this high. He was standing on top.

In 1859, Albert Pike published the Statutes, Regulations, Institutes, Laws, and Grand Constitutions of the Ancient and Associated Scottish Rite in French and English.

During the 1850's, Freemasonry took a drastic turn and Albert Pike was in the lead. It was incredible to read all the titles he accumulated in Freemasonry in many states and many other countries, all within this decade. The man far surpassed any other.

The Ley of the Land

The evolution of Freemasonry and the many branches of societies formed from its foundation, such as the Odd Fellows, Knights of Pythias, and Knights of the Golden Circle, etc. had grown from the roots of the Knights Templar in which grew and manifested it's full power upon this earth in plain sight. We learn about the powerful people involved, but what is their purpose, their beliefs, and their goals? We find many answers in the ley of the land.

The symbolism of Freemasonry is found in buildings in Washington D. C. as well as other cities built in this nation. Thomas Jefferson insisted that the Capitol building be named "Capitol" and not the "Congress House." The word Capitol is associated with the Temple of Jupiter Optimus Maximus on Capitoline Hill, one of the seven hills of Rome. President Washington and eight other Freemasons dressed in their masonic clothing, performed a masonic ceremony laying down the *cornerstone* for the Capitol building in 1793. Beginning with the presidency of Thomas Jefferson, church was conducted in the House and services would continue up until the end of the Civil War.

Freemasons claim that the Capitol building is a Masonic site, an American Temple of Solomon, a temple of Masonic mysteries. Looking up into the center of the dome, you will find a beautiful painting of George Washington who is depicted as sitting in the heavenly realm, highly exalted and becoming a "god-like" figure surrounded by figures of allegorical mythology. The painting is called The Apotheosis of Washington, painted by Greek-Italian artist Constantino Brumidi in 1865 after the Civil War. Brumidi had worked for three years in the Vatican.

It would take many years, many trials and arguments to create the capital city. Buildings had to be positioned in certain directions, along certain ley lines, and aligned astrologically in tune with the celestial architect composed of the sun, planets, moon, and stars. Occult numerology and spiritual energy were integrated into the design and the symbols had to be displayed within the art and architecture revealing the "keys to the Craft."

The design of the government, layout, and architecture, which was called "Sacred Architecture" was carefully constructed to adhere to the design of Freemasonry and Sacred Geometry. It was a connection to God and the Universe seen in nature and the celestial heavens. It was spiritual and sacred, first developed in designs by ancient civilizations such as the Egyptians and Greeks.

In Sacred Geometry, the focus is on the circle, being one of the more common shapes in nature, therefore all other geometric shapes can be formed from a circle or within. The use of the compass and a ruler is the key to the design within the boundaries of the circle, creating symmetrical components/shapes that enhance the original formation. It is quite interesting and also relates to the design of the human body. Freemasons believe that not only this concept should apply to architecture in buildings and symbols, but in the building of a man and his character.

What's disturbing is that Freemasons, as well as Occultists view the circle with a hole in the center as the "Reawakening of the Universe." The point within a circle represents the sun, while the circumference represents the universe. The philosophy involves sun worship, and in realistic terms, the sun is of phallic origin. The phallus represents the male generative organ.

The Washington Monument's cornerstone was placed down in 1848 when the Mexican American War ended, when Meriwether Lewis was properly buried, and when J. Frank Dalton said he was born.

The actual building of the monument would take 40 years and was completed in 1888 for public viewing. It had 900 steps inside to reach the top. It is basically designed as the point, the sun, the obelisk which sits atop on a circular foundation. It represents the god Osiris, the god of death and rebirth. The capstone atop represents the "all seeing eye" and weighs 3,300 pounds. On the east face of the capstone, it is positioned to face the rising sun with the Latin words "Laus Deo" which mean "Praise be to God." Twice a year, September 17th and March 25th, the sun lines up perfectly atop of the monument and produces a shadow that enters into the center of the steps of the Capitol building, as an arrow pointing to the door. There is another crude meaning to this alignment.

Careful study and analytical observation of these monuments dispersed throughout D.C. and other important landmarks throughout the world represent timelines in their architecture and symbols.

The Washington Monument's shadow, points and enters into areas including Lincoln Memorial on the exact day, April 9th, the ending of the Civil War in 1865. Its shadow also reaches the point of the National World War II Memorial, on the very day, August 15th in which was the day the Japanese surrendered in 1945.

The Washington Monument acts as a sundial with its exact astrological measurements. If you want to read more about it and other places it points its shadow, read "Washington DC's Chamber of Secrets" on www.washingtondcschamberofsecrets.com/absolute-proof.html. It is exactly 555, 5-1/8" feet tall, the tallest building in Washington D.C. It was hit by lightning several times, one on June 1885 which shattered the capstone on the northeast corner. In 2011, a 5.8 - magnitude earthquake impacted the building forming a crack large enough for light to shine through. In 2020,

June and August 2021, the monument was struck by lightning again. There are many instances of nature taking its course with the monument.

The Statue of Liberty was a gift from the French Freemasons that represents the goddess, Isis. The flames of the torch represent the Sun. The handle of the torch speaks for itself.

The heart of the capital city, Washington D.C. was carefully laid out in accordance to ancient occult principles. If one really looks into the design, the layout is found in numerous large cities of great power and government, found in the City of London; Paris, France; Sydney, Australia, and in St. Peter's Square at the Vatican. In these layouts, you will find a dome or a round structure, representing the womb of a woman and an obelisk, an ancient Egyptian phallic symbol, representing the male "principle" which is facing the dome. The union of the two represents the birth of a third entity that is described as "spiritual energy". The dome, arch, and pyramid are used widely in the secret societies and they potentially retain this energy.

This energy, the powerful meridian (longitude) and parallel (latitude) lines located geographically on this earth as well as ley lines were of the upmost importance to the Knights Templar, Freemasons and the Knights of the Golden Circle. There are ancient secrets untold to the common man. We have been kept away from this knowledge or maybe its by Divine protection. I don't understand the full extent of it, none of us do, but carefully we can find hints by digging and allowing the good Lord to guide us.

The first time I had heard of ley lines as a primeval line of force was from Dr. Victor Westphall who built a beautiful chapel up on a mountain outside of Angel Fire, New Mexico close to the area where Pike traveled across the mountains to Taos. I was privileged to meet Dr. Westphall in 1970 as he was finishing the chapel in honor of his son, David Westphall who was killed in Vietnam as well as more than 58,000 soldiers who died there. He described that the ground he built upon was sacred ground, spoken of by the Pueblo Indians of Taos explaining there was a direct line flowing from Wheeler Peak, the tallest mountain in New Mexico, through their sacred Blue Lake and down the valley to where the chapel rests. Dr. Westphall explained that when surveys are conducted in the area, the instruments go awry. If you are spiritually sensitive, you can feel a deep sense of a radiating energy of some kind that most often brings you to tears. Its hard to describe, but I definitely experience it every time I visit the chapel.

This beautiful chapel was the very first major memorial to honor those who served in Vietnam. It inspired the building of the Vietnam Veteran's Memorial in Washington D. C. over 10 years later. In 1985, they broke ground to build a Visitor Center near the chapel which contains pictures of servicemen who died, along with their bio in which families supplied, memorabilia, a library, and a theater. The center provides healing and comfort to so many who were affected by the Vietnam War.

When looking up the word "*meridian*" in the Merriam Webster Dictionary, the definitions vary: (1) A great circle on the surface of the earth passing through the poles (longitude), (2) a great circle of the celestial sphere passing through its poles and the "zenith" of a given place (zenith meaning "the strongest or most successful period of time, at the top, at the peak of prosperity), and the medical definition (3) an imaginary circle or closed curve on the surface of a sphere or globe-shaped body (as the *eyeball*) that lies in a plane passing through the poles…any of the pathways along which the body's vital energy flows according to the theory of acupuncture.

The meridian lines of the earth contain power and energy of some kind and possibly this is what Freemasonry tapped into and guided them, the All-Seeing Eye. Strangely in the dictionary, a description of the word "meridian" is used in the belief of Mormonism.

Joseph Smith (founder of The Church of Jesus Christ of Latter-Day Saints) interpreted his own translation of the Bible, in which he writes Pearl of Grace, including translations of Egyptian papyri containing the writings of the prophet Abraham which Joseph Smith obtained in 1835 at the time Freemasonry was moving into the West.

This is an excerpt from Smith's translation of Genesis, called the book of Moses. Chapter 7: 45-47 – "And it came to pass that Enoch looked; and from Noah, he beheld all the families of the earth, and he cried unto the Lord, saying: When shall the day of the Lord come? When shall the blood of the Righteous be shed, that all they that mourn may be sanctified and have eternal life? And the Lord said: It shall be in the "***meridian of time,***" in the days of wickedness and vengeance. And behold, Enoch saw the day of the coming of the Son of Man, even in the flesh; and his soul rejoiced, saying: The Righteous is lifted up, and the Lamb is slain from the foundation of the world; and through faith I am in the bosom of the Father, and behold, Zion is with me."[120]

The meridian of time means a precise **midpoint** of earthly time.

Joseph Smith became a Freemason in 1842, joining the Masonic Lodge in Nauvoo, Illinois and was greatly influenced by the philosophy. He started the Mormon Church shortly after that. Brigham Young would follow in his footsteps, becoming a Freemason and leader of the Mormon Church.

The importance of the story of Enoch, gods, and architecture fall within both infrastructures. Smith implemented LDS ceremonies which were copied directly from the rites of Masonry. The architecture of the Temple of the Mormons was influenced by the Temples of Freemasonry patterned after the Temple of Solomon. Many of the same symbols that Freemasonry use are also used in the Mormon Faith in the architecture, and many other items associated with Mormonism and their Temples. For instance, The All-Seeing Eye which is a prominent feature in the Salt Lake City Temple in Utah, the Compass and Square, and the Morning Star are good examples of the symbols they share.

Many believe that these symbols reflect Egyptian and Paganistic mythology in which Albert Pike embraced and built upon. The philosophy Pike attached to the All-Seeing Eye is the left eye of Horus, a Pagan god. The Mormons believe it is the "Eye of Providence," the all-knowing God and the triangle that the eye sits within is the Christian Trinity. The All-Seeing Eye is on the Great Seal of the United States and our currency. The seal also has the words inscribed, "Annuit coeptis novus ordo seclorum" which means, "he approves of this undertaking, a new order of the ages." This was the plan for America, a Grand Masonic Experiment, a Grand Masonic Republic.

Albert Pike's book "Morals and Dogma," published in 1871, was given to the Freemason candidate reaching the 14th degree in the Scottish Rite. The book was to be used as a supplement to his system of moral, religious and philosophical instruction that Pike had developed in his revision of the Scottish Rites' rituals. He describes the symbolism that connects the architecture in the Washington Monument, to the All-Seeing Eye of Horus, a Pagan God.

In Pike's book he writes, "the sun and moon represent the two grand principles of all generations, the active and passive, the male and female... both shed their light upon their offspring, the Blazing star, or Horus", (pg. 13,14). [121] Horus was a falcon-headed Egyptian god of light, the son of Osiris and Isis, the spiritual energy Pike spoke about and is outlined in architecture throughout the United States. Many believe that Horus is actually Lucifer.

In the Scottish Rite, there exists a level of degrees in "The Lodge of Perfection." The 13th degree relates to the legend of the secret vault and its contents of the Holy Royal Arch (of Enoch). Enoch was a very powerful figure in Freemasonry as well as Mormonism.

We know very little about Enoch in the Christian Bible, except that he descended from Seth, son of Adam and Eve.

In the Christian Bible, Enoch was the father of Methuselah and great grandfather of Noah. Enoch walked with God and lived 365 years on earth and never died. He was taken up into the clouds by God. He is mentioned in the book of Jude as a prophet, prophesying, "*Behold, the Lord cometh with ten thousand of his saints, to execute judgment upon all, and to convince all that are ungodly among them of all their ungodly deeds which they have ungodly committed, and of all their hard speeches which ungodly sinners have spoken against him.*" Jude 14-15.

Seth's two brothers, Cain and Abel were more prominent in the Bible as the story is told when Cain became jealous of Abel, the righteous one. Cain's offering to God was not acceptable, Abel's offering was. This enraged Cain, so he killed Abel. Cain left the "presence of God" and left the Garden of Eden. Cain had a son named **Enoch** and named a great city after him. Luciferians believe they are direct descendants of Cain who they believe was fathered by Lucifer himself.

This philosophy reminds me of when Eve was tempted by the devil in the Garden of Eden. He appeared to her in the form of a *serpent*, which is another strong symbol in Freemasonry, just look at the walls adorned with various sizes of serpents within the House of the Temple of the Scottish Rite in Washington D.C. Adam and Eve were instructed by God to eat of any fruit of the trees in the garden except the tree of knowledge or they would die. The serpent told Eve that she would not die, *"for God doth know that in the day ye eat thereof, then your eyes shall be opened, and ye shall be as **gods**, knowing good and evil."* Genesis 3:5

"For this is the message that ye heard from the beginning, that we should love one another. Not as Cain, who was of that wicked one, and slew his brother. And wherefore slew he him? Because his own works were evil, and his brother's righteous. Marvel not, my brethren, if the world hate you. 1st John 3:11-13

Luciferians believe that if they maintain the bloodline, the "demon seed", the Satanic energy will be passed on to other generations. They shall be as **gods**. The Mormons believe Lucifer is the brother of Christ Jesus, but they worship Jesus Christ as the son of God, "the Only Begotten Son in the flesh." [122]

Are there two Enochs; one from the seed of righteousness (Adam and Eve through their son, Seth) and one from the seed of wickedness (Cain's son)? The Bible states there was indeed. Which was the Enoch who was exalted so highly in Freemasonry and Mormonism? Why is the Book of Enoch excluded from the Christian Bible?

What scriptures have we lost in translations and powers that might be, keeping us from knowing the total Word given to the writers? We do know that those who came across the waters were given the exact tools and the Word that God provided to build a great Christian Nation, "Under God". We need to continue to *"study to show thyself approved unto God, a workman that need not be ashamed, rightly dividing the Word of Truth."* 2 Timothy 2:15. In other words, study the Word of God so that we know we are approved by God and not by man and the truth will be revealed.

Even though the Book of Enoch is not included in the Christian Bible, there has been evidence of Enoch's story in ancient Hebrew religious texts found in a cave in Qumran in the Dead Sea Scrolls in 1948 and now in the care of the Israel Antiques Authority. The fragments date back to the 2nd century BC. A more complete book of Enoch was discovered in the 18th century in Ethiopia.

The Book of Enoch contains material on the origins of demons and Nephilim, why some angels fell from heaven, the explanation of why the Genesis flood was morally necessary, and the prophetic exposition of the thousand year reign of the Messiah. Interestingly, the fragments found reveals that this book was known by the Jews and early Near Eastern Christians. Enoch describes his revelations and his visits to heaven in the form of travels, visions, and dreams.

The stories told in Freemasonry, depict Enoch as being inspired by the Most High by receiving a vision to construct an underground series of vaults to **hide** the wisdom, mathematical, arts, science, and treasures of the pre-flood era that he had accumulated. The legend explains that Enoch built nine brick perpendicular vaults inside Mount Moriah, that were joined by small openings. He used his masonry skills and carved out a stone for the door or entrance and attached a ring of iron to access to the secret tunnels/vaults. Enoch also designed and created a triangular plate of gold, each side a cubit long (18-21 inches), and enhanced it with precious stones. This plate was engraved with the name of God. It was sealed and above ground, he erected two pillars, one of marble and one of brass. He engraved the history of creation, the principles of the arts and sciences, and the doctrines of Speculative Masonry, practiced in Enoch's time span. On the pillar of marble, Enoch inscribed in hieroglyphic characters, information that precious treasure was deposited nearby.

As we get further into the book, we will discover how this legend applies to Freemasonry, the KGC, and how Jesse buried their treasures. Joseph Smith, the founder of the LDS Church believed in "money digging." Before he founded the church, Smith was involved in using "Folk Magic" to locate treasure. He used seer stones to receive revelations from God, translating the Book of Mormon, but documentation and articles support that he used the seer stone and magic to find treasure. "A **seer stone** in this culture was a prevalent **divination** tool used for a form of crystal gazing, or scrying." [123]

In Wikipedia, the word "Divination" is described as "the attempt to gain insight into a question or situation by way of an occultic ritual or practice. Using various methods throughout history, diviners ascertain their interpretations of how a querent should proceed by reading signs, events, or omens, or through alleged contact or interaction with supernatural agencies such as spirits, gods, god-like beings or the "will of the universe." [124]

An article explains the documentation and resources found on Joseph Smith's practice of "Money Digging." It was titled, "Joseph Smith and Money Digging," by Richard Lyman Bushman – rsc.byu.edu. [125]

The practice and procedures in the burial of treasure was derived from the occult, placing guards of evil at the entrance. This has been proven to be true in burial sites of the Spanish, Aztecs, and secret society caches.

The reason why the writer is going into so much depth and detail into the history of America and Freemasonry is to set the stage for what Jesse was drawn into at a very young age. Everything fits perfectly with what Albert Pike was building and grooming prior to the Civil War and thereafter which led Jesse down a lonely dark road. It all comes together here. Keep your eyes wide open as you discover the clues and reasons on why Jesse did what he did. "This was big," as Bud said.

The initiation into the 13th degree of the Lodge of Perfection in Freemasonry, is learning God's secret name: "Jahbulon." This was supposedly what Enoch engraved on the plate, the name of God. It connects the names of Jehovah (God) with two pagan gods, Baal (a Babylonian deity), and Osiris (the god of fertility and the most wicked god and father of Horus, their messiah). Jahbulon is the three headed god, the Great Architect's Trinity which is a perverted inversion of the Holy Trinity of Christianity, God the Father, the Son, and Holy Spirit.

Just prior to the prophecy of Enoch (descendant of Seth) in the book of Jude, the writer was speaking of evildoers and describing the path they were on to destruction. *"Woe unto them! For they have gone in the way of Cain and ran greedily after the error of Balaam for reward and perished in the gainsaying of Core."* Jude:11

The Grand Architect of Freemasonry is a combination of gods or deities that an individual Mason believes in. Freemasonry welcomes men of all faiths, including some wonderful Christian men.

The God of Mormonism is their Heavenly Father who was described in the original teachings as living on a planet. He was once a man amongst many other men who through their good works, tithes, and obedience became **gods** themselves. Men who are members of the LDS Church have a path of exaltation to godhood themselves. Those who fail in the process will be castrated in the afterlife. Women could not become gods, but they were deemed literally as sex slaves. The early Mormon church believed if you had one ounce of African American blood in your DNA, it prevented them from becoming a member of the priesthood. If mixed blood was found in a person, they were required to be killed on the spot. This racial theory was disposed of in 1978, only 46 years ago.

Both the Mormon Church (LDS) and Freemasonry were being developed widely in America in the early 1800's and was formed during the so-called Enlightenment Era. Their practices are parallel in nature, including striving to do good works to reach the light, secret handshakes, grips, secret words, rituals, and symbols. Howk stated that Jesse was a Methodist, then converted to Mormonism and then back to being a Methodist. I don't know if this is true. Remember, his father was a Baptist Preacher.

Is any of this revealed to the young man who wants to become a member of Freemasonry? This is not. This information is glazed over by a veil of falsehoods within the Lodge, dragging you deeper into the rabbit's hole. Way up the ladder, a member with the correct disposition, ideology, and a certain belief in a particular deity are identified, separated, groomed, and initiated into the higher degrees who go further into the deep dark side; A New World Order as described on our currency.

The requirement to join Freemasonry is simple: (1) Be of age (usually 18 years of age), (2) Believe in a Supreme Being, (3) Be of good character, and (4) Request the privilege of membership. Those who are allowed to join are initiated in a ritual and symbolic ceremony that involves dark, medieval reenactments, continuously reverberating that the initiate dies to self and is resurrected in the "light" and brotherhood. Those who are initiated into this society are required to take a blood oath, vowing to never reveal the secrets of masonry or his throat will be cut from ear to ear and his bowels will be cut out and given to the beast of the field.

The initiate starts their ascension in the Blue Lodge. Freemasonry has three levels to climb, 1st – Apprentice Degree, 2nd – Fellowcraft Degree, and 3rd – Master Mason Degree. Most men remain a Master Mason in the Blue Lodge and are satisfied in his service in the Lodge and his community. I truly believe their service is sincere and they are dedicated in helping mankind. If a member wishes to advance, he may petition for a position in the York Rite or the Ancient and Accepted Scottish Rite.

During the early years of the United States, I believe most of the Freemasons remained in the Blue Lodge as Master Masons, but there was an inner circle of higher degrees where the secrets were guarded more profusely and Albert Pike refined and defined those during the mid and late 1800s.

Albert Pike, "The Blue degrees are but the outer court or portico of the Temple. Part of the symbols are displayed there to the Initiate, but he is intentionally **misled** by **false interpretations**. It is not intended that he shall understand them; but it is intended that he shall imagine he understands them." Morals and Dogma (pg. 819).

The Freemasons maintained a façade within and without its organization, but the corruption invariably increased in the early 1800's and would continue to the time of the Civil War.

Albert Pike was noted as being extremely intelligent. He designed 30 initiation rituals for the advanced degrees that he created inside the Scottish Rite Freemasonry. Pike implemented a great deal of mystic and ceremonial magic into the rituals. The degrees he designed encouraged masons to work to advance their enlightenment. In the Scottish Rite, there are 32 degrees that a man can reach.

The highest degree achievable would be the **33rd degree**, an honorable degree not earned by works. A mason had to be selected by the Supreme Council in order to receive the title. It was reserved for outstanding members who had shown exemplary qualities in the Freemason's values. The number **33** is significant in Freemasonry.

There were higher levels unknown to Masons or the general public, a higher order within an order.

In "Lectures on Ancient Philosophy" by Manly P. Hall (1929), who was a 33rd degree Freemason wrote, "Freemasonry is a fraternity within a fraternity, an outer organization, concealing an inner brotherhood of the elect. Before it is possible to intelligently discuss the origin of the Craft, it is necessary, therefore to establish the existence of these two separate yet interdependent orders, the one visible and the other invisible. The visible society is a splendid camaraderie of free and accepted men enjoined to devote themselves to ethical, educational, fraternal, patriotic, and humanitarian concerns. The invisible society is a secret and most august fraternity whose members are dedicated to the service of the mysterious arcanum arcanorum. (mysterious or specialized knowledge) Those brethren who have essayed to write the history of their craft have not included in their disquisitions the story of that truly secret inner society which is to the body Freemasonic what the heart is to the body human. In each generation only a few are accepted into the inner sanctuary of the Work, but these are veritable Princes of the Truth and their sainted names shall be remembered in future ages together with the seers and prophets of the elder world. Though the great initiate-philosophers of Freemasonry can be counted upon one's fingers, yet their power is not to be measured by the achievements of ordinary men. They are dwellers upon the Threshold of the innermost, Masters of that secret doctrine which forms the invisible foundation of every great theological and rational institution." [126]

The inner sanctuary of Freemasonry replicates the most sacred Holy of Holies in the ancient Temple of Solomon. Notice they call it "of Solomon," but the most recognized term is the Temple of Jerusalem which God assigned King Solomon to build.

The temple was modeled after the original tabernacle built per God's holy instructions to the Israelites while wandering in the desert. God had released the Israelites out of bondage from the hands of the Egyptians and sustained them throughout their journey in the wilderness. He made a covenant with His people, *"I will be your God and you will be my people."* Jeremiah 7:23. God was faithful in His promises by forming them into a nation, building a place to commune with Him, continued to bless them and remain with them if they kept His commands and laws that He had given to Moses which included the rejection of other gods. *"Thou shalt have no other gods before me."* Exodus 20:3. God warned them of judgment and consequences if they turned from His ways He set before them.

The tabernacle was beautifully and intricately designed by God. The Israelites built it according to his instructions. It was designed for the place where God's presence would reside, and they would have a place to worship Him. This would be considered as their Temporary Tabernacle and was made of heavy cloth and timber.

The entry into the Tabernacle was of upmost importance. God required it to be on the **eastern** end of the tabernacle. In the outer court, an altar lay for the sacrificial animal, whether oxen, cattle, sheep, or goat. It was required by God, *"For the life of a creature is in the blood, and I have given it to you to make atonement for yourselves on the altar, it is the blood that makes atonement for one's life."* Leviticus 17:11. The offering had to be unblemished, only the very best would suffice.

Within the outer court was the bronze basin where the priests would wash, to purify themselves before entering the Holy place. The Holy Place consisted of the Menorah, a lamp stand made of seven branches containing cups which held the purest olive oil and a wick to be lit each day. It was the only light within the Holy Place (The Tree of Life and The Light of the Gospel). There was also within the Holy Place the Table of Showbread (The Bread of Life), and the Golden Incense Altar (The prayers of the Saints).

The final area, the Holy of Holies was behind a curtain or veil next to the Holy Place on the **western** side of the tabernacle. West has been known to be the direction representing the Holy Spirit and eternal life. It was the most sacred part of the Tabernacle, the inner most room, where the Ark of the Covenant rested, which contained the golden pot of manna, which was the bread from Heaven that sustained the Israelites in the desert, Aaron's budded rod (the rod of God), and the two tablets of the law (the Ten Commandments). Covering the Ark was the Mercy Seat.

Inside the Holy of Holies, God's Holy Presence dwelled within. The Holy of Holies was designed as a pattern of Heaven. Only the High Priest was permitted to enter the Holy of Holies, and only on Yom Kippur, the Day of Atonement. There the High Priest had to pour the blood of the sacrifices upon the Mercy Seat for atonement of the people's sins, as well as the sins of the High Priest himself.

In deeper study, it is clear that the symbolism that God designed for the Tabernacle was the beautiful body of Christ as our High Priest who was the unblemished lamb, sacrificed for the atonement of our sins.

When the permanent Jewish Temple was built, King Solomon's Temple, the contents of the Holy of Holies was transferred to the new area of the Holy of Holies deep within the Temple, separated by a heavy veil from the Holy Place.

Solomon's Temple is a vital part of Freemasonry regarding its architecture, symbolism and rituals. While God was showing us a glimpse of Jesus in His Tabernacle, which was a temporary place that the Israelites could take down and set up on their journey, the Freemasons set their eye more upon the permanent Temple thereafter which was built by King Solomon on Mt. Moriah, the "Temple Mount" in Jerusalem, the place where they believed Enoch had built the underground series of vaults to **hide** the wisdom of life, treasures, and where the name of God is engraved on a golden plate.

This sacred area was believed to be where the Knights Templar hid all the precious treasures of the temple in an underground vault.

The Temple was a masterpiece. The architecture was divine and enormously expensive. The Freemasons patterned their Lodges/Temples after Solomon's Temple except for one difference. In Speculative Freemasonry, they place their entrance on the **west** side of the temple and the Worshipful Master and inner temple (Holy of Holies) is in the **east.** Opposite of the tabernacle and opposite of Solomon's Temple.

This speaks volumes. Freemasons were adamant in following the design in strict adherence to Solomon's Temple for their lodges and temples, except for this one major variance. Why? It wasn't a mistake. After all, the positions of buildings, alignments and rules of the universe, and exact mathematical measurements were sacredly adhered to in other buildings they designed to retain their spiritual energy. We can see clearly the direction of the Freemason's spiritual energy. It comes from the **East**. Albert Pike calls Lucifer, "the Son of the Morning."

In their lodges/temples, Freemasons uses the term "inner sanctuary" or "inner temple" which is compared to the Holy of Holies. The Worshipful Master's chair or throne is placed in this area, with the symbol of the sun above him on the **Eastern** side of the Temple. Freemasons state that the architecture of the Temple displays the work that brothers coming together in their journey (from west to east) with the right tools can develop and perfect their temple, their body, their mind, and their spirit in making a better world. Through their journey, they seek light and the construction of a Spiritual Temple. The Ark represents the fountain head of wisdom per Manly Hall.

So, the focus of Freemasonry was Solomon's Temple, but it was destroyed. Looking into King Solomon himself, he was a King that asked God for wisdom and not wealth. God gave him wisdom and wealth and the opportunity to build the first permanent Temple. When the Temple was completed in all of its glory, God manifested his glory with His presence in the Holy of Holies. It was perfect.

After several years when Solomon's son was in charge of the Temple, God was disgusted with the people's desire to trust in deceitfulness of half-truths being taught in the Temple, and those who partook in theft, murder, adultery, burning incense unto Baal, and walk after other gods. There were depictions of idols being worshipped within the Temple walls.

God revealed some of the vile things that were occurring in His Temple to the prophet Ezekiel; the blatant idolatry, the abominations that were displayed within His Holy Temple. Ezekiel described what God said, *"Then He said to me, "Have you seen this O son of man? Turn again, you will see greater abominations than these." So, He brought me into the **inner court** of the Lord's house, and there, at the door of the temple of the Lord, between the porch and the altar; were about twenty-five men with their backs toward the temple of the Lord and their **faces toward the east, and they were worshiping the sun toward the east.***" Ezekiel 8:16. They were sun worshipers.

Remember, God's initial instruction for the tabernacle and Temple was that the entrance be on the **east** side and the Holy of Holies was on the **west** side. Why is this so important? The Eastern Gate in Jerusalem, facing the Mount of Olives, is the most direct route to the Temple Mount. This is the gate, many years later, that Jesus walked through to go to the 2nd temple that was built (Herod's Temple) and also will be the gate that Jesus will pass through when he returns to earth again. The Eastern Gate in Jerusalem was sealed shut in 1540 by order of Suleiman the Magnificent, a sultan of the Ottoman Empire. He wanted to prevent the Messiah from gaining entrance into Jerusalem when He returns.

After many abominations inflicted upon the Temple of Jerusalem, God departed and never again returned. Judgement came when the Babylonians attacked and destroyed the Temple.

The Temple was rebuilt and was called "Herod's Temple" during Jesus' time on earth. The Ark of the Covenant had disappeared, and God's presence was not there. Jesus and his apostles journeyed to Jerusalem to partake in the Feast of the Passover. This is the only time during the year when the sun is at its most accurate **eastern** point in the heavens that directly lines up to the Temple Mount.

As Jesus entered the Temple, he became enraged at the desecration of the holy place. In the outer court, there were animals everywhere being sold for sacrificial offerings. Imagine the sounds and smells that came from there. The courts were filled with people, animals, and money changers. It was more of a circus than a sacred temple filled with greed and profit. Jesus turned over the tables of the money changers, spilling all their precious coins upon the ground and drove out the men who were selling the animals, as well as the animals themselves. Jesus quoted from the book of Isaiah, *"My house shall be called a house of prayer, but you make it a den of robbers."* Matthew 21:13.

This began the plot to destroy Jesus by those who feared his authority and popularity; the High Priests who were getting a percentage of the profit.

The Freemasons only focused on Solomon's Temple, not the 2nd temple built. What did it hold?

Manly Hall wrote, "Solomon's temple, or the perfected temple of the human body, the perfected temple of the universe and the perfected temple of the soul, finally forms the perfect shrine for the living Ark. There at the head of a great cross it is placed, and there in man it becomes permanently fixed. The staves of polarity upon which it was carried are removed, and it becomes a living thing, a permanent place where man converses with his God. There **man**, the purified and **elect priest**, arrayed in the robes of his order, the garments of his soul, converses with the spirit hovering over the Mercy Seat. This Ark within is always present, but man can only reach it after he has passed through the outer court of the Tabernacle, after he has passed through all the degrees of initiation – not only ceremonial, but contemplative – and after he has taken the Third Degree and becomes a Master. Then and then only can he enter into the presence of his Lord, and there in the darkened chamber, lighted by the jewels of his own breast plate, he converses with the Most High, the true spiritual essence with himself." [127]

It is a philosophy that is very confusing and mysterious to the common man, whereas the Christian faith is simple. *"For God is not the author of confusion, but of peace, as it is in all churches of the saints."* 1st Corinthians 14:33

I may totally be wrong, but the Freemason's philosophy described above appears to be a belief that after many great works and proof of worthiness, going through all the steps of degrees and rituals, reaching a spiritual level or latitude, then one can become their own High Priest and can earn the right to converse with God, entering a new phase of spirituality. The right to be in God's presence is only reserved for those who follow these laws and is endowed with **his own** breast plate of glory. Could it also be a process of exaltation of a person reaching the rank of **a god**, reaching the most Holy of Holies such as the Mormon belief? I don't know, but I believe this belief speaks for itself.

*"Wherefore in all things it behooved him (Jesus) to be made like unto his brethren, that he might be a merciful and faithful **high priest** in things pertaining to God, to make reconciliation for the sins of the people."* Hebrews 2: 17

When Jesus, at the age of **33**, was crucified on the cross, the veil separating mankind from the Holy of Holies ripped from top to bottom, Matthew 27:51, a sign from God that the fulfillment of the purest sacrifice was met with His son Jesus, the ultimate unblemished lamb, slain for all of mankind's sins. The atonement would be everlasting.

God's purpose was to bridge the gap between man and himself, removing the veil, allowing access to the Almighty for **all**. Jesus as the sacrificial lamb was the only way for God to redeem our unworthy souls to be able to stand before Him in His presence.

Jesus said unto him, *"I am the Way, the Truth, and the Life; no man cometh unto the Father, but by Me."* John 14:6

God restored His presence with mankind through the life, death, and resurrection of His Son Jesus Christ who paved the way to eternal life, restoring communion with the Almighty.

Ceremonies

The ceremony of laying a cornerstone down in the construction of monumental buildings, such as Washington performed during the building of the Capitol, has great significance to the Freemasons. At the Capitol, the cornerstone was laid down on top of an engraved metal plate and with the president and three worshipful masters, the stone was consecrated with the "sacrifice" of corn, wine, and oil. A 500 lb. ox was barbequed thereafter. [128]

The stone masons or "builders" in ancient times used human sacrifices as their cornerstone, crushing a human under the stones to ensure that their spirit would dwell within the walls, enlivening and securing stability in the structure per Horace Sykes in the book, "Ancient Religious Traditions and Symbols of Freemasonry". [129] The human sacrifice was eventually replaced by corn, wine, and oil.

The Bible addresses the term "builders," "cornerstone," and "sacrifices" in several verses.

*"Therefore, everyone who hears these words of mine and puts them into practice is like a wise man who **built his house on the rock**. The rain came down, the streams rose, and the winds blew and beat against that house; yet it did not fall, because it had its **foundation on the rock**."* Matthew 7:24-25

*"Now to you who believe, this stone is precious. But to those who do not believe, "**The stone the builders rejected has become the cornerstone.**"* 1 Peter 2:7   Jesus is *"the stone you builders rejected, which has become **the cornerstone**."* Acts 4:11.

Jesus is the Chief Cornerstone and the rock. The number **33** which is very important to the Freemasons, is promoted as being the age that Jesus died, believing he was not the Savior of mankind and did not resurrect from the dead. If a Freemason reaches the **33rd** degree and claims he is still a Christian, he cannot advance.

The number **33** also represents the third of the angels that fell from Heaven with Satan. According to Manly P. Hall, **33** is the key to achieving immortality. I do know the **33rd** parallel on this earth is of greatest importance to the Freemasons. It is where life-changing events occur, good and evil.

The Georgia Guidestones were on the 33rd parallel, but were totally destroyed in 12 hours beginning at 4:03:**33** A.M.

Truth in Black and White

Throughout various books, writings of masonic leaders and those who left the Freemason's society, it is revealed that Freemasonry is a "religious" organization originating from Egyptian Paganism out of Babylon, Baal and sun worship leading to higher levels of the Luciferian religion.

There is controversy and questionable literature of course and one being a document that is titled "Instructions to the 23 Supreme Councils of the World," supposedly written and spoken by Albert Pike on July 14, 1889. Many, especially in the Masonic organization states that it is a hoax. I can not find a solid reference for this, supporting the document itself or the hoax, but it does appear to match other sources upholding these beliefs shown above.

This is the controversial statement supposedly written by Albert Pike, "Yes, Lucifer is God and unfortunately Adonay is also God. For the eternal law is that there is no light without shade, no beauty without ugliness, no white without black, for the absolute can only exist as two Gods: darkness being necessary to light to serve as its foil as the pedestal is necessary to the statue, and the brake to the locomotive. Thus, the doctrine of Satanism is a heresy; and the true and pure philosophical religion is the belief in Lucifer, the equal of Adonay; but Lucifer, God of Light and God of Good, is struggling for humanity against Adonay, the God of Darkness and Evil." [130]

Adonay or Adonai that Pike was referring to is another name for the God of the Hebrews, the majestic and sovereign God. He is Lord and Master. He is creator of all things. The darkness Pike refers to is the concealment of the one true God.

In the statement, supposedly made by Pike, he differentiates between Lucifer and Satan; Lucifer is the God of Light and the doctrine of Satan is a heresy. The best answer that I have found to support two different entities is found on a site, "This vs. That." "While both Lucifer and Satan represent evil forces in various religious and literary contexts, Lucifer is often associated with the initial fall of grace, while Satan embodies the ongoing temptation and corruption of humanity." Lucifer was a symbol of pride and rebellion and Satan is known as the adversary and accuser. [131]

Satan is a master counterfeiter presenting false teachings as enlightening and lifechanging. Lucifer is known as "the enlighten one." He uses many tools to masquerade as the angel of light, turning white to black and black to white. He portrays God as the liar and the source of darkness.

"For such are false apostles, deceitful workers, transforming themselves into apostles of Christ. And no wonder! For Satan himself transforms himself into an angel of light. Therefore, it is no great thing if his ministers also transform themselves into ministers of righteousness, whose end will be according to their works." 2nd Corinthian 11:13-15

The truth and the light are found in the Word of the one and true God. Without the Word of God, darkness can swallow us up.

"Your word is a lamp to my feet and a light to my path." Psalm 119:105

"For God, who commanded the light to shine out of darkness, hath shined in our hearts,, to give the light of the knowledge of the glory of God in the face of Jesus Christ." 2nd Corinthians 4:6

Manly P. Hall, (**33rd** degree) wrote, "When the Mason learns that the Key to the warrior on the block (a primitive ritual of human sacrifice) is the proper application of the dynamo of living power, he has learned the Mystery of his Craft. The seething energies of Lucifer are in his hands and before he may step onward and upward, he must prove his ability to properly apply this energy." [132]

They describe the power and energy as two parallel forces at play; Good and evil, Christianity and Paganism, truth and error, wisdom and ignorance, order and disorder, latitude and longitude, male and female, black and white, oppressor and the oppressed. The power lies within the fusion or balance of the two. The use of the two opposing forces are utilized to reach a goal: whether it be unity or division.

Albert Pike stated that all divine intelligence was divided into light and darkness. The best and the worst in humanity. The corrupt version of the good. Is this the same as "double-minded?" There are many symbols found in Freemasonry of a double headed eagle.

In the Renaissance Hall at the Masonic Temple in Philadelphia, there are two hexagrams located high above in the temple signifying the union of two principles or opposite forces. Remember, it's the union that creates the "spiritual energy". The symbol of the hexagram "was first used as a **mystic** symbol by Muslims in the medieval period, known as the Seal of Solomon, depicted as either a hexagram or pentagram, and which was later adopted by Jewish Kabbalists." ("Hexagram – Wikipedia") It has also been utilized in other religious sects and occults. The Pentagon in Washington D.C. is in the form of a pentagram, lined up perfectly with Washington's Monument.

This "so-called" divine intelligence is also symbolized in the black and white checkered floor that the Freemasons use in their buildings, reflecting a dual principle or yin and yang. Yin is the receptive and Yang the active principle, such as the female and male principle shown in Freemasonry Architect. The checkerboard or chess board and its philosophy is found hidden in plain sight in current movies, music and music videos, video games, celebrity venues, fashion, the media, books, cartoons, commercials, etc. If you analyze it carefully and use your God given gift of discernment, most of the scenes depicted are vulgar and disgusting.

The checkered board used in the game of chess is played out daily, even in the Super Bowl half-time show and the Olympics. The unenlightened man (defined in Freemasonry) is like a pawn in this chess game who is controlled by a manipulative master, fed propaganda, subliminal messages, false doctrines, false imagery, ideology, and rationalization of opposing doctrinal and spiritual beliefs. The pawn reacts only to what he can see, not beyond. This is a type of bondage or slavery to lies and control. The truth is concealed.

Can the two entities, good and evil become one? It muddles the two identities and becomes gray matter. The belief is that the good deeds balance out the bad deeds. That's the elite's grand scheme; to combine the two, creating a new spiritual energy, a New One World Order where we are one in religion, one in government, one in the economic system, and are slaves to the master. Albert Pike put this in motion in 1871. Out of chaos, there is order.

Albert Pike referred to Freemasonry as the custodian of these occult secrets. Pike's influence continued to swell within the organization and beyond, creating a whole new structure and philosophy that would eventually swallow up the original goal of Freemasonry.

A well-known Masonic leader, who followed Pike's direction in creating a new world, High Priestess of the New Age movement, and founder of the publishing company, Lucifer Trust/Lucis Trust, Alice Bailey (1880-1949) wrote out a plan.

Here is her ten-point plan of the New World Order, adopted by the United Nations to change Judeo/Christian tradition:

1. Take God and prayer out of the education system
2. Reduce parental authority over the children
3. Destroy the Judeo-Christian family structure
4. If sex is free, then make abortion legal and make it easy
5. Make divorce easy and legal, free people from the concept of marriage for life.
6. Make homosexuality an alternative lifestyle
7. Debase art, make it run mad
8. Use media to promote and change mindset
9. Create an interfaith movement
10. Get governments to make all these laws and get the Church to endorse these changes. [133]

Drip by drip, these points have all been met, hidden in plain sight, gradually fed to the masses, one spoonful at a time.

"For our struggle is not against flesh and blood, but against the rulers, against the authorities, against the powers of this dark world and against the spiritual forces of evil in the heavenly realms." Ephesians 6:12

"See to it that no one takes you captive by philosophy and empty deceit, according to human tradition, according to the elemental spirits of the world, and not according to Christ" Colossians 2:8

"And every spirit that confesseth not that Jesus Christ is come in the flesh, is not of God; and such is the spirit of Antichrist, whereof ye have heard that it should come, and even now already it is in the world. Ye are of God, little children, and have overcome them, because greater is He that is in you than he that is in the world." 1st John 4:3-4.

"These things I have spoken unto you, that in Me ye might have peace. In the world ye shall have tribulation but be of good cheer. I have overcome the world." John 16:**33**

Then said Jesus to the Jews who believed in Him, *"If ye continue in My Word, then are ye My disciples indeed. And ye shall know the truth, and the truth shall make you free."* John 8: 31-32

You decide for yourself. The information is out there, they have it in plain sight. Is the design of America and Freemasonry an occultists organization? If so, has it always been? Is it now? Did every Freemason follow Pike's lead?

What is not being revealed to the common man? All that glitters is not gold. Each one of us must use our moral compass and discernment and not shy away from the truth or ignore it. Our souls, our world, our country depends upon it.

"For God hath not given us the spirit of fear, but of power, and of love, and of a sound mind."
2nd Timothy 1:7

"Whoever is careless with the truth in small matters cannot be trusted with important matters."

-Albert Einstein

Chapter Nine: The Spy System and the Knights of the Golden Circle

The question now in the mind of the reader is this: Was Jesse James, the son of a Baptist preacher and described as a "Bible-toting" man by Jesse's cook and close friend, John Trammel, immersed in the philosophy of the Radical Freemasons led by Albert Pike?

Jesse Woodson James was naturally a perfect candidate to initiate into the secret organizations. During Jesse's service in the war, between the ages of 15 to 17, he had all the qualities of a valued surety. Being young and clinging on to a deep hatred for the Yankees, Jesse was the perfect subject to coerce, manipulate, and sway into an ideology that was branded into his very being through the emotions that flooded his spirit during the darkest days of America. He could never get over the abuse, loss, and suffering bestowed upon his family and the southern people.

The outlet for Jesse's emotions and his revengeful spirit was of course released in the brutal type of warfare he was involved in, but he wanted more. He was willing to believe and engage in any kind of activity to destroy the destroyer of his family, homestead and their way of life. During his time with Quantrill and Bloody Bill Anderson, he was being carefully watched and observed. The men were impressed with his fervor. They saw that Jesse's emotions could be funneled into a brotherhood whose mission met his passion, the South.

The secret societies that developed before, during, and after the war were filled with intrigue and mystery indeed. Many men joined just to know the secrets and to become a part of something greater than themselves and an opportunity to become a hero in the protection of the South. But were they given fiery propaganda and just enough of the mystical concealed knowledge to lure them in? In the last chapter, Albert Pike and Manly Hall confirms this.

If you can believe it, the Knights of the Golden Circle were more elusive and mysterious than Freemasonry. They were indeed connected to Freemasonry as many of the other secret societies are, but the KGC kept their mouths shut.

A book written by a former KGC member, R. H. Williams who had ties with the organization at the very beginning and throughout the war wrote, "In those days the Southern States, with their great "Institution," (slavery) were at the **zenith** of their power, and were ambitious of extending it beyond the boundary to which they had been restricted by the Missouri Compromise of 1820". [134]

Stephen E. Towne as a young man shortly after graduate school, discovered while working in the Indiana State Archive, a treasure trove of documents regarding uncovered truths of the Civil War. He came across information that had always been shoved to the back that was on a subject most believed to be a fairy tale, the secret society, the KGC, the Knights of the Golden Circle.

Bud Hardcastle fully understands the ridicule. In the early 1980's, Bud began publicly speaking of his discoveries of the secret society, the Knights of the Golden Circle. Ears were not ready to hear what had been kept secret for over a century. Bud was shot down numerous times by the media, and told, "There is no such thing." Bud proved them wrong. At the turn of the 21st century, others began following Bud's path and did a little research on their own, publishing their findings.

In Towne's book, "Surveillance and Spies in the Civil War: Exposing Confederate Conspiracies in America's Heartland", 2014; he writes that he has a profound sense of obligation and duty to document what he has found in his research. He particularly reviewed thousands of old documents in Illinois, Indiana, Ohio, Michigan, etc., the Northern part of the United States, that reveal there was a massive amount of secret societies promoting secession in the Northern states, persuading desertion from the Union army, and various plots to support the South.

There are several excellent books out there now that help prove the existence of the KGC and prove Bud was right all along, who was one of the earlier "truthsayers" to reveal this. I find the most accurate description of the society is on the website; https://knightsofthegoldencircle.webs.com. It was well written by Jay Longley, a good friend of Bud's, and Colin Eby.

Mr. Longley sought out the help of Bud Hardcastle in his long search for Confederate Gold in Brownwood, Texas and beyond. It is a very interesting website. Brownwood was a hot spot for the KGC and Knights Templar as we have already discussed, and we will further zoom in to the significance of that small town in Central Texas.

"Bud, he is the foremost historian on Jesse James more than any other one I know of. Nobody is more knowledgeable about Jesse Woodson James than Bud Hardcastle," said Longley to the writer.

Jay Longley is a historian, treasure hunter, and researcher. His interest began in 2006 when he read "Rebel Gold", by Warren Getler and Bob Brewer. Bud Hardcastle was mentioned in the book as being a valuable source on deciphering codes and signs in treasure hunting, providing maps, and the characteristics and path of Jesse James.

Bud told the writer that he highly respects Bob Brewer and Warren Getler, their research and the knowledge they gained over the years on treasure hunting. Bud was invited to Bob Brewer's home after Bob's friend, Stan Vickery paid a visit to Bud in Purcell, Oklahoma. Of course, Stan came to Bud to learn more about Jesse James. Bud shared his findings and documents with Stan and revealed his own discovery of Jesse's involvement with the Knights of the Golden Circle.

After Stan left and returned to his own home, he contacted his friend Bob Brewer and began telling Bob all that he had learned from Bud Hardcastle. Both Stan and Bob Brewer called Bud up and wanted him to come to Arkansas to learn more about what Bud knew on the subjects.

Bud went to Arkansas and met with them, explaining about all the information he had dug up on Jesse and the Knights of the Golden Circle, including the signs and symbols that they used to bury their treasure. Bud brought along maps and several documents to back up his statements. Bud stated, that on that visit, he learned Bob had never heard of the Knights of the Golden Circle until Stan came home with the information Bud had given him and what they learned in their meeting in Arkansas. Bob was only familiar at the time with Spanish symbols and Spanish treasure that his great uncle opened his eyes to which created a hunger for more. Treasure and gold have a way of getting into your blood.

Bud gave them plenty of information and maps, enough for Bob to write a book or two, and many clues leading them to treasures. Bob was involved in a few treasure expeditions with Bud. In one very complicated treasure hunt in Oklahoma, while working separately with a trusted individual, using Bud's maps, both Bud and Bob were burned. You will find that story in Bob's book and Bud's side of the story in a later chapter.

Back to the subject of this chapter; the Knights of the Golden Circle. What was their purpose? Jay Longley and Colin Eby's writeup on the KGC explained it in simple terms. Jay and Colin put out a website explaining the KGC and the stories caught the eye of the Texas State Historical Society. The Society contacted Jay and Colin, asking them if they could update the article they had on the KGC on their website because it was very outdated, had incorrect information, and a lot of it was hearsay.

The TSHS "fact-checked" it thoroughly, approved it, and published it on their website, exactly how Jay and Colin had written it. After three months of remaining on the website, Jay said they were barraged by naysayers and their enemies. Using fake names, these people began complaining to the president of the society that this was false. The president ordered it to be taken down and the old article, the one that had false information, was put back up.

With permission from Jay Longley, here is an excerpt of that writeup from his website describing the KGC's goal. "The Knights of the Golden Circle was to become the most powerful secret and subversive organization in the history of the United State with members in every state and territory before the end of the Civil War. The primary economic and political goal of this organization was to create a prosperous, slave-holding Southern Empire extending in the shape of a circle from their proposed capital at Havana, Cuba, through the southern states of the United States, Mexico, the Gulf of Mexico, the Caribbean, and *Central America*. The plan also called for the acquisition of Mexico which was then to be divided into fifteen new slave holding states which would shift the balance of power in Congress in favor of slavery. Facing the Gulf of Mexico, these new states would form a large crescent. The robust economy the KGC hoped to create would be fueled by cotton, sugar, tobacco, rice, coffee, indigo, and mining. The seven industries would employ slave labor." [135]

Jesse was fully immersed in the Knights of the Golden Circle. When he gave his oath, he gave his life. It is unknown when Jesse joined, but Bud believes it was during the war. There is evidence that the KGC supported Quantrill and his men. Bud stated that Quantrill was one of the original leaders of the KGC. The men who were in the KGC inner sanctum were Uncle George Payne, the secretary; Jesse James (the comptroller and paymaster), Frank James, Jefferson Davis, General Bud Dalton, Professor B E. Bedeczek, Cole Younger, General J O Shelby, Nathan Bedford Forrest, and Jack Brack Miller. Of course, some of these men were using an alias.

(Uncle George Payne)

Bud Hardcastle had no assistance from Ola or Aubrey Everhard on information for the KGC. Jesse rarely spoke of his associations with secret societies to Ola. The only thing that Ola knew was that he was a member of the Freemasons, the Odd Fellows, and Knights of Pythias Lodge whose motto was Friendship, Charity, and Benevolence. Ola described a watch charm that was attached to Jesse's watch chain holding a seven jeweled, white gold with yellow gold numbers pocket watch. It had the emblem, K.P. Lodge with the letters F. C. B. (Friendship, Courage, and Benevolence).

Bud worked extremely hard to decipher clues and hints of the Knights of the Golden Circle. It is truly amazing how keen and alert he was in his hunt for the truth. He followed every lead that would come across his path and was the first one to be able to decode the signs and symbols left behind from this clandestine group.

Bud discovered that the KGC did not allow Catholics in their organization for fear that their confessions to their priests would convey their secrets. Earlier we spoke of Albert Pike having the anti-Catholicism philosophy, but in recent years, many have proven that Albert Pike was very tight with the Holy Roman Empire within the secret societies he helped develop.

The KGC also did not allow a woman to be involved due to the danger and sacrifice it would entail. This is the reason why Jesse never shared his secrets of the knights or their treasure he had in his care. He did what any good knight would do, protect the women with his life, while protecting his secrets. Jesse possessed a very honorable and Medieval chivalry that stood the test of time.

Many believe that a Cincinnati doctor, George William Lamb Bickley, founded the KGC, Knights of the Golden Circle in 1854. Newspapers, mostly Union, speak of him as the founder and as "a scoundrel, a conman, a liar, etc." Bud Hardcastle believes he was just another pawn in the game.

There are many who agree with Bud, who believe there was a much bigger picture in the development of the Knights of the Golden Circle. Mr. Longley wrote that his research revealed that the K.G.C. started a whole lot earlier than what has been documented. Longley's article explains that it had its beginnings in the mid 1830's along with several "Southern Rights Clubs" that were formed to reestablish the African slave trade. The clubs followed the ideology of the secret organization called the Order of the Lone Star which had set the stage for the Texas Revolution, fighting for independence from Mexico. The KGC may have even been established further back to the Revolutionary War in which at that time, the organization was known as the Sons of Liberty.

John C. Calhoun (1782-1850) inspired the various Southern Rights Clubs towards the philosophy of preserving slavery and protecting the interests of the South. They believed that the Constitution was a tyrannical document, prohibiting slavery. They developed their own illegal slave trade along the African coast which later expanded into the Gulf of Mexico.

Calhoun was a huge political figure, serving as a representative in the House for South Carolina, Senator, Secretary of War under President James Monroe, and vice president for John Quincy Adams and Andrew Jackson. Strangely, Calhoun ended up butting heads with Adams and Jackson. Adams was strongly against slavery.

"It is among the evils of slavery that it taints the very sources of moral principle. It establishes false estimates of virtue and vice: for what can be more false and heartless than this doctrine which makes the first and holiest rights of humanity to depend upon the color of the skin?" John Quincy Adams [136]

Calhoun voted to censure President Jackson for his removal of the money from the Second Bank in 1834. He also became Secretary of State under President John Tyler who automatically became president after President Harrison died after one month of service. Calhoun created the *Bureau of Indian Affairs* within his department, without authorization from Congress in 1824. Do you see any similarities?

By 1844, when the Mexican American War was on the horizon, the Southern Rights Club was given a new hope that the war would give them an advantage in the direction of a new territory for slavery. Politicians within the club such as Calhoun, became an extreme coercive force in their efforts to create tension between the United States and Mexico, in hopes that a war would be the result which would increase their profit in slave trade. Slavery was always included in their vocabulary.

"Calhoun warned that the day "the balance between the two sections" (pro-slavery and anti-slavery) was destroyed would be a day not far removed from disunion, anarchy, and civil war." [137] President Andrew Jackson, on his deathbed, regretted that he had not had Calhoun executed for treason.

A few years after Calhoun's death, his spirit was still thriving within the secret societies who were pro-South. Some believe he was deeply involved in the establishment of the Knights of the Golden Circle. In 1854, the KGC organized or reorganized in Lexington, Kentucky. Bud had in his documents, a pamphlet, a brief section of the *Southwestern Historical Quarterly*, "Some Letters

Concerning the Knights of the Golden Circle in Texas 1860, 1861," compiled by Jimmy Hicks, July 1961 describe how the KGC was formed and how it spread in the South.

Hicks does explain that it was George Bickley who founded the KGC, Knights of the Golden Circle in 1854. By 1859, Bickley began to promote his ideology in the South. His main purpose was to preserve and protect the institution of slavery in the Southern States. Ideas began to accumulate in this mission to create a huge slavery empire which would include the Southern slave holding States, Mexico, Central America, the West Indies, and the northern part of South America; thus, the Golden Circle is created.

In 1860, prior to the Civil War, Bickley led men in the south to organize local chapters of the KGC, called castles. The State Headquarters in Texas was in San Antonio. Bickley had tremendous support and followers throughout the South. This organization promoted propaganda in secession and military organization throughout Kentucky, Tennessee, and Texas.

George Bickley refers to himself, KGC, President American Legion – police system. He also claimed in a letter that the KGC has the magic of Prince Arthur's horn, which could not only call his thousand legions at the blast, but before whose blast the enemy fell down.

Bickley stated, "As an organization, the KGC has no connection with the Government of the Confederate States, though its membership sympathizes deeply with the struggling people of the South, and hold themselves in readiness in most cases to lend the helping hand in the critical hour."

Bickley is noted in several writings that he met with four other unknown men to ignite the fuel within this secret society. Some researchers believe that one of the men was Freemason Killian Henry van Rensselaer (1800-1881) who was called the "St. Paul of Scottish Rite". He became the overseer of the Knights of the Golden Circle with the help of John James Joseph Gourgas. They supposedly maintained the Northern jurisdiction.

Van Rensselaer was a member of the famous Knickerbocker family and became involved in the Scottish Rite of Freemasonry organization. He began his life in New York and moved to Pittsburgh where he was named Deputy of the Supreme Council for Western Pennsylvania and Ohio.

He later became Sovereign Grand Commander who spread the rites west from Connecticut to the Mississippi River. He set up many Freemason lodges which included the first Scottish Rite body of Freemasonry west of the Alleghenies formed in Cambridge, Ohio in 1852. The KGC was formed in Cincinnati where George Bickley lived and was considered a Masonic organization. Cincinnati was where Van Rensselaer died. Strangely enough, Van Rensselaer was accused of being a longtime underground military operative for Britain in North America.

John James Joseph Gourgas (1777-1865), born in Switzerland and raised in London, was the founder and the first Secretary General of the Scottish Rite of Freemasonry Northern Supreme Council. At the age of 26, he moved to America and settled in New York. The highest award of the Scottish Rite of Freemasonry Supreme Council in the Northern Masonic Jurisdiction is named after him, the Gourgas Medal. He was known as the "Conservator of Scottish Rite Freemasonry."

Three other men who have been noted as part of the scheme to design the Knights of the Golden Circle were John Slidell, Judah Benjamin and Albert Pike who would be in control of the Southern jurisdiction.

Judah Benjamin, a Jewish senator for Louisiana and Albert Pike (1809-1891), the Scottish Rite of Freemasonry Southern Jurisdiction Sovereign Grand Commander, were noted as the "brains of the Confederacy." It became quite evident that these men and Freemasonry were the "brains, arms, and legs" of the Knights of the Golden Circle. These two gentlemen met frequently at the Pickwick Club in New Orleans. It is here that Pike has been noted as writing the by-laws and rituals of the Knights of the Golden Circle. Pike had already begun to revise the rituals, by-laws, and degrees of the Scottish Rite Freemasonry. The two orders were similar in nature, but apparently had different goals.

New Orleans was the leading *cotton* port in the nation. All the prestigious leaders of New Orleans were members of the Pickwick Club. The Pickwick had a sister club in London, named after the fictitious character, Samuel Pickwick in Charles Dickens book, "The Pickwick Papers." The New Orleans gentleman's club began in 1857. Its club was housed on Tchoupitoulas Street, but by

1858, its home was on No. 57 St. Charles Street. It was considered the most comfortable and cozy club house ever seen in New Orleans. A banker from Paris, Mr. Heine, who owned the lot on Canal and Carondelet became involved and helped build a new building in the year of 1882.

"Built of Philadelphia pressed brick of a rich deep red, its two fronts are set off by ornamental carved trimmings of Indiana limestone. Its roof rises with sharp slope high above the surrounding cornice and gives to the whole edifice an effect inspiring and lofty. Rising from a cluster of polished granite columns of almost diminutive length, and surmounted by a bowl-shaped stone support resting on the back of griffins, is a circular turret which extends to the roof and forms in its length place for oriel windows in each story. Jutting out as it does from the wall unsupported, it catches the *eye* at once." [138]

(The Pickwick Club, 1903)

The design followed the Ancient Greek Architecture. The griffins portrayed in statues were a mythical animal having the head, forepart, and wings of an eagle and the body, hind legs, and tail of a lion. Griffins have been known to represent the guarding of treasure and priceless possessions. They were sacred animals who manifested divine power to the mythical Greek god, Apollo. Symbolism was dispersed throughout the club, just as it was throughout the secret societies. Notice the "all seeing eye."

Judah Benjamin was later appointed by Jefferson Davis, President of the Confederacy, as Attorney General, Secretary of War, Secretary of State, and Chief of Intelligence of the Confederacy. Many believe that the Knights of the Golden Circle was formed into the Confederate Intelligence or Confederate Underground.

Judah Benjamin was known to have transferred Confederate money to personal bank accounts in Europe. It has been thoroughly documented that Benjamin had the backing of both the British and French Rothschilds. He was their agent.

Albert Pike was grooming himself as well to take control of the southern mission and its role in the Civil War. His philosophy now had an avenue or byway, creating an opportunity to expand throughout the country.

Prior to the Civil War, Pike's hatred for African Americans showed up in a signed pamphlet that proposed the expelling of all free African Americans from Arkansas. The pamphlet said, "evil is the existence among us of a class of free colored persons." It has not been proven, but many believe that after the war, Pike was head of the K.K.K. The mixture of his involvement and development of Freemasonry, slave trade, and his desire for land expansion made him the perfect leader in the move of domination of the South through the Knights of the Golden Circle.

John A. Quitman, father of Mississippi Freemasonry, a **33rd** degree Freemason was a Brigadier General of Volunteers commanded by Zachary Taylor in the northern part of Mexico during the Mexican American War. After the fall of Mexico City, he was named Military Governor of Mexico City and later became the Governor of Mississippi. He was the leader of The Order of the Lone Star that was formed September 1851.

Quitman thrived and hungered for military glory. He became wrapped up in a filibuster expedition encouraged by President Franklin Pierce to prepare to invade Cuba and remove the Spanish from that domain. This plan was dropped because the damage that it would do to the Democratic Party by adding another slaveholding territory. Quitman became an outspoken leader of the southern secessionists but was stopped short in 1858 when he died unexpectantly. Some believe it was poison, while others say it was a mysterious death from the effects of National Hotel Disease. This occurred during the inauguration of James Buchanan. Over 400 people got sick, while close to 36 people died.

Albert Pike took over Quitman's position, becoming leader of the Southern Secessionists. Pike increased the Supreme Council of the Scottish Rite Freemasonry branch in New Orleans to **33** members. The foundation was set for the strongest mobile force to infiltrate every inch of the country through an upcoming and carefully planned war to divide the country.

In the early part of 1860, when Abraham Lincoln was nominated for presidency at the Republican Convention, the Knights were holding their own convention in Raleigh, NC. In several writings, there is indication that the KGC wanted Lincoln to run and become president to create a fierce division in the country; creating an intense fervor and hatred in the hearts of the Southerners who wished to protect their freedoms and rights.

This may be one of the reasons why there were two Democrats; Stephen Douglas and John Breckenridge running in this election; to split the vote and bring Lincoln in.

The KGC began growing and organizing into a membership of 48,000. They were building their own army and recruiting rapidly in the north and south. The strength in this organization lay within the boundaries of Texas where 32 KGC castles were established which are similar to the Freemasonry Temples/Lodges. The numbers 32 and **33** are important in both Freemasonry and the KGC.

Marshall, Texas was claimed to be the capitol of Missouri during the Civil War with a heavy KGC presence in East Texas. In 1944, Frank Dalton (Jesse) told a newspaper reporter for the Marshall News Messenger, Aug 13, 1944 that "he was one of the escorts that helped Gov. Claiborne F. Jackson of Missouri move the official seal and many of the official records to a house which still stands at the southwest corner of E. Crockett and S. Bolivar. The governor took up his residence across the street east and made it the official governor's mansion." [139]

Prior to the Civil War, San Antonio was the headquarters of the U.S. troops in Texas where KGC members and secessionists stormed their fort in the bloodless takeover of San Antonio. The U.S. Troops handed over San Antonio which became the KGC's National Headquarters.

A plan to invade Mexico was on the KGC's agenda and approximately 1,000 Knights were willing to meet on the border in Brownsville to begin the invasion. A looming cloud hung over their heads as the threat of Civil War was nearing its opening stages within their own borders. The KGC changed their course and concentrated their fight to secede from the Union and sway the Southern governors to do the same. This new direction took them North where they would become agitators, starting fires, pro-secession rallies, and creating fear and uncertainty in the communities.

During this same time, Texas Rangers, whose many members were Knights, were coordinating an effort to cease U.S. Forts and take over D.C., preventing President Lincoln from taking office in 1861. The kidnapping of Abraham Lincoln was in the works. This never happened.

Members of the KGC began recruiting and forming units of the Confederacy and partisan rangers and raiders with many members, such as Quantrill Raiders. Pike's interest focused on using mighty warriors, who knew savage warfare tactics. He turned to the Indian nations in Indian Territory.

Albert Pike's good friend, Elias Rector had founded a new Indian agency called the Wichita Agency, established near Pond Creek and was the contact point for the Wichita and Kichai Indians. Pike had been named commissioner of Indian Affairs for the Confederacy and was appointed as Confederate envoy to the Native Americans.

Pike and Rector worked to negotiate treaties on behalf of the Confederacy with the Cherokee but was dropped due to the intensity of the war. It is unknown if Pike was involved in a scheme of embezzlement, but after the war, a report from the Federal government raised an issue involving Rector and the misappropriations of Bureau of Indian Affair funds. Rector may have used his influence in the prewar days to secure funds from the Indian Bureau that may have been shared among fellow Confederates.

An investigation into the accusations prompted Union forces to overtake Rector's home in Arkansas.

Rector's obituary was written by Albert Pike in the Daily Arkansas Gazette, Dec 4, 1878. He was the subject of Albert Pike's poem, "The Fine Arkansas Gentleman, Close to the Choctaw Line."

By November 1861, Albert Pike was commissioned as a brigadier general in the Confederate States Army and given command in Indian Territory. He trained three regiments of Indian Cavalry and negotiated an alliance with Cherokee Chief Stand Watie.

Pike put forth an effort to help Watie become a 32nd degree Scottish Rite Mason. Watie also became a member of the KGC and was commissioned to become a colonel in command of the First Regiment of Cherokee Mounted Rifles. He later would become a brigadier general in the Confederate States Army. Watie commanded units who served under Confederate officers Albert Pike, Benjamin McCulloch, Thomas Hindman, and Sterling Price. Price was the commander who ordered an artillery bombardment upon the Taos Pueblos during the Taos Revolt in 1847, leading U.S. troops along with Missouri volunteers.

The named Confederate officers led battles orchestrated in Indian Territory, Kansas, Arkansas, Texas, and Missouri. Pike utilized the high spirited Native American forces of Cherokee, Choctaw, Chickasaw, Creek, and Seminole to fight against the North, but during the Battle of Pea Ridge in 1862, the use of savage warfare would come back to bite him. The brutal tactics of the five tribes, including vicious mutilations and carving scalps off the Union soldiers, only led to severe criticism, allegations of treason and insubordination, forcing Pike's resignation. His property was confiscated, and he was arrested, and later released. He hid out in New York, Canada, Mexico, and Indian Territory until he was pardoned by his fellow Freemason, President Andrew Johnson after the war.

Tactical Warfare
The use of spies and secret societies in the Civil War

When I began researching the spy system and secret societies during the Civil War, I was generally surprised at the amount and the variety. Believe it or not, the "spy system" was very common during the war on both sides, as well as secret societies. It is documented in the book, "Notable Men of Tennessee," by Oliver Perry Temple, that Connally Trigg was a member of a secret committee with Temple after the Greenville Convention. Trigg used his influence through his committee to restrain Union men against violence towards the Confederates or resistance to their authority when they occupied Eastern Tennessee. Temple states that Trigg was able to suppress and prevent the outbreak of violence from Union men in a certain East Tennessee county. So not only were "secret" organizations emitting violence, such as we are familiar with, but many were also promoting non-violence as well.

For the most part, the secret societies were formed to encourage, support, strengthen, uphold order in chaotic conditions, promote and persuade others to follow their Northern or Southern ideology, to aid in their fight for the cause they believed in, and to create chaos for the enemy.

At the beginning of the war, some men with a fervent belief in the Union were forced to join the Confederacy by threats of killing their family or destroying their property. This was the same tactic used against those who were forced to join the Union, such as what Charles Hart (Quantrill) had experienced.

Those recruits, by forced enlistment, were not "in the fight," placing an awkward position for the units they served and proving to be a thorn in their unit's side. It would leave an open invitation to allow information to be leaked. The commanders on each side began using the leaks and information to their advantage.

The Union Army, who were on the battlegrounds, planning their next strategy, hired a network of spies, scouts, and guides who could provide intelligence on the enemy's movements, strengths, operations, and locations. They would hire both male and female, operating under the Union Provost Marshal. These men and women were required to venture in rebel-controlled areas at the very risk of their lives. They would also collect information from deserters or escaped slaves.

It was a massive network of spies. There were numerous stories of "double spies;" those who would relay information to both sides for a sizable sum.

Of course, the Confederacy had their secrets too and a certain backwood's style of spying. Bloody Bill Anderson's sisters were considered spies and one of Jesse's favorite spies was a young girl by the name of Myra Maybelle Shirley, later known as Belle Starr. Belle's father was a judge, Judge John Shirley who operated a tavern near Carthage, Missouri. The family welcomed Quantrill and his men and supported their cause.

Belle was very young when the war began, age 13, but felt very drawn into helping the south. She delivered bullets and messages in and out of Quantrill's camp, using a special bird call to allow her entry. Jesse told Ola that Belle never raised any suspicions amongst the Yankees. She was young, pretty, and innocent looking.

In their spy ring, they encountered Wild Bill Hickock who was a spy for the other side. They shared their camp several times but went their own way. I believe this is how Jesse knew so much about Wild Bill Hickock and his loyalty to the Union.

The KGC planted men in the Union Army, including officers of high rank to spy and plant seeds of ill will. They were given special insignias to wear to identify themselves to the brotherhood. One of these would be a five-point copper star pin worn on the left lapel. They also used forms of hand signals and other means to protect them in battle from the Rebel's bullet.

The secret societies became so much more powerful and successful than the spy system, but both worked hand in hand. The small clubs or societies began to develop within communities. The comradery was tight. It grew due to the active flame that was continuously fueled by propaganda and distrust of the enemy. Many towns and counties were split in their beliefs, which caused terrific strife between their citizens.

The enemy was not a foreign country whose warfare techniques or strategies were unfamiliar. Their enemy was their fellow American, their neighbor, their brother. The enemy knew you, knew where you lived, usually knew what you stood for, and knew your style of warfare. There had to be secrets for offensive and defensive maneuvers and for the protection of the family.

Men and women who never voiced their position, led many to become suspicious, creating fear that their neighbors were spies. Even though soldiers may have been wearing the blue uniform or vice versa, there was still some degree of caution regarding the true sentiment they were carrying.

It has been documented in books, that CSA soldiers stole Union uniforms to confuse the enemy. Jesse James himself speaks of doing this.

It is astounding to learn how intricate the web of secret networks merged and spread across the country during the Civil War causing the bloodiest and most catastrophic disaster in American History.

The Weapons of the Knights

Pike was heavily involved in stirring the flame during the war and the secret societies and spy rings evolved within themselves, expanding into others. It was all in the plan.

The organization of the Knights of the Golden Circle, which name would be changed several times to the "Order of American Knights" and "Sons of Liberty" was encamped in the North and the South.

Infiltration of spies began expanding into the organization, deeply embedded in the KGC who had various disguises, working their way into a number of lodges to learn of their secrets and plans. ("Spies Within;" In the Journal and Gazette, by Col. A.E. Redstone.)

On the other hand, infiltration of the Knights expanded into public offices, every known profession, behind enemy lines, and deep into the bowels of foreign affairs.

The Southerner's View

In the Daily National Democrat, Feb. 13, 1861 in Marysville, California, the paper stated that the KGC "were going to establish a Southern Republic, composed of Senora, *Chihuahua*, Lower California, Arizona, Mexico, New Mexico, Kansas, Missouri, Louisiana, a portion of Georgia, a portion of Alabama, and South Carolina, Mississippi, and Texas. The society has been in operation since 1855. The main reason why they formed was the election of a Republican President, just cause for the dissolution of the Union." [140]

Out of the La Grange *True Issue* (La Grange, Texas), it spoke of the KGC's members as being "the most respectable and enterprising citizens of that county." It was growing in leaps and bounds, fueling division and power amongst the citizens of this country. The newspapers were utilized to communicate between members in codes, numerology, and propaganda. David C. Jones, a surgeon in the 2nd regiment of the KGC wrote in the "Telegraph" that The KGC organization is composed of some of the most respectable and influential men of the South, and it is as true to Southern principles as the "needle to the Pole".

R.H. Williams in San Antonio who served in the Southern Committee of Safety, involved in the takeover of San Antonio with Texas Ranger Ben McCulloch in the lead, and a member of the K.G.C. stated in his book, "With the Border Ruffians: Memories of the Far West, 1852-1868", by R. H. Williams, that he was well-known, "**as sound on the goose**", meaning a good Southern man. As we read later, **"goose"** was a key word used in this time period and used quite frequently in the K.G.C.

These men were respectable and highly thought of in the South.

The Randolph Citizen – Huntsville, Missouri; April 20, 1860. Before the war started, they were in the news. "The current reports allege that the Knights of the Golden Circle number forty thousand men, scattered through the Southern States, who are well drilled and capable of furnishing, at a short notice, an army twenty thousand strong. From the outset, their contemplated field of operations is alleged to have been Mexico, where they propose to cooperate with the Juarez Government, obtain a complete triumph over Miramon, and then, as far as possible, Americanize the country, and make it an outlet for slavery, by preparing it for the establishment of that institution. The alleged design is to acquire a foothold in Mexico, and to give to it policy a proslavery cast, without any aid from our government, and, indeed, in despite of it, on the theory that it is necessarily, as a present constituted, hostile to the extension of slavery." [141]

"One regiment has been sent from this State, and others will follow soon; yet when Mr. Lincoln sends his Butler to arm our slaves, burn our dwellings, murder our wives and children, and lay waste and devastate our country, the "Knights of the Golden Circle", not of Kentucky alone, but of every Southern State, will meet him and his followers face to face, and test by the sword the justice of the cause we uphold. George Bickley, K.G.C., President American Legion (*Daily Missouri Republican* – June 4, 1861). [142]

In *The Wyandot Pioneer* in Upper Sandusky, Ohio, August 23, 1861 – Chronicling America: Historic American Newspaper, Lib. Of Congress: "The Disunionists bear the same relation. The Association is upheld and applauded as patriotic and noble, by the whole disunion press everywhere. The success with which the Knights of the Golden Circle have kept the secret of their order has been a matter of wonder to many. The Chief of the Order has pretended to publish all the written portion of the Ritual or Rituals, but we knew perfectly well that he was attempting fraud upon the community. Hundreds of members of the Order have sworn dreadful oaths that they would kill any one of their fellows who should dare to reveal, and any editor, or printer who should be guilty of publishing their mysteries. Probably the knowledge of these oaths has kept many persons silent who felt that they were under a solemn obligation to their fellowmen to speak what they knew.

"Three degrees 1st Military, 2nd Financial, 3rd Governmental. Ritual of 1st degree, it has a use of keys, a great many numerical figures being substituted for words.

"The first field of our operation is Mexico, but we hold it to be our duty to offer our services to any Southern State to repel a Northern Army. 'But whether the Union is reconstructed or not, the Southern States must foster any scheme for the Americanizing and Southernizing of Mexico so that in either case our success will be certain. Under the laws of Mexico every emigrant receives from the State authorities a grant of 640 acres of land. Under a treaty closed with Manuel Dodlado, Governor of Guanajuato on the 11th February 1859, we are invited to colonize in Mexico to enable the best people there to establish a permanent government. We agree to enter a force of 16,000 men armed and equipped, and provided, and to take the field under command of, who agrees to furnish an equal number of men to be officered by K.G.C." [143]

The Northern Perspective

In Stephen Towne's book, "Surveillance and Spies in the Civil War: Exposing Confederate Conspiracies in America's Heartland", 2014, he describes several incidents of spies or "traitors" (they were called), caught in the northern states. One story reveals a peddler who had come to a town in Ohio, who secretly was securing arms for the CSA and would hide them in his cart.

There was a man with his wife, posing as a photographer in northern Indiana. Local men became suspicious and began talking to them in a southern sympathetic tone. Believing that the men could be swayed to fight for the South, the photographer revealed to the men that he was there to recruit troops for the Southern Army. He was commissioned to organize the KGC in that area. The photographer revealed the organization was vast and was heavily concentrated in the South but spreading widely in the North.

The documents that Towne discovered show that the photographer revealed to the men the secret hieroglyphics they used for encoded messages that allowed easy passage of arms smuggled to the South. Needless to say, the governor was notified, and the couple was apprehended.

Not only was the KGC in the northern territory involved in smuggling arms, medical supplies, and recruiting for the South, but they recruited men to protect fellow "constitutional Democrats" and oppose the Lincoln administration. They were also promised that they would be protected from abolitionists who were making threats against the Democrats and to prevent volunteering or drafting.

Another tactic used by the KGC was dissention amongst the troops. Many Indiana, Illinois, and Ohio troops in the battlefields of Tennessee would receive letters daily denouncing the USA and encourage them to desert with an all-expense paid trip back to home.

Lincoln and the U.S. government knew very well what was going on. We find in the same article that published Bickley's letter earlier, the editor of the Daily Missouri Republican revealed "Startling Developments" describing a discovery of the Knights of the Golden Circle. "I find that the Union men are satisfied of the existence in Kentucky and in the States south of it, of a secret military organization, known as the Knights of the Golden Circle and that to this dangerous organization the otherwise inexplicable conspiracy against the Government may be traced such a military society, but which disclose its desperate objects and purposes." (*The Daily Missouri Republican of St. Louis*, June 4, 1861).

"Secret scouts" or "secret agents" were always in the crowd to wean out disloyal men, such as those in the KGC by intercepting mail, telegraph wires, and spying on citizens and newcomers in the area. Many were arrested and tried in court and court martialed for treasonous acts. When the cases came to court, many witnesses were intimidated by threats from the society, some refused to testify and others that did, died.

"There were men in high places who were KGC operatives, some were caught, some not. Judge and Congressman Hall in Frederick Court was charged with conspiring to overthrow the government of the United States. At the hearing, a witness A. H. Helper was asked about the KGC. His explanation helps us visualize the atmosphere at the beginning of the war and the tactics used by the KGC. This information was found in the newspaper, "Daily Ohio Statesman, Oct. 18. 1861". [144]

Helper was approached to join the KGC and stated the following during the hearing:
1. "The KGC was merely to strengthen the Democratic Party; It was organized by the Democrat Party to prevent volunteering and drafting; to keep down all mobs.
2. They had him sign a paper, a pledge, and an oath. He was required to pay a fee.
3. He was given signs and grips to identify members. Another identifying tactic was to ask the person in question if he was out last night. If the person said yes, then ask him what he saw. He should answer the North Star. The question would be asked "Which way was it traveling?" and he would reply "toward Bethlehem."
4. Another way to identify a brother in the society was to raise your hat three times with the right hand and the reply of the other party would be to raise his hat with his left hand."

In the Daily Missouri Republican, August 6, 1862:

"A recent act of Congress made it the duty of the Grand Jury to inquire into any combination or conspiracies formed by individuals within the jurisdiction of the Court to prevent the execution of any law of the United States. Having heard that organizations, with this object in view, existed in certain localities, witnesses were sent for, and brought before the grand Jury. These witnesses came from many counties and lived in various parts of the State. After a careful and diligent examination of the testimony from witnesses well acquainted with the facts deposed, and having a personal knowledge of the matters, said Grand Jury are constrained to say that a secret and oath bound organization exists, numbering some fifteen thousand in Indiana, as estimated by the members of the order, commonly known as Knights of the Golden Circle and even in the same localities by different names. One in particular that caught my eye was "They have signals by which they can communicate with each other in the day or the night time, and above all, they have a signal or sign which may be recognized at a great distance from the person giving it. This last signal, we regret to say, was invented for the use of such members as should, by means of the draft, or otherwise, be compelled to serve in the ranks of the army. In such case, members of the order serving in opposing armies, receiving the sign, are reminded of their obligation not to injure the member giving it. This signal is given in every instance upon the initiation of a new member, and its observance is strictly enjoined upon every individual belonging to the order. By the teachings of the organization, it is the duty of its members engaged in the present war, although arrayed on opposite sides, upon the signal being given, if they shoot at all, "to shoot over each other." The paper continued to state that when the organization originated it was to organize the friends of the institution of African slavery in the

United States, for the purpose of acquiring more territory in Mexico and the Central American State, and also for the acquisition of Cuba, thereby to extend and foster a great slave empire, even though it should dye those countries in human blood."

"The meeting of the Order referred to are holding in by places, sometimes in the woods, and at other times in deserted houses. Its members frequently attend with arms in their hands, and in a most every instance armed sentinel are posted to keep off intruders. **Youths not more than sixteen years of age are in many cases introduced and initiated into its mysteries.** The credulous and unwary are often allured into the fold of the Order upon the pretext that it was instituted for no other purpose than the better organization of their party. Its real character and teachings are sedulously concealed until the oath of secrecy has been in due form administered."

"Having taken the first degree, the initiate is familiarized with the obligations and opinions of his associates and is gradually prepared for the second degree. When he is further taught and found apt to learn, and ready to adopt its principles and teachings, he is obligated in the highest degree, and is turned out upon the country a thorough traitor, with the wicked purposes already specified. **Said Grand Jury are happy to know that in many cases individuals, after their first introduction into the Order, seeing its evil tendencies, have abandoned it, although unwilling, on account of their obligations of secrecy, and for fear of person violence are reluctant, to fully expose its treacherous principles.**

"For the purpose of evading any legal liability, in case of judicial investigation, it appears that their signs are to be used to enable them to get members of their order on the jury, in case of criminal charges being preferred against them, and by changes of venue, and appeals from a judge who does not belong to the order, to create judicial delays, until they can find a judge or juror belonging to this order, and thus escape all legal liability." [145]

There were indeed KGC members throughout the North and South Judicial arena. There was a member in every aspect of public office, churches, schools, military, and professions who would always come to the aid of his brother.

In the newspaper, *The St. Joseph Herald*, Jan. 15, 1863, an article titled "Genesis Chapter 1st", mocking the Bible reading of the creation by placing the lead players in the Confederacy within the text and proclaiming there were seven curses due to the creation of the Confederacy. In one part, the writer describes the KGC. "And Jeff (Jefferson Davis) said, let there be rich men in the system, to divide the people of the North, and let them be to fill vacancies in office, and the Congressmen in the United States, and let them be for Knights of the Golden Circle, and for editors of Democratic newspapers. And let them divide the people of the North and support the people of the South. And it was so. And Jeff made two creeping things, the **greater to rule England** and **lesser to rule France**, and he made Knights of the Golden Circle also. And Jeff sent these creeping things to Europe to represent the Confederate States. And to rule over England and to rule over France, and to divide them from the North, and Jeff thought it was good. And the negro and the Knights of the Golden Circle were the fourth curse." [146]

This write up has so many hidden meanings within its words. There was so much going on that the human mind could not comprehend, lots of "looky theres," but the reader will understand what all this means as they accumulate the clues Jesse has laid out for us.

George Bickley was carefully watched and followed. In July 1863, Bickley was arrested in New Albany, Indiana for being a Confederate spy and committed to the Louisville military prison. (*Alexandria Gazette*, July 24, 1863; Chronicling America: Historic American Newspapers, Lib. Of Congress).

This same month, Missouri was still sympathetic to the Southern cause. Jesse had pledged his service and had been in Quantrill Raiders for four months at the age of fifteen. He had seen the abuse of his family, the abuse of the South, and had witnessed the grief and pain of Bloody Bill

Anderson when he received the news of his sisters being rounded up and taken to a makeshift jail, suspected of providing aid and support to the Confederate guerillas.

The next month, August 1863, the tragedy of the collapsed ceiling and walls that killed one of Anderson's sisters and maimed the other two, had embittered Anderson and all his followers. There was blood in their eyes. Eight days later, the Quantrill Raiders responded with vengeance in Lawrence, Kansas in the Lawrence Massacre.

Jesse's young eyes, his hands, his body, and his spirit encountered some of the most gruesome types of warfare that would forever be branded into his mind. He was no longer a boy, but a man with blood on his hands. War indeed was Hell.

It was probably close to the time of these horrific events in the summer of 1863, that Jesse pledged his allegiance to not only Quantrill, Bloody Bill, and the Quantrill Raiders, but also to the Knights of the Golden Circle.

Many horrific battles incurred thereafter. The Raider's presence and type of warfare was encouraged to become involved in launching an invasion into northern Missouri, Arkansas, and Kansas, known as Price's Missouri Raid. General Sterling Price, the man heavily involved in the Taos Revolt, past governor of Missouri, and one of the generals who worked closely with Albert Pike, was commander of this invasion. In the Crittenden Memoirs, Jessie wrote that Jim Younger, Cole's brother was a scout for General Price from 1863-1865. The goal was to recapture all of Missouri from the Union's hands and renew the Confederate initiative in the larger conflict. One of his divisions was led by General Joseph O. "Jo" Shelby.

The Fall of 1864 was heavily saturated with more blood during this Missouri expedition, taking its toll on the guerillas. Bloody Bill's company became involved and was assigned to interrupt railroads. Many of the guerillas put on the Union uniform and swarmed the train passing through Centralia and supposedly brutally massacred Union men on leave, heading home. The Battle of Centralia followed as the newly formed 39th Missouri Infantry Regiment rode into Centralia and encountered the guerillas. The Union lost 147 soldiers that day.

Bud obtained a great map outlining the Confederate Guerrilla Theatre of War by P.B. Larimore. Shown below.

The many battles incurred during Price's Raid were failures. He left Missouri and Arkansas and went to Indian Territory and Texas. An unintended consequence was that the raids depleted the known Confederate guerrillas. The remnants went to Sherman, Texas to winter and regroup.

Price did not surrender at the end of war but went to Mexico with other Confederates who were interested in starting a colony of Southerners. He settled in Carlota, Veracruz where he sought service with Emperor Maximillan unsuccessfully. He ended back in Missouri.

Assassinations were planned, including one to murder Governor Oliver P. Morton of Indiana who had close ties to President Lincoln. In 1865, when the victor became all too obvious in this savage war, more and more assassinations were planned, including Lincoln, Vice President Andrew Johnson, Secretary of State William Seward, and Lt. General Ulysses S. Grant. These plans were pinned on the K.G.C.

John Wilkes Booth, along with many others were supposedly a part of the Northern units of the Knights of the Golden Circle. He was thought of as a spy for the Confederacy and met at least once with the Confederate secret service which held their meetings in Montreal, Canada. The British colonies included Canada.

Ironically, John Wilkes Booth and his friend, John Sarratt were Catholic which went against the grain of the Freemason's and KGC's philosophy but was that another falsehood fed to the masses? Jay Longley believes so, as well as the idea that Freemasons and the KGC were also anti-Black. We find plenty of evidence that this was not the case, even though Albert Pike claimed to be anti-Catholic and anti-Black.

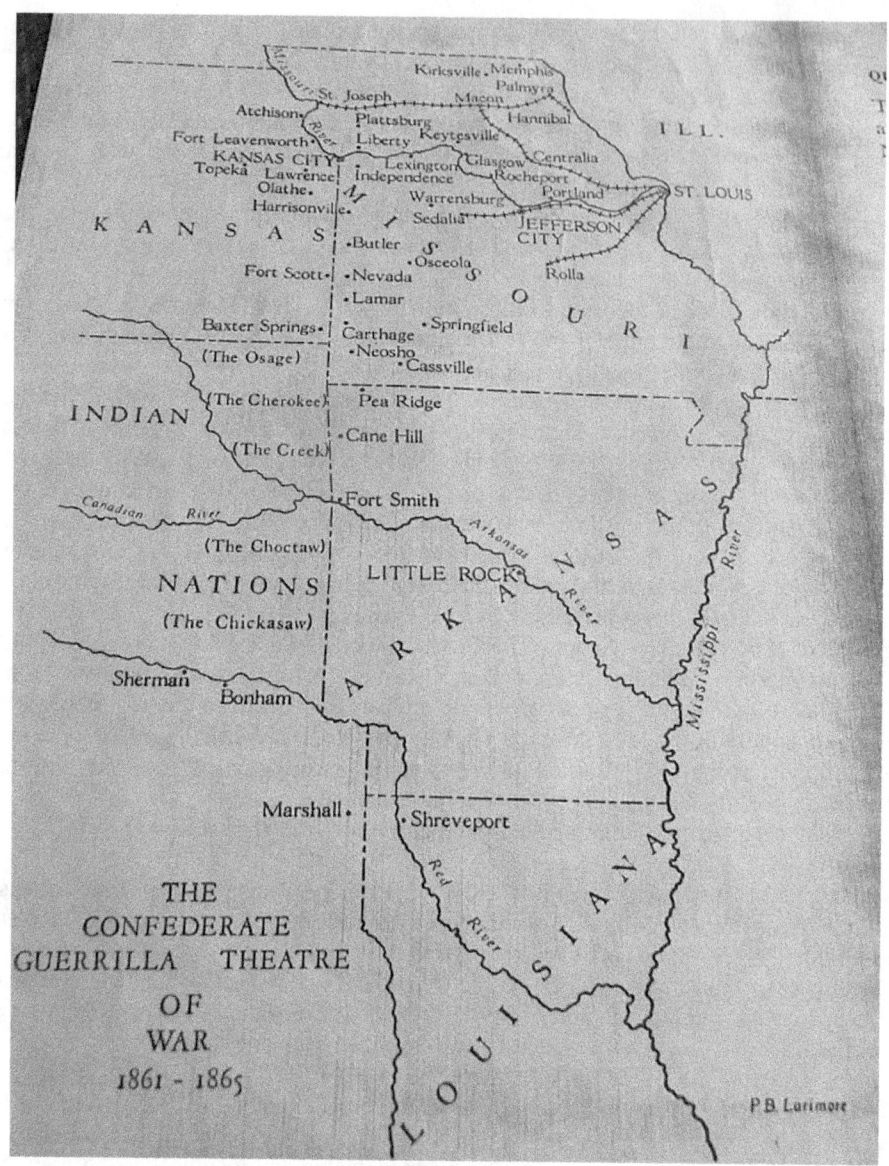

(Confederate Guerrilla Theatre of War by P.B. Larimore)

Was John Wilkes Booth planning from the very beginning to assassinate President Lincoln? We do know the original plan of the KGC was only to kidnap Lincoln and not kill him, but did Booth change the plans at the last minute?

Jefferson Davis and Judah Benjamin were accused of having plotted the assassination of Lincoln, but the biggest blame was aimed at the Knights of the Golden Circle. Follow the money. As Lincoln was dying, Judah, the Chief of Intelligence for the Confederacy, was burning the official papers of the Confederate Secret Service and fled to England.

Some believe that the Knights of the Golden Circle had plans from decades before to place a man, a pawn, in the Whitehouse in who they could manipulate and appear to be strongly against slavery, drawing the South further from the North and the North closer to their candidate. They further believe that the Pope of Rome took advantage of the Civil War, keeping the citizens and leaders of America focused on the war efforts while the Roman Catholic Empire set up a platform in Mexico. They sent Maxmillian, a Roman Catholic, under the protection of a French army to usurp dominion and take possession of the country. We definitely see an attachment to Maximillian by the K.G.C. members. This is also another example that the K.G.C. were not anti-Catholic.

The Roman Catholic Church seemed to be pulled into the circle. There are many references to support the connection to the Roman Empire. The Knights of the Golden Circle's symbols, as well as the Knights Templar include a Crown and Cross, representing a merger of government and religion.

The K.G.C. maintained a symbol of a triangle with a large R in the middle with the number 61 below it. This represented the Southern Revolution in the year 1861. There are also three numbers on each corner of the triangle, 3, 5, and 7, adding up to 15 states of the Confederacy. Those numbers also are used in Freemasonry, the number 3 -meaning rule, number 5-meaning law, and number 7- perfection.

There were several branches within the K.G.C. society: military, financial, and political. Jesse James's main duty as a K.G.C. member was in the financial branch, becoming the comptroller, but he was also involved in the military and political branches.

After the war, Freemasonry, the K.G.C. and many other secret societies were freed up to multiply and expand on corruption. The original 13th amendment was replaced with the new 13th amendment to abolish slavery in which was one of the greatest amendments of all times. With the new amendment in place, it quietly covered and terminated the "Title of Nobility" which restricted government officials from receiving gifts, offices, or titles from foreign states without Congress' consent. Those who participated in these acts would be convicted of treason. With the original 13th amendment hidden, it freed up the acceleration of corruption in the United States.

After the war, Pike was run out of his home because of threats of robbery, murder and other assaults to be inflicted upon him and his family at his country home in Arkansas. He was accused of dipping in the KGC money to live comfortably. People were coming to kill him. He was forewarned. He dug up his money and gold that he had buried, some that was buried under the front doorstep, Bud said.

Pike fled to the Creek Nation near Clearview, Oklahoma where the Creeks protected him. Bud has found near Pike's home, a hoot owl tree pointing to his house. He has also found many symbols and carvings on rock cliffs and trees near his home. There must have been very valuable caches and depositories near his home in Arkansas and Oklahoma. Jay Longley stated that Albert Pike master minded the placement of the KGC depositories throughout the country.

Albert Pike became a recluse and later moved to Washington D.C. and continued working for the Scottish Rite of Freemasonry in Washington D.C. In 1871, he published the book called Morals and Dogma of the Ancient and Accepted Scottish Rite of Freemasonry. That same year, he wrote a letter to an Italian politician, Giuseppe Mazzini, who supposedly was a member of the Illuminati, highlighting things that he is predicting, all having to do with three World Wars. He predicted World War III which will be against Islamic leaders, Christianity would be destroyed, and a one-world government established. That was his ultimate goal, more in the line of the Illuminati. Chilling.

Let me be very clear, as far as all of Bud's research and mine, and many, many others, this was not the goal of the Knights of the Golden Circle. Their goal was always for the betterment of their Southland and continued fighting for it. I believe Jesse began separating himself from Pike's radical philosophy.

Perhaps what Pike's goal in the development of the KGC and the real meaning of the Golden Circle had to be the obtainment of gold and the protection of it. Strangely, I was led to www.symbols.com/symbol/gold. "One of the main goals of the alchemists was to produce gold from other substances, such as lead, presumably by the interaction with a mythical substance called the philosopher's stone. Although they never succeeded in this attempt, the alchemists promoted an interest in what can be done with substances, and this laid a foundation for today's chemistry. Their symbol for gold was the circle with a point at its center, which was also the **astrological symbol** and the ancient Chinese character for the **Sun**." [147]

Pike died in 1891 and is buried inside the walls at the House of Temple, headquarters of the Southern Jurisdiction of the Scottish Rite. A memorial and statue of Pike was erected in 1901 in Washington D.C. The statue of Pike was pulled down and desecrated in 2020 by protestors whose sentiment was against the Confederacy and racism.

"For Israel and Judah have not been forsaken by their God, the Lord Almighty, though their land is full of guilt before the Holy One of Israel. Flee from Babylon! Run for your lives! Do not be destroyed because of her sins. It is time for the Lord's vengeance; he will repay her what she deserves. Babylon was a gold cup in the Lord's hand; she made the whole earth drunk. The nations drank her wine; therefore, they have now gone mad. Babylon will suddenly fall and be broken. Wail over her! Get balm for her pain; perhaps she can be healed." Jeremiah 51: 5-8.

"Truth is generally the best vindication against slander."

-*Abraham Lincoln*

Chapter Ten: Was JJ an Outlaw or Vindicator for his Beloved Southland

Bud said after the war, Jesse was very busy and became the comptroller or paymaster for the KGC. He was in charge of all the money and gold. He was one of the "top dogs" of the Knights. He was deeply involved in this clandestine organization more so than in a career of "outlawism." Both professions became one in the same. Jesse told Ola that he was an outlaw for 19 years, 1866-1885.

Many people believe Jesse and Frank were drawn into outlawry because of the sentiment against them after the war, especially since the guerillas were not recognized as legitimate Confederate soldiers, but very vicious animals. Many believe they had to make a living somehow, so they turned to outlawry.

In the Crittenden Memoirs, Dalto, aka Jesse, wrote that Quantrill Raiders disbanded in Louisiana after the war. He explains that General Jo Shelby went through their camp on their way to Mexico to fight alongside Maximillian. Cole and "John" Younger went, he stated. They fought in a few skirmishes and came back along the Sabine River and crossed the ferry where trouble was brewing. We do learn during one trip out of Mexico, Jesse and the group were escaping. They crossed over the Sabine River near St. Clair, Texas. It's no longer in existence, but in its location, *Clarksville* City was developed during the oil boom of the early 1930's. The town is just east of Gladewater. This area was Jesse's territory both then and into the 1930's and 1940's.

John Edwards went to Mexico with Shelby, as well as General Sterling Price. Edwards spent two years fighting for Maximillian's cause in which we will discuss in a later chapter. They established a colony in Vera Cruz and named it Carlotta after Maximillian's wife. Edwards and ex-Governor Allen of Louisiana printed the Carlotta Colony newspaper there, "The Mexican Times" and later Edwards would write his very first book, "An Unwritten Leaf of the War." But that's not the end of the story in Mexico as Jesse wanted us to believe.

Jesse was recovering from multiple injuries, with the last one being shot in the lung when he tried to surrender in the Spring of 1865 in Lexington. Throughout that summer he was transported to various places to recover. His family was in Nebraska since the first of that year. Per pbs.org, they were forced by Union forces to flee their home and were banished to Rulo, Nebraska. That's approximately 46 miles to the northwest of St. Joseph, Missouri, right on the border. It is said that Jesse traveled up the Missouri River on a steamboat to Rulo to recuperate from his wounds.

Dalton told Ola that he was injured in Nebraska in August 1865, was carried on a stretcher from a Missouri River steamboat to John Mims north of Kansas City. It would be in October when he was able to travel further to his home in Kearney.

Zerelda and her family returned to Missouri in October as well. Nebraska would become an important part of Jesse's life. It was 10 years later that Jesse was in Nebraska City having his famous portrait taken, but it was just 4 short years later that he would meet his first love in Nebraska.

(Jesse James in Nebraska City (1875))

What transpired after his war days were over? They weren't over. He had a lot of work to do. Jesse always said he could be anywhere in the country in 18 hours out of St. Louis. He covered a lot of ground and was an extremely fanatical patriot for the South.

Jesse stated that Quantrill did not die in a Louisville, Kentucky hospital. He was carried out in a coffin, presumed dead, and made his escape before burial. Quantrill was said to have stayed in Arkansas and "ran things." Remember, he was very high up in the KGC, one of the original leaders while Jesse appears to have been the front man, who took a lot of heat, a lot of bullets, and a lot of blame.

Dalton (Jesse) wrote, "We of Quantrill's militia have ever been a secretive bunch, and would tell nothing, so the writers of tales about us have had very little to go on in the way of facts, so they had to fall back on their imagination, but as that was usually in good working order they didn't need facts. Facts are sometimes bothersome things anyway in the making of a good story, so why use them? Or at least, such seemed to be the case with our biographers."[148]

Dr. William Tunstill stated that all the Quantrill men took an oath to protect one another and their families. He found 175 Quantrill men who spread out in Texas and Oklahoma. "They stuck together," said Ola. If anyone actually killed Jesse or caused him harm, one of the Quantrill men would of taken care of the killer. Same goes for Billy the Kid, whose father was a Quantrill man.

In one letter Bud has obtained, written by Mary Plina James' husband, Charles Norris, he explains there were two Jesses and two Franks, but the one who was the comptroller for the KGC was Jesse Woodson James. Jesse also played multiple roles and went under several different names and characters. Mary Plina James was the only daughter of Frank James. She was at Jesse's 102nd birthday at Meramec Caverns.

Bud believes that to be able to pull off what they did, they had to use doubles and hit multiple locations to confuse the enemy. Many movies depicted Jesse with a mission to destroy the railroads for what they did to the southern people, taking away their land. Ola stated that Jesse made clear to her that it was not just the railroads. The main goal of the members of the KGC was to hit the banks, railroads, stagecoaches, and businesses that were directly related to the Union, the North. Jesse and the men under him were gathering money, gold, and other valuables to finance a second Civil War against the North and expand the southern area of America, Central America, and South America into one Nation.

The majority of the KGC members followed the plan exactly, such as Jesse did, never taking anything for himself, except for expenses, but greed and cowardness settled amongst a few. They didn't live long.

In the year 1866 Dalton told Ola the bank robbing started. He said he had held up his first train at Clue Cut, east of Independence in 1863 during the war, so he was accustomed to that type of activity. He learned at a very young age. He never admitted to the robbery in Liberty in which many believe the Youngers were involved as well, along with Jim Reed. Jim was a captain under Quantrill. This man "Jim Reed" shows up quite a bit.

The train robberies were unique. Jesse told Ola that the Pinkertons and railroad men sent decoy trains to trick the outlaws, but Jesse outsmarted them. Jesse had learned the morse code while he was with Quantrill's Raiders and the KGC. Jesse would climb up a telegraph pole and would tap in with a telegraph transmitter device to learn which train was carrying the loot or gold shipments and which ones were the decoys. This was their information highway. This technique served them well during the outlaw days, receiving and transmitting messages themselves to fool their opponents. Jesse didn't miss a beat.

Jesse was known to be one who would go into a town and observe the layout, the lawmen, the banks, the citizens and the best road out. He also would return to the towns who were recently victimized with a robbery or the train station up ahead after a robbery. He observed the action of lawmen and posses to determine their actions and directions in locating the bandits. No one recognized Jesse, they didn't know what he looked like. Several times he was asked to join the posse, but he would reply that he was very timid and didn't feel adequate.

As an outlaw, Jesse said he was charged with 40 counts, ranging from stage to train robbery in places such as Minnesota, Arkansas, Missouri, Kansas, Kentucky and Iowa. He was tried seven times but beat the charges every time. He may have had KGC men on the bench.

Jesse says in the newspaper article in *The Kilgore Daily News*, October 13, 1939, "Were we guilty?" Dalton asks himself, anticipating your question. "If I said we were you'd say I was boasting and if I said we were not you'd call me a liar. So, I guess I had better keep my mouth shut and say nothing, just let you form your own opinion; which you'll do anyway. I'll say this though, Cole Younger and Frank James turned out to be good law-abiding citizens when given the opportunity and me, I was a peace officer in Texas and Indian Territory for many, many years." [149]

Jesse also says in article in an Austin newspaper, "There never was a James gang," the old man said as he lay in bed in his hotel room years later in the late 40's and 50's. "Ain't a farmer in the country in those days that wouldn't try to make a little more money if he got the chance. And that was the James gang."

"Let me tell you," he pointed with his left index finger, a finger with the tip end shot off. "I'd usually may have two or three experience men with me. But as the usual thing, I'd go around to farmers before the robbery and I told 'em: "If you want to go out and get a little piece of money I don't know, $50, $70, $100 you come with me and I'll take you and we'll get it. Didn't tell 'em what we were going to do. And we went." [150]

Jesse used many disguises, but he used one very cleverly, dressed as an old man with a hearing problem. He carried with him an ear trumpet, a funnel-shaped device such as a brass trumpet, held to the ear which collected sound waves, funneling them into the ear. He said he tried this one time with a disguise when interacting with Jay Gould, "a railroad magnate and financial speculator who was called one of the robber barons of the Gilded Age."[151] Gould was getting frustrated talking to him because the old man couldn't hear too well. Gould had no clue who he was talking to, neither did Allan Pinkerton when he was confronted in the bathroom at a gathering with Jesse, unbeknownst to Pinkerton. Jesse had the perfect opportunity to kill him. That would have never happened. Some believe they were brothers in the brotherhood.

The holdups continued by the gang at the rate of two or three a year. Bank holdups began with Liberty in 1866 where they got $70,000. Later, in October 30, 1866, Jesse and his gang were accused of hitting Alexander Mitchell Bank in Lexington, Missouri. On May 22, 1867 they supposedly hit the Hughes & Wasson Bank in Richmond, Missouri and Savannah, Missouri in 1867. On March 20, 1868 they hit the Bank of Russellville in Kentucky. When they were accused of hitting the Daviess County Savings Bank in Gallatin, Missouri on December 7, 1869 things became a little more serious. A cashier was killed.

Jesse claimed he was not there in Gallatin, but that he was there in Corydon Iowa and Columbia, Kentucky when a cashier was shot. He was very careful associating himself with the robberies where someone was killed.

Newspaper clipping in Bud's collection, *Gallatin Democrat* – "The Sheets Murderers," "$3,000 Reward: Is offered for the apprehension and delivery of the murderers of John W. Sheets, Cashier of the Daviess County Savings Association, to the Sheriff of Daviess County, Missouri believed to be Jesse and Frank James, of Clay County, Missouri, and described as follows: Jesse – About 6 feet in height, rather slender built, thin visage, hair and complexion rather light and sandy. Frank- About 5 feet 8 or 10 inches in height, heavy built, full in the face, hair and complexion same as Jesse." [152]

In a newspaper article in Corpus Christi Times, June 30, 1939, Frank Dalton's interviewer stated that Frank Dalton weighs 182 lbs. and 5'10 1/2" inches. [153]

"Who Was Murder Victim Capt. John Sheets and Why was he Shot?" (daviesscountyhistoricalsociety.com) says JJ mistook him for former Union leader Samuel Cox during the 1869 robbery of the Daviess County Savings Association in Gallatin.

In 1869, back in Missouri writing for newspapers, Edwards met with Jesse and Frank who were accused of the robbery of the Daviess County Saving Association in Gallatin, Missouri. It was the first time that Missouri introduced Frank and Jesse James as outlaws, but John Newman Edwards, editor of the Kansas City Times, contradicted the stories that placed Frank and Jesse as the guilty parties. He had gathered and printed signed affidavits of neighbors, friends, and family who swore that the two boys were at their home in Kearney on that date. He printed Jesse's letter to the governor of Missouri denying that they had anything to do with the crime.

But there is a larger story hidden. In the Lexington Weekly Intelligencer, August 25, 1883 when Frank James was being tried in Gallatin for the murder of Sheets, "the general opinion here seems to be that Capt. Sheets was killed by Jim Anderson and Jesse James. After the killing of Bloody Bill Anderson by Major Cox, of Gallatin, Jim Anderson, brother of the deceased, wrote to Major Cox, stating that he understood that he had the pistols taken from the dead body of his brother, and enclosing a check for $50 for the same, concluding the letter with the ominous statement, "If you don't send the pistols, by God, I'll come and get 'em." Cox who is a man of nerve, replied, "Damn you, come on." Jim Anderson on the receipt of Cox's letter hunted up his friend, Jesse James, and the two entered into a solemn compact to slay the man who had killed Jim's brother and refused to give up the revolvers." [154]

The story continues stating that Jim looked Jesse up and they both went to Gallatin and mistook the cashier Sheets for Cox. Captain Sheets served under Cox in the Union side during the Civil War. It was Major Samuel Cox who was the commander in charge of the Union ambush with John Sheets within the troops who ambushed Bloody Bill Anderson and killed him.

A detective for the bank had positive proof that the horse that got away after the bank robbery belonged to Jesse James. With a Police Gazette reporter, Jesse stated that he was not there. He would have still been in the Sioux Nation and in fact, the Quantrill men knew that Cox didn't kill Quantrill. He was still alive and well.

In another news article, titled, "A Double Crime", it states that the robbers sole objection was to only rob the bank, not kill anyone and as they were getting away, they conversed with people between Gallatin and Kidder and one of them introduced himself as Bill Anderson's brother.

In a Find a Grave for Bloody Bill Anderson's brother, Lieut. James Monroe "Jim" Anderson (1842-1871), we learn of his fate. Dave Pool, a former partisan ranger was working for the U.S. Army after the war, rounding up all the partisans, requiring their surrender or die. Jim Anderson was caught by Pool's brother, William Pool in Austin. Anderson's throat was cut on the Texas Capitol grounds.

Viewing the photo from Find a Grave on James Monroe Anderson, he could fit the description made of Frank James.

Frank James was tried and acquitted for the murder charge of Sheets. The defense rested on the possibility that the murderers were Jesse James and James Monroe "Jim" Anderson, Bloody Bill's brother. Quite convenient for two dead men to take the blame.

In the Kansas City Times, Edwards portrayed the brothers as "symbols of ex-Confederates "striking back" against the excesses and oppression of Republican rule in Missouri." He wrote about Jesse and Frank and declared them as Robinhood characters and heroes rather than vicious bloodthirsty outlaws.

Edwards was highly involved in the KGC. He had an unexpected death of "natural causes" at age 50.

The Youngers

Family members of the Youngers write that the Younger boy's mother was devastated toward the end of the war. She gave a brief interview to a reporter years later when she returned to her old homestead in ruins. Bursheba Younger related the story that during the heat of the war, under the order General Ewing of the Union Army, she was forced to burn her own home, with all the contents inside and vacate the premises with her children.

Cole, Bob, John, and Jim Younger rode with Jesse and Frank.

Cole Younger stated and wrote in his book that he had never met Jesse until 1866 when they hit the Liberty Bank. He rode with Quantrill and Frank James, but never met Jesse until after the war. Bud gets a good laugh out of that. Cole, continues to distance himself from Jesse by stating that "they were not on good terms." Cole made a point of writing that his younger brother, John hadn't seen JJ for 18 months before John's death. Cole also emphasized that John had never met Arthur C. McCoy, who was a well-known James/Younger Gang member. It appears that Cole was protecting not only his buddies, but his family. Why was Cole emphasizing on Jesse and his younger brother John Younger?

There was nothing written in Cole Younger's book about Jesse and Frank being involved in Northfield. Bob Boze Bell reveals that Cole Younger said that this raid was planned by Bob Younger and Jesse. Cole and Jim went along with it to protect Bob.

There are a lot of misconceptions around Cole Younger and Jesse. Ola heard many stories from Jesse himself about him and Cole, especially the story about him, Frank, and Cole riding up to a farmhouse to let their horses rest and get watered. Jesse went to the door and asked the woman there if they could water horses. She said, "Sure, help yourself."

While they were taking care of their horses, Jesse heard the woman crying and he went back to the house and asked if they could help her. She confided in Jesse saying that her husband had died in the war and she had no money to pay the mortgage. The banker was coming that day to foreclose on the mortgage. Between the three of the men, they gathered all that they had and gave to the widow.

She was very grateful and didn't know how she would ever pay it back. They told her when she makes a crop. Jesse helped her write out a receipt to have the banker sign, indicating that she was paid in full. They left, the banker came and was paid, signing the receipt to that affect.

Jesse, Frank, and Cole were waiting down the road for the banker and sheriff in the buggy to pass. The gang stopped them, got their money and a little extra and sent them on their way. Jesse turns around and goes back to the farmhouse and gives the woman more money to plant a crop with.

"We never saw her again, but her and her children had a place to live and something to eat. We seen to that." [155]

Cole and John were in the KKK until 1867 when their days of riding with Jesse really became heated. It was founded in 1865 and per Jesse, the KKK was started by himself to protect southern people from carpetbaggers. Howk describes in the book, "Jesse James and the Lost Cause", "The KKK was the secret military police of the old South, directly under the domination and scrutiny of the Knights of the Golden Circle at all times." [156] It was also said that they started the KKK near Gladewater, Texas and enlisted and trained nearly 20,000 black men to police their own.

"Not many people in either the North or South knew that right after the end of the Civil War we recruited twenty-thousand Negro KKK members. They were the most intelligent and reliable blacks we could find. Our theory was that Negroes would take orders easier from other Negroes. They weren't burning crosses or flogging, they were giving counsel and even financial help to the freed, but bewildered slaves. They kept busy knocking stupid ideas out of Negro heads put there by unscrupulous Carpetbaggers." [157]

In https://knights-of-the-golden-circle.blogspot.com, a post dated November 28, 2012, author unknown, titled, "Negros in the Ku Klux Klan" compares the stories supposedly of what Jesse told Howk to other books and articles that back up the theory of what the KKK was originally designed for. In the 1920's book, "The Ku Klux Spirit," by J.A. Rogers, a Black historian, writes, "A fact not generally known is that there were thousands of Negro Klansmen. These were used as spies on other Negroes and on Northern Whites." [158]

The other source found in this blog brings light to why there was such a hatred for Radical Republicans, especially those like Benjamin Butler who had a lot to do with the Northfield Bank Robbery that Jesse James was involved in. The book was "Nathan Bedford Forrest: A Biography," by Jack Hurst. Forrest was supposedly the man who started the KKK, but he didn't join the organization until 1867 when Cole and John Younger left the group.

In the book, "The Klan was reorganized to oppose radical proponents (the Radical Republicans) of what it perceived to be Black domination, NOT to scourge Blacks themselves. Although it has been written that Ku Klux Klan ranks were open only to the more than 100,000 honorably discharged ex-Confederate veterans, the hierarchy in some areas and some instances seems to have accepted and even recruited Blacks, provided they went along with Conservative-Democratic political philosophy. In Memphis of late 1868, 65 Blacks organized a "Colored Democratic Club" under the watchful eye of Klansman-editor Gallaway, who according to an account in the Appeal, "made a motion on behalf of the White men present, that they give employment and protection to Colored democrats." [159]

So, is this another fallacy we've been fed?

Bud has a letter, written by Jesse, verifying the KKK's original purpose. Jesse wrote describing his poor Southland being looted and stolen, both by whites and blacks. Jesse described in the letter the KKK then is not what it is known today.

Jesse also stated in the news article in The Kilgore Daily News, October 13,1939, titled, "Ex-Member of Dalton Gang Talks of Wide Experiences Here, Frank Dalton One-time of Quantrill's Outfit, Tells of Long Past Outlaw Life;" - "We were the beginning of a Ku Klux Klan in the Sabine bottom," Dalton sighs, "But our Klan wasn't like that thing you hear about today. We did good with our order and there was a need for it."

There is a lot more evidence to support this. Sadly, this organization also turned into something it was not intended to be. Evil and corruption slipped in and destroyed what was intended for good. They became a terrorist group. So many horrific and evil things came out of this organization towards the Blacks and some religious sects. Unspeakable and vicious acts of evil.

Both Albert Pike and Nathan Bedford Forrest were named as starting the KKK, and Forrest was the first Grand Wizard of the clan in 1867. Maybe this is when things were changing in the organization and Cole, John, and possibly Jesse left the organization. We don't know, but something interesting occurred.

"In 1869, Forrest expressed disillusionment with the lack of discipline in the white supremacist terrorist group across the South, and issued a letter ordering the dissolution of the Ku Klux Klan as well as the destruction of its costumes; he then withdrew from the organization. In the last years of his life, Forrest denied being a Klan member and, disturbed by anti-Black violence, made statements in support of racial harmony and black dignity." [160]

In 1868, Jesse was baptized in Muddy Fork and joined the Kearney Baptist church. The next year he was taken off the church roll. He joined the U.S. Army on March 10, 1868. Jesse mentions that John Younger was serving in the army in the Black Hills since 1868, but their outlaw days were just beginning.

In "Short Stories" by Frank Dalton; he wrote that on March 17, 1874, John Younger was supposed to be killed by Pinkerton men near his home in Monegaw Springs, St. Clair County, Missouri. It was another boy who was with Cole and Jim Younger who was killed on their way back to Texas.

Dalton writes in Crittenden Memoirs, "John was for several years a peace officer under another name of course and has led an honest and respected life. Little do the people think or realize that the erect, clear-eyed old man who is seen so often on the streets of various Texas towns is the former noted John Younger of Quantrill's band of the Civil War days. He would have a hard time proving his identity, even should he wish to at this late day, as all the people who ever knew him as "John Younger" are long since dead and gone."

"The leading papers of that day and time came out with various comments on John Younger's death, among the milder being (after stating the manner of his killing which they had all wrong, of course), "He was a perfect type of the genuine border desperado, and despite his age was the leader and guiding spirit of as ruthless a band of outlaws as the country has ever known." Another account had this to say about it: "John Younger, noted leader of the James and Younger band of outlaws and bandits, is laid low in death by the gallant forces of Allan Pinkerton. Now that the leader is gone the rest of the outlaw pack will shortly follow."

Papers say he was only in his teens and was in Quantrill's Guerillas. "In the meantime, the "life history" of John Younger was to be printed. It had about as much truth in it as had the account and manner of his death. Even his age, as well as the place of his birth were wrong." [161]

We will learn more about what happened to John Younger in future chapters.

During their outlaw days, they went to Mexico and along the Rio Grande. In 1874, they held up the Kansas City Agricultural Fair for $10,000. This was over a horse Jesse was going to race and the judge disqualified him at the last minute. He vowed to get his prize money anyway. They participated in holdups at Gads Hill, Muncie, near Kansas City, Huntington, West Virginia where a posse supposedly wounded JJ; but they did not Jesse said. Later, Jesse confessed to the bank robbery in Huntington, West Virginia in September 1875, getting $20,000.

The big bank robbery in Northfield will be discussed in another chapter.

In October 8,1879, there was robbery of the Chicago and Alton train in Jackson County, Missouri. In 1881, the Rock Island and Pacific Railway at Winston, Missouri was robbed. Jesse said he wasn't there.

We learn more of personal stories from those who new Frank and Jesse regarding their guilt or innocence.

Robert Hoag who lived in Anadarko, Oklahoma, born 1915, stated in a news story in the Wichita Falls Times on Dec. 19, 1982, that he was the son of the last Chief of the Caddo Tribe. His cousin, Salo Parker (Silas Silo "Ko-it" Parker), (1854-1932) always told him that he knew Jesse and Frank James well. They would always come to his house, only from the North, with fairly new horses, a pack horse, sometimes two, and mail bags. The contents were never discussed or revealed.

They would trade horses, get something to eat. "Jesse would just sleep over against the far wall, but Frank would sleep behind the door so if anybody came in, they couldn't see him. If there was any kind of noise at night, a dog barking even, they both were up and had their guns ready." [162]

During the day, Frank and Jesse would hide out in a cave, embedded in a cliff, not far from there. It had two entrances: at the top, and a ground entrance. He went on to say that Salo told him that Frank and Jesse were blamed for a lot of crimes they never committed but admitted to several train and bank robberies.

Shortly after the death of Frank James in 1915, people began to speak out about their knowledge of Frank and Jesse. Wiley Wyatt (1856-1932) was living in Wichita Falls, Texas and was raised near Kansas City, Missouri. His father was Solomon Wyatt (1809-1900). Wiley actually witnessed the aftermath of the Blueridge Battle between the Quantrill Raiders and the Federal troops. He also recalled several times when Frank and Jesse would make frequent visits to his father's home.

"I recall that the Quantrill troops were the most expert marksmen I have ever seen. They would practice near our house sometimes, each on running his horse around a tree and firing a pistol in each hand. They were such perfect shots that the balls cut down the tree almost as smooth as if it had been sawed down."

"Another favorite game of the James boys was racing their horses at full tilt and shooting each other's hats off. You know how dangerous that sort of thing would be, yet they practiced that way often to keep from getting careless with their guns, they said." Mr. Wyatt said: "Frank James never forgot a favor and never failed to resent an insult. He was a gentleman always, and I have heard hundreds of people declare, both in and out of Missouri, that the James boys were more sinned against than sinning, even when they were classed as outlaws."

"Mr. Wyatt told an amusing story of how the James boys and Sam *Vaughn* now of Fort Worth, put to flight about 3,000 federal troops near his father's home during the civil war. The soldiers were passing by and the three men mentioned hid in the woods nearby and shot so rapidly that the soldiers thought a whole regiment was lying in wait for them and so they double-quicked out of range. A few days later Vaughan wrote the commander of the troops that he might bring his army back if he wished, as the three would not hurt the army anymore."

Former Sheriff Randolph of Wichita Falls stated that Frank was a man of honor and integrity. "He thought anyone would have done about as the James boys did if they had been confronted with problems that the James boys were." [163]

Many people also met Zerelda and stated that she was a lady of refinement and of strong character. She was seen with only one arm and visited with her daughter quite often in the city of Wichita Falls.

Those who knew the James boys well in Wichita Falls, named a list of robberies that they were accused of, but even in 1915, they still claimed their innocence of the Northfield incidence.

Dr. Frank James

Bud had always heard that a Dr. Frank James was part of Jesse's circle who would patch them up when they were all shot up. After the Civil War, when Jesse went down to Mexico, per Howk, he got Dr. Sylvester Franklin James who Howk said was Jesse Woodson James' actual brother, to go down and help doctor Shelby's men to bring them back home to the states. Because of Howk's spin of this twisted tale, it is extremely hard to piece together the truth about Dr. Frank James, but Bud has done his best to unravel it for the family and for the historians.

Just like so many events in Bud's life when he started searching Jesse James, things just happen that you can't explain, it's like Jesse leading Bud to the truth. Bud was a guest on a radio program at the Black Angus Motel in Anadarko and it was about Jesse James. They got into a discussion regarding Dr. Frank James. Bud was looking for him. After the broadcast, Bud was on his way home to Purcell.

A lady called the radio station and said she was a granddaughter of Dr. Frank James and lived in Chickasha. Bud got a phone call from the station telling him about this lady who was kin to Dr. Frank. He had just crossed the Washita River bridge in Chickasha where gold was discovered by some young boys years ago, when he got the call. They told him where this lady lived in Chickasha, so he followed the directions he was given and was within a mile of her house.

The lady was amazed Bud was on her doorstep. She showed Bud a copy of a newspaper in Chickasha that had her and Dr. Frank's picture together. She told Bud the best one to talk to was another grandson of Dr. Franks, Fred Scott James (1914-1999) who lived on Gaines Creek east of Wilburton, Oklahoma. His father was Mack Scott James (1873-1956), son of Dr. Frank James.

In the family Bible and census records, Dr. Frank James date of birth reveals he was only 15 at the end of the Civil War, but his grave marker shows his date of birth as 1848. Bud received a letter dated January 9, 1993 addressed to his friend, Lou Kilgore who was a recipient of a letter directly from a granddaughter of Dr. Robert Franklin James. Her name was Velma Dorothy (James) Pelfrey. She stated that the doctor was born December 25, 1848. He would have been a year younger than Jesse and by the end of the war, he would have been 16-17 years old. I don't believe this was Dr. Sylvester Franklin James who Howk was talking about. Dr. Robert Franklin James became a doc in 1879.

Just who was the Dr. Frank James Bud was hunting? That wasn't his real name. He was born as Gabriel Marion *Scott* in Marshall County, Illinois to Flemmon Scott (1819-1884) and Phebe Ann James (1822-1886). His father was a circuit-rider preacher and was said to be very strict on young Gabriel. They moved to Falling Spring, Ozark County, Missouri before the Civil War by 1860. This was the area where young Gabriel grew up and met his first wife, Serilda Eslinger.

Young Gabriel would have been 12-13 years old when the war was starting. I don't believe he was in the war with Jesse, but he was heavily influenced by him and the war.

Looking into Gabriel's mother's family, Phebe Ann James, we find the connection to Jesse Woodson James' family and surprisingly another man who was with Jesse during the 1940's and 1950's.

Roscoe James (1890-1963) who Howk had pulled him into his own circle as a "relative" of Jesse or who made him believe he was the son of Jesse, went on various trips with Howk to see Jesse and locate treasure with him. Roscoe adamantly believed Jesse was his father, because of Howk's persuasion, but DNA by Roscoe's son, Robert "Bob" James (1928-2014) who wrote a letter regarding Howk, proved he was not, but he wasn't too far off.

Roscoe's father was Jesse Ballard James (1860-1904). Both Jesse Ballard James and Gabriel Marion Scott/Dr. Frank James shared the same great grandparents, Joseph J. James (1776-1838) and Elizabeth Garnet Ballard (1777-1808), daughter of Byrum Ballard (1740-1817) and Eleanor Candler (1740-1791). They were related to the Ballards spread throughout this entire book. They were related to John Tatum.

Also, the Ballards of Phebe James grandmother's line run in to my Thomason family line. Phebe's mother was Susannah Harless and lived with her son, Thomas during the Civil War and thereafter in the 1860-1870 census in Black River Township in Reynolds County, Missouri. The county seat of Reynolds County is *Centerville*.

Further up the line, Jesse Ballard James and Dr. Frank James shared 4th great grandparents with Jesse Woodson James, William G. James (1700-1753) and Mary Wheeler (1728-1755) through the Fields.

There is an unsettling tale related to Roscoe's great grandfather, Jesse Ballard James (1803-1861) which was Gabriel Marion Scott/Dr. Frank James' great uncle. He was hanged by Confederate bushwhackers for supplying grain to some Union Soldiers. This man's brother, William J. James' son, Jesse R. James married Serilda Eslinger (1841-?) in 1865. Jesse R. James (1834) fought for the Union side in the 16th Regiment in the Missouri Cavalry and died during the war. His wife, Serilda ended up marrying Gabriel Marion Scott/Dr. Frank James in 1868, living in Ozark County, Missouri. This was Serilda's 3rd marriage. Her 1st husband James Cunningham was killed by a bushwhacker in 1861 in Webster County, Missouri. They married in 1859. They had one daughter,

Arrena Jane Cunningham (1861-1948). On her death certificate, it refers to her father as Jess James, indicating it was Jesse R. James, but what the truth is, we do not know.

By 1870, Serilda and Gabriel were living in Richland, Ozark, Missouri. He was a farmer. During the 70's is when Gabriel must have met up with Jesse during the outlaw days. Jesse may have been traveling by or as several stories indicate that Jesse would go to farmers and see if they needed a few extra bucks and ask them to be part of his "gang" for a job or two. We do not have the full story, wish we did. During the 70's, Serilda and Gabriel Marion Scott, had 5 sons, Gabriel Marion Scott, Jr., Jasper Flemmon Scott, Silas Bloomer Scott, Mack C. Scott, Columbus Culley Scott, and Serilda's daughter.

This is when the story begins to get muffled. One man offered this assumption, stating that Gabriel Marion Scott was either caught in Northfield during the bank robbery with the James/Younger Gang in 1876 or was caught in counterfeiting and sent to prison for a short period maybe 2-3 years. Different family members say that he had told his family he was in prison for a shooting in Missouri and a woman was killed in the incident. If this really occurred, it had to of been an accident or unintentional for him to only serve just a few years in prison and not be hung. No records have been found on his imprisonment. He may have been going by a different name at the time. It was believed to have been in the 1870's and he even may have been sent to the Detroit, Michigan prison where so many outlaws were sent.

The event may have encouraged him to seek a medical degree while in prison or shortly after that. Is it possible he was encouraged by a doctor who worked in the prison to learn doctoring under an apprenticeship and then furthered his studies in a hospital? Not all the facts are there, but Gabriel Marion Scott obtained a medical degree from Saint Luke's Hospital in Niles, Michigan on March 30, 1879, only 150 miles from Ann Arbor, Michigan where Jesse was getting a medical and law education in 1872-1874. The name on the diploma was entered as Robert F. James, M.D. Lots of questions arise. Wish the answers would rise too, but Bud did all he could to find out the truth.

Gabriel Marion Scott must have traveled back home, a free man and a doctor to boot. We find him still under the name of Gabriel Marion Scott in the 1880 census living with his wife, Serilda and family in Bridges, Ozark, Missouri, in dwelling #**33**. He was a distiller. It is unknown what happened, but Gabriel and his family disappeared. Were they being ridiculed, were there issues with his stepdaughter, or was Gabriel still involved with Jesse and had to move on? It was about the time that things began to get a little "hairy." Jesse would be faking his death in 1882 and his gang needed to lay low.

No one knew where the family went. It would be years later that it was discovered that Gabriel moved his entire family to Arkansas, a little over 50 miles from where another man, Jesse Cole James lived in Barber, Arkansas. He was the son of Jesse Woodson James and a Cherokee woman who we will dive into later.

Gabriel changed his name to what was on his degree, Dr. Robert Franklin James. Serilda must have died during or after the move. There is a picture of her in Find a Grave, a pretty lady, but no gravesite or date of death. It was very strange.

It was learned by family, that Dr. Frank had a son with his stepdaughter, Arena Cunningham. She left home and Dr. Frank would marry again in Arkansas to Laura Heathcox in 1888. Dr. Frank would raise his son, Homer with all his other children and all their names would be changed to the surname, "James." Dr. Frank and his family moved to Indian Territory sometime before 1889. With Laura, he had many more children and lived in the Choctaw Nation.

By 1900, he was still living in the Choctaw Nation, Indian Territory under the name Frank James. He was a carpenter. He was buried with the tombstone, Dr. Robert Franklin James in the Sardis Cemetery in Pushmataha County, Oklahoma in **1933**.

This is such an amazing story. Bud is the only one to solve who Dr. Frank James was and how he was related and associated with Jesse. I don't believe he was in the war with Jesse, at the age of 13-17 but later he was a doctor for Jesse and his gang and may have even been in Northfield. That has not been proven.

Bud was able to go and visit Fred James, Dr. Frank's grandson with Burleigh Dale James, a grandson of Jesse's, son of Jesse Cole James and John and Jo Ella Tatum. Fred told them that Dr. Frank doctored him for his throat one time.

They had a wonderful time speaking with one another. Burleigh Dale and his brother had always heard of Dr. Frank James and likewise with Fred and his family about Jesse Cole James. Bud said Fred was open to a lot of things, but the entire family was very "closed mouth." They knew more than they really wanted to share.

Bud, John and Jo Ella Tatum, and Charles "Shorty" James and Jesse Quanah James, sons of Jesse Cole James were invited down to Tuskahoma, Oklahoma with Fred James to show them the grave of Dr. Frank and also to meet the other members of the family. They always had a James' reunion every year. Fred asked Bud to speak at the reunion. There was no hesitation on the invite.

Dr. Frank lived north of Sardis Lake back in the hills of Bolin Hollow. I believe it's now in the area called Gary Sherrer Wildlife Area. It was a very secluded place when he was living there. Bud found carvings on the side of the mountain. Bud recognized them right away as Jesse and the KGC's signature. He knew this was another secret that Jesse kept. Jesse never told Ola about Dr. Frank or his part in Jesse's life.

Fred took them to Dr. Frank's grave. They traveled on the roughest road which was properly named Savage Road. The cemetery was in its original spot that was established as early as 1875. It was outside the town of Sardis, which is no more. It's all under water except for the graveyard. The town was established in 1905, taking its name from the Sardis Indian Mission Church, named for the Biblical city of Sardis.

In 1980, the area was taken over by the U.S. Army Corps of Engineers who built Sardis Lake for flood control and tourism. They evacuated the town of Sardis and left the graves below the bottom of the lake. They filled the area of the cemetery with landfill making a small island and placing the tombstones many feet above the actual graves. There is a built-up causeway from the shore to the cemetery for easy access to the cemetery.

It makes one wonder, what was hidden under that lake or what was excavated. There are so many incidents where Jesse was involved in an area, that was completely flooded, a lake was built upon the land, or a lot of dirt work was done. Also, there is great importance of a cemetery to Jesse. We also see a lot of State or Federal parks being placed in these areas, such as wildlife preserves here in southeastern Oklahoma and in the Wichita Mountains. You will see this further as we go along.

On the tombstone of Dr. Frank, it was inscribed with the name of R. F. James, M.D. Bud has learned there was treasure 15 miles from where Dr. Frank was buried.

When Bud began speaking at the James' reunion, people were in awe of what he knew. A lot of it matched with what they knew, but many were amazed at Bud's details. One granddaughter, Joy, kept saying, "For Real?" Joy and her husband, Don Huddleston had Dr. Frank's medical degree over their fireplace. They were very proud of it.

Don Huddleston was a world champion bull dogger. Bud and Don hit it off right away. Don knew Bud's cousin, Todd Whatley. Todd was hazing for Don at Madison Square Garden. Bud and Don had a lot to talk about.

Bud met a life-time friend, Edwin "Eddie" Henry James (1899-1996) and his wife, Elizabeth Carter. Eddie was Dr. Frank and his wife Laura Heathcox's son. Elizabeth would always call Bud, Mr. Hardcastle. Bud said, "They were good people." As they began to feel more comfortable with Bud, they began to open up. Eddie told Bud that Dr. Frank would go for a couple of weeks at a time without telling anyone where he was going. He was in and out of Missouri, Arkansas, and Indian Territory. Dr. Frank would receive messages that Frank and Jesse were hurt, and he went immediately to them, didn't matter what he was doing, nor the time of day.

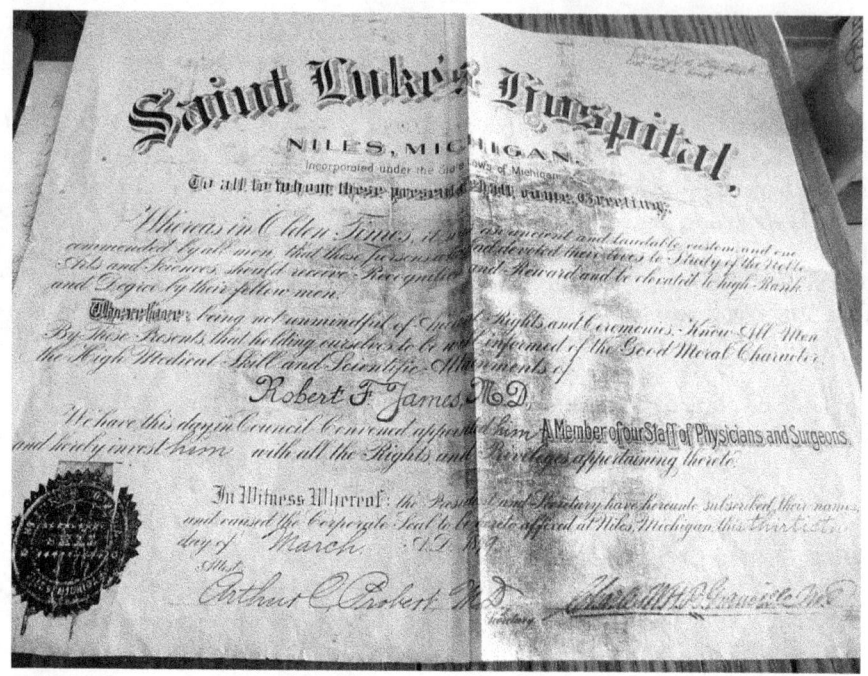

(R. F. James, MD medical diploma)

(L-R – Burleigh Dale James, Joy Huddleston, Charles James, and Bud Hardcastle.)

(Eddie and his wife, Lizzie)

(Lizzie, Bud, and Eddie in Nursing Home)

The family all knew that Dr. Frank was kin to Jesse James and ran with him. Dr. Frank even told some of his kin that he was first cousins to Jesse, but that wasn't exactly true. His grandchildren told Bud that Dr. Frank could quote Shakespeare, just like what was said of the real Frank James, Jesse's brother. Dr. Frank read all the time. He would drink a lot and cuss those Damn Yankees.

Some interesting stories came from the grandchildren. They all knew and agreed with Jesse Cole James' sons, that J. Frank Dalton was the true Jesse Woodson James. Eddie had actually seen Jesse James when he came to see his father one day. They were near Sardis Lake in a creek where there was a large pool of water. They were swimming and of course Jesse had his gun belt on at all times. They were swimming around and some men rode up, who appeared to be the law. They had their guns drawn and ordered the men out of the water. With pistols on Jesse's hips, he yanked those pistols out with lightning speed and "what happened wasn't very nice," Eddie's own words. They wouldn't be bothered no more.

Eddie told Bud that Jesse came there and had a bullet in his shoulder that Dr. Frank took care of. Eddie's half-brother, Homer was there when he removed the bullet. He said Jesse went by the name of Wild Bill Scott. The children of Dr. Frank would ask their father if they were brothers because they looked a lot alike. They were confused on the different last names though, "Scott and James."

In 1948, Homer wanted to take his son to Lawton to see if this man claiming to be Jesse had a bullet hole in his shoulder because he had actually witnessed his father remove the bullet. Sure enough, Jesse remembered Homer and the bullet hole was still visible in his shoulder. That man in Lawton, Oklahoma in 1948 was Jesse.

Another interesting story told to Bud was that Dr. Frank's son, Homer, was sent by his father to drive a wagon to where Belle Starr was and to bring her there so he could care for her. Dr. Frank took care of Belle Starr when he lived near Enterprise, I.T. which is in the valley of Brooken Creek which flows north to the Canadian River upstream from the Eufaula Lake Dam.

Close to Belle Starrs's house was Hi Early Mountain in Muskogee County near Eufaula Lake which had a great cave to hide out in. When she was hiding from the law, she would hold out there. Also, Jesse and his men would camp in the cave. It was in southeast Oklahoma.

Dr. Frank James lived out his days with his son, Robert Lee James in Sardis, Oklahoma. He died in **1933** at the age of 83.

Bud said that one day he went to the Choctaw Nation Tribal Council Chambers at Tuskahoma, Oklahoma near Sardis Lake. There he saw the prestigious portraits of former Chiefs of the Choctaw Nation surrounding the walls of honor. Bud was surprised to see Dr. Frank James' photo hanging along with the Chiefs. He was well loved and respected. He must have done a lot of doctoring for the nation.

Bud and the Tatums went 4-5 times to the Dr. Frank James' reunions and enjoyed themselves immensely. The family was extremely talented with music abilities through their instruments, voices, and dance. Bud said, "When the music started, their feet could not be still."

When Eddie's wife, Elizabeth died in 1994, Bud was honored to be an honorary pallbearer at her funeral. Eddie died two years from his wife's death in 1996 and Bud attended his funeral. At this last gathering, Bud said, Don Shaw, the husband of Zedith, the granddaughter of Dr. Frank James called him aside and said, "Hey, I want to show you something."

Zedith was the daughter of Dr. Frank James' son, Claude. Don Shaw took Bud to a back room where he pulled out the Family Bible. Don carefully pulled out an old map, carefully folded inside the pages. As he unfolded the map, Bud recognized symbols and the handwriting as Jesse's by his own hand. Don said that Claude's daddy was given this map by Jesse himself about money that he buried to the north, 15 miles from Dr. Frank James' grave. He said that not many of the family knew about this map and it was put up years ago. Don said, "Now don't mess with it now for a few years. It's still hot."

I asked Bud what he meant. He said at that time, in 1996, the government knew about the money and was looking for it, but they didn't have the map. They actively were searching for it. Don told Bud, "Wait a few years and if you decide to look for it, share a little with us." Don gave Bud the map, but he never did go back. Bud said on the map was a landmark showing the area where the New State School sat. Bud said everything on the map indicates Jesse drew this out in detail and that Jesse was extremely familiar with the territory. He left his mark down the Savage Road.

(Dr. Frank James at a young age)

(Dr. Frank James in Sardis)

"She was quite a woman, I had great respect for her."

-*Jesse James*

Chapter Eleven: The Starr that outshined them all

While Jesse was staying with Ola and Aubrey during some of the last years on earth, he carried an old photograph with him in his "purse." That's what the men called it back then, sort of like a drawstring pouch. The photo was fading, just as his life was fading before his failing eyes.

He told Ola that the woman in the photo was the love of his life, Belle Starr. Ola and Aubrey had the photograph blown up into a portrait size to be placed in a beautiful old-fashioned frame and hung on the wall for him in their home.

When he looked at it, or if someone asked him about Belle Starr, his eyes glazed over, as if swept away into another world of dreams of a happier time. You could tell, at that moment, he shunned reality, and went back in time.

Quantrill and Belle Starr were two of the greatest influences in Jesse's life. Jesse told a reporter, "they received little justice at the hands of historians."

For this chapter, we will honor the woman that meant so much to Jesse and respect Jesse in his privacy and protection he kept over her. Not much was let out of his heart about Belle, but what we will speak of in this chapter is his exact words about her, what Ola and Aubrey observed as well as others who spoke to him about Belle, and we will also bring in the book that Bud shared with me titled, "Doctor in Belle Starr County" by Col. Charles W. Mooney, son of Dr. Jesse Mooney, Jr. who was Belle's personal doctor who lived only 13 miles across the Canadian River from her in Indian Territory.

Bud was able to talk to Charles Mooney who wrote the book about his father's great adventures taking care of Belle. In doing so, he described what was actually taking place at her cabin, the character and talents of Belle, the people she associated with, and the hideouts she had spread all over Indian Territory. Mooney also adds interesting stories about Jesse within his book and told Bud himself he believed absolutely that J. Frank Dalton was Jesse Woodson James.

In his book, Mooney also reveals an ageless secret his family kept all these years on who the killer of Belle Starr was. Mooney's father was there. Was Belle really killed? Bud doesn't think so.

We will forego all the old stories of Belle that contradict each other. There's enough confusion as it is in the midst of the variations. I wish we had all the answers, but we don't. Like Jesse's family, he kept his stories and relationship with Belle private and protected.

Jesse told Ola, "Myra Maybelle Shirley was a wonderful person. I thought a mighty lot of her. She helped us a lot when I was with Quantrill during the war. She could ride like the wind and was brave. She was a wonderful woman, a wonderful rider, and a good shot with a gun." [164]

Myra's father, John Shirley acquired some fine-blooded Kentucky horses which influenced Myra in such a way that her love of horses was second to none. John bought a hotel and tavern in Carthage, Missouri before the war in 1858 which included a livery stable and corrals where he would rent out his horses and tack. During the war, this is where the James boys and Youngers, along with the Quantrill Raiders gathered due to Shirley's Confederate sympathy. Myra's brother, Bud was a member of the Quantrill Raiders.

Myra was exactly 5 months younger than Jesse, born in 1848 and was fascinated with the heroism the raiders exemplified while preserving the south. This is when the love affair or infatuation for these men started and the desire to serve in their cause. Belle became a hot shot spy for the Confederacy and supplied the needs for the guerillas.

Before the Civil War changed her outlook on life, she attended Carthage Female Academy and became a well refined woman drawing her interests and talents in music and education. The war, just like so many people who were in the heart of the conflict, affected the beautiful and talented lady.

In the Spring of 1863 is when Jesse really took notice of her, not just as a baby sister of one of his comrades, but a woman of great intelligence and talents. A friend of Ola's, Mrs. Frances Tiller, wrote Ola about the encounter she had with Jesse in Longview, Texas years ago when he was living near the Ford's grocery store. His deep love for Belle was quite evident when she asked for him to tell her about Belle Starr, the sweetheart of Jesse. "He looked out the door, and up towards the sky, and said, "Belle was a beautiful lady and was the smartest person I ever knew." [165]

In a March 1948 newspaper, the Houston Chronicle, when he was working on getting his pension, Dalton said, "In the Spring 1863, I was shot in the left leg during a skirmish (with roving Yankees) near Warsaw, Missouri, and took refuge in a nearby farmhouse until I was able to ride again. Skirting Osceola, county seat of St. Clair County and home of the Younger brothers (two of whom were in my company), I came to a schoolhouse. Here I stopped to get a drink at a nearby spring and to let my wounded leg rest. I had torn my shirt into strips and tied them around my leg, and I guess I had lost more blood than I thought, for I passed into unconsciousness. When I finally awoke, I was lying on a soft bed in a room filled with sunlight; looking up into the face of Myra Belle Shirley." [166]

She was an angel to Jesse. This is when Jesse's heart fluttered in the bright sunny place where he was being nursed back to health by the young teacher. Overwhelmingly, she captured his heart and she would become the love of his life. I believe this is when he received the photo of her at this young age of 15 before the harshness of life affected her. Jesse wanted to preserve her innocence and beauty in the photo he carried with him for the rest of his life.

(Myra Belle Shirley aka. Belle Starr)

The war was hard on both of them. The Shirleys lost their son, John Allison "Bud" Shirley who was one of Quantrill's Scouts. He was killed in Sarcoxie, Missouri, while he and another scout were being fed at the home of a Confederate sympathizer. Union troops surrounded the house and when Bud attempted to escape, he was shot and killed, June 1864. Dalton, before he was known as Jesse stated in The Intelligencer, April 19, 1890, that "Bud, he was as loyal a friend and comrade as I ever have known to this day."

It was either after Bud was killed or after the war, that Judge Shirley took his family to Sherman, Texas. This was where a lot of the Confederates went after the war for safety. The James boys and Youngers who knew the family well, would visit them often. The Youngers, especially Cole was extremely close to the Shirley family.

The Shirleys moved to Scyene, Texas. It is now surrounded by Dallas in the east central part of Dallas county. The town had 300 people, 6 saloons, a school, a church, and of course a Masonic Lodge and was named for a town in ancient Egypt. The Shirleys had a hotel and tavern bringing in income and outlaws. Belle owned and operated a livery stable there. It would become one of Frank, Jesse, and the Younger's hideouts.

The James-Younger Gang robbed their first bank in Liberty, Missouri on February 13, 1866. They fled to Scyene,Texas where Myra was living. Myra, later known as Belle Starr stated, "it was there that she became reacquainted with the first man she ever loved." [167] The three she had eyes for were Jim Reed, Cole Younger, and Jesse James. They were all in the running, literally, trying to escape the law, but Jesse had gotten shot in the shoulder, nearly taking his arm off, apparently during the robbery. The gang must have had to split up, because Jesse was taken by Wild Henry Roberts, a former Quantrill Raider to his home between Hamilton and Hico, Texas. The others apparently went to Belle's.

Many people were referring to Jim Reed as the one Myra really loved, but others said it was Cole Younger.

This is where it gets kind of fuzzy. The romance exploded in that small community, outside of Dallas. The one who had been documented as the lucky one who won Myra's hand was James Commadore "Jim" Reed (1845-1874). Reed helped with farm labor, the livery stable, and became a salesman for a Dallas saddle and bridle maker. The wedding was planned for November 1st, 1866. The marriage is documented in the Collin County, Texas records on that date.

Then we have the famous Eureka Springs, Arkansas wedding photo of Myra marrying Jim Reed on horseback. Some believe that this occurred in October or the first part of November 1866. Many stated that among the guests at the private ceremony was Frank and Jesse, along with Jesse's family, including a half-brother of theirs, Perry Samuels who wasn't born until 1868, General Joseph Shelby and John Newman Edwards who were supposed to be in Mexico fighting alongside Maximillian for two years after the war.

(The famous Eureka Springs photo)

There is no explanation on when this wedding took place and who the people actually were. From Scyene, Texas to Eureka Springs, Arkansas is nearly 400 miles. This has to be another wedding photo. It had to be a different year than 1866 and could have been a different couple. The St. Louis Globe-Democrat reported on March 15, 1903 that Cole Younger was the groom. "Mike Harrington of Fort Smith, Arkansas, declares that Cole Younger and the notorious queen of female bandits, Belle Starr, were once married. He says: I know they were married. I was present at the wedding and saw them married. It took place down in Texas and they were married on horseback. I had known both of them at sight for some time, and there was no possibility of my being mistaken. In her early life Pearl Starr, the daughter of Belle, was always known as Pearl Younger, and she was always referred to as Pearl Younger by her mother." [168]

We learn that Myra and Jim Reed tried to make a go of it in Scyene, but Jim was not one who could settle down. He was still involved in outlawry, some with Frank and Jesse, the Youngers, and Tom Starr and his boys. By the end of 1867, they moved to Missouri and it is here when Myra became pregnant with Rosie Lee, who Myra nicknamed her "pearl" born September 1868.

During the time that the family was in Texas, Myra's brothers became involved with trouble. Things went South. We find the information in www.findagrave.com. Myra's brother, known as Cravens (1858) and later as John Alva Shirley just disappeared without a trace. A slave for the family, Aunt Annie was interviewed in 1894 by the Dallas Times-Herald and she said the "boy had not been seen for years, and that Mrs. Shirley assumed he was dead." He was living with the family in 1870 in Texas. We learn that he had a son born in 1881, John Alva Shirley, Jr. so he was alive at least in 1880/81. [169]

Mansfield Shirley born in 1852 was shot and killed in 1867 in a fight with the law, possibly in Indian Territory or Texas. He too was listed in the 1870 census with his parents in Texas. Did he get involved in outlawry? Jesse speaks of a "Buck" Shirley, a brother of Myra Belle. Could this be Mansfield? Jesse said after the war, Buck went to Texas and stayed until 1867. He said Buck and he supplied buffalo meat to the railroad workers who were in grading camps as they built railroads from Kansas City to Denver, Kansas Pacific. They got 3 cents a pound, dressed, and the hides went for 75 cents to $1.50.

There was a half-brother, Preston Raymond Shirley who died in 1867 at Spring Creek, Collin, Texas. In the book, "Doctor in Belle Starr Country," Preston left farming and became a bartender in Spring Creek. He got into a gunfight with a disgruntled Texas cowboy who didn't like the price of a drink. Preston was killed by Joe Lynn.

Edwin Benton "Eddie" Shirley (1850) was always in constant trouble, arrested and charged with horse stealing. After they moved to Texas, he continued in this type of thievery and was charged on May 3, 1866 and again on October 24, 1866. He was shot and killed by a man named Palmer from Collin County in the Chamber Creek Bottom towards the end of 1866. [170]

Myra's husband, Jim Reed was drawn into the lifestyle of the James and Youngers and was hardly home while Myra was trying to raise Pearl. It wouldn't be too long before Jim was wanted for murder in Arkansas. They fled to California. He is shown in the 1870 census in Los Nietos, Los Angeles County with his wife Mary, which was the name she sometimes went by. She had a son named, James Edwin Reed in February 1871.

It wasn't long before Jim did something else where he had to hide from the law. Some believe that he was found with counterfeit money as he gambled in California. They went back to Texas and Indian Territory.

Reed fell in with Tom Starr, who pulled him into bringing whiskey into Indian Territory, murder, rustling, and counterfeiting by March 1871. At times, Reed would live with Tom Starr and it is believed that Myra did at various times.

Myra and Jim had a mutual love for horse racing. She ran her thoroughbred horses in Dallas, spurred on by Reed. Some have stated that this was the beginning of horse thievery brought on by the James/Younger gang bringing horses from Missouri and Indian Territory to ramp up her stock. Jim didn't like to stay in one place but got involved in racehorses and took up with a Dallas socialite, Rosa McCommas.

Jim and Belle were both in and out of Texas and Indian Territory, separated most of the time. Belle had enough and left Jim Reed for infidelity. They were together a little more than 7 years.

In 1873, Cole Younger went to get her and her children and brought her back to Scyene. Jesse told Ola, "She was a good friend of Cole Younger." [171] In the book, "Doctor in Belle Starr Country," the author emphasized that Cole Younger was Belle's first lover and father of Pearl. The author also stated that Cole Younger was a cousin of Jesse's.

(Cole Younger)

(Pearl (Younger))

In August 1874, Jim Reed was shot near Paris, Texas and killed by a former acquaintance, John T. Morris who had been deputized to capture Reed. Belle denied that the dead man was her husband.

During this time, we find that Myra, getting into the role as Belle, was running with the James/Younger Gang in the mid 70's through the 80's. She was seen with the James/Younger gang when they robbed the stagecoach in January 1874 near Hot Springs, Arkansas. "Jesse James and four members of the gang robbed their first stagecoach near Hot Springs, Arkansas, taking cash and jewels valued at approximately $3,000. No one was injured. After Jesse's death, (1882) a gold watch taken from one of the stage passengers was found among his effects." [172]

In the Spring of 1874, we find Belle was living with the Starr gang near Briartown, Indian Territory. She was there most of the time, collecting money from the outlaws who were bringing in loot and horses. We know this because of a story Billy the Kid told. You will read more in the next chapter on his visit to Belle's cabin.

It must have been somewhere in the mid 70's that Belle was going back and forth from Indian Territory and Texas. There are times that Jesse spoke of her in Texas during this time.

Jesse had told Ola that while Frank was living and working at a store in Wichita Falls, Jesse was staying at Belle's house in Scyene which is verified by a family story of the Hite family. Jesse would visit near Dallas in Scyene and gave the young boys a gold dollar to make sure horses were hidden. [173]

Dalton told newspaper reporters in March of 1948 in the article titled, "Quantrill Raiders Added To Civil War Pension List" before he told who his real identity was, he had an encounter with Belle Starr. "She was an adventurous spirit, taken from the profession of teaching school through days as a woman spy for the South, as the wife of a hunted man, and back to teaching, part of which was spent in a school near Dallas." Dalton stated in that same article, that "He knew what it was to be a hunted man."

So, Belle was teaching and maintaining a decent life. At one point in Jesse's life, he stated that he became a teacher at Calico Rock, Arkansas. Bud has been there. It sounded as though no one else was teaching the children there, so he stepped in. This was sometime in 1875. He said he called upon Belle Starr to come help him out. Frank James went to teaching in Red Rock, Texas.

(It is believed this photo was of Belle during this time)

While Jesse was living with Belle in Scyene, he told Ola a story that explains a lot. It was included in the book, "The Hoax that Let Jesse James Live," by Bud Hardcastle. "Belle was known for her elaborate clothes she wore, but lacking in women friends, though she always conducted herself as a lady. Bob and Jim Younger moved to Scyene and with them was their sister, Henrietta who was the housekeeper and cook. All of them attended church and Bob sang in the church choir. Frank was working at a store in Wichita Falls, Texas and I was staying there at Belle's house.

A Pinkerton Detective got to snooping around and I knew something had to be done. So, the Pinkerton man named Nichols was shot and killed. Belle told the folks that he was her husband. I left out and headed for the Indian Territory. Belle had seen that the Pinkerton man was buried then sold her livery stable and went out to the home of the Travis family at Lancaster, Texas. She stayed there for six weeks. They were close and longtime friends of Jesse and the Shirleys. Mrs. Travis had gone to school with Jesse in Missouri and knew that he was Jesse James." [174]

Mrs. Travis' son, DeWitt Travis, told Ola, "While Belle was there after Pinkerton Nichols was killed, she stayed six weeks then she got a letter from Jesse. He told her where he was, so she caught the train and headed for White Horse, Indian Territory. Arriving there she went to a hotel and there met a nice-looking young man named Mr. Bruce Younger. He courted her and then they were married. A big wedding and a fancy one, there in the hotel lobby. Mr. Bruce Younger was none other than Jesse W. James." [175]

This was Jesse's story told directly to Ola and seems to check out along with DeWitt Travis' story told to him by his mother. DeWitt's father, Elbert Dewitt Travis married Martha Patterson in Navarro County, Texas on August 13, 1874 and had no children. Travis must have moved north to Lancaster, which was in Dallas County, approximately 20 miles south from Scyene. The Travis family moved to Van Zandt County, by 1876/77 when their first child was born. So, the time period would have been around 1874-1877 when Belle stayed with them in Lancaster.

Another version, in which I debated to add here, is the story told by Howk that he said he heard from Jesse and was told to Del Schrader, the author of "Jesse James Was One of His Name." Take it with a grain of salt, but there may be some truth to it and explain a few things. Howk never did read Ola's manuscript to coincide this story with his, so it appears that Jesse did tell them both of this same story.

Howk's version was this in Del Schrader's book, "As much, as he liked adventure, Jesse had hated to leave ravaged Dixie. His wife, Myra Belle, and her father, Judge John Shirley, had accompanied him to Cyene (Scyene), Texas, 14 miles east of where Dallas now stands, and they had established a home. They lived as Mr. and Mrs. Dick Reed, but when a horse thief with the same name had been hung, Myra Belle and he had hastily remarried as Mr. and Mrs. Bruce Younger. Poor Myra Belle fretted about not being able to have babies and she began to nag her young husband. Jesse began playing around with every pretty girl that came along. Myra Belle found out and divorced him. Jesse said half a century later, "Myra Belle Shirley or James or Reed or Younger was the only woman I ever loved." [176]

Well, we know Belle had two babies, and maybe had lost one before Pearl was born in 1868 as indicated in some stories. Does this suggest that Jesse was Jim Reed? Some people believe that. This could explain the wedding in Eureka Springs with all the James' family there. It also explains the part regarding Belle leaving Jim Reed for infidelity. Bud had told me that Jesse's grandsons told him that Jesse was married to Belle and she left him for "infidelity." Here is a picture that is supposed to be of Jim Reed and Myra Belle Shirley and the one picture believed to be the true Jesse. You decide.

(Jim Reed and Myra Belle Shirley)

(Jesse James)

Also, as we go through the book, you will see a lot of times that Jesse used the name of "Jim Reed," Dick Reed, and J.D. Reed. Coincidence?

When we look into a man who later in life said he was Frank James, using the name of Joe Vaughn, the possibility of Jesse James being Jim Reed seems plausible. Joe Vaughn said that his father was Edd Reed and was brother to Jim Reed who married Belle Starr. Vaughn also stated that he went by Edd Reed. Was this another cover name for both Frank and Jesse James?

Howk said that Jesse Woodson James was the son of George James, brother of Robert James, but no such brother of Robert's has been found. Howk said that George changed his name to Jim Reed. Maybe Howk changed this when he read the book Joe Vaughn wrote and wanted his story to fit Joe Vaughn's story. It gets stranger by the minute.

In Howk's book, "Jesse James and the Lost Cause," Jesse used the name Jack Reed. He wrote "They killed him off." He also said there were two Belle Starrs, one was an older sister of Henry Starr. We don't know if this is fact, but Belle Starr's looks changed dramatically through her older years. Bud said she was shot in the jaw, which certainly could change a woman's look. We don't know the answer.

It is documented in many sources, including newspapers that Bruce Younger, supposedly the son of Charles Lee Younger and Permelia Dorcus Wilson (mistress) married Belle in Chetopa, Labette, Kansas on May 15, 1880.

We know Jesse was in Brownwood, Texas in November 1879 with his wife???. He wrote this in a letter that we explore later. Jesse was supposed to be married to Zee Mimms with children. In fact, his daughter was born in April 1879 and Zee and the children were living in Nashville.

In the same year, we find Jesse as Bruce Younger and Belle in Galena, Kansas where they were enjoying the night life on Red Hot Street in 1879. They were also possibly in Joplin, Missouri living together before their official marriage date. [177]

Some newspapers speak of Bruce Younger named by Hobbs Kerry as one of the perpetrators of the Missouri Pacific Railroad robbery in Otterville in 1876. He was captured and detained in Sedalia, Missouri." In Kerry's confession, documented in the "Western Spirit", August 18, 1876, he speaks of being with the "boys" meaning Bob and Cole Younger (who most of them called Bud), but Kerry stayed with Bruce Younger in Joplin in the winter of 1876. Kerry then met up with Charles Pitt and Bill Chadwick, but I believe he meant Bill (William) Chadwell. They eventually met up with Frank and Jesse. He then speaks of meeting with Clem Miller, which I believe was Clell Miller. He named Cole and Bob Younger, Frank and Jesse James, Hobbs Kerry (himself), Clem Miller, Charlie Pitts, Bill Chadwick who were in on the heist. No mention of Bruce Younger. The rail was sabotaged, and the train stopped. Hobbs remained with a few in the back of the train and it took about an hour before the James and the Youngers were riding hard towards the back, leaving the scene in a hurry.

They went down the road for about 20 miles and then went off the road. "Clem Miller carried the bag with the money in it part of the time, while Cole Younger and Jesse James also took turns."

"About 200 or 300 yards from the road we stopped and divided the money. They tore all the envelopes open and put the money on a pile. Frank James counted it and gave each one his share. They left the envelopes there when they divided, someone carried off the sack. My share was $1,200. After the divide, we scattered." Kerry met up with Bruce Younger in Joplin. Bruce Younger was picked up the same time Hobbs was, but no one could identify Bruce as a participant of the train robbery. He was released. [178]

Another story is printed saying that Bruce Younger was amongst the 12 that robbed the train and he had been caught with Carey with $4,700 in their hands. [179]

Hobbs then blamed Bruce Younger for inducing Hobbs to "form a conspiracy to rob the company's safe" of Hobbs employer, the Granby Mining and Smelting Company. Hobbs described the involvement with Cole Younger and the James boys. He said, "Cole Younger is a brave and generous man, cool as an iceberg, while the Jamess are impulsive." [180]

The rest of the stories attached to Bruce Younger are quite strange. One was regarding his sister, Sophronia who wrote a letter to the Kansas City Star after Bruce's death. She said there was a publication of a story that a fossilized body supposed to be that of Bruce Younger had been found in a cave in the Guadalupe Mountains in New Mexico which had been a hideout of Jesse's for a long time. Bruce's sister rebukes the story and said that Bruce lived with her for a while and that he died in 1889/1890 and never was an outlaw. [181] He had been a horse trader and gambler.

I believe Jesse, being a family member and a close associate of the Younger family, borrowed Bruce Younger's name to marry, recorded it, and then borrowed his name to print these wild stories and to kill him off.

Bruce Younger and Myra Belle Shirley were only married 3 weeks and she left him because of his "infidelity".

Shortly after that short-lived marriage, Belle married Sam Starr on June 5, 1880 in Cherokee Nation, Indian Territory. He was son of Tom Starr and she had known him through Tom and Jim Reed. Sam was Cherokee and had acquired the nice 62-acre ranch from his father. Belle named the area, "Younger's Bend." It is believed she named it after Cole Younger. The area was where a sharp southerly bend was in the Canadian River which has changed course when the construction of the

Lake Eufaula Dam was constructed in 1964. Their cabin was six miles due west of Briartown. The town Briartown was east of Wilburton, just north of Whitefield, Oklahoma.

The property was north of the Canadian River. Of course, today, the area to the west has been swallowed up by Eufaula Lake and the area to the east which runs into the Arkansas River was turned into Sequoyah National Wildlife Refuge established in 1970. It was an overlay project of the U.S. Army Corps of Engineers, Robert S. Kerr Reservoir.

The ferry that Belle frequented was six miles upstream from Briartown. Jesse told Ola that he was on a ferry going across the Canadian River to Briartown. He could tell an officer was following him, and Jesse warned him not to follow. The officer didn't heed Jesse's warning and Jesse shot a button off of his coat. After that, the man minded his own business.

Bud had a story of Tillden Cramp, the ferry man. In the 1950's the public began hearing about Mr. Cramp. A reporter by the name of Sam Campbell who worked for the Lawton Constitution in 1948 was one of the investigators who was hired to check out J. Frank Dalton's story. He moved to Muskogee, Oklahoma and really began to delve into the history of Dalton and those who knew him. He found Mr. Cramp, still living who knew Jesse James and Belle Starr as well.

Sam Campbell interviewed Tilden Cramp and came away with a fascinating firsthand story. Tilden verified in writing that J. Frank Dalton was the real Jesse James. Bud was able to speak with Sam Campbell who was living in Arkansas in 1990. Campbell stated that in his interview with the spry and alert Cramp, he was given a very thorough painting of the man who rode his ferry many times and was very close to Belle Starr. The man was Jesse James himself who was the same man who came out in Lawton in 1948 as Jesse James. [182]

Tilden knew many intimate stories between Belle Starr and Jesse James. Jesse drove cattle for Belle to Dodge City. They were in the business of rustling cattle and horses. Jesse tells Ola about this trip himself. "Belle took some of her cattle to Dodge City, Kansas one time. The men that worked for her drove the herd and Belle rode in the chuck wagon. When they got to Dodge City, Belle told Blue Duck to sell the cattle so she could pay the men, while she went to town to do some shopping, then she walked off to town. When she got back to the wagon, she asked Blue Duck, "Did you sell the cattle?" He said, "Yes I did." She asked, "Where's my money so I can pay the men?' Blue Duck said, "Well, I got in a poker game and lost all of it."

"That made Belle mad as hell. She said, "That's my money and I'll get it!" She got her gun, went to the saloon and gambling place where he'd lost it, walked in and there was two men sitting at a table playing poker that had been in the game with Blue Duck a little bit before. She walked over to the table, pulled her gun and got her money back, plus a little extra for her trouble. I was standing across the street watching, just in case she needed some help. She went back to the wagon, paid the men then started in on Blue Duck and really raked him over. He sure didn't make that mistake again." [183]

Sam Campbell published his article on January 19, 1950 in the Muskogee Morning News. The title of the article was "Shucks, Tilden Cramp Could have Told Them." Of course, Bud had a copy of this article in his hands.

Sam found Tilden in Muskogee at 234 South "B". He was a full-blooded Cherokee. He ran the ferry that crossed the Canadian which is now Highway 2, just north of Whitefield. He began learning the ropes of running a ferry when he was 14. This was approximately in the year of 1880. Belle was one of his regulars on his ferry.

Tilden remembered as a young boy the many times that Belle would wake him out of bed to get her and her gang across the Canadian. There were only two keys to the lock that kept the ferry close to the riverbank; Tilden had one and Belle had the other. She used it when in a hurry.

Tilden described Belle as having red hair and wore it short in a bob, not like the photos shown of her with it wrapped up upon her head. Tilden always saw Jesse ride across in the ferry with Belle's gang.

We learn a lot from Sam Campbell about Dalton/Jesse in his article. He wrote that Jesse was a painter as well as a writer and expert pistol shot, a multi-talented man.

A letter from a man, James McKnight verifies this very thing. McKnight wrote Bud on March 26, 1991 after seeing an article in the *Jacksonville Daily Progress* out of Jacksonville, Texas of Bud's interest and hunt for Jesse. McKnight wanted to pass on a story about Jesse. He describes a unique painted sign in a store window in Gallatin, Texas that he saw as a kid. Gallatin is southwest of Longview and Henderson, Texas. The kid was fascinated with the sign, especially seeing that it was signed, J. Frank Dalton and the store owner said it was painted by an old timer who claimed he used to be an outlaw. He thought that it could have been done in the early 20's. Well indeed, that area of Texas was one of Jesse's favorite places to live and was a place of protection.

This story prompted another story of a Cherokee woman who lived in Porter, Oklahoma. Her name was Kathryn "Katie" E. (Vann) Brown. Samuel G. Campbell, same man spoken of above, from Fayetteville, Arkansas interviewed this lady on January 23, 1950. Katie was 77 years old. Bud had a copy of the interview and was well documented. Katie was born in 1873 in Muskogee, Oklahoma, and died 9 months from the time of the interview.

Katie's father was Joseph Vann and it appears that her mother, Jennie (Waters) Roe died during childbirth in 1873. For a young girl with no mother, life was hard. "For a time, as a child she lived with her great uncle George (Kysuk) Waters who operated a ferry across the Arkansas at Brewer Bend. Katie said Belle Starr used to ride up to their place to see her great uncle and would ask to take Katie home with her, in fun."

Katie described Belle in this manner, "Belle was slender, sat very straight in the saddle, never dismounted at their place, was dressed in men's clothing, including chaps, wore a pistol on each side, and carried a Winchester across the saddle." [184]

Belle's hideaway was a perfect hideout for the desperadoes of the James and Youngers. It was secluded within lots of trees and brush. They had plenty of wild meat and wild whiskey they got from Fort Smith or Fort Gibson. There were caves to hide out in if necessary. There was a big cave on the west side of Grand River, above Fort Gibson. [185] There was Hi Early Mountain close to Belle's house, close to Eufaula Lake where the James/Younger boys would hideout with a huge boulder that would block the cave.

Belle had horse stealing stations about 50 miles apart all across the plains. One such station was at old Keokuk Falls in the Sac and Fox reservation, in Pottawatomie County, Oklahoma and another at old Chisholm Springs, 2 miles east of Asher, Oklahoma. It is believed that they had one in Mayes County, Oklahoma that John and Jo Ella Tatum found. All that was left was an old barn and, in the loft, were round holes drilled out every few feet for their guns.

"Belle Starr Journal," *The St. Joseph Herald*, February 18, 1889.- The journal was found on the Starr Ranch in which she intended to publish. She described crimes committed in Texas and Indian Territory. *The Ponca City Daily Courier*, Sept. 16, 1908 said that Belle Starr was a whiskey peddler at times. She raided the country from the Kansas border, invading Texas crossing into the Llano Estacada.

Bud received a typed written account of an interview conducted by his friend Samuel G. Campbell from Fayetteville, Arkansas with Bennett (Bennie) Patty (Mrs. William Tipton Patty) of Porum, Oklahoma on November 25, 1949. She lived in the original Belle Starr cabin southwest of Porum for 26 years, coming there from Johnson County, Arkansas about 1909.

His interview: "She was living there when the cabin burned, which date is apparently about 1935. She was absent from the premises at the time, but said her grandchildren set it afire. She described the cabin as being about 12x12 feet, the sides of logs, and the floor of wide planks. The door was built of 2x4 boards and hung to an upright pin by twisted hickory bark hinges. It had a latch on the inside. The ceiling was low. Beneath the floor was a dirt cellar, which Mrs. Patty cleaned on her arrival. She said she found a great deal of dusty debris and the handles of probably 300 suitcases.

(Belle's Mayes County horse stealing station (courtesy of John and Jo Ella Tatum))

The south side of the cabin site slopes to the Canadian River, and formerly a path led from the cabin to a spring on the bottom. Mrs. Patty said there were four lilac bushes along the path, two on either side. Two black walnut trees stand north of the cabin site.

According to legend, she said, Belle and her boys kept cattle in the vicinity. Mrs. Patty said she had heard a lot of talk about haunts about the place of Belle's ghost riding a ghost horse across the countryside. But she herself put no stock in that kind of talk. In all her 25 years of living in the cabin, she had heard no sound and had seen no thing that she could not account for, except once:

One night she went out of the cabin and saw a light hovering over Belle's grave (just to the south of the cabin). "It wasn't like moonlight and it wasn't like starlight," Mrs. Patty relates, "It was more of a golden light. First it would dazzle up and then it would dazzle down." She did not mention the experience until a few days later when other members of the family had testified to the same. Mrs. Patty does not believe Jesse James was killed at St. Joseph." Signed Samuel G. Campbell, 5/27/91. [186]

Belle must have really liked robbing the stagecoaches and trains and the passengers of their belongings. A man who betrayed Bud while treasure hunting, found an old rusted Derringer within the foundation of where Belle's cabin was and gave it to Bud to entice him into helping him find the good stuff.

In the book, "Doctor in Belle Starr County," by Col. Charles W. Mooney, we learn a great deal about Belle and Jesse. It is a story about Charles' father, Dr. Jesse Mooney. The doctor was a neighbor and personal doctor of Belle's, just south across the Canadian River about 13 miles from Belle, close to Briartown. Dr. Jesse Mooney (1866-1915) was the son of Major Jesse Mooney (1818-1884) who was a Confederate officer in the Civil War. The Major's closest friend was also his senior superior officer, General Albert Pike. Myra Belle Shirley had to report to him during the Civil War at Yellville, Arkansas and General Stand Watie in Indian Territory who was known as the Red Fox of the West. She was his eyes and ears. Her duties appeared to be much more than just a spy and a messenger. She was working for the "big dogs." This makes one wonder, what position did she really have alongside Jesse and these top-rated officials?

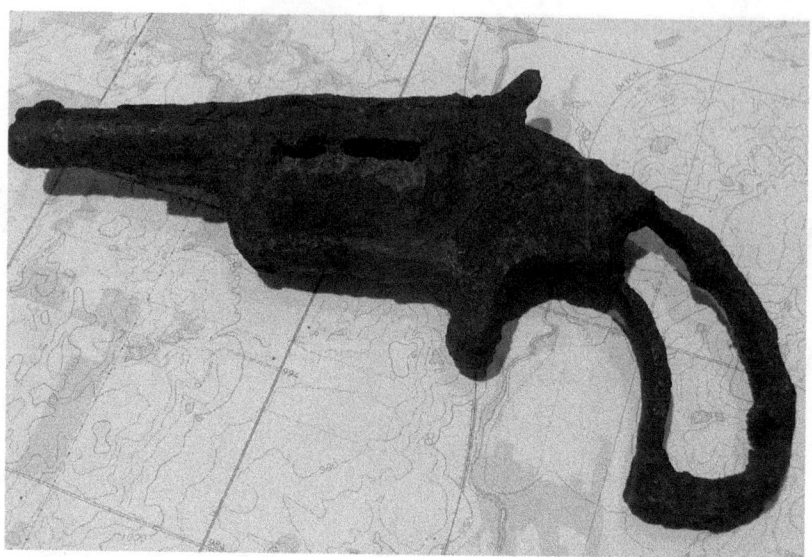

(Derringer found within Belle's foundation of her cabin near Briartown)

Major Mooney told his son, Dr. Jesse Mooney that Belle actually rode with the James/Younger Gang during a stagecoach robbery out of Hot Springs in 1874 that Major Mooney was riding in. After introducing himself, Mooney was given the pleasure of conversing with Cole Younger, Belle, and Jesse. They gave back Mooney's watch, wallet, and masonic ring.

Clayton Mooney, the Major's other son was also a spy for the Confederacy. He as well as many others tracked down and killed bushwhackers who killed their families and manhandled their women folk. He saved Belle's life one time.

Charles Mooney wrote in his book, stories that he heard from his father and his mother. His mother, Ella Ridley (1867-1951) was the first woman pharmacist registered in Indian Territory. "It was generally known that Jesse and Frank James had been good church members of the Baptist faith before becoming outlaws. Their father was a Baptist preacher in Missouri. Jesse James, blue-eyed and sandy-haired, had a peculiar idiosyncrasy of blinking his eyes noticeably and frequently. But he always carried his Bible with him and prayed often, even during his long years of robbery and crime. He was exceptionally good to his mother." [187]

One time, Belle was hurt bad by a bullet lodged in her shoulder from a gunshot during a heist. Dr. Mooney was summoned to come to her and help. The doctor traveled 90 miles or more to reach her in a cave, which was later known as the Starr Spring and Dugout northeast of Atoka, Oklahoma. He successfully removed the slug and got her back on her feet. She was forever grateful. Her payment to the doc was in $20 gold pieces.

She wasn't known just for her banditry, but also for her talents. In her home, the doctor said he had witnessed her playing exceptionally well on an upright piano. She had a library of books and was extremely intelligent. She had a well-worn confederate flag attached to a cavalry wooden staff in a corner of her living area.

When Belle and Sam were home, an old friend came to visit. "This is an old friend of the family from Missouri, Mr. Howard," Belle said. "Fact is, we grew up purty close, and our families know'd each other well."

"The stranger had blonde hair, a light sandy mustache, and bright blue eyes. His eyelids blinked noticeably. Sam was by now used to "old friends" dropping in, and thought nothing about the stranger wearing guns, as seldom did any ever come without their brace of six-shooters.

"Belle's friend stayed for several weeks (6 weeks) using their extra bedroom instead of the cave in Hi Early Mountain, but never left the premises. This suggested to Sam that the blinking blue-eyed man who was never without his pistols at his thighs was a personal friend rather than an old outlaw from the past, or just an acquaintance from back in Missouri.

"On one occasion the soft spoken, quiet mannered man aroused some suspicion in Sam's mind, and in fact, disturbed him. One of Sam's brothers came riding up to the secluded cabin one morning, breaking the serene silence. Then quick as a flash the blinking-eyed man was out of his chair and on his feet like a spring tiger. All Sam saw was the lightening-fast motion of both the man's arms and two blurs as both colts simultaneously came out of their holsters into his hands. The man peered out the window cautiously, his blue eyes cold as ice, his eyelids blinking fast, as the lone rider approached. Belle calmed the situation with her low-pitched voice. "It's just one of Sam's brothers."

"Slowly, Mr. Howard let both long barrelled pistols drop back into their holsters. But he remained standing at the window until Sam's brother left, his eyes twitching more than usual.

"Sam Starr never knew the fast-drawing man was none other than the notorious Jesse James. Nor did he ever know Belle took some of Jesse's hard cash for his keep and protection. There were but few Jesse James could trust, and Belle was one of them. They both rode together in an outlaw gang after the Civil War, and rumors still floated about they buried a large cash loot somewhere in the Wichita mountains." [188]

In this book, the author states "Pearl's admitting that her mother told her that Pearl's "real Pa" was Cole Younger, and the story of Cole and Belle's love affair and the trysting place where Pearl was conceived both are new revelations." [189]

Sam Starr and Belle were convicted of horse theft in 1883 and was sent to the Detroit Prison, serving 9 months. Sam Starr was the son of the famous Tom Starr who was a scout for General Stand Watie and became one of the guerillas. He was the father of the Oklahoma Starr outlaws and was known for a lot of killing and a lot of crimes. He was a Cherokee and had first obtained the property where Belle and Sam Starr lived on the southern end of the Cherokee Nation. Earlier, Jim Reed hooked up with the Starrs, living with them and is assumed how Belle became acquainted with them.

Sam Starr (1853-1886) was killed in the Briartown area, killed by a cousin, law officer Franklin Pierce West in a gunfight. Belle remarried Sam's adopted brother, Jim July to be able to keep her home and the 62 acres of the land, since she was not a Cherokee.

Belle was ambushed on Feb. 3, 1889 shot in the back, neck, shoulder, and face. Dr. Mooney got there too late, but Bud believes and heard from a lot of sources, including her family, that it was not Belle that got killed and he believed the doctor was in on the hoax to let Belle live. Her tombstone reflects that. No one was ever convicted, but both the doctor who heard directly from Pearl herself and in a news article of Jesse's, the murder was blamed on Belle's son, James Edwin Reed. Jesse told this story to a newspaperman in the 40's about his encounter with Belle during his marshaling days. "I concluded to stop on my way back home from taking prisoners and give her the "once over." She knew him at once. They cried like a baby. Jesse said Belle possessed a jovial and pleasing personality and great musician. He had a different story on her death. The son came home who was an outlaw and thinking his mom was a marshal looking for him, he killed her instantly. The article came out with a picture of Dalton and Mrs. Flossie E. Hutton, daughter of Pearl Starr standing together at Belle's Grave. [190]

Belle's children:

Pearl was sent to live with her paternal grandparents, and she became pregnant when she was 17 with Flossie in April 1887. Pearl became a prostitute in Van Buren, Arkansas. She did that to help get her brother out of prison. She was able to get a defense team rounded up and secured a presidential pardon for him in 1893. She moved to Fort Smith and had a prosperous brothel business.

James Edwin Reed (1871-1896) had quite a hard life. He lived with his paternal grandparents while Belle was settling in the Cherokee Nation. He resented that and he was convicted of horse theft and was to serve time in an Ohio prison. In 1889, he was suspected as being the killer of his mother whether it was by accident or intentional. After three shots to the back, shoulder, and face, you would think it was intentional or it was to hide the identity of the woman.

In 1895, he killed the Crittenden brothers per *The San Fransisco Call and Post* newspaper, December 16, 1896. The Crittendens were lawmen in Oklahoma. Reed began living right and became a Deputy Marshal but died in Claremore at the hand of either a bartender or by another deputy. The Cochran Cemetery where his wife's family was buried, was where he was laid to rest. He was only 25 years old. The cemetery was moved by the Army Corps of Engineers to it's present location when Lake Oologah was built. This was close to where Belle had a horse station in Mayes County.

Dr. Jesse Mooney ended up in Purcell. His son, Charles W. Mooney (1911-1982) became a colonel in the U.S. Army in World War II and was a **33rd** degree Mason. Bud Hardcastle knew the Mooneys in Purcell and they ended up being kin to the doctor.

Belle was remembered as an accomplished teacher, guitarist, pianist, and in "Belle Starr, Woman Bandit," in *the Kansas City Times,* May 9, 1919 stated that "Belle Starr had much sympathy for person in want. She would sit hour after hour singing old-fashioned Christian songs, such as "Jesus, lover of my soul" and "There is a fountain filled with blood" and telling stories to children."

She is described as a fine-looking woman, 5'7". She was very quick and graceful. She loved the old-time square dance. Her voice was soft and pleasant and had extremely good manners."

She wanted to ensure her children and the Indians received a decent education, so she built a school and church within three miles of her home. The Younger Bend School stands today near Porum, Oklahoma.

Bud said that Frank James had the tombstone made for Belle, while others say it was Pearl. Belle Starr, the "Bandit Queen" left her mark on Jesse's heart and the world for that matter, but also left us a mystery to solve as her life continues to sparkle into eternity.

Tombstone Inscription:

> Shed not for her the bitter tear,
> Nor give the heart to vain regret
> Tis but the casket that lies her,
> The gem that filled it sparkles yet.

(Painting of Belle, believed to be the most accurate portrayal of her)

"A people without a history is like the wind over buffalo grass."

-*Sioux*

Chapter Twelve: The Sioux who captured his heart

Jesse's charismatic and diplomatic characteristics plus his daring courage, allowed him to go where most men would not tread. He and Frank were known to be friends of the Indian. Jesse could speak 5 different Indian languages, including Indian sign language. Ola Everhard said that Jesse would take her hand and sing love songs to her in the Sioux Indian language.

Jesse learned from the Sioux, how to disguise himself by changing his looks. He would take leaves and berries, crush them into a dye that would color his hair brown, sandy colored, black, or white. It is possible that they also taught him ways of hunting, tracking, maneuvering, and using tree saplings to make hoot owl trees. Jesse may have taught them something himself.

His connection with the Indians, evolved into a spiritual kinship, an ally that would always have his back. This was proven with his relationships with the Apache down south, the five tribes in Indian Territory, but most especially with the Sioux Nation.

Bud was able to follow the trail of Jesse into the Sioux Nation because of a 5'4" lady named Grace Hopkins, who Bud fondly calls, "Blanket-assed Sioux Indian", "Blanket-butted Indian," and "Damned 'ole Sioux dog." All in fun of course. She calls him, "Old Fossil Fart."

Grace had an amazing story to tell about her great grandfather, Joseph Jesse "Tazmawaste" Chase (1870-1940). She was told all her life that her great grandfather was the son of the "famous" Jesse James. I had the honor of speaking with Grace who had met Bud in 2002 and after that had met with her 4-5 times more. "We became instant friends," Bud said. Throughout most of his research, he had never heard of her, but knew the story about Joseph Jesse Chase, the firstborn son of Jesse's. He was able to contact her and connect her to some of her family she had never known and the rest is history. Every bit of her story was true, and Bud has the evidence to back it up. Here is the story of Grace and the things her and Bud discovered together.

The story told to Joseph Jesse Chase by his mother, Margaret "Maggie" Hanyatusnawin Wabashaw (1851-1909), a full-blooded Santee Sioux Indian, tells him that Jesse James was his father and the young girl, Emma who lived with them as a sister, was actually Frank James' daughter.

In the beginning of the spring/summer in 1869, Jesse and Frank robbed a bank in South Dakota, believed to be in Yankton just north of the Missouri River near the border of Nebraska and South Dakota. They headed south and made it across the Missouri River as they were being *chased* by lawmen. They made it through some pretty rough terrain, but they had done it before during their Civil War days. No landscape was too hard for them.

They came upon a dense hedge of overgrown vegetation, populated with scrub oak, briar patches, crooked trees, and heavy brush which fell deep into a treacherous ravine or canyon that seemed to drop off the face of the earth. They drove their mounts into this great abyss called "Devil's Nest."

Many men, such as surveyors and lawmen, or any white man for that matter were leery of stepping into that dark overgrown belly of brush for fear of outlaws and Indians who blended in naturally in their new habitat called, the Santee Sioux Indian Reservation that was just recently established after a horrific slaughter of Minnesota settlers. In turn, the Sioux had just experienced their culture and heritage ripped apart and the punishment for a few, spread to many.

It was only seven years that had passed since the United States-Dakota War of 1862 in southwest Minnesota. It lasted six weeks, resulting in the deaths of hundreds of white settlers and

Dakota Indians. It was brought on by several eastern bands of the Dakota's who were struggling severely with starvation and displacement.

The Dakotas of the Sioux Nation had a beautiful wild and serene area in what is now Minnesota, with plenty of wildlife and rich dark soil to sustain them for centuries. When the white settlers moved in, the Dakotas were forced from their ancestral home to be placed further south along the Minnesota River. They were promised treaties and payments/annuities for the land they left.

Traders also moved in and set up trading posts. The Dakotas very seldom received payment from the government nor did the government pay the traders to provide food for the Indians, a promise they had made. It was in the middle of the Civil War, so money was tight.

The land they were forced to live on was not as fertile as the land they came from, nor the game plentiful. Food became sparse. The promises of the government did not fill their children's stomach and the traders took advantage of the situation by giving their goods to the Indians on credit. The Dakotas were soon controlled and enslaved by their debt to the traders.

The Sioux sold more land to the government, but never received pay or if they did, it all went to the traders to pay off the debts. This in turn set off a chain of events. The Dakota Sioux Indians could not stand for their people to go hungry, especially the children and the elders. The Indians tried to raid a storehouse where food was kept.

One of the traders who had two stores there was Andrew Myrick. He married a Sioux, Nancy Stone Wapaha (1840-1929) who was Grace Hopkin's great, great grandmother. Andrew was called "Wacinco", meaning "hothead." On August 15, 1862, Andrew called a meeting of the traders, the Dakota leaders, and the Bureau of Indian Affairs agent to help resolve the issues of the unsettling Indians. Andrew, getting madder by the second stood up and said, "As far as I'm concerned, if the Indians are hungry, let them eat grass, or their own dung!" [191]

This very vulgar statement prompted the Dakota War, sending the warriors in a rage against the white men. It also led to Andrew being killed and his mouth stuffed full of grass.

Andrew's wife, Nancy was only 22 at the time and was in the middle of this major conflict. Many settlers, nearly 400, lost their lives, their homes, and their families, killing as many Dakotas as they could. Hostages were taken by the Indians. At the end of the uprising, 303 Dakotas were sentenced to death by hanging by the U.S. government. After hearing protests from many citizens and missionaries, President Abraham Lincoln reduced the number to 38. They were hung on a huge platform outside Fort Snelling. It was the largest mass execution in American History.

The Santee Sioux were moved to another location which still proved fruitless and then shipped to the area they would finally call home which lay south of the great Missouri in the northeastern part of Nebraska. They settled in the area that intertwined into Devil's Nest. This was in 1867 and the reservation was officially established in 1869, the year Frank and Jesse appeared.

When Frank and Jesse entered the Santee Sioux reservation, 1869, a transformation was in the works to bring civilization and Christianity to the Indians. President Ulysses S. Grant announced the Peace Policy that year to accomplish these efforts through missionaries.

The Peace Policy was also intended to expose corruption and fraud in the distribution of goods to the Indians by Indian agents. As we learned earlier, the corruption was rampant before, during, and after the Civil War.

At the time that Jesse and Frank came onto the scene, there were not many white men in the area of Devil's Nest, but they loomed near the boundaries, just itching to change the Sioux's society, culture, language, and religion. The Episcopal Church had already sent missionaries to help the Indians in this process. Over 1,000 acres were designated for an Indian Agency, School, and Mission. The mission became the church which was built by Samuel D. Hinman. The mission also served as the first Agency school in 1867.

An interesting fact on Samuel D. Hinman. He had been appointed as a missionary to the Sioux Indians in 1860, sent to establish the Mission of St. John in Redwood County, Minnesota. He married Mary Ellen Bury (Berry). He was priest of the church, but he fled the mission during the uprising in 1862. The mission was destroyed. He then later served the Indians at Fort Snelling and then was assigned to the Santee Agency in Nebraska. His wife died in 1876. Hinman remarried to

Mary Myrick, the daughter of Andrew Myrick (Let them eat grass) and Nancy Stone Wapaha, Grace Hopkin's great, great grandmother.

Many older Sioux told the story of Frank and Jesse coming to Devil's Nest. They said they were brothers, with the last name of "Chase," the first name that popped into their heads. Hmmm? They came in driving a herd of cattle, giving the appearance of a peace offering. Were they trying to help feed the Sioux? I feel sure they were. Was it their cattle they were driving? I kind of doubt it. Both Frank and Jesse really liked the area and were hoping to settle there. They carried with them money belts full of gold and gold dust.

Frank and Jesse became involved in the community. With the money they had, the James' financed a trading post for their own convenience, but maybe also to help the Indians. The man running the post was a Frenchman by the name of Anthony Jaenecque who had no means of support except his blacksmith business. The James were considered "silent partners" with Anthony.

JJ and Frank became involved in the logging field. They hired several Indians to cut the cedar trees that were so thick in the community and sent them down the Missouri river to Yankton, South Dakota.

It wasn't long before two beautiful Sioux sisters caught their eye. The young ladies were Wabashas from a family of "chieftainship" within the Mdewakanton Santee Sioux Tribe. The girls were the cream of the crop of the Santee. Jessie fell in love with Maggie and Frank fell in love with her sister, Mendoza.

It was a whirlwind of a romance that struck the foursome. For the Sioux who desired a bond of marriage, a beautiful Indian custom allowed the couple to take a blanket, go off into the woods together, staying for a few days, and then come back to the village for a celebration of marriage. A priest, by the name of Good Teacher, in the Episcopal Church who served in Santee and was a Sioux himself told Grace about this tradition and he said, "it's the white man who needs the piece of paper", referring to the marriage license. The church allowed this tradition. It was beautiful and it was sacred.

Jesse married Maggie and Frank married Mendoza. The women became pregnant right away. Jesse and Frank had everything they could ever want and were wholeheartedly accepted into the Sioux Nation. They made long-lasting friendships, grounded in trust.

The Episcopal Mission books kept excellent records of births and marriages. One thing though that was found in the books stated Maggie was born in 1851, which would have made her 18 at the time of marriage, but her grave stone was showing she was born in 1856, making her only 13 at the time of marriage.

The mission books were the only way to keep records of the people in the reservation and in the family bibles. For instance: Near this area, was where Lewis and Clark (Meriwether Lewis and William Clark) camped near the Missouri River on their expedition in 1804. Meriwether Lewis also intermingled with the Teton Sioux (Lakota) and built great relationships with them, including a beautiful Sioux woman named Ikpsapewin "Winona." They would have a child, Joseph DeSmet Lewis (1805-1889). It was established in stories and genealogical records that were corroborated by entries in church mission records that this was so. The Yankton Mission of the Episcopal Diocese of South Dakota had entries that would confirm this.

Grace had in her possession, an old large family tree handwritten with Jesse and Maggie's marriage and a birth of a son, Joseph Jesse "Tazmawaste" Chase, born March 13, 1870. A Father Daniel who was a priest in the Santee Episcopal Mission during the life of Joseph Jesse Chase, confirmed this and wrote it out in the family bible and in the records of the Santee Episcopal Mission. In the Family Bible, Father Daniel wrote out the genealogy and underneath Jesse's name was printed, "famous." Father Daniel preached at Joseph Jesse Chase's funeral in 1940 in the Santee Episcopal Church, the Church of Our Most Merciful Saviour, rebuilt in 1884. The original mission church built in 1867 was completely destroyed along with the Agency school by a tornado in June 1870 at the time Frank and Jesse were there.

Grace went to the James/Younger reunion held in Missouri and took these records to the National Archives in Liberty. They were very excited to get to have a copy of the records and are now on file.

Grace's great grandfather, Joseph Jesse Chase was born March 13, 1870 just as the snow was making its last stand upon the reservation. The little boy inherited his father's eyes, beautiful crystal blue eyes. A few weeks later Emma, Frank's daughter was born. With all the reports found, both Frank and Jesse remained there.

Before Joseph Jesse "Tazmawaste" Chase passed away, he told his story to the white men in the town of Niobrara. ("Is This Nebraskan a Secret Son of Jesse James?" - *Omaha World Herald*, Nov. 6, 1938).

Joseph could speak very little English, so he had his daughter-in-law, Evelyn Chase interpret for him while talking to a newspaper man from Omaha in 1938. This was against the tribal rule, but apparently this was important to Joseph and for his children to understand the complete story. Why else would he risk his association with the Santee.

Joseph told the reporter that Frank and Jesse practiced "horse and pistol work" night and day. They would ride hard, over logs, through ravines while shooting their pistols in the air. When one of them threw a snowball up in the air, the other would shoot it with a pistol, saying to the spectators, "That's the way Jesse James would do it." Joseph Chase confirmed that man, his father, was Jesse. It's a big possibility that Joseph Jesse's Indian name, "Tazmawaste" meaning "Good Iron" was referring to Jesse's pistols he brilliantly performed with. This is also what Grace believed.

Three times, marshals came into Devil's Nest looking for the James, but never found them. Zerelda, their mother used to come to Obert, Nebraska, about 20 miles from Devil's Nest and the boys would ride over to see her.

Four months after Joseph was born, July 4, 1870, nearly the whole community of Devil's Nest went to Niobrara to celebrate the 4th at a packing house and brewery. Something bad happened at the James' trading post. Jaenecque was shot in the head and the gun lay on the bed nearby. It appeared to be suicide, but the Sioux believed he was taking more than his share of the money from the boys. As they were getting their gear and saddling up the horses, the James boys gave the girls lots of money and said they would be gone a long time.

Frank and Jesse wrote the girls and said they would come and get them. They had escaped to Devil's Tower in South Dakota, but the mother of the girls would not permit them to go or respond to their letters. Grace wishes that she had the letters.

Their mother had the girls keep quiet about the two white children. She was afraid the government would come and get them and place them in a government school. She had the children hide when white men came around.

Maggie's sister, Mendoza went to Minnesota and was never heard of again. The child, Emma, was left behind and taken into Maggie's home with her family. It is unknown what happened to Emma as she was growing into womanhood. Maggie stayed true to Jesse, but as years went by she knew he would never be able to settle down. Maggie would marry Hanwakanhdi William Goodteacher in 1879 when Joseph was 9 years old.

The older Sioux believe and support this story. Father Daniel did also and then there was a Paul James, no relation, who was a Santee Sioux. He told the family and the press that he later met Frank James after his acquittal in Kansas City. Frank asked Paul what kind of Indian he was, Paul said Santee Sioux. Frank and Paul talked for two hours about their (Frank and Jesse's) adventure in the Sioux nation and Frank asked about Joseph Jesse and Emma, never stating that Emma was his daughter. Grace went up to where Paul James was in Haskell, Kansas and found out that this was true.

Frank James, while talking to Paul stated that the Frenchman was shot by a James' gang member because he was stealing from them.

The James boys stayed from the summer of 1869 to July 4, 1870; except maybe for a bank robbery in Gallatin, Missouri in December 1869, but Devil's Nest was their home base for over a year.

The rest of 1870-71, the boys traveled quite a bit. We know that in 1871, Jesse had his photograph taken in Long Branch, New Jersey. This is where President Grant had his summer home. Ola mentions it in her manuscript and states Jesse gave her the photo, but she stated it was in Long Branch, Kentucky. There is no Long Branch in Kentucky, she just was confused on the state it was in.

(Jesse and Frank James in Long Branch, New Jersey in 1871)

During this entire time, they didn't sit idle. They had a lot of work to do and a lot of gold to gather. It was said they returned to Devil's Nest in 1873 and again in 1876.

In the book, "Echoes of the Past Along Pioneer Trails in Pierce County, Nebraska", written by Esther Kolterman Hanson in 1967, born in 1894, relates the story of Joe Jesse Chase and the news article out of the Omaha newspaper. She was close to the people who were directly connected to the Santee people and those who knew Joe. She said Joe never wanted to talk about it until he was getting on up in years. Grace said that this book was all true, except for the story on Jesse's death in 1882 as told to the whole world.

Another insert in Esther's book reveals why Frank and Jesse may have been back in Devil's Nest in the year 1873. Approximately 3.5 miles west of Adair, Iowa, there was a train robbery thought to be pulled off by Frank and Jesse, Cole, and Jim Younger on July 21, 1873. There was supposedly $75,000 in gold on the Rock Island passenger train, east bound. The gang derailed the train by pulling out the spikes in one section and pulling it over with a rope and attaching it to the end rail. It was a new technique in train robbery. It worked and the train went off the track. The robbers took what they wanted from the passengers but found the safe which only to their dismay had $2,000 inside.

After this incident, Esther wrote, "According to the people living in the Devil's Nest country, the James brothers were hibernating in this place." It was a perfect spot to hideout once again and a perfect time to visit their children and their women. The children would have been around three years old.

In the Spring of 1874, Frank eloped with Anna Ralston and they were married in Omaha, Nebraska. Jesse married Zerelda Amanda "Zee" Mimms, his cousin in June 9, 1874 in Excelsior Springs, Missouri. This is what he told Ola. Other sources say that they were married in her sister's home in Kearney on April 24, 1874. There is no marriage certificate found for Zee and Jesse. Ola did not write much about Zee in her manuscript, apparently it was a subject Jesse did not talk much about. That's another sad story. Zee's sister-in-law who married her brother Robert Mimms was Martha Ann Thomason (1841-1919) the daughter of Robert Thomason and Zerelda James' mother, Sarah Ann Lindsay. Zee's mother was Mary James, sister of Robert James and her father was Rev. John William Mims whose mother was Lucy Poor, and father, Robert Mims.

The other time that Frank and Jesse were back in their old hideout of Devil's Nest was in 1876. They were busy that year. The children in the Santee Sioux Reservation would have been six and Jesse Edwards was a year old, son of Jesse and Zee. It has been documented that Jesse shirked his responsibilities for his family, especially taking care of Zee and the children, but Bud found a lot of evidence that Jesse took care of them, one way or the other, even though his presence was very sporadic and his taste for women spread across many boundaries.

What were the boys doing in 1876? They were conducting and orchestrating the biggest event of their careers. It was not just one thing that spurred their involvement in this life changing event, but a cumulative series of events beginning in 1868.

The Battle of the Washita River

Events leading up to 1876, didn't sit well with Jesse. Just 6 months prior to the time Frank and Jesse arrived in Devil's Nest in 1869, the Battle of the Washita River, November 27, 1868, played out on the white crusted snowy fields along the Washita River in Indian Territory. It occurred in the area of present-day Roger Mills County, Oklahoma, in the far western part of the state. It was a slaughter of innocent and peace keeping Southern Cheyenne women, children, and men, led by Black Kettle who had been agreeable with the U.S. government since they and the Arapaho had signed the Medicine Lodge Peace Treaty, requiring them to move south from present-day Kansas and Colorado to a new reservation in Indian Territory.

The treaty negotiations "guaranteed the Cheyenne their traditional hunting lands as long as there was sufficient buffalo to justify the chase, a crucial treaty stipulation which was tacitly dropped in the subsequent ratification process. This forced them to give up their traditional territory for one, with little arable land and away from buffalo, their main source of meat and a center of their culture." [192]

One by one, the whites had been shuffling the Indians into specific corners of the nation, some had plans in exterminating the Indians and the buffalo all together. The buffalo was the most important element in the world of the Indian. It was used for food, fuel, clothing, shelter, weapons, utensils, medicines, and so much more. General Sheridan and General Sherman were adamant on having a massive buffalo hunt to destroy the Indian's food supply. They couldn't beat them otherwise.

In 1868, General Sheridan wrote Sherman "that their best hope to control the Native Americans was to make them poor by the destruction of their stock, and then settle them on the lands allotted to them." [193]

Six-thousand members of various tribes, Cheyenne, Arapaho, Kiowa, Comanche, and Kiowa-Apache made their winter camp along the Washita River. Black Kettle took his Southern Cheyenne tribe to the southern portion of the Washita River and desired peace. He began to prepare them to travel even more southward to the reservation near Fort Cobb in compliance with the U.S. government.

Just a few days before the long journey south, on November 25th, 1868 a small band of young warriors from the different tribes banded together and raided white settlements up north, even into Kansas. Several warriors came through Black Kettle's camp which created a trail by the robbers, leading directly to the Southern Cheyenne.

Lt. Colonel George Armstrong Custer was in charge of the 7th Cavalry Regiment, headquartered at Fort Riley, Kansas. He took part in Major General Winfield Scott Hancock's expedition against the Cheyenne in the summer of 1867.

That fall, Custer was court martialed for "absence without leave, conduct to the prejudice of good order and military discipline, and the unmerciful treatment of deserters." He was found guilty and sentenced with a suspension of his rank and pay for one year.

Before completing his sentence, Major General Sheridan reinstated Custer to command the 7th Cavalry and gave Custer the assignment of a winter campaign against the Cheyenne in 1868. Custer was to take on the raiding parties that played havoc in Kansas and Indian Territory. Custer's earlier focus was on the Cheyenne and Lakota warriors. This new uprising was an opportunity for him to finish what he had started.

Custer was proud of his service to the U. S. government. He had just seen his glory days, fighting as Major General under General Sheridan for the Union cavalry during the Civil War. Custer wanted to become president, so he began planning his career ladder toward that goal. His ego was growing day by day.

After the Civil War, Custer was offered $10,000 in gold to become an adjutant general in the army of Benito Juarez of Mexico, who was fighting against Maximillian. President Grant and Secretary Stanton endorsed it, but General Sheridan, U. S. Secretary of State William H. Seward, and Mrs. Custer opposed. General Sheridan had other plans for Custer.

On November 27, 1868, Custer led his cavalry, following the trail of thieves to Black Kettle's camp. What is so odd, instead of leading the men as a commander, Custer was promoting himself as leader of a parade. He had the cavalry musicians riding alongside the soldiers and were ordered to play the song, "Garryowen" to signal the attack.

As the music was still playing, the soldiers swooped down at daylight, killing everyone in sight, including women and children. There was no mercy. It was a horrific scene. It was a massacre. Black Kettle was holding his peace treaty when they hit the camp, but the soldiers didn't pay him any mind. He and his wife, Medicine woman, were shot in the back. Fifty-three of the women and children who were not shot were taken captive and used as human shields to escape the band of Indians who were forming over the horizon for a counterattack. The Indian tribes knew if Custer did that while they were under a peace treaty he would continue.

The Cheyenne hostages taken from the Battle of the Washita by Custer, were brought to Fort Supply, 75 miles north from the massacre site. Then Custer's troops went back down to the battlefield, buried the dead, picked up stray Indians, and traveled on to Fort Cobb, staying there from December 18, 1868 until January 6, 1869, 19 days. All inhabitants of Fort Cobb were moved to an area, 30 miles south that would become a new fort, more abundant in water resources, trees, "green grass", and areas of protection.

Fort Cobb was abandoned by March. The area where they had moved was indeed a more suitable place but was in the heart of Indian country. The area was home to the Comanche and Kiowa prior to the Civil War, making their camp near Bluff Creek. This was the place Randolph Marcy had found and wrote about on his expedition in 1852.

Marcy and Sheridan were involved in the establishment of this new fort, Fort Sill, near Lawton, Oklahoma, 30 miles south of Fort Cobb. Tents and teepees began to decorate the landscape. Custer stayed there, bound and determined to find the escaped Cheyenne who fled the scene of the massacre.

The interesting thing that came up with research was that some of the Southern Cheyenne who escaped from the battlefield of the Washita River, was known to be somewhere in the Wichita

Mountains and some in Texas. The Wichita Mountains was just a short distance to the west of Fort Sill.

Custer and his troops found a large group of Cheyenne near present-day Wheeler, Texas by Sweetwater Creek in the Texas Panhandle and took three chiefs as hostages. Custer negotiated a return of two white women the Cheyenne had kidnapped but Custer did not return the chiefs. Later, while in prison camps, the chiefs would be killed in an "accident."

Five years after this horrendous event, the same year that Jesse had hid out again in Devil's Nest, 1873, Lieutenant Colonel George A. Custer was assigned to take 6 companies of the 7th Cavalry to Fort Abraham Lincoln. It was situated on the river bluffs of the Missouri River across from present-day Bismarck, North Dakota. It would have been a straight shot up the Missouri from Devil's Nest; approximately 400 miles.

Custer's mission was "to further the advancement of the Northern Pacific Railroad and open the westward expansion of the American frontier. In addition to protecting the railroad, the troops accompanied the Yellowstone Survey Expedition of 1873. This was the year that 70 Santee Sioux died in a smallpox epidemic, blamed on U.S. issued blankets given to the Sioux that were laced with the smallpox virus.

The following year, in July 1874, Custer would lead an expedition into the Black Hills, "an event that would change the history of the region." [194] Gold had been rumored to have been discovered in the Black Hills but was not yet publicized.

Calamity Jane was on the expedition with Custer as a teamster and they discovered rich minerals, including pure gold. The Black Hills would be known as the next *El Dorado*.

Custer sent word back to General Alfred Terry confirming the evidence of gold and a land of abundance near the present-day town of Custer, South Dakota. Word spread, creating a mass of miners, investors, and land speculators to swarm the area. The town of Deadwood was formed. This movement and infringement violated the 1868 Fort Laramie Treaty with the Sioux. It started the Black Hills War, known also as the Great Sioux War of 1876.

The U.S. government offered the Sioux 7 million dollars for the land in the Black Hills in Western South Dakota. Sitting Bull and Crazy Horse and other chiefs said, "no, not for sale."

The Sioux saw the writing on the wall. They knew if they didn't fight, they would lose their land once more. They were already preparing for war.

Preparing for The Battle of Little Bighorn

This next part will describe a very controversial subject, The Battle of Little Bighorn, also known as The Battle of the Greasy Grass, or Custer's Last Stand that took place on June 25-26, 1876. The preparations for this confrontation started early for both sides.

Jesse never told Ola about this story, nor the story of Joseph Jesse Chase, but had implied about his good relations with the Sioux and other Indian tribes. However, Jesse told Howk.

The story of the battle and Jesse's involvement, was told to Bud from several creditable sources and he knew there must be some truth in it because it was also included in Schrader and Howk's book, "Jesse James Was One of His Names". The story claims Jesse supplied guns, ammunition, and other goods to the Indians to kill and destroy Custer. In the book, Schrader not only had Jesse's account per Howk, but quoted men who were there also. That was quite a statement.

The story is too incredible to believe. If this was true, Jesse's involvement would be considered one of the most treasonous acts ever committed in the United States at that time in history, next to the assassination of President Lincoln. As you remember, Jesse told Ola and Aubrey Everhard, that if he had told people who he was, before 1948, after he had turned 100, he would have been hung for treason.

Bud kept an open mind but could not rest until he found evidence that supported the story. He hesitated to add this story in the book, but after seven years of working with Bud on this book, he wants it told. He said it's part of the story.

Bud went to reliable sources to weigh facts from fiction, those whose fathers were connected or related to Jesse, those who had been in contact with Jesse and gang members, treasure hunters, a boy scout leader who was in charge of a boy scout camp near where Jesse and the Cheyenne met to exchange gold for weapons, and native Oklahomans from native tribes to pale faces who knew the land, and its history passed down from generation to generation.

Bud was told an incredible story and his confidence grew as everything began to check out with what he was told. With the clues, Bud's research, and lots of foot work he said, this story appears very creditable. Bud has found the evidence which leads to a multitude of treasures, both in the people and the gold that Jesse gained. In my own research, I too find evidence of this in so many different sources scattered about. You just have to pull them all together; "put 2 and 2 together" as Bud says.

Even of greater importance, Grace Hopkins, the great, great granddaughter of Jesse James and the Santee Sioux Indian woman, Maggie Wabashaw believes that the story is true. Her Santee Sioux people participated in the Battle of the Little Bighorn.

How did Jesse get involved?

During the Civil War, Jesse made many friends with the Indians in Indian Territory and they protected each other. "They had more of a Confederate-way of thinking," Bud said, and many fought with the Confederacy. Jesse had a love for the Sioux and bonded with their spirit and their way of life. They both had grievances towards Custer, during the Civil War and thereafter. Jesse was aligned with their sentiment, especially when it came to people's rights and the destruction of their livelihood. He had experienced it firsthand.

As the Sioux started preparing for war, which included the Lakota and Dakota, others joined in a coalition of different tribes, the Cheyenne and Arapaho. Many of the Cheyenne and Arapaho, were those who were victims and family members of the Sand Creek Massacre on November 29, 1864 in southeastern Colorado Territory. They witnessed the massacre at the Battle of the Washita River and had a vendetta that would follow them to Montana. They had escaped from Custer during the Battle of the Washita. They sought out a meeting with Jesse, asking for his help to prepare for battle against Custer and those who wanted to exterminate the Plains Indians. They knew Custer was coming for them.

Why Jesse?

It wasn't just Jesse who was involved in supplying the Indians, but the mighty underground organization of the KGC. There were lots of men involved and lots of coordination within the society with men planted in different areas, businesses, military, and government positions. This story remained very guarded and secret for over a century.

Custer was wanting to be glorified in controlling the Indian population, just as the government was doing in downsizing the buffalo to extinction. To get his glory in history, he had to win great battles against the Indians. He wanted to use his accomplishments as a great leader to win the presidential election, succeeding President Ulysses S. Grant in 1877. The KGC did not want that, they had someone else in mind.

Bud discovered with the help of Lou Kilgore, missing pieces to fill in the story, making more sense to this scenario. It all fits perfectly. The following information came from a man who lived in Arkansas and had partnered with Jesse. He outlined what Jesse was doing in 1870-71. We will introduce you to him in Chapter Twenty-One.

After Frank and Jesse left the Santee Sioux Reservation in 1870, they had a $10,000 reward on their heads for shooting a man in self-defense. He was referring to the Frenchman who ran the trading post in Santee.

Jesse was described as a peddler with a wagon full of goods in Johnson County, Missouri in 1870 where Frank and Jesse were both laying low. Jesse was going by the name of *Jim Reed* at the time. He described himself as a "railroad hand" on the 1870 census. His brother Frank went into the coal mining business with another partner. Jesse must have secured several wagons because the partner of Frank, a very prominent man, wanted Jesse to help move him to Kansas. He did help the man move, and it appears that Jesse had access to wagons and the railroad.

After traveling in 1871, and pulling off a bank robbery in Iowa, Frank and Jesse would both end up in Indian Territory.

Schrader wrote in his book that Jesse had a very successful freighting service. Bud had researched this extensively and discovered, he definitely was a freighter who was hired by the U.S. government to take supplies to the army at Fort Sill which was established in the Spring of 1869. Remember, Marcy in 1852, predicted that the very spot where Fort Sill was established in 1869 was near the area in the Wichita Mountains that Marcy said would become a productive mining district.

During the years between 1869-1875, the Buffalo Soldiers were breaking ground at the future home of Fort Sill and per instructions from General Sheridan would be building a quadrangle for their fortress with the officer's headquarters on the *northside*. Sound familiar? They not only needed food, weaponry, ammunition, blankets, etc., but building material as well. They also needed supplies for the thousands of Indians who were coming to the reservations. The government promised in their treaties that they would supply their every need if they remain peaceful and remain on the reservation.

From the wonderful website of the Cowley County Historical Society Museum out of Winfield, Cowley County, Kansas, we see a glimpse of what was occurring around Fort Sill. There are actual letters and reports from and to Fort Sill, describing the environment, hostiles, and depredations in that part of the country. It also describes the transportation of goods throughout Indian Territory.

In the latter part of 1871-1872, Jesse was indeed partnering with the railroad and the government. The freight would be shipped on the railroad to Caddo, Oklahoma, and then be transported by freight wagons to Fort Sill.

The first train to cross the Oklahoma plains was the Missouri-Kansas-Texas Railway (MK&T) which entered Oklahoma in 1871 and established a station in Caddo, Oklahoma in 1872. It originated near Fort Riley, Kansas and was first established under the name of Union Pacific, Southern Branch. The railway company received land grants to build this railway with the initial plan to supply frontier military posts, eventually reaching Fort Worth. The U.S. government made a contract with the railway company to transport a large amount of supplies to Fort Sill. The load of supplies would come from St. Louis and Fort Leavenworth, Kansas. The supplies for Fort Sill would consist of "Indian Goods" and stores for troops stationed at the post, weighing 3-4,000 tons.

Since no other railway was up and running in Oklahoma, the fort had to have the supplies taken off the train in Caddo and transported in large dray wagons to the fort, requiring overland transport, 180 miles. They could travel up to 24 miles per day. It would take 7 ½ days to get to their destination.

The government put in charge for the overland transportation the company of Messrs. Maurice & Graham, of St. Louis. They were highly recommended.

Another freighting company, not utilizing the railway, was Bernard, Irwin & Co. of Westport, a suburb of Kansas City which started out of Arkansas City, Kansas with 25 wagons and 350 cattle with 500,000 lbs of freight. Westport is near the area where the Younger's father was killed and also was where Quantrill's Raiders were stationed for a while during the Civil War. Another company was Neal & Co., led by Moses Neal, of Humboldt, Kansas. He specifically took his goods to the Cheyenne and Wichita Agencies. It is unknown if Jesse was working for one of these companies, or like Schrader and Howk said, he could have owned one of them under another name of course.

We learn more about the area from a family that Bud knew well that were pioneers. Bud had a book that the patriarch of the family wrote about her life on the Oklahoma prairie. The book was

"From Pioneers to Progress" by Anita Lindsay, published in 1957. Mrs. Anita Lindsey as a little girl, lived right on the wagon road to Fort Sill. The town of Lindsay, Oklahoma was named after her husband, Lewis Lindsay. The town Lindsay is 65 miles northeast of Fort Sill.

Mrs. Lindsay's family was one of the first to settle on Elm Springs, now known as Erin Springs, south of Lindsay. It was a natural spring that ran between the stage depot and the Washita River.

Anita Lindsay, born in 1869 was the daughter of Alzire McCaughey and William Powell. Her father died when she was only two months old and an Irish immigrant, Frank Murray stepped in to become her father two years later. In 1871, they moved to Elm Springs where there was only a "stage stand" and a one room shack on the banks of the Washita River. They were the very first settlers in the area. It was a quiet place in Elm Springs with the nearest neighbor 25 miles away. The stagecoach ran from Caddo to Fort Sill, passing by the house, carrying mail and maybe two or three passengers. They ran only twice a week. They were a welcomed sight, bringing news of the country as well as news of outbreaks of Indians or outlaws. This was also the route for the freight wagons to travel. Anita said, "There were not many settlers between Fort Sill and Caddo."

From her own words, "The Government route crossed the Washita at Cherokee Town, a small settlement across the river from Pauls Valley, and came up on the south side of the river, between here and Pauls Valley, never crossing it. It crossed Cabell Creek at about the present crossing and came on past the north side of our house and along this side of the river, on west to Rush Springs, and then on to Fort Sill.

"The Washita River didn't have too many crossings. We had no bridges and very few fords. We had to go along the river and cross where we could, the river was deep in those days. The shallowest crossing on the river was at *Rock Crossing*, which was this side of the present railroad bridge east of what is now the town of Lindsay, but while it was the best crossing on the river, it was too far to use all the time.

"Long trains of wagons drawn by oxen came past our house along the Government route, carrying food, ammunition and other supplies from Caddo to Fort Sill. Quite a small army of soldiers were kept at Fort Sill and it required a quantity of food to supply the needs of both men and horses. The freighters who drove the supply wagons for the Government were from everywhere and often adventurers. They were a fearless lot. There would be several together. Each driver had a dozen oxen yoked together in pairs, with wooden yokes. Wagons would be coupled together, as many as twelve. These freighters walked along with their teams. Jesse James was one of the freighters. He was a young man then, before he became an outlaw. He sometimes stopped by the house. I do not remember him, as I was very small at the time." [195]

Anita's family grew corn and was selling it to Fort Sill. They utilized the freighters in delivering their corn. They made a lot of money during those days.

Bud discovered that Jesse was also driving freight wagons through Johnsonville, Indian Territory which was a stage stop east of Fort Sill. This was where my 2nd great granduncle, who supposedly rode with Jesse, was gunned down by a Deputy U.S. Marshal in 1885. There is nothing much left of Johnsonville, but it is along the banks of the Canadian River. It is north of Byars and was close to the site where the initial Camp Arbuckle was established by Captain Randolph Marcy of the Fifth Infantry. Because of the location, malaria became an issue and they had to move to north of the present-day Davis, Oklahoma to establish Fort Arbuckle.

At one time, there was a workable gold mine 10 miles from Johnsonville and 5 miles west of Byars.

"I've heard all my life there was gold found near Byars," Bud Hardcastle said, "I found that proof in the 1980's." Bud told the story in The Purcell Register, October 19, 2006. He said a Spaniard came from Ada in the early 1800s to the site now Byars and discovered the mine, containing gold and silver. Bud found assay reports and documentation proving it was true. Bud set out to find the mine and he did. The entrance was blocked with a boulder. Bud also found the old Spanish arrastra located near the mine.

Bud said there are significant carvings around the mine and on the Canadian river that indicates Jesse was there.

The Johnsonville stage/freight road through Johnsonville may have been the "Johnson Trail" that was up and running in 1871, "fully open for all teams coming from Cottonwood Falls, Kansas and points further east." [196] It had an excellent ferry and was the quickest way to Fort Sill. I believe it must have been established by Montford T. Johnson who in 1868 created a ranch two miles northeast of present-day Washington in McClain County. He expanded his ranches to Johnsonville, Chickasha, Tuttle, Silver City close to the Chisholm Trail and just northeast of Fort Sill. He had cattle to move. Montford was known as a very generous man, helping and supporting all races that were settling in Indian Territory. An excellent book on the Johnson family is "The Chickasaw Rancher," by Neil R. Johnson, 1960 and an excellent documentary called, "Montford Johnson: An Original Brand", 2022 on Prime Video.

While all this movement of goods was going on in Indian Territory, many wagons, stagecoaches, and white settlements were being attacked by bands of raiding Indians. In July 1871, a letter sent to Washington from Fort Sill; "Kiowa Indians have made efforts to induce the Cheyenne and Sioux to join them in a war against the whites, but thus far they have failed." [197]

Texas was becoming a slaughterhouse with the raiders crossing the Red River, killing, stealing, kidnapping families, and burning new settlements at every turn. At one point, the Texas governor accused someone out of Fort Sill as being gunrunners for the Indians as they had weapons of all kinds in their hands. Schrader even puts in his book that Jesse, long before Custer's demise was a gunrunner for the Northern Plains Indians. Not sure if this was so, but as Bud always says, "It's a possibility."

Fort Sill hired independent scouts to keep an eye on the restless Indians. They hired Buffalo Bill Cody and Wild Bill Hickok. Wild Bill was also driving a freight team in 1860 from Independence, Missouri to Santa Fe, New Mexico. Hickok was a spy and teamster for the Union Army during the Civil War. Buffalo Bill claimed that he saw Hickok disguised as a confederate officer in Missouri in 1864. Hickok eventually was a scout for Custer. In Wikipedia, "Henry M. Stanley, of the Weekly Missouri Democrat, reported Hickok to be "an inveterate hater of Indian People." [198] Jesse always had a problem with Wild Bill.

Not much is said about Buffalo Bill and Hickok at Fort Sill, but the Oklahoma documentary, "Historically Speaking" in Episode 4, Season 1, "History of Ft. Sill, Oklahoma" on youtube.com, revealed the amazing history of the fort and Historian Frank Siltman, Regional Museum Director at Fort Sill did an excellent job narrating the story, confirming Buffalo Bill Cody and Wild Bill Hickok were there.

I feel sure that Jesse James knew them well way before this time. Buffalo Bill Cody became a Freemason in Platte Valley Lodge No. 32, in North Platte, Nebraska on March 5, 1870. He became a Knight Templar in 1889 and received his 32nd degree in the Scottish Rite of Freemasonry in 1894. Jesse had a long-standing friendship with Cody.

Buffalo Bill had been working with a freight caravan that delivered supplies to Fort Laramie in Wyoming. In 1863, he enlisted as a teamster in Company H, 7th Kansas Cavalry and was discharged in 1863. He became a buffalo hunter and supplied railroad construction workers with beef. In 1868, he went back into the army and was stationed at Fort Larned in Kansas. He rode as a lone dispatch courier to Fort Zarah, Fort Hays, Fort Dodge, and back. He rode hard through hostile country and part of the time on foot. General Sheridan was so impressed that he assigned Cody as Chief Scout for the 5th Cavalry.

Cody was asked by General Sheridan if he would take the Grand Duke Alexis from Russia on a buffalo hunt in January 1872. Going along with them was Brevet General George Custer. Surprisingly, Sheridan wanted to add an extra punch to the party and invited the famous Sioux warriors, Spotted Tail and Whistler with 100 braves. To ensure there was no firing of weapons in the direction of the dignitaries or army personnel, a body of U.S. Cavalrymen came along. It was quite a successful hunt where Buffalo Bill Cody really put on a show.

Buffalo Bill Cody's philosophy is pointed out in Wikipedia and agrees with Jesse's. "As a frontier scout, Cody respected Native Americans and supported their civil rights. He employed many Native Americans, as he thought his show offered them good pay with a chance to improve their lives. He described them as the "former foe, present friend, the American" and once said that "every Indian outbreak that I have ever known has resulted from broken promises and broken treaties by the government." [199]

During the construction of Fort Sill, Jesse became a Deputy U.S. Marshal in Indian Territory during the period of 1872-1874 under Chief Marshal James Jackson McAlester. Jesse was going by the name of John Franklin. Bud verified this in the Fort Smith records.

In June 6, 1874 to May 31, 1875, Jesse was a Texas Ranger in Company E in the Frontier Battalion of the Texas Rangers. He was a freight driver, verified by the Texas Rangers Hall of Fame in Waco, Texas. He was going by the name of Benjamin Franklin Johnson.

Jesse had a lot of experience as a freighter and apparently, he was well respected in Indian Territory from the highest of authorities, to the little children in the reservations. His work would come in handy for the long drive up to the Dakotas wouldn't you say?

There is not much information on what Frank was doing, but he was in Indian Territory. Around March of 1872, Frank had a love affair with Josephine Welch, a Cherokee woman who ended up giving him a daughter, Dec. 29, 1872 in Vinita, Indian Territory. Her name was Mary Plina (James) Norris. There is an affidavit to support this, signed by L. H. Tackett of Claremore, Oklahoma, signed on August 31, 1908. He was the ex-husband of Mary Plina Norris. [200]

Frank also had a son with another woman, and on the verge of marrying another Indian woman, but she died the day of their wedding. He met another lady in Indian Territory, and they worked together at a trading post. He stayed close to Fort Smith and Hackett City, Arkansas. Frank was in the trading business, which could have really helped the cause of the KGC. He also was working alongside a family who were heavily involved in Freemasonry, the Williams' family. Frank was taught surveyorship and became a skilled surveyor which was also much needed in the KGC.

I am sure Jesse had several things on the side he was doing beside his jobs as a freight hauler, "rangering", and marshaling, but you can just imagine what some of that was. Him and Frank were noted as being responsible for the following jobs during 1871-1875:

<u>1871</u> *Ocobock Brother's Bank robbery in Corydon, Iowa – June 3, 1871

<u>1872</u> *Bank of Columbia robbery in Columbia, Kentucky - April 29, 1872 *Robbery of the Kansas City Exposition Ticket Office at the fair – September 26, 1872

<u>1873</u> *Genevieve Savings Bank robbery, Genevieve, Missouri – May 27, 1873
*Chicago, Rock Island, and Pacific Railroad Train robbery outside Adair, Iowa – July 21, 1873 - when they hid out in Devil's Nest

<u>1874</u> *Stagecoach robbery near Hot Springs, Arkansas - January 15, 1874
*Held up the St. Louis Iron Mountain & Southern Railroad Train at Gads Hill, Missouri - January 31, 1874. They hid the money at Meramec Caverns. Gold coins were discovered on February 4, 1941.
*Stagecoach robbery in Austin, Tx. – April 1874
*The Kansas Pacific Railroad Train robbery in Muncie, Kansas – December 8, 1874

<u>1875</u> *Huntington Bank robbery in Huntington, West Virginia on September 5, 1875, on Jesse's 28th birthday

There were many others that the James/Younger gang were accused of, but both Frank and Jesse said they were innocent on a lot of them and guilty of those that weren't blamed on them.

Who knows the real tales of the James' and the Youngers? They were certainly busy as freighters, traders, lovers, outlaws, and lawmen during this time. We will go further into Jesse's time as a soldier and lawman in another chapter, but this is important to introduce this here to give the reader the idea of how busy Jesse was and why he was partnering with the Indians. He had the skills, the leadership ability, the manpower and the contacts within Indian Territory, Texas, Kansas, Missouri, and Nebraska to complete the mission, but most of all he kept his word. Both the Indians and Jess knew each other well and knew each other's business. It was a solid trust, like no other.

Jesse was also the man in charge of the money and wealth of the KGC, which was a huge organization, and he would be the one to trade with. The Indians had something of value to trade and knew Jesse would be most interested. What they had was gold. They planned a meeting.

Gold meant trouble to the Indians. It was worthless to them. When they robbed settlers and travelers, they took what they could use and would bury the gold they had stolen

Fort Sill was approximately 18 miles to the South of the place where the Cheyenne would meet Jesse. Surrounding the fort, was a reservation for the Comanches, Kiowas, and Apaches. Also, there were displaced tribes in the mix from the past battles and skirmishes.

Custer never found the other Cheyenne that slipped from his grasp after the Battle of the Washita River. He would end up going back to Kansas. The Cheyenne had teamed up with the Sioux in Indian Territory and Texas. There were several camps near Adobe Walls near the Canadian River in Texas. It is very possible, that many Southern Cheyenne, Sioux, Arapaho and Kiowa warriors remained hidden in the Wichita Mountains as well and this may have been those who met with Jesse. We don't know.

More information from Fort Sill from the Cowley County Historical Society Museum out of Winfield, Cowley County, Kansas:

On December 9th, 1874, the 8th U.S. Cavalry commander, Captain C. A. Hartwell reported from the Indian Expedition Camp on the Washita River in Texas, near the present-day town of Miami, Texas that they began traveling on the Canadian River, 5 miles north of Adobe Walls. They were scouting that area since the Second Battle of Adobe Walls occurred less than 6 months ago. The battle was between civilians living at the Adobe Walls trading post, traders, buffalo hunters and a war party of Comanche, Kiowa, and Cheyenne, 250-700 warriors led by the Comanche Chief Quanah Parker. The white men established this trading post, mainly for the buffalo hunters to come into the ripe and fruitful areas of the panhandle to hunt buffalo, sell the hides, and pick up supplies. The Indians felt threatened. The buffalo hunters were breaking the Medicine Lodge Peace Treaty, which allowed the Indians to continue using this land as their hunting grounds. Between 1872-1874, 3,000 buffalo per day were killed. By this time, the buffalo population was dwindling in number as well as the Indian's way of life. In 1840, there were 60 million buffalo, by 1890, there were less than 500. Thousands, upon thousands of their horses were killed also.

The soldiers vs. the Comanche, Kiowa, Southern Cheyenne, and Arapaho were in battle mode. The Red River War was in full swing to displace the tribes and forcibly relocate them to the reservations. George W. Arrington joined Company E in August 1874.

The Battle of Palo Duro took place in September 1874 when the U.S. Army led by Ranald Mackenzie, attacked a large Indian settlement at the base of Palo Duro Canyon. They had left the reservations and were hunkering down for the winter with supplies and nearly 2,000 horses. The battle was won by the army and the horses were slaughtered.

While scouting in late December 1874 near Adobe Walls, when things were still hot, the U.S. Cavalry spotted a **Mexican bull train** (a wagon train pulled by oxen) which consisted of 19 wagons and 70 men, and 100 head of cattle. They said they were hunting for buffalo, but the officers believed they were trading with the Cheyenne. The Mexicans were in the camps of the Cheyenne and the Cheyenne were in their camps.

There was lots of trading going on, from the Mexican border to the top of the Texas Panhandle. Reckon Jesse was a trader with the Cheyenne and the Mexicans?

On December 31st, 1874, a letter from Charlie Mann who was in the surveyor's camp on Elk Creek on the Kiowa and Comanche Reservation wrote that Fort Sill had "2,500 Kiowas and Comanches camped at the agency, drawing rations. There were about 500 ponies that were taken from the Indians, shot <u>according to orders</u>, and about fifteen hundred sold at auction. The greater part of these were bought by Texans at an average price of $5 per head. That will probably cripple the Indians on the warpath to some extent." "All of the Indians on the warpath have fled to the **Guadalupe mountains** for protection." (Cowley County Historical Society Museum out of Winfield, Cowley County, Kansas)

This statement caught my eye. The Guadalupe Mountains are bordered by the Pecos River valley and Llano Estacado, jutting out of West Texas and southeastern New Mexico. They were near El Paso. This area was also an important spot to Jesse. To the south, was the Mexican border.

Fort Sill, January 23, 1875, General Miles who had camped west of Adobe Walls rounded up 400-500 Comanche and Kiowa and made them march for 25 days in the dead of winter, without stopping to secure meat for their people. Miles led them back to Fort Sill. They were in terrible shape. "**It was over a country never ventured upon by whites at this season**, will be put down as one of the most remarkable on record as illustration the hardships and privations men are capable of enduring." Their route was from the Canadian River, straight south through the North branch of the Red River down to the Prairie Dog Town Fork of the Red River, basically the area that frames the eastern portion of the Texas Panhandle and then they turned east heading to Fort Sill.

This statement leads us to believe that this trail was not traveled much by the whites, but as you can see, it was a main thoroughfare for traders, buffalo hunters, Indians, and Mexicans. It was unheard of to be traveling during winter.

Fort Sill, January 24, 1875 – "The present has been an uncommonly severe winter, but I am told that the climate generally is mild and equable." It was a bad winter, and no one was traveling. What perfect timing for Jesse to travel.

On January 25, 1875, Frank and Jessie's mother Zerelda was severely injured when the Pinkertons threw an incendiary device into her house. It exploded, severing her right forearm and killing Archie, their half-brother. Pinkerton denied that the raid's intent was arson, but biographer Ted Yeatman located a letter by Pinkerton in the Library of Congress in which Pinkerton declared his intention to "burn the house down." [201]

Ola asked Jesse where they were when this happened. Jesse told Ola that him and Frank were in Louisiana and Texas teaching school at the time, but nothing has been found to substantiate that. I feel sure Jesse did not want Ola to know what he was involved in, instead of protecting his family, which I'm sure weighed heavy on his mind.

I believe during that time, January and February of 1875, Jesse and some of his men were in Texas, down on the border near the Guadalupe Mountains. In the company of Texas Rangers that Jesse was a part of during that period, was previously led by Captain William Jeff Maltby under Major Jones. In early June 1874, Maltby recruited men from Burnett, Brown, and Coleman Counties of Texas. The quota of men needed was filled the 2nd day of the organization in *Brownwood*, June 5, 1874. Jesse signed up the following day. The unit was assigned scout duty, in Brown, San Saba, and Lampasas counties of Texas. The Llano/San Saba area was known to be a hotbed of silver. If you remember the story on the San Saba River, it was important to Albert Pike. Pike was told in 1831, presumably while in Taos or Santa Fe on his expedition trip, of the story of Spanish miners who were working on the San Saba River in Texas.

Maltby's unit was called upon to help during the 2nd Battle of Adobe Walls in June 27, 1874. By Dec. 13,1874, B.S. Foster became commanding officer. Their assignment was to track down fugitives and outlaws in the Rio Grande valley. This must have also included renegade Indians.

This puts Jesse in the very spot where the Cheyenne were hiding in 1874-75. Jesse must have had word of a gold shipment, possibly from a mine around Chihuahua, Mexico that would be loaded on burros, led by many Mexican guardsmen heading north. They would be in a pack train similar to the one that was traveling up into the panhandle, reported on December 9, 1874.

These stories place Jesse near Adobe Walls in the Texas Panhandle and now in the Rio Grande Valley. It is unknown for sure where Jesse had planned to overtake the pack train, but it would have been one of the two areas noted. The writer's supposition is that Jesse had contact and help from the Cheyenne in the panhandle with information from the Mexicans in their camp, leading Jesse to the border where he received help from the Cheyenne renegades in the Guadalupe Mountains. It would have taken a lot of men to pull this heist and a lot of trust on both sides.

Most of the stories of the Mexican pack train, place Jesse near the border and near Chihuahua, Mexico.

In the dead of winter in 1875, Jesse and his men attacked and overtook the Mexican pack train, packed full of gold. As they had done before, they may have taken the Mexican's clothes and sombreros and disguised themselves as Mexicans and followed the trail up to Indian Territory. They could have also been dressed as rangers or militia.

There were gold bars on the 18 burros valued up to $2 million dollars.

Jesse and his men took the burros to Indian Territory, most likely on the Dona Ana Trail where they knew they could bury it and keep a watchful eye on it. The Dona Ana Trail was a little known trail that Jesse utilized a lot, starting in Chihuahua, Mexico going up through El Paso into Dona Ana County, New Mexico east of the present-day town of Las Cruces through the Organ Mountains, through Texas, across the Red River and just west of the Chisholm Trail. During their trip, a blinding blizzard hit them hard. They had 18 burros loaded down.

The story goes that burros became extremely burdened and Jesse and his men were following East Cache Creek, where Lake Elsworth lies today in Oklahoma. The lake wasn't there during Jesse's days, but was built by the City of Lawton for a water supply source in 1962. East Cache Creek is its stream source. It is south of the present-day town of Apache.

They were heading to their old hideout in the Keechi Hills, nearly 20 miles away to the northeast, but they weren't going to make it in the shape they were in. It was near here by a creek that Jesse had to put down a burro and left his mark pointing the direction they would be going with the gold. Jesse placed a burro shoe in a tree and emptied both his six shooters in a nearby cottonwood.

They traveled 3 more grueling hours to the northeast and seeing that they nor the burros could continue, they temporarily buried the gold in a ravine, kicking off the soil from the canyon walls and covering the rest with boulders and rocks. They let the burros go and the men gathered at a place where they could burn the pack saddles to keep them warm.

Many historians and treasure hunters have their ideas where they got out of the weather. Bud knows. He told me he had been looking for it for 20 years. He had the map which was drawn out by Jesse himself and Bud showed me the map on our first meeting. The reason you know it was the horse and saddle cave is that it has a saddled horse in front of the cave.

Right now, the cave is on private property and Bud has been there many times with the permission of the landowner. I was very honored that Bud took the writer to this very place where he believes it is the long-lost Horse and Saddle Cave that so many men have been looking for. I said, "Wow Bud, how did you ever find it?" Bud replied, "Getting out and looking hun, whatcha gotta do. It's the only cave out here to get horses out of the weather. They got several in there. You are one of the very few that knows where it's at." I felt very privileged and honored that Bud trusted me with this information.

(Bud believes this to be the Horse and Saddle Cave (Bud standing at the entrance, 1989))

There are some carvings in the cave and a back entrance like Jesse liked. Bud said, "He wasn't going to be in a cave that didn't have a rear entrance to it. He didn't want to get caged up.

After the weather cleared, they could travel on to the Keechi Hills, but not before they buried some of the gold and other items they collected. Bud believes there is buried gold on the outside of this cave. In Steve Wilson's book, he stated that Joe Hunter had this map of the Horse and Saddle Cave, but never quite figured out where it was. On the map, "it showed a grave, a horse and saddle, a cave, various symbols, and five caches of buried loot, with the descriptions: "$32,000 in gold, 136 paces north of cave; $28,000 in gold, 76 paces west of cave; $18,000 in gold, 72 paces north of cave; $38,000 in gold, 42 paces west of cave, and greenbacks and jewelry, 142 paces west and 11Hbg."
[202] The map was shared with Steve Wilson and with Bud from an interview with Wells Blevins, a very good friend of Bud's. You will learn more about Wells throughout the rest of the book.

Jesse and his men left the gold and would later come back to retrieve it. They headed to Lone Hill in the Keechi Hills.

Many stories found in newspaper clippings describe tales of Indians attacking Mexican pack trains who were carrying gold on the backs of burros near the Red River, Oklahoma, Texas, New Mexico, Kansas, Colorado, and Missouri. This was occurring even before the Mexican American War in 1846-1848. They stated that they used the Santa Fe Trail, Pike and Marcy's trail, the old Dona Ana Trail, and sometimes the Chisholm trail to move shipments. Could they have been moving gold for Montezuma as we explored earlier? There was and still probably is a lot of Spanish gold in the Wichita Mountains. Bud stated that the Indians would take the gold and bury it. Bud said that a lot of gold that Jesse dug up and reburied was first buried by the Spanish/Mexicans. Jesse had obtained maps and learned the symbols of the Spanish to lead him to the treasure, such as "Oro" inscribed on a rock, meaning "gold."

In the Spring of 1875, April, Jesse was accused of killing Dan Askew, a neighbor in Clay County, Missouri who was suspected as being a spy for the Pinkerton's. It was just a few months after Zerelda's forearm was blown off and little Archie was killed by the incendiary device that was pitched into their house. It was a hot subject. Jesse was in Texas at that time, finishing out his ranger duties. But an old Confederate told a news reporter that at the time, Jesse was in the cattle range near the Arkansas headwaters and about 120 miles southwest of Pueblo, Colorado. [203]

A few months later, Jesse writes a letter from Comanche, Texas, which was 26 miles from Brownwood in June 1875 to a "Jim" and the letter was intercepted by the law. "Dear Jim: Its one of old Penk's lies, circulated by his sneaks. I can prove I was in Texas, at Dallas, on the 12th of May, when the killing was done. (The event actually occurred April 12th). Several persons of the highest respectably know that I could not have been in Clay County, Missouri, at that time. I might name a number who could swear to this, whose words would be taken anywhere. It is my opinion that Askew was killed by Jack Ladd and some of Pinkerton's men. But no meanness is ever done now both the James boys must have the blame for it. This is like the balance of the lies they tell about me and my brother. I wish you would correct the lies the Kansas City papers have told about the shooting of old Askew and oblige. Yours faithfully, Jesse." Jack Ladd was the hired hand of Dan Askew.

A few months later when summer came, Chief Quanah Parker of the Comanche tribe, surrendered at Fort Sill, June 2, 1875. Just a few days before this on May 19, Quanah came to the post and desired to find out the whereabouts of his mother, Cynthia Anne Parker who was captured in 1836 by the Comanches during a raid at Fort Parker at the age of nine. She married Peta Nocona, a Kwahadi warrior chief. She had children, with one being Quanah Parker. She loved the Comanche way of life and loved her family. She was rescued by American forces of the 2nd U.S. Cavalry and the Texas Rangers in 1857. She did not want to return to her white family but was placed into the white world. When her baby, Topsana became ill and died in 1863, Cynthia took a turn for the worse. She died of self-starvation in March 1871.

At the time of Quanah's inquiry, neither the army nor Quanah himself knew that she had died. After Quanah had surrendered, President Grant decimated the treaties, and seized the unceded land because it did not support the buffalo. Grant allowed settlers to go into the land.

Jesse, as a freighter and lawman in Indian Territory, was trusted by the authorities of Fort Sill and was not ever questioned. Jesse agreed in helping the Cheyenne, Sioux, and the Arapaho to supply their every need to fight this northern philosophy of dumb downing the weakened and lifting the Powers That Be. If you really think about it, Jesse's philosophy was totally different from the Powers That Be. It was all about justice. Nothing like Albert Pike.

Jesse, with the backing of the KGC met with the Cheyenne at the sacred spot and agreed to help in exchange for 11 million dollars in gold coins and bullion. They were to meet again with the goods at the very same spot. This had to be sometime in early spring or summer of 1875.

The sacred place where they met had great spiritual significance and was used for healing or to prepare for the afterlife with their Creator. It would be where a blue and red granite rock lay. Bud knew it had to be in the Wichita Mountains, Jesse's favorite place and it truly was.

Bud set out to look for the meeting place. He knew Oklahoma like the back of his hand, knew from his past treasure hunts and exploration, the terrain, the mountains, caves, creeks, and crevices where Jesse left his mark. Bud said he just "put 2 and 2 together."

The clues led Bud close to Medicine Park, a small community north of the town of Lawton, Oklahoma and Fort Sill. This is the small town where Bud established great friendships with Rex and "Grandma" Ruby Leath who ran the Old Plantation Restaurant and Wells Blevins, a treasure hunter who himself had inherited some of Jesse's maps.

Blevins' grandfather was a full-blooded Eastern Cherokee, George Blevins. Wells came down from North Carolina to Indian Territory in the early 1920's and started working on the maps he received. He carried with him, much information about Jesse. In fact, Bud finally stated that it was Wells and "Grandma" that first had told Bud of the story of Jesse coming to the rescue of the Indians against Custer. They were a huge help. Wells married a full-blooded Comanche woman, Maude

Tocsi Chahtinneyyackque in 1927 in Comanche County, Oklahoma. She too, had a wealth of information to share.

The Blevins and the Leath's would always call Bud to come to the restaurant, "we want to show you something" or "we want you to meet someone" or "Bud, come on down, we got stuff to do." Bud had met them at the very beginning of his hunt for Jesse. Their friendship grew immensely. In 1984, Bud was asked to be honorary pallbearer for Maude Blevins which was a great honor to him.

(Bud and Wells Blevins at the Old Plantation Restaurant, 1991)

Medicine Creek runs through Medicine Park and flows for 30 miles within Comanche County, Oklahoma. Of course, the town of Medicine Park wasn't there in 1876, the area was remote and wild, known to be filled with outlaws, Indians, and soldiers. There was a lot of history, especially near Medicine Bluffs, that run parallel with Medicine Creek.

Bud said that he set out on his own, on foot, from Medicine Park, following Medicine Creek. He was close to Mount Sheridan and Tarbone Mountain. Walking several miles on Medicine Creek, approximately 5-6 miles from Medicine Park, Bud found in the middle of the creek, the sacred rock. It was actually two separate rocks, one of red granite and the other blue. They were prominent in the middle of the creek as the crystal-clear water splashed against their base. It was a very serene and sacred place within the Wichita Mountains Wildlife Refuge.

What a find. This was definitely the meeting place. Evidence of Jesse being there was an old gun and a horseshoe embedded in a tree, pointing out directions. It was not too far from where Joe Hunter dug money up in the old brass bucket found in front of Tarbone Mountain in 1934.

Traveling back in time, between 1871-1876 was a long span of time to prepare for war. It is unknown when the Cheyenne met Jesse at that sacred place, but it would have had to of been close to 1875 in order to gather all the supplies and travel 1100 miles to be prepared for what was coming. In the meantime, we learn what was happening in these years to escalate this meeting between the two great nations.

We do know that Jesse was in the middle of finishing up his duty as a Texas Ranger that ended May 31st, 1875. The summer of 1875 was close to the time Jesse was in Nebraska City, having his famous picture made. I'm assuming that during this time in Nebraska, he was getting things organized for the following year as well as visiting his family and his growing boy of 5 years old.

In Schrader's book, he writes that "months before" the supplies were delivered to the Sioux and Cheyenne, Jesse and other Confederate officers, including a general who possibly was General Shelby, were training the Sioux in the use of the new Winchester repeating rifle. The summer of 1875 may have been the time that this occurred. It's a possibility. This was also what Bud was told and that they were teaching all the tribes on how to fight using guerilla maneuvers and techniques. Their method was to hit hard and fast, yelling to induce fear, and retreating quickly after the first blow to stun the enemy before they had time to recover and defend themselves.

December 1875, Grant issues a deadline to the Lakota Sioux. By January 31st, 1876 all must be on the reservation. If found off the reservation, they will be shot like "unruly buffalo." It was the dead of winter and many were out hunting off the reservation. They weren't going to budge.

By Spring 1876, the Sioux began seeking alliance with other tribes. Sitting Bull was not going to allow the U.S. Army to take their freedom. They continued to go west to hunt, to defile the order. A coalition of the Lakota, Dakotas refugees, Arapaho, and exiled Cheyenne band together, totaling close to 8,000-10.000, setting up a massive Indian camp near the Little Bighorn River in Montana.

In the meantime back in Indian Territory, the Cheyenne, Sioux, and Arapaho were digging up the gold that they had hidden in caves and burial sites in order to pay for the guns and ammo and for Jesse's help. Between December 1875 until March 1876, Jesse had a massive job to accomplish with a few of his most trusted men. During the harshness of winter, when less travel and less scouting was being conducted, Jesse must have moved a majority of the gold they had left behind in the ravine near Apache from the Mexican pack train into the Keechi Hills of Oklahoma. It was quite a magnificent task. Jesse used his expert skills, Frank used his skills as a surveyor, and the other men had special duties as well to masterfully bury the gold in all directions from a center point designated as "Lone Hill."

They had their final meeting with the Cheyenne on Medicine Creek and was paid in full; 11 million dollars in gold. It was monstrous load, more than 5 times the amount they had to move from the Mexican pack train. Not far from the meeting place, they began to plan out their grid and technique. The gold was extremely heavy, so the center point had to be close by. Trusted individuals marked the locations of where they planted the gold, following an intricate grid with symbols, carvings, hoot owl trees, horseshoes, and guns.

Not far from the meeting place was where the brass bucket was found that Joe Hunter dug up in 1939. In the bucket was a small fortune and carved on the outside was a contract between the men who were there burying the treasure. Jesse James was one of the names. It was dated, March 5, 1876. That had to of been the completion date of the reburying of their cache. Directly to the northeast, approximately **33-35** miles, was another cache, connected to the bucket. The point of interest was Lone Hill.

From a letter from Lou Kilgore to Bud, she wrote that she had heard this story directly from Howk. "*The brass kettle (bucket) was a contract carved into it between the K.G.C. and the Indians. It guaranteed that the K.G.C. would support the Indians in knocking out George A. Custer, you know the rest of the story. Between Fort Cobb and Fort Sill on a cold winters day $16,000,000 was brought in and handed to the Confederate Underground by the Indians as their contribution to knocking out Custer.*"

Bud Hardcastle: The Truth Tracker

(The Brass Bucket)

Bud said that the gold that Jesse acquired from the Indians was buried near Tarbone Mountain, El Reno where the Cheyenne Agency was, and where the 5th Cavalry was stationed. We learn about this time that Jesse would become a part of the 5th Cavalry as told to Ola. Buffalo Bill Cody remained as the Chief Scout for the 5th Cavalry. The other part of the gold went to an area near Chickasha.

Around the turn of the century, there was flooding along the banks of the Washita River near the rock crossing east of Chickasha. Parts of the riverbank was washed out and some young boys found gold coins in a chest that was partially uncovered by the washout. It was the gold that the Indians gave Jesse. The boys took it to a bank in Chickasha and sold it to the bankers. The boys did well, and the bank also profited off of it.

We don't know if Jesse took the guns and ammo all at one time up north or just a partial load at a time. In Schrader's book it says that they took 150 wagons with some that were extremely heavy, in which they had to pull with 8 teams of horses. There were fifteen crews that would handle 10 wagons each. I am assuming there would have been at least 2-3 men per wagon and 20-30 per crew, which would make a total of men to be at 300-450 men. Incredible. It would be less noticeable if he had taken a little at a time, but all we know is that he got many wagons and men up to the Sioux Nation. But again, the number of wagons and the amount of men may have been an exaggeration from Howk. We don't know.

In Schrader's book, it says that Jesse got the supplies legitimately at Camp Worth, Fort Worth. Bud believed it was somewhere in Texas they got the guns with a payment of pure gold. I wonder if Jesse represented himself as an officer of a military regiment, a Texas Ranger, or had disguised himself as one. They loaded dray wagons with the supplies. Dray wagons were a heavy type of dead-axle wagon used for heavy freight loads. They had smaller wheels with a flat level floor, some with short sides and some with tall.

Inside the wagon, they would carefully conceal the weapons, ammunition, and gun powder within other supplies such as clothing, several tons of food, cans of pork and beans, and Pet milk. I had no idea that these can goods were in existence back then, but in research, they definitely were.

Bud said the Cheyenne didn't ask for anything except for the guns and ammo and Jesse took it upon himself to provide extra supplies for their immediate needs and health.

Bud understood from his source that there were thousands of repeating rifles, Winchesters and Henrys, as well as pistols delivered to the Cheyenne and Sioux. Some believe it was just 200 repeating rifles.

It would look like an entire battalion with that many men and that many wagons. They had to travel through some pretty rough and raw territory. If they did appear to be an army, they would need some protection from the Indian raiders who were still scattered across the plains. The Cheyenne and Sioux had that covered. Word spread between the nations to not attack the men who were coming to help. Bud learned that they wore gold and white bands on their arms and gold and white flags on the wagons to secure safe passage.

Jesse had the finest of men with him. They were mostly KGC operatives, ex-Confederates, Cheyenne, Arapaho and Jesse's trusted friends such as John Trammel and Lucky Johnson.

Not only did Jesse have 17 specialized soldiers with him to train the thousands of Indians how to use the repeating rifles, but also remained during the battle, wearing their gold and white arm bands so that they would not be a target. They apparently wore the army uniform.

Schrader writes in his book that some of Jesse's agents stole 6 Gatling guns from the U..S. Arsenal at Rock Island, Illinois and that they devised a way to strap them on mules to use at the battlefield. The Gatlings would use the firepower of .45-70 caliber rounds at a rate of 350 per minute. I'm not sure if these Gatlings were there. No evidence has been unearthed of a Gatling gun on the battlefield, not even one from the army. Custer chose not to take one.

The Battle is On -The Battle of Little Bighorn

The battle began and ended on June 25-26, 1876.

Custer took his troops after many days of traveling from Fort Abraham Lincoln in Bismarck, North Dakota, to where the Crow scouts said the Indians were camped in southern Montana. The scouts saw right away the huge encampment of the Indians and the many thousands of ponies grazing in the fields. They tried to warn Custer of the massive number of redskins they would be facing. Custer had to get closer to confirm. Even knowing this, he went ahead with his plans.

The Indians stated that they were totally surprised by the attack, but they were prepared. They had to of seen the soldiers smoke of their campfires and the dust made by their horses.

The Indians were organized and were meticulous. From Crazy Horse, leader of the Lakota Oglala band through Horned Horse as his spokesman and an interpreter, confirmed a story told of the great battle at Little Bighorn. It was just under a year since the battle when this interview was conducted. It was published in *The Bismarck Tribune*, June 11, 1877. "The Custer Fight."

From Crazy Horse's rendition of the fight, "The village was divided into seven different bands of Indians, each commanded by a separate chief and extended in nearly a straight line.; First the Uncpapas, under Sitting Bull; second, the Oglalas, under Crazy Horse; third the Minneconjous, under Fast Bull; fourth, the Sans Arcs, under Red Bear; fifth, the Cheyennes, under Ice Bear, their two principal chiefs were absent; sixth the **Santees** and Yanktonais, under Red Point, of the Santees; seventh, the Blackfeet , under Scabby Head. The village consisted of 1800 lodges, and at least four hundred wickayups, a lodge made of small poles and willows for temporary shelter. Each of the wickeyups contained four young bucks, and the estimate made by Crazy Horse is that each lodge had from three to four warriors."

Custer rushed into battle, in the wee hours of the morning and that was why he was called "*son of the morning star*" by the Indians. They knew he was coming. Custer split his units into three battalions to cover different areas within a 5-mile range. He had approximately 700 soldiers versus 1,100-2,000 Indian warriors. Custer, as he did at the Battle of the Washita River, first went after the noncombatants, the women and the children and was planning to take them hostage and use them as human shields. It didn't work out that way. There were too many of them and too many who were protecting them. The soldiers got pushed back up the hill from the camp. Within Custer's immediate command, Custer led them to Last Stand Hill. There were 210 soldiers spread out for ½ mile and the Indians had between 700-1500 following them. The U.S. Army was outmanned and outgunned. It was a slaughter of the white men.

The Cheyenne and Lakota were given the last part of the battle. They had the fiercest hatred for Custer and the government. Shortly after, when the battleground was silent, the warriors fled. Five of the twelve companies under the command of Custer, including him, were totally wiped out. Many sources agree that it only took less than ½ hour to completely annihilate Custer's forces. Altogether across the five-mile area of the entire battlefield, there were 268 soldiers killed, 55 wounded, and 6 of whom later died. Unknown how many Indians died.

Sitting Bull would not allow any of his tribe to mangle and mutilate the body of the soldiers or take anything from the bodies, but the Cheyenne women did per Sitting Bull's story.

Custer was warned not to do battle with them, but the Cheyenne said he didn't listen, so the women took long needles and reamed out their ears and maybe in the afterlife he would learn to listen. Most of the men were stripped, teeth and skulls bashed in with clubs, legs and arms were cut off. Sticks were jammed down their throats and in their eye sockets, and other unspeakable mutilations. Any of the wounded who were still alive were finished off with clubs and arrows. They took everything from the soldier, including their dignity. Only 55 men were recognizable by the army in Custer's unit the next day. Custer was found with two gunshot wounds, one to his left chest and one in his left temple. Per Wikipedia, Some Lakota oral histories assert that Custer, having sustained a wound in his chest early on, committed suicide to avoid capture and subsequent torture. [204] This goes along with what was in Del Schrader's book written in 1975.

Grace Hopkins stated that they took Custer's right arm from the elbow to the wrist off so that he would never have the opportunity to saddle a horse to go into battle again. They also reamed his ears out with arrows. Most documentaries suggest that Custer was not mutilated. Some believe the warriors did not want to touch his body because of the evil spirit within him. They did not want the spirit to enter them by touching him or taking any possessions from him.

Many people believe the army tried to keep the gory details from Custer's wife, Libbie, including the possible suicide. They preserved his dignity with stories of his bravery at the last stand. Libbie promoted Custer's bravery and his heroism in books and lectures. She defended his legacy until the day she died. Did she ever really know the whole story? We know now that the world never knew the entire story. We only had the accounts of the Indians and many whites brushed them off as being incorrect back in the day, but until the 1980's they found that the Indians were telling the true story.

People are releasing information that they have found from credible sources such as the surgeon who was with Custer's unit during the battle, the various tribes of Indians who independently stated that Custer got hit in his left chest while down at the river at the very beginning of the fighting when they were going after the women and children and later, after on the Last Stand Hill, took the fatal bullet to the head. Either Custer committed suicide or had his brother who was standing near him issue the fatal blow with the preserved bullet saved for situations of dire consequences.

Mounting evidence with today's new technologies and highly qualified men in science, specialists in ballistics and archeology have proven that Bud's evidence and stories he had gathered are credible. Many historians state that Sitting Bull had no way of securing the weapons they had that day. "Custer's highly regarded guide, "Lonesome" Charley Reynolds, informed his superior in early 1876 that Sitting Bull's forces were amassing weapons, including numerous Winchester repeating rifles and abundant ammunition." [205]

The weapons used by the Sioux and Cheyenne far outnumbered the military issued guns of Custer's regiment of 5 companies. To verify what the Indians used, an historic excavation of the Little Bighorn Battlefield was conducted by archeologists Douglas Scott and Richard Fox, Jr. in 1984-1985. They discovered that the Indians possessed 371 different guns of 47 different types.

In all, in Custer's field, there was evidence of at least 134 Indian firearms vs. 81 for the soldiers. The cavalrymen were armed with 1873 Springfield carbine rifles, Colt .45 single-action army revolver in .45-55 or .45-70 caliber carbines with only 100 rounds of ammo per man. They could only carry 50 rounds in their gun belt and had to leave the rest in the pack on their horse. They had an option to purchase their own weapon and ammunition. Custer carried a Remington .50 caliber sporting rifle with octagonal barrel (bolt action) and two revolvers that were not standard issued.

The Warriors used brand new, recently produced 1873 Henry repeating rifles, Model 1866 Winchester repeating rifles, Model 1872 Colt open top .44 caliber revolver, Sharps hunting rifles (sometimes known as the .50 caliber buffalo gun which could shoot the farthest), Spencers, Muzzle loading guns, Remingtons, Smith & Wessons, Ballards, Starrs, Evans, Maynards, Enfields, Forehand & Wadworths, bows & arrows, clubs, knives, and spears. The Battle of Rosebud, only a week before the Battle of Little Bighorn also indicated that they were using the same type of weapons.

Amazingly, in 1883, a rancher, Willis Spear collected several items off the battlefield. He recorded his findings in his diary. He found an 1874 Sharps rifle with serial number C54586 which used a .50-70 caliber. It would have been shipped new from the factory in 1875. It was found where the Indians were positioned during the fighting around Calhoun Hill. [206]

The Henrys were 3x more effective than the Springfield Carbine. The Springfield was more accurate, but at the rate the Henrys could get off a bullet, one after the other, proved to be more deadly for the soldiers in the skirmish line. Men who have been studying the battlefield for over 40 years who are forensic scientists stated that there were at least 200 repeating rifles and maybe more in the hands of the Indians. They were better armed 4-1, better than Custer's armory. The archaeologist stated that they only examined a fraction of the battlefield, but they recovered 2,361 cartridges, cases and bullets.

The young men who were led by Custer were between the ages of 17-18 years old, malnourished, inexperienced, with very little ammo to practice their shooting skills, and were scared to death during the battle. There were so many army issued cartridges that were unspent to testify to this. The Indians claimed many were running for their lives, terrified, with some committing suicide.

An incredible statement was made by Douglas Scott, the archaeologist who very meticulously examined the battlefield of Little Bighorn recovering over 5,000 artifacts also examined the battlefields of the Battle of Sand Creek and the Battle of the Washita River. He stated that the warriors that were connected to those two battles were at the Little Bighorn. They were all interrelated as family members of those massacred in the two previous battles that had destroyed their very existence.

Jesse told Ola that he joined the U.S. Cavalry, Company C, 5th regiment (5th Cavalry) in 1876 and they were sent to help Custer, but too late. One day too late. Bud believes he was already there. Jesse helped bury the bodies. Later Bud said that in recent times, people excavating the battlefield found bodies up there that they didn't know about.

Jesse had written a letter to Howk, that he never was able to give him. Aubrey Everhard still had it in Jesse's possessions. Aubrey let Bud read the letter which is on video. He was describing the aftermath of the battle. Jesse stated that he was in the 5th Cavalry and came late to the massacre of Little Big Horn.

The 5th Cavalry came from Forts Dodge and Leavenworth, Kansas under Lt. Col. Thomas Neil and was assigned to the Darlington Agency established in 1870 on the Cheyenne and Arapaho Reservation near Fort Reno which is located near El Reno. The Cheyenne Agency was 75 miles north of Fort Sill. Close to where Jesse buried the gold from the Indian payment. The 5th Cavalry was immediately sent to the Little Bighorn battlefield.

"After General Custer and 264 men died at the Battle of Little Bighorn, troopers of the 5th rode after the Sioux to avenge the deaths of their fellow cavalrymen. The punitive ride quickly became known as the Horsemeat March, one of the most brutal forced marches in American military history. Men and horses suffered from starvation, but they eventually caught up with the Indians. Under the leadership of Col. Wesley Merritt, a Civil War veteran, the 5th was instrumental in defeating the Indians at the Battle of Slim Buttes. It was the first significant victory for the army following Little Bighorn. [207] Jesse was at Little Bighorn but wasn't at Slim Buttes which was fought on September 9-10, 1876. He was elsewhere.

Sitting Bull and his people went to Canada and Crazy Horse surrendered in Nebraska on May 5, 1877.

Crazy Horse was killed by a guard during a scuffle on September 5, 1877. Jesse's birthday.

Seven million acres of land are ceased by the Federal government.

Red Cloud – "I, who used to own rich soil in a well-watered country so extensive that I could not ride through it in a week on my fastest pony, am put down here. Now, I, who used to control five thousand warriors, must tell Washington when I am hungry. I must beg for that which I own." [208]

While still up in that country, the question is, did Jesse Go to Deadwood?

In Howk's book, JJ had told them that Hickock got to asking too many questions, possibly about the Battle of the Little Bighorn. Jesse stated, "Jack McCall, contrary to what historians claim, did not shoot Wild Bill Hickok in the back of the head any more, than Charley Bigelow, using an alias of Jesse James, was shot in the back of the head. You see, the historians didn't see what actually happened, but we did, we saw these men shot, and not from the back, like historians state, but now get this… both Bigelow and Hickok were shot right over the right eye in both cases. Need I say more?" [209]

Also, Howk wrote that "Hickok was on our dangerous list. He had been not only a Union Army spy, but also one of General Jim Lane's Kansas Redleg outfit."....."It was perhaps six weeks after Custer's last fight and Bill Hickok was asking entirely too many pointed questions for us to swallow, so Hickok died!" He was shot and killed on August 2, 1876. [210]

Jesse was in Northfield – September 5-7, 1876

After the horrendous events that occurred, Jesse headed back to Missouri. In just two weeks after Custer's defeat and the celebration of our country's centennial, Jesse and his gang, Frank, Cole and Bob Younger, Clell Miller, Charlie Pitts, Bill Chadwell, and Hobbs Kerry were noted as robbing the Missouri-Pacific Railroad train in Rockey Cut, Missouri on July 7, 1876. It was near Otterville. The only one that got caught was the new man, Kerry and he named all the outlaws involved.

Jesse never slowed down, but he had to of been exhausted. Being with the Sioux Nation recently, he was reminded of the stories of what they had gone through since the Minnesota removal back in the early days of the Civil War. They treasured the land of their ancestors and desired to return, but it now was impossible. The Santee Sioux had to stay put in their reservation. Being fresh on his mind, Jesse began to look at Minnesota.

Jesse and Frank, along with Cole, Jim, and Bob Younger, Charlie Pitts, Clell Miller, and Bill Chadwell took the train to St. Paul, Minnesota around the first of September 1876. They divided in two groups and scoped out areas of Mankato and Red Wing, on either side of Northfield, Minnesota. Jesse found some of Maggie's family living in Mankato and decided he definitely didn't want to rob there, concerned about Maggie's family members who could get in the crossfire. This was told to me, the writer, by Grace Hopkins, Maggie's and Jesse's gg granddaughter. The gang chose Northfield which was 2nd on their list.

Ola said, "Jesse, I've read that you and Frank were both in that robbery at Northfield (Minnesota) but both of you got away." He said, "Oh honey, they write lots of things and they don't know anything about it. They are wrong. That was a Cole Younger project. Me and Frank was miles away from there. I was in Henrietta, Texas at that time with a leg injury and Frank was in Louisianna. No! Me and Frank was not in that robbery. They are all wrong and don't know what they're talking about." [211]

Frank Hall and Lindsay Whitten, reporters for the Lawton Constitution who interviewed Jesse in 1948 wrote the book, "Jesse James rides again." Jesse revealed many things that he and his gang did, but as he did with Ola, he said the Northfield Bank Robbery was strictly a Cole Younger project. Jesse said he was at a ranch near Henrietta, Texas, at Allan Palmer's home with his sis, nursing a leg wound. Frank was in Louisiana, working at a store.

Bud said Jesse was protecting Ola and his pride from the truth. Bud said, "Jesse was in Northfield." It was verified by Cole Younger, Frank James, and Grace Hopkins. Jesse didn't want to admit he was part of a heist that went badly wrong. It was not like him, especially because of the blunders, 3 deaths of his comrades (Clell Miller, Bill Chadwell and later Charlie Pitts), and his buddies, the Youngers were sent to prison for life. The guilt of leaving those men while Frank and he escaped must have been too much to handle. The gang had an agreement that if anyone got shot up and couldn't go on, they would leave them. Cole Younger was shot in the hip, and his brother, Jim was shot in the jaw, and Bob shattered his elbow.

Jesse and Frank obtained horses and escaped. The Youngers and Charlie Pitts were on foot, drained of blood from their wounds and their energy. When they were captured near La Salle, Minnesota, two weeks after the robbery, they were in an intense gun battle with their pursuers. They were shot up pretty bad. Cole had 9-11 bullet holes in him. Charlie Pitts was shot dead. All three Younger brothers were sentenced to life imprisonment in the Minnesota Territorial Prison at Stillwater.

Another fella who was very close to Jesse known as "Joe Vaughn" alias for Frank James, writes in his book that on September 3, 1876, they completed their plans for Northfield. The three that rode into town who had first dined, and then rode over to the bank was Jesse, Cole Younger, and Frank. He claimed Jesse had killed the cashier when after the 2nd time of demanding the opening of the vault, there was still no response. Jesse responded with a fatal bullet. Many stories and documentaries suggest Frank shot the cashier. We don't know.

The story above from Vaughn seems to be the most accurate. It was Jesse's birthday on the 5th. Bud said the gang partied up for two days celebrating. One movie depicted that they partied hard at a Cat House in the general vicinity of Northfield, not sure if this was true. On Thursday, September 7, 1876 they were still suffering from a hangover. At the trial of the Youngers, Northfield residents stated that they "had seen the gang leave a local restaurant near the mill shortly after noon, where they dined on fried eggs." They testified "that the group smelled of alcohol and that the gang was obviously under the influence when they greeted General Ames." [212]

The mill mentioned above was General Ames' father's mill. Jesse Ames was a sea captain and built the Ames Mill in Northfield. It would later be known for the product, Malt-O-Meal. Mr. Ames' son, Adelbert Ames served as a merchant seaman on his father's ship. Adelbert became a colonel in the Union Army and in 1864, his division, the X Corps of the Army of the James, served along the James River during the final operations of the Civil War, under Major General *Benjamin Franklin* Butler in the Bermuda Hundred Campaign and Siege of Petersburg. He received a brevet promotion to major general in the Union Army and brigadier general in the Regular Army. During the Reconstruction period he was an avid supporter of political equality for African Americans. He became governor of Mississippi as a Republican with a close political battle with a former Confederate General who was an actual Unionist, James Lusk Alcorn.

When Alcorn's Brigade entered the Confederate Army, Jefferson Davis refused to commission him on account of political differences. He was elected in the Mississippi legislature, but became a critic of President Jefferson Davis. The Republican Party at that time, was supported by Black voters. Those in the Confederacy and so-called White Southerners who supported the Republican party were called "scalawags." The Southern Democrats said these scalawags or carpetbaggers were traitors exploiting the Southern United States and trying to set up "Negro rule." Alcorn was supported by the scalawags, which were considered moderate Whiggish whites. Ames was supported by the Radicals and most black voters. The Radicals are who Jesse didn't get along too well with.

The Republican Party promised to rebuild the Southern United States, restoring public schools, railroads, and prosperity. By election time deep Democratic bureaucracy threw multiple arrows at Ames and terrorized the Republican voters to stay home, driving voters from the polls with shotguns and cannons, in which allowed the Democrats to gain full control of both houses of the legislature. Ames was on the verge of being impeached when he resigned on March 29, 1876.

Adelbert Ames became the son-in-law of his commanding officer, Major General Benjamin Franklin Butler. He joined his father and brother in the flour-milling business in Northfield and was there at the time of the robbery. Bob Younger stated that one of the outlaws in Northfield, "had a spite" against Ames. Cole said the same thing.

It had been rumored that Ames had deposited $50,000 in the First National Bank of Northfield. Bud had investigated Ames' role up there and found that he had a position in the bank, whether it was a stockholder or a member of the Board of Directors, we don't know. Bob Younger continued to point out after the Northfield robbery "that they had selected it (the bank) because of its connection to two Union generals and Radical Republican politicians: Benjamin Butler and his son-in-law, Adelbert Ames." [213]

Bud really emphasized that Butler was a crook. He too had a lot of money invested in the bank. Bud verified many things in the historical archives that connected Jesse's hatred toward Butler, and it appears that there was animosity towards both of the men. Everything Bud has stated and verified over 30 years ago was exactly what has been found in a document written and edited in 2023 in Wikipedia, "Benjamin Butler."

As a Union general, Benjamin Butler was known for ordering raids upon the south during the Civil War, taking the wealth and possessions from the southerners. His victims named him "spoons" because of his fondness of silverware.

During the Civil War, Confederates were naturally a huge part of New Orleans, their homeland, and were a strong force which included many ports that the Union wanted. By April 1862, Union fleets arrived in the bay and issued heavy and continuous bombardment towards New Orleans, Fort Jackson and Fort St. Philip. The city had to surrender. The federal forces entered New Orleans. While on duty in New Orleans, General Benjamin Butler, the Federal Commander seized a 38-piece set of silverware from a woman who was attempting to cross the Union lines. The woman had permission to pass but could only carry clothing. Butler accused her of smuggling contraband and declared that she was aiding the Confederacy.

Butler was horrific to the citizens of New Orleans. He imposed martial law upon the city. The citizens of New Orleans were being humiliated and taken advantage of. They became hostile towards the Federal government and women began expressing their disgust, verbally and apparently physically. One of Butler's rules over New Orleans was called Order #28.

"As the Officers and Soldiers of the United States have been subjected to Repeated Insults from the Women, calling themselves 'Ladies,' of New Orleans, in return for the most scrupulous Non-Interference and Courtesy on our part, it is ordered that hereafter when any female shall by word, gesture, or movement, insult or show contempt for any Officer or Private of the United States she shall be regarded and held liable to be treated as A WOMAN OF THE TOWN PLYING HER VOCATION. By command of Maj. Gen. Butler." [214]

Basically, she would be treated as a "low life", a prostitute and this order would permit the soldiers to punch back if needed, removing any restraint they had before in treating these women as ladies. This enraged not only the citizens of New Orleans, but all of the south, north, and countries overseas.

Butler was suspected of continuing the practice of engaging in "looting the household valuables of New Orleanians." Butler created a census on 4,000 of the city who failed to pledge loyalty to the Union. They were banished, some jailed, and property seized. The property was sold at a low auction price in which Butler's brother, Andrew was often the "prime buyer." Benjamin Butler sought out cotton plantations of those who were disloyal and confiscated their cotton. The cotton would be sold in a rigged auction which supposedly went to Butler's textile mills in Lowell, Massachusetts. This practice went beyond New Orleans.

Quite interesting that Butler was a big stockholder in several mills in Massachusetts that was supplying heavy cloth to the militia. He began receiving military contracts, a huge source of profits during the war. His brother Andrew was profiting off of lucrative deals which included bribes, use of military equipment, and use of his brother's authority in the military for their financial gain. Andrew's profits in New Orleans was near $200,000, equal to over $4 million in today's dollars. Butler was also accused of seizing $800,000 from the office of the Dutch consul. The war was a big money operation for the Butlers.

Lincoln felt it necessary to recall Butler in December 1862, after eight months in New Orleans. In 1865, Butler was again recalled per General Grant's appeal to Lincoln for not following through with orders to attack the Confederate Fort Fisher. It was appearing like Butler was playing both sides of the war. Money? You bet.

Butler was also known as the "Beast." "His commands were marred by financial and logistical dealings across enemy lines, some of which may have taken place with his knowledge and to his financial benefit."

"A very extensive trade with the Confederacy was carried on in Butler's department, profitable for Northern merchants and help to the Confederacy in which his relatives and supporters played a major role".

"Butler was dismissed from the Union Army after his failures in the First Battle of Fort Fisher. He went on to win the seat of the House of Representative from Massachusetts. He advocated "harsher punishment of former Confederate leadership and stronger stance on civil rights reform." [215]

He also led in the impeachment of U.S. President Andrew Johnson after the war who was a Freemason. Butler was the lead prosecutor in the impeachment trial proceedings of the president.

After the war, Butler continued in several different businesses and became extremely wealthy with a portion of his money in Northfield. When he died, he was estimated at a net worth of $7 million, which would be worth $230 million today. The source of his income remains a mystery, but it is believed to have come from New Orleans.

With Jesse's connections in New Orleans and his love for the Southerners, he had a multitude of reasons to afflict pain upon Butler, but it also had to of been personal. When it came to the Southland, Jesse took it personal. There is for sure something more to this story.

The bank robbery in Northfield only gained them a bag of nickels and a barrel of bullets. Frank and Jesse were shot up pretty bad. They both had leg injuries but were able to flee on horses and flee Minnesota. They knew where the safest place to hide would be …. Devil's Nest.

A legend exists that has not ever been proven but suggests that Frank and Jesse, running from the law, split up and Jesse was heading west towards Devil's Nest. Jesse reached the area near Garretson, South Dakota where Split Rock Creek actually splits two rugged steep cliffs in half, creating a narrow gorge of 20 feet wide. From the top of the cliffs to the creek is a drop of 60 feet. It was called Devil's Gulch.

Jesse was being chased by a posse of men who were probably farmers and townspeople who found out Jesse was in the area. As Jesse reaches the gorge, he had confidence that he and the horse could make the 20-foot jump across. Jesse was an expert horseman and knew the capability and strides that a horse could perform. He only rode the best horses and knew them all well. As Bud puts it, "It's a possibility."

I believe it could be done with Jesse's expertise in "horse sense" and guts. The world's record of a horse jump over a wide span of water is 27.6 feet in 1975 by Andre Ferreira. [216]

Needless to say, the posse stopped dead in their tracks. They could not believe the feat that they just witnessed. They did not follow.

The area was made into a beautiful park with lots of waterfalls and hiking trails, and of course a bridge over the gorge where Jesse jumped. Amazing. The locals believe wholeheartedly that this legend is fact. Jesse and Frank met up again south of Garretson, South Dakota.

(Devil's Gulch)

From Grace Hopkins, gg granddaughter of Jesse and Maggie – "With a posse trailing them, Frank and Jesse crossed over the Floyd River, which is a tributary of the Missouri River near Sioux City, Iowa. They traveled to Greenville, a suburb of Sioux City and stayed at a house a couple of days. They left. Apparently, someone within the city thought that a drunk who was passed out in an alley was Jesse. The law was informed and "Boy, they thought they had Jesse," said Grace. Well, they found out that it wasn't him."

Frank and Jesse made a direct line to Devil's Nest where they knew they would be protected. Their reputation and the care that they gave in supporting the Sioux in the Battle of Little Bighorn made them both heroes to the Sioux Nation. They also had many friends and family there.

They made it to Devil's Nest and found Maggie at home with their son, Joseph Jesse and Frank's daughter, Emma. When they heard that the posse was close by, Jesse jumped under Maggie's mattress and she jumped on top. Not sure where Frank went to hide. Maggie stayed right where she was on that fluffy goose-down feather bed. When the posse came, Maggie pretended to be very sick with the flu and could not get out of bed for nobody. They left her alone.

No one else came around to check on their whereabouts. Bud believes that Frank and Jesse stayed with the Sioux for over a year at that time.

This story was also verified by a letter Bud received from a woman named Kay Loraine Chrestman Johnston from El Paso, Texas. She stated that her maternal grandmother was Nanny (**James**) Ferguson, married to James Allen Ferguson. Nanny was related to Jesse. They were farmers around Graham, Texas and Portales, New Mexico. Their daughter, Lou Ella Ferguson married Tommie Jake "T.J." Chrestman who was also related to Jesse. Lou Ella and T.J. were 4th cousins.

Finding Kay's father's obituary in the El Paso Times, May 13, 1986, we learn that he worked 42 years with the El Paso Natural Gas Company. He was living in Las Cruces, New Mexico. "He was an active member of the Optimist Club and a member of the Masonic lodge AF & AM Wallace Houston #1393." [217] His father was Marion Columbus Chrestman (1882-1951) who was born to in Stephenville, Erath County, Texas. Marion's mother, Lavisa Frances **James** (1853-1945) was born in *Van Zandt County, Texas*. Her father was Elijah Columbus James (1816-1878) who in some ancestral trees, appears to be related to Jesse along with the Youngers.

The family rarely spoke of Jesse, protecting the family name. Kay wrote that in May of 1967, her and her husband in the first year of marriage were sent to Isanti, Minnesota with the Army. She said her husband came home one day and said he had met a cousin of hers with the last name of "James." Her husband took her to the cousin, who was a Lakota Sioux Indian from South Dakota. "He told me his family had always talked about the Northfield, Minnesota Raid the James Gang and the Daltons?? pulled together, and how those Minnesota farmers shot them all up so bad nearly all of them were killed."

"As they ran back south to escape the law, they passed through Dakota Territory, and the Sioux took them in and nursed some of them back to health. During that time, the James boys married Sioux women, and had several children from those marriages." [218]

Grace Hopkins is a delightful character and her stories were extremely interesting. Margaret Hanyetusnawin "Maggie" Wabasha, her great, great grandmother was a beautiful woman. Their son, Joseph Jesse "Tazmawaste" Chase married Martha Adelaide Wakute (1874-1915) in 1892. She was the daughter of Thomas Wakute and Nancy "Wiyangewin" Stone Wapaha who was previously married to Andrew Myrick (Let them eat Grass).

(Joseph Jesse Chase and Martha Adelaide Wakute)

(Nancy "Wiyangewin" Stone Wapaha)

Grace Hopkins descends from Joseph and Martha's son, Joseph "Joe" Nelson Chase, who was born on the Santee reservation and murdered in the same community when he was only 42 years of age. He was married to a beautiful lady, Grace Emily Campbell (1903-1998) who stepped up and became a welder on huge tanker ships during World War II. She never remarried but raised 5 children on her own. Her daughter, Constance Muriel Chase (1929-2000) was Grace's mother.

In 1961, Howk tried to write a story about Maggie in his book, "Jesse James and the Lost Cause", but the only similarity to this story was her name, her first name. He said, Maggie and her sister were adopted by a cowman. They were just Indian girls out of school. Howk wrote that Maggie's last name was Matuska instead of "Wabashaw". He writes that Jesse married Maggie and Frank married the other sister. In a photo in the book, he sways the reader to believe that Jessie and Maggie's son, Jesse James II was his (Howk's) father, making Jesse James Howk's grandfather.

Howk wrote these stories stating that Jesse said these things or was in his diary. Bud has also uncovered two affidavits that Howk had notarized stating two other different lineages from Jesse to prove that Jesse was his grandfather; one was completed in Tulare County, California in 1976 stating that his father was Jesse Barnhill James. The other one was completed in El Paso County, Colorado stating that his father was Jesse Franklin James in 1961. All three stories turned out to be bogus.

How did Grace meet Bud?

Grace said that she finally decided to go public with her story and began posting information on geneforum, a group on genealogy.com who were focused on the James family. Right away, she was contacted by Bud and Lou Kilgore, introducing themselves. Bud said that he knew of Joseph Jesse Chase and had been looking for his family for years. He was anxious to meet her. Bud called her up one day and wanted her to meet him and Lou in Kearney, Missouri for the James/Younger Reunion in September 2002 that commemorated Jesse's birthday. Bud would bring her lots of documents, pictures, and video tapes of his extensive research on Jesse. Grace was a little leery and got a friend to go with her. "I didn't know him.... he could have been a murderer or whatever," Grace said.

Grace said they got to Kearney and met Bud and Lou at Jesse's grave. Lou Kilgore knew Joyce Morgan, who was a well-known and respected psychic who lived near Kearney. She must have been there for the reunion and Lou asked her to come help them sort things out. Joyce told them that she can channel Jesse and Frank and the James family. Joyce knew about Bud and Grace ahead of time even though they hadn't met, and she knew that Grace thought Bud could be a murderer. Grace said Joyce Morgan and her husband, John were a hoot!

Bud said that he does not generally believe in psychics and doesn't really understand them, but he said Joyce showed him many things that made him a believer. Bud said they became great friends.

Joyce Morgan was a gifted lady. Her family shares this gift starting with her Cherokee great grandmother, passed down to her grandmother, her mother and then Joyce. Lola Joyce Otto Morgan (1936-2007) well known psychic, lived in Kingston, Caldwell County, Missouri. For over 20 years, she has used her gift for good, to help numerous law enforcement agencies to solve murder cases throughout the country. One of the police officers in Missouri said, "I don't know how she does it, not knowing the area or people she is zooming in on, but she's correct." Joyce was highly sought after to not only help solve crimes, but help finding missing persons and clear homes of ghostly activities.

Morgan appeared on Fox's "Sightings," The Family Channel's "The Scariest Places on Earth," "Psychic Detectives the Fugitives," found on youtube.com, and Court TV. Joyce also collaborated with a ghost-investigating group from Harrisonville, Missouri called Miller's Paranormal Research. Many Missouri newspapers are filled with her contributions in helping so many. Every article speaks very highly of Joyce Morgan with great respect for her gift. She predicted that the DNA test will prove the body buried in Kearney, Missouri is **not** that of Jesse James. [219]

What really impressed me, these articles state that she says prayer is the only thing that truly works in ridding people's homes of spirits. "She considers herself a spiritual and God-fearing person. She said she always uses her spiritual gifts for good." [220]

Bud described Joyce as super nice, and more of a grandmotherly type of woman who called everyone "honey" or "sweetheart" with a very gentle and soothing voice, but absolutely full of fun. Joyce is the one that gave Bud the nickname, "Fossil Fart" and Grace picked up on it. Joyce was a bigger kidder. "If she could get something on you, she'd do it," Bud said.

Joyce and her husband John, Grace and her friend, and Lou met in Bud's motel room to discuss Jesse. Grace said that Joyce was helping Bud with some treasure maps and Bud said to Grace, "You know I'm a treasure hunter. Grace, if I find anything, you are entitled to it. How much do you want?" Grace replied, "I just want a penny. I believe if God wants me to have anything, he'll put it in my hands." She was not after Jesse's money, but only answers.

Grace said Joyce came over to her and knelt down in front of her. Joyce asked, "Is there anything you would like to ask Jesse?" Grace replied, "Well ya." "What's that?" asked Joyce. Grace said "I would like to know if the story is true about my family. Is great grandpa his son?"

Joyce started in. "Joe Jesse, Joe Jesse, Joe Jesse Chase, Joe Jesse Chase, Tazmawaste, Tazmawaste. Is he your son?" As she was doing this, her blood vessels in her eyes popped out. You could see them! Joyce took on a whole different persona and in a strange voice, she said, "Hell ya!" The entire room dropped their teeth.

That was the only thing Grace wanted to know. Grace said after that, the blood vessels went down and the whites of her eyes returned. Joyce said, "Well you got your answer." Grace, in amazement, said, "Hell, ya!"

Bud's encounter with Joyce, the psychic, was similar. He had a lot of questions for Jesse. Joyce appeared to use all the energy she had, and her voice changed completely. It wasn't her voice he said. Bud was asking her about Jesse and there were several things that Bud would bring up that not many people knew about. The answers returned through her, came without hesitancy and coincided and confirmed what Bud had found through various sources through his research. Bud said, "I was hitting on some questions he hadn't heard in a long time. He answered quite a bit."

The atmosphere changed somewhat when Bud began to ask personal questions of Jesse. He wasn't used to questions like that, reaching deep into his personal life. Next thing Bud knew, Joyce was spewing out words in a very raunchy mad voice, "You are a nosy son-of-a-bitch."

Bud said, "That kind of rocked me backwards. I got the feeling I was getting close to home."

This caught Bud off guard. Bud said, "He got me straightened out in a hurry." Bud said the tension was high and he could hear in Jesse's voice through Joyce, that Jesse was pretty perturbed. Bud, trying to ease the tension said, "Jesse, yes I am nosy, but I'm trying to prove the truth same as you were trying to do. I promised Aubrey and Ola that I was going to prove the truth and would publish Ola's manuscript." Peace returned to the room and to Joyce's face, and the questions and answers continued. One of the questions Bud asked was, "Jesse, did you die in 1882?" – "No" was the answer. "Did you live the rest of your life after that as J. Frank Dalton?" – "Yes."

I asked Bud, "Did you feel like Jesse was speaking through her?" Bud replied after a long pause, "I did, I really did hun."

Joyce channeled Jesse 2-3 more times. Bud said she believed whole-heartedly that J. Frank Dalton was the real Jesse Woodson James. She helped Bud further by going to southeastern Oklahoma with him, Lou, John and Jo Ella Tatum. They were looking for a water well out in the middle of nowhere. Joyce had never been in this location, but she knew what to look for. She would feel things and receive visions of the past. She would bring up things that would fit the area and its history and would point them to the general area. Though, they never found the treasure, they found the well. Bud said she was amazingly useful. He said, "It's hard to believe that kind of stuff, but when it proves out, you believe."

Bud said they all became dear friends and went on many trips together, hunting clues and treasures of Jesse. They even stayed at Joyce and John's home. Sadly, Joyce passed away. She died in 2007 of cancer. "She was an amazing woman," Bud said, "she left this earth way too soon."

(Joyce Morgan at the Samuel's farm)

Bud treasured these two new friends that he met on the trip to Kearney and as a fond memory, Grace Hopkins always reminds him of his nickname Joyce gave him to this day, "You old Fossil Fart", in memory of the great friendships they share. Bud continued helping Grace dig into her family and to help her understand who her great, great grandfather, Jesse Woodson James really was. Bud opened many doors for Grace, including another branch of the family she never knew. You will find that in Chapter Thirty-One.

Thank you, Grace, for sharing your story. May God always bless you.

Thank you, Bud, for sharing this story, even though it touched on a lot of personal and controversial subjects. All through this book, you open yourself up, not concerned about the naysayers, but you want to tell the whole story, the truth and nothing but! I admire you greatly! You painted us a beautiful picture of Jesse throughout this chapter, a new glimpse of a man with a tender-heart for the weak and downtrodden, caught between two worlds. Jesse took upon the quest to defend them, to fight evil and wrongdoers in America, bringing justice in his own way. He never took his eyes off of his mission, he remained loyal to his cause and became a crusader for justice.

> "Justice is truth in action."
>
> *-Benjamin Disraeli*

Chapter Thirteen: The Man Behind the Silver Star

In an interview with Frank Dalton by Ron Buzbee with the Corpus Christi Times Newspaper, June 30, 1939, Jesse told him before he came out, that he served nine years in the U.S. Army, five years as a Texas Ranger, and 7 years as a U.S. Marshal out of Fort Smith, Arkansas. [221] On Frank Dalton's calling card, he listed he was a Peace Officer.

In January 1948, just a few months prior to Jesse's big reveal, an article in the Tyler Morning Telegraph described Frank Dalton, formerly of Gladewater, has proven his long and varied military record and has gained access to services in the Veterans Hospital in McKinney, Texas. Earlier, he was admitted to the Gregg Memorial Hospital in Longview with a broken leg. In order for Dalton to be admitted to the Veteran's Hospital, he had to prove that he had served in the military. The hospital officials checked with Washington and the War Department and confirmed that **Dalton served with the army from 1865-1874**. He was also **certified as a veteran of the Indian Wars** and was able to be admitted to the McKinney Veteran's Hospital. [222]

U.S. Army 1865-1874

Jesse told the reporter, Byron Buzzbee that he joined the U.S. Army March 10, 1868. His first official act was to marry the regimental colonel's daughter. We have no other information on that service, the location, or the wife he married, if this is even true. We may have one clue. In Frank Dalton's "Short Stories," he writes John Younger, the youngest brother of the Youngers, was serving in the army in the Black Hills since 1868. This was six years earlier from the time Custer scouted the Black Hills in 1874 with Calamity Jane and Buffalo Bill. Could Jesse have been in the Black Hills also when Younger was? There are quite a lot of similarities between Jesse and John Younger in which Jesse wrote about. At times it appeared as if he was speaking about himself.

Jesse said he was in the army for 9 years; 1865-1874. Jesse left no clue as to where he was stationed in his army service between the years 1865-1867. We do know he was rehabilitating after the war in Nebraska in 1865 due to the gunshot he took in his chest, damaging his right lung. He went to John Mimms home in August 1865 near Kansas City and was cared for by John's daughter, Zerelda Mimms who was Jesse's first cousin, later she would become his wife in 1874.

We start seeing bank robberies begin in 1866. On March 20, 1868, 10 days after he said he joined the army, Jesse admitted to a bank robbery. The robbery was at the Nimrod Long Banking Company in Russellville, Logan County, Kentucky. Jesse had told Ola that he did indeed rob this bank, but later found out that Nimrod Long helped finance his father's way through Georgetown Baptist Seminary. Jesse said, "I felt pretty bad about robbing it and I made it my business to see that the money was all returned." [223]

Would this imply that if he was in the army at the time of the bank robbery, he would have had to be stationed near there, such as in Kentucky, Tennessee, or Missouri? Is his army story true? We don't know, but apparently the war department had record of it.

We do know that Jesse and Frank were in South Dakota in 1869 robbing banks and they hid out in Nebraska with their Sioux wives. It makes one wonder if Jesse was in the army in the Dakotas or Nebraska in 1869. Was he a spy for the army, an undercover agent, or a freighter such as he was for Fort Sill? Wish we knew.

There is a possibility that he was stationed at Fort Sidney in Nebraska in 1869. We find that Fort Sidney was established to help protect the workers who were laying down the tracks for the

Union Pacific Railroad from the hostile Indians. The fort would later be the primary supply depot on the Sidney-Black Hills trail. Supply wagons and various travelers went on this trail to the Red Cloud Indian Agency and to the Black Hills onto the gold fields. [224]

In 1869 is when the KGC was really on the move. They were assigning men to different locations on the frontier. Jesse began his freighting business sometime in 1870. He worked for the government/army in the freighting business in Indian Territory at Fort Sill beginning in the later part of 1870 through the summer of 1872. In the Fall of 1872 is when he moved into the field of Deputy U.S. Marshal in Indian Territory.

In 1876, Jesse joined the U.S. Cavalry, Company C, 5th regiment. They were sent to help Custer but was too late, as Jesse put it. One day too late. They buried the bodies.

This is all that Jesse told us about his service in the U.S. Army. Possibly the reason we don't know more is that it involved clandestine activities.

Deputy U.S. Marshall 1872-1873

Ola wrote a letter to Bill and Fay, last name unknown, March 21, 1983. Bud had a copy. She explains Jesse was a Deputy U.S. Marshal in Indian Territory. "Now, Uncle Jesse was a Deputy U.S. Marshal the first time, from the fall of 1872 to the Spring of 1873, under the name of John Franklin. J.J. McAllester was Chief at that time. The 2nd time he was Deputy U.S. Marshal, he was Frank Dalton under Jake Yose. The last time, he was J.D. Reed as best I can recall. I have a copy of when he joined under that name, but I haven't found it yet."

Jesse had used the name of John Franklin in 1869 in Chicago to join the Masonic Lodge #60 and Odd Fellows #24. He also used the name John Franklin to publish several stories in the newspaper.

As John Franklin, Jesse went to Fort Smith in 1872 and became a Deputy Marshal before Isaac Parker was appointed judge in 1875. From 1870-1875, Indian Territory was a snake pit in which the most evil and corrupt outlaws dwelt. The vipers expanded into the law itself causing severe havoc amongst the citizens of the Five Civilized Tribes. The Judge and Federal District Attorney were known to "rig" court cases, freeing the guilty so that they could continue their work of criminality. There had to be mighty big payoffs. When Judge Parker was appointed, things changed dramatically. He put the fear of God into all the lawbreakers especially those who murdered or committed rape.

Jesse was only 25 at the time he first experienced what marshaling was like. He was no greenhorn by no means. He saw the worst of men during his days of Quantrill Raiders. He had the stomach for it.

Jesse said he worked as a U.S. Marshal under Chief Marshal James Jackson McAlester beginning in 1872. Before this date, Jesse and McAlester had a lot in common. During the Civil War, James J. McAlester, also known as "JJ" was in the 22nd Arkansas Confederate Infantry. He was raised in Fort Smith, Arkansas. During the Civil War he was with Brig. General Benjamin McCulloch during the Battle of Pea Ridge who was leading the right wing of the Confederacy, a cavalry brigade while Brig. General Albert Pike was in command of the Cherokee, Choctaw, Chickasaw, Creek, and Seminole cavalry at Pea Ridge. McAlester was a captain in that battle and escorted the body of McCulloch who had been killed during the battle.

McCullouch was as fierce a fighter as Jesse James was and wanted to be involved in all the wars. He had been in the Texas Revolution, in the Texas militia, a Texas Ranger with John "Coffee" Hayes, a surveyor for the Republic of Texas, was chief of scouts for Zacharay Taylor in the Mexican-American War, joined the gold rush fever in California, a U.S. Marshal, was in the KGC, and in 1862 he was in the Confederacy and died in the Battle of Pea Ridge.

After the Civil War, J.J. McAlester became acquainted with engineer Oliver Weldon who had surveyed land in Indian Territory and told McAlester of a location of coal deposits in eastern Oklahoma. McAlester took this information and began working at an Indian trading firm of Harlan and Rooks in Choctaw Nation. He later worked for Reynolds and Hannaford, a firm of post traders. Keep in mind, Frank James was also involved in the coal industry and began working at trading posts near Fort Smith during this time and in the Choctaw Nation. Belle Starr, Dr. Frank James, and Lee McMurtry were in the Choctaw Nation, all connected to Jesse.

I don't think it's a coincidence, but in 1869, J. J. McAlester began freighting from Fort Smith to several different locations in Indian Territory with an ox team. McAlester worked as a freighter for several years. Those were some dangerous times. [225]

Jesse became a freighter beginning 1870-1872 in Indian Territory in which we know he covered Fort Sill, but he also worked in the Choctaw Nation, where Caddo, Oklahoma is located. He ran his freighting business in the Chickasaw Nation around Johnsonville. I'm sure they all knew each other, in fact, from what Bud has gathered, it appears that Jesse may have been mentored by J.J. McAlester. He was an active *Mason*.

McAlester married a ¾ Chickasaw woman, named Rebecca Burney in 1872. The marriage took place in Tobucksy County, Choctaw Nation. The marriage allowed full citizenship and rights in both Choctaw and Chickasaw Nations, allowing McAlester to gain an excessive amount of land. This allowed for McAlester to gain control over the area's coal resources, first of its kind in Indian territory.

McAlester's records indicate that he was not officially a U.S. Marshal until later, but possibly his service may not have been documented at that time due to disorganization and much corruption but was much needed in the lawless land.

McAlester developed his own mercantile business near the coal fields. The town McAlester, Oklahoma was named after J.J. McAlester. He was a primary developer of the coal mining industry in eastern Oklahoma. When the arrival of the Missouri-Kansas-Texas Railroad was laid out through the Cross-Roads area (McAlester), his mercantile company and his coal production became invaluable. The railway was the same system that went through Caddo, Oklahoma just 65 miles to the south in 1872 when Jesse was using it to haul freight to Fort Sill that same year.

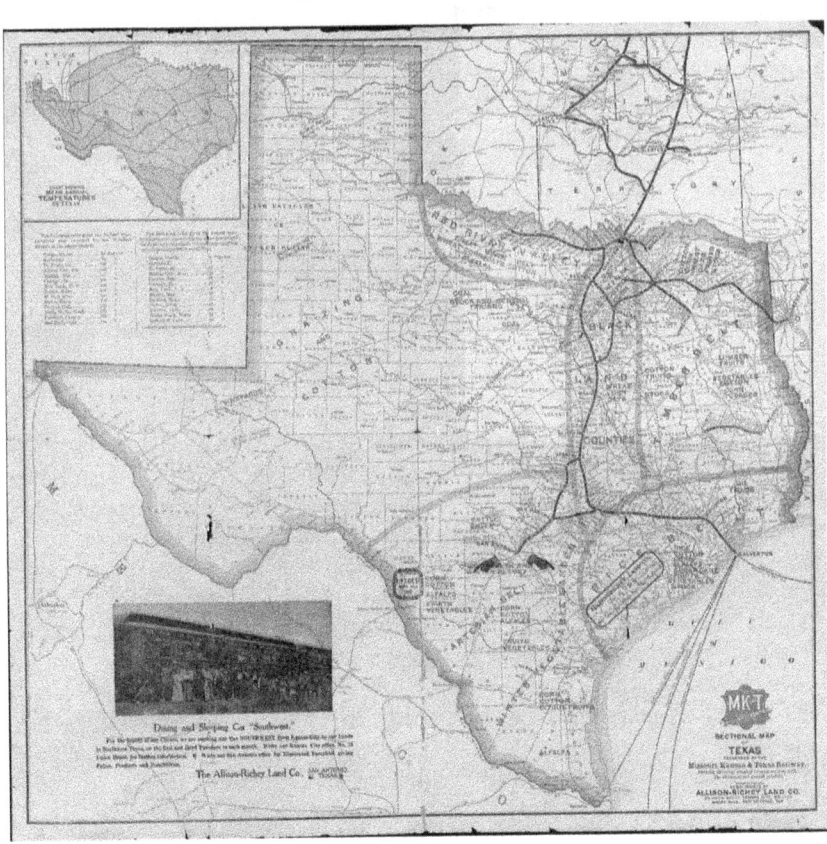

(1904 Sectional Map of Texas Traversed by the Missouri, Kansas & Texas Railway. Showing the crops adapted to each section, with the elevation ad annual rainfall. From The University of Texas at Arlington Libraries Special Collections published in St. Louis, Parker Engraving Company by unknown author. PD-via Wikimedia Commons.)

A little tidbit of information: J.J. McAlester's store was written about in the novel, "True Grit" by Charles Portis. U.S. Marshal Rooster Cogburn visited the store.

J. J. McAlester officially served as a U.S. Marshal from 1893-1897 in the Choctaw Nation and later became lieutenant governor of Oklahoma.

Rebecca Burney McAlester's mother, Lucy James descended from the James' family. Lucy James and Jesse shared their 3rd great grandparent, Thomas James (1674-1726). Lucy's great grandfather, Benjamin James (1756-1803) was a trader for the Choctaws. The writer shares both the James' and the McAlester/McAllister's ancestors.

Rebecca's stepsister, Emily Burney married Benjamin Jeremiah Vaughan who was a big cattleman near Ardmore. He was at one time one of Oklahoma's wealthiest citizen. He is mentioned in McAlester's obituary. He too was a Mason and the Vaughan name would cling to Frank and Jesse.

J. J. McAlester encouraged Jesse to better himself and reach for his dreams of becoming a doctor. Jesse only served one year as deputy and then enrolled in medical school at Ann Arbor, Michigan. He went by the name of John Franklin in school. He wasn't cut out for the medical field, he said "he couldn't stand the sight of blood." [226] Jesse changed courses, studied law, and passed his bar exam. He gained quite a bit of knowledge and skills. Ola, Aubrey, and William Tunstill all tried to verify his schooling and they could not locate the records that far back.

After his short education, Jesse went back to Fort Smith and served again under McAlester until 1874. In the Police Gazette files of 1882 titled, "Authentic Story Of The real Jesse James," outlined in the book, "The Hoax That Let Jesse James Live", Jesse told McGrath on his death bed, "About the war, I don't like to talk. It was war, and we perpetrated all the cruelties, I suppose, which soldiers have in all war. We were no different. But when the war ended, we hoped to be allowed to live in peace. I wanted to settle down and I started to study medicine, but it was too much for me. So I began to study law. But they wouldn't let us alone." [227]

He got a chance for his education thanks to McAlester and Jesse's encouragement to pursue education trickled down into the Texas Rangers.

Texas Rangers

Ola said that the first time she met Jesse in Centerville, she was drawn to him and felt a very tight kinship, but she knew there was so much more to this man after meeting him in person than she realized. As she was heading to the door to leave with her back to him, she said, "Now take care of yourself and we'll be back next Sunday." He said, "I always take care of myself." He repeated it again, "I always take care of myself." She "turned and looked at him and there he lay looking at me with a loaded .38 caliber special revolver six-shooter in each hand, leveled down on me." [228] The .38 six-shooters were used by the Texas Rangers and U.S. Marshals.

Jesse revealed to Ola, his time spent in the Texas Rangers. There are clues he left in the articles he wrote and the stories he told Ola, even though they may not have made sense to her. It's unbelievable and quite brilliant on Jesse's part to leave enough clues to pull together a story on who and what he was involved in; "Hidden in Plain Sight." The clues to look for is the territory that he covered in the Texas Rangers, the people, those who were ex-Confederates, Masons, the cattlemen, connections to John Chisum and Billy the Kid, cattle rustling, gun and ammo that the Indians had, the Mexican border, and the events that they were involved in.

I began to look through Bud's documents and did some research on my own. Both Bud and I have been to the Texas Rangers Hall of Fame and Museum in Waco, Texas at different times. Quite impressive. I went there to work on my family's book in 2017, trying to connect the dots and I believe that was the year that Bud and I started talking on the phone about Jesse and met in person later that year.

Bud had mentioned B.F. Johnson which was an alias for Jesse in the rangers and they had his record in the archives, an entire folder. When I asked the Texas Ranger archive specialist in the research center regarding alias' in the rangers, they said it was very prevalent in the Frontier Battalion. Most of them wanted to hide their true identity, some outlaws themselves.

I didn't know much about Jesse at the time. I knew my great uncle connected to the rangers, but until I met Bud, I had no idea that Jesse would be connected to the Texas Rangers. For some reason, I was drawn to the information on Arrington in the museum. I had a strong feeling that Arrington would be connected to both of these men we were researching. It all fits. Everything Jesse said to Ola or wrote about his service as a Texas Ranger, proved true as Bud said.

At the Texas Rangers Hall of Fame museum, there is extensive amount of surveyor equipment on display and a plaque that states "surveying was practiced by the *Egyptians* as early as 1400 B.C. for purposes of taxation." "During the colonial, Republic and statehood days of Texas, it was not unusual for a man to combine the duties of Texas Ranger and Surveyor. While on the wild Texas frontier, early surveyors had to defend themselves while practicing the science of land measurement, therefore it was logical to combine the two skills into one." These skills proved to be an extremely important factor for the Knights of the Golden Circle who were planted in many states and many organizations such as the Texas Rangers.

Jesse told the Buzbee reporter from the Corpus Christi Times that he was in the Texas Rangers 5 years. [229] What Bud and I have discovered was that he was in 1874-75 (Company E); 1877-1878 (Company C); 1879-?; 1886-?; and 1931-?. Bud said he used three different names, B.F. Johnson, Frank Dalton, and I believe it was John Franklin.

1874-75

Jesse enlisted on June 6, 1874, as *Benjamin Franklin Johnson* in Company E of the Frontier Battalion of the Texas Rangers under the newly appointed commander, Major John B. Jones who had served in the Confederacy, 8th Texas Cavalry (Terry's Texas Rangers) under the command of *Benjamin Franklin Terry*.

In May 1874, Captain William "Jeff" Maltby, was appointed as commander of Company E, Frontier Battalion of the Texas Rangers who had served in Gray's Battalion, Arkansas Volunteers in the Mexican-American War, a civilian employee as a teamster, wagon master, and scout for the U.S. Army in Fort Smith, Arkansas, and was a captain in the 17th Texas Volunteer Infantry during the Civil War. Maltby was the first to receive a commission as a captain in the Frontier Battalion. He was trying for the major's job as commander of the Frontier Battalion, with the amount of experience he had in Indian warfare and frontier life, and two petitions from outstanding citizens of Burnett County to support him. In Maltby's book, "Captain Jeff of the Texas Rangers: Fighting Comanche & Kiowa Indians on the South Western Frontier 1863-1874," by W. J. Maltby, he related that Jones received the appointment, without the experience, without living on the frontier, but was a personal friend of Governor Richard Coke who had seen his bravery on the battlefield in the Confederacy.

Captain Maltby served under General John R. Baylor in the Civil War who was a diehard Confederate soldier and requested to be buried in his Confederate uniform with the Confederate flag wrapped around him. He was a KGC member. Baylor led the 2nd Texas Mounted Rifles in 1861 to West Texas where forts had been abandoned by Union forces. He advanced into New Mexico to attack the Union Forts along the Rio Grande. He and his troops participated in the First Battle of *Mesilla* on July 25, 1861, which was in present-day Dona Ana County, New Mexico. The Confederates won and paved the way for the Confederate New Mexico Campaign in 1862 in which Josiah Dudley Doak (brother-in-law of Bloody Bill Anderson's sister, Mary Ellen Anderson Doak), General William Steele and the 7th Texas Cavalry took part.

Maltby helped build Fort Belknap, near Newcastle and Graham, Texas along the Clear Fork of the Brazos River which became the northernmost fort built in Texas at that time; Fort Clark, near the border of Mexico in Brackettville, Texas – the purpose of the fort was to guard the Mexican border and protect the military road to El Paso; and *Fort Concho* (San Angelo). Maltby served through the Indian Wars in the late 70's. He lived in Burnet County and was a cattleman who organized many cattle drives.

Maltby recruited men for Company E from Burnett, Lampasas, Brown, and Coleman Counties of Texas. From several accounts, he was placed in command in May 1874 and started recruiting in Burnett and Lampasas close to his home. In June, he concentrated on men in Brown and Coleman County. The quota of men needed was filled the 2nd day in *Brownwood*, June 5-6, 1874. Several accounts state that each company was enlisting at least 100 men, but some accounts state that Maltby's company enlisted 75 men, young, single, and of good character. Jesse joined on June 6th. He was 26 years of age, but undeniably, he was married to Zerelda Mimms, just less than two months from his enlistment date.

As we discussed before, Ola writes that he married Zee on **June 9, 1874**, but again, I believe she got the dates mixed up with the story about their marriage in the article titled, "Captured. The Celebrated Jesse W. James Taken at Last," published in the **June 9, 1874,** in the St. Louis Dispatch by "*Ranger*", which many suspect was written by Jesse's good friend and comrade, John Edwards. The article reveals the marriage took place on April 23, 1874 (not April 24, 1874 as most people list it) and married in Kansas City at a friend's house. The writer also reports that he met Jesse, his new bride, and Frank in Galveston and they were headed to Vela Cruz and then into the interior of Mexico. Jesse swore that he would return to the states when he could get a fair trial, "other than at the hands of a mob."

I believe this article was full of code words and secret messages; possibly a diversion from Jesse's new assignment with the rangers, promoting the idea that Jesse was leaving the country, hoping the law would take their eye off of him for a while. Notice the name or pseudonym of the writer, "Ranger." Edwards was known to hide things in plain sight in his articles. Jesse would already be a Texas Ranger when this article was published.

In the Ranger's archives for Johnson (Jesse) he had listed he was from *Coleman*, Texas.

Company E was assigned scout duty, in Brown, San Saba, and Lampasas counties. They would receive $40 per month, place to sleep, and feed for their horse. The rangers had to furnish their own horse, saddle, and firearms. The rangers were issued "Needle Guns," .51 caliber rifles. [230]

The rangers were required to protect the plains and settlers from the Comanches and the Kiowas who were still roaming the countryside, as well as thieves, renegades, and murderers.

Company E established a camp on Clear Creek just along the western border of Brown County. This was very near the geographical center point of Texas. The company moved to Home Creek in Coleman County, which was directly south of Trickham. Home Creek runs for 30 miles from southwest of Santa Anna to the southeast into the Colorado River.

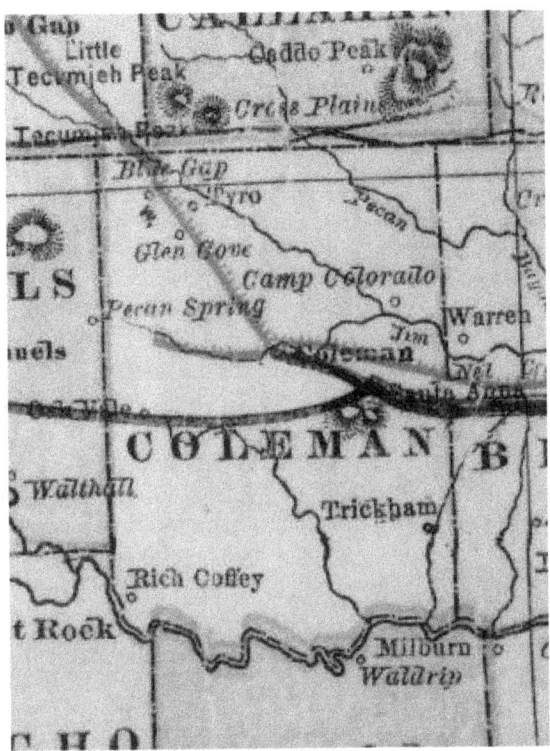

(Home Creek and Trickham in Coleman County, Texas (courtesy of Texas General Land Office)[231])

Adobe Walls

In less than a month, Jesse's company participated in the Battle of Adobe Walls in the Texas Panhandle when 27 men, some historians say 28 men held off a force of 700 or more Indians under Comanche Chief Quanah Parker, June 27, 1874. Some of the books regarding the Texas Rangers do not mention this, even the book Maltby wrote about his life as a ranger, but you would think that it was a fairly important task that they performed. Was it true? Here are a few hints that it possibly was, but for some odd reason the story of Company E being there has been quietly concealed.

In one book, "The Quirt and the Spur", by Edgar Rye, 1909 states that "Captain Arrington, with a squad of Texas Rangers trailing a band of rustlers, passed through Adobe Walls and reported that the Comanches, Cheyenne and Arapahos were concentrating for some purpose on the Deep Creek of the Colorado River." [232] Deep Creek is north of Snyder, Texas in Scurry County, approximately 200 miles away from Adobe Walls and approximately 165 miles from Home Creek. They would have been a long way from their camp or their assigned scouting area. Of course, at that time, there was no ranger camp in the panhandle. It was being handled by troops from Fort Dodge, Camp Supply and Fort Sill out of Indian Territory, but other incidents place them outside of their zone, so it is feasible that they could have been in the area. The men would break up into small scouting groups and go where needed, even if it was out of their territory.

We learn that Arrington was very fond of the panhandle but was not a captain yet as of June 1874 and he supposedly did not join Company E until August 1874, per the Texas Ranger's records. The only logical summation in this story is that Arrington was there as a private and the dates of his enlistment were wrong or at least his company was there. I think there is more to this story than what history has told us. Twenty-seven/twenty-eight men against Seven to Nine hundred Indians? We learn more.

Everything that has been written about the 2nd Battle of Adobe Walls state that there were a few of the shop/saloon keepers, a cook and his wife, but mostly were buffalo hunters at Adobe Walls. A team of wagons joined the group, including 20-year-old Bat Masterson and William "Billy" Dixon, who was a prominent Mason, a scout, and buffalo hunter who got a shot off, hitting a proud Comanche on top of a Mesa nearly a mile away.

Interestingly, Masterson and Dixon were part of Fort Dodge, Kansas' "firms" that were sent on expeditions with many wagons loaded with supplies instructed to locate in the center of the range. They were going to open supply stores. They became "a center for traffic in hides." [233] The night before the attack, Masterson got involved in a poker game and one of the players became irate and drew a gun on him. Masterson answered back with the first bullet out of his gun which killed a man. He became famous after this battle and went on to be General Miles' commander of "a body of scouts" and later became sheriff of Dodge City and marshal of Trinidad, Colorado. [234]

Adobe Walls was 15 miles northeast of the present-day Stinnett. It was two miles from the original mission/trading post that was taken over from the Spanish settlers by William Bent and Kit Carson. Another article that stated there were rangers in the battle was in J. Marvin Hunter's Frontier Times Magazine with the article, "The Battle of Adobe Walls", by Unknown; April 1947. It was written that "there were buffalo hunters with their curious rifles, seasoned Indian fighters, soldiers on furlough, trappers, gamblers, scouts, **rangers**, and camp hangers on, Americans, Englishmen, Germans, Mexicans, and what not." The article speaks of John J. Clinton, former Abilene, Texas Chief of Police who took part in Adobe Walls. Clinton was in the area hunting for his horses who had gotten away. He had taken a herd of steers to Dodge City and was accompanied by four Mexican vaqueros. When they saw in a distance a large band of Indians they headed for safety at Adobe Walls.

This story was published in the Fort Worth Record and Abilene Reporter. A response from Bat Masterson who was there, denied that John Clinton was ever there at Adobe Walls. Clinton stated that the battle was actually at the original site where a mission once was and where Carson and Bent tried to establish a trading post. [235]

But something that brings the writer to believe that the rangers were part of the many buffalo hunters at Adobe Walls, was a story in The San Angelo Weekly Standard, February 9, 1940, titled "Coleman Pioneer Recalls Concho As An Army Post." It was a story of an ex-ranger Noah Armstrong who lived in northern Coleman County. Two years after the Battle of Adobe Walls, Armstrong was a ranger under Captain John Sparks from 1876-78 with Jesse in Company C, but he gives us information on what some of the responsibilities were in the early Frontier Battalion.

In the article, Armstrong tells the reporter that "the killing of the buffalo was necessary for development of the country, as the shaggy animal provided meat and bread for Indians. The ranger company of which he was a member was sent out to protect the hunters from Indians, and it was their duty to call on the various camps, some of which were center of operations for killing of as many as 4,000 head in a single season." So, it can easily be said that the rangers were at Adobe Walls to protect the hunters. There were many buffalo hunter camps near Adobe Walls, indicating that this place was the main center of operations in the panhandle for the kill. How very sad. The buffalo hunters would come into the little community for supplies, socializing, drinking and spewing out tall tales of the hunts. They would take their hides to Dodge City and return for more.

Another clue may indicate that the rangers were with other buffalo hunters in the area and came to their rescue. In www.tshaonline.org – "Adobe Walls, Second Battle of," published 1976 and updated 2020 stated, "Hunters in the vicinity were notified of the attack on Adobe Walls, and by the end of the fifth day there were more than 100 men at Adobe Walls."

Was Jesse involved in the Battle of Adobe Wells? Weighing what information we do have, even though the men had only been in the unit for 21 days adjusting to their commander and their new duties, I believe Jesse was among the men who went to Adobe Walls. In the Daily News and Intelligencer from Mexico, Missouri, 1932; Frank Dalton alias for Jesse provided a story on this very event persuading the readers that he was there.

A month later, July 24th, Captain Maltby ordered Lt. B.F. Best to take 21 men to scout the Table Mountains in northeast Runnels county, which is south of present-day Abilene. They encountered a skirmish with a few Indians and did not give the Indians much of a chance.

On July 31, 1874, B.F. Johnson among many of the men in Company E requested in a petition for Captain W. J. Maltby to procure Colts improved Breech Loading Pistols of the latest and best improved quality. The men would pay for it out of each payroll due them. The man who signed his name above Johnson was James Knox Paulk. He was a Confederate soldier at the age of 15. The reader can find information on him and the company on usgenwebsites.org. James Knox Paulk enlisted on the same day as Jesse, June 6, 1874. He continued his service as a Minute Man in Coleman County, Texas in the Indian Wars.

**Camp Co. "E" First Batt
Home Creek Coleman County**

(B.F. Johnson's signature on petition for Colts improved Breech Loading Pistols)

In Paulk's obituary, in the Daily Tribune, March 21, 1932, it is stated that his company of 27 was involved in the Battle of Adobe Walls against 900 Indians (his account). He was wounded and several rangers were killed. Many accounts established that four white men were killed, and several were wounded. Some of the best marksmen were there and the battle went down in history as a remarkable and miraculous victory over the Indians, leading to the Red River Indian Wars.

The Kiowa soon pounced on Texas with a raid, while the Comanche attacked an army detachment at the Wichita Agency at Anadarko, Indian Territory. The final blow to the Texas Plains

Indians, those who were not willing to settle in the reservations, was at the Battle of Palo Duro, occurring Sept. 28, 1874.

Company E continually battled Comanche and Kiowa during this time. By Dec. 13, 1874, B.S. Foster became commanding officer and their assignment was to track down fugitives and outlaws in the Rio Grande valley. This is where we find Jesse when the Mexican pack train was overtaken in the winter of 1874-75.

Benjamin Franklin Johnson served from June 6, 1874 to May 31, 1875 in Company E under Maltby and Foster, serving with private George W. Arrington as of August 1874, maybe even earlier. Henry Sackett (1851-1928) was also in Company E, enlisted on the same day as B.F. Johnson. Sackett later became a Texas State Representative in the 33rd, 34th, 35th, 36th, and 38th Legislatures. He would become the owner of Camp Colorado where from there he with the Maltby's Rangers "pursued the bands of Big Foot and Jape, Comanche chiefs, and defeated them." [236] Sackett also was a county surveyor and laid out the town of Coleman.

Camp Colorado was moved several times. In 1855, it was near what is now Ebony in Mills County, northwest of Goldwaithe, which was in the territory of the military route connecting Fort Phantom Hill (north of Abilene in Jones County) and Austin. By 1856, Camp Colorado was near Mukewater Creek, just south of Trickham, and 6 miles north of the Colorado River on the route between Fort Belknap and Fort Mason in Coleman County. The next post was moved to the area which was known for Maltby's Rangers. It is located approximately 10 miles northeast of Coleman, Texas. [237]

Andrew Mather (1851-1929) was also in Company E under Captain Maltby. Mather became infamous as a Texas Ranger and was written about in books and articles, especially by author, J. Frank Dobie. Andrew or Andy as they called him was very good friends with Buffalo Bill Cody. Mather, Buffalo Bill, and J. Frank Dalton all looked alike, wide-brimmed hat, tailored clothing, beard or goatee, and long flowing white hair.

1875-1876

In 1875 and 1876, Jesse was busy with the Mexican pack train, burying gold, and helping the Cheyenne and Sioux on the Northern Plains.

In October 1876, after the Northfield bank robbery and time for Jesse to heal in the Sioux Nation, Captain John C. Sparks would take over the command of Company C of the Frontier Battalion after it was disbanded on December 1874. They would be stationed in Burnet County and cover Llano, Lampasas, Hamilton (where the towns *Hico* and Hamilton are located), Bell (Killeen), and Williamson (Georgetown) counties. These were all very significant counties in Jesse's and Billy's life.

John C. Sparks was born in Lawrence, Alabama. His father, Thomas was a merchant who had come from North Carolina. John would have been at the ripe age to be placed in the Civil War. In 1860, he was in Waco, Texas, living next to several young men, in their 20's, possibly a boarding house. The men's occupations varied with many identifying as young professional men; lawyer, merchant, mechanic, stock raiser, teacher, tin smith, and a Ranger, William Herring, age 27. John C. Sparks is listed as a clerk, age 19.

We find that Sparks enlisted in 1861 with the 6th Texas Mounted Cavalry, Company G in the Confederacy which appears to be under Stone's Regiment. Sparks was recruited in Waco, McLennan County by Captain Peter F. Ross, the older brother of Sul Ross. Brushy Bill Roberts father, J. H. "Wild Henry" Roberts, served under Ross as well until 1863 and then joined the Quantrill Raiders.

"The 6th Texas Cavalry received orders to march to Fort Smith, Arkansas in November 1861. The regiment marched in three echelons, the first was led by Ross, the second by Griffith, and the third by Stone. On 26 December 1861, the Texans took part in the Batte of Chustenahlah."

"The 6th Texas Cavalry joined a Confederate force under Brigadier General Benjamin McCulloch, who ordered Ross to take his cavalrymen on a raid behind the Union forces occupying the extreme northwest corner of Arkansas. Ross led his horsemen well to the west of Samuel Ryan Curtis' Federal army and struck the Union supply line at Keetsville, Missouri. On 25 February 1862, the Texans overpowered the Federal outpost, killing two and capturing one while losing two men wounded and one or two missing. Ross' men burned five sutler's wagons and captured 60 horses and mules. The raiders' return route went east of Curtis' army and south across the *Boston Mountains*; they arrived in camp on 1 March." [238]

The Boston Mountains would become a future stronghold for Frank and Jesse.

The 6th Texas Cavalry were also involved in the Battle of Pea Ridge as part of General McIntosh's Brigade under McCulloch's Division.

After the war, in 1870, Sparks is living in Navarro County, Texas, married with 3 small children. It appears that he was married in Mississippi and had one of his children there in 1866. On the 1870 census, it shows that John was a merchant, same as his father. Living next to them was his brother, Titus Clark Sparks, also a merchant.

Titus Clark Sparks' widow applied for a pension, Mrs. Mary Whitfield Sparks in the 1930's. Titus had died in 1895. Titus was in the 15th Texas Infantry under the organization and command of Col. Joseph Warren Speight. The companies were formed from Waco, Corsicana, and Velasco. Titus served in the Hospital Corps as a steward under Speight. He was a druggist by trade.

1877-78

In January 1877, under Captain John C. Sparks a Ben Johnson was mentioned who was at Ft. McKavett, which was 20 miles southwest of Menard, Texas. It is on the San Saba River and on the old trail to Fort Concho. Near San Saba River was the silver mine that Albert Pike was interested in and many others, such as the KGC. It was established by the Spanish and known and utilized by the Comanches. [239]

Johnson was a teamster for the Texas Rangers Frontier Battalion, Company C. I am not sure if this was Jesse or not. By this time, he should have been recovered from the bank robbery in Northfield after staying with the Sioux.

Ben Johnson was also from Coleman County, same as Benjamin Franklin Johnson. It would seem like he would be the same man. Coleman county only had a population of 347 in the 1870's. Ben Johnson is later mentioned at Fort McKavett, was noted as a wagon man and was black, but he and his partner, the cook, George Stevenson could pass off as white men, very lightly colored. Stevenson was noted as a mulatto. Was this another disguise for Jesse, or were they Jesse's right-hand men, John Trammel, his cook and Lucky Johnson, his horse handler? In their photos, they were dark skinned.

Jesse did tell Ola that he joined the Texas Rangers in 1877 and was stationed at Fort Concho. He was in Company C, Border Battalion. It is unknown when he joined and when he was discharged. His commander was Captain John C. Sparks, same company and same commander as Ben Johnson.

We know Jesse was in Fort Worth on March 10, 1877 when he wrote a letter that was intercepted by the law. "Dear.... the beeves will soon be ready. As soon as the roads dry up and the streams run down we will drive. We expect to take a good bunch of cattle in. You may look out. There will be plenty of bellowing after the drive. Remember it is business. The range is good I learn between *Sidney* and Deadwood. We may go to pasture somewhere in that region. You will hear of it. Tell **Sam** to come to Honey Grove, Texas, before the drive season comes. There's money in the stock. As ever, Jesse J." [240]

I believe "Sam" was Sam Skates who was actually John Trammel. This was the name he used when he was a bare-knuckle boxing champion. Honey Grove was near Sherman and where a good ole friend lived in 1930, Bob Goss. He mentioned Sidney, as in Sidney, Nebraska.

Later in October 1877, Ben Johnson would be chosen to be included in Company E under N.O. Reynolds, being paid $20 per month and would be discharged in February 28, 1878. He was stationed at Fort McKavett.

Fort McKavett was first established in 1852 and during the Civil War was used as an outpost for Confederate forces. During and after the war, it was used to help guard the upper San Antonio-El Paso Road. It was an isolated fort and materials and supplies such as tobacco, whiskey, and livestock forage were hauled by wagon from San Antonio. It was also a site where new weapons and equipment were tested.

Four regiments of Buffalo soldiers were stationed at Fort McKavett, one being the 9th Cavalry Regiment.

As far as we know, Jesse as Benjamin Franklin Johnson was in Company C during this time under Captain Sparks, who was commanding 14 men. The company stayed very busy in 1877 when a bloody feud between the Horrell brothers and Pink Higgins with his brother-in-law, Bob Mitchell flared up regarding cattle theft in Lampasas. Many counties in Texas were dealing with cattle rustling at that time and it would continue into the next century.

The Horrell brothers had all the makings and markings of cattle rustlers. It was documented that the Horrells were involved in numerous lawless activities. They had a cattle ranch in Lampasas and they started getting out of hand in 1873. They were depicted as five brothers who were always whooping and shooting it up at the saloons and brothels in Lampasas. They acted as if they were above the law, but was that the whiskey talking?

Now to be fair, you must dive into several sources to get the facts on the Horrell brothers, just as the story of Jesse and Billy the Kid. Some authors depict them all as vicious murderers. It was hard back then to tell who the good guys and bad guys were, and the authors could sell more literature on the "bad" in these men. One author, David Johnson has taken the time to research the truth on the Horrell boys. They did have a lot of meanness in them, but there were reasons, "not to defend them" Johnson writes, but to understand them just as Bud and I are trying to do. Johnson's book is *The Horrell Wars Feuding in Texas and New Mexico*, 2014.

One night in 1873, the sheriff of Lampasas came into a saloon to arrest some friends of the Horrells and some sources say that one of the Horrell brothers stepped between Sheriff Shadrick Denson and his prisoners-to-be and shot the sheriff of Lampasas, shot him dead. In other sources, the sheriff was severely wounded but lived. Johnson stated that it was other friends of the Horrells that did the shooting.

There were many other gun battles with lawmen who were attempting to arrest one of the Horrell brothers and his friends for the shooting of the sheriff. The lawmen were met with bullets and 4 state policemen were killed. Finally, after more state police arrived, one of the Horrell brothers was arrested with his friends and taken to Georgetown to jail. They didn't stay long; 30 men broke them out. The 5 brothers fled to Lincoln County, New Mexico. Billy the Kid was in Texas living with his father at that time, but John Chisum was living in Lincoln County, who owned the largest cattle ranch in the whole United States.

In Lincoln, the killing spree continued for the Horrell boys, but per David Johnson, the author, the Horrell brothers didn't invite the trouble, but they had plenty of trouble with them. Several versions of how many men joined the Horrells in New Mexico, relay that they may had up to 15-20 men with them.

Apparently, trouble had begun decades ago when the native New Mexicans despised the Anglos settling in their homeland near the Rio Ruidoso River in Lincoln County. Trouble grew between the two races over water rights. The Mexican inhabitants who initially settled in this area after the Apaches were placed on reservations, built irrigation ditches to supply the farmer's needs. When the Anglo Texans began moving in and settling, they built dams within the ditches to provide more water for their own needs. Greed and self-preservation took over on both sides. To make matters worse, the L.G. Murphy & Company, which included J.J. Dolan began organizing in 1866. The company was founded by two Union officers, one being Lawrence Gustave Murphy. They took control of trade with the Mescalero Apaches, Fort Stanton, and eventually the largest county in the U.S., Lincoln County, New Mexico.

Murphy & Company did not last long within the realm of Fort Stanton because of their corrupt practices. They were ordered off of Fort Stanton by the U.S. government. The company just took their business elsewhere and built, "the big store" in Lincoln. Their mercantile business grew until they maintained a monopoly overpowering the smaller business owners and government contracts. The Santa Fe Ring, made up of the most corrupt political and businessmen who controlled Lincoln County, welcomed Murphy & Company.

The trouble for the Horrells per Johnson started when the Mexicans began stealing from them, all of the supplies, livestock, and proceeds they received from the sale of their cattle to Clayton and Cooksey. This cattlemen's outfit, Clayton and Cooksey were deeply involved in buying and selling cattle near Lampasas, picking up the cattle in Coleman County, Texas near Trickham where John Chisum had his store. They had just hired young James Gillett to drive a herd of cattle from Coleman county to the Horrell brothers in Lampasas in 1873 and then turned around and bought them back when the Horrells had to leave town in a hurry. Gillett also worked for others who were part of Chisum's cattle camps around the Concho River where Jesse was later stationed near Fort Concho as a Texas Ranger in 1877. Gillett became a famous Texas Ranger during the time Jesse had been one, from 1875-1881.

Back in Lincoln County, New Mexico, the Horrells had settled on a piece of property that some believed was owned by Murphy and Dolan. They probably were the owners, as it was their practice to hold land loans to newly arrived farmers and if payments were missed, the company would foreclose on the land, the cattle, and the crops. The property was at the mouth of Eagle Creek on the Rio Ruidoso River.

It was no more than two months since the time they settled there that the locals began accusing the Horrells of murder when a Mexican neighbor was killed as he was "cutting" a water ditch.

In December 1873, the Horrells and their men shot up the town of Lincoln in a drunken state just as the brothers did in Lampasas. When Ben Horrell, former Sheriff of Lincoln County Jack Gylam, and Dave Warner were confronted by Constable Martinez, they were ordered to surrender their weapons. The three complied but gathered more guns and began shooting their guns in a brothel. When confronted again by more law officers, Dave Warner shot and killed Martinez. Warner was shot immediately, while Horrell and Gylam fled the scene. The lawmen caught up to them and shot and killed the guilty parties. Horrell was shot 9 times and Gylam 13 times. The bodies of the dead men, including Ben Horrell were mutilated by Martinez' loyalists. One cut off Ben's finger to retrieve a gold ring.

This left only 4 Horrell brothers.

Revenge overtook the Horrells and by the time they left Lincoln County, 13 Mexicans were killed by their guns. It was called the Horrell Wars. First, they killed two prominent Mexican ranchers. A new sheriff, Sheriff Alexander Hamilton Mills got up a posse and hunted them down. The Horrells got away.

Their next murderous trail landed at a Mexican celebration in Lincoln, killing four men and wounding a woman. The Horrell's friend, Edward Hart shot and killed Deputy Sheriff Joseph Haskins because he had married a Mexican woman. Less than a week later, the Horrells and friends came upon freight wagons outside of Roswell, New Mexico who were being driven by five Mexican men taking corn to the Chisum Ranch. All were killed by the brothers, but mostly by their friends. Their racial hatred for Hispanics followed them wherever they went, and their path proved deadly, setting the tone for an evil aura to surround Lincoln County.

That was one version, but David Johnson who wrote "The Horrell Wars: Feuding in Texas and New Mexico" outlines in detail what happened by several accounts of eyewitnesses and documents. He relates that the Mexicans did not like the Texans nor what they brought to their native land. There were accusations on both sides. Most of the killing done was in retaliation of what they did to Ben and those who were trying to force the Horrell's out of the area. Many Mexicans, several times came to their ranch and had shoot outs with them and threatened to burn them alive in their house. The lawmen didn't do anything nor investigate. The Murphy/Dolan clan got involved which only increased their power in politics, profits in the mercantile business, property, and their cattle industry. All this would lead to a more racially divided Lincoln County and the distrust towards

Anglos. The Horrell Wars would lead to the Pecos War, a range war between John Chisum and small ranchers/farmers/Indians along the Pecos River, and eventually it led to the Lincoln County War which would entangle Billy the Kid.

The Horrell Ranch was attacked by the law and sixty Mexican men who surrounded their house and drove off the horses. The Horrells escaped with only their lives. Horrell's friends who tried to go back and gather their belongings were stopped and all the goods were confiscated. J.J. Dolan got up another posse on January 25th and burned the ranch and all its contents to the ground after they stole all the crops. Men who had the most resistance to the vigilante groups of Dolans or the Mexicans, were being attacked, shot, and hung.

After the Horrell family members were safe, the Horrells and their men were going back to Lincoln to burn the town down, "killing and plundering indiscriminately, but the Harrold (Horrell) brothers did not want to do it, and fearing they could not control the party they turned back." [241]

An interesting note is that Roswell, Ruidoso, Fort Stanton, and Lincoln fall withing the **33rd** degree latitude parallel.

The Horrells returned to Lampasas like nothing had happened and continued to provoke authorities in February 1874. They were not welcomed by the town folk, but the Horrells put the fear in them.

The Horrells were arrested and tried for the murders of the lawmen in Lampasas, but the local jury acquitted them. Then the feud started building in 1876 when Pink Higgins accused Merritt Horrell of stealing one of his calves. The case went to trial and Merritt was found not guilty. In January 1877, the two met up in a saloon and Higgins outdrew Merritt Horrell, leaving him dead on the wooden floor of the saloon.

Another of the Horrells was down, leaving 3 Horrells left. Higgins and his brother-in-law surrendered to Captain Sparks of the Texas Rangers, who were called upon to get involved in February 1877. Higgins and his brother-in-law were jailed and bonded out with $10,000 each. Interestingly, a little later, the Lampasas courthouse was burglarized, and all the district court records disappeared, which held the bonds of Higgins and Mitchell. That was common in those days, as well as the burning down of courthouses to destroy trails of criminality.

Company C continued to remain on sight just to ensure the peace. They camped on the Lampasas fairgrounds. Civil unrest further north in Coleman, Mason, Comanche and Brown Counties was making Major Jones restless. In Brown County on May 11, 1877, 12 men forcibly broke out 6 prisoners. This prompted Major Jones to send Captain Sparks and Company C from Lampasas back to Coleman. He left three men of Company C in Lampasas. Jones writing to Sparks, "There are more desperate characters in this and adjoining counties than any section of country I know of now." [242]

After the majority of the rangers left in June, Higgins and his brother-in-law Mitchell met up with two other men of their clan and rode to Lampasas. The Horrell brothers and their friends were gathered in the town's square. An all-out gun battle began, leaving 2 dead: one from each group.

Major Jones went to Lampasas to negotiate peace between the two families and their clansmen. He placed Sergeant N.O. Reynolds in charge and prisoners were taken to Austin. That same day, June 7, 1877, Lieutenant B.S. Foster of Company E, the company that Jesse was previously a member, resigned from service.

Because of the many friends on both sides of the fence in Lampasas, the sheriff, Sheriff Sweet could not round up enough men for a posse to hunt these men down. Later, one of the Higgin's bunch was ambushed, shot and killed. Sargeant N.O. Reynolds and six of his men were able to surround the Horrell bunch in a cabin and took the three brothers into custody. They were later released on bond. By August of that year, Jones was able to persuade the two sides to give up their arms and make peace.

Later, two of the Horrell brothers who had left Lampasas, committed robbery and murder near Meridian, Texas. They were thrown in jail. Justice was served by a vigilante committee, both being shot and killed. Only one brother was left out of the five and he left the country. Peace returned.

We don't really know if Jesse, as Bejamin Franklin Johnson was involved in keeping the peace with the Horrell/Higgins feud since he was covering Lampasas in Company C with Captain Sparks, nor if he was involved in cattle rustling, Billy the Kid, or John Chisum, but the connections are there. Bud believes Jesse was heavily involved with Billy in the cattle rustling business in Texas, Mexico, New Mexico, and Oklahoma.

That summer of 1877, complaints began to pile up in Major John B. Jones' office regarding Captain Sparks. He liked his liquor, as well as the rangers in his company. Jones received a "disorderly conduct" and "discharging his pistol" complaint in Mason against Sparks. Later Jones determined after an investigation that Sparks was not personally involved. Joe Leverett, a sergeant of the company shot a member of the grand jury in the stomach in Mason, which may have been an accident and connected to the charge of "discharging his pistol." Major Jones could not have the rangers misrepresent their good reputation by their irresponsibility in their behavior or dereliction of duty, but at the same time, he couldn't afford to lose another ranger. The rangers were stretched thin as countless rangers were resigning. Now, it appeared there would be another feud in Brown County, like the one in Lampasas over cattle theft. That was in the jurisdiction of Company C also.

John Sparks was arrested October 4th in Austin for shooting a lamp in a restaurant within the city limits and was fined $25. Leaving the courtroom, Sparks used his cane to assault the person who filed the complaint. A new charge was filed for assault and battery and later a charge of carrying a concealed weapon. Sparks appeared before the mayor of Austin and almost had another altercation. The newspapers ran story after story of these events, calling Sparks a "bull-dozer and a bully." There was also a report out of Coleman that some of the members of Company C engaged in drunken and riotous conduct, firing shots in town and in houses.

In the fall of 1877, Captain Sparks led a detachment of rangers to Fort Concho. Ola wrote that in 1877, Jesse was sent to Ft. Concho, just 70 miles to the northwest from Fort McKavett. It was all within a 100-mile radius from Coleman County, Texas where Company C was headquartered. Fort Concho was situated at the junction of the North and South Concho Rivers. It was established in 1867 and the town of San Angelo was built outside of the fort.

The 10th Cavalry who had been stationed at Fort Sill was transferred to Fort Concho in 1875. They were known as the Buffalo soldiers who Jesse and his men John Trammell, his black cook and Lucky Johnson, his black horse handler knew well when they were freighters, taking supplies to Fort Sill.

It was well documented, that most of the soldiers in the southern part of Texas did not like the Texas Rangers. It must have been over who had supreme authority for that area. It also had to do with their racial differences. From what is documented most of the rangers had close contact with all the frontier forts and many were assigned to these forts. They made their camp outside of the fort, but it was their fortress and was designed for both the army and the rangers to support each other in fighting the enemy, but sometimes they were not clear who the enemy was.

The rangers experienced horrific encounters with the Indians and their style of torture and warfare. Their eyes had seen the worst of the worst inhumane techniques to destroy a human's soul and spirit, much less their body, piece by piece. The rangers were not totally innocent either in the treatment of their Indian prisoners or those whom they killed and tore off their scalps for trophies.

It was noted by Texas Ranger James Gillett that in the ranger's camp they would keep themselves entertained with music to counter the violence they incurred on the trail. Many men played musical instruments they had tucked away in their saddle bags. Jesse was known to play the fiddle and harmonica at the same time. They also enjoyed horse racing, making temporary racetracks wherever they were stationed, a favorite past time of Jesse's. They tried to enjoy their time in the midst of such turmoil in Texas. It lifted their spirits and you can bet spirits were involved overwhelmingly.

Some of Spark's rangers went into Nasworthy's Saloon off Fort Concho in San Angelo and did not like what they saw. Some of the Buffalo soldiers were dancing with the ladies. Per Colonel Benjamin Grierson and his Buffalo soldiers at Fort Concho, the rangers began shooting up the place.

Grierson expected an apology from Sparks, but instead, Sparks put out a challenge that "he and his little company could whip the entire post of Fort Concho."

"Troopers seeking justice returned to the saloon and a hot gunfight ensued resulting in the death of a bystander. Colonel Grierson, the commanding officer of the soldiers went to the Adjutant General of the Rangers in Austin to file a complaint." [243]

One fellow ranger who was in the same company with Jesse at Fort Concho related his side of the story of the incident. Noah Armstrong stated, "Finishing a round of buffalo camps, the rangers came into Fort Concho, ready for a little social life; entered one of the saloons, took a turn at Monte, and then enjoyed dancing with such girls as the settlement afforded.

The dance music was interrupted when 8 or 10 negro soldiers entered and attempted to dance with white girls. Mr. Armstrong says the rangers went into action and beat the negroes over the head with the butts of their guns. The post commander, hearing of the trouble, arrived and was rebuked by the ranger captain, Mr. Armstrong recalls, it being made known, without reservations, that the rangers would not permit negro soldiers to dance with white girls." [244] In 1949, Mr. Armstrong was named as the oldest living ranger, but little did they know that B.F. Johnson/Jesse was still alive and thriving.

From Major Jones' report in the book, "Texas Ranger, John B. Jones and the Frontier Battalion, 1874-1881;" by Rick Miller, 2012, the author writes that "on December 4, a citizen at Fort Concho wrote Major Jones that Sparks had broken up a "whorehouse dance" and threatened people with a drawn pistol. The observation was made that citizens of that place were glad twice when Sparks initially arrived there and when he left. This was apparently the proverbial last straw." [245] On December 10, Sparks submitted his resignation as commander of Company C. He was dismissed from the Texas Rangers and replaced by First Sergeant of Company A, George Washington Arrington.

Arrington would be appointed first lieutenant of Company C. This was a very unusual appointment, because of Arrington's past as a hothead, a murderer, a *spy* for the *Confederacy*, had been in *Central America,* and had been a drover who drove *cattle* from *Houston* to *Brownwood* and landed in *Company E* with Jesse James and three years later placed in Jesse's *Company C*? Do you see the chain of events that built Arrington's character? There was a reason. Arrington was in line for a promotion. Arrington was favored by Jones and was a part of his brotherhood. Arrington became a Mason and was a member of Samson Lodge, No. 231 in Lynchburg, Texas (10 miles east of *Houston*); Fort Griffin Lodge No. 489; Throckmorton, Texas, Albany Lodge No. 482; Albany, Texas, Miami Lodge No. 805, Miami, Texas, and the Knight Templar Commandry in Canadian, Texas.

Arrington was told by his commanding officer, Major Jones, that Company C, led by Sparks were their own men; no tight reins or strict demands should be forced upon them. "In light of the "slack rule" under which men in Sparks' command had been governed, it will probably be better not to be too rigid in the enforcement of discipline at first, as you are not acquainted with the men... As you become better acquainted with them you can draw the reins tighter and gradually bring them to proper discipline and duty." [246] Arrington knew Jesse as he served with him in Company E in 1874-1875, but now Jesse would be serving under him.

During the transition, Company C was ordered to Lampasas, to join up with Company E who was commanded by the newly commissioned First Lt. Nelson Orcelus Reynolds (N.O. Reynolds) who just received this promotion after he arrested the leader of the Horrell brothers and 10 of their sympathizers on July 28, 1877. Company C was temporarily under the command of Reynolds until Arrington could take his place.

In the official records at the Texas Rangers archives, Ben Johnson, a teamster was placed under Reynolds in Company E beginning Oct. 23, 1877 – Feb. 28, 1878. This Ben Johnson who had been at Fort McKavett earlier in Company C which was combined with Company E would be retained at Fort McKavett, now under the command of Reynolds.

Nowhere in Ben Johnson's records did it show him to be Black. Per the book, "Texas Ranger N.O. Reynolds the Intrepid," by Chuck Parsons and Donaly E. Brice, it states that Ben Johnson who was a teamster for Company E was black. This Ben Johnson would have the same experience at Fort McKavett as the brawl with the Buffalo soldiers at Fort Concho when Jesse was stationed there in the Fall of 1877.

The story of the McKavett brawl was on New Year's Eve 1878. The story was also in the book by Texas Ranger James B. Gillett, "Six Years with the Texas Rangers: 1875-1881," but he never wrote that Ben Johnson, the teamster was involved. He said the man who was involved was George, a mulatto, almost white. Of course, Gillett wasn't there, but heard this story from those who were. Henry McGhee was there and wrote to his brother that two black men in the company, one a cook and the other a wagoner were involved in the incident. The letter doesn't state their names. This is the only evidence that the "teamster" for the company may have been there.

At the McKavett brawl, on New Year's Eve, December 31, 1877, Lt. N.O. Reynolds and a combination of Company E and A had just came from scouting in Menard county and arrived at Fort McKavett to aid the county officers in the New Year's celebration. In the book, "Texas Ranger John B. Jones and the Frontier Battalion, 1874-1881", the black cook and wagoner went to a dance and met up with "drunken black men." Both the cook, George Stevenson and the teamster, Ben Johnson were "forced at gunpoint to hand over their pistols. There may have been some resentment of the light-skinned Stevenson, who could have been mistaken for white, and there was also the damning fact that both men were a part of the Ranger scout." [247]

The final outcome after heavy fire from several rangers into the house whose occupants refused to return the guns, resulted in the death of Texas Ranger Tim McCarty, three black men, and a young black girl who was accidently shot. Ben Johnson was not hurt nor Stevenson and Johnson would be discharged out of Company E as of February 1878.

Stories regarding N.O. Reynolds disclosed in the book, "Texas Ranger N.O. Reynolds, The Intrepid", revealed that Reynolds, instead of being an ex-Confederate from Missouri as he had said earlier and was documented in his records, was actually in the Union Army and fought against the Confederate guerillas. On his pension record after the turn of the century, he stated he was in the 147th Illinois Infantry Volunteers. His unit was assigned to Dalton, Georgia, which was where J. Frank Dalton said he was born. Was Reynolds a confederate *spy* embedded in the Union Army?

After the Civil War, in 1869, N.O. Reynolds moved to Roscoe, St. Clair County, Missouri, only 10 miles from where the Youngers lived. He stayed in Roscoe for 3 years and then traveled to Nicaragua in *Central America*. Was Reynolds a member of the KGC?

Another strange story found by the authors of this book was in the year 1886, there was a military encampment held in Lampasas. N.O. Reynolds was city marshal and sheriff of Lampasas County. In the heavily newspaper coverage of the event, it lists that Alexander Franklin "Frank" James was in attendance and was one of the speakers. This same year in 1886, Jesse was in Killeen, 30 miles away.

Reynolds had a heavy presence in Lampasas where Company C of Sparks covered earlier. An interesting note here, before Jesse came out about his identity, he, as Frank Dalton went to Lampasas, Burnett, and Marble Falls in 1943, his old stomping grounds as a Texas Ranger. He gave lectures at the schools and churches. In Lampasas, he talked two Saturdays on the courthouse square where the Horrell and Higgins had the shootout.

Both Spark's and Reynold's companies were camped at Hancock Springs to the south of Lampasas. Reynolds was not only the officer who arrested the Horrell brothers and calmed the feud in Lampasas, but was also involved that same year in 1877, in delivering John Wesley Hardin to trial in Comanche, 26 miles to the Northeast of Brownwood. Later, Reynolds had Johnny Ringo in custody, giving Ringo a bad taste of Texas and its lawmen. Ringo escaped and left Texas.

Reynolds was placed in charge of heading the company, Company A who would escort Major Jones around Texas to evaluate and inspect the camps and men under his care. Reynolds was allowed to choose men for the newly formed company from Company C and Company E. These two companies were valued by Major Jones and these were the initial companies Jesse was involved in.

After serving through January 1879, N.O. Reynolds would live out his life at Center Point, Texas in Kerr County. He was buried in Center Point, Texas in 1922. Forty Rangers are known to be buried there. Bud said Center Point is significant in the KGC as well as Centerville.

Major John B. Jones was an interesting character. He was a Confederate officer in the Civil War. He moved to Mexico after the war to establish an exile colony for former Confederate supporters, but after unsuccessful attempts, he came back to Texas. He accepted an offer in 1874 to become the commanding officer of the newly formed branch of the Texas Rangers, the Frontier Battalion. He was commissioned major of the command. This new battalion would enforce the law of Texas, stopping the Indian raids and quell the violent acts of badmen.

Jones lived in Corsicana, Texas in Navarro County. Interestingly, Jones with his brother-in-law, Robert Q. Mills organized a KGC castle in Navarro County before the Civil War broke out and prompted the state to secede from the Union. He was a *Mason* through and through and achieved the position of Grand Master of the Grand Lodge of Austin by 1879. He was engaged in several skirmishes with the Indians and the outlaws himself and respectively rode the trails of Texas looking after his men. It was said that he personally knew his men, not only the officers, but privates as well. He definitely knew who Benjamin Franklin Johnson was, as a member of the KGC and as a fellow Mason.

On the site listing the companies and officers of the Frontier Battalion (www.texasranger.org), Captain John C. Sparks was in command of Company C through November 1877 when G. W. Arrington took over command beginning November 1877 while he was still sergeant in Captain Neal Coldwell in Company A. Arrington was promoted to 1st lieutenant of Company C officially on Christmas Day, 1877. It was said that Arrington's bravery during missions against the "hostiles' was impressive. He was later assigned captain of Company C, in May 1879 stationed at *Coleman, Texas*. He served as captain of that company through 1882.

Noah Armstrong described that his company serving under Captain John C. Sparks and later with Lt. George Arrington, had an engagement with the Indians at Double Mountain Fork on the Brazos in Shackelford County. This was the spot that Albert Pike and Captain Randolph Marcy were interested in.

By 1880, John C. Sparks returned to Waco and was a grain dealer, living close to a cotton broker, railroad clerk, railroad engineer, editor, dental surgeon, and store clerk. Sounds as though he was near the railroad station, near several businesses in the town of Waco. His son, Charles Eugene Sparks became a railroad conductor for the Cotton Belt Railroad. He also had sons, Walter, a farmer, and his other son J.A. born in 1869.

An interesting note before we go any further, Ola stated that after Jesse had visited Buffalo Bill Cody in Chicago in 1893, he went to Frost, Texas which is in Navarro County to visit a close friend, John Sparks. She thought he was a Quantrill man, a marshal, or a Texas Ranger. Ola had no idea that Sparks was his ex-commander of the Texas Ranger's company he was in during the year of 1877. He never told her who Sparks was, just a good close friend. Captain Sparks' superior, Major John Jones lived in Navarro County, Texas also.

Frost, Texas was established in 1881 when the St. Louis Southwestern Railway was laid out on the way from Corsicana to Hillsboro. It is 20 miles from Corsicana. It hasn't grown much in population since it was founded, between 700-1,000 people. The small community where several of the Sparks lived was Dresden, approximately 10 miles from Frost, but only a population of 25 exist currently in that community. Dresden was a very early trading post and then developed into a small community that proudly built a Masonic Lodge in the center of town. [248]

What is strange is that John C. Sparks supposedly died April 9, 1883, an exact year from the time Jesse supposedly died on April 3, 1882. But yet, Jesse said he visited him in 1893. Sparks was supposedly shot by the Fuller boys, while Sparks was trying to arrest them for cattle rustling, but there is no indication he was a lawman during that time. [249] Did Jesse help him fake his death? We don't know. Were the dates wrong? Nothing else was said about Sparks but indeed Jesse was a good friend of his.

Ola stated that Jesse continued to be known as Benjamin Franklin Johnson in Company C, Border Battalion which coincides with everything in the official records. He remained stationed at Fort Concho. Arrington was still in charge of the company in 1878 and they went to Eagle Pass on several scouting expeditions on the border with a very small squad between 9-19 on each mission.

To show how accurate Jesse was in the information regarding his service in the Texas Rangers, giving hints here and there to Ola, you need go no further to verify it than the official records of the rangers, their stories, the old newspapers, and articles in which Jesse left clue after clue. We find this all to be true. What he was actually doing during those years, we don't know. Bud and I have a suspicion that he was working undercover for the KGC, fulfilling his duty assigned to him, the comptroller/paymaster.

1879

The same year that Major Jones became Grand Master of the Grand Lodge in Austin, Jesse stated that in 1879, he was a Texas Ranger, stationed in Abilene, Texas per Ola's manuscript, which was known at that time as Murphyville, Texas. I believe she meant Alpine, Texas. This town was known as Murphyville, not Abilene. He told Ola that he was going by the name of Frank Dalton. Unknown if he was still in Company C under Arrington, but by September 1879, Arrington established the first ranger camp in the panhandle, Camp Roberts, in Crosby County. At that time, he only had 28 men. The camp was on the **33-degree** latitude parallel.

In Murphyville, way down in south Texas, cattleman began entering the area and pitching their tents beginning in 1878. The name was changed to Alpine in 1888. It was less than 100 miles from Big Bend which sat on the border directly north of Chihuahua, Mexico. Not only cattle were drawing people there, but mining began springing up and the search for lost treasure. It was told that there were rich minerals in the ground. Many searched for gold and silver there, as well as the buried treasure in the mountains hidden by the previous inhabitants, the Spaniards.

Thirty miles from Murphyville, Camp Pena Colorado was established. It was near present-day Marathon, 30 miles from Alpine. It was first occupied in 1879 and was along a major stopping area along the Comanche Trail to Mexico. There was an excellent spring beneath a high bluff named Pena Coloroada, Spanish meaning "Red Rock." It was on the road connecting Fort Clark and Fort Davis. Company F and G of the United States Infantry were located there. It was founded the same month Victorio and his Warm Springs Apache escaped their imprisonment from the Mescalero reservation in New Mexico.

Colonel Benjamin Grierson who had severe issues with Captain John Sparks of Company C, Texas Rangers, was Commander of the District of the Pecos, headquartered in Fort Concho. His troops, the 10th Cavalry were assigned to Camp Pena Colorado in August 1879.

The 9th Cavalry who was stationed at Fort McKavett and the 10th Cavalry who were stationed at Fort Concho and now at Camp Pena Colorado were involved in the battle with Apache Victorio in 1879-1880 along with others, including the Texas Rangers. The battle was over a broken treaty by the Federal government with the Apaches in 1878 in the Hembrillo Basin near present-day Las Cruces, New Mexico.

The Camp Pena Colorado was just a temporary encampment or what they called a subpost to watch the principal water holes and trails. Grierson's soldiers patrolled the entire Big Bend region in which Howk said there were 92 gold mines near El Paso in the Big Bend. In 1881 to prevent Indian attacks, the fort remained to protect those who were building the railroad and protection for settlers and travelers in the Big Bend area. Is it a coincidence that the name of the camp coincides with the original Camp Colorado where the Texas Rangers occupied the buildings during the Civil War and thereafter in Coleman County?

Is it a coincidence that in 1855, in Coleman County, a little community named Trickham became a trading post for ranching activities of John Chisum? In 1862, Chisum raised cattle there to furnish beef for the Confederates fighting in the Civil War. Trickham was near Mukewater Creek that joined Home Creek which flowed into the Colorado River, a perfect area to establish headquarters for Company C Frontier Battalion. John Chisum also maintained ranch headquarters on Home Creek. Chisum had cattle in all parts of Texas, ranging from the Concho River, along the Colorado, and to the southern part of Cooke County which is in the area of present-day Gainesville, Texas.

There are so many clues and connections to all the characters of this book. Are they coincidences? Is it a coincidence that Coleman County and Brown County are the *"centerpoints"* of Texas? There is an historical marker between Brownwood, 26 miles south from Brownwood on Hwy 377 towards Brady that marks the geographical center of Texas. Ironically, it was close to where Trickham, Texas lays.

Jesse doesn't mention any other incidents or service with the Texas Rangers after 1879, until the year 1886. The name he took was not broadcast to the world like so many were. He quietly stayed in the background, maybe even in the underground for the KGC.

I do know one thing, I believe that the Texas Ranger's organization had the greatest influence on Jesse, along with the Quantrill Raiders, the KGC, and the War Between the States. We can see his pride in the way he stands tall in the saddle and upon the ground in the pictures we have of Jesse in the 30's and 40's before his broken hip. Many sources describe his posture, straight and erect.

The Rangers always had pride in their clothing, not only out in the field wearing high boots with their pant legs tucked in, wide brimmed hats, and cross-draw holsters under their coats to be able to draw their guns when riding a horse, but always after the hard work was done, many wore tailored vests and coats, and never forgot their tie. Does this all sound familiar? You bet it does. In his later years, Jesse never wanted to be seen without a tie. Ola saw to it that his ties were clean and ready for him.

The Frontier Battalion served a great purpose in civilizing the great State of Texas. With its strong leader's death in 1881, Major John Jones, the battalion eventually died out on its own. Many of its principal captains resigned that same year. Captain Arrington would resign the following year.

Even though these amazing men were hanging up their guns, their interest in the broad rangeland of Texas and its opportunities and resources kept their spirit alive. They were seeking their own fortunes. Many sought education in the field of prominent and professional careers. They became marshals or sheriffs, political leaders, doctors or lawyers, and many got into the cattle and ranching business, such as George W. Arrington in Canadian, Texas and James Buchanan Gillett in Alpine, Texas.

James Buchanan Gillett was one of the men who resigned in 1881. He was a famous Texas Ranger who had once served as a ranger beginning in 1875, in several companies, one being the infamous company under the leadership of N.O. Reynolds as an escort for Major Jones. Gillett's most memorable experience was in the pursuit of Sam Bass, the notorious outlaw.

Gillett was nine years younger than Jesse. His father, James Shackleford Gillett (1810-1874) came from Lincoln, Kentucky and his family moved to Boonslick Township, Howard County, Missouri close to the year of 1820. In 1827, his father Jonathan, brother Roswell, and sisters, Catherine and Sarah left Missouri for Texas with Henry Smith who was married to Elizabeth Gillett at the time. Jonathan applied for a land grant from Mexico, where the property was in present day Texas in March 1827. At that point in history, Mexico had claim to Texas.

The family headed back to Missouri but was never able to return to Texas. Jonathan and wife, Hannah died shortly after they reached Missouri in 1827. After this, possibly in 1828, James S. Gillett, age 17-18 had a wild hair and traveled to Santa Fe. This had to be close to the time in 1828 when Charles Bent and his brother, William from their headquarters in St. Louis took a wagon train of goods down the Santa Fe Trail just right after the Santa Fe trail was surveyed and outlined by Joseph Brown in 1825-27. The Bents established mercantile contacts and began a series of trading trips back and forth from St. Louis to Santa Fe. This is when Albert Pike jumped on the wagon. It is also the year when Kit Carson came to Taos. Charles Bent became the first Mason to settle in New Mexico.

On the trip to Santa Fe, James Shackelford Gillett was one of four youths who were captured by the Osage Indians along the trail. After two weeks, they were released unharmed. The Osage

Nation controlled the area between the Missouri River to the North and to the foothills of the Wichita Mountains and the Red River to the south. When the Santa Fe trail opened in 1828, the Osage Nation had to agree with the U.S. government to allow safe passage for travelers and traders. Gillett finally reached Santa Fe, where he lived for several years.

Henry Smith and his wife Elizabeth Gillett, sister of James went on to Texas. She died of cholera in Brazoria around the year of **1833**. Smith became a major surveyor in Texas. In 1836, Smith became the 1st governor of the provisional government of Texas. He then married his wife's twin sister, Sarah in 1839. Henry eventually was overcome by gold fever and left for the California Gold Rush but was one of them that never returned.

James Shackelford Gillett was in Captain John Coffee Hays' Second Regiment of the Texas Rangers during the war with Mexico and later appointed adjutant general under Governor Peter Bell. The family was living in Austin, and after he traded property in Grimes County for a herd of cattle from Brownwood, where Chisum had his holdings, Gillett became a cattleman in 1871. By 1872, he and his family were living in Lampasas.

In 1873, his young son, James Buchanan Gillett at the age of 17, set off on his own to Coleman County to join the Rangers, despite the wishes of his father. He was just following in his father's footsteps in becoming a Texas Ranger, with a future career as a cattleman. It appears that his father didn't want his son to go that route.

The wild frontier was enticing young Gillett, even though there was danger in the open plains. Indians were still heavily populated in all regions of Texas. On his way to Coleman County, he was sidetracked by Monroe Cooksey and Jack Clayton who were making their way through Lampasas and on to Coleman County to buy cattle. Gillett followed behind them for a chance to join them and learn about cattle and becoming a frontiersman. His Texas Ranger idea was put on the backburner. He wanted to be a cowboy first.

Gillett got a ride with Bob McCollum who was a freighter on the road just a short distance from the cattleman. McCollum was taking a load of flour to Camp Colorado, the ranger camp in Coleman County. The cattleman headed to Jim Ned Creek which flowed southeast into Coleman County. They made camp at Hord's Creek near the present-day town of Coleman.

After a "meet and greet" session with the drovers, young Gillett was put to a test after asking for a job. A known practice of cowboys was to shake down the greenhorns. The drovers challenged young Gillett to the wild horse test, placing him on the wildest horse they had. Gillett proved to have the "stuff" for a cowpoke and was hired by the cattlemen. Gillett remained with the drovers who camped at Home Creek where Captain Maltby's Company E established their camp, including Jesse and Arrington the following year.

Gillett's first job with the outfit was to gather and deliver a herd of cattle to the Horrell boys near Lampasas in 1873, the same year when the Horrells caused so much trouble in Lampasas. The cattle were delivered, but strangely, after Gillett and the drovers delivered the cattle to the Horrells, the cattlemen's outfit fizzled out.

We do learn that when the Horrell brothers left Lampasas, they sold their cattle to Cooksey and Clayton per "The Horrell Wars: Feuding in Texas and New Mexico" by David Johnson. They headed to New Mexico. They had a lot of money in their pocket.

Gillett continued working in the cattle business after Cooksey and Clayton sold out to Joe Franks. Mr. Franks may have been related to Bill Franks who ran the John Chisum store which was just a mile from the old Camp Colorado site in Coleman County, by Mukewater Creek. In the summer of 1873, Joe Franks and young Gillett were delivering cattle to the famous John Chisum whose outfit was camped along the Concho River where present-day Paint Rock is located, between Brownwood and San Angelo. There were four camps established with 75-100 men with 500 horses. The other men furnishing cattle for Chisum were John Hitsons and Sam Gholston, who knew Gillett's father and relayed a message to Gillett, stating that he saw his father in Lampasas and was asked to tell young Gillett to come home and go to school. His father was very concerned as well as Gholston.

They had to keep a close eye out for Indian raids who would try to steal the horses. In Gholston's camp, the Indians got away with 60 head of horses during a major shootout between the two. The cattlemen continued to gather and round up cattle and horses and were considered to be the first Coleman outfit to round up strays found in the San Saba and Llano country.

After working for these cattlemen, driving horses and cattle, Gillett went to Menard County and joined the Texas Rangers under Captain Dan W. Roberts in the summer of 1875. Gillett covered counties of Kimble, Mason, Menard, Kerr, San Saba, Llano, Lampasas, Burnet, and El Paso during the time Jesse was a ranger. Remember, San Saba was a hotspot for silver.

The ending of the Horrell Higgins Feud in 1877 scattered peace throughout Texas and New Mexico. Gillett would state in his book, "Six Years with the Texas Rangers, 1875-1881," that "from the spring of 1877 onward the rangers were transformed into what might properly be called mounted state police, and accordingly turned their attention to ridding the frontier of the outlaws that infested nearly every part of Texas." [250]

In 1877, Jesse was at Fort Concho, Captain John Sparks lost his job to Sargeant George Washington Arrington, Allen and Susan (James) Parmer moved to Clay County, Texas, Crazy Horse was killed, James Buchanan Gillett was chosen to be in the newly formed company of rangers who would escort Major Jones after a two year period of service for the rangers, and Billy the Kid kills his first man who was bullying and attacking him, Frank "Windy" Cahill. Billy fled the crime scene in Arizona and headed to Mesilla, New Mexico.

Billy would be drawn into strong relationships with good guys and bad at the young age of 18, but at this point in his life, it was hard to tell who the good guys were. He got a taste of both.

One of his best friends growing up, small in stature, was a fellow in Silver City, Jesse Evans, one of the top cattle/horse rustlers in New Mexico, South Texas, and Mexico. Billy learned the rustling trade from him. He also worked for the richest cattleman in the entire country, John Chisum at his South Spring River Ranch, south of Roswell, New Mexico. The ranch was later called Jingle Bob Ranch, the largest ranch in the United States.

Gillett in his book, "Six Years with the Texas Rangers" calls John Chisum, "old John" Chisum. Brushy Bill also refers to Chisum as "Old John." [251] Coincidence? Nah.

In 1891, Gillett started a new ranching career south of Alpine until 1904. It was near the border in the Big Bend area. He had seen that country, knew it well, had the experience as a drover, and had seen the great wealth cattle brought to John Chisum. In 1904, James Gillett moved to Roswell, New Mexico where John Chisum had created his dynasty.

1886

Jesse told Ola that in 1886, he was a Texas Ranger and was sent to Bell County in Killeen to "help out a situation there". At that time, the rangers were not considered to be in the Frontier Battalion, but more like Mounted State Police. I haven't found yet who covered Bell County during this time, nor have I found anything on the sheriff there, but Killeen was not far from Lampasas and 100 miles from Brownwood. It is in the same general area of where he was assigned before as a Texas Ranger.

Jesse rode on a train with Sheriff White of Bell County to Killeen, informing him of the situation. Reaching Killeen, while stepping off the train, the sheriff was shot in between the eyes. Jesse waited for the right moment, shot and killed the man who did the dirty deed. Jesse stayed there for three months in 1886 and went by the name of Benjamin Franklin Johnson and finally the townspeople felt safe to walk the streets again. After this incident, he headed to Brownwood.

We find one more year of service in the Texas Rangers for Jesse and that will be discussed in a later chapter.

"Coming together is a beginning; keeping together is progress; working together is success."

-Henry Ford

Chapter Fourteen: The significance of Brownwood, Tx. and Roswell, N.M.

Previously, we have discussed many things tied to Brownwood in Brown County and Coleman County, Texas. This is where Captain Maltby enlisted many men to form Company E in the Texas Rangers Frontier Battalion in 1874, it was a place where drovers took their cattle to buy and sell in the cattle industry, it was close to where John Chisum had a trading post and a ranch that held the cattle for widespread cattle drives, near the center point of Texas, and we later find that Jesse wrote a letter to the Editor of the Clipper-Herald. The letter was postmarked in Brownwood, Texas. From the Pen of Jesse James. "Brownwood, The Hardest Town in Texas," November 7, 1879.

"I am playing a square game and have settled down on a ranch about ten miles from this town of Brownwood and am no longer known as Jesse James. I am not ashamed of my name but want peace and quiet for my wife's sake. She has saved me from killing myself, and if I am let alone, I will be a good citizen and grow up in a new life with this great State of Texas.

"Tell your reporter to set 'em up to the boys around and send, the bill to me. I enclose a photo which was taken some years ago. It is not a really good picture but will pass muster. Believe me, yours in truth, Jesse James." [252]

Early in 1879, Jesse was in Murphyville now known as Alpine, Texas with the Texas Rangers. In May 1879, G. W. Arrington was officially Captain of Company C of the Frontier Battalion who had lived in Brownwood. In 1879, Major John Jones became Grand Master of the Grand Lodge of Austin, Jesse's baby girl, Mary Susan James was born on June 17, and Jesse met Billy the Kid in late July in Las Vegas, New Mexico.

By September 1879, Arrington had moved on up to the panhandle and within that month, Victorio's War began in New Mexico. In October 8, 1879, the Chicago, Alton & St. Louis train at Glendale, Missouri was robbed supposedly by the James Gang in which Jesse admitted to. In November 1879, George Shepherd, a former James gang member, orchestrated a hoax, saying he shot Jesse James in the head at Short Creek, Missouri on November 2nd in retaliation for the murder of his nephew, Ike Flannery which prompted a firm rebuttal from Jesse himself in that letter to the editor from Brownwood, 5 days later. Jesse was "back at the ranch" near Brownwood. He wasn't dead.

The ranch was 10 miles from Brownwood from the courthouse square in 1879. Was this his own ranch? No, many believe it was the ranch of his superior officer in Quantrill's Raiders, Bloody Bill Anderson. One historian out of Brownwood, Colonel George Day, a lawyer and DA, stated that he had found that Frank and Jesse lived with Anderson on his ranch close to the time of the letter in 1879. Day was in agreement that Jesse, Frank, and Bloody Bill Anderson lived in Brownwood as well as other KGC members. Day would later be bamboozled with criminal charges and legal matters regarding his practice in which he claimed his innocence.

What was it about Brownwood, the county it set in, Brown County, and Coleman County? Why did Jesse travel there quite frequently and all his war buddies assemble there? Those mentioned as being there who lived or visited there were Bloody Bill Anderson, Quantrill, Colonel James Russell Davis, John Trammell, Billy the Kid, Clay Allison, John Wilkes Booth, Frank James, Zerelda James, Cole Younger, and possibly even his younger brother, John Younger. Some of these men were supposed to have been killed.

(Brushy Bill Roberts aka. Billy the Kid. Ola said this picture was taken in 1904-1905 when he was 45. Taken in Brownwood, Texas. (Ola's collection))

John Wilkes Booth, for instance, spent a year in Brownwood in 1871. Very strong evidence support that Booth wasn't killed after the assassination of President Abraham Lincoln, but lived in Granbury, Texas and later in Enid, Oklahoma. Booth was supposed to have been killed in 1865 shortly after the murder of Lincoln in a barn. In the Fort Worth Star Telegram, March 6, 1984 an article stated that "Booth was discovered by federal troops in a burning barn in Bowling Green, Viriginia, 12 days after the Lincoln assassination. He was shot by an overzealous soldier and secretly buried under a warehouse floor at the old penitentiary building near Geeseborough Point on the Potomac River. Identification of the dead man was never conclusive. A reporter who viewed the body said the right leg was broken. But Booth broke his left leg in leaping onto the stage from the presidential box at Ford Theater. The legend of Booth ending up in Glen Rose and Granbury has never been proved or disproved." [253]

Bud traveled to Granbury and spoke with several of Booth's relatives. John Wilkes Booth had escaped and lived on.

Bloody Bill Anderson was supposedly killed in 1864, Quantrill in 1865, and Jesse in 1882, but yet they were all in Brownwood, Texas. What's so special about Brownwood?

As the reader can already tell, the area or territory described above was a safe haven, the hub or the zenith of the KGC. It became more connected and stronger after the Civil War.

The Brownwood Saga seems to begin in **1869** when Frank and Jesse were in Chicago joining other secret societies. They met up with Major John Edwards after this, co-founder of the Kansas City Times who was also involved in secret societies in Missouri. After the war, the KGC was outlawed, so the members of the KGC operated under various legitimate fraternal organizations including Masonic Knights Templar, Knights of Pythias, I.O.O.F. (Odd Fellows), and Woodsmen of the World.

In **1869**, future Texas Ranger N.O. Reynolds moved to Roscoe, St. Clair County, Missouri, only 10 miles from where the Youngers lived. In **1869**, J. J. McAlester began freighting from Fort Smith to several different locations in Indian Territory with an ox team. In the summer of **1869**, Frank and Jesse were robbing a bank in South Dakota and hid out in Devil's Nest.

What were these men doing? They were spreading out and the news spread as well that the rebels were on the move. News reports suggest Quantrill and Bloody Bill Anderson were not killed.

In a newspaper article, S. N. Wood writes from Fort Richardson Texas on the 29th of September **1869,** that Quantrill is yet alive. "He was badly wounded and ended up in the hospital at Louisville. A relative took him to her house to recover. A false report of his death spread like wildfire, his funeral was held with an empty casket and Quantrill went South through Texas into Mexico. He went into Brazil and Cuba." [254]

Fort Richardson is outside of Jacksboro, Texas, **133** miles from Brownwood. It had direct communication with its neighboring fort of Fort Belknap, 38 miles to the west, 115 miles from Brownwood, in which the two forts helped secure those along the Butterfield Overland Mail Trail coming from Fort Smith, Arkansas. It would be the information highway.

What was occurring in **1869** in Brownwood?

Jay Longley, treasure hunter, historian, and researcher who lives in Brownwood states that the Knights of the Golden Circle sent 12 families to settle there in **1869**. Bloody Bill Anderson was one, maybe one of the first arriving in the spring of 1865, going by the name of William Columbus Anderson, and a man with an alias of Henry Ford, who many believe was Jesse Woodson James came into the area of San Saba, Brown County from New Mexico in **1869**. Longley stated that Ford was a leader in the secret order of the Knights Templar and Knights of the Golden Circle. He was a trusted friend and confidant of Brown County's William C. "Bloody Bill" Anderson.

The KGC's plan was to rebuild the Southern Economy in full throttle. The KGC supported these men by placing them in high positions of government, law enforcement, banks, stores, hotels, livery stables, and some were placed underground in the bootlegging and counterfeiting rings. There were rustlers and outlaws spread far and wide, mostly coming in from New Mexico. The plan was to make money, big money. Half of it would go to the KGC and would be converted to silver and gold that would be transferred to KGC vaults underground. One being in Austin, Texas. The money would be used to fund a second Civil War and basically start their own country/empire. Cattle, railroads, mines, and the illegal rings were some of the biggest money-making schemes in their plan and you can bet, Jesse was smack-dab in the middle of it. He was the paymaster or comptroller of the KGC.

After the Civil War, the Federals were wanting to round up the members of the KGC. Knowing that deep in the heart of Texas where Indian raids were still prevalent, the KGC felt secure that the Feds were least likely to come into this wild country. The KGC built strongholds within Brownwood and a tunnel network underneath the downtown area with their own brilliant engineers and surveyors. It was a way of continuing their clandestine activities, set up treasure depositories, and provide an escape route if the Feds ever invaded.

Thanks to the precise and detailed information from Jay Longley regarding Brownwood and the KGC. He has lived there most of his life and has given us insight on what was going on in that neck of the woods. Jay's information matches perfectly with J. Frank Dalton's story told to Ola in the late 1940's and the articles Dalton wrote. Jay says that he has no doubt that J. Frank Dalton was absolutely Jesse Woodson James. Jay has given us permission to use his material which easily blends in with Bud's information and the research he has done. Take it for what its worth. It's worth its weight in GOLD!

Oh, there's plenty of naysayers and those who have tried to discredit Longley, but Bud has checked everything out that Jay has stood upon and has found nothing to be false information on Jay's part. Bud said, "It all fits." Each man had a puzzle piece to add and the truth is becoming stronger and more supported by their efforts. They have a great mutual respect for one another.

Jay Longley is very careful about stepping out with information unless he is 100 percent sure it is the truth. He discovered on very raw photos of Jesse, that have not used touch-ups to disguise blemishes, that Jesse had a scar running from the top of his left cheek, near his ear and sideburn, curving slightly toward the corner of his mouth. It is clear in the photo taken when he was 29-30 years old and it definitely is clear as an old man of 90.

(Young Jesse showing scar)

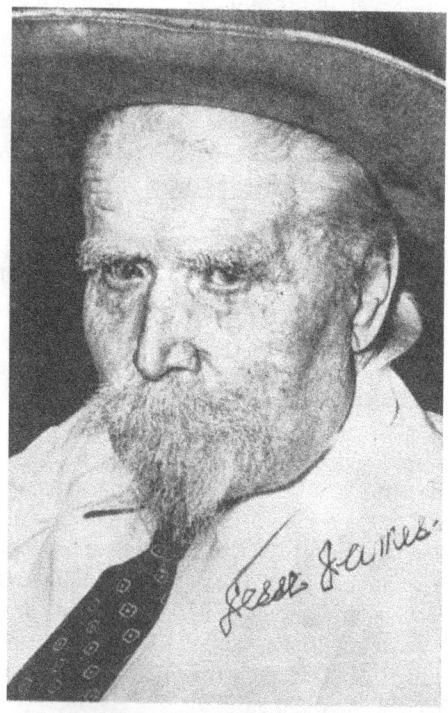

(Old Jesse with same scar)

(Jesse)

There is no doubt J. Frank Dalton was Jesse.

We will explore everything that Jesse told Ola, what Bud has unearthed, and what Jay has discovered in his research regarding Brownwood and its connection to the KGC. This is an amazing multifaceted story.

To set the scene, between 1869-1873 before the Texas Rangers took charge, Brownwood was in its rawest form, just as their citizens who were wild and untamed. It indeed was a hotspot for many *outlaws*, sympathizers of the *Confederacy*, and the *Masonic and KGC brotherhood*.

The population of Texas at that time was close to 800,000, but *Brown* County was just getting settled. In the 1870's, there was a population of 544 people in *Brown* County alone. Everyone knew each other well and knew their business.

I am very fortunate to have a letter that described Brown County and its people in 1872. It was a letter to Professor Washington Swisher Rector (author's 1st cousin 4 x removed) from J. B. Clack, a friend who wanted Rector to move to Brown County to start a college. Rector moved that year to

Johnson County, Texas instead and taught in Caddo Grove, while John James (distant cousin of Jesse James) taught in Alvarado the same year which was a short days-ride between the two.

The letter from Clack invites Rector to a buffalo hunt. He describes the people of the west in Brown County as the following: "The young ladies all look like mustangs – will weigh from 175 to 200 lbs. Never wear shoes and their feet look as though they had guts in them – while their legs have stripes on them which I imagine have been made by the "Piss Ants" traveling to water. They let their hair hang down and their heads resemble brush heaps made of blackjack of a dark night. You can scarcely find a man but what swears and drinks whiskey. Men shoot one another every few days for their meanness." J. B. Clack-October 1, 1872. Sounds real enticing.

Cattle Business - Between the years of 1869-1876

By 1873-74, the cattle business was thriving in and around Brownwood with the help of John Chisum who had partnered with Charles Goodnight and Oliver Loving in 1866/67. We discussed a lot about Chisum, but a strange story about him popped up in Howk's book, "Jesse James and the Lost Cause." John Chisum had his hands on cattle all over Texas, the cattle baron. "He was around East Texas and pulled a stagecoach robbery but did not turn the gold over to us or bury it, for us to weigh it later for our underground army. He took the gold and money on to Dallas or Fort Worth, and he made a deal to buy up a lot of cheap cattle at three dollars per head and started West with them." [255] If this was true, he was a part of the KGC and I'm sure they held him accountable for this in repayment.

Clay Allison

In Jesse's statement to Ola regarding meeting up with Clay Allison in Brownwood, I began to look into Allison to find the connection to Jesse in Texas and New Mexico. I was really surprised that it could have been cattle.

There were a lot of similarities between Clay Allison, Jesse, and Billy the Kid. They all had their hand in cattle. They all believed in justice.

Clay Allison, just like Jesse, had a father who was a minister. He served in the Presbyterian Church in Waynesboro, Tennessee. As soon as Clay was old enough, he joined the Confederacy, enlisting in 1861 under Captain W. H. Jackson's artillery. He had an old head injury which kept him from fulfilling his duties, therefore he was discharged. He still wanted in the fight, so in 1862, he enlisted in the 9th Tennessee Cavalry Regiment under General Nathan Bedford Forrest as a scout and spy.

After the war, Allison became a member of the KKK in Tennessee. He then headed for Texas. He may have been connected to Jesse through the KKK and the KGC in which both organizations were being led by Nathan Bedford Forrest, Allison's ex-commander. Several writings and speeches that J. Frank Dalton gave regarding the KKK includes these words, "Because of conditions in Texas in 1865, Mr. Dalton was one of the first members of the Ku Klux Klan. His experiences from then to the present flow against a background of Texas history and the old West." [256]

Clay Allison settled in the Brazos Valley of Texas in Palo Pinto County, 75 miles northeast of Brown County. General Randolph Marcy, who we have talked a lot before, established the Brazos Indian Reservation in 1854 in that county. Lawrence Sullivan (Sul) Ross signed on to become a leader of a band of American Indian auxiliaries from the Brazos Indian Reservation with the U.S. Army, stationed in Young County. Ross would become a mason and would eventually lead Ross's Brigade during the Civil War.

The Brazos Indian Reservation was to provide separate villages for the Comanche, Delaware, Shawnee, Tonkawa, Wichita, Choctaw, and Caddo to live peacefully along the Brazos River. The government contracted with the local cattlemen to provide beef for the reservation. It was a good idea, but it also created more Indian depredations between them and the settlers.

Cattlemen Goodnight, Loving, Marcus L. Dalton (who was a distant cousin of the Daltons), and Reuben *Vaughan* were some of the original settlers in Palo Pinto county. Marcus Lafayette Dalton or M.L. Dalton as he was called had a ranch in Sand Valley near the Brazos River in Palo Pinto County. He also had a ranch established in 1846, 7 miles West of Graford and 20 miles West of Mineral Wells. Interestingly, the small community, named "*Pickwick*" was not far from that site to the west. It now is completely submerged by Possum Kingdom Lake.

These cattlemen began seeing a great profit in the cattle business and provided the beef for the reservation and beyond.

For what's its worth, Jesse had a ranch northwest of Mineral Wells which would place it close to where Marcus Dalton's ranch was in the county of Palo Pinto in 1922, maybe even earlier, but it appeared to be an important asset to him.

Robert Clay Allison got to know these men in Palo Pinto County and got a job as a drover with Goodnight and Loving. In 1866, he was one of the 18 men who drove a herd, forging the new Goodnight/Loving trail. They traveled northwest along the Brazos River, picking up cattle along the way. They officially began the trail at Fort Belknap, 35-50 miles away. They then traveled to Fort Sumner, New Mexico and on up to Colorado. Later, Goodnight returned to Parker County, which was near Weatherford, Texas.

Goodnight traveled back to New Mexico in 1866-67, partnering with Loving and John Chisum near Roswell, New Mexico. Goodnight and Loving stayed on Chisum's Ranch, supplying cattle from the ranch to Fort Sumner and Santa Fe. Meanwhile, Clay Allison was back in Texas lining up work with M. L. Dalton. The goal for Dalton was a big one; take 800 head of Longhorns to New Mexico. It was a big undertaking. In one source, Dalton made Allison trail boss since he was already familiar with the Goodnight/Loving Trail.

In 1867-68, they drove the herd on the Goodnight/Loving Trail to New Mexico. Lucien Maxwell was one of the recipients of the Longhorns. He had contracts at Fort Sumner, Fort Union, Las Vegas, Albuquerque, and other military posts.

They returned to the Brazos Valley and Marcus Dalton had more cattle drives up into Kansas. Marcus Dalton sadly was murdered in an Indian ambush ¾ of a mile east and north of the present town of Salesville just north of Mineral Wells, Texas in November 1870.

Clay Allison developed a liking for the New Mexico lush grasslands, fresh water, and abundant wildlife. Several of the Brazos Valley cowboys and cattleman began moving with their cattle to Colfax County, New Mexico. The first one documented as moving there from the Brazos Valley of Texas was Thomas H. Dawson in 1867.

Allison continued on drives with his brother-in-law, Lewis Coleman and Irwin W. Lacy from Texas to New Mexico. Some have stated that Clay worked awhile in Lincoln County. With payment of cattle on a drive, 300 head, he obtained his own ranch near Cimarron, New Mexico and 9 miles north of Springer in Colfax County at the confluence of the Vermejo and Canadian Rivers. This was about 1869/70 when men were being moved around like cattle.

This also has an interesting related story. In Howk's book, "Jesse James and the Lost Cause," he speaks of Clay Allison working for Jesse in Cimarron, New Mexico. Allison was also wrangling horses for "them" at La Junta, Colorado, which was where Bent's Fort was located. Not sure who "them" were, but it is suspected as being the KGC. This was the time that men were being placed strategically. Jesse said they had to let him go because of his big mouth. He didn't fit in their "business affairs". "Too dangerous. Brother Frank and I simply had to let Clay go. When he was sober, he was tops; when he was drinking, he was terror." "Many wild tales spread about Clay, some were true, and some were fiction, same as with ourselves." [257]

So, the question arises. Was this really Clay Allison's Ranch or a ranch that Jesse claimed as his? Would it be a KGC Ranch? We don't know.

Clay was known to be a seeker of justice. He had the passion and drive to right the wrongs. In 1871, he was one of the leaders who had witnessed a woman so horrified and broken, stagger into a saloon in Elizabethtown, an old mining town north of Eagle Nest, New Mexico, to describe her husband as being a mass murderer. She had a gruesome story to tell as she tried her best to spit out the words of the horror she had lived through.

She had walked 15 miles east from her cabin in the high crusted snowbanks in that cold January night along the Moreno Valley. Her cabin was at the base of Palo Flechado Pass near Nine Mile Creek. This also may be a point of treasure that Jesse told Howk about, "Nine Mile Treasure." [258] The pass going West from their cabin was the beginning of a long trek over the mountain, at that time could only be traveled by foot or a horse/mule. It would take you to Taos. The other way to Taos was through Black Lake, over Osha Pass and into Apache Canyon. That route was used by those with wagons pulled by oxen, such as the trek Albert Pike took in 1831.

The woman's husband, Charles Kennedy lured travelers to his dugout/cabin, offered them drink and then murdered them viciously. Then he took the body and hacked away the body parts into pieces and burned all evidence of them except the bones which he kept behind the cabin. He took their belongings, money, and other goods and buried them around his property.

He had killed her son that day. The little boy had seen a traveler come by while his father was down the way a bit. The traveler drank from the creek and asked what that horrible smell was. The little boy said it was an Indian that his Papa hadn't cut up yet to burn. His Papa heard the boy tell the traveler that story and the traveler was dead in seconds. Charles grabbed the boy by the heels and bashed his head against the rock chimney. The two got the same treatment as the others. The woman watched from a dark corner in the cabin as she waited patiently and quietly for her husband to get drunk, giving her the opportunity to slip away for help.

Clay Allison was the first to help the woman and he became enraged over the story. He, along with other men went after Kennedy. They took him back to Elizabethtown for trial, but Clay Allison wasn't going to wait. Allison broke Kennedy out of jail and hung him in the cold January night. Allison then took a sharp knife and severed his head from his body. Allison road 29 miles back to Cimarron with the head in a gunny sack. He placed it on display upon a pole in front of the St. James Hotel.

Clay also took revenge on a man Cruz Vega, suspected of murdering Reverend F. J. Tolby, a Methodist circuit rider who was trying to help the settlers in the area against the monopoly of the Ring controlling the Maxwell Land Grant as of 1870. "Lucien Maxwell sold the grant in 1870 for $650,000 to the Santa Fe Ring. They turned it around and sold it to English investors for $1,350,000, who then found Dutch investors to issue $5,000,000 in stock in the Maxwell Land Grant and Railroad Company." [259]

The killing of the reverend in Cimarron Canyon in September 1875 escalated the Colfax County War, from 1873-1888. The suspects behind Vega appeared to be associated with the new leadership of the company, the new Maxwell Land Grant holders. They became violent against all the local original settlers and squatters, destroying their property and running them off. Clay stepped in once again and viciously hung the man accused of killing Rev. Tolby, Cruz Vega from a telegraph pole and dragged his body over the rough terrain.

Vega's uncle, Francisco Griego, out for revenge, tracked down Clay Allison in November of 1875 at the St. James Hotel and was out for the kill. Clay outdrew him and shot him twice in the chest. Clay got off for self-defense.

The Buffalo Soldiers of the 9th U.S. Cavalry were sent and got into a shootout with some Texas cowboys in the St. James Hotel. Three Buffalo soldiers were killed and Clay Allison himself shot and killed a sergeant in the bar.

A man by the name of Cardenas confessed to the murder of Rev. Tolby in which he was quickly given the noose. Sadly, this beautiful country was scared with the deaths of approximately 200 people during this period of time.

George Coe, a friend of Billy the Kid once said of Allison as a rancher and gunmen, "When Allison butted in, business started to pick up." [260]

George and Frank Coe, who were cousins and later would become good friends with Billy the Kid, once had a ranch near Fort Stanton in Lincoln County and later lived near Allison's ranch in Colfax County, outside of Raton, New Mexico.

Allison helped defend many ranchers and cattlemen in Colfax county as well as the townspeople in that area of Springer, Cimarron, and Raton. He didn't take nothing from nobody. He was a straight shooter. Allison even became a "special attorney" during a land dispute in Colfax County over land that the Coes had settled, in the Sugarite Valley whom another man stated that the Maxwell Land Grant company had allowed him to lease. The land disputes were stirred up and made to divide the people of the communities by the famous Santa Fe Ring having their hands in the Maxwell Land Grant Company.

The most respected lawyer, Frank Springer who arrived in Colfax County in 1873, became the lawyer for the Maxwell Land Grant Company. Springer, as well as other men, saw the writing on the wall and joined Clay Allison in taking up the battle against the Santa Fe Ring. There was a plot to assassinate Allison, Springer, and William Raymond Morley, an executive for the Maxwell Company, by Governor Samuel Axtell of New Mexico who was deeply embedded in the Ring. Springer took the issues all the way to Washington, on up to President Hayes.

Governor Axtell began his term as governor in 1875 and caused major havoc in Colfax County, as well as Lincoln County. President Rutherford B. Hayes replaced Axtell with the distinguished General Lew Wallace in 1878.

"As for the Ring: It is seldom that history states more corruption, fraud, mismanagement, plots, and murders than New Mexico has been the theater of under the administration of Governor Axtell." [261]

The Coes went back to Lincoln County, getting pulled into the Lincoln County War with Billy. The Coes would become one of the Lincoln County Regulators, riding with Billy.

Frank Springer wrote an affidavit of the character of Clay Allison, "a man of southern birth and education, of sensitive feelings and strong passions, quick to resent any indignities, and a man of well-known personal courage and determination."

Clay Allison left New Mexico in 1876 and went to Texas. He was an avenger there also, helping a family who was being raided by Comanches in the Texas Panhandle in Wheeler County in 1878. In 1881, he moved to an area 12 miles northeast of Mobeetie, Texas and established a ranch there. By 1887, he had obtained a ranch north of Pecos, Texas. He died that year by a freak wagon accident. He fell off of his wagon and the wheel of his heavy freight wagon ran over his neck, crushing his vertebrae into bits and pieces.

Many people look at Clay Allison as a vicious gunfighter and often mentally unstable, but he served justice his way.

Henry Ford

Who was Henry Ford in Brownwood? Per Jay Longley, noted historian, "many of the old timers (in Brownwood) thought he (Ford) was Jesse Woodson James because Jesse and Frank James' mother, Zerelda Samuels was seen at Ford's funeral in Brownwood in 1910 and Frank James spoke to the crowd at the funeral warning them that if they "put a marker on Henry Ford's grave, I will return and blow it to Kingdom Come."

In the book, "Jesse James and the Lost Cause" Jesse told Howk per say, "Why, do you know, some experts had me die at Brownwood, Texas, along about 1913, some such year. *I wasn't there either*. But my kin and my loyal friends let it ride, and never let on any differently. Just because the dead man going by the name of Ford happened to have a certain tattoo on his right forearm like many of us had, they once again presumed Jesse Woodson James died, and at Brownwood, Texas."

"That tattoo was on the right forearm of each and every member of the Inner and Outer Circle as well as upon the arm of each and every official of the International Anti-Horse Thief Association, of the old bunch. The tattoo was a thin ribbon affair with the letters "Tex-Y-S, in light blue ink, and tinged with red coloring; just a small insignificant narrow tattoo on the right, inside forearm." [262]

In the book, "Jesse James Was One Of His Names", by Dell Schrader, he wrote that Jesse had told Howk that he was one of the early backers of the real Henry Ford with his automobile industry and that Jesse borrowed his name, while in Brownwood, posing as a banker. Bud is not sure if this is true, but he said, "It's a possibility."

Henry Ford in Brownwood was definitely somebody.

Why was Jesse saying, "I wasn't there either?" I believe he was referring to an empty grave. In 1910, Henry Ford supposedly died. It was a closed casket. Zerelda and Frank James were there, and the exclamation made by Frank James was unusual. The family decades later placed a tombstone on his grave. Expert dowsers have gone over the grave site and have discovered there is no body or bones in that grave.

In a news article, "B'wood pioneer may have had outlaw's background. Was Henry Ford really Jesse James?" by Lex Johnston written in the Brownwood Bulletin, April 24, 1977, gives us clues about Henry Ford. Lex was a great grandson of Henry Ford. After his cousin, Henry Ford II got serious in learning the true story about their great grandfather, Lex who had been skeptical about the possibility that their great grandfather was Jesse, finally started coming around and looking into it himself. His article was very good. Lex Johnston was noted "as an avocation, Johnston is a columnist for the Brownwood Bulletin in his native home of Brownwood. Material for the column, "Old Brown Trivia," comes from Johnston's extensive studies and research on Texas history of which he is considered an expert." [263] Johnston helped organized the Prestonwood National Bank in North Dallas and the article presented him as being named president of the bank.

In the article about his great grandfather, Johnston explains that Henry Ford first was known as a stranger who showed up in San Saba and was hired by the Forsythe brothers as a cowboy on their isolated ranch in the southwest part of Brownwood. During this time, the article states that the "James brothers were hiding in southwest Texas and the Youngers were in Scyene, Texas." Scyene was where Belle Starr lived.

R.D. Forsythe stated that he had met Henry Ford earlier in 1869 in New Mexico and some believe he was briefly in Nebraska, Kansas, and Missouri. Sounds like Jesse, but in those days, especially after the war, men did not like to discuss their past. They had a code. "An unwritten code of the frontier was that no man should ask another about his background. Unless an individual volunteered such information, his past would never be discussed and, as in Ford's case, perhaps would never be revealed." [264]

Henry Ford worked as a cowboy for two years, 1869-1871. He was part of the drovers who pushed cattle to New Mexico. He could have also been on the Goodnight/Loving trail with Clay Allison. At times, he was placed in situations where he had to use his six-shooter. He was very familiar with the gun. When a poker game became violent, Ford whipped his pistol out from across the room and shot the perpetrator three times to save his friend Forsythe.

In 1871, Ford went to work with W. L. (Uncle Billy) Williams who had a very large cattle operation in Brown County. Between the years 1872-1876, Ford became a stockman. Later, his qualities and talents were unhidden. He was well educated, spoke several languages, including Greek, French, and Spanish and very prolific in math. His writing skills were excellent, and he produced literature in various subjects, especially for the business world.

In 1876, Ford sought after the county clerk position in Brown County. He won the election and moved to Brownwood. He was instrumental in bringing the Santa Fe Railroad to Brownwood and quality education, bringing schools to the prairie. He built a school, the Henry Ford School for all ages.

Ford joined a firm with the Coggin brothers, other highly successful cattlemen. They established a private bank. Sam and Moses "Mody" Coggin came to Brown County in 1857 and acquired large landholdings in both Brown and Coleman County. An excellent article in tshaonline.org relays the story. "They moved cattle to Home Creek in Coleman County in 1860. In April 1862 Sam and Mody Coggin joined the Confederate Army." "During the 1870's they engaged in money-making cattle arrangements with two of the state's most reputable cattlemen, John S. Chisum and Charles Goodnight."

Over the years, the Coggins "had ranches over much of Texas and what is now New Mexico and Oklahoma." They also grazed their cattle in the Concho country, the Panhandle, the Big Bend, Indian Territory, Kansas, Colorado, and Montana." [265]

The article describes the private banking firm called Coggin Brothers and Company. It was established on March 31, 1881. By November 1883, the firm would be changed to Coggin, Ford, and Martin. (Coggin – Biographies of Concho County, Texas, www.genealogytrails.com). The Martin side of the business was Colonel William H. Martin from Missouri who died early in 1886. In the article on tshaonline.org it states, "On December 12, 1901, the Coggins and Henry Ford entered a partnership with James M. Ingle of Abilene, Texas to form the Ingle Mining Company in Boise Country, Idaho. The principal mineral produced was quartz." Where there is quartz, there usually is gold.

(Construction of the Coggin, Ford, & Martin bank in 1874. Ford is just under the banker's sign. (courtesy of Jay Longley))

(Inside bank. Ford is the 8th man from the left, in the teller position with a beard. (courtesy of Jay Longley))

Many were connecting Henry Ford to the James and Younger Gangs. He was portrayed as a very quiet and private man. He became perturbed when asked about his past. When robbers rode into town and seized upon Ford's private bank, along with partners, Coggin and Martin, the robbers and Ford recognized each other. Ford and the robbers greeted each other warmly and carried on a pleasant conversation. The robbery was cancelled that day.

When Cole Younger or Frank James was in town, it was known that they were visiting their friend, Henry Ford.

Henry Ford was married three times. In 1880, he was married to a 21-year-old, Josephine Jones, daughter of James Jones and Rebecca Robbins. She was from San Saba, 50 miles to the south. Josephine died 1885.

In 1886, after Jesse, as a Texas Ranger, had taken care of business in Killeen, ridding the town of desperados, he told Ola that "I went to Brownwood, Texas and stayed a short time with Colonel James Davis and his wife. They were living there then and of course I also went out to see Bloody Bill Anderson. He lived out in the country from Brownwood." [266] He told Ola that Bloody Bill Anderson and Colonel James Davis had lived there for some time.

James R. Davis mentioned to Rudy Turilli that he had met Jesse in Brownwood in 1886. Quantrill, Billy, and John Trammell were there. What was happening in 1886 that many of the "gang" were there? It was either the death of Ford's partner in the banking business, William H. Martin or the wedding of Henry Ford and Mary Jane Mollie Couch, August 18, 1886. Brownwood was in the middle of a severe drought that year and the Coggins and Ford's firm helped the Brownwood citizens survive their financial difficulties. (Biographies of Concho County, Texas – www.genealogytrails.com)

In the news article, "Henry Ford Rose From Unknown Youth to Outstanding Leader" in the Brownwood Bulletin, April 8, 1956, the reporter stated that Ford took out a loan for $10,000 from a Fort Worth bank and loaned it to the farmers to buy seed and feed the year of the drought, 1886. They made a booming crop the following year and the loan was paid back, all but $2.50.

Mollie Couch Ford died in 1895. Mollie Couch's paternal grandmother was Jane Owen Couch (1796/99-1877) was the daughter of John William Owen and Mary Polly Byrd. She was related to the Owens, Byrds, and the Wheelers who were also part of the writer's family. The Wheelers were in the James' family.

Henry Ford married another woman in 1896, Sarah E. Porter, born 1869, 27 years old at the time of marriage. Ford was 20 years her senior. Sarah's father, Jonathan T. Porter was a trader living in Brown County and was from Missouri. There is no other information about him. The Porter name was in Jesse's family with the Woodsons.

Jay Longley was given a very special photo of a Knights Templar meeting in the old Henry Ford Schoolhouse, which was built on West Anderson Street in Brownwood. Jay believes that the school was the place where they also held their KGC meetings, having an escape route through tunnels underground if need be. Jay's friend who was a friend of the late Henry Ford II, a great grandson of Henry Ford, received a copy of this photo and gave to Jay. Henry II found it in an old museum. The photo was taken some time between 1880-1890. The man in white is a dead man. This must have been a ceremony to bid him adieu. The man standing, holding his hat against his left chest, is Henry Ford.

(Knights Templar/KGC meeting in Brownwood, Texas. (courtesy of Jay Longley))

Henry Ford was noted quite often in various newspapers across Texas as visiting San Antonio and Fort Worth and staying at the *Pickwick Hotel*. The word Pickwick has significant meaning in the Freemason society. There is no doubt that Henry Ford was in the Knights Templar, Freemasonry, Knights of the Pythias, and most definitely the Knights of the Golden Circle and had seen his days in battle.

Henry Ford II was very curious about his great grandfather. He had dug into a lot of things and had more access to the family's history and belongings than any other kin. Henry II had told Jay's friend that he had been in the underground tunnels that went under the Ford schoolhouse, the county jail, the courthouse across Center Street to the old Ford/Coggins bank building and under the old J. C. Penney building. It was also under the old Porter Insurance Building on Fisk Street. When they were demolishing that building, a heavy machine, such as a backhoe or bulldozer fell through the foundation into the underground tunnel in the 1950's. The city filled it up with concrete immediately.

Inside the tunnel, as a young man, Henry Ford II saw the plastered walls with a lot of Masonic symbols painted on them. The tunnels are now completely sealed up and hidden from the public. Jay had someone lined up who was going to show him the tunnel under the courthouse, but they backed out at the last minute.

Henry Ford II had no doubt who his great grandfather was and was close to revealing all that he knew. He was threatened by a man that if he didn't stop digging into Jesse James as being Henry Ford or the KGC he wouldn't be living long. Henry told his friend, a friend of Jay Longley's of these threats and it wasn't but a couple of days later, Henry Ford II died unexpectedly at the age of 59 in 1995.

Jay and Henry's mutual friend had been told by Henry Ford II that he was going to give his friend all of his information, books, documents, and pictures that he collected, put his name on the items to ensure they would go to his friend. When his friend asked the family for the items, they refused to give them to him.

After that, all of a sudden Jay's friend stopped being involved in the treasure club of Jay's, while his friend was president of the club at that time. He stopped pursuing any quest on anything that had to do with Jesse, Henry Ford, Bill Anderson, or the KGC. It was 15 years later, when Jay was interviewed by Gene Deason and the article was published in the Brownwood Bulletin about Jay and his research on Bloody Bill Anderson, Henry Ford, and Jesse James, that Jay's friend finally told him of the severe threats to him and his family from this same man who threatened Henry Ford II. He was told that if he continued his pursuit in this "Jesse James thing, being Henry Ford," he and his family would be killed.

This was some serious stuff. After that article came out of Jay's, he was thoroughly bombarded with a whole crew to destroy him and his reputation. It was the same people who hired a college guy to threaten Betty Duke with her life who was also looking into Jesse James and writing several books. The college guy finally came to Betty to apologize and to give her the names of who was involved. It was a group who was also involved in the exhumation of Jesse's body in 1995 in Kearney and who had hired the "forensic scientist" to perform the DNA tests.

The same group continued for years to fight Jay Longley through the internet and banned him and his group from historical groups. Jay was never threatened face to face, but he found a tracking device on his car, his phone was bugged, and his email was hacked. You had to be pretty brave to play this game.

Henry Ford was a Presbyterian and he also had a hand in establishing a grand college in Brownwood with other men such as the Coggins. It was called the Daniel Baker College, founded in 1888. The main building, named Coggin Hall was built in 1890. It was an elaborate building with several high triangular steeples. It was "founded by Dr. B. T. McClelland, fulfilling the plans of the Austin Presbytery to open a Presbyterian college for West Texas. He founded the first Presbyterian church in Brownwood in 1886." [267] The college mascot was a *goat*.

(Daniel Baker College (c. 1895) in Brownwood, Texas)

The school was plagued with financial issues and in 1929, the Presbyterian Church withdrew their support. They consolidated with Howard Payne University.

Another unusual death was the death of Henry Ford (1845-1910) on March 6, 1910 at the age of 65. From several points throughout Texas, including large cities such as Austin and El Paso, the word spread. Out of *the Fort Worth Record and Register,* March 8, 1910 – "Henry Ford, Brownwood," - "Henry Ford, for the past twenty years one of the most picturesque and stalwart figures in West Texas banking circles, died here suddenly at midnight last night of heart failure. The entire city will close business doors tomorrow to attend his funeral. He was cashier of the Coggin & Ford company banking house."

From the *Wichita Weekly Times,* March 11, 1910 – "Bank Cashier Dies." "Henry Ford, the well-known cashier of the Coggin and Ford Bank died here suddenly last night. After returning from a drive he complained of a pain. A physician was summoned, and the banker died in his arms, soon after his arrival."

The funeral was quickly organized, the casket lid sealed tight and Frank and Zerelda James Samuel were in attendance.

Bud had a certified copy of Henry Ford's death certificate. It shows that he was born in 1847 in Richmond, Virginia when Jesse was born, not 1845 as engraved on his tombstone that his family finally erected several decades later. Shows his age as 63. The attending physician documented that he was with him from 10 P.M. to 11 P.M. Time of death, 10:30 P.M. "Died suddenly, Cardiac Neuralgia, contributed by indigestion.?????" The certificate was not complete, or not fully shown in its entirety. Information on his family…unknown, unknown, unknown………

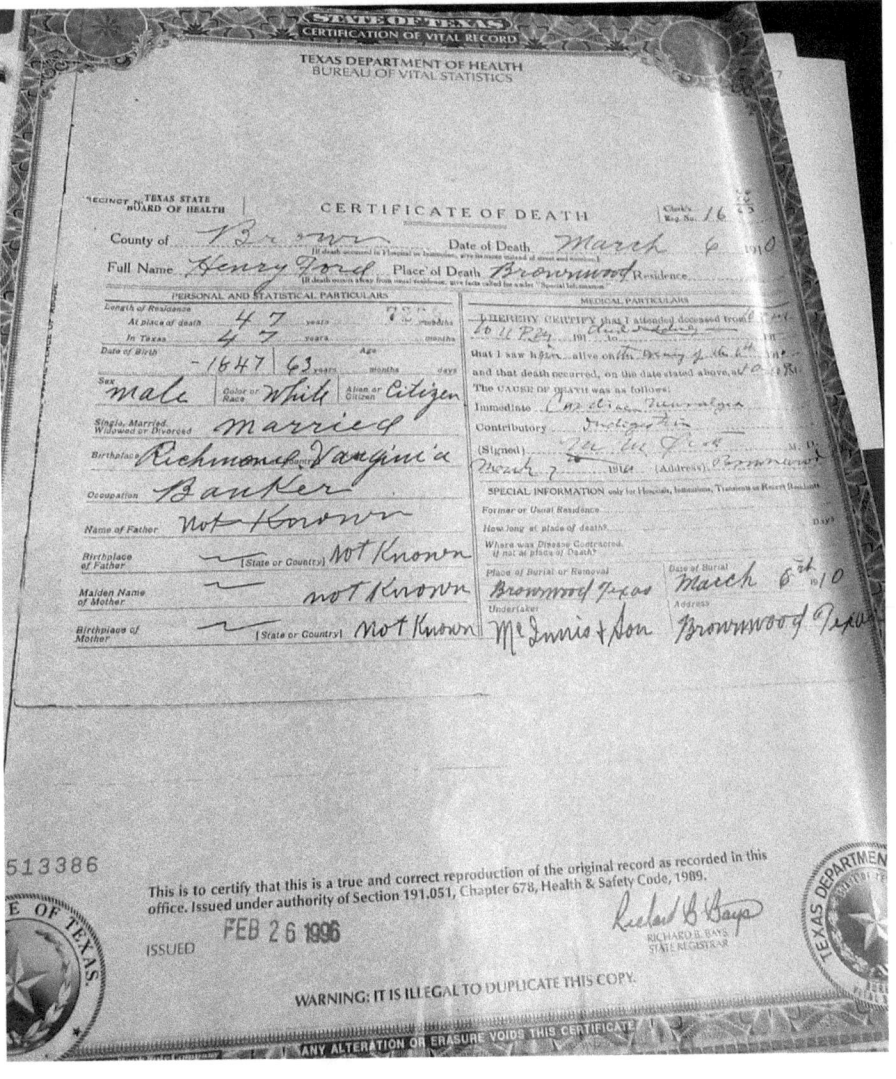

(Henry Ford - Certified copy of his death certificate obtained by Bud)

Forty-six years later he is still remembered. During the Brown County Centennial in April 1956, an article came out in the Brownwood Bulletin about Ford. He was very well educated, highly talented in mathematics, and spoke Latin, Greek, French, and English. "Henry Ford was one of the most respected and influential citizens who pushed forward the development of Brown County." [268] A special historical plaque was erected in honor of him.

Was Henry Ford Jesse? Look at his hair, his cowlick, and hairline. Look at his eyes? Like Jesse, he had the brains, the common sense, the talent, the work ethics, the education, fluent in different languages, business-wise, and was an excellent writer. Jay Longley said as of 2024 after years of research, that the jury is still out on this one. We don't know, but as Bud said, "It's a possibility".

(Henry Ford (courtesy of Jay Longley))

(Jesse)

Quantrill

Jesse stated that Quantrill was in Brownwood at certain times. <u>He</u> lived on. Many reports state that he was shot in the back and paralyzed from the chest down by a U.S. Army band who set up an ambush for Quantrill and his small followers in Wakefield, Kentucky. He was taken to Louisville, Kentucky to a military prison hospital and died later from his wounds on June 6, 1865. He was buried in an unmarked grave and later moved, supposedly. Jesse said he was actually in Mexico with him at the time he was supposed to be dead.

Jesse said Quantrill lived in Canton, Texas where Jefferson Davis was. Quantrill then moved to Osceola, Texas and taught school there, a very small community. Dr. William Tunstill discovered his father, Charles P. Hart was granted two tracks of land from the Texas Republic in Navarro and Hill County. Osceola is 15 miles north of Hillsboro, Texas. Sometimes it appears as if these small towns just popped up everywhere to hide KGC men in plain sight. Jesse told Ola that Quantrill, "Was living under his own name, Charles Hart and was highly respected by all who knew him. None of the townspeople suspected that he was once the much-feared Quantrell, leader of Quantrill's guerilla band. I visited him many times and so did Frank and other Quantrell men." [269] How ironic that the small community was named *Osceola* after the community that was destroyed by their arch enemy, Jim Lane during the war.

James Russell Davis

Colonel James Russell Davis was one of Jesse's most devoted friends. In several newspaper articles such as *Evening Star*, March 14, 1950 he claimed to be a first cousin of the James family. [270] We will learn more about him, but he too was in Quantrill Raiders. In the *Ada Weekly News*, March 16, 1950, he told a newspaper reporter that he used to ride in the Pony Express from Texas into California. I believe he was referring to the Butterfield Mail Route through Texas into California. He stated he was an Indian Scout and was once a Methodist preacher. [271] In *The Tennessean*, June 16, 1949, James Russell Davis said he knew Jesse since he was 14 years old in 1861. He said, "At my home I have a picture of me taken with Jesse James in 1886, and that's four years after Jesse is supposed to have been killed," Davis added. [272] Wish we had that photo. Maybe we do and we don't know it. This would have been in Brownwood.

Colonel Davis and his wife lived in the town of Brownwood and had lived there for some time. It is not known if he went by another name, nor do we know his wife's name or his occupation.

In Bud's book, Jesse revealed that after the Spanish-American War in August 1898, Jesse visited Frank in Dallas who was working for the Sanger Brothers Clothing Store, and then he went to Brownwood to visit Colonel Davis and Bloody Bill Anderson. On Colonel Davis' death certificate, it also showed that he fought in the Spanish-American War. His certificate showed that his father was "Gov. Davis." ???

(John Younger)

Jay Longley believes that James Davis was in Brownwood after the turn of the century. He found some old county paperwork that showed he lived on Fifth Street in 1910.

It appears that the two, Anderson and Davis could have possibly lived in Brownwood for over 30 years or more. I don't believe either one of them were stagnant. We find Colonel Davis in Indian Territory in 1899 at Fort Sill in a meeting with Jesse on "secret mission." In one newspaper, Colonel James R. Davis said he was a US Marshal for the Cherokee Indian Nation. [273] The Cherokee Nation is where Belle Starr lived and where a lot of the outlaws mingled and communed.

Colonel Davis told a newspaper reporter in Nashville that "he made his home in Nashville since 1924 when he came here on a case during his days as a private detective." [274] The year 1924 was a turning point for both Davis and Bloody Bill Anderson. As Bloody Bill Anderson was revealing who he was to the world, Colonel Davis left town for good.

Colonel James Russell Davis would marry Elizabeth DeLozier on October 21, 1925. Her great grandfather, Asa Delozeair (1762-1822) was a brother of Edward H. Delozier II (1774-1858) who married Frances Dyer whose mother was Rachel Dalton (1759-1862) and her sister Pheby Dyer (1782-1871) married into my Thomason family. Rachel Dalton's brother was David Dalton Jr (1752-1835) who was James Lewis Dalton's great grandfather, who was the father of the Dalton Gang and supposedly Zerelda James' brother. If James R. Davis was a first cousin, he had to either be a Younger, Dalton, James, Mims, Poor, Hite, West, Cole, Woodward, Barnes, Dunn, Cohorn, Maret, Thomason, Estes, or Patton.

(James Russell Davis)

Ola said after James Russell Davis' death, his children would call her and ask her who he really was. She had no clue.

This is just the writer's supposition. Oddly, James R. Davis relates the story of being wounded in the war through the shoulder, into the neck. Shot in the left shoulder. It was very similar to how John Younger received his wound when he supposedly was killed. John was the youngest brother of Cole Younger who visited Brownwood often. Brownwood was where James R. Davis lived for a while.

Frank Dalton describes in the Crittenden Memoirs that John Younger did not die by the hands of the Pinkertons as described, but lived a normal life in Texas????? Dalton mentions John quite frequently and his fondness for him was revealed in the words describing his character. Through several stories told by Dalton and Cole Younger, comparing them to stories told by the men most closest to Dalton, it appears that John Younger did live on and would take on the identity of Colonel James Russell Davis. We don't know that for a fact. Compare the two. Howk wrote in his book that John Younger became Judge Isaac Parker in Fort Smith, but the comparison does not come close. Some have believed Colonel Davis was Cole Younger, but he was too large of a man to be Davis. You decide.

William Columbus Anderson

Speaking to Ola about his ranger's days, Jesse followed up with stories about Brownwood which at the time, I don't believe Ola fully understood the magnitude and influence Brownwood had on Jesse. He was enlisted and stationed there as a Texas Ranger in Company E and the headquarters for Company C would eventually be at Camp Colorado, just 25 miles away in Coleman County.

Bloody Bill Anderson, per Jesse, did not die as was reported near Orrick, Missouri. Orrick was the legal name of George Washington Arrington who also lived in Brownwood and who became commander of Company C of the Texas Rangers stationed in Coleman County. Jesse told Ola that after the war, Bloody Bill Anderson moved to Brownwood and bought a ranch there. Bud and Jay Longley both strongly believe through their research, that Bloody Bill Anderson was going by the name of William Columbus Anderson. Jay said there is no doubt in his mind.

Jesse told Ola that "Back in my outlaw days, I went to Brownwood, Texas. I went there fairly often because Bloody Bill Anderson, under whom I'd served while I was with Quantrill, lived a short distance from Brownwood and had for some time. Had a nice place there." [275] We know he went to see Anderson in 1886. In 1898, after the Spanish-American War, Jesse went to see Anderson again in Brownwood and Anderson lived out his life there. Anderson is shown to have died on November 1, 1927, buried in Brown County.

There is much to this story. There are those who claim that the man in Brownwood, going by the name of William Columbus Anderson was not Bloody Bill, but a man who came from Cole, Missouri. The story goes that he, like so many, were disgusted with the Dutch farmers, "Home Guard" on their raids upon many farms in central Missouri. We hear this exact same story from another man close to Jesse. This Anderson joined Quantrill in the fall of 1861 but dropped out of the war and moved to Brownwood in 1863. This does not jive with the story told by this man himself to a reporter in the summer of 1924 nor the Oldtimers/Pioneers of Brownwood or his descendants. Over 21 ex-Quantrill Raiders were still alive that year and no one debunked this man or his life's story during this period of history. It would nearly be a century later when all the naysayers came out of the woodwork.

Anderson was a very well-respected man in the community of Brownwood. A street was named after him, but he was a feisty fellow and took up justice on his own. In December of 1902, Mr. Anderson had a land dispute with J. R. Thomas, a neighbor. It was regarding land that Thomas was living on. The two of them ended it with a shotgun duel. "Both were hit repeatedly with charges of buckshot, but it is thought Anderson will recover." (Fort Worth Star-Telegram – December 30, 1902). In the Marshall Messenger, Feb. 28, 1904 it appears to have happened again. Anderson was shot twice, once in the stomach and once in the leg. J.R. Thomas was shot in the stomach, arm and hand. It is unknown if there was any repercussion. The law apparently was on Anderson's side.

Jay Longley had a personal interest in the Anderson family of Brownwood. His great grandfather, Napoleon Bonaparte Longley, came from a family who had come all the way from Massachusetts and settled in the very deep part of south Texas in Calhoun, County prior to the Civil War. After his father died, in 1865, Napoleon had to take his father's place and began working as a farm laborer at the age of 14 in Lavaca, Texas. Napoleon married and moved on to Travis County, near Austin and became a farmer and then he is listed as a farmer in 1900 in Fanin County, Texas, near the mighty Red River. It is here that he and his wife, Cornelia had a slew of kids, one being Jay's grandfather, Clem Longley (1893-1965) born in Bonham. His sister, Letha (1889-1979) was 4 years older than Clem. She was born in Burnet, Texas where the rangers were stationed under Captain John Sparks with Company C. It was also where Captain Maltby lived while commanding Company E, both companies in which Jesse was a ranger.

(Napoleon Longley's family – Letha is on the back row, far left and Clem is right below her. (courtesy of Jay Longley))

It had to be around 1906/1907 that Napoleon took his family south once more to Brown County. They first made a dugout to live in and later built a home on their land which was just down the road from William Columbus Anderson and his family outside of Brownwood. Letha met Storm Anderson (1877-1935), son of William C. Anderson when she was 17. Storm would have been 30 years old when he met Letha.

Storm and Letha married in May of 1907 in Brownwood, Texas. This is the year Cole Younger came to Brownwood in August. Cole was traveling with a carnival, around 1907, the Cole Younger and Lew Nichols Theatre Company. Cole also joined Frank James in Frank's Historical Wild West.

In the Kansas City Star, May 25, 1924 a Dr. L.E. Skinner who was an optometrist of Longview, Texas stated, "Several years ago Cole Younger came to Brownwood with a carnival show. Bill Anderson met Younger, the latter did not know him, as he thought he was dead as reported. Anderson established his identity beyond question with Younger. It was a great meeting and they spent much time together while Younger filled his engagement."

This meeting between Cole and Anderson continued at Anderson's home at Salt Creek. Many Brownwood citizens document this meeting as well as a meeting with Frank James. Those who wrote and documented these meetings were Charles Tongate, Carl W. Breihan (Old West author),

Brownwood historian Dr. T.R. Havins, Brown County historian and author Tevis Clyde Smith with the account from John Water Tabor.

In the book, *From the Memories of Men* by Tevis Clyde Smith, 1954, a first-hand account told by John Water Tabor, an early resident of Brownwood. "I saw Cole Younger, in Brownwood after his release from prison. He was on Center Avenue and was talking with some Civil War veterans. (Center Avenue was where Coggins & Ford's bank was located) On another occasion, I saw Frank James, after he had given himself up. It was in Dallas, and he told me that he had spent the night in Brownwood a short time before. Later, back home, I mentioned this to a man who ran a blacksmith shop. "Yes, he was here," said the man, "He spent the night at my house." At the time he spent the night here, there was a $10,000 reward on his head, a fact well known to his Brownwood host.

Another old timer came to Brownwood, after the Civil War, from Missouri. The state of Missouri had been a hotbed of warfare, much of it irregular, in which men were forced to choose sides. He was a Southerner and rode with Quantrill. I asked him, once, why they burned Lawrence, Kansas. "Because," he said, "they burned one of our towns. We did to them as they did to us." There were a lot of fine men in those days, and those days were interesting."

The town the guerilla was referring to was *Osceola*, Missouri. On September 23, 1861, after James Henry Lane was appointed by President Lincoln to become brigadier general of volunteers in Kansas, the Kansas Brigade took action in western Missouri and Kansas, raiding and confiscating property of Missouri slaveholders, including slaves. Lane, known as "Bloody Jim" targeted the economy and assets of the enemy. He became the leader of the "Jayhawkers" in the Free-State Movement.

Lane informed his troops, "play hell with Missouri. Missourians," Lane said, "are wolves, snakes, devils, and damn their souls, I want to see them cast into a burning hell. We believe in a war of extermination. I want to see every foot of ground in Jackson, Cass, and Bates Counties burned over, everything laid waste." [276]

Lane had heard that the Confederates were hiding supplies and money in Osceola and they wanted to make their next raid in that town, stripping the town of its goods, and taking the cache out in wagon loads. They used cannons and torches to burn the town to the ground. Nine townspeople lost their lives. This was one of the many reasons why Quantrill's raiders hit Lawrence, Kansas, Lane's hometown. Lane escaped.

Many of Quantrill's raiders settled in Texas after the war and many settled in Brownwood. In the 1910 census, Storm and Letha Longley Anderson were living in Brownwood, close to his father's ranch/farm. His father, William Columbus Anderson was "Bloody Bill," fondly called "Uncle Bill." Storm and Letha Anderson were Jay's Great Aunt and Uncle.

Napoleon Longley was a farmer. He and his wife, Cornelia made a home near Letha and her husband, Storm Anderson, his father, William Columbus Anderson and his wife, Elizabeth. They were neighbors.

The Longley's son, Clem "Clemmie" at the age of 19 in 1912 got a job as a mail carrier. In 1914, Clem married a young girl, Beulah Faye Littlefield (1896-1972) who was living with her mom and stepfather, John Malone and Sallie Adams Littlefield Malone just ½ mile from where the Anderson's farm was on Salt Creek. Clem became a postal clerk at the Post office in Brownwood with a service in that position for 39 years. Clem and Beulah Faye Longley were Jay's grandparents.

(Clem and Beulah Faye Longley (courtesy of Jay Longley))

Jay remembers Letha very well, a very nice woman who would come over to their house to visit. Jay lived with his grandparents mostly when he was growing up. Letha never spoke about her father-in-law being "Bloody Bill," nor did her brother, Clem. But Clem's wife, Beulah Faye, Jay's grandmother, spilled the beans quite often. His grandmother, Beulah Faye would always point to the house where William Columbus Anderson lived, along Salt Creek, which was a magnificent house back in the day. It had a five-point star on one of the eaves of the house. She would tell Jay that this house was where Bloody Bill Anderson lived or that's where "Uncle Bill" lived. She told Jay that a lot of outlaws would come to stay there. Uncle Bill kept a register of his visitors in which the list included some pretty famous people. She had known "Uncle Bill" for 31 years.

(Storm and Letha Anderson)

Before 1920, Letha and Storm Anderson had moved to Corona, Lincoln County, New Mexico and by 1930 they were living in Roswell. After Storm died in 1935, Letha moved back to Brownwood.

What really opened a lot of people's eyes was the story that came out in the newspapers. By 1924, William Columbus Anderson began to talk of his past, but only to a select few. He knew his life would soon reach the end, so he wanted to get a few things off his chest while he had a sharp mind and memory. He was one of the first to reveal his true identity and his connection to Quantrill's Raiders. Did he have permission to reveal his true identity? Jay Longley said no, he was high enough in the KGC that he didn't require permission, but he only could reveal that he was Bloody Bill and nothing, I mean nothing about the KGC or his death would be at the doorstep.

The reporter who interviewed William Columbus Anderson numerous times that summer, Henry C. Fuller, wrote an article in the Brownwood Banner-Bulletin in 1924, relating the story told to him by Anderson, claiming to be "Bloody Bill" Anderson, using the name of his father, William C. Anderson. His father was a "hatter" who was killed in a dispute over a horse in 1862 by a friend. His mother, Martha Jane Thomasson was struck by lightning in 1860 and had died. His sister, Josephine died in the Union prison that collapsed in 1863 and two other sisters were severely injured. His life was extremely sorrowful and his whole motive for his bloody past was revenge.

(William Columbus Anderson)

Bud Hardcastle: The Truth Tracker

(Bloody Bill Anderson)

(Bill Anderson – during his later years (All photos courtesy of Jay Longley))

    The story in the newspaper set off a firestorm. Fuller wrote that he spent several hours with the famous old warrior and talked at some length of the eventful and tragic past in which Uncle Bill, as a young man, played an important part." ("Last of Quantrell's Band, "Uncle Bill" Gone," *Abilene Daily Reporter*, Nov. 6, 1927). The article was published in the *Houston Post* on January 27, 1924, "Daring Pioneer Dreams of Past of Tragic Times." The reporter said he had a "remarkable memory" while Anderson was relating his time as a lieutenant for Quantrill." Newspapers nationwide began printing the story with more detail and depth. The Missouri papers didn't believe it was so. Some people had actually seen Bloody Bill get shot and those that saw his dead body that was paraded in the streets.

The Houston Post's story on Bloody Bill in 1924, stated that "In 1863, Bill Anderson and Quantrill had a disagreement. Anderson left Quantrill and came to this part of Texas, where he settled and once turned his attention to the pursuits of life, and since that time, 60 years ago, he has been a most useful citizen, known and loved by all as a friend and neighbor, and although he is a great joke teller, many of which are on himself, he rarely talks of the stirring days with Quantrill in Missouri, and Kansas." The story was confirmed in the *Richmond Missourian*, May 22, 1924. [277]

In the Schulenburg Sticker newspaper, April 3, 1925, by Henry C. Fuller, they ran a more enlightening story about the ambush the Feds set up to capture and kill Anderson and his men in October 1864. One of the guerillas was on Andersons' horse, in which was a Black Stallion, who had just ridden him to water and was caught up in the chase and ambush. He was falsely identified as Bloody Bill, because of the horse he was riding and the clothes he was wearing. Most of the guerillas had quite lavish embroidered uniforms sewn by their mothers or sisters, such as Bloody Bill.

Documents that were found on the horse and in the pocket of his jacket, and personal affects, indicated it was Bloody Bill. He was killed, shot in the head and the rest of the men were killed. They took the body of the man whom they thought was Anderson and took photos, mutilated his body and cut his finger off for a ring. They cut his head off, putting it on display on a telegraph pole. He was buried in an unmarked grave in Richmond, Missouri.

It wasn't him the reporter said. Jay Longley believed it was another guerila by the name of William Smith. Bloody Bill Anderson escaped and headed south into Texas and found the Salt Creek valley in Brown County, a very pleasant place to settle.

In the San Angelo Evening Standard, "One of Quantrill's Bravest Men Lives in Brown County", by Henry C. Fuller ran on October 17, 1926 describes Bill Anderson and his home which was built in the Autumn of 1865. He fell in love with the area around Salt Creek and Jay said he named the creek himself. The news article stated that Anderson does not like to attempt to resurrect the war or the stories. "He is spending the evening of his days quietly, and never talks of the tragic past in which he played so important a part, unless questioned by a close personal friend."

The Texas State Historical Association website (www.tshaonline.org) mentions the story of William C. Anderson under the title, "Anderson, William (Bloody Bill) T. (ca. 1839-1864)."

Strangely, after 1907 when Cole Younger met with Anderson in Brownwood and confirmed who he was, Cole, during one of his tours in 1908 with the Col. Lew Nichols and Cole Younger Carnival Show was performing in Richmond, Ray County, Missouri in June and wanted to pay homage to his fallen comrade who was buried in Richmond. This town was where the Federal troops took Bloody Bill Anderson's body and buried it in an unmarked grave. It was said the Union troops took turns urinating on the grave and continuously rode their horses over the grave to hide it. (https://raycountyhistory.webs.com).

In 1908, with the grave being 44 years old and neglected, could Younger even locate it? True West Magazine suggests that after the body was placed at the Richmond Courthouse, his corpse was buried in a nearby field, not the cemetery.

In the Richmond Missourian, June 11, 1908, "Younger Here", relates the story. "When the cars of the Greater Nichols Amusement Company rolled into town, and Cole Younger knew that he had reached Richmond, he helped to put into execution a resolve that he had doubtless formulated long ago to help decorate the grave of his friend and loyal companion in arms, Captain Bill Anderson. A *remarkable coincidence* was the fact that Jim Cummins, another old comrade and soldier, was here. Jim Cummins was better acquainted here and managed the details of the joint tribute of respect for other days.

"Monday afternoon, the Band of the Amusement Company struck up a funeral march and, with solemn tread and bowed heads, Cole Younger, Jim Cummins, representatives of the Amusement

Company and others made their way to the Old Cemetery north of town. The grave had already been beautifully decorated with flowers.

"Arriving at the Old Cemetery the crowd gathered around Cold Younger while he, in a reminiscent yet withal reverent way, addressed them in a few short sentences. He said that as a soldier, prior to 1863, he had known and served with Captain Bill Anderson as a soldier, that he was a fearless man, standing back for nothing in the performance of his duty as he conceived it. As such, Mr. Younger said he knew and loved him. He (Mr. Younger), knew personally nothing of his work in 1864 north of the river, but that up to that time he was a conscientious man and a brave soldier."

"Mr. Younger was followed by honorable James L. Farris, son of the late Captain J.L. Farris of the Confederate Army. He spoke for some 20 minutes, paying high tribute to the power of endurance, courage and daring of the dead soldier." Farris stated, "the War had not been in vain; that the conditions and circumstances of the time of Captain Bill Anderson demanded just such a man as he; that if he went to extremes, it was because it was the inevitable and necessary result of war, which Sherman properly and aptly called "Hell". Farris saw it that it was time to cover the dust of the hero with the flowers of affection and honor."

Cole concluded, "Cole Younger cleared up a misunderstanding. He made it plain that at the time of his death Captain Bill Anderson was acting under orders direct from General Sterling Price. This he had heard for some years before he knew it." Did Younger learn this was true from Anderson himself in Brownwood? We did find earlier that the Quantrill Raiders were involved in Price's Missouri Raids.

"In the calm light of history, the deeds done by Anderson do not meet the same sort of condemnation which the hasty judgment of a strenuous and perilous time accorded him."

This event in Richmond occurred before William Columbus Anderson came out with who he was to the public. Do you think Cole Younger was directed to put a final closure on Anderson's life, allowing him to live nearly 700 miles away? Was there anyone in that grave in Richmond?

Jesse supposedly told Howk, "The easy way out of trouble in our day, if trouble dogged our trail too closely, was to have our closest friends conduct a funeral for us. Then, in those days, it was easy to pull a hoax, and once dead, the public was so sorry, and thus another legend started to grow and grow." [278]

When Jay Longley started the Bloody Bill Anderson mystery group on yahoo, 18 years ago, the intent was to uncover Bloody Bill's true story in Brownwood, Texas. Jay had the support of many old timers, historians, and direct descendants who stated that Bloody Bill Anderson lived out his days in Brownwood and never was killed. This was confirmed by Ola when she typed out the manuscript writing word for word from Jesse's own mouth also revealing that Bill Anderson lived outside of Brownwood. There's just too much evidence to ignore.

Bud was one of the first members of Jay's group. Jay became well acquainted with Bud and they worked together on several research projects. Per Jay, Bud was the main source of information that was contributed to Jay's websites:

https://bloodybillanderson.webs.com
https://knightsofthegoldencircle.webs.com

**The writer was able to access these sites in 2022 and with Jay's permission was able to retrieve the information and photos to enhance this book with Jay's great collection of items on Bloody Bill Anderson and Jesse James. Sadly, the sites have been taken down as of 2024. Jay was kind enough to share more information and photos in 2024. We owe Jay a tremendous amount of gratitude for his preservation of history and searching for the truth.

With all of Bud's research and knowledge of Bloody Bill and Jesse, he had to go to Brownwood himself to investigate. He drove from Purcell to Brownwood, 300 miles to look things over. He drove to the Staley Cemetery outside a small community of Early, Texas in Brown County. It was not far from where Anderson lived. Letha Longley Anderson was buried there. Bud asked two women to help him find William Columbus Anderson's grave. They knew right where he was buried and knew, beyond a shadow of a doubt he was "Bloody Bill" Anderson.

Bud did a lot of walking that day, near Anderson's homesite. He found many carvings on rocks, carvings on trees along Salt Creek. He recognized a lot of symbols of the KGC that were not noticeable to the human eye unless you knew what to look for. They were there. He firmly believes that William Columbus Anderson was "Bloody Bill." Many people he spoke to in Brownwood confirmed the stories.

Every time I, the writer traveled to Austin for my job or to Fredericksburg to visit my grandmother, I would always pass through Cisco down Hwy 183 to Brownwood. I would always try to stop at our favorite barbeque place, Underwoods. I had no idea that Brownwood held many secrets especially on the east side of Hwy 183 near Salt Creek.

I had a 3rd cousin who moved to Brownwood in 1918, Eula Mary Haskew (1890-1986) who joined the faculty at Howard Payne College in 1920 as a Professor of English. She started teaching classes on genealogy also and was very passionate about history. I would have loved to learn what she knew about the men who we are addressing in this chapter.

Howard Payne University was founded at Indian Creek on June 29, 1889, by members of the Pecan Valley Baptist Association and Rev. Noah Turner Byars and Dr. John David Robnett. [279]

The Anderson house that Jay remembers all too well was built first with material that was available at the time and then later lumber was hauled from Fort Worth. Sadly, the house burned to the ground in the 1980's turning all its secrets into ashes. This was about the time Jay Longley and too many others were asking a lot of questions and finding a lot of answers. It was suspicious. The log "dog run" house, next to it that consisted of two log structures attached by a breezeway in the center, was also torn down.

(Anderson's house)

Jay said the house had interesting signs upon it, especially the five-pointed star. He gave me a lesson in what it meant. Ah yes, the five-pointed star, a symbol of the Lone Star State, an emblem chosen by the Freemasons who developed Texas which established one of the largest grand lodges in the world.

The five points symbolized "the five points of fellowship" for the Freemasons. The five-pointed star is also considered Venus, the Great Goddess, also called Isis. It is the third brightest celestial body in the heavens behind the sun and moon. Venus is considered both the Evening Star and Morning Star, the first and last star to be seen from evening until morning. Venus' path as it appears from the earth, outlines a five petalled rosette at the completion of its course, appearing as a pentagram which is found in nature also. This is the Freemason's belief which includes their sacred geometry and the pentagram is seen in many of their symbols and designs.

The leaders of the Republic of Texas utilized the star in their flag, then it appears in the Bonnie Blue Flag used in the Civil War by the Confederacy, which all tie to the KGC which merged with the secret organization called the Order of the Lone Star, setting the stage for the Texas Revolution, fighting for independence from Mexico.

The five-pointed star was always worn on the brim of Bloody Bill Anderson's hat. Jesse also wore this five-pointed star on his hat when he was U.S. Marshal in Indian Territory. It was worn by the KGC during the Civil War on their left lapel or chest to prevent them from being killed by both brothers in the Union and the Confederacy. It was also adopted by the Texas Rangers, first appearing during the Frontier Battalion days. The rangers would have a silversmith or blacksmith make their badges out of 5- and 8-peso Mexican silver coins in the shape of an encircled five-point star.

With the five-point star prominently displayed on Anderson's house, it was important to him. You can also find these stars on old, old buildings throughout south Texas, especially old Masonic buildings and banks.

In 1927, William Columbus Anderson died. There is no indication that this too was a manufactured death. I'm sure Jesse attended his funeral. An entry in Bud's book has to be read very carefully, Ola said, "In 1945 was the last time Jesse went to Brownwood, Texas to visit at the ranch of a very good, longtime friend of his, Bloody Bill Anderson." Notice she didn't say he went to visit Bloody Bill, but only that he <u>visited the ranch</u>. Jesse told Ola, "Some of Bill's grandchildren are living on that ranch, if I'm not mistaken." [280] It sounds as though Jesse was checking things out, possibly treasure sites on Anderson's property in which he frequently checked on all the other cache sights. What secrets, what treasure is buried there?

The Treasure in Brown and Coleman County of Texas and Roswell, New Mexico

Brown and Coleman County, the center point of Texas. There is a reason why these counties were picked by the KGC. Remember these men were never individuals in their endeavors, nor were they a handful of men. It was a huge organization, and each were given a specific assignment. Jay Longley believes his great uncle, Storm Anderson, Bloody Bill's son was sent out to Roswell, New Mexico to be a sentinel to keep a watch on treasure buried there. Jay believes there is a large KGC depository there. Could it be on Chisum's ranch? Could be.

Jay Longley has been a treasure hunter for 54 years. Little did he know that when he got his first metal detector when he was 14, he would have an entire gold mine of treasures beneath his feet. He believes Brown and Coleman County, and central Texas contain more lost valuable treasure, than any other area of the U.S. or the world for that matter. There is more history, secret history that has yet to be uncovered.

Jay graduated from Brownwood and graduated from Tarleton State University. His studies included government and politics. He furthered his education at the University of Texas in pre-law. He worked as Assistant Sargent of Arms for the Texas Senate at the State Capitol and became fascinated in this field and history.

Jay was cofounder of the Central Texas Treasure Club in 1981 and was elected President of Central Texas Treasure Club in 2018. He has been involved with many treasure hunts, not only KGC gold, but other types of treasure and artifacts that were buried by the Spanish, Mexicans, Indians, and 49ers. As we have relayed earlier, many stories of travelers coming out of Mexico by the Spaniards, Mexicans, those hiding Montezuma's gold, military, outlaws etc. who hid their treasures because of imminent attacks by Indians or highwaymen, buried their items along the trail to keep it out of the wrong hands. Albert Pike and Randolph Marcy had heard of these stories and followed through with identifying hot areas. I believe that was why places, towns, and different landmarks were mapped out to help find and secure the treasure.

Jesse's job in the KGC as comptroller was to find and secure the treasures, relocating if needed and then burying the gold and silver gained in criminal activity along with the hard-earned money made in the business world of the KGC members. Why? To fund a Second Civil War. Jay believes that this answer was just a smoke screen. He believes that this may have been the intent at the beginning, but more knowledge and more prosperity turned their vision towards supporting the South and the Nation as a whole.

This would make a good ending to the story, but I don't think it's the end. There is more to it than we can ever imagine. But what happened to all the gold and treasure? Much of it is still underground, but I don't believe it was just abandoned. I believe there is still a purpose for it.

Jay Longley has located 3 probable KGC depositories, within a 100-mile radius from Brownwood. There is one he knows for sure of, as he has located one of the marker caches surrounding it. The depositories were big underground vaults where they kept the priceless treasure, not only precious metals, but weapons, and priceless Egyptian artifacts and treasures from around the world gathered in the 1800's. It may be much more than we realize. It's similar to the Oak Island treasure, which was buried in the 1600's-1700's or earlier. A good example of a depository is Victorio Peak in New Mexico which we will discuss later.

Jay located a marker cache with the help of an expert dowser. This was in 2009/2010. He contacted an old man who had learned the art of dowsing from his father who was a dowser. The art may have been passed down to him and also the dowsing equipment and techniques of old. The old man was extremely excited about the opportunity to do this. He told Jay he had been dreaming of these depositories every night for 20 years. He had knowledge of what could be under the earth in Brown County. The man used what Jay called were Spanish balls or marbles that he would hold. He would hold a certain color for whether you were looking for water or for precious metals.

Jay said the man was amazing. The dowser described treasures underground that were placed in extremely intricate designed vaults to sustain through the ages. It appears to be exactly like Oak Island in which there are 4 or 5 layers or levels under bedrock at least 20 foot down. Each level was supported by beams or planking of elaborate and exotic wood from Europe and all over the world. Jay mentioned they used Rosewood, but he couldn't remember what the other wood was. The only explanation is that the main depositories had to be treasure brought over and protected by the Knights Templar. Jay says that sacred knowledge was passed down, eventually reaching the Order of the Lone Star and then into the Knights of the Golden Circle.

There are depositories such as Victorio Peak that treasures of the world and many other precious metals were gathered and hidden in the 1880's. The depositories or treasuries are scattered all across this country. One such place is the Wichita Mountains in Oklahoma. A man from Brownwood, Dean C. Sayler was interviewed by Steve Wilson, author of "Oklahoma Treasures and Treasure Tales." Mr. Sayler told Steve that he knew for a fact that Jesse and Frank James buried $180,000 in the Wichitas. He learned this information from an old outlaw who lived in Brownwood, named "Conley." This man Conley was friends with Jesse and Frank and later Frank James came to see him quite often in Brownwood.

Conley told of being a lookout man for Jesse and had one of the three cowhide maps in existence of the treasure. He said the treasure was in a sealed cave near a natural stone corral, known by the outlaws as Horse Thief Corral and a cabin in Cutthroat Gap where Belle Starr stayed during their thievery. Could this be the cave with the Iron Door?

Jay believes there is also a large depository on Salt Mountain near his home. His friend Colin and him were climbing the mountain one time with metal detectors and other equipment and out of the blue, they were buzzed by a helicopter very close to their heads where they could see every detail of the pilot. It shook them a bit, more ways than one. The sight was being protected. Jay believed it was Masons.

A friend of Jay's has discovered that one of the large depositories is on the land that the Coggin brothers had owned. It is unknown which vast number of acres that it is located on.

A very interesting YouTube video was recently posted titled "Did the Knights Templar Secretly Discover and Found The USA?" A lecture by Scott Wolter, *The Cosmic Summit*. It is very detailed, but it helps one to understand the philosophy and the mindset of the Freemasons and the Knights Templar. It will blow your mind and take you into a new direction regarding the hidden secrets of America. It is far above my head. It was fascinating to hear a different version of history that we have never been taught. It suggests that the Knights Templar brought all the precious treasure over from Europe over 400 years before Columbus, such as the Lord's Supper Challis, the skull of John the Baptist, ancient relics, spiritual knowledge and enlightenment, sacred feminine, the divine bloodline, alchemy/science, and the foundation for the New Jerusalem or the Free Templar State, the United States.

What was incredible to hear was that the indigenous people who lived many moons before all of us in the U.S., knew the Knights Templars, intermarried with one another and guarded the treasure for centuries. This coincides with many treasure maps and information that Bud has obtained, noting that the Indians were guarding the treasure.

There are a few aspects included in the video that speak about the Great Goddess, Venus, the giver of life who balances the dual divinity. She represented the five-pointed star we spoke of. The video gets in deep regarding the philosophy and belief of the dual-gendered Godhead which reminded me of the Baphomet symbol representing the "equilibrium of opposites, half-human and half-animal, male and female, good and evil, etc." [281]

I don't completely understand this philosophy, but it concerns me greatly. I never was raised in it nor was I fed it, but I have to point out that it appears that this philosophy of the Knights Templar/Freemasonry manipulates creation from its original unadulterated form, creating something to be worshipped. Is this a form of blasphemy?

It appears that the focus is on the magnificent creation in nature and the heavens, rather than the Creator. This is only a slice of the Freemason's philosophy. Although God's creation is His signature and we are in awe of his handiworks, the more focus we place upon nature, we could find ourselves worshipping nature and the heavens instead of focusing on our omnipotent God Almighty, Creator of Heaven and Earth.

Also, Jesus was definitely mentioned in the video, but not much. The stories and new narrative presented, taken off of ancient documents, places Jesus more as a human than God's blessed son. This bothers me and nothing will make me change my faith in believing in God the Father, the Son, and the Holy Spirit. It is worth your time though to listen, to get a better understanding of what the Knights Templar and secret societies kept in their bosom and their minds for thousands of years.

The mysteries of this earth do certainly lie beneath the surface and have remained there for centuries, only known to a certain elect. What was the reason? Why wasn't it shared? The Knights Templars were severely persecuted by the Roman Catholics and for what reason? Did the Knights Templar have something to hide or was it the Roman Catholic church have something to hide? So much to explore and expose.

Knights Templar from France and Spain who originated from the Ancient Holy Land were trying to clean up the corruption of the Catholic Church. They were fervently protecting the 2nd Temple, Herod's Temple and it is believed during the destruction of the temple in the 11th century that they began excavation under the temple mount, hiding treasure maps, genealogy, sacred knowledge and treasure. But there is so much more, and I'm not equipped to write about it in truth.

We may all learn things, including the writer in this video. The next few years, more history, more treasures, and hopefully more truth will be uncovered.

"See to it that no one takes you captive by philosophy and empty deceit, according to human tradition, according to the elemental spirits of the world, and not according to Christ" Colossians 2:8.

Scott Wolter contacted Jay Longley several years ago, after learning Jay published many articles about the KGC, the tunnels under Brownwood, Henry Ford, and Bloody Bill Anderson.

Wolter was very interested in what Jay and Brownwood had to offer. The producer called several times begging Jay to do the show and after several promises from the producer, Jay decided to do this as long as his words would not be twisted, and the truth would be told. It was in 2013 when Scott Wolter and the crew from the History Channel came to Brownwood and the filming of "America Unearthed" began.

The program is found on You Tube, "America Unearthed: Lincoln's Secret Assassins Exposed (S2, E12). Jay said that there was a lot of filming and many cuts made that had more information to conclude the KGC was definitely embedded there.

Jay said that he and Wolter were both allowed to go into the basement of the county jail and actually see the sealed entry of one of the tunnels. At the sealed opening, an old rusted drill cable was sticking out. Someone tried their best to drill a big enough hole to look inside, but the drill bit became stuck inside the opening which was just big enough for the cable to go through but not the bit. They had to cut off the cable and just left it in place. You could move the cable back in forth through that hole, indicating a hollow area behind the sealed and plastered entry. For some reason, this was not shown in the documentary. Jay said the film crew were all excited and wanted to film it, but were told no.

Oh, if they could have had a full hour on just Brownwood and used a lot of the film that was cut out, it would explain a lot to the whole world. Wolter used ground penetrating radar to determine that there was evidence that there were manmade voids underground and could have been the KGC tunnels underneath the pavement and the buildings. Jay said Scott Wolter who is a Freemason didn't mind talking about Henry Ford or the KGC but did not want to talk about Bloody Bill Anderson or J. Frank Dalton.

When Jay first started corresponding with Bud Hardcastle, Bud sent him a large packet of information on Jesse and the KGC. Jay took that knowledge, information out of treasure books, and Bob Brewer's skills in deciphering codes and symbols of the KGC and put it to good use. With this knowledge and Jay's own research, natural skills, being familiar with the land, using expert dowsers, the depositories and marker caches can be found, Jay said. If you can find a marker cache, you can pretty much find the main depository that is usually 20 ft deep. This is the big prize. It takes a lot of work, mentally and physically and a lot of guts.

The KGC used an underground grid, designed by Albert Pike to lay out their caches, Sacred geometry. The marker caches are around the main depository in certain points within a circle, like a spider web. Marker caches are found around the perimeter of the circle and along the lines that form triangles similar to a slice of pie, pointing towards the center point where the main depository is. Each marker cache is a certain distance between the other, usually appearing to be equally distanced apart.

The marker caches may be 3-5 feet deep and contain gold, silver, small treasures and sometimes a trinket to indicate a clue. If a person came onto a marker cache, not knowing the complex system or layout of the entire design or those who are without this knowledge, then to the untrained eye and mind, they would think this is all there is and be satisfied with the treasure that was found. But those untrained in this magnificent skill and knowledge would be disturbing the design, the clues, the direction and location that has been superimposed upon each detail. I know this has to be frustrating to those serious treasure hunters when several marker caches are disturbed and the clues have been destroyed, including symbols, carvings, etc.

As one gets closer to the treasury, the depositories, the danger increases. The danger could be in the form of booby traps of all kinds, and from those who lay watch over them for whatever motive or purpose they have. Many treasure sights, not all that are buried under ground, will have a cap stone or a form of concrete/masonry poured on top to conceal it. Jay said the marker caches from each other and from the main depository or vault may vary in distance between yards or miles. They can be in the flat ground or up on a hillside.

Jay said he and Colin were in the process of retrieving 3 mason jars of gold coins in a marker cache around a depository outside Brownwood, an estimated value of $250,000. With the expert dowser who came to help, they were able to locate the area, got a good reading from their detector and had marked it. They started digging and was able to get down 3.5 ft and hit rock or old concrete. They busted through the concrete and were off a bit, but to the side, you could hear the rattle of mason jars. It was getting late, they covered it up and marked it inconspicuously. Jay came back later, and someone had been there. Whoever it was, dug 6 inches more to the south, with a post hole digger and took the jars. The cache was gone as well as any clues. They had been watched.

Jay said he saw two Masons watching them as they were digging. They wouldn't even say hello or give them a time of day. Jay said he shared some information he regrets through his email and treasure sites on the internet and he was hacked, tracked, and bugged. When the writer asked Jay if he thought those who were doing this were still the KGC sentinels, Jay replied that he does not believe there are any more sentinels guarding the treasure. He believes that when the KGC closed their books in 1916, they had their sons, and descendants become the sentinels just as Storm Anderson was sent to Roswell to watch over the large depositories in that area. Jay believes that after their children, even maybe their grandchildren fulfilled that position, the desire or need to continue phased out. He believes the caches were abandoned.

Jay believes that those who were watching his every move were those who were hired by big time Treasure Hunters. A lot of them are high ranking Masons.

Jay continues in his hunt, more on a smaller scale because of the loss of his most trusted friend, Colin who died of Lou Gehrig's disease in 2011. He keeps himself busy being the President of Central Texas Treasure Club and loves what he does. Thank you, Jay Longley, for your help and support of Bud and contributing to the uncovering of truth in History.

"You may have a cowboy hat, spurs, chaps, and a horse but you're not a cowboy till you can ride like one."

-Unknown

Chapter Fifteen: Billy

Just as the men of Brownwood, Texas had changed their identity to cover their past, Brushy Bill Roberts emerges in the 1880's covering himself in a new persona.

Who was Brushy Bill….really? The Texas Kid? Jesse told Ola he was the real Billy the Kid.

Bud pointed something out to the writer that makes one really stop and think. J. Frank Dalton never spoke of Billy the Kid as "Brushy Bill," but always called him "Billy" or "Poor Billy." He was fond of that young man, 12 years younger than him, and 2 inches shorter. They had history together.

Did their history begin in the Wild West days or down the cattle trail during the cattle rustling days? I think the reader will be surprised as I was to learn the truth from Bud.

Bud's greatest possessions he has gathered are letters from Brushy Bill to Ola Everhard and Jesse. Aubrey Everhard was kind of enough to allow Bud to have them. Brushy was two months away from his death, when his wife was writing these letters for him. He was working with a lawyer, Morrison, and the truth was still not out about his true identity.

Brushy's wife knew J. Frank Dalton was Jesse since 1948 when Brushy went to Lawton. Brushy identified Dalton to be Jesse and his reasoning was said that his father was in the Quantrill Raiders with Jesse. He told reporters that his father, "Wild Henry" Roberts was there when Jesse pulled the hoax on his death in 1882 and his father told him about it. Brushy also told the reporters that whenever Jesse got wounded, he would come to his mother's house and she'd take care of him. "Roberts said he had visited with Jesse off and on ever since, and that he and his wife took care of him for several weeks in their home after he had broken a leg at Gladewater, Texas." This would have been in 1937. This statement from Brushy was in the newspaper article, "More Proof That Dalton is 'Jesse'," *The Guthrie Daily Leader*, July 7, 1948.

Brushy never stated that he was Billy the Kid to anyone publicly until William V. Morrison came to his door in 1949 and it would be several visits later when he finally admitted to it. He kept it under the covers. Lizzie Roberts, his wife did not know he was Billy the Kid until just before he died. She admitted this in a letter to Ola in 1951. (See Appendix A-11)

(Envelope of the letter from Lizzie Roberts to Ola in 1951)

    The earlier letters from Brushy Bill are dated 10/27/1950. It would be a month later, 11/29/1950 that Brushy would be facing the governor of New Mexico for his long overdue pardon that he longed for.

    Here is one of the letters from Brushy Bill or "Billy" as we will refer to him from now til the end of the book, the way he was called by Jesse. Again, he's still not admitting being Billy the Kid. Lizzie wrote these for Billy, but her penmanship was not good enough for the writer to translate. Bud had studied them enough that he was able to. Here is the copy of the letter and the translation, written two months before he died.

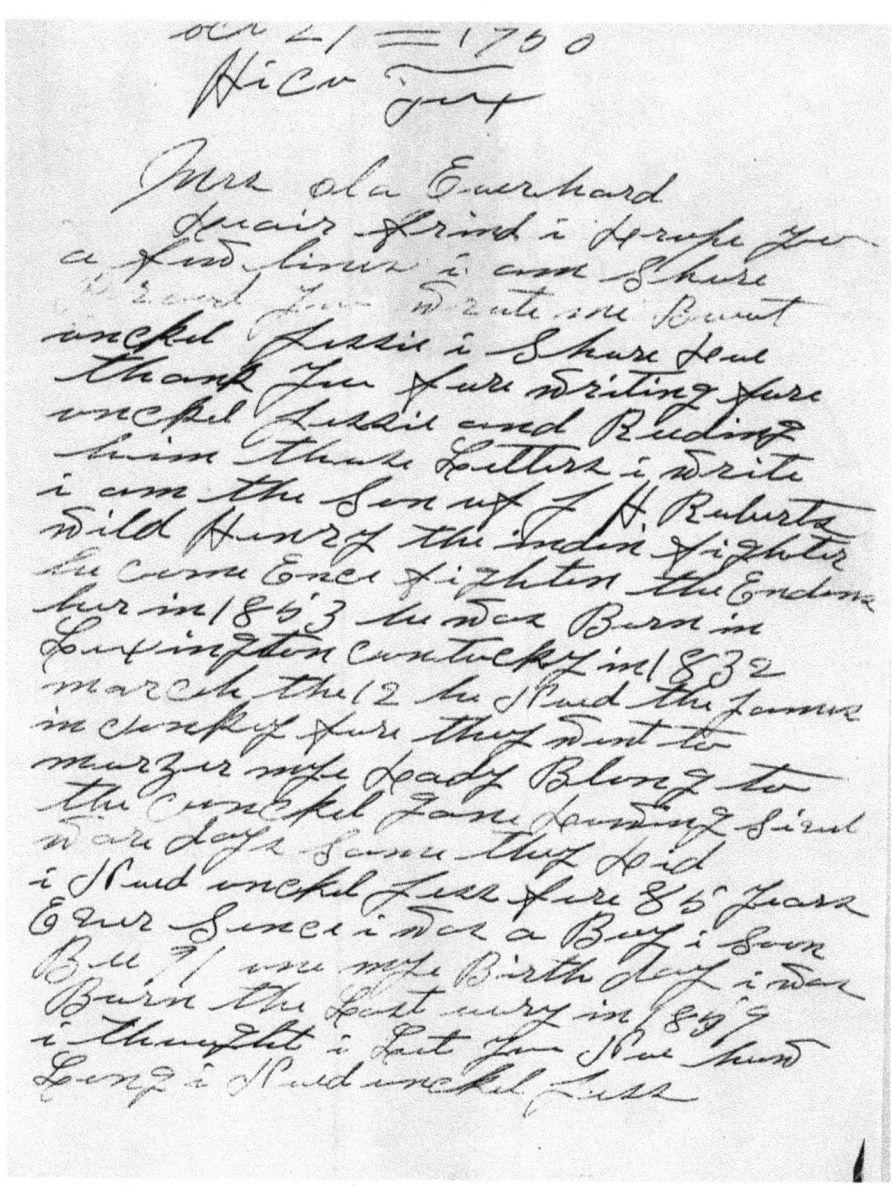

(Letter 1st page)

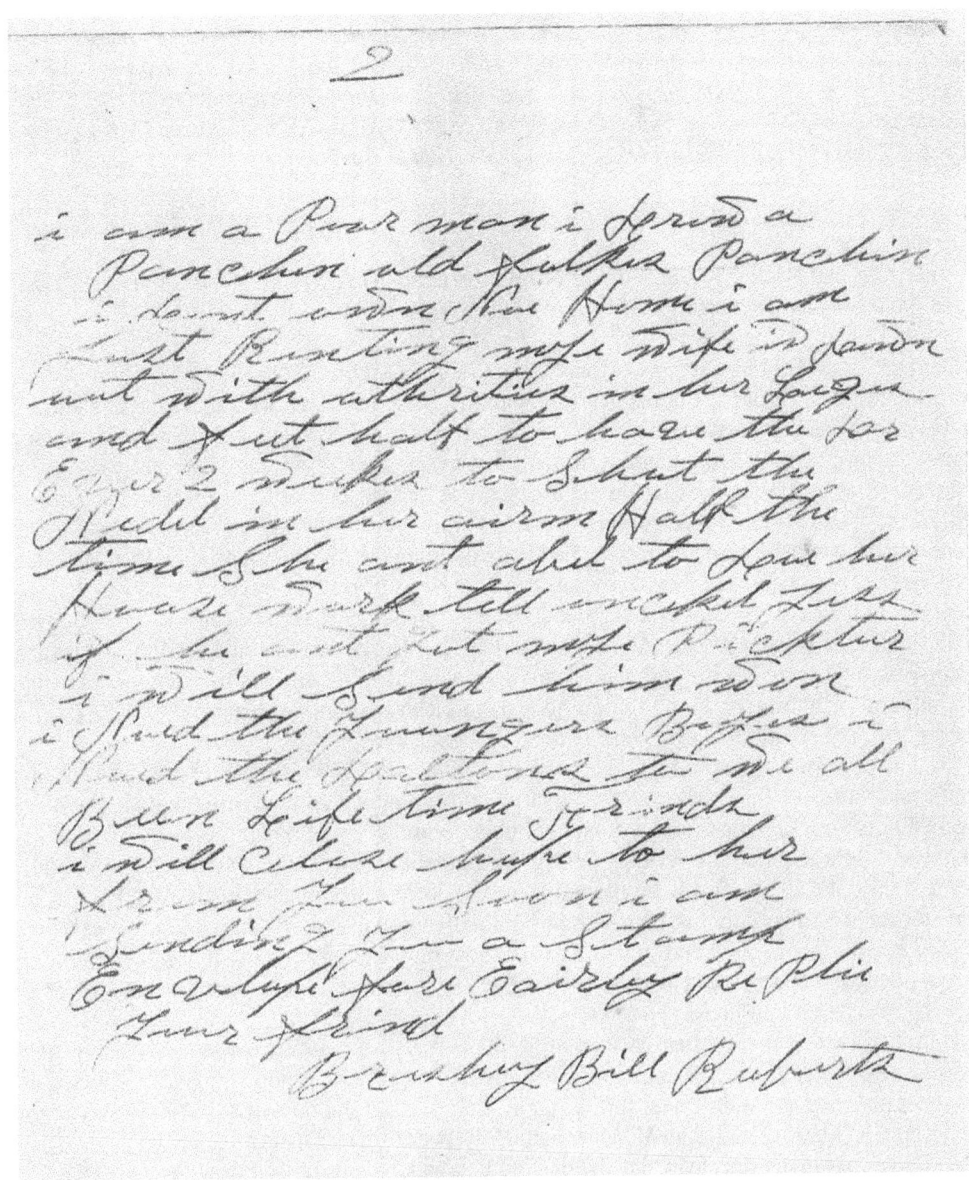

(Letter 2nd page)

October 27, 1950 – Hico Texas
Miss Ola Everhard,
Dear friend,

I drop you a few lines. I am sure proud you wrote me about Uncle Jesse. I sure do thank you for writing for Uncle Jesse and reading him these letters I write. I am the son of J.H. Roberts, "Wild Henry", the Indian fighter. He came out fighting the Indians in 1853. He was born in Lexington, Kentucky in 1832, March the 12th. He knowed the James in Kentucky before they went to Missouri, my daddy belonged to the Quantrill Gang, same as they did. I knowed Uncle Jesse for 85 years, ever since I was a boy. I soon be 91, my birthday. I was born the last very day in 1859. I thought I'd let you know how long I knowed Uncle Jess.

I am a poor man. I draw a pension, old folks pension and don't own my home. I am just renting. My wife is down with arthritis in her legs and feet have to have the ?? every 2 weeks to ???? in her arm half the time. She not able to do her housework. Tell Uncle Jess if he can't get my pictures I will send him some. I loved the Younger boys. I loved the Daltons. To me all been lifetime friends, I will close. Hope to hear from you soon. I am sending you a stamp envelope for early reply.

Your friend, Brushy Bill Roberts.

Billy also had a letter in the same envelope for Jesse. This will be shown in another chapter, written the same day October 27, 1950.

Sadly, Billy would be saying his final adios to the world on 12/27/1950, two months since he sent this letter, and a month after his meeting with the governor. The meeting was overwhelming to him. He was expecting a private meeting with the governor, but he was met with a packed room full of the pressing press, flashing camera bulbs at his every move, blinding him, and causing much confusion. They were eager to get his story, same as the relatives of Pat Garrett, the Coes, and Sheriff Brady who Billy had killed during the Lincoln County War. What alarmed Billy the most were the many lawmen present whom he had been dodging for 69 years with their pistols packed in their holsters. Billy just knew they were going to drag him off in shackles as he once was and would be hung from the neck 'til he was dead, dead, dead as one judge said in the past.

This terrified Billy at the age of 90. He had kept his secrets to himself for all these years, now it was going public. All he wanted was a pardon so that he could end his life in good standing. In his mind, and many others, he had done his part to clean up Lincoln County, but he admitted to Morrison, "I done wrong like everyone else did in those days." [282]

He was promised a pardon by Governor Lew Wallace in 1879 if he would give himself up and help the law prosecute those who were truly guilty of horrendous crimes. Billy kept his promise. He appeared before the Lincoln grand jury and with his testimony he helped put at least 50 behind bars, charged with murder and other crimes during the Lincoln County War. The local district attorney refused to drop the charges on Billy though. Promises offered to him were not kept. He was never given amnesty nor a pardon, but was kept in jail, hunted down like an animal after his escape, and was over zealously plastered and branded as the most blood-thirsty outlaw in all of the southwest. The most wanted man known in history. He was used as "a main attraction" to draw the guilt towards him away from the Santa Fe Ring.

Billy had carried this burden long enough. He had a stroke during the governor's meeting in 1950 and was unable to clearly explain his life in great detail. Governor Thomas J. Mabry seemed to have no patience and didn't hear him out, nor look over all the documents and photos provided by his friend and lawyer, William V. Morrison. Billy ended up collapsing.

Billy was not given the clean slate he desired that had been promised years ago from Governor Lew Wallace. The pardon was denied by Governor Mabry in 1950. It literally broke Billy's heart.

Billy and his wife, Lizzie were planning a trip to go see Jesse and the Everhards in Austin with DeWitt Travis. They were looking forward to it, but it appears that Billy just wasn't in good health. He had gone from his home in Hico, Texas to mail a letter addressed to Ola and Jesse in Austin when he died in front of the post office on 12/27/1950, just shy of 4 days turning 91.

When Ola told Jesse that Billy had passed, Jesse was in the hospital in Austin. Ola said he responded with, "Well, well, I've lost a mighty good friend." Tears were just rolling down his face as Ola stood by patting his arm. It was heartbreaking to see Jesse go through that, she felt helpless. With tear-filled eyes and a choking voice he said, "Poor little Billy. He was a good boy. He had a mighty hard time growing up. I've lost a mighty good friend. It hurts me mighty bad. I'm sure sorry he's gone." [283]

When Bud started revealing to the world that Jesse and Billy the Kid were very close friends, it brought out people who tried to shoot the friendship down. A newspaper man from St. Joseph,

Missouri called Bud and said "Jesse and Billy didn't even know each other." He didn't believe Bud. The reporter said, "Do you know someone with a PhD in History to verify that?" Bud told him to call William Tunstill who had a PhD in history. The reporter called Tunstill and asked the question about Billy the Kid and Jesse knowing each other. He needed to talk with someone who knew history with an educated mind. William Tunstill said, "Why, that's Bud Hardcastle, he is the PhD on the subject."

From many sources, Bud gained a lot of knowledge about Billy. He spoke with those who knew him personally; Aubrey Everhard, Francena Turilli, Joe Wood, and a lot of Oldtimers. It was Joe Wood that gave Bud lots of photos of Brushy Bill and Jesse in 1949. Aubrey and Ola Everhard had lots of photos of Billy and Lizzie and many letters verifying his connection to Jesse and revealing his true identity.

Bud went to Hico, Texas and saw Brushy Bill Robert's homemade tombstone. Bud became sad and very moved. It was just a piece of concrete someone took a knife or stick to scratch in his date of birth, which was wrong and date of death, December 27, 1950. He didn't have a proper tombstone. Bud went back to Hico later to buy one for him and someone had already bought a more appropriate one.

With all that Bud had and William Tunstill's knowledge of what he learned from Ola Everhard about Brushy Bill; Bud was able to put the story together. To embellish this story with more facts, filling the missing pieces, we are able to tell the story of Brushy Bill thanks to Bud and W. V. Morrison who actually investigated Brushy Bill's story with him, from 1949-1950. We are in deep gratitude for Morrison to tape these interviews with Brushy and for those authors who transcribed and documented the entire story that Brushy did provide. One of them, we are very grateful to have is Dan Edwards book, "Billy the Kid, An Autobiography."

Billy the Kid is a very hot subject! So many experts and amateurs alike are drawn into this mystery. It gets even hotter when discussing his death. Was he gunned down at the age of 21 by Pat Garrett in 1881 in Fort Sumner like history tells us, or was it in 1950 in Hico, Texas as an old man of 90? So many opinions, so many theories. Was Brushy Bill truly Billy the Kid? Bud and I definitely believe so.

In the interviews in 1949 with Brushy Bill Roberts, William V. Morrison was amazed at all the vivid details that he had spoken about in his early days of life and the Lincoln County War. Brett Hall, an author and detailed researcher of Billy the Kid/Brushy Bill Roberts who has many interesting and fact-based YouTube videos on the subject, enlighten those who are not familiar with the debate on the subject of Brushy Bill Roberts being the true Billy the Kid. He delves deep in research and dissects every detail, every clue that have been overlooked mistakenly or purposely.

We also have extremely enlightening videos from Dan Edwards under "Alias Billy the Kid/Asocial Media, LLC., who received the actual reel to reel tapes of the interviews with Brushy from Morrison's daughter. There is one more book I really desire to have. It is William Tunstill's book, "Billy the Kid and Me Were the Same."

Bud admired Dr. Tunstill. He was a very well-respected historian, who put his entire retirement years into researching Brushy Bill. He even received death threats when he was pursuing this. He gathered documents, speaking to Brushy Bill's relatives, the Everhards, Morrey/Maury/Maurey Davidson, and many others to get down to the truth. Mr. Davidson gave Tunstill a copy of the tapes recorded at Jesse's birthday party on Sept. 6, 1949, which include Brushy Bill speaking, along with Jesse, John Trammel, and Colonel James Davis. Tunstill put forth the effort to transcribe them. Bud has a copy of these and has shared them with the writer.

(Original tombstone of Brushy)

(New tombstone for Brushy)

I am in no way qualified to be among these great historians and researchers, much less enter this debate between them and other investigators who have reached a different conclusion. I don't care to get in the heated discussion. The arena for this debate has become a den of vicious slander and disrespectful innuendos between many who have a difference of opinion and believe they are right and the others wrong. Has anyone got the story completely right after nearly 150 years? Many think they have, who have their own egos or agendas. We all in a way, including myself, get blinded in our research, driving deep in our own tunnel vision where we can't see the forest for the trees.

Bud said, "Its plain and simple. Everyone is trying to make this harder than it really is. It could be right in front of our eyes if we just stop and look around and open our bullheaded minds." Bud promotes research on your own and not just looking in old books that has told the tale of Billy the Kid for so long that is ingrained in all of us. It was a tale, spun into such a tight web, it's hard to unravel. Things have been covered up. "Let us keep ourselves humble and "open-minded," as Bud says, "to truly find the truth. That's what we all want. We are all on the same team here."

I'm sure we don't have all the facts we need to claim complete truth. Neither Jesse nor Billy liked to talk about any type of involvement in killing and many things in their lives were kept private, but what they have given us is more truth than we can ever find in dime novels.

In this book, we are presenting what Bud has discovered and we're focusing on Jesse and his friends. The reason why we place the information in this book about Brushy Bill Roberts is that all of Bud's research, interviews, letters, and documents prove that Brushy Bill Roberts was one of the closest friends to J. Frank Dalton. In our eyes, and in our research, Brushy and Dalton have revealed to us that they were the real Billy the Kid and Jesse James. They were a huge part of each other's lives and lived long enough to tell about it. We should be ever so grateful for that.

Brett Hall describes in his video, "Brushy Bill Roberts in His Own Words: The Lincoln County War and Debunking The Saga of Billy the Kid" that according to C L. Sonnichsen and Frederic Bean (authors) who painstakingly transcribed the recordings of Morrison interviewing Brushy, stated, "Roberts spoke confidently, answering all of Morrison's questions, without hesitating and compromising and that Roberts spoke authoritatively." "When Roberts spoke of killing someone, or discussing the death of a friend, he would often become emotional and weep."

Let's go back to the beginning.

In 1859, Billy wasn't born in New York, he was born in a small community by the name of Buffalo Gap, which is 14 miles to the south, southwest of Abilene, Texas. It was not an established town at that time, but more like a winter camp for buffalo hunters. The gap was a thoroughfare for buffalo which drew the hunters and Indians to this runway of buffalo hides strutting their stuff. It was an area where Texas Rangers were in force, such as Charles Goodnight in the late 1850's. He began to establish a herd of cattle near Fort Belknap and were gathering as many mavericks as he could in this region. He would later establish the Goodnight/Loving Trail right through Buffalo Gap and his first run was in 1866. The town of Buffalo Gap began to take shape in the mid-1870's when it was designated as the county seat of Taylor County in 1874. There was no other town in Taylor County at that time.

The Butterfield Overland Mail Company which was a stagecoach service operating from 1858-1861 was just west of the area of Buffalo Gap. It would handle the mail and passengers from Memphis, Tennessee and St. Louis, Missouri and stops in between such as Fort Smith, Arkansas, into Indian Territory, down through Texas, New Mexico, Arizona, Mexico and ending in San Francisco. Dr. Tunstill and Ola both agree that Buffalo Gap at that time was a relay station and had a cabin and stables. Maybe the Roberts were the ones who ran the relay station.

We don't know if "Wild Henry" Roberts, Billy's father was a Texas Ranger, a cowboy, a soldier at Fort Phantom Hill, a relay station host, or if he and his wife were passengers on the stage. The two forts in that area were Fort Phantom Hill and Fort Chadbourne used as way stations for the Butterfield Overland Mail Route. This area was where Billy's mother, Adeline Dunn and father, "Wild Henry" Roberts stayed for a brief time, and had little Billy in the dead of winter, December

31, 1859. The story is not completely known, but I'm sure it wasn't where they intended to be when little Billy was born. Certainly not a place for a lady nor a baby.

Buffalo Gap is a very unique town with lots of history and lots of old buildings. It's a great trip to visit and go back in time. One of my favorite places to eat there is Perini Ranch Steak House that not only host a most casual rustic atmosphere but has the best steaks in all of West Texas.

J.H. Roberts, James Henry Roberts, known as "Wild Henry," Billy's father was born in Lexington, Kentucky in 1832. His family knew the James while living in Kentucky. His father, Ben/Benjamin Roberts took his family and moved to Nacogdoches, Texas in 1835. Ben participated in the Mexican American War.

"Wild Henry" Roberts grew up in East Texas. He met his wife, Adeline Dunn, who some believe was half Indian. Her folks were from Kentucky also. Billy was born with the legal name, William Henry Roberts. It is not clear where they were living when the war broke out. The Civil War was starting in 1861 and Texas was seceding from the Union. Roberts was off to fight with the Confederacy. We don't know where Adeline and her child of three were at the time her husband enlisted under Sul Ross' brother Captain Peter F. Ross. Sul Ross enlisted in this regiment as well as Jesse's friend and commander, Captain John S. Sparks. It was incorporated into the Sixth Texas Cavalry. The enlistment took place in Waco, so we are assuming the family lived nearby. William Tunstill suggest that the Roberts lived between Hamilton and Hico, Texas. At this point, it would be 70 miles to Waco which would make sense.

Adeline was on her own from 1861-1862 with her small child. She died in 1862, some believe she died in 1863.

William Henry Roberts age 3, was taken in by Adeline's half-sister, Catherine Ann who many believed she was married to William Bonney at that time. Ola and William Tunstill said on tape that Bonney was Catherine's maiden name. Billy told Morrison in a letter near the time of his death that the name Bonney was fabricated. This seems confusing, but maybe Billy was using his aunt's name as a cover. There are those who believe Catherine was married to William McCarty which seems to hold up. Catherine goes by the name of McCarty in 1873. It gets extremely confusing with so many different stories swirling around, but we are going to stick with what Billy told Morrison and Ola, backed by what Jesse said.

Per Billy, his Aunt Catherine had come from Indian Territory. Adeline's mother was supposedly a Cherokee. Did Adeline and Catherine have the same mother? Most likely, since Adeline's maiden name was Dunn and Catherine was supposedly Bonney as William Tunstill said. It is clear to me, that Catherine and Adeline were close, for Catherine would have never been able to locate the young boy after his mother's death if they had not been. We find information that Catherine had her mother living with her and supposedly Catherine's husband, William McCarty.

There are two different scenarios. One is that Billy, his aunt, his young cousin, Joseph (Catherine's young son), his grandmother, and Mr. McCarty went to Trinidad, Colorado. This had to have been during the Civil War. Trinidad was founded in 1862 after coal was discovered and drew many immigrants to that area for mining. There are those who believe that Mr. McCarty died in 1863 during the war, such as Ola stated, dying in Chattanooga with a gunshot wound. If this was true, Catherine Ann had more on her hands than expected. Per William Tunstill and Ola, they move to Cincinnati, Indiana.

Wild Henry Roberts would leave Ross's Brigade and join the Quantrill Raiders in 1863, the same year Jesse did. They became blood brothers.

Dr. William Tunstill believed that after Cincinnati, Indiana, they went to Kansas where Catherine ran the Wichita Kansas hand laundry and received land in Kansas from the government, part of the Osage Nation's Land. She met William Antrim, a "gentleman farmer."

In Billy's statements to Ola, Billy moved back or was forced to move back with his father after the Civil War around the latter part of 1865, maybe even staying through 1867. In 1950, Billy said he first met Jessie when Jessie was severely injured. His arm was nearly shot off. Ola said that it was in 1866 and Jesse got hit in the left shoulder during a bank robbery, which would have been at Liberty. Billy says he was seven years old (December 1866/1867) and his father, Wild Henry

Roberts brought Jesse to Billy's home where his wife and children were living in East Texas. He was cared for. Billy stated that he had known Jesse for 85 years, which would make it in 1865 using the end of the Civil War as a timeline. After several weeks passed, Jesse and Billy had become close friends. Jesse made a huge impression upon Billy. "When he got well, Frank taken him away."

During this stay with his father may have been the time that Billy learned to ride a horse. "From the time I was big enough to ride, I've been in the saddle. Beginning by riding behind my father on the old Chisholm trail on cattle drives, seeing thousands of head in a single drive." [284] The Chisholm Trail started to be used in 1867.

It is not known when Billy went back to live with Catherine Ann McCarty and her mother, but he did and had a fairly good education. Billy lived with them until he was 12 years old. This would be in December 1871-1872. Billy then left to find his father.

Billy found his father in Carlton, Texas, 60 miles from Brownwood and started living with him and his new wife, Elizabeth Ferguson. He said that his father owned a lot of horses and he learned how to shoot, rope, and ride especially on the deadliest of broncs. Billy learned how to break the most stubborn horses and by the time he was 14, he perfected the art. He had grown up hard and fast and he began to realize that he needs to be paid for his work. His father didn't like that none too well, took a bullwhip and whipped him unmercifully.

"Wild Henry Roberts was the meanest son of a bitch that ever was." That statement comes directly from Jesse James himself to Mitch Graves. [285] When Ola and Jesse were talking, Jesse said, "Old man Roberts, Wild Henry, Billy's father was as mean as hell to poor Billy." [286]

Thankfully, Billy had his stepmother, Elizabeth to nurse his wounds. He would always refer to her as "Mother" in later years. It took weeks, maybe months to heal. When he was well enough to travel, in May 1874, he left on a trail drive beginning in Sulphur Springs, Texas up the Chisholm trail on his own, wanting to be as far away from his father as he could. He rode along pushing the cattle but hiding in a wagon when they went through a town or met up with the law. He had been threatened by his father if he ever left, he would have the Texas Rangers after him who he had close ties to. This made me wonder if he was in the rangers under a different name. This year was when the Frontier Battalion was organized.

Billy had continued on the cattle trail as far as Briartown in Indian Territory and he decided to quit for some reason. He was on foot and that is when he ran into a man on a horse that took him on into a ranch house. There he met the owner, Belle Reed as he called her, none other than Belle Starr. Billy stayed there, somewhat as a chore boy and used as a lookout. He met all kinds of outlaws and got well acquainted with the James boys. Apparently, they were there often.

Belle took up for Billy and trusted him. He was a witness to a lot of things. He had observed how the outlaws brought in a load of loot, threw it on the bed and Belle counting it out for each member who were part of the robbery or heist. Cowboys were on standby with their six-shooters if there was any foul play or grievances. This is what Billy described to Morrison.

"In my practice Belle discovered I was a good shot with a rifle or six-gun and offered me a job as her right-hand man. The offer I at once refused, as I told her I did not like the outlaw trail. She saw that she could not make an outlaw of me and told me when I got ready to go, I could go. At the end of three months, she gave me nice clothes and fifty dollars in money, saying "Texas Kid, any time you want to come back, you have a home with me." [287]

Belle was the one that gave Billy the alias of William H. Bonney. Was this the name of his Aunt Catherine? Was the name derived from the Confederate song, "Bonnie Blue Flag" in which was a favorite song of the Quantrill Raiders. Her fondness for Billy would be with him always as well as her music. I believe Belle's home is where Billy was introduced to music. Belle was a master at the piano and per many who knew her says there was always music surrounding her place. When Jesse was there, I'm sure he picked up his fiddle and harmonica and played right along with her.

Staying three months, Billy must have been there in the Spring/Summer of 1874, May through July or August. He said he went back to New Mexico at his aunt's house, this time in Silver City. Catherine, shown as Mrs. Catherine McCarty on the marriage license, married William Antrim in 1873 in Santa Fe, New Mexico. They had moved to Silver City because of the new mining opportunities that had erupted there; silver. While William Antrim worked in the mines, Catherine ran a boarding house. Billy worked in a hotel.

Aunt Catherine died on September 16, 1874 with consumption, tuberculosis. Billy would continue to live with William Antrim and go by the name of Henry Antrim. William Antrim worked in the mines and put Billy to work. In one book, he helped make some money by singing, playing the piano, and dancing at Morrill's opera house in Silver City. [288]

In September 1875, Billy got into some trouble in Silver City. Sheriff Harvey Whitehill arrested him twice for petty theft. The first time was theft of food. The second time he was arrested, he was only helping a friend hide property stolen from a laundry and some believe it was just a prank. He may have just gotten in with the wrong crowd. The sheriff later stated that "the young man was a likeable kid; whose stealing was a result more of necessity than criminality." [289]

While in jail, Billy escaped through a chimney. He tells Morrison that he went to Indian Territory, possibly going back to Belle's place and got in with some cattle rustlers. They beat him up quite frequently except for one man and the boss who took up for him. Billy left for Dodge City and ran into some cowboys who were going to the Black Hills in South Dakota. It was a good thing that he did as one of Billy's father's friends recognized him in the cattle town and notified Wild Henry that Billy was in Dodge. Wild Henry sent word to the law in Dodge to lock him up until he gets there. Luckily, the law picked up someone else who fit the description, enabling Billy to travel North.

Billy met up with a man by the name of Mountain Bill who took advantage of Billy and his ability to ride broncs. He would showcase Billy, taking bets from ranchers and towns to challenge him on any horse. This Mountain Bill was putting lots of money in his own pocket. He took Billy to Montana, Nebraska, Oregon, Wyoming, and Arizona. Mountain Bill put him through 4 months of training with the Cheyenne and Arapaho. This all would have occurred between 1875 through April 1877.

Brushy never stated that he had killed a man, "Cahill" in Arizona. Brushy did state that he was in Arizona in April of 1877, working at the Gila Ranch for a few months with "Mountain Bill". William Tunstill states that Billy was at Fort Grant in Arizona, tending to the horses.

Billy came back to New Mexico alone. He must have first gone back to Silver City where he knew a lot of old friends, such as Jesse Evans. He took a chance going back, but apparently the law didn't bother him. He stayed outside town just in case he was recognized. He was on his own at age 17.

A Friend in Elfego

It is learned in a book, *America – The Men and Their Guns That Made Her Great*, in Chapter Nine, that Billy as a cowpuncher met Elfego Baca who was a young whippersnapper at a roundup 12 miles northeast of Socorro at Ojo de Perida Ranch. Elfego recognized Billy as the one who sang, danced, and played the piano in Silver City. Billy made quite an impression upon Elfego.

This book was very interesting. I found it 20 years ago in a pile of books that our local school library was giving away, when they were cleaning their shelves for newer books. I picked it up one day, just wanting to know more about the guns in the old west and I found the story on Elfego Baca who had mentioned Billy the Kid. The chapter was titled, "Elfego Baca: Forgotten Fighter for Law and Order," by Lee A. Silva. Baca was not a well-known old west legend. The more I looked into his story, the more interesting and creditable it became. It helps to understand the people who knew Billy, personally, in order to understand what these characters were all about. Later we will find connections to Baca not only with Billy, but also Jesse.

Elfego Baca was born in Socorro, New Mexico. His father, Francisco Baca took his family from there into Topeka, Kansas. After Elfego's mother and two siblings died in 1872, his father sent Elfego and another brother to New Mexico to where their grandparents were running a ranch outside of Socorro. He must have been with the other cowboys during the roundup and got acquainted with

Billy. This had to be in the summer of 1877 after Billy had returned from Arizona. In the book, it stated that Billy met Elfego prior to turning outlaw. Billy worked as a "nondescript cowhand."

Some of the stories told of Baca and sometimes Baca himself stated that he was around 16 at the time he met Billy and Billy was 17, but that would not be correct as they were 5 years apart. Elfego was born in February 1865. This would have made Elfego 12 ½ years old when he met Billy who was 17. The author of the chapter we are speaking about concurs that the year had to be 1877 when they met. I'm sure Billy took a liking to him as he himself was about his age when he started learning the ropes as a cowhand.

Elfego's father Francisco joined them in New Mexico. He became the town marshal in Belen. That town was heavily influenced by a political family and soon Francisco was stepping on toes. He was accused of murder and then thrown in jail. Elfego and his friend, *Chavez* helped break him out of jail and his father fled to Mexico for seven years.

Elfego was being influenced by many men and friends along the way. Was Chavez the same friend of Billy's? Jose Chavez? We don't know. We don't have the dates. In 1877, Jose Chavez was a constable and justice of the peace of San Patricio in Lincoln County, New Mexico. He became a founding member of McSween's Regulators in the spring of 1878 along with Billy the Kid. That's a whole 'nother story.

In the book about Baca, we learn that Elfego and Billy bonded and became great friends. Baca always credited Billy for teaching him how to be lightning fast with a gun. He told the stories of Billy being one with his gun, being able to pull it out when needed, whether it would be from his holster or under his derby hat as Baca described. Baca would tell his nephew that Billy was not a gunfighter at all. He was too nervous and anxious to use his gun, but he could use it when needed and his quickness kept him alive.

It is unbelievable how God's timing is perfect. In 2023, Dan Edwards, the author of "Billy The Kid – An Autobiography," did extensive research on a photo sent to him that identified a young man as Billy the Kid in Silver City. A NYPD detective who is a forensic facial recognition expert, analyzed the photo, not knowing who the photo was of and compared it to photos of Brushy Bill at different stages of his life and the famous photo of Billy the Kid. Dan never told the detective who the men were. In every instance, the detective ran several tests and software comparisons and was positive that they were all the same man.

In the YouTube video titled, "Billy the Kid: The Silver City Photo" with Emilio Estevez and original music by Tim Montana, 2023 it goes into great detail on the hows, whys, and whos. It was amazing. In the photo, Billy is wearing a nice suit with vest and a derby hat. This attire was spoken of in books regarding the rumble with Cahill in Arizona, when he made fun of Billy and his outfit and nearly beat him to death. The way Billy was dressed was also described by people who had seen Billy when he returned to Silver City. This photo is believed to be about the time that Elfego and Billy became good friends, August 1877. At this point in Billy's life, he was teetering on a precipice between getting his life together, or following a trail leading to trouble.

Elfego and Billy would go on several adventures as Billy was teaching him how to shoot. One time, they rode a railroad section cart all the way up the rail to Albuquerque. While resting on the way, they saw a policeman shoot a man in the back, who later claimed that it was self-defense. "The injustice of the act planted a seed inside Elfego that began to ferment into a lifelong desire to see that justice was done whenever it was needed." [290]

Elfego and Billy both adopted this philosophy, but it was mingled with trouble. Elfego, in his obituary in *The Capital Journal, out of Salem, Oregon, August 28, 1945 –"Old Frontier Gun-Fighter Dies in New Mexico Home"* lists that he was a cowboy, sheriff, lawyer, tried three times for murder, and once for conspiracy against the U.S. government. Another article in newmexicomagazine.org, states that Baca was a store clerk, a Deputy U.S. Marshal, county clerk, Mayor of Socorro, county school superintendent, an assistant district attorney, a District Attorney for Socorro County, a special agent for a cattlemen's association, a miner, bouncer, private detective, a publisher and editor, and a restaurant operator. When he was 19, in the village of Frisco, New Mexico which is now called Reserve, he disarmed an unruly cowboy from Texas who him and his followers were viciously oppressing the Hispanic population. One of their victims was castrated in a saloon.

Since Elfego was Hispanic, he took matters into his hands, not being satisfied with the justice in that town. Baca single-handedly stood off 80 of this cowboy's angry friends while barricaded in an old adobe house with a thatch roof. Over 4,000 bullets riddled the walls and items inside, including silverware. The next morning, as bullets were flying, they found him making tortillas on the grill inside. Somehow, someway, Baca did not get one scrape of a bullet, but he handed out a few for the mob. The cowboys finally backed off. He was bound to be a lawman for sure.

He later got to know Texas Ranger James B. Gillett through his uncle, Judge Joe Baca. Apparently, he learned a lot from all these influences.

In 1910, when the revolutionaries began to rise against the dictator, Porfirio Diaz in Mexico, Elfego became Colonel Pancho Villa's American agent for purchasing arms and supplies. They became friends exchanging jewels, gold, and money for weapons. They had a falling out and later became bitter enemies. It was learned that Pancho Villa was a cattleman, who stole livestock and sold them for a huge profit. Both Jesse and Billy the Kid were also tied in with Pancho Villa as we will learn later.

I truly believe that a lot of Billy rubbed off on Elfego. "In the telling of his (Baca) story, let it be said that there was never much very normal about the life of Elfego Baca. He was impulsive and hotheaded, and he attacked life as if it were a rampaging bull charging at him, yet when he was not aroused, he was disarmingly mild mannered and gentle. Things were either black or white to Elfego Baca. There were no gray areas with which to wrestle. The direct, simple way was always his way. His most important rule of life was that when trouble is looking for you, you don't wait for it, you go find it and finish it." [291] Sounds like the author is speaking of Billy. They were two of a kind.

Surprisingly, I was briefly looking through the book, "Jesse James Was One of His Names" and Elfego Baca was mentioned as being amongst many who visited the Pigeon Ranch in Glorieta Pass, where one of the famous battles played out between the Union and Confederates. This was along the Santa Fe Trail, approximately 30 miles southeast of Santa Fe. From 1865 until 1887, George Hebert owned the ranch. By 1880, the Atchison, Topeka & Santa Fe Railroad ran their trains through Glorieta Pass. Jesse owned a lot of stock in the railroad companies as well as the KGC. He had his eye on Glorietta Pass. In Howk's listing of treasure sights, he listed "Confederate Army Paymaster Cache (Glorieta, chest)." [292]

By 1887, Walter M. Taber bought the Pigeon Ranch from Hebert. It was at this time of the purchase that the ranch was a wild place of gamblers and tough characters. Howk would tell Del Schrader that Jesse kept the Pigeon Ranch in the early 1900s. The ranch house was used as one of the meeting places for the Confederate Underground. Those who met there were mentioned using alias', revealed as Jesse R. James, Cole Younger, Jefferson Davis, Butch Cassidy, Sundance Kid, Pancho Villa, Bill Roberts (Billy the Kid), Dr. Frank James, Bob Dalton, Kit Carson, and *El Fago Baca*.

By 1906 the ranch house would be greatly in need of repair. The ranch was sold in 1926 to Thomas Greer, a Pecos Valley cowboy. In the book, "Jesse James Was One of His Names", it states that the Green family took it over, but I believe it was actually the Greer family as documented in "Pigeon's Ranch, New Mexico" – https://www.legendsofamerica.com/piegeons-ranch/.

(Pigeon Ranch, 1880, by Ben Wittick)

Even a newspaper photo that was very low quality was in Del Schrader's book including a descriptive typed entry of a reunion in Harris County, Texas in 1931, identifying the men as Elfego Baca, Pawnee Bill, Kit Carson III, Jesse James III (Howk), Captain Roy Aldrich (Texas Ranger beginning in 1915) and DeWitt Travis. It also appears that Al Jennings was there also as you can identify him easily. I'm not convinced that DeWitt Travis was in the picture. I believe the one identified as Dewitt is actually Chris Masden. There are people dressed in Indian garments with colorful feathers and beadwork in which we learn were descendants of famous Indian Chiefs and warriors.

After careful search, the only reunion that this could be was the one held in Houston in November 1937, not 1931. It was called the Old Timers annual convention or the National Frontiersmen's Association annual convention. It was a fairly new organization in 1937. This association filed as a domestic Nonprofit Corporation in the State of Texas on Nov. 6, 1937. Jesse had severely broken his leg 6 months earlier, so I don't believe he was there, but Howk said, he himself was there.????

Newspaper articles mentions attendees as Elfego Baca, Al Jennings, Colonel E. D. Nix (Evett Dumas Nix) and Chris Madsen, both U.S. Marshals of Indian Territory and both serving around the time that Brushy Bill says he was a deputy marshal in I.T. Chris Madsen is described as being in the 5th Cavalry during 1876 for 15 years.. He was in the 5th the same time Jesse said he was. Madsen was a deputy marshal in Indian Territory beginning in 1891, bringing down the Doolin and Dalton Gang. He also joined Teddy Roosevelt's Rough Riders, same as Brushy.

Baldwin Parker, son of Quanah Parker was also there at the convention. There were approximately 50 members attending. In that same page of the newspaper, Ben Harbert from Taos, New Mexico stated that he was a businessman and he saw the young desperado (Billy the Kid) on the streets of Taos. He had known Billy earlier and was convinced he was still alive. [293] We find Mr. Harbert continued his pursuit in trying to find out the truth about Billy the Kid by going to Elfego's office in Albuquerque in the summer of 1938 with Pawnee Bill, Rev. J.W.E. Airey, president of the National Frontiersmen's Association, and Eddie Botsford. "They want to verify the Kid's death for the records of the association. Some have reported The Kid was still alive." [294] Elfego Baca received the men well in his office but was firm in the decision that Billy the Kid was killed by Garrett in 1881 and he knew two of the pallbearers. In my opinion, it was a cover for his friend.

At this convention in 1937, they honored May Lillie, the only woman who ever outshot Annie Oakley. She was the wife of Pawnee Bill. She died from injuries in a car accident in Taos, September 17, 1936.

So, with this information, it appears that Elfego knew Billy the Kid very well as well as others who were in the association. It also brings out that Howk was there at the convention since he had given the picture to Del Schrader and said that was him in the picture, but at the time of the convention he wasn't identifying himself as Jesse James III. At that time in 1937, Jesse was back in Gladewater with a broken leg, the time that Brushy Bill said that he took care of Jesse. It doesn't make sense why Howk was there at the reunion. He barely was acquainted with Jesse.

Interesting note: After Elfego's death in 1945, Disney picked up his story and used it in the TV series, "The Nine Lives of Elfego Baca" and it later became a movie.

A strange event occurred in 1972. The major source of information on Elfego Baca's life that was archived in the library of the University of New Mexico had disappeared. Was it stolen or misplaced? What was there to hide? Possibly something the family or someone didn't want out in public. A clue as to Billy's death or other mysteries that has been hidden from us? We don't know.

The story about Elfego and Billy, as well as Jesse, describe active and hardy men. They didn't sit still. It's amazing to me how Jesse, Billy, and Elfego didn't miss an opportunity to get in the fight, and most certainly, finished it.

Billy's Hardest Fight

Sometime after August 1877, we learn that Billy fell in with some fellows that made him feel like family. They took him down the wrong trail. Brushy Bill stated that him and Jesse Evans went down to Old Mexico quite a bit, his old friend from Silver City. They had a hideout at their compadre, Mel Segura's uncle's ranch in Chihuahua. During that year, they broke a friend out of jail in Mexico. Billy then traveled to Mesilla, New Mexico and met some friends there, one of them being Tom O'Keefe. Mesilla was a solid and secure base for Brushy/Billy and the men who he was involved with.

Tom O'Keefe and Billy traveled through the Guadalupe Mountains, the highest peak in Texas, 8,751 feet. This is the same area that Marcy traveled back in the 1840's. In 1958, American Airlines erected a steel pyramid on the highest point of the Guadalupes to honor the Butterfield Overland Mail trail that passed through south of the peak. The three sides of the pyramid represent the AA logo, the Boys Scout logo, and a tribute to the Pony Express Riders by the U.S. Postal Service. Its prominent position on top of the peak has a commanding presence and appears to represent a **zenith** of progress and power.

While in the Guadalupe Mountains, Billy and O'Keefe were attacked by Apaches. They got separated and they both had to find a way to survive. Billy had lost his horse and his boots, so his feet were cut and gouged by the rough terrain. He made it to a home on Seven Rivers which happened to be the Jones family who nursed him back to health. Later he would learn his new friends, the Jones' brothers were with the Seven Rivers Warriors gang.

The Seven Rivers Warriors gang were men made up of small disgruntled ranchers who felt victimized by the large cattle holdings of John Chisum. They sided with the Santa Fe ring's front men, Murphy and Dolan thinking they were backing the little guy, but instead, they found out later, they were backing a much bigger monster. They had the backing of corrupt politicians, businessmen, including lawmen such as Deputy US Marshal Bob Olinger and Texas Ranger Lon Oden.

Earlier in 1876, before Billy joined up with them, the Seven Rivers Warriors gang joined Jesse Evans, a friend of Billy's back in Silver City. Jesse Evan's and "The Boys" were rustlers and killers. They rustled cattle from Chisum. It was during this time, April 1876, that Evans rounded up 50 hard-hearted men who were good with their irons to join him on a cattle drive. They were headed to the Pecos Valley and would be driving 20,000 head of cattle to Dodge City. Billy was not with them at the time.

(Steel Pyramid erected on the highest point of the Guadalupes. Attribution (CC By 2.0) https://creativecomons.org/licenses/by/2.0/– Looking up the summit marker, Guadalupe Peak Trail @ Guadalup Mountains Nation Park, Texas, creator, daveynin – flickr; 2012 – no changes made)

It was a well thought out plan by Robert Hunter and Jesse Evans. Chisum had a lot of enemies in New Mexico and Texas. While Chisum was in Texas from Cooke County, Brown and Coleman County, down to the Concho River, he gathered cattle of his own as well as other rancher's, with a promissory signed note, giving him power of attorney over the cattlemen's herds in exchange for him to be in charge of fattening the cattle on New Mexico's grasslands, taking care of all the legal formalities, and selling them in the Denver market for miners, various forts, and other ranchers. This entire process would take up to two years. Chisum promised them big money in return. Between the two of them, they had a copy of the note. Chisum's way of doing business was known as "a mouth full of gimme and a handful of much obliged." [295]

After several years, they got no money. Tom Catron who was a lawyer, representing the Texans, filed a lawsuit against Chisum, but with the notes, the case was dismissed. Catron and the Texans were made to look like fools, with Chisum laughing all the way to the bank.

Robert Hunter devised a plan to make Chisum have a taste of his own medicine. He would handle negotiations with Chisum to purchase the cattle. Hunter went to Texas and bought all the notes from the ranchers that he could find, who had seen no money from Chisum. It was all in his pocket. Hunter paid a nickel for every dollar that was promised to the ranchers. He then contacted the lawyer, Catron and began to work out the sting. They included Hunter's friend, Jesse Evans, the small young man who could handle the toughest and raunchiest bunch of cattle and men on the prairie. Evans would stay in the background.

John Chisum was sitting on his "high horse" with cattle on his range who were yearlings during the fear and panic of 1873 when most cattlemen, such as the Horrell's were selling off their herds. Chisum had agents all around Texas to buy out the herds or give the rancher's promissory notes for future sale. After three years of good grazing and the cattle prices were at an all-time high, Chisum was eager to sell.

Hunter and Catron went to Chisum's Ranch and made an agreement for 15,000 head of cattle. Hunter made sure that only the cattle with the brands of the Texans were in the sale. Chisum, with his lawyer present, made out the Bill of Sale and gave it to Hunter and then Hunter in return handed

Chisum a black satchel. As Chisum opened the bag, his mouth dropped. It was full of all his promissory notes with his signature. Chisum's lawyer said it was all legal. Karma came back to bite him.

The Big Bend was a haven for unclaimed cattle and for outlaws who wished to take them off the hand of the drovers. Jesse Evans and Dave Rudabaugh, friends and comrades of Billy the Kid, rustled cattle there and hid out in Fort Stockton. Rustling was extremely prevalent in this region. There were many unbranded longhorns roaming in this area as well as the ones with brands that could be altered.

In the Fall of 1876-1877 is when the Pecos War in Lincoln County, New Mexico flared up. The Seven Rivers gang was able to block Chisum's expansion of land along the Pecos River for his cattle. The small ranchers had once occupied that land as well as the native Apache. The small ranchers won, but at a cost. This led to the Lincoln County War.

So, after the Pecos War ended, we find Billy taken in by the Jones family after his narrow escape with the Apaches and this is where he met Jim and John Jones who were working for Chisum. Billy went along with them to work. That fall, 1877 the Jones brothers and Billy made a cattle run up the Goodnight/Loving trail. The route they took would go in reverse from what Charles Goodnight had originally used it for to go from Fort Belknap (Newcastle/Graham) in Texas to Fort Sumner (Bosque Redondo where the Navajo and Mescalero Apache were forced to live in the reservation until 1868) in New Mexico.

Billy and the Jones started from southeastern New Mexico, near the Seven Rivers Ranch, south of Artesia, along the Pecos River, up the old Butterfield trail, through Fort Concho, Buffalo Gap (where Brushy Bill said he was born) and it is more likely they went to hook up on the Great Western Trail to Fort Griffin (outside of Albany). From other sources, they may have joined the Great Western Trail at Eden, Texas, just south of present-day Paint Rock near Chisum's string of cow camps along the Concho River. Chisum had established a ranch on the Concho near its confluence with the Colorado River in 1862-1863. [296]

There is evidence that Billy the Kid, Dave Rudabaugh, and Pat Garrett stopped at Fort Griffin. [297] Doc Holliday and Wyatt Earp met for the first time there, the same time Billy was there in 1877-1878. Bat Masterson was there also. Fort Griffin was situated on a plateau, a perfect spot to overlook the countryside and to observe the meandering Clear Fork of the Brazos down below. Many soldiers were stationed there, drawing many settlers in for protection, but as it began to expand, the protection was not so much from the Indians, but from the "Flats" below.

Fort Griffin not only drew in all types of families to this location, it also drew in the undesirable. Almost immediately after the fort was completed, a new settlement began at the bottom of the hill, first called "The Bottom", The Flat", "Hidetown", and gradually received the name, "Babylon of the Brazos." It was a place for buffalo hunters and cowboys to come through and live it up a little before hitting the dusty trail again. It was also a major supply center for the buffalo hunters.

This Wild West Shantytown naturally attracted horse thieves, cattle rustlers, fugitives from justice, highwaymen, swindlers, gunfighters, and gamblers enabling them to mingle with the population and secure supplies between rendezvous. It was the wildest, most violent, meanest place, surpassing the wicked communities of Dodge City, Deadwood, and Tascosa.

The Great Western Trail that took many drovers through the area on up to Dodge City was first used in 1874 and by 1879, it was the most traveled cattle trail in U.S. history. From South Texas, it went to the Llano River, the San Saba River, and Brady Creek west of Brady. There were feeder trails from Mason, San Saba, and Lampasas. It traveled through Coleman where a feeder trail came from Trickham, Texas, the area where Chisum had his store and in the area of one of his ranches.

One of the first stone built dipping vats for cattle was located along the Great Western Trail on the Hashknife Ranch, located 35 miles north of Fort Griffin. Fifteen more miles to the north, the trail meets the Salt Fork of the Brazos River out of Seymour, Texas. It was a favorite camping spot for the cowboys and a favorite locale for buffalo hunting. The writer was incredibly blessed to live right on the trail for many years and found several artifacts and remnants of the old western trail.

Doan's Crossing in Wilbarger County near Vernon, Texas was another popular spot for the drovers on the trail. It would be the last supply post to stop at before entering Indian Territory.

The cattle trails held many adventures and dangers but were very important during the 1870's and beyond. They were indeed the road to wealth if you could survive. They would also be used for KGC activities such as burial sites of caches per Bud and various sources.

Very good evidence of the trail drive that Billy was on, is the picture taken after the run in Dodge City. When Brushy Bill was being interviewed, Brushy told Morrison about the photo. William V. Morrison was able to verify who and where the man was who held the original tin type photo. Morrison and Brushy Bill visited Sam and Bill Jones in the home of Sam's daughter in Carlsbad, New Mexico in 1950. They were the brothers of Jim and John Jones. Sam brought out the photo that Brushy Bill had told Morrison about and Sam identified the men as Bob Speaks, Chisum's trail boss, Jim Jones, John Jones, and Billy the Kid. Some believe that instead of the presumed Billy on the far right in the back, it was actually Deputy Marion Turner who was indicted with John Jones for the murder of Alexander McSween. The photo is in New Mexico State University Library Archives and is titled Marion Turner, Jim Jones, John Jones, and Bob Speaks, but there is a possibility that the men were misidentified.

Author/Historian, Eve Ball is the one that claimed it was Marion Turner, saying that she was given this picture by the family, but Marion Turner would be in his forties at the time the photo was taken in 1877. This man was a young man between the ages of 18-25. The identities of these men may still be questionable as I find no other source to verify who they were except for Brushy's statement. I tend to believe him. Why would you go to a home where the people knew Billy the Kid if you were a fraud? Brushy described the photo to Morrison in great detail.

Brett Hall brought this information out in his video on YouTube, "Brushy Bill Roberts in His Own Words: The Lincoln County War & Debunking The Saga Of Billy The Kid." The trail drive was described by a man who knew Billy, Charles Frederick Rudulph in the book, "Los Bilitos: The Story of Billy the Kid and His Gang," by Louis Leon Branch. Charles Rudulph was a member of the posse that captured Billy the Kid in 1880. He wrote about Billy working for a short time for Chisum and about the cattle drive that Billy was on with the two Jones brothers and Bob Speaks.

A most interesting find in my father's bookcase was the first edition book of "Maurice G. Fulton's History of the Lincoln County War;" edited by Robert N. Mullin, published 1968. An excerpt in the front of the book reads, "Colonel Maurice Garland Fulton over a period of years acquired a remarkable collection of interviews, photographs, maps, documents, and other source materials which established him as the foremost authority on Lincoln County, New Mexico." He was unable to complete his meticulous manuscript, but Mullin was able to fulfill his promise to his friend to edit and skillfully preserve what Fulton had gathered. The new edition printed in 2008 has the picture mentioned above on the cover.

Billy left Chisum and went to work for Julian Maxwell at Bosque Redondo (Fort Sumner) for a short time, then stayed at Frank Coes' place. Billy ran into Jesse Evans, his old buddy from his childhood and from earlier rustling days. Evans was working at the Seven Rivers Ranch. They went to Murphy's cow camp and worked with them in the winter and stole Chisum cattle. The saga would continue between the two ranches, both stealing each other's livestock, horses and cattle.

Billy had a falling out with Evans and began to see what kind of men they really were, so on a last drive of cattle where they were picking up more than they started with, Billy left "The Boys" and was hired back by John Chisum once again. Billy could see what was happening. John Chisum teamed up with John Tunstall and Alexander McSween. When Billy wandered upon Tunstall's ranch, needing a bite to eat, Tunstall welcomed him and put him to work. Billy worked for John Tunstall and began to be drawn into a war between good and bad. Billy loved Mr. Tunstall, like a father he always longed for.

(Men on the Dodge City trail drive in 1877. Per Sam Jones, these men are identified L-R as Jim Jones, Bob Speaks (Chisum's trail boss), John Jones, and Billy the Kid (far right standing in the back))

Murphy and Dolan and all the men behind them, including the Santa Fe Ring tried to destroy Tunstall because of his success in his land holdings, his ranch, his livestock, and most especially his mercantile business in Lincoln, placing competition against their monopoly. They murdered Tunstall, igniting an explosion in Billy. He was out for justice and this is when Billy and others formed the Regulators to seek those who were involved in the murder and take on the Santa Fe Ring. The rest is history.

If the reader doesn't truly know the history of Billy the Kid, especially the younger generation, I'm going to step aside and allow the more qualified authors to tell the rest of the story from the point of view from Brushy Bill Roberts in books written by Dan Edwards, Brett Hall, W.C. Jameson, Frederic Bean, C. L. Sonnichsen, William V. Morrison, William Tunstill, Judge Bob E. Hefner, Dr. Jannay P. Valdez, and the videos mentioned.

You can read the other renditions from other authors and you will see a different take on the story who paint Billy as a vicious killer and outlaw. It's a true western tale, some true, some not. Sometimes you have to read between the lines. Many say Sheriff Pat Garrett, who was a friend of

Billy's, and who was hired by Chisum, killed Billy in Fort Sumner with several witnesses who can back the statement up on July 14, 1881.

Ola Everhard was very firm when she told Dr. William Tunstill that she had a very good friend who was a good friend of Pat Garrett's daughter, Elizabeth in Roswell who was blind and taught piano. "My Daddy never killed Billy the Kid; they were good friends." Ola had a letter from Garrett's daughter stating the fact. Jesse said Billy wasn't in that grave in Fort Sumner.

But there is more of a detailed rendition of the story told by Brushy Bill Roberts himself, stating that he, Billy the Kid was there that night in Fort Sumner, but wasn't the one shot and killed. He escaped from the scene and as he was running, a bullet creased his scalp in which was still visible when Morrison examined his bullet riddled body.

There were 26 scars from bullet and knife wounds, matching those documented that Billy the Kid had incurred on Brushy Bill himself. One bullet was still lodged in his calf muscle. A statement Brushy made to Morrison written in the book, "Billy The Kid, An Autobiography," by Dan Edwards, emphasizes his quickness with the gun. "I emptied this one in a fight once," he explained, patting his left hip, "and had to draw the right one. I wasn't as fast with my right hand as I was with the left. I could fire the pistol with both hands. I fired the Winchester and both pistols from the hip. My left hand was never hit because the man never lived who could beat me to the draw with the left. I wore my pistols in the scabbard with the butts toward the back. I fanned the hammer at times. I have been ambidextrous all my live, but I am left-handed naturally." [298]

Billy said that Garrett actually shot his partner, Billy Barlow that night. The name "Billy Barlow" was a common name many cowboys used to hide their true identity during those years when working for an outfit. This was verified when I was researching my great uncle, the outlaw, John Wesley Haskew. His sons worked for F. D Hendrix who started the Hook Nine Ranch in 1890. It was located to the northwest of Ardmore, Oklahoma near Hog Creek, close to where Ola Everhard's mother, Bertha lived. The ranch spread just below the Arbuckle Mountains into the area called the Eph James' pasture. On that ranch, there were several Billy Barlows working with the Haskew brothers. This was a common name used when you didn't want anyone to know your business. Its been stated in many non-fiction western books.

Brushy said he ran out into the yard when he heard the shots, and through the gate, men were shooting at shadows. He was hit in the lower jaw, shoulder, and then across his head. He lost consciousness on the run and found himself in a lady's home who was caring for him. This is when Celsa, his lady friend came and told him what happened. As soon as he was well, he fled to Mexico.

Brushy gave Morrison details on his escape and also how he could escape any kind of handcuffs with his small hands and large wrists.

On the episode of Unsolved Mysteries by Robert Stack; Season 1, Episode 20 found on youtube.com they introduce the mystery about Brushy Bill Roberts and William Tunstill speaks in that episode. It's worth your while to view it.

Who was Billy? Was he really an outlaw? He didn't think so. Let's look at Billy's description of those who knew him and encountered him.

In the book, "Wranglin' the Past," by Frank M. King, 1946, he states he was living in the days of Billy and had seen him and Dave Rudabaugh together. He wrote, "Billy the Kid was a small, light complexioned young feller of rather prepossessing appearance. He dressed immaculately when in town from his raids, attended dances, gambled, and had a general good time. He was always smiling and goodnatured, and was always polite and courteous to the ladies, among whom he was a great favorite." [299] His personality was enormous.

"There had been hundreds of stories written about Billy the Kid, but most of them so highly colored that they seem devoid of facts. I know many of the incidents of the Kid's operations, and personally was acquainted with many of the participants on both sides of the war. During the years I rode the ranges of Lincoln County, I met and talked with many who had taken part in the Lincoln County War, and heard many versions on both sides."

In a short sentence, with no explanation following, Frank King wrote, "Billy was just a gunfighter hired by John Chisum." [300]

In "Billy the Kid, A Short and Violent Life," by Robert M. Utley, 1989, the author implied that "Chisum did not promise Billy wages for his service as a McSween gunman, nevertheless, Billy blamed Chisum for all his troubles." [301] In "Billy The Kid, An Autobiography," by Daniel A. Edwards, Brushy Bill tells Morrison, "I tried to get him (Chisum) to pay us. I told him the quickest way he could do it was too slow. I had my six-shooter in his ribs, and I don' know why I didn't put him in a six-foot grave. From then on **Old John** was our bitterest enemy."

"The country was full of bad men in those days. We were not by ourselves. The only difference was they had the law and the politicians on their side. The law was just as crooked as the rest of us." [302]

After the burning and killing at the McSween home by the Dolan/Murphy/Seven Rivers cowboys, in July 1878, Billy managed to escape and became a fugitive. With not much support or pay by Chisum, Billy took a notion to follow a Chisum herd up to the panhandle of Texas in 1878. He wasn't a part of the drovers, but took four men of his own, and stole some cattle from Chisum in exchange for what was owed to Billy and approximately 125 horses to sell to the panhandle ranchers. They followed behind the Chisum drovers so it would appear all was legit. They stopped in the beautiful Canadian Valley near Tascosa.

Billy made a lot of friends in Tascosa and one became extremely important to him, a young physician entering the West, Dr. Henry Hoyt. Per Utley's book, we learn more about Billy. Frenchie McCormick, said about Billy, "he was the best natured kid and had the most pleasant smile I most ever saw in a young man." [303]

Utley also captured what Hoyt said. "Billy was an expert at most Western sports, with the exception of drinking." [304] Billy did not indulge in that. "He was a handsome youth with smooth face, wavy brown hair, an athletic and symmetrical figure, and clear blue eyes that could look one through and through. Unless angry, he always seemed to have a pleasant expression with a ready smile. His head was well shaped, his feature regular, his nose aquiline (like an eagle), his most noticeable characteristic a slight projection of his two upper front teeth. He spoke Spanish like a native, and although only a beardless boy, was nevertheless a natural leader of men." [305]

We have a magnificent rendition of the frontier doc, Henry F. Hoyt meeting both Billy the Kid and Jesse James, seated at a table in the Old Adobe Hotel outside of Las Vegas, New Mexico near the hot springs. It happened in late July 1879. *The Las Vegas Optic*, December 8, 1879 describes "Jesse James visits at the Las Vegas Hot Springs from July 26th – 29th."

Dr. Hoyt started his doctoring career in Deadwood in 1877 and then eventually moved to the gold fields in the Black Hills. He then moved to Ft. Sumner and his first patient was William Maxwell, son of Lucien Maxwell. The boy was suffering from malignant smallpox and he could not be saved.

He traveled further south in John Chisum's country and was advised by Chisum to go to the Texas Panhandle. There was a need for a doc there. This is how he got to Tascosa. Hoyt also worked on the side as a cowboy for the LX Ranch. In the Fall of 1878 is when he met Billy in Tascosa.

In Las Vegas, he knew Billy the Kid from their old friendship back in Tascosa and saw him sitting at the table with other men. Dr. Hoyt had gotten into some gambling issues with the game of Faro and had to work his way out of it by bartending at the hotel.

Dr. Hoyt went up to Billy and struck a great conversation with him. Billy introduced one of the men as Mr. Howard from Tennessee. Just as he described Billy meticulously, Dr. Hoyt described Mr. Howard in great detail. "Mr. Howard had noticeable characteristics. He had piercing steely blue eyes with a peculiar blink, and the tip of a finger on his left hand was missing. I mentally classed him as a railroad man. He proved to be congenial, was a good talker, had evidently traveled quite a bit, and the meal passed pleasantly. After dinner we separated and Billy, taking me to his room, gave me, after pledging me to secrecy, one of the surprises of my life. Mr. Howard was no other man than the bandit and train robber, Jesse James. I was skeptical, but Billy soon convinced me it was true." [306]

Hoyt revealed that Jesse had made Billy an offer to join up with him on bank and train robberies, but Billy wanted to continue to be into cattle rustling and horse stealing. I feel sure they were in something else together.

The story was also collaborated with Miguel Antonio Otero, the son of a wealthy merchant and would later become the governor of the New Mexico Territory. In the news article, "Old Memoirs Say Jesse James Paid NM a Visit," (*El Paso Times* – August 16, 1992), it relates the story. Otero was a frequent visitor at the Las Vegas hotel and knew the Moores who ran it. Otero stated that Scott Moore was a boyhood chum of the James brothers back in Missouri. Jesse found the hotel as a safe haven. Jesse, along with his comrades were there quite often.

Otero describes Jesse as "In appearance and dress, the man I saw was far from suggesting a noted desperado. He was of medium height, his eyes were blue and rather severe, and he wore a Prince Albert coat. His manner was pleasant, though noticeably quiet and reserved. And his demeanor was so gentlemanly that I found myself liking him immensely."

On August 28, 1881, Jesse James checked into the St. James Hotel in Cimarron, New Mexico, just a month after Billy was supposedly killed, and registered under the name of R.H. Howard. In the hotel registry, his residence was shown as living in Cimarron. If you remember, Jesse supposedly had a ranch in Cimarron and had Clay Allison as a wrangler early on, but by 1881, Clay had gone back to Texas. Many believe the man who called himself Dave Crowden and preferred a certain room at the St. James; room #5, was also Jesse James. He attempted to buy a ranch on the Rayado River, south of Cimarron, close to the area where Albert Pike traveled and where Lucien Maxwell and Kit Carson established the settlement of Rayado. There is an excellent vintage map of this area titled "Sectional Map of Colfax and Mora Counties, New Mexico" printed in 1889 and reproduced on https://tedsvintageart.com.

(JJ's room at the St. James Hotel)

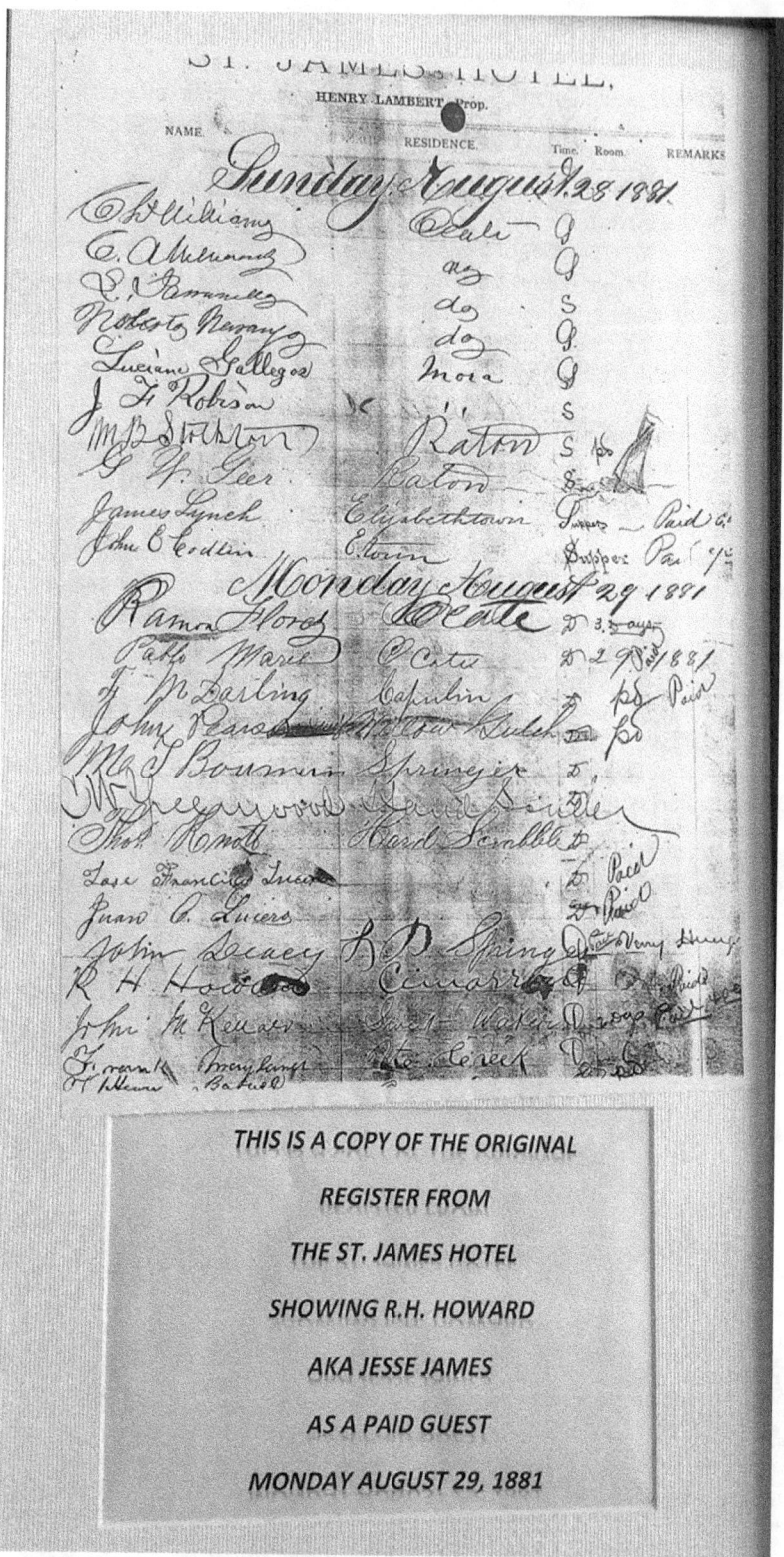

(The hotel registry at the St. James Hotel in Cimarron, New Mexico with Mr. Howard's signature)

He Lives

In 1926, Leland V. Gardiner of Santa Fe believed Billy was still alive. In an interview with the El Paso Herald Post, dated June 23, 1923, he stated, "I am told that he is on an isolated ranch within 500 miles of El Paso." "One thing that leads me to believe the Kid still lives, from what I have read, there was a big standing reward for Billie the Kid, and Sheriff Pat Garrett did not collect the reward after he was supposed to have killed the Kid at Socorro." "The Kid was not an outlaw by choice. The first killing he committed was forced upon him, and after that he was forced to kill in self-defense."

We have another witness that Billy was alive, James C. (Jim) Herron (1865-1949).

Jim Herron was born in Ellis County, Texas near Waxahachie. His father was one of the early cattlemen of Texas. In 1879, his father moved a herd to Coleman County, near Santa Anna mountain, west of *Brownwood* and put his son, Jim to work taking care of the cattle along with his cousins. He was only 13 at the time. He watched many cattle; longhorns especially being run from the Trickham feeder trail to connect to the Great Western Trail in Coleman County which indicates they were close to the Chisum ranch. It sounds like the boys stayed there through the summer and winter. The next year, in the Spring of 1880, he was ready for the thrill of a cattle drive up north. Jim and his cousins went into a camp of cowboys who were pushing cattle up to the Black Hills. The trail boss was Mr. Quinlan. The man gave that young boy a chance and Jim started on his first trail drive at age 14.

Everything was going well until they reached the Wichita River north of Seymour along the Great Western Trail. Quinlan went ahead to scout the area near the river, but when he did not come back with his drenched, lame horse, men took out to see if there was trouble. The river was mighty high at that time and for two days, men searched for Quinlan. When the water began to subside, they found Quinlan lying dead on a sandbar three miles down the river. It appeared that he had drowned. He was buried on a knoll, one hundred yards south of the river. It was a shock for his young drovers and those who had hit the trail with him many times.

Jim Herron loved the land he saw and the money he could make with cattle. He settled in the barren land of the territory called, "No Man's Land." He became the first sheriff of this Cimarron Territory in the Oklahoma Panhandle and at the same time he became a Deputy U.S. Marshal in the "Strip" under Marshal Chris Madsen who we spoke of earlier in the Frontiersmen Association. This was a favorite place for outlaws to roam.

As several lawmen did in those days, such as my 2nd great granduncle, who also settled in No Man's Land after his trouble, Herron found himself involved in cattle rustling and horse stealing. He claimed his innocence but was convicted of his crime in Kansas in 1893. He fled and began the trail of the old "hoot owl trail."

Herron worked with Billy the Kid after this time, purchasing or "acquiring" cattle in Mexico and selling them in the states, basically in Arizona, New Mexico and Texas. One place that they took the cattle to was Wilcox, Arizona from Mexico. This occurred after Billy supposedly was dead. They both had a hefty price on their head and took care of each other and their identity.

This may have been the time Herron was taking cattle herds out of Mexico and was dealing with Pancho Villa for safe passage for the sum of $5 in gold per head to drive the cattle out of Mexico.

How do we know this story? It is out of *Fifty Years on the Owl Hoot Trail - Jim Herron*, by Harry E. Chrisman, 1969, but also embellished by a wonderful video by Brett Hall, "Melton F. Hailey Interview with Dr. Jannay Valdez on Billy the Kid/Brushy Bill" on YouTube.com.

Dr. Janay Valdez interviewed Melton Hailey in Ft. Sumner, New Mexico where Billy was supposed to have been killed by Pat Garrett. Mr. Hailey was married to Jim Herron's granddaughter, Emma Frost. Melton knew Jim Herron and spoke with him many times when he had a ranch in Superior, Arizona. Jim told Melton and all his family, stories regarding his partnership with Billy. The book mentioned above, protected Billy's name and his association with Jim Herron because of their loyalty to one another.

Jim had quite a story and would always ensure that his family knew that Billy was not killed in 1881, that Billy was Brushy Bill, born in Buffalo Gap, and that he was not a criminal, but a victim of circumstance.

Melton Hailey was born in Dalhart, Texas in 1928, just south of No Man's Land. He was born the same year and lived in the same town as my mother. Hailey moved to Fort Sumner and worked in underground mining. He believes as well as many Oldtimers in Fort Sumner, that Billy the Kid was not killed in 1881 and is not buried in Fort Sumner. He said that New Mexico and the town hold on to this story as a "commercial deal" to make money. "If they told the truth, why didn't they dig him up?" It's never been attempted or allowed.

As we finish this chapter, not the complete story of Billy, we go to the article in the New Mexico Magazine published in April **1933** titled, "The Amigo of 'Billy the Kid', "The Man Who Fought Side by Side With Lincoln County's Outlaw Character Tells About the Days of 'Judge Colt's Rule'," by Wilber Smith, highlighted on the Roswell Daily Record website; https://rdnews.com. George Coe and Ygenio Salazar were still alive who had been a part of the regulators in the Lincon County War. Salazar described Billy as "He fought face to face with his enemies. He gave them a chance to draw. There was nothing about him to suggest his steel nerve. He had the face of an angel; the soft voice of a woman; the mild blue eyes of a poet. He had an unfailing sense of humor. He was always ready for some horseplay, to give a joke or to size one. His laughter was as spontaneous as a child's. He made you ashamed of yourself to lose your temper in his presence."

Billy was basically a scapegoat, while others were given amnesty. His boyish, trusting attitude made him a target, as he was trying to do good and fervently seek justice. Billy is characterized as a young man, a pawn used for turning the attention away from the big political monster in New Mexico which eventually placed the blame and bloodshed upon his shoulders. A heavy load to carry for a young man of 21 years of age.

"There was a saying in them old days that a man "had seen the elephant and heard the owl holler." It meant that he had been around a lot and slept out, maybe hid out when he got tangled up with the Law a bit. If he was wanted real bad by the Law, we'd say he was "ridin' the Owl Hoot Trail."   Jim Herron

"He did a good job at faking his death, cause the whole world bought it"

-Bud Hardcastle

Chapter Sixteen: Dead or Alive – 1881-1882

The whole world bought Billy the Kid's death in 1881 and 9 months later, the whole world would buy the story that Jesse James was dead, April 3, 1882.

This was not the first time a report was posted in the papers declaring the desperado was dead. After the Russellville, Kentucky bank robbery in 1868, blaming Jesse and his gang, George Shepherd who was part of the gang was captured and spent a short time in the Kentucky pen. Supposedly after he was released, he went straight. Shepherd went to work in the lead mine in southeastern Kansas at Short Creek, not far across the border from Joplin, Missouri.

Kansas City Marshal, James Liggett was bound and determined to seek out Jesse and his gang because of another robbery that occurred. He enlisted Shepherd to infiltrate the gang and help round up the notorious outlaws.

Shepherd tried to set up a fake death attempt in the Fall of 1879. It is unclear if Jesse was in on it, but it doesn't appear that he was, not even present for the event. Rumors were spreading that Jesse was killed near Short Creek, seven miles from Joplin, Missouri. The executioner was named as his comrade in the Confederacy and his gang, George Shepherd. The Kansas City Journal began spreading the story. "With His Boots On. Jesse James the Notorious Missouri Outlaw Meets His Fate." Kansas City Journal, Nov. 4, 1879.

It was an elaborate story; how Shepherd had been away from the gang and had pledged to remain clean. He was accused of several robberies, so he went to Marshal Liggett to clear his name and assist in the capture of the outlaws. They made a plan and Shepherd followed through. He presented himself to Jesse and the gang, stating that he was being accused of the robberies and even showed them a fake newspaper clipping of his name pinned to them. He wanted back in.

Shepherd was welcomed back in the gang and they headed to Texas in 1879. On the way, they decided to hit the bank in Empire or Galena, Kansas on the bank of Short Creek. At the bank, Jesse's keen eye noticed a guard that had worked for Marshal Liggett before. Jesse called off the heist. Leaving town, they noticed Shepherd was not with them. When Shepherd finally caught up, there was a confrontation. Whether a betrayal had occurred or if there was a chip on Shepherd's shoulder for having to pay a price on his prison stay and also the death of his family and friends during the holdup, the reason behind the fight is unknown.

Shepherd supposedly shot Jesse in the head and galloped back in town and spread the news that Jesse was dead. He produced a bloody mangled leg for evidence. [307] The authorities never found the body, but one witness came forward and said that they had seen the gang in a wagon that had something covered up in the back with a foul odor. It was assumed it was Jesse and they were heading to Clay County to bury the body.

"The body was never found and the story rests only with the one witness, Shepherd." [308]

But Jesse responded in a letter to the Editor of the Clipper-Herald, postmarked in Brownwood, Texas. From the Pen of Jesse James. Brownwood, The Hardest Town in Texas, November 7, 1879 in its entirety.

"Your reporter and George Shepherd have the most brilliant imaginations in America. They ought to pull in double harness at the boss hypothecators. They can lie with more appearance of truth than any two men in Missouri. Mark Twain's boss liar, who walked twenty miles to show a man a tree 100 feet around, and when he reached the spot where he said the tree was found only a sage-brush, and explained by saying that the tree had shrunk during the dry spell, was nothing to them.

"I never saw your cave, and never expect to. The man who runs me into a hole will do more than 'Pink's' detectives could, as *Louis J. Lull* can testify. Lull was game, though; the gamest man that I ever met, and I am glad that he pulled through. I read your reporter's yarn, and myself and wife laughed heartily over it.

"The description of my appearance, rather of my features, eyes, hair and beard was accurate. Where did your reporter get it?

"I have just read a telegraphic account of the way George Shepherd got the drop on me, and I'll be damned if I believe it. George Shepherd would never treat me in that way. I shot his nephew because I had to, and he knows it. Besides George is no coward and would never have shot me in the back. I wish you newspaper men would charge me with every train robbery and outrage that is committed in Missouri or the West. I had no more to do with the Glendale robbery than you had. The bungling manner in which the robbers allowed the 'dust' to slip through their hands shows this. I would have known what train the bullion was to be forwarded on from Kansas City, and would have stopped that train and no other, bet your life.

"But the very thoughts of the old days and old deeds make my heartbeat fast, and I long for the wild and reckless past, and but for my wife and boy would again take to the road. As it is, however, I am playing a square game, and have settled down on a ranch about ten miles from this town of Brownwood and am no longer known as Jesse James. I am not ashamed of my name but want peace and quiet for my wife's sake. She has saved me from killing myself, and if I am let alone, I will be a good citizen and grow up in a new life with this great State of Texas.

"Tell your reporter to set 'em up to the boys around and send, the bill to me. I enclose a photo which was taken some years ago. It is not a really good picture but will pass muster. Believe me, yours in **truth**, Jesse James." [309]

This letter from Jesse is full of clues and messages if one will take the time to decipher. It is strange that he brings up *Lull* and that he was able to pull through. Louis John Lull was a Mason. He was a detective of the Pinkerton's and was dispatched to Missouri to track Jesse in 1874. When he and other detectives, heavily armed went to a farmhouse, he didn't realize that John and Jim Younger were there eating supper with the Snuffers. The Youngers suspected something awry, so they followed the detectives down the road. They overcame the detectives and that is when Lull pulled out a Smith and Wesson, No. 2 pistol and shot John Younger through his throat. "In a split second, Younger (John) fired his shotgun and the blast shredded Lull's right arm. Jim Younger reacted immediately, firing his pistol and hitting Lull in the side." [310]

Lull's horse took off and John Younger followed and shot Lull in the chest. The story goes that John Younger fell dead off of his horse and Lull managed to hide out in the woods. After being found by a farmer who took him to a doctor, Lull was able to tell his story, but died three days later. But per Jesse in the letter above, 5 years from this incident stated that Lull survived. It also implies that it was Jesse who was at the scene instead of John Younger, another clue that Jesse was the man in John Younger's shoes. Another hoax in the making. It is another strong clue that J. Frank Dalton who fervently told this story over and over again and had stated that John lived and was living in Texas, refers to the same story Jesse is telling here. Were they one in the same?

Nothing came out of Jesse's death in 1879. No death certificate, no body, no grave, but only hearsay. This is the first hoax pulled on the death of Jesse or at least one written about. With the rebuttal, Jesse wasn't in on it, but maybe Shepherd was wanting a pardon or maybe a reward. This story didn't fly.

This was about the time the rumor of Frank James was dying of consumption. In an interview with Zerelda Samuels, she believed that Frank had died sometime in July of 1879 with consumption.

In the letter Jesse spoke of his wife and boy in Brownwood in November 1879. Remember he was quite busy that year. We find little clues here and there that they were in Nashville before that time in April 1879.

Nashville

Jesse and Zee Mimms had a son Jesse Edwards James (aka Charles "Timmy" Howard) who was born in August 1875 in Nashville. I believe this was Jesse's home base and he felt secure to keep his family right there in order to protect them from the bullets that would be trying to find their way into Jesse's flesh.

Jesse had a nice piece of property outside of Nashville which included his racehorses. He built a track to race his horses against others.

Jesse's son was named after his good friend John Edwards, his comrade in Quantrill Raiders, and the newspaperman/editor who supported him throughout his life. In his youth, Jesse's boy used the name of Timmy Howard or Tim Edwards. Later, we learn that Jesse himself was quoted as saying his son is Jesse Edwards, with his surname as "Edwards." We will see variations, but the one man who lived as Jesse James Jr. or Jesse Edwards James was the son of Bigelow.

After little Jesse was born, Jesse didn't waste time. He was on the road again or on the rails. On September 5, 1875, 340 miles away the Huntington Bank in West Virginia was robbed with a member of the gang shot. Jesse confessed to this robbery, but said it wasn't him that got hit by a lawman's bullet.

In 1878, Jesse is believed to still be in the Texas Rangers. The Ben Johnson we had spoken of earlier was discharged in February 1878 from the Rangers, the same month that Zee had twin boys, Gould and Montgomery. Sadly, the twins died after two weeks from their birth. It was heartbreaking to Jesse as he told Ola. They were living in Humphreys County, Tennessee and buried in New Johnsonville. A story later, in 1910, describes Jesse's twins who were working on Jesse's ranch in Mexico. It is unclear who these men were and if they were truly the twins that supposedly died.???? Another mystery.

Stories were told to Ola about Nashville by Jesse and also by a man who owned a store close to where they lived in Nashville, Henry Priest. Mr. Priest was in Lawton, Oklahoma in 1948 when J. Frank Dalton stated that he was Jesse James. Mr. Priest, with no hesitancy, verified that he knew Jesse and verified J. Frank Dalton was the man. He even appeared as a witness in J. Frank Dalton's hearing in March 1950 to identify him as Jesse James.

In Nashville, Jesse went by the name of Jesse Howard or Jess Howard. Sometimes he went by the name of John D. Howard. He loved to gamble. Mr. Priest remembers a very hot game of serious poker. Henry Priest ran a store nearby and was summoned to that game by a note delivered by a boy written by Mr. Howard. He was requesting that Mr. Priest bring him money to finish up a card game. By the time Priest got to the gambling table, he witnessed Jesse pulling out his six shooter in an unbelievable quick draw to keep the game clean and with his pistol directly pointed at his opponent saying, "don't let me catch you cheating again!"

After the game, Mr. Howard came to Mr. Priest's store and paid him back every cent.

In the Police Gazette, George McGrath documented that when Mr. Priest met up with Jesse in 1948 he asked about the Nashville card game. Jesse related the story in great detail. It was him alright. Priest knew both Jesse and Frank. He heard the children always call Frank, "Uncle Frank" even though he was going by the name Ben Woodson. Some folks called Frank, "Buck."

Jesse must have had several loans he borrowed from the people of that small community of Edgefield in East Nashville. Bud had in all his documents, a letter from Jesse, signed as "John D. Howard" of Nashville on April 24, 1879 to Henry.

It was transposed, and Bud had the last page of the original letter in his files:

Eaton Creek, Tenn. – April 24th, 1879

Friend Henry,

Your welcome letter of the 19th to hand and ___Henry. I hope you be sure to come up the 29th and stay all the week as the races will be very interesting. I am sure you can make more than your expenses. If my creditors will compromise with me at 50 cents on the dollar the prospects are very flattering for me to get money enough soon to pay all my debts off. Bring up the Larking note and hopefully we can trade on it. Also bring up the following notes that I owe.

Amos Corbit.....$12.00; Henry Warren.....$4.00; Robert Clark.....$15.00; ____ Warren....$2.25; ????.....$4.00; Joe_____.....$1.70

And I will try to pay those small debts off in full. Get those gentlemen to permit you to give me their receipts as some things have transpired recently. I do not propose to pay Mr. Jackson until after the _____ is resolved. I will explain fully to you. Be sure to come up Tuesday the 29th. I will be at the races. _____write at once on the arrival of this letter and let me know if you will be up. Address to John D. Howard – Nashville, Tenn. I will get your letter sooner as I am in the city every day.

Your Friend JDH

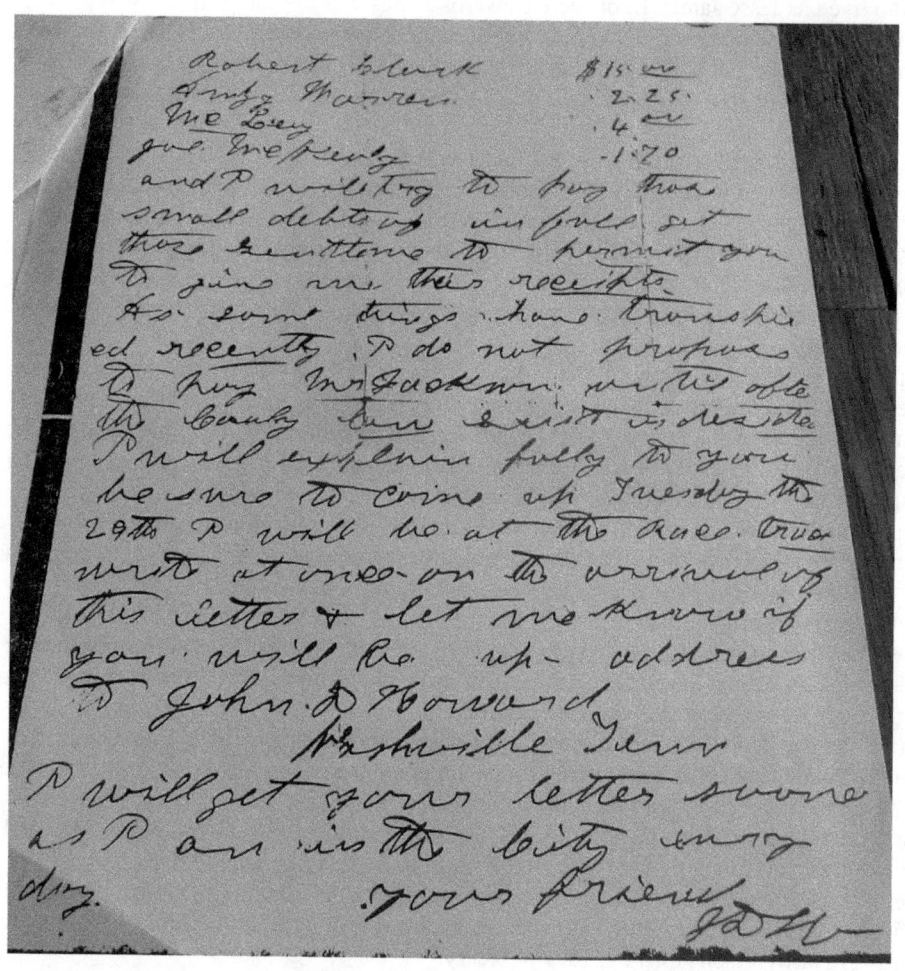

(2nd page of letter to Henry Priest from J. D. Howard (Jesse), April 24, 1879)

This letter is amazing to have, thanks to Bud's pursuit. It gives us a lot of information. Jesse was heavily involved in horse racing, gambling, living in Nashville, and also did not have a lot of money available to him as he had to "<u>borrow</u>" from Peter to pay Paul." It never sounded like he <u>robbed</u> Peter to pay Paul. All the money he gained from robbing went to the KGC and maybe covered a few living expenses, not his gambling expenses. He did pay his money back.

After April 1879, we see their daughter Mary Susan being born in June in Nashville. Jesse again was enlisting in the Texas Rangers in the fall, robbing a train in Glendale, Missouri in October, and was mailing a letter from Brownwood, Texas in November 1879 which only mentioned his son and wife, not his daughter.

Ola said that Jesse moved his family to Nashville in 1880, but I believe they had been there since the birth of their son in 1875 and remained there while Jesse was traveling.

When JJ lived in Nashville, he was highly thought of. He and his wife were very hospitable. Those who knew him as Mr. Howard noticed the chivalrous attitude towards women and children. One lady, Mrs. Alice Kate Roland of Nashville speaks to a reporter in St. Louis close to the turn of century. She said, "In the year 1879 or 1880, I boarded on South Cherry Street in Nashville. Among the families inhabiting the house during my several months' stay there was that of a Mr. Howard. He had a wife and child-a boy about 4 ½ years old. (No mention of a baby or a daughter) Mr. Howard was at home but little. The other boarders knew him as a horse trader, and none of us suspected that the tall, plainly dressed man was leading a double life."

Mrs. Roland stated that she had observed several men who came into the dining room with Mr. Howard who appeared to be "mudbespattered", booted and spurred, as if just from their saddles after a long and tedious ride. "When going downstairs one evening, I noticed that the door of my neighbor's room was ajar. The sound of voices, almost low enough to be called whispers, attracted my attention. With a swift glance I saw a bag, having the appearance of a mail sack, emptied upon the table which stood in the center of the room. The contents of the sack were gold and silver coin." [311] This may have been in October 8, 1879 when the Chicago, Alton & St. Louis train at Glendale, Missouri was robbed supposedly by the James Gang in which Jesse admitted to.

We find Jesse traveling back and forth in Missouri in 1880.

A newspaper article appeared May 21, 1948 in the Mexico Ledger. It told a story of a Callaway County, Missouri stock-raiser and farmer who had been in the business operating with his brothers, who specialized in saddle horses, mules, and shorthorn cattle. They were the Womack brothers. James Womack was retiring.

This story came out as a result of Jesse's coming out party in 1948, freeing up the mouths that were told to keep shut for nearly a century. James Womack revealed that Jesse was in their house as a guest during the summer of 1880. James Womack would have been 20 years old at the time. Womack stated that Jesse went by the name of John Franklin. They were told to keep their mouths shut. Two ex-Confederate soldiers, J.W. Pace and John Maloney who were in several engagements with Jesse in the war procured Jesse's lodging with the Womacks. It was secluded and the Womacks were southern sympathizers.

The newspaper article stated that "Acting as hosts to Jesse James was not, according to Womack, looked upon as the harboring of a notorious bandit, but as extending hospitality and security to a persecuted Southern soldier. Womack recalled the constant alertness of James, his skill as a croquet player, his good singing voice and his large repertoire of gospel hymns." [312]

In September of 1880, Jesse was accused of robbing a stagecoach in Mammoth Cave, Kentucky. I believe some of these dates could be off somewhat of what Jesse told Ola. He had confided in her that he went to Excelsior Springs in 1881, but I believe it had to be in 1880. Jesse had told her that he visited Thomas T. Crittenden, a family friend who they had known since Kentucky, who was running for governor at that time. Jesse just knew that he would listen to what he had to say, possibly give him a pardon if he won the election. Jesse said he gave Mr. Crittenden $35,000 towards his campaign. On November 2, 1880, Crittenden was elected governor. "As governor, Crittenden wanted to suppress the robberies and violence committed by the James Gang. He authorized a reward of $5,000 (which was paid for by railroad corporations) for the capture of Jesse James and also $5,000 for his brother Frank." [313]

Crittenden was noted in a book, "During the years from 1865-1870 – known as the "test oath" or disfranchisement period" in Missouri, Mr. Crittenden was the staunch friend and defender of disfranchised ex-Confederates." [314] His great grandfather was General Benjamin McKinley Logan of Kentucky fame. Both Bud and I are related to the Crittenden family through Thomas T.'s grandmother Harris' and Woodsons. I also am related to the Crittenden's through the Hackley family. They tie into our famous Lee family and the Webbs. Of course, the Woodsons are in Jesse's family.

We find Jesse back in Nashville, disguised as John Davis Howard visiting his brother, B. J. Woodson in February 1881. It was during this time Jesse, dressed as an old Quaker preacher, was spreading the gospel in Nashville. He was going by Elder Hopkins. Sometimes he would use "a whang" in his voice, talking through his nose. I think he really enjoyed these escapades.

In March 1881, Jesse was accused of robbing a paymaster, who was leaving a bank in Muscle Shoals, Alabama.

A very interesting story involving Jesse and Frank in Nashville sheds light into their activities besides gambling and preaching. An ex-Confederate Captain James Daniel Koger who served under General Joseph E. Johnston, Cheatham, and Hood knew Jesse and Frank well while they lived in Nashville and later in St. Louis. In the article, "The Rise and Fall of Jesse James," by Robertus Love in the Tulsa World newspaper, August 28, 1925, the reporter interviewed Mr. Koger about his stories on the James boys. The reporter stated that Mr. Koger was "erect as a sycamore sapling," a description often said of Jesse. They were proud men and always straight in the saddle.

The reporter, Mr. Love was able to get a vivid picture of Jesse and Frank during their stay in Nashville, a period in their lives which is not commonly known. Mr. Koger, who knew exactly who they were, had many dealings with the men going by the names of Mr. Howard and Mr. Woodson. This story was told by Mr. Koger in the year before his death, in 1925.

James Koger, after the war, became a clerk for 17 years for the company Rhea, Smith, & Company in Nashville through 1882 dealing with grain and flour. He became general manager and part owner of the St. Louis and Tennessee River Packet company, which operated freight and passenger steamboats on the Mississippi and the Tennessee. The headquarters was in St. Louis. He had known Jesse in 1876 in Nashville and had also known that Jesse lived in Humphreys County to the west. He said that Jesse lived in Humphreys County for a couple of years on a farm in the Big Bottom country.

Koger described Jesse as "with full-face whiskers of a dark brown color, worn rather short. He had snappy blue eyes. His face was of the roundish pattern, with a sort of stubby nose. He was not a large man, as I recall, medium height and weight. He dressed well and was a fairly good-looking fellow, and good natured enough except when he got excited. He seemed to have a very hot temper."

Koger described B. J. Woodson (Frank) as tall, older than Howard, **blue eyes**, his face was an angular shape, and thinly built. He wore "a beard of the sideburn cut," smooth chin, his sideburns, moustache, and hair were a sandy color. Howard and Woodson did not resemble the other indicating any kinship.

Captain Koger stated that both Howard and Woodson did a lot of business with the Rhea House which was a grain and flour business. Isaac T. Rhea was the head of the business in Nashville. Howard "had a bunch of steers and several horses, who bought a good deal of feed for them."

Woodson appeared to be "engaged in teaming and hauling saw logs," which if you remember, Frank and Jesse did this outside of Devil's Nest in Nebraska during their logging business. They utilized the river and steamboats to transport their freight.

Howard and Woodson rarely appeared together but were known in the community as strangers to one another. They were introduced to each other in the Rhea House and struck up a conversation talking about general things and the weather, but it was evident they were strong Democrats. After the discussion in public, they exited the area, and ducked behind a high stack of sacked grain and spoke in very low tones. They talked there for nearly an hour, Koger said. It seemed strange to Koger that these men were strangers to each other and then suddenly dived into a deep private conversation with one another.

Captain Koger observed Howard (Jesse) loving his Draw Poker games, but he didn't win very often. "He always played on the square and if anybody tried to cheat, Mr. Howard got quite indignant." Howard was also known as paying his debts as stated by Henry Priest. Evidently, Howard owed Mr. Rhea $265 and as a honest good fellow would do, he confronted Mr. Rhea and said he was the only one that treated him as a gentleman and wanted to pay him back what he owned, even if he had to work on the streets for a dollar a day. He paid him in full that very day. Captain Koger believed Howard was an honest man.

Captain Koger was a staunch ex-Confederate and was heavily involved in the Confederate soldiers' reunions and was a trustee to the Confederate Home in Pewee Valley, Kentucky. He would move to Hickman, Kentucky and was involved in the grain business there, connecting to the Nashville, Chattanooga and St. Louis Railroad.

St. Joseph, Missouri

Jesse was in Texas around May and June of 1881. He had a short love affair with Emma Anders, a young girl, age 13 going on 14 who lived in Marlin, Texas, southeast of Waco. She became pregnant. He left Texas and was back in Missouri, apparently close to St. Joseph.

In July 1881, the town of St. Joseph was putting on a parade for the 4th of July. Ozark Jack Berlin, also known as Pres. (Preston? Presley? Prescott?) Webb and Billy were visiting Jesse. A local leader saw them in town and invited them to join in the 4th of July parade. Apparently, the three looked like colorful characters. They got on their horses and rode in the parade session.

"So, as the parade moved slowly down the main street, there, riding along, was the much wanted Jesse James with a price on his head and on each side of him was Brushy Bill and Ozark Jack, while the Pinkerton's and other laws were as busy as bees looking for him. But they didn't know how he looked. There he was, well dressed and gave the appearance of a well- to-do cattle buyer, with no thought by the on-lookers of him being the much wanted outlaw and that under his nice dress coat that reached almost to his knees, which was the apparel of the well-dressed gentleman of that day, was a shoulder holster holding a fully loaded pistol." [315] I'm sure they all had a pretty good laugh.

From there, Billy would travel back down to New Mexico. It would be another 10 days that Billy was back in Fort Sumner for his so-called attempted assassination and the announcement of his death on July 14, 1881.

Eleven days later, Jesse was accused of the robbery of the Chicago, Rock Island & Pacific Railroad train near Winston, Missouri in July 15, 1881. Frank was accused of murdering Frank McMillan and the conductor William Westfall was also killed. Frank was charged for the murder of Frank McMillan, was tried and acquitted in 1883. Jesse insisted he was not there; he was with his family settling in at St. Joseph.

On August 28th, 1881 Jesse was checked in at the St. James Hotel in Cimarron, New Mexico under the name of R. H. Howard. He may have been inquiring about land to buy near Rayado.

Just 10 days later there was a train robbery of the Chicago and Alton train at Blue Cut, near Glendale, Missouri. Jewelry was taken from the passengers and $3,000 in cash, but the conductor was leary of the leader who kept saying he was Jesse James, but he didn't think it was Jesse. This may have been a robbery with others using Jesse's name. It was getting to be a habit, a bad habit.

Jesse's timeline on legendsofamerica.com stated that he rented a house on 1318 Lafayette Street, in St. Joseph, Missouri for $15 per month on Christmas Eve, 1881. Jesse told Ola that he owned two horses that he was preparing for a big race and wanted a good barn and an area where he could train them. This property was ideal for this. It had a nice barn and a good house which sat upon a hill.

I don't believe he ever intended to have his family there in St. Joseph with him but left them in Nashville per Ola. Jesse met up with Charley Bigelow and whether this was planned at the beginning or not, Jesse allowed Bigelow to stay at his home on Lafayette Street because "he had no other place to live." I believe this statement was just a cover for Jesse's true intentions. This was the usual pattern of Jesse's operations; buying places, ranches, businesses and placing men, members of the KGC to run them.

Charley Bigelow was an outlaw and a former Quantrill Raider. Jesse suspected Bigelow as using his name to pull off bank and train robberies. When one of the robberies went south, Bigelow shot a small boy on their way out of town. This infuriated Jesse and he was not going to have any more of this. As much as Jesse hated to speak of any killing, he was devastated to know that a murder of a little boy was pinned on himself.

Jesse had written earlier a letter criticizing the Pinkerton agents for the persecution of guerrilla fighters and their families. He wrote," We the James and the Youngers, were blamed for all the criminal acts committed from the close of the Civil War until 1882 when we were granted amnesty. While we had been fighting to protect our homes against northern invaders, all the bank and train robberies that were committed were laid to us whether guilty or not."

It was two months after he had rented the house in St. Joseph that an illegitimate son of Jesse's was born in Texarkana, Arkansas to the young mother, Emma Anders. His son would be named Jesse Cole James on February 13, 1882.

Another letter that surfaced depicting Jesse's frame of mind on possibly starting a new life or moving to another area is shown on https://sites.rootsweb.com/~nefrankl/JesseJames.html – "Jesse James Gang in Franklin, Nebraska." We find Thomas Howard, 1318 Lafayette Street in St. Joseph, Missouri answering an ad in the Lincoln Journal. Mr. Howard, Jesse, became interested in buying 160 acres in Franklin County, Nebraska near Lincoln, Nebraska.

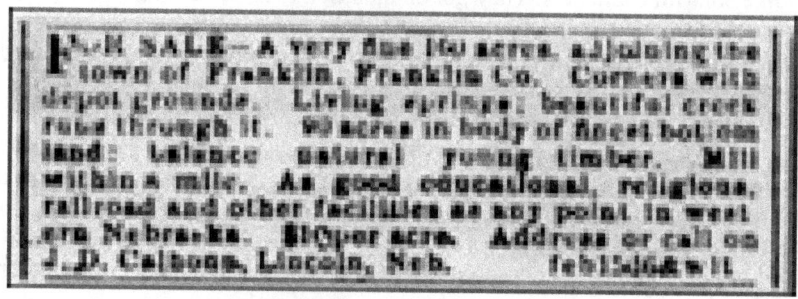

(Ad in the Lincoln Journal)

Mr. Howard answered this ad in this way:

Mr. J. D. Calhoun, Lincoln, Nebraska

Dear Sir: I have noticed that you have 160 acres for sale in Franklin County, Nebraska. Please write to me at once and let me know the lowest cash price that will buy your land. Give me a full description of the land, etc.

I want to purchase a farm of that size, provided I can find one to suit. I will not buy a farm unless the soil is No. 1.

I will start on a trip in about eight days to Northern Kansas & Southern Nebraska, and if the description of your land suits me, I will look at it, and if it suits me I will buy it. From the advertisement in the Lincoln Journal, I suppose your land can be made a good farm for stock and grain.

Please answer at once.

Respectfully, Tho. Howard, No. 1318 Lafayette St, St. Joseph, Missouri – Dated March 2nd, 1882

(Jesse's letter answering the ad)

(2nd page)

The answer came from the owner, "speaking in most glowing terms of the land, and of the social, religious, and educational advantages of the neighborhood." [316] Mr. Howard never followed through with his plans to start a new life in Nebraska. The next month, he would be assassinated by Bob Ford's bullet.

With this letter, written by Jesse, along with the letter he wrote to Henry Priest, and an unbelievable pocket notebook that Bud was able to obtain in Evening Shade, Arkansas, indicate the same man wrote all three. In all three sources, the writing is identical. The way he wrote the letter

"I" looks like a "P." There is a letter of authenticity to prove that this was JJ's handwriting by a man who ran the bank in Liberty, Missouri and his folks owned that bank when it was robbed. He had things to compare to.

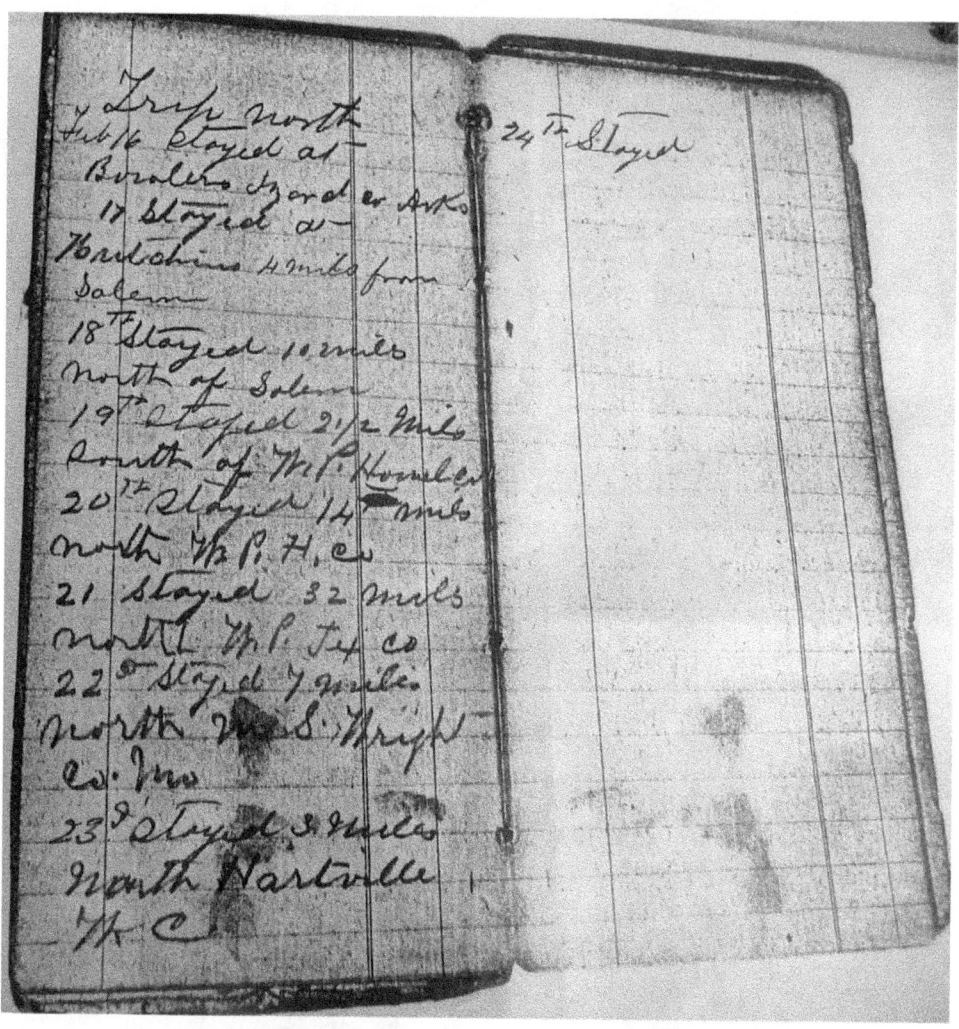

(Daily pocket notebook)

Here is the actual copy of the booklet and a letter of authenticity by Jack Wymore, Founder and Owner of Jesse James Bank Museum. The holder of this gem was Eva and Lonnie Haley of Sidney, Arkansas. Bud himself acquired another date book.

An interesting note: The pocket notebook shows a daily log of Jesse keeping track of his daily travels. He was on the move constantly. A feat, not many could achieve in this day and time, especially on horseback or foot, but that kind of life, Jesse was used to, in order to stay alive. Quite interesting. He also traveled frequently on railroads and steamboats. He stated that from St. Louis as the center point, he could get anywhere in the United States within 24 hours.

The little black weathered pocketbook listed a trip on February 16th titled "Trip North" It appears they were in Arkansas and had mentioned being 4 miles north of Salem, assuming this was Salem, Arkansas. They moved daily. On the 17th, they were 4 miles from Salem. The next day they were 10 miles north of Salem. The 19th, they were in Missouri in Howel County. Three days later they were through Texas County and into Wright County, north of Hartville. It was a full week of travel; close to 100 miles. Usually the average distance a horseman could travel would be close to 12-15 miles per day. The travel shown in the pocketbook was true to this calculation.

> August 17, 1991
>
> To Whom It May Concern:
>
> Numerous notations recorded in a small pocket size notebook which I have examined, were in my opinion, written by Jesse Woodson James, the notorious outlaw who was born in Clay County, Missouri in 1847. I have compared the handwritten letters and numbers with those in two copies of letters written by him and found them to be identical in all instances. There is no possibility of the two letters in my possession of having been written by any person other than Jesse James.
>
> Some similar entries found in a second notebook of similar size were also, in my opinion, written by the same person, Jesse James.
>
> The notebooks at the time of my examination on August 10, 1991 in Liberty, Missouri, were in the possession of Eva and Lonnie Haley of Sidney, Arkansas.
>
> As owner of the Jesse James Bank Museum building in Liberty, Missouri, including all of the various items housed therein, I have been a James historian before and since the museum was established by me in 1965.
>
> I have never known of any such record being made by Jesse James and I consider this to be an extremely rare James item.
>
> Yours truly,
>
> *Jack B. Wymore*
> Jack B. Wymore
> Founder and Owner
> Jesse James Bank Museum
> Liberty, Missouri 64068

(Letter of authenticity)

April 2-3, 1882

The general story told in all the books and movies throughout the years, was that Jesse, known as Mr. Howard was living in a house on Lafayette Street in St. Joseph with his wife and two kids. He was trying to get another group of men to join with him to continue his robbery schemes. He had Charley and Bob Ford, young brothers in his home who were joining his gang. When the Ford brothers heard of the reward for Jesse, they met with Governor Crittenden and devised a plan to kill Jesse.

On April the 3rd, Jesse and the Ford brothers were eating breakfast together and something unusual occurred. Jesse never let his guns leave his holsters tucked inside his coat. They were always with him. He was out of character that morning, taking off his guns and laying them on a bed. He noticed a picture on the wall that was crooked and got up from the table, with his back turned, and climbed up into a chair to straighten the picture. Bob Ford picked up Jesse's gun and shot him, killing him instantly. End of story? Not on your life and not on Jesse's!

This story has a lot of holes. Bud went to St. Joseph, Missouri to the house where Jesse was killed. "It's a farce," Bud said. "First of all, the ceilings were low and if you were 5'10" as Jesse was, you certainly would not need a chair to stand on, to fix a picture." One man who was with Bud said he was 5'4" and could reach the picture without a chair. Jesse himself, told Ola that he could stand on his tip toes and reach the ceiling.

(Picture at St. Joseph house)

The general story told by many, state that the bullet that killed Jesse went through his skull into the wall. Bud said the bullet hole that was in the wall was not at a level where a person standing would be close to head level. Bud stated that the autopsy report of the dead man shows that the bullet lodged into a bone and did not penetrate out of the skull into the wall. There was no exit wound and there was a deep bruise on his forehead. Many newspapers reported that the bullet entered the base of the skull and made its way out through the forehead over the left eye, leaving a wound on his forehead.

As stated before, does it make sense that Jesse, who was the most famous outlaw in American History, was shot down in his own home in St. Joseph, Missouri, with both of his guns laid down, when he was known to always have his side arms around his waist at all times, even when swimming in swimming holes? Does it make sense, that he was straightening a picture that was at arm's length above him, but he chose to stand up in a chair with his back to men with guns at their fingertips?

The story of Jesse's death was written out exceptionally well by Frank Hall and Lindsay Whitten in the book "Jesse James Rides Again" that Bud had in his possession. The story was told to them by J. Frank Dalton when he met with the newspapermen from the Lawton Constitution in Lawton, Oklahoma in 1948. Dalton was ready to reveal his true identity for the first time to the world. The same story has been told to many since that time, including Ola. Did we listen or did it fall on deaf ear?

As Hall and Whitten wrote, many players were involved in this hoax. "It required the cooperation of many persons." They explain that many people were led to believe that Jesse James used the name of Mr. Howard and set up a home in St. Joseph, Missouri. Rumors spread that Mr. Howard was the real Jesse, opening up a new pit to trap Jesse. Would Jesse James be this careless?

The man who took on the identity of Mr. Howard in St. Joseph was actually Charley Bigelow, a former member of the James' Gang who took on Jesse's name and activities for his own gain. Bigelow ran with the Slade Gang. Suspicions were mounting against Bigelow, amongst Jesse and his closest friends. Bigelow was believed to be informing the law and Pinkerton's Detective Agency of Jesse's whereabouts and schemes. It was mentioned that Bigelow was responsible for the child's death in a holdup, using the name of Jesse. This infuriated Jesse to no end.

It became obvious, that Bigelow was going to have to go. A trap for this traitor was being set.

During the same period, Jesse was going by the name of Jim Crow, portraying himself as an eastern land buyer. This name came up often in Indian Territory. One of Jesse's friends in I.T. was a blue-eyed Black man named, Jim Crow.

Details were not quite freely given by Dalton in the matter of the relationship between Bigelow and Jesse, but there was a lot to be hidden. One thing that Dalton told the writers is that there were two men named Johnson that always hung around Bigelow and were later penned by the press as being the Ford brothers. Jesse told Ola they were the Ford brothers going by the names of Charlie and Bob Johnson. They were staying in the house with Bigelow.

Dalton/Jesse told Hall and Whitten that he was out in the barn, tending to his horses when he heard the shot and knew his freedom was opening within a small window. Jesse said to these writers that Zerelda Mimms James, the mother of Jesse's two children, played the part well.

Some believe that this grieving widow at the time of the killing was actually Bigelow's wife and their children. In the article, in the St. Louis Post Dispatch, dated November 27, 1949," Still Insists He's Jesse", by Dickson Terry, Dalton is quoted as saying that "his wife" identified the body as me." In court testimony in 1950 the story changed. Dalton stated that it was Bigelow's wife.

Dalton told Ola himself that it was actually Bigelow's wife and children. Bud believes through his research, that it was Bigelow's family in that house who later went on to claim heritage to Jesse. The family, now going by Mrs. Jesse James, Jesse Edward James, Jr. and Mary James were brought out into the public eye and easily tracked from then on. This was not Jesse's style. He protected his family and their identity. They weren't his.

In Orvus Lee Howk's books, it suggests a totally different story, published after JJ/Dalton was dead. With Bud's research and gathering of many documents and statements, he feels confident that the story of Jesse's supposedly death would involve several murders in which Jesse never spoke of to Ola.

Crittenden met JJ on the night before the execution behind the house on Lafayette Street in the woods. Colonel James Davis guarded them so that they would have no interference. This was verified with Col. Davis in 1948 and 1950. They sat talking for more than an hour. Jesse had contributed $35,000 in campaign funds to Crittenden and he expected a favor in return. Jesse's plan was laid out to the governor. Within this plan, it would free Jesse from those who had hunted him, those who had butchered his name and reputation in the newspapers and enable him to become a normal citizen. He was planning to settle somewhere in Nebraska.

The plan could only enhance Governor Crittenden's reputation and make him a hero as the man who conquered outlawry in Missouri. They could both win. Afterall, they were in the brotherhood together. Governor Crittenden was a strong Mason, belonging to several Masonic bodies in Kentucky. [317]

Ola said, "It stands to reason, what took place from then on, the governor was in on the hoax." [318] She was quoted in the Lubbock Avalanche, "Outlaw's Kin Says Death Faked," by Jack Hartsfield, September 1983, that "James, she claims, may have been among the federal government's first "protected witnesses."

Jesse kept the gory details of the murders from Ola and never implied to her that he was the one who shot Bigelow. John Trammel, Jesse's most devoted friend, his black cook, his bodyguard who had been with him for many years stated that Jesse was in the barn that morning when Bigelow came outside. "I knew it was going to be done." Trammel said, "Jesse done the shooting. He shot Charlie Bigelow, one of the gang." [319]

The story that Bud believes is that Jesse was in the barn early the morning of April 3, 1882. Both John Trammel and Col. James Russell Davis were watching outside. They knew that every morning Charles Bigelow and his two brothers, John and Bert who were visiting would be coming out of the house to relieve themselves. Charles came into the barn where Jesse was, and they began to argue. Jesse hit Charles on the head with the butt of his gun, leaving a mark on Bigelow's forehead above his eye. Charles got a shot off, hitting Jesse in the shoulder and Jesse shot and killed Charles in the barn.

While all this was happening John Trammel shot John and Bert Bigelow with his Over and Under shotgun. It is a shotgun with two barrels; one over the other. Two triggers execute the bullets; one shoots a 410 gauge in one barrel and the other a 20 gauge. While Trammel, Davis, and Bud Dalton (as told by Howk) took care of the two bodies of John and Bert Bigelow, burying them in a shallow grave, Jesse had some of his gang take Charles Bigelow in the house and set up the hoax. Bud Dalton supposedly shot bullets into the wall to appear as if those were the bullets that killed "Jesse." At one point, Jesse stated that Bud Dalton was his uncle. The only uncle of the Dalton's Jesse would have, per Ola was the Dalton boy's father, Lewis Dalton. Was he still alive? Did he too, fake his death years ago? Bud Dalton is listed in the inner most sanctum of the KGC and on the brass bucket.

Bigelow's wife was in the house with their children. She was told to keep her mouth shut and to play along. She received a large sum of money plus a strong threat of death if she ever revealed the truth. She would assume the name of Mrs. Jesse James and her children would take on the name of Jesse James Jr., and Mary James.

Jesse confirmed over and over with Ola that the children who were noted as Jesse's children, Jesse Jr. and Mary were actually the Bigelow children who continued to claim Jesse was their father. Do we really know what happened to Jesse's wife Zee and his own two children, Jesse Edwards and Mary? Ola said they were in Nashville, but after that, it is a mystery. From then on, the woman portrayed as Mrs. Jesse James continuously wore black and fell into a deep state of depression.

Charlie and Bob Ford were in on the whole thing. Jesse and Ola both communicated that the Ford boys were Jesse's first cousins. They said that their mother was a "Dalton" and sister to Zerelda, Ola's great grandmother, and Lewis Dalton, the father of the Dalton brothers. It could be a possibility. There is no information to prove that. The Ford's mother was using the name of Mary Ann Bruin married to James Thomas Ford (J.T. Ford).

Bob Ford would be deemed as the "fall guy," the one who shot Jesse James. Sheriff Timberlake showed up to the scene right away. I believe he was in on it also. From Jesse's own words, "But I will say this, my disappearance was not my own idea. Other people were in on it. The Governor of Missouri, for one, and the sheriff for another." [320]

Sheriff James "Jim" Timberlake was a 2nd lieutenant in Joseph Shelby's Brigade in the Confederate Army and after the war traveled with Shelby and Price to Mexico to join allegiance with the Emperor Maximilian. Timberlake was noted in the Kansas City Times as standing over 6 feet tall and broad in proportion. "He was a magnificent specimen of manhood. With the strength of three ordinary men and the courage of a lion he combined all the graces of an Apollo and was noted as one of the handsomest men in western Missouri."

"Along in the seventies, when the James brothers were in the zenith of their fame, Timberlake was elected sheriff by the democrats of Clay County. He inaugurated his term of office by a fierce, unflagging and determined warfare on Jesse and Frank James and their gang, of whom nearly every other officer in the west stood in deadly fear." [321]

Sheriff James Timberlake was highly praised by Governor Crittenden. We learn later in the Kansas City Star, August 18, 1940 that "Timberlake planned with Governor Crittenden to catch the bandits and contacted the Ford brothers to help in the capture. Mr. Timberlake operated the old Arthur House Hotel in Liberty at the time and kept Bob Ford there three weeks after the shooting at

St. Joseph. The townspeople did not approve of this as many Clay Countians considered Ford a traitor as well as an outlaw." [322]

James Timberlake had been appointed Deputy United States Marshal for the western district of Missouri after the war. In 1874, he married Anna Mary Katherine "Kate" Thomason, daughter of Grafton Thomason who founded the town of Liberty, Missouri. Grafton's father was "Wild Bill" Thomason who taught Frank James how to shoot and ride like the Comanches. Wild Bill's brother was Robert Thomason who married Sarah Lindsey, the mother of Zerelda (Cole) James Samuels. Grafton was the brother of Martha Jane Thomason Anderson, the mother of Bloody Bill Anderson. This would make Kate Thomason Timberlake first cousins to Bloody Bill.

Another brother of Grafton's was John Samuel Thomason (1818-1905). He was captain in the "Paw Paw" militia in the Civil War with a reputation of bravery, defending the residents of Clay and Platte counties against the Redlegs and the Jayhawkers in the Kansas/Missouri border war. John was one of four Thomason men who were sheriffs of Clay County, Missouri. He claimed after the robbery of the bank at Hardin (some accounts said after the Gallatin robbery), that he went to the James' home in Clay County and in a skirmish with the boys, Jesse shot the horse out from under Thomason; killing the horse. Jesse would later pay them back for the horse he had killed.

John Samuel Thomason's son, William H. Thomason (1855-1947), who was also sheriff married Willie Ann Timberlake. Her Uncle and Aunt were James R. Timberlake and Kate Thomason Timberlake.

So, the reader can get an idea of how much family surrounded Jesse, especially those who served law and order. Whether or not they supported Jesse or firmly stood by the law, it is unknown, but what Bud has revealed indicates that Jesse had a lot of help from friends and family. Let's not forget those in high places, the KGC brotherhood that stood by Jesse as well. Sometimes their blood ran thicker than kinship.

Harrison Trow was summoned by Governor Crittenden to the Sidenfaden Funeral Parlor where they took the body, placing him in a casket. Trow was a former Quantrill Raider and many believe he was actually Jesse. The tall mortician standing above the casket along with two other Quantrill Raiders was Frank James per Jesse. "Wild Henry" Roberts, Billy the Kid's father was also there to identify the body.

The authorities sent Zerelda a telegram on the death of her son. When she arrived, after a 50-mile trip on the morning of April 4th, she wasn't prepared and was not in on the hoax. She immediately said, "Gentlemen, this is not my son." Colonel James Russell Davis guided her to the next room and explained the situation to her so that Jesse could be set free. He asked her to go along with it and identify the body as her son. She went in next to the body, and produced an act of a tearful, mournful mother, stating that "Oh yes! That is my boy Jesse."

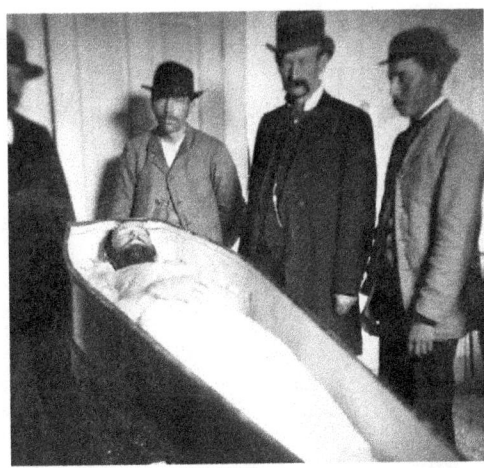

(The dead man, referred to as Jesse, and Frank James as the mortician)

"Jesse told Ola, laughing as he talked, "My mother just hadn't been briefed quite enough and she almost gave the whole thing away. So, she had to be taken out and briefed some more. She was a good actress. She just cried and carried on." 323

Zerelda, Wild Henry, and Harrison Trow were the official identifiers of the body of Jesse. Ola said that Jesse told her, "Those who knew me, kept their mouth shut. Those who didn't, accepted the man that was killed as being Jesse James. So, I, Jesse James, was officially proclaimed dead. Shot by Robert (Bob) Ford on April 3, 1882." 324

There was so much commotion in the streets and many people were coming from all over to see where Jesse lived and where he was killed. Jesse told Ola that him and Frank went to town and mingled amongst the men and women who were telling the story. They did this quite frequently when big events, such as robberies occurred to hear the comments and direction that the conversation was going. Many times, they were gathering information on the actions of the law to ensure their cover and escape. I am sure they were amused at all the gossip that was being spread.

It's amazing to find the actual logbook from the Funeral Parlor in St. Joseph listing, "Mr. Jesse James - Killed." A description in the newspaper, Independent-Courier in November 20, 1929 stated that on the ledger, it listed the casket made of steel was $265, but it was actually $250.00 plus $10 for the shroud. That was a mighty high price compared to the others and it may have included the funeral itself and the train trip from St. Joseph to Kearney for the funeral and burial.

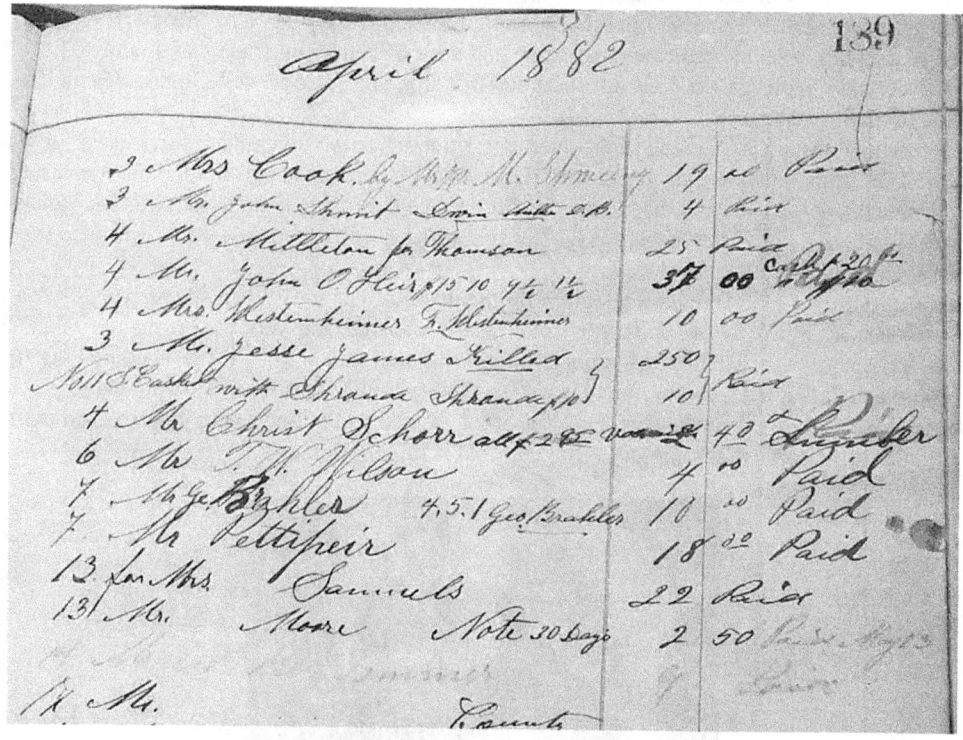

(The funeral home ledger for Jesse James' burial expense
https://www.onlyinyourstate.com/missouri/mo-funeral-museum-st-joseph/

Photo provided by Joseph Stone)

For some odd reason, the Coroner refused to sign the death certificate for Jesse James after the Coroner's inquest. He must have known.

The train took the body of Jesse from St. Joseph to Kearney with mother Zerelda, and Mrs. Jesse James and the children along with Sheriff James R. Timberlake. It arrived in the wee hours of the morning.

Sheriff James Timberlake went to the Reverend Dr. Flack on the morning of Jesse's body's arrival on the train. Timberlake suggested that it was not the intentions of the widow to exploit the opportunity for people to contribute donations to view the body, but if anyone wanted to volunteer a contribution, that would help her as "she was in straitened circumstances." [325]

Passenger trains coming through Kearney in the early morning hours stopped long enough to view the body. It was described as a "swarming fair day." The top of the casket was removed, and the body was displayed in the hotel office. "The funeral procession left the hotel at 2:00 P.M. First came the wagon with the corpse and next the family; next mounted officers; and last the wagon with reporters. An immense crowd on horseback and on foot and in wagons followed." [326]

The Baptist Church where the funeral was, could only hold 300, but there was over 500 people there: many out in the yard.

Five of the men who were pallbearers were identified as J.D. *Ford*, Deputy Marshal *J.T. Reed*, Charles *Scott*, James Henderson (J. B. Henderson), and William Bond. One newspaper, Henry County Democrat – April 13, 1882 added Sheriff Timberlake, Ben. Flanders, and James Vaughn to the list of pallbearers. [327] It was also confirmed in the Daily Charlotte Observer, April 6, 1882. No one knew who this James Vaughn was. He was deemed as a mystery man. The name *Vaughn* is significant in the saga of Frank and Jesse James. Could it be that it was James Monroe Vaughn?

In a story printed in the Falls City, Nebraska newspaper, June 1903, it states that a Mr. J.J. Tanner from that city was working in the area near Kearney as a railroad tie contractor and had some off time waiting on a train and decided to go to Kearney to witness the funeral of Jesse James. Tanner's great grandson, Stephen W. Tanner stated in genealogy.com that Tanner was a member of the Masons, German Society and GAR Post 84 in Falls City.

J.J. Tanner was pulled in during the procession going from the church to Zerelda's home for burial. When the procession got to Zerelda's gate, they were lifting the coffin over the gate and those carrying the body needed assistance. That is when J.J. Tanner was asked at the last moment to be a "pallbearer" as he said. He helped them move Jesse's body across the gate into her yard. The article stated he was the mysterious stranger everyone had spoken about at the funeral. It doesn't explain who this James Vaughn was inside the church acting as a pallbearer and who was listed in the news article in the Henry County Democrat and Daily Charlotte Observer.

Ola's story told by Jesse: At the funeral, "The sixth (pallbearer) was a man whom no one had seen until just as the procession was about to start; he then came forward, his countenance stern, his eyes bright and piercing. Moving to the head of the casket he directed the movements of the others quietly, dumbly, yet with a countenance sad and commanding. His apparent age was about forty years, but his lithe, muscular figure seemed to deny such age. The real Jesse James was the sixth pallbearer. Then Jesse decided to sing at the funeral, and did, while Colonel Davis stood at Jesse's back to protect him. In the vast crowd at the church were several Quantrell men." [328]

Bud said, Colonel Davis was there watching Jesse's back and if someone came up that they didn't know, Davis would touch him on the back. Jesse was James Vaughn.

Many people believed that Frank wasn't there at the funeral. Some believed he was still in hiding. One newspaper printed that "Frank James, it is believed, is not in Kentucky, but in the panhandle section of Texas, where he and Jesse invested in a ranch some years ago." [329]

A well-known citizen, not named in the newspaper, "The Chilicothe Constitution-Tribune," Feb. 22, 1891 stated "I was at the funeral of Jesse James. Jesse was buried in his mother's door yard, on the Samuels' farm, about three miles from Kearney, Clay County, Missouri. Sheriff Timberlake was master of ceremonies. The train on which the body was brought from St. Joseph arrived in Kearney about 2:00 in the morning. Sheriff Timberlake, Mrs. James, the widow of Jesse; Mrs. Samuels, Jesse's mother; Luther James and Tom Mimms, his cousins, were upon the train. The casket containing the body was taken to the Kearney House, where it lay in state until 10:00 a.m., when it was taken to the Baptist church, where the pastor of that church delivered a sermon upon the brevity and uncertainties of human life. The funeral procession from the church to the Samuels farm was fully a mile long. It was the oddest turnout of the kind that it was ever my fortune to witness. There were men and women on horseback and in every kind of vehicle to be found in the country. Sheriff Timberlake headed the procession and superintended the burial. Mrs. James and Mrs. Samuels created considerable excitement at the grave by asserting that Jesse's legs were cut off while his body was in St. Joseph and for a short time it looked as if there was going to be trouble. In anticipation of an attempt upon the part of friends of the dead bandit, Sheriff Timberlake had taken Dick Liddel and about twenty other men upon whom he could depend and each of whom was armed with two "long 45's. Before they would permit the casket to be lowered into the grave, Mrs. Samuels and Mrs. James insisted that it be taken into the house and turned upon one of its sides, so that Johnny Samuels, Jesse's cousin, could take a farewell look at the corpse. Their request was complied with." [330]

Jesse told Ola that after the funeral, he and Frank stayed in the Blossom House Hotel in Kansas City across from the depot. They had an adjoining room with Charlie and Bob Ford. Many newspapers had stated that the Ford brothers were in jail. Another story reveals that the Ford brothers were skirted away to the Arthur House Hotel in Liberty by Sheriff Timberlake and kept there until the trial on April 17, 1882. So many stories were being swirled around. It was hard to discern which story was correct.

April 17, 1882, Robert and Charles Ford plead guilty before the court and were indicted and convicted. Judge Sherman sentenced them to hang. That afternoon, Governor Crittenden issued unconditional pardons for the Ford Brothers.

On Oct. 5, 1882, Frank James surrendered himself and his famous Remington revolver, 44 caliber to Governor Crittenden. Bud was able to see the actual gun himself at the Jesse James Wax Museum in Stanton, Missouri. Here is a snapshot of Bud's video showing Francena Turilli holding the actual gun surrendered by Frank James.

(On the right, Frank's .45 Colt with a long barrel. This is the gun that he surrendered to Crittenden. On the left, Jesse's .44 Remington that he had at Meramec Caverns and the one he died with. He had it for 65 years. It had a very good balance. Bud was able to visit with Francena Turilli who had these guns at the Wax Museum in Stanton, Missouri, May 15, 1993)

The trial for Frank James was held in Gallatin, Missouri, Sept 6, 1883. The trial was quick, and Frank was acquitted on all three counts after only 5 minutes of deliberation.

Some rather interesting stories came out of this event.

Bud had heard a story about some bricks that were found by a boy in St. Joseph, that were unearthed at the original site of the house on Lafayette Street. It seemed like the story would go along with the story that was in Del Schrader's book describing Jesse's dedicated friend, John Trammel who wanted a record of what transpired at that little house in St. Joseph. Jesse had taught Trammel well on how to use carvings and symbols on rocks to tell a story or direct those "in the know" to treasure. In Schrader's book, it tells the story how Trammel took six freshly formed bricks and with the help of Bud Dalton, carved the story into the wet bricks. They then laid them in the burning embers of their campfire. Before the break of day, Trammel buried those bricks hoping that one day that this would prove it was Bigelow that died that day. "Jus' wait til dey find dem St. Jo bricks!" [331]

Well in Schrader's book, in the summer of 1966 a Charles Mason, a great grandson of Jesse's (unable to find the kinship) found the first one.

Bud wrote to River Bluffs Regional Library in St. Joseph in April 1991 and requested a copy of an article about the brick.

There was a brick found up there on the hill, known as "Jesse James' Hill" where the house stood on 1300 block of Lafayette Street in St. Joseph, Missouri. The house was moved to more of a secure location for a tourist attraction in 1939 to the Belt Highway location and then later moved in 1977 to the Patee House.

The news said the brick was found by a twelve-year-old boy, Danny Hargrave in 1967. Schrader listed a Charles Mason found it. Charles would have been Danny's brother-in-law's, brother. Finley Phillip Mason had married Danny's sister, Shirley. Danny had been staying with them when he found it.

The brick was buried deep in the old lot on Lafayette Street. The hill where the house had sat was lowered 10 feet due to the move of the house to another location. It had to of been buried very deep or moved while the ground was being excavated to level the ground. What else was buried under the house if that much excavation was going on?

The inscription on the back of the brick is extremely important, but the newspapers back in 1967 said "the inscriptions are largely meaningless and indicate that somebody buried the bricks in hopes that they would be dug up later and that it would be regarded as a mystery of history. At any rate, the finder, Danny Hargrave, will have an interesting doorstop." [332]

(Trammel's bricks (courtesy of the St. Joseph News, July 12, 1967))

Other Sides of Carved Brick

These pictures show more of the great amount of carving on the brick pictured on page 1. A lot of effort apparently went into the work. The inscriptions are largely meaningless and indicate that somebody buried the brick in hope that it would be dug up later (kids have always loved to dig in the loess soil back of the old Jesse James home) and that it would be regarded as a mystery of history. At any rate, the finder, Danny Hargrave, will have an interesting doorstop.

(Same as above)

On one side of the brick was carved "3 killed here April 3, 1882 and the other side had the names of John Bigelow, Chas. Bigelow, Bert Bigelow." On the back side, on the left hand lower corner of the brick are the initials "J.J." Filling the rest of the space was a carving of a horseshoe, key, star, which was the sign for the KGC, 777, a cross or dagger, a cobra snake, representing John Trammel who was called the "Black cobra".

Danny Charles Hargrave was born in 1955 and died young at the age of 24 in 1979. He was a welder at St. Joseph Structural Steel. He was involved in a shooting incident. [333]

Another story Bud found quite interesting was the story of a doctor who knew Jesse well. He was familiar with Jesse's conjunctivitis in his eyes. It was a chronic and painful condition of "pink eye." He had examined and treated Jesse for this condition. Dr. James Sanford Preston (1843-1916) who lived in Armstrong, Howard county, Missouri, receiving his degree in medical school after the war in St. Louis, stated after looking at the photo of Jesse in the coffin, that "if that was Jesse James... he was the Queen of the May."

Dr. W. D. Chesney, Wallace *Dalton* Chesney (1880-1977) wrote the article referring to Dr. Preston who was his father-in-law. His daughter, Mae Vonceil Preston (1883-1958) was Chesney's wife. The article was "Who Lies Buried in Jesse Grave?" As you notice in his full given name, the word "Dalton" appears. Dr. Chesney's mother was a Dalton, Mahala Emma Dalton. Her father was "Lewis Dalton (1826-1893) who was 2nd cousin to James Lewis Dalton...

Chesney's father, Judge Ezra Eramus Chesney was assigned a task from President Lincoln to squelch the lawlessness in "Bleeding Kansas." He became the County Attorney of Shawnee County, Kansas. He opened up a law firm in Topeka and later in Kansas City, Missouri. His son, Wallace described his father's law office just two blocks from the cigar store and gambling den operated by Frank and Jesse James.

Bud gave this article to the writer out of his collection. Bud had stacks upon stacks of newspaper and magazine articles as well as photos and letters. This particular article had a wealth of information from a man who knew the James' and other well-known western characters, such as Wyatt Earp, Calamity Jane, Billy Tilghman, Bat Masterson, Kid Curry, and Al Jennings. Apparently, he knew a lot about the Dalton family.

Al Jennings told Wallace Chesney that Harrison Trow was part of the plot to "kill off" Jesse and the whole thing was a plot to get Jesse safely to Texas.

Timidity and the fear factor prompted most of the citizens of St. Joseph not to speak regarding the possibility that this was not Jesse. In *The Missouri World Newspaper*, "So great is the terror that the James' and Youngers have instilled in Clay County that their names are never mentioned save in back rooms and in whispers."

Dr. Chesney always had a question on why Frank was never called in to identify the body of Jesse? He finally got to ask the question one day to Frank. Brother Frank replied, "Doc, you're in dangerous territory. Better mind your own damned business and maybe save your own hide." Chesney also had an opportunity to ask Billy Tilghman, a fearless lawman if he believed Jesse was truly killed. Tilghman responded, "Doctor, I just don't know. There is just as good evidence that it was not the real Jesse James, as there is that it was." Tilghman invited Chesney to go with him to the Kansas City Times and the Journal Office and read what they had to say in '82. Not much more did they dig up.

Dr. Chesney chatted with Dunt Ford, a druggist and a big politician in Excelsior Springs and he also wanted his opinion. "There are many who knew Jesse James who believe he is still living some place in Texas. Mysterious letters addressed in a printed scrawl come to Frank James, and they are from some town in Texas." [334]

Bud went to the Oklahoma Historical Society in Oklahoma City and found this article. On the front page:

"Shelby Don't Believe it"
Special Dispatch to the Kansas City Journal
Lexington, April 5, 1882

"As the Evening Star and other papers have commented on the recent interview I had with your representative, I desire to caution the public against swallowing all the reports relative to the death of Jesse James. It is barely possible that Jesse still lives and that the affair at St. Joseph was a preconcerted and prearranged matter by parties who seek to obtain a great reward offered for the gold raider dead or alive. The Evening Star calls upon me to write the obituary of Jesse James. Before I engage in it I shall await full evidence that he has been overreached and his death accomplished by the aid of the executive power of the state and misplaced confidence in those whom he believed his friends, I will say again that in the light of the knowledge now before me I shall continue to doubt whether the treasury of the state and its employees have captured their victims,

and it will be well to examine carefully and see if an innocent man has not been murdered. The express and railroad companies should require the most positive proof of Jesse James' death before they pay over their money. There may exist a combination between the robber and the officials to secure the money. Identification by citizens of Missouri, whose word will not be questioned, should be required."

Joe. O. Shelby

(General Joseph Orville Shelby)

Joseph Orville Shelby was a leading member of the Blue Lodge, a quasi=Masonic organization formed by prominent Missourians. They stood on pro-slavery. Shelby moved up into the ranks of the Confederate Army, becoming a Brigadier-General. After Robert E. Lee's army surrendered, General Edmund Kirby Smith appointed Shelby a major general, but was never formalized. Shelby's adjutant at the time was John Newman Edwards, who became editor of the Kansas City Times and was largely responsible for creating the legend of Jesse James and his fellow Confederate guerrillas.

Shelby did not surrender after the war, but took approximately 1,000 (some accounts say 500, up to 5,000) of his troops to the south into Mexico to fight along with Maximilian. Shelby's men earned the name "the undefeated" in which the movie of the same name with John Wayne and Rock Hudson was filmed.

Shelby was a critical and vital witness for his former fellow Confederate soldier, Frank James when his trial would come up.

Jesse said after the funeral he went to New Orleans and then on to Buenos Aires in South America. He was buying and selling cattle there, a known practice of his. He stayed there a little over a year.

The Ford brothers after being fully pardoned by Governor Crittenden, only received a small portion of the reward money. Sheriff James Timberlake and Marshal Henry H. Craig were awarded the majority of the bounty.

The Ford brothers tried their darndest to go forward as heroes, putting on plays, depicting the act of the assassination of Jesse. Their shows were named, "The Brother's Vow" and "The Bandit's Revenge." They made a lot of money out of the people's curiosity. They spent it freely and continued in this fashion until they began to see the money dwindle, causing severe stress and pressure. Their theatrical venue began to show and uncover their fear and anxiety. Audiences began seeing the farce in their presentation and when the Ford boys were using their real firearms in the act, the show became toxic. (*The Dallas Daily Herald, March 9, 1884*). Most of the sympathizers of the James' boys turned against the Ford brothers. The Ford brothers were booed off the stage many times.

This wrecked their psyche. Charles Ford was in deep despair and battling tuberculosis. He committed suicide with an overdose of morphine in 1884 in Richmond, Missouri. (*The New York Times*, May 7, 1884). Another article in *The Galveston Daily News*, May 7, 1884 reports from St. Louis that he shot himself through the heart. The story in *The Kansas City Times*, May 7, 1884 describes that apparently both methods of suicide were used.

This was about the time that Frank, a free man was running for sheriff in a New Mexico town. It could have been Las Vegas, New Mexico as we find Bob Ford and Dick Liddell in Las Vegas in the Fall of 1884. When Frank lost the race, Ola said he became a Texas Ranger and was stationed near Tascosa. Both Ola and William Tunstill have a picture of Frank James and Pat Garrett in Tascosa. The picture and explanation of their business will be revealed in a later chapter.

We find Bob Ford and Dick Liddel being run out of town in Las Vegas, New Mexico by vigilantes for the suspicion of a planned bank robbery. [335] In the El Paso Times, September 27, 1884 the story expands stating that a tunnel, 60 feet long underneath the town that was aimed toward the bank vaults was discovered. The "conspirators must have been employed three months in excavating it." [336]

From The Weekly Chieftain, October 2, 1884, "The vigilants of Las Vegas have offered Bob Ford and Dick Liddell to "shake" that town at once and forever. When the James gang in Missouri became demoralized these once prominent members transferred their affections to New Mexico."

In 1889, John Shevlin, who was a former U.S. Marshal saw Frank James and Bob Ford together in Colorado City, Colorado. They owned and operated the Grove Theatre there together. This just goes to show that either Frank was the forgiving type or this whole killing of Jesse was a set up with many players involved.

Something happened and Ford sold the theatre out from under Frank. Bob Ford moved to Creede, Colorado where the town exploded during a silver boom. It went from 600 to 10,000 people by 1891. Bob set up a tent saloon and dance hall in Creede, Colorado when the Cripple Creek Goldfield opened. Bob began doing too much talking while drinking, telling the tale that Jesse was still alive. A man by the name of Edward Capehart O'Kelley was hired to shut him up permanently, June 8, 1892.

Just before the killing, a day or two before, Jesse was spotted at his own establishment/saloon outside of Pueblo, Colorado on the road going toward Trinidad with O'Kelly. John Tatum told Bud that he had verified the building in which this speaks of and was turned into a Jesse James' museum. It's on the left as you are leaving Pueblo on the road towards Trinidad.

Strangely, Bob Ford, which not many people know, had a building for his saloon before his tent saloon was in place. It mysteriously burned to the ground on the Sunday before his murder on June 5, 1892. He then erected a tent to keep his patrons coming. [337]

The story in the newspapers describe the murderer as Edward Kelly, not O'Kelley. He was selected as Marshal of the town of Bachelor, Colorado in April 1892 and shortly after that, he became Deputy Sheriff of Hindsdale County, Colorado. In June, Kelly was seen standing at the entrance of the Bob's saloon. After a short time, a cowboy rode up to Kelly and handed him a shotgun. Kelly went in and Bob was standing at the end of the bar and not knowing if Ford saw him or not, Ford quickly turned and headed for a back room. Did he recognize this fellow? With Ford's back turned, Kelly said, "Hello Bob," and as Ford turned, Kelly blasted away his jugular and carotid artery. Kelly shut up Bob Ford for good. [338]

O'Kelley was convicted of Bob Ford's murder and was given a life sentence in the Canon City, Colorado Prison. He asked for a pardon in 1894. His sentence was reduced, and he was able to be released in the Fall of 1902. He got in trouble with the law in Oklahoma City and after a hefty struggle, was shot and killed by a policeman in 1904.

In Find A Grave, it states that O'Kelley was a friend and a cousin by marriage to Jesse James. He had married a "relative of the infamous Younger Brothers Gang." We find he married Mollie Caroline Jarrette whose mother was Mary Josephine "Josie" Younger (1841-1880) and father, John G. Jarrette, who was a sergeant in Quantrill's Raiders. Josie was the daughter of Henry Washington Younger and Bursheba Fristoe. Her brothers were Cole, John, Charles, Jim, and Bob Younger. Josie Younger Jarrette had moved to Louisianna after the war by 1870, but apparently her husband's reputation as a Quantrill man followed him. Josie was burned alive when men who were enemies of her husband burned down their house with her in it. [339]

(Edward Capehart O'Kelley)

Looking at this whole picture of all the characters involved and the drama that followed, the truth was stranger than fiction. It involved a lot of people, those related by blood and brotherhood. Jesse had many people in his corner.

Does it make sense that Frank James, or any of Jesse's closest friends did not seek to avenge his death as Ola would say? Maybe they did.

At the St. Louis Post-Dispatch Newspaper office, a letter was received, "As to the Death of Jesse James, it is a Dam lie. He is still alive and at large and wishes you to publish this note and relieve the people. I remain as ever, his brother, Frank James."

Bud has in his possession, a letter from Karen Fite of the Oklahoma Department of Libraries in Oklahoma City. Bud had requested any information from this department on the papers of Thomas Crittenden they had and if anywhere in their files from Missouri to study to see if there were any notes of Crittenden's involvement. Ms. Fite stated in her letter that they do not have the records for that time period. She called the Missouri State Archives regarding the papers of Thomas Crittenden and stated that she was told they do not have them. Fire at the Capital building had destroyed the records. Very convenient.

After the funeral and burial of Jesse, Governor Crittenden and Sheriff James R. Timberlake were ridiculed in calling this a legal execution. The people of Missouri were not happy with this action. Both of their political careers were over while Jesse was branded as a "hero."

At Timberlake's death, Crittenden stated that Timberlake was "the truest and bravest man that ever lived." "He was a man who knew absolutely no fear and whose loyalty to the state and his office rid this country of the most dangerous and lawless gang of desperadoes and robbers that ever infested it. In Sheriff Timberlake's death Missouri lost one of the principal factors in the extermination of the James' brothers' gang and the killing of Jesse James, the noted leader, by Bob Ford." [340] Timberlake died of an overdose of Morphine. That makes two, Charles Ford and Sheriff Timberlake.

In Governor Thomas T. Crittenden's obituary in the St. Louis Dispatch, May 29, 1909 we learn that Jesse James Jr. became an office boy for Crittenden and helped him to get started in becoming an owner of a cigar stand. This may have been the cigar stand that we spoke of earlier connected to Frank and Jesse. Crittenden also encouraged the boy to study law in which Jesse, Jr. was admitted to the bar in 1906. Crittenden also supported "Young Jess," advancing him money when he was tried and acquitted on a charge of train robbery. [341]

Per Jesse, in the stories told to Ola, the Jesse James Jr. spoken in Crittenden's obituary was actually Bigelow's boy. Jesse said, "Bigelow's boy was about the same size and age of my boy. There never was a Jesse James, Jr. My boy was Jesse Edwards. Bigelow's boy wanted to be a lawyer. So, I made it my business to see that he got to be a lawyer. I helped him and Governor Crittenden helped him too. He was a lawyer in Kansas City a good while, and from what I heard, had a good practice there." [342]

Jesse James, Jr. lived out his life in Los Angeles, California. He did go to the reburying of Jesse's body, which was actually Bigelow, his father, in 1902. They were moving the body from Zerelda's home to the Mount Olivet Cemetery where Mrs. Jesse James was buried in 1900, Bigelow's wife.

Rudy Turilli told Ola, "Ola, I went to Los Angeles, California to this Jesse James, Jr.'s home and looked him right in the eye and told him, "You are not Jesse James' son. You are Bigelow's son. He never replied. He just looked at me as if he was stunned. But never denied what I said." [343]

Moving the body

The reburial of Jesse Woodson James was quite odd. In the Kansas City Journal – June 30, 1902, it describes an array of people, just a small group who were at the old Samuel's homestead where it remained vacant after Zerelda could no longer stay there by herself. Her husband, Mr. Samuels was existing in the St. Joseph Insane Asylum.

They gathered to dig up the body of Jesse James. Among them was Jesse James, Jr. and several ex-Quantrill Raiders. There were also newspaper reporters. Frank James was in the hotel, in bed sick and unable to get out in the cold drizzly rain. Zerelda, also in the hotel insisted on being there to determine if the body was that of her son. Frank would not permit it. Frank said, "I am afraid of the consequences. If it isn't Jesse's body and she should know it, she would drop dead over it. And if it is I'm afraid it would kill her anyhow. No, it must not be."

In The St. Louis Republic, July 6, 1902 the story, "Where Jesse James, Guerrilla Rough Rider Rest Now," is told. When they dug up the casket where Jesse was buried, the place where Zerelda watched over it day and night, was not the nice heavy ornate metal casket that they paid for. Some newspapers reported it to cost $500. The coffin fell apart after 20 years and was made of cheap tin, badly soldered together. When the men began to lift the coffin out, the bottom dropped out and the remains dropped to the bottom of the grave. The skull fell to one side and was placed back in the collar portion of the preserved black broadcloth suit which was in excellent condition. The skull still had the dark brown hair and beard attached. The teeth were intact, showing many gold fillings. The teeth are shown in a display case at the house of Jesse's in St. Joseph. Jesse James Jr. was the only one who examined the skull, the teeth, and the body.

The newspaper implied that the body had not been embalmed.

The corpse was the right height, 5'10" and placed in a new cedar coffin. Some sources stated the coffin was black. It was placed inside the house with two or three relatives guarding it.

A small party of the family, friends, and Quantrill men traveled to the old homestead the next day. Several photographers were there as seen in the newspaper clipping. "The mud-bespattered hearse backed up to the gate with its sign: "Admission to strangers 25 cents." and the undertaker busied himself with badges and gloves." (Kansas City Journal, June 30, 1902).

Frank, his wife Anna, and Zerelda were able to be there to rebury Jesse, but the coffin had already been sealed. The newspaper men noticed that everywhere they went Zerelda was calling the man, known as Frank James, her son, "Mr. Frank." Besides holding an umbrella over Zerelda's head, Mr. Frank didn't show much affection toward her.

A silver plate was intact on the coffin inscribed with "Jesse James." The pallbearers lifted the heavy casket and placed in a pine box and lowered in the open grave. "There was not a word spoken; not a prayer offered; not a remark made; there was an utter absence of any religiosity about the whole event. It was strictly an act of routine, so far as any sign was concerned, either of feeling or emotion; the stoicism which has characterized the Samuels-James family ever, did not fail even at the grave." "So silent was it that it made one think that it might be almost *clandestine*."

Frank was heard saying, "Well, that's all we can do for him." (Kansas City Journal, June 30, 1902) They left with no sound, no feeling, no nothing.

As we will learn in Chapter Thirty-Two, the way the body was buried in 1902 was revealed in 1995. There was no respect for the dead.

A post card arrived on June 29th, the day of the reburial. It was from Kansas and was received by the marshal of Kearney. It read, "I will not be buried in Carny next Sunday. I am not dead. I was shot by Bobie Ford. Tom Howard was shot by Bobie but I wasn't there, you can't bury me." [344]

Lots of controversy and drama in this whole story of Jesse's death in 1882 and again in 1902. It doesn't end there. What do you believe? Are you willing to hear more? Was it the hoax that let Jesse live?

The lives of Zerelda and Frank James took a turn after this. Zerelda rented out her homestead to Alva Merritt while she lived in a hotel in Kearney. Frank and his wife lived in another hotel in Kearney for at least a year. (Kansas City Journal, June 30, 1902) Alva's grandfather was Alvah Merritt/Maret (1804-1880) a judge in Clay County for 8 years and lived in Kearney. He was buried at the New Hope Cemetery where Jesse's father established the New Hope Baptist Church. His daughter, Louisa (1829-1870) married Jesse R. Cole (1826-1895), Zerelda's brother. Alvah's sister, Nancy Merrit/Maret married John "Jack" Dever (1783-1843) whose grandchildren became heavily involved in the Confederacy, which evolved into Quantrill Raiders and into the outlaw gangs with Jesse, the Shepherds, and George Todd.

Frank James was seen in Fletcher, Oklahoma after this period. He began spanning the territory into Apache, Cyril, and Cement. He was looking for something, signs and symbols of any kind. He spoke to a Mrs. Hedlund who owned property around Buzzard Roost near Cement for rocks with any markings. He was able to find one cache we know of in the amount of $6,000. With that money, he and Annie bought 160 acres of land outside of Fletcher, Oklahoma in 1906. He built a home there and grew a peach orchard.

Many people knew Frank wasn't much of a farmer who broke land for crops, but he was seen breaking land in search of more treasure. He appeared confused, bewildered, and lost at times, going over the same area many times. Some believe he wore out 6 horses looking for treasure. Zerelda was seen there visiting Frank and Annie several times. In 1914, Frank and Annie moved to Missouri and sold the Fletcher farm to the Gossett's. They were Annie's aunt's family. Bud found there are Gossett's near Frank and Annie's grave in Independence, Missouri. The house in Fletcher was moved to Cache, Oklahoma, west of Lawton; moved it to Eagle Park in 1964.

Quite a performance by many actors to bury old Jess. Many still believe that was the end of the story. That's not the half of it. There are many acts to follow and the big finale will reveal the truth of this complicated tale.

"Those who stand at the threshold of life always waiting for the right time to change are like the man who stands at the bank of a river waiting for the water to pass so he can cross on dry land."

-Joseph B. Wirthlin

Chapter Seventeen: In and Out of the Red

With Jesse James buried and Frank living as a good, fruitful citizen, many believed peace would return and prosperity would flourish in this country. But there were still the badlands to conquer.

The Red River was a dividing line between the lawless and the lawful, but it never held the one or the other. It became a highway of highwaymen who peddled whiskey to the Indians, cattle rustling and horse stealing among other things.

This had been Jesse's playground. The Red River was his gate to freedom from both sides of the law. He had plenty of help, partners, and protectors. His favorite crossing was on the Little Wichita River that flowed into the Red. This was a known fact in the history of Clay and Montague Counties in Texas. I discovered this fact as I was researching my great uncle who supposedly rode with Jesse. These two counties lay just south of the Red River Station, along the Chisholm Trail. We know that Jesse was definitely there in Montague County (Montague and Bowie), Cooke County (Gainesville), Clay County, (Henrietta), Denton County (Denton), and Wise County (Decatur) Texas.

This crossing was along the Dona Ana Trail, D.A.T. Not many people knew about this trail, nor the name; only those who were in Jesse's brotherhood. The Dona Ana Trail was utilized by Jesse starting in Chihuahua, Mexico going up through El Paso into Dona Ana County, New Mexico east of the present-day town of Las Cruces through the Organ Mountains, through Texas, running parallel west of the Chisholm Trail, along the Little Wichita River and crossing the Red River just west of Terral, Oklahoma.

The map below, which Bud allowed me to show, indicates the trails that paved their way up into the heart of Indian Territory from the Texas border on the Red River. The darker line to the west is the D.A.T. trail and the one to the east is the Chisholm trail with vast acreage, shown in gray, depicting the area needed to move the cattle. Where the marked area for the D.A.T. trail stops is where Chickasha is located, directly west of Purcell. The trails continue north, past what is shown.

After Frank James' trial and he was in the clear in September 1883, we have signs that Jesse was heading back to the states. Just four months later into 1884, the Dona Ana Trail was being used once more.

Shortly after his staged death, Jesse went to South America to Americana, Brazil, South America and Buenos Aires. Three or four hundred people migrated there after the war and it was a welcome mat for the diehard Southerners. The community in Americana honored each year, the Confederacy. They put on their Confederate uniforms, long, colorful dresses and ate southern fried chicken, cornbread and apple pie. They danced under the Confederate flag.

Jesse came back to the states and was sighted with Frank in Searcy County, Arkansas. There was an eyewitness who told the story in 1948. He wrote an affidavit to verify J. Frank Dalton's claim of being Jesse James.

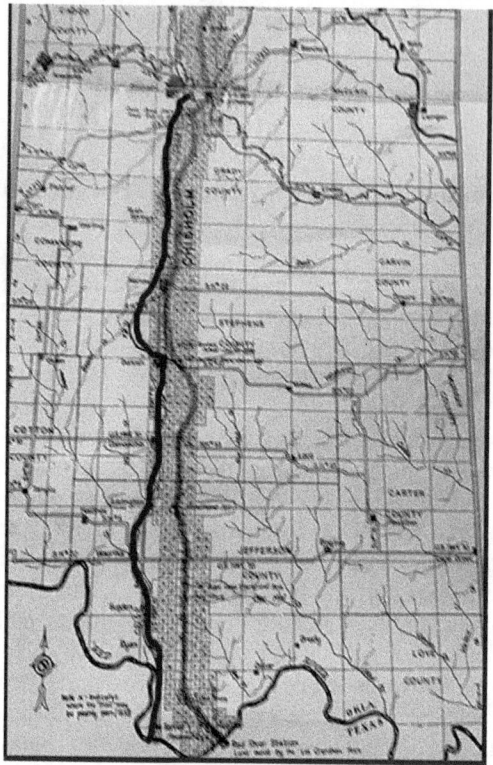

(Dona Ana Trail)

James Henry "Toss" Ingram – Toss was born in Trace Ridge, Searcy County, Arkansas in 1878, near the present town of Marshal. It was in the *Boston Mountains*. It was about 40 miles from Wayton, Arkansas where the man named Joe Vaughn lived. In February 1884, Ingram remembered the big snow that had covered the ground. He was six years old. "My dad was well acquainted with Frank and Jesse James. They were swapping horses and cattle. I sold Jesse James a pot-bellied calf for about $2.50 with which money I bought my first suit of clothes. They had good cartridge guns and shot up a lot of shells at some big red oak trees near our big house."

Toss Ingram's father was John Duncan Ingram. He was a Mason. John's father, William Timothy Ingram was in the Confederacy with the 5th Regiment of the Mississippi Infantry. Toss said, "We moved to Texas, then Oklahoma. I met and knew Frank James around Ardmore. About 16 or 18 years ago two men showed up at Ardmore, Oklahoma. One was, I think named DeWitt Travis. The old man I remembered as the one with Frank James back at our old home in Arkansas when I saw them many times. My father always said Jesse James was not dead but would not say much more. So along about 1930 and 1931 this old man gave a few lectures around Ardmore and *Wilson*. I hauled him out to visit Old Lady Jones. We talked about my father and my father's old place and I knew he was Jesse James. To the best of my knowledge and belief Jesse James is still alive in 1948 staying over around Lawton, Oklahoma at this time." [345] Ingram had lived in Ringling, Oklahoma since 1892.

(John Duncan Ingram in the Masonic Lodge in Simon, Oklahoma (c. 1905). John is the one seated on the left)

This area was very significant, Ardmore, Wilson, and Ringling in Indian Territory. It proved to be a safe haven for Jesse. He was back there by the Fall of 1884.

The next portion of this chapter will pull in stories from this area regarding Jesse and those who he associated with beginning in 1884, after he was supposedly dead. The stories are tied to the writer's 2nd great granduncle whose stories were uncovered in 2012-2014 and the book, *The Haskew Brand* was written. They validate Jesse's locations and activities.

My 2nd great granduncle used the Dona Ana trail to escape the law who was chasing him and 9 others out of Texas into Indian Territory. He was Bowie, Texas' city marshal, Captain John Wesley Haskew who "performs the duty of marshal, to the terror of all evildoers, arresting rich and poor without distinction." [346]

The town of Bowie was only two years old. It had its beginnings when the rumor of gold and coal were in the small mountains surrounding the area. The Fort Worth and Denver City Railroad was interested in running their rails through there. The grading and formation of the railroad beds began in 1881 stretching from Fort Worth to Wichita Falls. It is documented that Allen Parmer, Jesse James' brother-in-law worked on building the railroad in the northern part of this area. By July 1882, the train was ready to roll and Bowie became the railhead until the tracks reached Wichita Falls in September 1882.

By 1883, John Wesley Haskew was elected the 2nd city marshal in Bowie in this newly formed tent city with several buildings that began lining the streets. Haskew was a big son of a gun. It was noted that he had huge arms, the size of a normal man's thigh. He was as stout as an ox. He had to be. He and his brother Newton handled cattle, hogs, and what have you in their butcher shop in the middle of town.

Books relate that the area was filled with outlaws, cattle thieves, horse thieves, whiskey peddlers and cowboys who were familiar with the Chisholm Trail, making up a rowdy brew. John Wesley Haskew was reelected in 1884 with the town's people very pleased. It was a close race, but some hard feelings were brewing.

The Fall of 1884 was when all Hell broke loose. Jesse was in the area. Haskew somehow got mixed up with a robbery of a dry goods store where 6 saddles, boots, clothing, watches, and other items were stolen. It was like someone was trying to outfit a gang of some sort. Haskew was also suspected of whiskey peddling, cattle rustling, and horse stealing, but never charged with those offenses. He was only charged and indicted with theft when the merchandise was found in his home after he was arrested. He never had a chance to prove his innocence. He was caught by the Texas Rangers and former Ranger G. W. Campbell who was the commander of Company C in the Frontier Battalion. He was in command of the Montague County Texas Rangers and worked alongside a unit of the Tenth Cavalry. In Dec. 1873, he was ordered to establish a camp on the Little Wichita River which would remain until February 1874, Campbell was now sheriff of Montague County.

Many family members heard the story that Haskew got caught when he was heading out to warn Jesse that the rangers and sheriff of Montague County were on their trail. Jesse was known to have a campsite not far from Bowie, about 25 miles to the south in Wise County on Dan Waggoner's Ranch along Catlett Creek, close to the present town of Decatur. Mr. Waggoner frequented Bowie quite often. Here is a photo of Dan Waggoner in a Bowie saloon, the man who started the famous Waggoner Ranch which with the help of his son, William Thomas "Tom" Waggoner built the largest ranch in the United States under one fence. He was another cattle baron in the making.

(Dan Waggoner on the far right in a Bowie, Texas saloon. (courtesy of Max Brown))

The Waggoners

In 1869, the father and son team of the Waggoners wintered their cattle in Clay County, Texas on the *Little Wichita River*. By Spring of 1870, Tom at the age of 17 was placed in a man's world as his father put him over the management of the cattle operation. Tom headed his first trail drive up the Chisholm Trail, driving cattle to Abilene, Kansas. He netted a profit of $55,000. They were on the way to making their fortunes. They moved their headquarters to Clay County in 1871 but continued to live outside of Decatur on the ranch even after Tom was married in 1877. Tom lived there during his early married life and had his three children there.

An historical marker near the Decatur Ranch is planted alongside U.S. 380 pointing in the direction 1 mile south from the highway, the area where Jesse and Frank James had their campsite. They would have a line of campsites on those properties where they felt safe and secluded, trusting in the property owners who could keep their mouths shut. The line camps basically extended from the Rio Grande to the Red River, through Indian Territory, and up into Missouri and Arkansas. They would use these line camps to hide their stolen horses or cattle, get fresh horses, and pick up supplies. No doubt, there was a line camp on the Little Wichita River in Clay County near Henrietta, where the Waggoners had their headquarters. It was along the Dona Ana Trail.

There is evidence that Jesse was in the vicinity in 1884.

Bud had spoken and corresponded with Jack Loftin, a great historian in Archer City, Texas that is 40 miles from Henrietta, Texas in Clay County. Both of these towns, as well as Wichita Falls were where Susan James Parmer, Jesse's sister lived. Loftin worked on the book, "Trails Through Archer." Loftin confirmed that one of Susan's descendants, I believe it was the beautiful Feta Parmer Rose, had a letter postmarked in Henrietta from Jesse to Susan in Archer City in the Fall of 1884. He was in Clay County, Texas. Jesse had several hideouts in this area and visited his sister quite often.

In the writer's own research, back in 2012, I too was able to confirm this story with Mr. Loftin who was at that time in the Archer City Nursing Center. Jack Loftin was an amazing man and is sorely missed. He lived just 38 miles from the writer, and I was privileged to get to meet him.

W. T. Waggoner "Tom" had hired Brushy Bill Roberts/Billy in 1883/84 to break horses on the ranch just outside of Decatur. It was the same time that Jesse said that Billy was in the Anti-Horse Thief Association; 1883, 1884, and 1885. It is very possible that Jesse and Billy were there about the same time.

Tom Waggoner must have really liked Billy. During a roundup in Cheyenne Wyoming in 1889, a contest was being held to see who could ride the fiercest bronc of them all, "Cyclone." Waggoner put up the money for Billy, as the "Hugo Kid" to enter the contest, covering all bets. Well Billy did not let ole' Tom down. Billy won the contest, won respect from all the cowboys and was paid well for winning the contest for Waggoner. Billy received $10,000 from Tom. When Brushy Bill was telling Morrison this story, he stated that Tom Waggoner knew exactly who he was.

(Bronc Busting, an example from Quemado, New Mexico by Russell Lee, Library of Congress)

In the same year, 1889, Dan and his son, Tom Waggoner began taking the ranch land that Dan had bought in North Texas in 1852 and expanded upon it. The ranch spread out into several counties covering Wichita, Wilbarger, Foard, Knox, Baylor, and Archer County and covered more than a million acres of land. Tom was trying to drill for water on his ranch and struck oil instead in 1902. At the time I think he'd rather have had water for his cattle as the land was pretty rugged with very few fresh water sources.

W.T. Waggoner, as most people called him developed a natural love of cattle and horses. He learned how to preserve strong bloodlines in breeding with foundational stallions. The result was exquisite quarter horses, which brought worldwide recognition. One of the most famous characters of the ranch was Poco Bueno or "Pokey" as they called him. He was an amazing stallion and cutting horse. Poco Bueno became a Hall of Fame sire which achieved several awards and championships. He was insured for 1 million dollars. It all paid off. His offspring served the ranch well. They even had a stud named "Jesse James" who left his mark in the pedigrees of many fine horses.

W. T. loved to race his horses; therefore, he constructed the Arlington Downs racetrack between Dallas and Fort Worth and persuaded Texas to allow pari-mutuel betting. Wagering on races became legal after the track was completed. This was right up Jesse's alley.

W. T. Waggoner was not only good friends with Billy the Kid, and most likely Jesse James, but he was friends with Teddy Roosevelt and once went on a wolf hunt together. He also was friends with Will Rogers. I was very fortunate to learn more about the Waggoner Ranch living next to their fence, getting to visit often during the 17 years my son-in-law worked and managed one of the Waggoner's camps of 35,000 acres, and watching our grandchildren grow up amongst the hard working cowboys who did everything the old fashioned way. They learned life out on that rugged piece of land where the west had no end as well as the work that had to be done from sunup to sundown.

W. T. Waggoner died in 1934 and left the ranch in a trust divided amongst his three children, Guy Waggoner, Electra Waggoner Wharton, and E. Paul Waggoner. Little did I know until I started writing the books on my family, did I learn that my grandfather's 2nd double cousin, Robert Bernard Anderson became an attorney in 1937 for the ranch and later in 1941 became the general manager of the W.T. Waggoner Estate, the largest ranching estate under one fence in America which included oil and gas properties, cattle, and quarter horses throughout six Texas counties.

"He (Anderson) negotiated oil and gas leases with various Texas Oil Companies. This caused him to take an active interest in the Texas oil industry. In the late 1940's he served as an officer of the Mid-Continent Oil & Gas Association of Texas." (eisenhowerlibrary.gov) [347] This brought Anderson in touch with many businessmen and politicians who were supporting Dwight Eisenhower for president in 1952. It appears that the Waggoners were supporting Eisenhower also.

Dwight Eisenhower was very impressed with Anderson. Eisenhower was encouraged by Lyndon Johnson to strategically place Anderson as Secretary of the Navy since he knew the oil business well and an oil businessman was needed in the Navy since they used the biggest surplus of oil in the country. In January 1953, President Eisenhower appointed Robert Anderson as Secretary of the Navy. Anderson resigned from the Waggoner Ranch and headed to DC to serve his country in this position.

I'm sure the reader is wondering what this story has to do with Jesse. Look at the clues, look at the connections. It is the people, the locations within his brotherhood who stuck together and supported one another to no end. They would continue to grow and grow into a monstrous power that infiltrated every business, every political position, every institution, every entity that developed in this country, spreading into foreign nations. Keep an open mind and at the end, it will all make sense.

Indian Territory, a structured safe haven for the lawless

Robert Anderson and my grandfather shared the same great uncle, John Wesley Haskew, the lawman who turned outlaw and was said to have rode with Jesse in North Texas and Indian Territory.

It's a fascinating story and will be covered in another book that I have written, but the writer will preserve these pages and limit the story, only to allow the story of Jesse, hidden underneath and protected, to shine through revealing Jesse's whereabouts and activities he was involved in.

Why was Jesse in Clay County, Texas in the Fall of 1884? We have evidence of Billy the Kid and Jesse in the same area. We follow their path. There were some shenanigans going on and Marshal Haskew was in on it. It appears that Haskew was supplying Jesse James' line camps in Clay County and the general area. Haskew was caught. Some of the men who were captured with Haskew were men using the names of Clark, Dalton, and Franklin. Sound familiar? The previous marshal of Bowie, John Brooks was accused of theft of property also and taken in. It was a big affair. They were all thrown in the Montague County jail. The newspapers read, "This Town Has An Air Of Unwonted (unusual) Life and Animation Today!"

The Montague County jailhouse was filling up fast. It was close to election day in the county for the sheriff's position. A new sheriff was elected, L.L. McLain, a former deputy. It was only 13 days from his election that things took a drastic turn. On the night of November 24th, 1884 just after the prisoners were fed and the sheriff made the last round, he checked the guard and made sure all things were in order. At 8:00 P.M. that night, he was settling down in his quarters when he became aware of a thunderous roar in the streets. As he jumped to his feet, he saw for himself out the window, a mob of 50 masked angry men coming straight for the jailhouse. The mob broke through the door and stormed up the stairs. There were 12 prisoners crammed into the jail cells, 10 left with the masked men and 2 stayed.

The escaped prisoners headed to Indian Territory via the *Little Wichita River* in Clay County, Texas. It would be close to 30 miles of traveling at night from the Montague County jail to the camp on the Little Wichita. They were later spotted on a sand bar out in the middle of the Red River. Many of Haskew's descendants heard from tales past down that Jesse was amongst them. Someone had to be pretty important for a jailbreak like that. No one suspected Jesse to be amongst them, he was dead, or was he?

The desperados crossed the Red and fled north on the Dona Ana Trail. They first went to the Stephen Walker Ryan's ranch, outside the town which was named after Mr. Ryan, Ryan, Oklahoma. This is where Chuck Norris, the actor who portrayed Texas Ranger Walker was born and grew up.

Stephen Walker Ryan was a Master Mason. The escapees met up with Meredith Crow who was a former Texas Ranger and a Deputy U.S. Marshall in Indian Territory who had a place on Mud Creek. The newspapers stated that Meredith Crow wanted to the burn down the town of Bowie for what they did to Haskew, maybe he also wanted to seek revenge for Jesse. They also met up with Billy Wilson. The group split up; Billy Wilson taking Frank Wilbur, Joe Franklin, and Jim Smith with him to Billy's father's place, but I believe it was actually to John Means place, a partner of Billy Wilson's. They crossed the prairies to the east and met up with John Means who had a place between Mud Creek and the Reck community along Bear Hollow Road just southeast of Ringling, Oklahoma. Was that another line camp for outlaws?

The rest of the group camped at "Sugg's Ranch," but I believe it was officially named, "Old Suggs Campground and Tank along Mud Creek close to the Chisholm Trail. Jesse was known to have stayed at the 1-B Ranch between the Red River and Mud Creek in Indian Territory, straight north from Montague and Cook County, Texas with Bill and John Boone.

I was so grateful, through hard research, the help of my family, the wonderful Montague County Historian, Max Brown, the old newspapers, and the Fort Smith, Arkansas records to piece together Haskew's escape route and learn the identities of the men Haskew rode with. It's an incredible story and reserved for another book put on the back burner to finish Bud's story, but it all coincides together beautifully. "It all fits," as Bud says. The research has given us more credibility on the story of Jesse.

What I'm most thankful for, is meeting Johnny Means over the phone who was related to Billy Wilson. Johnny lived in Bakersfield, California. He was the grandson of John Means, the man who they sought shelter with and Laura May Wilson, John Mean's wife whose brother was Billy Wilson. We will be looking at Johnny's paternal grandfather, John Means, his maternal great grandfather,

William B. Wilson, and his Great Uncle Billy Wilson whose official name was William David "Billy" Wilson.

Johnny was so excited about talking with me and sent so many photos and documents to help substantiate the characters in his family who my great granduncle buddied up with. Johnny was so thankful that someone was finally going to be writing a book about them. Sadly, Johnny died in 2021.

Johnny's great uncle, Billy Wilson was born in 1862 in Collin County, Texas, right smack dab in the middle of the Civil War. He didn't know his father too well; he was gone most of the time. Billy's father, William B. Wilson enlisted in Weston, Texas near McKinney, in the Texas 6th Cavalry, Company K in 1861 under Captain James W. Throckmorton, composed of Collin County men. They would be ordered to move to Fort Smith to join General Ben McCulloch's Army of the West, where General Sterling Price and his Missouri troops would join them. They would be divided into 3 divisions, with Major "Sul" Ross commanding the first, Lt. Col. John S. Griffith commanding the 2nd, and Col. Warren Stone commanding the third. Stone's Regiment, was the same regiment Jesse James' friend and Ranger commander, John Sparks was in. It was also the regiment Wild Henry Roberts, Billy the Kid's father was in. Wild Henry Roberts joined Quantrill in 1863 and Wilson chose to do the same per his great grandson, Johnny Means.

It was fascinating to learn from Johnny that William Wilson was in charge of gathering the horses for Quantrill, possibly gathering the horses of the dead soldiers during the skirmishes. He was required to take care of the horses and developed a strong love for them.

After the war, Willian Wilson did not come home for at least 10 years. He was wrapped up in other things. When he did come home, he'd be gambling or at the racetracks.

Billy Wilson, William's son grew up in a hard period of his life as the oldest child, trying to keep the family together with a mother who was going blind. One of Billy's nieces, Maymie Wilson Martin, said Billy became an outlaw, loved to gamble, and killed his first man when he was 12 years old. He had 22 or 23 notches on his gun.

In his early teen years, Billy Wilson joined cattle drives and was found even working on the 101 Ranch in the Oklahoma Panhandle. He was fond of horseracing just like his Dad. They raced horses around Denton County, Texas with their friend, Sam Bass.

It was about 1878, the year Sam Bass died, that Billy Wilson joined up with a man by the name of John Means (1852-1936), Johnny Means' grandfather who eventually would become Billy's brother-in-law. Billy was 16 at the time. Johnny Means told me that this was about the time they were rustling cattle/horses and taking them to New Mexico. Johnny said that they were both involved in counterfeiting schemes. William Means (1836-1882), the brother of John Means who was 16 years older than him, was charged with counterfeiting in Indian Territory in 1876. He had hightailed it out of the territory, never to be found. Bud always believed Jesse and Billy the Kid were also involved in counterfeiting.

Billy Wilson would also be involved in larceny and introducing liquor in Indian Territory. He was sent to Leavenworth twice. I sent for his records in Leavenworth and received a photo of him, charged with introducing liquor. I am no photo expert, but the photo sent to me from Leavenworth appears to be the same man identified as the Billy Wilson who rode with Billy the Kid. You decide.

(Billy Wilson who rode with Billy the Kid)

(Billy Wilson of Indian Territory in Leavenworth Prison)

The Billy Wilson that was friends with Billy the Kid, were chained to each other as described in the (The Las Vegas Gazette, March 1, 1882) when they were taken from the Las Vegas jail and then on to Santa Fe. One of the great nieces of Billy Wilson in Indian Territory stated that Billy "was arrested in New Mexico for passing counterfeit money and was shackled with Billy the Kid in the back of a wagon going to Las Vegas, New Mexico to be put in jail." – V. Wilson Mueller, great granddaughter of William B. Wilson. This is what Johnny Means has provided to the writer.

Billy Wilson and Billy the Kid were taken further south for trial at Mesilla. Billy the Kid was found guilty of Sheriff William Brady and Andrew L. "Buckshot" Roberts death, and he was transported to Lincoln while Billy Wilson was taken back to Santa Fe for his trial. Wilson was held in the Santa Fe jail and was convicted in March 1882 for passing counterfeit bills. It was over a counterfeit bill $100 that Wilson had received when selling his livery stable business and he passed it to **William Robert** who then passed it to John Chisum and in return, Chisum passed it on back to Robert claiming it was counterfeit. "the note you sent me was counterfeit I send it back." "Thus far the evidence is clear enough, but there is no testimony to show that the note returned by Mr. Chisum was the same one sent to him, and therefore a serious break in the chain of evidence occurs." ("Wilson's Ways," The Santa Fe New Mexican; Feb. 18, 1882) Sounds like a set up to me. He was convicted of the crime and was to serve seven years in the Missouri federal prison.

Oddly, the Billy Wilson in Indian Territory had a uncle named William Robert and there was a William Henry Roberts (Brushy Bill) in the mix.

By September 1882, while still in the Santa Fe jail, Billy Wilson and another prisoner overpowered the guard and escaped. The story goes that he went to Texas and took on his real name, David Lawrence Anderson, started a ranch in Uvalde and became a lawman. Pat Garret was instrumental in getting a pardon for him by President Grover Cleveland. With Pat Garret involved, it may have also been a coverup. This story has too many holes in it like all the rest.

In 1884, is when Billy Wilson of Indian Territory said he had first met Haskew the last part of October of 1884. This would have been the time that Haskew was arrested in Montague County, Texas. Billy Wilson "hung around" the Younger and James Gang, per his niece, Maggie Means Williams. Johnny Means told me that his Aunt Maggie was the one who told him all these stories about Billy Wilson and his grandfather, John Means. They ran together and were in the criminal business together.

Johnny Means was born in 1937 and his father was John Means' son, Joseph Bailey Means. Johnny's mother died of tuberculosis when Johnny was only two, so he was raised by his mother's sister, Johnnie Rowe Kerr while his father went off to war. He remained in the Kerr's household throughout his life and would see his father often. Bailey, his father, as well as Bailey's sister Maggie continued to tell Johnny the stories of the outlaw days.

Johnny's brother, J.B. Means wrote a short story about their grandfather. John Means was born in 1852 and as a young man hooked up with the cowboys on several ranches near Tussy, Oklahoma which was northwest of Ardmore. He learned the ropes quickly by pushing cattle up the trails to Kansas and Missouri. It was along these trails that he ran into many outlaws. He was invited into the Dalton gang and became their cook. Means, who was raising his nephews, Jack and Louie Means because of their father's early death, William in 1882, took them along several times with the Dalton Gang. Johnny told me John Means was known to have pulled several jobs with the Daltons.

John Means brother, William A. Means was in the 6th Arkansas Infantry in Company H. He was previously living in Polk, Calhoun County, Arkansas in 1860 and joined the Infantry in Pocahontas, Arkansas. He was charged with utter and passing counterfeit U.S. Treasury notes and National Bank Bills in February 1876 in Indian Territory. He died in 1882, the year Jesse supposedly died. There is no record of his death date or his burial.

Johnny told me that his grandfather, John Means had a wonderful musical talent and even wrote songs. He was able to entertain the cowboys who could listen for hours. He had a pretty clever way to notify the gang that he was coming into camp by using a reed or taking a leaf and blowing into it as a whistle. It was very similar to how Belle approached the raiders during the Civil War.

John Means was charged with manslaughter which occurred on January 3, 1884 against Henry Persinger (some newspapers spelled his last name, "Serenger") who was the sheriff in Pickens County in the Chickasaw Nation. Means used the butt of his pistol and hit him over the head, cracking his skull. The sheriff died a few hours later. (Austin Weekly Statesman, Feb. 21, 1884).

He was arrested in Cooke County, near Gainesville, Texas. His father had once lived in Montague County, Texas, so he was familiar with the area.

In 1889, Deputy U.S. Marshal John Swain, Bud's relative, under Joseph Yoes had a warrant for the arrest of John Means for the charge of Larceny, stealing 11 cows in the Chickasaw Nation. A James Abel wrote Swain a letter stating, "I send you the particulars against John Means. I have saw all the witnesses and am satisfied it is a good case. John Means has a bad reputation and people would be glad to have him brought to justice. He has been stealing for some time." (Fort Smith, Arkansas, Criminal Case Files)

I don't believe John Means was ever convicted of anything. He always had a "way out."

John Means married Billy Wilson's sister in 1890, Laura May and had accumulated enough beef from strays, and it appears rustling, to set up a nice ranch. They had a beautiful place just north of Orr, Oklahoma. John had a contract with the U.S. Army to supply beef for the troops. He also had a racehorse track southwest of Wilson, Oklahoma which is 18 miles to the West of Ardmore. People for miles around would come every Saturday, match up their horses, camp for the night, and race on Sunday.

(John Means (courtesy of Johnny Means))

John Means, most people called him "Uncle John," had strong connections to the Dalton gang and the Marshall Gang. In the newspapers, the cattle and horse thief gang, assuming the Marshall Gang, was made up of J. M. Ryan, Tom Marshall, William Roberts, and George Hogan. (The Indian Journal, Feb. 21, 1884). Is it possible that the William Roberts listed in this article, supposedly Billy Wilson's uncle was the one named as being involved in the Billy Wilson's saga in New Mexico also? Could it be that this William Robert/Roberts was actually Billy the Kid? "It's a possibility," as Bud always said. Stories told to me by Mean's grandson is that several gangs rode in during the night at various times to John Means' ranch and spent the night out on the porch. The next morning, they would leave and Mrs. Means would always find something very valuable left for her under the pillows. Bud told me that this action sounds like what Jesse would do.

It was the dead of winter, January 3, 1885 and the winter winds were whipping through the rolling hills of Oklahoma. Haskew and Billy Wilson, who were wearing disguises were seen at Wild Horse Creek by Indian Police James Guy of the Chickasaw Nation, raising his suspicion.

James Harris Guy served as a Deputy U.S. Marshal and sergeant in the Indian Police at the same time. He was a Chickasaw, growing up in the Choctaw Nation. Guy's uncle, Cyrus Harris was the first governor of the Chickasaw Nation and James' brother, William Guy later became governor of the Chickasaw Nation. The family was highly regarded and respected. It is said that Gene Autry's character in the movies was actually portraying Deputy U.S. Marshal James Guy. He was known as brave, even to the point of rashness.

The outlaws were planning to get supplies for the group at Doak's Store in Velma. A list was written out of what they needed and signed it, "Please fill this order for moonshiner and oblige, your shifty friend. Another list had names written out that were there at the store, John Hascue, Billy Wilson, Frank Wilber, *Clark*, and *Franklin*.

James Throckmorton Doak owned the store the outlaws had their eye on, whose Uncle Alexander Doak married Bloody Bill Andersons' sister Mary Ellen. Doak was a Freemason and his father, Josiah Dudley Doak went to Mexico and fought with Maxmillian and took quinine down there. In the Dallas Weekly Herald, May 13, 1863, Doak was in charge of 250 "fine mules" from Mexico, designed for General William Steele's Division of the army in the Indian Nation. Interesting note: Steele was in the 7th Texas Cavalry and his first assignment was leading the Confederate forces in Mesilla during the New Mexico Campaign in 1862.

James Throckmorton Doak was a pioneer in banking, lumber, general mercantile, cotton ginning, cattle, and farming. The desperadoes must have felt that Doak was their friend. The incident didn't turn out none too friendly. Deputy U.S. Marshal James Guy, with several men, chased the desperados for several days and had them held up along the Canadian River, west of Johnsonville, where Jesse was known to visit at the stage stop when he ran his freighting business. It was probably another dependable line camp.

There were 13 men all together that began emptying the wagon at the cabin when Deputy James Guy surrounded them. Six of the men escaped and were not caught. Their identity was not known. Before any shots were fired, Guy saw Haskew through the doorway picking up a rifle. Haskew was a big man, an easy target. Guy thought Haskew was going to start shooting, so Guy shot and hit Haskew in the gut, the "kiss of death."

After the blast that stunned both sides, many men gathered around the cabin. Some believed it was more gang members, but their guns remained silent in shock.

Haskew laid in the cabin in disbelief. A doc was called to the scene and he did not have good news. He did not think that he would last another day. James Guy left him in the hands of a black family to care for him and bury the remains. Haskew's family told me that he did not die, he recovered and lived a long life, with another name and another family. Many say he rode off with Jesse James after he recovered and settled in No Man's Land. Haskew's son went to find him later. He was living just on the other side of the fence to Jesse James. This would have been in the late 1880's – 1910's.

James Guy was charged with manslaughter due to "maliciously slay and kill one, John Hasque." It gets very interesting in the criminal records in Fort Smith but is all laid out in the coming book. Guy never did face any convictions or jail time; he was killed 4 months later by the Lee Gang.

Billy Wilson was taken to Fort Smith where he answered to charges of larceny before Judge Isaac Parker. On February 25, 1885, he was sent to the Detroit House of Corrections, same place where Belle and Sam Starr were taken to in 1883, serving nine months.

This didn't stop Billy from outlawry. He would continue with charges of larceny and introducing liquor. His nephew, Bailey Means, Johnny's father said that Billy was caught with Frank Younger and served 5 years in Leavenworth. I don't believe there was a Frank Younger, but maybe it was another Younger he was speaking of. Last record we have of Billy, or that of his legal name William D. Wilson, sentenced to the Leavenworth prison was for introducing liquor in Dec. 1895 - Oct. 1896 and another charge of larceny with a sentence from February 1898 - Dec. 1898.

When Billy got out, he had a huge fight with one of his family members and took his saddle, his horse, and gear and left, never to be seen by the family again. This was in 1899. They thought he had gone to Mexico. Was he the real Billy Wilson who was with Billy the Kid or was the man David Lawrence Anderson, who started a ranch in Uvalde, Texas and was pardoned, the real Billy Wilson. We don't know.

Johnny Means told me that when his father, Bailey was a little boy, his father, John Means took him to Ardmore to see a Wild West show and little Bailey was introduced to Cole Younger. It appeared as though they were long lost friends.

Bailey grew up in a pretty rough environment. He saw everything such as gunfights, outlaws, horse racing, and everything that goes along with these type of activities. Bailey saw on numerous occasions, the bulge under his father's coat or overalls where he packed his pistols. His Dad always had them on him, especially after he had a squabble with his neighbor and received a slug, living to tell about it.

"Bailey witnessed the Indians gathering around their home, waiting on their beef that John Means was to provide to them through a contract with the government. They were hungry. When an impatient Indian, could not stand the wait no more, he tried to kill John Means with his knife, but Billy Wilson shot him down before he could do so.

Bailey also saw that once the Indians received their beef, they slashed the cow's throat to drink the blood and ate their raw intestines. Not a regular childhood.

Bailey said one time his father took him to the bank in Orr, not far from their house and once they got inside, his father said, "If you were a little older, we'd rob this bank."

Unbelievably, robbers blew up the bank in Orr and the town went downhill from then on and never recovered. [348] The newspapers didn't say the bank was blown up, but did name one of the suspects, Roy Means, a great nephew of John Means.

To lasso this story in with Jesse, if we hadn't already done so, we look at the Mean's neighbor. When Johnny Means was visiting his brother in the 1960's, they went to their grandfather's old home place. Fortunately, on a trip when I went to visit Bud, I was able to drive to the place where all this action occurred. Johnny gave me excellent directions and I saw the beauty of this country with so much history in its soil.

A neighbor who had known their grandfather, tried for years to get the boys to come over and hear the stories about their grandfather, John Means. Finally, when Johnny and J.B. were together, they went to talk to the old man who was 90 years old, born in 1878. The old man told them many stories about John Means, his run in with the law, the leniency he was given with noted lawmen such as U. S. Marshal James Mershon, and his great musical ability that got him off the hook many times.

This neighbor also stated that he had been in the neighborhood near Wilson, Reck, Ringling, and Ardmore, Oklahoma since 1892. He stated that he knew John well and used to go on cattle drives with him, possibly he was referring to roundups that John did in his cattle rustling days. John was still being charged for larceny in 1899. The thing that his neighbor remembered the most was that John would always wear his gun and holster under his overalls. You could hear the swishing and the creaking of leather rubbing against leather and metal underneath. Just like Jesse, he was concerned about self-preservation.

Just as God's hand has been in this research and this book that Bud and I have been involved in, God surprises me again. The neighbor who knew and worked with John Means was a dear friend of Frank and Jesse James in Arkansas and Indian Territory. The neighbor was Toss Ingram, the man who came to Lawton to identify J. Frank Dalton as Jesse James in 1948 who knew him in Arkansas and when he was in Indian Territory in Ardmore giving lectures. They all knew who the strangers were who roamed the rolling hills of Indian Territory, but they kept their mouths shut until the time was right.

Butcher Knife

We do know that Jesse was in Indian Territory in 1885, but was back in Texas in 1886 in Killeen, performing Texas Ranger duty for three months and then he went to Brownwood.

Shortly after he was in Brownwood, Jesse was working on the railroad construction around Granbury under an assumed name, J.W. Gates. It appears that he worked into 1887 and then was helping in Ardmore with the establishment of the Atchison, Topeka, and Santa Fe Railway. The tracks were laid strategically through the Roff Brother's 700 Ranch. The town of Ardmore exploded and became a site for cattle transportation, trading center for farmers and ranchers, and a great market for cotton.

Jesse seemed to gravitate more to Indian Territory. Jesse tells Ola he was in and out of Butcher Knife on Mud Creek in Indian Territory between 1887-1888. Not a very pleasant name, and I'm sure there is a story behind it. This is in Jefferson County, Oklahoma. This very small community is southwest of Ringling and directly west of Wilson in the neighborhood of Toss Ingram and John Means. The writer has been studying this area for ten years and it was deadly back in those days as the story was told earlier. Toss Ingram could testify to that. Just two years earlier is when Jesse, my 2nd great granduncle, John Wesley Haskew, Billy Wilson, and John Means were roaming that particular area and hiding out at some of the line camps there.

Ola Everhard's mother, Bertha lived in Butcher Knife as a child and relayed stories to her daughter about J. Frank Dalton (Jesse) as marshal coming to visit her father often, always concerned about the family. Butcher Knife was known as the "Home of Outlaws." It was rough.

When James Underwood, Bertha's father brought his family from Tennessee into Oklahoma in the Fall of 1888, they first rode the train to Ardmore, Oklahoma. Jesse was closely attached to Ardmore. It was if Jesse wanted the family there. James Underwood was first cousins to Jesse.

Underwood found a job with the Freeman Brothers who just so happened lived in Butcher Knife which was close to 25 miles to the west of Ardmore. He took his family to Butcher Knife and they lived in one room of the Freeman's house. He worked there taking care of the horses. Bertha was about 5 or 6 at this time.

Jesse referred to James Underwood as "Toby." Dalton would stay for hours talking with her father, but she could tell her mother didn't like for him to come around. Her mother, Savannah (O'Daniel) Underwood only knew that he was a former outlaw and she kept her distance. James Underwood never went into detail about his folks, especially to his wife, but deep down, I believe she knew.

Bertha recalled a time when the marshal came to their home in Butcher Knife warning the Underwoods that they were living in an extremely dangerous area. The town would later be known as Atlee.

Jesse and family named "Akers" helped move the Underwoods to a safer place in *Woodford*, further east, 22 miles northwest of Ardmore. *Woodford* is another name connecting Jesse to his mother, Zerelda, where she was born in Kentucky. It was a small community but a safe haven.

Frank Dalton

The **real** Frank Dalton (1859-1887), older brother of the Dalton Gang and Jesse's first cousin, was the only one who continued to be on the right side. He was a Deputy US Marshal in Indian Territory and died an early death while performing his duty in Indian Territory.

Several stories came out about Frank Dalton's death in 1887, some claiming a horse thief killed him and another story was by a bootlegger. Ola and Aubrey had a picture of Frank Dalton on their dresser, her 3rd cousin also. Aubrey told Bud that the outlaw didn't kill Frank, but when Frank was wrestling with an Indian and began taking him out of the gate, the Indians' wife picked up a Winchester and shot Frank. Bud never heard of this story except from Aubrey who heard it straight from Jesse.

The Parmers/Palmers

Through all the reports and documents that Bud has accumulated, we find Jesse in and out of Indian Territory and Texas before 1887. We know he was in Clay County, Texas in the Fall of 1884 and possibly earlier than that to be near his sister, Susan who had lived in *Clay County* Texas.

One article that Bud had from the *Quarterly of the National Association and Center for Outlaw and Lawman History* indicates that Allen and Susan James Parmer married in 1870 in Clay County, Missouri, leaving the state soon thereafter to Arkansas where Allen's parents lived. This was after the Civil War and they may have had to leave Missouri to escape a lot of backlash, just as the James had to go to Nebraska temporarily.

Allen's father, Isaac Palmer (correct last name, not Parmer as Allen used) was living with his wife and family in Platte, Clay County, Missouri in 1850. Isaac was a teamster in Independence, Missouri in 1860. He was in the 4th Missouri Infantry CSA during the war. Allen, taking after his father, became the youngest of Quantrill Raiders and was there during the Lawrence Raid, just a year younger than Jesse. It appears that after the war, they all moved to Arkansas.

Some descendants indicate that Allen and Susan Parmer lived in Cane Hill, Washington County, Arkansas after the war. I believe this was true as we find evidence that Allen and Susan's first-born son, Robert Archie Parmer was born in Cane Hill. In 1872, Susan taught at the old Bethesda School near Cane Hill.

Allen and Susan moved to Sherman, Grayson County, Texas in 1873. Records suggest that Allen's parents sold their property in Arkansas in 1874 and moved to Texas. Isaac and his family are found in Pilot Point, Denton County, Texas in 1880, shown that Isaac was a teamster on the census. Three years later, they were in Sherman where Isaac died.

It appears that Allen and Susan Parmer, by 1876, moved to a farm on Gilbert Creek in Clay County, Texas, near Henrietta. As you can see, they all moved quite frequently, trying to find a safe haven. We know Sherman in Grayson County was a safe place for the Confederates and Texas certainly was, especially around Wichita Falls, Texas where many ex-Confederates and ex-Quantrill Raiders landed.

My dear friend and ex co-worker, Ellen Jahnke, a Wichita County Heritage Society board member in Wichita Falls said "There are almost 150 Civil War veterans (in Riverside and nearby cemeteries), and for a very small town, that's quite remarkable." ("Here Lies City's History," by Lana Sweeten-Shults, 2011 – https://archive.timesrecordnews.com)

By 1882, the year of Jesse's death, the Parmers moved to Wichita County where Parmer got a job moving dirt and hauling freight for the construction of the Fort Worth and Denver City Railway through Wichita Falls. The following year, they lived near the Stone Ranch, owned by Stone Land and Cattle Company, also known as the T-Fork Ranch. A portion of the ranch was purchased by Luke Wilson who formed the Wichita Land and Cattle Company. Allen Parmer became the foreman. This was on Beaver Creek in Wichita County, which also runs into the Wichita River. We spoke of this earlier, where the trails of old that Pike and Marcy were interested in earlier and Jesse was very fond of.

Traveling due east along Beaver Creek that runs into the Wichita River, you will learn of Horseshoe Lake. The writer read an article in the Wichita Times, "Coming of Movie 'Jesse James' Stirs Memories Here," dated January 22, 1939. It spoke of the stories the old timers used to tell regarding the James boys. One story indicated that a certain hideout was at a house and a barn. This is possibly close to where the Parmers lived in Wichita County close to where Beaver Creek ran into the Wichita River.

The legend claims the old barn had a high tower on top, allowing a perfect lookout tower. There was a man in Wichita Falls in 1939 that stated he found a tunnel "a horse could be led through," which went from the barn to the bank of the old Horseshoe Lake, more than 200 yards away.

Living only 50 miles from Wichita Falls, I had never heard of the Horseshoe Lake. My dear "ole" husband knew exactly where it was. It is 5 miles southeast of Iowa Park, Texas. It runs parallel to the Wichita River and is within the 33rd degree latitude parallel. The Wichita River is where one of Allen and Susan Parmer's sons drowned.

The newspaper clipping also refers to young boys who were swallowing up stories right and left regarding Jesse and Frank James. One of the young boys came to Wichita Falls when they had just experienced the bank being robbed there. As the newspaper describes, the Horseshoe Lake was close to downtown Wichita Falls, not at the present site of Horseshoe Lake several miles away we had mentioned. The paper stated it was where Memorial auditorium is, right downtown.

The boys began to dig a tunnel on the bank of the lake and found a hollow space which appeared to be the tunnel you could lead a horse through. They had to terminate their quest, so they decided to explore the old barn 200 yards away and found a large cistern with a tunnel of the same magnitude and put the story together.

Sometime near the year of 1883/84, Allen became manager for the Stone Land and Cattle Company. The company built the house for the Parmers to live in Archer City. The town lies in Archer County which at one time had a copper mine where gun caps were made during the Civil War. There was also a Confederate Camp called, Camp Cureton. It was the hometown of the famous author, Larry McMurtry, where his novels came to life in the movies, "The Last Picture Show" and his Pulitzer Prize novel, "Lonesome Dove."

Frank and Jesse James often hid out near the Parmer's home. They were known to have well-hidden hideouts near Lake Creek near the present-day Hwy 281. This creek is located in northeastern Archer County and runs northeast for nineteen miles to its mouth on the Little Wichita River in western Clay County. This information lays out how Jesse traveled to and from Indian Territory in those days. His favorite path was noted through the Little Wichita River to the Red River.

There was a dugout where they also hid, per Jack Loftin, 10 miles south of Wichita Falls. August George Maag (1851-1892) befriended Frank and Jesse, as well as Allen Parmer and allowed the James boys to stay at his house, but always warned the kids to be quiet about this and never tell anyone. Mr. Loftin was able to get several interviews with the Maag children.

In Loftin's book, "Trails Through Archer," he writes that "Many of the early settlers knew both Jesse and Frank James as they made north Texas their area of recluse. They were wanted by the law but no county citizen, not even the sheriff, Bill Mann wanted to know their whereabouts. They were the Robinhoods of the frontier, having many friends and family members living in the area; thus, when told of their whereabouts, many local sheriffs just laughed it off as a joke. This writer does not believe that Jesse was killed in St. Joseph, Missouri, in 1882 but believes that an act of masquerade was set up to quiet the situation."

Allen and Susan Parmer continued living in Clay, Archer, and Wichita County. It was very interesting to find a newspaper clipping in a very old newspaper, "Wichita Falls. Attacked and Shot at by Enemies Lying in Wait – A Close Call with Winchesters" (Fort Worth Daily Gazette, April 06, 1884). Allen Parmer was described as one of Wichita's most prominent and enterprising citizens. He was cautiously returning from a Stock Convention in Seymour, driving his buggy, keeping an eye out for any trouble. Apparently, he had received threats from several parties in the area.

When he reached 12 miles out of Seymour, he spied a man who stood up in a ravine with a rifle. Parmer took up his Winchester and then noticed that there were actually three men trying to ambush him. The firing began with a massive number of bullets exchanged. Several bullets planted holes in his buggy, one in his pant leg, boot top, and in his coat.

Parmer never backed down. After injuring one of the "highwaymen," the other two backed down and allowed Parmer to pass.

There was tremendous support from Jesse's sister, Susan Parmer in North Texas. Susan was described as "a quiet, refined woman." Ola stated in a newspaper article that "Susan was one of five persons listed as charter members of the First Baptist Church in Wichita Falls." [349] Jesse spent one winter with her. One of Susan's granddaughters, Feta Rose's daughter, Mrs. R. M. Higbie, said she has a letter that Susan James Parmer wrote to her mother, Zerelda stating that "the boys are safe in Gainesville." The town of Gainesville is in Cooke County, Texas where several men who were hooked up to Jesse were hiding also, one being John Means. It was approximately 65 miles from Clay County. Thereafter, Jesse wrote his sister a letter from Clay County, Texas in the Fall of 1884.

With connections interlaced with the James there also seemed to be a steady influx of past Quantrill Raiders living in the same proximity of these families. There were two sheriffs in Wichita County in those days who were good friends to the Parmers and Frank James. Sheriff "Lee" Boon McMurtry was one of them. He was a Quantrill Raider. Sheriff McMurtry, not related to the award-winning author Larry McMurtry who grew up in Archer City, was there at the massacre in Lawrence Kansas during the Civil War. "The Company," he always explained, "was raised of fearless and daring men of the frontier who were accustomed to ride and shoot and was intended as a light horse attachment of the Confederate Army. Their recklessness led them into trouble with the leaders of the Confederacy and before they were aware of it, they were declared outlaws and the hands of both the Federal and Confederate governments were against them." [350]

McMurtry ran with the James brothers and escaped to Mexico and later went to Las Vegas, New Mexico where he was engaged in merchandising for two years. Others say Jesse did also.

McMurtry got into the cattle business and by 1871, he moved down into Choctaw Nation, Indian Territory. He did very well. McMurtry settled in Wichita Falls in 1883 and became a successful cattleman. McMurtry became a powerful sheriff in Wichita County for four years. He was noted as fearless and enforced the law to the letter. In the fall of 1907, Cole Younger visited him. McMurtry passed away the following year. McMurtry was a member of the Royal Arch and the Masonic Wichita Lodge No. 202. [351]

Eventually, Allen and Susan moved into Wichita Falls. Susan had many children with Allen, but sadly, the little baby boy she was carrying, died with complications on March 2, 1889. Susan died a day later. She had her funeral and burial in Wichita Falls and both Frank and Jesse were there.

In 1892, Allen Parmer remarried to a woman named Sarah Catherine "Kitty" Ogden. By 1905, Allen Parmer was a railroad contractor, working in Missouri, Mississippi, Arkansas, and Texas. Parmer may have given Jesse an opportunity to get involved in the railroad or vice versa. Parmer and his wife moved to Alpine, Texas.

Another interesting note about Allen and Susan Parmer. A wonderful newspaper story, "Frank and Jesse James are Uncle to Wichitan" by Martha Steimel; written for the Wichita Falls Times, July 20, 1969. In the story we find information about the families. It is noted that J.A. Kemp, an extremely well-known leader of the city of Wichita Falls, spoke at Allen Parmer's funeral. It was at Mr. Kemp's home that Allen had traveled from Alpine, Texas back to his hometown to see and visit some good friends. He died while on that visit. Mr. Kemp stated that Parmer was probably the first resident of Wichita Falls.

A former mayor of Wichita Falls, John T. Younger during 1934-1936 was said to have known J. Frank Dalton, who without a doubt was Jesse James. Frank and Jesse rode by his family farm in Missouri in 1879, ate supper, and spent the night in the hay loft. While mayor, Jesse came to visit him in Wichita Falls and reminisced about the past. [352]

In this same article, Jesse was speaking at the Princess Theater in Wichita Falls at that time and another fellow who the newspaper stated was Jim Marlowe was there at the theater and "set out to prove J. Frank Dalton was a liar and a fraud. He called out "Do you know a fella named Jim Marlowe?" he asked. "I ought to," Dalton replied. "He's my brother-in-law, How're the folks, Jim?" The newspaper stated that Jim was married to the James brother's sister. This was not Susan, so this implies the James had more than one sister, maybe three including Mary who died at the beginning of the Civil War.

It is not clear if this article was referring to the former mayor in the years 1918-1920, J. B. Marlowe (James Beard "Jim" Marlow, Sr. (1873-1952). At the age of 25, he married Sophia Mataska in 1898. He possibly was married before, but it is unknown. Jim's father was from Carthage, Missouri, Pleasant Monroe Marlow (1841- ?) and was 1st Sgt. in the Confederate Missouri 6th Cavalry, Company H.

Frank James was a shoe clerk in a Mercantile Store owned by Mr. Kemp in Wichita Falls.

Feta Rose, Allen and Susan Parmer's daughter, stated that she has very fond memories of her father, Allen, "wonderful – no human ever had a more generous nature or kinder heart. He was never with the James boys when they were in the outlaw band." She had wonderful memories of Uncle Frank and Aunt Anna. She had said that Frank and Anna had no children. Was Robert James adopted or was he someone else? Will explore this later.

"Both lawman and outlaw defend or violate the same moral codes and there is never a question as to the outcome of a career of crime or ultimate punishment of the outlaw because of the strength and solidarity of frontier law."

-Helen Hoffsommer Stout *(The writer's grandmother)*

Chapter Eighteen: Taming the Territory

The Run

April 22, 1889, a month after his sister, Susan died, Jesse was poised to make the land run along the northern boundary of the run in Guthrie, Oklahoma. The town was once called Deer Creek and was just a water stop for the train.

The heart of Indian Territory of nearly two million acres of unassigned land was being allowed for settling. The southern boundary for the land run was Purcell. Bud Hardcastle's grandfather, John W. Hays started out in Purcell, but ended up going to Guthrie for the run.

The eastern boundary was approximately 10-12 miles to the East of Guthrie along the Indian Meridian. This longitude line is 97 degrees 14'30" surveyed by Marcy years before and somehow miscalculated it, when his intention was to pinpoint the 100-degree meridian. The Indian Meridian extended from the Red River to the Kansas border. It was what governed the surveys in Oklahoma, agreed upon with the Choctaw and Chickasaw Nations. It established an intricate grid in which to lay out towns and sectional acreage. Another example of exquisite "order out of chaos" applied in this new wild territory.

Fifty to Sixty Thousand settlers were ready to grasp their chance for free land. Jesse told Ola that he saw to it that John Trammel would have a piece of this pie, his most trusted friend and confidant. Jesse made sure John Trammel had a farm and a nice home to live in near Guthrie. He or another one of his buddies staked a claim for Trammel, free and clear. Bud verified this and knew where the land and house was. He was able to go there and see for himself. There were signs/symbols only the KGC would use around his place and evidence of traps set if you got a little too noisy around the property. We will go into that later.

Amongst the settlers who started out from Guthrie was a man by the name of Allen McDaniel. Ola believed that this man was actually Jesse, but we find him in the census in 1890 indicating he was 27 years of age. Jesse looked very young for his age, but not that young as he was pressing 43 years of age. It could have been him, using the name or someone who did all the leg work to get the land for Jesse, but there was a real Allen McDaniel. He was the brother of a man whom Jesse also claimed to be, James Ira McDaniel.

This story really has puzzled me. All I can say is, I will present the story to you and you can decide how it all fits together. I do know that when Jesse told this story to Ola, he knew more about these people than anything written about them, but all the census and land records support Jesse's story. He was involved somehow. Jesse was either playing the part of these individuals or they were playing their parts well for Jesse and the KGC.

Jesse was a genius. As I have dug further into what Bud has gathered and in my own research, it is very obvious, Jesse was acquiring land for farming, ranching, mining, railroading, and you name it. He would have others do the work on these places and the money earned went to the KGC.

Jesse told Ola that he was able to stake out a claim for land, a farm located eight and a half miles southeast of Guthrie. Jesse said a John W. Pierce, also got land later, about ½ mile from his place. Allen McDaniel and John William Pierce lived side by side shown in the 1890 census in Logan County, outside of Guthrie. We find both of them in Township 15 in the far northwest corner. It was in the township labeled "Iowa" for the Iowa Indians who lived there. The land that Allen McDaniel obtained, had to be the land Jesse was referring to.

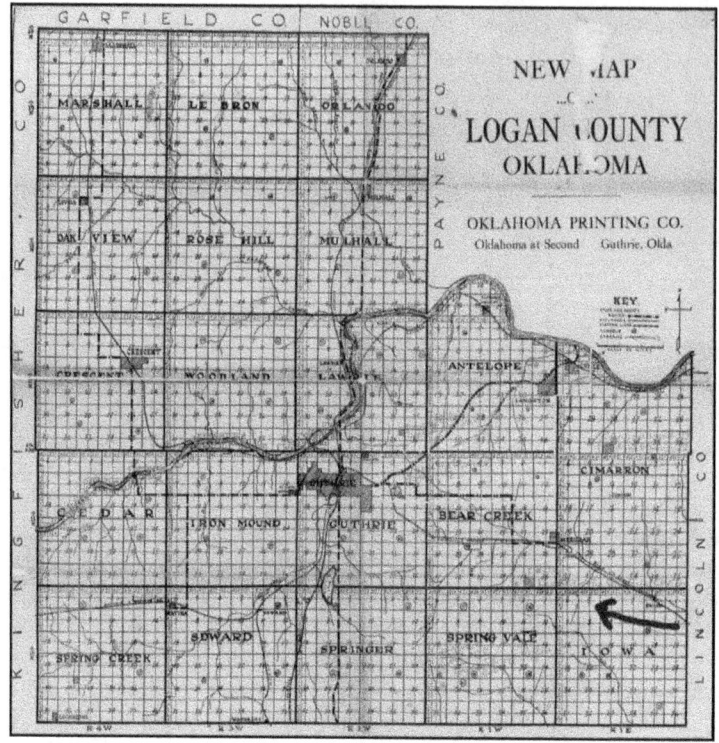

(Property claimed by Jesse and his cohorts)

This John William Pierce was quite an interesting man, a shadow in the background. William Pierce, as he was called was 35 years old, married to a 32-year-old woman, Mary with 3 children. Ola said Pierce worked for Jesse putting up hay on his place in Logan County, Oklahoma. Jesse said Pierce worked 7 out of the 8 years he kept the place. The last year Jesse had the property was in 1897.

We still find John W. Pierce living on his piece of land in 1900. He was a witness to prove continuous residence for William H. Dewitt on land near Pierce's, which was in Section 8, township 15, range 1 west. James I. McDaniel also testified on this man's continuous residence. [353] William Pierce would later be a witness to testify who Jesse was in a court of law in 1950.

In Pierce's obituary in the Daily Standard out of Excelsior Springs in 1952, he died at the age of 97. He was the son of Martin and Martha Arrell. He was living in Orrick, Missouri at the time of his death and had lived there for some time. He was born in 1854 in Valley Falls, Kansas and became a farmer. William went blind sometime before 1910. He was divorced and living with his son, John W. Pierce, Jr. in Hulen, Comanche, Oklahoma in 1910. So, he didn't stay long on the farm just as Jesse said.

How did Jesse know this man? John William Pierce had known Jesse for a long time. Per Ola, they first met in the early 1860's when Pierce was only 8 and Jesse 15, about the time Jesse had joined Quantrill. They met again in Excelsior Springs, Missouri in the early 1870's. William's cousin, Charlie Pierce was a member of the James Gang. It is unknown if William was in the James Gang or just a friend, but he sure was meeting up with Jesse a lot in St. Joseph where he was a brick layer and then again in the newly settled township of Logan County, Oklahoma in 1890.

Pierce signed an affidavit in which was addressed in The Police Gazette, by George McGrath in January 1952, "John William Pierce, of Orrick, Missouri, another of those "in the know", signed an affidavit that, as a confidante of the James gang, he knew Bigelow was to be slain instead of Jesse. "I was laying stone on a piece of ground about 200 feet from the house where the shooting took place at St. Joseph. That morning Jesse was supposed to have been killed," he asserted. "When I heard the shots, I ran to the house and saw the dead man lying on the floor. That man was the one I knew as Charley Bigelow." Pierce revealed that Jesse came furtively to his home around noon, and told him, "The job has been done. Now I will have to leave the country." The Missourian said that he saw Jesse again in 1893, and that James confided he had just returned from South America." It was in the town of Guthrie where they met again.

I'm curious, if Pierce was a brick layer or stone mason, living in St. Joseph, would he have been the person who provided the bricks for John Trammel to carve out the real story of Bigelow's death in 1882?

The other man who lived next to Pierce in Township 15 in Logan County was Allen A. McDaniel. He was born in Iowa and married Keziah Elsie *Campbell* in Council Bluffs, Iowa. Campbell is a name that Jesse used frequently. McDaniel is listed in the 1890 Logan County census in Township 15 as 27 years old, with his wife Elsa at 18. In one of the stories told in Elsie's obituary, they lived in Meridian, Oklahoma and lived there 8 years, until 1897 (Hill City Times; January 1, 1959). The year 1897 is when Jesse left his farm in Logan County.

Land records indicate McDaniel was issued a land grant, June 17, 1895 on the Indian Meridian, Township 15 N, Range 001W Tract 3, Tract 4, and Tract 5 in Section 6, proving that he had resided there and improved the land after five years. This gives us a better idea of where the land was exactly.

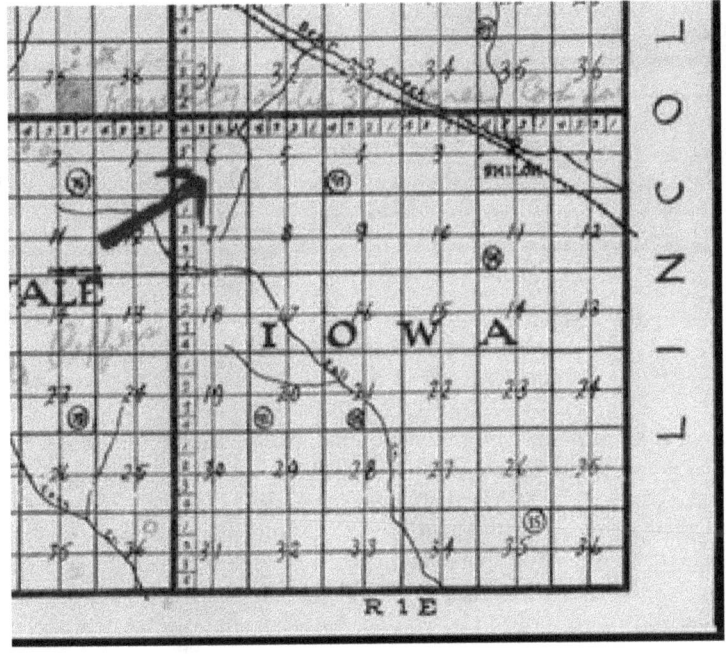

(Section 6 in Township 15)

This had to be farmland. The family lived in Meridian which was due north along the Indian Meridian. It must not have been the perfect place to live as we find Allen Andrew McDaniel (1862) and his family moved to Spring Creek, in Graham County, Kansas in 1897.

In 1902, after Allen had moved away, he was mentioned in a public notice for a hearing involving him, his father, Lewis McDaniel; his two brothers, James and John; and his sister Rebecca. They were all part owners of other property in Township 16, the northeast quarter of *section 33*, north of range one, east of Indian meridian in Logan County which involved the Fort Smith and Western Railroad Company in a land dispute to build and construct a railroad over the land. (*The*

Guthrie Daily Leader, June 10, 1902). On the map it looks like the railroad got their wish as well as the M.K. & T. which went through the same country parallel to each other.

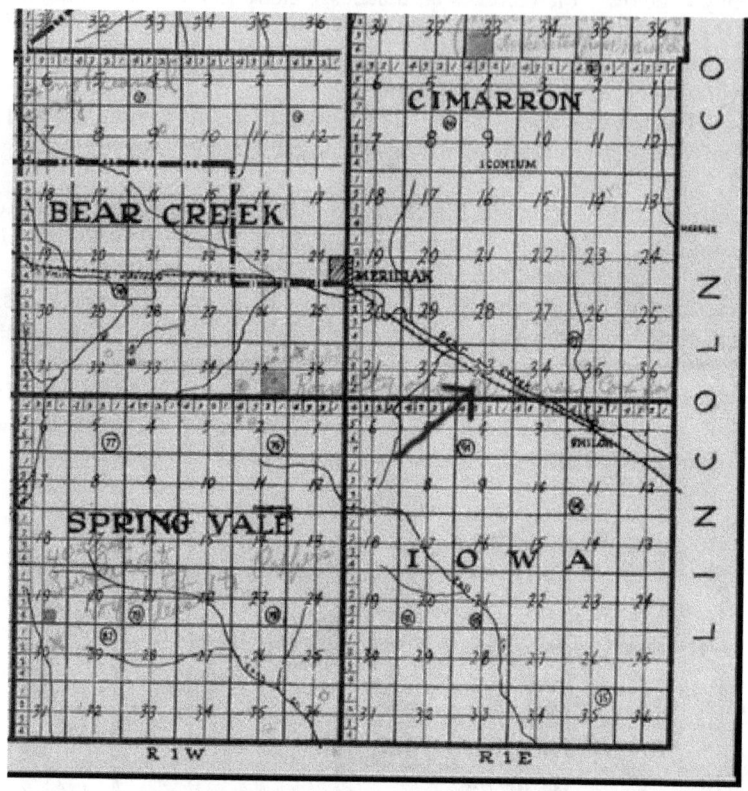

(Section 33 in Township 16)

Then Allen Andrew McDaniel faded out into history. Something happened to him. The 1920 census shows his wife was widowed. His wife remarried in 1922. There is no newspaper article, obituary, nor are there any family stories about him and no specific date of his death, only a death date of 1912.

We do hear about his brother, James Ira McDaniel. Ola was told by Jesse that he became James Ira McDaniel. He too was a real person with a creditable background and ancestral trails. What kind of clues was Jesse leaving us by saying that he was these two brothers? Many will say, "oh that's another false statement made by the old man J. Frank Dalton," but there was a good reason why he was telling Ola this. Jesse was good about leaving little morsels here and there as well as codes and clues. Keep an open mind and maybe some of this will make sense.

So how was Jesse involved? I don't have all the answers, but I believe he was right in the middle of it. Guthrie was important to him. Many people and agents of the KGC/Freemasons/I.O.O.F. members/Knights of Pythias and other secret organizations were involved in the grand scheme of things.

After the Run of 1889, the height of the "Gilded Age" began to penetrate into the South. Masonic lodges formed in the territory in Oklahoma City, Edmond, Guthrie, Kingfisher, Norman, and Purcell. [354] It was incredible to see the explosion of organizations and businesses of all kinds establishing their base in Guthrie. It's as something surely lit the fuse to start the chain reaction. It wouldn't surprise me if it wasn't Jesse with the power of the secret societies.

In 1889, after the run, the Knights of Pythias had grown in this country to 2,724 lodges and 263,847 members. By 1910, Oklahoma had 153 lodges and the lodges exploded nationwide to 7,895.

The huge magnificent Scottish Rite Temple in Guthrie was built with an elaborate design, Neo-Classical Revival style. The original part was built in 1908 to have a meeting place for the Oklahoma State Legislature. By 1910, when the state determined Oklahoma City was going to become the State Capital, the Scottish Rite Masons took it over and designed one of the world's largest Masonic Center in Guthrie.

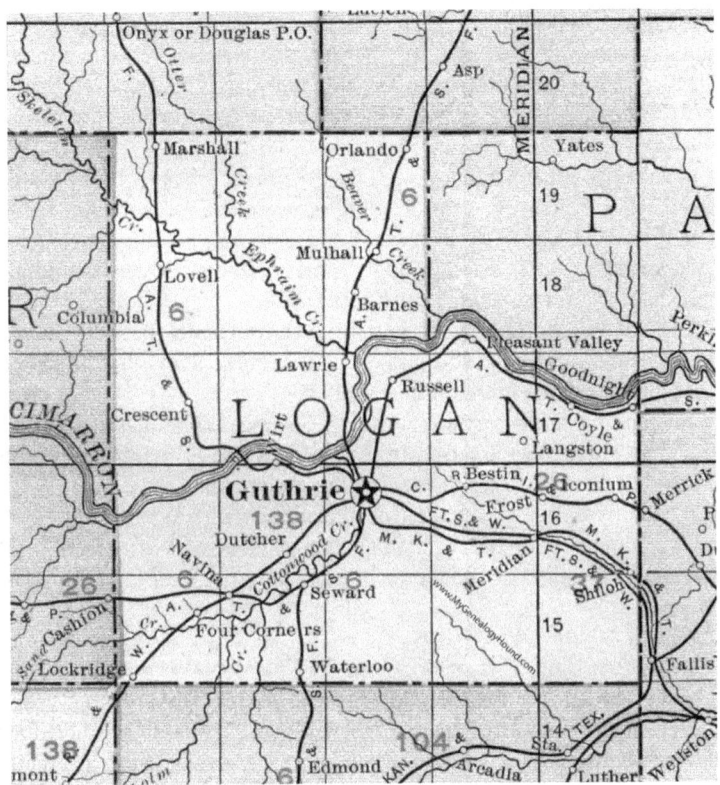

(Fort Smith and Western Railroad (FT.S. & W.) and M.K. & T. railroad)

The growth of Guthrie was overnight. After the run, the area had to corral and support 10,000 settlers. Tents lined the town upon each settlers' claim. Within a month after the run, buildings were erected in downtown. A massive amount of labor and material poured into the town. The buildings were not made of shiplap or wooden materials, but glorious use of brick and stone with colored glass framed within the *arched* windows. The Victorian architecture was the theme displayed in over 2,000 buildings which has endured the test of time. The buildings have been designated as National Historic Landmarks in the Guthrie Historic District. The buildings are beautiful and uniquely designed. It's worth a trip to go to Guthrie.

"Within months, Guthrie was developed as a modern brick and stone "Queen of the Prairie" with municipal water, electricity, a mass transit system, and underground parking garages for horses and carriages." [355]

There were a lot of tunnels underneath the town, the capital, and the Scottish Rite Temple, just as there were many under Oklahoma City, Tulsa, Brownwood, and I'm sure many more towns. A friend of Bud's had been down in the tunnels of Guthrie, Bob Beckenhauer. He found much of it sealed off. It is believed that the KGC dug it out. Bud said it was where they took their oath.

The maneuvers of Jesse were very well planned out in Guthrie. He wasn't settling down, he was in that area to help establish town sites, masonic organizations, the KGC, railroads, and a political foundation for Oklahoma. Jesse's enduring mark on the areas he concentrated on was identified in and around Guthrie. His first step was to establish a prosperous farm, a good repertoire, and get involved in the political arena. Where there is Power, there is Politics and vice versa.

In a fantastic website of the Oklahoma Historical Society, https://www.okhistory.org, I was able to find concrete information of what Jesse told Ola about the political career of James Ira McDaniel, whether he was the real James McDaniel or Jesse portraying him. I had been interested in Oklahoma legislators since 2008 when I was researching on another book regarding my 2nd great grandfather, John O. Baker who was a legislator in the 4th Legislature (1912-1914) from Wagoner County in the Oklahoma State Legislature. During that period, Lt. Governor James Jackson McAlester served as the President of the Senate, the man that had mentored Jesse James. My 2nd great uncle, Jacob Charles Hoffsommer was a state representative from Grant County, Oklahoma (1941-1947).

A year had passed since the run and the need for governance was required for this newly settled land in the heart of Indian Territory. In May 1890 is when the Organic Act for the Territory of Oklahoma became the foundation for a framework of territorial government. The president could appoint a governor, secretary, three federal judges, and a marshal. Voters would get the chance to elect their own legislators and lawmakers on August 5, 1890.

In the 1890 census in Logan County, we find James I. McDaniel, but he wasn't with his brother in Township 15, but in the town of Guthrie itself. The records show that he was the head of his family unit and had with him, his grandmother, Rebecca Graves (age 74) and his sister, Rebecca. Those were very raw and harsh days in the new city. Seems strange that he would have these two women with him. They must of rode the train. Later, their father, Lewis and mother, Sarah, and brother, John all traveled from Iowa to Logan County, Oklahoma

James Ira McDaniel was making a name for himself, appears to be living in town. In 1893, in the House of the Oklahoma Territorial Legislature, James McDaniel was elected, a Populist for the 26th district. The designated capital of Oklahoma became Guthrie. This was before Oklahoma gained their statehood in 1907. [356]

We are so fortunate to find a newspaper clipping of Honorable James I. McDaniel in *The Oklahoma Representative*, October 1, 1896; "James I. McDaniel, Sketch of the Free Silver candidate for Sheriff of Logan County." In the newspaper, it stated he was running for sheriff in 1896 in Logan County. It stated that "he bears the reputation of being honest and industrious, and his ideal seemed to be to develop into a successful farmer and a good man." McDaniel stated that he got involved in railroad construction and was very successful. He began on the Chicago and North Western, then Maple Leaf, and Missouri Pacific in the Cherokee Nation. He entered the land rush in 1889 and settled in Bear Creek township which is outside of Meridian. He was elected in 1892 for the '93 legislative body of the territorial government of Oklahoma. "He was close to be the winner for speakership and his clear intellect always forced a place for him on prominent committees, and in the consideration of the most important measures of that session." McDaniel was recognized as having "commendable ambition and pleasant manners." It was a great surprise that in this article was a picture of McDaniels. Was he Jesse?

(James I. McDaniel (courtesy of "The Oklahoma Representative," October 1, 1896))

(Jesse Woodson James)

Jesse stated that it was during his time as a legislature that he was up in Chicago on business and decided to stop at the World's Fair in 1893. It was also known as the World's Columbian Exposition from May to October 1893. The massive fair was one of a kind and its theme was to celebrate the 400th anniversary of Christopher Columbus' arrival in the New World in 1492. The layout and design of the Chicago World's Fair followed the Beaux-Arts design, "namely neoclassical architecture principles based on symmetry, balance, and splendor." This was the principles and layout design used in building great cities across the country, including Guthrie and

Ardmore. It resembles the Freemasonry design. "It became a symbol of emerging American exceptionalism."

"Although denied a spot at the fair, Buffalo Bill Cody decided to come to Chicago anyway, setting up his Buffalo Bill's Wild West Show just outside the edge of the exposition." [357] By August, they added a new attraction to the program, a reproduction of the Battle of the Little Big Horn. I wonder if he sought out Jesse's advice for this segment of the show.

Buffalo Billy Cody had Brushy Bill/Billy the Kid and Calamity Jane in the performance that year, and many other times. He knew Billy's father, "Wild Henry" Roberts when they were Indian fighters together and knew Billy's mother well. Cody had Billy work for him on his ranch in North Platte, Nebraska. Cody felt a strong attachment to Billy just as Jesse did.

Well, Jesse was not going to the World's Fair without seeing his friends. Remember, Jesse was portraying legislator, James McDaniel and looked quite distinguished and well dressed, not like an outlaw of the past. He was exceptionally clean shaven, with no hair out of place. It had been 11 years since his reported death. No one expected Jesse to be walking around in the fairgrounds.

Jesse walked to the private railroad car that Buffalo Bill was staying in after the show one night and was met at the door by a young man called Robert E. Lee. This young man was also taken in by Buffalo Bill due to his circumstances as a youth. He put him to work as his doorman and bodyguard, packed with two six-shooters. Lee wanted to know his name and his business. Jesse said, "I don't believe Buffalo Bill would want me to tell a kid like you, my business." [358]

Lee was finally persuaded to at least let Cody know about this man, just in case they were truly friends. With caution, Lee directed Jesse in to where Buffalo Bill was sitting. Bill didn't know Jesse right off. Jesse said, "Colonel, don't you know me?" After several minutes passed and he began to notice the index finger that was "buggered up" and asked Jesse to remove his shirt, Buffalo Bill immediately recognized the severe scars of the rope burns around his neck and the bullet holes. "My God man! You ain't nobody but Jesse James," said Cody.

From that moment on, Lee, the bodyguard said that they talked of the past nonstop. He said Buffalo Bill continued to call him "Old Jesse." In the National Police Gazette after the interview with Robert E. Lee, wrote, "If the world knew what they talked about, people would be dumbfounded," Lee insists. "At that time Dalton discussed with Buffalo Bill whether he should reveal his true identity of being Jesse James and the famed scout advised him to "leave well enough alone!" Good advice from an old friend.

The distinguished gentleman stayed a week there with Buffalo Bill Cody and returned to Guthrie and served out his term. From what he witnessed at the World's Fair in 1893, I'm sure he took some of the rich culture back with him and influenced the town of Guthrie and even the new state that would be developing; Oklahoma.

McDaniel moved to Meridian about 1907, the year that Oklahoma reached statehood. "Meridian citizens were successful in having some political influence in Oklahoma's territorial government. James Ira McDaniel, a Meridian area farmer, was elected to the Second Oklahoma Territorial Legislature in 1892." [359]

We learn from the Encyclopedia of Oklahoma History and Culture website, that the little town of Meridian, right along the Indian Meridian, and 12 ½ miles southeast of Guthrie, the county seat of Logan County, was where James Ira Daniel resided, first in the Bear Creek Township, to the west of Meridian. He was shown as a boarder by himself in the 1900 census. Later, in 1910, James (age 55) would be found in the Cimarron Township, to the east of Meridian with a wife, Mary (age 42). They had two white servants living with them, James Willis (34) and Charles Ferguson (30). James McDaniel and his family accumulated a lot of land in the townships around Meridian.

Meridian, in which the word has a significant meaning in surveyorship and the Freemason/KGC philosophy which go hand in hand, point to a site that was very important to Jesse, close to the 100th meridian. We had discussed earlier about Rector who became superintendent of the Five Tribes agency and in 1855 led a survey of the Washita Valley adjacent to the 98th Meridian to establish a reservation in Indian Territory. The meridian lines of the earth contain power and energy of some kind and is what Freemasonry tapped into and guided them.

Within the small community of Meridian, a general store, serving as a post office was established in 1893/94. The town never had an existing highway that reached it. In 1903, the Missouri, Kansas and Oklahoma Railroad constructed a line through there to Guthrie as well as the Fort Smith and Western Railroad. These lines went through the McDaniel's property. They were paid well.

By 1910, he and his wife, Mary lived east of Meridian in the south Cimarron district. He was a teacher, a farmer, a landowner who promoted the railroad expansion, and 1.0.0.F. member.

In his obit., *The Daily Oklahoma*, Sept 5, 1939 – "J.I. McDaniel, 85, Veteran Educator of State, Is Dead" lists his accomplishments. McDaniels helped develop Oklahoma with the railroad system. From Lee, Iowa he was a railroad contractor. He homesteaded southeast of Guthrie. He farmed and was a schoolteacher. He was involved with the state school land as an appraiser and adjustor. He had a wife, Mary and sister Rebecca. No mention of any other family members.

Howk revealed in Del Schrader's book, "Jesse James was One of His Names," a chilling story about James "Jim" McDaniels. He was only mentioned two times. Schrader never mentioned that McDaniels was a legislator in Guthrie. In 1903, Jim McDaniels, being called colonel, was reviewing reports of John Wilkes Booth, who was still alive. After he shot Lincoln, Booth fled to Texas and what Howk revealed was that they hid John W. Booth at Joe Vaughn's (Frank James) farm in Leon County, Texas for a few weeks and then to the house of Quantrill near Canton, Texas. Booth went to Glen Rose, Granbury, and Brownwood in Texas and then ended up in Enid, Oklahoma. He had "strict Confederate underground surveillance" upon him and was paid $3,600 a year to keep his mouth shut.

Being an actor and an orator, he began letting things slip from his tongue. "Texas Rangers and lawmen, mostly former Confederate soldiers, filed reports with the Knights of the Golden Circle telling about the strange behavior of John Wilkes Booth, alias James St. George. The actor-assassin was drinking heavily, bragging about being the man who shot Lincoln, and boasting about his knowledge of Confederate underground secrets." [360]

This did not set too well with Jesse or the KGC. What made the final decision of disposing Booth was when Booth published a book. "There's a lot of dynamite in the book. We're still preparing for the Second Civil War and Booth is busy revealing a lot of our secrets. He knows more than any of us ever thought." [361] The KGC bought up most of the books before they were consumed by the public.

In the Spring of 1903 when McDaniels was living near Guthrie, he planned on making a trip to Enid, Oklahoma with several KGC operatives to pay a visit to John Wilkes Booth going by the name of St. George. It was only 65 miles and, on a train, would take no time to get there and back.

Booth was surprised by the visit and he was a little leery that the colonel was there and called him by name, not McDaniels, but Jesse James. Jesse fixed Booth a glass of lemonade and poured a bottle of arsenic in the drink. Booth drank it down and began gasping for air. He was a goner. It was said that Booth was so full of arsenic that it preserved his body as if he was professionally mummified.

Another place in Schrader's book mentions that Billy the Kid "had known Myra Belle's husband (singular) as Dick Reed and Bruce Younger. This same man was called Jim McDaniels in the Indian Territory." [362] This meant that all three of these names were used by Jesse James. Dick Reed could have been the name "J.D. Reed" Jesse was using in Whitehorse, Oklahoma as a Deputy U.S. Marshal in 1898. I don't think that these stories were made up, because they were very similar to what Jesse told Ola. They had a commonality to the people and places where Jesse walked. It had some substance to it. Just how much substance and truth to it, we don't know.

Jesse also was under the alias name of Jess Wilson and was elected to the State Legislature in 1907 which would have been the First official Oklahoma Legislature as a state. There was a Ben Wilson in 1907, but, Bud nor the writer have been able to verify if this man was Jesse or not. Ola stated that she had a picture of Jesse as Representative Jess Wilson.

One thing is for certain though, Jesse helped form Oklahoma into a prosperous state.

The Significance of Guthrie, Oklahoma

Guthrie was truly a town for the elite, but we find incidents that prove it was a rough area to live. In the days of Jesse's big reveal in 1948-1951, Trammel said that the James boys slayed 7 Chisholm brothers who were thought to be stealing the James' cattle. They hung them from a big old oak tree near Guthrie, Oklahoma and then shot them through the head. Trammel explained that Jesse not only corroborated this story but led a party straight to the old oak with its hanging branch in the wild brush country, about 16 miles outside of Guthrie.

Per Howk's book, "Jesse James and the Lost Cause", he wrote that Jesse told him this story. "I saw Red Lucas and talked to him several times in 1889", [363] (the same year as the run) when he was made first Fire Chief at Guthrie, Oklahoma.

Orrington "Red" Lucas was an 89'er. He was able to stake down two town lots. Law and order were not in the cards in early Guthrie, with those taking advantage of situations and those who were claim jumpers. Orrington and his twin brother, Worrington, Bob Dalton, and four others were deputized to keep the peace. The streets were full of tents, so this was the first job, to get the tents down. Lucas called Guthrie, "a hell-roaring town." [364]

In his own words, during an interview with journalist Effie Jackson in 1937, Red became an official officer which included being the fire chief. He served until 1893. He then became a Deputy U.S. Marshal under Marshal Grimes. His headquarters were in Guthrie until 1895. He knew the Daltons well, "There were four of them, as fine fellows as I ever knew, Bob, Emmett, Grat, and Bill.

Lucas stated, "Fees for services were slow pay in those days and the boys used that at first as an excuse to go against the Government. I think the true reason for their going "on the scout" was the same that drove so many former cowboys to do the same thing – love of adventure. Tales of Jesse James, the Younger boys and the old Quantrill Gang had kindled their imagination. It seemed so easy to try it out in this "No Man's Land" where the fear of the "outlaw" paralyzed every storekeeper.

"Ranch houses were even a kind of rendezvous, they fed the outlaws and let them go on unquestioned. Even prosperous farmers found it easier to feed them and their horses or even to let them have their best horses than to ask questions. It didn't pay to ask questions. In fact, it seemed that these "protective" citizens were more afraid of the outlaws then they were of the law. So with all these things in their favor the Daltons chose what seemed to them the "easiest way" and left a short daring career of crime which other outlaws, Doolin and his gang particularly, tried to follow.

"I remember the day the Dalton boys decided to "go on the scout" or as they called it "going to the brush." Bob came to me and asked me to join them; he thought because I liked adventure, I would seek that kind of a life with them. I refused and tried to argue the law and order side of life. But it was useless. They said they were leaving that night, the four brothers. We were in Guthrie. I asked them where they would be that night and they told me they were going to camp at the Big Spring, 1 ¼ miles north of Tohee, a post office eight miles southeast of Guthrie." [365]

Tohee, back during the run, was in Logan County, just south of Meridian, but 18 miles southeast of Guthrie. I found an old map with it shown. They were camping 1 ¼ miles north of Tohee. This was very close to the land that Allen McDaniel had and very similar to where Jesse described his land. Possibly another line camp for the outlaws.

Tohee was formerly called Jackson. It was established November 13, 1890 and was discontinued January 31, 1906 when the mail went to Meridian. Map is located on https://gateway.okhistory.org (First Post Offices Within the Boundaries of Oklahoma, by George H. Shirk) Current day Tohee is in Lincoln County.

Another story that Bud had was regarding the Charles H. Anthis family who lived in Township 18 in Logan County in 1890. They encountered the Dalton Gang camping near their home in the Fall. "Father went down to their camp and visited with them and sold them corn for their horses.

They told him who they were and said they would do him no harm. Not long after that, Jesse James and his gang camped over night, bought feed for their horses and seemed like 'very nice fellows'. They told father they would not bother him and would be gone by morning. Mother and Father both were somewhat uneasy about those visitors. [366]

Not only did Red Lucas know the Daltons in Guthrie, but he knew Jesse as well. His first encounter with him was back in 1879 in Missouri. In an affidavit, Lucas stated that he was employed as a detective and sent to Southeast Missouri to locate the "general whereabouts" of Quantrill who was **supposedly still alive** and the James brothers in 1879. Lucas and his partner were in a swampy area and ran into some wild hogs that had them up a tree. As every inch of the bark was being pulled off by the hogs to get to the invaders of their mud hole, Lucas and his partner were using every means to shoot as many as they could. Shortly, they came face to face with their rescuers which so happened to be Frank and Jesse. Lucas said "I will never forget those cold blue eyes."

"I was with the U.S. Marshalls a long time in the Oklahoma Indian Territory days, I knew personally many famous outlaws, the Doolin, the Daltons, the Jennings Gangs and others. In all my record shows that I have arrested over 3600 badmen in the I.T. alone. I was Chief of Police in early day Tulsa when it was real bad. I had charge at or the first Fire Chief of Guthrie, Oklahoma at the opening of the strip. I was in charge of police work at Anadarko at the same time Heck Thomas was in charge at Lawton, Oklahoma. Heck Thomas knew Jesse James very well. [367]

Well, in 1902, Red Lucas met those cold blue eyes once again. Bud had an old newspaper clipping dated June 21, 1950, titled, "Former U.S. Marshall, 92 Recalls Famous Outlaws." The newspaper it was published in was not identified. It read, "It was in 1902 at Fort Gibson that he disarmed James. A deputy reported a stranger wearing a shoulder holster under his coat and Lucas asked about it. The desperado grabbed his arm, he said, and a deputy held a gun on him while Lucas disarmed him. "He said his name was Frank Dalton," "Lucas relates." But I told him he didn't favor the Daltons. I knew those eyes and the mouth, but I couldn't remember where I'd seen him."

"Lucas still has the gun he took from James. He says the outlaw is still living."

(Federal Officer, Orrington Red Lucas)

John Trammel

Guthrie appeared to be another safe haven for the outlaws. John Trammel was right at home in the place Jesse provided. His story was incredible. He honored and respected Jesse and would do anything for him. The same went for Jesse, he would do anything for John Trammel.

John would go when Jesse said go and would do when Jesse said do. He never would question Jesse. Most of the time John never knew where they were at, didn't care, as long as he was with his "boss", Jesse.

In the Colorado Springs Gazette Telegram, November 28, 1954, the article, "116-Year-Old Jesse James Gang's Cook Visits Region" speaks of Trammell traveling to Denver at the Spears Clinic for an examination of his longevity. John was 1 of the 25 oldest people in the world. He was involved in the Spears Longevity Research Study. John maintained his stamina with a lot of exercise, a lot of traveling on foot, running and dodging the law with Jesse. He attributed his good health to a diet of bacon and greens. He was asked if he smoked or drank, John said, "Everytime he could get 'em."

Before meeting Jesse, he was a slave in Georgia. John was flogged when he unintentionally killed another slave. Trammell escaped during the flogging and found himself living in the woods and learning how to forage for himself. He lived this way for over 4 years. He was captured by being roped as a cow. His new master, Ike Porter trained him to be a fighter for sport. John had incredible strength and perfect timing. He was six feet tall.

Trammell fought under the name of Sam Skates and was known as the bare-knuckle champion of the world. His nickname became the "Black Cobra." This was his insignia that was on the brick found at Jesse's St. Joseph homesite.

People called him "Uncle John" as did people call Jesse, "Uncle Jesse." Trammel met Jesse as he was escaping the life of slavery and making money for another man in his fighting career. It was in 1863 that they crossed paths. John stated in the interview that he was riddled with bullets as a head cook, camp tender, forager, and general handy man for Jesse James and his gang. He also stated that he was a "pigeon picker," a designation which, he said was given to a sort of early day bodyguard who stood nearby to protect a member of a gang from the fire of "snipers." [368]

Trammel stated that he was with Jesse until the hoax in 1882 and then he went to Texas to stay. It is rumored that he went to Brownwood. Trammel stated in an interview that he moved to Guthrie, Oklahoma where he operated a turkey farm. [369]

When John was 114, he married a lady of 67, Mattie Moore, his fourth wife. He outlived the others. She was from the town of *Meridian*. [370]

John Trammell lived just down the road from Dorothy Sears. They knew each other well. Bud Hardcastle was blessed to get to talk with Mrs. Sears on her front porch in Guthrie. She knew just who Trammel was and knew he was a close partner and friend of Jesse James. Mrs. Sears had a lot in common with John. He was born in 1838, born into slavery before the Civil War. Mrs. Sears' grandmother also had been a slave during that time. Lots of stories were told between the two. She directed Bud to Pollard's Funeral Home where John's burial was handled.

When Bud got to the funeral home, it was hard to find John Trammel's information or where he was buried. He finally found the issue. They had his name listed on the burial records and on the death certificate under "Tramble." He was then directed to his grave located in Gravel Hill Cemetery, a black cemetery.

Bud went to the cemetery and he met a black man there. He questioned him about John and the man said, come to my office. He kept a special tribute to John Trammel. Under the glass on his desk was a newspaper article he had about John. He was a celebrity in these parts. Bud found his grave and verified with the tombstone and his death certificate that John Trammel was born January 15, 1838 and died January 17, 1956; 118 years and 2 days old.

Bud obtained a letter written by John Trammel's friend Rev. James B. Ellis who went with John to Zanesville, Ohio on the treasure hunt. Ellis was writing a friend of John's, Floyd Champlin to inform him of the passing of John. Ellis stated that he put "Uncle John" in Edmond's Hospital and then later received a call of his death. The funeral was going to be January 21, 1956.

Bud and his friend, Ted Weichel were working together on treasure hunts in and around Guthrie. Bud found a lot of carvings north of Guthrie and found one of Jesse's hideouts near the Cimarron River. They were able to visit the site of Trammel's homestead. One time when Bud was not with Ted, the man went to Trammel's home and discovered a chain going down into the ground. Ted dug around the chain. He continued to dig, believing there was something valuable at the end. Once he got deep enough, he found the chain was attached to dynamite in an old pot. The digging stopped, needless to say, and the hole was carefully filled back up with dirt. Dynamite is more dangerous the older it gets. I'm sure old Uncle John had lots of interesting things planted in his yard and secrets buried for good.

John was said to have been extremely intelligent and very loyal, even to the very end, outlasting all his comrades and taking all the secrets of the outlaws to the grave.

Calamity Jane

During the year of the run, Jesse met up with Calamity Jane. Calamity was quite a gal. Bud gave me a copy of the letter that she wrote to James O'Neal the man who was taking care of her daughter, Jenny in England. The letter is in Bud's book, "The Hoax That Let Jesse James Live."

The letter was written November 30, 1889 and was within the year of the famous Run of 1889 that Jesse claimed to be on. The part of the letter that was interesting is that she had just recently seen Jesse James. "I met up with Jesse James not long ago. He is quite a character; you know he was killed in '82. His mother swore that the body that was in the coffin was his, but it was another man they called either Tracy or Lynch. He was a cousin of Wild Bill. You won't likely care about this but if Janey outlives you and me, she might be interested. He is passing under the name of Dalton, but he couldn't fool me I know all the Dalton's and he sure ain't one of them. He told me he promised his gang and his mother that if he lived to be a hundred, he would confess. You and me won't be here then Jim. To make it strange, Jesse sang at his own funeral. Poor devil he can't cod me – not even with a long hair and a billy goat's wad of hair on his chin. I expect he will start preachin'. He is smart maybe he can do it." [371]

So, in 1889, Jesse was already wearing the long hair and beard like Buffalo Bill. He must have been rough looking and trying to disguise himself.

Calamity joined Custer as a teamster in the early 70's and "gained the distinction of being the first white woman to enter the Black Hills country of South Dakota." This, with the rest of her story is found in Dan R Conway's article, "Calamity Jane, Unique Character of Old Frontier," October 8, 1926 in the *Bozeman Courier*.

The article defines the raw beauty of this rugged pioneer woman who dressed like a man. "Since her career reveals many acts of kindness and a heart that was charitable and considerate of the sufferer, the question often arises: "Was Calamity Jane a good woman?" This we cannot answer squarely. It all depends upon what "goodness" in its broadest interpretation, means whether character and morals are the same thing. If character and morals are the same, then Calamity Jane was a paradox. On the one hand, it can only be said of her that she drank, swore, stole, gambled and associated with desperadoes. On the other hand, it was proven beyond shadow of doubt that she thought straight and shot straight; she never turned down a friend or anyone in need. She lived according to the code of the plains. She left no personal history. Consequently, no one can explain her. She was simply "Calamity Jane."

On her card she advertises that she is a Pioneer New Woman Calamity Jane, Scout, Trapper and Indian Slayer. She was also considered a sharpshooter, storyteller, teamster, dance hall girl, gambler, and nurse. "During the smallpox epidemic at Deadwood, it has been stated of Calamity that she turned into a regular "female Robin Hood," going into the homes of the afflicted, taking food to them and administering to their needs."

She was completely infatuated with Wild Bill Hickok. Calamity claims Hickock was the father of Jenny born 1873 in Montana. She said she had Jenny when she was a scout. Jenny was put up for adoption by Jim O'Neil and his wife. The letter that Calamity wrote was to O'Neil.

After Wild Bill Hickock was killed in 1876, Calamity was known to "drown her sorrows in the wild excesses of the frontier camps. She became a confidante of all the outlaws of the west, yet she seems never to have broken the law openly enough to lose her liberty." [372]

She was lost without Bill. It is said that she went in saloons and sold photos of herself to gain money to support herself.

In 1893, she appeared in Buffalo Bill's Wild West Show as a storyteller in Chicago, the same time Jesse was there to see Buffalo Bill at the World's Fair and at the same time Brushy Bill/Billy the Kid was in his show. Three years later, she joined the traveling Kohn and Middleton Dime Museum as a performer, appearing on stage in buckskins, reciting her adventures.

Calamity Jane died August 1, 1903. She insisted to be buried by Hickok. Bud went to Deadwood and found her buried like she had requested, by Wild Bill. Her real name is engraved on her tombstone, Martha Jane "Calamity Jane" Canary (May 1, 1852-August 1, 1903).

An affidavit of birth of Jenny was obtained, which was in Calamity's diary, her "confession" in 1912, after the death of her father by adoption, James O'Neil. Jenny, Jean H. Hickok McCormick lived in Liverpool. She was in Butte, Montana in 1898 to 1902 teaching penmanship in schools.

On Sept 6, 1941, the U.S. Dept of Public Welfare did grant old age assistance to Jean after receiving evidence that her mother was Calamity Jane and Wild Bill who had married at Benson's Landing, Montana Territory on Sept 25, 1873. On Jenny's grave, it shows Jean H. McCormick, Daughter of Jane "Calamity Jane" and James Butler "Wild Bill" Hickok.

In an article, shortly after Calamity's death, one of her ex-husbands told the story of Calamity Jane claiming to be married to six men. Lef Smith was a policeman in Cincinnati. He had come to America from Australia and became a cowboy in the West. He met Calamity at Fort Dodge, Kansas where she was with Billy Littleford who was one of Jesse James' main men. Calamity was always known as the female counterpart of Jesse James.

Jesse was asked on the "We the People" radio program in New York City in 1950 if any historical person knew who he was. His reply was, "I met Calamity Jane." Also, in the court hearing in 1950 when asked, "who he saw that knew him and knew who he was when he came back from South America." His answer was, "I saw and talked with Calamity Jane."

In a newspaper article, "The Real Calamity Jane" by Stewart H. Holbrook, *Chicago Tribune*, Dec. 5, 1948, states that Calamity appeared at different times under the title of Hunt, Blake, Burke, White, Dorsett, and **Dalton**, but who these gentlemen were, if they even existed, has been lost in the imperfect records of the time and place."

Law in the hands of an outlaw

While Jesse had things under control in Guthrie, he served again as Deputy U.S. Marshal between 1894-1896 in Indian Territory. He was under Chief Marshal Jake (Jacob) Yoes, who was also over John Swain. Jesse was marshal in and around Ardmore, Oklahoma assigned to what was then, the Chickasaw Nation, White Bead, *Woodford*, Paul's Valley, Fort Arbuckle and the surrounding area. He was using the name, Frank Dalton.

White Bead was an important stage stop on the military/government freight road from Caddo to Fort Sill, the same freight road we spoke of earlier when Jesse was a freighter taking supplies to Fort Sill. Woodford is where Ola's mother grew up and saw Jesse many times when he checked on them periodically. He was very familiar with this area.

Even after the turn of the century, robberies were still occurring in and around White Bead and Cherokee Town. A stagecoach was held up in White Bead and Bud learned from a lady that her grandfather who was with Quantrill Raiders, rode with Jesse and held up a stage in Paul's Valley.

Her grandfather had a pistol belonging to Jesse. I too, was able to interview the lady. She lived in Chickasha.

Marshal Yoes, whose nickname was "Big Jake" was an ex-Union cavalryman. He enlisted late in the war into the First Arkansas Cavalry, Company D and got shot up pretty bad by Confederate bushwhackers and then was taken to prison. The movie, "Big Jake" was based upon Jake Yoes.

Yoes was a Mason. After the war, he opened many stores, hotels, flour mills, and a canning factory in Arkansas at various towns. He placed a lot of his businesses along the Frisco Railroad. He also owned many plantations along the Arkansas River. He went into mining. He became a Republican Senator. Yoes was appointed Deputy U.S. Marshal in 1889 to cover the western district of Arkansas out of Fort Smith. Ironically, it was Yoes who was approached by Bob and Grat Dalton to hire them as deputies. They wanted to follow in their brother's footsteps, Frank Dalton who served from 1880 until killed while on duty in 1887.

Yoes hired Grat Dalton, but not Bob due to his young age. Yoes offered Bob and Emmett positions as posse men for Deputy Floyd Wilson. One by one, the Daltons were making trouble for themselves; Bob was posing as a deputy and was seen with bootleggers enjoying the goods. Emmett was involved somehow, and warrants were issued for their arrest. Grat committed an assault against a man after waking up with a hangover from the night before. Grat was fired immediately by Yoes.

The situation and strife between the Daltons went from bad to worse. They had a tremendous amount of revenge against the law in which their older brother fought so hard to keep. The Daltons began their gang of outlawry.

Yoes would get the best of them. I'm assuming he learned their tricks early on and with the help of a U.S. Jailer Pape, learned of the plans of the Dalton Gang to rob the bank at Coffeyville, Kansas, which enabled the authorities to set a trap, ending the life of the Dalton Gang in October 1892. Yoes was documented as being part of the men who took them down.

Yoes' top deputy was Heck Thomas and two months later from the Dalton's raid in Coffeyville, Heck was given the assignment to go after Ned Christie who was accused of the murder of a Deputy U.S. Marshal Daniel Maples. They attempted to smoke Christie out of his home, but the cabin caught fire and having believed he died, they ended their pursuit. Later, they learned he had lived.

In December 1892, Yoes sent out another posse and designed a military style raid. They came upon Christie's fort, protected by two solid log walls with rock in between. Using a cannon and dynamite, they were able to penetrate a portion of his walls, catching the place on fire. When Christie came out, the posse fatally shot him. Sadly, Christie had always claimed his innocence and in 1918 a man came forward to prove that Christie was telling the truth of his innocence.

After all this, Jesse came on the scene and worked for Yoes from 1894-96. It makes one wonder if Yoes was leery of another Dalton under him, but I'm sure Yoes knew who he was.

Jesse was talking with Ola's mother, Bertha while staying at Ola's and Aubrey's house. They were reminiscing about the different events that occurred in the area where they lived, Woodford and Ardmore. There were still a lot of crimes being committed in 1895. They both remembered the times when farmers would take their cotton crops in wagons to sell in Ardmore. They worked doubly hard to make ends back in those days. Their crops were very valuable to them.

A pattern of crimes against these farmers were adding up. After they would get paid for their crop, they headed back to a place called Rock Creek before heading home. They would make camp there for the night. Farmers were being robbed at that very spot when they had cash in their pocket from the sale. This would continue during harvest time.

Bertha's house was just below this one farmer friend's house and as he was coming back from town he stopped and told Bertha's parents what had happened to him and his little girl on their trip. They had sold their crop and camped on Rock Creek. Out of nowhere came a woman dressed in a Mother-Hubbard dress and bonnet. She began to dance around their campfire. The man told his little girl that she was crazy but wouldn't hurt them. They went on to bed in the wagon. The woman continued to dance.

The little girl was still scared and kept an eye on that woman. She suddenly said, "Daddy, that woman's got on boots." The dad got his Winchester ready and just about that time, the woman was climbing aboard and was shot before she got to them.

The dad took the little girl to Ardmore and got the marshal, who happened to be Jesse James. He examined the body and found that it was no woman. It was a man dressed as a woman and was the president of the bank in Ardmore.

John Franklin Anderson and son, Charley Lee Anderson were the first men to open a bank in Ardmore in 1890. It was a private bank to begin with, but later began operating as a government charter under the name First National Bank. It was the first nationally chartered bank in Indian Territory. John Franklin Anderson was a member of the Odd Fellows. In 1895, fire destroyed it.

There was also another bank established in the 1890's which was the City National Bank. The president of the bank would be Dr. A.J. Wolverton, who came from Montague, Texas. He arrived in Ardmore in 1891. He died suddenly at the age of 49 because of an illness in 1901. I don't believe either one of these men were the robber.

The fire also destroyed the newly built three story Masonic Temple on the town square next to the courthouse. The Lodge meetings were held at the Odd Fellows Hall while a new building was being constructed. The Masonic meetings began again in the new temple by May of 1896. They had the upper floor and the First National Bank occupied the first and second floor. This all occurred when Jesse was marshal.

Sam Daube was another man who moved from Montague County, Texas to Ardmore. His story is quite interesting.

He was the one who leased out his building in Bowie, Texas to my two 2nd great granduncles on Mason and Montague Streets in Bowie for their butcher shop. In the 1883 directory in Bowie, this was the place that Daube had his "Red Store" which was a dry goods store. It was a wooden building and they moved further north downtown where a meat market was and built a nice new brick store in 1886.

The Daubes made hats upstairs and downstairs was a dry goods store, handling clothes, boots, and shoes. The Daubes were from Germany and were Jewish. The Jewish community out of Dallas brought in Aaron Miller to work with Sam Daube in his store. Miller would eventually take over the store.

The Millers were related to the Neimans, co-founder of the luxury clothing store, Neiman-Marcus which was started in 1907 in Dallas. The other co-founder, Herbert Marcus was working with Frank James at the Sanger Brother's store before he ventured into his new business with Neiman.

By 1900, Sanger Brothers was one of the state's greatest institutions and perhaps the single most important business in Dallas. In addition to retail and wholesale trade, Sanger's provided banking services and financing to other independent entrepreneurs.

Aaron Miller stayed in Bowie and maintained a fine clothing store while Sam Daube ventured north into Indian Territory. When Miller died, the Neimans brought his body to Dallas to be buried in a private Jewish cemetery.

"Ardmore had the first Jewish Community in the Oklahoma Territory, formally organized in 1890. Sam Daube was born in Germany in 1859. He came to the United States in 1877, first working in New York City and then Texas. He arrived in Ardmore, Oklahoma in 1885, where he opened the Westheimer and Daube Store with his brother, David Daube, and Max Westheimer. They also raised white-faced Hereford cattle on the thousands of acres they owned." [373]

Sam Daube's move to Ardmore, was the same time that City Marshal Captain John Wesley Haskew was overseeing the town of Bowie and had gotten into some trouble. The store in Ardmore sold groceries, hardware, household goods, and implements. It was located east of the Burlington Northern Santa Fe Railway tracks. It became an extremely important trading headquarters. [374]

Daube accumulated vast amounts of acreage for a cattle ranch, the Double O Bar, north of Ardmore near the Arbuckle Mountains. It was established in 1886 and he became an oilman. Anything he touched turned to gold.

We all have our skeletons in our closet, but in military intelligence records, Sam and his brother David Daube were under suspicion of being involved in espionage and sabotage. [375] There is no evidence if they ever went to trial or were found guilty. Sam did travel quite extensively overseas which may have put up a red flag.

Even though Ardmore was extremely populated with Masons, I could not find a complete list of Masons in Ardmore during that time, only a partial list. It did show that Sam Daube was a Shriner. Just as Guthrie was born with its foundation upon Freemasonry and extravagant architecture, Ardmore was not too far behind.

If you are interested in the Oklahoma Masonic History, check out, https://okmasonichistory.glogspot.com/2022/09/three-grand-lodges-one-state-how.html.

"The masons in Ardmore were striving to achieve in becoming "rightfully ranked" as the Masonic capital of the entire southern half of the state. They built a huge Temple in 1930 described as costing $300,000 that consisted of several floors with the fifth floor reserved for "the Gothic Hall of the Knights Templar. This is one of the most beautiful rooms in the entire temple. As large as the blue lodge rooms on the lower floor, this magnificent division of the temple with its peaked ceiling, arched windows and doors give one the feeling of entering into a medieval castle. The entire room is built with an *eye* to the needs of Knight Templar ritual and should inspire a general reawakening in that organization." [376]

Both Guthrie and Ardmore had a Carnegie Library designed as a Renaissance Temple with its arch above the pillars.

In 1890, the Pickens County Anti-Horse Thief Association is formed. The association would gather dues from its members and hire armed riders to track down horse thieves using federal warrants. They would carefully pinpoint suspicious violators of the law, placing them under surveillance and trailing them across the wide-open country. Once they got enough evidence, they would bring the criminals in for justice. It was no easy job.

Brushy Bill said he joined the association, focusing on Texas, riding up and down the Red River, in East Texas, and eventually into Indian Territory. Jesse told Ola that Billy was in the association in 1883, 1884, and 1885, but I believe it had to of been 1893-1895. He was also working for the Pinkertons. In 1894, Billy was up in the North Canadian River in Indian Territory.

After his duty as a deputy marshal, Jesse traveled back over the Red in 1897 to Wichita Falls visiting his brother-in-law, Allen Parmer and friends.

In 1898, Jesse was supposedly in Indian Territory as a Deputy U.S. Marshal near Whitehorse per Ola, for three or four months as J.D. Reed. Whitehorse was a very small township in Wood County, Oklahoma, north of the Cimarron River and just northeast of Freedom, Oklahoma and approximately 30 miles from where the writer's family homesteaded.

What was unbelievably surprising to this writer is when rereading the book I had written in 2014, "The Haskew Brand," I found that my family was in that same area of Whitehorse in 1898-1899. They had been living in the small town of Lahoma, west of Enid, but wanted to venture west. In late summer 1899, my great grandfather, Rufus Kelly Stout, his cousin William "Big Willie" Lafayette Haskew, nephews of John Wesley Haskew, the outlaw, and Rufus' brother-in-law, Bill Blevins set out west on horseback leaving the women folk behind. By the way of Waynoka, just south of Whitehorse, they traveled over rutty trails and roads carved out by Indians and cattlemen. They crossed treeless plains, then traveling through rugged hills and valleys until they came to the Cimarron River. They would find the right time to cross the big river, remembering those travelers who had disastrous troubles in crossing due to the mighty currents and quicksand. Not only was the land and river unforgiving at times, so were the outlaws who called this country their home.

The following story was written by the Bill Blevins family: "As they were traveling west, they crossed the Cimarron River south of Waynoka. Rufus, Big Willy, and Bill came out north of Curtis. The first guy they ran into was a cowboy on horseback, **Jim Dalton**. The men said, "We were looking for some new land to file. Where would you go?" Dalton said, "Go North." "As they began to move out and head north, Dalton and the cowboys told them to take plenty of nerve along, which they did. They had their shotguns and Winchesters by their side. So, they went north into country where they settled in late fall of 1899."

I don't believe this "Jim Dalton" was Jesse, but probably someone with the same type of caliber.

It would be their own little community that laid upon a hill amongst many little rolling hills. These three men would be the founding fathers of this very spot. They pitched a coin to determine what name they would call it. W.L. Haskew won, and they were all honored to call this community, "Haskew Flats."

Another interesting story written by my grandmother, Helen Hoffsommer Stout regarding this area as the men folk went back for their women to settle the ground they had found. "The character of this rugged country with its many caves, mountains, and valleys, made it an advantageous and popular place for cattle rustlers, a place of hideouts for gangs of thieves and outlaws. Many stories are told of the outlaws of western Oklahoma and the lawmen who apprehended them. Some of them are filled with folklore. This one is known to be true.

"The R.K. (Rufus Kelly, my great grandfather) Stout and Blevins' wagon train, guided by W.L. Haskew, had been traveling almost two weeks. They would soon reach their destination, stake land claims and establish new homes. They had not foreseen what was to happen that evening the rainstorm threatened them. It was necessary that they seek shelter. A short distance ahead, they saw what appeared to be a deep canyon; a likely place to make a camp. They pulled into it. Lo and Behold! It was indeed, a shelter – one already occupied by a band of notorious outlaws and their horses, led by Sam Green. They were cattle rustlers and horse thieves.

"There must have been a time of bewildering fear among the members of this little group. It is not known exactly what sort of confrontation ensued, but they stayed there together through the night. The next morning the outlaw gang rode out, only to return in two days with pack horses loaded with food and supplies for all. It was indeed a strange brand of western hospitality by a ruthless gang of outlaws. Perhaps when they saw the two young mothers with their four young children, their hearts softened, and good will dominated the scene. At this time, even bank robbers never aroused public hatred as did the common thief or cattle rustler because of the Westerner's dependence on the horse and on cattle for his livelihood. Both lawman and outlaw defend or violate the same moral codes and there is never a question as to the outcome of a career of crime or ultimate punishment of the outlaw because of the strength and solidarity of frontier law.

"Sam Green was an unsavory character. Occasionally, he had been known to walk into a mercantile store, brandishing a long knife while pilfering and stealing anything he wanted. Green had a claim in the Haskew community and lived there part time as a neighbor of Rufus Stout. Stout once bought a calf from him, then inquired, "What if someone claims it? Green's reply was, "Damn it, if they do, I'll give you another." He had assured Mr. Stout that he would never bother his livestock for he respected him and knew him to be an honest man."

Sam Green "led an outlaw gang in Oklahoma. He killed Sheriff Jack Bullard and Deputy Sheriff Cogburn in Roger Mills County, Oklahoma." [377] It was in June of 1902 when Sheriff Bullard attempted to arrest horse thieves near Dead Indian Creek in Roger Mills County. There were 7 of the outlaws, including a woman, Mrs. Sam Green and their two children. The Greens came from Woodward County where Sam worked on a ranch 20 miles north of Woodward. He was 5'8", 200 lbs., sandy mustache, yellowish hair and red face. [378]

"Pete Whitehead and the Green boys, Sam and Richard, with Mrs. Sam Green and a confederate named Otis Stuhl, were in hiding near Cheyenne, having in their possession a bunch of alleged stolen horses. Bullard learned of their whereabouts and with Cogburn, went to arrest them. As they approached the underbrush, where Green and his partners were in hiding, the latter opened fire on the officers, instantly killing Bullard and fatally injuring Cogburn." [379]

"Sheriff Bullard was lying dead with eleven bullet wounds in his body and holding in his hand a six-shooter from which two shots had been fired. Four of the wounds entered from the back, six from the front, and one ranging downward in the head. His deputy received one shot only, and this from the back."

"The outlaws had in their possession three wagons, twenty-one head of horses, fourteen head of cattle, and a lot of miscellaneous articles." An examination shows that Sheriff Bullard had been shot by three different caliber guns or pistols, some of which were unusually large. One gun fired an explosive bullet." [380]

Green held out at the "Bert Casey-Ben Cravens gang's headquarters on the boundary line between Indian Territory and Texas, and whose rendezvous is at the Hughes ranch in southern Comanche County." Deputy Sheriff Nell Morrison of Washita County stated the facts regarding these gangs which were aiding and abetting the fugitive, Sam Green and Whitehead. Morrison stated, "This is the worst gang in Oklahoma, but the members can be run to earth if the federal and territorial authorities will cooperate. Casey has sworn to have my life, but if he gets me he will have to beat me to his gun." [381] Green and Whitehead fled north and some believed they were in North Dakota in 1904 and others believe them to be in Portland, Oregon in 1905. Authorities traveled to both states with no such luck in getting their men.

In 1906, the law received word that Sam Green was in British Columbia, going by the name of G. McGiven, living in Vancouver. [382] It turned out that the man they arrested in Vancouver and brought back to Oklahoma, was not the wanted Sam Green. The authorities had another lead in Durant, Oklahoma in 1915, but that turned out not to be their man either.

In 1915, a well-dressed man came to the home of one of the peace officers of Cheyenne and stated that he represented Sam Green and wanted to know what kind of charges were on Mr. Green. "Green is tired of being on the dodge and he has come back to fight his case."

After not finding the charge in the courthouse, which just disappeared as most legal documents on criminals did back in those days or the courthouse burned down with the records, the lawyer produced Sam Green. He told his side of the story. He didn't know they were lawmen and it seemed odd to him that the two guys who rode up on them wanted to trade his fine "prize animal" for any of Sam's stolen stock. Sam thought they were fixing to hold them up. His wife delivered a pistol to Sam as he was washing his feet in the creek. The gun was covered with socks. He deeply regretted it, but again, disappeared.

Green was known as quick tempered who would shoot on proper provocation. The defense that the wife made was that Bullard and Cogburn had called the women of the gang, thieves and outlaws, and that the members of the gang fired on the officers to protect the honor of their women. But little credence was ever given this story, however." [383]

Finally, in 1935, the story broke on what actually happened. It was in the Elk City Daily News, August 29, 1935. The crime was known as one of the most notorious killings in old Roger Mills county. Whitehead died in Montana, but by 1935, Sam Green dropped out of sight. [384]

Armed and Ready
Spanish-American War 1898

I feel sure, Jesse had his brush with these gangs near Woodward and Western Oklahoma, but something caught his attention in the Spring of 1898 that drew him away from the marshal service. He was drawn to fighting in the Spanish American War, beginning April 24, 1898. Jesse signed up in Wagoner, Oklahoma, east of Tulsa under the name of J.G. Hood or Frank Dalton. Brushy and his friend, Jim signed up in Muskogee. Colonel James Davis also signed up to be in the war. They were going to get in the fight. It was in their blood and always would be.

In The Encyclopedia of Oklahoma History and Culture on www.okhistory.org site, we find under "Oklahoma Territory" that a "majority of Oklahomans of all political parties rallied around the war against Spain. Hundreds of young men hurriedly volunteered for Theodore Roosevelt's famed Rough Rider regiment, and other units organized for the conflict in Cuba."

The war did not last long, it ended a little over seven months due to the U.S.' intervention on behalf of the Cuban revolution in the Cuban War of Independence. It brought the United States into the forefront, becoming a predominant source of strength in the Caribbean Region. In a news story we find that Jesse told the reporter that he had a brief service in Puerto Rico during the war with the quartermaster corps, handling horses. [385]

The U.S. would acquire Puerto Rico, Guam, and the Philippines. More territory for the U.S.

Jesse confessed to Howk that with the blessing of the "Inner Sanctum" of the Knights of the Golden Circle, they helped the Cubans win this war. The Cubans had helped the Confederacy during the Civil War. The Cubans despised their Spanish rulers and called them "Sadists." Jesse and the KGC supplied the Cubans with guns and military officers to train them in guerilla warfare. Jesse had their backs. [386]

Jesse, after the war, went to see Frank who was working at Sanger Brothers in Dallas. He then went to Brownwood to visit Anderson and Colonel Davis. His visit would lead him into more secret missions. In 1899, he went to Fort Sill on an assignment that only he, Frank, Sam Todd, and Colonel James Davis knew about.

Boer War 1899-1902

On October 11, 1899, Jesse entered the Boer War, fighting along with the British. Why Jesse was involved in the Boer War is quite uncertain, but it appears that he had many ties to Britain and hid out in the British colonies of Canada. He became a British Army Colonel in October 1899. He traveled to Africa and was involved in hand-to-hand combat with the Hottentots. Jesse told Ola and Aubrey, "That's the only assailants I ever fled from. Their method of combat was not those of the white man." [387]

The Boer War, as stated in the New World Encyclopedia, "was over territory, power, and culture fought by European settlers and troops on foreign soil." There was no regard to the African Natives and their claim to the ownership of the land. Gold was discovered in the Transvaal, which caught the eye of the British.

"In reality, the British aim was to exploit Africa's resources more efficiently by building and controlling railroads. To the Boers these were wars against imperial oppression. In some respects, with troops from Australia, *Canada*, and New Zealand contributing to the British victory, these wars prepared the British for involvement in World War I and World War II, during which time she was supported by these former colonies." [388]

Does all this sound familiar with what happened in the previous war? The Boer War paved the way for the British to control more territory and more valuable resources within.

Mexican Revolution 1910-1920

The next conflict Jesse and his buddies were in, was in Mexico. Billy had been in Mexico where he had established a ranch. After Fort Sumner, he had gone to El Paso and then to Sonora, Mexico. He had lived with the Yaqui Indians for two years into 1883. It was at this moment in time that Billy went back to the States and worked for Tom Waggoner. He then was in and out of Indian Territory and joined the Anti-Horse Thief Association. In 1893, Billy was in Chicago entertaining with the Buffalo Bill Wild West Show at the World's Fair.

In 1895, Billy goes to El Paso and meets up with 10 cowboys who he knew well. They had heard of a great opportunity to start a ranch down in Mexico. I believe it was in Chihuahua as some of Billy's friends had connections there.

President Diaz of Mexico had allowed that area to be used as grazing for anyone who wanted to pay a small fee. If it wasn't for Billy's story he told to Morrison, the story would be confusing. Jesse had supposedly spoken of this to Howk but its more elaborate and unbelievable. The two stories will be presented, but the one Bud and I feel is more creditable is the story from Brushy Bill.

In the book, "Billy the Kid, An Autobiography," by Daniel Edwards, Billy tells the story. The boys pitched in and bought 1,000 head of cattle and 50 pony mares. Billy was going by the name of the "Hugo Kid" in Mexico and had a nice spread. Billy went back and forth from Mexico to Indian

Territory during this time. They continued ranching on this place in Mexico during the years 1896-97 and were raising mules and *Steel Dust horses*.

In one of Howk's books he said the Mexicans were impressed with the Steel Dust horses Jesse had, so it is believed that Jesse was a partner in this ranch in Chihuahua in which Howk identified the location as being in Chihuahua. Billy, or Bill Roberts, as Howk says was the ranch manager. Whether this was Billy's own ranch or one that Jesse or the KGC set up for him is unknown.

Jesse supposedly told his Chihuahua story to Howk, translated in Del Schrader's book, but Jesse never told Ola about his time in Chihuahua; only the time in Torreon, Mexico in 1910-1912 when Jesse and Billy both lived across the road from one another on a ranch with Luz Villa, Pancho's wife as a neighbor. This clue indicates that the ranch was in Chihuahua as this was Pancho Villa's headquarters and where Luz lived.

Jesse told Ola that Billy made a lot of money down there, had money in the bank.

It does get very confusing, so there may have actually been two ranches. I believe Brushy speaks of this later. We learn more details through Brushy Bill regarding Chihuahua. Both Jesse and Billy went to the Spanish-American War in 1898 and we know Billy was in Teddy Roosevelt's Rough Riders. It was said in Edward's book, "Following the Rough Riders, Brushy says he **returned** to his ranch in Old Mexico." [389]

Billy described in detail, what occurred on the ranch in Mexico. Howk had his own version, but what he described was slightly different, dates different, and the numbers killed were quite different. We find the date through Brushy regarding the invasion of the ranch.

It was June 1899; President Diaz of Mexico was seizing property right and left. How Brushy described it was in Edward's book, "They would not let us ship or drive our cattle out of there. They sent soldiers down to drive our stuff off. We asked for thirty days grace. We thought we might get some help from the U.S. If not, we could get some ammunition. About fifty soldiers came there to round up our cattle and horses. We sent an interpreter down to talk to them. They said it was Diaz' orders. We had 36 cowboys. We fired into them with .30-.30 rifles and picked them off like blackbirds." [390]

It was standoff. On the 4th day of the siege, 2,000 soldiers surrounded them. "Each man (Brushy and the ranch hands) packed his horse like he was going off for a ride. We agreed to fire into them in the weakest spot, then make our getaway if we could. We fought for twelve days, living on wild game and trying to escape into the U.S. On the thirteenth morning, we crossed the Rio Grande below Del Rio. I had a cousin there on the Ranger force. He helped us with food. I was supposed to be worth about thirty thousand dollars but came out with one horse and saddle." [391]

Bud heard several stories from the family members of Jesse and putting two and two together, it appears that Jesse may have been there during part of the siege. He may have gotten word to come and help them out. Jesse saw the troops of Diaz coming back to the ranch. Jesse told the men to "get out of there or we will all be killed, including my son, Jesse." (It is unknown if this was Jesse Cole James, or the other Jesse Howk has named, Jesse F. B. James). Jesse said he never had seen so much gunfire at play, even in the Civil War. Jesse and his men were in a running gun battle with the Mexicans as they fled to the U.S. Jesse used a lot of fire power from his own hand-designed shoulder holster, that would carry 6 pistols at one time that he carried during the Civil War. He knew how to get out of tough situations, especially when his son was with him. They got out of there.

Schrader's book states that "Under Diaz direct orders his federal troops attacked Jesse's ranch without warning and slaughtered a couple of hundred cowboys and workers. Only three escaped the massacre. They were Jesse's son, Jesse F. B. James, an Indian servant, and Brushy Bill Roberts, alias Billy the Kid." [392]

Billy said two other buddies were with him when he went back to Mexico to get another ranch in 1907. It was called the 3 Bar Ranch. They raised *Steel Dust horses*. I believe this is the ranch that Jesse told Ola about in Torreon, but still there is not much evidence of where it truly was.

In Schrader's book, Jesse had told Howk that him and Billy were in Van Zandt County, Texas and Jesse was encouraging Billy to connect with old Confederate officers and KGC agents to learn military strategy and tactics to avenge the Chihuahua Ranch. "You go on The Organization payroll tomorrow as a captain." Billy agreed. [393]

By 1910, Jesse was in Mexico, trying to convince Pancho Villa to take a leadership role in overthrowing the government of General Porfirio Diaz. The Mexico dictator, Porfirio Diaz, had been in complete control for 34 years, serving 7 terms over the Mexican people. Diaz began to feel pressure from the revolutionaries, including Pancho Villa. Diaz was not serving the people, but those in his circle of allies and foreign investors. The rich got richer and the poor got poorer.

"Despite public statements in 1908 favoring a return to democracy and not running again for office, Diaz reversed himself and ran in the 1910 election. Diaz, then 80 years old, failed to institutionalize presidential succession, triggering a political crisis between the cientificos (scientists) and the followers of General Bernardo Reyes, allied with the military and peripheral regions of Mexico. After Diaz declared himself the winner for an eighth term, his electoral opponent, wealthy estate owner Francisco I. Madero, issued the Plan of San Luis Potosi calling for armed rebellion against Diaz, leading to the outbreak of the Mexican Revolution." [394]

Of course, Jesse wanted in the fight. Per the book, "Jesse James Was One of His Names," by Del Schrader, Diaz was a part of the Mexican force in the Mexican American War and fought against the rule of Maximillian. Diaz was determined to overthrow the emperor and was the one who ordered Maximillian's execution. Diaz also knew who headed the removal of Maximillian's treasures. He kept his eye out for Jesse and knew about his ranch. Jesse also had his eye on Diaz, a bitter enemy from the past.

During that period, Pancho Villa was considered a bandit, living up in the mountains of Mexico. Pancho was the one who introduced Jesse to the Yaqui Indians. It is believed that Pancho was living amongst them, hiding out, just as Billy did after his supposed death.

Pancho Villa had the same philosophy as Jesse. He sought justice for the peasant's rights of land and redistribution of wealth for those impoverished people who have been enslaved by their government and the Catholic Church. Jesse said that Villa's most bitter grand fight was against the Catholic Church, who were stepping a little heavy on the rights of the people and their pocketbook, who couldn't support the church financially.

Raids and ferocious acts were part of the scheme of Diaz. Jesse didn't speak much of this, but we get little bits and pieces of how dangerous it was to live in Mexico, especially Chihuahua and the northern part of Mexico where most of the battles were fought.

The Mexican Revolution was in full force by 1910. Jesse was right in the middle of it with the KGC. In Schrader's book, it was said that Jesse had told the incredible story of the whole affair. The KGC and Jesse invested millions of dollars for this entire uprising, backing Pancho Villa all the way. He was a good friend of Jesse's. Pancho made Billy a captain in Pancho Villa's Cavalry.

Jesse set up his own army to help Pancho Villa with manpower, smuggling arms, ammo, supplies, food, mules, horses, etc. to Pancho's army. In Howk's book, "We gave it thought, so hired out to fight under General Pancho Villa, with us were the two twin boys of Jesse's, Billy the Kid then known as the Texas Kid." [395] So here, we learn that the two twin boys of Jesse may have lived and were working with Jesse in Mexico. We don't know for sure about the twins or if they really grew into manhood. No other evidence exists that Bud has found.

Brushy was in the fight also. In Edwards book, "We (Brushy Bill) joined with Carranza's men, and later with Pancho Villa. I was captain of 106 men, all mounted on *Steel Dust horses* from our ranch. Our *Steel Dust* horses could outdistance the Spanish ponies of the Federals." [396] This coincides with Del Schrader's book.

Also in Edward's book, it speaks of the time when William Morrison, the lawyer was helping Brushy tell his story in the late 40's and 1950 and was striving to receive a pardon from the New Mexico governor. Morrison pursued evidence and confirmation from those who knew Billy the Kid and his story, who could identify and verify who Brushy Bill was, along with his story. "Morrison and Brushy Bill went back to El Paso, where there were more old-timers to see, Luis Martinez, of Parral, Mexico, and Hernando Chavez, of Torreon, stated that to their knowledge Billy the Kid had lived in Mexico after his supposed death. "We were told," said Chavez, "that Billy the Kid fought with Carranza and Pancho Villa during the Revolution." [397]

In Schrader's book, he describes that Villa persuaded Jesse to trust Carranza, but later Carranza turned on them and became their enemy.

Jesse told Howk that they, the KGC continued to supply Pancho Villa from 1911-1918. Jesse was well paid by Villa. Per Howk, some of the group that helped this cause were ex-Texas Rangers and peace officers of the South and Southwest. We know that Elfego Baca became Colonel Pancho Villa's American agent for purchasing arms and supplies. They became friends exchanging jewels, gold, and money for weapons.

Another way of financing the effort, Pancho became a cattleman, who stole livestock and sold them for a huge profit, using the proceeds to benefit the war effort.

The Mexican Revolution involved fierce fighting with many raids and mercilessness deaths. Pancho would kill the oppositional men and steal the women. He had several wives and many women fought with him. Pancho became a mercenary and soon became the Robinhood of Mexico when he would redistribute the stolen goods from the raids of the wealthy to the poor peasants.

Pancho Villa legally married Senora Dona Maria "Luz" Corral on May 29, 1911 right in the heat of the battle. They were living in Chihuahua City and Jesse said his and Billy's ranch were down the street from Luz Villa's home. The Villa's home was a 50-room mansion, which is still there today as a museum. Pancho was not home very often. The Federal forces targeted this neighborhood. Schrader's book describes numerous attacks on the Chihuahua ranch of Jesse's, but apparently, they stood their ground. Luz Villa never left her home.

(Luz and Pancho Villa)

By 1911, Diaz began to see the writing on the wall and went into exile overseas, but the revolution continued. Pancho Villa kept pouring it on, night after night and by 1914, Pancho Villa and his forces were in control of Northern Mexico. He fought hard to take over the hills surrounding Torreon and the city itself, which was completely devastated. He never let up.

In those years, power exchanged hands between parties and the revolutionists. It was mass chaos in Mexico and caused a Civil War from 1914-1915. Pancho asked the American President Woodrow Wilson for aid to continue his mission. Villa would continue to sell his livestock, mostly stolen, to buy weapons and ammunition.

It appears in all books, documents, and statements from Jesse's family that Jesse had more irons in the fire elsewhere, so he must have left Pancho's army and his men in charge to fulfill their goal. Bud had found information just how far the KGC went with financing the revolution after Jesse left the scene. In a map drawn out by Howk with Jesse's instructions, there is an inscription that indicates a place where Jesse stashed a lot of items to have if times get tough. Copper, gold, lead, and silver bars, as well as canned milk, pork and beans, saddles, and blankets were stashed along with a lot of guns and supplies to be issued to General Pancho Villa in Chihuahua, Sonora Mexico 1915-1922. The secret hiding place was a hollow mound, location unknown.

Finally, the entire Federal Army collapsed. Pancho Villa became the hero of the Revolution, but it wasn't over. The revolutionary armies then turned on each other for power. Pancho turned on America. Elfego Baca and Villa had a falling out and later became bitter enemies.

Anger toward the United States was ignited in October 1915, when President Wilson recognized Venustiano Carranza as the new ruling authority over Mexico and legitimized his constitutional government. The access of support and arms from the U.S. began to open back up for Mexico, but at the same time it caused anger from Carranza's opponents, which included Pancho Villa.

Pancho Villa would take his anger out on Columbus, New Mexico, driving his forces into the United States and raiding the town in March 1916. President Wilson retaliated and sent 5,000 troops into Mexico to capture Villa. It was an opportunity for the U.S. forces to utilize their new weapons and practice maneuvers that would help them in World War I. They had new steel-plated armored vehicles and several bi-planes for surveillance.

After a year of not finding Villa in the secluded northern mountains, Carranza forced the U.S. to withdraw.

Villa was assassinated in an ambush in Parral, Mexico in July 1923. But wait. Jesse told Howk, written about in Del Schrader's book, that Jesse smuggled Villa out of the country and gave him a place in New Mexico to live on a trust fund set up for him for life. The man who was shot to death was Villa's double.

Another confession from Jesse, in both Howk and Schrader's books, stated that Villa did not raid Columbus, New Mexico. It was Carranza who staged the raid in order to stir up anti-Villa sentiment in the United States and to take him out.

If all that Del Schrader wrote from Howk's information in the book, "Jesse James Was One of His Names" and Howk's own book, "Jesse James and the Lost Cause" are factual, the story is bigger than you could ever imagine. If it is possible, get a copy of Del Schrader's book, "Jesse James Was One of His Names." Read it with a grain of salt and a lot of research. It reveals the intricate power of the KGC and its leader, Jesse Woodson James in all aspects of war, politics, and secret societies. Your mouth will drop to the floor in most incidences. I guar-an-tee!

What drama that took place in Mexico at the turn of the century. All during this time, Zerelda, Jesse and Frank's mother died on the St. Louis and San Francisco Railway (Frisco) train, 15 miles north of Oklahoma City in February 1911 per the Washington Post, February 11, 1911. [398] She had been visiting Frank and Anna for two months in Fletcher, Oklahoma. A newspaper clipping Bud had out of Anadarko, February 11, 1911, titled, "Mother of Frank and Jesse James dies," stated that her and Anna were on their way to Kansas City to visit Jesse James, Jr.

In this article, there seems to be some discrepancies. The Frisco Train route on the 1910 map showed that it went from Lawton, to Cement, Chickasha and Tuttle which would be approximately 20 miles from Oklahoma City. The article said Zerelda Samuel died at 3:00 about 20 miles west of Oklahoma which would have been near Tuttle. The body, verifying with other news sources was brought to Oklahoma City to immediately prepare her for burial and then shipped on the 7:00 train for Kansas City.

Ola stated that Jesse was living in Torreon, Mexico at the time that his mother came to Frank's home, but Jesse made a special effort to go to Fletcher to see his mother. On her trip back home with Anna, she died from a heart ailment.

Brushy, in his own words in the book, "Billy The Kid: An Autobiography," by Daniel Edwards: "We left Mexico in 1914, coming across the border at Brownsville, Texas. The Mexican Revolution broke us up. We lost everything we had, about $200,000 between the **three of us**. In 1912, I met Mollie Brown of Coleman, Texas, and we were married. She was a member of the old Brown family, of Brownwood, Texas. We went back to east Texas and then into Oklahoma, in the trading business again." [399]

In that statement from Brushy, he too states there were three of them, which coincides with the statement in Del Schrader's book, "Only three escaped the massacre. They were Jesse's son, Jesse F. B. James, an Indian servant, and Brushy Bill Roberts, alias Billy the Kid." [400]

An interesting fact that Dr. William Tunstill researched and verified is that Brushy, after crossing the border went to his cousin's, John Heath. He was a Texas Ranger. Dr. Tunstill was able to speak to the family about Billy and the events in his life.

World War I

With major events occurring in Jesse's life, we see another conflict rising before the one in Mexico had settled down. Jesse said he tried to enlist in the U.S. military, but was 70 years old and was refused, so he says he went to Canada and got in by concealing his age and was sent over to Europe." [401]

Britain declared war against Germany during World War I in August 1914 which pulled in all their colonies and dominions including Canada, Australia, and British India to fight. Jesse enlisted in the Canadian Army and became an officer. He was in Company C, 126th Battalion, Heavy Artillery. He said he was an interpreter, speaking French, Spanish, Portuguese, German and Indian Sign language. Jesse had said he was in there between 1915-1916.

During this conflict in February 18, 1915, Frank James died of a stroke.

J.R. Flynn in Waterloo, Iowa stated that he had known Jesse under a different name, which was John Franklin in the Canadian Army at Camp Sewell in 1916. He was 68 years old and "awful handy with a pistol or rifle. A powerful man for that age. We knew he had a past, but he was supposed to have had a parole from the Mounted Police." [402] This was revealed in 1948.

Jesse stated that he was discharged because of his injured lung and the effects of the mustard gas used by the Germans. He then went into the Royal Canadian Air Force R.A.F. in World War I, flew a plane for 22 months. He was made captain and earned the title of a decorated Major, but he declined. He was out in December 1918. Jesse told Ola, "World War I was four years of hell." [403]

Jesse's days of participating in war was coming to an end. As an organizational entity, the KGC officially closed the books in 1916, never to open or operate again for 50 years. Most of them would be dead by then, 1966. They knew all too well, that their goal of starting a 2nd Civil War and breaking off into a whole new country was not in the future for them, but America, the United States was.

World War II

When he was 96, he was working during World War II as a volunteer for the 6th War Loan Drive. It was one of eight drives to bring America to the war front by contributing to the war effort. An excellent article, "Loans & Bonds – Brief History of World War Two Advertising Campaigns War Loans and Bonds," from the Duke University Libraries, lays out the campaigns. "The war bond campaign was a unique fusion of nationalism and consumerism. Seeking to stir the conscience of Americans, it invoked both their financial and moral stake in the war. The sale of war bonds provided a way in which patriotic attitudes and the spirit of sacrifice could be expressed and became the primary way those on the home-front contributed to the national defense and war effort.

"The Sixth War Loan – "Attempting to capitalize on the surge of patriotism following Allied successes in Europe, November 20, 1944 marked the commencement of the Sixth War Loan. Promotion of this program was reoriented to appeal to American's perception of the Japanese as primary enemy, and well over $11 million of advertising was donated toward these ends. By the end of the Sixth War Loan on December 16, 1944, $21.6 billion had been raised." [404]

Jesse was part of this. He never stopped.

"The only difference between try and triumph is a little umph!"

-*Marvin Phillips*

Chapter Nineteen: Wranglin' the Range

Ranches

Jesse had his hand in everything. Ranches were a big priority to him. What were they being used for? We don't know the extent of their purpose, but it appears some were used for KGC business and some were used as personal. We have hints of Jesse being a cattleman, horseman, and farmer. Nearly every one of the ranches had a racetrack. As we dig a little further, we find evidence that the ranches were also used for hiding caches.

In this chapter, we will list ranches he owned and ranches he was associated with. We will also bring in information on Billy. It's by no means a complete list and I suspect Jesse had hundreds more, especially in Oklahoma and Texas, but this will give us some insight into his operations.

MEXICO

Coahuila, Mexico, Torreon - Mexico meant a lot to Jesse and the KGC. The area was connected by rail to Mexico City by 1883 and became a very lucrative location by the Nazas River for livestock and mining. Many came to the area to homestead and it would be known as Torreon Ranch for the entire community. It became a declared village in 1893 and a city by 1907.

In 1907, when Brushy Bill said he went back to Mexico after the raid in 1899 on the Chihuahua Ranch, he said he started another ranch, the 3 Bar Ranch. He does not say where that was. It possibly could have been in Torreon. Jesse only told Ola about his ranch in Torreon, not Chihuahua. Ola was very adamant about this location and the period of 1910-1912. It may have been here, that Jesse found Billy to be very popular and could have run for any public office he desired.

Chihuahua, Mexico - Howk never spoke of Jesse's ranch in Torreon, Mexico, but of a very large ranch in Chihuahua. In both "Jesse James and the Lost Cause" and "Jesse James Was One of His Names," he relates stories that Jesse supposedly told him of hundreds of ranch hands who worked there and his ranch manager was Bill Roberts, Brushy Bill. The *Steel Dust horses* were raised there along with mules and cattle. It was discussed in the last chapter.

In the early 1920's "Chihuahua City point to the increasing tide of mining men coming to the state looking over new properties abandoned during the revolution. These mining men, most of them from the United States, and many representing large interests, are not content to look at close-in properties near the state capital but are penetrating far into the mountains in every direction. Just at the present time, considerable interest is taken in reports of valuable ore discoveries in the southwestern part of Chihuahua." [405]

They were still using the Mexican pack trains to transport the ore through the mountains and long distances to a point of transfer in 1922.

CALIFORNIA

San Luis Obispo County - Paso Robles - Between 1868-1869, Frank and Jesse headed out to their Uncle Drury Woodson James' ranch outside of Paso Robles which is approximately halfway between Los Angeles and San Francisco. It was in the Spring of 1868, after the Russellville robbery that Frank set out on the train and stagecoach to reach his uncle's ranch. Jesse, on the other hand, traveled by a steamer, Santiago de Cuba to Panama and then on to San Francisco on another steamer. They separated, as not to draw attention and it was a bit easier and smooth sailing for Jesse who was still recovering from his gunshot wound in his chest. Jesse told Ola that while there, he took many hot springs mineral baths which seemed to help him in healing.

Drury James had traveled with his brother, Robert James in 1850 to California during the gold rush. They settled in a place known as Placerville. Arthur McCoy settled in a place called *Centerville*, California within the same county of *El Dorado*. Supposedly, Robert died in California, but with Ola and William Tunstill's research, it appears that Robert did not die, but left his family and started a new life. Drury, with partners, James and Daniel Blackburn purchased the Rancho Paso de Robles Mexican Land Grant in 1857 in California. The site of Paso Robles was a stop along the el Camino Real trail.

Paso Robles was founded by these men and grew into a community similar to what we find in Guthrie, Oklahoma and many new towns that were born in 1889. Paso Robles was incorporated as a city that same year. The architecture and stonework arches were very similar to the Oklahoma cities that emerged. The town included a Carnegie Library, same as Guthrie and Ardmore, as well as many other cities. It also included a Masonic lodge. Drury and the Blackburns built a massive, exquisite hotel and spa, drawing thousands of people to the area to partake of the Sulphur-rich healing waters.

Find-a-grave goes into great detail of Drury James' life. Among many other things, Drury gave land to the railroad, he carefully subdivided the 5,000 acres into city blocks, and "attracted selected business owners through a secret society." He also became involved in politics.

Drury became a very successful cattleman and rancher. He maintained a 30,000-acre ranch. Many sources state that Frank and Jesse worked on the ranch during their stay in 1868/69. One of the working cowboys stated that Jesse was going by the name of "Scotty." He stated that Scotty was a loner and not very sociable with the other cowhands. Scotty wasn't good at roping, but sure was an excellent shot with a six-gun.

Frank and Jesse stayed there throughout the winter of 1869 and then left. No one knew where they went, but by June 1869, we find them in Devil's Nest in Nebraska. Their timeline fits perfectly.

NEBRASKA

Lincoln County - We know that Buffalo Bill Cody had a ranch in North Platte and Billy had worked there several times, but there is a possibility that Jesse also had a ranch there.

TENNESSEE

Humphreys County – Jesse had a ranch/farm we spoke of earlier that was in *Humphreys* County. Jesse had a racetrack on the property.

NEW MEXICO

Colfax County - Jesse is thought to have been going by the name of Dave Crowden who attempted to buy a ranch on the Rayado River, south of Cimarron, close to the area where Albert Pike traveled and where Lucien Maxwell and Kit Carson established the settlement of Rayado. It is also believed that he had more land in the county that other men were managing for him, such as Clay Allison.

Santa Fe County - In Del Schrader's book, it mentions that Jesse had the Pigeon Ranch at Glorietta Pass, New Mexico in the early 1900's. The ranch house was used as one of the meeting places for the Confederate Underground. Those who met there were mentioned using alias', revealed as Jesse R. James, Cole Younger, Jefferson Davis, Butch Cassidy, Sundance Kid, Pancho Villa, Bill Roberts (Billy the Kid), Dr. Frank James, Bob Dalton, Kit Carson, and El Fago Baca. This information coincides with many sources that Pancho Villa went into Texas and New Mexico during the revolution to escape for brief periods of time. He was running a fairly large cattle operation. Surprisingly, my father had kept old X.I.T. booklets that his mother had, which told stories of the old cowboys of the X.I.T. ranch which were distributed during the X.I.T. Rodeo Reunion. He had kept the 1939 and 1940 edition. What a treasure. Inside the 1940 issue were different brands used in the area. It included the brand that Pancho Villa used.

(Pancho Villa's brand found in the old X.I.T. booklet, 1940)

Chaves County - The Bottomless Lake, 14 miles southeast of Roswell, which lays on latitude, **33.34417**, -104.35472 and longitude of **33** degree 20'39"N, 104 degrees 21'17" W is where Billy the Kid used to water his cattle/horses. This is a mysterious place and possibly was another place that was important to Jesse. A charcoal portrait of Jesse, Mother, and Frank was found in an old cabin near the lake. The portrait is done from pictures, possibly around 1890-1893 as others are found similar with this date. There was one done on Quantrill, William (Bill) T. Anderson, Alexander Franklin James, Cole and Bob Younger, Charles Fletcher (Fletch) Taylor, and Harrison Trow. I'm sure there were others. Most of them were done by Elmer Stewart and Anna Lee (Dillenbeck) Stacey found on The Kansas City Public Library site, https://kchistory.org.

WYOMING

Sheridan County - A Mrs. A.J. Cooksley of the Flying C Ranch in Clearmont, Wyoming wrote a letter to Carl Breihan, sharing a story regarding Jesse and his gang, including John Trammel. Mrs. Cooksley heard from old timers in the area that Jesse spent two winters in a dug-out hideout near the foot of Big Horn Mountain. "Jesse was known to be a gentleman. When ranchers had to leave their wives to hunt for cattle and get supplies, etc., Jesse and one of his companions would see that these ladies were kept supplied with firewood, water, and heavy chores taken care of." They were all gentlemen in front of women and children.

Johnson County - In "Jesse James Was One of His Names," Jesse was right in the middle of the Johnson County Cattle War in northern Wyoming in 1892. Jesse had purchased what he named the Shamrock Ranch along Crazy Woman Creek in 1874 or 1875. The ranch was southeast of the newly formed town of Buffalo in 1879. Jesse was amongst the big cattleman who in 1892, "were alarmed by the farmers who built fences and the Johnson County nesters and small ranches." The large cattle ranches banded together and organized the Regulators to settle the issues military style, hanging or shooting, whatever was required. "They hired gunman from Texas, Idaho, and Colorado and placed a former army officer in command." That my friend was the former Confederate Colonel, Jesse Woodson James. [406]

ARIZONA

An interview with Ozark Jack Berlin with the newspaper from Veedersburg, Indiana on August 19, 1949 stated that before Jesse went off to the Boer War, he owned a ranch in Arizona under the name of Jesse Williams.

SOUTH DAKOTA

Ranch near Bruce, South Dakota

OKLAHOMA

Logan County – Jesse supposedly raised horses on his ranch that he received after the Run of 1889 southeast of Guthrie.
Cimarron County – This would be part of the Diamond Ranch in which both Ola and Howk stated Jesse told them about.
Texas County – Jesse supposedly had a ranch outside of Texhoma in the Rice Community or what they called Stratton Township. nearby. They may have been connected to the Anchor D Ranch, but it is unknown.

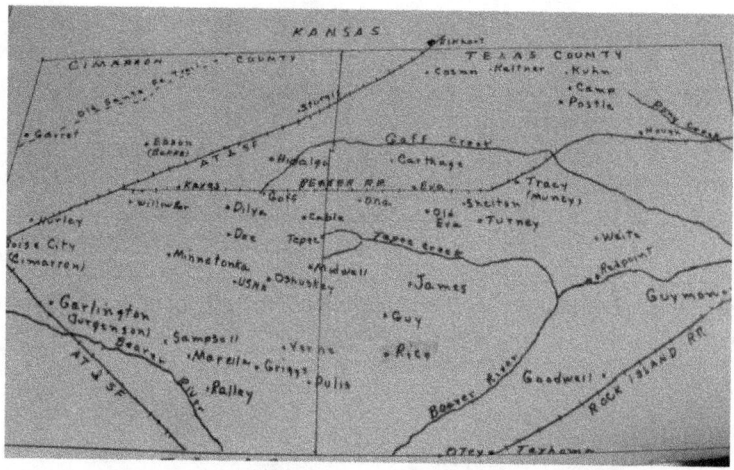

(Rice Community in the Oklahoma Panhandle where Jesse supposedly had land (courtesy of the Texhoma Museum))

Starr ranch – Close to the Canadian River, Belle Starr had a ranch on what was called Younger's Bend, near Briartown. This is where many an outlaw hung around and worked for Belle. Frank and Jesse, along with Billy, and the Youngers frequented the secluded ranch where many a night was filled with music and dance.

WASHINGTON

Kittitas County - In Del Schrader's book, "Jesse James Was One Of His Names", While Jesse was going by the name of Senator William A. Clark, per Howk in 1920 he was on his Wiscom Ranch, south of Ellensburg, Washington. [407]

MONTANA

Same book as noted above, stated that Jesse had a ranch named Bull's Creek Ranch in Montana. Maybe also the Two Dot Ranch. A man by an alias name Jack Longley who was very close to Senator William A. Clark, knew the senator was Jesse Woodson James. He came out and told Longley while in a merry way on the Bull's Creek Ranch. This was in 1927. Senator William A. Clark supposedly died in 1925. Longley was a bronc buster for the Miller and Lux ranches from Mexico to Canada. His father was a confederate officer and a member of the KGC. [408]

TEXAS

Dallas County – 1864 -The Shirley Ranch where Myra Belle Shirley's (Belle Starr) parents lived in Scyene, Texas after the Civil War. It is now surrounded by Dallas in the east central part of Dallas county. The town had 300 people, 6 saloons, a school, a church, and of course a Masonic Lodge and was named for a town in ancient Egypt. The Shirleys had a hotel and tavern bringing in income and outlaws. It was one of Frank, Jesse, and the Younger's hideouts.

Llano County – In "Jesse James was One of His Names," it was told that Jesse was a silent partner of the Bragg Ranch in Llano County. General Braxton Bragg was indeed known to have gone to Texas in 1874, during the height of the Texas Rangers Frontier Battalion. Bragg became chief engineer of the Gulf, Colorado, and Santa Fe Railroad and later served as the chief railroad inspector for the state of Texas. As you remember, Llano County is where Jesse served in the rangers and was a very important place. In the book, the story explains that the KGC learned of a huge amount of gold that was being shipped by Union soldiers in wagons from Sacramento to Fort Leavenworth. Once they reached the Western Oklahoma Panhandle on the Santa Fe Trail, the Confederates, General Hood's cavalry, led by Captain John Lamb and 60 Texas Rangers attacked and overtook the wagons. The wagons were taken to Llano County to the Bragg Ranch and gold coins worth 18 million dollars were buried in the *Camel and Straw Cave*. Booby traps were laid for those who came a visiting. [409]

Brown County – November 1879 – Jesse wrote to a newspaper that he, his wife, and son have settled on a ranch 10 miles outside of Brownwood. After the Mexican Revolution, Billy went to Coleman County, Texas and met his future wife who was from Brownwood in 1912, Mollie Brown.

Wichita County - Stone Ranch on Beaver Creek. This is where Allen and Susan James Parmer lived and worked. Jesse visited them often and had several hideouts in that area.

Winkler County - Jesse Cole James, born in Texarkana in February 13, 1882 was Jesse's son. When he was 18, he was a ranch laborer in Winkler County, Texas. In 1900, is when the State of Texas ended the free use of land and ranchers on this public land were required to pay rent. There were 12 ranches in Winkler County at that time. There were only 60 people living in Winkler County which the county seat became Kermit, 45 miles west of Odessa, Texas close to the New Mexico border. In 1910, he was in Cass County, Texas working as a Farm Laborer. Cass County was just south of the Red River on the Texas, Arkansas and Louisiana border, close to where he was born. In 1920, he was in Lawton and was a laborer. He was where Jesse needed him to be.

Near the Mexico border - Somewhere near the border Jesse had a ranch which was a secret training ground for Pancho Villa's men and those who volunteered from his other Texas Ranches.
410

Van Zandt County – Brushy Bill/Billy the Kid bought a ranch in Van Zandt County before the trouble started in Mexico. On the census in 1920, Billy was living there as Ollie Roberts indicating he was widowed, so his wife, Mollie Brown passed away within 7 years of their marriage. 1920 is when DeWitt Travis was living in Van Zandt and remembers Jesse being in his home, hiding out that year. DeWitt was 29 at that time. He was born in Van Zandt County. Billy married Loutecia Ballard in 1929 in Van Zandt.

Palo Pinto County - After the war effort, Ola said that Jesse went back to Texas in 1922 to his ranch, 25 miles northwest from Mineral Wells, using the name of Frank Dalton. This was in Palo Pinto County where Clay Allison became a drover and where Marcus Lafayette Dalton was one of the cattle kings.

West Texas - C Dot E Ranch – Al Jennings owned this ranch at some time. It was said that he had a chicken ranch at one time, but unclear if this was it. Jesse and Al once had a shooting match there and to both of their surprise, Al Jennings won. That was one of Al's greatest moments and memories.

Denton County– In 1906, Jesse had a ranch about 8 ½ miles south of Denton. (Notice the distance from town, same as what he said about his ranch in Guthrie, Oklahoma). Sometime after 1914, they drilled for oil and hit a fine producing well.

Collin County – Not far from Denton, Frank and Jesse James had a hideout at Captain Francis Marion "Tuck" Hill's home in McKinney on 616 West Virginia Street. Hill served in Gordon's Regiment under General Sterling Price for three months and was given an honorable discharge so that he could join the Quantrill Raiders. He was a cousin to Frank and Jesse. Hill's mother was Susan E. Poor and her parents were Drury Woodson Poor and Elizabeth Ellen Britt. Tuck Hill was very well thought of and made a profitable living by livestock breeding, mostly mules. When Frank and Jesse were in the area, they would always go to Hill's home and hide in the attic if a posse were on their tail. They were well liked in McKinney.

Schleicher County – Is a very small county with the county seat, *Eldorado*. It is close to Fort McKavett. Per Howk, Jesse had a ranch near El Dorado, Texas called Al Parmer's Ranch. I have not been able to substantiate it, but it appears that the ranch was named after his brother-in-law, Allen Parmer. A story out of the Fort Worth Star Telegram, June 4, 1948, titled, "It Would Be Easy To Determine If Latest 'Jesse James' Is Imposter" is written about Dr. Jim Dan Hill (1897-1983), a former Texan who lived in Leon County (the county of Centerville) and who at that time was president of Wisconsin State Teachers College. He went to college at Baylor University in Texas and was the president of the Press Club. At the time of the article he was a contender for presidency of Texas Technological College at Lubbock, which later would become Texas Tech University.

Dr. Hill stated that he knew and worked for Allen "Palmer" who was running a "first class ranch just northwest of town for many years when we moved to Eldorado in 1910." Hill stated, "During the summer, between high school sessions, I worked on Allen Palmer's ranch."

Dr. Hill had a lot of accomplishments in his life, not only as an educator, a writer, and an historian, but served in the U.S. Navy in World War I, Officers Reserve Corps, and National Guard. He was a Commanding Officer, 190th Field Artillery Regiment in World War II where he received many decorations, (1) European theater medal with five campaign stars and arrowhead (Omaha Beach), (2) Bronze Star, (3) Legion of Merit (Battle of the Bulge), (4) Chevalier de la Legion d'Honneur, and (5) Croix de Guerre with palm. In 1956, he retired as a Major General. He lived out his last years in Abilene, Texas and was buried in the same cemetery as his wife who was from Wichita Falls, Texas along with Allen Parmer and Susan James Palmer in Riverside Cemetery in Wichita Falls, Texas.

Brazos County and Leon County – There are hints about ranches owned by Francis Claude Wilson in Brazos County and Joe Vaughn owning a ranch in Leon County where Centerville is located. There is no substantiating evidence of this, but Howk stated that these were friends and kin to Jesse who owned these.

Gregg County – This was a ranch that was in Gladewater, owned by Jesse's good friend, DeWitt Travis who took great care of both Jesse and Billy. In 1942, this photo was taken of Jesse and Billy on the ranch.

(Jesse and Billy on DeWitt Travis' ranch, 1942)

CANADA

Dryden, Ontario, 1928 – 1930 Jesse was going by the name of Frank Dalton. He went to Brighton, Ontario, then bought a ranch in Dryden, Ontario where he had fine Percheon or draft horses. They were known as well-muscled, intelligent, and hardy work horses. He also had some saddle stock. Later, he sold it to the man that was renting from him.

Lea Park, Alberta, 1933- After selling oil leases in Texas, Jesse went back to Canada and bought a ranch near Lea Park, Alberta, Canada. It was said to be 320 acres, half a section. He had cattle, horses, wheat, and oats. The Lea Park Rodeo grounds were a ¼ mile away from his place. He left the ranch in 1935 to go back to the States to write the Crittenden Memoirs. The eyewitness to all that took place in Lea Park was a young man who worked and lived with Jesse on this ranch. The witness was Mitch Graves who wrote many letters to Ola. Bud Hardcastle had the pleasure of speaking with Mitch over the phone and corresponded with him and his wife. What a treasure. I had the pleasure in speaking with a relative over the phone in Alberta and she confirmed what Mitch revealed to Ola and Bud. Jesse and Dewitt came back to the Canadian ranch in 1936. That's the last time Mitch Graves saw Jesse. The ranch was sold in 1946 and 1947.

(Mitch Graves, 3rd man standing on the left (courtesy of Concetta Phillipps, Mitch's great niece))

(Mitch and his family in the 1930's (courtesy of Concetta Phillipps))

Saving the best story for last -

PANHANDLE OF TEXAS/OKLAHOMA –

Shortly after Jesse was supposedly killed in April 1882, a newspaper article was naming the different associates of Jesse and their whereabouts. "Frank James, it is believed, is not in Kentucky, but in the **pan-handle section of Texas**, where he and Jesse invested in a ranch some years ago." (Atchison Daily Patriot, April 7, 1882). The investment must have been in the late 1870's or early 80's when they "invested" in this ranch.

Ola stated that in 1884, Frank James went to Tascosa in the Texas Panhandle and became a Texas Ranger, fighting against the cattle rustlers. She said that Pat Garrett was there too as a ranger. She had a picture dated in 1886 with Frank and Pat Garrett together in Tascosa. Garrett served as captain of the LS Texas Rangers; an independent ranger company paid by the panhandle's larger cattle operations. It was described as "a group of rangers sent by Governor John Ireland to the Panhandle to protect ranchers from rustlers." [411] Garrett served a full year and the ranger's band was dissolved in the Spring of 1885, but many of the rangers stayed on with the LS Ranch at various camps. They frequented Tascosa.

(Photo that Aubrey and Ola had and is also shown in Maverick Town, by John L. McCarty, 1968. Standing l-r: W. S. Mabry (William Spark Mabry - surveyor), Frank James (merchant), C. B. Vivian (county clerk), I.P. Ryland (attorney). Seated from l-r: Jim East (sheriff), James McMasters (county judge), and Pat Garrett (captain, Texas Rangers))

That does not look like the Frank James we all know, but I think you will see who he favors as we continue in the book.

So, two years after Jesse's death, Frank was in the Panhandle. Tascosa was one of Billy the Kid's hangouts. Its where Frenchie McCormick, a dance hall gal called home. The writer's grandmother and great grandparents who worked for numerous Texas Panhandle ranches, including the Bivins Ranch, the L.I.T. Ranch, and the Buffalo Springs headquarters of the X.I.T. Ranch where Ab Blocker designed the X.I.T. brand, were able to meet Frenchy and had quite a colorful visit.

We also have evidence that Jesse was in the Texas Panhandle. Ola Everhard once said that Jesse told her that he had a ranch that spread from the Texas Panhandle into "No Man's Land," the strip in the Oklahoma Panhandle.

Per Howk's book, "Jesse James and the Lost Cause," he wrote that Jesse told him this story. "I saw him (Orrington Red Lucas) about 1890, when he was Chief of Police at Tulsa. We met out at Kenton, Oklahoma (northwest corner of the Oklahoma Panhandle near the Cimarron River), and he and I rode down to **Diamond Ranch**, which belonged to us (unknown if the ownerships was referring to him and Frank, or him and Red, or if he was referring to the KGC), between Boise City and Dalhart. I had given Red a fine *Steel Dust* horse from that particular ranch in 1910." [412]

The Steel Dust horse was named after the Greek mythical wonderful winged horse named Pegasus. It was a breed all of its own and was the cowboys favorite amongst ranches and trail drives. "They were heavy-muscled horses, marked with small ears, a big jaw, remarkable intelligence and lightning speed up to a quarter of a mile. Steel Dust was an American Quarter Horse. He and his kind would achieve fame in proportions every bit as magnificent as that of the mythical Pegasus." [413]

"After the Civil War, cattlemen moved into the area. Gradually they organized themselves into ranches and established their own rules for arranging their land and adjudicating their disputes. In 1886, Interior Secretary L.Q.C. Lamar declared the area to be public domain and subject to "squatter's rights". [414]

In the Oklahoma Panhandle, it was truly "No Man's Land." The land was flat as a pancake, not much water, no trees, just land and sky. The winters were harsh with blizzards that could wipe out cattle in an instant as well as families unprepared. The spring and summertime would also be treacherous with the dust storms and violent thunderstorms leaving many without proper shelter to protect them. But the new pioneers of that area and era were tough and hardy.

No Man's Land opened for settlers in 1890, but before this, ranches had been established along the creeks. The area where Jesse was speaking of, Boise City, the Corrumpa Creek which began in Union County, New Mexico, traveling east into the Oklahoma Panhandle close to where Felt, Oklahoma now sits, became the Beaver River which flowed south of Boise City. Now, its dry as a bone.

The origin of the Corrumpa Creek just inside New Mexico was where the McNees Crossing was on the Santa Fe Trail, near Rabbit Ears Mountain. This was pretty much the only water source in No Man's Land except for the Cimarron up north. Sometimes if you were lucky, water stood in the old buffalo wallows. So, with a little bit of effort, a rancher could benefit from the closeness of the Santa Fe Trail, the creeks and the rich tall Buffalo grass. That's why the buffalo roamed throughout those plains.

In the Texas Panhandle, near Dalhart was the Rabbit Ear Creek, later known as Coldwater Creek that meandered from New Mexico and in and out of the Texas and Oklahoma border. There was Buffalo Springs Creek, 30 miles north of Dalhart where the headquarters of the X.I.T. ranch was located. My great grandparents were asked by the former foreman of the northern division and later the assistant general manager of the X.I.T. ranch, Bob Duke, to work at the Buffalo Springs headquarters in 1930 in which he was still overseeing the remnants of the X.I.T. estate. Duke was the last original X.I.T. cowboy to actually work for the estate.

My great grandparents said the cowboys at the ranch would always tell them that there is one very deep hole in Buffalo Springs creek that was bottomless, indicating a deep-water basin below the surface. There was the Rita Blanca Creek. Another creek most vital to the ranches in the

Panhandle was the Red Cow Creek. Water was one of the most important assets for a cattleman to have besides the grass and his horse.

Ranches began to spring up and the cowboys had an opportunity to start owning land in 1890, but it appears that the James brothers were one of the first on this land in the Panhandle utilizing its natural resources, earlier than the X.I.T. Ranch which was established in 1885. The famous X.I.T. Ranch rose into being when two brothers, the Farwells from Chicago were interested in land in the Texas Panhandle that was set aside by the Texas Legislature to finance the building of a new capitol in Austin. The old one burned down in November of 1881.

A man named Mathias Schnell of Rock Island; Illinois accepted the contract to build the capitol in return for the land. He transferred ¾ interest to several men, including the Farwells, who formed the Capitol Syndicate out of Chicago. To secure a huge portion of money to be able to develop the land into a workable ranch, the Syndicate looked to London. The Farwells and many other wealthy and notable investors from London and the United States formed the Capitol Freehold Land and Investment Company. Farwell returned to the States with roughly $5 million dollars in his pocket to establish a huge ranch on the Western edge of the panhandle. The land of the X.I.T. expanded over 10 counties and consisted of over 3 million acres. This land was not on the land where Jesse owned, but it appears that it bordered it.

This transaction was similar to the Syndicate who were involved in the purchase of the Maxwell Grant in New Mexico.

We find that ex-Texas Ranger George Arrington began to develop property to the East of Jesse's land in Hemphill County near the Washita River in the Texas Panhandle. Captain Arrington was assigned the Texas Panhandle in September 1879, establishing the first ranger camp in the panhandle, Camp Roberts, in Crosby County. "Arrington resigned from the rangers in the summer of 1882 to take advantage of Panhandle ranching opportunities." He became the sheriff of Wheeler County and he and his family lived in Mobeetie. "During his service he filed on choice ranchland on the Washita River in Hemphill County. After first living in a dugout he erected two cabins as his home and headquarters and in 1885 registered his CAP brand." [415]

The man who identified Jesse James' body in 1882, Harrison Trow also had a ranch in the Texas Panhandle beginning in 1900. Some believe Trow was Jesse. In 1920, Harrison Trow sold his ranch in Deaf Smith County, between Vega and Hereford which was 8,610 acres; sold to Sandy Murchison of Amarillo. Trow owned it for 20 years. It was a big cattle and agriculture ranch. [416] Trow was in Quantrill Raiders and later published a book of his adventure. Mrs. Trow gave land in Castro County to Wayland College. [417]

With Jesse telling both Ola and Howk about this ranch in the Texas Panhandle, plus the newspaper article, the timeline of Jesse's ownership and management of the ranch in the Texas Panhandle was somewhere in between 1880-1910 or earlier. Jesse gifted a Steel Dust horse from this ranch of theirs, in 1910 to Red Lucas. It appears that it was a working ranch, a horse ranch.

To add more validity to this story of Jesse having a ranch in the Oklahoma and Texas Panhandle, I learned several years ago from a great grandson, Donald of the Haskew outlaw who rode with Jesse James, that after Haskew recovered from the gunshot wound, him and Jesse both left Johnsonville, Indian Territory and headed for No Man's Land. This was in 1885/86. They had a place to go, to the Panhandle where very little settlement was established. Haskew never went back to the family. He remarried and lived to a very old age. It was told that John Wesley Haskew and Jesse remained close friends, even though Haskew's older brother, William Haskew who was in the 4th Tennessee Union Cavalry was killed viciously by the Confederates led by Nathan Bedford Forrest at Sugar Creek, Alabama the day after Christmas 1864.

At the turn of the century, the outlaw's son, Aaron Haskew went looking for his father. Aaron went up to the Texas and Oklahoma Panhandle on a lead. In 1905, Aaron settled there and was the 2nd person to file for land in Texas County, Oklahoma in No Man's Land. It was near Texhoma that straddled the Oklahoma and Texas border about 55 miles from Boise City, Oklahoma, 323 acres. It was close to the Rice Community or what they called Stratton Township and a plot of land there was named, "James." Aaron was overheard by his grandson, Donald saying that they lived right over the fence from Jesse James.

John Wesley Haskew's brother, Newton Haskew who helped his brother escape from the Montague jail was apparently there in Johnsonville himself to see the shooting of his brother in 1885. He told the family, the last time he saw his brother was when he left him at an old man's house. He had been wounded, but not seriously. Newton also told the story that he sat close to Jesse on a train in the later part of 1885 after he himself escaped from jail. Both knew each other and kept their tales to themselves with a nod of recognition.

Another one of Haskew's sons, Ransom was quoted as saying that his father got in trouble for horse rustling and they "knocked" the "H" out of Haskew, going by the name of Askew or Akers. Akers was the name of the people, the kin, who helped Ola's family move from Butcher Knife to a safer place with the help of Jesse. James Akers was also found in the small town of Texhoma in 1905, living next to Aaron Haskew, the son of the outlaw.

This information was shared with Bud and right away he told me a story connected to Jesse regarding the "The Treasure of the Tall Tombstones." Even Howk listed this one in the treasure caches in Del Schrader's book. [418] You wouldn't think that this would lead us to information regarding ranches in Jesse's pocket, but it does.

Bud said that he had been trying to uncover this story for several years regarding huge tombstones that are in line with the Wichita Mountains in Oklahoma, that point to possible treasure. He found the cemetery off in a very remote area of southwestern Oklahoma in *Humphreys*, Oklahoma, 7.5 miles southeast of Altus. The word "Humphreys" stands out because Jesse, as you recall, had a ranch in Humphreys County, Tennessee.

In Humphreys, Oklahoma, the old Missouri-Kansas-Texas Railroad passed through the small incorporated community. Very unusual that the major railroad we have been writing about went through this spot in the road. The only thing left of the town currently is the Co-op and cotton gin mill. There are a few houses and most of the roads are unpaved.

Bud told me to go and see for myself, the tall tombstones about 8-10 feet tall, as it was not far from where Bud and I had met in Altus. I drove down a dirt road, not sure if I was in the right place, and sure enough I crossed a railroad track that was embedded in the dry earth with no barriers or mechanical gate arms to warn me if a train was coming. It was pretty primitive, but I'm sure it served its purpose and I'm sure it still transports cotton. I had to stop by the cotton gin to ask someone where the cemetery was. They pointed me in the right direction.

The Francis Cemetery was very well kept, but I could see from the road, the gigantic tombstones. They were at least 10 feet tall. I carefully stepped out of the car and made my way through the gate. My mouth dropped when I saw the names on the huge tombstones. It was people named "Askew." Yes, in research I found that they had big ties to the Confederacy in Alabama, and they came from the same family as mine, many, many years ago, William Dekalb Askew (1834-1912). This is what Bud said he wanted me to see. They were the most massive monuments that I had ever seen in a cemetery. The alignment of these were strategically placed. The tombstones were recently placed there, within the last 30 years or less I would say.

(The Tall Tombstones outside of Humphreys, Oklahoma)

    The name Askew also comes into the story of Jesse. Those who know history or what has been told, was that Jesse killed Daniel H. Askew, a neighbor in Missouri who supposedly was working with Pinkertons. The murder occurred 3 months after Jesse's mother lost her arm and his little brother, Archie who was killed in the explosion caused by the Pinkertons in their home. The explosion occurred in January 1875 and the killing in April 1875 of Askew. Jesse stated in a letter that was intercepted by the law, that he was innocent of Askew's murder and that it was Jack Ladd, Askew's hired hand along with the Pinkerton's detectives that did the murder. The poor man was shot in the face three times. He was unrecognizable.

    The Askews lived ¼ mile west of the Samuels home in Missouri. Jack Ladd, tied to the Pinkertons, was spying on the James, and revealing their location. In the old newspaper article, at the inquest of Askew's murder, no one was blaming the James boys in Kearney or within the vicinity, but those in Liberty were. A neighbor, Henry Sears, heard the gunshots and shortly thereafter, a man on a horse came to his house. In the dark, the man screamed out, "We have killed Dan Askew tonight, and if anyone wishes to know who did it say that detectives did it." He yelled out a detective's name, but it was not recognizable. "Tell his friends to go and bury the damned son of a bitch tomorrow." [419]

    Many of the neighbors believed it was Jack Ladd who did the killing and he hadn't been seen since the killing. Jesse stated he was in Texas and had many alibis, but yet his name would forever be branded as the killer.

    Mr. Daniel Askew is buried in the same cemetery as Sarah Lindsay Thomason, Zerelda's mother, some James,' and Mimms' in New Hope Cemetery in Holt, Clay County, Missouri. From what I have learned, Daniel Askew and the Askews on the tombstone in Humphreys were not related, but Daniel Askew was related to another family just a few paces from where the gigantic tombstones were.

    Bud said there was a lot of symbolism and signs in that cemetery. He told me to go to a gated portion of the cemetery and there were James buried there. "Look at the names," he said.

    Andrew Andy *James* (**1833**-1901) who married Susan C. <u>Cole</u> (1842-1930) – Andy <u>*Frank*</u> James (1903-1925) – Dorcas McClure James (1844-1925) - <u>*Frank*</u> Matthews James (1876-1909) – <u>*Jesse*</u> Campbell James (1868-1890) – Dr. John Thomas James (1836-1915) – <u>*Robert*</u> Lee James

(1864-1913) – Sue James *Richardson* (1883-1978) – who died in Gladewater, Texas, buried in Humphreys). All these names were names from Jesse Woodson James' family.

This was amazing to me and I too, as Bud did, felt like the people buried there were trying to tell us something or point us into the right direction. Yes, there were many symbols and signs of the Confederacy, masonic symbols, and how the graves were placed or laid out in the Francis Cemetery. Some graves had the head to the east and the feet pointing west. Christian tradition is based on placing the head and marker of the deceased to the west while the feet points east, enabling those that have gone before us to face the rising sun as the Lord Jesus returns for his people.

Bud has found at many different cemeteries, signs as these, placed in plain sight. They are directional and symbolic signs to locate treasure. This has been evident in *Baxter* Cemetery, 5 miles north of Zanesville, Ohio, Wapanucka Academy in Oklahoma, Monument Hill in Oklahoma, and Waco, Texas. Look at the writings, the numbers, the names on the tombstone, the placement, and any directional markers that point the way. For the untrained eye such as myself, you can pick up a lot of clues, but for the expert, like Bud, it was very plain to see what the clues were revealing. He didn't share what the clues meant, but he told me that some of the tombstones were perfectly in line with the Wichita Mountains which held more gold than you could ever imagine.

(Tombstones lined up perfectly with the Wichita Mountains)

Who was this James family, so carefully placed in a beautiful iron fence within the Francis Cemetery? This is when I really began to see how God's hand was in everything that Bud and I were doing. As I researched this family, everything began to become clearer. The family and their descendants passed on the names of Jesse, Frank, and Robert quite frequently.

Andrew "Andy" James (**1833**-1901) came from Virginia. His parents were John James (1790-1871) and Clarissa Taylor (1793-1876). Clarissa's family stems from the famous Taylor and Hubbard family, James Taylor (1732-1814), whose uncle was President Zachary Taylor and Ann Hubbard (1738-1789). Ann Hubbard's uncle, Moses Hubbard (1709-1780) was Daniel H. Askew's maternal 2nd great grandfather. Jesse Woodson James' also had a branch of Hubbards in his tree.

"Hard to make this up," as Bud always says. The James family of course is directly related to Jesse James. Andrew "Andy" James and Jesse Woodson James share the same 4th great grandfather, Thomas James (1674-1726). Both the writer's maternal and paternal family intertwine with them.

Andrew James joined the Confederacy force during the Civil War. The papers for a widow's pension show that he was in the 21st Virginia Cavalry, McCausland's Brigade, Lomax Division, Peter's Regiment, in Company K, which later changed to Company A, and also was in the CSA Army. He was on the firing line the morning General Robert E. Lee surrendered.

Dr. John Thomas James, his brother served as CSA 2nd Lt. in Company A, 23rd Battalion in the Virginia Infantry.

The story of Andrew "Andy" James is quite interesting. After the Civil War, about 1871/72, he brought his family to Texas by boat through Galveston. They traveled over the great state of Texas in ox-driven wagons and went as far as the northern boundary of Texas just shy of Indian Territory. There, they set up house at Spanish Fort, just south of the Red River, near Red River Station in Montague County, Texas. In 1877, a Masonic lodge was erected in Spanish Fort, one of the first buildings to be established.

Just as a lot of ranchers did during this time, such as the Waggoners and Burnetts, Andrew leased land from the Chickasaw Nation to establish a very profitable ranching operation. It was here that young Walter Peleg James was born in 1878 in the Chickasaw Nation.

Andrew James' son, Andrew Marmaduke "Andy" James (1882-1958) was born in Spanish Fort. He was named after one of Robert E. Lee's generals. At the age of five, his father took the family in 1887 and moved further north into Greer County, Indian Territory. They made winter camp near the North Fork of the Red River next to the Navajoe Mountains.

Nearby, W.H. Acers and H.P. Dale had built a general store to enable trade with the Indians and cattle drovers heading north to Kansas. The Indians were still very prevalent in that area. They would call the little community, Navajoe, named after the nearby mountains, adding an "e" to distinguish it from Navajo, Arizona. It would eventually become a part of Jackson County and lies 5 miles northeast of Headrick, Oklahoma.

With a little bit of research and clues that Jesse gave us, the whole picture comes to view. This little community or camp that the James were staying at in 1887, had a very interesting beginning. It was no ordinary town; it was developed as a "company town."

What was a company town? The only thing that came to my mind was the song, "Sixteen Tons." The town companies began in the 1880's – 1935 and a business or organization would own all the buildings, houses, and businesses. "In some situations, company towns developed out of a paternalistic effort to create a utopian worker's village. Churches, schools, libraries, and other amenities were constructed in order to encourage healthy communities and productive workers. Saloons or places or services believed to be negative influences were prohibited." [420]

These company towns were created to house and utilize the working class for a particular business, such as textile mills, coal, steel, railroads, etc. It is not clear what Navajoe was established for. The company towns were built near natural resources so it could have been for gold mining as there were a lot of prospectors and miners that moved into Navajoe. The King Solomon Mining Company was very interested in the prospects of gold in the mountains, creeks, and riverbeds. The Otter and Cache Creeks were of great interest.

The reason for the desire to make Navajoe a "company town" may have been for what was promoted in the papers and pamplets, a farming community, claiming the land for farmers and not the elite cattleman who thought all the land was theirs for the taking as the newspapers stated. Sadly, it was also specified to be for Whites only.

Joseph Spaulding Works, known as "Buckskin Joe," was a Texas land promoter out of Fort Worth, Texas. He was born in 1847, same year as Jesse, and stated in the newspapers that he was in the Union Army during the Civil War. [421] He played a major role in the development of communities in Texas and Oklahoma.

Bud Hardcastle: The Truth Tracker

J. S. WORKS.

(Joseph Spaulding Works aka. "Buckskin Joe." (courtesy of The Daily Oklahoman, Jan. 2, 1915))

Several news articles explain what was occurring in the far corners of southwestern Oklahoma in 1887. A Captain *Payne* had a scheme to move bands of squatters into that area of Indian Territory, before any of the unassigned lands were open for settlement, but that part of Oklahoma belonged to Texas at the time. The borders and land were being disputed.

Payne and several men, including Buckskin Joe established the organization, Texas-Oklahoma Homestead Colony in 1885. Payne, the president in his pursuit to open up settlements for nesters in Indian Territory was kindly escorted by the military out of that region. President Payne was charged with planning and operating a grafting scheme and was arrested by Federal officers. He was acquitted.

The company that Payne started didn't die, it just reformed. They began to look to the Texas Panhandle where the Fort Worth and Denver Railroad was being built. It could be a "company town" to support the railroad. [422]

The first rail in the Panhandle of Texas of the Fort Worth and Denver Railroad was laid on February 27, 1882. In 1901, the Chicago, Rock Island, & Pacific, crossed over the Fort Worth and Denver Railroad, making it an ideal spot for a prosperous town. The town of Dalhart was born on that junction in 1901.

The leadership changed in the Texas-Oklahoma Homestead Colony organization. "T.C. Carlock was elected president and Joseph Spaulding Works, a picturesque character known far and wide as "Buckskin Joe" was elected vice-president, secretary, and general agent for the Texas Oklahoma Homestead Colony." [423]

Buckskin Joe was quite a character. He was not going to give up in Indian Territory. His story is found in newspapers and out of his diary kept at the Oklahoma Historical Society. He called a meeting at the Central Hotel in Terrell, Texas on January 6, 1887 to start the process of organizing a town company to go to Greer, Lipscomb or Wilbarger counties in Oklahoma and Texas.

Buckskin Joe and others scouted out the area that would become Navajoe. He found the main camp where the trade store was and thought that area was perfect for the town, good water resources and a beautiful mountain to the East. Buckskin published the *Emigrant Guide* to promote new settlers to come. His words were enticing to those who were looking for a new way of life. "The immigrants were routed through Vernon, Texas, up by Doan's Crossing and almost due north to Navajoe." [424]

Plans were in the works. By July 4th, 1887, a celebration at the Navajo Mountains included the Greer County residents and Quanah Parker with 300 braves to welcome all the new immigrants. Joe and Quanah made speeches. "Joe said that day, that he was going to found a town on the site of the picnic." [425] It would be Navajoe.

This company town was somewhat different than others. Buckskin Joe received half of the lots of the community in exchange for his promotion of the new town in the *Emigrant Guide*. A fee of $5 was charged to each member of the community.

A family member of Buckskin Joe wrote this, "He became a moving force in colonizing Southwestern Oklahoma and Northwestern Texas, publishing a newspaper and found several towns, including **Navajoe**, Comanche, and **Altus** in Oklahoma, and Oklaunion in Texas. He participated in the run for unassigned lands in Oklahoma, claiming a town-site and naming it Union City." [426]

The little town of Navajoe began to grow which included a horse racetrack near the public square. It must not have fit to Andrew James' liking possibly because it was turning into a farming community and the sentiment towards cattleman/horseman did not follow his path.

In the Spring of 1888, Andrew James took his sons, 45 miles south to Vernon, Texas to haul wood to the place they would homestead, somewhere in that general vicinity near Humphreys, south of Navajoe. It is unknown how many acres Andrew had there, but the parcels were large enough to establish good rangeland for his cattle and horses. In one of the son's obituary, Bob James, (Robert James) it stated that their homestead was 9 miles southeast of Altus. [427] This would be close to Humphreys. It was near Doan's Crossing as this was where Andrew's children went to school.

Bud found that in 1888, Charles Hart moved to Navajoe. This was another name that Quantrill used.

In the late 1890's, the pursuit of gold in the Navajo Mountains was finally satisfied as well as gold found in the Otter and Cache Creek nearby. "Navajoe was the headquarters for gold seekers, who prospected in the Navajo mountains and other peaks of the Wichita Range." [428]

An interesting note from Bud. He said there is something definitely there in the Navajo Mountains. This was another sight that Howk pointed out in Schrader's book where treasure is, suggesting there are gems and gold. [429] To the north of the North Fork of the Red River lies a very small community of *Centerville*. Bud found on a large rock there, carvings indicating gold on Navajo Mountain. Centerville was only 30 miles from Humphreys and a very short distance from Navajoe. Towns named *Centerville* come up quite frequently in Jesse's path.

By 1890, the town of Navajoe had 150 people living there. The other small communities in Greer County were Mangum and Fraizer. The community of Frazier would be moved due to flooding and renamed, Altus in 1907. The bulk of the wealth was in cattle, not farming. After the decision to not place the railroad near Navajoe, the town died. Andrew made the right choice.

Andrew would keep up the ranching business and did a lot of trading with Quanah Parker. In the family stories, Andrew had lots of horses. It was said that the horse country was on Otter Creek, where the gold was found, the cattle ranch was on Boggy Creek, and sheds near Davison. Otter Creek is just east of Humphreys.

Andrew was a trader and blacksmith. What is interesting is that everywhere that Jesse had any ties, there was always a blacksmith or a livery stable that he was connected to. Howk also listed treasure of the Government Blacksmith Shop. [430] This is true with Myra Belle Shirley's father's ranch in Scyene, Texas where he owned a livery stable; Brownwood, Texas where Frank James sought lodging from a friend at the livery stable; the Frenchman in Devil's Nest was a blacksmith who went in partners with the James Brothers in the trade store; Billy Wilson, friend of Billy the Kid owned a livery stable; Jesse staying close to Smith Paul who owned a blacksmith shop when Jesse was Deputy U.S. Marshal in Paul's Valley; and Bud himself told me that livery stables were very important to Jesse, most importantly for his horses, but they may have been a common meeting place or a location where a KGC operative or treasure could be found. Ironically, Andrew's son Andy had a livery stable later in life.

One of Andrew's sons, Jesse Campbell James worked at a camp on the Waggoner Ranch until he died at the age of 22. Another son, Robert "Bob" James was considered very wealthy. He worked with Tom Waggoner, near Doan's Crossing per his obituary. In the family story, Bob was the boss man on the 3 D (Waggoner Ranch) in the Mangum Division in Oklahoma. He was threatened by the Indians to pay up on the lease of the land. They gave Bob James so many days to bring the money to them or they would start a prairie fire. Bob rode all the way from the Mangum Camp to Decatur, Texas to get the money and return to Mangum before the fire would be lit. It was a round trip of 370 miles.

Bob James is also listed as being a member of the Altus Lodge No. 62, A.F. & A.M., Altus chapter R.A.M., Frederick Com. Knights Templars, and the Oklahoma City Temple Nobles of the Mystic Shrine. Walter Peleg James, another son of Andrew was a Mason, belonged to the Woodmen of the World, and Odd Fellows. Walter was able to meet and ride in a buggy with Dan Waggoner as he was checking the camps on the Waggoner Ranch. Dan had found no one at a particular camp and wanted to leave a note. Dan started to try to write something out on paper but handed the paper to Walter and said "Hell, I can't write, Walter, I will tell you what to write."

Walter went to school at Doan's Crossing and became good friends with the lawman, Eugene Logan (1848-1935) who oversaw the herds that crossed the Red into Oklahoma. He was a cattle inspector in New Mexico, Texas, and Oklahoma and later became a member of the Texas Cattle Raiser's Association. Logan was a Texas Ranger in the Frontier Battalion, Company B; 1892-1897 under Captain Bill McDonald. He was a Young County, Texas Deputy Sheriff, Young County Constable, the Mayor of Dalhart, and a Deputy U.S. Marshall. The town Logan, New Mexico was named after him as he took part in the construction of the Chicago, Rock Island, and Pacific railroad bridge that was built over the Canadian River in that area.

Eugene Logan was quite a man, and his great grandson, Captain Robert Stout followed in his footsteps in law enforcement, another remarkable man. Robert worked for the Dalhart Police Department for 32 years and was an incredible public servant to the community. He was well loved. His uncle, W.L. (Dick) Stout, my grandfather, also guided Robert in law enforcement as the Dallam County Sheriff for 10 years. Both Robert's father, Roy and Dick Stout's great uncle was John Wesley Haskew. Strange how everything ties in together. It truly is a small world.

Andrew James, in 1898, must have had another opportunity arise for him and his family. I'm sure he was thinking of his boys and he may have been encouraged by Eugene Logan. His determination and the knowledge he received about rich property in the Texas Panhandle, drove this 65-year-old rancher to seek the greener grass on the other side. He rode horseback to the very far northwestern point of Texas to Texline, nearly 300 miles. He rode to the east and northeast of Texline. There he could see miles and miles of rich grassland, perfect for grazing cattle. The grass in the Panhandle of Texas into Oklahoma was known to be belly deep to a horse, and in virgin, untouched land where the Indians roamed and hunted years before. The James family described it as "waist-high bluestem, interspersed with rich gramma and buffalo grass." It was very rich in nutrients.

Andrew couldn't wait to get back and tell his family. "They'll never put a plow to that land," he said. It was ready for the taking and the grazing. When Spring came in 1901, it was a perfect time to travel. Sadly, on the trip to the Panhandle, Andrew died in April 1901. The family turned around and took his body back to be buried in the Francis Cemetery near Humphreys. Andrew's dying wishes for his family was to go to the country to the north. It will serve them well. "It will never be turned by a plow," Andrew's famous last words. The family never forgot his words and they kept their word to uphold his wishes; to keep the rich grassland intact.

Andrew's tribute in The Altus Plaindealer, April 12, 1901 states this, "Whereas, it has pleased the Grand Architect of the universe to call from labor to rest our beloved brother Andrew James." "Resolved, that in death of Bro. James his family have lost a kind and devoted husband and father, the lodge a faithful and useful member and the community an upright and honored citizen. Resolved, that we will endeavor to bear in grateful remembrance the zeal and fidelity with which Bro. James discharged all his duties as a Mason, and will try to imitate his devotion to the grand principles of our fraternity." He was thought of very highly and with his fidelity, I feel assured his family was well taken care of.

Andrew's future son-in-law who would marry his daughter, Sue was Marvin Winfield Richardson (1880-1963) who was also a very devoted Mason. Marvin was noted as being elected as a guard at the El Dorado Commandery, No. 27, Knights Templar, regarded as Jackson County's Highest Masonic Body. [431]

To fulfill Andrew's wishes, Susan Catherine, his wife, his sons, Walter and Andy, and two daughters, Vergie and Sue took the map that Andrew had drawn out and rode the rails to Texline in 1901. Once in Texline, they hired a team of mules and a buggy and drove out to the general area that was marked on the map. They were only allowed to buy 4 sections at $1.25 an acre. The land was purchased from Joe Sneed. Walter went back to Altus. He and Bob, his brother added to their herd and drove as many as 200-500 head of cattle to the new Panhandle homestead. Catherine, their mother was said to have brought 10 mares. Walter, his brother Andy, and a cousin, Joe Taylor would travel to Arizona and round up wild horses, drove them to their Panhandle ranch, broke 'em and then traded them for cattle. In 1903, they loaded up two freight cars of wild horses in Arizona and took them to Trinidad, Colorado, a popular hangout for Jesse. From there, they were broke and taken to Arkansas and to Altus to trade.

In 1909, they bought a carload of mares from the Chiricahua Cattle Company, the most revered name of the cattle industry in Arizona. They were branded with "CCC" and moved to Wilcox, Arizona, the same area that Jim Herron from No Man's Land claimed to have moved Mexican cattle to Wilcox, Arizona with Billy the Kid. They bought 2 carloads of horses and mares branded script W and 20 branded PB connected from a Mexican at Romero. (Assuming Romero, Texas, just west of Hartley).

The horses consisted of one stallion, one American saddle horse, one Quarter horse (Steel Dust), one Hamiltonian (buggy horse), and the rest Persian broncs.

Andy was known to have loved horses. He was a bronc rider. His nephew, Jesse James said, "There wasn't anything too wild or too mean for Andy to get on." Early on, in his ranching days, Andy raised horses sired by Steel Dust. The family stories tell of the great and masculine horses, useful for a lot of things, one being they were a mighty good racehorse in a ¼ mile race.

The James Brothers continually increased their territory by buying more land, placing four section plots in different family names, and buying and leasing water rights. They began to obtain a monopoly of water rights in the Panhandle. By 1914, the ranch was comprised of over 400 sections of land extending from near Dalhart into Cimarron County, Oklahoma with about 17,000 head of cattle, mostly steers. Upon that sacred land, became one of the largest ranches in the Panhandle except for the famous X.I.T. Ranch. The James Brothers Ranch as they called it, stretched from south of Dalhart, all the way up into Oklahoma near Boise City, Oklahoma. This was exactly the area Jesse had spoken about. No other ranch was in that territory during that time.

Andy took care of the South Ranch and Walter took care of the North Ranch into Oklahoma. Andy too was a Mason in the Rock Island Lodge 869 of Dalhart. Their grandchildren still to this day preserve their heritage and are good stewards of the land.

Jarret Bowers, a great grandson of Andrew Marmaduke "Andy" James is the Operational Manager of the ranch currently consisting of a partnership with his brother, Chip, and sister, Nicole, and was gracious enough to allow the writer to post a map of the ranch. They controlled nearly all the water rights and leases of the Texas and Oklahoma Panhandle, over 318,000 acres. By 1916, they owned or held under lease nearly 500,000 acres of grassland and 20,000 head of cattle. Andy even tried to drill for oil, but never did reach it. The ranch consisted of 7 camps all together.

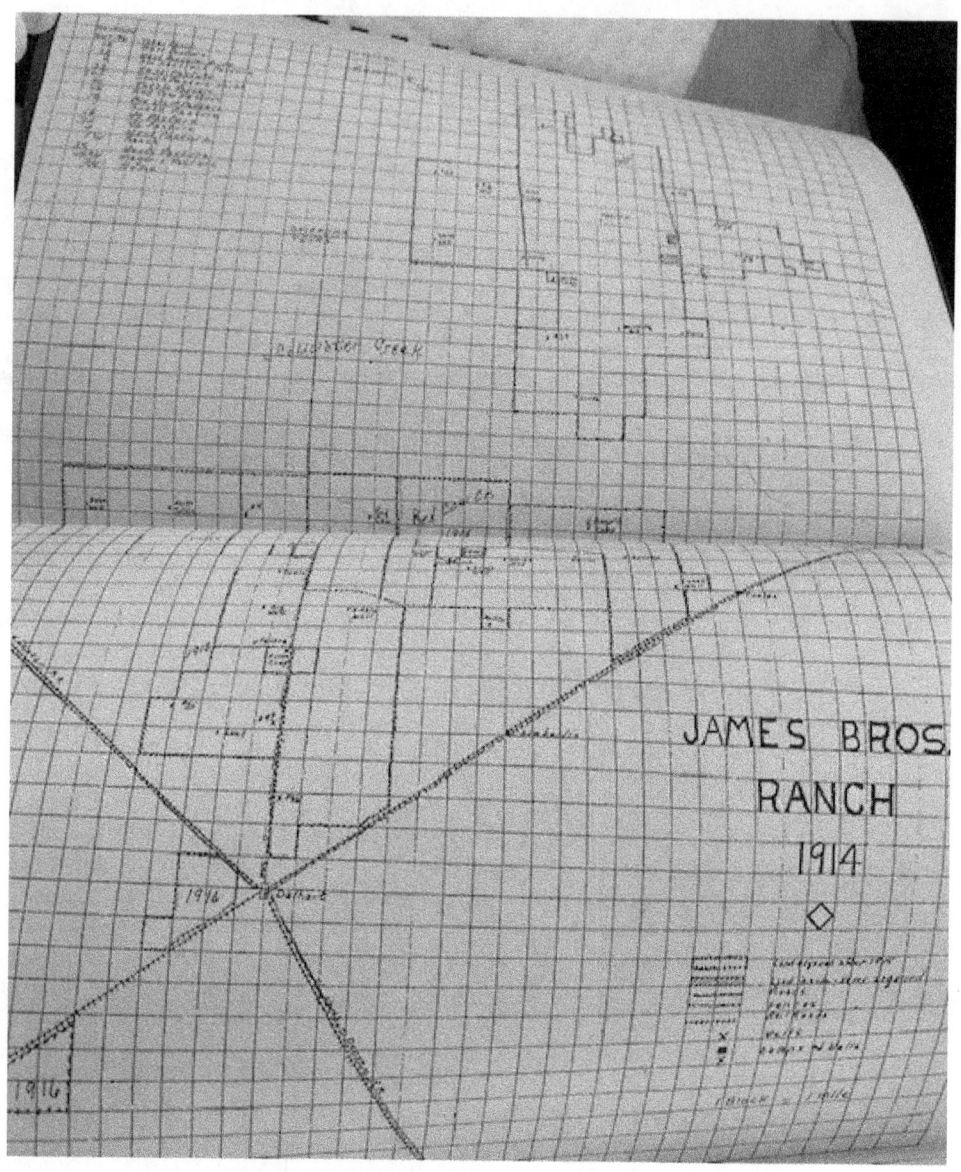

(James Ranch map)

(Current photo of the James Ranch – (Both photos, courtesy of Jarret Bowers, great grandson of Andrew Marmaduke "Andy" James))

Tragedy hit when one of those famous blizzards hit the Panhandle. "In 1882, the Panhandle Stock Association ranchers erected a drift fence that ran from the New Mexico line east through Hartley and Moore counties to the Canadian River breaks in Hutchinson County. Over the next few years more sections were added, so that by 1885 barbed wire drift fences stretched across the entire northern Panhandle, from 35 miles deep in New Mexico to the Indian Territory. These formed an effective barrier for northern cattle attempting to drift onto the southern ranges. Beginning in late December of 1885, a series of blizzards struck the southern plains. Cattle retreating to the south were stalled by the drift fences and unable to go any farther. They huddled against each other along the fence line in large bunches, some of them 400 yards across. Unable to stay warm or escape the crush, these cattle either smothered or froze to death in their tracks within a short while." [432]

This is exactly what happened to the James Brother's cattle in 1918. My dear grandmother, Ruth wrote about the Blizzard of 1918. She was only 12 years old but heard stories of the storm from Oldtimers. She wrote, "The wind blew so hard it drifted the snow as high as the roof tops. So many cattle just drifted up to the fence and the snow piled up on them and they froze to death." [433]

The blizzard began in December 1918 and would continue snowing off and on throughout that winter, covering the ground with several feet of snow and no grass to graze for the cattle. Up to April 1919, the James lost 3,000 head of cattle and thought the worst was over. Green grass was finally peeking through the snow-covered landscape.

On April 9, 1919, at the break of dawn, a northerner hit, a deadly blizzard was in the making. The snow was wet and clung to anything it touched including the hide on the cattle and filling their nostrils. When the temperature dropped to 17 degrees below, the snow began to freeze and the cattle, only knowing how to breathe through their nose, suffocated and died. The storm lasted 30 hours. Once cleared, the cowboys were able to realize the damage. Out of the 17,000 head of cattle, another 5,000 died during that storm. Their loss was horrific; 8,000 cattle in all.

It was devastating and to top it off, the expense to feed during the storms, what was left standing was enormous. Cottonseed cake that the James used to feed went from a dollar a sack to a hundred dollars a sack. The feed bill mounted to over $1,000 a day. "The terrific death loss and sudden drop in prices, brought about the breakup of the James Brothers Ranch." Lois James Garner 1997.

The James lost most of their property and had to utilize what they could to save the rest. Then the Dust Bowl hit, the "Dirty Thirties" and the family was hit hard. The James family is featured in the book, "The Worst Hard Time," by Timothy Egan 2006.

Andy James had to watch his lush grassland dissipate before his eyes. The Black Blizzards took a toll on his ranchland, which accumulated mounds and mounds of sand covering his grass and sweeping away the rich topsoil that provided nutrients for the grass to grow. Andy became quite a leader in finding a solution and being totally honest in public meetings. No one took the blame, not the nesters, nor the farmers, but blamed it on the weather, the drought. Andy was bold in seeing it was caused by man and that they must seek help from the government.

A man by the name of Hugh Hammond Bennett was head of the Soil Conservation Service for the United States at that time and made it his project to examine the cause and effect of these massive dust storms that covered the Texas and Oklahoma Panhandle. No one had ever seen anything like it. He traveled down to the depleted areas and began to contemplate the steps that could be done to stop the erosion of the greatest breadbasket of the country. He blamed it on the ignorance of the people for the way they were plowing up the earth. His hands were tied until the majority of the farmers and ranchers of the affected areas agreed for the government to step in.

Andy wrote many letters to Washington expressing the dire situation and the need for a solution. Many of the area landowners joined Andy in asking for help from the government. Andy's effort "was instrumental in developing a five-state agriculture and livestock organization to present the plight of farmers and ranchers to Washington. He was elected president of the organization." [434]

All worked together with Bennett to restore what was lost with a new concept of soil conservation. With the help of Franklin Roosevelt, Hugh Bennett, and men such as Andy James, the largest soil conservation project in the nation was able to return life back to the Texas and Oklahoma Panhandle.

This story was fascinating to me because of it involving my hometown, Dalhart. It was like a western novel, following this family of Andrew James from Montague County, Texas, where we know Jesse and Haskew were, Humphreys, Oklahoma (same name *Humphreys* where Jesse lived in Tennessee), and then Dalhart, finally settling on land that Jesse James said he owned in the 1880's-1910. Is it all a coincidence?

What really blessed me though, were the remnants of this hardy James family. I didn't know any James' who lived in Dalhart, but yet I hadn't lived there in 50 years, only visiting my family who are now since gone.. "Many still live there and continue ranching on this sacred land," I was told by my very best friend's sister, Lisa who works at the X.I.T. Museum in Dalhart. What was the most exciting part is when Lisa told me who the family was. They are the most well, respected, and upstanding citizens of Dalhart. Our families grew up together and went to school together, not realizing the history of our past which finally all comes together. The two daughters of Andy James whose family still works hard on the range, were Helen James Priestly and Mary Patricia James Bowers.

Wow, had to be another God thing! But what validated the entire story after speaking with one of the descendants, Jarret Bowers, is when I asked if the name "Diamond Ranch" or diamond had anything to do with their ranch. The answer flabbergasted me! Jarret's answer, "our brand is the diamond." What? Jesse's story was true.

The first brand they used was the "locked J" which is a symbol of two J's lying on its side interlocking one another. It was the mother of Andy James, Catherine whose favorite brand they chose to use in 1903, the "Diamond" brand.

Jarret had a book that his great aunt, Helen James Priestly had written about her immediate family that provided so much information. The proof of occupancy of the land was recorded in the Dallam County Courthouse on February 22, 1905. The original name of the ranch was the **Diamond Ranch** but was also known as the James Brothers Ranch. The Diamond brand was officially registered in the Dallam County Courthouse under A. M. (Andy Marmaduke) on June 11, 1910. This would remain the official brand throughout his lifetime and would continue to this day.

(The Diamond brand and the locked J Brand of the Diamond Ranch (courtesy of Jarret Bowers))

Later, some of the family members adopted this familiar brand; one that Jesse used often to make his mark.

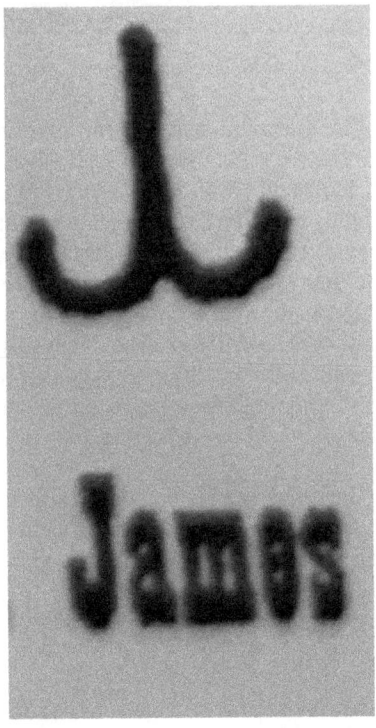

Pic 119 B – Back to back J Brand (courtesy of Jarret Bowers)

Jarret sent me a photo of the jacket he was wearing as we talked on the phone when he shared this information. *The Diamond*. Just below the diamond, are the words, "Est. 1910."

(The Diamond Brand on his jacket. (courtesy of Jarret Bowers))

Gathering up my wits after all these coincidences, I was grateful to God for this revelation and for the family to be able to share this with me. The family always heard they were related to Jesse James and Jarret's grandmother, the daughter of Andy, Mary Pat Bowers confirmed it in a joking manner to her daughter, Trish as they passed a Jesse James' museum in Arkansas. Trish said, "We need to stop there because we may be related to Jesse." Mary Pat replied, "Probably more than you know, and that's probably why so many of mine act the way they do."

Mary Pat James Bowers was a wonderful woman. She was always doing something for the community. Mary Pat was the mother of 11 children. The ranch was extremely important to her and impressed upon her children, the value of it and their heritage that remained deep within the sacred soil. Her words to her children still remain in their hearts passed down to her grandchildren. "The ranch should always stay as one, never to be sold and only owned within the James' family bloodline."

Is it ironic that Andy James, in his early ranching days raised horses sired by Steel Dust? The year 1910 when Andy officially established the ranch as the Diamond Ranch was the date that Jesse gifted a Steel Dust horse from this ranch to Red Lucas and then he was off to Mexico to supply the Revolutionaries with Steel Dust horses.

(Photo of Andrew Marmaduke "Andy" James (1882-1958) (courtesy of Jarret Bowers))

The last coincidence: Andrew Marmaduke "Andy" James had a wonderful photo made of himself during his prime of life, looks as though he is in his thirties, very handsome, and possibly taken in the 1910's-1920's. In the photo, on his left lapel of his suit was a pin. Jarret Bowers pointed this out to me. What he told me, gave me chills down my spine. He and his family had been enlarging the photo to determine what kind of pin it was. You could tell that there was a cross on the upper portion of the pin, tilted to the right and a mass on the lower side of the pin. Jarret showed me what he thought it was. It was a pin that had the tilted cross and what looked to be a crown. Jarret had found a similar image of a pin which turned out to be an emblem for the Knights of the Golden Circle. It's very similar to the Knights Templar pin.

The family did know that Andy was a Mason, but there is no other evidence of any other association to other organizations. But even so, there was a lot of history in Andy's family of their connection to the brotherhood that Jesse was a part of. There was a common bond not only through their bloodline, but also their bond of fidelity to the brotherhood. They had each other's back.

Many thanks to the Priestly and Bowers family, especially Jarret Bowers. Jarret was so kind in loaning me the book that his Aunt Helen Priestly contributed to with other stories told by family members, "History and A Few Tall Tales of the James Brothers Ranch 1901-1936 and on through 2001." It is from this book and Jarret's family stories, that this story can be told. The family had such rich western history that could curl anyone's toenails. I want to thank the family of Walter and Andy James for allowing us to share this amazing story which helps validate the stories told to Ola and Howk by Jesse himself. Wow! Just Wow!

*Note – An amazing end to this story puts the icing on the cake. No one, but no one, can tell me any different, that this was another incredible "God thing." Just a month before I completed this book, I received a text from Jarret Bowers. He couldn't believe what just happened. His cousin decided to up and move from his home and gave a very special treasure of Andy's to one of Jarret's uncles. Jarret was unaware what this would be. Remember, there were 11 children of Mary Pat's and other aunts and uncles who inherited Andy's possessions as well as many other members of the family. Jarret was actively trying to locate something to connect Andy's involvement with Jesse or the brotherhood. Well, this was it.

Jarret began unloading pictures, sending one after the other of this magnificent sword that Andy had kept in his possessions. The handle was made of pure ivory and the scabbard and sword itself was made of gold and silver. Its surface was engraved with many intricate signs and symbols of Knighthood and Christianity in which it bore a "red passion" cross. Jarret thought it might be related to the Catholic fraternal service order of the Knights of Columbus. Andy's son, Joseph was ordained in the Catholic Priesthood in Rome in December 1957 and the family remain faithful members. ("A. M. James, 75, Rites in Dalhart"– The Amarillo Globe-Times, March 4, 1958)

I sent the photos with Jarret's permission to Jay Longley in Brownwood, Texas and he confirmed that was the sword of the Masonic Knights Templar. Wow! Jarret is allowing us to share these photos with the readers. It is beautiful and such a treasure for the family to have. Jarret also has the sash and hat to go with it.

(Knights Templar Meeting (courtesy of Jay Longley in Brownwood))

(Knights Templar Sword and Hat of Andrew M. James (courtesy of Jarret Bowers))

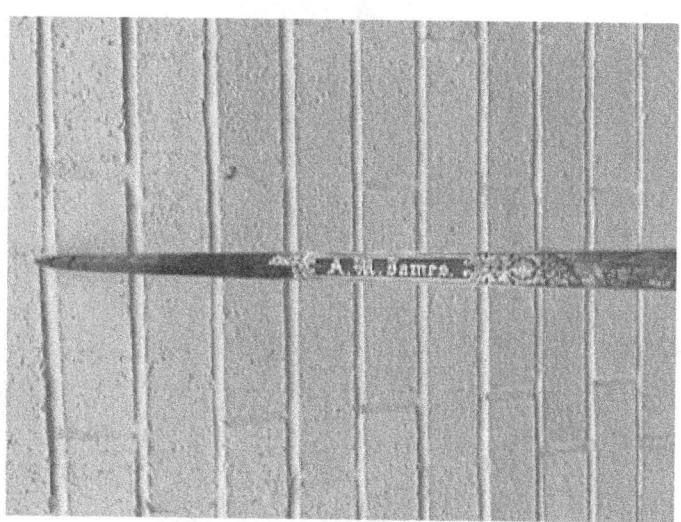

Jarret was amazed at the photo Jay provided of the Knights Templar meeting in Brownwood. They were wearing the same attire as what Andy left for his family.

The sword was made by The M.C. Lilley & Co. in Columbus, Ohio which indicates it could have been made as early as 1882 and no later than 1925. The sword, below the ivory handle is the five-point star with each point embossed with letters spelling out T-E-X-A-S. It also has Andy's name beautifully inscribed, "A.M. James."

We are so blessed to have information on this particular ornate sword which is found on https://www.md-mrs.com in the article titled "The History and Symbolism of the Knights Templar Sword from the 11th to 20th Centuries, by Norman Williams Crabbe. I believe Andy's sword is the one designed in circa 1890, "styled for the Texas and Iowa Regulations." The crosses are all embossed with a deep red color.

From the article above, we find explanations of what some of the symbols represent:

On the scabbard: Appearing on "the foot" are two unclothed women facing opposite directions and represent the Zodiac sign of Gemini. They represent the "Universal Duality" and a Karmic Principle. In the center of "the foot" is the sunburst which represents God. His right hand is shown, raising through the sunburst holding onto the cross, which represents Christ with light rays and flames shooting out. "Above the flames is the lighthouse at Alexandria, Egypt: the ancient entry port to the Holy Lands and esoterically symbolizes Christ's words: "I am the Light of the World" and esoterically means "I am the pathway to Wisdom and also means "I am the Son/Sun."

Grapevines and grapes adorn the scabbard to represent Christ as the vine and the harvest. The grapes are there to remind us of the "Holy Blood" served at the last supper.

The crown and the cross are in the design of the scabbard, the crown meaning immortality and the cross represents the way to reach immortality. The article suggests this: "With a bit of imagination we can see in the crown and cross, the symbol of the female principle as well as the symbol for the planet Venus."

At the top of the scabbard, is a Knight with heavy armor of protection depicting a "pinecone seed" design on his breast plate. The pinecone is very important in this society. Their belief is that the pinecone represents the "Pineal gland, the Sixth "Chakra", the Chakra of Wisdom and the Kabbalahic Sephiroth "Cochma", located in the human skull, the location of the Third Eye of Man; the mystical center of insight and clairvoyance."

There are two spears that jut out of the breastplate on opposite sides. Spears symbolize a Christian Mission. Below that is the Templar's Cross.

On the sword: There is the logo of skull and crossbones with "Memento mori" inscribed meaning, "You must die." Reminding the living that death is inevitable. The article states that words are translated to mean, "Ego, Falsehood, and Death."

On the top of the sword, above the handle, which is known as the pommel, sits a Knight's head covered with a metal helmet in which a dragon sits upon: "a symbol of destruction for all who oppose this knightly sword and, like the snake, mystically symbolize the wisdom of the ancients."

The Masonic square and compass are in the design, but instead of the "G" in the center, a pentangle is there. The article describes the symbolism: "The Masonic square symbolizes virtue by squaring our human actions thereby maintain the harmonic balance of good and evil. The Masonic Compasses symbolize morality by circumscribing the human passions thereby keeping good and evil within the circle of our outward bodily manifestations. The pentangle star is used in many mystic rites and is the mystic symbol for man. Each point symbolizing a human appendage, as well as each point representing one of the five human senses. The pentangle also represents the five occult elements and elemental essences: earth, water, air, fire, and aether." Aether is described in the dictionary as "a medium that in the wave theory of light permeates all space and transmits transverse waves."

I wish I understood the Knights Templar and their mission. I wish I could understand the purpose and their reasoning behind the secrecy that they held so sacredly. Their lips were sealed regarding ancient knowledge and they were persecuted and tortured by the leaders of the Catholic Church in ancient days because of it. What was there to hide?

The Knights Templar started the first banking system, an underground system, and a gold network, thousands of years ago. Their ability of being able to maneuver, ship, and protect their wealth was highly successful. Jesse James' philosophy and actions coincided with these techniques. He didn't believe in banks, he couldn't trust them, but trusted the underground banking system that the KGC put in place which I believe was designed by the Knights Templar.

Was Andy a part of Jesse's circle? It appears that he was. There are too many coincidences involved in both of their lives for them not to be. They were related through blood and brotherhood.

I pray someday, we will all understand what's been kept from the common man. I pray it was for the good of mankind. Men associated to the Knights Templar were leaders and upstanding citizens, making a difference in their community such as Andy. We do know that it was quite an honor to be a part of this organization and even though we don't understand it, we trust that its longevity and strength to survive all these years was for a purpose that God had in mind.

> "Merely stating a truth isn't enough. The truth has to be made vivid, interesting, dramatic. You have to use showmanship."
>
> *-Dale Carnegie*

Chapter Twenty: The Art of Horsemanship/Marksmanship/Showmanship

Horse Trainer/Breeder/Racer/Shooting Exhibitionist/Performer in Wild West Shows

Lou Kilgore, a very dear friend of Bud's and great researcher said that the North had their agenda and the South had theirs. When they saw that it was not possible to start another civil war, the KGC decided to build up the South and West. They would use the money and the gold they collected for that very purpose, to outdo the industrialized North. In the book thus far, we see the evidence in the building of architectural masterpieces, building of modern cities with all the fancy amenities, colonization, the construction of railroads, establishing various organizations, and the development of land for mining, farming, and ranching. They put their money and energy into the Southwest and succeeded beautifully.

Jesse focused on breeding horses, perfecting their bloodline, training them in the most expert way, and giving many people "starts" of the famous Jesse James' horse, the Steel Dust. It is very evident in the ranches discussed thus far.

In this chapter we will discuss Jesse's various skills and talents in the field of horsemanship, marksmanship, and showmanship. They all go together.

Jesse was incredibly one with a horse. He could outride just about anyone. Whether his skills were learned with what "Wild Bill" Thomason, the grandfather of Bloody Bill taught him and Frank to ride like an Indian, becoming the "horse boy" for Confederate Generals, the riding techniques he learned as a Quantrill Raider, or if it was the skills he learned in the getaways. Let us not forget the skill of maneuvering his horse across Devil's Gulch that was at least a 20-foot-wide gap.

His skills as a rider, having "horse sense" and comradery with a horse, speaks volumes of Jesse. His technique was a very valuable asset in his line of work. Beside the horses, one other great asset to Jesse and his horses was John Trammel, his Black cook. John looked after the horses for Jesse during his outlaw days and beyond.

Mitch Graves, in a letter to Ola related the story of Jesse at his ranch in Canada. Mitch witnessed Dalton/Jesse treat horses extremely well. Dalton, at the time was raising and selling work horses for a living, as well as raising thoroughbred racehorses on another ranch nearby. Mitch also witnessed how Jesse loved to pull pranks on people and one time it was in front of an entire rodeo audience who were in fear for his life. The announcer over the loudspeaker said, "Frank Dalton from Lea Park on Black Dynamite." The name spoke for itself and no man could ride Black Dynamite. The audience knew old man Dalton and couldn't believe what they were hearing. He would be killed. Jesse played along and the rodeo hands made all sorts of racket in the chute, making the audience think the horse was going wild and trying to pitch. Jesse got on top of the horse where the audience could see him and made out that he was holding on for dear life. When the chute opened, he wasn't on Black Dynamite, but on his own horse, Black Prince, who was broke by Mitch. Jesse just strutted right out in the arena and the crowd went wild. They loved him in Canada.

Ola had stated that her husband, Aubrey and Jesse were talking one day. They had a lot in common regarding horses. Aubrey was a former jockey, who trained and rode thoroughbred racehorses. Jesse told him that his favorite racehorse was Queen of Hearts. Jesse liked the Kentucky Thoroughbreds and the "copper bottom strain" of Palomino, which had good feet. Copper Bottom was an incredible Quarter Horse in which General Sam Houston brought to Texas in 1839. Jesse's favorite of all times was the horses sired by Steel Dust. Steel Dust was a progeny of Sir Archy, as well as Copper Bottom. He was an undisputed champion of Texas horse racing.

A fantastic story in *True West Magazine*, titled, "Steeldusts on the Chisholm Trail," by Darley Newman, states that the Steel Dust was foaled by a Kentucky thoroughbred mare in 1843 and brought to Texas by Middleton Perry and Jones Greene. "This roughly 16-hands-high champion quarter-mile match racer was so fast that his jockey reportedly coated the stallion's back with molasses in order to stay on."

"Steel Dust was described as a muscular blood bay with small ears and a large jaw, which, to many, symbolized his tenacity and determination. Richard Chamberlain, senior racing writer for the American Quarter Horse Journal, tells me what made his horse special was he wasn't just a racer. He had intelligence and a down to earth sense that's not always found in racehorses, and these traits – speed, intelligence and endurance-were passed down to his progeny, making them tractable saddle horses.

"After the horse suffered an injury in 1855, Steel Dust's owners offered him up for stud. Ranchers, who needed quick horses to work cattle and to earn them extra money in match races, where they could win or lose anything from a drink to a whole plantation, sought out Steel Dust as a sire." [435]

In Howk's book, Jesse supposedly told the story of actually purchasing the stud. "Steel Dust was the name of a famous racehorse that I bought, who made fine records on the track. I bought him at Old Cyene, near Dallas, Texas, as a stud horse. Brother Frank and I hired one of our brother-in-laws to oversee the breeding of these Steeldust horses. He arranged contract breeders amongst the German and Bohemian farmers of Central Texas, to raise these horses for a good profit, selling the prize and best ones only to our buyers. Our brother-in-law's name was Tom Houston, and he ranged from Fort Bend County, Texas, to Mason and Llano County in Texas." [436]

It is unknown if this story is true. Steeldust did live out his days in Texas as a stud and supposedly died between 1864-1874. He was last seen in Dallas County near Ten Mile Creek which lies near Lancaster, the area between where Belle Starr lived at Scyene and where Elbert DeWitt Travis lived. This would be in the era of Jesse's days in and out of Scyene and Lancaster. It's a possibility, as Bud says.

In the same article, it told the story that occurred from 1895-1910, that a Steel Dust progeny was being ridden on the LX Ranch in the Panhandle of Texas. This fits into the time when Jesse had ownership of the ranch in the Panhandle we spoke of and gifted a Steeldust horse to Orrington Red Lucas in 1910 on the Diamond Ranch.

Confirming Jesse's various horse breeding ranches, such as the Diamond Ranch who raised the Steeldust horses, John Gibson, a Black man from Colorado Springs who knew Jesse in his days in Fayette County, Arkansas stated in an affidavit, "Old Jesse had thoroughbred, standard-bred, Steeldust racehorses by the dozens down in Arkansas. He also **was a silent partner in many old-time livery stables, horse ranches, and farms.**" [437] This is another validation of Jesse's activities in the last chapter.

Jesse's love of horses and racing began during the Civil War when he learned how valuable a horse was. He only wanted the best that could endure the hardest and roughest terrain, as well as the fastest.

After the war, we find Jesse, going by the name of Howard in Tennessee. He had a nice piece of property outside of Nashville which included his racehorses. Sometime around 1877, he built a track to race his horses against others. "Howard had some racehorses on his farm, and he had fixed up a sort of temporary track on which races were run. He associated with some gamblers of notorious reputation, who also were interested in horse racing. I recall that one of them tried to cheat Howard out of a race in which the wager was $500. Howard got hopping mad, He rode up to the miscreant and plucked out a big pistol. "Hand over that money," he demanded, "or you'll be a dead man in two seconds." The cheater handed over the cash, and Howard cooled down." [438]

Ola had received a letter from a friend, Eugene Huff that had sent her a newspaper clipping regarding Mr. Koger and how he described Jesse. Mr. Koger stated, "I think it was in the fall of

1878," said he, "when the State Fair was being held at Nashville. A handsome cash prize was offered in a competition to determine the most graceful rider. It was the gentlemen rider's event. I recall that there were about thirty entries. I sat in the grandstand with thousands of others as the riders passed in front.

"Mr. Howard, mounted on his favorite horse, was one of the contestants, and he rode well up toward the front. Knowing him to be a most skillful rider, I took particular interest in watching him." [439] Mr. Koger goes on to say that Jesse did not show his full ability of horsemanship, because the Pinkertons and the Nashville Police were there, watching for the most expert rider to come forth the winner who could very easily be Jesse James. He just fit into the crowd of contestants, but he definitely could have really won the huge prize.

Ola stated that "Jesse James frequently rode as his own jockey in horse races at county and neighborhood fairs." She continues, "None of them would suspect that the notorious bandit would have the nerve to appear thus at a public event. For that matter, throughout his career, this man mingled with the general populace, wherever he happened to be, going and coming as other men go and come. In his way, Jesse was a wise man." [440]

Ola had written that in 1909, Jesse went to Alexandria, Louisianna as Jesse Redman and raced horses. [441] There are numerous tales of his participation in racing, any chance he got.

Bud's dear friend, John Tatum (**1933**-2012) was a man who had history with Jesse. Through his mother, Rachel James, he said he was a third cousin to Jesse. I do find she was the gg granddaughter of Rev. Jesse James (1771-1836) who was the brother of William "Thomas" James (1775-1840). This man was the great grandfather of Nancy F. James (1839-1916) who married Adam Van Buren Haskew (1839-1913), 1st cousin of the Haskew outlaw. In our family, Nancy James, was always said to be related to Jesse James, the outlaw. Her past was very elusive.

The blood connections have not completely been validated. The ancestral line can be very tricky and sometimes it really is hard to connect with your family, but in today's world, there are more tools that are more accurate through DNA if you don't have substantial family records. What we have been told regarding Jesse's true ancestry may not be accurate. What we have been told within our own families may not be the complete truth. It's the same with Ola Everhard's family with the Daltons. Not much evidence is left behind, same as Bud and my family. As Bud and I have learned, documents and validations have been construed, distorted, or destroyed when a family has something to hide.

John Tatum was always told by his family that Jesse was their cousin. Jesse had a lot of ties to this family for sure. He stayed at their house in California twice, the first time was when John was 14 years old and shared a bedroom with him for six weeks.

John Tatum and his beautiful wife, Jo Ella Wilson were quite a pair. They were as solid as they come and deeply devoted Christians in the Freewill Baptist Church. Lou Kilgore knew of John and Jo Ella Tatum and told Bud about them. Bud didn't hesitate to contact them, went to their house and they became extremely good friends. They teamed up together and took a lot of trips exploring the past involving Jesse. They were as eager as Bud to hit the road to solve mysteries about Jesse and follow clues to treasure. "We are ready to go tomorrow, come on." They traveled a lot to Southeast Oklahoma, and was there with Bud at Kearney, Missouri during the exhumation of Jesse in 1995. Bud told me quite frequently, "Haven't met two better people."

Rachel James, John Tatum's mother's maternal family are the Ballards who intermarry with the James and the Thomason family. Their family also share the families of Hubbard, Fields, and Ironmongers with Jesse.

There truly was a strong connection between John Tatum's parents, Emmett Tatum and Rachel James, as well as John's wife's family, Jo Ella Wilson to Jesse. They were connected, as well as many others, as descendants of members of the Quantrill Raiders, the Confederacy, and the Mason brotherhood.

In John Tatum's mother, Rachel James' paternal family, her father was Jacob Colston James (1852-1916) who lived in Valliant, McCurtain County, Oklahoma. He followed in his father's footsteps, who was William Mayfield James (1829-1909). William raised Steeldust horses for Jesse James. He lived in Saline, Arkansas and later moved to Valliant, McCurtain County, Oklahoma. This was convenient for Jesse when he was in need of fresh mounts in that particular area, Arkansas and Oklahoma. Once they were in Oklahoma, the family raised the Steeldust horses in the mountains of Southeast Oklahoma. This was Jesse's planned out scheme throughout the country. He would set up a rancher, a livery stable, or a camp that would keep horses available for him at any given moment.

William Mayfield James was a Mason and joined the Confederate Army in Company C, 3rd Arkansas Cavalry. He participated in a number of battles: Iuka and Corinth, Mississippi; Atlanta, Savannah, and Dalton, Georgia; Chickamauga, Knoxville, Pigeon River, and Thompson Station, Tennessee.

John Tatum's father, Emmett Tatum Sr (1900-1982), was the son of John Wesley Tatum (1868-1939) and Rebecca Markham (1874-1939). The Markhams and the Greenleafes are in the writer's family tree. John Wesley Tatum and his family came from Lewis County, Tennessee in 1883 to Indian Territory. His parents were Reuben Moses Tatum (1850-1920) and Irene Starr (1852-1913) who left Tennessee and established a home in Valliant, Oklahoma. John Wesley Tatum married Rebecca, who was part Choctaw Indian, in 1891. All things indicate that Rebecca was living in Tuskahoma, in the Choctaw Nation. This would be the same area as another man, who chose a wife for himself. That man will be discussed in the next chapter, who was very close to Jesse. This was a very important and protective country for Frank and Jesse James. The people loved them, and they kept their mouth shut.

Reuben Moses Tatum's father, Thomas Thernas Tatum (1826-1900) came to Texas sometime around 1880. Thomas was a miller, a Free will Baptist preacher, and justice of the peace in Lewis County, Tennessee and was sometimes called "Tatumas." He also farmed and raised racehorses. He was southwest of Nashville, just shy of 50 miles from Humphreys County where Jesse had racehorses and a racetrack. In 1871, Tatum became Deputy Sheriff in Lewis County, Tennessee. By 1880, his family moved to Red River County, Texas which basically placed them at the three corners of the border of Texas, Oklahoma, and Arkansas. They would eventually move back to Arkansas.

Reuben Tatum stayed in Oklahoma and was thought to have been in Quantrill's Raiders, but I believe he was too young. His brother, William B. Tatum was in the Confederacy, Tennessee 11th Infantry, Company K.

John Tatum, as a young boy, lived in Valliant, Oklahoma. He was born in **1933**. His father, Emmett was a farmer and a stone mason. In 1930, they lived in El Reno, Canadian County, Oklahoma and in 1940, they lived in Kirk, McCurtain County, Oklahoma. He knew Jesse very well. When World War II ended, John's brother, Oscar who had fought in the war, moved to Nipomo, San Luis Obispo, California. Oscar was 10 years older than his brother, John. Oscar must have encouraged his parents to move to Nipomo, as we find them living there by the middle of the '40's. Ironically, this was the same county as where Drury James lived, and the towns were 50 miles apart. Jesse had many, many ties in that entire area and it is thought that he had many, many caches buried in that area where his uncle lived.

When John Tatum was 13 or 14 years old, in 1946/47 he got the surprise of his life. An old gentleman rode up to their home in Nipomo in a taxi. His parents were expecting him and told John that was his Uncle George Motley. With Uncle George, was a black man named Griggs from McAlester, Oklahoma and a Hispanic man. John was totally captivated by Uncle George. He hoped out of the taxi with no problem, straight as an arrow, and was a very proud man, full of confidence from his toes to the brim of his hat. The Tatums had a tall porch off the ground and Uncle George had no problem in climbing up and down the stairs, back and forth to get his things. John described him as very agile. The men with him were very respectful of him.

Uncle George had with him two footlockers and a long trunk that he kept books and papers in. Tatum called him, "the most intelligent man you ever met."

John said the old man, who would have been 99/100 years old was very likable and had a good sense of humor. He brought his dog with him. He was so kind to the dog. While unloading things onto the porch, the Hispanic man started kicking the dog and Uncle George got extremely upset and told him in a very stern voice, "don't kick my dog." The Hispanic man looked more like a whipped pup, than the dog did.

John's mother, Rachel James Tatum treated Uncle George like a king. He trusted her with everything he had. When they were alone, George gave her a homemade cloth pouch that was stitched by hand to secure the contents. He asked her to put it in a very safe place where it would keep until he was ready to leave. Curiosity got the best of Rachel and when the men were gone for the day, she very carefully unstitched the pouch and found a stack of hundreds of $100 dollar bills. That was extremely hard to come by in the 40's. Rachel was just amazed. She meticulously sewed the pouch back up and placed it in a secure place. When George was leaving, he retrieved his money and Rachel kept his secret.

Uncle George shared John's bedroom for six weeks with him. John got to know him well and greatly admired him, not really knowing who he was at the time, just an uncle from Oklahoma. George fondly called John, **"Tator Tatum."** Uncle George even bought John his first bicycle. John said that Uncle George was extremely talented in many aspects. They would go out on the porch and George would sing and play the fiddle and harmonica all at the same time. John was mesmerized watching George play his instruments and the folks sang along. Uncle George really had a good singing voice. Many a good time was had on that front porch.

George had a lot of good philosophy and stories to tell John. He could speak Spanish. He taught John how to play the harmonica and Bud said John continued to play the harmonica throughout his adult life. George was a good man and good hearted. He wasn't mean at all. The Tatums were extremely religious and I'm sure George felt right at home with them. They hosted prayer meetings of the Whosoever Will Mission in Nipomo in their home.

Uncle George was so fond of John's father, Emmett, that he bought him a car. A few months after that and Uncle George had left, the family picked up and moved to Oregon. Emmett became involved in the timber business for a company in Oregon.

John Tatum was used to work and helped his father in the timber business. Out of the blue one day, Emmett told his family that they were going to a fair. That was so unusual for the family as they were used to hard work and no play. Emmett was part Indian and he was usually solemn, focused, and work driven. They went to a big park which hosted the Oregon State Fair with many vendors and activities being performed. Emmett directed his family to a shooting exhibition. The man who was performing at the shooting exhibition, called himself, Otto Garner. He didn't charge anything for the shooting exhibition, just did it for show. John Tatum was still a very impressionable young man and described what he saw. Bud told me the details, but Bud videoed a lot of what John said. Incredible.

The man going by the name of Otto Garner was an older gentleman, wearing a fancy Western outfit with long white hair and a goatee. At first, you would think he was Buffalo Bill. An Indian was narrating stories and describing the old west before and during the performance. You could tell this old man had done this for many years. John said he was a crack shot with a pistol.

With eyes glued upon the man, John, his sister, brother, and a cousin watched as the Indian described what the gunman was about to attempt. The Indian said, "I am going to throw up this tin can and watch as the Wild West star unload both pistols into the can spinning it clockwise." With great amazement and gasps from the audience, Mr. Garner began shooting the tin can and sure enough it continued like clockwork to spin clockwise continuously while he unloaded every bullet into the can high up in the air with both pistols. The audience was astonished. John's father, nudged John and said, "How did you like that Johnny?" John said, "Pretty good Dad! Never seen anything like that."

The Indian continued with his stories of the Wild West and said, "Now, I will throw up another tin can and watch Mr. Garner spin the can counter-clockwise. Sure enough, he unloaded his bullets into the can making it spin the opposite direction. Oh my! Can you imagine what thrill that gave John, age 14 and the rest of the children. John said that when the performance was over, they all got to go up front and meet the gunslinger. My, my, they recognized him as Uncle George! His eyes gave him away.

John said they had a wonderful reunion and the family adored Uncle George. He loved them back, a very caring and loving man. Uncle George showed John and the other older children how to shoot, spending as much time with them as they desired.

That would be the last time that John Tatum saw Uncle George. A few days later, John asked his father, "Was that Jesse?" Emmett didn't say anything for a while, both he and Uncle George were the same way. They thought before they spoke. There was always a hesitation before they would talk, to ensure what would be coming out of their mouths wouldn't get them in trouble. Emmett looked at his son John and said, "You don't need to know."

John said, "You don't question your father," so he waited a few days later when they were alone working in the timber. They took a break and were eating their lunch on a log. John asked his father again. "Are you sure that wasn't Jesse James." His father turned to him and said, "Yes, that was Jesse, Jesse James, but you be sure and call him Uncle George and treat him with all respect." That's all John wanted to know.

Jesse went back to Texas and John had a memory to last him a lifetime. Once in Texas, towards the end of the summer of 1947, Jesse was trying to get help to secure a Civil War Confederacy Pension in Texas and he succeeded just in time for his 100th birthday. Sadly, in October 12, 1947, he broke his hip. It was about half an inch from where he broke it earlier in 1937. He would remain a cripple for the rest of his life.

John's family moved back to Nipomo, California where Emmett continued in the timber business by 1950. John was reaching manhood at that time and beginning to have his eye on a young 14-year-old girl, Jo Ella Wilson. It is not clear if the Tatums knew the Wilson family when they lived in Oklahoma, but it certainly appears that they did, as well as coming to California in the mid to late 40's together. The Wilsons moved less than 100 miles from where the Tatums lived in Nipomo, settling in Kern County, California. It bordered San Luis Obispo County where the Tatums lived and where Drury James had established Paso Robles.

(John and Jo Ella Tatum (young))

(John and Jo Ella later in life)

Jo Ella Wilson's parents knew the Tatums well and knew Jesse. Joseph Hulvatus "Joe" Wilson (1892-1982) and Fannie Dora Frazier (1893-1967) were farmers in Oklahoma in various locations, moving quite frequently. They came to California and in 1950 on the census, Joe was not working, 57 years of age, and claimed to have other means of support.

Joe Wilson was born in Aurora, Wise County, Texas, 16 miles from Decatur, Texas where Jesse and Frank had their camp on Waggoner's property. Joseph's father, William Samuel Wilson (1855-1911) married Cornelia "Olive" Anderson in 1882 in Wise County. By 1900, William Samuel Wilson later moved his family to Wharton, Texas southwest of Houston. He was a farmer. By 1910, they moved to Memphis, Texas and thought it would be a great adventure to go to Oregon and live. They were on a train and stopped in Denver to spend the night and he died in the Oxford Hotel in 1911. He was only 56 years old. He wanted to be buried in Memphis beside his daughter who had recently died, Dillie Alila, but he wanted the rest of the family to continue to go to Oregon. One train took the body back to Memphis and the other train headed Northwest to Oregon. It didn't take long to decide that was not for them. They headed back to Oklahoma after a brief stay.

Joe married Fannie in Palmer, Oklahoma in 1912 and they lived in Fitzhugh, Oklahoma by 1920.

William Samuel Wilson's father was John McHenry Wilson. He had strong connections attached with Jesse. He was born in Alabama and before the Civil War, he was living in Neshoba, Mississippi. He was a merchant there. Per Find a Grave, John McHenry Wilson was 1st Sgt., Company D in the Neshoba Rangers. He was also 1st Sgt., Company D, 26th Mississippi Infantry, and 2nd Lt. Company G, 40th Mississippi Infantry. In 1880, he was living in Navarro, Texas and working as a Mason.

If you remember, Jesse was in Navarro, Texas quite a bit during his Texas Ranger's days. It was where Major John Jones lived. It was also where Jesse's former commander lived, John Sparks in the Frontier Battalion of the Texas Rangers near Frost, Texas where Jesse made a special trip to see him in 1893. John McHenry Wilson lived in Frost at that time. He died in 1912 and is buried in the Frost Cemetery.

(John McHenry Wilson)

John Tatum and Jo Ella Wilson married in 1952 in Nipomo, California. He was 19 and she was 16. They lived mostly in Oklahoma. Gerty is where they raised their children. Bud said she made the best fried apple pies. "John worked in the oil fields, painted cars and raced cars, operated a bulldozer, and worked in construction. He worked for Hughes County District #3, where he was employed for 32 years and served as Sunday School Superintendent at the Free Will Baptist Church." [442]

John and Jo Ella were the best partners in tracking Jesse besides Charlie Holman. Bud loved them as family. When John knew he could trust Bud, is when he told him about his father, Emmett Tatum and his father-in-law, Joe Wilson. They knew Jesse in Oklahoma and Jesse had known their families for years and knew that he could trust the two. We find so much evidence that Jesse depended on family and those of the descendants of the KGC, Quantrill Raiders, Confederates, or Masons.

Jesse asked Emmett Tatum and Joe Wilson to help him rebury some gold. It is unknown when this occurred, but it was sometime in the 30's. Jesse had known that the cache he buried earlier in North Texas had been compromised. Jesse took them to a place southeast of Quanah, Texas where the sacred Comanche Medicine Mounds lay near the Red River. There are 4 mounds there. From the top, you can see the Wichita Mountains in the distance, only 75 miles northeast from there. It was indeed a landmark, but most especially it was a healing sacred place for spiritual renewal for Comanche Chief Quanah Parker and his people, centuries before him. After the unrest between the Comanches and the Whites, Chief Parker surrendered, and peace returned to the land. The mounds were preserved for the Comanches. A small town was erected in 1907 called Medicine Mound near there, but it is a ghost town today.

Jesse promised to pay Emmett and Joe $5 an hour to dig up the gold/money in the area of Medicine Mound and rebury it. It is unclear if it was in the town itself or another location that was near the mounds. Jesse had close ties to Quanah Parker.

While the men began digging, Jesse was off carving something in trees or rocks to indicate the treasure was moved. We don't have a clear picture where they moved it to. It may still be there on the premises and Jesse would have had to leave some sign only known to the KGC of its new location.

That was really good money back then. Jesse offered them $10 an hour if they would move some gold for him in Louisianna. Although it sounded good, they turned him down.

John Tatum later learns that in the area where they were living, in Gerty, Oklahoma, about 85 miles away to the southeast was another family who was kin to Jesse, Dr. Frank James who worked with Jesse back in the Wild West days. Bud introduced John to his descendants. The older family members of Dr. Frank James knew John Tatum's father-in-law, Joe Wilson. Quite a story. They all lived in southeastern Oklahoma, Valliant, Felker, and Sardis Lake. The Choctaw Council at Tuskahoma, Oklahoma is near Sardis Lake where Dr. Frank James' photo was hanging along with the chiefs. He did a lot of doctoring for the nation. Tuskahoma is also where Rebecca Markham Tatum, part Choctaw, John Tatum's grandmother lived.

John Tatum was honored when he received a special gift from Jesse after he had been dead for many years. Jesse had given a beautiful gold pocket watch, with the inscription of "With Love" to his 1st cousin, Sarah James. It opened on both sides. That side of the family kept in touch with John's family. Sarah's grandson and his son would go hunting wild hogs with John Tatum in the mountains. The son, great grandson of Sarah's had become a minister. He heard the wonderful stories regarding John and Jesse and instead of passing the watch down to the rest of the family, the minister gave the watch to John Tatum. Bud had a videotape of the beautiful gold watch in mint condition. John was forever grateful and proud to have a piece of Jesse to carry him and the memories of him.

(Gold watch given to John Tatum of Jesse's as Bud dangles it in front of Ralph Swaby who was the pilot for Jesse in 1948)

Sadly, both John Tatum and Jo Ella have passed on, but Bud's fondest memories in treasure hunts with the Tatums for a period of 10 years, was finding the treasure in Jesse and the Tatums. One of his greatest friends and times in his life. "It doesn't get any better than this," Bud said.

Marksmanship –

Jesse's shooting ability was remarkable. He had a lot of practice. There are various stories of his marksmanship in which we have touched on. He used his unique abilities for showmanship and preservation. In the later season of his life, he focused his talents on entertaining folks and teaching the values of life.

Jesse loved his guns, there is no doubt about it. As he was one with his horse, he was one with his gun. He always kept them with him. In Howk's book, 'Jesse James and the Lost Cause," Jesse stated, "I was always armed. I carried small pistols, butts forward and I carried 'em high for a fast cross-draw. I also had a .32 caliber Smith & Wesson pistol stuck in each boot, just in case I ran into some ambitious detective seeking to make a reputation for himself." [443]

Even in his twilight years, he demonstrated his readiness for trouble. Many stories depict that Jesse was on guard at all times. His guns were ready. Francena Turilli from the Jesse James Wax Museum in Stanton, Missouri visited with Bud at her business. I was able to capture photos off of Bud's video tapes of him interviewing Francena with her showing Jesse's .44 Remington, the one he had over 65 years. He had it with him when he died. She said it had a very good balance. Francena stated that he had it with him when Jesse stayed in a cabin near Merrimac Caverns.

One story that Francena told was that Jesse was bed ridden because of his broken hip. He was close to 102 years old. When the nurse went to go get some food at the cave, Jesse heard a knock on the door. It was a tourist who had parked outside his door wanting to come in and speak with him. Jesse didn't respond. When the knocking continued and the man outside kept insisting on coming in, Jesse pulled out this .44 and shot a hole in the door. The bullet grazed the back seat of their car, missing a baby by a few inches. Needless to say, the man didn't wait around and left, but Rudy, Francena's husband found out the next day. When Jesse wasn't near his gun, Rudy went and took out the bullets and replaced them with blanks. Four or five days later, Jesse was messing with his gun and noticed the blanks. He threw that gun clear across the room and cussed Rudy to no end. He wouldn't speak to Rudy for a week at a time.

Jesse loved the pistols and rifles that used the .44 caliber bullet which could be interchanged between the two firearms, allowing the gunman to only carry one form of ammunition. Jesse designed the holster and harness to carry five or six guns at a time.

Bud found a pistol in one of the caves he was exploring following the trail of Jesse. It was used as a directional marker.

(Pistol found in cave (appears to be a Colt-Single Action, "Peacemaker" c.1874))

Bud told me one day a man came into his restaurant and wanted to show him a Smith and Wesson Schofield that he had bought at an auction. The man said the auctioneer had stated that it was associated with the James Gang, but he didn't have any papers or documentation to support it. The man was a gun collector and acquired the gun in western Oklahoma. Under the ivory grip, there were blood stains and five signatures carved inside. One was J. James. The History Channel had taken up his story and placed experts on the case to match those signatures and possibly pull DNA off the old blood that was caked between the grips and the frame. The handwriting appeared to be a match with Jesse's, but the blood was too old to collect any DNA. The blood was literally like glue, binding the ivory grips to the frame. The gun was determined to be issued to the military in 1875.

(Another gun authenticated as being Jesse's)

Witnesses state that they have seen Jesse shoot a button off of a Union Officer's coat, shoot three nicks in a squirrel's tail as he ran up a tree, and drive nails into a barn with his bullets. "Not too long ago, witnesses testify that he used only a single shot in bagging a mud hen at the range of 125 yards." [444]

In 1910, a couple, Mr. and Mrs. Arthur A. Beville, living near Harrisburg, Oklahoma, 20 miles east of Duncan had a visitor one night. He called himself Mr. Kelly. He was carrying with him a Winchester rifle with no sight at the end of the barrel. When Mr. Beville mentioned it, the visitor said nonchalantly that he could shoot just as good backwards as forward, and that he didn't need any sight. When Jesse came out in Lawton in 1948, the Beville's identified him as the man who called himself Mr. Kelly and was an excellent marksman.

Jesse, in 1901-1904 received a license to run a shooting gallery in Hot Springs, Arkansas by John Shevlin, a most dedicated and abrasive detective and chief of the government reservation at Hot Springs. Shevlin had many detectives and Pinkertons under him and not one of them knew that the man running the shooting gallery was Jesse going by the name of Frank Dalton.

Shevlin had many long conversations with Cole Younger who told him a story will come out that will rock the nation. Shevlin admitted that he always believed the white-headed gentleman with Frank and Cole was Jesse.

Ola said that Jesse entered shooting exhibitions in Corpus Christi and East Texas.

In 1931, Jesse was in Gladewater, Texas with the Rangers, the same time Bob Goss and Tom Hickman were in. Hickman was over Company B of the Rangers who were stationed in Gladewater.

In **1933**, the former Texas Ranger since the early 20's, Bob Goss, had gotten in the East Texas Oilfield business and became Chief of the Kilgore Police Department. In 1936, in the town nearby, Gladewater, Chief Goss, who was the State Pistol Champ, was selected as the judge of the pistol contests. In his obituary, he is noted as an expert marksman with .45, .38, and .22 caliber weapons and was a member of the East Texas Rifle and Pistol Club. They had a range 5 miles East of Kilgore. Frank Dalton (Jesse) was selected as Master of Ceremonies for a pistol shoot held for peace officers. Neither Dalton nor Goss could join in the contest because of their extreme accuracy and reputation. They did show off a few trick shootings. One of Goss' best exhibition of pistol shooting was to stand a playing card on the ground, the edge facing him, he walks back 30 feet, and cuts the card in two edgewise, knocking the top part into the air.

Dalton's tricks were taking his two six-shooters, tossing a can into the air and kept it up until the six-shooters were unloaded. "If you miss once you might as well let her come down."

We find an extremely interesting story about Bob Goss before he moved down in the Kilgore area. He was certainly well known in Texas and Oklahoma as a Texas Ranger. In 1930, he was living in Honey Grove, Texas, just 43 miles east of Sherman. He owned and operated a 15,000-acre farm which extended into Southern Oklahoma. He not only had his special Texas Ranger Commission, but also was a member of the Oklahoma Peace Officers Association. He was known as the best pistol shot in Texas.

Goss along with his famous Texas Ranger friend, Captain Tom Hickman traveled all over Texas and Oklahoma, entering pistol shoots. Hickman was a Ranger Captain over the oil fields, maintaining the area of Borger, Ranger, Kilgore, Burkburnett, Mexia, Desdemona, Breckenridge, and Wink.

Hickman was a rodeo judge and also a contestant in rodeos throughout the West. For a short time, he was a member of the Miller Brothers 101 Ranch Show and performed with the Wild West Shows. He always made his home in Gainesville, Texas.

Getting back to the story about Goss and Hickman, who became extremely good friends, had very similar experiences as did Dalton. In a statement made by Hickman in the Fort Worth Star Telegram, February 14, 1930, "Goss and I attended one of the shoots given by the Oklahoma officers. When they found out who we were, and knowing how well we could shoot, they barred us on the grounds that we did not hold an Oklahoma commission. Goss then secured one, claiming that right, because he lived a portion of his time on the 5,000 acres of his farm which extended into that State." [445]

After his resignation from the Kilgore Police Department in the same year, Goss returned to the Texas Rangers, serving in the southeast Texas division. [446] In his obituary, it listed that he had been a Mason for 50 years, since 1928.

Mitch Graves who worked at Jesse's Canada Ranch told Bud that Dalton/Jesse had numerous buddies come to his ranch to visit and were excellent horsemen and marksmen. One of them was called Jim Sidner, who Mitch knew well, but he was actually William Henry Roberts, Brushy Bill Robert's father.

They would often have a shooting match. Dalton would have Mitch throw a tin can into the air, only to be shot all to pieces in a matter of seconds with two long-barreled pistols he carried in holsters underneath his long coat. Using the cross-arm draw technique, Dalton would fire his Frontier Model Smith and Wesson revolver and his Colt 45, continuously keeping the can in the air until all the bullets were dispensed.

When Mitch saw the Police Gazette, he verified that the picture of J. Frank Dalton holding a gun was indeed Jesse and the picture was taken in Canada.

Jesse gained a lot of respect from those who witnessed his horsemanship and marksmanship, but after they found out who the man was, the respect tripled.

Showmanship

Wild West Shows - Bud received a letter from a lady regarding when Cole Younger was released from prison in 1901. Jesse brought Cole to Lexington, Ok, just across the Canadian River from Purcell. On the Purcell side, he dug up $40,000 for Cole. Frank and Cole started a wild west show. Bud thinks the money was initially buried on Red Hill.

Jesse participated in a lot of wild west shows, but no one knew it was Jesse. Sometimes he would be the ticket taker at the Jesse James Show in which Frank James and Cole Younger would display Jesse's personal effects. They made a killing off of that.

The Cole Younger-Frank James Wild West Shows - In the Stroud Star, Sept. 18, 1903 describes the show; "quadrilles on horseback, mimic attacks on settler's cabins and stage coaches by bands of Indians, dances that are a part of the religious rites of the Sioux and other Indians; feat of horsemanship by Cossacks and Mexican Vaqueros in competition with American cowboys and other features of the wild west. The display is so large that thirty-three railroad cars are necessary to haul it about the country. In it are 700 horses, 500 equestrians and equestriennes and 300 Indians." [447]

Fairs - Jesse loved the World and State Fairs. I'm sure he loved the county fairs also, but there was something mysteriously attracting him to them. We know he performed at the Chicago Fair in 1893, the Oregon State Fair in 1947, the Alabama-Mississippi State Fair, and took an active part in the St. Louis Fair in 1904. He was also at the fairs in Kansas City, Nashville, and Pensacola, Florida.

At the fair in Kansas City, Jesse told Ola about preparing to race his horse. Frank and Cole Younger were with him, but the officials would not allow him to race. It is unknown what the reason was. This infuriated Jesse and he said, "By God I will get the money I could have won." "I walked up to the ticket window and said to the young man that was selling tickets, "What would you say if I told you that I am Jesse James and to hand over that money box?" The man said, "I'd tell you to go to hell!" I said, "Well that's just what I am saying!" [448] Jesse went home the winner. The money box had $10,000 in it.

Another time that Jesse mentions going to fairs was with Howk and they were making money, either by racing or shooting. I believe he could have made more money by racing. He told Ola that they had made $32,832.00 at three fairs and all Jesse received was a mere $14.00; Howk got the rest.

A Dempsey Biggs who lived in Granbury, Texas, stated that definitely, J. Frank Dalton was Jesse. "In 1907, when he was just a boy, he went to the Alabama-Mississippi State Fair. A man, later identified as Frank James, said "My brother is a living man. I could produce him today if the law would guarantee his immunity." [449]

These were nothing compared to the World Fairs which exploded before the turn of the century during the Gilded age, spreading into the new century. The fairs were to motivate and transition the world and America into a new type of Utopia. Symbolism, persuasive new inventions, and a view of the different world cultures and history were introduced to coax and influence the mind of the fairgoer.

Millions and millions of dollars were spent excavating and reforming the landscape, creating a world that was far above the imagination. "Just what were they all about? I never discovered," said a worker at the St. Louis Fair." In St. Louis in 1904, it was the first-time buildings were electrified.

This St. Louis Fair was to celebrate the centennial of the 1803 Louisiana Purchase. It featured the amazing feat that Lewis and Clark had performed that started to open a new civilization. It was an amazing show of new technology and science with a cultural flair all decked out in extravagant and majestic architectural structures. Buildings began springing up everywhere that much thought and handiwork was carved into its exterior and interior. The St. Louis Fair was patterned after the Chicago World's Fair in 1893. Waterways, rivers, and lakes meandered around the huge property with expert landscaping. Gardens, plaster statues of Grecian and Renaissance persuasion, and an assortment of European culture exhibits.

The fair was an eye-opener to many various cultures around the world. Exhibits featured how pygmies, cannibals, and Filipinos lived in their own setting, displayed for all to see. It promoted colonization with many innuendos and symbols suggesting how primitive they were, separating the wheat from the chaff. They placed Blacks only in the exhibit featuring the "Old Plantation," working in gardens, singing minstrel songs, etc. The propaganda was everywhere.

It was called "The Babylon of the New World." "Expositions are timekeepers of progress." [450] President David Roland Francis said, "For more than a generation to come, it will be a marker in the accomplishments and progress of man. So thoroughly does it represent the world's civilization that if all man's other works were by some unspeakable catastrophe blotted out, the records here established by the assembled nations would afford all necessary standards for the rebuilding of our entire civilization." [451] Francis was the mayor of St. Louis and governor of Missouri at the time of the 1904 St. Louis World's Fair. He was a member of George Washington Lodge No. 9, St. Louis. Also, Francis was a member of Oriental Chapter No. 78 Royal Arch Masons and Ascalon Commandery No. 16 Knights Templar.

The first ice cream cone and iced tea were introduced there. The Pike was a street that ran for a mile, offering food, amusements and entertainment. The phrase, "Coming down the Pike" originated there. The official song for the St. Louis World's Fair was "Meet me in St. Louis, Louis (Louie)."

John Shevlin who had previously been a chief detective in St. Louis, before taking on the job as Chief Detective, was there at the fair to assist the local force during the World's Fair. [452] He would later be one of the witnesses to verify J. Frank Dalton's identity as Jesse in 1948.

The St. Louis World's Fair lasted for 7 months. It had everything you could imagine. Jesse said he wrote several articles during this major event and I believe he also participated. He would have been 43 years old and in good health.

The World's Fair was full of interesting subjects, but the ones that would have stood out for Jesse and his knowledge of the subject would have been the Cummins Wild West performances, which performed "extremely vivid reproduction of an atrocity which was a common ordeal in the early days of frontier life." [453] Many exhibitions included Geronimo who was considered a prisoner of war at that time and heavily guarded. Jesse told Ola he knew Geronimo and showed her a picture he had of them together. There were many trick riders, sharpshooters, and roping events on display. It was noted that "50 of the most noted cowboys and Wild West performers in the country will participate and the performance will be under the management of the Gabriel Brothers, known the world over as daring riders and expert lasso artists." [454] The exhibition included a "Cattle Show," exhibiting fine and quality bred cattle from Texas and Indian Territory. The Cummins Wild West outfit placed an ad shortly after the exposition, offering the entire Wild West show up for sale.

The Cummins show got tangled up with the Humane Society, stockholders, and other legal battles. In the St. Louis Globe-Democrat, August 15, 1904, the news read, "Arrest Col. Cummins Amid Much Excitement"– "Humane Society people declare concession employees were cruel." The Humane Society watched with great empathy for the steers, as they watched them being roped in the arena, declaring it was cruel and unusual. They never had seen anything like that before in the protective "Gilded Age" that they lived in.

"Then, when one of the steers was thrown with a lasso about its horns and one leg, drawing the two together, while the cowboy handling the rope galloped across the arena pulling the unhappy animal along the grounds, the Humane Society people believed they had their "cue" to "go on" in the performance, and go on they did. Entering the arena, they instructed the detective with them to arrest the cowboys who had roughly handled the steers. This was the signal for almost a riot. The first cowboy Mr. Meigs reached for his gun. He set up a lusty shout of "Hey Rube," which, in tent-show parlance, means that one of the showmen is in distress. That brought cowboys hustling from all parts of the Cummins concession."

Weapons and blows were exchanged between the cowboys and Indians up against the society and spectators. It began to get pretty serious and then Cummins stepped up and offered a surrender to the police. He was arrested. It definitely defined a border between the past and the present at the turn of the century. Two worlds collide and I believe that was what Jesse was going through. So tied to the past and unwilling to move forward. The west and the past were still trying to be tamed.

One interesting note that ties Jesse to this World's Fair is in the Lawton Constitution, May 19, 1948, "Many Oldtimers recall now that at the world fair at St. Louis in 1904 there was a show of Jesse James' personal effects. Some of them recall too, that a whitehaired gentleman was selling tickets." [455]

Another amazing find was that Frank James had the original cabin that Reverend Robert James built, disassembled and moved to the St. Louis World's Fair. There is an original picture of the cabin on "canteymyerscollection.com." The writing on the photo states, "Old house where Jesse James was born near Excelsior Springs, Missouri." After the fair, it was never seen again.

At the World's Fair, there were thousands of men, representing the Knights of Pythias who marched in the parade and camped on the grounds. Jesse was a member, but the lodge or location of his membership under an alias is unknown. He did join the Masons and Odd Fellows in Chicago.

The Knights of Pythias was the first fraternal organization and secret society to receive a charter under an act of the United States Congress, founded in Washington D.C. by Justus H. Rathbone in

1864. Rathbone lived 17 miles from Albert Pike. In 1889, after the Run in Oklahoma, the Knights of Pythias had grown to 2,724 lodges and 263,847 members. In one news article that year in the St. Louis Globe-Democrat, August 17, 1904, it was reported that there are "546 lodges in Illinois, 446 in Indiana, 400 in Iowa, 206 in Kansas, 247 in Missouri, 237 in New York, 647 in Ohio, 453 in Pennsylvania, and 323 in Texas. By 1910, Oklahoma had 153 lodges and the lodges exploded nationwide to 7,895: a difference of 5,171 from 1904." [456] It was the hottest thing for men to join at the time.

Many military regiments from all over the world, including the Spanish American War and the Boer War vets in full uniform and garb were there. Black soldiers were not allowed to participate. They performed drills and marched in parades around the fair. There were exhibits of the wars and also reenactments. It too may have been propaganda, not getting to the heart of the subject and reasoning for the wars.

"The Boer War makes the average circus or Wild West look like a cheap imitation of open-air amusement." [457]

The Boer War exhibit was the most popular show at the St. Louis World's Fair. It depicted a reproduction of the many battles fought during this war. It brought the battles to the people. It too had violence within its performers, with one being fatally shot with a real bullet.

An article in the Pineville Herald, Oct. 14, 1904 speaks of a Frank Dalton who possibly could be Jesse. Not only did he participate in St. Louis, he was having his own fair in Anderson, Missouri which was 300 miles away. "Frank Dalton, oldest brother of the famous outlaws, has been in Anderson (Missouri) for several days this week painting signs and giving exhibitions on the streets at night. He showed his wonderful strength by pulling against eight heavy men with his teeth and against Van Carnell's big black team of horses." [458] The real Frank Dalton had already been dead for 7 years. This had to be Jesse.

In 1906, Jesse told Ola that him and Frank went to the Dallas State Fairgrounds. There they met David Walker Farris (1854-1916), who was a Deputy U.S. Marshal in Indian Territory. He lived in Colbert at the time. Also, one of his brothers was with him and David's son, George who was 18 at the time. Jesse's story is validated by a write up in a newspaper.

The story told by George (1888-1989) David Farris' son was the most revealing. It was published in *The Marshall News Messenger*, February 19, 1982. "My daddy (David Walker Farris) was a deputy U.S. marshal in Indian territory," Farris recalls. Every year they had the fair in Dallas, my uncle and I would catch a train and come to Dallas for it."

"In 1906, Farris, his uncle and father stepped off the train to find Frank James, Jesses' brother, and a former member of the gang, among the crowd. Farris and the James' family were not strangers. His grandfather had grown on a Missouri farm adjacent to the James' family farm, and when Farris was born in 1888 it was Dr. George James, a cousin to Frank and Jesse, who helped him fight for life for three days and nights.

"Frank James accompanied the Farris party out to the fairgrounds, and the entire group was about to enter an exhibit featuring John L. Sullivan, the boxer when Farris noticed his uncle was missing. "I looked around and my uncle and a man were standing together. He had his arm on my uncle's shoulder, talking," Farris said. "My Uncle was facing the other way." I said, "Come on they want us to go in", but he didn't come. So, I went over and hit him on the back. About that time that fellow wheeled around and walked away. That man, Farris is for certain was Jesse James."

Going in to see the boxer Sullivan, Farris introduced Sullivan to Frank James. Sullivan asked Frank, "Why don't you have a show? People would pay more to see you than me, since Jesse's dead." Frank said, "You give me $10,000 and give him a pardon and we might be able to turn him up pretty quick."

This incident is another example of Jesse still being alive in 1906. He and Frank knew the Farris' well, even though David Farris was a Deputy U.S. Marshal at that time and knew Jesse before, during, and after the time they were both Deputy U.S. Marshals. His son, George Farris became a lawman and had a farm southwest of Mead, Bryan County, Oklahoma in the Washita riverbed. He later became a judge in Carrizo Springs, Texas and served for 30 years. George firmly believed Jesse was J. Frank Dalton and buried in Granbury, Texas in 1951.

In 1910, again George Farris and his father, David was on a train and met Dr. George James. David told Dr. James about the encounter with Frank James in Dallas just 4 years earlier. The doctor asked if they saw Jesse as well. David's reply was no he hadn't seen him, but the doctor said, "I bet he was there. He lives south of Denton." [459]

> "The James family was a mystery to the people of Missouri, they went by several different names."
>
> *-From "The Only True History of the Life of Frank James," written by Himself.* [460]

Chapter Twenty-One: A Brother from Another Father or Mother?

Joe Vaughn, a man who was the county surveyor for Newton County, Arkansas for 38 years beginning in 1887, finally unwrapped his history in 1925. He had ties to J. Frank Dalton and John Trammell, who always said there were two Frank James. John Trammel in the Denver Post said there was a "double switch with Sam Collins." What does that mean? Who was this Joe Vaughn?

The three had a secret meeting on the huge flat rock, high off the ground with KGC markings engraved upon it, which lay in front of Vaughn's house in a secluded wooded area outside of Wayton, Arkansas. Joe Vaughn's dying words, "I am Frank James."

Not as many researchers hunt out the detailed life of Jesse's brother, Alexander Franklin James, as much as they do Jesse's. There is more than meets the eye and it appears to be another wild tale of sorts, but he definitely was connected to J. Frank Dalton and John Trammel.

Bud had never heard of Joe Vaughn, but one day an old school buddy that worked at the airport in Oklahoma City led him to a man who carried clues of connection to Jesse and the man called Joe Vaughn. He directed Bud to the "lady in the know," Betty Lou Kilgore in Jasper, Newton County, Arkansas.

This is the first time Bud had heard of Lou Kilgore, as she prefers to be called. She was a hard worker and researcher. Bud gave Lou a call and she invited him to Arkansas to open a whole new world of Frank and Jesse to him. It would give them an opportunity to learn from each other. Bud said she became a big part of this hunt for Jesse and had been doing it for years before she met Bud.

Lou had lived most of her life in Newton County, Arkansas and at one-time lived-in **Holden**, Missouri, giving her a fantastic opportunity to research the James boys. They were supposedly living there after the Civil War. She kept getting deeper and deeper into the subjects. She moved back to Newton County where the story of a mysterious man who her grandfather knew, kept tugging at her mind to investigate.

She remembers vividly, the stories told to her as a young girl, as she would sit for hours listening to her grandfather tell the stories of Frank James who was his neighbor. The warmth of the old wood stove and the unbelievable tales of the Wild West kept her glued to the floor.

Lou's grandfather, James Buchanan "Buck" Wilson was born in 1885 in Parthenon, Newton County, Arkansas and lived there all of his born days in a very small rural area in the backwoods of the Boston Mountains. He got to know his neighbors well and they depended upon each other. A well-grounded and well-watered trust was planted upon that fertile soil.

(James Buchanan "Buck" Wilson (courtesy of Betty Lou Kilgore))

One of his neighbors was Joe Vaughn. Buck knew 'ole Joe early in his childhood, his teens, and young adulthood. Joe was two generations older than Buck.

Joe was the county surveyor for years and would be out and about in the woods with his surveyor equipment, his compass and staff. It took a highly skilled person in science, mathematics, and physics to map out an accurate ley of the land. This art is what the Knights Templar, Freemasons brought to America and the KGC used this system to bury their treasure. It was their underground banking system developed thousands of years ago. There is evidence all over Joe Vaughn's property that Joe was a member of the KGC. This made Joe Vaughn extremely useful in a primitive and remote area of Arkansas. That was his assignment.

Howk wrote that Alexander Franklin James/Joe Vaughn headed one section of Arkansas and Missouri with "secret police," the KKK, receiving complaints and conducting makeshift courts to dish out justice to the injustice. The KKK, at that time, helped those impoverished with food, clothing, deeded them a tract of land, built houses, and helped people find jobs who were impoverished by the war and the bloody aftermath of the war which was sometimes worse than the war itself. [461]

Joe Vaughn was in other places, saying "While the Pinkerton detectives professed to be hot on our trail in some big city, we would be punching cattle on a western ranch." He also said he was in the South, looking after the interests of a timber company. [462]

Howk had also stated that Joe Vaughn had a farm/ranch in Leon County, Texas hiding John Wilkes Booth. Vaughn had a family there also. Howk was familiar with Joe Vaughn. There was a J.D. Reed who lived in Leon County at the time. The Reed name ties to Vaughn. Could that be a name Vaughn used in Texas?

Buck, Lou's grandfather had many conversations with Joe Vaughn, his family, and his friends. He went to church with Joe and watched him as he helped build the school and even was a teacher. Joe was well respected in those mountains. Joe Vaughn actually told Buck that he was Frank James, the famous outlaw. The majority of that entire backwoods' region knew who Joe Vaughn was, but he wasn't ready to tell the world until the walls and his health started closing in on him.

Lou spent much of her life investigating Joe Vaughn and J. Frank Dalton. She knew many people who actually were kin or interacted intimately with Vaughn and Dalton. She became an expert in their secret history and teaming up with Bud, made their path to the truth more fruitful.

This chapter opened the writer's eyes even further and helped explain some unanswered questions. Until you can research it for yourself, using all the clues given, the story becomes clearer and starts to make sense. But again, it uncovers more questions in which I don't believe will ever be answered.

The story of Frank and Jesse James is the most complicated tale in the history of the world. No wonder Anna Ralston James said, "the truth about the James boys will never be known." Agreed.

This portion of the story could not have been possible to unravel, not completely mind you, without Bud's thorough research and documents; Lou Kilgore's persistent investigation, letters collected, Lou's grandfather, Buck and their connections to the family of Joe Vaughn; and the autographed signed book from Joe Vaughn's descendants; Sarah Snow, Lester Snow, and Columbus Vaughn, authors of the book, "This Was Frank James"; the people interviewed who knew Joe Vaughn; Del Schrader/Howk's book, "Jesse James was One of His Names", Howk's book that came out in 1961, "Jesse James and the Lost Cause", Find a Grave.com, and ancestry.com.

As the writer, I will lay out what we all have discovered about Joe Vaughn and his connection to Frank James the outlaw. Whether he really was Frank James, the one and only, or another man who was deeply involved with Jesse and carried out his cause, portrayed as Frank James, we do not know for certain. It appears that he was with Jesse through the Civil War and outlawry.

Lou said Joe Vaughn was known as a kind, gentle caring person and truthful as well as honest. Apparently though, he was leading a double life, as most of the men did in this organization, the KGC.

Alvin Seamster who owned the Seamster Museum, south of Garfield, Arkansas and north of the Pea Ridge Battlefield told a newspaper reporter in an article out of the "News-Gazette" that he had an affidavit in his museum from a man who said Jesse James stayed at his father's barn after 1882 when he was supposedly dead. Mr. Seamster, a widely known historian did a lot of research on the James' subject and he came to the conclusion that Frank and Jesse settled in **Jasper, Arkansas**. "Frank unwittingly gave away his true identity there when he showed his marksmanship, he said. He shot in rapid succession five agates tossed in the air, and his expertise caused people to ask questions that led them to the conclusion that he was Frank James." [463]

Sarah (Vaughn) Snow, born in 1888, daughter of Joe Vaughn and Nancy Richardson had always thought her father was keeping things from the family. There were many incidents in her father's life when he was elusive and cautious. Watching his reactions to people, places, and things created a sense of mystery surrounding her father's past.

The family says there were many nights people would come to their gate, and a voice from the dark would say in a low cautious tone, "Hello", exchanging code words with their father such as a phrase using "the wild goose". Joe would meet the men outside and would camp out for 2 or 3 days in front of the house on this large flat rock.

Other times the meeting would lead Joe to packing his horse with food and blankets and heading out with these strangers. He would be gone for days, sometimes weeks. He would come back with loads of cash; "enough to fill a wash basin to the brim." [464] Joe Vaughn's son, Ebb saw his father with $500 in gold coins once. [465]

Columbus Vaughn, grandson of Joe's said that they actually lived in poverty, but when things got bad is when he would leave. Columbus' grandmother would ask Joe, "Where did you get this?"

Joe's reply, "Now the less questions you ask, the better it would be, and he said we'll have just as much money if you keep your mouth shut." [466]

There were times in town that Joe had confrontational scenes with men and during one certain encounter, he and the other man he was conversing with backed away from each other, not for a second wanting to turn their backs on the other.

Joe was a sharpshooter. His son Will threw six green walnuts in the air and from his hips, he pulled his gun without sighting and burst every walnut except one that slit the nut in two. His children said that they saw his shooting ability this one time, otherwise Joe did not allow sidearms in the house.

Joe Vaughn would take his daughter, Sarah to Indian Territory to visit relatives, claiming they were her mother's relatives. Sarah's mother, Nancy Richardson's mother was a Daniels, Phebe Daniels and they visited "Uncle" John Daniels. She was ten at the time, 1898.

Sarah's father then said he was going to go a little further and visit someone else. They traveled all day and all night and after the 2nd day, reached their destination. A large cabin, with two large rooms separated by a breeze way. Inside was an old lady with only one arm, who was living in the home, a teenage boy and a tall sickly man.

Years later, Joe told Sarah that the old lady was the stepmother of Frank and Jesse James. The boy, named "Little Frank" was Joe's own son, born to his Indian sweetheart, Ann Ralston. The tall sickly man was Sam Collins. He was given the duty to raise Frank's son. We learn from Jesse's own words that Robert James who always had been known as Frank and Annie's son, was actually an adopted son. Robert is shown in the 1880 census in Tennessee under the household of B. J. Woodson, an alias that Frank James went by. Was Robert really "Little Frank"?

We also learn in a newspaper clipping that Bud had, from "The Times," dated July 2, 1979 [467] that Columbus Vaughn, grandson of Joe Vaughn, stated that Ann Ralston revealed before her death that she lived out the lie with Sam Collins as Mr. and Mrs. Frank James and that Sam received $35,000 and the James' Farm for portraying himself as Frank James. This goes along with what John Trammel always said, as well as Joe Vaughn.

Also, it is not clear if this is true, but a piece out of the *Folktales* booklet, titled "Outlaw Stories" that Bud had in his collection, stated, "Sam Collins, a neighbor to the James farm, had secretly been courting Frank's wife Annie Ralston during Frank's many years on the outlaw trail. Frank had made a deal with Collins whereby Collins would "become" Frank James and would receive $25,000 from Frank as well as title to the James Farm and to Annie. After being pardoned for all past crimes the real Frank left Missouri and went to Arkansas under the alias of Joe Vaughn." [468]

Sarah (Vaughn) Snow took care of her father and towards the end of his life, he requested that his real name be engraved on his tombstone. He wanted his name to be declared in stone who he really was, "Frank James, Alias Joe Vaughn." He presented to her a manuscript that he had been working on for four years. He started it in 1921 and finished it in December 1925. He asked her not to publish it until after his death. On his deathbed, he confessed to his family, "I am Frank James." Everything was now making sense, or was it?

What was really surprising to me, the writer, is a quote I had written in a book in 2011, before I met Bud that I used from a newspaper article. It was published in 1915, before Joe Vaughn's book was finished. Many people knew the James' in Wichita Falls, Texas. In "Many Wichitans Recall Frank James Noted Bandit" in the Wichita Falls Times; **February 21, 1915**; "Squire Howard remembers as far back as 1880, Frank would visit Sheriff McMurtry who was another ex-Quantrill Raider. Squire said Frank would come by possibly to rest after a heist, but he called him "a brave man and a gentleman, and I would have taken his word or his paper for any amount at any time. He was honest and honorable. I have often thought that there are many people who have never been charged with any crime who are infinitely worse than Frank James ever was."

Squire continued, "On one occasion, I drove Frank all over West Texas where he sold shoes. On that trip I only saw him angry at one time. I had introduced him to a cattleman in Vernon, when the cattleman very unthoughtfully said, "oh yes, I have read your history." Quick as a flash, James' face went white with wrath and he retorted, "no you have not read my history. You have read a pack of damnable lies, gotten up by a bunch of people who have slandered my family and me, for no other reason than to make money." That right there says it all.

Squire Howard says, **"The only true history of the James boys** has been written, but it has never been published. It was written by Frank James and he told me the last time that I saw him that it would be published by his family after his death if the family thought proper. The James history will show that Frank and Jesse James were forced into outlawry after the civil war and they could not have done otherwise if they had tried." [469]

This seems like it fits the story of Joe Vaughn. His family stated that Joe was gone often from the family. He was heavily involved in Freemasonry and the KGC. Was a shoe salesman and department store worker a cover for his KGC activities or was this the real Sam Collins who was doing that? The article about Squire Howard's statement was written in February 21, 1915, 3 days after Frank James, supposedly Sam Collins died. No book was ever published that I know of, that came out on this Frank James' life, but a man going by the name of Joe Vaughn, back in Wayton County, Arkansas was writing with an old lead pencil on thin tablet paper, an autobiography, **"The Only True Story of Frank James."** This title was very similar to the one that Squire Howard spoke of in 1915 of the book that Frank James was writing.

Shortly after Joe presented the manuscript to his children, he died in 1926. It was within a few months within that year, 1926, that Sarah took the original manuscript of 134 pages to Norton Printing Company in Pine Bluff, Arkansas. Before the company could distribute the books, the place was burned to the ground. Only twenty-five copies were saved. One of the copies is located in the Jasper, Arkansas museum per Lou. One is found in the Library of Congress.

Later, Sarah learned that the fire appeared to be arson. She believes it was set by a man who had visited their home multiple times and was thought to have been Joe's brother, a very mean-spirited and spiteful man. For some reason, he or someone didn't want that book published.

In the meantime, Sarah and her son, Lester went on many trips to places her father had mentioned in the manuscript, even to Mexico, and sought out the people who were mentioned. They were starving for information to validate his story. The story was materializing before their very own eyes.

The stories, the secrets, and the statements from family to friends persuaded the family that yes indeed, he was Frank James. His son, Marion said he was Frank James, but there were **three or four**. He was the Missouri Frank. Marion told the family that his father told him to go to Camp Wood in Texas and dig up some money buried there, $1500 worth of gold and silver at the foot of the Bullhead Mountain. It was there alright. This mountain peak is in south Texas, west of Bandera and north of Uvalde.

After 20 years of research, Sarah received surprising answers to her questions.

In 1948, after J. Frank Dalton told the world that he was Jesse James, he contacted Sarah Snow via a letter. Columbus Vaughn showed the letter during his speeches at historical meetings relating the Vaughn story. Dalton was living in Van Nuys, California with Howk, validated with one of the letters Lou had. Dalton wanted to meet Sarah in California where she was living. He knew exactly where she was. He told her that he has been keeping up with the family and knew about her father's death. He knew about Joe's book, and what she was planning to do with it. He was very concerned when it went to the publisher in 1926 because it was too early for the information within those pages to be revealed. Was he threatening? No, it sounded as if he wanted to help her and protect something very dear to him, his family.

When Sarah met J. Frank Dalton, memories flooded in like a wall of water. She recognized him as that man who was extremely interested in her father and appeared in their backwoods two times that she could remember. The first time she had remembered him, was in the dead of night. Sarah heard an old hoot owl outside. She heard her father slip out of the house. Sarah got out of bed and peeking through the cracks of the log walls of her home, she saw this man talking with her father and a black man. They were talking on the big flat rock in front of their house where many a night her father would lay just thinking and pondering on some pretty serious stuff.

Another time, this same man, Dalton was that old cantankerous fellow who was trying to find her father once again. The event Sarah remembers was during the years between 1910-1920, after she became married to her husband, Wiley Snow in 1906. Dalton was found stumbling around on the old dirt road close to their home, calling himself Mr. St. Myers. He said he was from Missouri. He gave Sarah's family and brothers fits because of his dramatic display of being old and decrepit. He was on foot and had nothing nice to say, quite the contrary. He said, "Joe Vaughn is a damn liar. There never was a man named Joe Vaughn." [470]

He cussed up a storm, even when they gave him a ride, their ear, something to drink, supper, and offered to take him to see Joe Vaughn. By trying to help the old man up and around, they could feel multiple concealed guns under his coat. He was armed and ready. For what?

They all braced themselves when Sarah's brother, Will asked the old man since he was from Missouri, if he ever knew the James' boys. St. Myers went into a mad rage over the question. The cussing continued.

When the men of the family had enough, they talked tough to him and wouldn't allow anymore of his sassy words and attitude. The old man did calm down a bit and became more pleasant. "…with an admiring smile he said, "I can tell you one thing, the first wild goose I ever killed, I did it while sitting on Jesse James' pony." Sarah and her brother both said they had heard their father say the same thing, except Joe Vaughn said he was on Frank James' pony." [471] The "wild goose" showed up in a lot of the James' boys' phrases, used as a password.

It was just a show, just a game the old man was playing. When not looking, the family noticed he was more agile than what he was putting on. He was trying to see how far he could go and, in the meantime, get to know his brother's family a little bit better. He knew them all. He knew where they lived, he had for the past forty years.

The old man apparently stayed the night at Sarah's house or slept outside. The next day, Joe's son, Will found Joe and told him about the old man. Will suggested it may be Joe's brother, who he called Bill (William Nelson Vaughn). "If I knew it was Bill, I wouldn't go see him for my right arm." [472] Joe's brother had threatened him, saying that if they ever crossed paths again, he would kill him.

The next day, St. Myers and a few of the family were outside of Sarah's home when Joe Vaughn boldly walked through the yard and through the gate. Both men's penetrating eyes pierced through each other as if they were daggers. They never took their eyes off each other as Joe passed by. No words spoken.

Joe went through the house and was gone out the back. The next time they saw their father, he denied knowing the old man. Sounds like brothers, sibling rivalry, or brotherhood rivalry at the least.

Dalton confirmed with Sarah in California in the year 1948, that the old man was him. He confirmed he was Jesse James and her father; Joe Vaughn was his brother, Frank James. Dalton also answered her questions about the fire that destroyed the publishing company. His reply, "Sometimes it's best that things get stopped before they get too far." [473]

He told her to follow through with her research and speak with a man named John Trammell who was Jesse and Frank's cook in the gang. He was the black man with him when they were speaking with her father on the flat rock outside their home when Sarah was a little girl.

Dalton also told Sarah Vaughn Snow to see Carl C. Clark in Death Valley. He was another son of Frank James from another mother. He would have been a half-brother to Sarah and happened to be half Indian, conceived in Indian Territory.

Bearing in mind that Howk was with Dalton in California when Dalton met up with Sarah Snow, we do understand that Howk was fully aware of the meeting and possibly encouraged it. In the Del Schrader book, "Jesse James Was One of His Names", he writes, "And old white-haired Carl O. Clark, Box 86, Death Valley, California, who died in 1967 in his 90's, admitted, "For many years I served as Jesse W. James' double as copper king William A. Clark in Montana, Arizona and Utah." [474]

Even though this was Howk speaking, it still may have had some credence. Just briefly we will later explore William Andrews Clark, the copper king, who many believe was actually Jesse James himself. He looked like him and had the same cowlick. But all along, it could have been Frank's son, Carl Clark working for the KGC. The only picture we have of Carl Clark is from Sarah's book. His stature is comparable to William A. Clark. Could it be possible that Howk's story is true regarding Carl Clark as a stand-in for Jesse, when he was unable to attend the social and political affairs of Senator William Andrews Clark? It's possible, we don't know.

Carl O. Clark may or may not have been part of this Clark family or a "stand-in" for Jesse as Clark, but many people believe, even some family members, that Clark was really Jesse. Even though it may have not been him, Clark had to have help somewhere and Jesse could have been the man behind the scenes, involved in some way. We don't know.

Carl Clark also told Sarah Vaughn Snow, author of "This Was Frank James," that he was her half-brother, admitting he was an illegitimate son of Alexander Franklin James.

There apparently were several illegitimate sons of Frank's and we know of one daughter, Mary Plina Norris, from a Cherokee woman, Josephine Welch.

The Family

If Joe Vaughn was Frank, Alexander Franklin James and J. Frank Dalton was Jesse, Jesse Woodson James, who was their father and who was their mother? They shared only one as Joe Vaughn stated he was a half-brother of Jesse's. Another complicated story.

The choices for their father: Ebb/Edd Reed, James Vaughn, George James, or Robert James.

The choices for their mother: Zerelda (Dalton) Cole, Mollie Dalton, Mary Adeline Cole, or Agnes Collins.

There may be more that we don't even know about, but keep in mind, Frank and Jesse used a lot of different family names to hide behind. That has been proven. Remember, these were brilliant men and involved deeply in the clandestine organizations.

Howk also wrote about the encounter with Sarah Snow regarding her father, Joe Vaughn, whom Howk confirmed with her that he believed Joe was Alexander Franklin James. Howk claimed that "Alexander Franklin James" had a "batch of kids" in Newton County, Arkansas and another family in Leon County, Texas. Howk wrote in "Jesse James and the Lost Cause," that Jesse said after the meeting with Sarah Snow, "When we were out in Van Nuys, California, his (Joe Vaughn) good and loyal daughter, Sarah, came from her home at Farmersville, California, and, along with her good husband, had a lot of time with me and talked some things over. We concluded that there were still some facts and secrets best left as they were, let alone until after I'm dead." [475]

This is an important statement, because the original manuscript of Joe Vaughn's published in 1926 has a few different things revealed in it that the 1969 book does not.

Howk wanted us to believe that Alexander Franklin James was the son of Zerelda and Robert James and that he had a brother Jesse R. James. They were the Missouri Frank and Jesse. They were with the Quantrill Irregulars. Howk believed Jesse Woodson James/J. Frank Dalton was a 1st cousin to them and was the son of Mollie Dalton and George Strother James, Robert Sallee James' brother. He believed that Jesse Woodson James' brother was Dr. Sylvester Franklin James. They would be the Kentucky Frank and Jesse. Howk stated that Zerelda was Jesse Woodson James' aunt. Presumably through marriage by the two brothers, Robert and George James, but it also could be by Zerelda Dalton and Molly Dalton as sisters.

Howk went so far as to write and sign an affidavit on October 12, 1978 describing this entire relationship and outline of Joe Vaughn/ Alexander Franklin James and his brother, Jesse R. James. It was shown to be in the county of Tulare, California.

Ola denied this extensively and stated that Jesse Woodson James alias J. Frank Dalton's mother was Zerelda (Dalton) Cole and his father was Rev. Robert Sallee James. Jesse never told her otherwise. So why would Howk have a completely different story? Was this something Jesse told Howk? We don't know how he came up with this.

Bud has a letter that Charles Norris wrote to Howk about 2 Jesses and 2 Franks. Charles was the husband of Frank James' only daughter, Mary Plina Norris. Charles Norris wrote about Alexander Franklin James, but Howk, very obviously scratched it out and put Sylvester Franklin over the name Alexander. Hmmm? The letter starts out as "Well Folks," similar to some of the letters Bud has that Howk wrote. Did Howk write this? Is this letter authentic or just a ploy to direct people into believing the story that Howk created? We don't know.

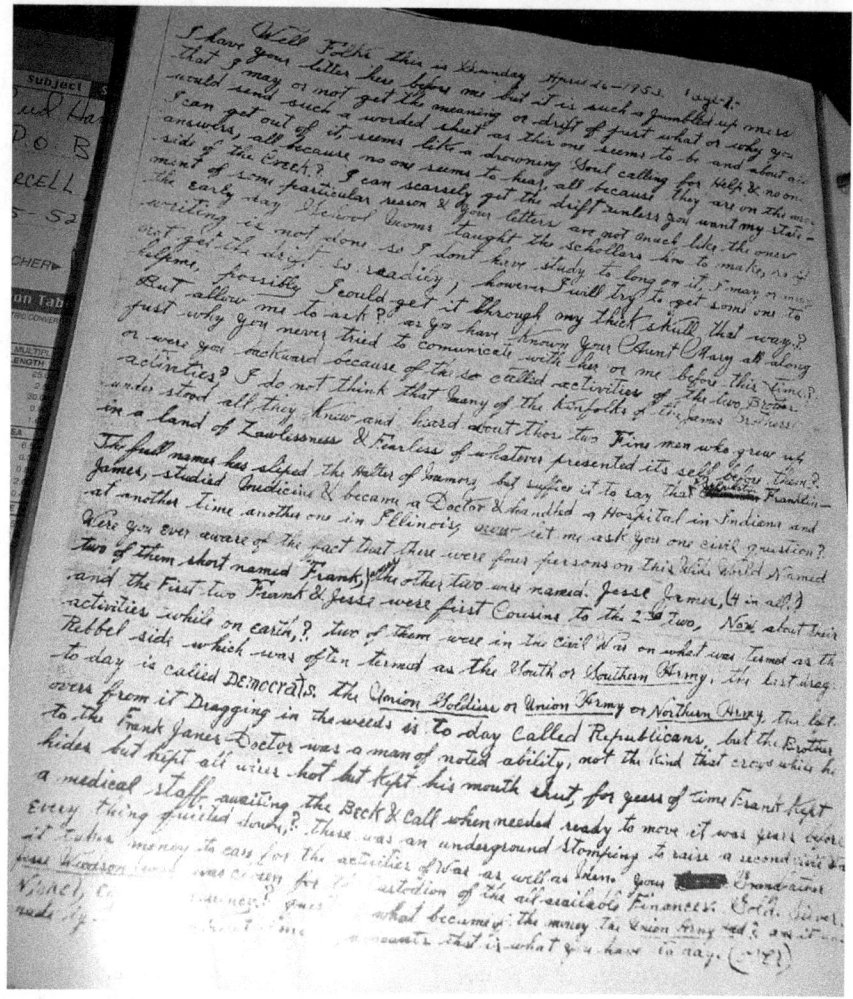

(Charles Norris' letter)

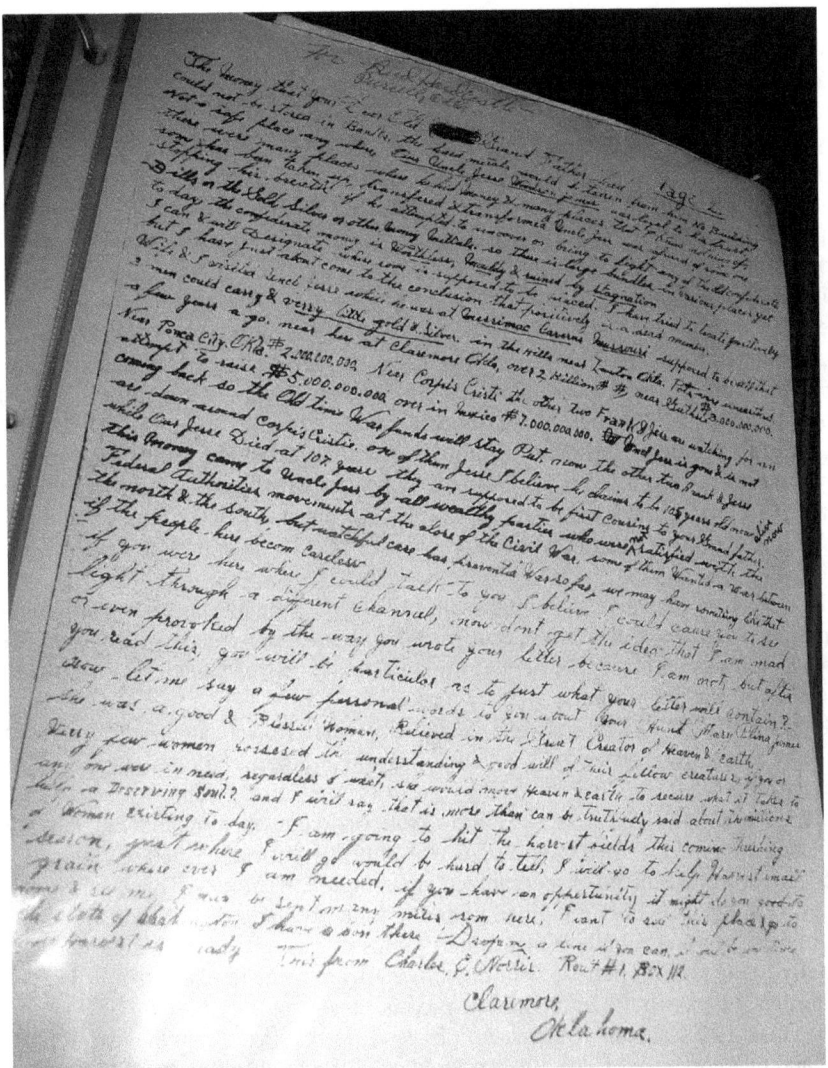

(2nd page)

In 1948 when Jesse came out in Lawton, Oklahoma, Mary Plina Norris, her husband Charles, and son, Henry came to see him. They identified him right away as the real Jesse Woodson James, Mary's uncle. Even Henry stated in a newpaper that "he recognized the 100-year-old city visitor as soon as he saw him here as the former outlaw. "I went to Ellensburg, Washington about 28 years ago with Jess James, Jr. to see his father, and this is the same man," he declared. "I was with him for about nine months then." Norris explained his mother is listed on the Cherokee Indian rolls which show her father's name as "**Alexander Frank James,** the bandit." [476]

The suggestion in the book, Sarah Snow and her son, Lester, and her nephew, Columbus Vaughn published, "This was Frank James" in 1969, leans toward Zerelda as the mother of Alexander Franklin James. They include Joe Vaughn's own story, "The Only True History of the Life of Frank James" at the end of the book. Joe Vaughn outlines it in his book, though very hard to follow. The book has clues, puzzles to solve, and riddles scattered throughout, similar to the way Jesse wrote his stories. I believe it was the clandestine style of writing.

On page 96 of this part of the book that goes into Joe's manuscript, he speaks of "Father", a very honorable man who was in *Lexington*, Kentucky studying to become a minister when he met Zerelda Cole, a girl who was pregnant by **Ebb** Reed. Joe doesn't call Zerelda his mother, but he is calling his Father, Robert James, the minister.

Oddly, in the original 1926 book, "The Only True History of the Life of Frank James," written by Himself, on page 9, he writes, "Father emigrated from the State of Tennessee to Missouri and married Miss Agnes Collins. Three children were born to them, one being William Nelson, alias Jesse James, **myself**, and James Monroe. A short time after Jim was born, Mother died with consumption. Father soon married Miss Malinda Rymel, and to them five children were born, being George, John, Marion, Marguerite and Sarah-Agness."

In the 1926 book, Joe Vaughn writes on page 117-118, "When the Civil War was over Bell (Belle Starr) married Jim Reed, a noted highwayman, who had served under Quantral. Jim Reed and my father were brothers. I was a base begotten child. It was never known to the world. My parents came from Tennessee to Missouri. I was born a short time after they arrived in **Clay County, Missouri**, and the people never knew or thought anything about the child that was called Frank James. My mother was promised to be married secretly to a man named **Edd** Reed. He was killed before I was born, and to save the disgrace, my mother married Robert James and then moved to Missouri. So, the people of this old world did not know that Frank and Jesse James were only half-brothers."

I believe Robert James was the man who raised Joe Vaughn, possibly going under several different names, such as James, Reed, and Vaughn. Joe highly respected Robert James. It was obvious in his writings and I'm sure he was the only father he had known. But who really was his mother, Zerelda or Agnes Collins?

I think we have to go back to *Lexington*, Kentucky where Robert James was studying to become a minister. It was the very center of Kentucky and was the best choice to secure a Freemasonry Lodge. Lexington Lodge No. 25, chartered by the Virginia Grand Lodge was established in 1788. It was the first lodge west of the Allegheny and Cumberland Plateau mountain range. It later became Lexington Lodge No.1 when the Grand Lodge of Kentucky was established in 1800. [477]

In 1854, the KGC organized or reorganized in *Lexington*, Kentucky. This is where James Henry "Wild Henry" Roberts was born and lived up to the time of this reorganization and then headed to Texas before the Civil War. I believe that Robert James was caught up in Freemasonry in *Lexington* and eventually in the KGC. I believe with the moving from place to place, the different names, the different families, he passed the tradition down to his sons.

In "The Hoax That Let Jesse James Live", by Bud Hardcastle, "From the research that William A. Tunstill and Ola conducted since 1981, it looks as if their father Reverend Robert James didn't die as reported by Mr. Sallee. He deserted his family in Missouri, but Frank and Jesse never knew it." [478]

I believe they did know it. Bud at first was teetering on the idea that Joe Vaughn was Frank James, but he told me a story similar to what Joe Vaughn wrote. Bud was seeing evidence that Robert James did not die in California, but remained alive and remarried a lady, but later was killed in the Civil War in Missouri. Bud believed that his sons knew it.

I can't explain the ins and outs of this, but I will address what has been written and what we know.

Thank goodness Bud was given a personal copy of the original book that Lou Kilgore had, given to her from Sarah Vaughn Snow herself, in which explains in greater detail of the family, very well written, but still it is filled with hard to follow information and inconsistencies in the section that Joe Vaughn wrote himself. It seems as though something has been left out. Did Dalton/Jesse require Sarah Vaughn Snow to change a few things, remove things, especially about the family at the last moment, such as the mention of Agnes Collins? Maybe so and that was where the confusion lies, in the family. Maybe Howk pressured her. We don't know.

Joe Vaughn said himself that he was a "base begotten child" and his father was **Edd** Reed in the 1926 book and in the book printed in 1969, it was **Ebb** Reed. Joe was known for a time as Frank

Reed and Ed Reed. The Reed name was used quite often between Frank and Jesse. Joe said that Jesse went by Jim Reed. Joe also brings up the statement that Jim Reed who married Belle Starr was the brother to his father which doesn't seem plausible at all. Was he actually referring to himself and Jesse as brothers under the name of Reed, another cover name for both Frank and Jesse James? Many people believe that Jesse was actually the "Jim Reed" who married Belle Starr.

I can find no evidence that an "Edd Reed" was the brother of James "Jim" Reed who married Belle Starr. Oddly, Joe Vaughn named one of his sons, "**Ebb**," but his first son was named **James R.** Vaughn. His 3rd son was named **William Nelson** Vaughn. You can learn a lot of the sentiment a person has by the naming of their children.

One thing in the book, "Jesse James and the Lost Cause," written in **1961** Howk writes as if Jesse was speaking about his Aunt Zerelda and Uncle Robert James, "He was a Baptist preacher, but she was of another religion. Bless her soul, she was a big woman, and, in many ways, she was a good woman. But I know that even patient Uncle Robert, although a preacher, finally had to desert her and call it quits. He then changed his name to **Reed** but made himself known to his sons." [479] Howk stated he remarried, and his new wife's name was Martha Hines. I find no evidence of that marriage, but we do find something interesting about the double life that Robert James supposedly had.

Joe Vaughn has gone by the names of Edd Reed, Frank James, Frank Vaughn, and Joe Vaughn. He said the James family used many different names in their life spans. "I am the only Frank James that ever existed, and that there never was a real Frank James, that the boy Frank James was none other than **Edd Reed**." [480]

The explanation Joe Vaughn gave as being a "base begotten child," conceived out of wedlock was this in the 1969 book, "They were married (Robert James and his mother) and shortly afterwards, moved to Missouri. To them was born three children I, **William Nelson (alias Jess James)** and James Monroe." Vaughn states, "Father and Zerelda Cole (he doesn't call her Mother) separated and he soon married Malinda Rymel. To them, five children were born, George, John Warren, Marion, Marguerite and Sara **Agnes**." [481]

The 1969 book implies Zerelda as Frank's mother, but then he describes his mother dying before his father did in 1864. Joe Vaughn stated that his father died during the Civil War and that he was buried next to Joe's mother. So, since Zerelda lived for a long time past the Civil War, Zerelda was not his mother, but had to be his stepmother as he told his daughter and Agnes Collins had to be Joe Vaughn's true mother. That would point to Joes' father as Robert James, going by the name of James Vaughn and possibly went by the name of Ebb Reed. It would mean that the preacher led a double-life and had another family in another location. This type of life had to of been related to clandestine activities.

Remember James Vaughn was the 6th pallbearer who no one knew who he was at Jesse's funeral in 1882. It apparently was the real Jesse, using his Father's alias name or it could have been James Monroe Vaughn, the youngest brother mentioned. Howk also stated in one of his letters that James "Jim" Vaughn was at the big reveal in Lawton, Oklahoma in 1948. He died in 1952.

Another thought would be that Agnes Collins was an alias for Jesse Woodson James and Frank James/Joe Vaughn's true mother. There are no records of history or ancestral lines for Agnes Collins.

Joe wrote a lot about his brother, **William Nelson** or "Bad Nelse" (note that he stated that he used the "alias of Jesse James"). Could this be the Jesse R. James that Howk mentioned? It appears that Joe and William played the part of Frank and Jesse at times, but certainly the real Jesse James was heavily involved with them and the family. I believe the two families were heavily intermingled.

In the census records, we find the following family that fits what Joe Vaughn was saying regarding his family.

1840 – James Vaughn (the father) was in **Cole** County, Missouri. James Vaughn's land ran between Jefferson City and Kansas City, Missouri.

*In December **1841** is when Zerelda married Robert Sallee James.*

In Feb. 19, **1845**, we find James Vaughn married **Agnes Collins** in Cole County, Missouri. Agnes Collins has no records, nor a grave marker has not been found.

1850 – James Vaughn is still living in Cole County, age 29 born in 1821 and Agnes Collins, age 22 (born 1828), **William** age 4 (born 1846), a daughter, Rachel, 2 years old. There is no Joe Vaughn listed. A William Swearingame age 16, a laborer was also included in the household. This census was recorded in August 1850 and Robert James supposedly left Zerelda and her children for California in April 1849. * Also, Joe Vaughn mentions in his text that Mr. Swearingame was still close to the Vaughn family during his days in outlawry and beyond when Joe asked him to take him from Cole County, Missouri to Springfield, Green County, Missouri to buy a horse for a trip down to Texas. This was indeed the right family.

*In the **1850** census in Platt Township in Clay County, Robert James was still listed with Serelda even though he was supposedly dead. Listed also was a son, **Franklin** born in **1840**?? Was this Frank James?" Joe Vaughn always said that he was a "base begotten child," born out of wedlock and Robert James married his mother to "save disgrace." Bud found this original census and raised this question. This would fit if Joe's father was really Ebb Reed and Zerelda was his mother and she had the baby in 1840 before her marriage to Robert James in 1841. The other people listed in the household in 1850 were **Jesse R. James** born in 1846 and Susan James, age 9 months.*

Isaac Parmer, father of Allen Parmer also lived in Platt Township in 1850.

***Also, the census record in 1880 shows Ben J. Woodson, who supposedly was the real Frank James, living in Nashville with Mr. Howard reveals Ben's year of birth shown as **1840**.*

1851 – Joseph Frank Vaughn is born to James Vaughn and Agnes Collins. This age for Joseph contradicts numerous dates in Joe's writings.

1851-1852 – In Joe's book, he told of Robert James separating from Zerelda. She remarried to Benjamin Sims in 1852.

1853-1854 – James Monroe Vaughn is born in 1853 to James Vaughn and Agnes Collins. She died in 1853 and James Vaughn (the father) married Malinda Rymel in 1854 in Cooper County, Missouri.

1855 –*Zerelda married Reuben Samuel in 1855.*

1860 - In Moniteau County, Missouri, in the city of California, it lists the Vaughn family exactly as Joe wrote it out in 1925. James Vaughn, age 38 (born 1822), Malinda Rimel/Rymel, age 27 (**born 1833**); children W.N. (William Nelson), age 14 (born 1846); **Joseph Frank, age 9 (born 1851)**; James Monroe, age 7 (born 1853); then lists George and John.

1860 – *In Zerelda's household; Reuben Samuel, Zarilda, Alexander born in 1844, Jesse W. James born in 1848, Susan L. James born in 1850, and Sarah Samuel, born in 1859.*

Go figure. Were the real Frank and Jesse using the names of these families for cover or were they two different families? I believe they all were in on the scheme and were all part of the family. Was James Vaughn, the father really Robert James? It's a possibility. Was Ebb/Edd Reed really Robert James? That's also another possibility. I do believe the only father that Joe Vaughn/Frank James knew and was raised by was Robert James whom Joe called "Father."

Of course, I don't believe the Joseph Frank Vaughn listed in the census was who we're focused on. In Joe Vaughn's manuscript when he was just beginning his writing in 1921, said that he was 78 at the time he was writing his first chapter. This would put his date of birth at 1843 in which supposedly is the real Frank James date of birth; Ola and Jesse stated it was 1843. Joseph Frank

Vaughn, per the census was born in 1851, which would make him too young to be involved in the Civil War as Joe writes in his book. Would Joe Vaughn in Arkansas, just be using his name?

It is unknown if these discrepancies were placed in the census or in the book unintentionally, if a writer/editor made a typo, or if Joe, like his proclaimed brother Dalton/Jesse, intentionally used a myriad of names and stories scattered throughout the book to throw the reader off or reveal hidden secrets in plain sight for his clandestine buddies. Another game of "Hide and Go Seek."

Maybe, its simple. Its all been manipulated to hide the truth, especially if it's about family.

Using what Bud has discovered and Lou Kilgore's personal knowledge of the family and locations of Joe Vaughn, we will not let the discrepancies stand in the way of the truth. Everything coincides with Bud's research except for the information Joe gives us on his family tree. It's always been a touchy subject for Jesse and now it appears to be Frank's philosophy also. We will move on.

Joe Vaughn stated that he was 16 and Jesse was 14 "when they were **treated so badly by the Home Guard.**" (The Only True History-1926). In another section, Joe wrote that he was 16 and Jesse 14 when the **Civil War broke out**. It must have been in 1860 which would place Joe Vaughn, born in 1844 and Jesse or William Nelse, born in 1846. Joe then explains what happened to their father, James Vaughn. At the beginning of the dark days of war, the Dutch neighbors wanted the Vaughn's farm because it was in the center of the colony and choice land. He had 160 acres. The Dutch belonged to the Home Guards who felt that they had full authority to do what they wished.

The Dutch Home Guards wanted to buy the Vaughn's land. If he did not sell to them, they threatened to kill him. James Vaughn had no fear and stood ground. At one point, he was stabbed in the side by Major Dunn of the Home Guard.

Things became heated. General Rosecrans began ordering Home Guard captains to kill and burn all the rebel sympathizer's property. I believe this is when Frank James/Joe Vaughn decided to fight and joined the Missouri State Guard who took part in the siege of Lexington, Missouri.

Major Dunn was later killed in the Battle of Lexington which was led by General Sterling Price in September 1861 along with the Missouri State Guard who sieged upon the Federal military post in the old Masonic College in Lexington. [482] Jesse described this in one of his writings we discussed earlier. Frank James supposedly attended the Masonic College in Lexington when the war broke out.

To enforce harder restrictions on all the Southern sympathizers of their community, an indemnity tax of $1,000 was levied on the Vaughns. The tax collectors drove off a yoke of steers of the Vaughns. Joe Vaughn said he and his brother ransacked the tax collector's property, and the Home Guards went into a rage. James Vaughn was accused of being an accessory in the killing of **Jake Bower.**

This brings me back to the story that Jesse wrote in the little booklet, "Quantrell...In the Civil War. Reminiscences of Civil War Days," by Frank Dalton, published May 20, 1935. He had one story about the Battle of Bowers Mill. Unfortunately, I didn't get a copy from Bud on this particular story, but Jesse does talk about it in the Crittenden Memoirs. It was something important to him. Would this be connected to the killing of Jake Bower? It definitely was connected to Frank and Jesse James, especially if Jesse wrote about it in two books.

Bowers Mill was located in Lawrence County, Missouri, east of Carthage. The operating owners of the mill were George Bowers, and his two brothers. It was a grist mill and the site became a town.

"While other towns were raising Confederate flags and furnishing Confederate officers, Bowers Mill was recruiting for the Union army. On account of the extreme loyalty, Bowers Mill became a marked town, and as war progressed, raids by bands of bushwhackers and Confederate soldiers became a frequent occurrence. In August 1863, during one of General Shelby's raids with a section of his army, he visited Bowers Mill and burned the grist mill and every building in the town except two." [483]

George Bowers had joined the 7th Provincial Militia at the beginning of the war, serving 11 months. He was promoted to the rank of 2nd lieutenant in the 15th Missouri Cavalry, a rather strong Union regiment. He was severely wounded in a fight with bushwhackers on July 4, 1864 and traveled home to recover. He came home to a destroyed mill and a ruined home. The loss was valued at $50,000. [484]

Jesse revisits in his mind the cruelty that was "practiced on both sides." In the Crittenden Memoirs, he expands on the story of the Battle of Bowers Mill. "Some of these stories are true, but the most are not. For instance, it was reported after the Battle of Bowers Mill that Cole Younger, in order to try out a new rifle that we had captured, lined up twelve of the twenty-two prisoners we had captured, and taking careful aim, fired killing two of them and stunning the third. This was even printed in a supposed "history" of the Youngers brothers. There is not a word of truth in it. I was there and know all that took place, and as the twenty-two men were all executed, it was done because they belonged to "Jennison's Jayhawkers," a bunch of rabid Kansas abolitionist, "red legs" we called them, and our bitterest enemies. Jennison however, retaliated by visiting the home of the James brothers."

Jesse again tells the story that his Aunt Zerelda, the mother of Jesse and Frank, their sister, and his own mother and sisters were in the home when Jennison came to visit. "… and taking the women, stripping them to the waist, they tied them to trees, and taking a blacksnake whip that they found in the stable they whipped them until they got tired and then they rode away, leaving the women and girls to be cut down and carried into the house by our negro slaves, who washed and bandaged their bleeding backs and bodies and put them to bed."

With great emotion, he continued, "Yes, sometimes the war was rather cruel! That we afterward exacted a terrible revenge for this inhuman treatment of our mothers and sisters goes without saying. We surrounded Jennison's men when they were in camp one night shortly after that and shot into them from the brush until we ran out of ammunition."

"It was said afterwards that we killed or disabled over two-thirds of them. And so it went. First one side being the aggressor and then the other." [485]

*Note – Charles R. Jennison "was considered the most brutal and unscrupulous of the jayhawkers. He served as a Union colonel and as a leader of Jayhawker militias during the American Civil War, until being dishonorably discharged for murder and robbery." [486]

This horrific event against the women of Jesse's life must have occurred in the Summer of 1864. It was noted that "Jennison made a foray into Platte and Clay Counties, Missouri against bushwhackers committing depredations in Kansas during the summer of 1864." [487] This is when Price's Raid became a must through Arkansas, Missouri, and Kansas. Quantrill Raiders took part.

Jennison hit the Homefront. I believe that this was the time that all the men were gone, and all the women came together for greater protection. In this group of women, Jesse listed his mother and sister, separate from his Aunt Zerelda who he said was Jesse and Frank's mother along with Jesse and Frank's sister. The women and the sisters were together when Jennison attacked their home in 1864. Could the mother of Jesse as he describes here, refer to Mollie Dalton who was possibly Zerelda's sister? It seems as though these families were all connected in relationship, the James/Samuel/Dalton families and the Vaughn family. Joe Vaughn stated that his stepmother was Zerelda, sometimes called "Mother" and then he had another stepmother, Malinda Rymel Vaughn during this time in 1864 when trouble came for his father.

Everyone has their own view of who's who and what the truth is, but sadly, I don't think everyone knows the whole truth. Trying to make sense out of this whole story is impossible. There are so many roads and rabbit holes to follow.

This is just my belief. I have no solid proof to back this up, but I believe James Vaughn, was the father of the two families spoken here: the James and Vaughns. I believe James Vaughn and Ebb Reed were cover names for Robert James. They shared a bond, especially during the Civil War that could not be broken. Both the real Frank and Jesse were in no way orphans as depicted when their father went to California. They were raised well in Bible knowledge and received an excellent education from both families. Frank James loved Shakespeare and Jesse loved the Bible, carrying it at all times and reading it to his raider buddies and gang members. Jesse had an excellent literary ability and a large vocabulary. They would have had to receive this type of training from both a father and a mother who was knowledgeable in the Bible and education. If you remember, Frank James was going to the Masonic College in Lexington until the war broke out.

Apparently, Frank and Jesse were living at both residences during the war; in Clay County and in Cole County, about 150 miles apart. The Union soldiers and the Jayhawkers (Redlegs) had their eye on James Vaughn though, even though he was trying to remain neutral. He was a peaceable man, a preacher man who had turned farmer. They were watching him closely. James was summoned to court to answer charges of feeding bushwhackers. He was found innocent.

Very late in the game, James Vaughn joined the militia, in the Fall of 1864, just to stay alive, but being on duty for only a week, he was shot and killed while returning from picket duty. This was October 9, 1864. "He was laid away to rest at the Mt. Lebanon cemetery, beside "my mother," Joe Vaughn said. [488] This would be the Old Lebanon Cemetery in McGirk, Moniteau County, Missouri.

A few days after he was buried, a squad of Dutch Home Guards rode into the field, tied plow harnesses around Frank and Jesse's necks (Joe Vaughn and William Nelse) and drove them like yearling calves. They were in the presence of their stepmother, sisters and brothers. Their stepmother would have been Malinda Rymel. Malinda filed for a pension in 1868, which reveals James Vaughn was with the 1343 Ensign Missouri Militia.

Joe blamed the barbaric behavior of the war to the State Militia and the Home Guard of Missouri who were too cowardly to fight for their country. They robbed from the Missourians while the men were off to war.

In Joe Vaughn's manuscript – (Speaking of Jesse) "My brother would not allow a word about **our** mother. He loved **his** mother, and the way Mother was treated caused us to do many things that we would have left undone." [489] This suggests they had the same mother. Would this be Zerelda, Mary, or Agnes? Joe had a tendency to use the word "Mother" respectfully towards his mother and stepmothers, as he did his father or stepfathers. We don't know really who he is referring to, but we do know the real Jesse Woodson James was indeed very protective of his mother.

Who knows what happened to their real mother? We have the story put out in books on what happened to Zerelda. Jesse's writing in the memoirs of how his mother, during the war, received such harsh treatment, was put in jail and his sister Mary died. We learn of the abuse his mother sustained and the Pinkerton bomb that blew a portion of her arm off and killed her son, Archie.

In an article, from the JCHS journal (Jackson County Historical Society, Jackson County, Missouri) in June 1976, it states that Joe Vaughn's stepmother lost her arm by an incident with the Home Guard, no mention of the Pinkertons. Was this another occurrence with another woman such a Malinda Rymel or was this a clarification of what happened to Zerelda? Was he speaking of Zerelda as his stepmother which coincides with what he told his daughter, Sarah? We just don't know.

To any son who has a loving mother, their protection goes beyond the physical. Being rebels, being outlaws, they did everything in their power to keep her from hurting. I believe they put their mother in Jesse and Frank's "witness protection program." That is why the truth regarding their mother will never be known in its entirety.

In Joe's book he said, "After Centralia, Frank James, Clell Miller, Oll and George Shepherd, and **Jim Reed** hid out in the Kentucky mountains." [490] His father, James Vaughn was killed the month after, October 1864. After his father was killed, Joe/Frank James went to Fort Smith, went into Indian Territory and lived with the Indians for 15 years.

In Indian Territory, he spent most of his time in the Choctaw Nation in the Kimichia Valley. He had a store in Culla Chihi, a little village on Riddle Prairie in the Choctaw Nation which was six miles west of Hackett City which was 20 miles southwest of Fort Smith. Many people would bring their racehorses to Culla to race. He also drove cattle.

He fell in love several times and had three children that we know of with the beautiful Indian maidens of Indian Territory and one we know of in the Sioux Nation. He loved their way of life and defended them to no end. They in return defended and protected him. He wrote that the Indians were "wronged and forgotten people."

He never betrayed anyone he says. They were never guilty of insulting women. Joe Vaughn also began to be in the business in helping traders, especially for the Indians around Fort Smtih.

This was the time he met Hamp Williams. Joe writes about him in his book. Hamp Williams was born in 1858, lived in Hacket City, Arkansas. His full name was Hansford Alonzo Hamp Williams. His father, James Alexander Williams was the news editor of the Hackett City "Horseshoe." Hamp later lived in Hot Springs, was a war time food distributor in World War I, best friends with Herbert Hoover, and served three terms as a director of the Federal Reserve Bank of St. Louis. He was a senator and president of the National Hardware Dealers Association. He became a grand master of the Free and Accepted Masons of Arkansas. [491] He also was a 32nd degree Mason and a Knight Templar. [492]

Hamp's father, James Alexander Williams (1836-1889) and mother, Malvina Flanagan Kelley (1840-1920) (born in Missouri) married in 1858 in Crawford County, Arkansas. James grew up in Jasper, Arkansas. They moved to Hunt County, Texas in 1862. He enlisted that year with Martins's Cavalry (Fifth Partisan Rangers) and became a captain in Good's Battalion Texas Cavalry, Company A, stationed at Camp Earle. After the war they left to go to Owensboro, Kentucky. They came back through Arkansas and settled in Sorrells Prairie in Sebastain county, Arkansas in 1866. He was elected as a representative of Sebastian county in the State Legislature two times.

The Williams family went back to Hunt Texas in 1867. In 1868, they moved to Griffith Mountain in Sebastain County, Arkansas on the William Ramsey place who were kin. They moved quite frequently and in 1871, they were in Fort Smith and sold goods then moved again.

Joe Vaughn said Mr. Williams "always seemed like a father to me." "He is the man that educated Frank James." [493] Joe said he went to school with his children. This statement doesn't fit in here because James' first child, Hamp was so much younger than Joe Vaughn. Maybe he was referring to another type of school or college.

James' grandfather, Hansford Williams (1811-1894) served in the Confederacy in Arkansas. He was living in Texas, Hacket City and Cole, Arkansas. The family came from Overton and Weakley, Tennessee into Texas near Camp Arbuckle, Texas. James' great grandfather, Thomas Nathaniel Williams (1775-1848) served in the Mexican War with Texas Military in Victoria, Texas.

It's a possibility that since Joe Vaughn/Frank was in this particular territory after the war, it must have been James Alexander Williams who taught Joe the art of surveyorship and drew him in the secret societies he belonged to. James Alexander Williams had masonic emblems on his tombstone and his son was heavily involved in Freemasonry. Joe Vaughn/Frank James' tombstone, as well as the cemetery, reveals strong ties to the clandestine society.

Also, another tidbit to pass along that may mean nothing, but in a video tape that Bud has, Ola Everhard said that Quantrill was in Arkansas after the war and he and his wife had a daughter. The daughter ended up marrying a "Williams." Would this be James Alexander Williams' family? We don't know. Ola also stated in writing that Judge George Farris who knew Jesse well, told her this and they ended up moving to Tolbert, Oklahoma.

If Joe Vaughn was indeed Frank James, he was also on the move during his outlawry days with his brother, Jesse James, whether it be William Nelson Vaughn, Jesse R. James or Jesse Woodson James. I believe their home base was in Indian Territory, but they were in and out everywhere.

Joe said that him and his brother were on the run and they stayed in **Holden**, *Johnson County*, Missouri. They had a $10,000 reward for shooting a man in self-defense. Joe said Jesse became a peddler, going by the name of **Jim Reed**. I believe this must have been the time that Jesse got into the freighting business. Frank invested in a coal mine, going by **Ed Reed**. Joe's partner, Mr. Green was going to hire Jim Reed to help his family move to Kansas and have Joe Vaughn buy his portion of the mine. Joe turned around and sold all his mining interest to a neighbor and they moved on, possibly back into Indian Territory.

Interestingly, William Nelson Vaughn was also living near Warrensburg, (Washington Township) *Johnson County*, which was 70 miles from California, Missouri to the West and 19 miles to **Holden** where Joe Vaughn said Frank and Jesse were. In 1870, William Nelse was with a wife, Nancy and a daughter, Susan. William was a "railroad hand." A marriage certificate is on file in the county of Moniteau, Missouri on April 15, 1867, marriage to Nancy Wisdom. She also went by the name of Nancy Elizabeth Wisdom. Nancy was living in Cooper, 30 miles away from California, Missouri in the same county as Moniteau. Nancy is the descendant of the Lees and the Buford/Beaufords. The Wisdoms also marry into the **Collins**, Lewis, and Bradley family. The **Collins** marry into the Taylor family.

J. Frank Dalton told Sarah Snow, that Frank James in Fletcher, Oklahoma was actually a stand-in for Frank, who turned himself in after Jesse James' death in 1882. The stand-in's name was Sam **Collins**. Was he related to Agnes Collins or to the family of William Nelse Vaughn's wife? Hold on to your seat if you haven't already fell out of the chair.

During their outlaw days, Jesse, Frank and the three Younger brothers were in and out of Arkansas, Colorado, Missouri, Texas, and Indian Territory during the years of 1866-1879. Joe Vaughn had written in his book that he was meeting up with **Jesse James**, Cole, Bob, and Jim Younger, George Shepherd, Clell Miller, Jim Cummins, and **Jim Reed**.

They were accused of holding up a stagecoach south of Eureka Springs, Arkansas. On the Newton County, Arkansas Chamber of Commerce site, an article states that "Legend generally holds that the James brothers came here to cool their heels between robberies and maintained a low profile while frequently using eastern Madison County and western Newton County as a resting place. After Jesse was killed, Frank worked out a surrender agreement and dropped from the public eye. About the same time, Joe Vaughn settled on a farm at Wayton where he kept to himself and raised his family. There were, according to family historians, some in the county who knew his identity, but in the mountain tradition he was left alone. One of those to whom he revealed his identity was "Yank" Sutton, who worked with him surveying all over the county. Just before he died, Joe gave his family a short autobiography. Descendants say a look alike was persuaded to surrender for Frank James and he changed his name and moved to Newton County." [494]

Sam Collins went through the trial of Frank James and was acquitted. It was all worked out so that the real Frank James could have a peaceful life. I believe this is why Jesse was so angry with Frank. When the old man, the mysterious visitor at the Vaughn and Snow home in Arkansas, was leaving the small community, he said to Joe Vaughn's son, Ebb, "You be sure and tell that Joe Vaughn to try to work some in his old days, as he sure didn't do any in his younger days." [495] Jesse continued working for the KGC and building up a huge empire for the south, while Frank was enjoying the good life since 1885 in the Boston Mountains. But per the family, Frank was still doing lots of things in his line of work as a surveyor. For whom?? I think we know, and I believe he was overseeing the treasure in those mountains. His family describe Joe Vaughn living his life out in Arkansas, not in peace, but in "fear and restlessness." [496]

Sam Collins continued life as Frank, but it is more complicated than you think. He was paid $35,000 to take on the life of Frank James. He was given maps to find treasure in the Keechi Hills in Oklahoma. Bud believed that he was paid as a sentinel to watch over the Oklahoma area as well.

He bought land outside of Fletcher which the "Hills' were directly north of his place. It took him a long time to find the treasure that we know he found. He dug up $6,000 close to Buzzard Roost. If he was the real Frank James, he would have known exactly where it was and could have gone right to it.

Bud gave me a gift by taking me to where "Frank James" house was outside of Fletcher and showed me the place where the hole was dug to uncover the money near Buzzard's Roost.

The book, "Cow By the Tail", by Jesse James Benson, the author stated that he had evidence and knowledge that after they gave up outlawry, the James boys settled in the Ozark Mountains under the name of the Vaughn Brothers. Frank and Jesse were good friends of his father back in

Kentucky. Benson was born in 1864 and Jesse James said to his dad, "If you name the kid after me I'll give him five dollars in gold."

"Dad was agreeable, as he liked Jesse. Mother kept the five dollars for me for five years, but then we spent it."

"Frank and Jesse James visited our place about twice a year. We children did not know anything about their being bandits, as they went by the name of the **Vaughn brothers**. They would stay five or six days. When they rode up, if a stranger happened around, they told him they was looking for a place to settle down. My dad and them would hold long talks to theirselves. They never made any display of arms and took pains to talk to strangers like they was afraid of outlaws and Injuns – especially outlaws. They never slept in the house. They camped outside in a concealed place, not by the spring, and every night or so they would change camps. This puzzled me. But I didn't suspect them because they acted kind to everybody. Dad subscribed regular to the Courier Journal, printed in Louisville by Henry Waterson, and he kept the papers till they come, and they spent a lot of time reading them papers. I am almost sure there was thousands of dollars buried on our old homestead somewhere. After Jesse were killed, Dad said, I don't know where their cash is buried. It might be here. They never did say.

"They both was riding their thoroughbred Kentucky horses last time I seen them. Jesse's horse were a gray named Skyrock and Frank's a sorrel named Jim Malone. Jesse had a dark or black beard and Frank's were sandy. Neither ever shaved. They wore long coats and high leather boots. There were two sets of saddle pockets in their saddles. I never did see them with a Winchester or gun of any kind, but each packed two silver-mounted pistols that I admired very much. When they come, they used to give me a gold piece, so I were always glad to see them come. Jesse James were a man with a big kind heart. Dad never told no one that the Vaughns that visited our home were the James brothers, or that I were named after one of them." [497]

This story is confirmed in a news article in the *Des Moines Tribune*; March 3, 1964; "Iowan's Problem, Frank James' Kin or Not?" It was a story put out before the new book was published by the family of Joe Vaughn. An interview was conducted by Herb Owens with Columbus Vaughn as the subject. Columbus Vaughn stated, "My information is that around 1872 two brothers came to Wayton and settled under the names of Bill and Joe Vaughn: at first spelled "Von".

In the original manuscript, Joe Vaughn talks about his brother Bill, also going by the name of William Nelson Vaughn, "Bad Nelse," alias Jesse James. His brother was about the same age as Jesse. His brother Jesse/Bill/William Nelson didn't stay around too long, but Joe Vaughn stayed and raised a family in Arkansas, believing it was in 1885 that he settled in the Ozarks.

If he was Frank James, we find Frank, just 5 years earlier, under the alias of Ben J. Woodson in 1880 on the census in District 23 (Nashville), Davidson County, Tennessee with a wife Fannie, and a 2 year old son, Robert. This Ben was listed as 40 years old making his birth as 1840, just as the census showed in 1850. It also showed that living in the home was Geo. D. Howard, brother-in-law, age 32, which would indicate he was born in 1847, which would correlate with Jesse's birth. Under Howard's name was his wife Josie and children Charles, in which we know Jesse's son used that name and his daughter, Mary.

In the 1880, William Nelson Vaughn was living in Pettis, *Dresden* County, Missouri, with wife and three children and was a "jeweler." *Dresden* was the community that Jesse's Texas Ranger Captain John Sparks was living in Texas.

Then in 1910, William Nelson Vaughn is found in Roc Roe, Monroe County, Arkansas and was a laborer as a "boat builder." In 1920, he was a "farmer," dying in 1925, supposedly buried in Roc Roe Cemetery in Monroe County, Arkansas, but there is no grave marker.

William Nelson Vaughn was apparently a "jack of all trades". I believe he was a real person, taken on the identity of Jesse James in various degrees. Was he the real Jesse James or Jesse R. James? We don't know.

The story that the Vaughns and Snows tell, says that Frank was living his last 40 years in the Ozarks at Wayton, Arkansas. After Jesse was supposedly killed in 1882, Frank went underground to Hackett, Arkansas, and then to Wayton. He took on the name of Joe Vaughn, and married Nancy Richardson, raising nine children. He died in 1926. Years before he died, he spent most of his time writing "The Only True Story of Frank James." Lester Snow, Sarah Vaughn Snow's son gave rights to Lou to publish the original manuscript, but the written story in a letter has disappeared and she didn't get that opportunity.

Speaking with Lou on November 6, 2023, reaching the age of 90, she told me that she still is not 100 percent on Joe Vaughn's story. There are still a lot of "I don't knows." She said the Snows and Vaughns were very honest people and she believed what they had told her.

Lou Kilgore knew the family of Joe Vaughn's well. Her sister-in-law was Joe Vaughn's 3rd great granddaughter. Lou heard many of the family stories and spoke with Sarah (Vaughn) Snow and her brother Ebb. They took Lou to the old homeplace where only the foundation was left. They showed Lou all the incredible sights around the property that indicated very clearly that it was a fortress with symbols engraved in the landscape of the KGC. They took her to the cemetery where he was buried and revealed things to her that has not been made public.

Lou in turn took Bud to the homeplace and the cemetery. Bud described Joe Vaughn's gravesite. The tombstone held a masonic emblem. The cemetery gate itself was made of stone with pillars on each side of the entry way. It was decorated with an inlay of stone and pebbles in a design of turtles. Bud said it was obvious that you're in a place where the people buried there were part of the secret society. It also had the "all-seeing eye" included in stone. Joe Vaughn was a Mason, joining the Buffalo Lodge #366.

Lou took Bud to where the house was located, but only the foundation remained. Vaughn built his home himself and laid out hand-hewn planks of wood for his flooring, cut himself and shaved down smoothly with a horizontal ax. It was called a puncheon floor and underneath the flooring and the joists, was a rough dugout cellar. He would lift one of the planks to access the cellar, but most importantly to access his escape route. There was a drainage ditch running from the cellar to outside in heavy brush, meandering a ways toward a hidden cave. The ditch also provided a route to a creek. Once he could make it to the creek, no one could find him.

Bud was able to locate the ditch that was under his house and followed it to a 7'-8' tall rock wall that covered an entrance to a hideout cave behind his house. There were a few symbols there, but nothing substantial. It was a small cave.

(Joe Vaughn and his surveyor equipment)

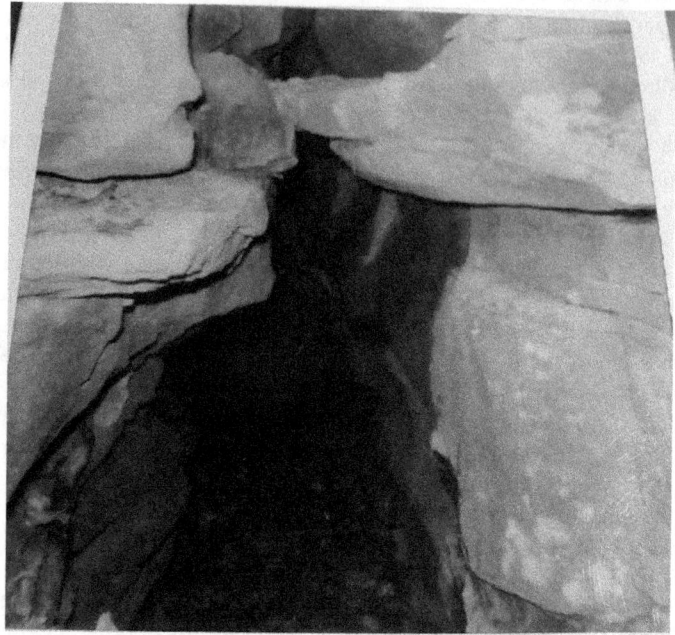
(Tunnel behind Joe Vaughn's house)

In Joe's house, he left a row of chinking out between the logs in his cabin at eye level, which enabled him to see from every direction.

Lou wrote an excellent article on Joe Vaughn in the newspaper. She has had offers of doing two documentaries for PBS and several authors wanted to write her book, but she was not through with her research of Joe Vaughn. She had to have the whole picture. She never really felt it was complete and is still researching. She said the family had pictures of Joe Vaughn's mother, that is said to be Zerelda which leads credence to the story. Lou said there's something there, but she just doesn't have the whole picture. She knows the who but doesn't know the why.

The frustration that Joe Wood felt, hits hard on Lou, Bud, and me when searching for the truth on Jesse's family. It's frustrating and yet again, Jesse wins with his secrets kept intact. He didn't want us to know.

In a newspaper article that Bud had when Frank and Jesse were on the run, it states that Frank James was described as square-jawed and stocky built. In the book, "Jesse James and the Lost Cause," by Howk, he speaks of Jesse and the KGC hiring a "stooge" Sam Collins to play the part of Frank James. Howk called him "Big Nose Frank" who lived in Fletcher, Oklahoma and had brown eyes. Some news articles, one in particular out of Henrietta, Clay County, Texas that I found in the museum there said he had black eyes.

In the news article, "The Rise and Fall of Jesse James," by Robertus Love in *Tulsa World*, August 28, 1925 described Frank James, using the name of B. J. Woodson in Nashville, as having an angular face with blue eyes. Clearly, these were two different men.

The famous cedar barrel factory picture, taken in 1880 in Nashville that Bud had a copy of, shows the men designated as Jesse James and Frank James. Bud believes this was the real Frank and Jesse as many others do. They appear to be the same men in the threesome picture. Frank has the angular and square jaw described.

Jesse James appears, fifth from the left, sitting, in a group of employees at a Nashville, Tennessee, cedar bucket factory in 1880. Frank James also appears, fourth from the right, standing, on the back row. This is believed to be the last photo of Jesse James a

(Nashville photo at the cedar barrel factory)

(Jesse, Mom, and Frank)

When Lou published her story in the newspaper and highlighted Joe Vaughn's picture in his latter days, it shows the angular, square-jawed man.

(Lou's Newspaper article (courtesy of Lou Kilgore))

When the Frank James who lived in Fletcher was asked about his life as an outlaw, he answered, "That was another life." Indeed, it was.

Zerelda made several trips to Fletcher, with one of those trips as her last. She passed away on the train back to Missouri in 1911 with Annie Ralston James by her side. Zerelda had more ties and connections to the Frank James who lived in Fletcher. Frank and Annie moved back to Kearney in 1913. Bud had said that one of the things that this Frank James inherited was the Samuel's farm.

Bud found that the Gossetts had bought Frank's place in Fletcher, Oklahoma after this period. Frank requested his son, Robert to come operate the Samuel's farm because his health was declining. Frank died on February 18, 1915 in Washington Township in Clay County, Missouri. Bud received a certified copy of Alexander Franklin James' death certificate, labeled "Registered **No. 33**." His date of birth is shown as January 10, 1843 born in Clay County, Missouri. He was cremated.

Robert, the son and his wife Mae inherited the farm, staying on the Samuel's Farm until 1947 and then moved to Excelsior Springs. [498]

Bud had some of the letters from the Gossetts to Robert and Mae, sending them some of the royalties off of the property in Fletcher. Bud was on the trail of the Gossetts. Just who were they? Bud went to Missouri. In Independence, Missouri at Hill Park Cemetery where Frank James' ashes are buried, on the other side of him were the Gossetts. The nearest Gossett grave was Ann Elizabeth Gossett (1850-1880) who married William Moberly Hill.

William Moberly Hill was the uncle to Annie Ralston, Frank James' wife. Mary (Hill) Ralston was Annie's mother. So there definitely was a connection between the Collins, the James, the Vaughns, and Ralstons. Did the real Frank James marry Annie Ralston or had that always been Sam Collins? Another mystery to solve. We know that the real Frank James in Nashville was with his wife and son, Robert, born February 2, 1877 in Nashville, Tennessee. Was Robert "Little Frank" as Jesse called him?

Bud told me, just like everybody else, for a long, long time, he didn't believe the story of Joe Vaughn being Frank James. Things just didn't add up. Toward the end of writing this book, Bud believed that he is swayed more into believing Joe Vaughn was indeed the real Frank James.

Joe Vaughn was also a writer for news articles, in different newspapers and called himself, "Rattle Head" or "Hill Billy." One article of local gossip was signed "Rattle Head" and was in the *Osceola* Times: April 2, 1898.

Bud and Lou went to many locations connected to Joe Vaughn and talked to many Oldtimers who knew Joe Vaughn and they had no doubts that he was Frank James.

Just like Jesse, Joe Vaughn/Frank pondered upon his life towards the end, "there are crimes laid to the James boys that they never committed." He wrote that if they were left alone, they would have been different men. He never thought he had a bad disposition. "My brother, he was called Bad Nelse, that was the name he went by, was a bad man. No fear of beast or men. Kill was his aim."

Joe's last words, "Let me say to the young boys of today, don't ever start out through life wanting revenge. Don't ever think about leading the life of a desperado, for it is not a pleasant life to live. It is true, I have made my escape, but do not ever undertake the things that I have done." [499]

Who was Joe Vaughn? I wish we could clarify it in this chapter and be confident in our findings, but its just not meant to be. He had a hand in it all, but what hand he was dealt and what hand he played, is still a mystery in the Dead man's hand.

"So exact is his information."

-(Corpus Christi Times - June 30, 1939)

Chapter Twenty-Two: Word of Mouth/Word of Honor

Author/Lecturer/Politician/Movie Man/Preacher/Teacher

Author

He loved to talk. He loved to write. When Bud went to visit Francena Turilli on May 15, 1993 she said Jesse was a History book within himself; very intelligent man, self-educated, spent time in England, South America, and Canada. He had a lot to say.

In 1882, when Jesse faked his death, it was the first time that Jesse was able to take a hold of the reins and write his own story. Many times, he would tell the Turillis', Joe Wood, and Ola Everhard that the writers got a lot of Jesse's history wrong. It was time to set the record straight.

The first indication of his career as a writer was when he told Joe Wood that he used to write stories for the St. Louis Globe Democrat during the St. Louis World's Fair in 1904. Jesse knew exactly where the newspaper office was located on 6th and Pine. This was the same newspaper that Joe Wood wrote for, and indeed that was where the newspaper office was located at that time but had moved in 1931 to its new location.

The writer is unable to find any articles by Frank Dalton or John Franklin in the St. Louis Globe-Democrat, the aliases he used in many of his articles, but certainly he could of used others. Many articles did not reveal the author's name. Other newspapers do reveal interviews with Frank Dalton and stories he provided that were published.

A journalist, Bryon Buzbee, from the Corpus Christi Times, June 30, 1939 described Dalton as weighing 182 pounds, "and is proud, in his casual sort of way, of his 5 feet, 10 ½ inches, and his mop of white hair that falls over his shoulders. The hair formerly dropped to his waist, but when he broke his leg in 1937, it was cut off while he was in a Gladewater hospital.

"Dalton has proof of all his statements, too. But the way he talks leave little room for doubt, so exact is his information." "He doesn't look within 25 years of his age. He talks like a veteran of the lecture platform." [500]

Major John Edwards had to of been an inspiration to Jesse by his writing ability. Edwards was part of Joseph Shelby's Iron Brigade. He definitely was tied to Jesse in many ways. John Edwards wrote for many newspapers around Missouri and was co-founder of the Kansas City Times. He wrote about the James Gang and their brazen leader, Jesse James.

Jesse had an opportunity to tell his stories in many ways. One of his greatest accomplishments was to write articles in the Crittenden Memoirs. Of course, he was using the name of Frank Dalton to write these and not revealing that he was the real Jesse. Dewitt Travis and Jesse met with Hugh Crittenden, son of Governor Crittenden, to begin the process in 1935. The newspapers all said they had never met before, but Mitch Graves who had known Jesse and Dewitt and who corresponded with Ola told Bud that they all knew each other. Dewitt told Ola, "When we got to Kansas City and went to the home of Hugh Crittenden, someone else let us in the door and when Hugh came walking in he said, "Old Jess, I'll be damned, ain't you dead yet?" Then walking up to Jesse with a smile on his face, took hold of his hand and looking at him said, "Well, old Jesse, my goodness alive, you don't look much older than you used to." [501]

Jesse mainly wrote, as Dalton, stories of Jessie James in his days with Quantrill and stories of his outlaw days, claiming to be amongst these men. He never, never wrote of his clandestine activities.

Crittenden Memoirs, by Frank Dalton, "It is of no difference how I know. That I do know is sufficient. There are lots of incidents of those days, however, that have never been told at all or greatly misrepresented. This was unavoidable, as we, who knew the truth, were necessarily silent and for obvious reasons, while the chroniclers of that time took the few facts they could muster and let their imagination do the rest. As a whole the men of Quantrill were a secretive bunch and would tell nothing. But the need of secrecy has passed as to the things I shall tell about here." [502]

During this time of writing the stories for Crittenden, possibly the same publisher printed a small booklet of articles penned by Frank Dalton with the subjects of Quantrill, the Civil War, the Battle of Bowers Mill and John Younger, the outlaw and peace officer. It was twelve pages long with Frank Dalton's picture on the cover. Bud had a copy, possibly got it from the University of Oklahoma. I was fortunate to find the booklet online on "Buckingham Books", a dealer in rare and first-edition books. The title, "Quantrell…In the Civil War. Reminiscences of Civil War Days," by Frank Dalton, published May 20, 1935. This particular book had been sold, but it had a personal note to whomever bought the booklet in Jesse's own handwriting.

(Jesse's booklet, 1935)

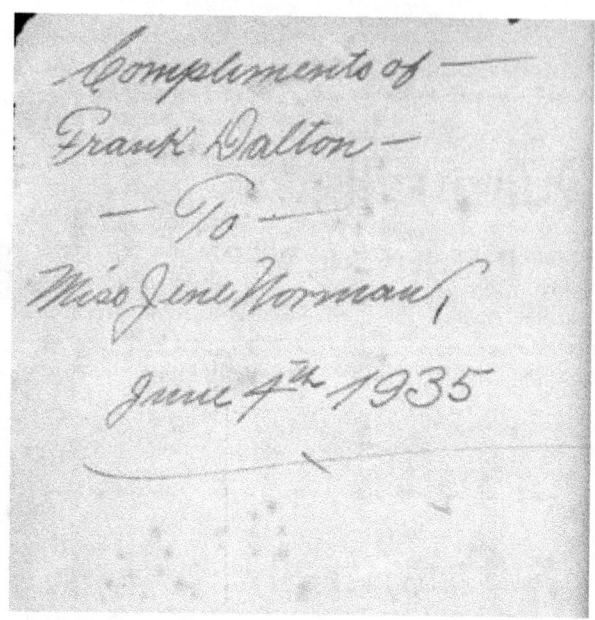

(Personal note from Jesse inside book)

Jesse stated that he wrote for the Daily Picayune Newspaper in New Orleans using the alias of Frank Dalton or John Franklin.

Bud had an article from *The Cattleman Magazine*, Vol. XXXI, June 1944 in which Frank Dalton wrote "Military Escort For A Trail Herd." His writing skills were very polished and was an extremely interesting article, very well written. He described himself as enlisting in Quantrell's militia at 15 years old. He does not reveal he was Jesse James but stated that he later joined the U.S. Army and was part of the Army patrol on a major cattle drive taking beef from South Texas to Fort Reno in Indian Territory. The beef was being provided to the Indians on the reservations and the soldiers overseeing them.

Jesse wrote that he was in charge of a dozen soldiers to ensure their safe travels. For the government, he purchased 2,000 head of young steers from the King-Kennedy Ranch in the Spring of 1873. He hired a good trail boss, Doc Manahan from Fairfield, Texas to handle the cattle and the cowboys. Dalton's story was filled with the trail traumas such as the weather, rustlers, swindlers and wild rivers. He knew the country well.

Garland Farmer, publisher of the Henderson Times in Henderson, Texas took Jesses' stories and forwarded it to newspapers such as St. Joseph News Press, The Whitewright Sun in Whitewright, Texas, Evansville Press in Evansville, Indiana, The Paris News, The San Bernardino County Sun, Arizona Republic, The Akron Beacon Journal, Long Beach Press-Telegram, The Salt Lake Tribune, and The Montana Standard. Garland was so intrigued by Dalton's stories.

Garland Roscoe Farmer was very well thought of in the world of journalism not only in East Texas, but around the world. His obituary in The Kilgore New Herald, July 19, 1956 stated he was a Mason. He died at the young age of 59. His son worked for the Counterintelligence Corps in Germany. [503]

Farmer had known Jesse for 20 years while he was in East Texas, mentioning Henderson, Longview, and Gladewater. It was in March 28,1948 when Farmer wrote the article, "Frank Dalton Finds Peace" in the Houston Chronicle Magazine. Jesse had not come out with his identity yet, only that he was a past Quantrill Raider and had just gained a military pension as a Confederate soldier.

"With long hair, tied in a knot and tucked up beneath his white 10-gallon hat; mustache and goatee that reminds you of such frontiersmen as Buffalo Bill, Frank Dalton has crammed more excitement and adventure in one lifetime than a dozen average persons." This pretty much sums up Jesse to a "T". Even the way he wore his hair in a knot above his head, tucking it under his hat. This picture, which has been authenticated as Jesse, shows the way he wore it and wore it in 1948 when he didn't have his hair down.

(Bob Ford and Jesse James)

Garland Farmer writes a story told to him by J. Frank Dalton. The man claimed he was the Dalton Brothers' uncle. He said the Dalton boys began to get in trouble with the law after a Faro game in Silver City, New Mexico, the old stomping ground of Billy the Kid. Dalton said Bob, Grat, and Emmett went back to Oklahoma and made their headquarters in a cave near the South Canadian River in the Creek Indian Territory. They were joined by old friends, Bryant, Newcomb, Powers, Doolin, and Broadwell. This may have been near Belle. "Men shot straight those times" per Dalton.

Garland Farmer finally stated in an article, "Although I have known him intimately for about 20 years, of course I cannot say what his true name is, but I do believe he knows more about the James, Dalton and Younger families than any other living person." [504] Farmer also said, Dalton never seemed to have much money.

J. Frank Dalton's stories were incredible that Garland Farmer published. In 1941, Farmer published a story that he had written, told to him by Dalton regarding Quantrell. It was in The Whitewright Sun out of Whitewright, Texas (between Sherman and Bonham, Tx) in August 7, 1941. This story was of great interest to Garland Farmer and so to authenticate it, he wrote the words of Jesse himself, even though he did not know his real identity, or did he?

"Quantrill thought he had a rightful cause for everything he did while carrying on his guerilla warfare in behalf of the South," Frank Dalton said, "and when he was repudiated by the South's leaders, he went right on fighting in their behalf. Of course, Quantrill, and the remainder of us, did things in the hot rush of the battle we might not have done if given time to think them through, but Quantrill was blamed with many things he did not do, and his own men did things he never knew about nor would he have countenanced."

"My Chief Quantrill was a man you both loved and feared. His tall, angular form towered above and inspired you, but his piercing eyes looked a hole through you and you dared not tell him a lie.

The public was allowed to believe he had died in Kentucky at the end of the Civil War, because there was a price on his head, just as there was on the rest of us who fought beside him, but he recovered and for the second time changed his name and moved on. I can't give you the name he used this time, son, for he died only a few years ago. I can tell you, however, he came to Texas following the war between the states and there with his wife, again took up his old profession of teaching school, and many of his students grew up to be leaders in the nation."

Farmer stated in the article, "This revelation by Frank Dalton of the personal life story of the noted Quantrell is of interest to the writer of this article because he happened to be a student of the Texas school teacher who Dalton says was the famous Civil War Chieftain, Quantrell!" [505]

Wow, what a story! Farmer was a student of the Texas schoolteacher, Charles Hart, the mild-mannered man, well-liked by his pupils, respected in Osceola.

"A one room school registered 116 students and employed two teachers in 1905-06". [506] This was written by Brian *Hart* on the town Osceola, Texas on the TSHA online website. Notice the author's name. Osceola is 15 miles north of Hillsboro. Garland Farmer would have been 8 and 9 years old.

None of the townspeople suspected that Hart was once the much-feared Quantrill, leader of Quantrill's Guerrilla Band. Bud went to Osceola to check it out and was looking for Charles Hart's grave. He later found a Hart/Kennard Cemetery near there, closer to Rio Vista, Texas but was not able to go back and find the grave, but on a monument, listing all those living there, was Charles Hart's name.

We find articles in The Journal of Tyler, Texas in 1932 that Jesse wrote. There were a series of articles and poems which also appeared in the Troup Banner and The Overton Press. This was in The Daily News and Intelligencer; March 30, 1932 out of Mexico, Missouri. It was also in the Mexico Weekly Ledger, March 31, 1932.

In 1926, the Dude Ranchers Association was formed in Montana and Wyoming. Its purpose was to preserve the life of the West and promote tourism in mountain resorts and dude ranches. They worked closely with the Northern Pacific Railroad to transport guests to these venues. They also were heavily involved in conservation of the land. A quarterly magazine called the "Dude Rancher," featuring life, business, and the history of Dude Ranches came to life in 1937, published by Dude Ranchers Association. It would continue printing the magazine up to 1971. Jesse said he wrote stories for the Dude Rancher.

Jesse wrote an article in True Magazine, "The Aftermath" in 1937/38, after the recovery of the Great Depression for The Kilgore News Herald, October 15, 1939.

The Journal out of Tyler addressed the correspondence regarding a man who lived in Mexico, Missouri stating that he believed he was the only surviving member of the Quantrill Raiders, Dick Worsham. Both Jesse and Dick Worsham respond. "Mr. Dalton, now past 85 years of age, is for the time a resident of Smith County. He was a member of the famous "Quantrell Band," one of the younger members. You would enjoy meeting him personally. He is a typical plainsman, loving the open spaces and true to the type of those great pioneer Indian fighters and soldiers of fortune that were more common back in the last quarter of the last century. He is well preserved for a man of his years, reads without glasses, prefers to live by the campfire and spend his time in the open places."

Frank Dalton/Jesse remembers "Dick" Worsham, mentioned in the above quotation as a resident of Mexico, Missouri and also recalls William F. Hopkins and the Black man who are also mentioned. "Dalton did not want to go into his relationship with the Daltons just yet, "That's a minor matter and of no significance now." [507]

An incredibly interesting news story in the Mexico Weekly Ledger, March 31, 1932 mentions Frank Dalton. "We have from the doughty old pioneer two stories which will appear soon. One of them is *"Buckskin Joe*'s Last Ride" and the other is "The Battle of Adobe Walls." [508] When I saw this, I remembered that Buckskin Joe was the one who established that small community of Navajoe, Oklahoma where Andrew James was. Could it be a possibility that Jesse was Buckskin Joe or an associate? There was some kind of connection or Jesse wouldn't have been able to adequately write about this man. Also, looking back at Adobe Walls, Jesse James and his company of the Texas Rangers were supposedly there. You've got to be alert for Jesse! He drops clues everywhere!

Lecturer

Jesse could hold an audience's attention. He spoke for hours on the Civil War, Quantrill's Raiders, and other wars he had been in. I feel sure he intrigued his listeners with tales of the Wild West also. Some of his words were hard to hear, while others were placed appropriately to lighten up the heaviness of war. His sense of humor was a breath of fresh air.

In 1930/31, he performed lectures in Ardmore and Wilson, Oklahoma, his old stomping ground.

Jesse tells the Cameron Herald (Cameron, Texas), October 28, 1943 that he was lecturing on the town square of Cameron about the war. [509]

He told Ola that he also lectured in 1943 in Lampassas, Burnet, and Marble Falls, Texas, places he knew extremely well in his Texas Rangers Days. He lectured in the courthouse square, schools, and churches.

He traveled to Sweetwater, Texas and lectured at the City Auditorium twice. He was deathly ill at the time.

As a lecturer in 1944, he was described as a big man with a broad hat, blue eyes, long flowing white hair and a moustache. He claimed to have written for the New Orleans Picayune, the Chicago Interocean and the New York World. He claimed to be the uncle of the Dalton boys. He served in World War I as a captain in the Canadian Army's artillery, transferred to the air corps, learned to fly and was retired at the end of the war as a major. He was discharged in 1916 because of his injured right lung. He had written a letter to Lindley Beckworth, a United States representative from Texas in 1947 that Bud obtained, stating that he was gassed in France while in the line of duty during World War I. Ola believed he went by the name of John Franklin in the Canadian military.

In a newspaper article that Bud had, Jesse stated that "Being a cripple didn't stop him from making a nationwide tour in 1949 and 1950. Among other things, I appeared on a nationwide radio network broadcast to recite his life story." [510]

Politician

Jesse always spoke of being in politics in the Old Populist Party. They were able to elect several governors, but no President.

Jesse told a reporter, Byron Buzzbee that he did get in politics as a politician and as a supporter through his speeches for candidates. Jesse said he gave 12 campaign speeches for Jerry Sadler who was running for Railroad Commission and Pierce Brooks for Lieutenant Governor in Texas.

In Howk's book, he stated that Jesse had held at least 4 political offices at one time; from Oklahoma, Colorado, and Wyoming. We know Jesse told Ola that he was one of the representatives in the legislature in Oklahoma. In 1893, in the House of the Oklahoma Territorial Legislature, James J. McDaniel was elected, a Populist for the 26th district. It is shown "The Oklahoma Territorial Legislature: 1890-1905 by R. Darcy – Oklahoma State University. [511] The designated capital of Oklahoma became Guthrie. This was before Oklahoma gained their statehood in 1907.

Jesse also was under the alias name of Jess Wilson and was elected to the Oklahoma State Legislature in 1907 which would have been the First official Oklahoma Legislature as a state. There was a Ben Wilson in 1907, but, Bud nor the writer have been unable to verify this or find his name listed as Jess Wilson, unless he was using another name. Ola stated that she had a picture of Jesse as Representative Jess Wilson.

Jesse's office that he held in Colorado and Wyoming have not been uncovered unless this is false, but curiously and mysteriously, there may be truth to a man who ran for Montana State Senator by the name of William A. Clark. Ola never spoke of Clark, but Howk did, as well as others who heard it from Jesse himself.

<u>William A. Clark</u>

In one of Howk's books, "Jesse James and the Lost Cause", Jesse tells Howk, "I owned some interest in a few mines around *Butte, Montana*, same as I did around Leadville, Breckenridge, Fairplay, Central City, and Black Hawk, Colorado. I had holdings in Idaho, Utah, New Mexico, and Black Hills. I had interests down in Texas, coal and quicksilver. I had some stocks in mines in Oklahoma." [512]

William Andrews Clark was an amazing entrepreneur and built an incredible empire in America from scratch. He had moved to *Butte, Montana* and started in the mining business (copper mining mostly), was in the banking business, electric power companies, newspapers, railroads, and became a senator for Montana in the years 1901-1907.

Las Vegas, Nevada was created as a maintenance stop for Clark's railroad; the San Pedro, Los Angeles, and Salt Lake Railroad. It ran from Utah to Los Angeles. Clark created 1200 lots of prime real-estate around Las Vegas, making a huge profit. They named the county after Clark where Las Vegas sits. The glam and the glitter speaks for itself.

Also, Clarksdale, Arizona was named after Clark who had smelting operations for his copper mines in Jerome, Arizona, an intriguing mountain community to visit. Jerome was Clark's Copper Queen as he was always referred to as the Copper King. In 1888, he bought out the United Verde Copper Company in Jerome and brought in a railway system, the Verde Canyon Railroad in which today is a popular 4 hour scenic ride. Clark added new updated equipment to improve the mining company, making it more efficient. Clark was taking in $1 million per month in Jerome.

After Montana organized their state government in 1889, Clark put in his hat to run for United States Senator for the state of Montana in 1890. It didn't work out for him then, but he pursued a stronger foundation and many more assets in the financial and economic growth of his political theatre. He had a strong rival pushing towards the top seat, Marcus Daly, another copper magnate. In 1899, Clark won the seat, but his rival filed a petition that charged Clark with bribery to win the election. Ninety-six witnesses came forth during an extensive hearing and Clark was found unfit to hold office.

Bribes up to $100,000 were discovered. Clark's son was named as the one who coordinated Clark's agents to "pay off mortgages, purchased ranches, paid debts, financed banks, and blatantly presented envelopes of cash to legislators." There was also corruption on the side of Clark's opponent's team.

"Predictably, Clark complained about the procedures of the committee, the admissions and omissions of evidence, and the machinations of Marcus Daly. He contended that the Senate had lost sight of the principle of presumption of innocence and concluded that the committee had not shown that bribery sufficient to alter the election results had occurred. At the conclusion of his remarks, Clark, clearly aware that he did not have the necessary votes to keep his seat, resigned."

Conveniently, Marcus Daley died in November 1900 and by January 1901, a new state legislature was elected with most of the winners receiving financial support from Clark. They elected William Andrews Clark to fill the seat he initially set out for. He took his place on March 4, 1901. He remained in office through 1907. This incredible story was published in the senate.gov site in the article, "The Election Case of William A. Clark of Montana (1900)." Issues: Electoral misconduct: bribery. [513]

In 1907, the New York Times estimated that Clark was wealthier than John D. Rockefeller. Not everyone adored him, it seems as though he made his profits off the hard-working people who had no other sources available except through him, especially in the mining camps, who sold goods at extreme prices and had total control of the assets and money. That sounds just like a "company town" as we discussed earlier.

Mark Twain, speaking of William A. Clark wrote in an essay in 1907, "He is as rotten a human being as can be found anywhere under the flag; he is a shame to the American nation, and no one has helped to send him to the Senate who did not know that his proper place was the penitentiary, with a ball and chain on his legs. To my mind he is the most disgusting creature that the republic has produced since Tweed's time." [514]

Was William Andrews Clark actually Jesse in disguise? If so, it would have been one of the greatest feats of all time in a drama played out by hypocrisy. Only Jesse could pull it off.

Bud believes it's a possibility. Several things indicate that it was Jesse. Bud told me to contact his old friend, Ralph Epperson.

I had the pleasure of talking with Mr. Epperson. He called Bud the "Father of all knowledge on the subject of Jesse James." Epperson believes wholeheartedly that J. Frank Dalton was Jesse James. He said that he has mounting evidence that supports Jesse was Senator William Andrews Clark. He advised me to watch his videos on YouTube.com, "Jesse James Lived to be 103: Part 1-4." [515]

Ralph Epperson says that Jesse after seeing that there would be no Second Civil War, he took the $7 Billion in gold the KGC collected and went to work to invest in many areas of the country. He established many businesses that could make a substantial profit. Jesse got into the copper mining business because of inside information received from Thomas Edison and Henry Ford when the need for copper would be in high demand with the invention of the light bulb and the automobile.

The Clark family put out a book, "The Clarks: An American Phenomenon," by William Daniel Mangam, 1939 to explain the man, William Andrews Clark. The man who wrote the book was a general business manager for Clark's son. Epperson said that the words he wrote, leave clues inside for one to figure it out on their own on just who this man was. It's exactly Jesse's style in his writings and lectures. Epperson stated that he was convinced that the author was writing in a way to tell the family and the world just who William Andrews Clark really was.

Clark played a beautiful Stradivarius violin and looked so much like Jesse James, who also played the violin and fiddle. Their hairline and cowlick were identical. Clark had his own family and several children. What has really pulled me in to believing Clark may have definitely been Jesse is a fact that Bud pointed out to me. Bud said look at the photo of Clark's first wife, Katherine Louise "Kate" Stauffer Clark.

Studying Katherine's photo, I turned to the portrait of Myra Belle Shirley (Belle Starr) that Jesse always carried in his wallet. It was a tin type and Ola and Aubrey had it copied and blown up. Ola had the portrait hanging on her wall, the same photo Jesse would always have near him. It was the same woman in Bud's eyes, and my oh my it just wasn't a coincidence. You be the judge.

(Katherine Clark's photo)

Ralph Epperson said after he had written books and produced videos, he has had many calls and visitors in Tucson where he lives. He said he got a call one day from a man named Clark, asking for a copy of his catalog. Ralph asked several questions: "You're a Clark?," "Did you have a family member in your family, William Andrews Clark?", "Was your Clark a railroad builder and a Senator of the United States?" The answers were all "Yes, he was our great grandfather."

Mr. Epperson said that he began to tell the story about his theory and all the clues leading to believe that William Andrews Clark was actually Jesse James. The young man on the phone was totally enthralled with what Mr. Epperson was saying. While talking, they heard a loud shriek and Ralph asked, "what was that?" Mr. Clark said, "I don't know, let me check." Epperson heard people talking and when the man got back to the phone, he was stumbling with his words as in shock and said, "My wife found a picture of Zerelda James, Jesse's mother and said, "That's Grandma Clark!"

The wife pulled out a family picture of William Andrew Clark's mother to compare and she said it again, "That's Grandma Clark." Mr. Epperson said "Double check to see if Grandma Clark was missing her right forearm. The Clarks then said, "Yes, Grandma had told the family many years ago, that part of her arm was blown off in an accident and in that accident her young son was killed. Coincidence?

Ralph Epperson has no doubt that William Andrews Clark was the real Jesse James. He said that Jesse killed him off in 1925, had a doctor who was paid to pronounce his death by pneumonia. Epperson said Clark went into hiding in Paris for several years and came back to the States. He believes that Clark confronted his family with the news that he was alive and was Jesse James and advised them to keep their mouths shut. Epperson believes this big reveal is why one of his daughters became a recluse for many years thereafter.

MYRA BELLE SHIRLEY — Better known as
BELLE STARR.
Taken from old tintype, Jesse W. James' collections

Bud Hardcastle: The Truth Tracker

(Myra Belle Shirley)

This is another story to weigh your own judgement upon. If William A. Clark was Jesse, he was an incredible brilliant and intelligent man as many who knew him personally said. He did more for this country than any man could in building this great nation into the powerhouse that it was.

In the political world back in the days of the outlaws and at the turn of the century, there were plenty of political favors handed out by politicians to help Jesse and others connected to him, starting with Governor Crittenden. The pardons extended to Frank James, the Fords, and the man who killed Robert Ford, O'Kelly who was earlier convicted and sentenced to 40 years in Canon City, Colorado Pen, but pardoned within 30 days by Gov. Waite. Cole Younger was pardoned in 1901 after he had been in prison, sentenced to be imprisoned for life. Even the most revered Freemason in the country, Albert Pike was pardoned by his fellow Freemason, President Andrew Johnson after the war.
Where there's Power, there's politics and where there's politics, there's Power.

In the Movies

1928 – Ola said that Jesse didn't tell her much, but he was really wanting Hollywood to pick up his story. He went to California and did some work at the movie studios, but Ola didn't know what kind of work he did. He did tell Ola that he met Juliette (Judy) Canova and really liked her. She was just starting her career and her loud dominating voice took her far. She had her first solo recording in 1928, "I Wish I Was A Single Gal Again." She was considered a country bumpkin and her talents included singing, acting, and was a natural comedian. [516] Jesse didn't stay too long in California at that time and came back to Texas.

Preacher/Teacher

Jesse was a great orator, especially when it came to the things that mattered the most to him; his life stories and lessons learned, and the Bible that he continuously read and leaned upon.

By just listening to Jesse, you knew that his faith in God was huge. Why else do you think he survived what he did. So many actions spoke in volumes of kindness and concern for others. I believe that was the real Jesse, not the ruthless, egotistic madman that he has been portrayed as. Even the character he played in William A. Clark, did not fit Jesse's true character. Was that really him or Carl Clark who claimed to be the son of Frank James? It was only when he was threatened or his family or friends were in danger that he turned to violence, but it was to preserve life, mostly his.

Jesse shared the Bible when he could to others. John Trammel and Mitch Graves testified to that. Others stated that he was always reading the Bible around the campfire of the raiders and the outlaws. Calamity Jane even stated in her letters that Jesse could be a preacher. She must have been on the other end of his preaching.

A beautiful story told by Ola, reveals what a kind and gentle soul he was. In March 1949, "Thank the Lord, Jesse was getting better daily. Ola was out to see him as she was every afternoon. She was standing by the bed and she and Jesse were talking when a little boy about ten or twelve years old, a pretty little fellow, came rolling into the room in a wheelchair. Ola said, "Hello! What do you want son?"

He said, "Well, I heard that Jesse James was in here and I wanted to meet him." Ola said, "Well this is him honey." She turned to Jesse and said, "Jesse, here's a young man that wants to meet you."

Ola heard the little boy, as he rolled up to the side of the bed as close as he could and say, "Mr. James, this is ……." Poor old Jesse almost fell off the bed reaching down to shake hands with the little boy. The little fellow sat there a little bit and then said, "You was an outlaw? The outlaw Jesse James?"

Jesse replied, "Yes, that's right. But listen son, I want to tell you something. That is a bad way to live. It's the wrong road to travel. I know how bad it is." Then he talked on so nice and kind and Ola thought as she listened, "I have never heard a preacher in a pulpit preach a better sermon to a congregation in a church than the way he was talking to that little boy."

Then he added, "Now son, pay attention to your parents, live a law-abiding life, get a good education and you'll be a fine man when you get grown. I'm glad you came to see me."

The little boy said, "Thank you sir. I'm glad to meet you." Then he left. Ola never saw him again, but she thought many times about when he visited Jesse and how Jesse talked to him." [517]

Bud always said, "you can find out pretty quick about a man the way he treats children and dogs."

Jesse was a natural and knew his Bible well. His father and grandfather on the James side were preachers. His story telling pulled the listener in and the scriptures he spoke of gave the story depth, applicable to life. In 1880/1881, Jesse dressed as an old Quaker preacher and was given the opportunity to preach in Nashville.

In the Mexico, Missouri Evening Ledger Newspaper, October 11, 1948, "In 1910 Jesse taught Bible classes and served the old Unity Church as Sunday school superintendent for a month and taught classes of little children in the open air. He was known as "Brother Johnson." [518]

Jesse preached for an hour and half at a Burnet, Texas at the Baptist Church on a Sunday night in 1943. He had an attentive audience, not knowing who he really was.

In 1924, Jesse was in Wichita, Kansas for a short time, preaching in a big tent revival. He spoke in a deep, rolling voice. A friend of the Everhards, Allen Mozingo was there to hear him preach. Jesse told his audience that he was the youngest member of the James Gang. Allen later saw him in the hospital in Austin under Ola's care and said it was the same man.

Jesse's influence had a big impact on his closest friends, Colonel John Davis, Ozark Jack, Al Jennings, and Cole Younger. They followed in Jesse footsteps to make things right in this old world.

Colonel James Russell Davis became a Methodist Preacher.

Ozark Jack Berlin gathered large crowds to listen to him speak, aimed at reaching the young ears. They were "campfire talks" regarding his days with Western bad men and Indians. Crime doesn't pay he told them. He taught them how to be "temperate and live a Christian life, which is the happiness of the world." In the article on "Find a Grave," titled "Wanted! Ozark Jack", the writer states that "It has been remarked by ministers of various denominations, "If we had more men like Ozark, we would have less of our boys and girls in penitentiaries and jails."

He carried with him large pistols and leg irons; the kind used on Billy the Kid. At the end of the article, "Ozark Jack stands among the best as a citizen in his home community and always stands for law and order." [519]

Out of the Lawrence Country News, September 27, 1934 titled "Ozark Jack Berlin Saved Truck Driver Not Jack Glosser", a story relates of the hero effort by Ozark to save men who were involved in a horrific wreck at a railroad crossing who were in a truck hit by a passing train. Ozark was on the train and jumped out to save the men. He would have been 67 years old.

Al Jennings was another outlaw "gone good." In an interview with Al Jennings he spoke words of wisdom. "Talked all over the land, trying to tell boys that it doesn't pay to commit crimes. I don't want them to be criminals. I don't want them to be anything but law-abiding citizens. And I'm giving my every effort to help throughout the United States in dissipating the great crime wave that's now sweeping over the country." [520]

Also, in the newspaper, "Evening Times" in Grand Forks, North Dakota, on April 2, 1910, the title reads "Cole Younger, Ex-Bandit, to Become Lecturer Missourian Who Was Intended For the Ministry will Preach". Thomas Coleman "Bud" Younger became a reverend.

Cole said, "I will say just one thing in my own defense. During my career of outlawry, I rode into town under the glare of the noonday sun, and all men knew my mission. No man can accuse me of prowling around at night or of ever having robbed a lone man or the honest poor. Yet there is no heroism in outlawry and the fate of each outlaw in his turn should be an everlasting lesson to the young of the land."

By July 1903, Cole Younger was deemed as a "philosopher" in the State Journal, of Mulhall, Oklahoma, July 24, 1903. "Younger's speech is now polished with quotations from the classics. The Scriptures, Shakespeare, Emerson, Indian legends, French phrases, Greek and Latin proverbs are part of the every-day speech of this one time "bad man." One of Cole's sayings: "Get into partnership with God, but don't try to be the leading member of the firm. He knows more about the business than you do. You may be able for a time to practice deception upon your fellow men, but don't try to fire any blank cartridges at the author of this universe." [521]

"There is nothing wrong with men possessing riches. The wrong comes when riches possess men."

-Billy Graham

Chapter Twenty-Three: Black Gold, Texas Tea

In the oil boom years, Jesse was right there at the beginning. In 1914, Jesse claims as Frank Dalton, he served as a peace officer in many towns connected to oil; one being Burkburnett, Texas. Oil was being produced as early as 1912 in Wichita County, Texas, but several years earlier in 1907, it was being pumped out of Oklahoma.

This statement that Jesse made, leads us to several clues about his days in the oil fields. Open your eyes and you will see in plain sight the coincidences and clues. It was in 1931 that Jesse went to Gladewater, Texas, using the name of Frank Dalton serving as a Peace Officer in the "first oil booms in Texas." In one newspaper article, he had told a reporter that in '31 is when he joined the Texas Rangers again. The Rangers, Company B stationed in Gladewater were under the command of Captain Tom Hickman. Bob Goss and Tom Hickman were some of Jesse's buddies especially when it came to shooting matches. Goss and Hickman were both oil men.

In The Kansas City Star, March 14, 1939 article, "A Member of the James Band Still Tells of Group's Exploits", it is written that Frank Dalton was the marshal for many years in Gladewater and had oil interests in Texas.

Jesse was also back with his old buddy, Brushy Bill/Billy the Kid in Gladewater.

After the chaos in Mexico, Billy went to Van Zandt County where he supposedly had a ranch. He had several wives earlier, but under the name of Ollie Roberts, he is shown to be widowed in 1920. Dewitt Travis had lived in Van Zandt County most of his early life and in 1920, he too was living in Van Zandt County and stated he had known Brushy Bill as long as he could remember in an Abilene, Texas newspaper. We find Jesse also in Van Zandt at Dewitt's home when he was a young man. Dewitt was born in 1889. In the 1930 census, Dewitt was in the oil business in McCamey near the Pecos River, between San Angelo and Odessa. He would later join Jesse and Billy in Gladewater.

In some of Frank Dalton's news articles, we see another mention of Van Zandt county. Dalton writes that his father was Lawrence Dalton born in Dalton, Georgia. They were living in Goliad, Texas when Frank Dalton was born in 1848. Lawrence fought in the army of General Zachary Taylor in the Mexican American War in which the real Lewis Dalton did, father of the Dalton brothers. Frank Dalton stated that they moved to Missouri, settling at Monegaw Springs, west of Osceola. This was the area where the Youngers lived. He returned to Texas in 1864, living in Van Zandt County. [522]

Of course, this is the ancestral line Jesse was using before he came out with his real identity, but apparently Van Zandt was another important point in Texas, another clue, another possible stronghold for the KGC. It was a strong Confederate county and later would be highly connected to the KKK.

Van Zandt County is the county where the famous town of Canton, Texas lies. It is where the largest flea market in the world is held on the first Monday of the month, started back in the Confederate Days during the war used for bartering goods and surplus. Dewitt Travis was buried in Myrtle Springs, between Canton and Wills Point. The writer was able to travel to those towns in search of my 3rd great grandmother's grave outside of Wills Point. She had an Indian background and buried in 1914 in a cemetery known for outcasts. She was not allowed to be buried in the town cemetery. The others who were buried there were considered the wrong color or white trash. There is a lengthy story of a lady's research of her white ancestors buried there during the same era. One was a falsely accused murderer, so they could not be buried in town, but buried in this same cemetery, Howell Cemetery. Shortly after they were buried, the cemetery was ransacked, and the tombstones were demolished; some believe it was the KKK. This lady found also that Blacks were hung and buried there. Racial tensions divided the population back in those days. It was sad to see my great grandmother's grave amongst strangers, buried alone.

It was a beautiful part of Texas, very wooded with plenty of water resources. The Neches River runs through the eastern portion of the county and the Sabine River forms part of the northeastern county line which was mentioned several times by Jesse. Following the Sabine River to the East, 60 miles, is the town of Gladewater in Gregg County.

In the 1930's, Billy was working in the oil patch. A lot of the Gregg County Oldtimers remember him as Ollie L. Roberts. He was a popular figure in Gladewater and Longview as a storyteller, bringing folks into the Wild West adventures. He was very good with his six-shooter and gave shooting demonstrations wearing his well-worn leather buckskin jacket with the fringe, boots, and hat to fit his character. He also worked for the city of Gladewater and was an undercover cop there. Both Jesse and Billy were the upper hand of the law there in the 30's and very well respected.

Gregg County, where Gladewater and Longview sat, just 12 miles apart, came alive while the nation began facing the Great Depression. "On April 7, 1931, the first Gladewater oil well blew in. It was located one mile outside town in the Sabine River bottom." [523] The discovery of oil in 1931 brought farmers to turn from crops to oil. The population of the county increased in a short amount of time from 16,000 to 100,000.

Jesse doesn't go too much into detail about this time of his life, but being in Gladewater and associated with Robert "Bob" Goss, who was in charge of the Texas Rangers officers who oversaw the oil fields, I'm assuming that this was what Jesse was involved in. There was an incident on May 1, 1931 when the Mounted Texas Rangers, led by Goss and M.T. "Lone Wolf" Gonzaullas were summoned by the Sinclair Oil company to patrol the area four miles from Gladewater. A horrific oil fire, described as "a burning geyser" on one of their wells caused several explosions, killing eight men. The rangers were there to keep nonemployees and newsmen out. [524] Nitroglycerine was used to cause an explosion to snuff out the fire. It would separate the flame and the atmospheric oxygen away from the fuel.

While in the oil game, Jesse was at Overton, Kilgore, Longview, Carthage, Greggton, Hallsville, Jefferson, Daingerfield, and Marshall, Texas. Goss and Manuel Gonzaullas, who was later made captain of Company B of the Texas Rangers were in Overton also, sent there June 1931 to take charge of policing the area around the Tulsa Oil Company's flaming well. Jesse told Ola and to newspaper reporters that he didn't do so well in the oilfields and those fumes were hard on him, especially because of his lung injuries which bothered him for the rest of his life.

In August of that year, the oil scene was overflowing with zealous producers and workers. This was all new to them. They were not prepared. As the gold rush was to California, the newly discovered oil was to East Texas. The oil brought an overflow of people and with that comes greed, fraud, crime, carnival activity, power, and the desire for more. The town began to fill up with vagabonds, Pleasure Palaces, gaming, and plenty of whiskey and oil to go around.

This is exactly what occurred just a few years earlier in Borger, Texas in 1927. Another town promoter, A.P. (Ace) Borger who was known throughout Texas and Oklahoma had purchased a 240-acre townsite near the Canadian River in the Texas Panhandle. "Within 90 days of its founding, sensational advertising and the lure of "black gold" brought over 45,000 men and women to the new boomtown." [525] The Sante Fe Railway created a spur line to the new town, named after its founder, Borger. It appears as it too, was a "company town."

By the Spring of 1927, Governor Daniel J. Moody sent a detachment of Texas Rangers under Captains Francis Augustus Hamer and Thomas R. Hickman to quell the crime situation that was mounting. Hickman was stationed in Borger in the early years when it was a rough old oil town, which was at one point, under martial law. In one newspaper article, in Hickman's obituary was quoted as saying, "Borger in the early 30's was the roughest town ever created by an oil boom. More citizens were killed, more peace officers were killed, and more men were slain in holdups." [526]

"Borger's wave of crime and violence continued intermittently into the 1930's and climaxed with the murder of District Attorney John A. Holmes by an unknown assassin on September 18, 1929. This episode prompted Moody to impose martial law for a month and sent state troops to help local authorities rid the town of the lawless element. This goal was eventually achieved, but not before Ace Borger was shot to death by his longtime enemy, Arthur Huey on August 31, 1934." [527]

As a Ranger Captain over the oil fields, Hickman maintained the area of Borger, Ranger, Kilgore, Burkburnett, Mexia, Desdemona, Breckenridge, and Wink. In Kilgore, the rangers used an old abandoned church for the jail and a bible stand for the fingerprint desk. [528] Hickman was also a special officer for Gulf Oil Company.

The over production of oil, issues of storage, and other problems began to surface. Martial law was put in place to shut down the East Texas oil field, after Oklahoma and Borger left them an example to follow, encountering the same issues oil brought. The order and proclamation were made by Governor Sterling. The oil fields were being patrolled by guardsmen, 800 of them; **13 were Texas Rangers**. The area they covered was over 600 square miles. Sixteen hundred wells were shut down. [529]

By the end of August 1931, State Troopers joined the law enforcement teams. The Texas Rangers wore civilian clothes, who mixed into the crowds and were unnoticeable, even with their white high-crowned Stetsons. There are a lot of pictures of Dalton with a dark, wide brimmed western hat, but in one news article, referring to Dalton as being a very familiar character around Henderson, Longview, Gladewater and other East Texas points, he (Jesse) fashioned his long hair into a knot, and tucked it up beneath his white 10 gallon hat. They were the highest respected law enforcement present and with their seasoned knowledge and experience, handled the situation well.

In the *Longview News Journal*, Nov. 22, 1931 – "Gladewater Road is Colorful Spot with Nightfall in Sway" sets the scene. "Gladewater – passing derricks that in spots rival the trees in number. Closer one approaches the sister city, thicker and more hectic is oil activity. Right on the eastern edge of Gladewater, big trucks, heavy teams, and other activity attendant to drilling, actually menaces and impedes highway traffic, so intense is town lot development. The stranger or transient is surprised to see the front campus of the Gladewater high school converted into a mire of mud and water – slush pits for an oil well in the school's front yard. In fact, this institution of learning is right in the middle of a hotbed of derricks and roaring rigs."

For a child, there was nothing but black mud, slicker than snot to play in with very little signs of green grass.

The smell of the piney woods in the communities of Kilgore, Longview, and Gladewater were replaced by the smell of putrid gas. The smell was repulsive. I remember going to Borger as a young girl, just 30 years from this time in history. The smell of the community left a deep memory of wanting so bad to leave. It was the smell of something rotten, pure and raw Sulphur gas.

Jesse said of the oil fumes, "It got me," he said. "Those oil field fumes were hard on me and we didn't do so good, my partner and I." [530] We are not sure, but his partner may have been DeWitt Travis since he was in the oil business or it could have been Brushy Bill.

By **1933**, in Gladewater, Jesse was selling oil leases. This must have been the time he met Howk. Howk claims to have worked and cured titles before drilling, while Jesse got involved with the leases. Could it have been Howk that was his partner? In the Lawton Constitution, Howk explains that his grandfather, Baxter told him about an old gentleman that he needed to meet. He met J. Frank Dalton in a café in Gladewater. An exchange of the rebel password opened up the conversation.

Shortly after this meeting, Jesse went to Canada on his ranch. This is when he met Mitch Graves. Mitch wrote Ola and stated that Jesse during that time, was really having trouble with his chest, caused by a bullet wound in his lung that he received in the Civil War and the oil fumes irritated it badly. He had to get away from that, but after Jesse wrote articles for the Crittenden Memoirs in 1935, he went back to Gladewater.

In March 25, 1948, noted in *The Paris News*, a J.E. Bunch said in 1934-35, that a man claiming to be Jesse James came to Tyler, only 25 miles from Gladewater. Mr. Bunch stated that Frank Dalton and Bill Rakestraw (William "Buddy" J. Rakestraw) of Gladewater had seen circulars that an imposter was putting out in area towns, claiming to be the real Jesse James. They wanted to confront this man. This was many years before Jesse came out with his identity.

Bunch took the two men to Tyler and right off knew that this man was an imposter. He was a very small, weak man; nothing like the real Jesse as the newspaper relayed. The stories told by this man was a little off, but some of it was true.

Frank Dalton wanted to immediately go to the sheriff. The sheriff said that the man was harmless but was a fake. Dalton went to the room of the man calling himself Jesse. Frank Dalton was able to speak with both the imposter and his manager for some time. The manager then wanted to see Frank alone. Dalton finally came out and told Mr. Bunch and Rakestraw that the imposter was a cousin to Jesse and to just leave him there and go on. Dalton had made some type of agreement with the manager and came back to Gladewater with plenty of cash in his pocket.

Mr. Bunch stated in the newspaper account that "Frank Dalton loved booze. He drank a lot, so after Gregg County went wet, he moved from my place over on the road to Kilgore, as there was a liquor store near there. He continued to drink a lot and one evening when he started back to his camp after he had taken too much he fell and broke his left hip. He laid there on the ground several hours, about four or five miles from my place. I heard from him a few times, but I never saw him after he got hurt." [531]

It was within a year or two that Jesse took a fall and Mr. Bunch blamed it on the booze. "On May 12, 1937, I slipped on some steps and broke my leg, then broke two ribs and my wrist due to the slippery mess (the oil). The doctor said if I didn't get out of there, I would only live two months."

Jesse stayed in the hospital for several days and then went to live with his dear friend and his wife in Gladewater, Brushy Bill. He stayed with them for several weeks until he could maneuver around well enough on crutches. Jesse really began writing more and more stories for various media organizations and that is how he was able to pay off his hospital bill.

Dalton was known all over East Texas as well as his stories. In Gladewater he was known as Major Frank Dalton. He accumulated many friends there and much respect. The population at that time was less than 6,000.

Two clues that Jesse left behind in Gladewater were letters he wrote in 1938. It was addressed to Stillwater Prison in Minnesota. It was regarding a concern about Thomas Coleman Younger who was either in the prison in 1876 and 1877. He wanted to know the prisoner's height and weight. He also requested to know how many bullet holes Younger had. The questions were numerous and varied in the subject matter.

Bud Hardcastle: The Truth Tracker

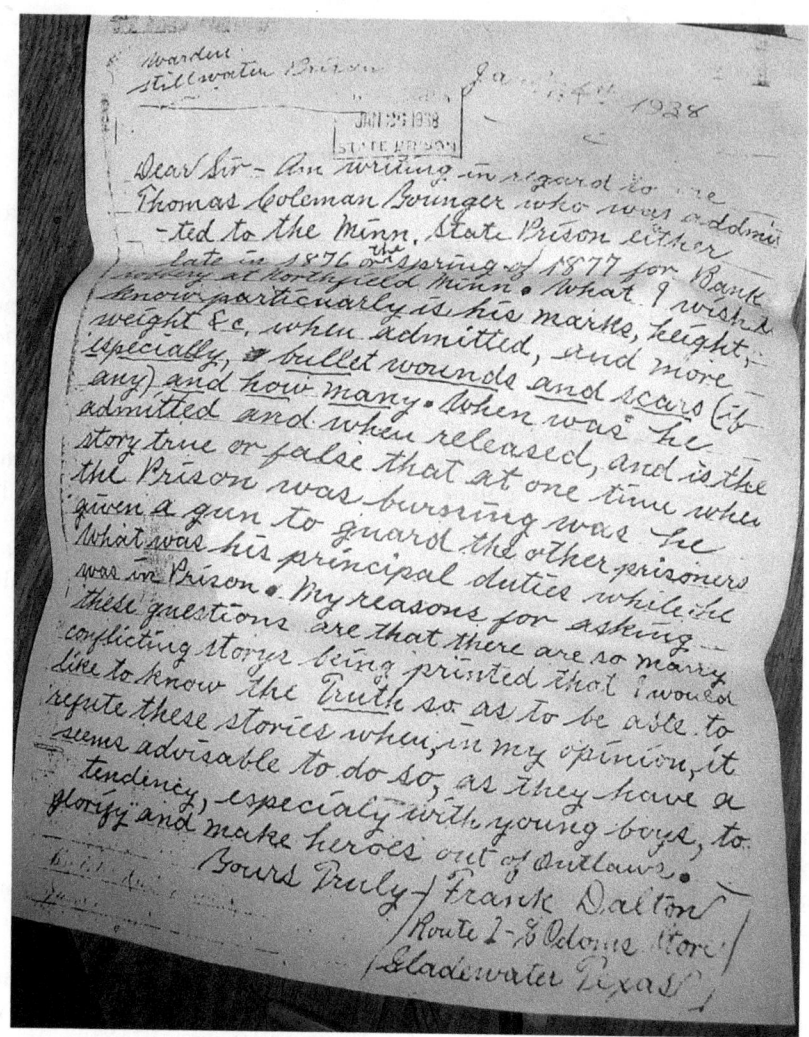

(Letter from Dalton to the Warden of the Stillwater Prison, January 24, 1938)

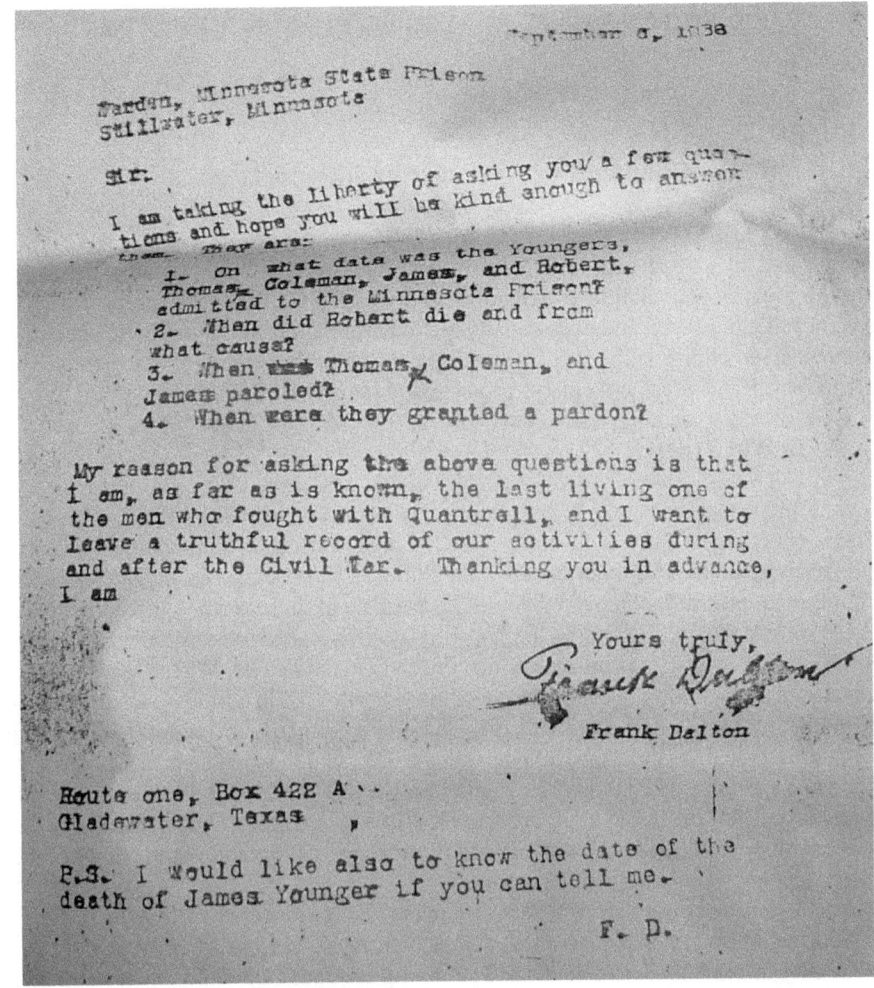

(Letter from Dalton to the Stillwater Prison in Minnesota. September 5, 1938)

Was he concerned who was really there? John Trammel told a newspaper reporter of the Denver Post, Robert Byers in 1954 that the Younger Brothers were captured in the aftermath of the Northfield Raid, but "because of politics," the three were set free and three other men posing as the Younger brothers were tried, convicted and spent 25 years in the Minnesota prison for the crime."
532

In the December 26, 1945 issue of *The Amarillo Globe Times* titled "Guerrilla Leads Life of Peace," a story from Gladewater, Texas, writes, "He's back." We know he stayed in Gladewater for a while and then went to Longview in 1946. He was living in a motel near a restaurant when Slim Williams met him that year in Longview.

"A rich man buying you something means nothing, but a busy man giving his time means everything."

-Anonymous

Chapter Twenty-Four: Buddies in Texas

In the 30's and 40's, Jesse continued to stay near Gladewater and Longview which was only 24 miles from the town of Marshall in which Jesse said was the Capitol of Missouri during the war. Jesse stayed near Tyler as well and occasionally moved around the country until he became crippled for life in 1947. Even after that, he still crossed the country with the help of his friends. They were like family to him. His dearest and closest friends were Brushy Bill/Billy and DeWitt Travis.

Billy and DeWitt Travis

Billy, as Ollie Roberts and his wife, Loutecia Ballard were still living in Gladewater in 1940. Dewitt Travis encouraged Billy to go to Dr. C. C. Crews, dentist in Longview to fix his teeth in 1932. This was why the only publicly confirmed photo of him back in the early 1880's shows the prominent upper lip protruding above his lower lip because of those teeth. Ola said he had like two "tusk teeth." He had them pulled and it helped Billy's looks and his occlusion or biting plane.

Dewitt Travis always stayed in close contact with Billy and Jesse. When DeWitt was living at his own ranch and still working in the oil business in Longview, Billy and Jesse would visit. Possibly they had stayed there for long periods of time. There is a wonderful picture that Ola had of Jesse and Billy, photographed in 1942 on DeWitt's ranch. Ola said it was taken in Gladewater. When William Tunstill and Ola were talking, they said that DeWitt took it upon himself to see that both of them were taken care of. In the 1950 census, DeWitt was living in Longview, Gregg County as an independent oil operator. He was well off, but as you can put two and two together, in their later years, neither Jesse nor Billy had much income.

Billy's wife Loutecia died in Van Zandt County in 1944 and Billy would marry Malinda Elizabeth "Lizzie" Murrell Allison who was a widow in 1945. He and Lizzie would move back to Hamilton County in the late 1940's to his old stomping grounds as a child when he lived with his father. They lived in Hico, Texas, in a small house and didn't have much to live on. He came to Lawton, Oklahoma when Jesse revealed himself in 1948, and again in Guthrie, Oklahoma. He didn't let anyone know who he was. In 1949, he attended Jesse's 102nd birthday party at Meramec Caverns in Missouri. He had begun working with Morrison at that time, but still did not reveal who he was.

Dewitt Travis' father was Elbert Dewitt Travis (1847-1894). He was born in Mississippi and lived in Perry, Mississippi in 1850 before the war. He was in Company E, 3rd battalion in the Mississippi Cavalry Reserves, enlisted on Aug 15, 1864 at Augusta, Mississippi. He was taken prisoner and paroled May 16, 1865. DeWitt's father fought with Wild Henry Roberts, Billy's father.

Ola said DeWitt's mother, Martha Ann Patterson went to school with Jesse and knew him well. Dewitt Travis signed an affidavit to help Jesse (Frank Dalton) with his pension, speaking of his mother, Martha Ann Patterson Travis who knew Jesse since the early part of the war. She and her family lived just across the river from where the Battle of Jenkins' Ferry was fought. Frank Dalton helped move her family to safety before the battle started between Quantrill's Raiders and the Northern Invaders. Her two brothers Neal and Duncan Patterson were with the Quantrill Raiders. "All through my childhood days, Frank Dalton was a frequent visitor at our home. I have listened to them discuss different battles and incidents many times that occurred while they were fighting with Quantrill." [533] DeWitt's parents were heavily attached to Jesse in more ways than one.

From records, we find Elbert Travis and his family were living in Van Zandt County, Texas in 1880, near Wills Point and was a farmer. DeWitt Travis told a newspaper reporter in New York,

H.D. Quigg that he remembers sitting on Jesse's knee when Jesse was in hiding at his family's home and had been associated with him since 1920. [534]

In DeWitt's obituary, it stated that he belonged to the Castilian Lodge No. 141, Odd Fellows Lodge, and Rebekah Lodge of Canton, Texas earlier. He became **a 33rd** degree Mason.

Dewitt's nephew, Arlo Norman (1918-1998), was a very interesting fellow. Both he and DeWitt were at Jesse's funeral in Granbury in 1951. Bud was able to go to his house and speak with Arlo in Arlington. Bud said that Arlo was not very open about some of the questions Bud was asking of him, but when Arlo's son came in, who was a doctor, he said "Now Dad, open up, it's about time to tell what we know. Bud said they did open up and told what they knew. J. Frank Dalton was truly Jesse James. Arlo said that it definitely was Jesse/J. Frank Dalton in the casket at the funeral in Granbury, Texas in 1951. The casket was a wooden one and opened to view the body. Arlo was an aeronautical engineer and was a 32nd degree mason of Arlington. I think Arlo still had a lot of secrets to tell, but he never let go of them.

Loy Lee and Nan Gamble

In Longview, Jesse mentions he and DeWitt would visit L.L. Gamble. This man's full name was Loy Lee Gamble (1899-1960) who lived on Hudson Street in Longview. He was the son of John Lee Gamble and Ella Doyal.

Loy Lee Gamble's maternal grandfather, William Balie Doyal (1851-1938) was a brother to Ellen Doyal who married Christopher Woodall. They all lived in the Doyal Township, St. Clair County, Missouri, only seven miles south from where the Youngers lived. The Woodalls connect to Robert Thomason who was the stepfather of Zerelda Cole (Dalton) James and Wild Bill Thomason, grandfather of Bloody Bill Anderson. The Woodalls connect to the Faris' and the Woodsons.

L.L. Gamble's maternal great grandfather, Hugh Lee Martin Doyal (1828-1887) was in the K-9 Missouri Militia. This was a state militia, Company K in the 9th Provisional Regiment for the Union. He enrolled in 1863 in Maries County, Missouri. Their mission was to serve as garrisons and oppose the guerillas. After the war, in 1870, we find him and his family living in Osceola, Missouri, the town that was burned to the ground by Lane in 1861. In 1872, the Doyal Township was established just south of there.

Loy Lee Gamble was born in Denton, Texas and by 1918, he was serving in the military and living in Las Vegas, New Mexico. In the 1930 census, he was living in Eunice, Lea County, New Mexico.

Gamble was living in Longview as early as **1933**. Gamble was a surveyor for Perry Thompson Surveying Company who had worked on the Big Inch and Lake Cherokee projects and later worked as a civil engineer for the city of Longview. He was one of the pallbearers for Brushy Bill Roberts.

Gamble wanted to be buried in Tishomingo, Oklahoma. He died of a sudden heart attack while fishing at the Lake of the Pines. He was 61 years old. [535]

Mrs. Gamble wrote out a letter for Frank Dalton as a witness to confirm his military service with Capt. William Anderson. L. L. Gamble wrote out an affidavit stating that Dalton helped his family evacuate from the Jenkin's Ferry Battleground. This battle was April 30, 1864 with E. Kirby Smith and Sterling Price leading the Confederates. It was fought southwest of Little Rock, Arkansas. The battle was one of the deadliest battles during the Civil War.

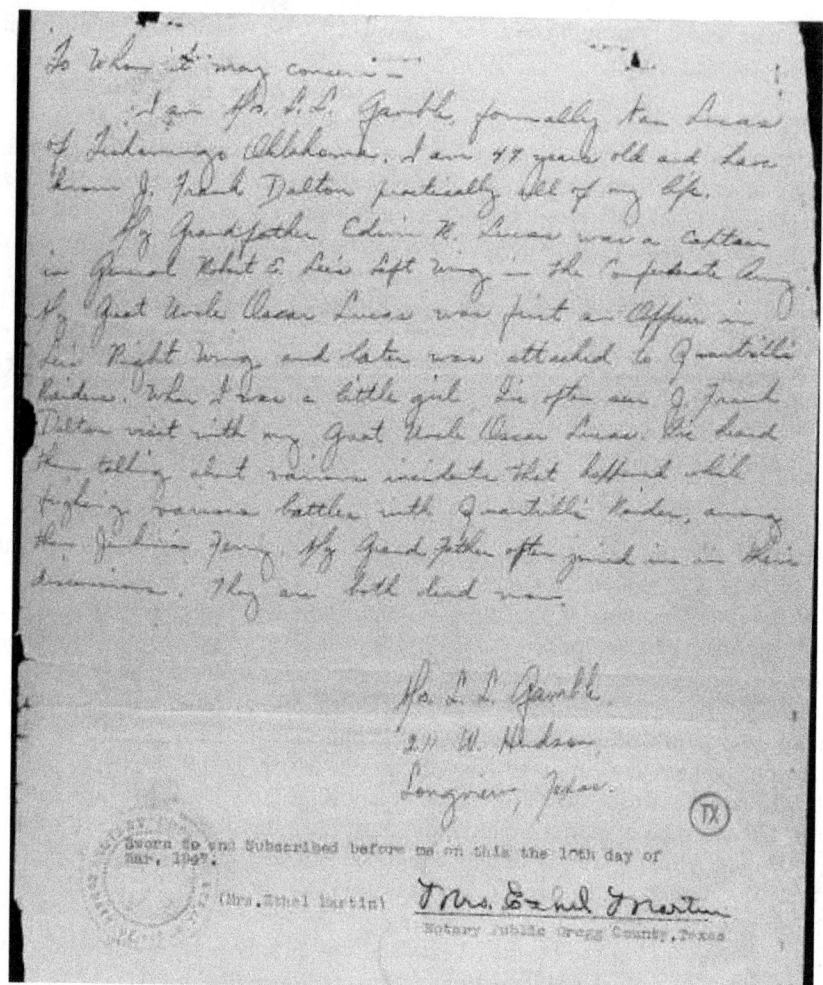

(Letter from Mrs. Gamble for Frank Dalton (From Frank Dalton's Pension file, "Alabama, Texas and Virginia, U.S. Confederate Pensions, 1884-1958 – Ancestry.com))

Mrs. L. L. Gamble, who was Nancy "Nan" Lucas before marriage wrote that she knew J. Frank Dalton all her life. Her grandfather, Edwin R. Lucas was a captain in General Robert E. Lee's Left Wing in the Confederate Army. The obituary of this man states that he was in 24 "pitched battles." Earlier, he had enlisted as a private in Company K of the 11th Alabama regiment, but later became captain of the company. [536]

Nan Gamble stated that her Great Uncle Oscar was an officer in Lee's Right Wing and later was attached to Quantrill's Raiders. When she was a little girl, Dalton would come visit with her Great Uncle Oscar. They would talk about various incidents, including Jenkin's Ferry; apparently Oscar and Jesse were both there.

Oscar Madison Lucas (1838-1920) was a reverend. He was licensed as a Baptist preacher in December 1862 and was ordained after the war. He preached in Alabama, Mississippi, Arkansas, and Louisianna. His war days are stated as enlisting in Company G, 5th Alabama Infantry in April 1861, previously known as the Cahaba Rifles. He was involved in many battles and after the Battle of Gettysburg he was transferred from Company G to the 11th Alabama, Company K.

Charles Coleman Ford, the Keys, and Frances Tiller

It's amazing how many people were touched or attached to Jesse. I'm sure there are so many more that we don't know about and never will. A rather interesting story comes from Longview, Texas in the 30's and 40's.

There are several indications that Jesse was amongst the most elite, as well as the common country folk. He had no societal boundaries and as far as Bud has found, he had no racial tendencies. It was the character he judged.

In Longview, next to the Santa Fe railroad track on the outskirts of town, was the old Ford "Last Chance Grocery Store." It was a great location for the store, close to the Santa Fe Depot and Round House on E. Cotton Street. In the 30's and 40's it was a place where you could get your groceries, but also where you could chew your "baccy", spit on the old wooden floor, and get a belly full of laughs. There was also a back room for a little bit of gambling on the side. Sounds like Jesse's happy place. Well, indeed it was.

It was owned by Charles Coleman Ford (1883-1950) who had a huge sense of humor and was full of practical jokes. He was called Pop Ford.

Bud first learned about this story from Ola's manuscript and Aubrey. Ola had written that Jesse and DeWitt Travis went to the grocery store on East Cotton street in Longview quite often. Ola said that the owners were Charles Coleman Ford and his wife, Lola Belle Foster. "He (Charles Coleman Ford) was the son of the late D.C. (Cap) Ford and wife Mary Owen Ford of Missouri, brother of Charlie and Robert Newton (Bob) Ford." [537] Ola stated that a friend, Frances Tiller wrote to her when Charles Coleman Ford died in 1950 and Ola took the news to Jesse in the hospital. Ola heard from Jesse directly that Charles was Cap's son who Jesse said was his 1st cousin along with the Fords boys, Bob and Charlie who played out the hoax for Jesse to die in 1882.

Part of this story about Charles Coleman Ford being the son of Cap Ford was not completely true per the granddaughter of Charles Coleman Ford, Karen Ford. She has meticulously researched her family going back through the Ford's ancestral line. Charles' father was Dempsey Coleman (D.C.) Ford who was a sawmill owner in 1900 in Gregg County, Texas. He grew up in Georgia and his father, Norman M. Ford went into the Confederacy during the war in March 1862. Sadly, he died of the measles just two months after his enlistment.

Both Bud and I had the pleasure in speaking with Karen Ford. She was a joy to speak with, full of life and personality, just as her father, George Kenneth Ford who Bud was able to meet back in 1996 at the old Ford's homeplace in Longview. Bud said he was a very nice man and he really enjoyed talking with him, but Bud too said they talked about Cap Ford. Bud remembers that Kenneth had told him Cap was his grandfather, but after hearing Karen's story, Bud said, "well she should know."

It is only one of the two stories that Bud has run across from Ola's stories that did not "jive" with his findings. The other story that Jesse expressed again and again was that he was not in Northfield at the time of the bank robbery. It is not clear why he spun these two stories. Bud remains cautious with every story told until he has enough evidence to prove the truth.

Bud really delved into the story of Charles Coleman Ford and his grocery store where Jesse hung out in Longview. There is enormous amount of evidence that Jesse was truly there at the grocery store and I believe he was there long time before the store was in existence. He spoke a lot about the Sabine River which is near there and the town of Longview which became a big railroad town in 1870 when the process began to roll in the Southern Pacific Railroad.

"It checks out," Bud said. The years that Jesse spoke about was in the 30's and 40's just as the population was doubling during the oil boom. By 1942, construction started on the Big Inch pipeline in Longview. Jesse wrote a letter in 1942 from Longview to Howk.

Aubrey Everhard gave Bud a letter from a lady that included a map of the area where Ford's grocery store and the railroad depot for the Santa Fe Railroad was. The lady had family there, living by the Fords and encountered Jesse.

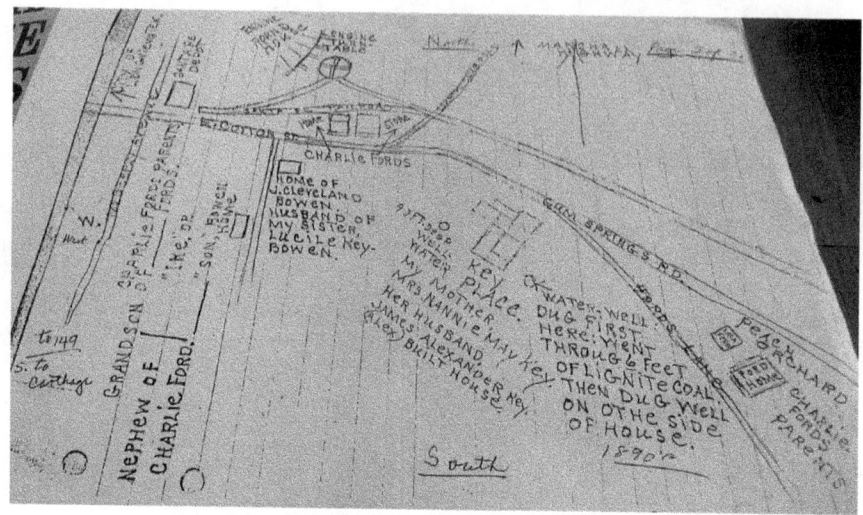

(Map of Ford's Grocery Store)

The wonderful letter written to Ola was from Frances (Hull) Tiller (1904-1994), wife of Willis Tiller from Carthage, Texas, 35 miles from Longview. [538] She was a dressmaker. Frances' mother was Nancy Elizabeth "Nannie Mae" (Hensley) Key Hull Rowe (1875-1963). Nannie Mae had first married Alexander James Key, a railroad conductor. In 1890, he was able to build a very nice, big and beautiful home on the intersection of Cotton Street, Gum Springs Road and Fords Lane. Karen Ford said it was heavily wooded on both sides of Fords Lane when she was growing up.

Alexander James Key first dug a well on the southeast side of the house but hit lignite coal at 6 feet. He chose another site on the west side and dug a 90 foot deep well. Alexander died at a very young age of 32 in 1902. They were married only 5 years.

Alexander's father William Hurbert Key was in the Louisiana 19th Infantry, Company C in the Confederacy, He was captured by the Union Army in Citronelle, Alabama and paroled at Meridian, Mississippi on May 13, 1865. [539] After the war he moved to Gregg County, Texas. The Keys intermarry with the Daltons. On Alexander's very large tombstone, beautifully carved stone, reveals that he was a Knight of Pythias.

Nannie Mae married again in 1903 to Dr. Charles Frances Hull, father of Frances Hull Tiller. He was a long-time practicing physician in Carthage for more than 50 years. He was a member of the Odd Fellows Lodge in Carthage. After he passed away, Nannie Mae remarried to Frank Rowe and they moved to Longview.

While Frances (Hull) Tiller was living in Carthage and Mom, Nannie Mae was only 35 miles away in Longview, Frances would ride the Santa Fe passenger train to Longview to take care of her mother when the need arose. Her mother lived only a short distance from the Ford Store. She describes her trip to Longview in a letter to Ola Everhard. Excerpt from "The Hoax that Let Jesse James Live," by Bud Hardcastle:

"I shall never forget my "visit" with an elderly white-haired, fine-looking man at the little country store of Charlie Ford, in Longview, Texas around 1944. His soft, wavy hair, shoulder length, and white, and his clean white shirt and blue or grey trousers, gave him the appearance of "stepping out of a picture! I had made the trip to Longview on the Santa Fe passenger train that day and was to return to Carthage the next morning. My mother lived a short distance from the Ford Store. She was sick, and I had gone to the store to buy some groceries to make some soup for her. Mr. Ford was waiting on me, when he said someone was in the store and he wanted me to meet. I turned around, and saw that fine-looking elderly man walking towards me from the back room. Mr. Ford said, "Mrs. Tiller, I want you to meet J. Frank Dalton," I said, "You mean The Frank Dalton?" Mr. Ford said, "Yes!" I shook hands with him, I could hardly believe my eyes! I told him, "I thought you died, a long time ago!" He said, "No, I'm still living!" Then added, "And, if there are any questions you would like to ask me, I will be glad to answer them." I told him I would like to hear something about Belle Starr, that I knew she was the sweetheart of Jesse James. "Well! He looked out the door, and up towards the sky, and said, "Belle Starr was a beautiful lady and was the smartest person I ever knew." I told them I would have to leave and prepare the soup for my sick mother. They followed me to the door, and Jesse James asked me if I could sit down and talk, for a few moments. So, I sat down on a step and they sat in cane-backed straight chairs. I asked Jesse James if all of the stories I had heard about the James and Daltons were true. I thought I was talking to J. Frank Dalton you see. He said, "No!" After I had talked with J. Frank Dalton, I said to myself on my way to my mother's house. "Well, I sure found out something! Frank Dalton was in love with Jesse James' sweetheart." Imagine my surprise, while I was listening to the radio one night in May 1948, I heard a man say he had a big surprise announcement to make! He turned the microphone over to his guest, which happened to be Jesse James! He said yes, he was still living and was born September 5, 1847. That the dead man who was buried in the yard of Jesse James' mother, was Charley Bigelow. Mrs. James knew that Jesse had not been killed. Jesse James lived until August 15, 1951." [540]

What a great story. Frances apparently had heard of J. Frank Dalton in the area and knew he had a connection to Jesse James. What a surprise for her and what a great story for us to get a clear picture of how impressive he was. There is no doubt in my mind that Charles Coleman Ford also knew who he was. How could you not.

Bud didn't have the opportunity to speak with Frances Tiller, but the letter was quite a gift. Frances Tiller died in 1994 and was buried in the Odd Fellows Cemetery in Carthage.

Aubrey Everhard made Bud a copy of the letter and the map that explained a lot of things. Bud called up John and Jo Ella Tatum and said, "We're going to Longview." They were ready to go. Jo Ella took her video camera.

They arrived in Longview and found the area with no problem. The map was very precise. The old store had been torn down. Aubrey had told Bud that Jesse had stayed in Charles Coleman Ford's trailer for a while that was parked next to the grocery store. Of course, it was not there either. On the map, Bud was curious about certain things that Jesse usually utilized in burying treasure. Is that why Jesse hung out there? Bud told me he had found signs and other sources pointing to a possible treasure site involving the well that Alexander Key dug. Key may have been a sentinel for that area.

On the map, it showed the family homes of the Fords along Fords Lane. Bud took a chance like he always did and knocked on a door at one of the homes shown on the map. It would be a miracle if he could locate any of the family after 50 some odd years. A man appeared at the door. As Bud was explaining to him what his purpose was and to find anyone of the Ford family, to Bud's surprise, the man said he was Charles Ford's son.

George Kenneth Ford (1921-1998), son of the original owner was standing in front of Bud and the Tatums. Kenneth, the name he went by, told them that there was an old man that would visit on different occasions when he was a little boy. That would have been in the 20's and 30's. He had no idea who the man was. He was told to keep his mouth shut about what he saw and heard.

Kenneth talked about Cap Ford, and recalled Cap was a brother to Bob and Charlie Ford, but Bud believes that Kenneth stated that his grandfather was D.C. (Cap) Ford. Bud said to be sure that's what he said, he would have to go back and review his video tapes. Bud hasn't been able to do this, but per Karen Ford, who was the daughter of Kenneth, Bud and I prefer to believe her and her research on the family that proved he was not Cap Ford, the brother of Charlie and Bob Ford. Who knows, we may all have been fooled.

Bud explained the entire story to Kenneth and the three men had a lot to say to each other while Jo Ella was videoing. Bud really liked Kenneth. When Bud told Kenneth who the old man was, Kenneth replied, "You mean that's who that old man was?" He told Bud that now, things make sense.

Kenneth graduated from Longview in 1940 and we still find him in Longview on the census that year. So, even as a young adult, he knew about the old man who came quite often with DeWitt

Travis. Kenneth remembers him staying in the trailer for a while. What a blessing it was to find and speak with Kenneth's daughter, Karen who had this wonderful photo of Charles Coleman Ford on the porch of the old Ford's Last Chance Grocery Store, taken in 1940, and low and behold, there was the trailer where Jesse stayed.

(Charles Coleman Ford on the porch of Ford's Last Chance Grocery Store- (trailer on the side where Jesse stayed for a while) (courtesy of Karen Ford))

Karen remembered stories told by her father and aunts that their dad, Charles, would allow workers or those in need of a place to stay, to use the trailer. Charles had received a lot of money from his father, D.C. Ford, but Charles spent it all by the time he was 25, in the year 1908. Charles married Lola Belle Foster, whose father also had some money and land. Both Charles and Lola Belle split up and she lived in the home where Bud found Kenneth until her death.

Karen was a delightful lady, she was a school teacher for years. She said her grandfather had a huge sense of humor and played a lot of practical jokes. He and her father, Kenneth would always spew out great words of wisdom or clever puns. They were both "people persons." Karen had the personality of both of her father and grandfather. Full of life. Bud thoroughly enjoyed speaking with her and her father. Bud told Karen, "Kenneth was a nice man, I enjoyed visiting with him. He certainly had a charming personality." It was August 1996 when Bud met him. Kenneth died two years later.

(Kenneth and Bud on the front porch having a good visit)

Karen, born in 1950, explained that her father was the only one of his siblings who left Longview and made a big name for himself. He made it big, but it appears that it was at the cost of his family. Karen said he became a hermit the latter part of his life and just stayed in that little house on Ford Lane. Now the house is gone, and the landscape has changed. There are two huge factories or industrial buildings sitting on top of where the Key's well was located, across Ford Lane where Kenneth spent his last days.

Karen explained to me how important the military and teaching was to Kenneth. He was a brilliant man and you could tell by Karen's voice; she was one smart cookie herself. Sadly, her father was not home much for her. He married her mother twice and divorced her twice. He became estranged from her mother and Karen. He chose to live his last years alone to deal with the "inner demons" he was carrying per Karen.

I found the obituary for George Kenneth Ford in the Longview News-Journal, Feb. 22, 1998. Kenneth "earned degrees from the University of Maryland in College Park, Maryland, and Louisiana State University at Baton Rouge, Louisiana. He did additional post-graduate studies in Taiwan and Mexico and at Cambridge University in England. Mr. Ford was a combat veteran of World War II and the Korean War. In World War II, he flew *33* bombing missions in B-17 bombers from England and later served as technical intelligence officer in North Korea during the Korean War. He earned the following combat decorations: Distinguished Flying Cross, six Air Medals and the Distinguished Unit Citation for bombing Brunswick, Germany on Jan. 11, 1944. During his 20 years in the U.S. Air Force, he served primarily in the field of intelligence. After he retired from the U.S. Air Force, he taught political science at the University of Maryland, Louisiana State University, and Del Mar College in Corpus Christi. Mr. Ford had been a member of the Longview Masonic Lodge since 1947 and was a 32nd Degree Scottish Rite Mason and a Shriner of Sharon Temple in Tyler. He is survived by his nephew, Michael Fitzgerald of Longview." [541]

There is no mention of his children. Not only did they not receive the recognition of their father, but he chose to leave everything to organizations. Kenneth Ford gave $100,000 to the Masons, left property to them, and some went to an Arab organization. Breaks my heart for Karen.

Kenneth's father, Charles Ford and his grandfather, Dempsey Ford may have been Masons and may have connected with Jesse that way. Charles' daughters were in Eastern Star and their husbands were Masons.

This was one of the most interesting trips that Bud and the Tatums took and to find Kenneth Ford was indeed a rare and special opportunity. Bud and I want to thank Karen Ford for her graciousness and willingness to help tell the rest of the story.

(Kenneth Ford, 1962 (courtesy of Karen Ford))

(George Kenneth Ford's Tombstone (courtesy of Karen Ford))

Solomon (Sol) Bedford Strickland

In 1947, Jesse went to Austin to apply for a pension in person. Jesse would soon be 100 years old in September. He went to see the one man left in Texas that he could depend on who knew his history well, Solomon (Sol) Bedford Strickland. Jesse knew Sol for years, fighting with Quantrill and knew he would back him up to pursue a pension that Texas was offering Confederate soldiers, especially the guerillas. Jesse could see his life changing especially after the fall in 1937. Jesse may have felt the need for a little help financially and physically. He was pursuing a small pension and a nice rest home to be cared for.

Jesse had visited Strickland in 1939 when he was living in Corpus Christi, but now Strickland was staying at Mrs. Danielson's home in Austin when Jesse reached out to him. A letter provided to Bud written by J. H. Taylor from the Texas Comptroller's office indicated that both Strickland and Dalton stayed in a nursing home on 1303 Canterbury Street in Austin for a short time.

In the Alabama, Texas and Virginia, U.S., Confederate Pensions, 1884-1958 we find Frank Dalton's official application for the pension. Dalton lived in Travis County, noting the address above, and in handwriting, it states he was in Elgin at the Johnson Nursing Home. The pension was filed March 19, 1947. On the application it said his age was 99, which goes along with his actual date of birth, September 5, 1847. He enlisted on March 8, 1863, served 2 years, 1 month, and 1 day. This is exactly what Jesse said as his enlistment date in all of his publications. He listed that he was under Captain William Anderson serving in "general service" (mounted).

Sol Strickland helped Jesse by writing out an affidavit verifying Dalton's service in the Civil War. Remember, at this time, Jesse was still going by the name of Frank Dalton and hadn't come out with his true identity.

Bud received from the Texas State Archives, a letter that was written by J.H. Taylor, Clerk Confederate Pension Division Comptroller's Department in December 11, 1947 to Harold Preece who was inquiring about Dalton. J.H. Taylor's response to Preece. "The last address furnished this office by Mr. Dalton was General Delivery, Longview, Texas. From different addresses furnished this office since he has been a pensioner, it appears he spends much of his time going from place to place. At the present time he is one hundred years old, and the last time I saw him he was very feeble physically, but his mind was very alert and communicative. As to whether or not he has kept any sort of personal journals or records, I am not informed. He likes to talk and seems to enjoy conversation and has a very ready recollection of matters which concern his past life. The application for pension of Mr. Dalton was approved on the testimony of one Solomon Bedford Strickland who was more than 100 years of age and had been a resident of this city for many years."

Mr. Taylor included the Strickland affidavit:

"When I first met applicant, Frank Dalton he was located at Lone Jack, Missouri. I know that he was in Bill Anderson's Company during 1863, when I was chief scout for Chas. Quantrill of the Quantrill's Gorillas. We were located at that time in the State of Missouri near Westport, known as Kansas City. Frank Dalton was in the first battle known as the Battle of Lone Jack. I was known as the "Red Wolf" also as the Mysterious Rider," this name having been given me by General Ewing of the Union Army. He offered a reward of $1500 for my body. I was born in Montgomery County, Texas on June 15, 1839, it was then known as the Harrisburg Land District. My father was a soldier of Sam Houston."

Signed Solomon "Sol" Strickland [542]

Note – Notice Sol used "Montgomery County, Texas as his birthplace, but remember James Lewis Dalton was born in Montgomery County, Kentucky in 1826. The county in Texas is where Conroe, Texas is located, near Lake Livingston.

Just really who was Strickland?

In the Civil War records on Strickland, it shows that he was in Waul's Texas Legion, formed in 1862 in Brenham, Texas between Austin and Houston. Strickland was in the cavalry and in Company F in the infantry division. They were first assigned to Arkansas and Louisiana and later transferred to Mississippi. They then fought with Nathan Bedford Forrest in Western Tennessee and Kentucky. We also show a Solomon Strickland in the 8th Louisianna Confederate Infantry. He was also known as the Chief Scout for Quantrill.

In his obituary, he is shown to be a Cherokee Indian, son of Princess Wildflower Ward and Chief Ward. [543] In the El Paso Herald-Post, August 15, 1947, He boasted on "aiding the Cuban Revolution in 1884 which resulted in the overthrow of the ruler, and often recounted his experiences as captain of a small band of Indian guerrillas in the Civil War." "His prize possession was a silver-cased watch he said Sam Houston gave him on his 20th birthday in 1859." [544]

At one time, after the war, Strickland was living in the area of Arkansas where Joe Vaughn and Lou Kilgore's grandfather did. Lou told the writer this story. He became friends with Lou's grandfather, Buck Wilson. They went squirrel hunting together many times. The Indian (Strickland) said, "I like you and you're my friend." He blindfolded Buck and turned him round and round and took him on a long journey down the Buffalo River during the dead of night. They reached an area where there was a concealed cave. They went down steps and the old Indian took the blindfold off. Buck saw stacks and stacks of sliver bars, as high as he was tall, and Buck was tall. The old Indian placed one silver bar in his hands which was very heavy. The Indian put that blindfold back on and took him back. He told Buck, do not try to find this location or you will be killed. There was always someone watching it such as a sentinel, which probably was the old Indian. Lou said that her grandfather broke limbs to try to find it again. He never found it.

Later, Lou was talking to Joe Vaughn's son, and she told this story about the old Indian showing her grandfather sliver bars in a secret cave. He said, "Don't you know who that was?" He said, "That was Red Strickland."

In the Amarillo Daily News, Feb. 18, 1941, Strickland is described as" living with the Indians in Texas, fought a duel with a Yankee captain, was a member of Quantrill's guerillas, was a personal friend of Jesse and Frank James, knew Bat Masterson and Sam Houston, and ate dinner at the White house with President Grover Cleveland." [545]

Solomon later moved to the Texas Confederate Men's Home in Austin. The picture Bud got from Aubrey Everhard of Sol was in front of a home, with busts of George Washington and it appears to be Sam Houston.

(Solomon "Sol" Strickland)

Sadly, Strickland died at the age of 108, August 14, 1947, before he received his own pension. (*The San Angelo Weekly Standard,* "Quantrill Raider, 5-War Vet Due for Confederate Pension," October 24, 1947). Strickland is buried in the Masonic Cemetery in Austin.

With Strickland's help, Jesse/Dalton was approved the pension by Geo. H. Sheppard as of September 1, 1947 before his 100th birthday. Dalton was named as 1 of the 13 Confederate Veterans still alive in Texas. He was given the number "13", a lucky number considered within the secret societies, befitting for Jesse. In the Texas Confederate Home in Austin, where Strickland had stayed, they had a hospital there and bed number 13 was reserved for Dalton, along with the rest of the surviving members.

Dalton finally started being recognized as a member of the Quantrill Raiders and began the process for allowing this band of Confederate heroes a chance for compensation. Dalton was the first Quantrill Raider to receive a pension. Another man whom I believe helped Jesse obtain that honor was Major Horace Shelton. He was a retired military major and a topnotch attorney. He was the Commander of the Texas Division, Sons of Confederate Veterans. After JJ came out, 8 months later, he never accepted another pension check.

In October 08, 1947, we find a newspaper clipping in the Kansas City Star that headlines, "Quantrill Raiders Recognized by Texas as a Confederate Unit". "Still spry, he can give a confederate yell that would scare a Yankee out of his britches today. Dalton was found eligible for $100 along with 13 other surviving veterans. The application stated that he enlisted at Boonville, Missouri under Capt. William Anderson of the mounted service and was discharged when Gen. Robert E. Lee surrendered. The statement of Solomon Bedford Strickland, also identified as a Quantrill Raider was known as "Red Wolf" and Mysterious Rider." Several other newspapers stated that Strickland was known as "Red Wolf", but other documents state that he was called "Red Fox". Ola also backed that up and in Arkansas, he was known as "Red Strickland."

The newspapers went viral as you would say in this day and time. Dalton's pension story prompted Harold Preece (1906-1992), to continue to correspond with J.H. Taylor, Clerk of the Texas State Comptroller's office, to retrieve more information on Dalton. Another letter from Preece to the comptroller was found in the Texas State Library and Archives Commission/Alabama Department of Archives and History on Ancestry.com. In his last paragraph, Preece said, "I hope to get back to Texas in 1948 and follow down a number of leads. I have the idea that much fine historical material is going to be lost if it is not taken down from the lips of the few surviving old pioneers or their immediate descendants. And I'd like, as a Texas writer, to preserve as much Texana as possible." 546

Preece loved to write American folklore and Western histories. He started out as a young reporter for the Austin Statesmen in 1922, wrote for magazines in 1925, and then became a freelance writer. He moved from Texas to Tennessee and wrote fervently for civil rights and the support for all races, especially the black community. He tackled the Ku Klux Klan in 1946 in a magazine article and he and his family were chased out of the state. They moved to New York, then Massachusetts and would continue to contribute his work to the Texas Rangers and Zane Grey's Western Magazines. 547

Another writer, Richard S. Brownlee saw an article in the Kansas City Missouri Star regarding Dalton getting his pension and having served with Bill Anderson. Brownlee was writing his Master of Arts Thesis for the History Department of the University of Missouri on the Irregular Confederate Forces in Missouri between 1861-1865. He wrote this letter to the Texas Comptroller office on November 21, 1947.

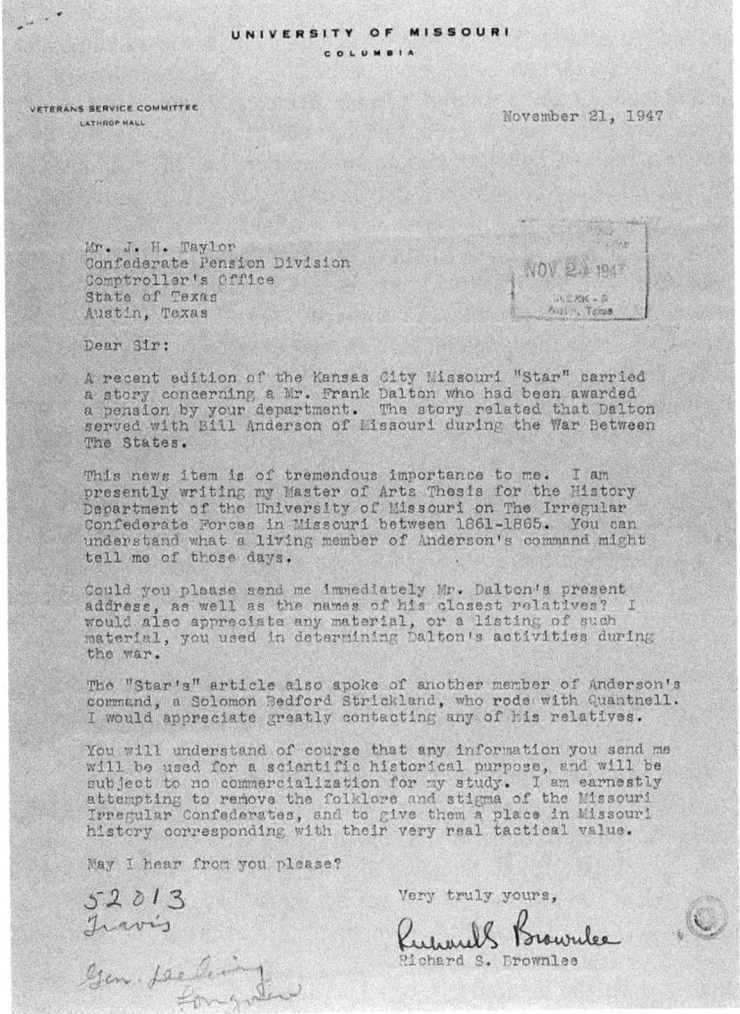

(Letter of Richard S. Brownlee (Image from the Alabama, Texas and Virginia, U.S. Confederate Pensions, 1884-1958. Ancestry.com.))

Dr. Richard Smith Brownlee II (1918-1990) was the author of "Gray Ghosts of the Confederacy: Guerrilla Warfare in the West, 1861-65," published in 1983. He was noted as "the finest public historian the state of Missouri has ever known." (Quoted from Representative Francis Bud Barnes III in 1985.)

Brownlee's words within the letter, "I am earnestly attempting to remove the folklore and stigma of the Missouri Irregular Confederates, and to give them a place in Missouri history corresponding with their very real tactical value."

Back in Longview

Just after a month from the celebration of his 100th birthday and receiving the recognition he desired, Jesse was back in Longview. His life and independence would change overnight. He told Ola, "I was living in a hotel at Longview and I was walking on crutches then because I'd broke my leg not too long before, and I had to be careful. I went up town and was talking with some men. I was a big talker, when I could talk and before my throat started bothering me. I met a man that I knew pretty well, and we got to talking and he wanted me to go home with him and eat supper. So, I did. And that night I got a taxi and went back to the hotel. Some men had been working on the front of the hotel and the light out in front of it had been changed and wasn't very bright like it had been. I couldn't see very good when I got out of the taxi. I took about two or three steps and my crutches gave way and I fell. A bunch of people ran out there and the men put coats down on the ground for me to lay on. I said, "The dickens, don't do that! Just call an ambulance. I'm broke all to pieces." So, some woman called an ambulance and I was taken to the hospital and they found that my hip was broken. This happened on the night of October 12, 1947." [548]

The break was about half an inch from where he broke his leg near his hip before in 1937. He was taken to the Gregg Memorial Hospital in Longview.

This must have been about the time that Howk enters the picture once again, at Jesse's weakest point. In Howk's book, "Jesse James and the Lost Cause", he was speaking of how tough Jesse was. Howk said at the time of the 1937 break, "We thought most surely he would die both these times (1937 & 1947), but somehow he would manage to stay in the land of the living. None of us ever had the slightest idea he would even live for a month.

"About the time he broke his hip in Longview, in October 1947, in True Magazine, issue September, 1947, as I recall there was a picture which True represented therein, and proved it to be a picture of Frank James on one side, Jesse Woodson James on the other side, and their mother behind them. It was a great picture and had been discovered by a man named Clarence N. Bouyer. Bouyer had found the picture in an old cabin, he said near Bottomless Lakes, New Mexico. It was this photograph which started a series of incidents and revelations going that since have never once stopped, not even for a good breath. From then on, things started falling into their natural places. One after another they came and started off with bits of real proof, facts, legal evidence, and so on. Jesse remained in Gregg Memorial Hospital in Longview, Texas for several weeks. It looked as if the rugged old warrior would surely die, but he didn't." [549]

A cold heart Howk had. He was more interested in the notoriety, the fame, and fortune of the man that he could collect himself, rather than concern for the well-being of the man himself.

Jesse was having a pretty rough time. Of course, back then, they couldn't perform a hip replacement. With Jesse at 100 years old, there was not much they could do for him. Usually, once a hip was broke, especially for a 100-year-old man, their life expectancy fell drastically. He was one tough man.

Jesse was transferred to the Veteran's Hospital in McKinney, Texas sometime in January 1948. An article in the Tyler Morning Telegraph described Frank Dalton, formerly of Gladewater, "has proven his long and varied military record and has gained access to services in the Veterans Hospital in McKinney." In order for Dalton to be admitted to the Veteran's Hospital, he had to prove that he had served in the military. The hospital officials checked with Washington and the War Department and confirmed that Dalton served with the army from 1865-1874. He was also certified as a veteran of the Indian Wars and was able to be admitted to the McKinney Veteran's Hospital. This helps to solidify Dalton's stories of being in the army and the Texas Rangers. [550]

Jesse was transferred again to Dallas Veteran's Hospital in February 1948. When he was received by the hospital, he told the staff that he was a Confederate veteran and a former Texas Ranger. They had no proof at the time and didn't know if these were facts. The papers were never transferred from the hospital in McKinney. It prompted Zuleika B. Hicks, Director of Home Service with the American Red Cross of Dallas County Home Services to write a letter requesting more information from the Confederate Pension Division. They wanted to know more about his next of kin. [551]

I believe the hospital found out rather quickly that he was a confirmed vet and he was admitted to the Dallas Veteran's Hospital. They took his guns away from him.

During this time, Dalton's stories continued to be told. "Dalton says he was with the cavalry troops in the South Dakota Bad Lands that found the bodies of General George Custer and his men the day after the Sioux Indians under Sitting Bull had killed and scalped them all in the battle on the Little Big Horn River in June 1876. The detachment with which Dalton rode was expecting to join Custer, who was known to be somewhere in that part of the territory. They reached the river, above where Custer was supposed to be, and camped for the night. Early next morning two Indians who served as scouts for Custer came into camp and told about a battle that had been fought and that all the soldiers were killed. Nobody put much belief in the story, Dalton said, because Indians were not remarklable for telling things straight, but the troop saddled and rode down the river. They saw smoke and thought it was a village Custer had burned. Then they came on a village the Indians had deserted, with a few dead bodies laying about. Riding on they came to the real battlefield, where Custer and his men were laying where they had fallen, each one scalped clean and the Indians gone. It was a dreadful sight, and one that Dalton says he will never forget.

"The Veterans Administration checked Army files to establish Dalton's right to a bed in a Veterans hospital, and found the record entitled him to the service. He says he had brief service in Puerto Rico during the Spanish-American War, but it was with the quartermaster corps, handling horses. He tried to get into World War I, but was 70 years old and was refused, so he says he went to Canada and got in by concealing his age and was sent over to Europe." [552]

Another story printed and spread throughout East Texas was that he was a private operative for a famous detective agency. [553]

Jesse had plenty of time to think during his stay in the hospitals. Supposedly, with the encouragement from Howk, he teeter-tottered on the idea of revealing who he really was. Jesse had told Howk, in "Jesse James and the Lost Cause" that "The leaders (of the KGC), every one of them, had each taken the bloody oath of loyalty instigated from the beginning of the hostilities by Quantrill himself. Every man who took this oath was well informed about what disloyalty, violation of oath, and violation of orders would mean. It also meant, that if any man or men ever disclosed a single secret or talked or wrote without specific permission from headquarters, the first member of the Circle who could reach that violator would kill him on the spot. Up until October 1947, I Jesse Woodson James, dying then with a broken hip was given permission to talk." [554]

Jake Wilson and Howk

While Jesse was suffering in the hospital, Howk and his friend Jake Wilson were brainstorming at Wilson's home in Rye, Texas 235 miles away.

Jake Wilson's family went way back with Jesse. Good ole Jesse used to come to their ranch where they had built a racetrack just for Jesse. The ranch was either in Brazos County or Leon County, Texas.

Jake's grandfather was Francis Morgan "Frank" Wilson (1844-1931), born in San Augustine in the Republic of Texas. His father was Reverend Francis Wilson and mother, Harriet Brown. They moved to Newton County and then Livingston, Polk County, Texas. Livingston is where supposedly Maxmillian was taken. On Frank's gravesite there is a Confederate Flag, indicating he was a Confederate soldier. A Confederate Pension was filed on Oct. 19, 1909 in Leon County and it was learned he was under Captain W.C. Gibbs in Company "E" in the Spates Battalion in the infantry. In Frank Wilson's pension, the State and County Assessor for Leon County, *J. D. Reed* signed the affidavit. Jesse used the name, J.D. Reed.

There was a J.D. Reed who in 1870 lived in *Leon County* and was a farm laborer in *Centerville*. He later was found in the 1880 census as a farmer whose wife was John Ella and they lived in dwelling *#33*. The number **33** comes up quite often, even in addresses.

Frank's son, Francis Claude Wilson (1870-1951) married Mary Thomas in Polk County, August 31, 1870. They moved to Brazos County in the late 1870's, then settled near Leona, in Leon County. His 2nd wife, Jane Wingfield who was a widow, was buried by her first husband, near Centerville, Texas.

Jake, whose full name, John Jacob Aster "Jake" Wilson (1912-2005) ended up in a very small town of Rye, Texas, way down in South Texas, northeast of Houston in the hot, humid and boggy part of Texas. Jake owned and operated Trinity River Sand and Gravel Company.

Lou Kilgore found out about Jake Wilson and Howk who took care of Jesse during his last years and began writing Jake. He invited her to come to Rye, Texas. She did and they got engaged. Lou met Howk through Jake Wilson. Both Howk and Jake took care of Dalton in the 40's and 50's. Both Howk and Jake knew Dalton very well. Howk stated that Jake Wilson was a grandson of Jesse, per Lou Kilgore, but she said he wasn't. She was more comfortable with Jake than Howk, Lou said.

Jake told Lou that Howk thought it would be a great idea if they showcase Jesse. They went and talked to Jesse in the hospital about a big reveal and the excitement of going on tour with him as the real Jesse James. Jake said that later Jesse had said something like, "They're going to do something, I guess that's alright." Did not sound like he was all in at the time.

Leon County was the county where the town, Centerville was located. A very important hot spot and safe haven for Jesse. It was also noted by Howk, that Joe Vaughn had a farm/ranch in Leon County there where he hid John Wilkes Booth for a short time. I don't know if that was true, but Leon County was a place that definitely should be placed on the map, as well as Brazos County, and the Houston area.

In the meantime, Jesse was loving all the attention from the nurses in Veteran's Hospital in Dallas. He was definitely a lady's man, even at the age of 100. He had listed his birthday as March 8th, 1848. Bud stated that Aubrey Everhard told him that Jesse left Quantrill on March 8th, which was a momentous date for him. He used that date as his birthday when he was going by the name of Frank Dalton/J. Frank Dalton. Jesse told the Everhards that he changed names and date of births just as he would a dirty shirt.

Many people were informed of this big day for him, his 100th birthday. He was going to have another party.

Major Horace Shelton said "he participated in Dalton's 100th birthday party in Dallas, when Dalton was made commander of the Texas Division of Confederate Veterans. Dalton was recognized as a veteran of Quantrill's Raiders and as such was admitted to the Texas Confederate Pension rolls." [555]

Major Shelton did so much more than that. Ola said, "Jesse received a Confederate Service Commission. The promotion jumped him from the rank of a Private to that of General, Jesse said." [556] Several letters from the Confederate Pension Division and newspapers began calling him, "General."

(Major Horace Shelton (Ola's collection))

Major Horace Shelton's father, Dr. James Knox Polk Shelton (1845-1884) lived in Nolanville, Bell County, Texas, 8 miles East of Killeen where Jesse was. He was a former captain in the Confederate Army. He served in Terrell's Regiment, 34th Texas Cavalry, Company H. His son, Horace was greatly influenced by his father and a tremendous supporter for the South and Confederacy. He had a Confederate flag beside his American flag in his law office. Shelton also was a reporter/writer and wrote for the Austin Statesman. He later became city editor for the Statesman and for State Topics. He became a correspondent for the Hearst Newspapers and established the San Antonio Gazette.

Shelton was heavily involved in Mexico as President Diaz' press agent and then became Madera's until his assassination. "He served in World War I as a lieutenant, ended up in France and stayed after the armistice to sell horses and mules to Belgium and supervise feeding of Russian refugees. He was decorated for the latter task." He was promoted to a Major. He had 30 years of being a Legionnaire, a VFW state commander, State's outstanding Legionnaire and was chosen as the No. 1 Legionnaire in the nation. [557]

Jesse and Horace Shelton had a lot in common as you can see. I'm sure they enjoyed each other's company and conversation. Great respect was had between the two and there's no doubt in my mind that Horace knew who the old man was. In Horace Shelton's family, we find the Sheltons and Daniels who connect to my family and also most importantly connecting to Elbert, Georgia and the Lindseys and McGeehees who were a part of Zerelda's family.

"I want it brought out so that the people will know some facts, the truth. They have lived under an umbrella of fiction for too many years and its time for some of these people that have been making money and still making money and I can name them, some of them, are stopped from writing a bunch of baloney. It is time the truth came out."

-Ola Everhard

Chapter Twenty-Five: A New Woman in His Life

Ola Everhard had read in the Austin newspaper that Frank Dalton was in the Dallas Veteran's hospital and had turned 100 years old. He was awarded a Confederate pension and was recognized as a Quantrill Raider. Ola and her mother, Bertha were following some of Dalton's articles in the newspaper as early as 1939 and became very interested in the old man. She was curious to know if this is the same man her mother, Bertha knew and claimed kinship with. They planned to go see the man who was drawing much interest.

As recognition and notoriety was all around Jesse, Howk wanted to reel him in to protect his own interest and plans he had for Jesse. Howk came to the Dallas hospital and whisked him away to Centerville in Leon County, Texas, 125 miles, whether he was ready or not.

After the Everhards found out Dalton was moved out of the hospital and into the Sullivan Hotel in *Centerville*, they went there to see him. *Centerville* is a very small community, southeast of Waco in Leon County. Howk was caring for him at that time and said Jesse had lived there in Centerville since 1944. It was only one of the few places he was living during that time period. We have evidence he was in Longview in 1944 and 1946/47.

When Ola and Aubrey entered the room, Ola explained to Dalton whose daughter/granddaughter she was. He lightened up and said, "Is that a fact, I knew them all, I knew them well." [558] That was the beginning of a wonderful relationship.

We touched a little on Ola Everhard's mother, Bertha, who was related to Jesse and knew him when he was in Indian Territory, but little is known about Ola's father. He was a cowboy, named Archie Cimmons "K" Maddox. Census records show different dates of birth, 1883/1885/1887. His date of death is not found, nor the location of his burial. His census records show that he was born in Texas and his father born in Missouri. His parents are unknown. He's another man who's mysterious and lived on the edge; moving from place to place, changing his name and any identifying aspects of himself. Many researchers show him connected to the Maddox family in Rusk County, Texas, who had an Archie G. Maddox in their household, but the dates and locations do not fit, nor the census records. This Archie died in 1920 and he was related to Jesse through the James and Wheeler family.

Ola had written in a letter to Cowboy Williams that her father was a cowboy for the famous X.I.T. Ranch in the panhandle of Texas near Channing in Hartley County. This was probably in earlier years between 1900-1912. Maddox also worked on the Edmonson Ranch near Claude, Texas, a foreman for various ranches in that region. Ola had a wonderful framed photo of her father wearing a cowboy hat on her wall in her home in Lovington, New Mexico.

Ola's father was going by the name of Arch Wynn in the 1910 census in Carson County, Texas which is within the towns of Panhandle and White Deer in the Texas Panhandle. This is where the JA Ranch was located. Also, there was the *Diamond F Ranch* near White Deer. The town of White Deer began in 1882 when British-owned Francklyn Land and Cattle Company bought up railroad land. On the 1910 census Archie was married and had a baby girl age two, Ollie, Ola Mae's oldest sister. Archie was shown to be a farmer.

After the cowboy life, he is shown as a Track Foreman for the Panhandle and Santa Fe Railway Company in 1918. This is shown on his Draft Registration Card during World War I. This railway system ran through Pampa, Amarillo, and *Hereford* which became a major part of the Santa Fe's freight route from Chicago to California. It also ran a disconnected line from the Texas-New Mexico border south of Carlsbad, New Mexico, to Pecos.

The Maddox's were listed in the Carson County, Texas census in 1920, listing Archie as A C Maddox. It shows he was a carpenter. Ola was three at the time, born in Ardmore, Oklahoma in 1916. That's about all that is publicly known of Archie. This may have not been his real name.

Bud heard about Ola and Aubrey Everhard from his good friend Joe Wood, the newsman and investigator for the *St. Louis Globe-Democrat*. Joe spent several months with Jesse at Meramac Caverns and knew the Everhards. They had come to Missouri and met him. Joe put a story in his book about Ola and Jesse.

When Bud and his cousin, Kenny Brown met with Aubrey Everhard on April 3, 1990, after Ola had passed, Aubrey stated that after the introduction of themselves to Dalton in Centerville, the tension eased up a bit. Aubrey lured Howk to town to get items for Dalton on false pretense, allowing Ola and Dalton to talk amongst themselves.

During the time Dalton and Ola were alone that evening, he told Ola how he was kin to her and her mother's family. He said to Ola, "By now, I guess you know who I really am." Ola answered, "Yes I do." Dalton stared intensely with his piercing blue eyes and said, "Look, whatever you do, my name is J Frank Dalton." "I know that", replied Ola. Dalton firmly said, "Well, when you talk to me or about me, my name is J. Frank Dalton." With a smile, Ola said, "I'll remember that." She kept her word.

They had a great visit, all the while Dalton laid in bed with a sheet pulled up to his neck. When they were leaving, Ola said something to Dalton, such as "be careful" as she reached for the door. When she turned for one last look, Dalton stared her down and said, "I'm always careful." He had two loaded .38 Special Revolver six shooters pointed straight at Ola and Aubrey. He kept them along each side of his waist under the crisp white sheets. They never left his side, except when he was in the hospital. He also had two pistols, loaded in a suitcase under the bed and two in the dresser close by. Who would do that? Only Jesse. He was always prepared for trouble. He had seen plenty and expected plenty.

It is funny, Aubrey learned from the best. When Bud and Kenny went to see Aubrey for the first time, he too had a pistol with a long barrel in his hand, possibly a .44 caliber, pointing in the direction of Bud and Kenny. Placing it on the table between him and his visitors, Aubrey stated, "Now you boys are both pretty big and I don't know you, so right now I'm going to lay this up here for protection until I get to know you a little better, I'm going to keep this right here".

(Gun that Aubrey kept on hand)

Well, it didn't take long for Aubrey to feel at ease with the two and the gun remained untouched. Aubrey, Kenny, and Bud became great friends, staying for two days. Aubrey was a great host and even paid for their motel room.

Bud said that Aubrey's home in Lovington, New Mexico was like a museum, full of photos, memorabilia, antiques, and even a pair of Jesse's pajamas. All this and Bud's interview with Aubrey were captured on video. Aubrey at the age of 84, was still sharp as a tack and his memory was excellent. The writer was given privy to the tape and was able to retrieve snapshots from the video to share with the readers. Bud and Kenny left with a newfound friendship and a wealth of information. Sadly, Aubrey died a year after their meeting, July 29, 1991, three years from Ola's death, November 27, 1988.

(Aubrey and Kenny)

(Aubrey and Bud)

    Thankfully, Ola was interviewed on March 6, 1986 by William Tunstill, Jr. while working on his book, "Billy the Kid and Me Were the Same", published in January 1988. Tunstill spent six years working with Ola regarding the connection between Jesse James and Billy the Kid. She was able to have Tunstill's book on hand before she died. Ola and Aubrey thought very highly of Mr. Tunstill and he did of them. He stated, "I have yet to find her in error on anything she had from Jesse," he said. "I have nothing to gain by chasing rainbows. I was so enthralled with this setup that I went hook, line and sinker. She's 100 percent." [559]

    Mr. Tunstill has been noted as "a recognized authority on the life of Billy the Kid." He set out to prove that Billy the Kid was William Henry "Brushy Bill" Roberts, born in Dec. 31, 1859 in Buffalo Gap, Texas near Abilene and died in 1950 in Hico, Texas. Tunstill's interview on Unsolved Mysteries, Season 1, Episode 20, he said, "There were 17 points of identification between Brushy and Billy the Kid."

    Ola and Tunstill worked extremely hard to pull all the evidence that they each had to confirm that Brushy was who he said he was and who was a great friend to Jesse. As we explored earlier in the book, we see how close Jesse and Billy were even though they were 12 years apart.

    We have all been misled, missing out on knowing the truth of the extreme suffering both Jesse and Billy endured, and how they developed into men who were willing to take on justice upon their own shoulders for someone who they deeply cared for. We missed out on knowing their true character and what they had to do to survive. Tunstill stated, "We need to do away with all these legends that have poisoned the true facts of history."

    William Tunstill was a very credible man, born in Big Springs, Texas who later became a teacher and administrator in the Fort Worth school system. His interest in Billy the Kid was his passion, becoming a great historian of his time. He moved to Roswell, New Mexico where he pursued the outlaw in Billy's own territory. He wrote an article for the Lovington Newspaper, searching for someone who had info on Billy the Kid. Ola called Tunstill and explained her story and the connection that Jesse and Billy had. Tunstill did not hesitate for one moment and drove from Roswell to Lovington, 92 miles, that very day.

    Tunstill gave Bud a copy of the video tape containing Tunstill's interview with Ola, including Ola describing and showing some of the photos and keepsakes she received from Jesse himself and

Brushy Bill. Aubrey supplied both Tunstill and Hardcastle letters between the two. Jesse and Brushy were dear friends to the end.

As the reader has seen throughout this book, the evidence that Bud himself has uncovered, proves the devoted friendship between Jesse and Billy. It's a fascinating story. Whether or not your strong opinion goes against this path is the reader's prerogative, but all Bud asked is for the reader to keep an open mind, gather the evidence, and do your own research.

Aubrey and Ola developed an incredible relationship with Dalton. They were family. In the first year of knowing each other, they respected J. Frank Dalton's wishes and addressed him as he requested. Ola was a third cousin to him, but out of her southern ways of respect for the elderly, she called him "Uncle Frank."

The Everhards began visiting him every Sunday in *Centerville,* which was 150-mile trip one way. They took care of his needs. One Sunday when they went, they found that Howk was tearing up pictures, letters, and other documents and throwing them in the waste basket next to Jesse's bed. Ola cringed thinking that these items were valuable to Jesse, but Jesse must have asked him to do this. What was he hiding? Ola said that Jesse had several albums of photos and scrapbooks just pouring out the history of his life. She said, "No one knows what old Howk did with the albums and scrapbooks of Jesse's, but Ola heard that he pawned the guns and watch. What a shame!" [560]

The photos and scrapbook were probably put together by him and someone who meticulously followed his life story and was going to give them to someone to write his story or for Metro-Goldwyn-Mayer (MGM) studios to produce a movie with. Aubrey gave Bud a letter that Dalton wrote to Lucille Mahaffey in Longview, asking her to write his story. Lucille met Dalton at the Ford's Grocery Store in Longview. John Shevlin was going to write Jesse's Memoirs. And of course, Ola did indeed write his story and Bud vowed to prove the truth with her story and his.

Ola said that Jesse gave her copies of several pictures and signed them J. Frank Dalton. The photo of Jesse and Frank with his mother in the middle was given to her by Jesse. He showed the Everhards a picture of him and Geronimo together, probably was shot at the World's Fair in St. Louis in 1904. He also showed a photo of his mother at the James' farm, not the Samuel's farm.

Things appeared to be changing for Jesse. Howk and him were going through everything he had, piece by piece. Jesse personally gave Ola a special gift when they were alone. It was an old tarnished coin. Jesse had carried this old coin with him always, which meant a lot to him. He placed it in her hand without any explanation. Ola took it home, placed it in a special clear container and set it in her glass showcase. She never knew what she had nor did Aubrey.

When Bud was at Aubrey and Ola's home in 1990, Aubrey showed them the coin. Bud had never seen anything like that, but knew it was something valuable to Jesse. In the video that Bud's cousin Kenny took during their visit at the Everhards home, Bud was able to examine it. The coin read, "Confederate States of America Half DOL." At the time of the visit, Bud didn't know the history of the coin, but said it was tarnished and very heavy. It was definitely old and made of silver.

With further research, Bud and I discovered it was a very valuable coin. It was the only coin produced by the Confederacy from the New Orleans mint. The mint prior to the war was under the control of the United States. In March 1861, at the beginning of the war, the CSA seized the mint. They used some of the dies that were originally there, but took the design and altered it with their own CSA coin with 13 stars surrounding Lady Liberty, representing the 13 states which the Confederacy was born and the date of 1861. On the reverse side, there is a shield with seven stars representing the 7 seceding states and a liberty cap entwined with a stalk of sugar cane and cotton.

(Confederate States of America, 1861 original Half Dol. Coin (This original coin shown on Professional Coin Grading Services, PCGS, a division of Collectors Universe, Inc. https://www.pcgs.com, was auctioned and sold at $960,000))

(Bud examining coin at Aubrey's home)

Due to the war and other factors, there was very little bullion left to produce any coinage. The CSA were only able to make 4 coins of the original revised die. The original 4 coins were made of 93 percent silver, 6 percent copper, and 1 percent trace element.

The New Orleans mint was shut down late in May that year, only being utilized for a few weeks. Union forces took it over in 1862.

There are several inconsistencies regarding where the four coins went or if there were truly only four. The four have apparently been found. Jefferson Davis claimed to have a Confederate coin that was stolen after his capture. A great article on this is found on *Heritage Auctions* – https://coins.ha.com - "1861 Original Confederate Half Dollar PR40, Only Official Coin of the Confederacy." Something that came out of this article raises a flag. "Researcher George Corell, coauthor of *The Lovett Cent; a Confederate story*, has advanced the theory that the Confederate half dollars were actually **clandestine striking**s." This may explain why Jesse had one and carried it with him always.

The story came out after the war, 18 years later after the coin was minted, written by Dr. Benjamin Taylor of New Orleans. He had one of the original coins and who was Chief Coiner of the Mint for the Confederacy at the time this story broke.

There were restrikes made of the coin which are nowhere close to the original. The images are not clear, very distorted and flattened. [561] We will never know the true value of what Jesse gave Ola, but it was worth its weight in gold to Ola because it was a gift from Jesse.

Jesse was getting things tidied up, just as a person prepares for substantial changes, a move, or death. The change that was coming would change his life forever. There was no turning back. It was inevitable.

One Sunday in Centerville, Jesse told Ola, "Ola I'm fixing to leave here in a few days. I promised my mother that I'd come out in the open with my true name when I got to be a hundred years old. I'm a hundred now so I'm going to keep my promise to my mother. I will shock a lot of people when they learn who I really am. Of course, there's a lot of people who already know. When I get where I'm going, I'll let you know where I am and when I do, you come to me, you hear?" [562]

Dalton wrote them a letter, requesting Ola and Aubrey to meet him in Lawton for a special event in 1948 to declare an important message to the world. They went and supported Dalton who informed the world he was the real Jesse James. From then on, Ola called him "Uncle Jesse."

"Someday there'll be a story that will rock the nation. You'll know it when it breaks."

-Cole Younger

Chapter Twenty-Six: The Coming Out Party

When Joe Hunter began to publicize in 1948 that he had found the brass bucket back in the 30's, leading to Jesse James' gold, the newspapers exploded. *The Lawton Constitution Newspaper*, February 29, 1948, printed the article just before Jesse's celebrated birthday party was held on March 8th at the Dallas Veteran's Hospital. The title of the article was, "Lawton Trio Believe End of Trail is Near In 16-Year Search for Fabulous Treasure in Expansive Wichitas." The trio was Joe H. Hunter, Herbert Penick, and his son, Archie Penick.

Joe Hunter was stumped after 16 years of searching with the clues he had, to find the big cache of the century. He needed help and he turned to the media, hoping that someone would come forward to help him decipher the clues to reach the treasure.

Jesse saw the news article. Jesse and Howk wrote Joe Hunter with codes placed in the letter to check Joe out to see how much he knew or if it was all fake. Joe wrote back and placed codes within his letter to also do some validating himself. Both letters proved that both sides knew what they were talking about. Joe discussed maps that he had.

The more Jesse learned what the man knew, and having his hands on the maps, Jesse became furious. Jesse was ready to go kill the man. Bud said, "Jesse buried all the money, gold, and priceless items with intricate details for the South, not for some greenhorn to dig it up for himself."

Howk and Joe Hunter continued to correspond with each other. After Howk and Jake Wilson moved Jesse to Centerville, the writing became clear on the wall. It was now or never. It was time. Jesse felt the pressure building and he knew that the time was right to reveal who he was.

Frank Hall and Lindsay Whitten, journalist and investigators for the Lawton Constitution of Lawton, Oklahoma encouraged Hunter to go to Centerville to influence Jesse to make a trip to Lawton. Hunter made a trip to Centerville with the newsmen, Whitten and Hall. Jake Wilson was there. Howk said he did not want any money??? He only wanted to "present his elder friend to the world in a fashion not embarrassing to him, to present to the public a person who already had become immortal."

The first thing they noticed when meeting Jesse was the piercing, chilly, blue eyes, and his keen intellect. Hall and Whitten noticed the photo of him, his brother and mother compiled together on the table. They were curious about the photo laid before them. The photos they had always seen depicting Jesse and Frank were not like the men that were in the photo.

JJ said, "There was lots of gold hidden in the Wichita mountains area, plenty of it, but unless they have the right information no person will ever find it." Joe Hunter discussed what he found with JJ, but as the pictures show on the front page of the *Lawton Constitution*, May 19, 1948, JJ was hesitant and a little perturbed of the intrusion into his gold fields.

The maps to where the brass bucket was found and other areas in the Wichita Mountains that Hunter obtained were stolen from Jesse in 1882 after his alleged death. JJ told of being on a trip to England, aboard a ship and was seriously ill. They were stolen at that time and made their way back to the U.S. to an aged man in eastern Oklahoma. They were hidden in a concealed bottom of a chest. Hunter became the custodian. The maps were made out of a huge cowhide and the other on the tongue of Jesse's boot.

Hunter said he got the maps from an aged man who was a friend of his father's, by the name of Cook. The man said, "We buried it there about 62 years ago and I hope you can find it." He was able to find clues and a rock on which another map was carved into it. Hall writes that Hunter learned that the codes and markings coincide with the codes first established by the Spaniards and English. Codes were confirmed by Jesse per Hunter. The code breaker was the direction the pick head was pointing. Hunter in the newspaper article in February 1948 said the code breaker was the direction of the pick handles. Somebody was misleading somebody.

Frank Hall and Lindsay Whitten really set out to investigate Dalton's story. It was incredible. Their interview with Dalton left them wanting more. Dalton's mind was sharp, and he never hesitated in answering their questions. The photos, documents, guns, and other items that they were shown, blew them away. It would have taken many decades to accumulate what this old man had collected. Those eyes, they never seen such eyes that could see right through a person.

Howk took Jesse to Lawton and began preparing to be exposed in living color.

Hall and Whitten talked to many people, to people who Dalton said knew him. They went high and low in validating this man from libraries to checking fact against fiction, and finally came to the conclusion that Dalton was the real Jesse James. The story that they would be putting together would either put their names in the limelight or ruin their reputation. They did not care; it was the story of a lifetime and they truly believed this man was Jesse James.

At midnight, May 19th, 1948 Hall and Whitten began to construct the unbelievable tale of Jesse James. They gathered staff and had an all-night vigil. The stories were complete by morning. It was considered a "World Scoop."

"Jesse James Is Alive! In Lawton" – The Lawton Constitution; May 19, 1948. "Jesse James, the famed Missouri outlaw, is still alive and riding the trail again. The two-fisted, gun-slinging Robin Hood of the post-Civil War era was revealed today to be officially alive and residing in Lawton." [563]

"Rare in the annals of newspapering, an occupation inoculated to the unusual, have reporters had the privilege of recording a story of such historic character as has been the lot of members of The Constitution Staff. The story of Jesse James defies imagination. The fact that The Constitution, in this edition, is "scooping the world" on a story destined to be carried to the far corners of the earth within the next few hours is, in itself, the realization of a newspaperman's' dream." [564]

(Front page Headlines from: Lawton Constitution, May 19, 1948)

From this story, people began to write saying they knew the real Jesse. One in particular from Robert E. Lee, from Baton Rouge. He was 78 at the time and from the famous Lee line. He was sent for to identify JJ. He arrived in Lawton, 4 days afterward. Before Robert E. Lee could say anything when he entered the room, JJ said, "Haven't I seen that nose of yours somewhere before?" Jesse remembered Robert.

"Boys! It's him! I can hardly believe my eyes, but that man is truly JJ. I can't be mistaken. It's the old bandit himself," said Robert E. Lee.

Lee had joined Buffalo Bill Wild West Show in 1893 in Chicago during the world's fair. Lee was Buffalo Bill's bodyguard. Brushy Bill was also up there at that time. He was doing something with horses for Buffalo Bill, riding in the Wild West shows. In Howk's book, "Jesse James and the Lost Cause" said that Jesse helped Cody finance his Wild West Show and put it on the road. Jesse performed in these shows as a rider and as an expert shot. He said that Jesse had stayed there for three weeks performing.

Buffalo Bill allowed Robert E. Lee to be in part of the conversation, but most of it was private between the two aging men. It was at this time when Jesse asked Buffalo Bill if he thought he should let the world know of his identity and Buffalo Bill's reply, "No, just let it ride for now," but that was back in 1893 and many things had changed since then.

One man, Leo W. Park from Lawton went to see Jesse. He had been told by his father about Jesse James and that Jesse had saved his life one time. Mr. Park visited with Jesse but did not mention the story. When Jesse learned of his name, Jesse said, "Why Thunder, and the Dickens. I knew a boy named Park back in Missouri. In fact, when the Yankees burned the schoolhouse and killed the schoolteacher, I went back into the schoolhouse and carried that little boy out. I also took him home to his mother." Mr. Park was stunned. That's exactly what happened.

In the Lawton Constitution, May 19, 1948 the newspaper was filled with stories of intrigue about Jesse Woodson James. It would take up two or three chapters if they were quoted in this book, but one particular story titled, "James' Identity 'Known' Secret," by Emmett L. Keough relates what Bud has fully discovered about Jesse.

"With his cold-blue eyes beaming, Jesse himself has confided to his intimates that "a half million people in Texas alone" knew for all these years that Colonel J. Frank Dalton of Centerville was none other than the man who was feared in some corners as a ruthless desperado in the '70's and respected in others as a man who never turned down a friend in need.

"But there's a code among the kith and kin of that lost generation of Americans who lived by the staccato bark of a flaming six gun as they took from the people "who had it, and distributed their loot to those that didn't."

"That code, never spoken but always understood, makes it an offense punishable by death to reveal the hand of a man whose past failed to meet with the dictates of the law.

"For Texans of that generation judged a man "for what he is, not what he was." And Col. J. Frank Dalton, is a man with a generous heart. And sons of Texas pioneers love the man they know as Colonel Dalton.

"Known as a "soft touch" by his associates, the tales of J. Frank Dalton's generosity are legend even as were the earlier stories of the man known as Jesse James, feared as an outlaw, but loved by man, with the icy eyes and the booming voice, now in Lawton, near the heart of his former Wichita Mountain hideout, is Jesse James, living-not dead."

From the Lawton Constitution, May 19, 1948, written by Lindsey Whitten, "Jesse declares that there still are many of those caches untouched by human hands since they were buried years ago, but he is an old man and money no longer means anything to him. Besides, too much blood has been spilled already over the inglorious gold which sets the very blood of mankind racing with greed. Leave it for the individuals who are capable of working out its puzzles and solving the secrets of nature's most severe problems, Jesse confides. Men like Joe Hunter."

Jesse knew, now that Joe Hunter has come out, there would be many more treasure hunters to follow. All Jesse desired now was peace, recognition, and the truth to come out of this reveal.

Ola and Aubrey were notified by Jesse to come to Lawton. They came and were overwhelmed by the people that began to fill the motels, and streets to see if they could catch a glimpse of Jesse. While visiting with Jesse, Ola could tell that Jesse was having some regrets about his life as you can tell by the statement he gave above. He was examining his life, the good and the bad.

In Ola's own words, she described what Jesse confessed to her with a true sense of shame, humbleness, and sincerity, "Back in our outlaw days, me, Frank and our men were in the state of Louisiana riding along when we came upon some Yankee soldiers and learned that they were coming from New Orleans. And, that while in New Orleans, they had gone into a Catholic Church and stole a diamond-emerald studded gold cross from the church." 565

He didn't say how he and his men managed to get the cross. Just that they did and intended to return it to the church where it belonged. But they couldn't right then. So, they rode on to the little town of McCombe, near the Mississippi River and just a ways from there, stopped and buried the cross so they could come back later, dig it up and return it to where it had been stolen but they never got a chance to.

After Jesse came out with his true identity in Lawton, Oklahoma in 1948, he still wanted to go get that cross and return it, but he couldn't because of his age and a broken hip. In 1951 when he was there at home with the Everhards in Austin, Texas he told Ola, "Ola honey I sure would love to go get that cross and get it back where it belongs before I die." Bless his heart, he never got to fulfill that wish." 566

Hall and Whitten gathered many affidavits from various people throughout the country confirming that J. Frank Dalton was truly Jesse James. Many newspapers were filled with these.

John Shevlin and his wife had come all the way from Chicago to see the man who was calling himself Jesse. Ola and Aubrey were in Jesse's motel room and witnessed Shevlin coming to the room to see Jesse. First words out of Jesse's mouth was, "Well John, you shaved your mustache off." Shevlin was taken back a bit, but sure enough, he recognized Jesse as the man he had dealt with in Arkansas and Missouri. Shevlin was known for that bushy mustache of his.

(John Shevlin (courtesy of Daily Arkansas Gazette, Sept. 25, 1903))

Shevlin – John Winfield Shevlin, known by his fellow comrades as "Jack." He was chief of the government reservation at Hot Springs, Arkansas and licensed Dalton to run a shooting gallery there. This was in 1901–1904.

In the *St. Louis Post-Dispatch*, July 30, 1899, "A Detective Story Founded on Facts," Shevlin was praised as being a keen investigator and solving the Brant murder case while he was suspended as a probational officer. He was also on the detective force. During his lull time, he became a freelance writer. Shevlin was known as the "Sherlock Holmes" of the St. Louis department. He later became Chief Detective in St. Louis. In 1903 he was Chief Detective at Hot Springs, Arkansas. "The position was especially created for him by the City Council because of the ability to handle the class of crooks which make their headquarters at that Health Resort." [567]

He had four local detectives and six Pinkertons on his staff. By 1916, he was an attorney in Winner, Iowa and became a candidate for attorney general on the Democratic ticket. He edited the only Democratic newspaper in Tripp county. Shevlin also was engaged in publishing the Rosebud Monthly Review, a 110-page magazine, designated to further the historical interests of the middle west. Shevlin (C.C.) was a member of the Acme Lodge, No. 219, of the Knights of Pythias. [568] He was handpicked to be an officer of President Teddy Roosevelt's bodyguard in the inaugural ceremonies on March 4, 1905. [569]

John Shevlin, during the time he was in St. Louis, was witness to the pardon of Cole Younger in 1901. Shevlin in 1903 was sent to Frank James and Cole Younger's Wild West show where pickpockets were prevalent. Jesse James was selling the tickets. By the end of that year, Shevlin left for Hot Springs and Jesse did also. Jesse was under the close eye of Shevlin. It sounds more like Shevlin was Jesse's bodyguard. Bud believes that Jesse was never caught by the authorities or the Pinkertons because of their comradery in their brotherhood.

Shevlin traveled to Lawton to identify Jesse and write his memoirs. "The entire story will be published for the world to absorb. The entire facts about one of the west's most beloved, but feared characters, will be revealed in full." [570] It is unknown if he ever finished that story.

All sorts of characters showed up at Jesse's door. Ola said at the motel, they were standing at the door of Jesse's room when a psychiatrist went to see and examine Jesse. Ola said that man came out of the motel room, saying "My God, there ain't a thang wrong with that man's mind. He's got the mind of a 35-year-old. He's smarter than I am."

Bud was speaking one time at a Treasure Hunter Club meeting in Oklahoma City. He brought up the big Lawton reveal. After the meeting was over, he met a nephew of the man who owned the motel Jesse stayed at in Lawton. It was the Star Auto Courts. It was about 6-8 blocks from downtown. The man had stories to share with Bud.

Lawton was extremely excited to have Jesse James there in 1948. They wanted to highlight Jesse as much as they could. The city established a "Jesse James Day." Jesse desired for it to be on Saturday when most everyone would be off work and those traveling would have time to get there. It was a huge gala event.

Jesse was picked up in a cream colored 1948 Cadillac convertible. He was escorted to the downtown area where 30,000 people waited to see and hear him over the loudspeaker from the sound truck that was following him. A very short film was captured by a reporter and is shown on YouTube.com, titled "J. Frank Dalton – 1948."

Jesse had many followers and many who believed he was Jesse James. In June 9, 1948 in the *Odessa American*, Homer "Dusty" Dalton described Jesse as a "big, barrel-chested man with piercing blue eyes and a Buffalo Bill type beard and mustache. "He's as sharp as a lawyer." [571]

Paramount Studios and many media sources flooded the streets and buildings, pushing their way to the front to get his story. Jesse made a short speech and then was taken back to the motel which was also swamped with people.

Ola and Aubrey left to go back to Austin. Many people came to see Jesse and verified who he was. They would start stories with first-hand knowledge of Jesse, and others would come with stories told by their relatives. Ironically, Jesse could always finish the story, adding credence to their connections. Of course, there were naysayers saying that he was fake, including the Pinkerton's who said Jesse was dead.

Sadly, in the *Springfield Leader-Press* on May 20, 1948, an article expressed that Robert James, son of Frank James said "Phooey". Robert never admitted that Dalton was a phony but stated that "Everytime he gets low on money; he cooks up a new angle and then sells his story." [572] Also, the people in Centerville has heard the rumors, but they were not convinced and treated it as a laughing matter.

In the Lawton Constitution, May 20, 1948, the newspaper exclaimed that there were many from Fletcher who had known Frank James when he lived there, and several were very close to him. They all confirmed and was assured that Jesse was still alive. [573]

Jesse stayed for a few more weeks and by June, Howk had another appointment set up for Jesse in Pueblo, Colorado.

Jesse could not escape the crowds as he did back in the old west. A man by the name of Ralph Percy Swaby was called upon to take him out of there in a private plane, avoiding the chance of people following old Jesse.

Ralph Percy Swaby (1907-2008) had a private plane taxi service in Lawton and was called to take Jesse, Nadine, Howk's wife, and their child to Pueblo, Colorado. Bud had heard of this plane trip, and the man who flew them, but did not know much about him until one day, Bud had a phone call from Pilot Swaby himself. He had heard about Bud and wanted to come and visit. Bud called John and Jo Ella Tatum to come down to his Used Car Sales business in Purcell and visit with the man who flew Jesse James.

It was shortly after Bud's attempt to exhume the grave of J. Frank Dalton in Granbury in 2000 that Bud had this elderly man walk in his office. He introduced himself as Ralph Swaby, the man who flew J. Frank Dalton twice in his private airplane in 1948. Bud couldn't believe his eyes and ears. Bud said, "Things like this just happened." What a gift this man turned out to be for Bud. Mr. Swaby was living in a nursing home in Oklahoma City and had read and heard all about Bud and his connection to Jesse. He drove himself all the way from OK City to Purcell, 50 miles on a heavily traveled interstate. Bud asked him how old he was, and he told Bud he was 93 ½ years old with a big old smile. I was blessed to get a copy of the video of their meeting.

Mr. Swaby had an extremely sharp memory and told his story. He also had photos with him of the event. His story was incredible.

Mind you, this was in the middle of summer where it gets extremely hot and the temperature can range from 100-110 degrees if you're lucky. Howk and his wife, Nadine were preparing Jesse for the trip, but before they left, they ate a lunch consisting of spaghetti. Mr. Swaby arrives with his car to pick them up. He said going into the motel room, he saw the threesome picture of Jesse, Frank and Mom and he said that was the same man he was looking at in the bed. No question on that. He said that he would never forget those sharp, piercing, steely eyes.

There is no room for Howk in the plane, so he apparently drives to Pueblo and he puts Nadine and the child in with Mr. Swaby while Jesse rides out to the airport in an ambulance. They drive to the airport and a huge crowd was waiting on them there to send him off. Of course, Jesse was still stoved up and could not walk, so they manage to get him aboard with a stretcher in the very small plane. With him laid out and Nadine and child squished in the back with him, it was none too comfortable. These are the photos Mr. Swaby gave Bud of the back seat of the plane. Mr. Swaby said, "I have no idea how we ever got him in that plane. Well, of course, Jesse had a pint of whiskey with him and started drinking to calm his nerves. That was his favorite drink.

(Jesse loaded in the plane with Nadine Howk and child (courtesy of Ralph Swaby))

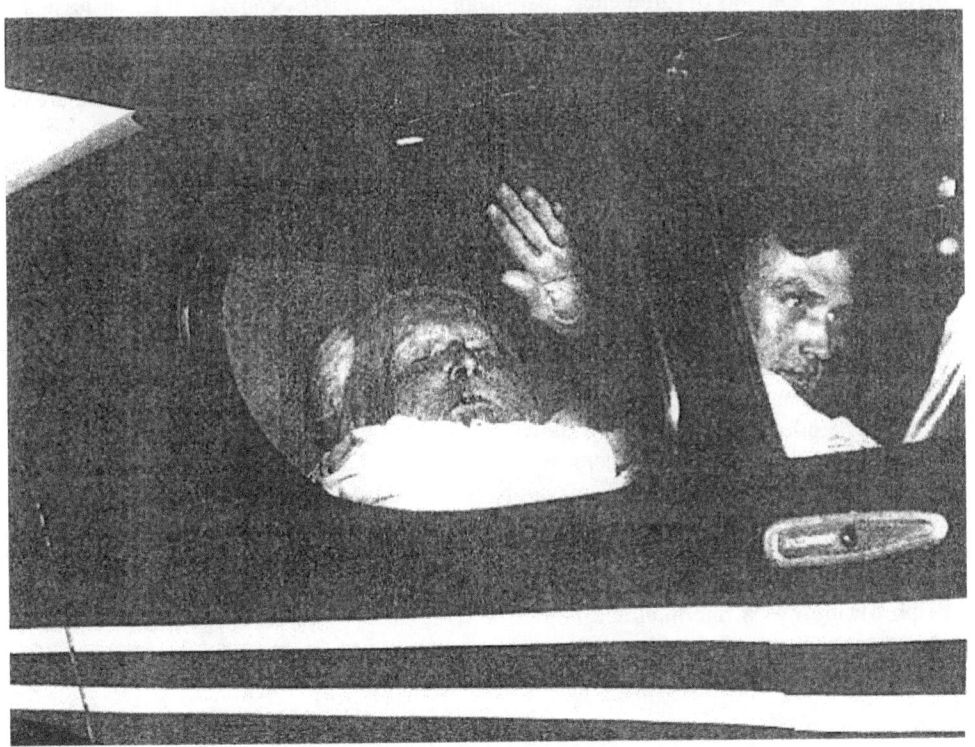
(Jesse in the airplane with pilot Ralph Swaby (courtesy of Ralph Swaby))

(Ralph in Bud's office in Purcell)

They got off the ground. It was stinking hot and they had to fly low. It was a rough ride. It's not known if this was the first time Jesse ever flew on a plane. It may have been the first time for Nadine and her child. It turned out to be quite an experience.

Flying along, with lots of turbulence, that spaghetti and whiskey came right up on Jesse's nice new white coat. He was sicker than a dog. The young child, next to Jesse had to join in after seeing Jesse's upchuck. Mr. Swaby said there was spaghetti all over the place with a strong smell of liquor. They had to make an unexpected stop in Canadian, Texas to get everyone cleaned up and the plane aired out. Ralph Swaby chuckled through the whole story.

He flew them on to Pueblo and made it safely. It is not known why they went to Pueblo, but John Tatum believed he went to see Bob James. Pueblo was also where Jesse loved to have his saddles made. He wrote in a letter that Bud has that his saddles were made in Pueblo, best saddle company in the West. Pueblo was also where Jesse had his honeymoon (unknown which bride) and had a saloon or establishment that was turned into a museum. Ola said they then went to Rye, Colorado. The name "*Rye*" is also a noteworthy name for Jesse. Mr. Swaby later flew Jesse to Waco and then on to Kansas.

Ralph Swaby was an incredible man. In researching him and also through the information he gave Bud, we were able to learn he was a pilot at an early age. In the 1930 census, at the age of 22, he was already a pilot. In October 1928, He was flying a plane at an airport dedication. They had a diving air meet in a balloon busting contest in the sky. His plane went into a tailspin and crashed while he was diving for balloons. He amazingly survived the crash. After that he started his own private airlines, which was actually just basically a small plane to taxi people from place to place.

He went to battle in World War II and knew General George Patton really well during the war. Mr. Swaby said he was honored to get to teach Patton how to fly a plane and sold him two airplanes.

Ralph Swaby was a fine man and before he left Bud's office, he said that one day he was walking down the street in Lawton and ran into Lindsey Whitten. Ralph said, "Just between you and me, was that really Jesse?" Lindsey said, "Absolutely, I know that was Jesse."

We later find Jesse in Guthrie. Ola said Jesse was in Guthrie staying at the Ione Hotel. She said it must have been July 1st, but I believe it was in the later part of June. He stayed for several days and his dear friend Brushy Bill, who hadn't come out with his identity, went to see Jesse. Lucky Johnson, Jesse's friend who took care of his horses was there, along with Eugene Robertson, John

Trammel's nephew who was a bell hop at the hotel. John Trammel was there also. It was an incredibly special reunion and Ola had the picture.

What is so funny, Guthrie was opening a movie at the movie theater on Billy the Kid. Jesse and the men were asked to be in the parade. The townspeople didn't know that the real Billy the Kid was actually riding along with Jesse James in the parade. Billy had not come out at that time.

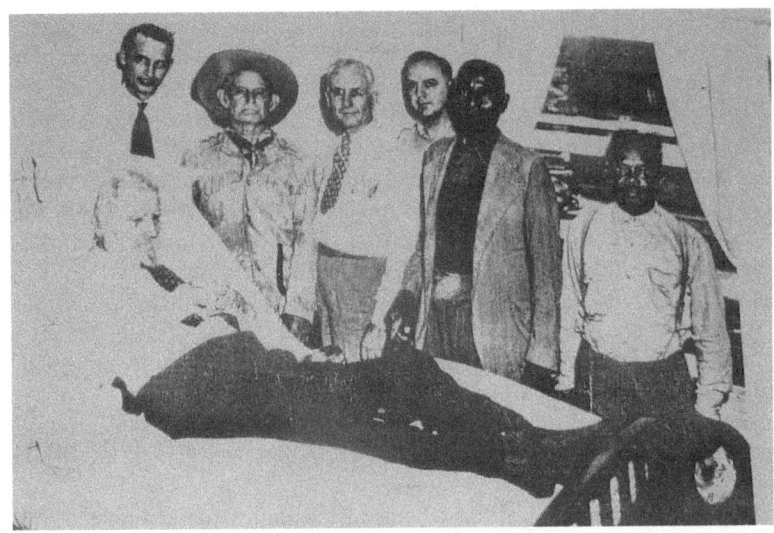

(Jesse at the Ione Hotel in Guthrie, Oklahoma. On the bed, Jesse James; standing L-R, Henry Norris (Mary Plina Norris' son), Brushy Bill Roberts, an Oklahoma historian, Orvus Lee Howk, John Trammel, and John's nephew, Eugene Robertson. (Ola's collection))

(L-R, Jesse James, John Trammel, Lucky Johnson, and Eugene Robertson at the Ione Hotel. (Ola's Collection))

On July 2, 1948, Howk loaded up Jesse and traveled to San Francisco, California to attend the Fourth of July celebration at San Leandro. In *The Ottawa Journal*, July 5, 1948 reveals that those who knew Jesse during the Civil War and his outlaw days were emotionally attached to Jesse. Al

Jennings who lived in southern California was taken to the man who was flown in to be featured in San Leandro's Independence Day rodeo. As soon as both men saw each other, their eyes welled up with tears. Jennings, all choked up, said "It's Him!" That's the face. My word of honor. Boys, there aint' a bit of doubt on earth. This here is Jesse James. Jennings asked Jesse, "Do you know me"? Jesse said as his voice was broken said "you bet. You won a shootin' match on the old C.E. Ranch." 574

In a newspaper article, "Al Jennings, Once Fastest Gun in West, Scoffs at Modern Television Badmen" – *Tulsa World*, June 16, 1957. He said he was 14 when he met Jesse and Frank in Dodge City. He said, "I had a .45 strapped on each side of me. Jesse asked me if I could shoot and I said, 'purty fair.' Jesse said he'd bet me 50 cents that he and his brother could outshoot me. We put a bottle on a rock and Jesse and Frank both missed. I hit it the first shot." The tale of two guns.

Al Jennings and Jesse knew each other from the time Al was a young lawyer in Indian Territory. Jennings practiced law in Comanche County in Lawton and Woodward where his brother was shot down by Temple Houston during a very heated trial. There was a quarrel in a saloon soon after because of the outcome of the trial. This was the time Al turned to outlawry.

Some suggest that Al Jennings was just seeking adventure with the notorious outlaw, Richard "Little Dick" West, but their outlaw days were full of blunders. West's family derives from the Cole family and intermarries with the McGehee family and the Thomason family. It is the same Thomason family of Robert Thomason who married Zerelda's mother. One of "Little Dick's" distant cousin was Almeda West, who married my 3rd great grandfather, Ransom Haskew (father of the outlaws) in Johnson County, Texas. Almeda West's mother was Nancy Ann *Woodson*.

The story about Jesse going to California to see Al Jennings sparked another story. A woman claiming to be Jesse's great granddaughter in Ottawa, Canada; Bessie Reid.

In *The Ottawa Journal*, July 6, 1948, the writer stated that once Jesse shook off the posses with his quick burial, he lit out for the Canadian border. He went specifically to Kemptville, Ontario where he went into the horse raising business. He settled in Debell Junction and raised and raced his horses. He was so successful that he laid down red velvet carpet in his stables. The article states that his son joined him, and son married Jenney Hemingway and they had a son named Dalton O'Brian. Jesse's son tragically died when a horse kicked him in the head. 575

After Jesse opened up the door to his past, people came from all around out of the woodwork who took the opportunity to exploit Jesse. He was taken all around Oklahoma to Colorado, Illinois, Arizona, California, Tennessee, and Louisianna. Ola kept up with him through telephone, telegram, and letters.

In July 1948, Jesse was in Oklahoma City and around 350 persons gathered around him at the edge of the civic center. Everyone was climbing over everybody to get a chance to meet the man and discuss their kinship with him. They also traveled to Tulsa where Ola said that they were not welcomed there. He was being dragged here and there. He was like a side show and Howk was making money off him.

By the end of July, they traveled to Chicago and stayed there through September. Jesse was being interviewed for the radio program, "The Big Story." Frank Hall and Lindsay Whitten also went, but the strangest thing was that an actor played the part of Jesse. "Some man that was an actor played the part of Jesse. He had a high silly voice. Jesse had a loud deep voice, not a squeaky one." 576

In October, they were in New Orleans and by November 20, 1948, they were in Van Nuys, California. On December 12, 1948, they were back in New Orleans. Jesse was plum tuckered out. We find him back in Van Nuys, California.

Tug of War

Everyone wanted a piece of Jesse. Was it about the money that he could draw in or the treasure secrets he kept safely in his mind? December 31, 1948– Howk said that while they lived in Van Nuys, California and had Jesse in his care, a woman who claimed to be Jesse's cousin came to the home with her husband who was a preacher, and a "holy roller talker" demanded that all Jesses' records be given to them. Then a Supreme Court judge came in and they whisked old Jesse away. Howk claimed he didn't call the police but called Jesse's men, Jesse Cole James, Jim Cooper, and John Trammel.

We know about Trammel, but we don't know much about Jim Cooper. I believe it could have been J.D. Cooper who helped Trammel in treasure hunting. He also wrote for Trammel. Below is a letter written by Cooper for Trammel to Mr. and Mrs. Floyd Chaplin. The date is not clear but appears to be close to Thanksgiving that year. The letter describes about treasure hunting and includes a map on the 2nd page. Could Copper be referring to treasure in Johnson County, Texas as Bud stated at one time that Trammel knew of treasure in Johnson County?

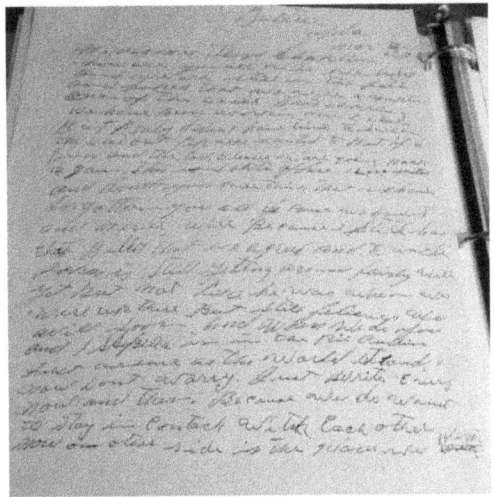

(JD. Cooper writing for Trammel to Mr. and Mrs. Floyd Chaplin)

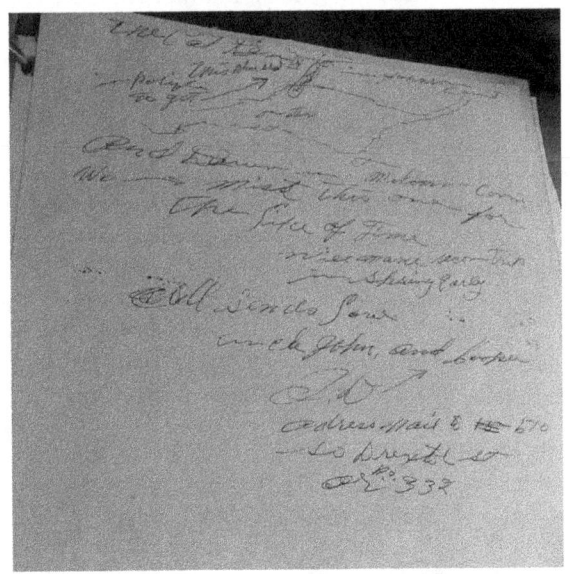

(2nd page)

(Howk, Roscoe James, Trammell, Cooper,... etc. I believe this was in Guthrie (Ola's collection))

Who was Jesse Cole James? There were two. This one was the son of William Martin James (1859-1947) and Mary Marindia Christie James (1867-1953). Jesse Cole was born in Centralia, Trinity County, Texas in 1893 and was living in Kennard, Texas in 1948/1950 which was approximately 85 miles north from Rye, Texas and was 50 miles to the West of Centerville.

Jesse Cole James' grandfather was Benjamin Martin James (1825-1864) and was a Confederate soldier in the 21st Mississippi Infantry, Company G.

Jesse Cole's mother Mary M. James was one of the people who wrote out an affidavit stating who J. Frank Dalton was during his big reveal. It was recorded in the Lawton Constitution, May 19, 1948.

"My name is Mary M. James widow of William Martin James, deceased. My husband passed away during the months of August 1947. My father was Joe Christie, he married Mary Louise Pate (my mother) and I was born not far from where I live now on January 3, 1857. I married William M. James. When I was about 10 years old a man calling himself, Jesse Redmond came to our home and stayed. (1867) He was hunting a place to rest up and hide out for a while. While with us a few weeks he helped us pick cotton and do other work about the place which was on the Neches River. I had many opportunities to get a good look at this man who wore long hair, which was more or less wavy, he had blue eyes, fair complexion. I recollect then that he left a steel bullet proof jacket when my brother carried him to Lufkin, Texas. We found an identification card in the jacket naming him as Jesse James. My brother carried him on to Lufkin and he sent a gallon of whiskey back by my brother for my father. I do not recall seeing him anymore until the week of April 8th, 1948, at which time this same man came for a week's visit with my son and his wife. My son's name is Jesse Cole James. I would be willing to swear that this man now going by the name of J. Frank Dalton is the same man who we knew years ago as Jesse James alias, Jesse Redmond." [577] Jesse told Ola he was going by the name of Jesse Redman in Alexandria, Louisianna, racing horses.

Mary's father, Joseph Christie (1825-1885) was a farmer in Sabine, Louisianna when the war started. In 1870, when this encounter occurred with Jesse, they were living in Cherokee, Texas which was in San Saba County, where Jesse was quite frequently. Cherokee was approximately 65 miles south of Brownwood, Texas. Joseph was listed as a farmer. This may be the reason Mary named her son, Jesse Cole James. By his mother's affidavit, Jesse Woodson James was keeping in touch with Jesse Cole James, who went by Cole James.

The "kidnappers" of Jesse, the Highleys took Jesse all around the country by train to make public appearances and I'm sure to make some money and they ended up in Zanesville, Ohio. This town was important to Jesse and important to Howk.

Cole James was one of the first ones who found Jesse with double pneumonia when the caravan with Jesse reached Sweetwater, Texas. Schrader put in his book that the Highleys wanted Jesse to sign all his fortune over to them. [578]

The story must be true, but there are several versions, with fingers pointing in all directions. Ola's story is that Jesse and Howk went to New Orleans on December 12, 1948. By the end of December, they were back in California. She was told by the Highleys that they removed Jesse from the clutches of Howk due to his distraught condition. Ola said that "they brought Jesse away from old Howk because he was being so badly neglected, lack of food and care. Jesse had known preacher Highley for some time and he told Ola, "He's not much of a preacher. Fact of the matter, I've preached better sermons myself." [579]

After a full month of dragging Jesse around the country, Reverend Robert E. Highley, Mrs. Highley and Ira Mann took Jesse to Sweetwater, Texas and had him give lectures twice at the City Auditorium while the preacher collected and kept the money. After Cole James caught up with them, they took Jesse to Aubrey and Ola's house in Austin on February 5, 1949.

Rev. Robert Earl Highley (1895-1993) was an author of the book, "Jesse James: Though Officially Dead Lived on for 65 years", 1981 and was an evangelical minister. When he and his wife Helen Thirwell got married in Chanute, Kansas following a public meeting, the lights were turned out and the ceremony took place beneath the fiery cross of the Ku Klux Klan. [580]

Ola said Jesse was extremely sick with pneumonia when they got to their home. They called an ambulance to take him to the hospital immediately. Ola said that Rev. Highley told her that they first took Jesse to Cole James' house in Kennard, Texas, but the real truth was that Cole went all the way to Sweetwater to meet up with the Highleys and joined them there to take care of Jesse and bring him to a place he could be taken care of. It was about a 350-mile trip on a bus from Cole's house in Kennard to Sweetwater. I'm sure Jesse demanded to be taken to Ola's. Cole spent the night with the Everhards and got a bus to go home the next day.

Visiting with Jesse, Ola said, "Cole James went back home this morning. He seems like a good man." He said, "That so." Ola said, "Yes sir." Jesse said, "Well he don't know nothin." She said, "Well I don't know about that. All I know is he seemed like a good man from what little I was around him." He said, "Oh well honey, they won't pay him to be good, so he has to be good for nothing."

"Cole's mother knew Jesse James back when he was an outlaw. He spent the night at her parent's home when she was quite young. He was using the alias name of Red Buck and when he left the next morning, he left a bulletproof vest in the bedroom. When her mother looked it over, she found a card in a small inside pocket and on it was the name Jesse James." [581] In this statement from Ola, it validates the affidavit of Cole's mother in the Lawton Constitution.

It was the following Sunday when Ola saw the true Rev. Highley. Ola stated, "Preacher Highley rubbed his hands together and said, "Where's a Baptist Church around here that a person can go pick up a few quick bucks?" [582] She found out that he had lied to her about bringing Jesse from Kennard.

Since the Highleys had been with Jesse for a full month and had met up with Jesse Cole James, I'm sure the Highleys had some questions about Cole. Who was he? Ola said that Rev. Highley popped off saying, "I guess you know that there's lots of bastards in the James clan and their kin." I believe he was referring to Cole James.

This statement from the Reverend, made Ola "mad as a wet hen and she replied as she looked at him straight and hard, "Well, let me ask you something? Can you prove, beyond all shadow of doubt, that you are not one?" Looking a bit stunned, he said, "Well-no." She said, "Well!" [583]

There was another Jesse Cole James born in 1882 who is not the same one we have been speaking of but was one who was very close to Jesse. We will speak of him in Chapter Thirty-One.

Jesse had to stay under the oxygen tent in the hospital for seven weeks. His pneumonia was severe because of his right lung injury. During the Civil War he was shot in the right lung and under the right lung. Per Dr. William Tunstill, the Union Army have records of shooting Jesse James in the right lung and right side.

Jesse was really having a challenging time breathing. He became riled up when an orderly began speaking of California. "That's what's wrong with me now, and that's how come me to be here like this, because of that trip I made to California and back." [584]

This was a very special time for Ola to be with Jesse. She went twice and sometimes up to five times a day to be with him or bring him things like his favorite chaw of tobacco, Tennessee Twist. Jesse got his tobacco from Tennessee which came as "a hand" of tobacco, several leaves cut and tied together. Ola's mother used to pour sweet warm water over it to soften it.

Jesse and Ola were very fond of each other and compared the traits of her family to his. Both had those beautiful piercing blue eyes and dark auburn hair.

Jesse was aggravated with his "granulated eye lids" that would never heal. He had suffered with it for years. Ola told Aubrey, "Bless his heart, as sick as he'd been and still was, he had his sense of humor. His wonderful sense of humor, quick thinking and ability to cope with any situation, kept him going, and had for many years." [585]

By March 1949, he was feeling somewhat better and improving in the hospital. Something that Ola wrote really sums up what Jesse had experienced throughout his entire life and would forever be branded into him. He was always on guard, always had his pistols with him except in the hospital, and his trust in people was very carefully guarded. One day, he had an orderly to pull down the shades, saying "he couldn't be too careful." When Ola got to his room, she raised the shade and he told her that he was concerned someone would be watching him through the window or crawl through the window. Ola assured him that it would not happen, they were on the 2nd floor.

Ola said her thoughts with this were, "Bless his heart he's been through so much in his life and has always had to be so watchful and careful and he's aware that at present, he's totally helpless and also that he's unarmed. Something he never was without until now was his six-shooters." [586]

While Jesse was suffering in the hospital after the escapades that Howk and the Highleys took him on, Howk was up to no good in March 1949.

A letter that Bud Hardcastle obtained written by Howk was to a Russell E. James in 1949. Russell was in Guthrie when Jesse was there in 1948. The letter speaks volumes of Howk's true colors and his real reason for getting involved with JJ. Howk doesn't call Jesse, Grandpa in this letter as he does in public articles.

In the letter, Howk was complaining that JJ ran up his beer bill; over $20 weekly while he took care of him in 1948. He requires whiskey, buttermilk, beer, tea, and coffee. For breakfast, he eats a heaping bowl of oatmeal, scrambled eggs, hot cakes, ham or bacon, French-fried spuds, and coffee. For lunch, he eats cake or donuts. For supper, he has more oatmeal or cornmeal mush, chicken dumplings without the chicken or meat. He was extremely finicky. He ruined his sheets with tobacco stains and refused to use the bed pan. By 1949, JJ was slowing down, crankier, having hearing loss, and can hardly see.

Howk stated that he has got to do something fast because he was flat broke and going deeper in debt. "JJ being crippled made it bad and a dead weight load to carry. We could have made a lot of money had he been on his feet. I can write a book and devote my time to research work and eventually get my investment back." His investment was in JJ making money for him. How sad, how really sad….

Howk took the opportunity while Jesse was laid up in Austin, to use some of the maps and knowledge he had obtained from Jesse on the treasures Jesse had buried. Howk and Roscoe James took John Trammel to Zanesville, Ohio to dig for treasure in 1949. The trip was unsuccessful. There was reportedly $1,500,000 buried by Jesse there in the mid 1880's. They unearthed a rusty strong box in an old abandoned cemetery (Old Black Log Cemetery) but was found empty. "Either Jesse got scared and moved the money, or he needed some and got it up," he theorized. "But he didn't take it all. That's the gang's money. Jesse wouldn't have taken it." [587]

In the Kansas City Times, March 14, 1949, out of Austin, "A white-bearded old man who claims he is the real Jesse James said today the Zanesville, Ohio treasure hunters are wasting their time. They aren't going to find it. It wasn't put there to find," Frank Dalton, 101, hooted after hearing that four men with a mine detector began a search for the treasure Saturday. Until recently he has been on the Texas Confederate veteran pension rolls as Frank Dalton, but asserts he is the Missourian who fought the Yanks with Quantrill's guerrillas."

"It's not 1 ½ million," said Dalton or James. "It's about $52,000. I'm not worried about anyone finding it. Howk just knows enough to think he knows, but he doesn't." Trammel said, "He (Jesse) told them that he'd bury the treasure so no gadget would ever find it." [588]

Howk stated in the papers that he was a private investigator for the James' family and began using Trammel at age 111. He used Trammell after Jesse died. In 1953, Trammell goes to Arkansas to hunt for the treasure. In 1954, at the age of 116, Howk took him to Colorado. Trammell was to show Howk the location of two caches of gold coins, gold and silver bullion, that was buried by Jesse in the Ute Pass area in 1876. In 1954, John Trammel goes back to Zanesville with Rev. James E. Ellis from Guthrie.

Howk stated in that letter, that JJ really throws curves. At that time, Howk believed that JJ's case was only 65% proven. "There is a lot more to be done. We will have to take care of JJ anyway." He was 2nd on their list.

First on Howk's list was to use, Roscoe James, Jake Wilson, Russell James, and himself to figure out the maps they had, especially leading to treasure around Guthrie. Howk was working on places beyond Oklahoma, and Jake Wilson was working on places on the Gulf Coast.

Howk wrote, "So we'll just have to look out for one another of those caches in Oklahoma and Colorado. Anyone of the big ones will be enough for all of us to buy a big ranch and settle down and run it."

He then goes on and states that Hunter, meaning "Joe Hunter" has the maps, "JJ eased around and destroyed markers or moved the big ones. Hunter is a slippery fellow and certainly caused us some static. While he has found some caches, he may never find a big one."

They all began to realize that the door that they had opened, could never be shut and they, like Jesse would have to watch their back. "Our every move with JJ will be watched and spied on."

"A friend is one that knows you as you are, understands where you have been, accepts what you have become, and still, gently allows you to grow."

-William Shakespeare

Chapter Twenty-Seven: Back to His Old Hideout

Still in the hospital, Jesse continued to improve. He was challenged in several duels, not with swords, or pistols, but with words.

In April 1949, Ola had received a call from Ray Chitwood who was the manager of the Jesse James Hotel in St. Joseph, Missouri. He challenged Jesse to come back to St. Joseph, Missouri, stay at his motel, and be proven to be a fake in two weeks' time. Well you know, Jesse wasn't going to back down on a challenge, especially when he knew what the outcome would be, the TRUTH!

Ola asked Jesse if he was interested and he gave a definite "yes" without hesitation if he can go by plane, on an empty stomach of course.

Mr. Chitwood requested a letter signed by him on the agreement to come back. I guess they were going to compare signatures with documents they had. Ola called Frank Hall, who always kept in touch and asked if he could arrange a private plane for him with his wife, Fern to go along as an escort.

Before the trip, Ola requested a professional photographer to come out and take their picture. That was the picture she had hanging in her home. She was very proud of it, her and Jesse, friends and kin for life.

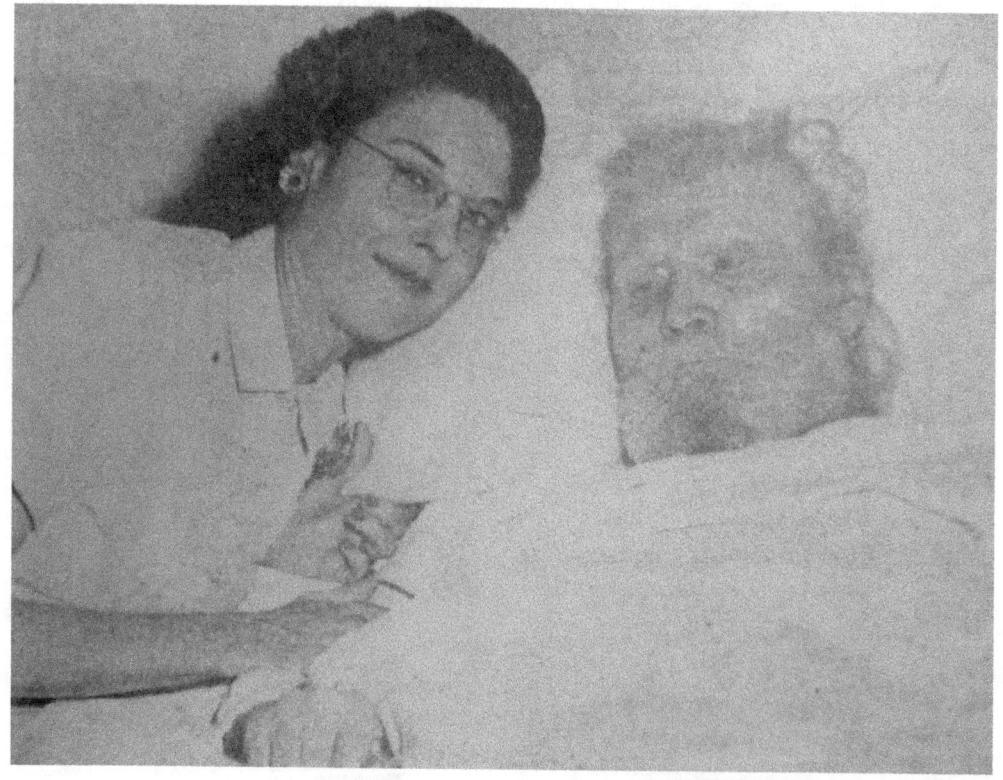

(Ola and Jesse(Ola's Collection))

The next day, they all loaded up, while Jesse was checked out and taken by ambulance to the airport. Ola went with them to the airport and sent them off. Ola waited and waited for a call from Mr. Chitwood to assure her that they made it ok. He never called.

Finally, Ola called Mr. Chitwood, and he was overwhelmed with the circus-type atmosphere around Jesse. He said, "Yes they are here and, oh my God, this hotel is in such an uproar I can't even think." [589] All you could hear on the other end was noise and people chattering with excitement.

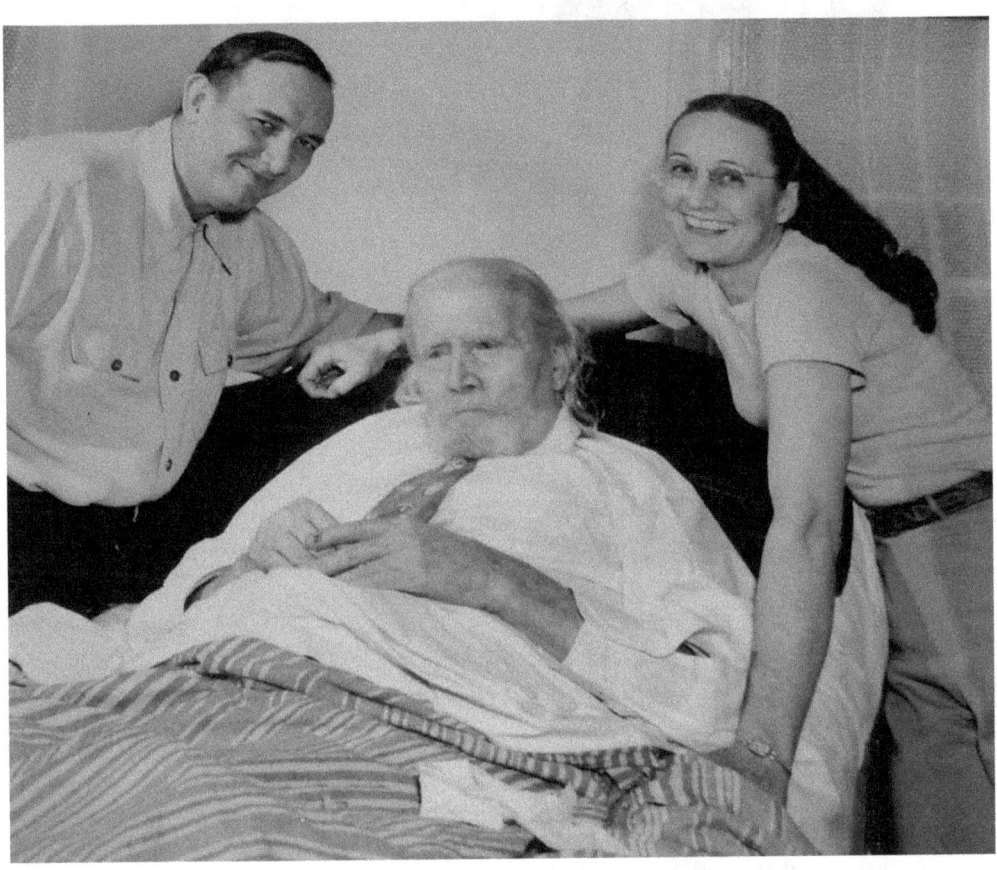

(The Halls with Jesse at the Jesse James Hotel)

After six weeks, St. Joseph, Missouri and all those who challenged him could not come up with an answer if he was or wasn't. No one could prove he ain't.

Frank Hall had brought Dalton to St. Joseph, Missouri to contact the Chamber of Commerce, Historical Society, or major newspaper to finance further investigation etc., but nobody wanted anything to do with him. They ran into a brick wall.

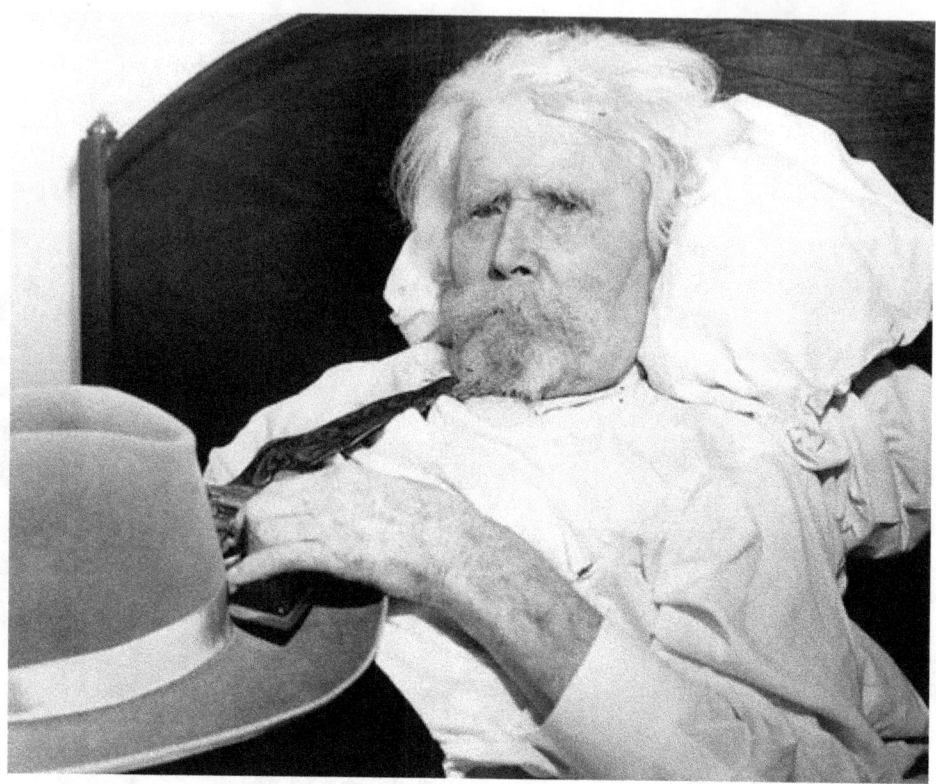

(Jesse was not happy there. You can tell from his picture and he was ready to go, gun in hand)

I believe it had to of been about this time that Jesse made a trip up to the farm in Kearney, Missouri. The only place that I could find this information was in the Lubbock Avalanche, Sept. 1983 from a statement made by Ola. Jesse went to talk to Frank James' son, Robert James. Possibly the Halls took him, but it is unknown how he got there or if it was a surprise visit. Robert was running the family farm after Frank died and Ola describes the meeting. "After the quiet meeting with his uncle, Robert closed the family farm to all tourists and didn't reopen it for visitors until after Jesse died in 1951," Mrs. Everhard said. "Why would Robert James have closed the family farm to visitors after that meeting unless he himself was convinced that this elderly man who had come to see him was, in fact, Uncle Jesse," she said. [590]

Just as Hall, the editor of the Lawton Constitution and his wife, Fern spent their careers and money investigating J. Frank Dalton, seeking to prove his real identity, many others followed.

Lester Dill came into the picture. He was the owner and operator of Meramec caverns near Stanton, Missouri. Dill had heard the old man's stories and the Hall's layout of the big story in the Lawton Constitution. Dill had learned that Jesse James was a frequent visitor in the cave when it was the perfect hideout during many of his rendezvous. A story had surfaced that a Confederate group of guerillas dynamited the cave during the Civil War.

Dill thought Jesse would bring a lot of publicity to his tourist attraction. He sent his son-in-law, Rudy Turilli to check him out and to extend the invitation to the Halls and Dalton to come to Meramec Caverns. Rudy went to the Jesse James Hotel in St. Joseph to meet this man and was quite delighted to meet the old fellow. He was impressed. Rudy offered the invite, face-to-face to the dignified gentleman who claimed he was the most feared outlaw in all the West, Jesse Woodson James.

While Lester Dill was skeptical, his son-in-law, Rudy Turilli became extremely convinced he was the real deal.

To help in this venture and to investigate this old man further, Rudy called upon Joe Wood, a very well-known newspaperman and photographer. At first Wood was not willing, "He's just another phony," but Rudy begged him for a personal favor. If Joe was going to get involved, he would have to put everything into it and other things aside. Go all the way. Joe took leave of absence from his job in the newspaper business and traveled to St. Joseph to see Jesse James.

Rudy and Joe went to see Jesse, and Frank Hall was there also. Frank showed Joe all the evidence and spoke with Joe for two hours and then they went in to talk with Jesse. Frank introduced Joe as a newspaperman. Instead of Joe interviewing Jesse, it became the other way around. Jesse asked Joe, "What newspaper do you work for?" Joe's reply, "St. Louis Globe Democrat." "Is that still on 6th and Pine?" Joe was really thrown off balance and surprised the "hell" out of him. He was amazed this old man knew where the old newspaper office was before it moved in 1931. Jesse said, "Well, when I wrote stories for that paper, in 1904 during the St Louis World's Fair it was still on 6th and Pine." That broke the ice.

That man was sharp as a tack.

Joe Wood – "I associated with Jesse, with J. Frank Dalton from the summer of 1949 until September 1950 when Jesse went back to Ola Everhards. As a newspaperman, I spent over a year investigating him. I started out disbelieving him, I wouldn't believe he was Jesse James, I thought he was just another imposter. I never form an opinion until I have all the facts."

Joe Wood was in, and in for the long haul. Rudy Turilli hired an ambulance to take Jesse to Meramec Caverns at Stanton, Missouri. They had fixed up a nice cabin there for Jesse to stay in comfortably and hired a nurse to look after him. Lester Dill paid Joe a salary and paid for his expenses.

Just reading the personal letters that Joe Wood sent to Bud, the photos, the news articles, and the video of their meeting with Vincel Simmons was enough for the writer to truly see a clear picture of who Joe was. I'm not even sure if Bud really knew Joe's entire background. He was such a humble man.

The meeting with Vincel Simmons and Joe was an extremely enlightening one. Vincel believes his grandfather was Jesse James/J. Frank Dalton. He had a lot of evidence to prove what he was saying and even rode in the same car with him at one point in his childhood. Bud believed that Vincel was indeed Jesse's grandson, but there were several issues that they couldn't come to an agreement on, mainly pertaining to his death. Vincel certainly looks like Jesse.

(Meeting with Vincel Simmons, Joe Wood, and Bud Hardcastle)

Bud first met Joe Wood when Lou Kilgore thought a trip up to Missouri would enlighten the mystery somewhat. Lou had told Bud that Joe Wood had a lot of information regarding Dalton at Meramec Caverns and was there at his birthday party in September 1949. Joe and Bud became the dearest of friends.

Joe Wood was an exceptional and accomplished photographer for the St. Louis Goble-Democrat for 27 years. He had experienced life in America during its heyday before, during and after World War II. In 1936, he was honored to spend 10 hours with President Franklin Delano Roosevelt as a photojournalist when Roosevelt was on the campaign trail in St. Louis.

Joe served in the Merchant Marines and became a champion boxer. Out of the Marines, he developed his skills as a photographer and possessed a very personable personality. He fit right into the newspaper world. He photographed news stories including politics, sports, and celebrities such as Judy Garland, Spencer Tracy, Katherine Hepburn, Clark Gable, and Dizzy Dean. In his obituary in 1996, it was listed that he was a personal friend of President Harry S. Truman who he played poker with on occasion, one being at the Jefferson Hotel in St. Louis.

Joe was also an accomplished violinist and played with the St. Louis Philharmonic Orchestra. Many of his comrades note his integrity and honesty. In his obituary, December 5, 1996 in the St. Louis Post-Dispatch, a friend and colleague resonate the summation of Joe, "Joe was a real professional, an outstanding and trustworthy individual. He looked for the facts and didn't go for the fluff." [591]

Joe was inducted to the Photojournalism Hall of Fame of Missouri in 2007. A photo of a young and vivacious man is shown on his inductee photo into the Missouri Photojournalism Hall of Fame. www.photojournalismhalloffame.org/joe-wood.

Joe was the real deal. As a newspaper man, he sought out the truth. You could not fool him. Jesse was up against the best.

When Joe started investigating Dalton, Rudy and he went to libraries and started reading books on Jesse, but the confusion it created became unsurmountable. Joe said, "To hell with this, I want to take it from here. Because of phonies out in the world, Joe went to Bob (Robert) James, the son of Frank James. Joe asked Jesse if he'd mind if Bob James came to see him, to verify who he was. Jesse said, "Of course, I wouldn't mind, but Bob would never agree to see me. But go ahead, it will be an interesting experience for you." They knew each other. Jesse had nothing to hide. What did Bob?

Joe Wood told Bud that every time that there was a new man coming out to reveal another imposter of Jesse James, it would be Robert "Bob" James who would expose them. Wood always wondered why Robert James had never debunked Dalton as the real Jesse James.

Lester Dill wrote out a check for $10,000 to offer Bob James. Rudy and Joe traveled to Excelsior Springs to offer his check. They found him on the golf course. Bob wasn't interested in talking with them. Joe said, "Just come and talk to this man." Bob said, "I will not see this man under any circumstances." He walked away. Why would he refuse just to see this man for $10,000? It may have had something to do with their visit on the Samuel's Farm.

Lester Dill, too, spent thousands of dollars trying to prove the old man's true identity. He told the papers he had spent $17,400 in rounding up testimonies, affidavits, and many travels to verify claims of those who knew this man as Jesse James.

Francena Turilli, Rudy's wife and daughter of the owner of Meramec Caverns stated that her and her father, Lester Dill were not convinced as much as Rudy that the old man was truly Jesse James. Francena was the most skeptical. In a newspaper article in the Kansas City Star; January 10, 1988, she was noted as saying that she had her private doubts for at least two years, but what finally convinced her that he was the real Jesse James "is the way the old man talked to people who came to visit him. They'd come and say that their grandfather or uncle had known Jesse James, and the old fellow would tell them about how he remembered their folks, or about a night he'd spent on their place. And then he'd describe the place, telling them how many acres it was and talking about the location of some tree or rock. And when those people went back to check, sure enough, he'd been exactly right. That must have happened at least a dozen times. How could he have known those details if he wasn't who he said he was?" [592]

She also said that when Oldtimers who knew Jesse in his outlaw days would come and try to trick him, by mixing up dates of events, the amount of money stolen in robberies, and secret passwords, Jesse was quick to correct them and set them straight. There was no fooling Jesse.

Rudy continued to travel, and research traveling 98,000 miles and was financed by Lester Dill, amounting to $35,000 while Joe Wood was doing his own research. Joe was the one who always told Bud to "Research, research, and then research some more."

Jesse's birthday, September 5, 1949, turning 102 years old was coming. Joe Wood joined Rudy in a quest to find anyone that knew Dalton as Jesse and invite them to the birthday party.

Joe Wood said there was so many dern arguments with Jesse, he was hiding some information at times, especially about his family and his very close friends. Joe would ask, "Is there any members of your gang that are still living that we can collaborate your story with?" "No, boys, you don't think any of the members would have lived to be a 100, do you?", replied Jesse.

Four months into the investigation, it was affecting Joe and Rudy's relationship, putting a wedge between the two. Rudy was convinced Dalton was Jesse and Joe was not. It was becoming too serious and the difference of opinion was overwhelming. Joe was going to bow out.

Rudy went to talk with Jesse about their rift. Jesse, being the negotiator he was, insisted on seeing them together. Jesse, full of wisdom and like a father-figure said, "Now you boys, I've become fond of you and I don't want to see something happen between you, it would be my fault. I'm going to answer a question you are always asking me. Yes, there is a man still alive and I knew him since I was a little boy. His name is Colonel James Russell Davis, who lives in Nashville. He was instrumental in getting me in the Quantrill Guerillas."

James Russell Davis

Jesse knew Davis would still be alive; if not, he would have been notified by various channels. Jesse and those of his close-knit comrades kept up with the whereabouts of the other.

Jesse told them that he would write a letter to Davis explaining to him what the situation was and that it was ok, to come with these men to where he was at in Stanton, Missouri, **330** miles away. Jesse wrote the letter and gave it to Rudy and Joe. They set off to travel to Nashville.

When they learned of Davis' address from the newspaper office, they were told that Colonel Davis was a pretty feisty old fellow. In the Tampa Bay Times; June 17, 1949, James Russell Davis came into the driver's license office in Nashville and listed his age at 108. The curious clerk asked, "How come you've lived so long?" "Tending to my own business," was his reply. [593]

Rudy and Joe came upon Colonel Davis' doorstep and knocked on the door. Davis answered the door and the men quickly gave him a letter that Jesse had written to verify who they were and what their reason was for coming. Col. Davis took his glasses off to read the letter and said, "this doesn't mean a damn thing." "What do you mean?" said Rudy. "I'm too old to go cross country on a wild goose chase," said Davis. He slammed the door in their faces. After a second knock, they were met with a .38 revolver in between their eyes and was told to get off his porch in 30 quick seconds or their brains would be blown out.

If Jesse wanted to mend the rift between Joe and Rudy, it just made it wider. They were furious. They both knew that Jesse was playing another game with them. He loved practical jokes, but this time he went a little too far; 660 miles too far. They were devastated.

When they got back to Missouri, 10 hours, Rudy went to Jesse and started cussing Jesse out. They were beyond angry. Jesse listened to their outburst of anger and then he let out a good belly laugh. "Now boys you can't stay mad at an old man for having a little fun once in a while." He gave them another letter which contained something secret between the two that would give Davis a sign that it was from the real Jesse James. The first letter did not contain the secret sign. Joe said he examined both letters and could not tell any difference, not to the naked and untrained eye.

Jesse said, "I want you to go back and tell Colonel Davis I want him to be up her in 24 hours but give him the password."

Joe Wood was pretty upset with Jesse and refused to go, but Rudy set off again, only this time with the magic password. The password, "The Goose Flies High." Rudy got to Davis' door and knocked, with a little bit of fear in his heart.

Colonel Davis answered the door and before anything was said, Rudy quickly blurted out, "The Goose Flies High." Colonel Davis with a different tone replied, "Everything is lovely. Where is Jesse?" Rudy told Davis where Jesse was and gave him the letter. Even after a slight heart attack, Colonel Davis wanted to go right then. Bud said that was "extreme loyalty to one another. Under Quantrill, they had agreed to go to their comrade in need, even if it cost them their own life. This is exactly what he did."

Rudy called Joe from Nashville and he said they were on their way. Joe could not believe it.

When Colonel James R. Davis arrived at Meramec Caverns, Joe positioned himself to watch each other's reactions when they met up. Joe was a firm believer to validate everything with facts as a newspaperman, but he said at this moment, when the two old gentlemen met, his belief changed with emotions. Joe Wood said, "It was against all my ethics, my experience, and professionalism to go with my gut, my emotions on a subject, but at this remarkable moment in time, I knew I had been wrong all this time." Joe was now convinced, the old man he had been investigating was the genuine authentic Jesse Woodson James.

Joe captured the moment in the photo below. "You had to be there," Joe said. Colonel Davis walked into the room of Jesse's, shifted his right arm towards him and as Jesse was reaching with his good hand, the kindred spirits that they shared overwhelmed the room. "Hello James, it's good to see you," said Jesse. "Hello Jesse," said Colonel Davis.

Joe Wood said, "Something came over me, there are no words to explain what happened to me. I began to perspire uncontrollably, and I thought, my God, it's true." Just the shaking of their hands, tone of their voice, and their weary teary eyes of their souls connecting, radiated the bond and the history they shared. It was powerful.

Joe Wood just experienced the true inner soul of Jesse that Bud had been hunting.

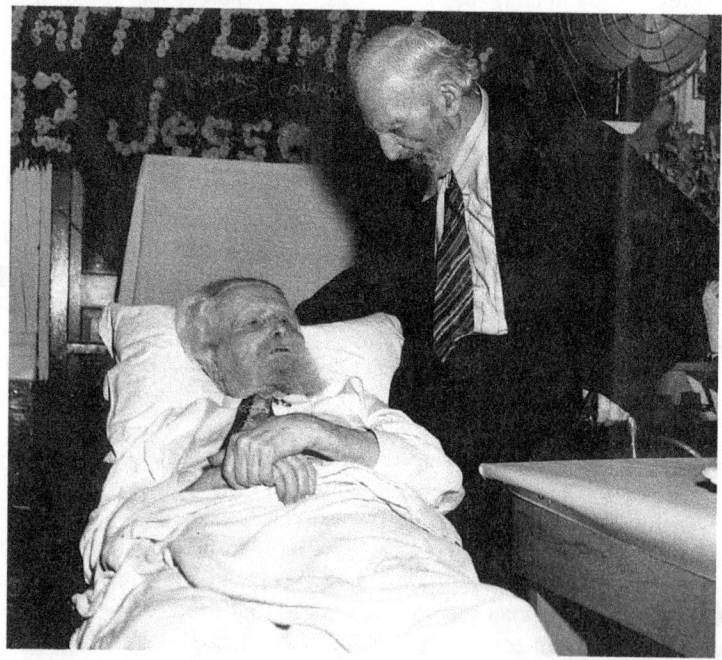

(Picture of Colonel James Russell Davis and Jesse at Meramec Caverns)

In the St. Louis Post-Dispatch, published, November 27, 1949, "he differs from most claimants to the title, in that he seems to generate a sort of Jesse James fever among those who come in contact with him and, at present, is the center of a veritable epidemic." [594]

While Jesse and Colonel Davis were enjoying the visit privately, Rudy and Joe gathered more names of men that they both knew who were still alive and could vouch for Jesse on his identity. The birthday was soon to be celebrated for his 102nd year on this earth, so they began to reach out to Brushy Bill (not known at that time to be Billy the Kid), Ozark Jack Berlin, and John Trammel.

Jesse told Rudy and Joe that Old John Trammel lived 10 miles outside of Guthrie, Oklahoma. This was about the area where Jesse had his ranch after the run of 1889. It may have been the exact place.

Rudy and Joe went to the Guthrie Hotel where Eugene Robertson, Trammell's nephew worked as a bell hop. After he got off work, Mr. Robertson drove them out to the farm. When they got to John's home, Rudy told John that Jesse James had sent for him. John Trammel said, "I don't know any such person." After several attempts and coercing, Rudy finally said, "The goose flies high." John Replied, "Everything is lovely, where's Jesse?" John insisted that they leave immediately.

This password must have meant during their guerilla war days and outlaw days, to come quickly to the aid of their comrade.

John Trammel and Colonel Davis didn't know the other would be coming. They too broke into tears with a heavy embrace. They had a few years between them. Davis wanted Trammel to tell the story of what happened close by there in one of their days of running. Trammel first wanted permission from the boss, Jesse.

Trammel rolled into the story with no hesitation after he had gotten the ok from Jesse. They all shared this story and in great detail, describing a time they were running from a posse. Col. Davis got shot and was knocked off his horse by the blow of the incoming bullet. "Jesse took a quick look at him; said he would die anyway, and they couldn't stop. Cole Younger got off his horse and said either they pick up Davis or he was staying and ordered Trammel to put the injured man on his horse. Jesse and Cole flared up in disagreement, and after a little argument, Jesse backed down. They took the colonel to the cave and there he recovered from his wounds." [595]

Oddly, James R. Davis relates this story as being wounded in the war through the shoulder, into the neck; very similar to how John Younger received his wound. Many people believed that Colonel Davis was really Cole Younger, but Bud said he wasn't tall enough and big boned as Cole. Davis was about 5'7 or 5'8". Would he have been really John Younger?

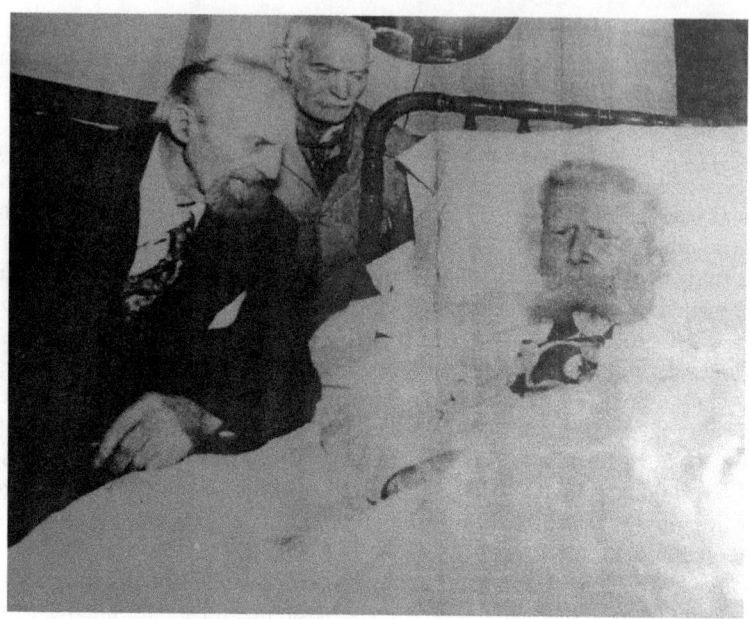

(Colonel James R. Davis, and Brushy Bill behind him)

James Russell Davis was noted in his obituary in Springfield News-Sunday, March 14, 1950, that he was one of the oldest Civil War vets. Lester Dill spoke with the reporter, who was the operator of Meramec Caverns, "Davis was wounded during the Civil War and also wounded by an Indian arrow during the uprising in 1857. Dill said, "There was a lot of history packed in that man. He was with the Quantrill Raiders during the Civil War. He also used to ride pony express on the southern route from Texas to California. He was a Methodist preacher at one time, and I believe the oldest Mason in the country, joining that lodge in 1862. The Jackson Sun, March 14, 1950 shows that he was 109. [596]

In The Wheaton Journal, March 16, 1950, Davis claimed he was a first cousin of James. He was born in the Austin Colony, Columbia, Texas on Oct 1, 1840. He participated in the construction of Union Pacific railway. The newspaper also stated that he was acquainted with Kit Carson and a friend of Sam Houston. He too was a sheriff and U.S. Marshal, civil engineer, receiving his degree at Cornell University, and a private detective. [597]

Davis was featured in a newspaper article, March 1950 that Bud had, titled, "Is Jesse James Dead or Alive? Nashville Citizen to Testify." In that article, it is mentioned that Davis was a scout for General George Crook's army when Fort Yuma, Arizona was established. Part of his story "Jim Davis' adventures has been recorded in a book published in the last century, "Thirty-one Years in the Mountains and on the Plains" by William F. Granan." [598]

Davis stated in The Tennessean, June 16, 1949, that he knew Jesse when he was 14 years old. That would have been 1861, at the beginning of the Civil War. He was convinced that the man who appeared at the state fair in 1948, under the billing of "Jesse James" was the true outlaw. He claimed to have a picture of himself taken with JJ in 1886 in Brownwood, Texas, four years after JJ was supposedly killed. [599]

Davis married Susan Elizabeth DeLozier. Susan's great grandfather, Asa Delozeair's brother married Frances Dyer whose sister married into our Thomason family. Frances and sister, Pheby Dyer's mother was Rachael Dalton who was a sister of James Lewis Dalton's great grandfather, David Dalton, Jr. James Lewis Dalton was the father of the Dalton Gang and was allegedly the brother of Zerelda James.

Colonel James R. Davis at the age of 109, John Trammel at the age of 111, Brushy Bill at the age of 89, were there for Jesse for his big 102nd birthday party. Mary Plina James Norris, daughter of Frank James was there from Claremore, Oklahoma, DeWitt Travis from Longview, Texas, Ozark Jack Berlin of Veedersburg, Indiana, John Shevlin and his wife from Chicago, Illinois, Robert E. Lee from Baton Rouge, Louisiana, Henry J. Walker of Iowa who was writing a book about Jesse, and Morrey Davidson of New York City. Ola and Aubrey Everhard could not make it because of her elderly mother, Bertha who was ailing a bit. There were many others such as reporters, Joe Wood, the Dills, the Turillis and many others tied to Jesse. Francena Turilli told Bud that Howk was there, but he was stirring up so much trouble, he was asked to leave.

Ozark Jack Berlin

His real name was Andrew Jackson Berlin, born 1867 and died at the age of 86 in Veedersburg, Indiana in January 1954. The first indication of his association with Jesse was at Jesse's 102nd birthday party at Meramec Caverns. He was there with the rest of them who were close to Jesse.

Ozark Jack stated earlier that he, as a fourteen-year-old boy, was hiding out at Meramec Caverns before it was a tourist attraction, sometime in 1881. He may have "run away and joined the circus" as his obituary states that he was associated with the Adam Forepaugh Circus when in his teens." [600]

Adam Forepaugh was a horse trader and a circus owner. Mr. Forepaugh became very wealthy during the Civil War by selling horses to the U.S. government. This may have been how Jesse and Ozark Jack connected. Forepaugh operated his circus venue between the years 1865-1890 which became one of the largest circuses in the country alongside P.T. Barnum's circus. They were fierce competitors. In 1877, he had the first Wild West show. [601] With the outfits that Ozark Jack wore, he surely was a Wild West performer.

The Meramec Caverns was used by the Union soldiers during the Civil War and was a favorite hiding place for Jesse and his gang during the outlaw days. Ozark tells the story that he met Frank and Jesse James in the caverns and became life-long friends. Jesse must have taken him under his wing, because we find him with Jesse in St. Joseph, Missouri where Mr. Thomas Howard lived. Jesse gave him the name of "Press Webb" who was actually a scout for Quantrill. Webb was noted as having the "eye of an eagle and the endurance of the deer." [602]

St. Joseph's city leaders had a Fourth of July parade in 1881, and without knowing his real identity, asked Mr. Howard to ride in the parade. Alongside with Jesse was Ozark Jack and Brushy Bill as the story is told by Jesse to Ola. Jesse was being hunted down during that time, but his portrayal of a very well-dressed gentleman wearing a nice dress coat stretching to his knees was never suspected as being the famous outlaw. Under that coat was a fully loaded pistol housed in his shoulder holster.

Ozark Jack told Ola about being in Round Top Mountain at a dance in the Creek Nation with Jesse and Frank, Brushy Bill, and Al Jennings. Ozark said this was in 1888, when he was 21. Ozark got hit by a stray bullet in a saloon and Brushy rushed to his side, giving him a drink of water from his old stained and dusty cowboy hat. Ozark credits Brushy as saving his life. Ola tells the story that this occurred in Tascosa.

Ozark Jack Berlin, later worked for the New York Central Railroad, working on the bridges and building department. He lived in Veedersburg, Indiana. He became a hero when he, as a passenger on a train was involved in a collision with a truck. Ozark jumped off the train and rescued the two men out of the burning truck cab. He rubbed out the flames and then ran to the train's engine and helped firefighters who were in danger.

"Ozark Jack is a native of Richland Country born south of Sumner but has spent the greater part of his life in the wilds of the Ozark Mountains in Missouri. He carries a scrap book filled with the exploits of his colorful life, wears more medals than Andy Stiner and his costume is one to attract attention when he appears on the street." [603]

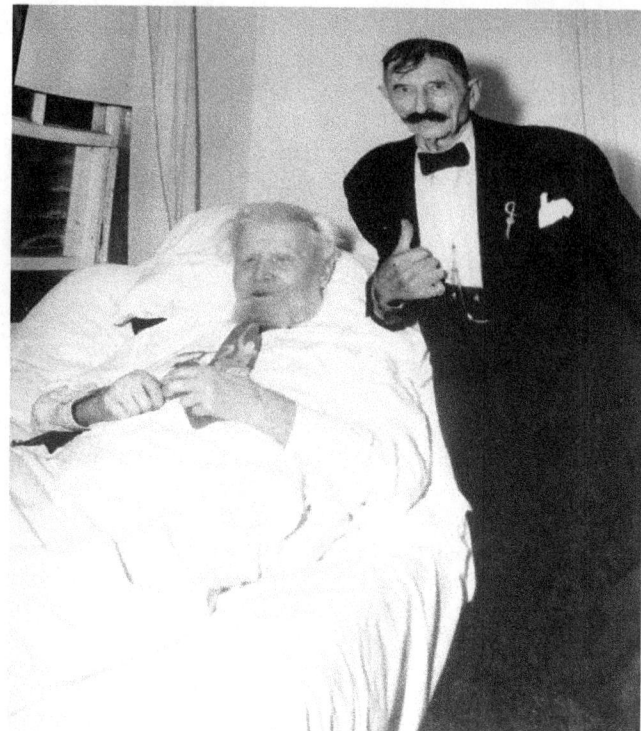

(Ozark Jack Berlin)

Jesse's nurse stayed by his side constantly in his small cabin and of course at the party. Mrs. Alvie Baker was Jesse's nurse while at Meramec Caverns. She believed wholeheartedly that he was JJ. Her father-in-law was a minister of the Assembly of God church in Lansing, Michigan, Rev. R.E. Baker. He and his wife spoke with JJ at the caverns and they too are convinced. [604]

Rudy had a 100 lb. cake for the celebration. Jesse told Ola that he got $500 for his birthday. He said that his nurse got part of that. She had confided in him that she really didn't want to be a nurse, apparently Jesse was a handful to her, which I have no doubt. She said she wanted to be a beauty operator. Jesse said, "Well why don't you?" She said, "I haven't got the money." Jesse ended up giving her money that she needed to go to school and said, "Now, get out of here and go be a beauty operator." Ola said that Jesse offered her the rest, $45, that was all he had left. "It ain't much but it's all I've got and it's for you." [605]

He truly was a generous man. Every act of kindness and generosity proved beyond a doubt that he was not made of money nor was money his idol.

They all learned a lot about Jesse at Meramec Caverns. Robert Ruark from New York City, leading journalist in the country was there. He was a novelist and columnist for the New York World-Telegram. Joe Wood told Bud that Mr. Ruark was thoroughly convinced Jesse was the real deal. He stayed three days interviewing him. He also interviewed the others who were his old buddies from the Wild West days.

Robert C. Ruark wrote in the Buffalo Courier Express, July 8, 1949, "Called Uncle Jesse by the people who look after him, he is bedridden by a broken hip, but at the age of 102 his mind is still whip-sharp, his memory remarkable and his arguments convincing. He is nearly blind and a touch deaf but is handsome still and full of scrap."

"Even at his age, his resemblance to the authenticated photos of the outlaw is amazing. There are the same cavernous eyes, the same sharply cut nostrils, the same sweep to his hair, the same scraggy growth of beard, the same set to the ears. Jesse James was supposed to have lost a fingertip in a gun accident. Old man Dalton's left hand shows a ruined, twisted nail.

"The resemblance to the young James is more striking than the resemblance of the photos of the dead Jesse to the live Jesse. The live Jesse had the lean look of an ascetic, and he was sparsely whiskered. The dead Jesse's photo showed a heavy, dark-bearded man of a definitely burly look. On coincidental resemblance, the old boy could easily be the man he claims he is. His age is exactly right."

The story on Jesse being killed in 1882 created many doubts for Ruark. "There was written expression of doubt at the time of the killing. The body was hurriedly identified by a few intimate, swiftly buried in Jesse's mother's yard, and disinterred a full 20 years later for burial at Kearney, Missouri. Former City Editor Hall (Frank Hall) believes there were some peculiar political doings at the time, and that a deliberate hoax was worked to allow James to escape. It is odd that the Ford boys, the killers, gave themselves up, it was odd that they should have been pardoned immediately by Gov. Tom Crittenden; it was odd that Frank James should have turned in his guns a short time after to receive full pardon. His story is remarkably tight." [606]

The highlight of the celebration was when Morrey Davidson interviewed, Jesse, Brushy Bill, John Trammel, and James R. Davis on the following day, September 6th. Morrey Davidson was a famous NBC radio announcer in New York City who had come to interview Jesse. Morrey was vice president of International Artists Corporation. He recorded the interview and gave the audio tapes to Dr. William Tunstill and Morrey Davidson, himself brought the tapes to Ola in 1982. Dr. Tunstill gave Bud a copy of the tapes and Bud allowed me to have a copy. Pretty fascinating to hear these men speak. Jesse had a raspy, deep voice and Brushy Bill had a high pitch voice and talked very fast spewing out electric energy.

The Meramec Caverns was a happy place for Jesse. He did indeed know that area well, including the extensive limestone cave system which was known as the Old Saltpeter Cave. It was used to extract saltpeter, the key ingredient to manufacture gunpowder. The Union Army used the cave for this purpose and to store ammunition. The guerillas discovered this and secretly infiltrated the site as workmen and destroyed it with dynamite. This would become the hideout for Quantrill Raiders and Jesse during his outlaw days and now it was becoming another safe haven for him. He knew the ends and outs of the caverns. Jesse asked Lester Dill if he ever had found the rear entrance and outlet in the cave. It was always a must for Jesse to have an escape route.

Lester Dill had no idea there was any back entrance. He hired men to locate it. The entire cave system was very intricate with tunnels, leading to rooms of all sizes from small to massive rooms, and water ways.

In the Police Gazette, January 1952, Special Investigator George McGrath wrote the words of Jesse when he interviewed him just before his death. "One time, while making a getaway, we were being pressed close by a posse of Pinkertons and we made for the caves with them at our heels," old Jesse recalled. "They didn't try to come into the caves after us. They figured we would have to come out eventually because they thought there was only one entrance. They holed up at the mouth of the cave for days." He added.

"But I knew the cave like the back of my hand for I had been there with Quantrell and many times afterward. We knew of an exit, about eleven miles back from the mouth of the cave, which came out on the other side of the mountain. The opening was just big enough to allow a man and a horse to squeeze through single file. We all escaped."

McGrath wrote: "The operators of the caverns at that time, in 1950, knew nothing of another exit from the caves. Old Jesse made a crude map of the interior of the caves for them, and after considerable exploring, the exit was found hidden in underbrush and rubble – just as the old man had explained." [607]

This was "dead on" proof that Jesse definitely was there and utilized the cave quite frequently. Not many would know about the escape back door, not even the owner of the caverns since he had purchased them in **1933**.

Lester Dill also discovered a special room that was only able to be entered when the water table was low during the drought of 1941. He discovered a small sliver of an entry way, uncovered by the shrinking pool of standing water. He slid under and found many artifacts appearing to be those of Jesse James. Several guns were found along with gold coins, believing they were coins from the Gads Hill robbery. Lester took one of those coins, dated 1854, and had someone make it into a watch charm for Jesse. Ironically, this was the year that the KGC is noted as being established or reestablished.

Jesse felt at home there at Meramec Caverns. He was totally amazed at how the caverns were "electrified." He asked Dill how far back they went. I believe, the deeper into the cave, the deeper the secrets were held. Back in his war and outlaw days, they had to use lanterns to move around in there.

He was well taken care of and was able to see visitors easily, but there were times he became pretty disgusted or irritated with all those sightseers who wanted to get a glimpse of Jesse, such as the time he took his six shooter and fired at someone knocking at his door insisting on coming in to see him, missing a baby in the back seat of the car they were in. This was the story from Francena Turilli, Rudy's wife.

Bud Hardcastle was able to travel to Meramec Caverns and to the museum in Stanton, Missouri to visit with Francena and Joe Wood personally several times. All these stories related to Meramec Caverns and Jesse's life were from Joe Wood, Francena Turilli, Ola and Aubrey Everhard who were all there to witness it.

Catching her on tape on May 15, 1993, Francena used words of admiration and respectfulness regarding Jesse. You could see in her eyes the many stories that flooded her memories of Jesse. Some of the stories reflected his humor and rashness, while others painted an amazing man. She said Jesse was a History book within himself. He was very intelligent man, self-educated, spent time in England, South America, and Canada. Francena, with a cautious look, said he could be very cantankerous, depending on what kind of mood he was in.

Rudy spent 23 years of research on this man. He was worth every minute of it. Both Joe Wood and Rudy called Jesse, "Uncle Jesse." At times, Jesse would call Rudy, "you damned old Yankee" and Rudy would call him, "damned old Rebel."

Francena stated that John Trammel was also a very intelligent man and self-educated. She was very impressed with Trammel. Very loyal to Jesse. In her museum, they have wax figures of Trammel and Jesse.

Bud's greatest treasure found at Meramec Caverns were indeed Francena Turilli, but most of all Joe Wood.

Lou Kilgore and Bud, on their first visit to Meramec Caverns, stayed two days. They met Joe Wood. Joe told Bud about Ola and Aubrey and that is when Bud knew he had to meet Ola. Joe said there was nothing wrong with Ola. She was a very sharp woman. No crippled mind as Howk said. Wood also had published a book about Jesse and wanted Bud to have a copy.

Both Joe Wood and Rudy Turilli wrote a book about their adventures with Jesse. They included stories from those who knew Jesse, then and now. The best one I believe is the affidavit by Orrington "Red" Lucas. "I positively identify this white-headed and bearded old gunman to be Jesse James, the man as I knew as such back as far as 1879, by virtue of many intimate things that nobody else could exchange with me, by his eyes, his hands and manner of talking, plus many other things any police officer who has ever hunted outlaws would know and never forget," wrote Orrington "Red" Lucas in a signed affidavit.

This affidavit, signed and notarized in Franklin County, Missouri, on July 6, 1950, tells of knowing this old man in 1879 as Jesse Woodson James and then in 1949, knowing the same man who was at Meramec Caverns portraying Jesse James.

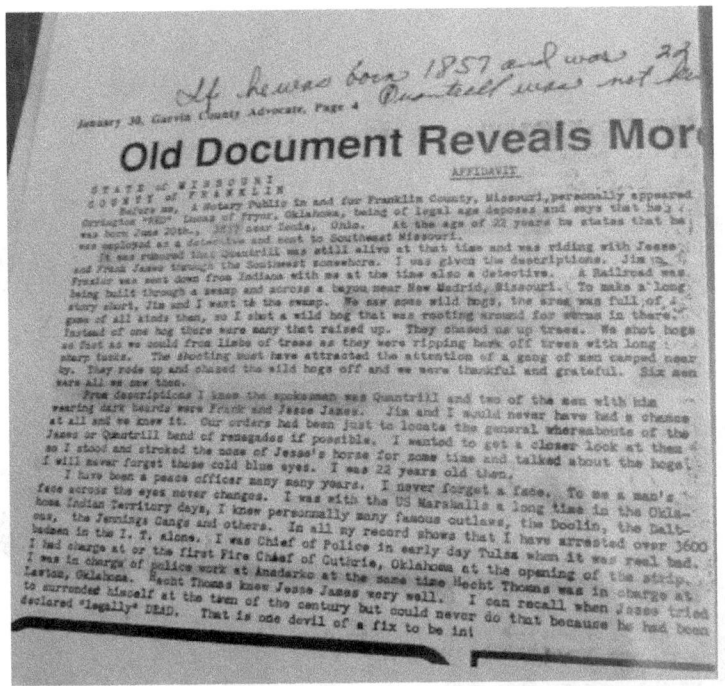

(Orrington "Red" Lucas Affidavit (courtesy of Garvin County Advocate))

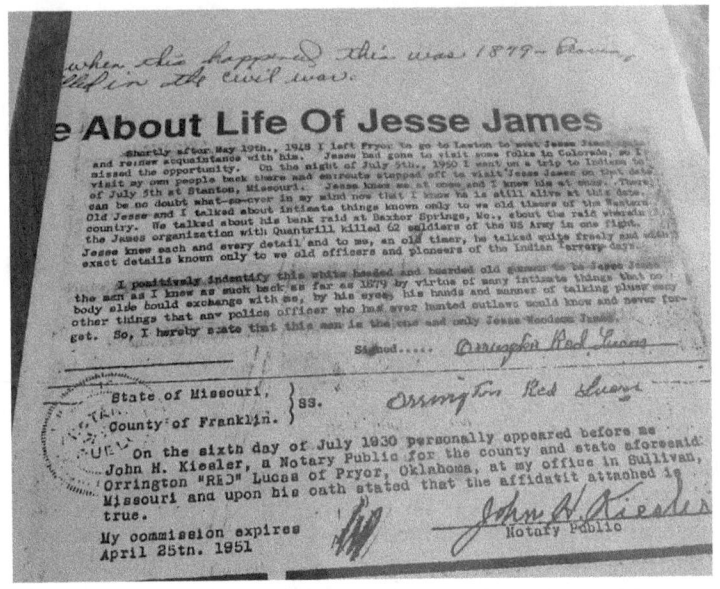

(Page 2)

Red Lucas was putting up $100 to anyone who could prove that J. Frank Dalton was not Jesse. No one came forward. Red definitely knew who he was.

Joe had the actual newspaper that announced Jesse James was alive, the Lawton Constitution. Bud and Lou wanted a picture with Joe Wood holding the newspaper. What a great picture.

(Joe Wood with the original news story in the Lawton Constitution)

Bud is on the left, Lou standing behind him, and Joe Wood in the middle. The lady and man on the right were Mr. and Mrs. David Moellendorf who were treasure hunters from Walatosha, Wisconsin. David was with the International Museum of Myths, Mysteries, Legends & Lost Treasures in Milwaukee. He got in touch with Bud and Bud told him about Joe Wood. David wanted to meet Bud in Missouri and for them to get to know Joe Wood. They did and Joe shared a lot of things and video tapes with them.

David had written Joe later and said they were connecting with "séance" people. David said in his letter that he learned that Bud is a reincarnation of one of the original knights of the Golden Circle. Bud did not know whether to be honored or laugh it off. This man was serious. Joe Wood wrote Bud on Sept. 26, 1991, and told him this and said, "Read on, noble knight, read on."

They all went to Meramec Cave and saw where an old mine shaft was. There were carvings on both sides of the entry way. There were secret passageways all through that cave network. Bud would continue to correspond with Joe Wood, and Bud continued to travel up there to see him. They both began to know and memorize each of their stories.

On tape, Bud captured Joe Wood saying, "The encounter with Jesse was a remarkable experience, but even being with him for 18 months, I learned more about Jesse from Bud Hardcastle than I had from the man himself." Joe said Jesse was very protective of many aspects and avenues of his life, especially his family.

Joe said, when a question was asked, he never had to think about nothing, he spoke without hesitation. He was solid as a rock.

Joe took many priceless photos of the man during his 18 months with him. We are ever so grateful. He gave many to Ola and many to Bud to share. One picture really stood out to Bud. It was the photo at the 102nd birthday party. Jesse was in a hospital bed with many of his friends surrounding him with the huge birthday cake. At the edge of his bed, the solecs of his feet were uncovered. It appeared as if Jesse was wearing black socks.

(Jesse's 102nd birthday. Rudy Turilli is making a speech)

(Far left Mary Plina Norris, one in front of Mary could be writer Robert Ruark, next is John Shevlin, nurse Mrs. Alvie Baker, John Trammel, Brushy Bill, Harriet Redding, Col. James R. Davis, Ozark Jack Berlin, DeWitt Travis, and unknown)

Bud asked Joe, "Were those socks Jesse was wearing?" Joe said, "No, they were his bare feet!" Oh my, these were solid black as you can see in the photo. This was his blackened feet, scarred so severely that they remained black throughout most of his life. This was from the torture he sustained as a young boy at age 14 by the Yankee soldiers. Oh, what pain this man has lived through.

    Joe had such great respect for the man and even more so as Bud revealed his discoveries of the truth about Jesse. Joe said that everyone at Meramec Caverns loved Jesse which caused great friction and jealousy between Howk and those who were caring for him. Francena Turilli had told Bud that during Jesse's 102nd birthday party, Howk caused so much trouble and strife, they had to ask him to leave. This in turn provoked Howk to start rumors and lies of the mistreatment of Jesse by Rudy and Francena Turilli.

Bud was able to locate some of Howk's letters describing the mistreatment, but Joe Wood cleared this up right away in a letter to Bud.

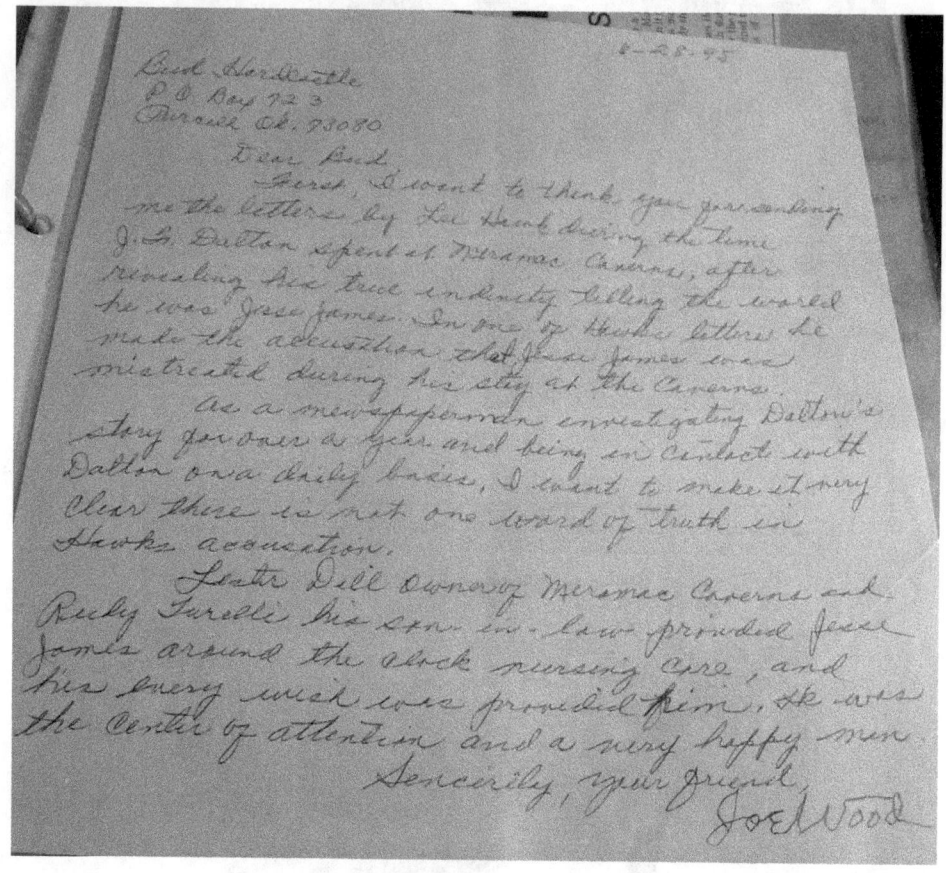

(Letter to Bud from Joe)

Nuff said!

"The beginning of wisdom is to call things by their right names."

-Unknown

Chapter Twenty-Eight: Taking the Stand

From the words of Joe Wood, "If he was a fraud, why did not someone, in the months that this story received worldwide notoriety in the papers, on the radio, and on television, come forward and expose him? All the others before him had been exposed almost immediately."

There were many naysayers, but no one, I mean no one came up with any hard evidence to prove that Jesse was not who he said he was.

Joe Wood, after hearing the story from Homer Croy, self-proclaimed authority on JJ went to see him in St. Louis. Croy wrote a book called, "Jesse James Was My Neighbor." Joe asked Croy if he would go and see for himself, the real Jesse James to identify him. Croy refused to go see JJ. He said, "I talked to the man in Oklahoma when he couldn't answer questions that only Jesse would know. His favorite horse, he couldn't tell me." Bud said that the question asked by Croy was "Who is Red Fox?" This was indeed the name of one of his favorite horses, but the answer Jesse gave Croy was "He was an old Indian." Croy was waiting for the answer of his horse, not a person, but he didn't make that clear.

Jesse's answer involved his good friend and scout for Quantrill, whose nickname was "Red Fox." His name was Sol Strickland who helped Jesse get his Confederate pension from Texas. Jesse told Wood that to him, the man was more important than the horse. Wood asked JJ did you have a favorite horse? Jesse said, "My favorite horse was always the one between my legs at the time."

Carl W. Breihan wrote a letter to Ola in 1949 wanting more information on Dalton and said if she had any doubts on who he was, to write him. Carl Breihan was the president of the Missouri Division of Longstreet Memorial Association, Inc, that honored and memorialized General James Longstreet in the Confederacy. Breihan wrote a letter to the Confederate Pension Fund Division in Austin on April 4, 1950 saying that Dalton was a fraud. "I have learned that this Dalton is a member of the Daltons of Arkansas, and was supposed to have used the sobriquet of "Arkansas Tom", and also that Roy Daugherty of Dalton-Doolin fame, is this same Dalton. Some claim this Dalton is a member of the outlaw band of Daltons of Coffeyville, Kansas bank robbery fame. But I am not sure of this yet." [608]

Breihan even wrote the Chamber of Commerce in Austin on April 18, 1950. [609] By June 1950, he wrote another letter to the Comptroller stating that he talked to Dalton in Stanton, Missouri and "he did not seem to mind that He was checking up on him." [610] I believe he came up empty.

Bud said that Ola was told by Jesse himself, that "what Carl Breihan didn't know would write a book." Bud has caught Breihan in several errors. He contradicted himself in his own handwriting when he wrote Lou Kilgore when she posed many questions to him under two different alias' names.

Roy Daugherty, known as Arkansas Tom Jones (1870-1924) was an Old West outlaw with the Wild Bunch Gang led by Bill Doolin. Wikipedia has an article on him, but you can see there is no comparison to J. Frank Dalton.

(Arkansas Tom Jones)
(http://trianglecranch.com/catalog/default.php?cPath=21)

There was a lot of undercover investigation on Jesse, but nothing was found to contradict who he was. In the Confederate Pension files, it shows that a N.K. Dixon, Special Investigator of the Texas Department of Public Safety was notified to check Dalton out. This had to be Texas Ranger Norman K. Dixon. His son, Kemp Dixon, used his father's diary to tell his story in "Chasing Thugs, Nazis, and Reds, published in 2015. Nothing was found in this book about his investigation into J. Frank Dalton. The Texas Rangers knew who Dalton was per Bud.

While Jesse was at Meramec Caverns, they were all trying to get the word out about Jesse's true stories and give back the honor and his original name that he deserves. They wanted to put all this negativity to rest. Rudy Turilli came up with an idea. Go to court.

Why would anybody go to the trouble and humiliation of court, in front of numerous onlookers to plead for restoration of his full Christian-given name. Jesse did in 1950. It was Rudy Turilli's idea and he must have thought he was really helping Jesse in order that he could wear his name proudly again. After years and years of using a host of various names, Jesse was ready to live out his life with his real name, Jesse Woodson James. Ola disapproved of it, as well as many others who cared for Jesse.

Wood told Bud that after gathering evidence of who he was, they were really trying to have the court declare that he was Jesse James for the whole world to know and believe the story. Rudy hired a lawyer.

They hit a curve ball when Rudy got a telegram from "We the People." Morrey Davidson, the NBC radio and TV announcer who was there for the interview with Jesse and his friends at the birthday party at Meramec Caverns wanted to know if Jesse would be interested to be on the very popular radio show, "We The People." Davidson spoke to Jesse about it, and they agreed. Morrey would make all the arrangements for the appearance.

We do find that Morrey Davidson had connections. He had written a letter to J. Edgar Hoover on November 22, 1949, fifty-three days before this broadcast. Bud had a copy of the response from J. Edgar Hoover, dated November 28, 1949. The letter is shown below, and Morrey Davidson typed in another response that Hoover gave him personally over the phone.

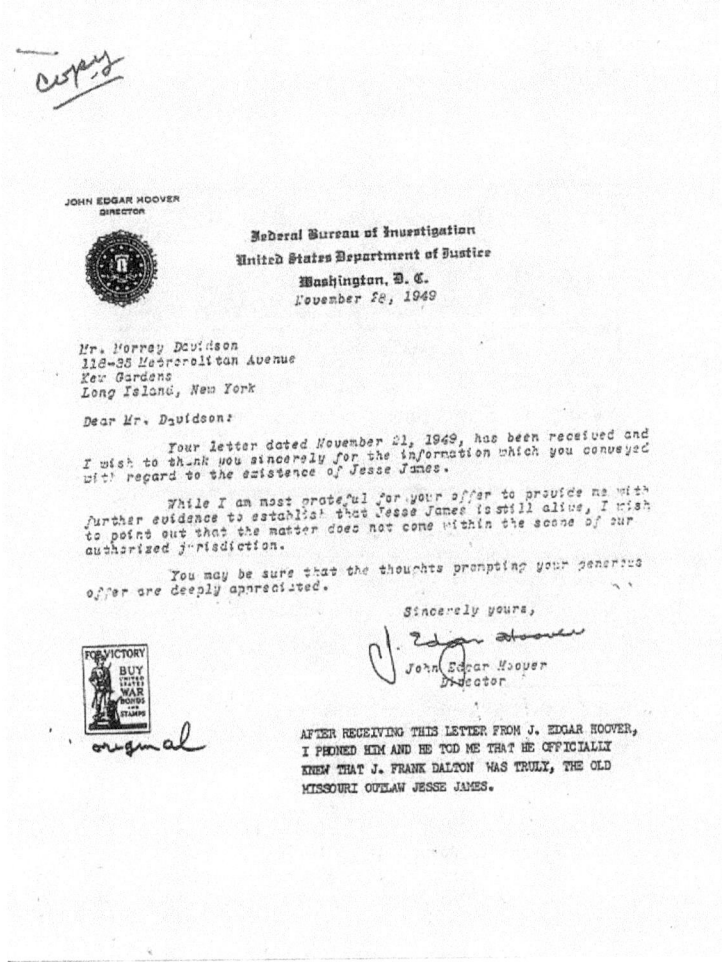

(Letter from J. Edgar Hoover to Morrey Davidson)

Joe Wood said he was against doing the radio show, "We were close to our goal in proclaiming Jesse as the real Jesse James in court, and the main concern was the danger of the trip, and how hard that would be on Uncle Jesse." Wood refused to go; he was mad as hell.

Rudy and Jesse took a plane to New York and Lester Dill paid for the expenses. Jesse called Ola just before he was to go to the news station and was asking several questions of her and asking for moral support. It was the morning of January 11, 1950.

It was aired on January 13, 1950. Jesse was interviewed and he went into the hoax of all times and the robberies they committed. The interviewer was amazed of his accuracy in details. The NBC investigators concluded that he was none other than Jesse Woodson James.

Ola's friend, E. T. Huff from Toledo, Ohio wrote Ola and recalls reading newspaper articles in 1929 that described contradictory evidence that Jesse was not killed but was a hoax. He stated in the letter that the articles have disappeared from the St. Joseph, Missouri Public Library and the

Missouri State Historical Society at Columbia, Missouri about 1950. He was led to believe someone didn't want any evidence to support the new claims of Jesse still being alive in 1950.

As far as we know, the "We the People" interview was not transcribed into print, nor is there a copy of the broadcast. Strangely enough, the writer has been unable to find anything on Morrey Davidson. His records or history of him cannot be found in the old newspapers, documents or anything of his family history. Maybe that was his stage name, but he is the only one that I cannot find a paper or computer trail on in this entire research that I have done. We have pictures though that Joe Wood provided of Morrey Davidson.

I did find an article in the New York newspaper notating the "We the People" program and Jesse's scheduled appearance.

(We the People program (From the Daily News, New York, New York, January 12 & 13, 1950))

Joe Wood said Jesse was an overnight sensation in New York after the program. The next day, a National Press conference was called to put Jesse through a test. The Associated Press and United Press Writers were there.

Joe Wood told Bud that famous columnists lined up to have a chance at an interview with Jesse while he was in New York. Among the list of award-winning writers who interviewed Jesse were Hal Boyle, Dorothy Kilgallen, Eleanor Roosevelt and Bob Considine.

Hal Boyle (1911-1974), who was a prolific, Pulitzer-prize winner in journalism for the Associated Press, was best known for his work as a war correspondent during World War II in the European and Pacific theatres. His articles were the only ones I was able to locate describing the man who was claiming to be Jesse James. In it, he was very skeptical and added snide remarks about the old man. [611] There are no other records of Jesse's interview or anything that would confirm who he was. Dr. William Tunstill stated when interviewing Ola, that around 1950, newspaper articles regarding Jesse were disappearing in the archives. Ola said Fern Hall brought some old papers that the Lawton Constitution had in their archives from 1882 and she was able to copy them by hand, but there is very little left of the 1882 newspapers regarding Jesse.

The other columnists' articles were never found, but their credentials are below:

Dorothy Kilgallen (1913-1965) was a columnist, journalist, and television game show panelist for "What's My Line". She wrote many controversial articles including an article on Frank Sinatra, Sam Shepherd, and one on the Kennedy Assassination, addressing concerns and skepticism on the conclusion of the Warren's Commission's report and the killing of Oswald by Jack Ruby in 1964. Tragically, she was found dead in her Manhattan townhouse in which it was believed she died of a possible accidental overdose of alcohol and barbiturates at the age of 52. [612]

Eleanor Roosevelt (1884-1962), of course was the wife of President Franklin D. Roosevelt, serving as first lady of the United States from **1933**-1945. She was an excellent writer and columnist for newspapers, magazines, and other news media. She was active in numerous organizations and "President Harry S. Truman later called her the "First Lady of the World" in tribute to her human rights achievements." [613]

Bob Considine, Robert Bernard Considine (1906-1975) was an American journalist, author, and commentator, known to co-author Thirty Seconds Over Tokyo and The Babe Ruth Story. He also was a panelist for the television show, "Who Said That?" [614]

The Police Gazette had in their files, all the identification marks of the real Jesse. They gathered their findings from the Pinkerton Agency Detective Reports that originated in 1874. The reports revealed and identified Jesse with 7 bullet wounds, a rope burn around his neck, a missing lung, a damaged fingertip, and severely burned feet. Jesse allowed them to undress him to reveal all the wounds he had on his body, to give him a complete exam, to Xray his chest and to everyone's surprise, he had all of these identification marks as listed. The story broke Nation Wide. "Jesse James is Alive in 1950."

This story sparked others. In "The Norman Transcript" in an article titled, "James Story True?" dated January 15, 1950, Sheriff of Cleveland County in Oklahoma, Jess Jack stated that his uncle, Harrison Everett, formerly of Lexington which is over the Canadian River from Purcell, Oklahoma was married to Catherine Isabel "Belle" James, who was supposedly Jesse James' second cousin. Harrison Everett was a preacher. Isabel told Sheriff Jack that Jesse was never shot as the legend has it. "She asked me not to say anything about it, and I never did except to members of my family until last night when I heard this fellow on the radio telling the story in almost the same words as my aunt did," Jack said." [615]

Catherine Isabel James was buried in the area of "The Masonic Home Family" plots at Summit View Cemetery in Guthrie, Oklahoma. Her father was Marmaduke Michael James (1826-1879) This appears to be the line of John Tatum's mother and Nancy James in my family.

In The Decatur Daily Review, May 11, 1950, another woman was claiming kinship to Jesse in Decatur, Illinois. Her name was Harriet Redding. She stated to the newspaper reporter that she was a 3rd cousin. She attended Jesse's 102nd birthday at Meramec Caverns and she also attended his funeral the following year after this article came out. [616]

At the funeral, Ola stated that Harriet claimed to be Jesse's daughter. Aubrey wrote a personal letter to Bud describing that at the funeral home, the sheriff of Hood County, Texas, Oran Baker spoke to Harriet Redding. He said he saw in the newspaper that she was a daughter of Jesse's. He asked her how. Aubrey said she stuttered and stammered and could never tell him how they were related.

Bud had a copy of Harriet Redding's obituary in the Decatur, Illinois newspaper dated 10/7/75 and it listed Harriet's parents as John and Isabelle Rush Ray. [617]

Joe Wood told Bud that while in New York, influential people advised Rudy and Jesse to go back to Missouri and fight in court to change his name back to Jesse Woodson James, when their initial petition was just requesting a declaration that J. Frank Dalton was Jesse Woodson James with all the evidence they had. It was two different things.

There was some confusion to this and the petition to the court in Union, Missouri was to change his name back to Jesse Woodson James. This really made Joe Wood mad because he knew this would complicate things with what they had already prepared. A hearing was set.

Judge Henry M. Priest, who we spoke of before who lived in St. Louis and served on the bench in St. Louis, Missouri for 25 years wrote Rudy and Joe. He said he knew the man who was claiming to be Jesse in the newspapers. He had lived in Nashville under the name of Howard. Priest rented a house to JJ at 411 Fatherland Street. Priest recognized him immediately as Jesse Howard. He was invited to come testify along with John Trammel, James R. Davis, and Robert E. Lee.

When they all arrived at Union, they talked and reminiscence. Joe Wood asked Judge Priest, "What are our chances in court?" Judge Priest replied, "Good. Trammel does not know how to lie. Davis is so old he does not have a reason to lie. Before the hearing started the two attorneys spent two hours with the judge. All the evidence had been discussed.

It was March 10, 1950 when the courthouse was filling up with people in Union, Missouri. Ola had wonderful pictures of the scene that she got from Joe Wood and Bud saw them at her house. It was packed. Jesse had to be carried up three flights of stairs in the Franklin County Courthouse to the courtroom where Judge Ransom Albert Breuer, age 80, presided. Jesse fervently held on to his blanket and tomato or coffee can used for a spittoon for his chaw of Tennessee Twist.

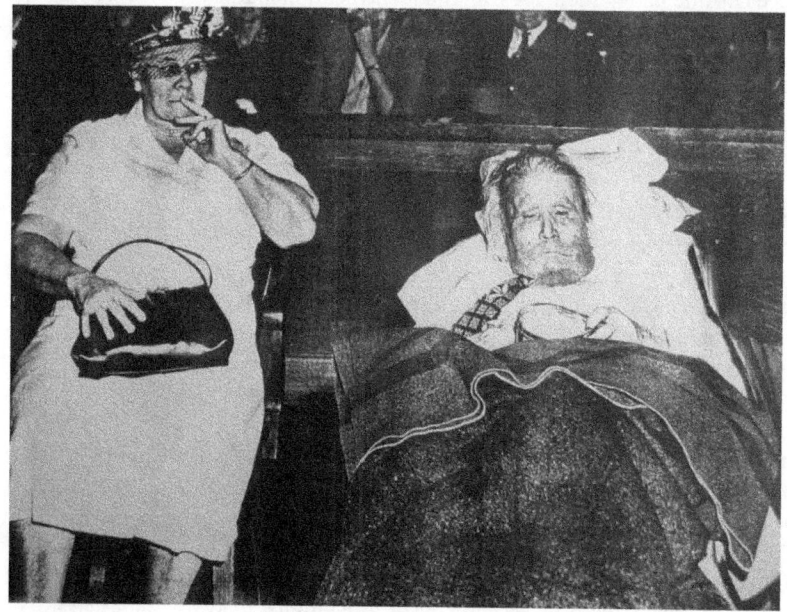

(Jesse in the courtroom with nurse. Has his spit can firmly on his lap, with his other hand on his pistol concealed under the blanket)

There were many, many newspapermen anxious to get the story. It became a circus with newspaper reporters, photographers with their large flash bulbs going off at every angle, and jeering lawyers who tried to discredit Dalton.

When things began heating up and photographers were bombarding him with bright flashes of cameras from every direction, Jesse pulled out his pearl-handled .44 caliber pistol from underneath his army blanket in disgust and shouted, "____those pictures!" Those standing close to the door amongst the crowd to get a glimpse, stepped back in fright.

A motion was made by Jesse Edward James and his wife's attorney, the supposedly only son of Jesse James, to throw the case out. It was not quickly considered, but overruled. If you remember, Jesse Edward James was given the title of Jesse's only son with Zee Mimms, when in actuality was Charley Bigelow's son per many investigators in which Bud believes.

Judge Ransom Albert Breuer, age 80 and spectators began to listen intently to the witnesses that would last 6 hours while Jesse laid on a stretcher with a horse pistol beside him. Reaching the age of 102, the old man was claiming he was the real Jesse Woodson James and wanted to restore his name and identity.

The witness who presented the most impressive testimony was that of James R. Davis who upon being cross examined, became extremely infuriated by Jesse Edwards James' attorney, who was implying Davis was well compensated to testify for Jesse. Davis hit his cane on the floor and leaning forward said, "Young man, I have one foot in the grave and the other on a banana peel under oath to this court and to my God, to tell the truth and that's what I've done. If one of these whippersnappers thinks he can twist me around his thumb, he's not going to do it!" The crowd broke out in laughter while the judge and bailiffs were trying to subdue the spectators. "I'm here to tell the truth and not be led by some attorney," Davis stormed. "I'm too old to be messed with. I've got one foot in the grave and the other on the brink." (Eyewitness account of Joe Wood and the Tyler Morning Telegraph- March 11, 1950) [618]

The next witnesses called were Robert E. Lee of Louisiana, bodyguard for Buffalo Bill Cody; William Pierce of Ray county, Missouri; and Judge Henry M. Priest of St. Louis, formerly of Nashville who was a storekeeper there and knew this man as Mr. Howard, an alias always used of Jesse's.

John Trammel presented his testimony and said he had worked for Jesse for 17 years cooking hoe cakes. "All I know is when the boss say come, I come. When he say go, I go." [619]

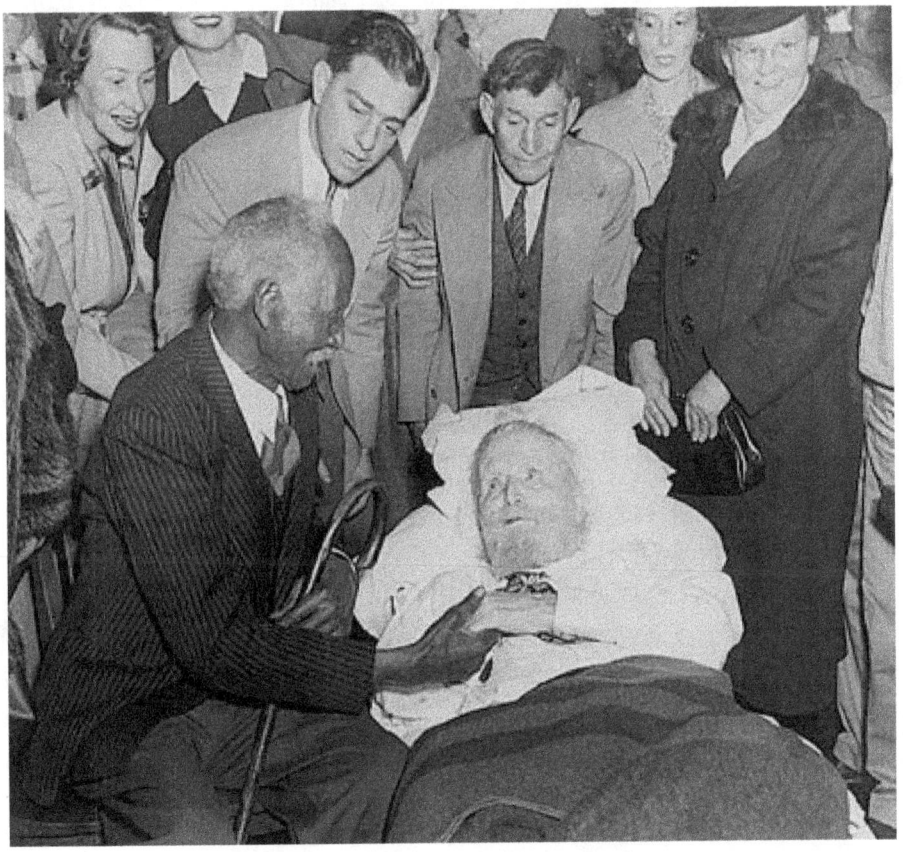

(The sweetest picture showing their love and devotion to one another. John Trammel and Jesse at court hearing. (Harriet Redding in the dark coat))

It was Jesse's turn to talk. He was rolled over in a gurney to an area by the witness stand. He had a loud and shaky tone. During the opposing lawyers questioning, Jesse became unglued. "All

I'm here to do is testify that I'm Jesse James, and I'll refuse to answer questions about anything else."

Judge's response after the witnesses had finished: "For a quarter of a century almost, what is known as the James gang murdered, robbed and burglarized the people of Missouri in defiance of the people, the laws and the courts of this state. Now, after almost three quarters of a century, one who claims to be one of the main leaders of the gang comes into a court of equity, in the same courts that have been defied, asking for some relief. The people of Missouri and the courts of Missouri have always been liberal, tempering justice with mercy, but there is too much innocent blood crying from the ground of Missouri to be forgiven."

He considered Jesse James and all outlaws were a "Black spot on Missouri." The state turned their back on Jesse. Judge Ransom Breuer stated "There is no evidence here to show that this gentleman, if he ever was Jesse James, has ever changed his name. If his name has never been changed from Jesse James, he is still Jesse James in name, and there is nothing for this court to pass on. If he isn't what he professes to be, then he is trying to perpetrate a fraud upon this court. If he is Jesse James, as he claims to be, then my suggestion would be that he retreat to his rendezvous and ask the good God above to forgive him so he may pass away in peace when his time comes to go." [620]

After the hearing, Morrey Davidson went in the Judge's private chambers. He asked the judge if he did not believe that the petitioner was the real Jesse James, the former outlaw? The judge's reply, "Hell yes that's him! But I ruled the only way I could."

About two weeks later, Judge Breuer speaks again on the subject to a reporter. "As for the crimes committed by Jesse James, Judge Breuer says he does not know of any charge of murder ever having been made against him, but if there is such a charge it could be pressed, as the statute of limitations doesn't apply to murder." [621]

Rudy describes what a verbal beating Jesse took in the hearing to claim back his original name. The judge did not want any part of it or the exhumation of the ills and cruelties that the James Gang brought to Missouri. "It was a mess," Jesse said.

A day later after the hearing, Colonel Davis went into a coma and died in Stanton at the age of 109. Colonel Davis fought alongside Jesse most of his life and in the end, he fought for him with his dying breath. What devotion, respect, and comradery they shared.

This must have devastated Jesse. I'm sure it broke his heart.

They came from such excitement in New York to such a letdown in Missouri. The loss of a mighty good friend took the air out of Jesse. His right arm became paralyzed and he was losing his eyesight, but he chose to stay at Meramec Caverns.

Six months later, September 1950, Rudy loaded Jesse into an ambulance, and they were heading to Texas. Jesse was wanting to go back to Ola's to stay. Rudy wanted Joe to go with them, but he didn't, and Joe regretted that for the rest of his life. That would be the last time he would ever see Jesse.

Eighteen long months with Jesse; Joe would not take anything for that remarkable experience.

Joe wrote a book on all his research and investigation of Jesse James in 1989 called "My Jesse James Story." He gave Bud a copy.

Bud admired Joe so much and their friendship was so important to him. The last time Bud saw Joe Wood, Joe was in a wheelchair and he kissed Bud on his cheek. Bud knew he was saying goodbye for the last time. When Joe died Dec. 3, 1996 at the age of 82, his wife called Bud and told him the news. Bud honored his dear friend, attended his funeral and retold his story for this book.

(Joe wood with wife, December 1995 in Kirkwood, Missouri near St. Louis. Bud said, "Joe was as fine a man as you could ever want to meet.")

    Just another reminder of what Joe was all about; From the words of Joe's friend and colleague at the Globe-Democrat, Herb Waeckerle said, "Joe was a real professional….an outstanding and trustworthy individual. He looked for the facts and didn't go for the fluff." [622]

    A very special letter was found in Bud's collection. It was a letter to Bud from Joe, expressing his philosophy. "In my 77 years of life experiences I have developed a simple philosophy regarding my fellow man. To me – the total worth of a man is based on his work. No greater epitaph can be given a man than these words chiseled on his tombstone. "He was a man of his word."

(Photo of Joe Wood)

"A blessed thing it is for any man or woman to have a friend, one human soul whom we can trust utterly, who knows the best and worst of us, and who loves us in spite of all our faults."

-Charles Kingsley

Chapter Twenty-Nine: Trust

Rudy took great care of Jesse and personally took him all the way to Ola's house by ambulance from Stanton, Missouri to Austin, Texas, 765 miles. Destination: Ola and Aubrey's home, it is where Jesse wanted to be.

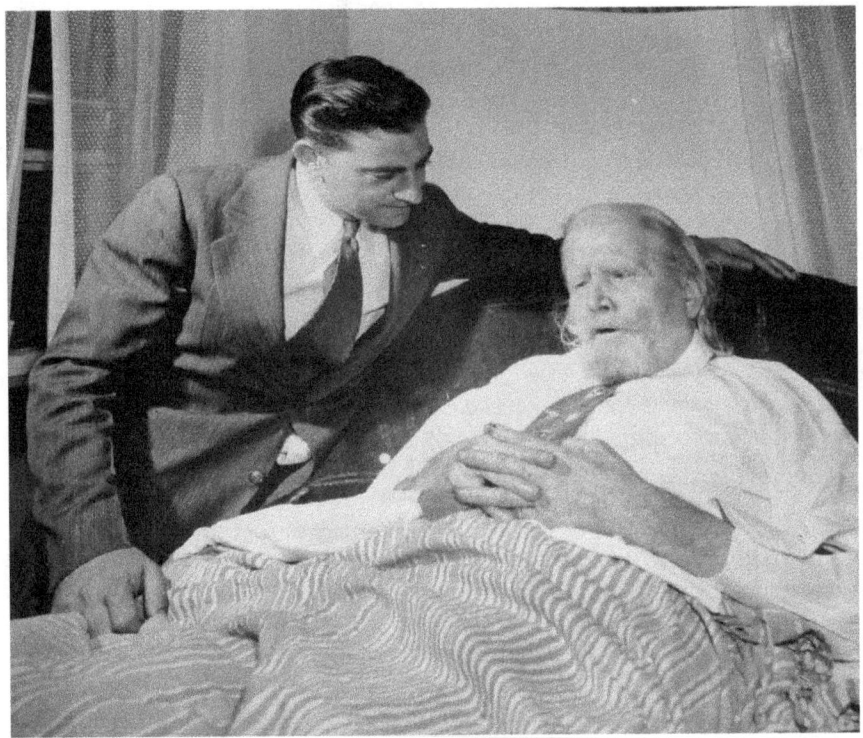

(Rudy Turilli and Jesse (notice his "buggered up" left index finger))

Up until now, Jesse had possessed a young vivacious spirit trapped in an old man's body, living in the past, but yet put his heart and soul in building the future for this great country that once was extremely divided. He was finally slowing down and reflecting what he had accomplished. "He did a lot of bad things, but he certainly did a lot of good things," Ola said. He manifested the brotherhood's "Universal Duality."

Aubrey was a very small man, but a good man and a good heart. He helped Ola care for Jesse and also hired some black women to help bathe Jesse. Aubrey told the story to Bud that none of the women would stay very long. They would find out who he was and were too frightened to come back.

Aubrey said he had one lady who had come to bathe Jesse and when Aubrey went the next morning to pick her up, he asked her if she was ready. She said, "No." Aubrey looked puzzled and said, "What's the matter? Didn't we pay you enough?" She answered, "Yes'm, yes'm, but knowing who that man was, I never slept a wink all night long." She wasn't about to go back.

These women, along with many others saw all the years of abuse to Jesse's body, the rope burns around his neck, the badly burned and blackened feet, the mangled fingertip or "buggered up" (as Jesse said), and the many deep gunshot scars, dimpling a third of his body. Aubrey said he had 28 bullet wounds and showed Bud where they were located. Jesse not only had scars on the outside, but deeply embedded scars within. Jesse shared his story with Ola; a woman of kin, not after his gold, and about the only one left he could trust.

Ola took down everything Jesse said. She typed up her notes on an old typewriter next to her day bed. She was an endearing woman who was crippled in both of her legs and at the same time cared for her mother, Bertha.

Bertha thoroughly enjoyed having Jesse live with them from time to time. There was no question in her mind who he was. They would talk for hours about the family and the events that occurred in the rough territory of Oklahoma. Ola enjoyed listening about their days growing up near Ardmore.

The Everhard's extensive care for Jesse was never about money, never about buried treasure, but the sincere concern for Jesse's wellbeing and protection. One day Jesse asked Ola, "Ola, do you think I've got money?" She said, "No Sir." He said, "You don't?" She said, "No sir, I don't." He said, "Well why don't you? Everybody else does." Ola said, "Well Jesse, you've got a lot of years on your head and my common sense tells me that what money you had, you had to use it to live on over the years because you had to live." He said, "Well honey, you're right. But you'd be surprised how many people never think of that." Ola said, "Well Jesse, the way I see it, when you were younger and in your outlaw days, what money you got wasn't all yours. It was equally divided between you and your men. So that means that none of you got much at a time after it was divided." He said, "Honey you're right." Then she said, "As you told me, it took more money for you and your men to live on than just ordinary people." He said, "That's right too. For when we were out on the road and people were nice enough to give us food or took us in for the night and gives us shelter, we always seen that they were well paid for their kindness when we left." [623]

That last statement was certainly true, verified by a multitude of witnesses.

Aubrey was a very humble man, and of good character. Aubrey was never boastful about any of the things he did for Jesse during his care or things he learned about Jesse. Aubrey was not the type of man that sought out recognition or fame, or anything that would elevate his status in knowing Jesse himself.

Not once did Aubrey ever suggest that they spoke to Jesse about buried treasure. In fact, in one part of Bud's visit with Aubrey, leading up to the story about Howk, Bud asked Aubrey about Jesse's funeral in Granbury in 1951. Aubrey said that Howk threatened Ola that if she came to the funeral, she wouldn't leave alive. Aubrey explained that Howk had an assumption that Jesse had told Ola about buried treasure but didn't tell him. Howk had it in for Ola with extreme jealousy and the sense that he lost complete control of his exploitation of Jesse.

Aubrey said that the buried treasure was the reason Howk stuck around. The man was crazy with greed and envy. Aubrey said there was no buried treasure. Apparently, this was a subject rarely discussed between the Everhards and Jesse. Ola was more fascinated with the man himself, his stories, and the truth rather than what glittered in the bottom of a hole.

Oh, "there is gold in them thar hills." Bud can attest to that. He knows a few people that are living comfortably now because of Jesse's gold. Jesse didn't make it none too easy to find. It is not known if Howk found any buried treasure and I'm sure Jesse didn't make it any easier than he would have for the other guy. Jesse gave him just enough to tantalize his appetite for wealth.

Keep in mind, Jesse was very cunning, cantankerous, and outsmarted most of his opponents at one time or another. In so many instances, he pulled off a lot of monkey business in his days. To get the full picture of Jesse's sense of humor and demeanor, I must quote him exactly, word for word when he spoke to Ola and Aubrey, and others. Some words are a little bit spicy and crude but shows the true character of the man. He wasn't aiming to please anyone but told it like it was.

An example of his pranks, wit, and character is as follows: (told to Bud by Aubrey Everhard):

Aubrey and Ola were in the hospital visiting Jesse. A man came in Jesse's room one day and claimed to be a relative. The man was very interested in buried treasure. He stated that he had heard that Jesse had buried money by a long rock wall near Big Springs, Texas. He asked Jesse if this was true. Leading him on, Jesse stated, "yes I did." Jesse continued, "you follow that rock wall and go about 30 feet out to a small tree, then go 10 ft. south of that, and you dig, and you'll find it." When the man left, Ola said, "What made you lie to that poor man like that?" Jesse said, "Well, the son of a bitch wanted to dig, let him dig."

Aubrey said Jesse was very funny and kept them amused. He gave Bud several letters from Jesse and within those pages, you could hear the wit just flow from his thoughts, as well as the horse sense he possessed. He brought a new sense of purpose to Ola and Aubrey. They would do anything for Jesse and Aubrey said Jesse was willing to give his last $45.00 to them. It's very evident that the endearment was felt on both sides. When Jesse went completely blind, the last six months of his life, he asked to be taken to Ola and Aubrey's house. That speaks volumes.

Ola said Jesse liked "an egg, a couple of sausage patties, a cup of coffee and two slices of light toast for breakfast. Ola's mother would cook it and Ola would feed him. Then, at night, he wanted a cup of milk and two doughnuts put on a nightstand by his bed to eat during the night. The next morning after breakfast, Jesse told Aubrey to go get him a pint of whiskey. Aubrey did and when he got back, Jesse told him to pour half of it into another bottle. Ola didn't recall where he got another bottle, but he did and poured half of the whiskey in it. Then Jesse said to Ola's mother, "Bertha, if you don't mind, will you boil some tea and when it gets done and cool, pour it in the two bottles of whiskey so they'll be half whiskey and half tea so I can take a swallow every once in a while to clear my throat. It helps me." [624]

Jesse spoke of a lot of things to Ola that he hadn't before and said that Frank, his brother only had one son, Alexander Frank Jr. Jesse would call him "Little Frank" but in 1950, he was in a mental hospital in Los Angeles. Jesse told Ola that Robert James, who Joe Wood and Rudy tried to get to come see Jesse for $10,000 was an adopted son. The next part is contradictory of other statements. Jesse said there was never a Jesse James Jr., but the one you hear about is the Bigelow boy. Jesse said my boy is Jesse Edwards who was the County Attorney in Wyandotte County, Missouri, which actually is in Kansas right on the border of Missouri.

Jesse only stayed for 3 weeks at Aubrey and Ola's and then he had to go back to the hospital. Ola was up there every day like before. Jesses' right arm was paralyzed, so he had to write with his left hand. Writing became hard and unreadable. Jesse requested Ola to write letters for him to Billy, Ozark Jack Berlin, and Al Jennings. His eyes were getting worse, he was nearly blind because of the chronic conjunctivitis. Ola said, "Oh well, I've got eyes, we'll just use mine."

Ola wrote a lot of letters and answered a lot of letters. One was from Mary Plina Norris.

(See Appendix A-**10)**

Jesse enjoyed hearing Ola read the letters and when Brushy Bill wrote, Jesse was all ears.

(Brushy's letter to Jesse, Oct 27, 1950)

(2nd page of Brushy's letter)

Bud had to help me decipher the letter. Lizzie wrote it for Brushy, but she didn't use the correct punctuation or spelling.

Dear Uncle Jesse,

Hope this will find you feeling good. I ain't been well for a month. I ate some Chili. It didn't agree with me with this high blood pressure. I liked to died before the doctor got here. I had the doctor 5 times. I'm feeling better now. I was sure proud to hear from you. I was sorry to hear the way they treated you in Missouri. They got all the money out of you and throwed you away. That's the way it looks. I got a letter from Travis, he said the last time he heard from you, you was getting along alright. I wrote "Dill" (Lester Dill) four letters sent him stamps and envelopes to see how you was. He never answered, never heard a word, just quit writing. I wrote Roscoe James he didn't write either.

I wrote to John Trammel that old Negro in Guthrie. I didn't hear from him either????? I sent you something for your birthday. I sent you something some of those days I send you some white socks to keep your feet warm. I heard you was at the old Soldiers Home at Austin, Tex. ……… I hope to hear from you soon.

Your lifetime friend, Brushy Bill Roberts
Write soon

Ola said Frank and Fern Hall still kept in touch and would come to visit as often as they could. Ola said that children of Col. James R. Davis would call her and want to know who their father really was. They knew he was not who he said he was.

Ola said while in the hospital, about October 1950, Jesse desired to see and visit with Masons and Odd Fellows. Ola and Aubrey rounded up a few and Jesse enjoyed their visit. This is when Jesse revealed he was a **33rd** degree Mason. Of course, secret handshakes and questions posed from the visitors was a way to check this old man out to see if he knew all the secrets of their organizations. Jesse answered all the question without wavering a bit.

Ola made Christmas 1950 as special as she could for Jesse. He was in the hospital and by that time he was completely blind. She bought a small Christmas tree, and a little Santa Claus figurine. Ola guided his fingers across each branch of the tree and each curve of the little figurine. Jesse was receiving a lot of Christmas cards and she would read each one to him, describing the card's picture and colors. She made it as pleasant as possible.

Brushy and Lizzie sent a Christmas card the year before to Jesse at Meramec Caverns in which Aubrey proudly displayed. They were planning to come to see Jesse after Christmas 1950.

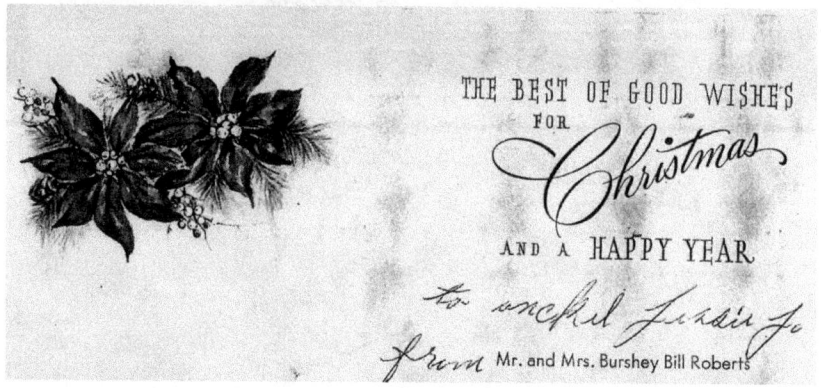

(Christmas card from Brushy to Jesse – (Also see letter inside in Appendix A-9))

Just a few days after the celebration of Christmas, Jesse was settling back down to his normal routine of being bed ridden. He had been this way for 3 ½ years. The only thing he looked forward to was when Ola came to visit. She was about the only one that he could trust at this time, and the only one who could really bring joy to his heart.

On December 28, 1950, Ola came to the hospital, but she wasn't bringing optimism and sunshine as she usually did, but quietly sat down and held Jesse's crippling hand and told him the sad news of Billy's passing on the 27th. Billy was just shy of turning 91 years old. Ola said he responded with, "Well, well, I've lost a mighty good friend." Tears were just rolling down his face as Ola stood by patting his arm. It was heartbreaking to her to see Jesse go through that, she felt helpless. With tear-filled eyes and a choking voice he said, "Poor little Billy. He was a good boy. He had a mighty hard time growing up. I've lost a mighty good friend. It hurts me mighty bad. I'm sure sorry he's gone." [625]

They sat in silence for a spell, soaking in the sad news. Jesse was getting weaker and frailer. Jesse was extremely heartbroken when Ola gave him the news of Billy's passing. Two of his best buddies were gone.

He began to talk to Ola more intimately. He said the one regret he had in life is not returning that diamond-emerald studded gold cross they stole from the church he had mentioned earlier. That weighed heavy on his mind. I'm sure his mind was taking him back to many regrets that were never voiced. He knew his days were numbered. When a person starts losing their family and friends, one by one in death, it has such a strong effect on the ones who are left.

He was in and out of the hospital and Ola's home frequently. His hip was extremely painful, but he was back in the hospital again as of March 1951. One night, as in their daily routine, Aubrey and Ola went to the hospital. They found Jesse extremely upset. "He was greatly disturbed. After a little bit he told Ola, "Ola, I'm fixing to leave here in the morning with old Howk." Ola said, "Jesse, I wish you wouldn't, because you're not able to be drug around by him like you have been. I wish you'd stay here where you can get good care because we love you."

He said, "Well honey if I go, it will save your life. Because old Howk has got it in for you so bad that you are in danger. Ola, Hawk, the son-of-a-bitch, is just crazy enough to be dangerous and I don't want anything to happen to you. So, I'm going with him."

"The next morning just at daylight, Aubrey and Ola went to the hospital with Jesse's clothes and hat, but he was already in an ambulance and they didn't get to tell him goodbye. Old Hawk, Jake Wilson and a man named Woodell were all out at the ambulance. Howk and Jake were wearing handguns, so they'd look tough. Jesse always called Howk, "Old Hawk the son-of-a-bitch." "In my opinion, he wasn't a hawk. He was a buzzard," wrote Ola. [626]

Howk and Wilson actually went into the hospital with guns strapped on to take Jesse out. What was their intent? Take him by force if need be? Holly Molly!

On March 24, 1951 at 5:50 A.M is the last time Ola and Aubrey saw Jesse alive. Ola noted the license plate of the ambulance, **J-J 3133**. How very odd.

By dark, they were in Galveston and then on to Gilchrist, Texas, 250 miles total. A person couldn't go any farther than Gilchrist, it was the very southern edge of Texas next to the Gulf of Mexico. There was no concern for his physical condition, food, clothes, and shelter. This tore Ola up. It was a kidnapping, no doubt about it, but we learn later that Howk had a binding contract with Jesse.

After four months, Howk had squeezed as much out of Jesse that he could and then became flat broke as said in one of his letters. Jesse was no good to him anymore. By August 1951, Howk called Golda (Rash) Burks living in Texas City, Texas who was a close family friend to Jesse. In 1935, Golda and her husband, Henry Edwin/Edward Burks lived at Gladewater where he got into the oil business. Jesse, DeWitt Travis, and Billy knew Henry well. Mr. Burks' father, John was a Methodist preacher and Henry was born in 1889 in DeLeon, Texas.

By 1951, Henry Burks and Golda were living in Texas City where her husband worked for Southport Petroleum Company of Delaware before World War II and later worked at the American Refining Company, transferring to Texas City in 1944. Mr. Burk was a Stillman Fireman in the Oil Refinery business, a professional who oversees and maintain safety and efficiency in the operation of oil and gas pipelines.

It is not known what was occurring, but it appears that Jesse was on his last leg, literally and wanted to go to the one place that he felt secure, protected, and within a realm of trust. It was where he wanted to lay his head down for all eternity. We assume this was Jesse's decision, nothing else indicates otherwise, but Howk needed some help, financially I'm sure to be able to get Jesse to Granbury. He knew Golda Rash Burk would help as she was financially able, and that Jesse wanted to be buried in the plot her father had reserved for him.

Golda Rash Burk drove down to Galveston and helped Howk to get Jesse on an ambulance and on a train traveling up to Granbury, 320 miles. Noone ever informed Ola and Aubrey that Jesse was going down fast, nor that they moved him to Granbury.

Golda's family, the Rashes go way back with Jesse. He wanted to go back to the old Rash home before he died. A photo of the Rash home is in the book, "Jesse James Was One of His Names," by Del Schrader.

Golda "Gola" Rash was the daughter of Samuel "Sam" A. Rash and Mary Alabama Thornton. Golda had married in 1911 to Theodore E. Renois. Their marriage ended, unknown if it was by death or not. By 1920 Golda was the wife of William Henry Holland who was 12 years older than Golda. Holland was born in 1882 to John Jay Holland and Margaret Towle. John Jay Holland was born in 1847 in Missouri and grew up in Missouri up to the time of 1867 after the war. He was the same age as Jesse. Military service cannot be found on him. John Jay Holland moved to Granbury in 1867. He became a well digger. One of the stories from the family said he was a grave digger, made headstones and some residents would hire him to clean the tombstones. There may be something more to this story that has yet to be uncovered.

His son, William Henry Holland was a manager for R. R. Pump Station, later we find that he worked as a pumper for the Frisco Railroad Company, pumping water for trains that ran through Granbury, Texas. Pete Galik from Louisianna wrote about his half uncle, William Henry Holland, stating that his arm had to be amputated after he had broken his arm when he was 13 from a fall from a pecan tree. The injury was so severe, the doctors at first thought they could amputate his right arm at the wrist, but gangrene set in and the doctors had to amputate up past the elbow. The family buried the arm in 1895 where the rest of the family was buried in Granbury.

It is not known what happened to William Henry Holland who was in the Fort Worth Hospital in 1927, age 44. He was having blood pressure issues. His wife, Golda came to the hospital to see him and bring him some fish she had fried for him. He sat up on the side of the bed and ate the fish and then fell back and died instantly.

Golda then married Henry Burks and was living a comfortable life. Now, Jesse would be spending his last days in Granbury at Golda's family home. He finally let his guard down and put his trust in another woman to take him down the last trail ride towards the eternal sunset.

> "Life is a succession of lessons which must be lived to be understood."
>
> -Helen Keller

Chapter Thirty: "I am Jesse James"

The man who wrote "To Catch the Wind," which the story was later produced into the movie, "Twister," was a good friend of Joe Wood. His name was Steven Kessler who was a writer, director, and producer. Joe Wood told him about Bud. Kessler was able to meet up with Bud and Joe and suggested to Bud to allow him to take the known photo of Jesse and compare it to a photo of J. Frank Dalton in a regression mode. Kessler had a professional studio with computer aging analysis software. Bud said, "I think that is a good idea."

The outcome was amazing. Kessler wrote, "The photo-image to the far right was taken by photographer, Joe Wood in 1949 and was posed to emulate the position of the photo seen at the far left. Working with a computer, KEPSFilms, Inc. simply matched the eyes, then overlayed one image over the other, increasing the amount of transparency between the young man and the old man. The only cosmetic changes between the two images was in "trimming" the excess weight off of the older face to help conform its profile to that of the younger face. The weight difference is seen in the finished photo. The chances of two faces from two different people lining up at the eyes, nose, mouth and shape of the skull are astronomical.   Stephen Burns Kessler, KEPSFilms, Inc.

(Steven Kessler's regression photos of Jesse. (Caption underneath reads, "The first photo has been authenticated as Jesse James, age 28, by James Family historians. Jesse was said to have been killed by Bob Ford in 1882. The final photo of J. Frank Dalton, age 102, was taken by Joe Wood at Meramec Caverns in 1949. J. Frank or Uncle Jesse, died in Granbury, Texas in 1951. He is buried there under the name, Jesse Woodson James. We matched the eyes of Jesse James with the eyes of J. Frank Dalton. No morphing or image altering program was used to distort the facial proportions." - (courtesy of Steven Kessler to Bud Hardcastle))

As life was fleeting from his body, Jesse's clues were multiplying, leading those who were willing to open their eyes to follow the truth. He was Jesse James. He would be content in Granbury and knew this was his last stop along the trail.

Howk was especially interested in Granbury where Jesse had one of his hideouts. Howk would have Noel Foreman take him around Granbury to look for spikes driven into oak trees and would look for maps carved in big rocks. Mr. Foreman remembers quite well, the old man who talked very little, but had a very deep voice.

The Fort Worth Telegram, August 16, 1951 stated that Frank Dalton/Jesse James came to Granbury the first week of August, about a week from this writing, traveling from Texas City where Golda Rash Burk lived. Jesse was accompanied by Howk and Golda. They boarded the train and headed to Fort Worth. There they took him by ambulance to Granbury where he wanted to spend his last days. "The porch of the house (on Sam Rash's property) to which he was brought was partially covered with clippings of publicity he had received and signs said Jesse James was living there and contributions would be gratefully accepted." [627]

Howk had turned it into a carnival. He had signs all over the place on the house. He was drawing a crowd to see the one and only, Jesse James for a price of course; 25 cents for adults and a dime for children to see the marks of the outlaw. "Step right up folks."

Jesse stayed in the Rash home for approximately 8 – 10 days.

Most of the family of the Rash's had been gone for some time. Sam Rash died in 1943 and Mary his wife, died in 1946. Their sons, Walter (66) and Needham (68) were still living there. The family had always reserved a cemetery plot in their family section for Jesse in the cemetery at Granbury.

(Sam Rash family from The Granbury Tablet, May 24, 1984)

In the Hood County News Tablet, in August 1966, Sheriff Oran Baker who spent every day with Jesse while he was in Granbury stated that Dalton worked the railroads near Granbury and fell in love with a girl whose father worked for him on the railroads. She eventually died, but he wished to return to that area at the end of his life and be buried next to her. Who was the girl? We don't know. Some speculate it was Belle Starr. Granbury citizens and historians state that "Belle Starr maintained a hideaway in northwest Hood County where she trafficked in horses that she repeatedly sold and stole." [628]

The Rashes moved from Hot Springs, Arkansas in 1891. Jesse may have met Sam Rash in Hot Springs. Sam and his wife, Mary Thornton married in 1882. Sam grew up in Jackson County, Alabama, but the connection to Jesse may have been through his father.

Sam Rash's father lived to be 100 years old, Wesley Allen Rash (1829-1929). When Wesley died, he was considered the oldest Confederate veteran in Jackson County, Alabama. "He was a noble and patriotic son of the Confederacy, serving with honor throughout the four years of strife" [629] In the "Alabama, Texas and Virginia, U.S. Confederate Pensions, 1884-1958," we find a report of an examination of Mr. Rash regarding a pension he was filing upon. The official form, Jackson County, Alabama, Pension Board was completed by E.R. Smith, M.D. and S. H. McMohan, J.P. stating that Wesley A. Rash worked in the "niter mines" during the war. His Pension Claim was **No. 33**. He served in Stevenson, Alabama. [630]

Looking further into "niter mines" during the war, led me back to the saltpeter caves. They were important to both sides of the war. An excellent article on the "principal ingredient of black gunpowder" in the 1860's is found in the article by Robert C. Whisonant, titled "Geology and History Of Confederate Saltpeter Cave Operations In Western Virginia," November 2001. "The use of this invaluable strategic material was to keep alive the dream of southern independence."

"In the 1860s, the principal ingredient of black powder was potassium nitrate, derived from niter or saltpeter as it was called. Each powder grain contained about 75 per cent niter, together with charcoal (15 percent) and sulfur (10 percent). When war began between North and South in April 1861, the Confederacy did not possess an adequate supply of gunpowder. Planned importation of powder could not meet all of the South's needs, as the Union blockade of Confederate ports quickly proved. Thus, the need for a strong, home-based gunpowder supply, and consequently a steady source of niter, became evident. Among the potential providers of niter were the numerous saltpeter caves in the limestone regions of the Southeast." [631] And as we know, Meramec Caverns provided the ingredients as well.

In the pension records it shows that Wesley Rash was working under Captain Gabbit in the mines and later cutting cordwood for the Confederate soldiers. He then worked on the Nashville & Chattanooga Railroad as a track hand. He was called "Uncle Wes" by those who knew him, just as Jesse was called "Uncle Jesse."

Sam Rash, his son was fondly called "Uncle Sam" in the community of Granbury. He was a tin smith by trade. He was later a constable and jailer. [632]

The Rashes lived next to the railroad in Granbury. When Jesse was coming and going as an outlaw, the Rashes' home was handy to hide out in. The relationship between Sam Rash and Jesse described by McGrath of the National Police Gazette after interviewing Jesse several times explains a lot. McGrath stated that the James gang would hop off the train, near Sam Rashes' home and stay. Rash would always keep his mouth shut for Jesse, a great mutual respect between the two.

In 1886/87, Jesse was known as J.W. Gates, working on the railroad construction in Granbury, Texas as a railroad contractor. The railroad did not reach Granbury until 1887. Jesse stated that he helped put up the dump for the Frisco, formerly the Fort Worth and Rio Grande Railway from Fort Worth to Brownwood. "With financial backing from the Vanderbilt railroad syndicate, construction of the FW&RG began at Fort Worth in November 1886, but proceeded slowly with many changes of route, reaching Granbury (40 miles away) a year later. It reached Comanche in 1890 and Brownwood, 144 miles from Fort Worth, in 1891." [633]

The headquarter camp for the railroad work crew was at Granbury, located near what is known as the Sam Rash home place, near the dump and spring on Lambert Branch. This site was chosen because there was plenty of water for men and the teams. The Granbury Tablet, May 24, 1984 stated that Sam Rash worked with Jesse on the railroad. [634]

Harry Huggins (1895-1972), a man who was very close to the Rashes went to visit Dalton on his death bed when he got back to Granbury to see if it was the real Jesse James whom he had known when he came to stay with Sam Rash. Harry was full of questions that only Jesse would know. This old man was sharp as a tack; Dalton answered all questions to Harry's satisfaction. He was talking to the real Jesse James.

Harry Huggins became motherless at the age of 7 and went to live with his older sister, Eva. Sam Rash's son Needham Leroy "Lee" Rash had married Eva Huggins and their sister Mary Ella Huggins, born 1870, married Daniel A. James (1866-1940). The Huggins father, Moses Elmer

Huggins (1838-1909) was a Confederate soldier in Company A, 8th South Carolina Confederate Infantry.

The Huggins lived in Acton, Hood County, same county as Granbury. Needham and Eva (Huggins) remained in Hood County. They were visiting their daughter Mrs. Burl Duncan in *Gladewater* for Christmas in 1938, during the oil boom. She became very ill and stayed with her daughter in Gladewater. Sadly, Eva died in Gladewater in February 1939 from Atelectasis, possibly caused by the oil fumes. She also had heart issues. She was taken back to Acton to be buried. Needham was still alive in Hood County when Jesse came back to Granbury. Eva was only 52 years old.

So, the Huggins were extremely attached to the Rash family, but also there within the mix was another "James," Daniel Azariah James. Mary Ella Huggins married Daniel in 1889 in Hood County about the time the railroad was going strong. Was he related to Jesse? Harry Huggins' daughter, Leta B. Hudson stated in a letter, outlined in a newspaper article "Letter reveals more new facts concerning the question of James", by Barbara Lancaster, *The Granbury Tablet*, May 10, 1984, that Dan (Daniel) was first cousin to Jesse James.

Mrs. Hudson believed that it was because of Daniel James and Jesse's relationship that Sam Rash got to be good friends with Jesse James. There are quite a few interesting connections with this James family that will help us to pull this story together. Bear with me as we put the new missing pieces of the puzzle that connects Jesse, the Rashes, the James, DeWitt Travis, John Tatum, and the Haskew family together.

Daniel Azariah James (1866-1940) was born in Bledsoe County, Tennessee to Azariah S. James (**1833**-1880) and Melvina Walker (1835-1925). Azariah was living in Coulterville, Hamilton County, Tennessee when the war started. Coulterville is between Dayton and Chattanooga, Tennessee. He was 28 years old. His father, William lived in Pikeville in Bledsoe County along with 2 daughters, Matilda and Mary and 2 sons, Tandy and John who were living with him. His wife had died in 1842. The other children, 5 more sons (including Azariah) and another daughter, Nancy F. James had married and left home. Azariah married Melvina Walker and Nancy James married Adam Van Buren Haskew.

While Azariah lived across Walden's Ridge to the east, Nancy and her husband lived at Fosters Crossroads in Bledsoe County and her father, not too far down the road. Adam Van Buren Haskew was 22 years of age. Azariah and his sister, Nancy are the two members of the family we will focus on and also their father, William who was 61 when the war began looming on the horizon in their beautiful neck of the woods.

I had studied this exact area in Tennessee since 2011 and have traveled there with my sister. This is where our family, the Stouts, Browns, and Haskews made their home in the early 1830's through the early 1900's. The Sequatchie Valley lying in Bledsoe, Marion and Sequatchie Counties to the west of Hamilton County over Walden's Ridge had held within its valley, the sadness and loss of those who traveled on its sacred ground during the Trail of Tears and those lives lost during the Civil War and after.

My sister and I were able to be taken on top of Walden's Ridge to get a bird's eye view of what the troops could view. While there, my sister and I could feel the heaviness of history that was still embedded deep down in the soil, but my sister and I felt we belonged there. It was home. It was a part of history and it was part of Azariah James and his son, Daniel's history.

(On top of Walden's Ridge overlooking the Tennessee River")

There was a total population of 200 living outside of Pikeville where the family lived. Just prior to the war, the families in Sequatchie Valley were flourishing with their farms and livestock and they had just established a private college in May 1860 which was nestled in the heart of the Valley. William Haskew, Nancy (James) Haskew's father-in-law, his brother, Ransom Haskew, my 3rd great grandfather, and John Jack Stout, my other 3rd great grandfather helped establish the college. Just as the school began its fine art of teaching, the rumors of war began overshadowing its curriculum. The year 1861 opened up to a world that was spinning out of control. The brand-new Sequatchie College had to close and the students had to choose sides of who they were going to fight for.

At the beginning of the Civil War, the Confederates had occupied East Tennessee by May 1861 before the official vote to secede was taken in Tennessee. Many young men were recruited by the Confederacy while other men who didn't want to join the Confederacy hid up in the caves of the mountains or traveled up to Kentucky led by guides to join the Union. Many young men went into the fierce guerilla groups on both sides of the fence. One of the worst of them was Champ Ferguson. They were banding together in rural areas, based in Sparta, Tennessee only 35 miles to the northwest of Pikeville. Ferguson claimed to have killed over 100 Union soldiers and Pro-Union civilians during the Civil War. It didn't matter if his victims were male or female.

The Union sympathizers or those who wanted to remain mutual such as my Stout family were targeted. Shortly after the war started and Tennessee seceded, my 3rd great grandmother Stout died at the age of 43 in June 1861 and a month later her daughter who had married a Haskew died at the age of 22, her husband wasn't at home, he was out fighting. In a photo taken in April 1861, the ladies were healthy, vibrant, nice looking ladies. It is unknown what happened to them and we may not want to know.

Azariah James, 28 had gone off to war with six of his brothers, leaving their father and two sisters at home. One of the sisters, Matilda who was living with her father, later married Joseph Brown who was in the Union 4th Regiment of the Tennessee Calvary, Company G. Matilda told this story and her husband Joseph wrote it down for the family. In October 1861, while her father, William was out working, he was attacked by rebels. They tied him to a tree and stole his horse, leaving him for dead. When it began to get late, the daughters went looking for him and found his body.

There were many skirmishes and movements of troops, foraging and thrashing, heavily populating Walden's Ridge and spreading down into the valleys on the east and west side. There was the siege of Chattanooga and the Battle of Chickamauga in their neighborhood. In Bledsoe County, Nathan Bedford Forrest and his men camped near Pikeville. There are many graves of his men who were planted there.

I cannot find where Azariah served in the Civil War, but his brother Tandy served in the Union Tennessee Infantry, his brother, Hezekiah in the Union 5th Tennessee Mounted Infantry, and his brother John was shown to also be in the Union Army.

Azariah's brother-in-law, Adam Van Buren Haskew has no military records found, but his brother Joseph Birdwell Haskew enlisted early in Pikeville, October 26, 1861 with Company C, 43rd Tennessee Infantry, Captain William J. Hill's Company, Gillespie's Regiment of the Confederacy. He became 2nd Lieutenant. He served in the Quartermaster Corps. Their father, William Haskew was a staunch Confederate supporter.

Joseph Birdwell Haskew was noted as in charge of purchasing horses and beef for the army. At one-point Joseph was in Florida on a mission and once he got into Levy County, he was in charge of requisitioning supplies for the troops. On today's map, it was just east of Chiefland. It was during the time when Cedar Key was being occupied by the Federals. Joseph was confiscating cattle on June 13, 1864 and was encountered by Jim Turner, the sheriff of that county. Jim told him he could have one of the steers, but not to take a heifer. A heifer was for milk. Lieutenant Haskew took a heifer, and Sheriff Turner shot and killed him. Turner was sent to Federal prison at Savannah and was incarcerated for over a year in a dungeon. He was released along with the rest of the political prisoners when the war was over.

Not too long ago, family members traveled down to Florida to view Joseph Birdwell Haskew's burial site. What they found took them back a step. Buried above Joseph was Sheriff Turner. The other odd story associated with this one comes out that Joseph Birdwell Haskew was a Union Lieutenant, but all records and family stories document he was in the Confederacy and the man who killed him may have mistaken him for a Union Lieutenant or hid the fact that he was a fellow Confederate comrade that he shot. The whole truth will never be known.

Since Sequatchie Valley was one of the main routes from the south to the north, whether by foot or rail, this sacred land would be scared heavily by the presence of Confederate soldiers now occupying the valley that once stood for peace, not war. Confederate provost marshals were assigned to every town in the East Tennessee region and were known as the fiercest men of the force. William Haskew, Adam Van Buren Haskew and Joseph Birdwell Haskew's father became a Confederate Provost Marshal when the Confederates occupied Bledsoe County at the beginning of the war. William Haskew was one of the higher authoritative figures for the Confederacy in Bledsoe County. He would later be sued for $20,000 for some of the actions taken on his behalf during the War of the Rebellion.

William Haskew, pro-Confederate, lost his son, Joseph Birdwell Haskew who was married to James Roberson's daughter, the son of the man who the Roberson's Crossroads was named for. This is where Azariah moved his family during the war. It was in Bledsoe County, south of Pikeville where my family had lived since the 1830's, right in the very small neighborhood of Roberson's Crossroads.

Ransom Haskew, my 3rd great grandfather, William's brother and his 3 sons were supporting the Union. Ransom's next to the oldest son, William B. Haskew, named after Ransom's brother was in the 4th Tennessee Union Cavalry and was killed viciously by the Confederates led by Nathan Bedford Forrest at Sugar Creek, Alabama the day after Christmas 1864. His body was mutilated, and his effects were stolen.

Ransom's two other sons were in the Union Army, Aaron Jenkins Haskew and Joseph Wilson Haskew who was a sharpshooter in a mounted infantry unit to combat the guerilla bands that were infesting the Cumberland Mountains and Northern Georgia. The younger Haskew sons, too young to fight became the outlaws in Texas and Oklahoma when they moved to Texas in the Fall of 1871. They settled in Johnson County, Texas, only 25 miles from Granbury.

John Wesley Haskew, born 1854, supposedly rode with Jesse James. Would they have met Jesse in Tennessee? He was known to be in Sequatchie Valley and the Haskews always believed that their cousin, Adam Van Buren married a cousin of Jesse's, Nancy James. Her family records have been very elusive, but just recently they came to light. She was the sister of Azariah James.

We only knew of our family the Stouts, Browns, Nails, Roberson's, and the Haskews living in Roberson's Crossroads and Adam Van Buren Haskew and his wife, Nancy James living in Foster Crossroads. We didn't know much about the James family who lived at Roberson's Crossroads. It literally was just a very small community where people settled near crossroads, having farms along the Sequatchie River. When my sister and I went to find Roberson's Crossroads, remnants of a church and a cemetery was all that was left of the community.

Azariah and Malvina had several children. Daniel Azariah James was born after the war in 1866 and grew up in Roberson's Crossroads. It has been said by the Bledsoe County Historian that it was so much worse after the war, than the war itself, neighbor against neighbor and family against family. You can see within the population of the county how many people moved off, while many stayed.

Azariah and his family stayed at Roberson's Crossroads. My Haskew family didn't stay, they first went to Marion County, Tennessee and then headed for Texas in 1871. My Stout family stayed and opened the doors back up to Sequatchie College. My 2nd great grandfather William Decatur Stout was a physician at Roberson's Crossroads and lived on the Sequatchie College campus. They welcomed and supported both Union and Confederate families to help heal their community. Several wonderful and endearing stories were discovered. I'm sure Azariah's children went to the college as this was the only school within their area.

Sadly, Azariah died in June 1880, just before the census was taken that year. He was only 47 years old. His son Daniel Azariah James was only 14. While his mother and several siblings stayed in Bledsoe County, Daniel took off for Texas. He landed in Hood County, just 25 miles from his Uncle Haskew's cousins in Johnson County. Daniel first married Nancy J. Davis in Hood County, in 1884 when he turned 18. This was the time that John Wesley Haskew was City Marshal for Bowie in Montague County, Texas and when Jesse was in Henrietta, Clay County, Texas, 88-110 miles away.

Jesse was in Granbury in 1886/87 working on the railroad. By 1889, Daniel James married Mary Ella Huggins in Granbury. They all knew each other well.

By 1920, Daniel and his family were living in **Polk County, Arkansas**. Daniel died in 1940 and Mary Ella died in 1941.

Interesting note – Bud had a newspaper clipping when Jesse came out in 1948. "More Proof That Dalton Is 'Jesse." *The Guthrie Daily Leader*. July 7, 1948. – "City Woman Sure It's Jesse." It reads, "Mrs. Nola Mayabb, 75, of 405 W. Washington, Wednesday also declared "I know its Jesse James," after visiting him. She said she saw Jesse when he was arrested in **Polk County, Arkansas** when she was 16 years old. "He knew all about it, and even the name of the sheriff who arrested him," she explained. That would have been about 1889.

Hoping to receive more of Jesse's fascinating story, George McGrath, from the National Police Gazette came to Jesse's bedside for the last of his final days. He published his story January 1952, a few months after Jesse's death. Bud gave me a copy of that article.

McGrath wrote that Daniel (Dan) James was a first cousin of Jesse James. He received this information from Jesse himself. Dan's brother-in-law, Harry Huggins had seen Frank James close to Dan and Ella's home near Acton in Hood County, Texas close to Granbury. He reported that he had seen Frank James ride up on a horse, never dismounting and staying in the edge of the woods. Dan went out to Frank but neither Harry nor Ella heard what was said. This occurred in 1905.

This was another very questionable supposition regarding Daniel being a cousin to Jesse as well as his Aunt Nancy (James) Haskew being kin to Jesse. Maybe this was all it was, a supposition, or maybe everyone has been given the wrong ancestral line of Jesse or we all have been fooled who the real Jesse James was. We don't know, but there are extremely strong connections to all of these folks. What we do know, is the man who was dying at the Sam Rash home was the real character who lived his life out as Jesse Woodson James and had his hand in everything that had Jesse James' name on it.

Daniel James was also a cousin to Dewitt Travis through the Harris family. Travis' 2nd great grandmother was Elizabeth (Harris) Chappell. Daniel James and DeWitt share 4th great grandparents, Robert Edward Harris (1663-1734) and Mary Turner (1667-**1733**) who were the writers 8th great uncle and aunt. We also share the Chappell family.

Daniel James and his Aunt Nancy F. James Haskew (1839-1916) were not only kin to my family through marriage on my maternal side, but also through my paternal side through the Harris', same as DeWitt Travis' family.

John Tatum shares 4th great grandparents with Daniel James, William Henry James (1734-1812) and Rosannah Waggoner (1740-1796). John Tatum's mother was a James and had always been told Jesse was his kin. He also shares the Ballards who marry into the James connecting into Jesse's family and into Roscoe James' family, who was around Jesse and worked with Howk.

So, it seems quite odd how everyone is related, one way or the other and were strongly associated to Jesse. Sam Rash and our family share the same ancestors through the Taylors, Warrens, Hackleys, Crittendens, and Thorntons.

Sheriff Oran Baker helped unload Jesse from the ambulance to the Sam Rash home. Sheriff Baker visited the old man every day for nine days. Baker was gifted with Jesse's spurs, hand cuffs, and his favorite necktie from Jesse himself. The conversations were extremely interesting. Bud was able to speak to Sheriff Baker's daughter and she said her father absolutely believed J. Frank Dalton was truly Jesse Woodson James.

Another portion of McGrath's story describes Jesse's last days: "The searing heat converted the tiny room into a scorching oven but the frail, white-haired man shivered. Gnarled hands clutched at the scarred, old six-shooter at his side and hoarse whispers clawed their way out of his throat in the rasping rattle which precedes death."

"It was August 15, 1951, and the old man who had lived almost 104 years was dying. He knew it. But his steel-blue eyes still glittered unafraid and for the last time, through thin, almost bloodless lips, the old man sneered at those who questioned his identity. "I am Jesse James," he declared. Then, grating out the words with painful effort, the man who had perpetrated the hoax of the century by masquerading for 68 years reiterated in a deathbed confession his claim to being the infamous outlaw supposedly slain by Bob Ford at St. Joseph, Missouri, on April 3, 1882."

"What they believe does not matter now," he panted as he faced his last ride. "Let them think what they will. But this I know, because of what I did, I lived 70 extra years."

At 7:30 P.M. on August 15, he uttered his last words once again, "I am Jesse James."

His last words. Why would anybody intentionally tell a lie on his deathbed? It had to be the truth.

August 15, 1951, Jesse was pronounced dead. He was 103 years old. He was taken to the Estes Funeral Home. People were calling Ola and Aubrey right and left to inform them of his death. They were never informed that he was in Granbury very sick. They saw it on the news. The only word they heard from Howk was a telegram informing them that if she came to the funeral, she would not leave alive. Ola said, "Well, I'm going to Jesse's funeral, you can bet on that! That's not going to stop me!" [635]

They left very early the next morning to go to Granbury, 175 miles away. Ola said when they got to the funeral home, "they were absolutely horrified when they walked in and saw pictures of poor Jesse all over the funeral home. Even in death, old Howk was displaying the poor old fellow like a freak of nature."

Shortly after Ola and Aubrey got there, DeWitt Travis arrived from Longview and they were sure glad to see him. Francena Turilli said DeWitt was the nicest man, very intelligent, and congenial. Ola said to DeWitt that she was very concerned about Howk, there might be trouble. The way Howk looked towards them was bitter hatred. "Ola thought about what Jesse had told her the last time they had talked, that old Howk was just crazy enough to be dangerous."

Ola had remembered how Howk was carrying pistols when she last saw him. She told DeWitt, explaining her concern and that she left her gun at home. DeWitt patted his boot where he was concealing his gun and assured her that he would take care of things if something were to happen.

Ben Estes, the funeral director would not dress the body until Dewitt Travis got there and gave Mr. Estes a Masonic handshake. Jesse's 3rd great grandmother was Susannah Estes (1706-1729) married to Thomas Poor who descends from Abraham Estes (1647-1720) and Barbara Brock (1662-1720). These were also Ben Estes' ancestors as well as the writers through the Thomason family.

Mr. Estes began to examine and prepare the body for burial. "The scars were counted by DeWitt Travis, Sheriff Oran C. Baker, and undertaker, Ben Estes." Ola writes that she was by the door leading into the examining room and Aubrey told Bud that he was at the door watching the entire process. The men in the room were counting all the bullet wounds, scars, burnt feet, and badly scarred tissue around his neck. They were also curious about the tattoo on his inner side of his forearm reading "Tex Ys." Bud said that he didn't know what it stood for but knew that it had to do with the KGC or Quantrill's Raiders.

Sheriff Oran C. Baker of Hood County stated that he was called to appear at the postmortem examination. Jesse, lying flat measured 5 feet, 8 1/2 inches, big broad and squared shoulders, counted 32 bullet wounds from his forehead to his knees. The body had badly burned feet, scar from a rope burn around his neck, the end of his left index finger was missing, and a one newspaper printed that Jesse James had scars indicating **33 bullet wounds.** [636]

Bud was able to retrieve the actual postmortem document. Also to support this was the article in the Garvin County Advocate, February 13, 1990 in Bud's collection, "Autopsy tells more of Jesse James."

Ola began describing Harriet Redding who was there while they were examining Jesse, claiming to be Jesse's daughter. She brought her son-in-law and daughter with her, but it was Howk who got her to come to the funeral. Earlier, she was bragging in the newspapers that she was a third cousin to Jesse. Ola said they acted like they were on a picnic instead of a somber event in respect for the dead. Harriet kept saying "Jesse this, Jesse that," not speaking of him in terms as a father. Ms. Redding was also at his 102nd birthday and the hearing that took place in Union, Missouri.

The funeral was on August 19, 1951. DeWitt and the Everhards sat together. Ola said that throughout the service, the phone was ringing at the funeral home and it was for her all the time. Someone was playing a nasty joke on her. She kept going to the phone and no one was there. This continued throughout the service and the preacher would stop the service for her to answer the phone. The body could be viewed after the service and both Ola and DeWitt Travis' nephew, Arlo Norman stated the casket was open for viewing. It truly was Jesse.

(Jesse's postmortem)

Sadly, Howk was the informant for the information of the deceased and the death certificate was completed with incorrect information. He listed his date of birth as April 17, 1844, making him 107 years old, born in Louisville, Kentucky. He listed his father as Robert James and mother as **Zerelton** Dalton, not Mollie Dalton.

"Old Howk made money off poor old Jesse, made the funeral home look like a carnival after his death then took his hat, guns, watch and chain, scrapbooks, photo albums, clothes and what he had in the way of personal things." [637]

The funeral bill was $150. Howk wrote a check that bounced, and the bill remained unpaid. Ola thought that DeWitt Travis paid for it, but it appears that Travis gave the money to Howk to pay for it, then Howk wrote a check and kept the money. Bud pulled the record at the funeral home and found the invoice, "not paid." Bud was going to pay it and the director said, "We didn't own the funeral home back then." The bill remained unpaid since 1951. Bud would have loved to pay the funeral bill for Jesse Woodson James.

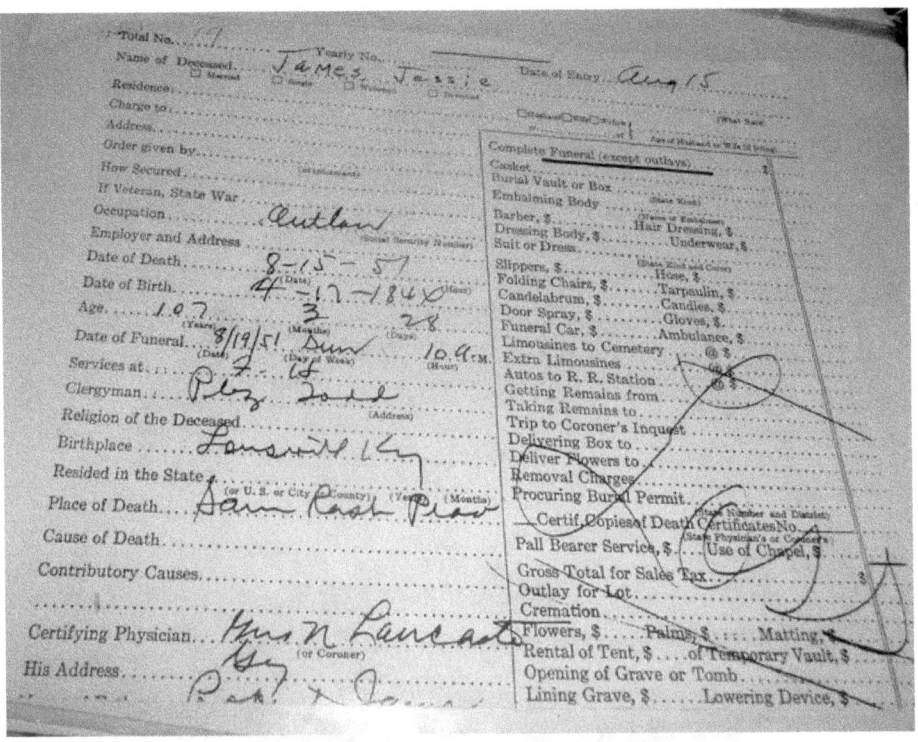

(Funeral bill on Jesse)

Sadly, two days after Jesse was buried, Howk began to make arrangements to drum up money to pay for JJ's expenses. He wrote a letter to Roscoe James on August 21st asking if he could pitch in. ($75 for doctor, $90 for drugs, plus $335). He was asking Roscoe, Dewitt Travis, Golda Rash Burks, and Bill Popenbarger for help. The Popenbarger mentioned in the letter was actually William Poffenburger, who was the son-in-law of Harriet Redding. A newspaper article in *Herald and Review* out of Decatur, Illinois - "Woman Claimed to Be Jesse James' daughter," Nov. 2, 1975, stated that Harriet Redding came away from the funeral with Jesse's hat and tie.

Was Mrs. Redding a daughter or 3rd cousin to Jesse? Her full name was Harriette Verna (Ray) Redding (1889-1974) from Decatur, Illinois. In her and her husband's obituary, Henry Lucius Redding (1885-1961) was a Mason and she was in Eastern Star.

Maybe Harriet Redding was a daughter, she was there at three major events of Jesse's life. There is nothing in her ancestry to indicate her connection to Jesse and her mother was from Illinois, married to her husband at the time Harriet was conceived. It's a mystery and may remain one.

The will was brought up in Howk's letter. Howk said, "The Shevlins had JJ sign a Last Will and Testament at Meramec Cave in 1949. They will never find a thing in real estate, oil wells, etc. They will make a big splurge. Let them look and if they should find it, I have a will hid back that will upset all the plans. Jake Wilson, DeWitt Travis and I could never find any record of JJ's real estate we could legally tie claim, but we have the buried treasure resources. JJ evidently from what we can gather, sold out 90% of all assets and took cash. Once JJ got the cash he took and buried it like he did almost everything else. JJ told me this himself. Jake and Dewitt checked and believe JJ told us the truth because he was liquidating his stuff in the 1920's and 1930's. The depression scared him stiff, so he got out, selling some stuff very very cheap. That's the story as nearly as we can figure out."

Who got what, we do not know? Howk also stated that Jake Wilson was a grandson of Jesse, but per Lou Kilgore, he wasn't. This shows how Howk was manipulating false relationships to serve his purpose.

It's very possible that Jesse put everything in DeWitt Trávis' name and may have planned together, Jesse's exit out of this world.

Mary Kate Durham was a well-known Granbury historian, a member of the Historical Preservation Committee, Granbury Cemetery Board, Museum Board, Daughters of the American Revolution, Daughters of the Confederacy and Colonial Dames. She has done much to preserve Granbury history. She gave Bud the original tombstone marker for Jesse's grave. Mrs. Durham said, "Bud I got something I want to give you. Now I want you to understand we didn't steal this, but my husband paid $5 to the man who did."

(Jesse's original grave marker)

Several years later, in 1983, Ola worked hard in getting a monument placed upon Jesse's grave in Granbury. She paid $467 for that monument. Ola had his death certificate amended to have the correct date of birth of 1847 instead of 1844 that Howk had written in.

In Bud's documents, he had letters to the Martin Funeral Home in Granbury from Ola, thanking them for their help and the ceremony that the Everhards and Dr. William Tunstill put together to honor Jesse and his new tombstone. Bud also had Dr. Tunstill's news release that he wrote, August 29, 1983. "A News Release" – For the Tombstone Dedication At Grave of Jesse James. Time: 9:30 A. M., Monday September 5, 1983, Granbury, Texas, Granbury Cemetery Meeting Place: Reception Room at Martin Funeral Home, Granbury, Texas. Visitors and public invited."

Dr. Tunstill then goes into the story of the Everhards and Jesse. Before this ceremony, Jesse had only a wooden marker, marking his grave that was stolen often. Maybe this is why years later, in 2000, it was discovered that the granite tombstone was placed over the wrong grave in an unintentional error.

(Wooden marker)

(Tombstone)

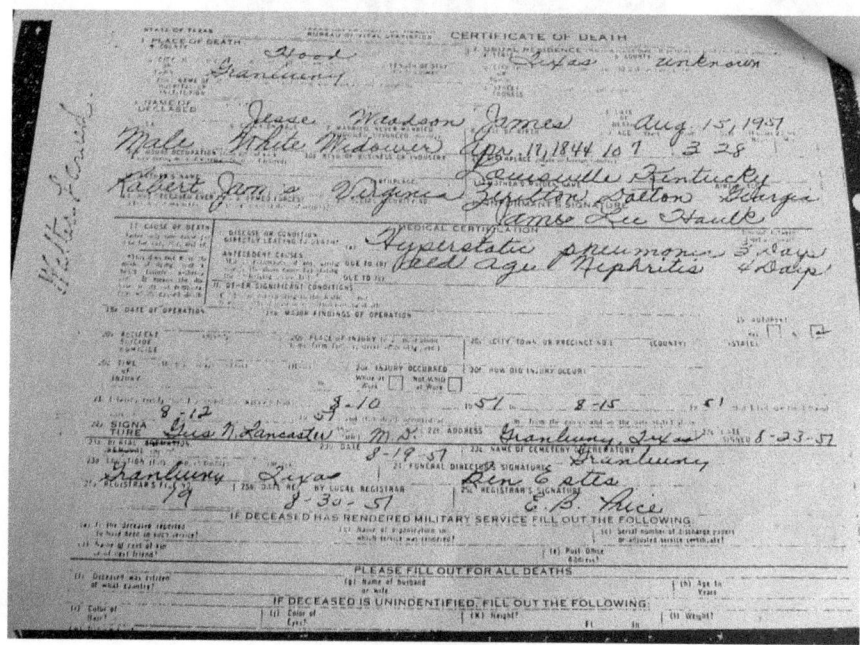

(Death certificate)

Bud was able to copy letters out of the Funeral Home's files for Jesse, mostly written in the 50's and 60's. They were from private individuals who were questioning who this man Dalton was and who his relatives were. One, Mr. R. A. Thrasher, a dedicated Mason in Las Vegas, New Mexico was inquiring if the Masons gave him a Masonic funeral.

After Jesse died, Howk kept looking for Jesse's gold. Francena Turilli at Meramec Caverns said that she couldn't count the number of times that people would come to her museum in Stanton and asked if they knew anything about Orvus Lee Howk/Jesse Lee James III. They all were bamboozled by him. "Howk was a fraud," said Francena Turilli. He took $1,500-$12,000 from several people to contribute in his effort to find Jesse's gold. Howk claimed that he knew where the treasure was, but he needed money for expenses to find it. Howk left them cold. He didn't follow through with his promises. Howk took the money and went to another state to continue his money schemes.

Bud had several letters that Howk wrote, one to "Dear Folks", Dated November 19th, 1953. He was living in Manitou Springs, Colorado and hunting treasure. He stated in his letter that Jake Wilson was down in Southern Arizona looking for treasure, while he was working Colorado.

As Howk as her encourager, Harriett Redding, still claiming to be Jesse's daughter had an attorney who wrote the funeral home, Estes Funeral Home, advising that Mrs. Redding's "desire for the body of her father, the late Jesse James, remain in its present burial plot. And that no one has authority from her to remove the body from Granbury Cemetery to any other place." [638] Rudy Turilli was in the process of moving the body to Meramec Caverns. Everyone still wanted a piece of Jesse even after he had been 6 feet under for two years.

While Howk was on the road, Ola Everhard was on her typewriter, typing out the story that Jesse had told her, inserting her research. Amazing Ola, you were quite a woman. They moved to Lovington, New Mexico and she continued her research. In Dr. William Tunstill's video taken on March 6, 1986, which is on youtube.com by Brett Hall, you can see Ola and Aubrey. Ola was near her typewriter which was always handy next to her day bed. She said in the video that what she wanted to become of her story, was she'd like the story to be a television series. Aubrey told Bud when he visited that they desired for this to be publicized, to prove the truth. Bud's intentions are just that and this book is what he promised as well as "The Hoax That Let Jesse Live."

Ola Everhard died in 1988, Bud went to visit Aubrey in 1990, and Aubrey died in 1991. Much gratitude goes out to Ola and Aubrey in the pursuit of the truth. Your work has paid off.

I never could understand why Bud wanted me to write his book. I told him, he needs a man and a man's perspective in writing such an incredible story about Jesse and all the fine details that Bud added to Ola's manuscript that he has dug up to prove the truth. I was no "blood and guts" type of girl. I told Bud he needs a professional writer, but Bud's answer was always, "I want you!" What an honor!

It began to sink in, that Bud and I were both called for a purpose here. We were a great team, feeding off of each other's strengths, knowledge, research, and passions, trusting God to lead the way. Bud was born and bred in Oklahoma, I in Texas, where Jesse's trails were hot.

My eyes really opened when I began reading Ola's manuscript that Bud had gotten from Aubrey. Ola had poured out her heart and love for Jesse. She was the first woman I know, who wrote about Jesse. She painted a different picture; it was as though she was not only connected to him through DNA, but through a kindred spirit. She saw his heart and opened up a part of Jesse that he never shared with anyone before.

The story she wrote down, opened up my heart, and as a woman, I understood Ola's great intuition of who the real man was behind Jesse James. Most women have a gift of intuition (in tune) placed within them by their creator. It's a phenomenon. Women tend to go deep down beneath the surface, layer after layer, to understand a person's inner soul and spirit. Men tend to only remain on the surface and concentrate on the actions of a certain person.

Traditionally, women throughout centuries were placed in roles as caregivers, homemakers, comforters, listeners, and as protectors of their offspring, having a precise instinct to protect those who are vulnerable from potential threats. They place their emotions and empathy into their surroundings and relationships. They have a built-in discernment for truth and underlying motives of the individual's spirit and character they encounter. If a woman allows this gift to flow through her, her moral compass will guide her into the right direction.

The relationship between Ola and Jesse was one of deep mutual love and trust for one another. Jesse didn't share everything with her; possibly to protect her, but he shared all that he had to give, the truth.

"When my Soul seeks range and rest beyond the Great Divide,
just bury me some place out West that's sunny, lone and wide.
Let cattle rub my tombstone down and kyotes mourn their kin,
let horses paw and tromp the mound, but do not fence it in."
Frank Dalton/Jesse James, June 4, 1935

"They were ready to talk"

-Bud Hardcastle

Chapter Thirty-One: The Hidden Sons Who Kept Their Mouths Shut

After the funeral of Jesse's, John Trammel went to Arkansas to the home of Jesse Cole James in Barber, Arkansas, Logan County near Booneville. It is approximately 27 miles southeast of Fort Smith. It is a very small township, isolated by rolling farmland, forested ridges, mountains, and lakes. As of this date, there are only 641 people living there. The Chicago, Rock Island and Pacific Railroad was established there after the turn of the century. Why would Trammel be traveling up to Arkansas at the age of 114 years of age. He had to fulfill his one, last mission for Jesse.

Bud said that when Jesse died in Granbury, his son, Jesse Cole James did not know he had died for six months. John Trammel, "Uncle John" went to their home in Arkansas and told them about his death. Shorty and Dale James, Jesse Cole James' sons said that Trammel stayed with them for two weeks. Four years later, Trammell, 118 years old and 2 days died in January 1956 after a long illness and was in the Oklahoma City Hospital. [639] He was loyal to the end.

Who was Jesse Cole James? It wasn't the man who came and helped Jesse when the Highleys kidnapped him, who lived in Kennard, Texas and stayed at Ola's house. No, this was another man by the same name. The man who truly was a son of Jesse Woodson James.

The only son Jesse spoke of was Jesse Edwards born in 1875. Jesse always called him Jesse Edwards without the James' surname on the end. This boy went by the name of Charles Howard and Tim Edwards. With Jesse's help he became County Attorney in Wyandotte County, Kansas, where the county seat was Kansas City.

It gets very confusing when the news media promotes Jesse Edward James as Jesse's only son, but throughout this story, we learn he was actually Charles Bigelow's boy and the one who tried his hardest to throw out the case of Dalton's when he tried to reclaim his name as Jesse Woodson James? It is very complicated and not clear who is who here, but Jesse Edward James died March 26, 1951, and less than 6 months later, Jesse died.

Jesse had told Ola that Jessie James, Jr. you hear about is actually Bigelow's boy. Jesse very rarely spoke of his family and was very hushed mouth about it to Joe Wood. Jesse was still trying to protect them at the end, but I believe he also had deep regrets about his life and his family. Bud stated that Jesse apparently had lots of families, lots of wives, and lots of children from his research. Another son, whom Bud discovered was Joseph Jesse Chase as we discussed earlier.

Jesse also stated in a news article prior to his coming out, a very strange statement that he had two sons who served in various wars, one born 1872 was a retired army doctor living in the Philippines and one born 1873/74 who is a retired army officer. [640] He also told Howk he had a son and his twins down in Mexico, working on Jesse's ranch.

Well, there is another son who Bud discovered with the help of Charlie. The man we will focus on here is Jesse Cole James, born in Texarkana in February 13, 1882. Genealogy records indicate that Emma Anders (1867-1930) was the mother of Jesse Cole James who lived in Marlin, Texas in 1880, southeast of Waco. Marlin is 55 miles from *Centerville* where Jesse stayed. Her parents were James Hammett Anders (**1833**-1897) and Martha Ann Yarborough.

The child between Emma and Jesse, Jesse Cole James, if full term, was conceived in May 1881. She would have been 13 years old going on 14. On Jesse Cole James' delayed birth certificate, it shows that his father was Jessie James, born in Missouri and was living in Texarkana, Arkansas at the time of birth as well as mother, Emma Anders, who was born in Texas. Jesse Cole James, nor his sons, ever talked about Emma Anders. Emma may have been at an institution for unwed mothers in Texarkana. Her family was still in Falls County, Texas at the time of Jesse Cole James' birth.

(Birth certificate of Jesse Cole James)

After seven years from the birth of her son, Emma married Charles. T. Hunter in 1889 in Falls County, Texas. Jesse Cole James is never mentioned in her household. The missing years of Jesse Cole James' childhood cannot be found. Was he raised by Jesse or someone close to him? It is unknown, but Jesse Cole James always told his children that Emma was a Cherokee woman. This makes one wonder if the Emma Anders or as some people refer to her as Emma Andrews in Texas was not the mother, but another woman who possibly lived within the Five Tribes of the Indian Nation. We'll never know.

When he was 18, Jesse Cole James was a ranch laborer in Winkler County, Texas. In 1900, is when the State of Texas ended the free use of land and ranchers on this public land were required to pay rent. There were 12 ranches at that time. There were only 60 people living in Winkler County which the county seat became Kermit, 45 miles west of Odessa, Texas, close to the New Mexico border.

In 1910, he was in Cass County, Texas working as a Farm Laborer. Cass County was just south of the Red River on the Texas and on the border of Arkansas and Louisiana, approximately where he was born. In 1920, he was in Lawton, Oklahoma and was a laborer. He married Ora Price in 1922. In 1930 he was in Boone, Arkansas as a farmer, and he died in Barber, Logan County, Arkansas in 1964.

From Bud's friend and partner, Charlie Holman, Bud had heard about this son and that his sons were still living. One was living in Oklahoma, and two in Arkansas. Charlie Holman, out of the blue called Bud one day and said "You know those grandsons of Jesses's we've been looking for, well, I got one of them up in my office making him a set of teeth. Burleigh Dale James (1934-2005) was his name. Bud said, "Hold on to him, I'll be right there."

Bud left immediately. It was an hour and a half drive, 89 miles to Perkins, Oklahoma. When Bud rolled into town, Burleigh Dale James was still there. When they met, they became "instant friends." Burleigh was very open and honest with Bud. They talked for a long time and Burleigh was proud of who he came from and for years was told to "Keep His Mouth Shut."

Charlie and Burleigh had known of each other, but not close at that time. They were members of the same church. They met at a church convention in Colorado. Burleigh had heard of Charlie making excellent false teeth, so he made an appointment to have his teeth done. Burleigh lived in Vici, Oklahoma, 142 miles from Perkins.

Burleigh was born to Jesse Cole James and Ora Price in Sugar Grove, Arkansas. He was a good man and worked for the County of Dewey, Oklahoma. He was in the Korean War in the U.S. Air Force, enlisted in 1952. After this initial meeting, Bud, Charlie, and Burleigh met frequently in Oklahoma and had amazing conversations.

Burleigh Dale James told Bud about two other brothers, Charles A. "Shorty" James and Jesse Quanah "Tubby" James, named after his grandfather and Quanah Parker. They lived in Barber, Arkansas. They made arrangements for Bud, John and Jo Ella Tatum to go and visit Jesse Quanah James. Barber was in *Logan County*, Arkansas, the same county name as Guthrie, Oklahoma.

Bud couldn't find Jesse Quanah's house in Barber, so he pulled up to men who were in their yard and asked if they knew where Jesse Quanah James lives. "No, we don't know any such man," they said. They talked awhile and then Bud said, "Well, he's going to think we're not coming." "Oh, do you know him?" the old man said. "Ya, he's waiting for me to get there today," Bud replied. "Is he expecting you? He lives right over there," the man said. Bud laughingly replied, "You weren't going to tell me anything were you." The man just grinned and said, "I sure wasn't." They evidently had a "neighborhood watch", protecting the James. The house was just a block away.

Bud said they sat out on the porch and talked for hours with Jesse Quanah James. Just like Burleigh Dale James, Jesse Quanah James felt free enough to talk about their Dad and Grandfather. They both stated that J. Frank Dalton was their grandfather who was the real Jesse Woodson James.

(On the front porch, John Tatum, Bud, and Jesse Quanah James)

Jesse Quanah was more of the quiet and simple man of the bunch, just a good 'ole boy. He was a "hill man," Bud said. He didn't want any publicity. He was also told to keep his mouth shut, but they were ready to talk. Jesse Quanah said, "We know who we are." Bud said, "What was on his mind, would come off his tongue." He was dadgum honest.

Charles "Shorty" James was living in Iowa, raising hogs, when Bud first met him, but moved back to Logan County, Arkansas. The brothers told Bud that they were told by their father, Jesse Cole James, stories filled with treasure and intrigue. They discussed the trails and places they traveled. They had maps of hidden treasure, photos, documents, and letters proving what they were saying was legit and proving who they were.

Jesse Quanah, also known as "Tubby," remembers a time when he met his grandfather. None of the other brothers got to meet him. Tubby was born in 1923 and he remembers he was 8-10 years old when he met his grandfather, Jesse James in 1931-**1933**. Jesse Woodson James was in Anadarko which is just West of Chickasha, Oklahoma. His Dad, Jesse Cole James took Tubby to a dance at Gracemont, just 8 miles away. Jesse was introduced to Tubby as his Grandpa.

Tubby remembers at the dance that his Grandpa was playing the fiddle, harmonica, and a French harp. A blue-eyed Black man was playing the guitar. His name was Jim Crow. Jesse had used this name before in St. Joseph in the early 1880's before his supposed death. At the time, Jesse portrayed himself as an Eastern land buyer in St. Joseph.

Little Tubby got an eye and ear full when a fight broke out at the dance. It must have been a pretty good one, because it made an impression on Tubby.

The next day, several men met with Jesse in Anadarko who Tubby, after he was grown, realized these men were of great importance to Jesse. They were setting up a horse race. They gathered their horses and Jesse kept his horses in Fred, Oklahoma where Bud's family once lived during the Wild West days. Bud had verified earlier that both Jesse and Frank were there in Fred, breeding horses at one time. It was not far from Anadarko.

Bud had received a letter from Mrs. J.W. Bess in Marlow, Oklahoma with information on the small community of Fred regarding Jesse and Frank's frequent visits there. It validated Jesse Quanah "Tubby" James' story. In an old store notebook kept by a Mr. Fletcher, who lived near Fred, was an entry of Frank James coming to his home to bring his horse "to stud" on March 22, 1889. The next entry listed Jesse James brought his horse "to stud" on April 8, 1889.

Tubby told Bud that Jesse had a young horse, "Patty Face." None of the other horses could catch him as they ran along the dirt track. Winding down to the last leg of the race, "Patty Face" ran into a fence and broke his nose, but it didn't slow him down. Patty Face won the race. It was a memorable trip for Tubby and a very impressionable one in which he never forgot.

Tubby told Bud that there was supposed to be money buried around Anadarko.

Jesse Quanah James was a World War II veteran in the Army. He served as Private First Class in the 542nd Engineer Boat and Shore Regiment. He was considered a "Marksman Rifle" in the campaigns in New Guinea and Southern Philippines. He received several medals and decorations including the World War II Victory Ribbon, Good Conduct Medal, American Theater Ribbon, AP Theater Ribbon, two Bronze Service Stars, Philippine Liberation Ribbon, and one Bronze Star Go 23 HQ USAFFE 45. (Army of the United States official Honorable Discharge papers for Jessie Q James 38 445 **033**). Many soldiers always asked if he was related to Jesse James and he would always say, "no, that is a different pack of dogs."

Bud devoted a lot of time with Jesse's grandsons. When they got together, they had fun pulling out items for both parties to look at and view. There was a lot that Bud learned from them, but there was a lot they learned from Bud.

There was a little booklet, "The Amazing Outlaw Life Of Jesse James", by Paul G. Howard, Edited by Gerald H. Pipes that Bud showed the grandsons, that had a picture inside with men lined up on horses guiding burros loaded down heavily with pack loads of goods or gold. The booklet indicates this was Jesse James and the pack train loaded with gold coming out of Mexico in 1875. Bud had gotten it at a little museum/shop in Branson, Missouri. One of the grandsons said, "Bud, where did you get that picture? We have the original. That is our daddy riding the horse right there with the arrow pointing down."

Well, sure enough, they had the picture Bud said. If this was their daddy, which I'm sure it was, it had to of been around the time that Jesse Cole James was in Texas and Oklahoma between the ages of 14 -38 (1896-1920). They were moving something. This was a common practice of Jesse's, moving treasure to more secure locations. It is unknown where this was actually taken, but we do know the photo and the mission was truly something that Jesse Cole James was proud of and kept for his sons.

(Photo of the booklet cover)

(Jesse Cole James shown by the mark on the photo, identical to the original photo that the James' grandsons had. Also, the photos on the next page, far right, Howk had this photo on the cover of his book, Jesse James and the Lost Cause. This photo was in J. Frank Dalton's collection Howk had access to. The photo on the left next to that photo has been tagged as the Texas Rangers, but many people, including Howk, state that Jesse is the man sitting on the left. Comparing photos of Jesse, that this is a possibility)

(Texas Rangers or JJ and his gang?)

(JJ)

    Bud seems to believe that the mule pack train photo may have been taken during the time when Jesse moved the gold that they hastily buried during the frigid snowstorm back in 1875. They had gone up East Cache Creek from the Red River, about 20 miles. Jesse and his gang held up in a cave 15 miles from Buzzard Roost at that time. They had 18 jack loads of gold. A jack load is considered around 150 pounds. Bud found that cave and was able to show me where it was located. The gang eventually moved the gold towards Buzzard Roost and the Wichita Mountains.

    Was this photo proof of the movement of gold to a more secure place? Jesse Cole James lived in Lawton in 1920 not far from this site. Could this photo have been taken somewhere else more secluded such as Victorio Peak? The grandsons knew where the Victorio Peak treasure was, and the information had to come from Daddy. Strange events occurred with those who were "in the know" of Victorio Peak. Jesse Cole James was "in the know" and he wound up with 11 bullet holes in him when he died.

    Yes, the grandsons knew about Victorio Peak and what was along the Dona Ana Trail. They said it was Jesse's and their daddy's favorite trail.

Bud pulled out a map he obtained that was supposed to have been drawn out by Jesse. It is known as the "Wolf Map" named by Bob Brewer, but Bud calls it "The grave is a witness." Bud showed the brothers the map, Dale (Burleigh Dale) immediately said, "the Dona Ana Trail" and pointed to D.A.T. on the map. No one else had ever known what those initials meant, but the brothers knew immediately.

The Dona Ana Trail was a very old trail, possibly made by the Spaniards and Indians. The creeks in that area were full of water and was a good place to camp.

On an old map that Bud found in Waurika, at the Chisholm Trail Museum, shows the Dona Ana Road that was established by Americans in 1852.

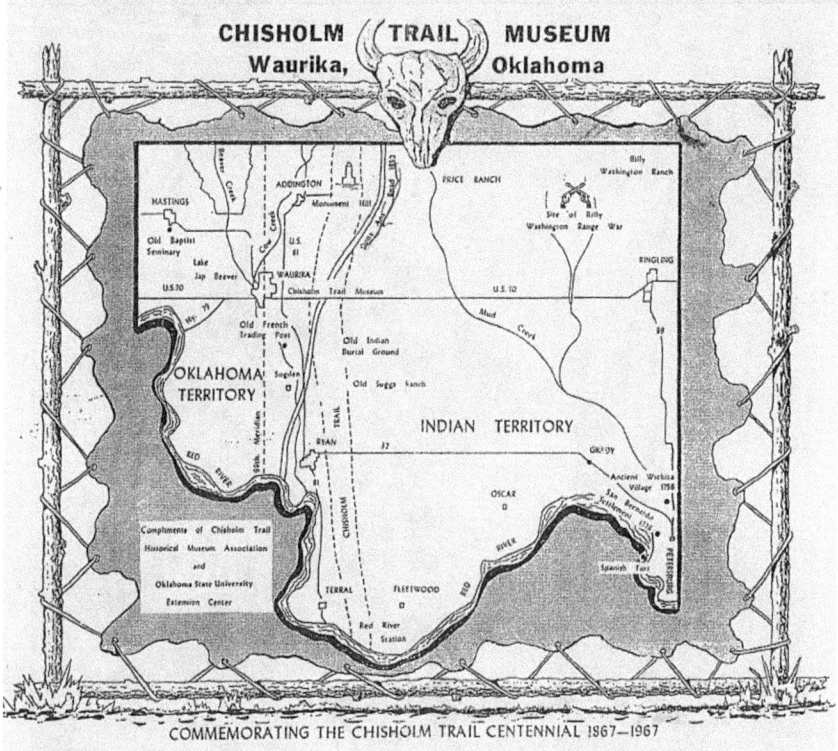

(D.A.T. trail in Indian Territory)

It started in Old Mexico, went through Dona Ana County, New Mexico, close to Victorio Peak, through Texas, went up the Little Wichita River crossing the Red River just below Ryan, Oklahoma. It was west of the Chisholm Trail, about a mile apart, but The DAT trail was there first before the Chisholm Trail. It ran by the "Big Tree Price" Ranch, north of Waurika and then moves across the Chisholm Trail, east of Addington and east of Monument Hill; slightly different from the earlier map of the Dona Ana Trail.

The Chisholm Trail splits going both sides of Monument Hill. This hill is significant. The cowboys pushing those "doggies" could see the hill twenty miles away. It was known as a *center point*, a look out, or a point that travelers, such as Jesse James could always come back to, such as Buzzard Roost. There was a Black man who worked as a trail driver for the Price Ranch, Tom Lattimore. He was born in 1865 and buried on top of Monument Hill in 1944. Bud had spoken to some of the family of the Prices and the family knew Jesse James. The Ranch was northeast of Addington, owned by Henry and Blanche Price.

Bud, and the two grandsons, Dale and Shorty, and Lou Kilgore traveled to five states; Oklahoma, Kansas, Missouri, Iowa, and ended up in Rye, Texas where Jake Wilson lived. The grandsons wanted to go there. They knew the whole story behind Jake Wilson, but they didn't like Howk, which he was supposedly dead by then. Bud had heard of Jake and Lou knew him personally.

Jake was still living, and each side, the James and Jake had a lot of questions and had a lot of answers. Jake never had a doubt that Dalton was Jesse. He stayed there with Jake on his place quite frequently. A funny story about this trip, Bud loves to tell. That country was very swampy being close to the coast. The men asked Jake if there were any alligators in the gravel pit about 100 yards away and Jake said yes, when it fills up with water. They asked if the alligators ever come around the house and he said sometimes. Well, Bud went to take a whiz out by a wagon. A dog came up behind him and rubbed up next to his leg and Bud jumped and hollered and just knew an alligator had gotten him. They all had a big laugh at the big man who thought he was a goner. Then Shorty had to go take care of business and the dog did the same thing to him and he about jumped out of his skin. Bud said, "No you're not scared of alligators."

Bud told me that Jake said towards the end of Howk and his excursions, he began to doubt Howk. It just got crazier as it went along. Lou ended up staying with Jake and they became engaged.

Back in Arkansas, the grandsons took Bud around where Joe Vaughn lived, close to the cemetery where he was buried. They showed Bud how they were taught by their daddy to form the hoot owl trees. This was a way that the Indians and later the KGC would direct their members to treasure. It was a unique system that would last throughout the years, unless they were cut down. They would take a young, flexible sapling on a tree and pull it over. They would stick the sapling in the ground to form a root in the direction they wanted to point to.

(John Tatum and Bud - hoot owl trees)

Dale and Shorty took Bud to an area indicated on a map that they had, that would hold treasure. It was very rough terrain and they came within a ¼ mile circumference of it but couldn't find it. A relative of the James Brothers, a young boy found it several years before. The young man, in his 20's, took a burro out a few weeks at a time. He had found the cave and said that the gold bars were stacked along the wall as well as artifacts and church related items, such as belonging to the Jesuits. The boy took the gold challis and some gold bars.

Learning of what the young man did, the father told him, "You best take that back and put it where you found it and don't you go back. You'll get us all killed." They described what was in this cave; lots of money, stacked rifles, artifacts, and gold bars stacked like cord wood. They didn't want to tell anybody, and they sealed it back up like they found it. They never went back. Bud had talked to the young man about what he saw. Bud invited him to go with him and the grandsons, but he was afraid and did not want to go back. He said he buried the challis near a tree close to the cave, but he always felt he was being watched.

Bud had received word from a treasure hunter who later betrayed him, that the grandson of Quantrill was living in Claremore, Oklahoma. His name was Michael Ragge. Bud went to see him and brought along Burleigh Dale James and Shorty. Michael stated that he had never heard that Quantrill had used the name of Hart and later lived in Osceola, but he did know that he was never killed in the war. He said what has been handed down to him was that Quantrill first changed his name to Cottrill/Cottrell/Catrell and lived in Arkansas which coincides with what Bud had discovered. He then must have moved on down into Oklahoma and Texas.

Bud said the conversation between Burleigh Dale, Shorty, and Michael was quite interesting to say the least.

(Charles (Shorty) James, Michael Ragge, Burleigh Dale James, 1992 in Claremore, Oklahoma)

(Michael Ragge and Quantrill)

One of the greatest joys and greatest treasure that came out of meeting the grandsons was Bud hooking up another relative with them. The grandsons had always heard growing up that he had some cousins in the Sioux Nation. They had heard the story of Joseph Jesse Chase being a son of Jesse with a Sioux woman. They had no doubt that this was true because it came straight from their daddy's mouth. They would be soon meeting the great granddaughter of Joseph Jesse Chase, Grace Hopkins.

I heard this story from Bud and Grace herself. Bud set this meeting up. Grace knew Lou Kilgore in Arkansas, not too far where the grandsons lived. Lou was not able to go to Barber, Arkansas, so her daughter, Gayla went with Grace.

When they got there, Grace said they were invited in and she met Shorty, but he remained a little skeptical and cautious. He fed them a few snacks, just briefly looked at her pictures and she felt he was ready to shuffle her out the door.

Grace then said to Gayla, "Get that newspaper article of Great Grandpa." Grace threw it down on the table, next to a photo of Jesse Cole James. Grace said, "That's my Great Grandpa and that's your daddy." The pictures were side by side, the two sons of Jesse Woodson James by two different mothers. Shorty froze, looked stunned and then yelled to Tubby, "you want to come in here and see this picture?" He immediately recognized the kinship of his father to her great grandfather.

(Joseph Jesse Chase)

(Jesse Cole James and wife Ora)

(Ora and Jesse Cole "Cowboy" James)

Everything changed from that moment on. Shorty knew she was telling the truth. He wanted them to stay after that. Shorty and Tubby took her to Jesse Cole's grave and then fed them the best prime rib that you could cut with a spoon.

Grace became very fond of Tubby and they talked a lot and shared things that were never told to anyone else. After Tubby died, Grace was in Barber and was speaking with Shorty's son. Shorty became mad because he was telling her lot of things, but she reminded Shorty how close her and Tubby were, and she already knew these stories.

The kinship with the grandsons was such a wonderful connection for Grace. They called her cousin. The grandson of Grace stayed with Shorty and Tubby for one summer and had the time of his life. The bond of family was certainly there causing Shorty to want to adopt Grace's grandson.

It was such a joy to hear this story from Grace and to validate even more the connection to Jesse. Bud was glad to be a part of it. Also, Bud learned that the grandsons knew Mary Plina James Norris was definitely a daughter of Frank James.

Bud would continue to stay in touch with all the grandsons and especially Grace. Tubby died in 2005, Dale in 2005, and Shorty, 2022, but before they left this earth, they committed to help Bud prove the truth one last time.

"If you have so many people tell you that your wrong and so many people tell you you're right, and you want to prove you're right, you got to put up or shut up. And I put up $10,000 and five years to get it done."

-Bud Hardcastle

Chapter Thirty-Two: Exhumation

Bud was in the fight of his life. He bet his life, his money, and reputation upon Jesse Woodson James. He was going to prove to the world that Jesse lived past 1882 and that J. Frank Dalton was the real Jesse. It would cost much more than he expected.

Bud was at the exhumation conducted in 1995 at Kearney, Missouri to exhume the body that had been reburied from Zerelda's yard in 1902 and transferred to Mount Olivet Cemetery in Kearney. If you remember the story, not much fanfare or respect was put forth in the ceremony that was held in 1902.

In 1995, the exhumation of the body of Jesse James, killed in 1882 and buried in Kearney, Missouri was due to a claim of a woman named Betty Dorsett Duke in Texas. She claimed that her great grandfather, James L. Courtney was Jesse James who lived beyond 1882 and the body in Kearney was someone else. The entire process did not unearth the truth as expected, but rather became a bumbling attempt to cover up the truth.

Before this event, Bud went to the James/Younger Reunion, Judge Ross promoted. Bud was on the program to speak in San Angelo, Texas. When he got there, he was told that he could not enter, because he hadn't registered or paid his entry fee. He argued that he did and that he was on the program. They were trying to keep him out. They finally let him speak, but he only did so for a short while, and then allowed Betty Dorset Duke to speak the rest of his allowed time. Judge Ross was a descendant of Jesse Edward James. I don't think Bud and Betty left on good terms with Judge Ross. The negativity didn't stop in San Angelo.

Bud, the Tatums, and Lou Kilgore were there at exhumation event in 1995 in Kearney. The grave was roped off from the onlookers and guards were surrounding the premises. Ironically, one of the guard's name was a Pinkerton. John Tatum, being a relative, asked the officials if he could go up to the dig area during the exhumation. John, Jo Ella, and Bud all walked up to the grave. As the coffin was being exposed, they noticed the casket was a badly decayed wooden box, which agrees with the 1902 version stating that the body was placed in a cedar casket when it was exhumed in 1902.

To their surprise, Bud said they opened the casket, which was falling apart, and the body was buried faced down. Bud said, they wouldn't have buried the body so disrespectfully if it was Jesse. It was a message to whomever was buried there, that they were sending him straight to Hell.

This was very odd. The newspapers in 1902 stated that Zerelda and Frank James were not at the disinterment on her farm but was at a hotel. Jesse James Jr. along with some of the Quantrill Raiders were there digging up the body. The newspaper reporters were there from St. Louis and Kansas City describing the entire ordeal. Jesse James Jr., who Jesse spoke of often, was able to examine the body and described the gold-filled teeth. The Kansas City Journal, June 30, 1902 stated that Jesse James, Jr. was the only one who viewed the body. "Frank never gazed on his dead brother, nor did the aged mother." [641] The Journal also said the body was placed in a black casket. The papers describe how very carefully and respectfully the men pulled Jesse's body out of the grave and placed in the new cedar coffin. Something just doesn't smell right.

During the exhumation in 1995, after seeing the body face down, Starrs, the forensic scientist hired by Judge Ross ordered the cameras to be shut off and no one was to say a word. There were lots of witnesses there. Bud was right there when Starrs said that. There was a guard there at the grave and made everyone back away. Bud said the guard was a Pinkerton.

Also, in some reports, it states that the femur bone was very small, indicating it possibly could have been a female. In one report, they saw two skeletons in the grave. The bones were waterlogged, making it extremely difficult to extract DNA. It indeed was not Jesse.

The ones in charge of Professor James Starr's examination presented their evidence as concluding the tooth they found in the grave revealed a match to Jesse James, but the report only included DNA retrieved from a hair sample. There was a hair sample, a tooth, and bones that was given to the professor in a Tupperware container that did not come from the grave.

Bud stated that the tooth that was supposedly from the original grave of Jesse's at his home was placed in a Tupperware bowl and was on display at the James farm museum. There was no indication or proof that these teeth were his.

Bud obtained a letter from Gene Gentrup, editor of the Southern Platte Press newspaper in Parkville, Missouri. The letter was dated and notarized May 27, 1999. During the 1995 exhumation in Kearney, he worked for the Kearney Courier during the exhumation. He wrote the article, "Special Collectors" edition in which Professor James E. Starrs said a tooth collected from the James Farm Museum provided the necessary mitochondrial DNA needed to prove that "with a reasonable degree of scientific certainty," the remains buried in Mt. Olivet Cemetery in Kearney are indeed Jesse James. "I never heard that any teeth found among the remains exhumed from Mt. Olivet earned sufficient mtDNA for the purpose of Starrs' investigation. Likewise, Starrs expressed his disappointment that no teeth were found in the "Tupperware bowl" unearthed from Jesse's original grave at the family farm. I did write a later story that Starrs credited the tooth from the James Farm Museum as being key to his probe. I never thought to ask about the contradiction."

Where did they come from? The bones were female. The findings appeared to be inconclusive, but the reports and newspaper articles projected the story that it was Jesse James.

Bud was on the program "Up to the minute" a national news program. They sent Bud to an affiliate at the University of Oklahoma, to discuss the exhumation of JJ in Kearney and what his opinion was. He didn't have anything good to say but said that they didn't prove anything. He knew he wouldn't be in there. This whole affair prompted Bud to take care of the matter himself. He started on the process to have J. Frank Dalton's body exhumed in Granbury to prove that he was Jesse Woodson James. It would take five years and $10,000 out of his own pocket to accomplish this.

Bud looked into what it would take to exhume J. Frank Dalton's grave in Granbury to prove that the man was none other than Jesse Woodson James. He had the support of many men such as John Helsley, Granbury Chamber of Commerce Manager, a lawyer who volunteered to help them through the process, Dr. William Tunstill and his wife, and Judge Bob Hefner. Mary Kate Durham, a well-known Granbury historian, a member of the Historical Preservation Committee, Granbury Cemetery Board, Museum Board, Daughters of the American Revolution, Daughters of the Confederacy and Colonial Dames helped and encourage Bud all the way.

Most of all, his support and foundation for this entire process stood upon Jesse's grandsons; Jesse "Tubby" Quanah James, Burleigh Dale James, and Charles "Shorty" A. James.

In August 1995, Bud wanted to check the temperature and the sentiment that Granbury had for J. Frank Dalton, Jesse Woodson James. Bud, Charles "Shorty" James, and Jesse Quanah "Tubby" James had a special question and answer session for the community of Granbury and the media. It was held at the Granbury Opera House.

With a full auditorium, the grandsons, up on stage didn't talk much, but later Shorty did. Jesse Quanah had his overalls on, and he wasn't there to try to impress anyone. Bud said there was a little newspaperman who was giving them fits and being sarcastic, smart-mouthed, and Bud looked down and said, "Son, are you a Yankee?" The crowd broke out in laughter. Charles and Jesse Quanah burst out laughing. And sure enough the man was one. "Yes, I'm a Yankee," the man said. Bud said, "When this is over I'm going to whip you." The Yankee called Bud later and they both had a big laugh.

In a newspaper article that Bud had from the *Fort Worth Star Telegram* " Jesse James' Family Tree Sprouts Two Arkansans, " by Barry Shlachter wrote that a crowd, at the Granbury Opera House "applauded the two shy Arkansans for coming forward, many readily accepting them as Jesse James' descendants."

(Newspaper clipping of the brothers on stage (courtesy of the Fort Worth Star Telegram))

"I believe them; I really do," said Leanna Jones, 36, a local resident who works in Fort Worth. The brothers say they descend from the bandit and a Cherokee woman named Emma Sanders (Anders), one of at least 13 women the bandit married, according to amateur historian Bud Hardcastle, who accompanied the brothers."

Myrtle Hensley was at the presentation and as a young girl, she went to see Jesse at the Rashes. She knew it was him then and when he was on his deathbed. Many others came forward and it appeared that the majority of the Granbury residents were behind Bud and the grandsons.

In the newspaper clipping Bud had said, "The two Arkansan James brothers said they had kept their lineage secret since the early 1950s because their father was badly beaten by abductors convinced that he knew where Jesse James buried his loot. "We've had our house broken into, and my father, Jesse Cole James, was kidnapped," said Charles James, 56, who now lives in Iowa. "That's kind of the reason we've been quiet, keeping our mouths shut…. It's a big relief to get this all out in the open."

The grandsons gave Bud proof of their daddy's kidnapping. The grandsons told Bud that in 1954, their daddy met up with some people, possibly in Guthrie, Oklahoma and he went missing after that for about a year. They said, finally the sons got this card from Daddy.

Bud Hardcastle: The Truth Tracker

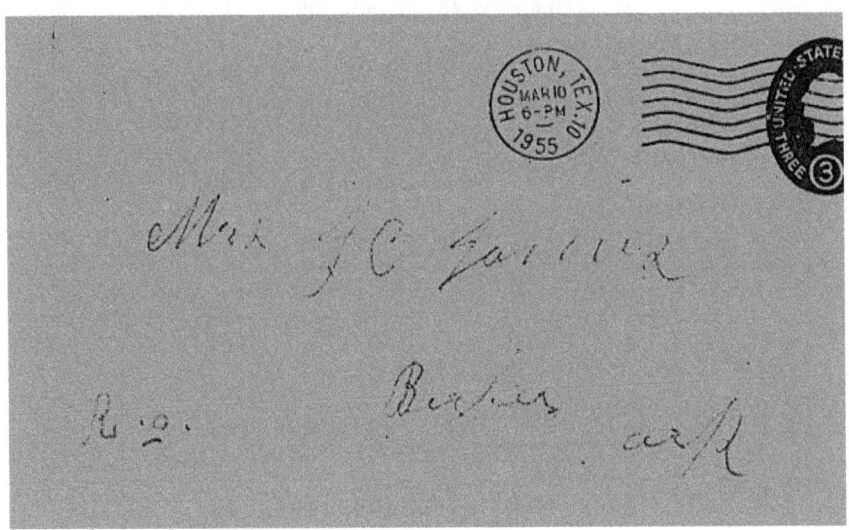

(Card from Daddy)

(Envelope)

March 10, 1955
From: J C James

    Dear wife, just a few lines to let you know, I am still living. Just got out of old Mexico, I have been kidnapped. But I am out. I will come soon home in a few days. I will leave here in a few minutes, so can't write. I will see you all in few days, so Daddy ain't dead yet. So bye bye to all. My love to all, J. C. James.

The grandsons showed this letter to Bud and told him their Daddy was kidnapped somewhere in Oklahoma and the abductors were convinced that he knew where Jesse James buried his loot in Mexico along the southern border. It was a man and woman. They held Jesse Cole in a cave and tortured him, trying to get him to tell, but he wouldn't. He had to endure this from August 1954 to March 1955.

Jesse Cole James told his sons, "they won't do that to anybody else." Apparently, he took care of his kidnappers.

In October 1995, Bud began the process to secure a court order to exhume the grave of Jesse. He traveled to Barber, Arkansas and retrieved affidavits and a power of attorney from the closest next of kin. All three brothers agreed in pursuing this, letting down their guard, even though they have been quiet all these years per their daddy's instructions. Their lives would be changing. No man would put themselves in the limelight if their story was untrue.

Bud had to prove that the grandsons were who they said they were by supplying the affidavits regarding the relationship to Jesse. Bud gathered and furnished documents to support the relationship to Texas in order to get a court order. "We proved it to the satisfaction of the State of Texas," Bud said. Shorty James said, "Call me the grandson of Jesse James or J. Frank Dalton, either one he is our Grandfather."

The next step was to speak with the funeral home who would be presenting this to the Cemetery Board for approval. Also, it was required to get permission to exhume the grave within the family plots of the Rash family from an actual member of the family. Bud was given power of attorney from David Burks, descendant and nearest surviving relatives of Sam Rash who owned the cemetery plot.

David Burks was Golda Rash Burks' son. He said he was in the photo as a little boy in the cowboy outfit next to Jesse that was shown in the Police Gazette magazine. The photo was taken in Galveston County, Texas. I have seen this photo, but unfortunately, I can not locate it.

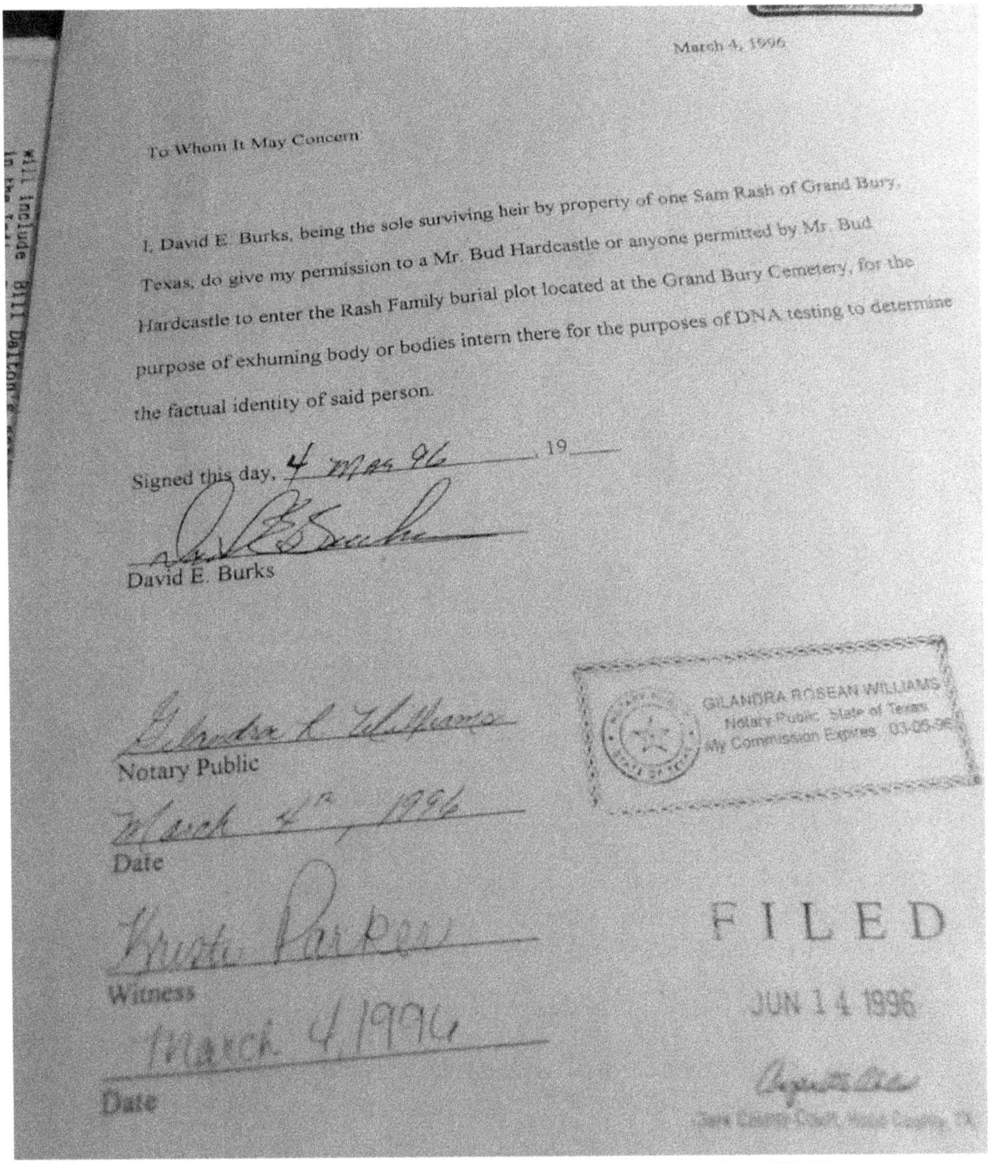

March 4, 1996

To Whom It May Concern:

I, David E. Burks, being the sole surviving heir by property of one Sam Rash of Grand Bury, Texas, do give my permission to a Mr. Bud Hardcastle or anyone permitted by Mr. Bud Hardcastle to enter the Rash Family burial plot located at the Grand Bury Cemetery, for the purpose of exhuming body or bodies intern there for the purposes of DNA testing to determine the factual identity of said person.

Signed this day, 4 Mar 96, 19___

David E. Burks

Notary Public

GILANDRA ROSEAN WILLIAMS
Notary Public, State of Texas
My Commission Expires 03-05-98

March 4th, 1996
Date

Witness

March 4, 1996
Date

FILED

JUN 14 1996

(Permission from Burks)

While in Texas, Bud went to the Billy the Kid, Old West Festival in Hico, Texas. There he met up with Dr. William Tunstill and met Janay Valdez and Judge Bob Hefner. The judge asked Bud whatever happened to Ola Everhard's manuscript and Bud said, "I've got it. I'll get you a copy and give one to the Billy the Kid Museum." Hefner, in 1987, opened the Billy the Kid Museum in Hico. He was a former newspaper publisher and Justice of the Peace in Hico. He was an extremely dedicated man to the community, his church, and to Billy the Kid. He was very respected amongst all who knew him. Bud said they became good friends and stood by him during the agonizing process of the exhumation.

(John Tatum, Dr. William Tunstill, and Bud Harcastle at the Billy the Kid festival in Hico, Texas)

In September 1996, Bud had everything ready to present to the Court of Hood County, the evidence to support the petition to exhume Jesse's body. He had a lawyer for the grandsons, Jan Barto of Granbury and Shorty and Burleigh Dale James would be there. Dr. William Tunstill was there with John and Jo Ella Tatum. Waggoner Carr was there representing Howk's son, but the sons did not show. The witnesses had to appear in court for the hearing in front of Judge Don Cleveland's bench. The judge had it in his court because he was expecting a large crowd.

It was a harrowing experience and a frustrating one at that. The judge didn't believe anything that Bud, the grandsons, Judge Bob Hefner, or any witnesses said or presented. "It was a gut punch," Bud said.

They spent 2 hours in court for the judge to come to the conclusion that he could not make a decision or ruling on the exhumation request. Jesse's grandsons were none too happy. Burleigh Dale James said, "It was important for them to know where their grandfather was buried. He's been buried in Missouri and here and there," James said of the legend. "He's our grandfather. People have called us liars. We need to get the matter straight." [642]

(Outside Hood County Courthouse – Standing L-R, Dale James, John Helsley, Charles "Shorty" James, Bud Hardcastle, Bob Hefner, and sitting, Dr. and Mrs. William Tunstill)

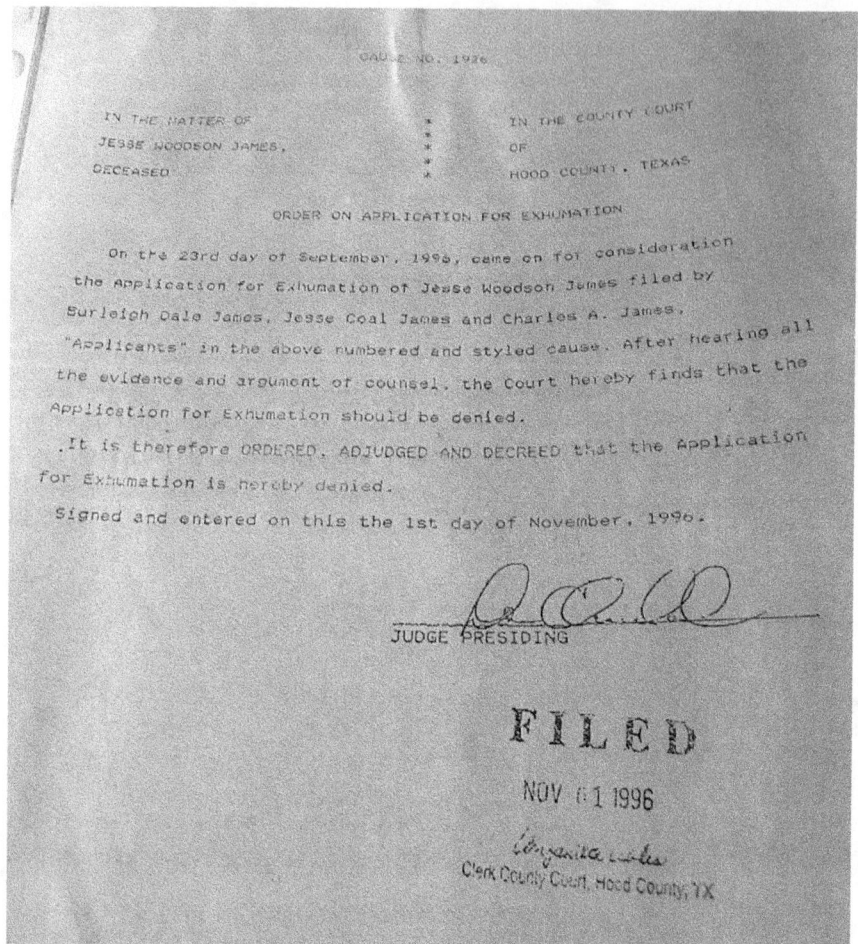

(Exhumation denial)

The judge stated in a newspaper article that "he would reopen the hearing if attorneys could produce more compelling evidence on why he should approve, or deny, the request. Opening a grave to prove kinship is not a compelling reason, Cleveland believes." He missed the point. The attorney for the James' grandsons, Barto said, "The wishes of the James' descendants to learn the truth was the most compelling reason to exhume the body." [643]

Judge Cleveland said, "that he had no legal guidelines to instruct him on whether he had the right to approve or deny the request." He advised the lawyer for the grandsons "to file a law brief, detailing the law in previous exhumation cases before he considers the case again." [644]

Bud said that after all this was said and done, the district attorney, Richard Hattox told them they didn't need permission to exhume and transfer Jesse's body to Barber, Arkansas like they had wanted. They could because they were his only closest living heirs, but due to complications brought up by Austin Attorney Waggoner Carr who were representing Howk's children, was threatening to stop the exhumation. They wanted to go through the courts and get the final reports first from the Missouri exhumation. [645] Bud also said that the examiner of Jesse's body who will make the final determination on the DNA requested that they go ahead with retrieving a court order to make it completely legal and done with integrity, especially if there were others who could later sue them for this act.

Another thing that threw a wrench in the process was Waggoner Carr wanting to have another DNA expert involved. He believed the DNA expert that Bud got would be biased because he was involved in the Missouri exhumation. The case was at a standstill.

Judge Cleveland decided not to run again in 1998, and Judge Linda Steen was elected to take his place as of January 1, 1999. She was a highly esteemed candidate who had 25 years of experience as a superintendent of juvenile corrections facilities. Steen was raised in Granbury and then worked in the Brownwood State School as their superintendent. She attended Texas Tech, graduated from TCU with an undergraduate degree in criminal justice and received her master's degree in criminal justice and public administration from the American Technological University in Killeen. 646

Bud was not going to give up, neither were Burleigh Dale, Jesse Quanah, and Charles James. Bud gathered his evidence and tried his presentation again, with the new judge. Judge Linda Steen was very open minded and had Bud just come to her office, not having to go to court, to discuss this and present a new petition. A new Granbury attorney representing Bud and the grandsons was Steve Reid. She examined the evidence and received the argument of the council, and she granted the application for exhumation in 2000.

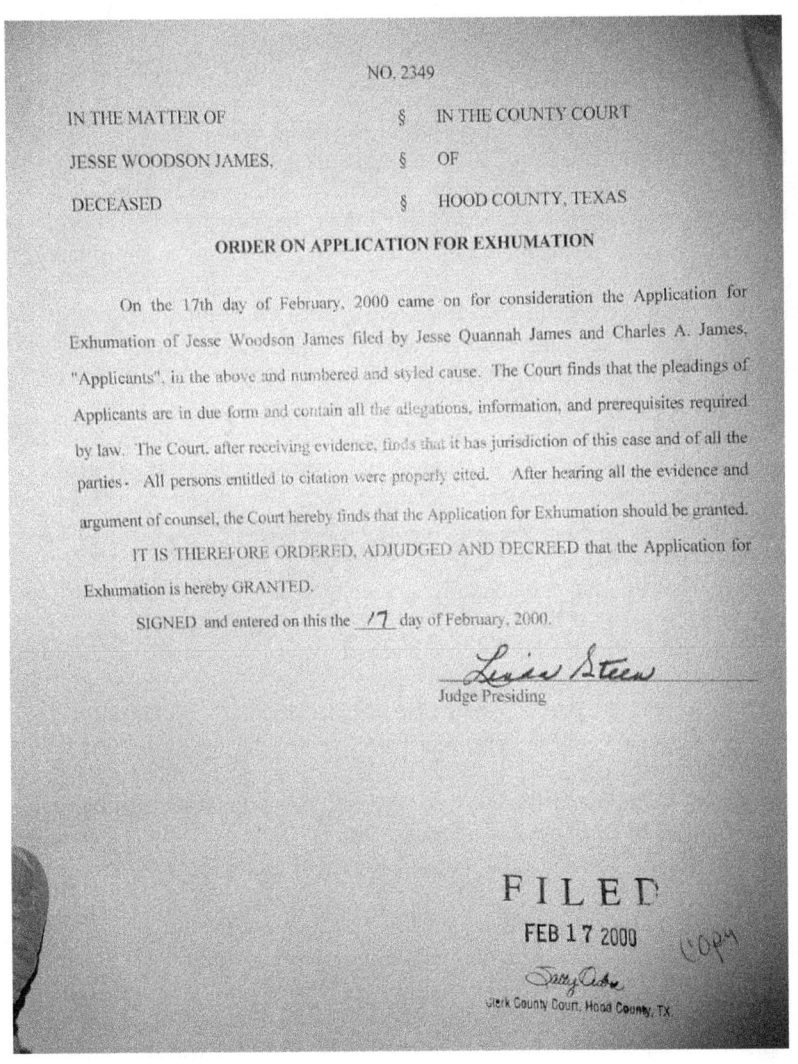

(Judge Steen granting approval for Exhumation)

"You don't know how much I appreciate it," Hardcastle told Judge Steen emotionally. "You've fought a good fight for a long time," Steen said. [647] Bud said, "She was a really nice lady, a sweetheart. I liked her alot."

Let the fun begin. The newspapers began reporting this new quest that Bud was endeavoring. Newspapers all over the country began to contact Hood County, Bud, and others involved. Even newspapers and the media from Australia and England wanted a piece of the story. But wait, there is another problem. The University of North Texas forensic expert Harrell Gill-King who had agreed with Bud to compare the remains to the DNA samples and complete the forensic testing all through this process up to 30 days ago has backed out. King complained to the Hood County News, "I do not appreciate my name being in press releases in newspapers across half the country."

Yes, Gill-King was hounded by the news media, but also what he says next shows that he thought it was best to leave well enough alone. "If the body in the grave isn't Jesse James, Granbury could receive much negative publicity," he said. Gill-King doesn't believe any evidence that is obtained from the exhumation will prove "beyond a reasonable doubt" that James is in the grave. Evidence is needed that would stand up in court, such as in a criminal trial, he said. "I think the same scientific yardstick should be applied," stated Gill-King." [648]

Bud said, "Somebody must be putting some pressure on him," who speculated about whether the scholar was nervous about the project. "Why would I go ahead if I didn't have him on board?" [649]

Bud always told me, "Loose lips, sink ships." That was the saying that my own father had told me regarding the sailor's motto when he was a flagman on an LST ship in the Pacific during World War II. Bud wasn't going to stop, and he wasn't going to name publicly who he would get to fill Gill-King's place. He did tell the news media that David Glassman, a forensic anthropologist at Southwest Texas State University will participate in the exhumation.

The DNA testing would be conducted by David Glenn Smith, professor of anthropology at the University of California at Davis.

Bud said, another thing that happened that went against the grain of his progress was Attorney Robert Jackson who was a descendant of Susan James Parmer who relented in providing DNA samples. There were a lot of bad things said about Bud and he was hurt by the accusations that his motives were not genuine in finding the truth.

"We've been called impostors and scavengers and this and that and people have tried to stop us from doing it," Hardcastle said. "It could have been a pleasure, and I'm still going to enjoy it, but I didn't appreciate being called some of those names." [650]

The day of the big reveal, May 30, 2000. It was a hot day, 100 degrees or more in the shade and the digging began at 8:30 A.M.

At the cemetery, only descendants, researchers, media, and regular visitors at the cemetery were allowed in. There was security at the gate.

Bud had his nephews there, Lou Kilgore and her sister, Geneva, Joyce Morgan, Judge Bob Hefner, Jannay Valdez, Ralph Epperson, and many more. Ralph Epperson, in his YouTube video, "Jesse James lived to be 103: Part 2," states Bud Hardcastle is "The Dean" of the Jesse James Researchers. Ralph Epperson sent Bud $1,000 to help cover the cost of the exhumation. Jannay Valdez told Bud, "You will never know how wonderful it was to meet Jesse's grandsons." Both Judge Hefner, Jannay Valdez, and Dr. William Tunstill planted a seed in a lot of people's minds regarding the true stories of Billy the Kid and Jesse James.

Of course, Charles and Jesse Quanah James were there. Burleigh Dale couldn't be there due to some health issues.

Everyone was talking about the man who was sitting on his wife's tombstone. Lou Kilgore went over, and the man shared his lunch with her. Bud didn't know him, but later found out it was Billie Sol Estes. He and his wife had moved to Granbury and she passed away just 3 months earlier. He shared ancestors with Ben Estes and Jesse James through the Estes family. Billie Sol Estes' great, great grandfather was Col. William Newton Estes (1831-1863). He was born in Tennessee and his family moved to Dekalb County, Alabama before the war. He was one of 5 men who served the

Confederacy as regimental Officer from DeKalb County. He was in the 3rd Cavalry, 2nd brigade in the Wharton S. Division and was killed in action on September 17, 1863 at the Battle of Chickamauga.

Howk's sons were there with an attorney, Waggoner Carr. At times they seemed to be working with Bud and other times they weren't. Howk supposedly had died in 1984, but one of the sons told Bud at the exhumation, who wholeheartedly believed Howk's story of kinship with Jesse, told Bud himself in Granbury, "I have yet to be at my father's funeral."

Attorney General Waggoner Carr was vested in Jesse James. Anything "Jesse," he was there. He was the guest of honor at a fund-raising open house at the Meredith Hart House near Rio Vista and Cleburne, Texas, April 11, 1965. Funds would be used in the markings of Historical Sites in Johnson County, Texas. Richard Meredith Hart was born 1811 in Hardin County, Kentucky and built this home in 1856. He was an Indian fighter, cattleman, Texas Ranger and patriot. [651] He died Dec 13, 1864 and is buried in the Hart cemetery near Rio Vista, Texas. This is where Bud suspects Charles Hart was buried. Were they related? It's a possibility. Bud has had his eye on Johnson County. He believes gold is buried there. That was also suggested by John Trammel.

Carr was elected as a Representative in the Texas Legislature in 1950, Speaker of the House for two terms, became attorney general from 1963-1967 and completed the prosecution of Billy Sol Estes and slant oil well cases. He and his wife were among those who ate breakfast with President John F. Kennedy and his wife, the morning of that fateful day in Dallas on November 22, 1963. When President JFK was assassinated, Carr led the Texas investigation and participated in the work of the Warren Commission. Carr wanted to conduct a state probe but was blocked by the Warren Commission which was appointed by President Lyndon B. Johnson. He was involved in the prosecution of Jack Ruby. Carr testified that Lee Harvey Oswald was working as an undercover agent for the FBI and was receiving $200 a month from September 1962 until November 1963. Hoover denied his claims.

Carr was very interested in Jesse James and was writing books about him. He died in Feb 25, 2004. His obituary states that he was a Mason.

Many, many news media showed up in Granbury, from national broadcasters, international broadcasters, radio stations to newspapers from around the country. The BBC was broadcasting live. Australia broadcasting company called during the exhumation and wanted an interview.

(Bud being interviewed by a news reporter)

(L-R, Bud giving another interview. The 2nd man sitting is Kenny Brown, Bud's cousin. The 3rd and 4th men sitting are Jesse Quanah James and Charles "Shorty" James and Lou Kilgore standing)

Bud Hardcastle: The Truth Tracker

(L-R, Two nephews of Bud's, Zach and Nathan, Bud Hardcastle, and John Tatum)

It was an all-day affair. David Glassman and his team began at the marker and started using a backhoe to dig. The team then began using shovels after they got down to three feet. Their shovels hit a metal vault and then a wooden casket, only 18 inches apart. For some odd reason, they began just focusing on the metal vault, but there was no other grave marker to indicate another body was there. Some believed that it may be Jesse' lady friend in the wooden casket. Bud saw the wooden casket and knew that one held Jesse. The cemetery records had shown the body was buried in a cloth covered redwood casket. Bud had told Mr. Glassman before it ever started, that Jesse was buried in a wooden casket.

(The metal vault to the left and to the right, the outline of the wooden casket with a piece of the wood that was stripped from it. Bud's nephews ran to the hardware store to get protective shielding to cover it and when they got back, the heavy straps were pulling up the metal vault)

Bud said he knew their focus was wrong. Bud called out, "That is not Jesse's coffin, he is buried in a wooden box to the south." The cemetery board did not listen to Bud. They didn't pay any attention. They kept going. Bud was sick. We don't know why they continued with the metal vault. Maybe it was easier to remove than an old decaying wooden casket. They told Bud later that the court order only allowed the removal of one casket. But it was wrong, all wrong.

(Metal Vault being pulled out. Bud in the background looking sick)

When Jesse's monument was placed on his grave, it was put in the wrong place. Ola had it put there in 1984, **33** years from the time Jesse died. Before that time, Jesse's markers were stolen for souvenirs, so the exact spot was just a guess. You would think the cemetery records would have the exact location of all burials, but it was not correctly identified. Apparently, there was no marker or record for the one who was buried in the vault, right under where the monument was located.

It took nine hours to dig out the metal vault. All those spectators were pretty well drained and were told that the body would be taken to an undisclosed place and the results of the test would take several weeks.

Bud said that the steel vault was taken to a warehouse to open and carefully remove DNA samples and examine the body. Bud, Judge Steen, Glassman, and others were there as they anxiously waited for the vault and casket to be opened. They found the body to be in good condition and as Glassman began to remove a few of the parts, he noticed that the body only had one arm. Glassman asked, if J. Frank Dalton had one arm. Bud just sank. He couldn't believe what he was hearing. Oh, my Lord! They got the wrong body!

Bud walked away feeling like he had just gotten hit by a train. A stab in the heart. He was mortified and embarrassed. God bless him. What a blow!

Judge Steen came over to where Bud was, checking on him. He was nearly in tears and he said how sorry and disappointed he was and "wouldn't do anything to embarrass Granbury." The kind judge said, "I'm not worried about Granbury, I'm worried about you."

The body they dug up was Golda Rash's husband, William Henry Holland. Bud hated that they had disturbed a grave that was not the right one and apologized to the family. As it turned out the family had no idea where he was buried. They knew where his arm was buried when he was a boy, but now they could put a marker on his grave. Holland was found, but Jesse was still in hiding.

Once again, Jesse was showing he had the upper hand when it came to his self-preservation, even in the grave.

"I feel like I've got the weight of the world on my shoulders," said a red faced Bud Hardcastle, the Oklahoma used-car salesman who has tirelessly championed the theory that Dalton was the legendary train robber. "You can't imagine what a bad day this is for me. It is not a happy day," he said from Purcell, Okla. David Glassman, a Southwest Texas State forensic anthropologist, said there were questions when two caskets were found so close together on the day of the exhumation.

But he believed that the court order only allowed his team to remove the casket directly under the headstone." [652] The wrong casket is the latest setback for Hardcastle.

Bud said, "I don't know how to quit." I'm not a quitter. I've gone this far; I think the truth needs to be proven, but financially it's not easy to do." Both Steen and Glassman were willing to do this again.

(Bud in the newspaper holding gun from a Metroplex paper)

After the attempted exhumation, many people had to rub the failure in Bud's face. From the Department of Forensic Sciences out of George Washington University in Washington D.C., Professor of Law, and Forensic Sciences, James E. Starrs, who oversaw the Kearney exhumation writes to the editor of The Washington Times, May 31, 2000 following a report in their newspaper about the Granbury exhumation.

"The escape theorists are on the loose once again, as per your report of May 31st on the Texas exhumation of J. Frank Dalton, who claimed to be the Jesse James.

"As the Project Director of the 1995 exhumation in Kearney, Missouri of the remains of the person historically reputed to be Jesse James, I am exceedingly skeptical of the legitimacy of the current exhumation. The exhumation I chaired in 1995 proved beyond a shadow of a doubt that the person buried in Kearney's Mount Olivet cemetery under a Jesse James inscribed headstone was, in point of scientific fact, the real and authentic Jess James."

He goes on to say how many people were involved in the Kearney exhumation who had high credentials in their field. Then he continued to make a mockery of Bud.

"It deserves saying that the escape theorists have struck out every time they have claimed a notable individual escaped a terminal event. Not Lee Harvey Oswald, nor John Wilkes Booth, nor Anatasia, the daughter of Czar Nicholas II, nor the Dauphin, the child of Marie Antoinette, nor Billy the Kid, nor numerous others escaped the death that history records they suffered...

"Who is next on the agenda of the escape theorists – Elvis Presley? Maybe not, since there continues to be as many sightings in as many faraway places of a still living Elvis as there were of Jesse James after his death in 1882. Notable people die like everyone else but the myths surrounding many of their deaths live on to confound both logic and science."

Signed: James E. Starrs,
Professor of Law, and Professor of Forensic Sciences [653]

The following year, in 2001, a final report of the DNA tests that were publicly revealed in 2000 on the 1995 exhumation in Missouri, indicated that the teeth and hair used for the testing was from the 1978 exhumation of the original burial place of Jesse's on the farm, and indeed they belonged to Jesse; 99.7 degree of certainty. But a wrench was thrown when the Deputy Counselor for Clay County, Stephen Caruso, who represented the James Farm and Museum said the entire report and DNA analysis were fraudulent. Caruso told NBC 8 KOMU TV anchorman Jim Riek that the teeth submitted "had nothing to do with the teeth that were dug up."

There were a lot of shenanigans going on at that time. Professor Starrs turned out to not be a forensic scientist. He was a professor of forensic law. He taught forensic science at George Washington University's National Law Center. His title was "LLM," Master of Law.

Bud stated that Sidney Kanazana, who is considered a mediator, arbitrator, trial lawyer for both plaintiffs and defendants, had an opportunity to cross examine James E. Starrs and determined he was not a forensic scientist, but a lawyer, professor, and writer. He was put in charge of the exhumation of the body in Mt. Olivet Cemetery in Kearney only because of his skills in applying exhumation and forensic concepts into criminal cases as a lawyer. Sidney practices law in Hawaii and California.

Sidney found that Mr. Starrs received grants for his very own nonprofit company, Scientific Sleuthing which his title includes, President, Vice President, and Treasurer.

Bud called the University where Starrs was employed, George Washington University and found out that Starrs in no way is a forensic scientist, and he did not represent the university in the exhumation. Starrs was hired by Judge Ross who claims to be a descendant of Jesse's under Starr's organization, Scientific Sleuthing. He descends from Jesse James, Jr. from California. Remember what Jesse said about Jesse James, Jr.

Starrs' interest in Jesse peeked in his own investigations and Bud stated that it appears that Starrs published a book regarding his findings on Jesse prior to exhuming the body. "It appears a predetermined outcome was already in place prior to the shovel going into the ground," said Bud.

Apparently, there were more ruthless naysayers regarding the exhumation in Granbury and the way it was handled. One of the professional board certified anthropologist, who has worked cases of skeletal recovery and identification for law enforcement agencies in Texas, David M. Glassman, PHD, was called upon by the Hardcastle team to be a part of the exhumation process to recover some of the bones, teeth, etc for DNA analysis. Robert A. Jackson, of Jackson, Hall & Associates, a law firm out of Oklahoma City, the direct descendant of Susan James Parmer, contacted Dr. Glassman and inquired about his study of the reports of the Starr Team's conclusion on Jesse's exhumation in Kearney, Missouri. Also, Jackson was questioning Hardcastle's integrity and professionalism.

Bud had the letter from Dr. David Glassman, Ph.D. to Robert Jackson in response to Jackson's letter questioning the Hardcastle team. Glassman stated in the letter, "I am truly sorry that your opinion of the Hardcastle team has not convinced you of their professionalism in handling this sensitive issue. I can assure you, however, that the exhumation I conducted in Granbury was done with professionalism in mind." [654]

An article came out on the Hood County News, www.hcnews.com, "A legend shrouded in mystery: Former forensic anthropologist recounts the 2000 exhumation of Jesse James' grave," by Ashley Inge on December 20, 2022. The article was incorrect, stating that it was a family member of Jesse James and his attorney, former Texas Attorney General Waggoner Carr that contacted Glassman to exhume the body of J. Frank Dalton. The article stated that they had interviewed Glassman, and these were his statements and that Carr and his client got the court order. This was false.

Bud Hardcastle is the one that put the money up and got the court order. Waggoner Carr and one of Howk's sons or grandson was there wanting to stop the exhumation, but they had no grounds. They could not prove kinship, but Bud could with Jesse Cole James' sons.

The article went on to report that Glassman said that when they were exhuming the body that a few pieces of rotten wood were found on plot over from what is now known as Holland's grave. But he also stated, "As a scientist, I'm totally unbiased," he said. "To me, I do this as a science, and the outcome is based on the science that's found. I have no opinion one way or the other. Some people thought I was on a team to help prove that the Missouri exhumation was correct. No, I was essentially hired to exhume a body and extract elements for DNA analysis to see if that was Jesse James."

He went on to say, "The mystery still continues and probably should remain a mystery," Glassman added. "This is part of the lore. It is part of the Granbury story, and I would suggest that it be left at that".

Another one suggesting to leave it alone.

Attorney Jackson, who was a criminal defense trial lawyer would not let "dead dogs lie." In March 7, 2001, he wrote to Bud after a phone conversation with him. Bud apparently told the attorney that he intended to get another court order to exhume the remaining wooden coffin from the Granbury cemetery. The attorney advised that he desired the examiner of any DNA analysis, Dr. Smith to review the Starr Team's reports of the Kearney exhumation. Jackson wanted written documentation of Dr. Smith's evaluation or analysis of the work conducted by the Starr team in Missouri.

The attorney included a genealogy chart from the Wellcome Wing of the London Science Museum in London; a chart verifying his direct link to Jesse's sister, Susan. He descended from Feta Rose.

Robert Jackson stated that there has never been a record of a divorce from Zerelda Mims, first wife of Jesse's, therefore making the three grandsons who were supposedly conceived with Emma Andrews, illegitimate, and if Emma and Jesse were married, it would be considered bigamy under Oklahoma law and the grandsons would have no legal standing. Has anyone found a marriage license between Zerelda and Jesse or for that matter a divorce decree?

The next few months it appeared that Bud was moving forward and even into 2001 he was working on doing another exhumation. We see items in the newspaper up to February that he was waiting on his lawyer to present the petition to the court, but the judge said she has never seen it. Something happened and Bud dropped it all together. That's not like Bud. I asked him about it, and he wouldn't say what happened.

I asked Bud's nephew, Zach what happened. He stated that Bud's lawyer kept asking for more money and more time, but very little action was taken. He said Bud was up against numerous injunctions that were obtained to prevent any further actions in this matter. It seemed that his support was falling out from underneath him and he was crushed from the weight of it all. It broke his spirit and broke his soul. It took a toll on him, and he was never the same after that.

This truly breaks my heart. Bud didn't deserve this after all the hard work, time, and money he put into this to only watch it all be buried in the grave with Jesse. The one piece of evidence that would solve the mystery for Jesse's descendants and the world, to prove beyond a doubt that Jesse lived beyond 1882, bringing final rest in the matter, was only 18 inches away, but yet unreachable.

Sadly, more and more evidence has been destroyed to prove the truth. Any evidence of what may have been buried on the Rash's property is all under water. It now is a part of Lake Granbury.

"All that glitters is not gold."

-*William Shakespeare*

Chapter Thirty-Three: There's Gold in them thar hills

The thing that kept Bud going, after such a letdown of not being able to recover the correct body during the exhumation, was the realization that he didn't need DNA to prove who J. Frank Dalton really was. He had all the proof he needed.

The documented postmortem at the funeral home revealed that Dalton's bullet-riddled body told of his physical toughness and stamina during many gun battles and abuse he sustained, but the body only told a portion of the story.

The real story behind the man in the grave next to Holland was treasure worth millions. While Bud was unable to uncover the body, the DNA, he was able to uncover the gold within Jesse, which was his unwavering and undying spirit to fight for justice. This fervor was one thing that Jesse could not hide.

The clues Jesse left behind revealing this explosive spirit are imprinted upon everyone who knew him, upon his love and protection of his family, upon the stories he told, upon the maps he drew, upon the trees, rocks, and caves he carved into, and the treasure he meticulously protected for his beloved Southland.

He left his mark in more ways than one.

Bud will now take us down the trail that leads us closer to what Jesse put most of his energy and time into, gold and the preservation of the South and its people. He staked his entire life upon it.

The immense treasure Jesse buried was unbelievably laid out in clues. Bud has proven beyond a doubt that the knowledge and maps that was passed down to Jesse Cole James and the maps J. Frank Dalton so intricately described in great detail to Howk whom he stayed with in his final days are legitimate, down to the last detail. Bud also has eyewitness accounts of Jesse/J. Frank Dalton, moving the money.

"We're getting into something really big," said Bud. When there's gold, there's danger. The stories he shared with me are unbelievable, but he can back up what he says. Some stories, some treasure sites, some maps, some symbols, he has asked me not to share, but Bud is willing to share a lot with the reader to encourage them to seek the truth and perhaps solve the unsolved mysteries that are still left buried.

Bud, to this day, continues to hunt for treasure. He has always been the "go-to" man when other treasure hunters need codes or symbols deciphered. He can spot a clue, a carving, or a cave before anyone else can. He knows where and what to look for with his keen eyes set on the prize. This has brought him closer to understanding Jesse and evidence proving J. Frank Dalton was indeed Jesse Woodson James.

If the stories Bud is sharing in this chapter doesn't convince the reader who Jesse Woodson James/aka J. Frank Dalton was, then they themselves need to dig up proof that will debunk Bud's 40 + years of research. No one has ever proven Bud wrong that the author is aware of and no one ever proved J. Frank Dalton was NOT Jesse.

The 1970's
The Superstitions

Bud's taste for treasure hunting and solving life-long mysteries began in the early 70's. He started in one of the most famous and largest treasure sites in the U.S., the Superstition Mountains in Arizona. His cousin, Tommy Hays worked for a detective agency in Oklahoma City and had been to the "Supers" with another professional private detective, Glen Magill who dedicated his life in finding the Lost Dutchman Mine. Magill was President of the Oklahoma Association of Private Detectives, a World War II and Korean War veteran, a candidate for the legislature, and the Oklahoma City Council. He was well respected.

Glenn Magill had organized many expeditions in the late 1960's and early '70's within the Superstitions. Tommy Hays was able to join him on some of the adventures.

After near death experiences of being shot at, dynamited, scorned, and stalked, Magill claimed in 1966 that he had identified the location of the mine, but later corrected himself as stating that he was mistaken or the mine had been "played out". He came out empty-handed each time.

"The Killer Mountains" by Curt Gentry, chronicles the many treasure hunting adventures of Magill. The title is very appropriate for the mysterious mountains that hold many secrets and death for many who venture within its core. Many people never return, or their remains are later found without their heads. Several corpses have been found with bullet holes piercing their skulls confirming the reports of a sniper who protects the gold.

The mountains and the legends are well preserved in this rugged terrain. There are no roads, only trails and those who maintain the trails cannot use anything but axes and hand saws; no machinery or motorized vehicles are allowed. Aircraft is also not allowed except during rescue operations. No insecticide can be used, or foreign material allowed in the air space or ground. It is to remain in its pristine state.

The Superstition Mountain Range draws many people into its grasp. The trails begin on a dead-end road outside of Apache Junction, Arizona, east of Phoenix. My daughter, who once lived in Apache Junction, took me where the road ends and trails proceed into the unknown, leading to the jagged rocks of the main Superstition Mountain. It is majestic and spellbinding, towering above the giant living cacti that appear to be people of all different shapes and sizes, frozen in time.

We were going for a short hike. My daughter warned me of several dangers such as the "jumping" cactus (Jumping Cholla), flash floods, snakes, Gila monsters, mountain lions, cats (not the domestic kind), and the hot sun that is extremely intense and appears to have several rings and layers within its white surface. The sun is totally different in this arid region compared to the Texas and Oklahoma sunshine that Bud and I were used to.

The Superstition Mountain Range also has its own weather system like no other place on earth besides the Grand Canyon. It can melt you like a candle or freeze you into an ice cube. It is another world of its own.

I was game for a hike, but halfway up the mountain, I was overcome by a strange sensation of not being able to breathe and my heart was pounding. I sensed a feeling of uneasiness. My digital camera stopped working and appeared as though the fresh new batteries were sucked dry. I myself was sucked dry. Needless to say, we didn't stay long after we made it to the crown of the Superstition Mountain.

We descended down the trail and I began to feel more at ease. When we reached the car, my camera came on with full battery power. I cannot explain it, but I knew these mountains, which were sacred to the Apaches, in which they called "The abode of the Thunder God", held energy that cannot be explained. I had my fill, but for many others, it only whets their appetite to explore further into the unknown.

Tommy Hays, cousin of Bud's, was one of the many treasure hunters who went with Magill into the Superstitions. Tommy asked Bud, the next time we go, do you want to go?" Of course, Bud wanted to go. The next time Tommy went, Magill couldn't go, but Bud did. They flew out there with another friend, Terry Hickman. The only experienced hunter in the bunch was Tommy Hays.

Arriving at Apache Junction, the three of them hired a guide to "pack them in" with pack mules, horses, and all the supplies needed to venture into the abyss. The guide left them in the desert, on their own, and would return at a designated time and place to guide them back to civilization.

As the guide was leaving, he left them with words of wisdom. "There is a man on Blacktop Mesa or Black Mountain who will be watching you. Just act like you don't see 'em. Just don't say a word." Bud said, "Sure enough, as we were making our way on Bluff Spring Mountain just across Black Mountain, ole' Crazy Jake with a rifle on his hip, was looking down at us, watching every move we made."

They learned later that just a week before they were there in the Superstitions, Crazy Jake killed a Mexican man working for him. Jake dropped him off in a canyon and put rocks on him. Jake went to tell authorities. Apparently, there was no trial or investigation, possibly claiming self-defense, and he was back on the mountain again.

Jake was very protective of his mines and his information. There were many stories of killings, shootouts, and strange events that were connected to Crazy Jake. A man who worked for Crazy Jake, whose real name was Robert Jacob, said that Jake conned a lot of people out of their money, claiming that he would invest it in the mine. Lots of promises with no profit gained. Sounds like gold fever got the best of him like many others. Their whole life was swallowed up in their dreams of golden dust that never materialized.

He ended his last few years on earth being involved in several scams, scandals, and serious charges against him including slavery, sex crimes, and other nefarious activities. He spent 8 years in prison.

It was 106 degrees in the shade. Terry was having a difficult time on the trail. As he poured water over his head, he said a line straight out of the movies, "Ya'll go on, I can't make it." Bud took his backpack, grabbed him by the arm and hoisted him to his feet. They took Terry on up the mountain to a shady spot where the wind was blowing. It felt so good and they stayed there for about 30 minutes until they cooled off.

They continued on the trail and found a wild area. Within its boundaries, there a freshwater spring pouring out from the rocks. Very few springs exist in those parts. The area is known as Bluff Springs Mountain.

The men filled their canteens along the cool water's edge. All of a sudden, Terry found enough energy to jump up and scramble all over the ground, picking up something. Bud and Tommy were puzzled, they thought Terry was exhausted and thought the heat was really getting to him. Terry's eyes widened as he focused his eyes on rocks that were sparkling in every direction around him. He had struck it rich.

Bud and Tommy looked at each other and burst out laughing. "That's fool's gold!" It took the breath and sudden burst of energy out of Terry. He just knew he hit the motherlode.

The trail was somewhat treacherous, being only 2-3 feet wide. If your horse stumbles, you tumble down the steep 400-500 feet drop, off the side of the mountain. There were snakes every 15 feet and they weren't too friendly; rattlesnakes and copperheads.

They had to make camp out in the open desert where it was pitch black at night. The team set up their camp site before dark, placing one large sleeping bag underneath them on top of the hard desert floor and placed their other sleeping bags on top for cover. When they finally settled in for the night, Bud said, "This boot don't make a very good pillow". Terry said, "You ought to try a pickle jar!"

Every morning bees would fly over their head. "What are we going to do?" Terry said. Bud chuckled and said, "You can do what you want to, but I'm going to hide my head under this sleeping bag." Eventually, the bees left. The boys had to continuously laugh at themselves to keep sane in this barren and unforgiving land.

They reached La Barge Canyon and came upon a creek. It was waist deep at one end and then shallow near the bank where rocks were stacked neatly by mother nature, but something caught Bud's eye. It did not look natural. The bank was lined with white rock and black rocks were placed where they shouldn't be. Bud just knew that it was a sign of something buried behind the rocks.

Tommy and Bud waded out into the waist deep water and got to the other side where the rocks were calling their names. Bud pulled one of the loose black rocks away from the bank and a "snake run his head out." Bud said we turned and just knew if we ran back through that high water, the snake would have them. They jumped the highest they had ever in their lives up over the tall rocks to get away. Bud said, "All the snake could see was my rear."

They stayed three days and left the fourth day. They found a few caves, but nothing to write home about. Bud said, "The guide looked better coming after us than he did taking us out there."

They had their fill. They were glad to get out of there. They still had their packing pistols on their hips when they reached civilization and went to a bar/saloon to relax and get a cool drink in Goldfield. "You boys packing pistols?" one guy at the bar said. Another one chimed in, "Does that make you think you're tough?" Bud replied, "I'm a lot tougher with it or without it." Bud told me, "I was up on that mountain, I didn't need a smart mouth. They didn't say another thing."

70's & 80's
Charlie and the Organ Mountains

Charlie Holman was just a good 'ole boy. He attended Oklahoma State University on a wrestling scholarship. Charlie was a three times state champion in wrestling between 1965-1967 in high school. He was short and chunky, but stout as an ox.

In 1988, Charlie's mother, who lived in Yukon, Oklahoma read an article in the Daily Oklahoman newspaper. The story was about Bud Hardcastle and his hunt for Jesse. She called Charlie, "There is another man who believes like you do."

Charlie was just as interested in Jesse James as Bud was and the buried treasure resting in the southwestern part of Oklahoma. Charlie also believed that Jesse lived beyond 1882 who was determined to store up wealth to help finance a second Civil War. It was a fascinating subject, creating a drive within Charlie to continue to quench his thirst for the adventure of hunting for Jesse's gold.

Charlie called Bud and wanted to come see him. Charlie did not waste any time. He traveled from Hobart, Oklahoma to Purcell, 100 miles and came knocking at Bud's door that very night.

Bud at the time was just piddling around in treasure hunts, but was mostly interested in the history of Jesse, but ole Charlie was deep into treasure hunting of all kinds. Bud and Charlie hit it off and became partners, complimenting each other. They were a pair. Charlie was a denturist, made false teeth and Bud was a used car salesman. Combining their skills and knowledge, they became experts in the art of treasure hunting.

Bud stated that the more he delved into research and partnered up with Charlie on treasure hunts, the more it kept "proving out" that Jesse lived on beyond 1882.

Bud's interest shifted from Oklahoma to the southern part of New Mexico when his research led to Jesse's involvement in Chihuahua, Mexico, Maximillian, and the Dona Ana Trail.

Charlie had a head start in exploring the southern part of New Mexico where lore and legends originated on the Seven Cities of Cibola or Seven Cities of Gold. Many men, including Albert Pike were on the hunt for the cities, but maybe, just maybe the gold was within the crude and wild mountains of southern New Mexico which was spread out in seven different locations just north of Chihuahua, Mexico, another hot bed for Jesse.

One of the mountain ranges that Charlie frequented and focused upon before he met Bud was the Organ Mountains which is east of Las Cruces, New Mexico. He confided in Bud on the things he had learned about the mysterious mountains. Bud, to this day, does not know the sources Charlie used on these hunts, but he knew a lot. Charlie's stories coincided with Bud's knowledge and research regarding Jesse and his connection to Victorio Peak which was only 7-8 miles to the north. Both set of eyes became intensely focused on both set of mountains.

1797-Early 1800's
Father LaRue

Charlie's interest began with Father/Padre LaRue who was a French priest assigned to agriculture work at missions in Mexico. Father LaRue was stationed at Chihuahua in 1797, which was during the last few remaining years of the Spanish occupation. He was designated as Priest #7. His parish was suffering and starving from drought and famine. When an old Mexican man, some believe a soldier who had been injured, stumbled into their parish, it was as if he was God's messenger of relief ahead. The padre served his needs, emotionally, physically, and spiritually. When it appeared that he was not going to make it, the man told Father LaRue that there was a place up north that could supply their every need.

The dying man spoke of a rich vein of gold in a mountain north of El Paso. He had been mining up there. It was laying within a rugged mountain range on the east of the Rio Grande River, past Mesilla, which was near today's city of Las Cruces. Mesilla was the capitol of New Mexico at one time. At Mesilla, which ran parallel with the Organ Mountains, was the area that the Father was told to look for three peaks. Once in sight, he said to turn east.

From this location, looking straight east would be the Organ Mountains running southward and the San Andres Mountains running northward. The two mountain ranges are divided by the San Augustin Pass, Hwy 70, the major U.S. Hwy that takes you from Las Cruces to White Sands Missile Range, White Sands National Park and Alamogordo, New Mexico. It's a beautiful drive.

The dying man spoke of a basin, which would later be known as the Hembrillo Basin. There he said you would find a spring at the foot of a solitary peak which held a rich history.

When the need for relief reached its peak, so to say, Father LaRue took those who wanted to go north to find better land and better water through the desert to the San Andres Mountains, but did he make a trip through the Organ Mountains also? Bud and Charlie found evidence that he did.

In the story told, most people believe that Father LaRue found the spring at the base of a cone-like mountain, unique in its shape. The spring was the only water source in a 40-mile radius. This is believed to be Victorio Peak.

Father LaRue settled in this area and named his new colony, Spirit Springs in Dona Ana County. The landscape was harsh but held priceless resources. They indeed found gold within the mountain and surrounding area. The gold vein within the mountain became richer the further down inside the mountain they explored.

The only human presence that they encountered were an ancient tribe of Apache Indians. Father LaRue enlisted many monks and Indians to mine the rich vein of gold. They used their own homemade smelter to mold the gold into bricks and stacked the gold along a cavern inside the mountain. They did this for two years.

The story goes, the Spanish Army became very suspicious when Father LaRue abandoned his assigned mission in Mexico. There was no trace of where the Father or his parishioners went. The army became aware of activity in Mesilla which pointed to the members of the parish. A red flag went up when the parishioners used gold to purchase items in Mesilla.

Word got back to Father LaRue, that the parishioners were uneasy about the whole incident in Mesilla. Father ordered all gold, smelters, and mines to be sealed up. One story stated that when all was concealed in the mountain, they rolled a huge boulder to cover the entry. There had to be other entries into the mountain in order to get carettas (carts) through when transporting the gold. All was concealed and Father LaRue went back to their camp.

The Spanish soldiers gathered a great force and found Father LaRue. One story states that the Father was in his church that was built in that area. They tortured Father LaRue into telling them where the gold mine was. He refused. They continued the torture until he was dead.

The soldiers then turned to the parishioners and began torturing them. They kept their mouths shut. It was a horrific massacre in the Hembrillo Basin, but the gold was never discovered.

The story doesn't end here, but it didn't start there either. There are many facets to this story. And it may go back as far as the Knights of the Templar, Montezuma, and Cortes. Then the story continues to include members of the Apache tribe, Maximillian, Jesse James, Doc Noss, and the U.S. military and government.

We will pause here to bring in Bud and Charlie's story. "It gets big hun," said Bud.

Charlie took this information on Father LaRue plus an old Mexican man who directed and guided him to the Organ Mountains. These mountains were directly due east of Mesilla and Las Cruces; more so than Victorio Peak as the Father LaRue story suggests. Charlie found strong evidence that Father LaRue first mined in the Organ Mountains and then later into Victorio Peak.

Charlie, with a crew of men from Oklahoma, traveled to the Organ Mountains with clues, the Mexican guide, and a lot of courage. The guide took Charlie and his men up the mountain to an old mine close to a waterfall.

This was the most rugged terrain that he had ever experienced. "It never did get too tough for Charlie," Bud would always say, but it was extremely tough on Charlie's crew who had to climb those angular, slick mountains where not many dared to tread. One man, who was carrying some of the equipment up the trail, broke down many times with tears in his eyes as his feet slipped under the heavy load and impossible rocky landscape.

Charlie found one of the mines and dug deep within its cavity with lots of hard muscle and back breaking maneuvers. Along the interior of the shaft, there were symbols. Not all of the markings were recalled by Bud, but the ones that stood out was a number 7 and a Franciscan Sword carved into the wall. Bud said the number 7 represents "gold", and possibly could have been referring to Father LaRue (Priest #7), or the 7th depository of the Seven Cities of Gold.

Charlie went back 3 or 4 more times and each time; he was escorted off the mountain by the White Sands Military Police. That portion of the Organ Mountains was within the boundary of the White Sands Military Missile Range.

This never stopped 'ole Charlie. It was in his blood. After Charlie met Bud, he told him of the excursions up into the Organ Mountains. He told Bud he didn't find anything, except the signs of a mine, the symbols and carvings. Charlie still believed there was something there.

In the 80's, a magazine article caught their eye, written by a man offering $1,000 to anyone who could find the word "*Cimarron*" carved on a rock in the Organ Mountains. There were clues.

Bud and Charlie took the challenge, left for the Organ Mountains and put their minds together to solve the clues. Charlie was awfully familiar with the area, where to go, where to avoid and was aware that they would be watched. The clues led them straight to the scene of where Charlie had dug within the mine years earlier across from a waterfall. The waterfall was one of the clues. Bud's built-in sonar and keen sense of discernment took him straight towards the waterfall that flowed between two mountains. The water of the falls fell down into a creek and flowed north towards a hill, in line with the waterfall. At that point, Bud spied a huge boulder. It caught Bud's eye and he knew that it had to be a landmark of some kind, which was often used by the Knights of the Templars, Spanish, Indians, the KGC, and Jesse James.

Bud climbed up to the rock and discovered a small crevice under the rock. He shuffled the dirt and rocks out of the way and found some very old burro shoes. Father LaRue and the miners had been there and supposedly packing something onto the mules and taken out of the area. Bud started to remove a rock that looked out of place that was sitting atop the boulder. There it was. Underneath the rock was the word "*Cimarron*" carved directly on top of the huge rock. Bud said it was written in fancy cursive handwriting. Someone really took the time to chisel it out. It did not appear to be ancient writing, but Bud thinks it was written by the Spanish and possibly sometime in the 1800's.

The carving apparently had been under the rock for decades or centuries, who knows, but it was not weathered or worn, very well preserved. Bud was proud that he found it and he said, "It was fairly easy." Bud believed that the inscription was indicating that treasure was near. The site was not far off the Dona Ana Trail.

Charlie said, "if it was worth a $1,000 to that man, it's worth a $1.000 to us." They covered it back up and soon thereafter, the White Sands Military Police road up on horseback and said, "Are ya'll a part of the Oklahoma group that had been coming in and out?" Bud said, "No, I've never been here before." Charlie said, "I'm a part of it." They were honest but were ordered out.

Bud and Charlie never called or contacted the author of the magazine article to claim the $1,000. Bud said, "We sat on it." It might come in handy someday. They never went back.

What did "Cimarron mean?" "*Cimarron*" is a Spanish word for wild and untamed. It was first recorded in **1840-1850** from Colonial Spanish. "Old Spanish – *cimarra* "brushwood, thicket," from *cim(a)* "peak, summit". [655] Some sources say the word means "bighorn," which are sheep that roam in the Cimarron Mountains in Northeastern New Mexico.

This is an extremely important clue. Bud said it was the start of clues directing one to treasure. It was exactly 25 miles from Victorio Peak. It also may have been a directional clue along the Dona Ana Trail leading to Indian Territory in the Wichita Mountains, to the Cimarron River, and it even could have been directing towards Northern New Mexico.

During the time this word became familiar and used, mid 1800's, the land around Cimarron, New Mexico was being developed. This time period was during Beaubien's land grab to utilize resources on the eastern slopes of the Sangre de Cristos in northeastern New Mexico. Charles Bent, as told earlier, received a quarter of that property to help establish ranches along the Ponil, Vermejo, Cimarron, and Rayado Rivers. When Beaubien died, the land went to his son-in-law, Lucien Maxell who founded the town of Cimarron.

Was the carving "*cimarron*" a clue to the next depository of the Seven Cities of Gold? Was it a clue of ancient treasures? Could it be a clue connecting the Organ Mountains/Victorio Peak, the Wichita Mountains, and Cimarron, New Mexico together? We don't know. So many questions.

Does this tie into Jesse James? Bud believes strongly that Jesse knew Kit Carson well who partnered with Lucien Maxwell. They had both founded Rayado, a community south of Cimarron. Was it Jesse or someone in the KGC that wrote the word "Cimarron" in the Organ Mountains, possibly moving the mined gold to a more secure area? That would be a wild guess, but I believe Jesse knew about it. He was in the Organ Mountains/Victorio Peak, the Cimarron River in Indian Territory, and Cimarron, New Mexico.

In Cimarron, Jesse stayed at the famous Santa Fe Trail hotel, called the St. James Hotel in 1881 under the name of R.H. Howard. This was after the Indian Wars fought near Victorio Peak in 1880. Why was Jesse in Cimarron? Was it on a business or pleasure trip? Bud has knowledge of a KGC deposit in Eagle Nest, the old Elizabethtown site, and Taos which were old western towns during that period near Cimarron. There may have been more locations Bud said. The grandsons of Jesse gave Bud the maps.

What's interesting is that in Howk's treasure list, he included a cache buried at Ojo Caliente ($1 million). [656] This was one of the oldest health resorts in North America, located near the Rio Grande River between Taos and Espanola, New Mexico. The Tewa Nation have a belief that its hot springs pools access the underworld. It is still in operation as a spa resort and many famous people visit there. My husband and I have visited the resort and it is everything it is advertised to be and more. Quite a place.

Not far from Taos is the small town of Chama which hosts one end of the historic Cumbres & Toltec Scenic Railroad. The rails were laid down in 1880 supporting the narrow-gauge train traveling from Antonito, Colorado to Chama, New Mexico. This is another treasure sight that Howk listed called, "Chama River RR Bridge Treasure ($250,000). [657]

Did Jesse's visit in Cimarron have anything to do with gold and treasures of the Knights of the Templar who were the very foundation of the Knights of the Golden Circle?

There is also evidence northwest of Cimarron, high in the mountains, of a very ancient Knights Templar's marker, meaning a carved stone pillar in the shape of an obelisk, sticking out of the ground *33"* high. It is an extremely older stone, not found in the environment from which it was planted and carved with symbols resembling the Knights of the Templar's symbols. It is in a very remote, "hard to get to area" surrounded by other grave markers which appears to be in a small cemetery.

Oddly, way up into the mountains on the Ring Place, within the Maxwell Land Grant, a small settlement established by Timothy Ring, has a mysterious history behind it. He bought the place to raise cattle, but now it belongs to the Philmont Scout Ranch. It is located in the Valle Vidal area that runs parallel with Cimarron Canyon on the northern side which meanders through the northern side of Red River.

("Looking up Caliente Rio at the Hot Springs" – photo by Dana B. Chase taken at the New Mexico History Museum exhibition, Curative Powers: Hot Springs in New Mexico, 1884-1892. Original photo taken by D. B. Chase, Santa Fe, New Mexico)

    The beautiful mountainside holds many tales. In 1844, Beaubien built a cabin close to this mysterious landscape on the Ponil River. "Charles Bent conspired around New Mexico Governor Armijo to ensure a settlement on Ponil Creek." [658] It was granted and became a center for logging and sawmill operations. I feel sure there was also mining going on. Lucien Maxwell, son-in-law of Beaubien's was ambushed on the trail up to the cabin when taking supplies and was injured. He obtained the land after Beaubien died and it was known as the Maxwell Land Grant.

    These men were very familiar with this area and this pillar. Many small communities erupted out of that mountain, Ring, Labelle, Bonito, Dawson, Anchor, Midnite, and Hopewell. There are very few remnants left of these communities, but the stone pillar remains, embedded deep into the soil.

    Another stone pillar was found, pulled out of the ground by a hunter in 1986 from an unknown location in those same mountains and taken to the St. James Hotel to be displayed. A native New Mexican historian, Louis Serna identified the marker in the hotel and has been researching who, what, and why regarding these stone pillars. Who put them there, centuries or thousands of years ago? What was it for? Very fascinating. You can find Mr. Serna's information, his books and videos on this fascinating subject on his website, www.louisserna.com. He has an amazing story and is strongly connected to this land. Ironically, Mr. Serna's mother-in-law, Tessie Maxwell, was a descendant of the famous Lucien Maxwell family. [659]

(On the stone are symbols from King Solomon's Temple. Notice the eight-pointed star which symbolized the star of Venus, the Morning Star)

1800's-1880's
The Apaches

   Bud believes that Father LaRue and his parish moved beyond Organ Mountains and settled near Victorio Peak where they found the spring, thus naming the land, Spirit Springs. The Mescalero Apaches called it their home; land given to them by their Creator. The land and its resources were sacred to the Apaches, but gold was not as important to the Apache as it was to the European settlers who were invading their land.

Supposedly, Father LaRue and his followers worked together with the Apaches and trust was built between the two. Out of the book, "True Tales of the American Southwest," by Howard Bryan, 1998, a man by the name of Maximiano "Max" Madrid, who was a young Spanish boy of 15 years old during the Civil War living in Paraje, New Mexico, saw many Confederate soldiers ride along the Rio Grande. In 1870, when age 23, he was living at the southern base of the San Mateo Mountains, Canada Alamosa later changed to Monticello at the southern edge of the Warm Springs Apache Reservation in the 1870's where he experienced the hostile Apaches.

Madrid stated that the Apaches had Indian sentries posted on the high peaks and trails surrounding Victorio Peak. No one could ever penetrate their boundary or would face grave consequences. Chief Victorio came down to their village and said that if the Spanish people would leave the Apaches alone, and not help the American soldiers, he would not bother them, but if they did support the soldiers, Victorio would come and destroy the town. He advised the villagers to wear something on their hats to identify themselves as non-threatening Spanish villagers and they would be left alone.

There were many incidents of raids and murders by the Apaches who stood strong in their promises. They stole many items from soldiers, settlers, and concealed them in Victorio Peak. Mr. Madrid stated that his godfather who spoke Apache and spent time with them described Victorio's secret hiding place. They scooped out on the mountain peak a deep hole and covered the hole with timbers, dirt, set fire and rode their horses back and forth over the spot to cover all trace of the secret entrance.

But one thought of mine was a possibility that the Apaches attacked Father LaRue, but Bud is positive it was the Spaniards who attacked Father LaRue. After the massacre of Father LaRue and his parishioners, the Apaches may have buried the dead within the tomb of Victorio Peak. Bud stated that there were lots of skeletons of women and children and another man, close to the insides of the peak claiming to be their priest.

There were numerous gold mines in that area. In Dona Ana County alone where the two mountain ranges are located, there are 163 mines. There is also a Merrimac Mine and Mormon Mine in this county.

The town of Dona Ana was founded on the eastern bank of the Rio Grande, a few miles to the northwest of Las Cruces. The town was started in 1839 by settlers from El Paso. Its included on the Dona Ana Bend Colony tract.

This was about the time that settlers came into the Apache territory as well as explorers and trappers. Earlier, they had put up with the Spanish, slave traders, and other foreigners, but more were coming of a different breed. This did not set well with the Apaches and they were seeing the white settlers abuse and rape the land.

Chief Victorio, born in Chihuahua, Mexico sometime around 1825, was chief of the Warm Springs band of the Tchihendeh, a division of the central Apaches. They lived in their ancestral homeland for centuries. The Hembrillo Basin was one of their strongholds and possibly a place they were guarding because of its value.

After the Civil War, more people began moving westward. The Confederate population lost all their homes and many resources were confiscated. Many relocated to Texas, New Mexico, and Mexico.

The corrupt Indian Affairs department did not keep their promises to the Native Americans and many treaties were broken. The Apaches as well as other Native Americans were forced off their land and removed to reservations. This spurred on the Indian Wars with Apache leaders like Geronimo, Cochise, Nana, and Chief Victorio.

Raids were common for the Apaches. It was a tradition that began with their ancient people in the raiding parties which devoured priceless items, clothing, jewels, etc. from the Spanish Conquistadors. In the l880's, raids on white settlers began to pick up as well as raids on caravans of wagons, mule trains, and stagecoaches. Shrewd white traders would trade guns for gold with the Apaches, while the Apaches learned great marksmanship and the art of guerrilla warfare from them. There were a lot of trade secrets passed amongst them by men who were interested in their gold.

1864-1867
General Shelby, Quantrill, Jesse, and Dr. Frank James, and the Guerillas in Mexico

After the war, the KGC were treasure hunters. Where was the treasure? The answer, south of the border. Bud said that the KGC did business with the Indians. They would give them money, goods, and guns for gold to refinance the 2nd Civil War. Who was the comptroller of the KGC? JJ of course. In Howk's book, "Jesse James and the Lost Cause", Jesse told Howk about the Knights of the Golden Circle, "The treasurer and comptroller, who had sole and complete custody of all gold and silver bullion, money, jewels and taxations, was one, one, and one man only…that man was myself…yes me, Jesse Woodson James!"

"We manipulated a lot of politics and dodges and subterfuges, hoaxes, and double talk. All we did was not accomplished overnight either. We had to be extra careful in order to secretly carry on these activities and remain uncaught. We went armed at all times. Being exceptionally broad-shouldered, I could carry several short-barreled pistols with ease, and sometimes wear a steel vest or even chain mail." [660]

During the Civil War when America was split and in utter chaos, Mexico too had many divisive powers seeking control. The fight was between the liberal and the conservative population, but also foreign powers. The country was being led by a non-elected President Benito Juarez, supported by liberals. Juarez put a strain on his fellow citizens by confiscating property, putting heavy restrictions on church attendance, and weakened the country by losing control of the mounting debts owed to foreign governments. The foreign creditors who provided financial support in past wars wanted to be paid, but Mexico had suspended payment due to their declining economy. Foreign troops began occupying the region, such as Spain, Britain, and France waiting for their chance to overtake the country and promote a regime change. They also had their eye on America who was at its weakest point during the Civil War.

The emperor of France, Napoleon III needed a "front man" to use to rule over Mexico with the discretion of France. Napoleon III invited Maximillian of Austria to rule over Mexico, with the support of conservatives, moderate liberals, natives of Mexico, and the ever-present French troops. Maximillian became Emperor of Mexico in 1864 and took his oath seriously. He did not sway to the desires of the French, but to the Mexican people. The only problem was that the United States recognized Juarez as the legal leader of Mexico, not Maximillian, but could not intervene in this takeover because of the American Civil War in progress.

After the American Civil War in 1865, the U.S. began supplying support and aid to Juarez's forces. Many American volunteers joined Juarez' Mexican troops, while the remaining dye-hard ex-Confederate soldiers and outlaws chose Maximillian's side. *General Joseph O. Shelby* and approximately 2,000 ex-confederate men went to Mexico to fight alongside the French troops and Maximillian's followers. *General Sterling Price* also went. They established a colony in Vera Cruz and named it Carlotta after Maximillian's wife.

The fight did not last long. The French troops began to withdraw, and sickness, smallpox, malnutrition, and dysentery spread far and wide. Shelby got word to Quantrill, who was still alive, that they needed help to retreat from Mexico.

Per Howk who stated that Jesse told him that Quantrill gathered some of his finest men in the KGC, Quantrills' words expressed in Oak Grove, Louisiana, "I first want men who do not fear death, I want men who have the skills to bring out Shelby's troops, I want seasoned rear-guard fighters who will turn the rivers of Mexico into blood if need be. There is no assurance any of us will ever get back across the Rio Grande alive. Some of you may be tortured by Benito Juarez' fanatics. All of us may and probably will suffer from the tortures of the damned. I want the best 100 men that the South can muster for this mission." [661]

Jesse, chosen as the joint commander for the mission, Quantrill and 96 other men went to help them get out. They picked four doctors for the mission for their shooting ability and skills in doctoring. Howk believed that Jesse's (supposedly) brother, Dr. Sylvester Franklin James went along. Bud believed that Dr. Robert Franklin James of Sardis went. This was before he became a doctor. Dr. Frank as he was called, would have been just shy of 20 years old and Jesse one year older. Dr. Frank (Robert Franklin James) was a part of the KGC's Inner Circle. He was a cousin of theirs who was always there to patch the boys up. Dr. Frank took quinine to the men and nursed them back to health. This story is validated with another man's descendants. Josiah Dudley Doak. He was born around 1830 in Doaksville, Oklahoma in the Choctaw Nation. His father, Josiah Stuart Doak established the trading post there in the early 1820's. The post was near Fort Towson for protection, and Doaksville became the largest town in Indian Territory by 1850 in the Choctaw Nation.

Josiah Dudley Doak was living in Collin County, Texas when the Civil War broke out and had been sheriff between 1858-1860. There are no solid records of his service in the war, but with family statements, he did support the Confederacy. He was noted in the Dallas Weekly Herald, May 13, 1863, that he was in charge of 250 mules from Mexico, designed for General William Steele's Division of the army in the Indian Nation. What else was tacked onto the mule train? Interesting note: Steele was in the 7th Texas Cavalry and his first assignment was leading the Confederate forces in *Mesilla* during the New Mexico Campaign in 1862.

Dudley's family records also indicate that he fought with Maximillian and smuggled quinine to and from Mexico during the war. Quinine was a rare commodity and needed to cure malaria and other type of illnesses. Both the North and South were struggling to secure it. There were those who smuggled it in doll's heads or animal intestines.

Doak acquired gold for his service but ended up trading it in for Confederate dollars which was of no use to him after the war. Doak's brother, Alexander Doak married the beautiful Mary Ellen Anderson, sister to Bloody Bill.

Bud said that Jesse, Frank, and Dr. Frank James were all down in Mexico to help Maximillian. After caring for and doctoring the sick, Jesse and Maximillian developed a strong bond. Jesse's courage, intelligence, and ambition impressed Maximillian and he had gained his trust.

Maxmillian was very protective of his wife, Carlotta, and the treasure he had accumulated from his beloved Austria and Mexico, which was more likely the treasure of the ancient Aztecs. He was entrusted with the House of Hapsburg crowns of jewels. The emperor began seeing the writing on the wall, and knew his time was short.

Jesse and some of the finest, strongest men out of Shelby's unit, around 50 were given the honor to help preserve and protect Maximillian, his wife, and the treasure. The next part is unclear, but Carlotta went to Europe to persuade men who had supported Maximillian in the past to help him. During this time, Jesse and the 50 men dressed in disguise, possibly as Mexican peasants or Indian servants came out of Mexico with 11-12 carettas of gold and treasure. They had a running gun battle with the Mexican militia. One story state that they had to retrieve some of the treasure that was secretly buried. A portion of it was taken to a mountain hideout. Was this Victorio Peak?

Another story relates that the Apaches targeted Maximillian's caravan treasures. It was lost. An estimated 28-billion-dollar treasure. There is no evidence that the Apache's overtook Jesse and his men, quite the contrary. The Apaches had to have worked together with Jesse to secure these treasures or Jesse and his men would have all been dead. It is documented that the Yaquis Indians who were tied with the Apaches were also good friends of Jesse.

In Howk's book, "Jesse James and the Lost Cause," he states Jesse said, "Pancho Villa made me personally known and acquainted with the powerful Yaquis Indians of the interior. Bucky O'Neil and myself were said to have been then, and even today, the only white men to ever penetrate into the inner Yaquis Indian country and come out alive and live to tell it. I still count them today as the most lovable and loyal, friendly Indians that I ever knew." [662]

Maximillian was captured and later executed in a firing squad by the restored Republican government in 1867. There are those who believe Maximillian was not executed and had entered a secret agreement with Juarez. He was thought to have lived in exile in El Salvador as Justo Armas until 1936. But what Howk revealed that Jesse told him was that Maximillian wasn't dead. One of the Indian servants saw his arm move after the execution. They asked if they could bury him. They took him out in a cart.

Bud said that he has documents with Jesse saying he brought the Mexican emperor and "the wealth of two nations back with us."

According to J. Frank Dalton's story, told by Howk, Maximillian was taken to Livingston, Texas, the Big Thicket, to an Indian Reservation by Jesse and Dr. Frank James. He was barely hanging on. Dr. James saved Maximillian's life. He recovered fully and took on the name of John Maxey/Maxie and went into the lumber business in East Texas, a place where he would be protected as well as Jesse.

In a letter from Howk written to Betty Lou Kilgore in 1979, Howk wrote that Maximillian "suffered extreme pain as a result of several chest bullet wounds." Howk had seen him on several occasions.

Jesse traveled overseas and hired a double to play the role of Carlotta, who was either in prison or a mental institution, and swept the real Carlotta away from her turmoil and returned her back to her husband in Texas.

Bud said that Maximillian paid the KGC 12.5 million dollars in gold for their deliverance, and a fair sum of 5 million to Jesse.

Howk wrote in the letter to Betty Lou Kilgore that the James boys returned to him (Maxmillian) every portion of his Crown, jewels, and bullion. Alexander Franklin James had a hand in it as did Jesse Woodson James.

The story goes, because of the removal of Maximillian and the treasure, the Rothschilds put up a $50,000 bounty on Jesse and $25,000 on the other men who helped.

1879-1880
War

After this huge endeavor, Jesse settled back into his normal life, or what most people would call living as a vagabond, but I don't think he was idle; never was. He had a lot of work ahead. Bud found evidence that he was involved in robberies, the U.S. Army, the Texas Rangers, and marshaling.

The west was still not settled by no means. The Federal Government was flushing out the Southern way of life and the Native American lifestyle. The government ordered the Apaches to move to the reservations, but they refused to leave and made the Hembrillo Basin their stronghold. Apache chiefs said, "if you will just leave us alone and let us live in our homeland, we will show you more gold than you would ever know existed, more gold than the great white father in Washington has."

A treaty was agreed between Victorio's tribe and the government allowing them to remain on this land. But when a rich vein of gold was discovered, the treaty was broken in 1878.

This again raised Victorio's fury, placing it upon the white settlers, wagon trains, mail coaches, and churches. It is also noted that he took prisoners from New Mexico and Texas to the Hembrillo Basin and subjected them to extensive torture before killing them, many who were searching for gold.

It took many rounds of skirmishes and chases by the 6th, 9th, and 10th U.S. Cavalry, the Buffalo Soldiers, 15th U.S. infantry, the Texas Rangers, and the Mexican Army to finally catch up to Victorio. The warrior finally gave up his fight and died during his last battle with the Mexican Army in October 1880. The movie "Buffalo Soldiers" made in 1997 was an excellent movie and brought to life the sheer bravery of the Buffalo Soldiers who fought against this brave warrior and his people.

The cavity of Victorio Peak, which the Apaches exclusively protected was never discovered, never disturbed until 57 years later.

1937
The Discovery
Victorio Peak (Solidad Peak)

Fifty-seven years after Chief Victorio was defeated and forced off his sacred mountains, a man had gained significant information about the legend of gold near the Rio Grande that piqued his interest. Milton Ernest "Doc" Noss came from the beautiful valley of Taloga, Oklahoma that is nestled within the horseshoe bend of the Canadian River. The Daltons as well as other famous outlaws were noted as having filed on lots in Taloga, using aliases.

Noss was known as a treasure hunter. He was ¾ Cheyenne. He would later be tagged with the nickname or alias of *Tom Starr*. Ironically, the real Tom Starr who died in 1890 in Indian Territory was Belle Starr's father-in-law. She was married to Sam Starr, his son. He was a Cherokee outlaw who was previously a guerilla in the Civil War under General Stand Watie. He was peddling whiskey into Indian Territory, and was accused of murder, rustling, and counterfeiting by March 1871. He was also known to be a member of the James Gang.

Doc Noss' grandson said Doc obtained important information in Oklahoma on a specific site for a large treasure in New Mexico. The story he told his wife was that they would become rich. He packed up his small family and headed to Santa Fe by 1934 and was listing himself as a Chiropodist and Foot Specialist. A newspaper article stated that he came from Oklahoma City where he had his office for a number of years. [663]

By 1940, they had moved to Hot Springs, Sierra County, New Mexico in which is now called Truth or Consequences.

Doc Noss did a little treasure hunting there, possibly discovering a cache of gold in the Caballo Mountains, but somehow, he ventured southwest into the area of Victorio Peak in the Fall of 1937. He and his wife Ova went on a deer hunting trip with several couples in the Hembrillo Basin. The men went out, while the women stayed in the camp near an old rock cabin, some believe it was remnants of a rock fort.

While hunting, Doc came up on a natural spring at the bottom edge of Victorio Peak and knew that if he climbed to the top, he would be able to see the deer that would be drawn to the natural spring. Reaching the peak, he sat down on a rock and felt cold air hit his leg. He looked down amongst the rocks and saw an opening.

He spied an old rustic ladder made from wood going down in a shaft. He went down the ladder as far as he could go and came out, elated on what he had found. He got back to camp and after supper, he called it a night. While in bed, he told his wife, Ova that he had found what he was looking for.

Several days later, they went back to the peak and had what they needed for Doc to go further down. Inside, there were fissures and tunnels and huge caverns containing nearly 16,000 bars of gold. There were 5 completely different sets of ingots, meaning they were produced in other areas and in many different periods of history. It was a huge depository, one of the biggest in the United States. It appears that many groups of people from various periods of time and cultures used the mountain for safekeeping of prized possessions, and as Bud says, Jesse James added to it.

There were jewels, chests of coins, swords, Conquistador armor, statues, chalices, gold crosses and other religious artifacts, crowns, jewelry, ancient antiquities and artifacts, part of a stagecoach, a Wells Fargo chest, Wells Fargo bags, packsaddles, letters, and of course gold; lots of it. This was huge. There were items that provided clues of Maximillian's treasure, such as an oval shaped box with the name of "Carlotta" stamped on the top and a 7.5 lb. gold crown with 243 diamonds and one pigeon blood ruby.

The most horrific find in the peak, were 79 skeletons, chained to posts. Other reports from the Noss family stated that there was a skeleton of a priest. Could this be Father LaRue? Bud's research also identified skeletons of women and children. Some skeletons still had hair and rotted clothing against their barren bones.

The shock of finding so much death in the peak's cavity caused a portion of Doc Noss' hair to turn white.

Could this change the story that was passed down about Father LaRue? Were they all hiding in the peak when the Spanish soldiers came, and a sudden landslide caused the peak to become a tomb? Were they buried within Victorio Peak by the Apache?

Were the skeletons chained to posts be the slaves of Montezuma, who traveled with the Aztecs into the United States to hide his gold from Cortes and then later were used as human sacrifices to guard the gold? Were they the victims of Chief Victorio's torture? So many unanswered questions.

Were the treasures from Cortes, the Incas from Peru, the Aztecs, Spaniards, Mexicans, Apaches, Jesuits, the Catholic Church, the lost treasure of Maximilian, or the one and only, Jesse James?

The answers could be found in all of the above. One thing is for sure, it was heavily guarded and monitored.

Doc Noss and Ova kept to themselves and later filed a claim on Victorio Peak and the mining rights in the state of New Mexico. Later they filed a treasure trove claim. They worked day and night retrieving items out of the mountain.

The progress came to a halt when Doc hired a mining engineer to help him remove the huge boulder that was blocking the entry way from the top which only allowed a very small crevice to slide through to reach the bottom. The idea failed when the engineer used too much dynamite and the entry was completely blocked.

Doc and Ova continued to work, hauling out the debris that the explosion caused, one five-gallon bucket at a time.

When World War II hit, things slowed down a bit and word was leaking out. Per Doc's grandson, Doc went missing around 1947-48 and was gone for weeks and then showed up on his front porch in a daze with the soles of his feet burnt to a crisp. Someone had kidnapped and tortured him into telling them where the gold was. This form of torture was used on Jesse Woodson James and his son, Jesse Cole James.

Doc got state and federal officials to come to Victorio Peak to validate his claim. They did and the race was on. New Mexico was in favor of the Noss', but the federal government, especially the military believed it should be in the hands of the government per the Gold Reserve Act of 1934 signed by President Franklin D. Roosevelt in January 1934, transferring ownership of all monetary gold in the United States to the US Treasury and prohibiting banking institutions from redeeming dollars for gold.

This caused Doc Noss to hide most of his recovered items.

Doc disappeared again in 1949, and later returned with a new wife, and business partner he picked up by the name of Charlie Ryan. The fear of conspiracy against Noss and losing his fortune to his partner, drove Doc to relocate the gold. Him and a friend, Tony Jolley buried 110 bars in various places in the desert.

When his partner felt deceived, he became enraged and Charlie Ryan picked up a gun and shot Doc in the back of the head and killed Doc Noss as he was running to his vehicle on March 5, 1949. Ryan was acquitted of murder on the grounds of self-defense????

Ova and her family picked up the pieces and continued what Doc Noss started. They worked the peak, but Ova was physically removed from Victorio Peak in 1955. The United States Army at the White Sands Military Base wanted to expand their territory due to the direction the army was heading in the Military Industrial Complex in which President Eisenhower warned about in 1961 in his farewell speech and shared his concern with President-Elect Kennedy.

The year 1961 was John F. Kennedy's first year of presidency. He was kept extremely busy with foreign affairs and it is unknown what he knew about Victorio Peak, but things began to look very dim for Ova Noss. A portion of the military were allowing military personnel and civilians to enter the area and penetrate the peak to find the treasures. Eyewitness accounts support heavy equipment, many workers and large trucks began to overtake the landscape, and new roadways around the peak were being constructed.

It was noted that a man by the name of Gene Erwin from Texas was a brother-in-law to Captain Orby Swanner, who was executive assistant to the provost marshal at White Sands in 1961. Swanner confided in Erwin about the removement of close to 300 million dollars' worth of gold from the peak. Swanner had left evidence in the peak that he was there. He wrote an inscription upon one of the walls, his name, Captain Orby Swanner, 7 October 1961, including his serial number. Of course, Swanner swore Erwin to secrecy and it was never spoken about again.

Many people believe and have written that Swanner was murdered by an unknown poison. Several men who were connected to this operation died unexpectedly or lost their military status and service records.

One hunter in the area signed an affidavit reporting that he saw men loading three old wooden containers which had to be reinforced with steel bands so the chests would not fall apart in transport. It appeared that the Dept. of Treasury and the Army were removing many items out of the peak at a lower elevation.

Ova Noss was allowed back in the area to be able to work on the peak for 60 days in 1963, but it was cut short to 10 days.

In the summer of 1963, some very interesting facts come together that is not just coincidence. President John F. Kennedy was serving in his third year and Lyndon B. Johnson was his vice president.

June 4, 1963, President John F. Kennedy signed the Executive Order 11110. This order would return to the U.S. government, the power to issue currency, without loans from the Federal Reserve with high interest. It would give the Treasury the power to issue silver certificates against any silver bullion in the Treasury. The silver backed currency of nearly 4.3 billion dollars in U.S. notes went into circulation. If enough of the silver certificates were to come into circulation, they would have eliminated the demand for Federal Reserve notes which is not backed by anything. Debt would have been paid off rather quickly. President Kennedy knew this was the right thing to do because he knew that the most successful vehicles used to drive up debt was war and the creation of money by a privately owned central bank.

The very next day, June 5, 1963, President Kennedy was at White Sands Missile Range, thanking all military forces and NASA connected to White Sands for working in the field of defense, securing and strengthening America. This was eight months after the Cuban Missile Crisis.

This was the first time any U.S. president ever stepped foot on the White Sands Missile Base. Several books and magazines relate that on that trip, Kennedy and Johnson were taken to Victorio Peak and were shown the treasures and the gold bars. John Clarence and Tom Whittle, co-authors of "The Gold House Trilogy" writes about the evidence they uncovered on this subject matter. Clarence interviewed a former CIA agent who served President Kennedy during this visit to White Sands. The agent confirmed that the president and vice president visited the peak and that Kennedy wasn't "too elated" over the gold, but more elated with the artifacts in the cave.

President Kennedy was briefed about the gold and treasures before the trip and must have been informed of the various cultures and periods of time that these items were produced in.

The speech Kennedy made at White Sands indicates his knowledge of that part of the world, southern New Mexico as "an ancient part of the United States, settled before all the rest." What he discovered or was made aware of, would change history.

Bud and several people of the media learned that Ova Noss had a secret meeting set up with President Kennedy in Denver after his trip to Dallas in November 1963. They were to meet at the Brown Hotel. One author, Jeremy Kuzmarov wrote an article, "Did Richard Nixon Secretly Steal 36.5 Tons of Gold Bullion from U.S. Army Base While He Was Telling America, "I Am Not A Crook?", November 3, 2022 on the covertactionmagazine.com website; claiming he has spoken to many witnesses who stated that the meeting was supposed to be with President Kennedy's brother

Attorney General Robert Kennedy who was planning to take custody of the Noss' gold and finally resolve ownership. After the tragedy in Dallas, the meeting was cancelled. [664]

The same article, which also directs you to the book, "The Noss Gold" by John Clarence and "The Gold House", by John Clarence and Tom Whittle, states that Lyndon Johnson was seen many times at Victorio Peak after he became president and pulled out many, many bars of gold and treasure and had them flown to his ranch in Chihuahua, Mexico and then on to Canada. The article is very interesting and mentions the relationship that Johnson had with Billie Sol Estes, whose name comes up quite frequently throughout this story and throughout this book.

Strangely, Victorio Peak was mentioned again in the Watergate hearings. Attorney F. Lee Bailey's name was mentioned when the question was asked of White House Counsel, John Dean if there were any irregularities in the Nixon Whitehouse. Dean stated that "Mr. Bailey had a client who had an enormous amount of gold and would like to make an arrangement, where the gold could be turned over to the government without the individual being prosecuted for holding the gold."

There were close to 50 clients who were represented by Bailey regarding Victorio Peak, but none were revealed. One of them was believed to be Nixon.

The publicity regarding the gold in Victorio Peak brought up in the hearings, perked up the ears of gold lovers across the country to pursue a piece of this pie. The army allowed all sorts of groups, claiming to rightfully own a part of the mountain, including the Noss family, to come and look for the lost treasure.

Groups and individuals along with their lawyers took up the invitation and came out to dig, observe, and take part in this opportunity. The year was 1977. The groups and individuals consisted of the Apache Tribe, the Noss Family, and of all people, Howk or as he called himself Jesse Lee James III. Howk claimed some of the treasure was Jesses' and he was rightfully his heir. Howk must have had extensive knowledge from Jesse on this incredible story and his involvement.

It was a circus with many newspaper reporters, including Dan Rather from the show "60 minutes". A surprise appearance of Howk being interviewed by Rather was televised at the Peak. The outcome proved unsatisfactory to all claimants. Nothing was found.

Ova died two years later in 1979 and her grandson, Terry Delonas was given the torch to carry and proudly he did. He went to Washington in 1988 with a 150-page petition asking for one more chance. Congress allowed him that chance by granting the army permission to issue the Noss Family Partnership a license to look for the treasure.

They were restricted in their process. During this period, in the early 90's, (1990-1995) and while they were involved in this new hunt, Terry Delonas and Bud's friend, Tom Jones who lived south of Weatherford, Texas on the Brazos River called Bud one day. Jones was a dowser and was helping Terry Delonas and the Noss family with this hunt along with many avid supporters of Terry with equipment, miners, engineers, and scientists. Terry and Tom asked Bud several questions on signs, symbols, and carvings they had found at Victorio Peak. Their description of the symbols fit perfectly with the KGC code system and the codes Bud found himself near there. One question was about the "Bloody Hands" that were found at the lower portion of the outside of the peak about a ½ mile from the peak itself. Bud knew right away that it was a KGC symbol, and possibly was an earlier Indian symbol found at many treasure sites. The red hand (bloody hand) meant danger, possibly a booby trap. A black hand means it is safe.

There was indeed evidence that Jesse was at the peak, including several symbols carved in rock by the KGC. Jesse added money/gold to Victorio Peak to hold for the time of the Second Civil War.

Both Terry and Tom wanted Bud to join in the search of the gold and treasure in Victorio Peak, so that they could be enlightened with Bud's knowledge of any connections to clandestine activities, the KGC, and Jesse. Bud was the right man who could help them in solving this mystery and guide them into the right direction. It was a big deal as Bud has always said.

Bud was never able to go to Victorio Peak. The military base shut them down when they began to find human bones in the mountain and near to the treasure cavern itself. An excellent documentary done so tastefully well, by Alex Alonso, tells the tale of the Noss family and his own incredible journey with them during the 90's hunt. The documentary is "Gold, Lies & Videotape" on the Discovery Channel aired in 2023. You can watch it on Amazon Prime Video.

Was this the biggest heist in American history? Were the bad players in the government, secret societies and Jesse James involved? You better believe it.

> "You make friends doing this and that's a treasure in itself."
>
> -Bud Hardcastle

Chapter Thirty-Four: Dropping Nuggets of Gold

Jesse never led Ola into thinking that he had treasure hidden. Ola didn't think Jesse had one red cent. She was curious though and asked him the question. "Why is it that when your name is mentioned, people immediately think of you having money buried from by gone days?" Jesse said, "Oh people say and imagine a lot of things and don't know what they're talking about." [665]

Ola said, "Old Howk, R.E. James and others are always talking about the Jesse James buried treasure, looking for it and digging for it." He gave the same reply he had given that day in the hospital, which was "Hell yes, they think me and Frank didn't have a damn thing to do but go rob banks and trains and bury the money so some of them could come along later and dig it up. Hell! Just let them go on and dig their damn fool heads off. They ain't gonna find a damn thing. Because there ain't nothing to find." [666]

In the St. Louis Post-Dispatch, November 27, 1949, "Still Insists He's Jesse James," words directly spoken by J. Frank Dalton, "Only thing I'm sorry about is that there's so many ignorant people in the world. And people still trying to dig up the money I buried. God-a-mighty." He chuckled and closed his eyes. "Oh, I got a little money buried." He said sleepily. But not where they're going to find it." And with a cagey smile on his face, he seemed to fall asleep. Comfortable in his secret knowledge of their whereabouts." This was in the end of 1949. He would pass, less than 21 months later.

So, what did Jesse leave us? Plenty. Bud, for nearly 45 years followed Jesse's path, the people he encountered and trusted, uncovering many hidden secrets that Jesse protected. He left us clues everywhere. Clues are throughout this book. Bud is freeing up some of his knowledge on symbols, carvings, directional guides, and maps that he has held close to himself for years. Many have slipped through his lips and many have been taken by bamboozlement. Bud said his special book that revealed a lot of the meaning of the codes was stolen from him. He knows who it was but wouldn't say.

Bud is willing to share these things to help the treasure hunters who are just getting started in the business. Bud said he's getting a little too old to continue to do this sort of thing and he is passing the baton to the younger generation of treasure hunters. There is still a lot of gold out there and are still a lot of secrets Bud is not willing to let go. He said, "You can't just give your information away."

From the Lawton Constitution, May 19, 1948, "Jesse declares that there still are many of those caches untouched by human hands since they were buried years ago, but he is an old man and money no longer means anything to him. Besides, too much blood has been spilled already over the inglorious gold which sets the very blood of mankind racing with greed. Leave it for the individuals who are capable of working out its puzzles and solving the secrets of nature's most severe problems, Jesse confides. Men like Joe Hunter."

Supposedly, Jesse was impressed by Joe Hunter, but little did Hunter know that Jesse was ready to kill him until he realized during their first meeting, that Hunter didn't know as much as he thought he did. Jesse spared his life. That may seem very harsh to some, but you got to realize Jesse worked all his life in accumulating wealth for the south and there were and still are secrets that had to be continually guarded. If Jesse was that protective of the Wichita Mountains and Buzzard Roost, you know that it was something huge.

After 1901, miners, treasure hunters, settlers began moving into Indian Territory.

We learned a lot about Joe Hunter and his search for Jesse's treasures, but we will dig a little deeper into this matter. As Bud always said, things just happened, like they were supposed to happen for a reason. He was talking one day to a young man in the restaurant and Bud began speaking of Joe Hunter. This young man said, "Well Bud, that's my grandfather." What do you know, this young man's name was Emmett Ward and he only lived a few miles away from Purcell. They had a great talk. Emmett now comes into the restaurant quite often.

Emmett helped Bud on a lot of questions he had. The maps that Joe had, went to his son, Kenneth who sold them to Ray Pack, a pharmacist in Ada. Ray purchased them at a price of $300 per Emmett. Quite a deal wouldn't you say. Bud also had the help of Archie Penick who was with Joe during the hunts. Bud also credits the help of author, Steve Wilson who he has spoken to several times and refers to his fantastic treasure book, "Oklahoma Treasure and Treasure Tales."

Bud met Steve Wilson at a Treasure Hunting meeting in Marlow, Oklahoma. He knew the work Bud had done.

While I was doing my research on my outlaw uncle, before I met Bud, I had found this very same book in Larry McMurtry's bookstore in Archer City, Texas. It was in McMurtry's vast collection within miles and miles of books that were cataloged and sitting on shelves that towered to the ceiling in three different buildings. That book, just jumped out at me, not really understanding the importance of it until I met Bud. It is a wealth of information.

Bud learned from Emmett that Jesse visited Joe Hunter's home and Joe Hunter visited him in Lawton, Oklahoma. There is a short clip on Youtube.com, "J. Frank Dalton – 1948," regarding this visit with Jesse and the brass bucket Hunter found that had several valuable items inside and the contract signed by Jesse and his inner circle.

Joe Hunter was a Mason and was in tune with the historic value of the maps and codes he received from this mysterious "Cook" character. This man had to of been one of Jesse's inner circle members to know what the maps and codes meant and had to of been there when the treasure was buried. The year that this man appeared was in 1932, admitting that he had helped bury the brass bucket 62 years ago, which would place the timeline when the bucket was buried in 1870, but the contract on the brass bucket was dated 1876.

Howk was very suspicious of Hunter and the way he obtained the maps. In a letter to Betty Lou Kilgore dated September 18, 1979, Howk believed a most gruesome story which may or may not be true. Howk believed the maps were obtained through torture among Jesse's old Black and Indian friends. He tells of murder and bobby traps that killed some of Hunter's treasure seekers. One in particular accident occurred at the Camel and the Straw cave. Howk said, "JWJ got revenge at that place." Now, I don't know if this was true. It may have been fabricated by Howk due to jealously of Hunter, just as he was of Ola Everhard and Rudy Turilli.

What's raising a flag here is that the Camel and Straw Cave is related somehow to a depository in Oklahoma. Howk drew a map showing two dead men who died in a booby trap there.

With the maps, Joe Hunter sought help from Herbert Penick and his son, Archie Penick. They began to hunt. Joe abandoned his job and his family life and spent his time searching for this treasure.

An exciting breakthrough occurred when a woman, living in the area around Cement, Oklahoma reported to a newspaper that she had found a rock with carvings that years ago a man was looking for. The stone had been buried to the southwest of Buzzard Roost which was on her property. There were men working on her place and they dug it up. She knew that was what Frank James was looking for. Mrs. Hedlund was interviewed by the newspaper and her story went out everywhere.

Hunter immediately met Mrs. Belle Hedlund (born in 1872) who had the strange rock now in her possession. She told the story when she was in her 30's, just shy of Oklahoma statehood when an odd fellow appeared and asked for her to show him the "old spring." This was an area where he and some other fellows camped. She took him there and he said that if this is the right place, this is Jesse's kitchen, pointing to a rock and under the rock was a spoon. He told her he was Frank James.

This was a fantastic find for Joe Hunter. The stone had a lot of markers and directional points. Carved into the stone was a profile of a man's head who had a pointed goatee. The lapel of his coat was pointed. It had a cross at the top, with numbers and letters and the date 1867. On the man's ear, it appeared to be a triangle-shaped earring. Bud said that the hole in the ear, with the earring dangling represented the hole in Buzzard's Roost, not the prominent hole in the massive mound that juts out of the landscape, but a smaller one on the side of the mound. In that hole was found the tea kettle which I believe was represented by the triangle.

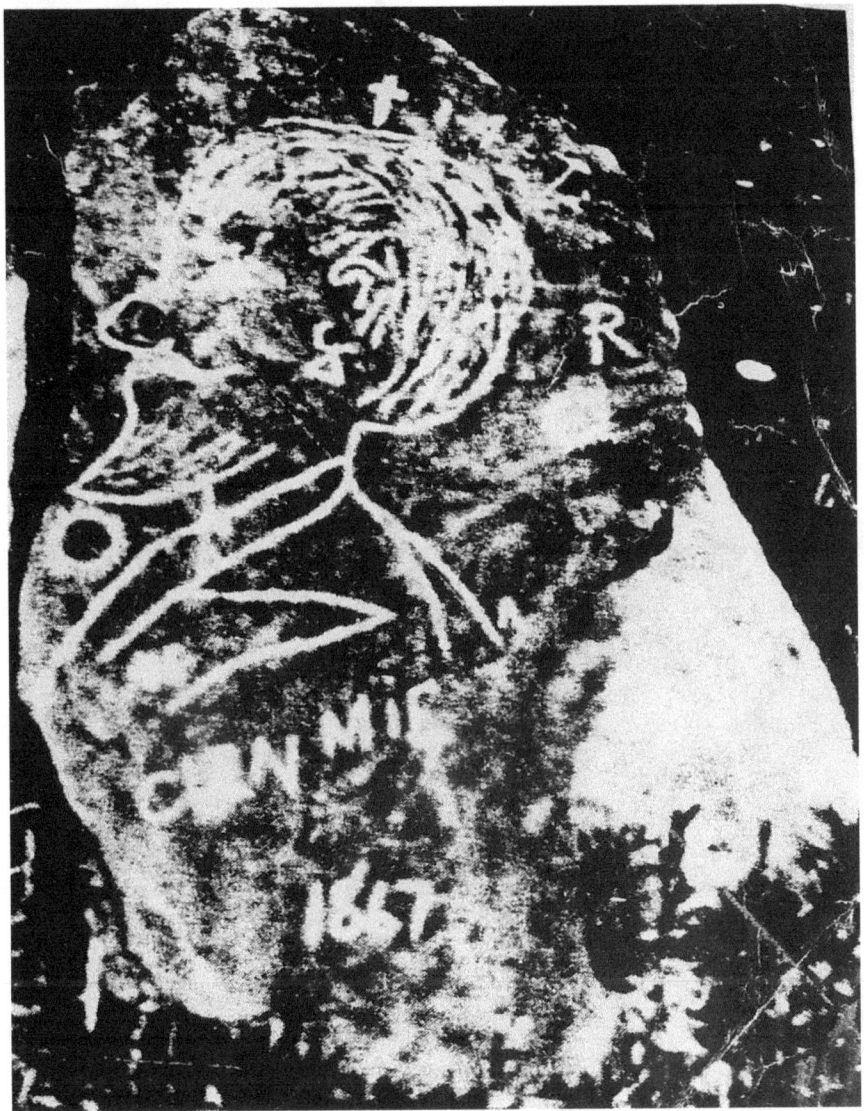

(Carved gentleman in the rock)

Bud said, there was a rock on the top of Buzzard Roost, in the same shape of the beard, pointing east. It was pointing to where Frank James dug up the $6,000.

When Bud took me to Buzzard Roost, my mouth just dropped. Looking at it, from the base, it does appear to be a buzzard resting on its nest. There was a large hole where the buzzard's mouth was, just below the prominent beak. Bud called it the "all-seeing eye." The place was so surreal and to make it even more spectacular, buzzards were flying all around there.

(Buzzard Roost)

Bud showed me exactly where Joe Hunter found the cast iron tea kettle. It wasn't buried but placed deep within a cavity of the old buzzard. Archie Penick was with Joe Hunter when it was found, and he told Bud this story.

Bud located Archie Penick, close to Wagoner, Oklahoma. He told Bud that they were on the north side of Buzzard Roost on the side of the mound, in a very, very small cave that you had to bend over to get into, close to the top. There was a ledge you could stand on which had some carvings on it to indicate "at or close by." They were walking and a pebble rolled from under their feet and went through a crevice. They heard "ping" and knew it hit metal. Bingo, they found the kettle.

They worked hard getting it out. The lid was stuck and had rusted over. Inside was a carved copper sheet map, gold coins, a 1841 U.S. penny, a French five-franc piece with a picture of Napoleon, engraved on it was "Dieu Protégé La France, 1811, a ring, 4 small rocks, a star, and a pocket watch. Everything inside had a special meaning. Some believe there were actually 4 copper sheet maps. Bud said one was the "Grave is a Witness" map, one was the Wapanucka site, and one was a site outside of Altus, Oklahoma.

The penny dated 1841 was very significant. It was larger than a normal penny of today's standard but was worn by KGC members. Also, the 5-pointed star was also an insignia of the KGC.

The watch was quite interesting. Bud said, "It was a witness of who it belongs to." Bud got to hold the watch. He was 150 yards from Buzzard Roost when he met up with Mark Pack, who now owns the watch and Monte Snider. Bud knew what the inscription should say on the watch, and sure enough, it was the genuine watch found.

(The watch out of the tea kettle from Buzzard Roost. Bud, Mark Pack and Monte Snider)

The inscription on the watch indicated it was the 3400th manufactured by the New York Watch Company of Springfield, Massachusetts. The name Theo E. Studley was engraved on it.

Searching for information on this man, we find he was born in Worcester, Massachusetts in 1831 and died in New York in 1908. Before the Civil War, he lived in New York and was a "Rubber Dealer/Merchant." It's quite interesting to find an IRS Tax Assessment List in District 8 of New York in 1866, requiring the taxpayer to list their taxable assets. Studley's list included, income - $4,400 and $9,097, carriage, **watch**, piano, and silver.

In his obituary, Studley was listed as the secretary, treasurer and director of the Vulcanized Rubber Company. He was a member of the New York Athletic, Arkwright and Twilight clubs and the New England Society. [667] He was an extremely wealthy man and traveled a lot on business affairs. He was issued a passport in 1896. Studley may have been robbed of this watch. Jesse always had the tendency to rob from the rich Northerners. He would have been on a train or a stagecoach. I am sure there was a very interesting story behind this. Maybe there is a hint in his name as Bud said.

Bud also says that the numbers where the hands are set on the face of the watch are clues also. The watch was set on 5 til 7:00. The most intriguing clue on the watch was the initials carved in the back, MAJ with a hangman's noose beside it. These same three letters are on a map that Bud has.

Sometimes they wrote words backwards. Could these initials mean [JAM]es??? Did it stand for [MAJ]or??? The meaning is unknown.

(A drawing Bud did of what was on the back of the watch)

There were numerous stories around Buzzard Roost that seemed to come out when Joe Hunter revealed his story in 1948. Many old timers with stories passed down, who lived in Cement, Cyril, Fletcher, Apache, and even Brownwood, all had a rumor or legend regarding Jesse being there. In the newspaper, *The Daily Oklahoman*, January 31, 1993, Monte Snider, the one in the picture, remembers a 90-year-old gentleman who claimed to have ridden with James and kept some of the loot. No one believed the old man and he became very angry, vowing to prove his story. He came back with a handful of double eagles, $20 gold pieces. [668]

Hunter gave Mrs. Hedlund the gold out of the kettle and he kept the artifacts and the map. The map was connecting to another treasure sight. With the help of the two Penick men, they followed the codes and symbols 30 miles to the southwest into the Wichita Mountains.

Archie Penick told Bud that they went on the northside of the Wichitas and north of Tarbone Mountain. The site where they looked for was not a ledge on Tarbone Mountain as some stories have said, but it was out in the pasture.

In the book of Steve Wilsons, "Oklahoma Treasures and Treasure Tales," Steve relates the story on how Hunter located the Brass Bucket. It also was noted in the newspaper article, "Kettle Bearing James Gang Names Displayed by Cityans" by Lindsey Whitten in the Lawton Constitution, February 29, 1948. The old man named "Cook" told Hunter that he would find a pile of rocks where another map was located in the Wichitas. Hunter found the pile of rocks, but didn't find any map, anywhere.

"Finally, he hit upon an idea, fantastic though it sounds. Looking off into the near distance he readily sited a prominent high point. Using the pile of rocks and the distant landmark as two points of an equilateral triangle, he located approximately a third point. It was an old scrub oak tree." [669] The map was found on a rock in the hollow trunk of the tree. This will help the hunters understand how the equilateral triangle was used to bury treasure.

Bud said that the triangles on all three sides were at 60-degree angles. (60°x60°x60°) Bud, working with Wells Blevins, learned this and Wells had many maps showing the triangles in these treasure sites. You can view some of them in the book, "Oklahoma Treasures and Treasure Tales," by Steve Wilson.

In the general area, two picks, a wedge, a three-legged Dutch oven skillet containing the chain and fob to the watch that was found at Buzzard's Roost was located near the brass bucket. This indicated these treasure sites were all connected. Every one of the items were placed strategically underground and marked in a certain way, in a certain position that would lead the hunter to the big one.

Another odd and strange thing that Hunter and Penick stated was that on one of the maps it suggested there was another map to be found by a grave, directing them to the treasure. They found after extensive research, partially exposed bleached bones of a giant of a man. They discovered a buried rock with carvings of a map which showed to be within the same code pattern that Jesse used.
670

With the maps and codes, they were able to pinpoint an area to dig. They dug down and found the brass bucket with the inscription carved on the side.

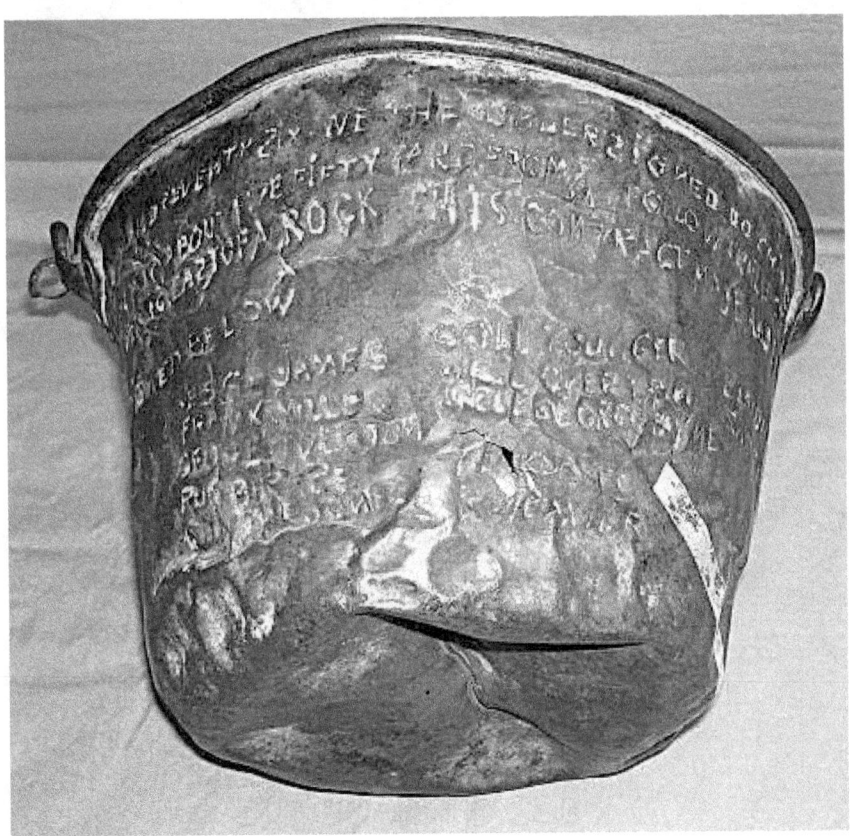

(Brass bucket)

Inside the brass bucket were gold coins, a gun, and unknown items. On the bottom of the bucket itself, there was what appeared to be a slit, such as someone took an ax and sliced a hole in the bottom.

When Bud was at Archie Penick's house, Bud asked, "Did you stop there?" Penick stated "Well we found the other items from that point." Bud had seen too many treasure sites like this that makes the hunter believe they found the ultimate treasure and would stop there. At times, Jesse put out decoy treasures to throw hunters off, leading them away from the big treasures they buried. The small treasures have enough value such as the loot from a train robbery to satisfy the hungry gold digger.

With Bud's keen mind, he told Archie, "I think the slit in the bottom of the bucket meant to go on down." Archie Penick's eyes at the age of 72 lit up and began to think about that.

Bud said the map in the tea kettle said go 11 feet down. The brass bucket wasn't that far down. Archie was ready to go. He believed that the mound of dirt they pulled out of there would still be visible to find. Archie was ready to go on down. Bud knew the owner of the property and received permission to go in there.

Bud said that when they got there, they couldn't find the exact area and Penick wasn't feeling very well and tensions were high. They shut it down, Bud said. He never went back.

Archie Penick told Bud that they truly believed J. Frank Dalton was Jesse James. He knew too much about the treasures and codes/symbols. Archie said that the picture with Jesse in the big hat and Joe Hunter was taken in Archie's living room.

(Jesse and Joe Hunter)

(Archie and Bud looking at the same photo above)

Jesse's response on how he came to chisel the contract. – "We had reburied the gold and felt that we should have a contract on it. We didn't have any ink or pencil and no writing paper. I found an old brass bucket in one of our wagons. It wasn't any good anyway, because it had a slit place in the bottom. So, I took a chisel and carved a contract on the bucket and then put the names of my friends and myself on the bucket. Then we buried it." [671] Jesse did not allow any other clues to escape his lips.

On the contract: "This the V March 1876 in the year of our Lord one thousand eight hundred and seventy-six. We the undersigned do this day organize a banty bank. We will go to the west side of the Keechi Hills which is about 50 yards from a crossed set of rifles. Follow the trail line coming through the mountains just east of Lone hill where we buried Jack, his grave is east of a rock. This contract made and entered into this V day of March 1876. This gold shall belong to who signs below."

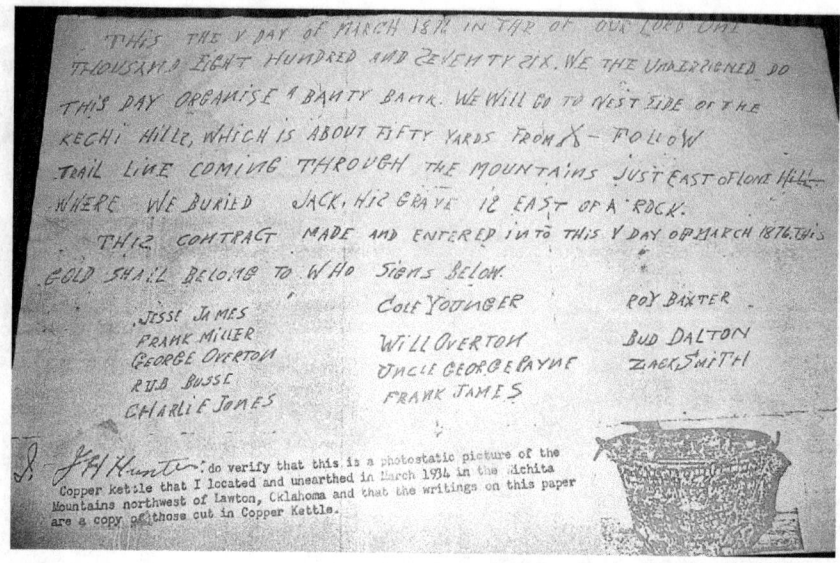

(Contract written on bucket)

Looking at the actual rubbed contract, you will see some of the letters written with flair, some backwards, some large, some small and some with extra lines attached, or a dropped line off of a letter, and a letter within another letter. This was another way of having a secret code in the letters, the same as the handwritten letter that Jesse wrote Colonel James Davis.

"They also relate how the once noted outlaw came upon the gold. It was gold brought into this country by the Spaniards, just as Hunter believed. The James gang found it while they were hiding in the Wichitas and they **"took possession" from others who knew its location.** Then they hid it, not too far from Lawton and then prepared their maps that would point to its locations." [672]

Who did they take it from? Bud knew the answer. It was from the Indians who used it to pay for the guns, ammo, and supplies for the Battle of Little Big Horn.

These news story came out before Jesse revealed who he was in May 1948. Once Jesse identified himself, he was able to prove to Joe Hunter who he really was, by testing the old man with the codes he found and the treasure that went along with it. Both sides were satisfied that each other knew extensively of the treasures of Buzzard Roost and the Wichita Mountains. Hunter was hoping he could get a little assistance from Jesse.

There is not much else that has been printed on what else was found, but it appears that they didn't find everything that they desired. Now the property is controlled by the Wichita Mountain Wildlife and Refuge and private land.

Last that Bud knew, the bucket is in private hands in California.

Bud had in his possession, a letter he received from his good friend, Lou Kilgore in 1991. She had heard this story directly from Howk himself. Whether it is completely true or not, it may shed some light on what happened to the rest of this treasure.

"Early in the Spring of 1894 the 16 million dollars was dug up. Jesse took 50 percent and divided the other 50 percent between various other men. (Supposedly members of the K.G.C.)

Each went their own way with Jesse hauling his half in chests of which he buried right near Fort Cobb on the Washita to lighten the load. Later J.W.J. unloaded another 2 million at another crossing where it remains today, going Northeast.

The other (rest) 4 million he hauled about 100 miles Northeast and unloaded just short of a once booming Oklahoma town (in a cave in boxes, entry filled in and hidden). So this is about all I have on the thing in your area."

This story was also verified in a letter that Lou gave to Bud written by Howk himself, dated September 18, 1979. The reason for the movement of the gold was during the Panic of 1894. It was performed by Jesse and the original Inner Circle of the KGC. The letters are in Bud's collection.

Lone Hill

This name, "Lone Hill" was described in the contract on the brass bucket of Jesse's. Bud searched for Lone Hill and the grave of "Jack," assuming that was one of the burros. It was right under his feet all the time. He worked it for years, almost 20," Bud said, and when he saw "Jack" from way up on top of Buzzard Roost, he knew he was standing on Lone Hill. He could clearly see the word "Jack" spelled out with white cobblestones. "It was plain to see, if you just pay attention," Bud said. Bud took a picture of the aerial view of Buzzard Roost showing "Jack."

(This is the photo Bud had that he said reveals "Jack," especially with the letter "c.")

Bud said Jesse and his boys would mark out spots with rocks that you could only see from a distance to recognize "in plain sight." They did that in a lot of places. You might see an arrow pointing in stacked rocks or shaped into something meaningful. You certainly had to of had a good eye. Bud did have. Can you find "Jack?"

The grandsons, Burleigh Dale, Shorty, and Tubby knew where Lone Hill was. Jesse Cole James was the one that told them that their daddy went to the Wichita Mountains and reburied the gold they hastily buried during the storm. Moved it to Lone Hill, 18 jack loads of gold. Was the word "Jack" spelled out in stone referring to the 18 jack loads of gold? We don't know. "Jack" was spelled out east of Buzzard Roost, 150 yards.

The newspaper, Lawton News-Review, May 20, 1948 also used Jesse's statement told to Howk and Hunter, "he moved some of the gold he had hidden in the Wichitas and concealed it at another spot in eastern Oklahoma. However, he told them he had left $500,000 in gold bullion as a "reward" for anyone who was successful in following the trail to the end of the treasure rainbow." [673]

Bud said one time, with permission from the property owner, he began to explore the area where "Jack" was. He said he got a very good reading several times over the area. He began digging and was still getting a good reading. He went as far as he could that day and came back the next day. The hole was already covered over with dirt. Bud just left it.

The area around Lone Hill is rolling hills with several mounds and some pretty rough country in between. Lone Hill juts out of the ground most proudly and Bud said the area around Lone Hill/Buzzard Roost was named after an Indian word meaning prairie dog, like mounds of prairie dogs.

Nearly to the top of Buzzard Roost is the word inscribed in the rocks as "Rex Pender", Latin meaning "Paymaster." That would be Jesse. He was the paymaster/comptroller of the KGC.

(Rex Pender)

Buzzard Roost, which Bud believes is the "center point" where they can always "come back to," is a landmark of distinction. From the top, you can easily see how they could radiate a grid in each direction, North, South, East, and West.

We spoke of the rock in shape of the man's pointed goatee, pointing east to the $6,000 Frank James dug up. It was about a ¼ mile from there. There is a section line in that pasture. Up the ridge, twenty feet was where the hole where Frank dug the loot out. Bud found the hole where the $6,000 was buried. Frank was able to buy 160 acres and built his home near Fletcher with the money. The house was moved to Cache, Oklahoma, west of Lawton where it sits in an amusement park. I was blessed to get to see where Frank dug up the money and the place, the land that Frank James bought and had his farm.

On top of Buzzard's Roost, there were carvings. There were directional symbols drawn out as a gun and a knife pointing to the north. Bud learned while he was hunting around there that ¼ mile North of there would be another treasure of gold. A man across the road, to the north who had a farm there, knew treasure was on his property. He saw Bud walking around Buzzard's Roost, and he came over to Bud and said he knew treasure was on his property, but he didn't know where to start.

Bud went to help. He used his metal detector and found a buried capstone, but his detector was picking up something underneath. Bud lifted the stone and digging in that spot, they found a Wells Fargo safe. They were able to open it and inside was numerous piles of gold shiny coins. The man said, "Thank you, I won't need you anymore." The man didn't share any of it with Bud, but Bud knew the man needed it more than him. He was glad he could help.

The man called Bud again a year later and said, "Bud, I think I found another one in my garden. It was in his potato patch. There was a flat rock on top. It was 50 feet from the safe they found the year before. Bud was able to take the flat rock off and there was a "wagon spring." Bud believed that was a sign to "go on down." Bud didn't get an opportunity to dig some more, but thought, "I'll outlive him, I'll come back and get that treasure." When Bud later went back, the man had built a brand-new house on top of where that wagon spring was. Good enough. Bud was happy for the man.

Another carving on the southside ½ way down Buzzard Roost, was a pistol barrel pointed south/southwest. Someone had broken the rock on it. Bud took the part that was broke to the JJ museum in Cement.

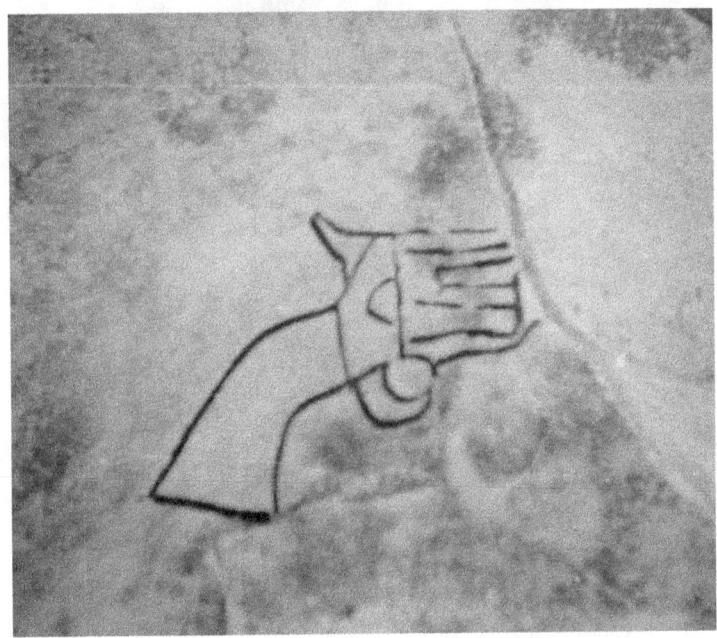

(Broken carving of the pistol at Buzzard Roost)

Charlie Holman and Bud followed the pointer going south looking around. They had separated and soon Bud heard a pretty powerful grunt and then an uncontrollable laughter. That was Charlie. Bud went down the bank of the creek to see what 'ole Charlie had gotten into. Bud found Charlie, drenching wet and muddied up. He had tried to cross the creek on a log and slipped and fell into the water. He was ok, but the sight of Charlie in that creek gave them a good belly laugh.

Signs were pretty precise on their directions. There may be a southern and western treasure from Buzzard Roost, but no one has spoken up about it if that is so.

Bud told me the story that there were some oil leases beginning to pop up on that property and some men running the pipeline, dug up some of the gold and they left the job that very day. They never came back to work.

Another interesting story to confirm Jesse James was in that area was a lawyer from Hobart, who was then living in Lawton, Oklahoma. He called Bud one day and wanted Bud to come see him. Bud took Charlie Holman with him and Charlie knew the man. This man's father and his uncle had land leased at Buzzard's Roost, running cattle. The property was north of Buzzard Roost.

His father told him that he found Jesse and Frank on the property on a ledge that went down into a creek. They were camping and had butchered a steer and were eating it. The camp was about a ½ mile north of Buzzard Roost. Now Hwy 19 sits close to there. The lawyer's father was a pretty tough cowboy himself and walked into their camp. The outlaws were very nice and paid his father $20 for the beef they were chewing on. They visited for quite a while and then paid his father for another beef for when they would be returning. Bud was able to find the area where they camped and saw where they had their campfire. I wonder if that was Jesse's kitchen Frank was looking for?

Also in these Keechi Hills, there was a white goat carved out on a steep cliff. It has faded through the years, but was very visible when Bud took this picture. It was a directional sign to go the way the goat was traveling. This was north of the town of Cyril.

(White goat carving)

Bud still believes there is a lot more treasure than anyone can imagine around there at Lone Hill, but sadly, a lot of the clues have been destroyed. He will continue to hunt there as long as he is able, and the property owners will allow it.

Treasure sites and the treasures they hold

Bud tells us that some of the treasures and gold were definitely from the Mexican Pack Trains, some were brought into the Wichita Mountains by the Spanish, and some from other sources such as robberies. Jesse, as the paymaster/comptroller of the KGC, was in charge of the money, the gathering, the storing, and the guarding. He had his own banking system, the ground. The system he used appears to follow the Knights Templar banking system.

Jesse and his men were treasure hunters, searching for gold and antiquities to collect and store for the future securities. There were numerous sites in the Wichita Mountains. They learned the codes and techniques of the Spaniards. When they found the gold, they would move it to a more secure location, placing it under their own code system, several miles within a circle.

Bud can recognize the Spanish symbols versus Jesse's system. It takes a good eye. Bud has been gracious enough to let us in on treasure sites.

Horse and Saddle Cave

This cave was of great importance to Bud. He had looked for it for years. This was the cave that Jesse and his men sought refuge in from the blizzard in 1875 when they were moving 2 million dollars of gold bullion stolen from the Mexican authorities. During our first meeting in 2017, Bud showed me the map. I remember it had a saddled horse pointing toward the cave. He said Jesse drew this map out himself.

Bud knew that from the Red River, they traveled up East Cache Creek. Bud would go often to try to trace the route that they would have taken along East Cache Creek. There were no towns when Jesse went through there, only landmarks. Bud began to place himself in Jesse's boots to see what stood out in the landscape.

The blizzard was horrific, and they dumped the gold in a ravine, marking the spot with a burro shoe nailed to a tree. Jesse emptied both of his six shooters in a nearby cottonwood. The mules were turned loose. Saddles were burned for warmth. An Apache doctor claimed to have seen the mules and the burned saddles. [674]

Bud said that he had some help locating the place where the burro shoe was embedded in the bullet riddled tree. "Grandma" Ruby Leath who ran the Old Plantation Restaurant knew exactly where the tree was. She had been there and saw it. Wells Blevins, the treasure hunter who had inherited some maps, had the Horse and Saddle Cave Map. He was extremely good friends with Bud and Wells showed Bud the map. Bud said, "I held it in my hands." Wells explained in great detail with Bud on what he knew about it.

Bud stated that he also had the help from Jesse's grandsons who had a map indicating a horse with a saddle on the side of it, and the horse was looking towards a cave. A creek ran out in front of it. The map indicated there were 5 caches of gold and jewelry near this cave.

Bud scoured the countryside and put two and two together. He knew about a cave that was on two of his friend's property throughout the years he has been searching, but never did realize that it was the Horse and Saddle cave. It was the only cave in that area that was big enough to put men and their horses in. It was 20 miles from the Red River and 15 miles to Buzzard Roost where they were heading. Bud knew they used this cave quite frequently.

The cave had a back entrance like Jesse liked and Bud found markings and carvings around there. To protect the owner of the property and its location, Bud asked me to only release a directional hint. "It is directly north of Frank James' property outside of Fletcher, Oklahoma."

(Horse and Saddle Cave)

A copy of the Horse and Saddle Cave map is found on page 144 in Steve Wilson's book, *Oklahoma Treasure and Treasure Tales*.

Mount Scott

Mount Scott is a very prominent mountain in the Wichitas and northwest of Lawton near Fort Sill. It lies in the Wichita Mountains National Wildlife Refuge. Bud stated that there are tunnels within and under Mount Scott.

Doolin/Dalton Hideout

The Doolin/Dalton hideout is northeast of Guthrie. Bud revealed to us that Jesse and the Daltons were around Guthrie quite a bit and also southeast of Guthrie. In the northeast location, Bud found a flat rock on the outskirts of Guthrie that was covered with vegetation and layers upon layers of dirt. Bud said it took a few days to clean that up to decipher what the years have covered up. It had the letter F carved inside a D and a 5-pointed star. There was a spring there and by the waterfall was some more carvings. He found a carving of a tomahawk ½ mile from the other carvings, showing a direction to go. It directed him to another flat rock. There was no cave, but it was leading you to either a meeting place, a hideout, or possible treasure.

Robber's Cave

Robber's Cave is 5 miles north of Wilburton, Oklahoma close to where Belle Starr lived. After the Civil War it was notorious for outlaw gangs to hide out there, including Belle Starr, Jesse James, and the Daltons. The Civilian Conservation Corps developed it during the Great Depression era under President Roosevelt's New Deal program. It became the Robbers Cave State Park, spanning

8,000 acres which includes a wildlife management area, 3 lakes, massive rock formations, hills, rugged cliffs, heavy woodlands, and of course caves.

Josh Gates, host of Expedition Unknown called Bud up one day and wanted to do a show with him on Jesse James and treasure hunting. Bud took him and his cameramen to Robber's Cave. Bud believed wholeheartedly there was buried treasure there. During the episode, they found carvings on a large flat rock, a horses' hoof, cross and an arrow. Josh said, "So you think that this indicates that some money was buried or moved in this direction." Bud said, "No, I don't think it, I know it. They wouldn't put that there for nothing." [675] I've heard Bud say this numerous times. His confidence was extremely strong.

Bud believed Jesse buried loot somewhere in the chamber of this cave. "Fiddlin' Jim" was killed at the entrance of the cave while he played his fiddle. He was a great admirer of Belle Starr and some say that jealousy by another man killed Jim. Legend has it that people can still hear a weird melody at the cave when the harvest moon shines.

Jester Cave

Charlie Holman contacted Bud and had told him that he knew of people who dug up treasure around Hobart, where he lived, but there was one cave they were both interested in northeast of there about 30 miles. Jester Cave was 8-9 miles northwest of Mangum, the 2nd largest gypsum cave in the world. It went back for at least 30,000 yards. Bud met a lady that said when she was a little girl, she went at the front of the cave and saw Frank and Jesse had carved their names on the rock with 1881 beside it. They were there alright.

Bud said that thing was huge. You could drive a truck through it in the front of it and a pickup and car the further back you went. Bud and Charlie went together to explore the cave. It was one of their first adventures together. Charlie surprised Bud by telling him that his cousin was hired by a man who had a map and wanted Charlie's cousin to help do some digging at Jester Cave. This was several years before this time.

As you start in the cave, there was a small hole to your right, that you had to get on your belly to get through. Once in that room, you go back about 40 feet. They had to do a lot of digging toward the back wall. They found an ore cart track that went into a secret room in the shape of a triangle. An ore cart would have been used to haul dirt and gold in and out. In that secret room, there were stacked rifles, forming a teepee. That is how the soldiers in the Civil War stacked their rifles in their camp. Charlie said his cousin told him after reaching that room, the man who had hired them, paid them and let them go. Bud said that the treasure was under the stacked rifles.

Bud said, further back, there was a very long message that Jesse inscribed on a wall using their code system. On the wall was the name of Frank and Annie. The place where the message was, has since caved in. We don't know if it did naturally or possibly was a booby trap.

A funny story Bud told me was when him, his cousin Kenny Brown, his younger brother Bill, and his nephew went to Jester Cave. Kenny was filming and Bill and his nephew decided to go through that small hole to explore that secret room. Bud laughed and said they came out of there with 40 pounds of mud on them. Kenny was filming while the two men jumped into the creek that was running through the cave to wash off. Kenny said in the video, "It's about 30 degrees and these boys decided to take a bath."

Bud's cousin told a reporter for Channel 9 news out of Oklahoma City about Bud and his effort to track Jesse. Bud was contacted and they wanted to do a weeklong special series with Bud during the nightly news. Bud took the TV crew to Jester Cave and Buzzard's Roost.

(Bud during the documentary)

The woman who owned the show, said that was the most interesting show they had done in a long time. She herself, wanted to go the next time. Bud had a lot of calls after that. A lot of people who knew Bud didn't know he was doing that. The TV series boosted him and his ego.

Wichita Mountains

This was the mother of all treasure hot spots. It is believed that this is where the Spanish brought their treasure and gold in the late 1500's. It was a place with lots of caves, deep ravines, and tall mountains. The caves in the Wichitas are natural, but many were made by the Spanish miners which sparked interest in Captain Randolph Marcy's mind who explored this area in the mid 1800's.

During that time up to the late 1800's, Indians were guarding the gold and burying it in various places. The Comanches were supposed to have robbed an Army paymaster and buried the loot near Treasure Lake. Various wagon trains, pack trains, and caravans were attacked, and items stolen. Of course, Jesse and Frank knew the Indians well and got along with them. They made a lot of good trades with the Indians in that area as we learned earlier.

Jesse made a lot of friends in those mountains and one was Silas Lee Ison, known as the "last of the old prospectors in the Wichita Mountains." Silas was born in 1870 and came to the Wichitas in 1901. This was the time that the Wichitas, the Kiowa, Apache, and Commanche territory were overrun by gold prospecting beginning in 1890-1901. Gold was determined to be there.

Silas' father, George W. Ison fought with Morgan's Raiders and served in the 16th Regiment, Company A in the Tennessee Cavalry during the Civil War for the Confederacy. After the war, he went west and prospected in Colorado and New Mexico. His attention turned to the Wichita Mountains as it was said that there was undiscovered gold there. He staked several claims in 1867 within the mountains and one was at the base of Granite Mountain.

George became friends with men, such as Quanah Parker, and those who leased land from Quanah to graze their cattle, such as W. T. Waggoner, Burk Burnett, Andrew "Andy" James, and Charles Goodnight. Eventually George moved to Wichita Falls, Texas and later Duncan, Oklahoma, but he never gave up his claims in the Wichitas. George saw everything you could imagine, but with his stubbornness, he held onto his properties even when he was being forced to leave. There was something there in the Wichitas that kept him there. Was he a sentinel to watch over the KGC's treasures?

Bud said both George and his son, Silas had several encounters with Jesse James. Bud said that Jesse, Frank, and Cole Younger visited with George, connecting with their Civil War sentiment with the Confederacy in 1867 in the Wichita Mountains. Jesse wanted to bury some things on his property and was allowed to. Bud said Jesse James rode up to George's son in the early 1900's and asked Silas "What are you doing?" Silas said, "I'm looking for gold." Jesse replied, "Well that's what we are doing too."

Bud learned a lot from Wells Blevins about George and Silas. George died in **1933** and his son continued to fight hard to remain on the land in which he built a cobblestone cabin upon. On Silas' property was an old smelter and the dam for mining. Blevins and Bud were able to go to the area where Silas lived. The smelter and dam were still intact.

Silas was able to stay on the land when the government took over the property converting it to the Wichita Mountain Wildlife Refuge, but with much legal court battles, fight and perseverance. It was finally settled and the court awarded him to stay on the land as a "legal squatter" in 1942. Silas lived 100 years and died in 1972. The Wichita Mountains Wildlife Refuge organization bulldozed the cabin down after his death.

One very interesting place where Bud and Wells Blevins went in the Wichita Mountains, was less than half a mile from Silas' place near Treasure Lake. Bud said Blevins was a dear friend of his and shared the same interest. Bud stated that Blevins was very good at landmarks and finding peaks, but he didn't know much about the carvings and symbols. That made them a good team.

Bud and Blevins were looking around for something else and stumbled on a site that blew Bud away. He saw a small rough mountain range that caught his eye. It was a huge formation on the side of the mountain that looked like the devil carved out of the rock with his gigantic hand curled up. Upon the devil's thumbnail was an X which Bud said is telling you something. It you scan the side of the mountain, the human eye does not see it right away, but Bud said you got to pay attention. It was put in plain sight and he believed the Spaniards put that there. Bud took a picture and sketched it out and there it is, in plain sight. Look at the far-left end going down to the ground.

(Carved out rock appearing as the devil with gigantic hand curled up. In Bud's notes, he writes "Payne and Buckner discovered in the Fall of '88.")

Bud said there is a cave near that area and he found a red seven, meaning gold and the red is "danger". Could this sign indicate that the area was one of the Seven Cities of Gold?

Wells Blevins and Bud did a lot of hunting in the Wichitas. Wells fully trusted Bud with some of the secrets he knew of the area, but he was very cautious with a lot of treasure hunters. Wells told Bud that some men came by and wanted to use some of his maps that he had inherited. Wells said they won't find anything. Wells said he changed the steps and directions on the map.

Jesse was most definitely the same with his maps. Bud said, that on Jesse's maps, he would never put the last sign to the treasure. He kept it in his mind. Sometimes he would use a separate piece as an overlay on the map to give a more exact location. You had to have both to figure out the location of the treasure.

No one really ever knew how Wells Blevins inherited Jesse's original maps, not even Bud. He told Bud that he received them from an original member of the outlaw gang. As I was writing this chapter and put two and two together, as Bud says, my summation is that Wells Blevins received them from Silas.

Silas knew Wells pretty well and knew that there would be many after the maps, especially those who were fighting him in court. Silas had to of had someone to trust with these. It makes sense that it would be Wells Blevins. But how did Silas receive the maps? The answer had to be through his father, George who Jesse trusted to bury money on his property. George had to be a member of Jesse's gang or was a KGC member, sent to the Wichita Mountains and strategically placed near Treasure Lake as a sentinel. I may be dead wrong, but this is the only thing that seems to fit.

Another prospect of who gave Wells Blevins the maps was an old fellow described in Steve Wilson's book, "Oklahoma Treasures and Treasure Tales," an old bandit of Jesse's, John Von. Would this man be part of Joe Vaughn's clan, whose name originally was "Von?" We don't know.

Wells talks of the man named Von/Vaughn who had lived in Lawton for several years. His name was John Vaughn. There was a man found in the Lawton Constitution, April 24, 1924 his name John P. Vaughan. He was born in 1841 and died in 1924. He was an early settler and employed by the U.S. government as a teamster at Fort Sill. He was a kindly gentleman and loved by all who knew him. [676]

It is another, "I don't know," but Wells said he knew too much about where to find things in the Wichitas and dug up the evidence. He knew where graves were buried up there, with one skeleton found shot between the eyes. This Von character certainly was involved somehow.

In a cave in the Wichita Mountains, Bud found an 1874 Colt .44 caliber pistol wedged in rocks and used as a pointer to signal members of the James gang where the next meeting location was. Gang members would look down the gun barrel to see the location the gun pointed to. It may have also been a directional sign, pointing across the canyon to another cave.

Bud took the gun to a gun smith to clean it up. The gun smith called Bud and said there were initials on the gun. Bud said, "I'll be right there." Sadly, by the time Bud got there, the chemicals used to clean the gun took off the initials and were unreadable.

(Gun found in cave, used as a directional marker)

Bud said the Wichita Mountains is very rough and full of rattlesnakes and wildlife in their natural environment. One time he was down in the Wichitas with his cousin and his nephews. They separated and Bud went up a little rise and there was a water hole down below. He looked down and thought he saw a big tan dog getting a drink about 30 feet from him. Bud thought well that's a good stout dog, I'll just take him home with me. Bud hollered at him. Turned out, it was a mountain lion. Bud said, "I frightened him, and he frightened me. He went one direction and I thought it was a good time to go the other direction."

Bud said that he had always been afraid of snakes, but he learned to get over his fear, maintaining a healthy respect for them. Back in those mountains was a spring and a little waterfall coming down the mountain. Bud was going towards the waterfall when he saw a rattlesnake getting a drink. Bud decided he would let the snake have all he wanted.

Channel Nine news who did the weekly news special, called and wanted to do an article on Belle Starr and Treasure Lake, as well as the cave with the Iron door in the Wichita Mountains. People have seen the sun reflecting on it. Bud said it is a railroad car door.

Bud's take on the Iron Door is that Belle Starr and JJ robbed a train and they took a door off the box car and put over a cave opening which secured many treasures. Some believe the Iron Door is on Elk Mountain.

Bud never told me about the hunt for the Iron Door, but his nephew Zach told a funny story about it. Bud met up with some men that had several clues where the Iron Door was. He took along his nephews who were between the ages of 10-12. They met up at Medicine Park.

A fella drove up in an old beat up pickup who was a "cross between the men of Duck Dynasty, an Ozark Mountain Hillbilly, and a Northern Colorado hippie," said Zach. His name was Ernie. Bud told his nephews; "You go with Ernie and I'll go with this other guy up over the hill there." To say the least, the nephews were a little concerned.

Ernie said, "Hop in the back and we'll go up this gully a way. When the boys climbed up over the side of the truck, there was another passenger in the truck bed which nearly took up the entire space. In one of those Walmart kiddie pools filled with water, was Ernie's pet 4-foot alligator.

Well, it was too late for them to back out now, Bud had already left and was on the other side of the mountain. They clung to the top rail of the sidewalls, watching their feet so that they wouldn't be near the gator's reach. Well, Ernie found every rock and hole on the way, causing a very rough ride for those boys.

They stopped many places, using old maps, looking and examining anything that glimmered, and walked til they could walk no more. At times, Ernie would go behind a bush and the boys could see puffs of smoke coming out of the branches. Ernie was smoking him a reefer. Oh Boy!

While still shell-shocked, the boys heard Ernie ask the question, "Ya'll hungry?" The boys looked at each other and said "no" even though they were starving to death. Ernie said, "Well, I am!" He reached in his pocket and pulled out a can of tuna fish and threw it out on a rock slab with a wrapper of crackers and said, "Dig in boys."

After 6-8 hours of this, they were ready to find Uncle Bud. Of course, nothing was gained on this trip except a good education of Wichita Hillbilly living. Bud never heard the end of it.

There were many legends within the legend somewhere in the Treasure Lake area. Why was it called that? It is obvious. Before the 1930's, the area where Treasure Lake is located was a very deep canyon before the Civilian Conservation Corp, established by President Franklin D. Roosevelt in **1933**, completely flooded the canyon. It became a small but beautiful dammed up lake. This Corp was established when Roosevelt enacted the Emergency Conservation Work Act during the depression, "caused by the Dust bowl, the stock market crash on Black Tuesday, and the reliance on credit instead of cash." [677]

In 1984, Wells Blevins' wife Maude, a full-blooded Indian, whose last name was Whitewolf, turned 100 years old. They were married for 57 years. She passed away and Wells Blevins asked Bud to be an honorary pallbearer. Bud was so honored to do this.

In 1986, Wells Blevins and Bud went on another adventure. They were looking around at the area where Silas lived. Both Blevins and Bud felt strongly that there is something buried here. They went by Treasure Lake and went west into the mountains. I asked Bud, "Did you find anything?" Bud said, "Well, we knocked on the door of it and know that something happened there. When they came out of those most intimidating rugged mountains, Wells said, "Bud, this will be my last trip." He was 89 at that time and within a few months, he passed away.

Other places for possible treasure

Not only was Southwestern Oklahoma hot with gold, but the southeastern part of the state was also. Bud, Lou, John and Jo Ella Tatum went with Bud to explore some maps they received from JJ's grandsons. There were a lot in the Choctaw Nation. From Purcell to the bridge at Lake Texoma, Bud said you are in the Chickasaw Nation. Across Lake Texoma, you enter into the Choctaw Nation. Jesse knew these tribes well, along with the Creek, Kiowa, and the Commanche.

The Apache medicine man says: "treasures are buried to await the coming of one particular person. If you are that person you will find it."

The KGC sent members out to protect the gold and would settle in these areas as well as gaining their trust with the Indians to guard their treasure. They were assigned these areas and paid very well. Bud said they were paid $200 or $300 a month. That was pretty good income back in those days. The location was watched at all times. If any of them double-backed to get a piece of the pie, other men in the organization was supposed to shoot the traitor on sight. Sentinels were very prevalent between the 40's and 50's. Bud has never had a problem with any of them nor have received any threats, but Jay Longley has.

Bud provided me a map that was fascinating. Howk had drawn out the map in great detail per instructions from Jesse himself. Bud had come across this map, either by the grandsons or from a museum. There was one museum Bud had visited where they had maps and letters written by Howk. Bud said he was able to copy 150 letters from Howk to compare with his information. I've seen a lot of them, but some are so outrageous and exaggerated that it's hard to tell if any of it is the truth. But this map, Bud said, there's no doubt about it, the map was legit and accurate with Bud's own discoveries.

Howk and Bud had no idea where this location on the map was, but knew it was in Oklahoma. Just like always, things were meant to be. Bud had numerous friends all around the country in which he could call on for help.

Bud attended the annual Waurika Rattlesnake Hunt held in Waurika, Oklahoma to learn more about rattlesnakes for him to be better prepared at dealing with them. He had met a snake hunter there, Bob Young and they became great friends. He was an expert snake handler and hunter. They both gained great confidence in one another and learned from each other.

One day, Bud was showing Bob the map and he said, "Bud, I know where this is. I have been "there". Bob was out snake hunting and found some carvings on top of a mountain and there was a hole in the ground going into a cave. It's very snakey up there.

Bob took Bud to this location. (Refer to Appendix B-4) Charlie came with them. Later, Bob Brewer would join in. Bud has been there 8-9 times. Bud told me that he was being very careful with the location. He said just let the readers know it's in the Slick Hills near Cooperton, Oklahoma. It was near the area where the James had the natural corrals for their horses and where Belle Starr stayed in a cabin in Cutthroat Gap. It is an extremely sacred and spiritual place for the Kiowa and must be respected. It is carefully protected.

The hoot owl tree at the top of the ridge was no longer there. They found a loose flat rock that looked out of place and lifting it, they found the hole. On the other side of the rock were the words, "Get Map."

They put a ladder down in the hole which was about 12 foot to the bottom from the top. Charlie began climbing down into the hole and all of a sudden, he stopped. Bud said, "What's wrong Charlie?" "I'm wedged," Charlie snickered. Bud, with all his might pulled out Charlie who weighed over 250 pounds.

They brought out the ladder, it was just in the way. The three guys, Bob Young, Charlie Holman, and Bob Brewer went down with a rope that was attached on one end to a strong metal bar laid across the opening of the shaft and attached to their waist. Bud stayed on top and helped lower them down.

Inside the cavern, in which are many chambers, there were a lot of cave-ins, blocking some of the rooms. Supposedly, someone had already been in there and removed the loot in that small area because it was picked clean. They did see carvings on the wall and saw the *camel* etched into the stone. They didn't see the two dead men who had died in there near the trap door leading to the air shaft, but they knew they were in the right place. Bud said, "It's just as real as can be."

As you see on the map, the air shaft goes further down vertically into the cavern. Bud said the men didn't find it, but Bud knows it's there. A man he knows went down in there and saw it. There are a lot of booby traps in there. On the map, it shows that Jesse himself put in blasting powder and dynamite next to the shaft in the 1930's. He would have been in his 80's. Apparently after he did this, he went back to check on it, as he usually did with all his treasure sights, and found that more men died in an explosion in the shaft.

Quite fascinating finds in both the map and the location. Now to get Charlie and the two Bobs out of there. To really prove how stout and strong Bud is, he pulled all three of them straight up and out, all over 250 pounds each with just a rope.

(Hole that Bud had to pull them up from)

(Charlie down in the hole)

    The air shaft goes down to another room. No one has gotten down in there who has lived to tell about it, but per the map, there is another entry way as Jesse always required.

    Interesting that the map indicates a wagon entry where they brought in the gold. Bud found the main entry at the bottom of the mountain where dynamite had blown up rocks to completely seal the entrance. Bud also found the creek indicated on the map.

    Bud said there is a huge amount of gold in there, coins and bars. There are coins stamped with SAC which stands for **Sacramento** where the mint was. Some coins are square cornered. This brought to mind of what Howk was told by Jesse relayed in Del Schrader's book, "Jesse James Was One of His Names." There was a massive amount of gold stolen from the Union soldiers, but Jesse had told Howk that was taken to Llano County, Texas to Bragg's Ranch, but was some of it or all of it taken to the location we have been speaking of? Possibly, Jesse gave him the wrong information to conceal its whereabouts as he did a lot with his treasures.

    This is the story Jesse gave to Howk that we discussed earlier: A huge amount of gold that was being shipped by Union soldiers in wagons from **Sacramento** to Fort Leavenworth. Once they reached the **Western Oklahoma Panhandle** on the Santa Fe Trail, the Confederates, General Hood's cavalry, led by Captain John Lamb and 60 Texas Rangers attacked and overtook the wagons. The wagons were taken to Llano County to the Bragg Ranch and gold coins worth 18 million dollars were buried in the **Camel** and Straw Cave. Booby traps were laid for those who came a visiting.

    Why was the **camel** carved on the wall in this cavern we are speaking of? Could it be that this is where the shipment was taken? Is there a connection to the cave in Llano County? Makes one wonder, especially the story that Howk told about Joe Hunter's men who were killed in the Camel and Straw Cave. Were they the two dead men shown on this map?

    Sometimes you really have to look at the words and the clues such as what is stated on the map, **"Indian Watchdogs looking over this."** Could Jesse be referring to the Kiowa who guard this mountain and consider it their most sacred place?

Sadly, again the government and corporations wanted their hands on the mountain in 2013 to be used for limestone mining and gravel pits. I am not sure who won this battle. I pray the Kiowa did.

In Schrader's book, he lists at least 100 Confederate caches and this was one of them, listing it as a large treasure. [678]

From the Wichita Falls Times Record News, in August-September-October 1956, a series of articles written by Jim Koethe about buried treasure sites found in the Texas and Oklahoma areas:

Atoka County, Oklahoma - Bugaboo Canyon near Atoka, Oklahoma where Belle held up when injured.

Comanche County, Oklahoma – On the banks of Cache Creek.

Jefferson County, Oklahoma - Big Rock – near Addington, Oklahoma. Monument Hill where Tom Lattimore was buried.

Logan County, Oklahoma - Jesse buried some money in and around Guthrie, which had numerous underground tunnels carved out by the KGC. There are carvings up there and the initials J.J. and J. Frank Dalton side by side.

Archer County, Texas - In the early 1900's a man using a team of mules dug a slush pit near Holliday, Texas and dug up $20,000 dollars in gold coins.

Knox County, Texas – Apparently there is an old gold mine where the Brazos River and Wichita Rivers run to a point. Very deep shaft, 80 ft. deep. A 100-year-old man remembers helping a man reach the bottom which held 3 vaults full of gold, silver, jewels, and copper. It supposedly was Spanish treasure. They removed lots of treasure and placed it in the Haskell State Bank vault. The man who hired the centenarian to work the mine ended up very ill before they could finish, died, and a fire at the bank in 1911 destroyed the treasures.

Montague County, Texas – In Montague, there is supposedly a large wooden box full of loot stolen and hidden in a cave by outlaws of the early days in Montague. The box was full of gold bars, bearing the stamp of United States government mint. An old man in Wichita Falls told the story. Years ago, when he was a small boy, his family had a homestead near a creek in Montague County. One day, shortly after supper, two men rode up on horseback to his family's house and asked if they could water their horses and spend the night. The boy's father told them they could and then one of the riders who was carrying a small leather bag on his saddle, rode off into the woods and returned a short time later, without the bag. The following day, the two men left, and the boy and his family forgot all about them. Several weeks later, when they were in a small town just across the Red in Oklahoma buying supplies, the two men who had visited their home were shot in Oklahoma and the boy and father identified them.

In a cave, near his home, the boy found two skeletons holding rifles guarding a large wooden box, 3 ft long, 2 ft wide, and 2 ft. deep. The boy found watches, rings, money, and other pieces of property. He left the treasure intact. He went back, but then lost his nerve. He covered up the cave. Placed a large stone to the cave entrance. It was south of Bowie.

A black man, working in the street department in Wichita Falls, knew where the treasure was in Bowie. He said that he would never go down there because of evil spirits guarding the treasure. The treasure is by an old barn on a rock hill. The man believed you could protect yourself if you sprinkle coffee, milk, and whiskey around the treasure. The spirits will not cross the mixture.

Spanish silver, gold and jewels lie in southeastern Montague County with markings carved on a tree to point the way at the headwaters of Clear Creek.

Another treasure of gold coins, $20 gold pieces, worth $10,000 was said to be buried close to the Rock Crossing along the Chisholm Trail on the Texas side. In 1894, bank robbers robbed the First National Bank in Bowie, Texas and one of the town's leading citizens was shot and killed. They were caught with the help of the City Marshal of Bowie and his posse, pushing them into Indian Territory to be apprehended by Deputy U.S. Marshal Lewis Franklin Palmore. The marshal was told by one of the robbers that the gold was hidden near their camp in the timbers. It was near the sandstone falls, 300 yards below the mouth of the Little Wichita. It was close to the old cattle trail, which sounds very likely to be the old Dona Ana Trail. [679]

Wichita County, Texas - Pot hole of gold in Wichita Falls, Texas.

Burkburnett, Tx – Outlaw cache near Burkburnett amounting to $7,000 – Bank robber in 1880's robbed bank and crossed over Red near Burk with gold coins and paper money. Riding on a road parallel to the river, he went 250 yards to a clump of cottonwoods and large flat rocks. Hid the money under the rocks and rode off, later caught. He wrote out a map and slipped it to a teenager of one of his relatives while in prison.

Buried treasure on the south bank of the Wichita River near the northeast corner of Riverside Cemetery in Wichita Falls. Large rocks there with markings showing the direction.

Clay County, Texas - buried gold on the banks of the Little Wichita River. A troop of soldiers from Fort Sill was transporting a load of gold across that area when they were attacked by Indians.

Hardeman County, Texas - Beryl Beach (1887-1973) who lived in Quanah whose grandfather was John Crockett (1839-1895), a member of Quantrill Raiders under Jackman, an officer of the raiders relayed this story. After the Civil war they went to Old Mexico with the James Brothers. If they found more loot than they could take, in their saddle bags, they would bury what was left and later return. Only once did the Indian beat them to the dig up and in retaliation, the outlaws captured the old chief's beautiful daughter and held her in a Wichita Mountain cave until the chief brought them much more gold than the Indians dug up. Crockett took the loot and bought land in Quanah.

Texas surveyor, E. A. Reiman in 1883 reported a party of surveyors had been working canyons and brakes north of the Pease River near Medicine Mounds, Tx. They found copper nuggets and happened upon an abandoned copper mine. Above the entrance of the old tunnel was scrawled upon a board: Mercia Costello, San Antonio, A.D. 1847. [680]

Bud wanted to also share these interesting treasure sites in Oklahoma and Texas.

Doan's crossing – Treasure is supposedly buried on both sides of the Red River at Doan's Crossing in the river hills. Look for 2 identical Hoot Owl trees, side by side, pointing towards river which would indicate a crossing or an old river ford. Look for large, out of place rocks and petroglyphs.

Marshall, Oklahoma – A possible treasure buried at a creek crossing on an old trail at the edge of Marshall.

New Mexico treasure sites that were included in Howk's list in Schrader's book that Bud and I have discussed and Bud has researched; those not mentioned previously: (This is just a handful compared to what Jesse shared with Howk) [681]

-Red River Ghost Town Treasure ($250,000)
-Old Raton Pass High Road Treasure
-Old Stage Relay Hotel (10 miles south of Raton) – This would have been the old Clifton House, very famous.

-Santa Fe Trail FF Treasure (near Watrous)
-Look at the Hill Treasure (west of Ft. Union)
-Old Santa Fe Trail Treasure (North of Ft. Union)
-Dim Trail Treasure (north and west of Ft. Union)
-Eagle Nest Treasure
-Taos Mission Treasure ($60,000)
-Elizabethtown Treasure
-Forks of Two Rivers Treasure (believed to be near Questa)
-Cimarron Creek Crossing Treasure
-Maxwell Trading Post Treasure
-Sangre de Cristo Treasures (5 or 6)
-San Luis Trail Treasure

Bits and pieces of Info:

*Bud learned that the KGC had gold miners around the country, especially in Colorado and Mexico, who little by little stole the gold and buried it under Jesse, the comptroller's directive.

*The Turtle Rock that was 1 mile from Joe Vaughn's house near Wayton, Arkansas had carvings on the turtle's back. A heart with an arrow through it, pointing southeast.

(Turtle Rock)

(Heart and arrow)

*Bud said the area where Joe Vaughn lived was full of treasures and secret depositories. One was the cave Lou's grandfather was taken to blindfolded that supposedly contained 80,000 silver bars inside. There is an area within a circumference of Wayton, Murray, and Parthenon (which means "a Doric temple of Athena built on the acropolis at Athens in the 5th century b.c.") [682] –which is a hotbed for treasure and it would have taken a very skilled surveyor to design and map out the area for treasure to be stored. This appears to be a massive KGC operation and depository in this particular part of the country. There is the Diamond Cave and the Treasure Cave in which have significance. Bud has been to the Diamond Cave and there were many signs and symbols to identify that the KGC was there. There is a cave that has a stone altar or what you would call a stone throne, possibly used in a ritual. The area is full of mystery and intrigue, including those who protect it.

Bud said the cemetery where Joe Vaughn was buried has extensive KGC and Masonic symbols all around. Someone spent immense time in creating rock walls and a rock entrance gate that has rock formations in the shape of turtles. There are clues everywhere in that cemetery as well as hoot owl trees nearby. There are cemeteries dotting the landscape in that area that Bud believes hold clues, directions, and possible treasures.

Bud went back to that area recently to continue his search but got into an extensive built up of vegetation and briar patches that put him in the hospital. He said he was getting pretty close and had to stop and probably won't ever be able to go back there again, but he found a lot that was leading him to a big treasure sight.

(Gate of cemetery where Joe Vaughn is buried. (Snow Cemetery))

*There were really several maps in the kettle that Joe Hunter found. One was a guide to 5 million dollars in gold. It directs the hunter to dig down 30 feet and then dig horizontal and you will discover the money. Bud is sure there are booby traps because it was backfilled in. Bud got to see the map, had it in his hands, and memorized it. Bud believes the area its referring to is out of Altus, Oklahoma.

*Rocky Ford is a crossing over the Washita River to get to the Lindsay Mansion in Erin Springs, Oklahoma. This is the crossing that Jesse went through as a freighter going to Fort Sill. There is supposed to be money buried there. Bud said there are a lot of Rocky Fords in Oklahoma.

*On a trip to southeastern Oklahoma, Bud, John and Jo Ella Tatum, and Joyce Morgan were trying to find Good Water Springs. Supposedly there was treasure nearby. They had a map of Jesse's titled, "Trail to Good Water." They were north of Fort Towson and saw a Choctaw Indian lady named Inez Taylor and the group mentioned the spring. Inez said, "its right out there," pointing not too far from them. "I used to carry water from it when I was a little girl," Inez said.

Reaching the springs, there was a hoot owl tree pointing to a cave. They got to the cave, but a cottonmouth water moccasin swam into the cave. Bud said, "I'm not going in." The owner was with them and said in the back of the cave, there is an open room and it's just filled with snakes.

They managed to get above the cave, away from the snakes and they noticed a limb on the tree next to the cave opening that was oddly formed into a circle pointing down to the ground. It was pointing to where treasure was buried. Someone had already dug a deep hole and retrieved it.

I asked Bud, "How did Jesse deal with all these snakes?" Well, maybe that's why the treasure was buried outside the cave, but they also would use snakes to guard their treasure. They would place snakes in caves sometimes to create a natural guard system. They would populate. If the caves were wet, the snakes wouldn't make a home in there, only water moccasins or water snakes would. Quite interesting what Bud has learned about snakes.

*Bud had another map of Jesse's which led him near Miami, Oklahoma. (See Appendix B-1) This was another place where Joe Vaughn frequented. There is a rocked-up water well where a big Indian boy, 6'6" lived. He played college basketball and Bud and him hit it off. Bud told him they were looking for a water well. The man said, "Bud, I got it hidden. There were others looking for it, one was Howk." The man didn't trust Howk, nor others who came a lookin'. Bud won't mention those who the man didn't trust, but he sure enough trusted Bud. The man took Bud and Charlie Holman to the well. It was plugged up with an old wringer washer machine, flush to the ground. It was camouflaged.

This was another treasure area that Howk listed as the Treasure of the Small Rocked-up Water Well. [683]

The man pulled the washer out. Bud said he lowered 'ole Charlie in it and boy the water was cold. Bud said that Charlie could hold his breath longer than anyone he knew. He was down there for a while and when he came up, Charlie said, "I'm Purple." He was frozen. Bud pulled him out in a hurry. Charlie was such a good sport. Bud said that there was supposed to be gold bars as false bricks inside that well wall, but all he found was an old wagon axle. The gold was supposed to be worth 2 million dollars.

(Photo of well flush with ground)

I asked Bud how he found this place. He said, "By knowing the Oklahoma Territory and knowing where Spring River is which was shown on the map."

*Bud has a map indicating 66 tons of gold buried near a tombstone in the southeast corner of Fairplay, Colorado. You can only get up there in the summertime. It's covered up in snow the rest of the time. It was a KGC site. (See Appendix B-7)

*In the Austin Statesman, January 10, 1950, [684] Jesse told the reporter, H.D. Quigg in New York that "he has 2 million dollars in loot buried near Fort Sill, Oklahoma."

*Known locations that the KGC focused upon to bury their treasure in numerous states and Mexico were: Permanent fixtures, such as courthouses, ferry crossings, two rail line crossings, right of ways, water towers, switches or switch stations, some landmarks along the track, layover stations, natural caves, old grist/grain mill sites, smelters or furnaces for gold, silver or coal, charcoal, coke ovens, cattle trails (most prominent trails), livery stables, blacksmith shops beyond the boundary of the structure, inns/taverns, cemeteries, landmarks by a river or forks in the river, and Indian mounds.

Known caves with hidden treasures were in Kentucky, Tennessee, Louisianna, Oklahoma, Texas, and Arkansas. Many, many more are out there.

Other treasure sites have been found at Old Spanish missions such as those at the Double Mountain Fork on the Brazos River and near Adobe Walls. Also, at Spanish Fort near the Red River. There were many sights in Texas and Oklahoma that those who were bringing in gold, artifacts, etc. those who were trying to protect their fortunes from the Spanish and Conquistadors and from the Indians were depositing their cache in many locations. Some had to do it on the spur of the moment, and some had time to meticulous hide it in miraculous and mathematical and geological ways.

Sadly, after writing about Adobe Walls, the entire area was completely destroyed by the largest wildfire in the history of Texas and was the 2nd most destructive wildfire in U.S. history, the Smokehouse Creek Fire. It started northeast of Stinnett and headed east, destroying the area of Adobe Walls and the Turkey Track Ranch. The fire also destroyed a lot of the Arrington Ranch.

Also, many fires have been set in known areas of treasure and also many places have been flooded intentionally. Land has been placed under Federal control.

*Take with a heaping tablespoon of salt, but Howk left us treasure hunting tidbits he learned from Jesse. Bud located a letter from Howk to "Folks", written from Gilchrist, Texas dated July 31st, 1951, just 15 days before Jesse's death. The letter started out very cold with Howk writing of "moving Jesse most conveniently and most efficiently the 400 odd miles northwest from here. That will place us almost centrally located to several places of interest. When JJ moved his stuff he apparently, according to what he now reveals, simplified his caches and system of locations.

"Some are only 3 or 4 feet deep. You look around, never go north, you know why, don't you?" (Bud said that it had to do with the Union being in the North and also I believe it had to do with Freemasonry, but Bud has debunked that theory. He has located treasure due north from a centerpoint) Howk continues, "Go S.E. first and look, then S.W. and look – go N.E. and last of all look to the Northwest from focal points of key points."

"When Jesse pulled a raid, his men and he would most generally take out in a SE direction if available and hardly ever go 4 or 5 miles to where they would stop long enough to bury a cache. When JJ buried $16,000,000 near Fort Sill on March 3, 1876, he returned along about 1888 and moved part SE. Part went NE and part SW and the last went Northwest toward Camp Supply in Oklahoma. About $4,000,000 in each treasure. One was found several years ago when it rolled down a hill after a rain storm had caused erosion. A banker found it when two boys came to him with gold they picked up down a draw below the site JJ hid the treasure. It brought over $4,000,000."

"So, from your old Milo Miller house you may find something along the East side – along the West side of the house or at the SE corner – never expect to locate a cache on the north side of the house or north side of the well if its Jesse's."

"You see – King Solomon's Temple had no north door. Therefore the Yankees from the north could never enter without going around JJ's own planned temple."

"If there is a hill within 2 miles going SE, look from ½ to 2/3 (rds?) the way around and up or straight up the hill near rock ledges. Look for maps and marks in top the hill on rocks if handy or on tree. JJ's own marks were the turkey track and turtle. If the turtle has his head up keep going. If the head is turned down look near the foot of the tree indicated by the sharpest pointer on the turtle's anatomy. Get it?"

"Read that over and over. The treasure may be at the foot of the tree if the head points down and is sharp. A foot may be a sharp point acting as an arrow but pointing out another tree where you find the cache nearby."

"Old Jesse James is smart but he greatly simplified his cache when he moved his stuff to new locations. In the deal at Joseph James' place, JJ may have simply moved it 5 or 6 foot to Joseph's wife's grave's headstone."

Howk implied JJ would sometimes move treasure "a grave away" from its original burial, "providing it was not the Northward." A creek or river, "look down along the water's edge." He drew out a map showing the treasure could be in between two forks or a creek running into a river.

Howk wrote, "JJ still has hundreds of rifles stored in limestone caves since the 1860's and 1870's, saddles and ammunition included. It is these secrets JJ revealed only recently.

"So, what are we going to do about them? Shall I return to Dakotas, Montana, and Wyoming, West Texas? What else has JJ revealed if vast historical importance? Why did JJ force us to approach his problems in exact reversal to that route we should have taken? Why? JJ could have made things a lot easier for himself as well as for those amongst us who fought his battles for the proof he is Jesse James!

"So, why worry? Why rush? But, time means everything and time is so short. We need money to get these things started off right now that JJ has given me the short cut. I think we can accomplish something.

"Adios, Jesse Lee"

*Caves where Jesse's treasure was buried, told to Bud directly from Jesse's grandsons, Burleigh Dale, Shorty, and Tubby James:

-Bear Den Cave – Blackjack Ridge, Le Flore County, Oklahoma near the Potteau River. This is in southeastern Oklahoma in the Ouachita Mountains.
-Daltons Caves – Pawhuska, Osage County, Oklahoma
-Lake Eucha Caves - Delaware County, Oklahoma- Lake Eucha was created to keep the Spavinaw Lake full
-Spavinaw Lake Twin Caves, northwest of Lake Eucha – the lake was built over an active gold mine
-Belle's Bluff Cave
-Belle's Bluff Annex
-Joe's Folly Cave
-Natural Bridge Quarry Cave
-Natural Bridge
-Bolton Cave
-Campground Spring Cave
-Flat Cave
-Butler Cave

*Names of towns that were used as center points or landmarks, possibly indicating a safe place for the KGC:

Centerville, Woodford, Montgomery, Osceola, Lexington, Marshal, Reed, Franklin, Scott, Clay County (Missouri and Texas), Johnson in the form of Johnsonville, Johnson County, Clark (Clarksville in Texas and Arizona)and Orrick (Orrick, Missouri where Anderson was supposedly killed and Arrington's real name).

Compensation for Cole Younger

*When Cole Younger got out of prison, February 1903, (from a pardon) he met Jesse. They dug up money between Purcell and Lexington, Oklahoma for Cole to live on the rest of his life. That same year, Cole Younger went to the Wichita Mountains, Lawton, and Ardmore in Oklahoma. Bud believed he was there, scouting out the areas where treasure was buried before Frank and his wife settled in Fletcher in 1907. Cole was noted as receiving $75,000 to sit in prison. Howk and Trammel spun the story that others were hired to sit in prison.

(See letter in Appendix A-4)

Techniques in burials (of treasure)

They used dynamite, hoot owl trees, which points you in the direction to go and may had a turtle carving on the tree. Usually carvings around the area.

Graves are of importance; treasure has been buried in graveyards to protect the treasure and with fresh earth stirred up, it would not raise suspicion.

Bud said that most of the buried treasure is not found in caves, but a certain distance from the caves. That theory has held up well, but it stands to reason that with Bud's tremendous experience as a treasure hunter and knowing Jesse so well, they certainly did both. Jay Longley wrote that the KGC buried their loot in "elaborate man-made mine shafts" which fits perfectly with what he has found and the treasures in the Wichita Mountains.

We learned about surveyorship with George Washington, but not much had changed from the 18th century to the 20th century except maybe the tools. It still required two men to run the chains to measure distance. The exact measurement had to be monitored at each location due to the fact that the chain could be easily stretched, especially in the rugged mountainous region.

Joe Vaughn was a surveyor and was excellently used by the KGC. The surveyor's chain was sixty-six feet long and each rod measured 16 ½ inches long. Two rods would equal **33** inches, Jesse's favorite number. The surveyor would use a point of interest or center point and go from that point in all directions, North, South, East, and West. From the point of interest, locations would be marked and then angles, and equilateral triangles could be drawn out to give a more detailed and accurate map of the land. The layout would appear as a grid or spider's web.

A fascinating connection to caches of gold and this grid pattern was brought out by Bud on the word and locations noted as "El Dorado." In the Merriam-Webster.com dictionary, the story is told. "In the early 1500's, Spanish conquistadores heard tales of an Amazonian king who regularly coated his body with gold dust, then plunged into a nearby lake to wash it off while being showered with gold and jewels thrown by his subjects. The Spaniards called the city ruled by this flamboyant monarch, El Dorado, Spanish for "gilded one," and the story of the gold-covered king eventually grew into a legend of a whole country paved with gold. These days, El Dorado can also be used generically for any place of vast riches, abundance, or opportunity. – A place of fabulous riches held by 16th century explorers to exist in South America."

There are cities and towns named El Dorado in California, Arkansas, Missouri, Oklahoma, Texas, Kansas, and Louisianna. El Dorado was the name of the county in California where Jesse's father, Rev. Robert Sallee James died in 1860 in the Gold fields. Harrison Trow lived in El Dorado Springs, Cedar County, Missouri in 1900.

With the help of Jesse's grandsons, Burleigh Dale and Charles James brought to Bud a map with descriptions regarding "El Dorado" that they had of Jesse's. They said if you can figure out the clues and secret messages encoded in the map; you will discover 20 triangles. If you find them all, you will get it right and be able to locate the caches.

With Jesse's map, spotting the locations named El Dorado on a map of the United States, and deciphering the secret message containing 72 letters, Bud found 17 triangles. One of the triangles includes the area south of Altus, Oklahoma.

Within the KGC, not only did they have surveyors, but they had army engineers that could dig tunnels and caves rigged with booby traps. On one map which Bud believes leads to treasure in Tennessee, close to Nashville, an intensive burial system was laid out in 1870. It took 18 months to dig and prepare the depository. The detailed burial map was so intricate, that it is very similar to the burial sites at Oak Island. Bud believes that the Knights of the Templar were so skilled that they had a part of burying treasure in America and passed down the techniques to the Knights of the Golden Circle. The designer of the Eifel Tower was brought into design vaults for the Knights Templar and the KGC. Not only was this done in America, but stashes of treasure are buried around the world, including England, France, Cuba, Mexico, and Canada.

Tips from Bud

Bud's rules in treasure hunting were to always ask permission from the landowner and consider them if treasure is found. Honesty is the best policy. Bud has never been turned down by a property owner. Also, if someone else is working the site, be considerate and step aside unless asked to help. If you do have partners involved, make sure you can trust them and be good at your word. If greed enters the picture, step aside. It is not worth it. He has known partners within his own circle that were ready to kill someone because of someone's greed. Bud told him, "If you kill him, his troubles will be over and yours will be just beginning."

Bud says, "Research is 80 percent of treasure hunting. The key to the whole thing. You need to know the general area." Somebody would have to have a map and focus in on landmarks designated on the map. Bud collaborated with friends and treasure hunters he could trust, as well as the locals in the general area where he was hunting. "You've got to understand where they (Jesse and the gang) were. For example, at Lake Texoma, with many creeks and canyons, they were there and research Sherman, Texas where they had their winter camp, north of there. Bud's given you plenty of clues.

"If you think that you're going to go out in the woods and find something, you're a dummy," Bud said. "Consider the area and the season you want to go. Copperheads, Rattlers, ticks, and chiggers are something you need to consider."

"Don't go with people you don't trust. Take people that are healthy that can dig and can walk. You need to wear snake proof boots, snake proof chaps, take your guns, dagger on your belt, shovels, canteen, a compass, ropes, and a pocketknife. If its rough terrain, you got to be ready for it. I used to go out there without that stuff and learned pretty quick that was not good."

Bud loved to take his nephews along, not only for the company and young strong muscles, but also to develop a strong bond and relationship between them. It was a great learning experience for all, and he wouldn't take anything for it. Many times, the trips were at the spur of the moment. Bud would say "let's go" and the boys would jump to their feet in excitement with no hesitation. One time, Bud came to the boys and said, "let's go." "Just leave your Momma a note and tell her where we're going." Zach said, "Well where are we going?" Bud said, "Mexico." Zach wrote his Momma a note saying, "Gone to Mexico with Bud." He didn't get a chance to say goodbye. Zach said his mother allowed this as she had complete trust and faith in Bud to take care of them.

Bud also suggests that if the place you are going to is grown up in weeds and lots of vegetation, take allergy medicine if you are sensitive to these allergens. Bud was highly sensitive to Cedar and Ragweed and after many treasure hunts, he would end up in the hospital.

Bud suggests using a metal detector that goes three feet deep. Bud uses the White's brand. Bud also suggests a metal detector that will cover 15 feet deep. Also use a dowsing rod. Load it for what you're looking for, such as gold, placing it in the end of the tube. When the dowsing rod starts going round and round, you are on top of it. This is what happened when Bud uncovered "Jack" at Buzzard Roost.

Snakes don't' hibernate. If it is 57 degrees in winter the snakes can move, but very slowly. If the temperature is above that, be ready and watchful for those low belly reptiles. At 64 degrees, the snakes come out in full force. Bud learned all he could about them. Always take a gun. "Them rattlesnakes got to be careful of me too," Bud said.

"When you go into wildlife's territory, you must respect that this is their home and your invading their territory."

Bud said in the Wichita Mountains, he met up with a Rattler and it raised up its head and started swerving. The snake was level at Bud's knees, and he just knew he was had. Bud slowly got his 357-pistol, lowered it down and both Bud and the snake let the other live and move on. Whew!

Bud said, "The bigger the treasure was, the more well concealed it would be, deeper or further back in. Some of the treasure sites are small caches, such as coins in fruit jars that the KGC hid for their expenses and some were used as decoy sites.

Signs and Symbols used:

Bud suggests try to get into their minds, what were they thinking. Bud had no book on symbols, nor anyone to show him what they meant. He learned on his own and had his own booklet of codes and symbols that someone stole.

Bud said there were a lot of symbols of the KGC that were merged with the Spanish symbols that the KGC discovered and used. Sometimes Jesse would change the symbols when treasure was moved or wanted to direct the treasure hunter in the opposite way of the treasure. Some symbols and carvings were destroyed by Jesse himself.

If you come across a sign, it may not be the first initial sign to follow, it may be in the middle of a clue or at the end. It could be a decoy; it could mean go in reverse of the direction it refers to. It could be a Spanish symbol indicating a Spanish treasure that was reburied to make it harder to find. The KGC would leave a signature on those reworked burials to indicate that they were the ones moving it around.

Large Templates were used especially for wide open spaces and smaller templates were used for dense foliage areas. Large symbols are carved into the rocks, sometimes the entire rock is carved into the shape of an animal. The entire symbols within that area must be considered to be able to efficiently interpret the symbols. Many KGC members were involved and each site will be different.

Tic Tac Toe

One of the most intriguing and simple symbols that Bud discovered on his own and shared with a few was the Tic Tac Toe sign that was used to decode letters, words, and sentences directing their path or another clue. A Tic Tac Toe playing field has 9 separate segments to enter an X or O. What they used to hide the message was the lines for a particular segment such as the first top left segment that forms a backward L, which the backward L would be the letter A. The next segment, forming a U, would be the letter B, and so on. The Tic Tac Toe playing field, would hold A-I. If you find a segment such as the backward L with a dot in the space, that would be the letter J. That playing board with dots in them would be the letters J-R. Then as you can see on the diagram shown below, the Tic Tac Toe playing field would change to an X and another X with dots to use as the last letters of the alphabet. You can then decipher what the message is. Sometimes it's only a direction, such as East. It really is a genius coding system that is as simple as Tic Tac Toe.

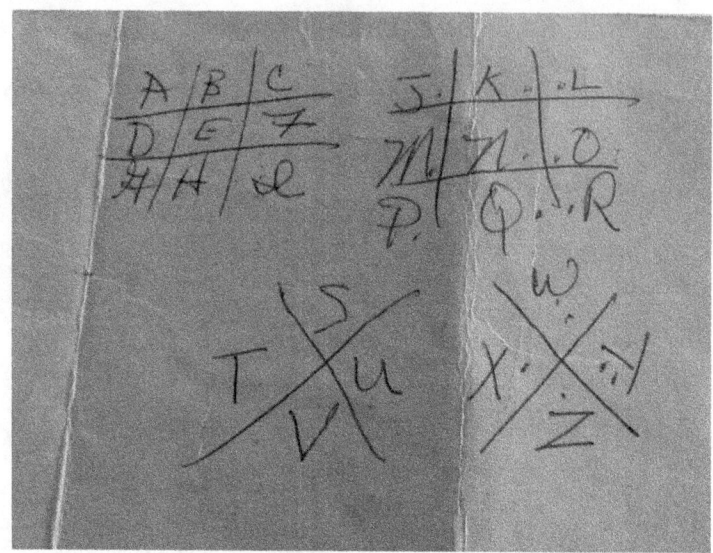

(Tic Tac Toe codes)

C G – carved into the stone. The C goes into the G, such as what is shown in the middle of the masonic emblem between the compass and the ruler. Sometimes the letter "I" would be used to point to a direction and the Big C with a little "i" that looks like a G, would also be a directional marker. Go in the direction of the dot in the i. Sometimes the symbols would appear as a Letter C coming up with a line and arrow, meaning "look up."

(C and i symbol)

(Box with cross - is a church symbol)

Crosses – The longer line in the cross would point a direction and sometimes there would be something tagged onto the line to indicate the direction.

Turtles – If the turtle got all his legs, head, and tail in, its where he needs to be. He can't go anywhere. If one leg is going a different direction, follow that. If the tail is curved, follow that direction. If the head is turned, follow that direction. If the neck has a squiggly line through it, which means a broken neck, it indicated the treasure was moved. This sign was seen by John and Jo Ella Tatum's parents at Medicine Mound in Texas when they moved the treasure there to another location and watched Jesse as he was marking the original carvings. They witnessed the ingenious procedures Jesse followed in the removal and the reburying of treasure.

Turkey Tracks – These were very popular with Jesse. Turkey track – follow the side of the track that is dug deeper into the stone or tree. If they are all the same go straight. A turkey track with a dot by the line is the direction to go. The turkey tracks mean go and a slash underneath is "West." Sometimes they are used to throw you off.

Symbol for Gold – Spanish word for gold is "Oro," sometimes seen in carvings. The number "7" means gold.

Paces - Sometimes you will see dots around a symbol which could mean how many paces from there you go – a pace is 30-**33** ½ inches and 2 rods is **33**" – such as 3 dots on a handle of a pistol could mean, 3 paces, 3 rods, 30 paces, 30 rods, 3 miles, etc.

Gun or daggers – points the way. If there is a dot on one end, follow that direction. Bud has seen more than one gun, pointing to treasure.

Buried clues – some clues are buried such as the bayonet at Wapanucka Academy pointing a direction or another clue to follow to the treasure such as the 3-legged Dutch oven that Joe Hunter found.

Triangle – most of the time, the smaller end of an elongated triangle is the pointer.

Letters – Sometimes there are letters spelled backwards, done on purpose. Smaller letters and smaller numbers printed alongside larger ones in a message.

There is also a certain symbol indicating the treasure "at" or "nearby" which has always proven to be correct. Bud did not want to disclose this symbol and I will respect his wishes.

JJ – many times Jesse would put his initials in various ways as well as members of the gang. Sometimes he would put an "F" inside a "D" in the name of Dalton. There were times when Bud found the names "Jesse James" and "J. Frank Dalton" close to one another within two inches and sometimes upside down on top of the other indicating that they are one in the same.

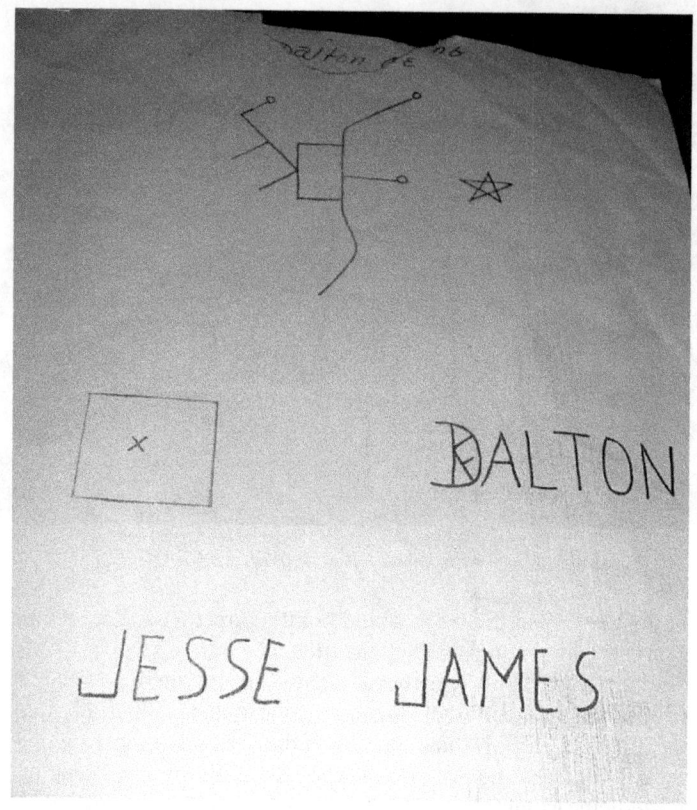

(Symbol showing F inside "D" close by the carved initials JJ)

There will be straight lines, an upside-down F attached to a box with a crooked line and along the line would be 3 different points. Bud could determine which point to follow.

Other initials - If the symbol was a "JY" it stood for Jim Younger, "CM" – Clell Miller, BA – Bill Anderson, "FJ" – Frank James, "CY" – Cole Younger, "HF" - ???, and CQ – Quantrill. Bud found all these initials carved on the side of a mountain in the Wichita Mountains along with a drawing of a pistol pointing a direction. Bud would later find exactly 30 feet from where the pistol was pointing, a rock carved with several letters which Bud was able to break the code. The treasure was nearby. Bud never got to finish the hunt of this treasure, due to a man he had helping him, who started seeing $$$ signs and went behind Bud's back. This created problems with the owner of the property. The owner would allow Bud to go in, but not the other guy, who later committed suicide. Bud said, you have to be careful who you choose to go on these hunts with.

(Letters carved on rock in the Wichita Mountains)

Rifle point – Near Carnegie OK., North of the Wichita Mtns and north of Slick Hills. Carved on rock with a snake with lines drawn inside the snake. Follow rifle.

Tomahawk - follow the handle or the head of it. A directional symbol.

Circle – May be the starting point or look for a circle of trees nearby and focus on the center.

Egyptian Hieroglyphics, Spanish, Indian signs, and cattle brands were used for KGC.

Horse- follow nose – this sign was found in the Wichita Mountains
   Broken lead rein –follow direction of longest portion of rein.

Indian chief – follow the most prominent feather in his headdress and check the Indian's hand, possibly there is a directional pointer there.

Anvil – directional marker

Beak of the Buzzard at Buzzard Roost, which is broke off now, pointed to treasure, Frank's cache.

Numbers in degrees – A measure in surveyorship. Bud has a special instrument to measure the degrees from a center point or direction.

Crossed Winchesters – Direction pointers. Go both directions where they're pointing. There are crossed Winchesters on one of the Tall Tombstones in line with the Wichita Mountains in the Francis Cemetery outside of Humphreys, Oklahoma.

Roman Numerals – Possibly how many paces to go.

Star – treasure marker, bottom point of the star will be the direction to go.

KGC liked to use snakes – when tail is up in warning; ahead was a booby trap site; a briar patch.

Head of snake crosses the body– that is a false direction, follow tail.

Snake carved 22 ft long, tail in warning position –large cache with booby traps.

Ace of Spades – point to next sign.
Rattlesnake – does not cross, not in danger position, pointing to next site; no danger
Spanish boot – point of boot is the direction you should go
Two snakes – two caches. One direction is a false trail and the other correct trail.
Star – 5-pointed means KGC. Bud has found carvings of 4 stars in a row by the Washita River with an arrow.
MAJ – Carved in back of the pocket watch found at Buzzard Roost. There is a MAJ on a map also with a Hangman's noose.
"Resume Interest" – Letters written out means, Go back to what you were doing – found down by Buzzard's Roost.

Booby Traps

Above all, you have to be extremely careful when treasure hunting. The men burying the treasure didn't want it to fall in the wrong hands, so they did all they could to make it hard for anyone to reach the treasure.

If it was a big cache, they are going to protect it. The more valuable the treasure, the more well concealed and further back in it was buried and the deeper and stronger the booby trap was. The traps were intending to stop the treasure seeker in his tracks. Sometimes they used a lot of briar patches to seal up a cave entrance or a dig, making it harder to get to. For a small cave, they would collect snakes and throw the snakes in the cave to ward off treasure hunters. At times, they would hide their stash in a poison water well.

They would also utilize decoy stashes with small amounts of money. They would dig out a shaft in a cave that had a dead end, or up the hill. They would very easily plant them with explosives, or a keg of Black powder. If explosives get wet and then dries, its more dangerous.

In a cave, there was always a front and rear entrance. The front would be covered with dynamite and contain booby traps. They would set the traps and move out the back. Sometimes they would leave signs such as a crescent moon near the traps to signal those in the know that there is a trap near. Some markings would indicate the nature of the booby trap.

Other booby traps that Bud has run into were heavy rocks stacked in a certain area and if you move one, they all fall on top of you, crushing you to death. Sometimes a hunter doesn't have a chance as there are very small spaces that you have to crawl through on you belly, 2.5-3 feet tall and there is no way to protect your head if you come across a booby trap or snake.

They also used water to drown an invader. If you move a heavy rock that was used to plug up a spring and you're in a small space, you may end up drowning. Bud knew of a man who drowned this way. Bud said, "You can't act like a fool and jerk things around. Every inch of a treasure site has to be handled with care to protect yourself."

Bud was explaining that sometimes they used wet rawhide placing it in mud and when it dried, the rawhide would draw up. When any kind of tension was released in this mud bomb, it would explode.

One-man Bud knew, recently was working near Robber's cave and said he was talking about going into a sealed cave. Bud warned the young man about going into an old sealed up cave which contains "Black damp" poison air. The young and healthy man, being anxious, went ahead and explored that cave and he died. Bud said, "You need to open it up and air it out for at least a day."

You got to know what you're doing for sure.

Wapanucka Academy

This next story, Bud told me over and over again. It weighed extremely heavy on him. You could tell it upset him quite a bit, but most of all you could see the hurt and pain in his eyes when he told it.

Bud has shared his life-long research with many treasure hunters whom he felt he could trust and shared a map or two in good faith. He has always tried to help those treasure hunters to decipher codes and symbols that were pretty complicated. But not everyone has the moral values and integrity to respect the hand that feeds you. Bud would later find out that those he shared his life's work in confidence and took them to treasure sites, went behind his back, using the information to contact Bud's own contacts, explore treasure sites on their own, sometimes without permission from the landowner, and illegally remove any treasure found and keeping it for themselves. This infuriated Bud to no end when the trust was broken and the so-called friend, he thought he had, didn't have the proper code of ethics to be honest, respectful, and good at his word. This caused friendships to be dissolved and placed Bud's reputation at stake being associated with the thief.

If the culprit was dealing with Jesse in these matters, he would be dead by now.

This very thing hit Bud hard, right in the gut. He received a call one day from a history teacher and a jr. high school football coach, telling Bud he needed help with deciphering some carvings he found on a site that Bud had shared with him. Bud, willing to help, opened up his knowledge and expertise to this man. Bud said the man told him they had complete permission to go on to the property where the map indicated.

The place was on the old grounds of the Wapanucka Academy, south of Bromide, Oklahoma. It was a Chickasaw Indian girl school, also known as the Wapanucka Female Manual Labour School. It was constructed by the Board of Foreign Missions of the Presbyterian Church in 1852, built near the Delaware Creek. A teacher and missionary, Mary Coomb Greenleaf died when nursing students back to health after severe issues of dysentery. She herself became ill and died in 1857. She was buried not far from the school.

The school closed because of lack of financial support in 1860 before the war. The Confederates took it over for a hospital and a prison for the Yankees. From the ruins of the Academy was a big rock, straight up and down, and had the carving of a box with a cross on top.

Bud recognized the carvings right away and had known about this location and had the map. The man had a copy of the map. As Bud was looking around the area, he found turkey tracks and other carvings. They also found old rusted handcuffs, a pickax, and a bayonet in a hole under a rock which were clues and directional pointers.

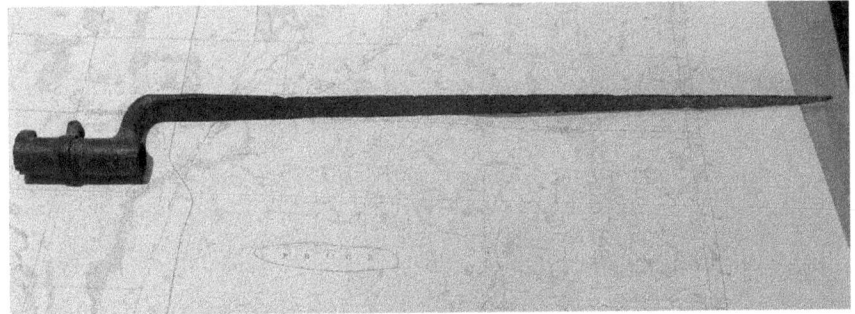

(Bayonet)

With Bud's great eye for recognizing Jesse's way of burying things, the symbols and signs, but most especially his intuition of how Jesse thought, Bud turned to the carving of a box or altar with the cross, leading them to another location, the cemetery.

Bud went to the teacher's tombstone and found an arrow on Ms. Greenleaf's tombstone, suggesting the direction of the treasure. Bud knew that Jesse liked to use the cemetery or tombstones to carve a clue or symbol. Jesse, like a surveyor, used surveyor's rods. Two rods would equal **33** feet. Bud suggested that the treasure probably is within the **33** feet.

They continued looking around the property with Bud suggesting several things. "I furnished him everything, the snake proof chaps and the metal detector."

Little did Bud know that the man was also using Bob Brewer.

Bud said the man came to him later and said he found the treasure, just right where Bud said it would be, **33** feet from the tombstone. He brought Bud one gold coin dated 1880, dug up near Delaware Creek in a fruit jar.

That's all. He didn't really say how much he had found, but the man acted like it wasn't much.

Bud said the next thing he knew, there was a huge newspaper write up in The Daily Oklahoman, September 6, 1995 that this man had gained financial wealth from treasure hunting by unearthing a Wells Fargo safe full of gold coins. He said, "he and two others decoded one of Frank and Jesse James' maps and unearthed a Wells Fargo safe full of gold coins. He won't say where because other excavations are planned near there." [685] Bud said he had phone calls from his friends who read about this and was very concerned that this man went behind Bud's back.

Bud found out later that this man had used Bob Brewer to help him in the Wapanucka site and that the man had given the "Grave is a Witness" map that Bud gave him to Bob to locate where this other site would be. All this was done without Bud's acknowledgement. The man supposedly never told Bob about Bud's involvement, nor about where he got the map. Bob would spend many hours on that map to decipher the extensive clues and finally decoded it. The map, as Bob called it, "The Wolf Map" was probably the hardest map to decipher which was drawn out by Jesse himself.

Bob made the mistake of sharing the new information with the man and taking him to the place where it was located. Bob laid down the rules of who was going to get what. The number one task ahead was to get permission from the landowner, give him a third, Bob a third, and this man a third. What about Bud?

This man didn't go by the rules or do a thing, except go to the property, without permission and dig up the safe with gold coins that he spoke of in the newspaper. He never shared one cent with anyone. You can read all about the story in "Rebel Gold: One Man's Quest to Crack the Code Behind the Secret Treasure of The Confederacy," by Warren Getler and Bob Brewer.

You can tell the character of a man by their actions. Bud learned of all this from the newspaper and when Bob Brewer called him and apologized for not knowing Bud was the one that supplied the "Grave As A Witness" map to this man in full confidence, the 'Wolf Map" as Bob referred to. Bud had obtained this map and had showed the map to Jesse's grandsons before all this had occurred. The grandsons recognized it immediately and said the D.A.T. at the top was referring to the Dona Ana Trail. The treasure was along the Dona Ana Trail. They also clued Bud into several other symbols on the map.

Both Bob and Bud were burned by this man. He was an amateur and didn't know much nor have the equipment to handle the jobs. He needed the "big boys" to do the hard work for him. The "big boys" received no credit and no profit that were due them. Bud said. "Don't even put his name in the book. His name is not worth mentioning in his book. He was a snake in the grass."

This incident devastated Bob Brewer and Bud did what he could to help him recover. Bud believed it was a hard lesson for everyone to swallow even the landowner, where the safe full of gold was stolen. The landowner died shortly after this incident. It is a deadly game of greed which can bury men in a hurry.

If you stop and think, just whose gold does this really belong to? Bud knows and that's why Bud maintains a healthy respect and philosophy to use the treasure sites to understand and prove the truth about Jesse and not focus on personal gain.

Here is a photo of what Wapanucka Academy once was.

(Wapanucka Academy in its heyday)

(The ruins of Wapanucka)

(See Appendix B-2 for map of Wapanucka Academy and Appendix B-5 for the Wolf Map)
Bud knows more about these two sites than ever before, but he is not trusting anyone with this information. I certainly don't blame him, do you?

Bud located treasure no doubt, but his integrity allowed others to enjoy the benefits.

"You can learn a little about people's principles by listening to their words and a lot by watching their actions. But you don't truly know what they stand for until you see their sacrifices. The ultimate test of integrity is what we're willing to risk to uphold our core values."

-Adam Grant

Code of the West: "These homespun laws, being merely a gentleman's agreement to certain rules of conduct for survival, were never written into statues but were respected everywhere on the range. Number one, don't inquire into a person's past. Take the measure of a man for what he is today."

"The Cowman and His Code of Ethics," by Ramon Adams

Conclusion

Many men in American History were put upon pedestals, made to look good when their heart and intentions were bad and there were those who were branded as bad, but their hearts and intentions were good. The latter describes Jesse.

Jesse's words left in Rudy Turilli's book: *I Knew Jesse James*, 1966.

A message to the Youth of America

"I am a perfect example that crime doesn't pay. I live in remorse because of some of my past. I appeal to the youth of America to stay on the right side of the law. There is no substitute for a good law-abiding citizen.

The youth of today will be our citizens of tomorrow. Upon their shoulders will rest the responsibilities of guiding the destiny of our nation.

They should be well prepared for the tasks ahead. One of the most important prerequisites is to obtain an education. Every boy and girl in America should attend the grade and high schools and if at all possible, enroll in a college or university.

Education is something you can always carry. It isn't heavy and no matter how you travel, you can always take it with you. You know, you can't even dig a good ditch without an education."

Jesse James

Bud's words about the man, Jesse Woodson James, who he had been studying and trailing for nearly 45 years: "Jesse was a good man. His first rule was self-protection. Somebody who was going to kill 'em, he would kill 'em first. Other than that, a good man. I know that's hard for a lot of people to understand, but they didn't find out things about him like I have." Bud stated, "I got as good a feel for him, as anybody alive today."

After going down this trail with Bud, I truly see a different Jesse Woodson James than I knew about before. Should he be exonerated? What would you have done in his shoes? His heart was good, but justice overtook his heart and he acted upon it. His fervor was intense and unstoppable. I hope others have opened their eyes and mind to get a better understanding of the man. We can all learn from him. As Ola said, "Jesse done a lot of bad things, but he done a lot of good things too that seem to outweigh the other."

Now, it is in the hands and mind of the reader to sum up their own conclusion. The evidence has been presented and hopefully will be useful for future researchers. Bud has done his job for you. Research, research, and do more research for yourself.

Sometimes it's the little things that matters in a person's character. Bud wanted us to see the good in Jesse. Here is a short list of good things Jesse did:

1. Staying at a farmhouse and noticing the family was very poor, he and his men came back to the house with two large tow sacks full of food.

2. If someone fed them, he would leave a $20 gold piece under the cup or plate. Staying overnight, they would leave a gold coin or jewelry under the pillow.

3. Returning the stolen money from the Nimrod Bank who had helped finance Jesse's father's schooling.

4. Giving the lady on the train money who was going to see her son who was injured in the war.

5. Paying the widow's mortgage.

6. After a Rock Creek robbery by a banker, Jesse helped the man and girl back to Ardmore, gave them money and bought the girl a new dress.

7. In 1926, going by the name of Jess Johnson stayed at the Camp Cottages in Brighton, Colorado. He was a very nice "old timer" and the children loved him. He had quite a bit of money on him and as he did with John Tatum's mother, he gave the woman who ran the cabins, Oshie the money to keep in a safe place. He was a wonderful babysitter for the children and at night he would play penny-ante poker with Oshie. When it was time to go after 10 weeks, he gave the children all the pennies he had won and gave Oshie a ring he was wearing on his finger. Oshie told Ola that he was so kind, and it turned out, she was a Dalton also.

8. During a train robbery, he gave all the Confederate veterans back their goods.

9. During another train robbery, he did not take from the men who had callused hands indicating hard working men, but the northerners, with smooth, soft hands, Jesse had no problem in taking from them.

10. After the turkey shoot in Canada, Jesse gave away the turkeys to families in need, while he settled for a prairie chicken.

11. At Jake Johnson's house in Austin, after a lengthy stay, JJ tried to pay for room and board, Johnson said no, JJ left a wad of bills on the gate post.

12. Jesse loved children and they loved him back. Many instances reveal this and especially the love for children was shown in the hospital in Austin with the little boy in the wheelchair.

13. Jesse wanted to give Ola his last $45.

14. Jesse was an honest man and paid back what he owed. He paid back a horse, saddle, and money borrowed.

15. He paid in full, money owed to a Mr. Rhea in Tennessee, describing how he was hard up at that time in the early 70's and would pay him in full even if he had to go out and work on the streets for a dollar a day. Honest and kept his word.

16. K.R. Ross, the James' neighbor in Cass County, and also related by marriage to the Younger family asked the boys not to come around so much, because the authorities were getting a little suspicious. Jesse was in need of help and sent a note, signed David Howard, wanting Ross to meet him. Jesse was lying on the ground with arms crossed on his chest with a pistol in each hand, ready for action. He was suffering from malaria and needed help. He had been down the Mississippi River. Ross described his words as desperate; no money, not able to trust anyone and was very sick. He showed Ross his wound he received in the right side of his chest in his lungs received in the Spring of 1865 and it was very inflamed. Ross brought him a horse and $40. Jesse returned the horse and the money, all within a month.

17. Jesse saved a black man from a whipping by two white men.

18. Whenever he stayed with someone, he helped with the chores. Bud verified with Mildred Kimball, schoolteacher, that Jesse came to her home, slept in their barn near Whitebead, Oklahoma. He helped with farm work. Ms. Kimball wrote two letters to Bud about this. She said her father owned the Kimball Ranch and Jesse gave him a pistol belonging to him. She said the woman folk were uneasy while he was staying there. In Whitebead, Jesse, as J. Frank Dalton, performed a marriage. Bud had a copy of the marriage certificate with Dalton's signature.

In the *Kansas City Times*, April 6, 1882, shortly after Jesse's fake death, the writer, which possibly was John Edwards wrote, "Jesse James had one of those peculiar organizations to which fear is unknown. An enterprise that required bold, courage and dash that not one else would think of attempting had the greatest for Jesse. He was impulsive and generous to a fault. Instances of his kindness to poor Missourians are absolutely innumerable. If he found a man that he had ever known so poor he could not put in his crop, his first inevitable act would be to put his hand into his pocket and give him the money he needed, though it be the last shot in his own locker. If a poor friend needed a mule and Jesse met him, he would dismount and give him his horse." [686]

In the *Lawton Constitution*, May 19, 1948, Dalton was known for his generosity. He was known as a "soft touch." A writer for the Lawton Constitution "Doc Dopey" stated, "Once you see J. Frank Dalton, all doubt is dispelled. His eyes are a frigid blue, steely in one glance and pools of affection in the next. He is barrel chested. His body is bullet scarred. His voice is one of authority. His very bearing is dynamic."

In the *Muldrow Press*, July 15, 1912; now the Vian Press, "The first negro school in Missouri was founded in Kansas City by J. Milton Turner in 1868. The school commissioners were ex-Confederates and refused to appropriate a salary for him.

"Every Saturday night or so, he says, Jesse James, the celebrated bandit, rode over from Liberty, Missouri, shot up Kansas City and robbed its citizens. Then he would gallop to the negro school, discharge his pistols in the air and shout: "Where's that nigger schoolteacher?" I would go out in fear and trembling, Turner relates, "and say, "Here I am boss."

"Haven't those commissioners done anything for you yet?" James would yell. And I would answer: "No Boss."

"Then I'll have to help you," he would roar, and give me $10, $15, or $20. But for Jesse James I could not have kept up the school." [687]

An affidavit from a Black man who knew Jesse from Arkansas, John Gibson who was currently living in Colorado Springs stated, "Not too many folks ever knew that Frank and Jesse James would come and go, move about amongst the Negro people, who saw to it that nobody sneaked up on them. They keep their mouths shut and their eyes open…they were fine white men, helped out many poor folks all around us and were the best friends we colored folks ever had. They will be loved and well-thought of as long as the world stands. They helped my father out. I don't know how much money they gave my daddy and mammy they helped pay off our debts and the mortgage on our farm." [688]

In the *Atchinson Daily Patriot*, April 7, 1882, shortly after Jesse's fake death, the paper printed a story that was told to the editor about another editor of a paper who reported the news of a train robbery. The news blew up and the suggestion was made that the James boys had assaulted or even insulted the woman on the train. The editor of this newspaper told a different story about the train robbery. Both Frank and Jesse rode to the newspaper office of the editor one night and confronted the editor, "For what you have said of the James boys as robbers and murderers I have no fault to find with you; my visit here is to thank you personally for saying what is true, that in the recent robbery we did not insult the woman. We have never been guilty of that crime. We want to pay you for what you said, and you will please accept this." Frank handed him a package of $3,000. The editor did not accept but was overly relieved that he remained alive. The James' boys wished him a good night and rode off in the darkness." [689]

Jesse paid for two horses that he had killed; one was to Clay Allison for his horse of his father's who he had killed and one to Oscar Constable Thomason, son of Captain John Samuel Thomason, son of Wild Bill. Captain John Samuel Thomason served in the Confederate Army and was a sheriff of Clay County. Jesse shot his horse out from under him.

After a bank robbery in Gallatin, Ex Sheriff Thomason thought he should lead a group of men to the James' home. His son, Oscar was with him. A procedure of trading words to have the James come to town to address the concerns of the citizens, Jesse refused to give in. They exchanged gunfire, not intending to hurt anyone, but to have it come to a conclusion, Jesse shot Thomason's horse in the head. Thomason walked up to the Samuels and borrowed a horse. [690]

In the *Kansas City Star*, August 18, 1940, "Oscar and a group of friends made a trip into the Southwest with team and wagon. One night when they stopped to pitch camp in Oklahoma, Jesse James rode up to them and asked Oscar if he was there in search of him? When told that this was not his mission, Jesse sat down and ate with the crowd. As he left, he gave Oscar, $50 as payment for the horses he had killed. [691]

"He (Jesse) had a tenderness in his eye that would contradict the fabulous stories afloat, but the eye also shows a sternness" .... Mary P. Norris, daughter of Frank James and Josephine Welch. November 6, 1950.

Jesse was noted in a book written in 1883, described by Ola that JJ was "Temperate by nature, easy, self-possessed, and gentlemanly in his demeanor. His dress was as modest as the man himself and he would never have been selected, so far as any outward indication went, as a bandit and desperado. In one thing, did he give way to temptation. Like most men of generous impulses, he was a born gambler. His nerve and judgement were both excellent, and in all games of chance he played with great skill." [692]

A great little newspaper clipping was happened upon unexpectedly. It was a story of a man who knew Jesse well. It was in *The Star-Journal* out of Warrensburg, Missouri, March 22, 1929.

"The death here of Dr. John Feathers, 85-year-old chiropodist, marked the passing of a man who for years fitted boots to the feet of Jesse James and who was a staunch defender of the notorious outlaw.

"Some days Jesse James would sit in my little shop in Monett (Missouri) and talk about the world in general." Dr. Feathers recalled before his death. "He talked boldly of his exploits. Then, the next day perhaps, we would hear of a bank robbery many miles away. A few days later James would drift back into town and into my place. But no one dared to touch him.

"Dr. Feathers referred to James as "a brave and honorable gentleman, who I knew and loved for 16 years during the time he was wanted by the law.

"The James were fine people and were leaders in community life and business. What Jesse was, he was because of the war. He was bold and daring but he never was a bad man." [693]

History has been manipulated, manufactured, distorted, and exhorted to direct a path for society to follow. Wars were created to divide and accumulate wealth and land for the elite. Very sound and creditable organizations and societies have been slowly infiltrated with evil. There was an ongoing power struggle between them to see who could be the "King of the Hill" and I believe it continues today. Albert Pike was on this path with the Scottish Rite Freemasonry society, the Knights of the Golden Circle, and took it beyond what it was intended for. He became involved in a much higher sect of orders.

Jesse was a very smart man and picked up on this. Jesse learned alot when he went to England and found the fuel and the motives behind the KGC, several secret societies, and most especially the European Bankers. He found out what they were up to and why they required a lot of the money/gold to be shipped overseas that the KGC had accumulated, which had not been placed in their underground banking system.

Jesse and those he could trust, began moving treasure/gold/money and liquidating it because he knew that the Europeans wanted it for themselves and not for the south, much less the United States. The Europeans wanted to keep control of the money system all over the world. They were creating a monster for themselves, but the people they were using such as Jesse and the KGC were nothing more than "front men" and pawns. England and France had lost hold of the United States in previous wars, but they wanted it back as well as its wealth.

Jesse never trusted banks that were being controlled by the European Bankers, controlling the Federal Reserve. Bud said, Jesse was actually doing his part at protecting the whole country from these thieves. He was a patriot and not many people knew this. Jesse, even at the age he was getting, did all he could to preserve the United States. The future was not to separate the country again, but to solidify its foundation based on faith and liberty.

This sentiment was felt in our country again during and after the most horrific war with the greatest generation fighting their hearts out during World War II. Finally, we reached peace and the world began to look brighter and seemed to be on the right path. Did the monster die?

After Jesse Woodson James died in August 1951, the world began to drastically change. The monster began to be fed through the Military Industrial Complex. I bring this to the reader's attention to understand what many great men, such as Jesse James, were doing to prevent our country's destruction. Why was Jesse moving around so much, staying with trusted friends and family, and always had his guns cocked, always on guard. He was not only watchful of kidnappers who desired the Confederate's gold, but he knew he was going against the "powers that be" or should I say, the "powers that want to be" and would be killed for his disloyalty to their cause.

Do I believe all secret societies and the men who join, mean harm against our nation? Certainly not, but I believe some have been deceived and there is no easy way out. The penalties of breaking the oath is death or total destruction of one's reputation and life. Some of the most intelligent and talented people of the world are being swallowed up into these societies. It doesn't matter how intelligent you are, which appears to be the ones who are drawn to this, but it is how the devil lures us all.

Jesse James was one of the most intelligent men on the earth. His wisdom was as solid as a rock, based on a foundational stone and corner stone of Biblical principles, that emerged throughout his life, but was hidden in plain sight to the public.

He may have put his whole life into these secret societies, believing strongly that it was for a good cause for mankind. Maybe the majority of it was, whom am I to judge. But I believe, even beyond the grave, Jesse was giving us clues of what his fight was based upon.

I found in Bud's notebooks, something that never really made sense until I was winding down the completion of this book. It was a note about the Civil War stating: "It was a war that should never have occurred. Its purpose was to divide the U.S.A. into 2 parts. South half going to France, placing Maximilliam to oversee that portion and the North half going to England and Canada.

Maybe this message was trying to be conveyed through the contents of the cast iron tea kettle found at Buzzard's Roost. It had (1) **1811** French Franc, with Napoleon's picture on it and (1) **1841** U.S. penny. What happened on these dates involving France, United States, and England? Were these clues also?

1811 - The nation's first *"centralized* bank" was created by Rothschild and founded by Alexander Hamilton, their agent in the Washington cabinet. Stockholders of the bank consisted of foreigners across the ocean. It was affiliated with the European Central Banks. They began to dominate the financial policies of every country in the world.

The first bank in America was called the First Bank of the United States. It was allowed a 20-year charter. During the 20 years, President Thomas Jefferson, the author of the Declaration of Independence, saw firsthand how unconstitutional this central banking institution was and would be in the time of a national crisis.

The charter was not renewed in **1811**, under the watch of President James Madison, who led in designing and creating the Bill of Rights which he introduced in 1789. This document spelled out American's rights in relation to their government. It was passed and ratified in 1791, the same year Rothschilds took over the money of America.

British financiers who owned two-thirds of the Bank's stock were extremely upset that the charter would not be renewed in 1811. By the wealth and financial power of the Rothschilds, the British declared war in 1812 against the United States. There are many opinions on why the war was started, just as those opinions about the Civil War, occurring 49 years later. I believe the reason is obvious.

1841 – Robert James and Zerelda (Dalton) Cole got married.

Prior to 1841, the national economy was booming under the leadership of Andrew Jackson and the federal government through duty revenues and sale of public lands, was able to pay off the entire national debt by January 1, 1835. Twenty-nine days later, January 30, 1835, there was an attempt to kill the sitting president of the United States outside the Capitol. By God's divine protection, the assassin's two pistols misfired. Jackson was spared. Jackson claimed Rothschilds were to blame.

By 1836, Jackson finally succeeds in removing the Rothschilds Central Bank out of America. The bank's charter was not renewed.

In **1841**, President John Tyler, who after just one month of becoming vice president to President William Henry Harrison, became president overnight when Harrison died just one month after taking the office. Tyler was an advocate of states' rights and citizen's rights. He vetoed the act to renew the charter for the Bank of the United States. He receives hundreds of letters of threats of assassination.

When the Civil War started in 1861, the economy was unstable. The Civil War was creating tremendous debt. The international bankers were eager to step in. Otto von Bismark, chancellor of Germany, 1876 was quoted as saying, "The **division of the United States** into federations of equal force was decided long before the Civil War by the high financial powers of Europe. These bankers were afraid that the US, if they remained as one block, and as one nation, would attain economic and financial independence, which would upset their financial domination over the world."

"It is practically certain that war between the North and the South was fomented by the money interest of Britain, the purpose being to divide the states, that the "old mother country" might profit thereby." ("Vindication," by Judge Joseph Franklin Rutherford)

During the Civil War when America was split and in utter chaos, Mexico too had many divisive powers seeking control. The fight was between the liberal and the conservative population, but also foreign powers. The foreign creditors who provided financial support in past wars wanted to be paid, but Mexico had suspended payment due to their declining economy. Foreign troops began occupying the region, such as Spain, Britain, and France waiting for their chance to overtake the country and promote a regime change. They also had their eye on America who was at its weakest point during the Civil War.

The emperor of France, Napoleon III needed a "front man" to use to rule over Mexico with the discretion of France. Napoleon III invited Maximillian of Austria to rule over Mexico, with the support of conservatives, moderate liberals, natives of Mexico, and the ever-present French troops. Maximillian became Emperor of Mexico in 1864 and took his oath seriously. He did not sway to the desires of the French, but to the Mexican people. This is why Shelby and many Confederates supported Maximillian.

Judah Benjamin was known to have transferred Confederate money to personal bank accounts in Europe. It has been thoroughly documented that Benjamin had the backing of both the British and French Rothschilds. He was their agent and stirred up the country to split and fight each other.

He or someone high in the authority of the KGC ordered the majority of vast amounts of gold, from the gold confiscated during the Civil War from the Union, to be shipped overseas to Europe. Some evidence found of this was included in a map Bud received from the grandsons. Massive amounts of gold, 66 tons, buried in Colorado seized from the "Vanishing Wagon (Union) Train," would later be shipped to Europe notated on the map in Appendix B-7.

Some of this was written in previous chapters, but it is just a reminder what America has gone through in the past centuries. Europeans wanted their hands-on America's land, money, and power and Jesse knew it. He never believed in banks, that's why he hid everything under the ground and kept it out of the hands of the Europeans. History and Jesse were teaching us in plain sight.

When I was looking up Robber's Cave, an important hideaway for Jesse James and Belle Starr, I was amazed at the extensive hills and woodlands spanning the countryside. As I was researching and watching videos of Robber's Cave, the YouTube video of the Robber's Cave Experiment appeared. Amazingly as God's hand was in on it, this summed up the story of Jesse's fight to save America.

The Robber's Cave Experiment was an experiment unbeknownst to the 10-11-year-old boys it involved. The Rockefellers gave psychologist, Muzafer Sherif, a Turkish-American social psychologist $38,000-$350,000 beginning in 1953 to study the effects of the "Group Realistic Conflict Theory". It was not about race, but grouping of young boys, within the same social status in an environment of competition and comradery. But how the theory was proven was in a devious and manipulative way.

The first attempt to prove this theory was in 1953 at Middle Grove, New York where Sherif brought these young men into a camp setting and allowed them all to get to know one another and they began making friends and build relationships between themselves. Then Sherif and the other researchers, only known to the boys as camp counselors, separated the group into two groups. The two groups would have their own cabin, their own territory, their own team name, and team flag. The boys prepared to compete against one another in a very provocative and manipulative way, with the "counselors' encouraging conflict and seclusion. They encouraged demonizing the groups against each other.

The so-called counselors would cause damage to each of the group's belongings, tents, and flags, blaming the other groups as the culprits. They would put the boys through tough competitions with games, tug of war, and other competitive stressful exercises.

This 1953 experiment failed because the boys could see clearly what the "counselors" were doing to provoke division and hatred towards the other group. They turned on the counselors as one united group of boys.

In 1954, Sherif again tried this experiment, but this time it was held at Robber's Cave Park in Oklahoma. The two groups came separately and never met one another. They were separated in their own territories and was not allowed to mix in the other groups. When the competition started, they were encouraged to be aggressive and promoted "the king of the hill" philosophy. The team that won would receive metals or trophies. The losing team received nothing. This went on for several weeks until resources, such as food, was reserved for the winners which caused great resentment.

This caused the groups to fight one another and burn the other's flag and ransack the other group's cabin. Well, this proved the theory that when it involved two groups who didn't have any kind of relationship with the other and the resources were limited, that the fighting and division mode took over. But the experiment didn't stop there.

When a common problem existed for both groups, demanding action to be taken by both groups, such as a water supply problem in the campground, the two groups united and fixed the problem. They began to realize that you can accomplish more as one unit and their comradery began to develop.

It goes along with a quote from Abraham Lincoln – "A house divided against itself cannot stand."

Be assured, that America has been tested, prodded, and experimented upon by forces created to divide and conquer, opposing God's full intention for this land and for His people, to be the light of the world. *"Let your light so shine before men, that they may see your good works, and glorify your Father which is in heaven."* Philippians 2:16

Since 2006, 18 years, I have been studying and writing about the European persecution of Christians, prompting the men and women of faith to seek a new world of religious freedom in their pilgrimage to America. What a fascinating and enlightening journey. No matter how much evidence is being revealed of the secret societies that infiltrated America, we must firmly believe that it was not them who established America, but is was God Almighty and He still stands on the throne.

The truth is hard to find these days and the destruction of America's past and its heroes is running rampant in our streets and parks. History is being torn down, rewritten and our Founding Fathers are being defamed, creating a fateful division in this country. It tears my heart apart to hear anti-Americanism which is being taught and used as propaganda to destroy what our founders/ancestors established.

I began noticing how our history was being rewritten, beginning in 2009. It was very evident. Digital historical books I had been using on the internet, suddenly became unavailable. Articles on major informational and historical sites were changing and depicting our national heroes as flawed slave owners, and of immoral character. We can never let their character be defamed. They were human of course, not perfect, but God used them in a great and mighty way.

Our Founding Fathers and all those who established this great nation were divinely called by the Almighty to establish a country where the citizens and their rights came first and were not subject of the elite. That was their goal. They deserve our honor and respect. We must cherish and honor what they established and not allow evil to tear us apart, for it is our foundation and our **unity** that is our strength.

We can learn a lot from the veterans of the Civil War who wore the blue and grey. At the turn of the century in 1900, they began a long hard process to heal. They put their differences, grudges, and suffering aside and placed a path for America to unite. They began meeting together at reunions, at memorials, at colleges to finish out their education, and at church. My great uncle remembers in a little town in Oklahoma, Hillsdale, just outside of Enid, that men, wearing both uniforms often came and worshipped together at their little church. Love for mankind was being restored.

In Jesse's own experiences and his maturity, he began seeing things in a different light and where his beloved country was headed. As Jesse said, the wars that began to fester up during the turn of the century were the deciding events that encouraged him and the loyal southerners to drop their hate and unite with the rest for the good of the country. A brotherhood formed that overcame the political, loyalties, and divisions.

Jesse was heavily involved in the building up of the south and contributed in the growth of America. Not many people knew that. He was indeed misunderstood and deemed as a blood-thirsty outlaw, out for his own self, even though he died penniless. He gave more than he took. Even in his last years, he had Howk deliver money to those who he knew were in need, verified by a letter written by Howk.

Jesse's actions and his words spoke for themselves. He pushed on, seeking the truth and doing his part to right the wrongs. He overcame the divisional propaganda and philosophies that were promoted to destroy this country. He put forth all his effort and intelligence into uniting the country. Jesse was truly a patriot for his country, preserving its wealth and building upon its foundational structure. He never forgot his own solid foundation in the Word of God.

Bud knew in his heart that this part of Jesse was hidden from the world. Jesse indeed had a good heart. It took a Patriot of Truth, my dear Buddy Bud, to uncover the real Jesse, the real truth. Let it be a lesson to us all. "We are one people," as Gary Bowen said. United we stand, divided we fall.

From the words of the "Bonnie Blue Flag," by Harry McCarthy – *"Like patriots of old we'll fight, our heritage to save."*

(Jesse)

(Bud)

In Andrew Jackson's farewell address in 1837, his words were powerful. "Providence has showered on this favored land, blessings without number, and has chosen you as the guardians of freedom, to preserve it for the benefit of the human race." [694]

Epilogue

Within the decade that Jesse left this earth, the 50's, the battle he fought so hard to overcome was still raging. He did his part, but one could not do it all.

This book has taken the writer into a deeper understanding of the so-called "Powers That Be", so my intent in this epilogue is to paint a broader picture of the patriots who followed Jesse into the latter part of the 20th century. I pray it will enhance Jesse's story and encourage others to preserve the blessings of liberty.

To be totally honest, I was very surprised to find out that my family tree had some mighty influential men in secret societies. I never really knew much about them until recently. I'm willing to open my family record such as Bud did to show their credentials, their successes, and sadly their vulnerabilities. It gives us all an idea of who and what they were involved in. The two I will introduce were connected to Jesse in various ways; the Thomasons and the Andersons. My 2nd great grandmother was first cousin to **Robert Ewing Thomason** (1879-1973) and my great grandfather was a double 2nd cousin to **Robert Bernard Anderson** (1910-1989). They both were **33rd** degree Freemasons. I never knew them, nor much about them.

Robert Ewing Thomason was nominated by President Truman to be a U.S. Federal Judge for Western Texas. They were both Freemasons and achieved **33rd** degrees. Thomason belonged to El Paso Lodge #130 A. F. & A. M. and belonged to El Maida Shrine, serving as Illustrious Potentate. Thomason was mayor of El Paso, Speaker of the Texas House of Representatives, and a U.S. Representative. He was district attorney in Gainesville, Texas. He ran for Governor of Texas but lost to Pat Ness. He was good friends to President Lyndon B. Johnson. One famous trial that Thomason presided over was that of Billie Sol Estes, convicted of fraud and conspiracy in **1963**. That year was quite eventful. [695]

Billie Sol Estes, "was an American businessman and financier best known for his involvement in a business fraud scandal that complicated his ties to friend and future U.S. President Lyndon Johnson."

In 1962, after information came to light that Estes had paid off four Agriculture officials for grain storage contracts, President John F. Kennedy ordered the Justice Department and FBI to open investigations into Estes' activities and determine if Secretary of Agriculture, Orville L. Freeman had also been "compromised". Freeman was cleared. Congress conducted hearings on Estes' business dealings, including some that led to Vice President Johnson, a longtime associate of Estes. Johnson had gotten Estes multi-million-dollar agriculture contracts with kickbacks to Johnson in **1963**.

Estes alleged in the 1980's that he had inside knowledge that Johnson was involved in the assassination of Kennedy in **1963** and the killing of Henry Marshall, U.S. Department of Agriculture investigator. Marshall was immediately designated as another suicide victim, but further investigations show that he was shot 5 times in his abdomen and chest and 4 times in his back. [696]

Its incredible how many of these characters all interact with one another in this story and Billie Sol Estes was at Jesse's exhumation in Granbury.

My mother did speak of Robert Anderson when I was very young. She told me about her cousin whose name appeared on U. S. currency and showed me a bill with his signature. His signature was found on U.S Currency of $5 - $100 bills. He became famous and was on the cover of Time Magazine in November 23, 1959.

At a young age, 22, Anderson received a law degree at the University of Texas and furthered his political career as a Texas state legislator, assistant attorney general, state tax commissioner, racing commissioner, member of the state tax board, chairman and executive director of the Texas Unemployment Commission, deputy chairman of the Federal Reserve Bank in Dallas, chairman of the State Board of Education, director of the Texas and Southwestern Cattle Raisers Association, president of the Texas Mid-Continent Oil and Gas Association, director of the association and the American Petroleum Institute, boy scout leader, owned KTBC radio station in Austin later sold to Lady Bird Johnson - Lyndon Baines Johnson's wife, ambassador to Panama during the Panama Canal negotiations. He was director of the *Vernon* (Texas) *Times*, served on boards of Texas Wesleyan College and McMurry College, and a law teacher. In 1937, he became an attorney and the general manager of the W.T. Waggoner Estate, the largest ranching estate under one fence in America which included oil and gas properties, cattle, and quarter horses throughout six Texas counties, Wilbarger, Wichita, Archer, Baylor, Foard, and Knox.

During the time at the Waggoner Ranch, Robert Anderson became a member of the Freemasons at the Vernon Lodge. He received a **33rd** degree in Freemasonry and became an officer of the Grand Lodge of Texas.

When Dwight D. Eisenhower came off the battlefield as a military commander after World War II, he was elected as our 34th President of the United States in 1953. He was encouraged by Lyndon Johnson, the Senate Democratic leader, who was a Freemason to strategically place Anderson as Secretary of the Navy since he knew the oil business well and an oil businessman was needed in the Navy since they used the biggest surplus of oil in the country. Johnson of course was very deep in oil himself and was deeply embedded within the Texas Oil Tycoons community, along with Ross Sterling, Hugh R. Cullen, Sid Richardson, Clint Murchison, and Haroldson Hunt who owned 500 oil wells in East Texas. Hunt traded poker winnings for oil rights and became the man who accrued the highest net worth of any one in the world. Columbus Marion "Dad" Joiner discovered the East Texas oil field based in five counties. Before he moved to East Texas, he was a member of the Tennessee House of Representatives and then in 1897, relocated to Ardmore, Oklahoma, became a wildcatter in oil and handled leases for the Choctaw Nation of Oklahoma. He was forced to sell his oil holding to Haroldson Hunt due to overselling interest and leases to multiple sources.

As you can see for yourself, so much of this is related to Jesse and the inner circles of Freemasonry, but there are no Masonic ties to President Dwight Eisenhower; none that can be found.

Robert Bernard Anderson was selected as Secretary of the Navy in 1953 by President Dwight Eisenhower. The president admired Anderson and his abilities and was highly impressed with him even though he was a Democrat and Eisenhower a Republican. Anderson's modest and intellectual approach to issues that were dear to Eisenhower created an extreme comradery between the two men.

As Secretary of the Navy, Robert Anderson ended the last formal vestiges of racial segregation. He was promoted to U.S. Deputy Secretary of Defense in 1954. His foreign affair policies included trips overseas from a request from President Eisenhower in 1956 to the Middle East to negotiate between Egypt and Israel. During this time, he changed his loyalty from the Democrat Party to the Republican Party.

Anderson became Secretary of the Treasury 1957-1961. As Secretary of Treasury, he helped to create the International Development Association which gives grants and loans to poor and underdeveloped countries. President Eisenhower said of Anderson, "perfectly wonderful young man. My God, he could run for Pope on the Presbyterian ticket and get elected." [697] He was Eisenhower's most trusted member of his cabinet.

President Eisenhower and Robert Anderson became one in their ethics and integrity. They shared in their beliefs and hope for the future. They began to see many issues facing this country that they knew only God could handle. They knew the importance of faith and the country's foundational principles in which to rely upon, in keeping America safe. Eisenhower added "one nation under God" in the pledge of allegiance and also "in God we Trust" on the U.S. currency.

President Eisenhower had tremendous confidence in Anderson as you can see with Anderson being placed in many roles in Eisenhower's Cabinet. He wanted Anderson as his running mate in 1956. Anderson declined and would take up the role as Secretary of the Treasury. Eisenhower wrote in his diaries that he would have complete trust and satisfaction to turn over the presidency to Anderson come January 20, 1961 if he would consider the presidency. Eisenhower did all he could to convince Anderson to run for President in 1960. The President vowed to offer "the full limit of his capabilities in every aspect to help Anderson get elected."

Robert Anderson declined. He did not want to continue in politics but wanted to go into private business. Also, he felt that it was only right for Eisenhower's Vice President, Richard Nixon, to be the candidate to run up against the young senator, John F. Kennedy.

Anderson had many honors; a building is named for him at the Harvard Business School. Anderson received many awards from around the world, amongst them were the highest awards the Navy, Army, and Air Force can bestow upon a citizen. The most prestigious award was the Medal of Freedom, given to him by President Eisenhower.

His achievements and high official positions led Anderson to be selected to become a Knight of Malta. [698]

The race for the presidency was tight in 1960 and Kennedy was the first Catholic to run. Oddly, the Freemasons endorsed Kennedy within their brotherhood, the same as when Abraham Lincoln was running. There are so many similarities between the two men: Kennedy and Lincoln. John Fitzgerald Kennedy won the presidency and would become the 35th President of the United States. Of course, there was controversary regarding the outcome, some believed the election was corrupt.

Before they left their post, Eisenhower and Anderson were becoming more and more concerned at where the country was headed. The military industrial complex was rising and growing after World War II and the atomic bomb. The Cold War was setting in. The monster was getting bigger and more aggressive. Eisenhower and Anderson saw this firsthand and was warning the American people. In Eisenhower's farewell address in 1961:

"In the councils of government, we must guard against the acquisition of *unwarranted influence*, whether sought or unsought, by the military industrial complex. The potential for the disastrous rise of misplaced power exists and will persist. We must never let the weight of this combination endanger our liberties or democratic processes. We should take nothing for granted. Only an alert and knowledgeable citizenry can compel the proper meshing of the huge industrial and military machinery of defense with our peaceful methods and goals, so that security and liberty may prosper together."

"Akin to, and largely responsible for the sweeping changes in our industrial-military posture, has been the technological revolution during recent decades. In this revolution, research has become central, it also becomes more formalized, complex, and costly. A steadily increasing share is conducted for, by, or at the direction of, the Federal government. The prospect of domination of the nation's scholars by Federal employment, project allocation, and the power of money is ever present and is gravely to be regarded. Yet in holding scientific discovery in respect, as we should, we must also be alert to the equal and opposite danger that public policy could itself become the captive of a scientific-technological elite." [699]

Several incites of President Eisenhower's administration indicate that the president began seeing an increase of infiltration of the military and industrial corporations, leading to a surrender of our constitutional government which he strongly tried to preserve. It was said that Eisenhower set up a secret plan with military intelligence to safeguard our constitutional republic for the future against a potential domestic enemy. It was put in place to become activated if in the future our republic was ever threatened. Eisenhower shared this with the new incoming president, John Fitzgerald Kennedy.

President Kennedy gave a speech, April 27, 1961, during his first year in office at the American Newspaper Publishers Association called "The President and the Press:"

"If you are awaiting a finding of "clear and present danger," then I can only say that the danger has never been clearer, and its presence has never been more imminent. It requires a change in outlook, a change in tactics, a change in missions, by the government, by the people, by every businessman or lay leader, and by every newspaper. For we are opposed around the world by a monolithic and ruthless conspiracy that relies primarily on covert means for expanding its sphere of influence. On infiltration instead of invasion, on subversion instead of elections, on intimidation instead of free choice, on guerillas by night instead of armies by day. It is a system which has conscripted vast human and material resources into the building of a tightly knit, highly efficient machine that combines military, diplomatic, intelligence, economic, scientific and political operations. Its preparations are concealed, not published. Its mistakes are buried, not headlined. Its dissenters are silenced, not praised. No expenditure is questioned, no rumor is printed, no secret is revealed. It conducts the Cold War, in short, with a war-time discipline no democracy would ever hope or wish to match." [700]

After leaving his White House position, Robert B. Anderson went into private business in mining, oil, real estate, investments, and banking affairs, but still helped to carry out diplomatic missions for the United States. In 1963, President Kennedy appointed Anderson to a special committee to study the U.S. foreign aid program.

In the private sector, during Kennedy's presidency, Robert B. Anderson continued to back President Eisenhower's philosophy and faith. Anderson wrote a highly recognized poem which later was published in a beautifully illustrated book titled, "A Nation Needs to Pray," which out of all his awards, he was most proud of.

I was so blessed to find a copy of the book in which the forward was written by Dwight Eisenhower. Eisenhower respected and admired Anderson, he was his right-hand man. Eisenhower's words reflect his admiration: "Throughout the nation's history, a deeply felt religious faith has been a powerful force molding Americans in uncounted ways. Robert B. Anderson's moving, and poetic statement of this deep-rooted national tradition is a stirring reaffirmation of the American faith. Most importantly, he demonstrates the strength which is found only with the realization of man's humble dependence on the Almighty."

In Anderson's book, "A Nation Needs To Pray:" "that in humility we see that greatness is not measured by industrial grandeur, or destiny achieved by things we touch, by things produced, nor things consumed, nor things we set afloat upon the sea, nor send in the air." His words speak of all the advancement America has achieved in its history, its wars, its technology and industrial revolution, but then directs our attention towards the human factor and the importance of respect for different cultures, races, and the concern and welfare of all people. "Our greatest need is for a wisdom that transcends our own; for devotion that insures there is no instant of neglect. For that, wherein is held the fate of all, this nation needs to pray." [701]

After Robert Anderson's book was published in **1963**, many great men began speaking out regarding the Military Industrial Complex and the danger, if it was placed in the wrong hands.

Suddenly, our world stopped and changed instantly. President Kennedy was assassinated. Along with many other conspiracy theories related to the JFK assassination, one theory points to the Texas Oil Industry as the fuel behind the assassination. Vice President Lyndon B. Johnson was sworn in as President.

Earlier, as a senator, Lyndon B. Johnson, under Eisenhower's presidency, became highly interested in the "Space Race." His ideas for national security was in the form of missiles and the complete control of space. In October 1957, President Eisenhower could see the writing on the wall and said the US was not in a space race and commented, "Lyndon Johnson can keep his head in the stars if he wants. I'm going to keep my feet on the ground." But Johnson was going to force Eisenhower into a space race, whether the President liked it or not." [702]

Members of the Senate Armed Services Committee conducted hearings, chaired by Senate Majority Leader, Senator Lyndon B. Johnson on this very heavy subject. It was reported in newspapers on January 8, 1958 regarding Johnson's statements to the committee. It was easy to find this information years ago, but now it is extremely hard to locate on the internet. Many sites have been taken down. It's no longer shown in the newspaper archives.

In a very excellent document written by Alan Wasser, I thankfully found the exact quotes of Johnson that coincided with my research in 2013-2014. Senator Lyndon B. Johnson's words were printed in the New York Times, "Text of Johnson's Statement on Status of Nations's Defense and Race for Space." Also, it was printed in the Washington Post on the same date, "Free World Must Control Space, Johnson tells Senate Group."

His words, "Control of space means control of the world. From space, the masters of infinity would have the power to control the earth's weather, to cause drought and flood, to change the tides and raise the levels of the sea, to divert the Gulf Stream and change temperate climates to frigid. There is something more important than the ultimate weapon. And that's the ultimate position. The position of total control over the Earth that lies somewhere in outer space."

While Johnson was vice president to Kennedy, the President appointed Johnson, Chairman of National Aeronautics and Space Council. This power or military industrial complex was in the wrong hands.

Robert Anderson was asked to carry out diplomatic missions on behalf of President Lyndon B. Johnson. He became involved in business interests in several international projects. In 1964, Johnson was elected as president with the help of the campaign of Robert Anderson. [703]

Anderson had a lot of political power, especially in foreign affairs. It was believed because of his status with President Dwight Eisenhower and his noble heritage, that he was invited to become a noble knight in the British Order of the Knights of Malta before or during the Eisenhower administration.

The *British order* of the Knights of Malta was formed over a thousand years ago and began as a humanitarian order and evolved into a military order. Robert B. Anderson was chosen.

The British Monarchy during the 1900's began issuing titles of nobility to Americans, bringing them into knighthood and merging them into the British honor system. Many men became knights, dukes, and earls. Many Americans in the upper echelon and high political and military offices, business enterprises, and bankers were targeted. The British goal was to create a new type of empire, seize the wealth of the planet, and reincorporate the U.S. They wanted the British military forces to combine with the U.S. forces, especially the Navy. The Navy was the primary mechanism of power. That is why Robert Anderson was swayed to join the Knights of Malta.

There are many in political and judicial positions in America that have "Title of Nobility." They were promised wealth, position and power.

This entitlement went against the original 13th amendment. The amendment (Title of Nobility) states, "If any citizen of the United States shall accept, claim, receive, or retain any title of nobility or honour, or shall without the consent of Congress, accept and retain any present, pension, office, or emolument (payment or stipend) of any kind whatever, from any emperor, king, prince, or foreign power, such person shall cease to be a citizen of the United States, and shall be incapable of holding any office of trust or profit under them, or either of them."

Between the years of 1811-1819, the 13th Amendment, "Title of Nobility" was ratified and placed in the Constitution to protect the country from espionage and treason.

The original 13th amendment was quietly replaced with a new 13th amendment during the Civil War, the abolishment of slavery. "Neither slavery nor involuntary servitude, except as a punishment for crime whereof the party shall have been duly convicted, shall exist within the United States, or any place subject to their jurisdiction."

Sadly, Anderson's last years of his life were plagued with private and business discord causing severe legal and health matters. Was he also a "pawn," similar to Jesse, whose intelligence and faith stirred them to not follow the loyalty of the secret societies which had been infiltrated with corruption and evil? As you can see, if you do follow their rules, you were highly rewarded with high positions, money, titles and ultimately protected. If you didn't play by their rules, you were defamed and destroyed, one way or the other.

"The very word 'secrecy' is repugnant in a free and open society; and we are as a people inherently and historically opposed to secret societies, to secret oaths, and to secret proceedings. We decided long ago that the dangers of excessive and unwarranted concealment of pertinent facts far outweighed the dangers which are cited to justify it."
President John F. Kennedy

This book was all about Jesse James, Bud's pursuit of the truth, but also the "Universal Duality" that is so often displayed through secret societies and the effect it has upon a person's soul. You either go along with what is fed to you, staying in the gray matter, or you break out of the stronghold and "do what's right."

By way of God's lead, I became aware through research of an extensive amount of information and proof of a scheme designed to try to destroy the Republic that our Founding Fathers created. It started with the schemes of high-level men in secret societies. They focused on the highly intellect, those with strict moral values, the young, the passive, and the oppressed.

We learn of a man, Jim Shaw who was a Freemason. It appears that he had been through a lot of trauma in his life, especially when he was young when he was very vulnerable. He was just recovering from his 2nd operation and discussing ultimatums with the doctor, but also the road ahead. Shaw began reading scriptures and tossing around his spiritual readiness. He received an elegant letter from Washington D.C. Shaw was being rewarded with a **33rd** degree. He was chosen by the Supreme Council of the **33rd** Degree in Washington D.C. and was requested to appear at the ceremony conducted at the House of the Temple. He traveled there and became amazed of the architecture of the Temple. The tall bronze doors had inscribed, "Freemasonry Builds Its Temples in the Hearts of Men and Among Nations."

The symbolism and magnitude of the structure was incredible. There are several videos that can actually take you to the Temple so that you can see yourself how powerful and monstrous this structure is, not far from the White House. Shaw writes that he was struck by the number of serpents embedded in the stone structure as decorative ornaments. He writes, "It was all most impressive and gave me a strange mixture of the sensations of being in a temple and in a tomb – something sacred but threatening."

Shaw was taken into a room the first day by three members of the council. The first question was "Of what religion are you?" Shaw stated, "Not long before this I would have answered with something like, "I believe the Ancient Mysteries, the "Old Religion," and I believe in reincarnation." However, without thinking at all about how to answer, I found myself saying, "I am a Christian."

"Then to my surprise and theirs, I asked them, "Are you men born again?" The man in charge quickly stopped me by saying, "We're not here to talk about that – we are here to ask you questions." After they sent me back out, I sat down and thought about it. When the next man came out, I asked him, "Did they ask you if you are a Christian? He said, "yes, they did." What did you tell them?" I asked, and he replied, "I told them Hell no, and I never intend to be!" Then he said a strange thing to me, "They said I'm going higher," and he left through a different door, looking pleased."

"During the actual ceremony, there were four books in the center table, as you can also see on the videos that these remain on the table. The books were, the Bible, the Koran, the Book of the Law and the Hindu Scriptures. Shaw was asked to kiss the book of his religion. He kissed the Bible and was made to drink wine out of a human skull. "May this wine I now drink become a deadly poison to me, as the Hemlock juice drunk by Socrates, should I ever knowingly or willfully violate the same." Shaw drank the wine and then a man came out dressed as a skeleton , throwing their arms around Shaw and was obligated to state "And may these cold arms forever encircle me should I ever knowingly or willfully violate the same."

"Shaw conducted a ceremony within his Lodge prior to Easter and was sickened to say the words he had said for years. He suddenly realized the blasphemous words he had just spoken, "I had just called Jesus an "apostle of mankind" who was neither inspired nor divine!" The ceremony he had been conducting all these years identified itself as darkness and black. "We had dramatized and commemorated the snuffing out of the life of Jesus, without once mentioning his name, and the scene ended with the room in deep silent darkness." He left Freemasonry. [704]

All of us, are in an important battle within ourselves and our world we live in. It's a choice in which each individual must choose the path to follow. The best illustration of this is told through a Cherokee Indian legend, "Two Wolves."

An old Cherokee is teaching his grandson about life. "A fight is going on inside me," he said to the boy. "It is a terrible fight and it is between two wolves. One is evil – he is anger, envy, sorrow, regret, greed, arrogance, self-pity, guilt, resentment, inferiority, lies, false pride, superiority, and ego." He continued, "The other is good – he is joy, peace, love, hope, serenity, humility, kindness, benevolence, empathy, generosity, *truth*, compassion, and faith. The same fight is going on inside you – and inside every other person, too." The grandson thought about it for a minute and then asked his grandfather, "Which wolf will win?" The old Cherokee simply replied, "The one you feed." [705]

"But if serving the Lord seems undesirable to you, then choose for yourselves this day whom you will serve, whether the gods your ancestors served beyond the Euphrates, or the gods of the Amorites, in whose land you are living. But as for me and my household, we will serve the LORD!"
Joshua 24:15

Final Thoughts

Looking back on this 7-year journey with Bud, I can see Jesse in him; his mannerism, chivalry, boldness, toughness, his cantankerous spirit, stubbornness, wisdom, wit, common sense, perseverance, sense of humor, and his charisma that draws so many people to him. Some of the stories and phrases that Bud would come up with were so funny, I cried. I wish I could tell them all. Aubrey Everhard said the same about Jesse.

Bud had a newspaper clipping that had no date, no name of the newspaper or title to the story, but it was in the Dennis McCarthy's column. There is a Dennis McCarthy who has a column with the Los Angeles Daily News. It is not known for sure if this is the same man who wrote this piece. He was speaking of Morrey Davidson who was a New York theatrical booker and songwriter who went to see Jesse, going in very skeptically, but leaving the meeting, he was convinced that Dalton was the real Jesse James. Morrey was the one who was at Jesse's 102nd birthday party and did a recorded interview with him. The article also speaks of Ola Everhard. At the end of the article, the writer wrote one of Jesse's remarks told to Morrey. "Like old Jesse says when asked if he has any special words for the youth of the land, "Don't take nothing from nobody, keep a hot poker and give 'em half a carrot."

*Sadly, the day I finished the conclusion of this book for Bud, June 8, 2024, he left this earth to go home. I learned of his passing early the next morning. Oh, how I loved that man. I had such a deep mutual respect and love for Bud. Like Jesse with his friend, Ola, he too didn't share everything with me, but what a blessing for him to trust me with his research and his words. We both had the extreme passion to make the truth come forward for Jesse and for dear sweet Ola.

Bud accomplished what he was here for, as we had discussed time and time again. This hunt for Jesse was miraculously orchestrated by God to prove the truth. Bud didn't go after the treasure for his own gain, he went after Jesse to understand him, to find the human side of Jesse, the real Jesse and his motives. Even though Bud never got to collect in any of Jesse's treasures, he found his treasure in his family, his friends, his new friends he met along the way, and in the truth he discovered that prompts us all to become a Patriot of Truth.

At Bud's celebration of life, his nephew, Zach summed Bud's life up in one sentence. "Everyone thought that Bud's life was centered around Jesse James, but in reality, his life was centered around his family."

Many stories were shared during his celebration of how people's lives were changed because of Bud's love and intervention. It was so heart-warming to hear these stories from a waitress, from the nephews who Bud took under his wing, and the joy that he brought to the stranger in town, giving them a warm welcome. He never met a stranger. Those he encountered were made to sincerely feel like Bud loved them unconditionally. He treated everyone like family, including me and my husband. He was one of the greatest men I have ever known. What an honor it is that I was able to complete this book for Bud, in God's perfect timing.

May you "Go Rest High on That Mountain" dear Bud, my Buddy Bud! Your story is complete! "Son, your work on earth is done." "Go Rest High on That Mountain," music and lyrics written by Vince Gill, 1995.

"Then you will know the truth and the truth and the truth will set you free" John 8:32

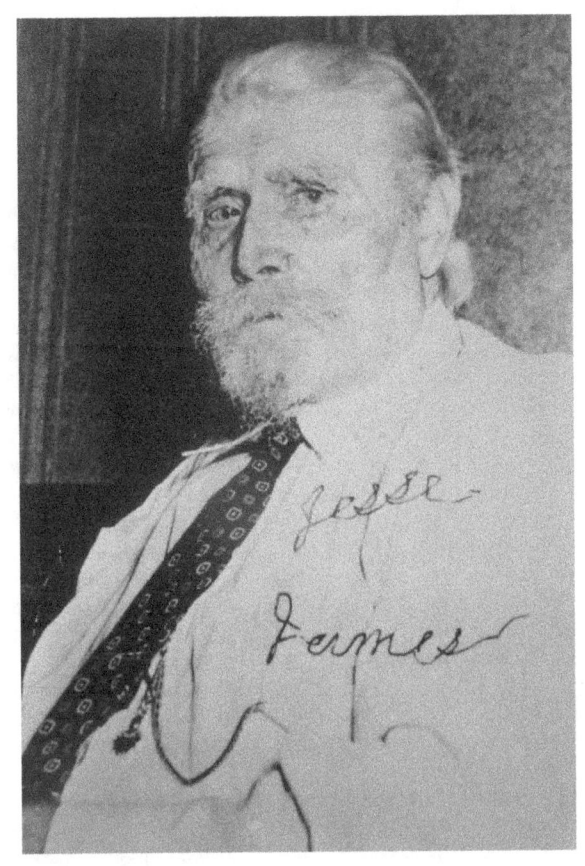

(Jesse was found (photo given to Ola from Jesse))

(Bud and John Tatum, riding off into the sunset)

Bud Hardcastle

Ellis Eugene "Bud" Hardcastle died June 8, 2024, in Purcell, at the age of 85 years 1 month 4 days.

Bud was born May 4, 1939, in Purcell, Oklahoma to Arthur "Buck" and Lola (Hays) Hardcastle. He grew up and attended school in Purcell, where he graduated high school in 1958. In 1959, Bud joined the United States Army and spent the next four years serving his country. He lived the rest of his life in the town that he loved and it was there that, on November 27, 2004, he married Barbara Fielder (Rains). Bud led a wonderful life full of love, family, and friends. Throughout his years, he explored a variety of jobs, including selling used cars, selling insurance, and, of course, taking care of the patrons of Ruby's Inn alongside Barbara. There were many facets to the man that Purcell knew as Bud Hardcastle. As many know, he was a social butterfly that had never met a stranger. He was a man that could and would strike up a conversation with anyone about anything. He genuinely enjoyed people and was always there to talk to, to lend a smile or a helping hand, and to support his local community. Bud was an avid sports fan who supported all levels of teams from his Purcell Dragons to the OU Sooners and beyond. Such was his love for football that he played semi-pro football in Oklahoma City when he was in his early thirties and even participated in a local alumni full pads football game at the age of 49. When not working or enjoying sports, Bud enjoyed spending his free time having morning talks at the coffee shop, loving his large family, and just enjoying life. He was a man of quiet strength who, along with his brother Paul, helped to raise their siblings after the deaths of their parents. The two brothers instilled a sense of family and created a bond that has lasted throughout their years and has been taught to their newer generations. Bud and Paul not only worked on strengthening their family in their youth, but also strengthening Purcell as pillars of our community throughout their adult lives. Bud was a "man's man" who considered himself a poet. He was a historical author with two books that are due to be published and an avid treasure hunter for anything related to Jesse James. Bud had an amazing sense of love and embraced those he cared for whole heartedly. Although he was not the best at keeping time, he knew how to spend it well. Bud shared his smile, his stories, his zest for life, and his love openly. He will be missed.

Bud is preceded in death by his parents, Arthur "Buck" and Lola (Hays) Hardcastle; his sister, Patricia Ann "Trishann" Taylor; his son-in-law, Dennis Beller; his niece, Liz Roberts; and his nephew, Ricky Hardcastle. Survivors include his wife, Barbara Hardcastle; his daughter, Debra Madden; his son, Curtis Fielder; his brothers, Paul Hardcastle and Bill Hardcastle; his sister, Carmen Mitchusson; his grandchildren, Chase Hudson, Chad Hudson, Aaron Hyde, Austin Carr, Staysha Beller, Erica Mills; his great-grandchildren, Jase and Charlie Mills; and numerous other family and friends.

(Bud's obit. Written by his family)

In Loving Memory

BUD HARDCASTLE
May 4, 1939 ~ June 8, 2024

Appendices

Appendix A: Letters
Appendix B: Treasure Maps
Appendix C: KGC Codes

<u>**Appendix A: Letters**</u>
A few letters that Bud has accumulated and are transcribed below.

(Bud's box of letters that Bud allowed me to use)

Appendix A-1 (1880)

Bud was able to get a copy of a rare letter sent from Jesse James to Isaac Milton, living in Laredo, Texas; April 16, 1880. The letter was authenticated and is part of the Charles Rosamond Collection. Look at the way Jesse writes the letter "I". Other documents that Bud has, indicate Jesse and J. Frank Dalton's handwriting, the way the letter "I" is written, is identical.

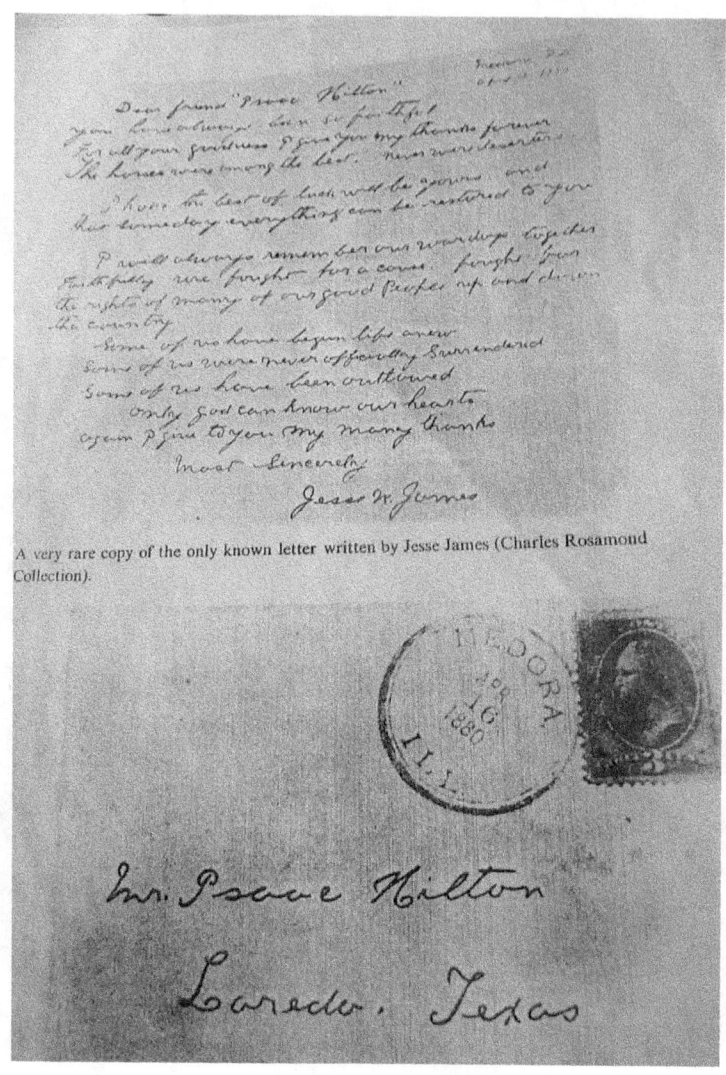

(Letter from JJ to Isaac Milton)

Appendix A-2 (1909)

A post card was sent by Jesse James to Ms. Bertha Dalton with an encoded message, January 10, 1909. The post card he had made, is believed to be a photo of the oil well, with the inscription on the front said "Shooting First Oil Well at Centralia, Illinois, January 10, 1909. Bud had the postcard which contained a secret coded message on the other side.

(Post card sent by JJ)

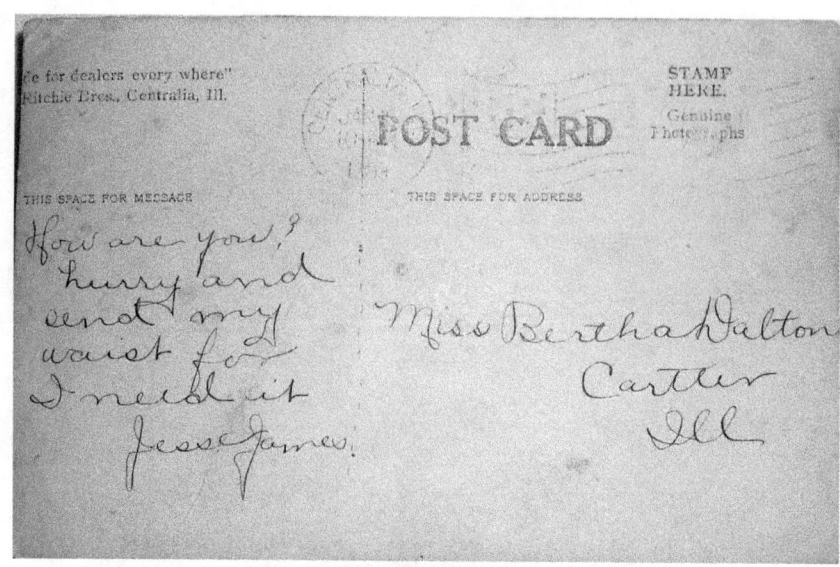

(Encrypted message to Dalton)

Appendix A-3 (1932)

We learned that Jesse was in Gladewater, Texas in 1931 when the oil boom exploded in East Texas, serving with the Texas Rangers. Because of a series of letters Bud had accumulated from a member of the James family in Missouri, we find valuable information regarding the activities of Jesse in the early part of 1932. In that year, Jesse was staying in Excelsior Springs, Missouri. This was before he met Howk and before he came out as Jesse James.

The letters were written in pencil, on the Blue Willow Café stationary. The owner of the Blue Willow was George Lieser. Jesse was using Rhodella Shepard to write his letters for him. The Shepard family rode with Quantrill and Rhodella, before taking on this task, had to verify that this elderly man was really who he said he was, Jesse James. Not explaining to Jesse who she was, she asked him if he remembered going to a farmhouse near Platte City, asking for shelter, food, and protection. He told her, yes, it was the Shepard's farm. She asked him where they hid the horses and without hesitation, Jesse told her that the barn was north of the house. There was a deep hollow just north of the barn and they hid the horses there.

Rhodella knew with no doubt, that this man was really Jesse.

Rhodella P. Payne Shepard (1884-1966) was born to Minor Payne (1845-1930) and Alsey Ann Porter (1852-1926). She married Paul Shepard (1880-1928) son of John Shepard (1843-1918) and Sarah E. Ashby (1854-1917). They lived in Platte County, Missouri.

Jesse was giving lectures during this time but going by the name of Frank Dalton. The public did not know him as Jesse James, but only a few were in on his secret.

Surprisingly, he let the governor in on the secret; Governor Henry Stewart Caulfield who was governor between 1929-**1933.** Jesse had Rhodella write him a letter. Jesse first bluntly states that he is Jesse James dictating this letter. He then begins to defend his family, his most prized possession.

To: Governor Henry Stewart Caulfield
From; Jesse James, by Rhodella Shepard, January 24, 1932:

"I have just returned from Kearney where my son-in-law lives (Henry Barr). He informed me that there was a man there in Kearney had wrote to you that he knew all about my family and that I was nothing but an imposter. I can't understand how that he would know all about my folks when he is not one-fifty at the furthest. When my father and mother were born in Logan County, Kentucky.

My Father, Robert James and Zarelda Cole were married December 1841 and that of this union there were Alexander F. James who was born January 10, 1843. Jesse Woodson James born Sept 5th, 1847. Susan Lavina James born Nov 25, 1849 and Robert James who lived but few days. Robert James, my father at the time of his marriage was a Baptist preacher licensed in May 1839. After settling in Clay County, he visited California and died there August 18th, 1850. Then I can't see how that man should know all about my family. After mother had lived five years single, she married Doctor Samuels, he was my stepfather. We boys didn't stay at home hardly any we were first here and there not going to school but very little. I went part of one winter to the Summerset School. John Biglow was our teacher. Maggie Kebron was going to the same school where I did. I liked the little girl, both mischievous in school hours. I sat behind her. I pulled her hair and sometime steal a kiss from her. I did not go the full term. I left the neighborhood and went down on the river bottom where Captain Rankins lived staying there the most of my time in and the latter part of 1861. I went back to my mothers in the 1861. The Yankee soldiers had some trouble with my stepfather. They overpowered me when I was out in the field plowing for corn and beat me til mother thought that they had killed me. When she got to me she fell upon her knee and begged them to spare my life. They even used her rough and then left. I lay in bed almost six months before I was able to be about. I left there went up in Iowa staying there til in June 1862. I returned to Clay County. I then joined Quantrills band with my brother Frank. We were called guerillas not being at home any more, only now and then so I can't see from my part how that man could know all about us boys. Now when you read this letter, please take it in consideration that this man surely has given you false statements. I understand that they told you that I was chased out of the Elms Hotel. I left there on my own accord. If I could, a few minutes on the phone at your town, I could explain to you beyond a doubt that I am Jesse James after that I will bring some parties to Jefferson City proving to you what I have said, thanking you for the kindness that you showed me.

I remain your friend,
Jesse James by Rhodella Shephard

Appendix A-4 (1932)

A letter addressed to Samuel R. Bogle in Yakima, Washington, dated Feb. 6, 1932. It was Samuel Reed Bogle (1851-1935). He was a dry goods merchant in the northeastern part of Indian Territory in the Cherokee Nation. He had a store in Grove, Indian Territory by 1900-1930.

Rhodella Shepherd did the writing, signed by JJ by RC Shepherd. They were still in Excelsior Springs.

To: Mr. Samuel R. Bogle – Yakima, Washington
From: Jesse James by R.C. Shepherd, Excelsior Springs, Mo. Feb. 6, 1932

"Dear Sir:
I am answering your letter this morning Samuel R. Do you remember that you have just stated about Waterville, Okla? We did not talk much in regard to that trouble in St. Joseph, Mo. But I seen by what you said that you thought you was riding and talking with Jesse James. I noticed that you kept watching my horse and saddle. You spoke about the money that was in my saddle pocket. If you had known at that time how much cash there was, you would have been sure that you was talking to Jesse himself. I was riding a horse at that time that you did often see in Oklahoma. After leaving you I went to a little town in the Choctaw Nation. There I went out into the canyon not far from Lexington, Oklahoma on the south Canadian River. There I buried the most of that money in a place where it never could be forgotten. After Cole Younger got out of the penitentiary in Northfield, Minnesota, he and I come into Okla together. We got it or a part of it. Belonging to Cole there was 40 thousand dollars in cash. I was carrying in my saddle pockets at the time we crossed the mountains. You know I rode the best of horse and was riding an extra good saddle that was made in Pueblo, Colorado. It was noted as the best saddle company in the west – we did not talk so very

much about the James on the trip we talked a good deal about a hundred and one others about your home in Oklahoma. Now if you think that I have explained enough for you, are you satisfied that this is the same man that you crossed the mountains with? Will you go before a Notary Republic and state as much as you can remember that this is the man you had that conversation with as we crossed the mountains. It would be one of the greatest proofs that I could have. Now when you get back to Okla., you write to me and I will try someway to get you here to the Springs. I could take care of you while we were having a long visit. This is a beautiful summer resort you sure could enjoy yourself. I am still tall and slender and straight as ever. People here don't think that I am as old as I am. Now I will close my letter hoping this will find you in good health and a good Christian believing in your maker and trusting in God for your health. I remain your true friend,
Jesse James by R.C. Shepherd

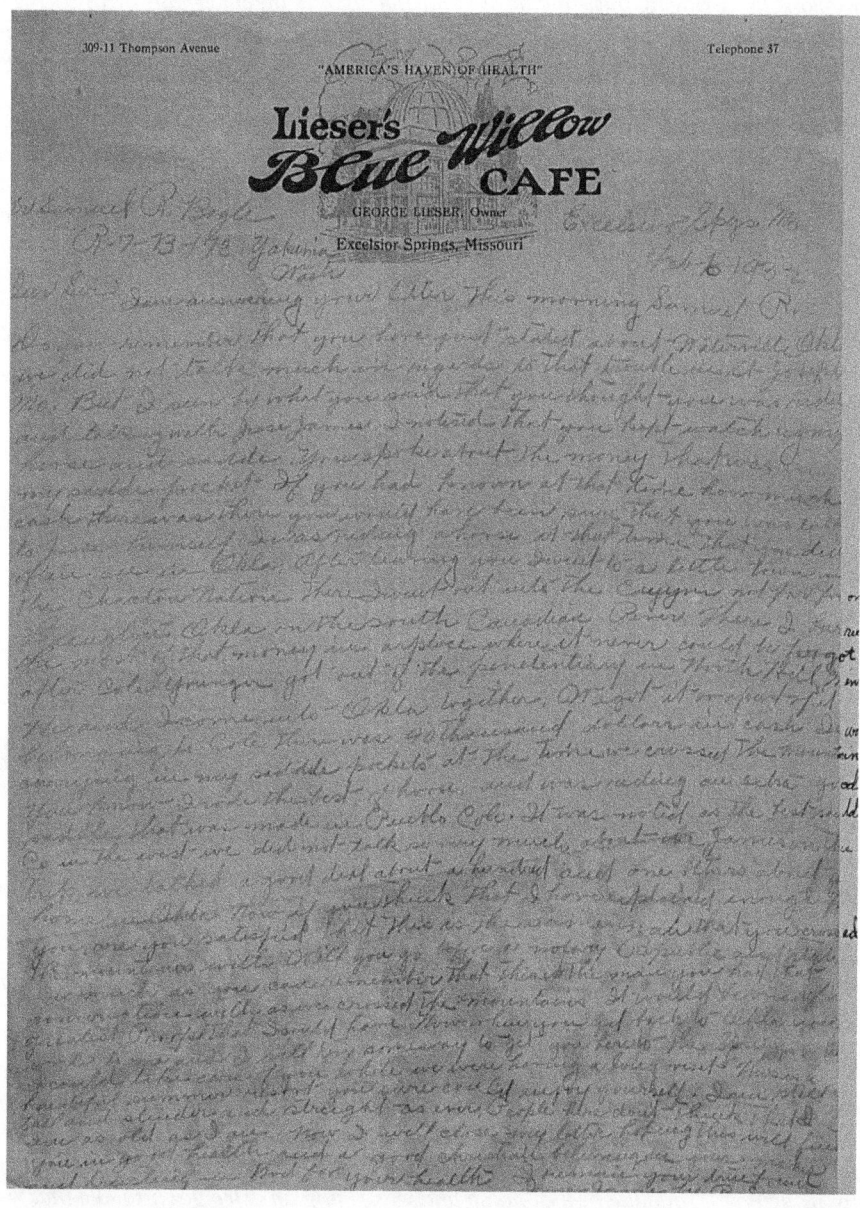

(Letter from JJ to Samuel Bogle, Feb. 6, 1932)

Appendix A-5 (1932)

The same day that the above letter was sent to Mr. Bogle, a letter was sent to L. C. Ackerman (Leland Callaway Ackerman), Rison, Arkansas, dated Feb. 6, 1932 from Lieser's Blue Willow Café, Excelsior Springs, Missouri. Mr. Ackerman was the editor of the Cleveland County Herald.

Mr. Ackerman had written the mayor of Excelsior Springs on January 16, 1932 speaking about the man in "your city" who is claiming that he is the original Jesse James and that he had a letter written over 50 years ago by Frank James that his father had which could "throw some light on the subject." The mayor must have contacted Jesse to respond to this letter. Bud had the original letter.

To: L. C. Ackerman
From: Jesse James, February 6, 1932

"I have your letter of Jan 16th, 1932, before me stating you would send me a copy of the letter written by my brother Frank James. If you would not trust us with the letter please take it to someone and have a photo taken so we may have a picture of it as it is written and whatever the expense is I will be glad to pay it. Notify us as to how much it will cost and send it C.O.D. I think this will be better than a certified copy. Just have it witnessed by a notary and please collect the plate from the photographer. I wish this to be done so nobody else can use it but ourselves. If you will trust us with the letter we will return it to you by Registered mail and we can have a picture made here. I am greatly interested since I found your letter among some unanswered ones. It is a great thing to know and see my own brother's handwriting for we never dared to correspond you know, written words never die. The only way I had any chance to talk with him it was hard to get to see him. Now, I am sending you a clipping that they give me while I was dictating my life as a rebel spy in the southern army. I was going under the name of Jesse James Cou? – (can not make it out, possibly "cousin") to Frank and Jesse James. Part of this clipping is false. Except one thing that is the name of my sister – Bessie. She was a well-known actress as we played in theaters. She was with me some of the years I was keeping under cover after my wife Zarelda Mims died. I then married her she was Amelia Cole, a fourth cousin of mine born in Kentucky and loved race horses. So you can see what my life was after the supposed killing of Jesse James, or Charly Howard. Now I will close my letter hoping this will find you well and thanking you for the interest you have taken.

Yours truly,
Jesse James by R/S

Appendix A-6 (1940)

Bud had a copy of a letter from Frank Dalton, from Wrights Camp in Kilgore, Texas written February 4, 1940 to Arlo Norman who lived in Austin. This was DeWitt Travis' nephew. Dalton/Jesse mentions his Aunt Zerelda whose arm got blown off. This would have been written after he was with Howk.

2-4-'40

Dear Arlo —

Just rec'd your letter. Also got a letter from your father. DeWitt has been laid up with the flu but is OK again. Arlo, I'm awful glad that you and Gene both received a chance to get an education (but trust your mama to see to that) for life holds nothing much that is worth while without one. About the movies you speak of — I hasn't saw "Gone with the wind" so know nothing about it yet, but "Jesse James" was pure fiction and done us a terrible injustice for it was so terribly misleading. For instance — it was not railroaders but Pinkerton Detectives who blew the house up. They killed Frank and Jess' seven year old half brother and blew Aunt Jerelda's arm off. She lived nearly 30 years after that. And Kit Dalton? Sure I knew him. I'd like to get his book, I knew he'd written one. About me getting killed — I've been killed so much that I'm getting used to it and don't mind it a bit any more. I let a girl — Miss Tuttle — have your address, she asked me for it and I suppose she's written you by this time, but say young man, watch your step! This is Leap year! The Tuttles are fine folks. Opal is doing my typing and we have a movie story in Hollywood. I have already signed a contract and the MS is in the hands of the re-write people. Nothing more of importance

(Letter to Arlo Norman from Jesse)

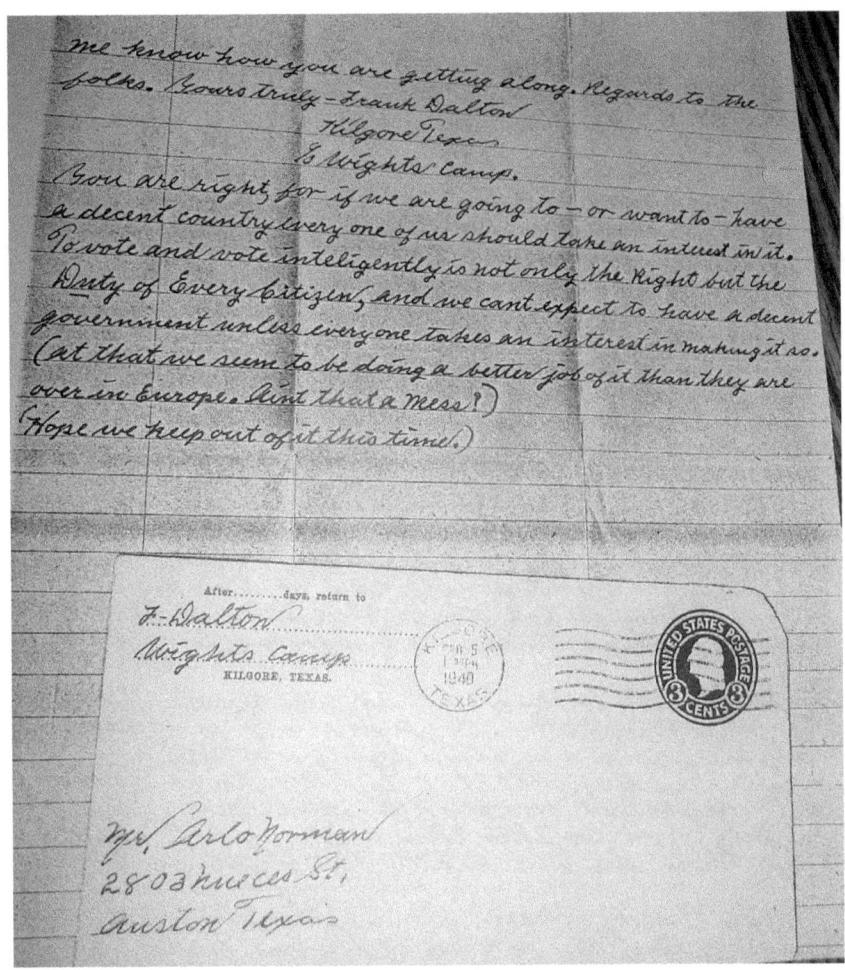

(2nd page and envelope)

Appendix A–7 (1942)

Bud also obtained a copy of a letter from Aubrey Everhard, written by Frank Dalton who was in Longview, Texas to Howk on September 12, 1942.

9-12-'42

Well, Howdy!

I'll bet this is the smallest letter in the biggest envelope you've got for a month of sundays, but its the only air mail envelope I've got till I go down town and get some.

We're going to have a local option election next saturday, the 19th and I look for Gregg county to go dry as H--l.

If it does I'm goin to buy me a teakettle an get me a piece o' corn bread an go to makin my own likker, for damd if I'm goin to do without! Heck No! Life's too short.

I got a write up in the Dallas News Aug 25th and as soon as they send me some papers I'll shoot me out to you.

They printed about a half page of crap about me, but they didn't do so bad at that. Not as bad as some of them do anyway.

Its still hot here. I thot I'd send you the temperature, so I hung a thermoter outside of my door, but the darn thing melted as soon as the sun hit it so I'll have to guess at it, and maybe you can do the same. But Its nighly hot for this time of the year. In fact we've had an unusually hot summer.

Say Howk, them pictures are simply swell, and I'm proud of them. I show them to all my visitors and they all admire them.

I'm having the Hotel to forward this if you've moved on.

If you visit the Custer Battle ground be
— over —

(Letter from Dalton to Howk)

sure to tell me about it. I was there by 10 oclock the next day and we helped to bury the men of the 7th cavalry. I believe they were most all taken up and buried some where else afterwards though.

Well theres no news, and if there was I wouldnt know it for Im in bed nearly all the time.

I dont take the local paper for it costs a nickel and a postage stamp only costs 3 cents, and theres more news in the postage stamps.

Write soon for Im always glad to hear from you.

          Yours Truly Frank Dalton,
               1007-E. Magrill St,
                 Longview Tx.

Lost! Strayed or Stolen!

A gal by the name of Jean Carlson

    Habitat,

Lewiston Idaho!

I received a letter from her and was chump enough to send her my picture and I guess she hid under the bed for I havnt heard from her since. Oh well! my hearts plumb busted, but I guess Il recover, I always have.

(2nd page)

Appendix A-8 (1947-48)

Waiting on the pension:

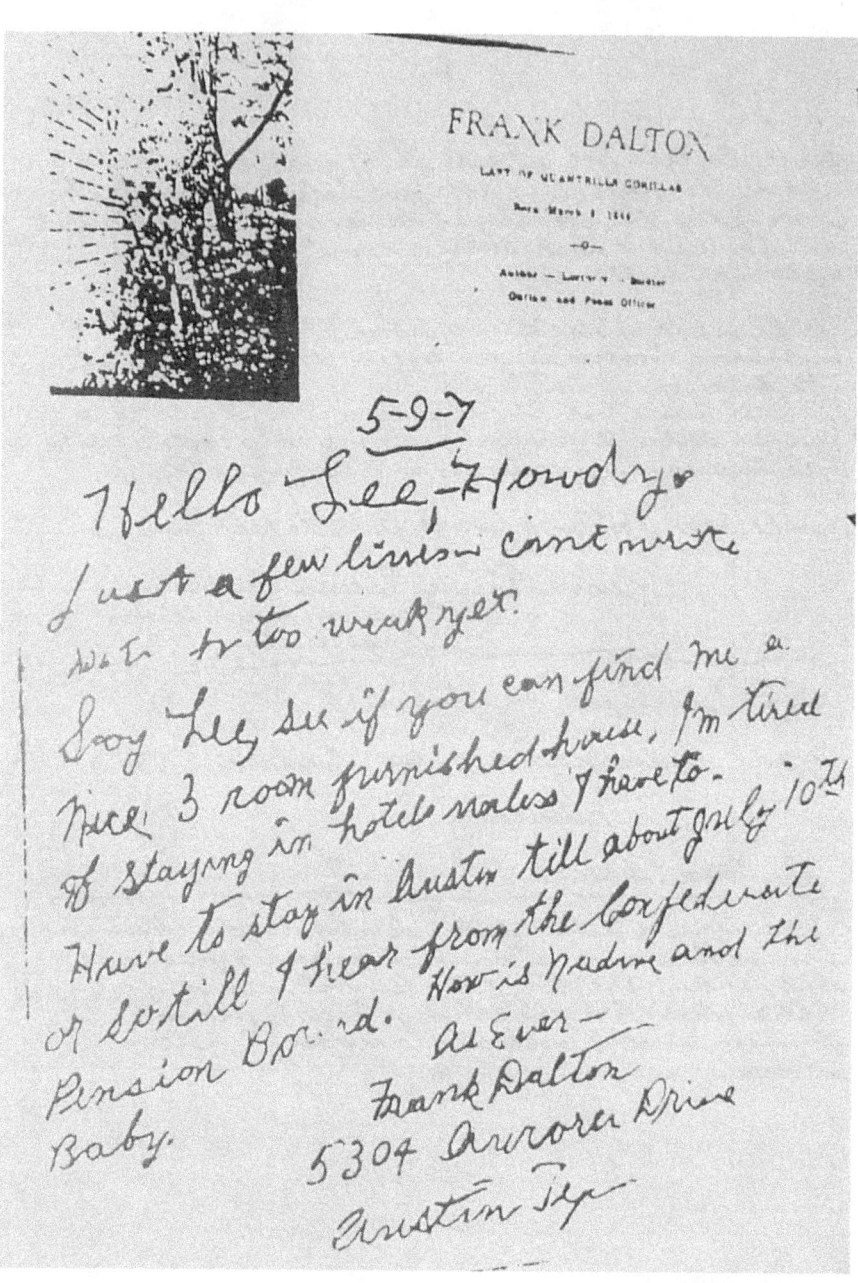

(Letter from Frank Dalton to Howk, May 9, 1947)

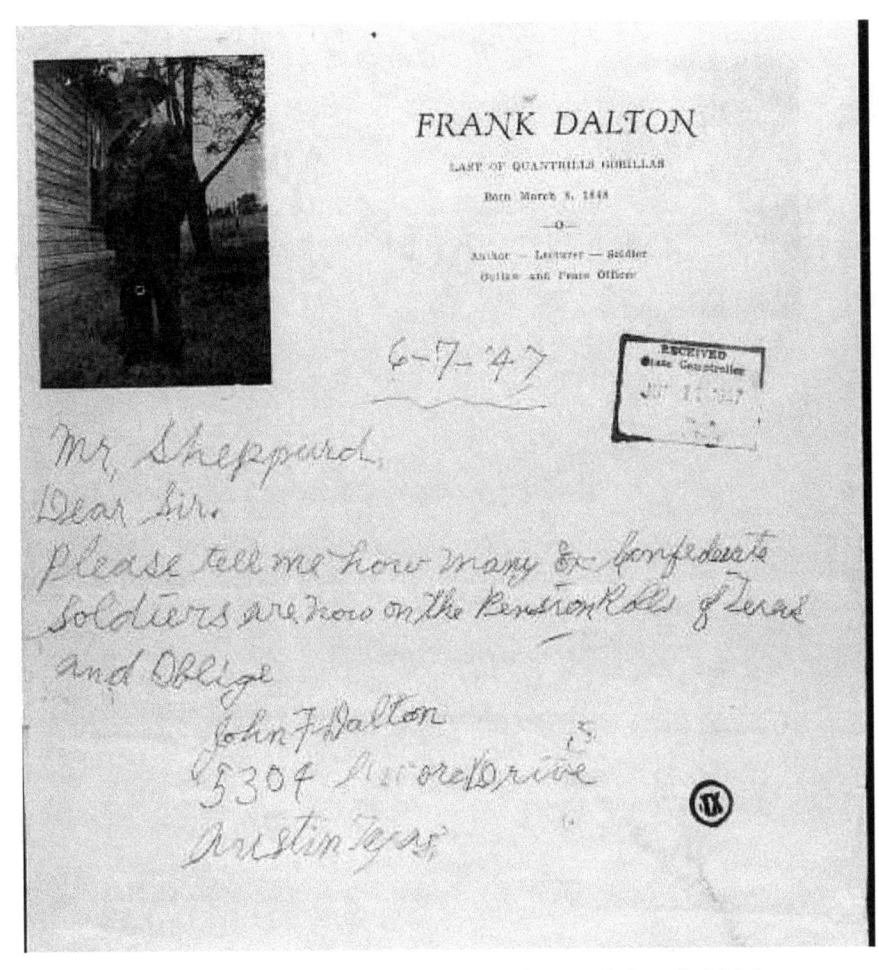

(Letter from John F. Dalton to Mr. Sheppard, June 7, 1947)

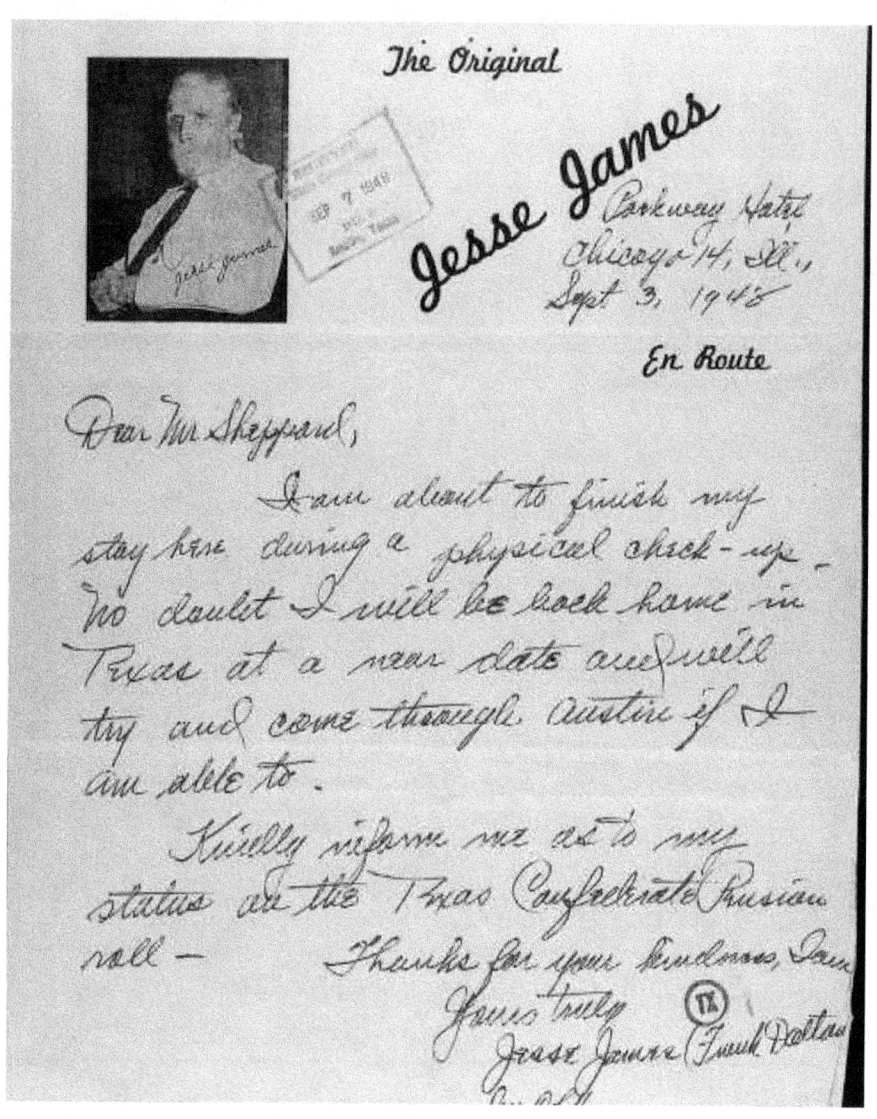

(Letter from Jesse James in Chicago, Illinois to Geo. Sheppard, Texas State Comptroller of Public Accounts, Sept. 3, 1948 before his 101st birthday.

Last two photos above are courtesy of the files of Alabama, Texas and Virginia, U.S., Confederate Pensions, 1884-1958, Texas Archives: Ancestry.com)

Appendix A-9 (1949)

Letter from Brushy Bill and Lizzie Roberts to Jesse that was in their Christmas Card to him.

Dec. 12, 1949

Mr. Jesse James -
Dear Uncle,
I drop you a few lines. Hope this will find you well. I ain't been well. I liked to died with the hiccups again. My wife is better, not well. I loved to hear from you. Sometime if I could help you out in any way about your records you been getting up when you get your book fixed up (Helping Ola

write the manuscripts) I loved to have one. I got a letter from Travis. He's alright now. You tell that man (Howk) to send me my pictures back to me when he has some taken up. Send me back the old pictures. I loved to hear from you all, if You are getting along. I got a lawyer working up my case what we was talking about. I got a letter from him yesterday. (Referring to Morrison) He seems to be getting along alright. I'd love to hear from Ozark Jack; he was up there this summer and was living in Indiana. I loved to get his address. I loved to hear from you, once in a while. Write soon, your friend, Brushy Bill Roberts

(Letter inside Christmas Card)

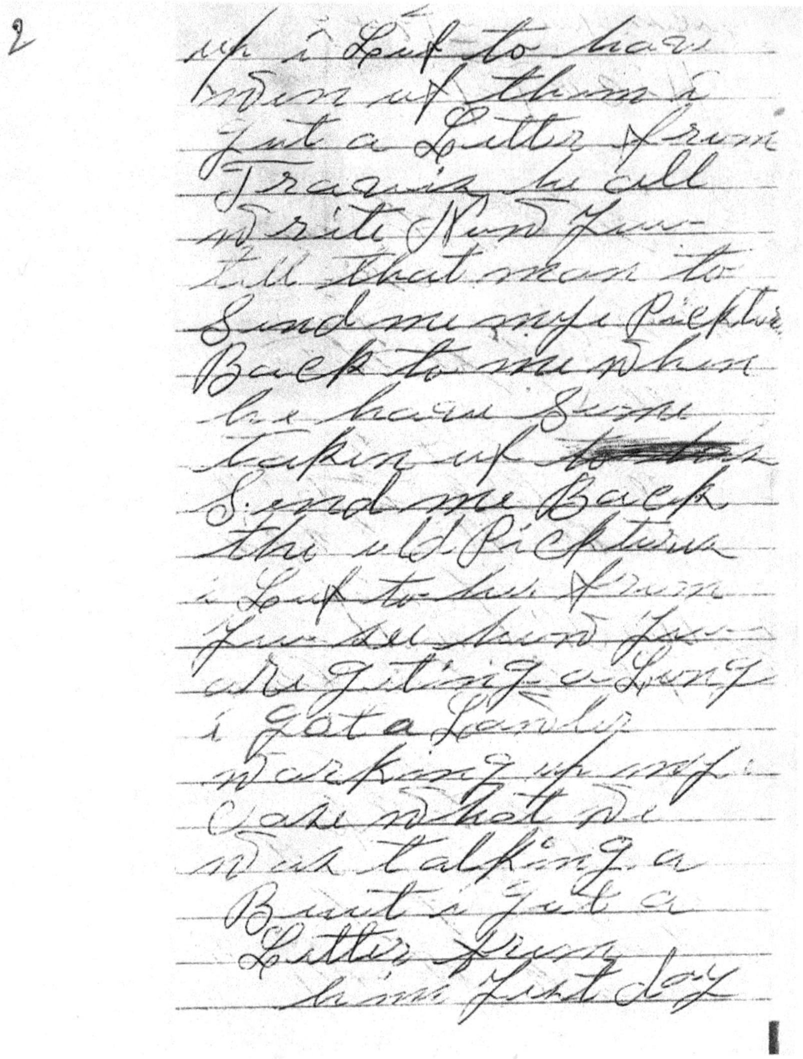

2

up i Sent to have
mom at them i
just a Letter from
Travis he will
write Now you
tell that man to
send me my Picture
Back to me when
he have been
taken up ~~to top~~
Send me Back
the old Picture
i Sent to him from
i we heard you
are giting a long
i got a family
working up my
case what we
was talking a
Bout i get a
Letter from
him just day

(2nd page)

Appendix A-10 (Nov. 6, 1950)

Letter from Mary Plina Norris, daughter of Frank James

Claremore, Okla
Nov. 6th, 1950

Dear Mrs. Everhard
Austin, Texas

I received your kind letter a few days ago. Was verry glad to learn of dear uncle Jesse James condition and to know he is being cared for by kind, tender and simpathetic hands that will make all comfort possible. I am excedingly please to learn of you being a family relative. Of course you understand I never had the pleasure of meeting you. I would have answered your letter sooner but I have not been feeling so well and just did not answer but hope to do better next time. I am sorry to hear of uncle Jesse's eye sight failing him. My own eye site is very poor and getting gradually worse so you know I can sympathize with him. Please tell me all about uncle's condition and how he is physically other than broken bones it sure must be a trying situation for him day after day to be forced to the confinement of his chair or bed. How is his appetite? Tell me all. I would like to go to him and see him but don't see how I can now.

Tell uncle Jesse that his grandnephew (Henry Norris) came to visit me and he wished he could get to Austin and have a visit with uncle Jesse. He said he can't help but like that old man, he has a tenderness in his eye that would contradict the fabulous stories afloat but the eye also shows a sturness .... to himself or immediate family would not be tolerated.

Now for myself I Mary P. Norris am a chip off the old block. I am a daughter of Frank James, a brother of Jesse James, the only daughter of Frank's. There are others who claim Frank James is their father, if that is true they are illegitimate. My eyesite is so poor that I have my husband to write for me but I would like to get down there to see uncle and bring a hen and cook it while I could be there so he could have chicken and dumplings, I know he likes them.

I am sending my love to uncle Jesse and you.

From Mary P. Norris (the only daughter of Frank James. Brother of Jesse James)

My prayers may
God bless you all.

(Letter to Ola from Mary Plina Norris that Ola typed out)

Claremore, Okla, Nov 6th 1950.

Dear Mrs. Everhard,
Austin Texas.

I received your kind letter a few days ago. was verry glad to learn of Dear Uncle Jesse James condition and to know he is being cared for by kind, tender and simpathetic hands that is all comfort possible. I am exceedingly pleased to learn of you being a family Relative, of course you understand I never had the pleasure of meeting you. I would have answered your letter sooner but I have not been feeling so well and just didnt answer but hope to do better next time. I am verry sorry to hear of Uncle Jesse's Eye Site failing him, my own Eye site is verry poor and getting gradually worse, so you know I can sympathise with him. I have told me all about Uncle's condition and how he is physically other than Broken Bones, it shure must be a trying situation for him day after day to be forced to the confinement of his chair or Bed. How is his appetite? tell me all.

I would like to go to him and see him but dont see how I can now. Tell Uncle Jesse that his Grand Nephew Henry Norris came to visit me and he wished he could get to Austin and have a visit with Uncle Jess. He said I just cant help but like that old man, he has a tenderness in his eye that would contradict the fabulous stories afloat but the eye also shows a sterness and inquiries to himself or imediate family would not be tolerated.

As for myself I Mary P Norris am a chip off the old Block. I am a daughter of Frank James, a brother of Jesse James, the only Daughter of Frank's. there others who claim Frank James is their father, if that is true they are illegitemate, my eye site is so poor that I have my husband to write for me and I would like to get down there to see Uncle and bring a hen and cook it while I could be there so he could have Chicken and dumplings, I know he likes them.

I am sending my Love to Uncle Jesse and you.
From Mary P. Norris. (the only Daughter of Frank James, Brother of Jesse James.)

My Prayer May God Bless you all,

(Original letter in Mary's handwriting (both in Ola's collection))

Appendix A-11 (1951)

A portion of the letter from Lizzie Roberts after Brushy Bill died, January 11, 1951.

Mrs. Ola Everhard,
"Bill thought a lot of Uncle Jessie. If Bill hadn't died me and him and Travis was coming down there to see you all. ....I guess you know Bill was Billie Kid he told me he was before he died. When he told me he thought I would quit him. I told him I was going to stay with him til he died. I loved him with all my heart. Nothing wouldn't turn me against him. He was so sweet to me. Uncle Jessie knowed Bill was Billie kid. Many thanks to you for everything you sent."
Your Loving Friend,
Lizzie Roberts

After this letter, Lizzie wrote another one, January 23, 1951 telling about her family and how much she missed Bill. He never said a cross word to her. He kissed her the morning he died, went to the post office to mail a letter to Ola and Jesse and never returned. He died December 27, 1950.

Appendix A-12 (1991)

Letter from "Margie" (1925-2008) in Hallettsville, Texas to Bud, 6/15/91 – "He (Jesse) lived with us for some time in the late '30's and he was very much alive at that time. This was in Houston County in East Texas."

Margie spoke with Bud on the phone and explained that her stepfather married a "James" in 1895 before marrying her mother. Her stepfather lived until 1952 and revealed several things to Margie. He was living in Houston County, Texas in Dwelling **#133** in 1900. His first wife's family descended from the same family as John Tatums' mother, Rachel James, Azariah James, and Nancy James Haskew. They all descend from William Henry Laban James (1734-1812) and Nancy Elizabeth Waggoner (1740-1796).

Margie's mother married her stepfather after his first wife died in 1929. Margie remembers as a young girl that Jesse stayed for a month with them and worked their farm in the late 30's. She remembers him well. He was very helpful doing the chores. This was the same man who identified himself as Jesse James in Lawton.

Appendix A-13

Another letter came to Bud from "Carolyn" from Dallas. The letter is not dated. "After seeing the Television interview on channel 4 Fox News regarding Jesse James, where and when he died and was buried triggered many conversations I had with my Grandmother. At the age of 14 she moved with her parents, from North Alabama to Southeast Missouri. This was in 1922-1923 during that year another sister was born July 4, 1923. During the time they were in Missouri, Jessie and possibly Frank James came and stayed with them, for how long I'm not sure. Jessie and Frank were cousins to my Great-great-grandmother."

**Note – For the sake of privacy, family names have been omitted, but the author has researched and found that their family histories indicate their connection to Jesse and their stories are validated.

Appendix 14 (1991)

Bud received a letter from Jill from Nevada, Missouri sent April 1, 1991 after reading the article in the Nevada Daily Newspaper on Jesse James.

"I had to write a genealogy paper in my College English Class and in my research I was speaking to my uncle about the story my mother had told me of an old man visiting them when they were children. My mother is 74 and my uncle is 81 and they both remember when an old man came to visit their grandma, Henrietta. He claimed he was a second cousin to their grandmother. He stayed with their grandpa and grandma for a short visit and while visiting told some interesting stories including old trails and hiding places that he and the gang used. I assume no one followed up on the stories because they probably didn't believe him, but my Uncle Floyd said that when he and my Uncle Harold took the old man to Springfield, they were talking to some old timers at a coffee shop and again the old man claimed he was Jesse James, so some of the men tried to confuse him on his stories, but Uncle Floyd said that they never did confuse him. My uncle and my mom have always thought the old man was the real Jesse James. Uncle Floyd recalls this happened around 1930, so if it was Jesse James, he would have been around 83 years old."

Grandma Henrietta and her husband lived 9 miles north of Liberal, Missouri, but within Vernon County, Missouri. Henrietta's great grandfather was the brother of William John James (1754-1805), Jesse's great grandfather.

Appendix 15 (1994)

A Letter was received from John Koweno from Indiahoma, Oklahoma dated Feb. 22, 1994 to Bud. John was a member of the Comanche Nation. He writes Bud regarding stories that were told to him by his grandmother who heard them from her elders. The family lived west of Lawton near the Wichita Mountains for centuries. Quite interesting. Thank you for sharing this with Bud, John.

"My grandmother, the late Edora Koweno, used to tell me stories which were told to her by another elderly Indian woman, about Jesse and Frank James. Jesse James is considered to be one of the most famous western outlaws of his time, during the mid-1800s to the late 1800s. It is said that Jesse would rob banks and trains in Kansas, Missouri, Louisiana, Texas and New Mexico, and would ride back to hide out in Southwest Oklahoma, then known as Indian Territory. (Oklahoma became a state, Nov. 16, 1907.)

The only lawmen allowed in Indian Territory were a U.S. Marshal and Texas Rangers and they would not come into the Territory for fear of being shot and killed by one of the many outlaws who hid out.

Jesse's gang included Jesse's brother, Frank, and a group of brothers known as the Youngers, with Cole Younger the most famous of the brothers. They were also cousins of Jesse and Frank, all of them being from the state of Missouri.

My grandmother told me the Indians of the area thought Jesse and his gang were crazy, so they left them alone. The Indians, according to Comanche law, would not harm or attack a crazy man or a very brave man who showed he was not afraid of the Indians. Which shows that he was crazy anyway if he was foolish enough to go to the Indians, his most feared enemy. Jesse and his gang also had mutual respect for the Indians, and they left each other alone.

According to my grandmother, a small group of Indians was camping on the south side of a small mountain southwest of what is now Treasure Lake Job Corps. It was late in the day, and the Indian women were cooking Indian bread—also called fry bread—for supper, when Jesse and his gang rode up to their camp. Jesse got off his horse without saying a word and walked over to where some freshly cooked fry bread lay, and picked up one piece. He threw it into the air, drew his pistol, and shot a hole in it. He then walked over, picked it up and go back on his horse, eating his fry bread as he rode off without a word."

"Another story my grandmother, the late Edora Koweno, told me was about Jesse James' gunfights in the late 1800's. According to her, Jesse James and another man got into an argument— about what, she didn't know. It was thought this other man believed he could out-draw Jesse with a gun and become famous for killing Jesse James.

The man argued, then the man challenged Jesse to a gunfight, and Jesse said he would meet him at a certain time in the late afternoon on a certain hill known to all the people who lived around the area. It was believed that Jesse was giving the other man time to think about what he was doing and gave him time to leave before he got killed.

The gunfight was to take place about two and a half miles west of the present Treasure Lake Job Corps Center. Word traveled quickly that there was to be a gunfight between Jesse and another man late that afternoon, so the Indians and the white settlers stared to come to the site early in the afternoon. My grandmother said it was like a circus had come to town, and the people who came early wanted the best seats. She said the people were lined up all on one side, with the white settlers on one end and the Indians on the other end.

My grandmother said the people came all dressed up for the occasion. The white settlers came in their horse-drawn buggies with their Sunday-best clothes, and the Indians did the same with all their Indian regalia. Also, some Indians at this time owned and came in their horse-drawn buggies. Grandmother also said people brought picnic lunches to eat while they waited for the gunfight.

As the sun got lower in the western skies, the man and his friends rode to the side and stopped on the north end, with the people on the west side. A little later Jesse James and his gang came and stopped on the south side. Then the men approached each other and stopped about 30 feet apart and stared to talk, with no one else saying a word but trying to listen to what was being said.

Grandmother said the other man drew his pistol first, but Jesse James was a lot faster. And a few seconds later the other man lay dying, with his friends trying to help him. Jesse and his gang got on their horses and rode off.

The people stayed around a little while longer. They talked about the fight, then they started for home."

Appendix A-16 (1990)

Bud's dear friend, Mary Kate Durham who was a well-known Granbury historian, a member of the Historical Preservation Committee, Granbury Cemetery Board, Museum Board, Daughters of the American Revolution, Daughters of the Confederacy and Colonial Dames, wrote him a letter on February 23, 1990.

"This Jesse James story never stops. After the local newsman put the story and my picture on the front page of the paper, I have had an interesting call or two. One lady called to tell me that she used to have breakfast at the Southern Hotel in Brownwood when she was a girl. She met Jesse James there. He always had beans for breakfast." Her name was Mamie.

Mary continues, *"An old friend suddenly came forth with all sorts of information. She said that she never knew that I was interested in this subject. She lived with her grandparents for the first 12 years of her life. She said that she heard stories of Jesse James from them forever. She always believed that her grandfather was a very close relative—cousin or even a brother. She said that he always seemed to have money when no one else had any. There is a farm somewhere around here that she called the old James place. I think she meant that it was in Johnson County near Cleburne. She spoke of a little place called Venus. She was telling me so much so fast that I didn't really understand all of it. There is a family reunion every summer."* Her name was Dorothy.

Appendix A-17 (1991)

In a March 27, 1991 letter to Bud from Peggy, she clues Bud in on some information her grandfather told her when she was young. Her grandfather was James.

James' grandfather, came from Mississippi, was married in Sabine, Louisianna and prior to the Civil War, they ended up in Texas. In Texas, he enlisted in the Texas Rangers in Jacksboro, Texas under Captain H.A. Hamner on January 14, 1860 for the protection of the frontier. (Texas, U.S. Muster Roll Index Cards, 1838-1900). He fought with the Confederate 9th regiment of the Texas Cavalry under Sims, Company B. He died shortly after the Civil War and was buried in Killeen, Bell County Texas. His son, James lived in Llano, Texas and then moved to Brady, Texas. James' son was James Jr. who was the grandfather of Peggy. They lived in Llano and then moved to Mason,

Texas. James Jr. died in San Angelo, which was close to where his brother, John lived for a while. By 1917, John lived in Brown County, Texas in a little town called Zepher, close to Brownwood and close to where "Bloody Bill" Anderson lived.

Notice that all these places were where Jesse roamed.

Peggy writes, "*The San Angelo Standard Times ran this small article in yesterday's paper, and I am writing in reference to the article. Perhaps what I am writing will help you. I don't know but I feel a need to share with you.*

My grandfather, James was quite a storyteller. When I was a child, he would sit on the front porch in a rocker and we would sit in the porch swing or the day bed on the porch and he would tell us stories about his life and people he knew growing up – cattle drives, etc.

One story he told in my presence several times was: "Jesse James is not dead like people think. He's alive and living over in Brown County under a different name and he would add "I know him or I've known him." This statement I'm not sure about the exact wordage.

My grandfather's younger brother (John) lived in Brown County many years and is buried there. He and his family lived in a small town named Zepher." The stories were told to her in the late 30's and early 40's."

Appendix A-18 (1991)

A strange and mysterious post card came to Bud stamped October 1st, 1991.

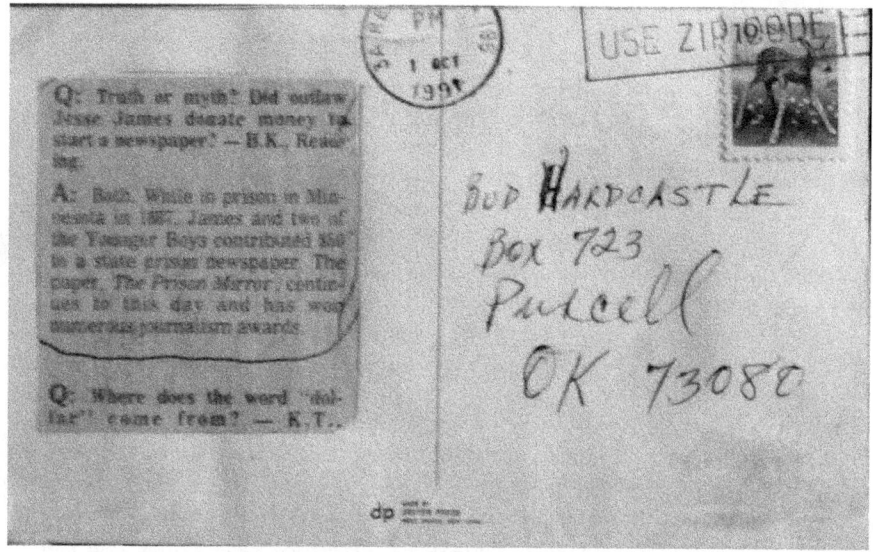

(Picture of post card sent anonymously)

Appendix A-19 (1995)

Letter from Francena Turilli to Bud stating facts about her encounter with Howk.

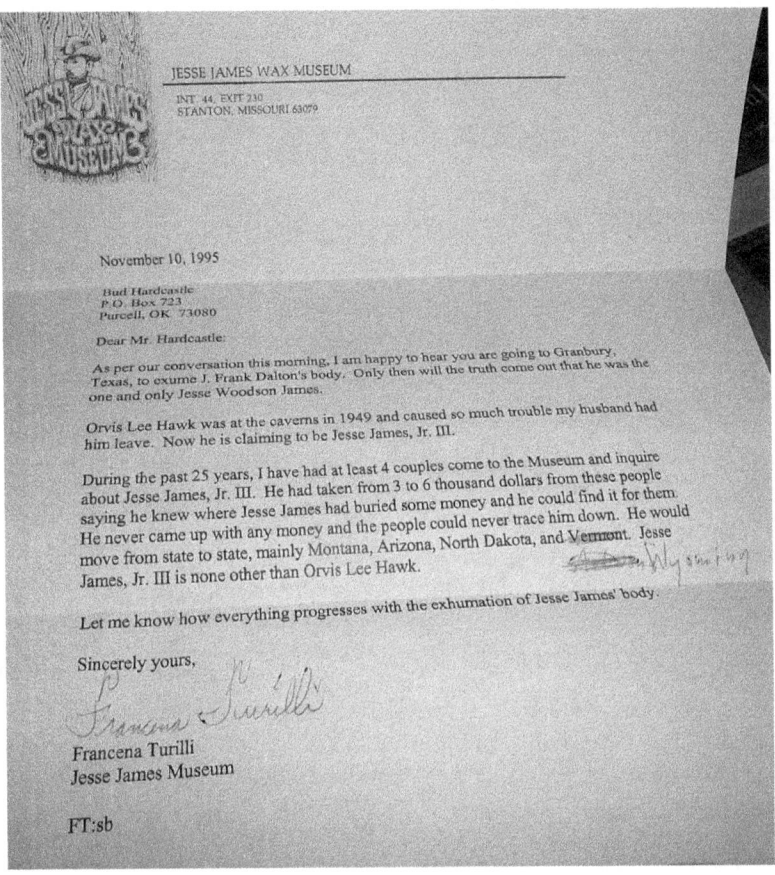

(Francena Turilli's letter to Bud)

Appendix A-20 (1995)

Letter from Mrs. Howk, Nadine to Bud.

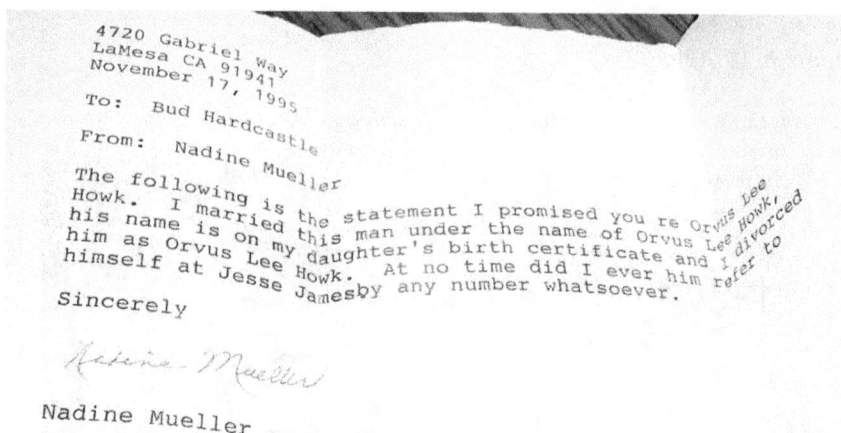

(Nadine's letter to Bud)

Appendix A-21 (1991)

A very interesting letter came to Bud from Glenn who lived in Keyes, Oklahoma on March 26, 1991.

Dear Sir,

Saw your article in the paper by Jim Etter, Staff Writer. A friend Mr. ____ and I used to take metal locators and go prowling. I had relation (relatives) down in Mineral Wells and I got to know a Mr. Y. that had checked all the treasure stories til they moved or died. Mr. Y. said Frank James was a cousin to his wife.

Note: He was speaking of Mr. Y. who was born in Seymour, Texas in 1882 and was raised in Palo Pinto County between Graford and Mineral Wells. He was a member of a pioneer ranching family of the county, postmaster, and owned a trucking company during the oil boom in the early 1920's. He was into ranching and a stockman. (*Remember, in 1922, Jesse had a ranch northwest of Mineral Wells which would place it close to where Marcus Dalton's ranch was in the county of Palo Pinto and near Graford).

We will continue with Glenn's letter:

Mr. Y said he (Frank James) used to come see them and stay a week or two, said he left a pair of glasses I could have but went off and forgot them. He told us about a cave on the Pecos River north of Horse Head Crossing South of Odessa, Texas – South to McCamey – Southwest to the Pecos River. Said there was a big rock around 12 to 14 ft. square with ____ leaning against it; in the opening there was a small room with a big room on back.

They went and got Belle Starr's ____ bed and fixed her a table. There was 4 men and her. Said they used it for seven years to rest in. Said there was Jessie and Frank and two others. There was a grandson or son came down there with a map to some cave west of McCamey and north ?? They or some guy built an Irrigation project in there. This relation (relative) came down to look and went into one cave and found piles of snakes, so he got the boss of the Irrigation project to help him and they found $3,500 after throwing oil on the snakes and burning them. All this I partly know from talking to Mr. Y. and he talked to Frank James when he would stay with him.

Mr. Y. said he and a friend went looking for the rock one time in their old car and had two flats close to a small town west of Odessa. I can't remember the name of the small town. Due to what he told me I feel there is a good chance all that stuff is still in the cave. He said they had an awful time getting a wagon close enough to unload all the stuff. I feel if you went to the Pecos River in the highest mountains you could find it. If you do? I want to know about it.

Mr. Y. has been back several years. I am in bad shape with my eyes, be a while before I can get them worked on. If you go down there, take a horse to ride along that Pecos River. I don't think it would be too hard to find the big rock. I don't think it is in the river much if any. Would like to talk to you sometime.
Yours Truly,
Glenn

Appendix A 22 (1949)
Letter addressed to Russell James, Roscoe James and Floyd from Howk regarding Custer's Last Stand, December 31, 1949

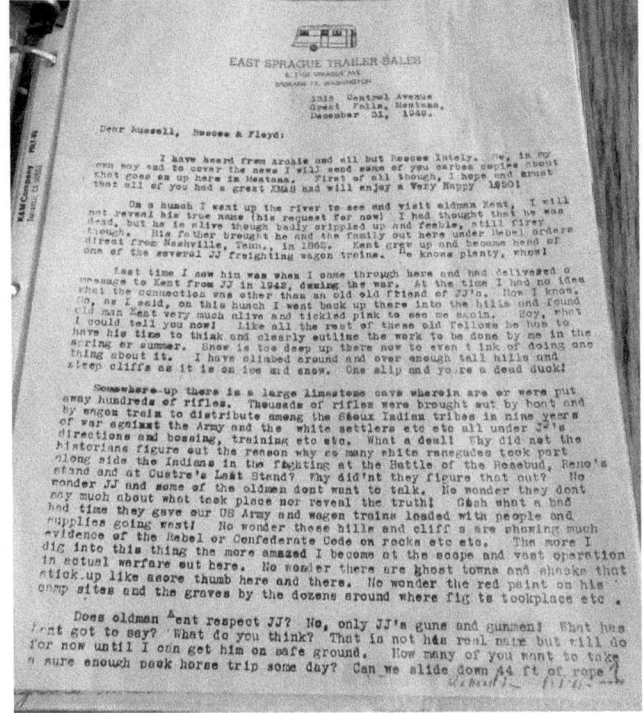

Appendix B: Treasure Maps

Appendix B-1

The Big Indian Well, also known as the "Rocked Up Water Well". It was in the northeastern part of Oklahoma.

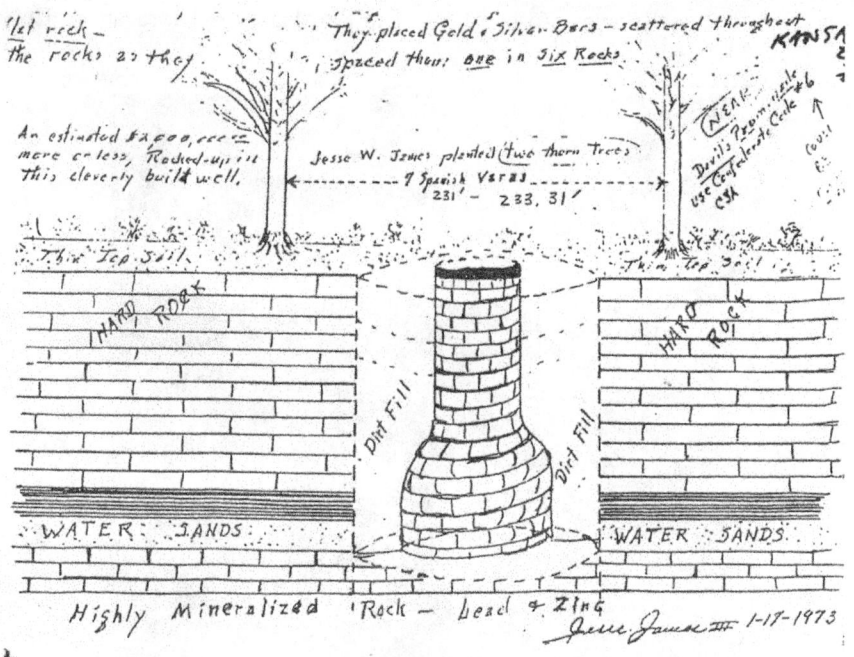

(Map of the Rocked-Up Water Well. Drawn out by Jesse James III (Howk))

Appendix B-2

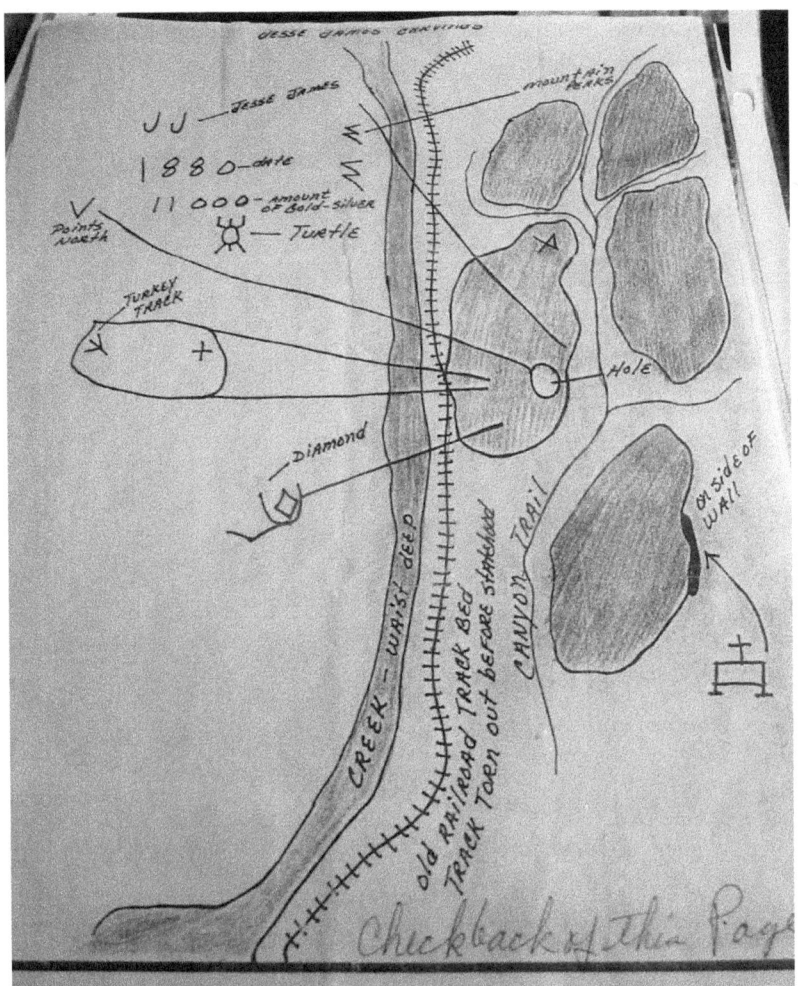

(Map of Wapanucka Academy)

Appendix B-3

Buzzard Roost. This was originally laid out by Jesse. Bud had in his possession a great map of the area around Buzzard Roost and hoping that it will be of some help to those who continue the search.

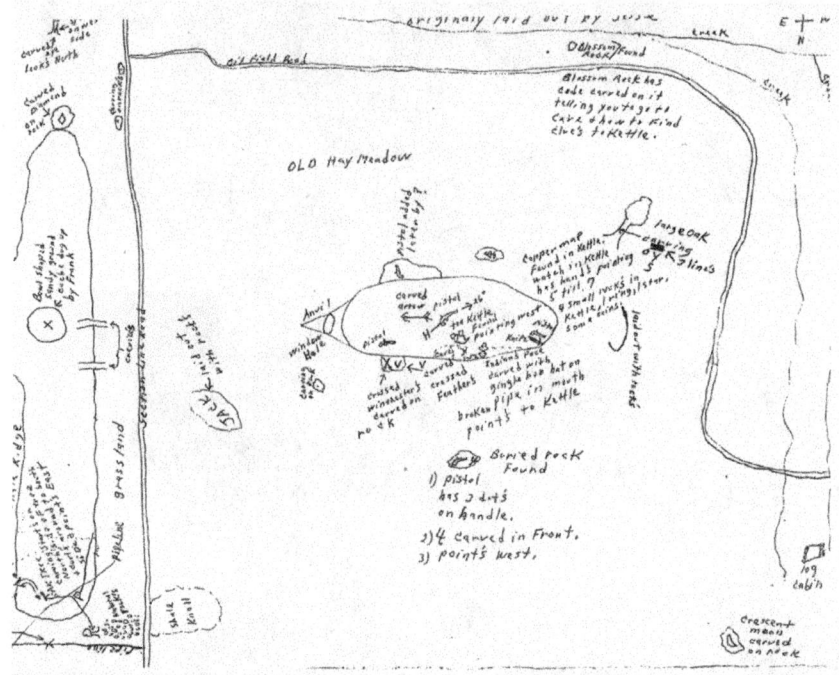

(Map of Buzzard Roost, Bud's friend drew this out)

Appendix B-4

Longhorn Mountain

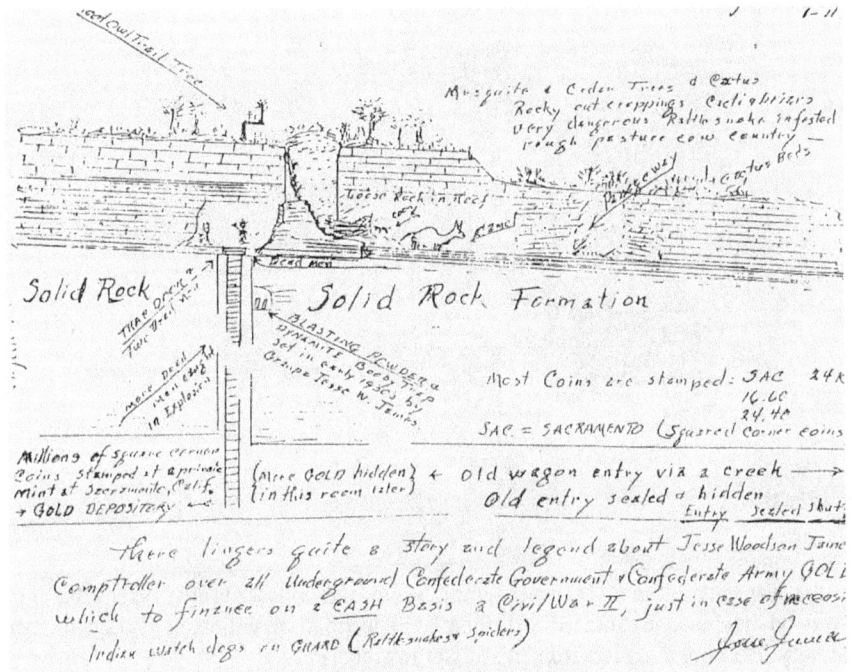

(Longhorn Mountain Map (drawn out by Jesse Lee James III – Howk))

Appendix B-5

The Wolf Map or what Bud calls "The Grave is My Witness," found as a copper sheet map in the kettle.

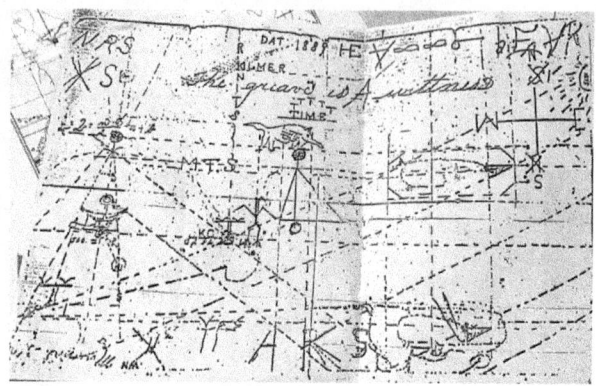

(Wolf Map without the overlay that goes with it)

Appendix B-6

Map of Tennessee treasure

When the war ended, the KGC moved money out of Tennessee, near Nashville and buried it along the way on their escape route towards their final destination, which, per Bud, was barely inside Indian Territory. Bud got this map from Jesse's grandsons.

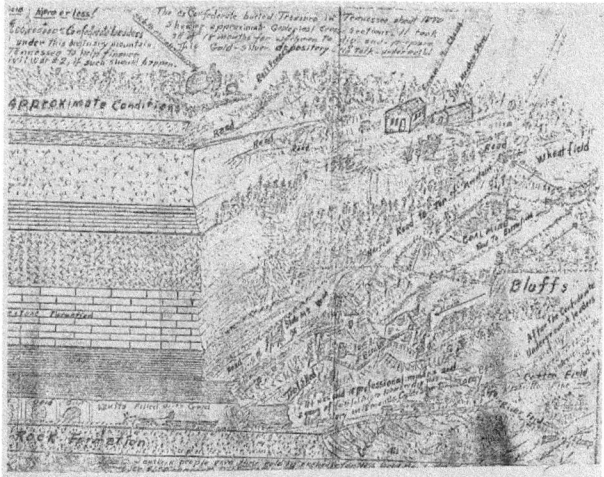

(Tennessee Map)

Appendix B-7

Treasure near Fairplay, Colorado in mountainous area. Bud received this map from Jesse's grandsons. It appears that this is only half of the map.

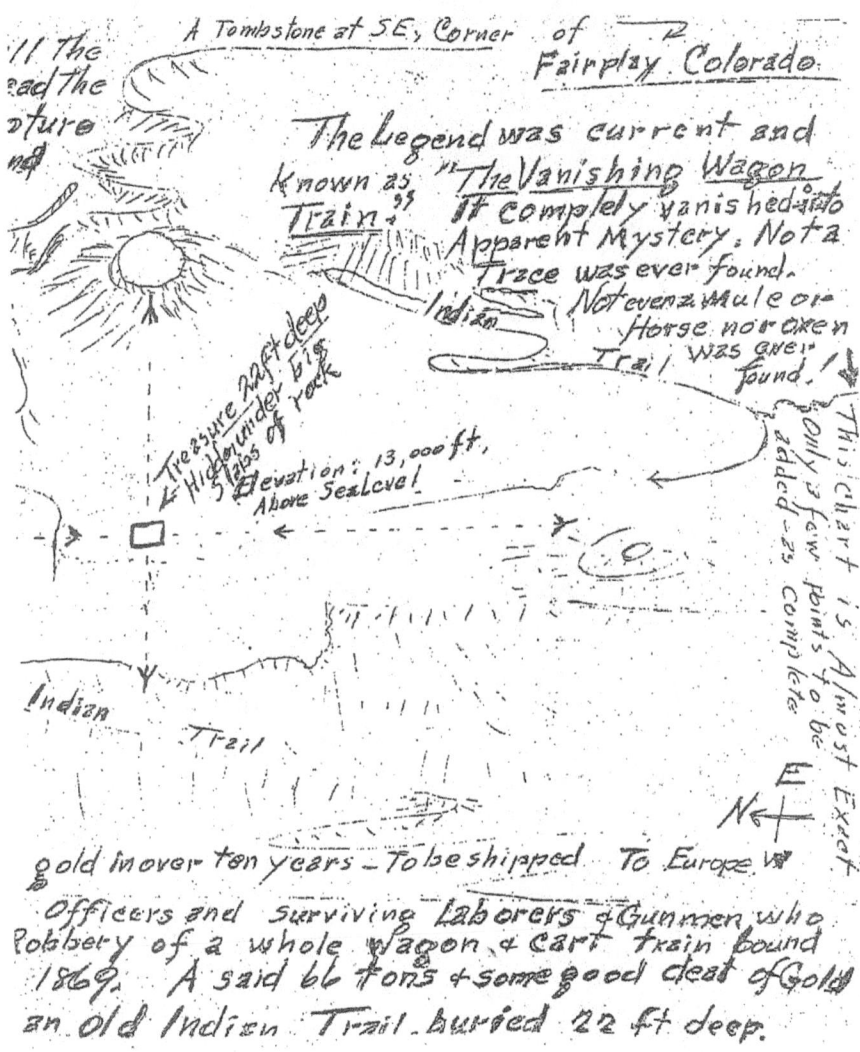

(Fairplay, Colorado map)

Appendix C – KGC codes

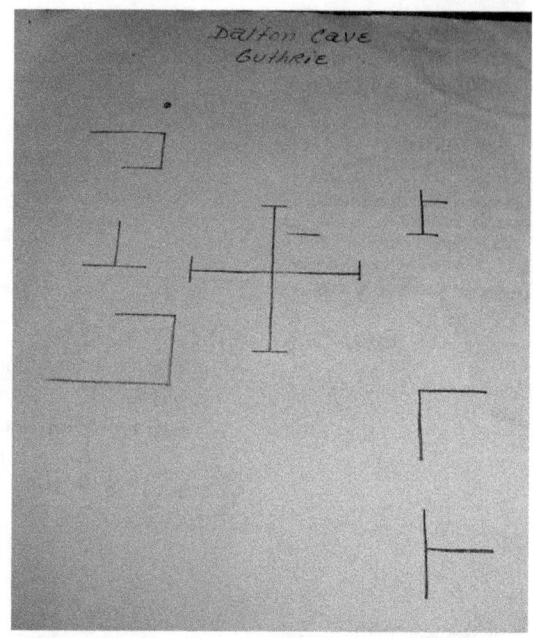

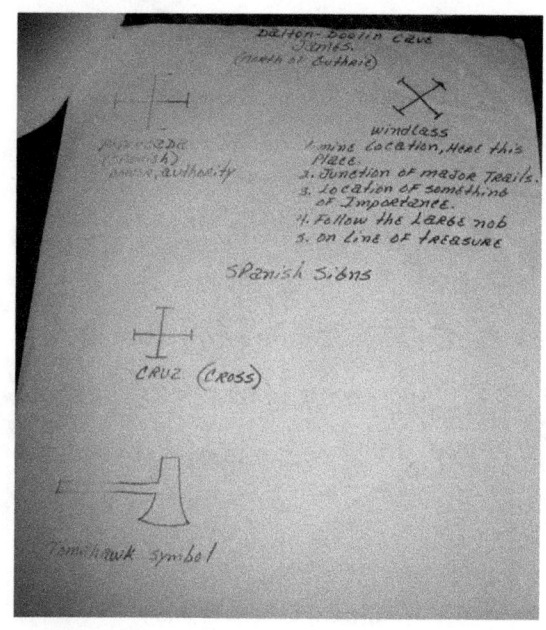

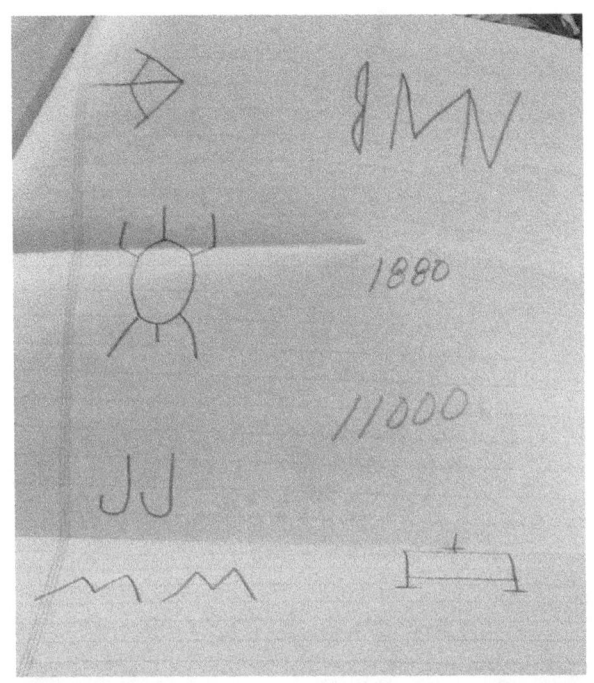

(Various codes and symbols)

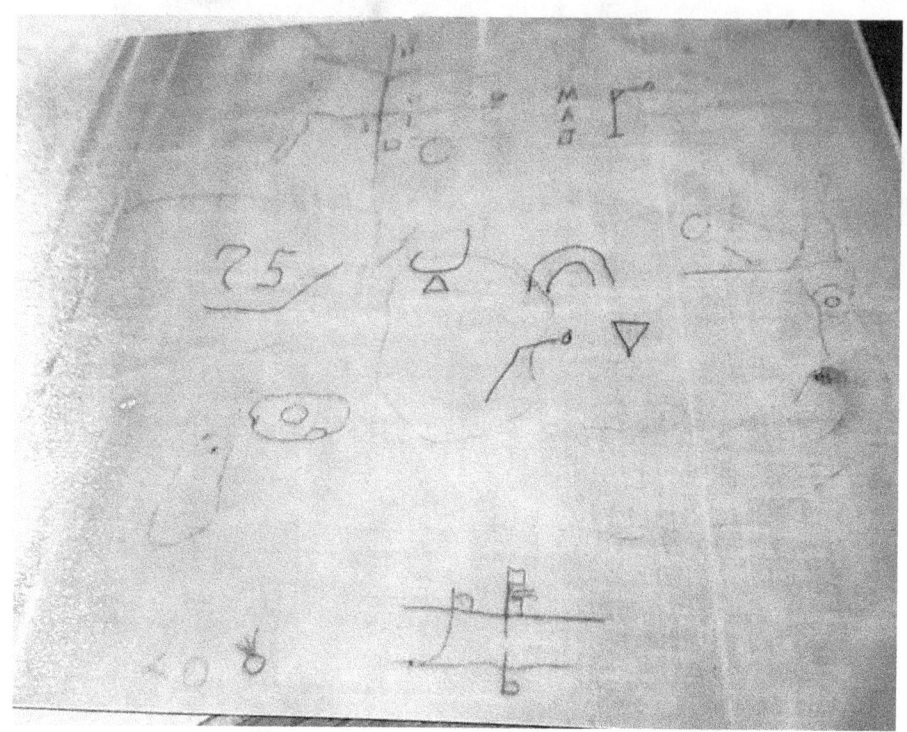

(Bud said this was actually a map which included the [MAJ] and hangman's noose that was on the back of the watch)

(Codes carved on Triangle Rocks which Bud said were distant apart which directed the hunter to treasure)

Appendix C-2

(Letter written in code (courtesy of Jay Longley))

Appendix C-3

(KGC codes (courtesy of the Louisville Journal))

Bibliography

Bud's personal collection of various news media, documents, maps, interviews, and photos: This is only a small portion of what Bud has accumulated. It would take volume after volume of books to reveal them all.

*Note – Several sources were not fully cited within Bud's collection. Author is citing what was available.

Books:

Booklet of Letters of the Outlaw Jesse James, Alias J.D. Howard – Letter from John D. Howard in Eaton Creek, Tenn. To Friend Henry; April 24th, 1879.

Crittenden, H. H. *The Crittenden Memoirs*. G. P. Putnam's Sons, 1936.

Dalton, Frank (Jesse). *Short Stories*. Date unknown.

Everhard, Ola. Original manuscript of *The Hoax That Let Jesse James Live*, given to Bud Hardcastle by Aubrey Everhard, April 3, 1990.

Folktales booklet with article, "Outlaw Stories."

Hall, Frank O., and Lindsey H. Whitten. *Jesse James Rides Again*. Lahoma Publishing Company, 1948.

Howard, Paul G. and Gerald H. Pipes, ed. *The Amazing Outlaw Life Of Jesse James*.

James, Jesse Lee. *Jesse James and the Lost Cause*. Pageant Press, New York; 1961

Lindsay, Anita. *From Pioneers to Progress*. 1957.

Loftin, Jack. *Trails Through Archer*. Eakin Publications. 1979.

Mooney, Col. Charles W. *Dr. In Belle Starr Country*. The Century Press, Oklahoma City, Oklahoma; 1975

Snow, Sarah, and Columbus Vaughn, and Lester Snow. *This was Frank James*. Dorrance & Co. of Philadelphia; 1969.

Turilli, Rudy, *I Knew Jesse James*. 1966.

Wood, Joe. *My Jesse James Story*. 1989.

Newspapers:

"116-Year-Old Jesse James Gang's Cook Visits Region." *Colorado Springs Gazette Telegram*. Colorado Springs, Colorado, November 28, 1954.

An interview with Ozark Jack Berlin. *Veedersburg, Indiana Newspaper* on August 19, 1949.

"Autopsy tells more of Jesse James." *Garvin County Advocate*. Paul's Valley, Oklahoma. February 13, 1990.

Caldwell, Bill. "Belle Starr Was Her Own Woman." *The Joplin Globe*. Joplin, Missouri. Feb. 29, 2020.

Chesney, W. D. "Voice of the People." *Janesville Daily Gazette*. Janesville, Wisconsin. August 26, 1958.

"Claim Badman Jesse James Living In Oklahoma Town." *Lawton Constitution*. Lawton, Oklahoma. May 1948.

Correspondence with Frank Dalton and Dick Worsham. *The Journal of Tyler*. Tyler, Texas, 1932.

Dalton, Frank. *The Intelligencer*. April 19, 1890.

Dennis McCarthy's column, possibly with *Los Angeles Daily News* regarding Morrey Davidson and Ola Everhard. Date and title unknown.

Dezort, Jeff. "Joe Vaughn (Frank James) Research is Outlined by 'Grandson' Columbus Vaughn." *The Times*. Newspaper title and city unknown. July 2, 1979.

Dittrick, Paula. "Cousin Claims Jesse James died in 1951 at age 103." *Sunday Advocate*. Baton Rouge, La. Nov. 20, 1983.

Farmer, Garland R. "Frank Dalton Finds Peace." *Houston Chronicle Magazine*. Houston, Texas. March 28, 1948.

"Federal Link Found in Bombing." *The Daily Oklahoman*. Oklahoma City, Oklahoma. Sept 14, 1992.

"Former Sheriff of Hood County Thinks Real Jesse James Died in Granbury." *Granbury Newspaper*. Date Unknown.

"Former U.S. Marshall, 92 Recalls Famous Outlaws." Newspaper unknown. June 21, 1950.

Hartsfield, Jack. "Outlaw's Kin Says Death Faked" and "James' Death Faked, Kin Says." *Lubbock Avalanche*. Lubbock, Texas. Sept. 1983.

In Ola's documents. The Nebraska City News. Nebraska City, Nebraska. April 29, 1882.

"Is Jesse James Dead or Alive? Nashville Citizen to Testify." Newspaper unknown. March 1950.

"James' and Youngers." *The Missouri World Newspaper*. Date Unknown

"Jesse James' to End," *The Independent,* Long Beach, California; August 17, 1951.

Lancaster, Barbara. "Alleged Grandson of Outlaw Dies." *Abilene Reporter News*. Abilene, Texas. July 29, 1984.

Lancaster, Barbara. "Letter reveals more new facts concerning the question of James." *The Granbury Tablet*. Granbury, Texas. May 10, 1984.

"More Proof That Dalton Is 'Jesse." *The Guthrie Daily Leader*. Guthrie, Oklahoma. July 7, 1948.

"Mother of Frank and Jesse James dies." *Anadarko Newspaper*. Anadarko, Oklahoma. February 11, 1911.

"Old Document Reveals More About Life of Jesse James," *Garvin County Advocate*, Pauls Valley, Oklahoma, January 30 ? - Affidavit of Orrington Red Lucas, Franklin County, Missouri. July 6, 1950.

"Quantrill Raiders Added To Civil War Pension List," *Newspaper Unknown*, March 1948.

"Redding." *The Decatur Daily Review*. Decatur, Illinois. October 7, 1975.

Regarding John Wilkes Booth. *Fort Worth Star Telegram*. Fort Worth, Texas. March 6, 1984.

"Services Tuesday For DeWitt Travis." Newspaper article from Unknown Source.

Shlachter, Barry. "Jesse James' Family Tree Sprouts Two Arkansans." *Fort Worth Star Telegram*. Fort Worth, Texas. August 18, 1995.

"Shucks, Tilden Cramp Could Have Told Them." *Muskogee County News*. Muskogee, Oklahoma. January 19, 1950.

Stansbery, Lon R. "Cops and Robbers." Newspaper and date unknown.

Story on Cole Younger. *State Journal*. Mulhall, Oklahoma. July 24, 1903.

Story on Sam Rash working for Jesse. *The Granbury Tablet*. May 24, 1984.

"The Sheets Murderers." *Gallatin Democrat*. Gallatin, Missouri. date unknown, c.1869-1870.

"Video Sheds Light on James Mystery." *St. Joseph News Press/Gazette*. St. Joseph, Missouri. June 19, 1991.

"Where lies Jesse James? Some say in Granbury, where he died in 1951." *Dallas Times Herald*. Dallas, Texas. Nov. 13, 1983.

Williams-Allen, Susie; "Fair values of gold, silver found in McClain County." *The Purcell Register*. Purcell, Oklahoma. October 19, 2006.

Articles/Periodicals:

Author unknown. "What Happened To Jesse James?" An interview with Alvin Seamster. *News Gazette*. Date Unknown.

Dalton, Frank. "Military Escort For A Trail Herd." *The Cattleman Magazine, Vol. XXXI*. June 1944.

Dr. Wallace *Dalton* Chesney article referring to Dr. Preston who was his father-in-law. The article was "Who Lies Buried in Jesse Grave?" Date Unknown.

Hicks, Jimmie. "Some Letters Concerning The Knights of The Golden Circle in Texas, 1860-1861." *Southwestern Historical Quarterly*. Number 12, July 1961.

Magazine Article from unknown source documenting Jesse's visit with Billy the Kid in Las Vegas, NM on July 26, 1879.

McGrath, George. "Police Gazette files of 1882 produced conclusive evidence that the famous Western outlaw was never killed." *The National Police Gazette*. April 1950.

Palmore, Frank E. "Gold At Rock Crossing." *Treasure magazine, October 1989, Vol. 20, No. 10*.

Stonum, Sally; "Story of Susan Peters (1873-1965)."

The American Barbed Wire Journal. Volume IX, Number 6, written June 1975.

The Parmers. *Quarterly of the National Association and Center for Outlaw and Lawman History*.

Tunstill, Dr. William. "A News Release" – For the Tombstone Dedication At Grave of Jesse James. August 29, 1983.

Archived Documents:

Army of the United States official Honorable Discharge papers for Jessie Q James 38 445 0**33**.

Certified copy of Henry Ford of Brownwood, Death Certificate issued Feb. 26, 1996.

General Affidavit in the State of California, County of Tulare by Jesse Lee James, April 20, 1996.

General Affidavit in the State of Colorado, County of El Paso by Jesse Lee James, April 15, 1961.

"Hite Family." Roots web by Patricia. Date unknown.

Pritchett, Lulu Anthis. "Fred Raymond Anthis Family," Logan County Historical Society book.

Records of Texas Rangers Ben and Benjamin Johnson. Frances T. Ingmire; Texas Ranger Service Records, 1847-1900, Vol. III; Printed by Ingmire Publications, 10166 Clairmont Drive, St. Louis, Mo. 63136, c1982.

"Shelby Don't Believe it." *Special Dispatch to the Kansas City Journal*. Lexington, April 5, 1882. Located at the Oklahoma Historical Society, Oklahoma City, Oklahoma.

Taylor, J.H. Clerk to Mr. Harold Preece with the attached affidavit of Solomon Bedford Strickland. Confederate Pension Division Comptroller's Department. *Texas State Archives*. December 11, 1947.

Letters:

Bess, Mrs. J.W. from Marlow, Oklahoma to Bud Hardcastle in Purcell, Oklahoma.

Breihan, Carl W. to Ola Everhard. 1949.

Campbell, Samuel to Bud Hardcastle. Interview by Samuel G. Campbell, Fayetteville, Arkansas conducted on 4/27/91 with Mrs. Katie Brown of Porter, Oklahoma. Witnessed to Belle Starr being on the ferry that her great uncle ran in Arkansas at Brewer Bend.

Carolyn from Dallas, Texas to Bud Hardcastle. date unknown

Chrestman Johnston, Kay Loraine from El Paso, Texas to Bud Hardcastle in Purcell, Oklahoma. Date Unknown.

Cooksley, Mrs. A. J. of the Flying C Ranch in Clearmont, Wyoming to Carl Breihan. "Letter to Carl Breihan concerning Jesse James/John Trammell" posted by Martha Swope, November 13, 2005. Accessed 2023. www.genealogy.com.

Dalton, Frank from Austin, Texas to Lee Howk, May 9, 1947.

Dalton, Frank from Kilgore, Texas to Arlo Norman in Austin, Texas, Feb. 4, 1940.

Dalton, Frank (Jesse) from Longview, Texas to Howk. Sept. 12, 1942.

Dalton, John F. from Austin, Texas to Mr. Sheppard, June 7, 1947.

Durham, Mary Kate from Granbury, Texas to Bud Hardcastle in Purcell Oklahoma. February 23, 1990.

Ellis, Rev. James B. Choctaw, Oklahoma to Mr. Floyd Champlin in Zanesville, Ohio informing about the death of John Trammel. 1956.

Everhard, Ola to Bill and Fay, March 21, 1983.

Everhard, Ola to Mr. Eugene T. Huff (a friend). June 24, 1981 provided by Marsha Swope.

Fite, Karen. The Oklahoma Department of Libraries to Friends (Bud) regarding the Crittenden Papers; Date Unknown.

Gentrup, Gene, editor of the Southern Platte Press newspaper in Parkville, Missouri to "Whom it May Concern." Dated and notarized May 27, 1999.

Glassman, Dr. David to Mr. Robert A. Jackson. July 9, 2000.

Glenn from Keyes, Oklahoma to Bud Hardcastle in Purcell, Oklahoma. March 26, 1991.

Graves, Shirley and Mitch from Iron River, Alberta, Canada to Bud Hardcastle, May 19, 2000.

Graves, Shirley from Iron River, Alberta, Canada to Bud Hardcastle, January 2001.

Hoover, J. Edgar from Washington D. C. to Mr. Morrey Davidson in Long Island, New York. November 28, 1949.

Howk to "Folks," written from Gilchrist, Texas, July 31st, 1951.

Howk to Russell E. James, 1949.

Howk, "Lee." from Great Falls, Montana. to Friends. January 28, 1950.

Jackson, Attorney Robert to Bud Hardcastle, March 7, 2001.

James, Jesse (Frank Dalton) in Chicago, Illinois to Mr. Sheppard, Sept. 3, 1948.

James, Jesse by R. C. Shepherd in Excelsior Springs, Missouri to Samuel R. Bogle in Yakima, Washington. February 6, 1932.

James, Jesse by Rhodella Shepard to Governor Henry Stewart Caulfield who was governor between 1929-1933. January 24, 1932.

James, Jesse by Rhodella Shepard to L. C. Ackerman, Rison, Arkansas. Feb. 6, 1932.

James III, Jesse Lee to "Folks" from Manitou, Colorado. November 19th, 1953

James, Jesse Lee, "The Hawk" in Bakersfield, California to Betty Lou Kilgore. September 18, 1979

James, Jesse Lee. "The Hawk" in Medina, North Dakota to Mrs. Clovis Byars Herring in Buffalo, Texas. August 24, 1982.

James, Jesse to Miss Bertha Dalton. Post Card titled, "Shooting First Oil Well at Centralia, Illinois. January 10, 1909.

James, Jesse W. Authenticated letter from Jesse W. James from Medora, Illinois to Mr. Isaac Milton in Laredo, Texas; April 16, 1880.

(James) Pelfrey, Velma Dorothy, granddaughter of Dr. Robert Franklin James to Lou Kilgore in Jasper, Missouri. January 9, 1993.

James, Roscoe from Pueblo, Colorado to the Russel family. May 18, 1949.

Jane, Calamity to James O'Neil. November 30, 1889.

Jill From Nevada, Missouri to Bud Hardcastle in Purcell, Oklahoma. April 1, 1991.

Kilgore, Lou from Jasper, Arkansas to Bud Hardcastle in Purcell, Oklahoma. March 6, 1991.

Koweno, John from Indiahoma, Oklahoma to Bud Hardcastle in Purcell, Oklahoma. Feb. 22, 1994.

Loftin, Jack from Archer City, Texas to Bud Hardcastle in Purcell, Oklahoma.

McKnight, James from Gallatin, Texas to Bud Hardcastle in Purcell, Oklahoma. March 26, 1991.

Margie M. from Hallettsville, Texas to Bud Hardcastle. June 15, 1991.

Mueller, Nadine from LaMesa, California to Bud Hardcastle in Purcell, Ok. Nov. 17, 1995.

Norris, Charles to Howk, April 26, 1953.

Norris, Mary Plina to Ola Everhard, November 6, 1950.

Numerous letters addressed to Estes Funeral Home, requesting information about J. Frank Dalton/Jesse James.

Peggy from Llano, Texas to Bud Hardcastle in Purcell, Oklahoma; March 27, 1991.

Priest, Henry to J. D. Howard (Jesse), April 24, 1879.

Roberts, Brushy Bill in Hico, Texas to Mr. Jesse James at Meramec Caverns, Stanton, Missouri, (Christmas card), Dec. 12, 1949.

Roberts, Brushy Bill and Lizzie from Hico, Texas to Mr. Jesse James in Austin, Texas, October 27, 1950.

Roberts, Brushy Bill and Lizzie from Hico, Texas to Mrs. Ola Everhard in Austin, Texas, October 27, 1950.

Roberts, Lizzie in Temple, Texas to Mrs. Ola Everhard in Austin, Texas; January 11, 1951.

Roberts, Lizzie in Temple, Texas to Mrs. Ola Everhard in Austin, Texas; January 23, 1951.

Rosenberg, Joseph L. of Rosenberg & Rosenberg in Decatur, Illinois to Estes Funeral Home in Granbury, Texas. Nov. 2, 1953.

Sheppard, Geo. H., Comptroller of Public Accounts in Texas to Honorable Lindley Beckworth, U.S. Congressman, Washington D. C. January 6, 1948.

Starrs, James E, Professor of Law, and Forensic Sciences, George Washington University in Washington D.C. to the editor of The *Washington Times*, May 31, 2000.

Thrasher, Mr. R. A. to the Estes Funeral Home in Granbury, Texas. April 30, 1962.

Trammel, John by J. D. Cooper to Mr. and Mrs. Floyd Chaplin, Nov. 23, ??

Turilli, Francena from Stanton, Missouri to Bud Hardcastle in Purcell, Ok. Nov. 10, 1995.

Wood, Joe from Kirkwood, Missouri to Bud Hardcastle in Purcell, Oklahoma. Oct. 18, 1991.

Wood, Joe from Missouri to Bud Hardcastle in Purcell, Oklahoma. June 28, 1995.

Wood, Joe from Missouri to Bud Hardcastle in Purcell, Oklahoma. Sept. 26, 1995.

Wymore, Jack B., Founder and Owner of Jesse James Bank Museum in Liberty, Missouri. Letter of authenticity of Jesse James pocket size notebook. August 17, 1991.

Videos:

Aubrey Everhard, interview by Bud Hardcastle, filmed by Kenny Brown. Lovington, New Mexico. April 3, 1990.

Francena Turilli, interview by Bud Hardcastle. Stanton, Missouri. May 15, 1993.

Joe Wood and Vincel Simmons, interview by Bud Hardcastle. Missouri. 1993.

John Tatum, interview by Bud Harcastle and an unknown reporter. Date unknown.

Ola Everhard, interview by Dr. William Tunstill. Lovington, New Mexico. March 6, 1986.

Ralph Swaby, interview by Bud Hardcastle. Purcell, Oklahoma. 2000.

Audios:

Howk speaking about Jesse. Date unknown.

Morrey Davidson interviewing Brushy Bill, Col. John Davis, John Trammel, and Jesse James. September 5, 1949.

Photos:
Accumulated by Bud through various sources;

Aubrey Everhard, Joe Wood, Lou Kilgore, Marsha Swope, Grace Hopkins, Jay Longley, John and Jo Ella Tatum, Mitch Graves, Eddie James, Burleigh Dale James, Jesse Quanah James, and Charles A. James, Charlie Holman, Eddie Schneberger, and Karen Ford.. Many, many more unknown contributors.

Interviews conducted by Bud Hardcastle:

Archie Penick

Arlo Norman and son

Aubrey Everhard

Bennett (Bennie) Patty (Mrs. William Tipton Patty) of Porum, Oklahoma, interviewed by Samuel G. Campbell from Fayetteville, Arkansas, November 25, 1949. Type-written interview sent to Bud by Samuel Campbell.

Betty Lou Kilgore

Burleigh Dale James, Jesse Quanah James, and Charles A. James

Col. Charles Mooney

Cowboy "Slim" Williams

Dorothy Sears

Dr. William Tunstill

Eddie James and family

Edward "Eddie" Schneberger

Emmett Ward

Francena Turilli

Grace Hopkins

Jack Loftin

Jake Wilson

Jay Longley

Joe Wood

John and Jo Ella Tatum

Joyce Morgan

Karen Ford

Kathryn "Katie" E. (Vann) Brown from Porter, Oklahoma interviewed by Samuel G. Campbell from Fayetteville, Arkansas, January 23, 1950. Type-written interview sent to Bud from Samuel Campbell.

Kenneth Ford

Louis Serna

Mark Pack

Michael Ragge

Mitch Graves

Ralph Epperson

Rex and "Grandma" Ruby Leath

Sam Campbell

Steve Wilson

Vincel Simmons

Wells Blevins

And a Multitude of others along the trail.

Maps:
Map of Longview Texas where the Ford grocery store was located.

Map for Wapanucka Academy

Map outlining the Confederate Guerrilla Theatre of War by P.B. Larimore

Map of Buzzard Roost

Map of Longhorn Mountain

Map of Tennessee treasure

Wolf Map

Others notated.

Sources of Further Research

Books:

Allsopp, Fred W. (Fred William). *The Life Story of Albert Pike*. Little Rock, Arkansas, Parke-Harper news service, 1920.

Anderson, Robert B. *A Nation Needs to Pray*, preface by Dwight D. Eisenhower, Publisher – Nelson, 1963.

Benton, Jesse James. *Cow by the Tail*. Houghton Mifflin Co. 1943.

Bizzack, Ph.D., John W. *How & Why Freemasonry Came to Kentucky: The Backstory*. CreateSpace Independent Publishing Platform, 2015.

Boehner Stout, Mildred. *More Ryan Roots: Descendants of William and D. Ryan of Viriginia Through Their Sons: William, John, Philip, Joseph, Thomas who Lived in Kentucky, Tennessee, and Alabama*. M.B. Stout, 1994.

Boyd, Maurice. *Kowa Voices – Myths, Legends, and Folktales*. Texas Christian University Press; 1983.

Branch, Louis Leon. *Los Bilitos: The Story of Billy the Kid and His Gang*. Published by Descendants of Louis Leon Branch, 2023.

Brock, Dr. R.A. *Descendants of John Woodson of Dorcetshire, England*. 1888.

Brownlee, Richard S. *Grey Ghosts of the Confederacy: Guerrilla Warfare in the West, 1861-1865*. LSU Press, 1983.

Bryan, Howard. *True Tales of the American Southwest*. Clear Light Publishers.1998.

Caldwell, Clifford R. *John Simpson Chisum – The Cattle King of the Pecos Revisited*. Sunstone Press. 2010.

Chittenden, Hiram Martin (1858-1917). *The American fur trade of the Far West: a history of the pioneer trading posts and early fur companies of the Missouri Valley and the Rocky Mountains and of the overland commerce with Santa Fe; Volume II & III*. Publisher - Francis P. Harper, 1902.

Chrisman, Harry E. *Fifty Years on the Owl Hoot Trail, Jim Herron*. Ohio University Press, 1969.

Chrisman, Harry E. *Lost Trails of the Cimarron*. Sage Books, 1961.

Clarence, John and Tom Whittle, *The Gold House, Soledad*. 2012.

Coleman, William Head. *Historical Sketch Book and Guide to New Orleans and Environs*. 1885.

Creasey, Sibyl (compiled by). *Civil War Veterans of Van Zandt County, Texas: Military and Pension Information, Biographies and Obituaries, Muster Rolls, Newspaper Articles*. The Van Zandt County Genealogical Society. c2005.

Curtis, George Washington Parke. "The Man Who Could Not Be Killed." *Recollections and Private Memoirs of Washington*, Philadelphia, J.W. Bradley, 1859.

Dalton, Frank. *Quantrell....In the Civil War, Reminiscences of Civil War Days. First Edition*. Privately Published, May 20, 1935.

Denslow, William R. *$10,000 Famous Freemasons*. Macoy Publishing & Masonic Supply Co., Inc. 1957.

Donald, Jay. *Outlaws of the Border: a complete and authentic history of the lives of Frank and Jesse James, the Younger brothers, and their robber companions, including Quantrell and his noted guerrillas.*" Coburn & Newman Pub. Co. 1882, Internet Archive. https://archive.org/details/outlawsofbordercoodona/page/442/mode/2up.

Dozier, Edward P. "Rio Grande Pueblos." Edward H. Spicer, ed. *Perspectives in American Indian Culture Change*, 1961.

Edwards, Daniel A. *Billy the Kid: An Autobiography*. Creative Texts Publishers, LLC, 2014-2021.

Egan, Timothy. *The Worst Hard Time*. Mariner Books, Classics. 2006.

Farr, Hon. F. C. "Thomas Theodore Crittenden." *Distinguished American Lawyers: with their struggles and triumphs in the forum by Henry W. Scott*. Charles L. Webster & Company, 1891.

Fox, Francis. *Sweet Land of Liberty: The Ordeal of the American Revolution in Northampton*, 1925.

Fulton, Maurice G. *History of the Lincoln County War*. Edited by Robert N. Mullin. University of Arizona Press, 1968.

Gentry, Curt. *The Killer Mountains*. Comstock Book Distributors, 1976.

Getler, Warren and Bob Brewer. *Rebel Gold: One Man's Quest to Crack the Code Behind the Secret Treasure of The Confederacy*. Simon & Schuster, 2005.

Gillett, James B. *Six years with the Texas Rangers, 1875 to 1881*. Yale University Press, 1925. Internet Archive. https://archive.org/details/sixyearswithtex00gill.

Grady Gay, Beatrice. *Into The Setting Sun, A history of Coleman County*. 1936.

Groce, W. Todd. *Mountain Rebels: East Tennessee Confederates and the Civil War, 1860-1870*. Univ. Tennessee Press, 1999.

Halstead Van Tyne, PhD., Claude. *The American Revolution 1776-1783; The American Nation: a History, Volume 9*. Harper & Brothers, 1905.

Halstead, Hon. Murat. *Pictorial History of the Louisiana Purchase and the World's Fair At St. Louis*, National Publishing Company, 1904.

Hardcastle, Bud. *The Hoax That Let Jesse James Live*. Creative Texts Publishers, LLC, 2021.

Hedgpeth, Don. *They Rode Good Horses: The First Fifty Years of the American Quarter Horse Association*. American Quarter Horse Association, 1990.

Howard, Paul G. *The Amazing Outlaw Life of Jesse James*.

Hutcheson Davis, Virginia Lee. *Tidewater Virginia Families*. Genealogical Publishing Co., Inc., 1989

James, Jesse Lee. *Jesse James and the Lost Cause*. Pageant Press, 1961.

Johnson, David. *The Horrell Wars: Feuding in Texas and New Mexico*. University of North Texas Press, 2014.

Johnson, Neil R. *The Chickasaw Rancher*. Revised Edition. 2001.

Johnson, William Jackson. *George Washington, the Christian*. The Abingdon Press. 1919.

Johnstone, William Jackson. *George Washington, the Christian*. Kessinger Publishing, 2007.

King, Frank M. *Wranglin' the Past: The Reminiscences of Frank M. King*. Trail's End Publishing Co., 1935.

Kolterman Hansen, Esther, *Echoes of the Past Along Pioneer Trails in Pierce County, Nebraska*, written in 1967, Self-published, Fourth Edition, 1976.

Maltby, W. J. *Captain Jeff of the Texas Rangers: Fighting Comanche & Kiowa Indians on the South Western Frontier 1863-1874*. Leonaur Ltd, 2010. Kindle.

Marcy, Randolph B. *The Prairie Traveler – A Handbook For Overland Expeditions*. Harper & Brothers, Publishers, 1859.

McKim, D.D., Randolph H. discusses the cause of the Civil War. *The Photographic History of the Civil War in Ten Volumes; Francis Trevelyan Miller, Editor in Chief, Robert Sampson Lanier, Managing Editor*. Review of Reviews Co. 1911.Meacham, Jon. *American Gospel: God, the Founding Fathers, and the Making of a Nation*. Random House Trade Paperbacks; Annotated edition, 2007.

Members of the Moreno Valley Writers Guild. *Lure, Lore, and Legends of the Moreno Valley*. Columbine Publishing Company, Inc. 1997.

Miller, Rick. *Texas Ranger John B. Jones and the Frontier Battalion, 1874-1881*. University of North Texas Press, 2012. Kindle.

Montgomery, Bonnie and Lois Garner, Mary Caye Judd, Jesse & Jess Jr, Virginia Minor, John Tom & Shuler Donelson, Johnnie Sue, Mettie Lee Brown, Barbara James Fretwell, Brad James, Carl Keith James, Tom Taylor James, Helen Priestly, and a whole slew of James' family members; *History And a Few Tall Tales of the James Brother' Ranch 1901-1936 and on through 2001*."

Parsons, Chuck, Donaly E. Brice, and Leon C. Metz (Forward), *Texas Ranger N.O. Reynolds the Intrepid*. University of North Texas Press, 2014. Kindle.

<u>Pike, Albert, 1809-1891. *Prose Sketches and poems: written in the western country*. Boston: Light & Horton, 1834. Internet Archive. Accessed 2022. https://archive.org.</u>

Pike, Albert. *Morals and Dogma*. The Council, 1871. Internet Archive. 2022 https://archive.org/details/MoralsAndDogmaAlbertPikeTheCouncil1871/mode/2up.

Pinkerton, Gary L. *Trammel's Trace, The First Road To Texas From The North*. Texas A&M University Press, 2018.

Priddy, Rosanne Wilcoxson. *The Haskew Brand*. Blurb, Inc. 2014.

Roberts, Archibald E. *Emerging Struggle for State Sovereignty*. (Betsy Ross Press, 1979).

Robison, John. *Proofs of a Conspiracy against all the Religions and Governments of Europe carried on in the secret meetings of Freemasons, Illuminati and Reading Societies*. 1798.

Rogers, J.A. *Ku Klux Spirit*. Lushena Books, 2021.

Rutherford, Judge Joseph Franklin Rutherford. *Vindication*. Watch Tower Bible and Tract Society and the International Bible Students Association, 1931.

Rye, Edgar. *The Quirt and the Spur*, Vanishing Shadows of the Texas Frontier. W.B. Conkey, 1909.

Schrader, Del. *Jesse James was One of His Names*. Santa Anita Press, 1975. Internet Archive. https://archive.org/details/JesseJamesWasOneOfHisNamesDelSchrader.

Shaw, Jim and Tom McKenney. *The Deadly Deception; Freemasonry Exposed By One Of Its Top Leaders*. Huntington House, Inc., 1988.

Shirley, Glenn. *Heck Thomas, Frontier Marshal, The Story of a Real Gunfighter*. Chilton Company – Book Division, 1962.

Silva, Lee A. "Elfego Baca: Forgotten Fighter For Law and Order." *America – The Men and Their Guns That Made Her Great*, edited by Craig Boddington, Petersen Publishing Co. 1981.

Smith, Tevis Clyde "TJ." *From the Memories of Men*. Self-Published. First Edition, 1954.

(Smith) Wilcoxson, Ruth Geraldine, and Rosanne Priddy. *The Would-Be Pioneers*. Xulon Press, 2011.

Stanley, F. *Clay Allison*. World Press. 1956.

Steele, Phillip W. *Starr Tracks: Belle and Pearl Starr*. Pelican Publishing Co., 1989.

Temple, Oliver P., compiled and arranged by his daughter, Mary B. Temple. *Notable Men of Tennessee From 1833 to 1875*. The Cosmopolitan Press, 1912.

Towne, Stephen E. *Surveillance and Spies in the Civil War*. Ohio University Press; First Edition, 2014.

Turilli, Rudy. *I Knew Jesse James*. Self-published, 1966.

Tyler, Ronnie C. *The Big Bend-A History of the Last Texas Frontier*. Texas A&M University Press, 1996.

Utley, Robert M. *Billy the Kid, A Short and Violent Life*. University of Nebraska Press, 1989.

Walker-Wyatt, Reggie Anne. *Chasing Rivers, Trains and Jesse James*, 2000.

Williams, Jonathan. *Legions of Satan*. 1781.

Wilson, Steve. *Oklahoma Treasure and Treasure Tales*. University of Oklahoma Press. 1989.

Yadon, Lawrence J., with Dan Anderson. *200 Texas Outlaws and Lawmen 1835-1935*, edited by Robert Barr Smith. Pelican Publishing Company, 2008.

Younger, Cole. *The Story of Cole Younger, by Himself*. The Henneberry Company, 1903.

Zimmer, Stephen. *For Good Or Bad: People of the Cimarron Country."* Sunstone Press, 1999.

Newspapers:

The majority of the newspaper articles were found at Newspapers.com, with a small amount found in chroniclingamerica.loc.gov.

"100 Per Cent Curb in E. Texas, Vast Field Is Inactive; Jobs Secure." *Fort Worth Star Telegram*. Fort Worth, Texas. August 19, 1931.

"108-Year-Old Man Renews License to Drive Own Car." *The Tennessean. Nashville*, Tennessee. June 16, 1949.

"109-Year Oldster Can Recall Days of Indian Wars." *Nashville Banner*. Nashville, Tennessee. Oct. 1, 1949.

"116-Year-Old Negro to Get Doctor Study." *Seminole Producer*. Seminole, Oklahoma. Nov. 1, 1954.

"1882 Magazine Tells Of James Gang Exploits." *Lawton News-Review*. Lawton, Oklahoma. May 20, 1948.

"33 'Bullet' Scars Found on Body of 'Jesse James.'" *Fort Worth Star Telegram*. Fort Worth, Texas. August 18, 1951.

"A Detective Story Founded on Facts." *St. Louis Post-Dispatch*. St. Louis, Missouri. July 30, 1899.

"A Good Citizen Gone." *Muskogee County Republican and Fort Gibson Post*. Muskogee, Muskogee County, Oklahoma. Sept 29, 1910.

"A James Boy's Story." *Atchison Daily Patriot*. Atchison, Kansas. April 7, 1882.

"A Member of the James Band Still Tells of Group's Exploits." *The Kansas City Star*. Kansas City, Missouri. March 14, 1939.

"A Necessity." *The Snyder Signal*. Snyder, Texas, Sept. 05, 1919.

"A Pallbearer at Jesse James' Funeral." *Falls City Daily News*. Falls City, Nebraska. June 5, 1903.

"A Sensitive Set, Contributions of Reminiscences by F. A. Mitchel of Chicago, History of Frank," *The Kansas City Times*. Kansas City, Missouri, April 6, 1882.

"A Sensitive Set, The Governor's Instructions." *The Kansas City Times*. Kansas City, Missouri. April 6, 1882.

"A Tussle With Casey's Gang." *The Norman Transcript*. Norman, Oklahoma, August 14, 1902.

"A.M. James, 75, Rites in Dalhart." *The Amarillo Globe*-Times. Amarillo, Texas. March 4, 1958.

A.W. Neville: Backward Glances. "Frank Dalton Lives One Hundred Years." *The Paris News*. Paris, Texas, March 9, 1948.

Abcarian, Robin. "Treasure or Treachery?: Did 'Doc' Noss Really Find Caverns of God or Did He Pull Off a Hoax That Has Plagued His Kin for Years?" *Los Angeles Times*. Los Angeles, California. June 16, 1991.

"Adventurer, Civil War Guerilla Dies at 108." *El Paso Herald-Post*. El Paso, Texas. August 15, 1947.

"Affidavits Submitted To Verify Outlaw's Claim." *Lawton News-Review*. Lawton, Oklahoma. May 20, 1948.

"After a Long Chase, Sam Green, an Alleged Murderer, is Taken in British Columbia." *The Guthrie Daily Leader*. Guthrie, Oklahoma. May 25, 1906.

"Al Jennings, Once Fastest Gun in West, Scoffs at Modern Television Badmen." *Tulsa World*. June 16, 1957.

Alexandria Gazette, July 24, 1863. 2022. Chronicling America: Historic American Newspapers, Lib. Of Congress. https://chroniclingamerica.loc.gov.

An Interview with Leland V. Gardiner of Santa Fe who believed Billy the Kid was still alive. *El Paso Herald Post*. El Paso, Texas. June 23, 1923.

"Anderson Items" *Pineville Herald*. Pineville, Missouri. October 14, 1904.

Anderson, Robert B. "A Statement by Robert B. (Bob) Anderson concerning the character of Lyndon B. Johnson and his qualifications as President of the United States." *Wichita Falls Times*, October 25, 1964.

"Another Member Of Quantrell's Band Is Found." *Mexico Weekly Ledger*. Mexico, Missouri. March 31, 1932.

"Another Pioneer Passed Away." *Jasper County Democrat*. Jasper, Missouri. April 13, 1909.

"Another Thomason Is To Be Sheriff of Clay County." *The Kansas City Star*. Kansas City, Missouri. August 18, 1940.

"Are the History Books Wrong About His Death? Jesse James More Than A Legend Here." *The Granbury Tablet*. Granbury, Texas, April 26, 1984.

"Arkansan Pal of Jesse James Dies. Aged Chiropodist Once Fitted Boots for Outlaw." *The Star-Journal*. Warrensburg, Missouri. March 22, 1929.

"Arrest Col. Cummins Amid Much Excitement"– "Humane Society people declare concession employees were cruel." *St. Louis Globe-Democrat*. St. Louis, Missouri. August 15, 1904.

Article on Jesse James funeral in 1882, describing the "mystery man," James Vaughn. *Daily Charlotte Observer*, April 6, 1882.

"Astounding Developments before the United States Grand Jury; A Secret Society of Traitors in Indiana. In the District Court of the United States, for the district of Indiana, May Term, 1862." *Daily Missouri Republican*, St. Louis, Missouri, August 6, 1862.

"At the Majestic." *The Shreveport Journal*. Shreveport, Louisianna. August 19, 1931.

"Bank Cashier Dies." *Wichita Weekly Times*. Wichita Falls, Texas, March 11, 1910.

"Barbara Fritchie and Quantrell." *Watonga Republican Newspaper*. Watonga, Blaine County, Oklahoma, April 28, 1920.

Bass, P.C., JNO. H. letter to the editor. *Our Brother in Red Newspaper*. Muskogee, Oklahoma, February 21, 1895.

Behymer, F. A. "Judge Who Threw Out Jesse James Case." *St. Louis Post-Dispatch*, March 23, 1950.

"Belle Starr Journal." *The St. Joseph Herald*, St. Louis, Missouri, February 18, 1889.

"Belle Starr, Woman Bandit," *Kansas City Times*, Kansas City, Missouri. May 9, 1919.

Bickley, Geo., K.G.C., President American Legion, letter to the Kentucky Legislature, *Daily Missouri Republican*, June 4, 1861.

"Bill" Anderson, The Guerilla, Still Alive, Texas Paper Says." *The Missourian*, (shown as Richmond Missourian). Richmond, Missouri. May 22, 1924.

"Billy Wilson." *The Las Vegas Gazette*. March 1, 1882.

"Bob Ford Again." *Austin American-Statesman*. Austin, Texas. September 25, 1884.

Bob Ford and Dick Liddell in Las Vegas, New Mexico. *The Weekly Chieftain*. Vinita, Oklahoma. October 2, 1884.

"Bob Ford and Dick Liddle Have got Orders to Go." *El Paso Times*. El Paso, Texas. September 27, 1884.

"Bob Ford Killed." *St. Louis Globe-Democrat*. St. Louis, Missouri. June 9, 1892.

Bob Ford's Saloon burnt to the ground. "Board of Pardons." *The Democrat-Herald*, Date Unknown.

"Bob Goss Takes Position With Texas Rangers." *The Kilgore Herald*. Kilgore, Texas. November 22, 1936.

"Bob James Dies at the Age of 82 Years." Obituary of Robert "Bob" James (1877-1959). *The Lathrop Optimist*. Lathrop, Missouri. November 26, 1959.

"Booming Bowie." *Fort Worth Daily Gazette*. Fort Worth, Texas. May 12, 1884.

"Bowers Mill Has Been in Existence Sixty-five Years." *Carthage Evening Press*. Carthage, Missouri. July 09, 1903.

Brice, Ed. "Booth," *Fort Worth Star-Telegram*. Fort Worth, Texas, March 6, 1984.

"Buckskin Joe." A Partner of Captain Payne, the Noted Oklahoma Boomer, and His Great Scheme." *Fort Worth Daily Gazette*. Fort Worth, Texas. April 1, 1887.

"Buckskin Joe" Returns; City Seems Like Dream." *The Daily Oklahoman*. Oklahoma City, Oklahoma. January 2, 1915.

"Burrell Whatley Kills Hardcastle." *The Valliant Tribune*. Valliant, Oklahoma. June 22, 1921.

Buzbee, Byron, "Last of Quantrell's Raiders, Now Living in Corpus Christi, Plans to Enter the Movies." *Corpus Christi Times*, Corpus Christi, Texas, June 30, 1939.

Byers, Robert. "Not Shot by Ford, Jesse James Died in 1950, Says Old Friend." *Denver Post*. Denver, Colorado. Nov. 18, 1954.

"Callaway Farmer, Host to Jesse James, Is Now 88 and Retired." *The Mexico Ledger*. Mexico, Missouri. May 21, 1948.

Capt. J. Dud. Doak in charge of 250 mules from Mexico during the Civil War for Gen. Steel's Division. *Dallas Weekly Herald*. Dallas, Texas. May 13, 1863.

Chapman, Art. "The 1999 Charles Goodnight Award, Saluting a Texas Legacy." (W.T. "Tom" Waggoner). *Fort Worth Star Telegram*. Fort Worth, Texas. December 5, 1999.

Charles Ford's Suicide. The New York Times, May 7, 1884. *The Galveston Daily News*, May 7, 1884. The Kansas City Times, May 7, 1884.

"Chihuahua, Treasure House of Mexico, Largest State Rich in All Resources; Development Fast." *El Paso Herald*. El Paso, Texas. June 17, 1922.

"Chiropodist Moves to Santa Fe." *The Santa Fe New Mexican*. Santa Fe, New Mexico. October 27, 1934.

"Civil War Vet Dies at Age of 109 After Amazing Life Story." *The Ada Weekly News*. Ada, Oklahoma. March 16, 1950.

"Cole Younger, Ex-Bandit, to Become Lecturer Missourian Who Was Intended For the Ministry will Preach." *Evening Times*. Grand Forks, North Dakota. April 2, 1910.

"Coleman Pioneer Recalls Concho As An Army Post." *The San Angelo Weekly Standard*. San Angelo, Texas, February 9, 1940.

"College Given Land Valued At $16,000." *Fort Worth Star-Telegram*. Fort Worth, Texas. Dec. 15, 1925.

"Coming of Movie 'Jesse James' Stirs Memories Here." *Wichita Times*, January 22, 1939.

Conway, Dan R. "Calamity Jane – Unique Character of Old Frontier." *The Bozeman Courier*. Bozeman, Montana. Oct 08, 1926.

"Crisp News Condensations from the Two Territories." *Indian Citizen*. Atoka, Oklahoma, January 17, 1895.

"Cupid's Arrow in the Shape of a Watch." *Fort Worth Gazette*. Fort Worth, Texas. April 27, 1891.

"Dallas." The killing of Sheriff Peringer by John Means. *Austin Weekly Statesman*. February 21, 1884.

Dalton, Frank as told to Garland Farmer. "Belle Starr Was Noted Outlaw of Early West," *St. Joseph New Press*, St. Joseph, Missouri, Jan. 21, 1940.

"Daring Pioneer Dreams of Past of Tragic Times." *Houston Post*. Houston, Texas, January 27, 1924.

"Days of Wooly Wild West." *The St. Louis Republic*. St. Louis, Missouri. July 31, 1904.

"Death Claims Indian, 108." *Austin American-Statesman*. Austin, Texas. August 14, 1947.

"Death of Bob James Ends Life Of Pioneer." *Oklahoma Democrat*. Altus, Oklahoma. August 14, 1913.

"Death's Door, It is Suddenly Opened for Daniel H. Askew by an Unknown Hand." *The Kansas City Times*. Kansas City, Missouri. April 14, 1875.

Debusk, Leland. "Jesse James, Researchers hope for exhumation this month." *Hood County News*. Granbury, Texas. May 4, 1996.

DeHaven, Jess. "Psychic views ability to 'see' as way to help," – Psychic predictions." *St. Joseph News-Press*, Nov 3, 1995.

"Denies Garrett Shot, Killed Billy The Kid." *El Paso Times*. El Paso, Texas. November 10, 1937.

Description of Jesse James' funeral expense in 1882. *Independent-Courier*. Clarence, Missouri. November 20, 1929.

"Detective Chief Named as Guard." *Newport Daily Independent*. Newport, Arkansas. February 10, 1905.

"Detective John W. Shevlin To Be Chief At Hot Springs." *The St. Louis Republic*. St. Louis, Missouri. September 27, 1903.

Dickerson, Argus. "Greer County." *The Gould Democrat*. January 21, 1932 and January 28, 1932.

"Digging for Lost Treasure of Aztecs in Taylor County, North of Abilene." *Fort Worth Star-Telegram*. Fort Worth, Texas, November 17, 1907.

Dittrick, Paula. "Cousin Claims Jesse James died in 1951 at age 103." *Sunday Advocate*. Baton Rouge, La. Nov. 20, 1983.

Dobie, J. Frank. "Indian Tales Lured Fortune Hunters On-Dobie Tells." *The Austin American*. Austin, Texas, September 17, 1931.

"Doggerel." *Tampa Bay Times*. June 17, 1949.

"Double Killing of Officers An Early Sensation." *Elk City Daily News*. Elk City, Oklahoma. August 29, 1935.

"Double Killing." *The Norman Transcript*. Norman, Oklahoma, January 11, 1895.

"Duel to the Death. John Swain Mortally Wounded-Kills Garl Vincent." *The Purcell Register*. Purcell, Oklahoma. January 4, 1895.

"Duel To The Death." *Purcell Register*. January 11, 1895. https://sites.rootsweb.com/~okbits/purcellregister.html

"Ex-Bad Man Scoffs At Idea Billy The Kid Is Alive." *The Paris News*. Paris, Texas. June 23, 1938.

"Ex-Confederate Soldier Dies at Ripe Old Age." *Tishomingo Leader and the Mannsville Herald*. Tishomingo, Oklahoma. April 3, 1914.

"Exhumation of 'outlaw's' grave on hold," *Hood County News*, Granbury, Texas. April 1, 2000.

"Ex-Ranger Hickman Dies In Gainesville." *San Angelo Standard-Times*. San Angelo, Texas. Jan 29, 1962.

"Ex-Sheriff Dead." *The Chillicothe Constitution-Tribune*. Chillicothe, Missouri. February 22, 1891.

Farmer Garland R. "A Dalton Tells The Story of Quantrell." *The Whitewright Sun*. Whitewright, Texas. August 7, 1941.

Farmer, Garland R. "Frank Dalton Or Jesse James, This Old Fellow Knows A Lot." *The Kilgore News-Herald*. Kilgore, Texas. March 19, 1950.

"Father of Arlington Resident Dies at 91." *Fort Worth Star-Telegram*, January 28, 1974.

"For County Judge, Retired Prison Head To Run." *Hood County News*. Granbury, Texas. Nov. 19, 1997.

"Former Sheriff of Hood County Thinks Real Jesse James Died in Granbury." *Hood County News Tablet*. Granbury, Texas. August 11, 1966.

"Fought Under Black Flag of Quantrill; Is Visiting in Cameron." *The Cameron Herald*. Cameron, Texas. October 28, 1943.

"Four Who Searched for Jesse James' Hidden Treasure in Ohio Stop Here." *Joplin Globe*. Joplin, Missouri. March 18, 1949.

"Frank James. His Trial Begins at Gallatin. Large Crowd in Attendance – Much Interest Felt." *The Lexington Intelligencer*, Lexington, Missouri, August 25, 1883, 2023, https://chroniclingamerica.loc.gov.

"Frontier Forces." *Austin American-Statesman*. Austin, Texas. June 10, 1874.

Fuller, Henry C. "One of Quantrill's Bravest Men Lives in Brown County." *San Angelo Evening Standard*. San Angelo, Texas. October 17, 1926.

Fuller, Henry C. Story on Bloody Bill Anderson's Ambush. *Schulenburg Sticker*. Schulenburg, Texas. April 3, 1925.

"Funeral Services for John P. Vaughan." *The Lawton Constitution*. Lawton, Oklahoma. April 24, 1924.

"Garland R. Farmer Dies In Henderson." *The Kilgore News Herald*. Kilgore, Texas. July 19, 1956.

"Genesis Chapter 1st." *The St. Joseph Herald*, St. Joseph, Missouri, January 15, 1863.

"George Kenneth Ford." *Longview News-Journal*. Longview, Texas. February 22, 1998.

"Gladewater Road is Colorful Spot with Nightfall in Sway." *Longview News Journal*. Longview, Texas. Nov. 22, 1931.

Glen R. Cooper, "'Jesse James Is Alive,' Decatur Woman Claims Kin of Outlaw James," *The Decatur Daily Review*, May 11, 1950.

"Got Their Man." *The Daily Oklahoman*. Oklahoma City, Oklahoma. May 26, 1906.

"Guerrilla Leads Life of Peace." *The Amarillo Globe Times*. Amarillo, Texas. December 26, 1945.

"Had Photo Made On Hundredth Birthday." *The Progressive Age*. Scottsboro, Alabama. November 28, 1929.

"Hamp Williams, 70, Dies; Was Arkansas Leader." *Chattanooga Daily Times*, Chattanooga, Tennessee. May 17, 1931.

Hanna, Bill "Grave Debate," *Fort Worth Star Telegram*. Fort Worth, Texas. March 14, 2000.

Hanna, Bill. "Dalton Search Finds Wrong Body." *Fort Worth Star Telegram*. Fort Worth, Texas. July 1, 2000.

Hanna, Bill. "Rift delays Granbury exhumation." *Fort Worth Star-Telegram*. Fort Worth, Texas. April 4, 2000.

Harrison Trow sells 8,640 acres to Sandy Murchison. *Fort Worth Record-Telegram*. Fort Worth, Texas. March 27, 1920.

Hartsfield, Jack. "Outlaw's Kin Says Death Faked" and "James' Death Faked, Kin Says." *Lubbock Avalanche*, Sept. 1983.

"Henry Ford Rose From Unknown Youth to Outstanding Leader." *Brownwood Bulletin*. Brownwood, Texas, April 8, 1956.

"Henry Ford, Brownwood." *Fort Worth Record and Register*. Fort Worth, Texas. March 8, 1910.

"His Bones are Dust." *The Kansas City Journal*. Kansas City, Missouri. June 30, 1902.

Holbrook, Stewart H. "The Real Calamity Jane." *Chicago Tribune*. Chicago, Illinois. Dec. 5, 1948.

"Hoots Accompany Affidavits as Paper Claims Jesse James Is Still with Us." *Austin-American Statesman*. Austin, Texas. May 20, 1948.

"Hot Springs Banker To Be Buried Monday." *The Commercial Appeal*, Memphis. Tennessee. May 17, 1931.

"Hundreds Amuse the St. Louis Public." *The St. Louis Republic*. St. Louis, Missouri. September 08, 1904.

"In Loving Memory of Attorney General, Waggoner Carr 1918-2004." *Austin American-Statesman*, Austin, Texas. February 27, 2004.

Inge, Ashley. "A legend shrouded in mystery: Former forensic anthropologist recounts the 2000 exhumation of Jesse James' grave," *Hood County News*. Granbury, Texas. December 20, 2022. Accessed 2023. https://www.hcnews.com.

Intercepted Letter from Jesse J. *The Kansas City Times*. Kansas City, Missouri, April 3, 1882.

"Is it really Jesse? Judge grants order to exhume reputed outlaw's bones." *Hood County News*. Granbury, Texas. February 19, 2000.

"Is Jesse James Alive? Lansing Pastor Thinks He Is." *Lansing State Journal*. Lansing, Michigan. August 1, 1949.

"Is This Nebraskan a Secret Son of Jesse James?" *Omaha World Herald*. Omaha, Nebraska. November 6, 1938.

"It Would Be Easy To Determine If Latest 'Jesse James' Is Imposter." *Fort Worth Star Telegram*. Fort Worth, Texas. June 4, 1948.

"J. Frank Dalton, Who Said He Was Jesse James, Dies," *Fort Worth Star-Telegram*, August 16, 1951.

"J.I. McDaniel, 85, Veteran Educator of State, Is Dead." *The Daily Oklahoma*. Oklahoma City, Oklahoma. Sept 5, 1939.

"James Boys' Mother Dead." *The Washington Post*. Washington D.C. February 11, 1911.

"James I. McDaniel, Sketch of the Free Silver candidate for Sheriff of Logan County." *The Oklahoma Representative*. Guthrie, Oklahoma. October 1, 1896.

"James I. McDaniel." *The Oklahoma State Capital*, July 13, 1900.

"James R. Davis Is Dead At 109." *The Jackson Sun*. Jackson, Tennessee. March 14, 1950.

"James Russell Davis, 109, Civil War Veteran, Dies." *Evening Star*. Washington, District of Columbia. March 14, 1950.

"James Story True?" *The Norman Transcript*. Norman, Oklahoma. January 15, 1950,

James, Jesse. Letter to the editor of The Clipper-Herald, Hannibal, Missouri. The letter was postmarked in Brownwood, Texas. From the Pen of Jesse James. "Brownwood, The Hardest Town in Texas," November 7, 1879. *The St. Joseph Weekly Gazette*, November 20, 1879.

"James' Treasure Hunt Continues." *The Wewoka Times-Democrat*. Wewoka, Oklahoma. March 14, 1949.

"Jesse James Fled to Kemptville Great-Granddaughter Declares," *The Ottawa Journal*. Ottawa, Ontario, Canada. July 6, 1948.

"Jesse James Funeral." *Henry County Democrat*. Clinton, Missouri. April 13, 1882.

"Jesse James Heard From. A Remarkable Letter." *The Ouachita Telegraph*. Monroe, Louisianna. December 12, 1879.

"Jesse James lived 'til he was 103, says JP who believes he met him." *The Marshall News Messenger*," Marshall, Texas. February 19, 1982.

"Jesse James visits at the Las Vegas Hot Springs from July 26th – 29th." *The Las Vegas Optic*, December 8, 1879.

"Jesse James." *Chariton Courier*. Keytesville, Missouri, November 8, 1879.

"Jesse James' grandsons threaten to move body." *Hood County News*. Granbury, Texas. September 28, 1996.

"Jesse James' Son Will Fight for His Name." *Austin-American Statesman*. Austin, Texas. January 1950.

"Jesse James' to End, Man Takes Outlaw's Name to Grave." *The Independent*. Long Beach, California. August 17, 1951.

"Jesse James" Case Witness Dies of Heart Attack." *The Wheaton Journal*. Wheaton, Missouri. March 16, 1950.

Jesse's Reburial. *Kansas City Journal*. Kansas City, Missouri. June 30, 1902.

"Joe Wood, 82; Photographer For 27 Years At Globe-Democrat." *St. Louis Post-Dispatch*. St. Louis, Missouri. December 5, 1996.

John Means and the Marshall Gang Arrested. *The Indian Journal*. Eufaula, Oklahoma. Feb. 21, 1884.

John Means killing the Sheriff of Pickens County, Indian Territory. *Austin Weekly Statesman*, Austin, Texas. Feb. 21, 1884.

"John W. Pierce's Obituary." *Daily Standard*, Excelsior Springs, Missouri. 1952.

Johnston, Lex, "B'wood pioneer may have had outlaw's background. Was Henry Ford really Jesse James?" *Brownwood Bulletin*. Brownwood, Texas. April 24, 1977.

Johnston, Lex. "Pioneer had outlaw past." *Brownwood Bulletin*. Brownwood, Texas. January 02, 1977.

Jordan, Jaime S. "Former State Attorney General Dies." *Abilene Reporter-News*. Abilene, Texas. February 26, 2004.

"Judge Denies Plea of 'Real Jesse James,' Blisters Gang as 'Black Spot on Missouri.'" *St. Louis Post-Dispatch*. St. Louis, Missouri. March 11, 1950.

"Judge R. E. Thomason, Public Servant, Dies." *El Paso Times*, El Paso, Texas. November 9, 1973.

"Judge wants better reasons for Jesse James' exhumation." *Hood County News*. Granbury, Texas. Sept. 25, 1996.

"Just A Joke To "Jesse." *The Kansas City Times*. Kansas City, Missouri. March 14, 1949.

"Kerry's Confession, Details of the Otterville Train Robbery, The James Boys and the Youngers in the Lead." *The Western Spirit*, August 18, 1876.

"Keziah Elsie Campbell's Obituary." *Hill City Times*. Hill City, Kansas. January 1, 1959.

"Killed by an Officer." *The San Francisco Call and Post*. San Francisco, California, Dec. 16, 1896.

"Knights of the Golden Circle-Frederick Court Before U.S. Commissioner White – Examination of Witnesses," *Daily Ohio Stateman*, Columbus, Ohio, October 18, 1861.

Koethe, Jim. "Lost Diamond Mine Object of Intense Treasure Hunt." *Times Record News*. Wichita Falls, Texas, December 6, 1956.

Koethe, Jim. A series of articles regarding treasure sites near Wichita Falls, Texas including Oklahoma. *Wichita Falls Times Record News*, August-September-October 1956.

Land Dispute between the McDaniels and The Fort Smith and Western Railroad Company. *The Guthrie Daily Leader*. Guthrie, Oklahoma. June 10, 1902.

"Last of Quantrell's Band, "Uncle Bill" Gone." *Abilene Daily Reporter*. Abilene, Texas, Nov. 6, 1927.

"Legends of Jesse James Live On in Minds of Many," *The Daily Oklahoman*, Oklahoma City, Oklahoma. January 31, 1993.

"Lex Johnston named head of Dallas bank." *Brownwood Bulletin*. Brownwood, Texas, Nov. 29, 1977.

"Longview Man's Rites Conducted." *The Kilgore News Herald*. Kilgore, Texas. November 14, 1960.

Love, Robertus. "The Rise and Fall of Jesse James." *St. Louis Post Dispatch*. St. Louis, Missouri. July 23, 1925.

Love, Robertus. "The Rise and Fall of Jesse James." *Tulsa World*. Tulsa, Oklahoma. August 28, 1925.

Love, Robertus. A story told by Captain James Daniel Koger (1845-1926), "The Rise and Fall of Jesse James." *Tulsa World*. Tulsa, Oklahoma. August 28, 1925.

Love, Robertus. Title unidentifiable. Jesse's Reburial. *St. Louis Post-Dispatch*, St. Louis, Missouri. June 30, 1902.

"M'Alester's Cattle Nearly Cost Life." *The Daily Oklahoma*. Oklahoma City. Jan. 11, 1920.

"Major Shelton Dies in Austin." *Times Record News*. Wichita Falls, Texas. December 29, 1952.

"Man Passes on Memories of Frank, Jesse James." *Wichita Falls Times*, Wichita Falls, Texas, Dec. 19, 1982.

"Many Detectives Arrive." *The St. Louis Republic*. St. Louis, Missouri. April 26, 1904.

"Many Wichitans Recall Frank James Noted Bandit." *Wichita Weekly Times*, Wichita Falls, Texas, February 26, 1915.

"Masterson's Death Brings Recollections." *Amarillo Daily News*. Amarillo, Texas, November 21, 1921.

Minco Minstrel, January 11, 1895.

"Missouri's First Negro School." *Muldrow Press*. July 15, 1912; now the Vian Press, Muldrow, Oklahoma.

"Monument to Mark U.S. Fort, Shaft to Be Erected At Camp Colorado in Coleman County." *Abilene Reporter-News*. Abilene, Texas. July 9, 1936.

"More Proof That Dalton is 'Jesse'." *The Guthrie Daily Leader*. Guthrie, Oklahoma. July 7, 1948.

"Mother of 'James Boys' is Dead." *The Choctaw Herald*. February 16, 1911.

"Mrs. Elsie N. Howk Granted Divorce." *Great Falls Tribune*. Great Falls, Montana, June 9, 1950.

"Murder!" The *Cheyene Sunbeam*. Cheyenne, Oklahoma. July 4, 1902.

"Mysterious Revelations, From the Louisville Journal. The Order of the Knights of the Golden Circle," *The Wyandot Pioneer*, Upper Sandusky, Ohio, August 23, 1861 – Chronicling America: Historic American Newspaper, Lib. Of Congress. 2022, https://chroniclingamerica.loc.gov.

"Navajo Picturesque." *Mangum Daily Star*. Mangum, Oklahoma. Nov. 16, 1932.

"Navajoe Established." *The Mangum Daily Star*. Mangum, Oklahoma. October 13, 1937.

"Needle Guns." *The Galveston Daily News*. Galveston, Texas, June 12, 1874.

Neville, A. W. "Bunch and Dalton See 'Jesse James'." *The Paris News*. Paris, Texas. March 25, 1948.

Neville, Maude. "Mailed Fist Shuts in East Texas Wells." *San Angelo Evening Standard*. San Angelo, Texas. August 31, 1931.

"New Officers Elected For Commandery." *The Altus Times*. December 19, 1912.

No title – Marriage of Mr. R. Earl Highley to Miss Helen Thirlwell. *The Humboldt Union*, Humboldt, Kansas. September 6, 1923.

"Obituary for Arlo Norman (1918-1998)." *Fort Worth Star Telegram*. Fort Worth, Texas. Dec. 22, 1998.

"Oklahoma Ex-Outlaw Identifies Texan As Jesse James." *The Ottawa Journal*. Ottawa, Ontario, Canada. July 5, 1948.

"Old Frontier Gun-Fighter Dies in New Mexico Home." *The Capital Journal*. Salem, Oregon. August 28, 1945.

"Old Memoirs Say Jesse James Paid NM a Visit." *El Paso Times*. El Paso, Texas, August 16, 1992.

"Oldster Loses Attempt To Claim Name of Notorious Desperado." *Tyler Morning Telegraph*. Tyler, Texas. March 11, 1950.

"Orvus Howks, Miss Redd are Wed Saturday." *Jacksonville, Journal Courier*. Jacksonville, Illinois, May 01, 1932.

Owen, Penny. "Search for outlaw turns grave, 2nd casket found at burial site." *The Daily Oklahoman*. Oklahoma City, Oklahoma. May 31, 2000.

Owens, Herb. "Iowan's Problem, Frank James' Kin or Not?" *Des Moines Tribune*. Des Moines, Iowa. March 3, 1964.

"Ozark Jack Berlin Saved Truck Driver Not Jack Glosser." *Lawrence Country News*. Lawrenceville, Illinois. September 27, 1934.

"Panhandle Hero Buried." *The Brownsville Herald*. Brownsville, Texas. June 27, 1929.

"Personal Appearance Slated For Saturday On Courthouse Lawn; Invitation Given Public." *Lawton Constitution*. Lawton, Oklahoma. May 20, 1948.

"'Phooey' Says Nephew of Famed Bandit." *Springfield Leader and Press*. Springfield, Missouri. May 20, 1948.

Pike, Albert. "Elias Rector." *Daily Arkansas Gazette*, December 4, 1878.

Pike, Albert. "Narrative of a Journey in the Prairie Series." *Arkansas Advocate*. Little Rock, Arkansas, 1835.

Plant, Geoffrey. "Plaza construction closures to extend into 2025." *Taos News*, June 22, 2023.

"Pythians Elect St. Louis Officer." *St. Louis Globe-Democrat*. St. Louis, Missouri. August 17, 1904.

"Quantrill Raider, 5-War Vet Due for Confederate Pension." *The San Angelo Weekly Standard*. San Angelo, Texas. October 24, 1947.

"Quantrill Raiders Recognized by Texas as a Confederate Unit." *Kansas City Star*. Kansas City, Missouri.

Quigg, H.D. "Latest, 'Real' Jesse James Declares $2 million in Loot Cached Away in Mountains of Oklahoma." *The Austin Statesman*, Austin, Texas, January 10, 1950.

Quinn, Harry. "96-Year-Old Frank Dalton Recalls Moving Missouri Capital to Marshall." *The Marshall News Messenger*. Marshall, Texas. August 13, 1944.

"Radio Programs." *We the People* program itinerary. *Daily News*. New York, New York. January 12 & 13, 1950.

Ranger. "Captured. The Celebrated Jesse W. James Taken at Last." *St. Louis Dispatch*, June 9, 1874.

"Rangers Ride At Well Fire." *The Amarillo Globe Times*. Amarillo, Texas. May 1, 1931.

Redstone, Col. A. E. "Spies Within." The Journal and Gazette. Date Unknown

Rev. Dr. Flack to Dr. M. Munford, *The Kansas City Times*. Kansas City, Missouri. April 12, 1882.

Ricks, Thad. "'Jesse James' Twist To Dalton's Stories Greeted by Smiles Here." *The Kilgore News Herald*. Kilgore, Texas. May 23, 1948.

Robert C. Ruark, "Jesse James, Alive or Dead." *Buffalo Courier Express*. Buffalo, New York. July 8, 1949.

Robertson, Mack. "Ex-Member of Dalton Gang Talks of Wide Experiences Here." *The Kilgore Daily News*, Kilgore, Texas, October 13, 1939.

Ross, Tamie. "Jesse James Remains Mysterious." *The Daily Oklahoman*, Oklahoma City, Oklahoma. September 6, 1995.

"Sam Rash Died Sunday At His Home Here." *The Hood County Tablet*. Granbury, Texas. January 7, 1943.

Scott, James H. "Odessan Looks Over New Jesse James Is Convinced He's the Real McCoy." *The Odessa American*. Odessa, Texas. June 9, 1948.

"Secret Societies. Knights of Pythias." *The St. Louis Republic*. St. Louis, Missouri. August 6, 1900.

"Services Are Held For Former Slave." *Lubbock Avalanche-Journal*. Lubbock, Texas. January 22, 1956.

"Services Monday for shooting victim," *St. Joseph News Press*. St. Joseph, Missouri. November 11, 1979.

"Shall Not Stay Here." *Brownlow's Knoxville Whig*. Knoxville, Tennessee, January 9, 1864.

Sheriff "Lee" Boon McMurtry. *Fort Worth Star Telegram*. Fort Worth, Texas. July 5, 1908.

"Sheriff Timberlake Dead." *The Kansas City Times*, Kansas City, Missouri. February 21, 1891.

Smith, George. "Former Navy Secretary Anderson dies at 79," *Fort Worth Star Telegram*. Fort Worth, Texas. August 16, 1989.

Steimel, Martha. "Frank and Jesse James are Uncle to Wichitan." *Wichita Falls Times*. Wichita Falls, Texas. July 20, 1969.

"T.T. Crittenden, Ex-Governor of Missouri, Dies." *St. Louis Post-Dispatch*. St. Louis, Missouri. May 29, 1909.

"Temple to Be Opened Southern Oklahoma Citizens Cordially Invited to Attend." *The Daily Ardmoreite*. Ardmore, Oklahoma. October 19, 1930.

Terry, Dickson. "Still Insists He's Jesse." The Everyday Magazine, *St. Louis Post Dispatch*. St. Louis, Missouri. November 27, 1949."

"Texas Horseback Wedding of the Long Ago. The Principals Were Cole Younger and Belle Starr, According to Mike Harrington of Fort Smith." *St. Louis Globe-Democrat*, March 15, 1903.

"Texas Ku Klux Member Speaks." *Dallas Newspaper*. Dallas, Texas. 1944.

"Texas News via Kansas." *The Galveston Daily News*. Galveston, Texas, October 23, 1869.

The Coffeyville Weekly Journal, Coffeyville, Kansas, July 18, 1890.

"The Cole Younger-Frank James Wild West Shows." *The Stroud Star*. Stroud, Oklahoma. September 18, 1903.

"The Custer Fight." *The Bismarck Tribune*. Bismarck, North Dakota, June 11, 1877.

"The Dalton Gang. They Hold Up the Santa Fe Train in Oklahoma Territory." *Austin Weekly Statesman*. Austin, Texas. June 9, 1892.

"The Golden Circle and the Pacific Republic." *Daily National Democrat*. Marysville, California, February 13, 1861.

"The Killing of Daniel Askew of Clay County," *Daily State Journal*. Jefferson City, Missouri, April 17, 1875.

"The Knights of the Golden Circle." *The Randolph Citizen*. Huntsville, Missouri, April 20, 1860.

"The Last Chapter Written For a Fighting Frontiersman," *The Kansas City Star*. Kansas City, Missouri, July 10, 1929.

"The Late Express Robbery, Bacon Montgomery's Account of It, Together with His Views, Based on a Variety of Evidence." *Columbus Courier*, Columbus, Kansas. September 7, 1876.

"The Quiet, But Mysterious Boarder Was Jesse James." *St. Louis Post-Dispatch*. St. Louis, Missouri. June 30, 1902.

"The Story Behind The James Story – News Vigil Is Long." *The Lawton Constitution*. Lawton, Oklahoma. May 19, 1948.

The story of Sam Green killing Sheriff Bullard. *Woodward Bulletin*. Woodward, Oklahoma. July 4, 1902.

"The Younger Brothers." *The Bismarck Tribune*, Bismarck, North Dakota, April 28, 1893.

"Theodore Earle Studley." *New York Tribune*. New York, New York. May 1, 1908.

"Thousands of Heirs Interested In Rich Conroe Field Acreage." *Amarillo Daily News*. Amarillo, Texas. February 18, 1941.

"To Be Avoided. Detectives and Desperadoes. The James Boys and Pinkerton's Detectives – Both Factions Are Daring, Desperate And Lawless." *The Indiana State Sentinel*. Indianapolis, Indiana, May 13, 1875.

"Tom Hickman Dies at 75." *The Marshall News Messenger*. Marshall, Texas. January 29, 1962.

"Tommy Jake Chrestman." *El Paso Times*. El Paso, Texas, May 13,1986.

"Tribute of Respect." *The Altus Plaindealer*. Altus, Oklahoma. April 12, 1901.

Use of Firearms in Bob and Charlie Ford's show. *The Dallas Daily Herald*, March 9, 1884.

Van Blarcom, W. D. "Best Pistol Shot Visits City." *Fort Worth Star-Telegram*. Fort Worth, Texas. February 14, 1930.

"Versatile Vet." *Tyler Morning Telegraph*. Tyler, Texas. January 22, 1948.

"Veteran Ranger and Indian Fighter Dies," J. K. Paulk's obituary. *The Daily Tribune*, March 21, 1932.

"Waco. News of the Day Gathered by a Statesman Reporter." *Austin American-Statesman*. Austin, Texas. April 8 & 10, 1883.

"Waggoner Carr to Be Guest At Dinner of Historical Unit." *Fort Worth Star-Telegram*. Fort Worth, Texas. April 6, 1965.

"Washington Monument Struck by Lightning." *The Dallas Daily Herald*. Dallas, Texas. June 9, 1985.

"Watch the Abolitionists" and "An Abolitionist Badly Whipped." *Squatter Sovereign*. Atchison, Kansas, August 7, 1855.

Watson, Elmo Scott. "He Dined With Jesse James and Billy the Kid!" *Okeene Record*. Okeene, Oklahoma. March 6, 1930.

Weston, Alonzo. "Research team takes paranormal seriously." *St. Joseph News-Press*, October 26, 2003.

"Where Jesse James, Guerrilla Rough Rider Rest Now," *The St. Louis Republic*. St. Louis, Missouri. July 6, 1902.

"Where lies Jesse James? Some say in Granbury, where he died in 1951." *Dallas Times Herald*. Dallas, Texas. Nov. 13, 1983.

Whitten, Lindsey. "Centenarian Tells Tale of Historic Ruse." *The Lawton Constitution*. Lawton, Oklahoma, May 19, 1948.

Whitten, Lindsey. "Kettle Bearing James Gang Names Displayed by Cityans." *The Lawton Constitution*. Lawton, Oklahoma. February 29, 1948.

Whitten, Lindsey. "Lawton Trio Believe End of Trail is Near In 16-Year Search for Fabulous Treasure in Expansive Wichitas." *The Lawton Constitution Newspaper*. Lawton, Oklahoma. February 29, 1948.

"Who Can Tell?" *Galena Miner*, Galena, Kansas, November 9, 1879.

"Who Carved This Brick?" *St. Joseph News-Press*. St. Joseph, Missouri. July 12, 1967.

"Wichita Falls. Attacked and Shot at by Enemies Lying in Wait – A Close Call with Winchesters." *Fort Worth Daily Gazette*. April 06,1884.

"Wild West Show At World's Fair." *The St. Louis Republic*. St. Louis, Missouri. November 12, 1904.

Wilson, Steve. "Four Decades of Searching Yields Clues, Little Treasure." *Wichita Falls Times*, Wichita Falls, Texas, July 28, 1963.

Wilson, Steve. "Two Maps May Hold Key To "Spider Rock" Gold." *Wichita Falls Times*, Wichita Falls, Texas, October 13, 1963.

Wilson's Ways," *The Santa Fe New Mexican*, Santa Fe, New Mexico. Feb. 18, 1882.

"With His Boots On. Jesse James the Notorious Missouri Outlaw Meets His Fate." *Kansas City Journal*. Kansas City, Missouri. Nov. 4, 1879.

"Woman Bandit Dies." *The Ponca City Daily Courier*, Ponca City, Oklahoma, September 16, 1908.

"Woman Claimed to Be Jesse James' daughter." *Herald and Review*. Decatur, Illinois. Nov. 2, 1975.

"Younger Here." *Richmond Missourian*. Richmond, Missouri. June 11, 1908.

"Younger's Bend," *Tulsa Weekly Democrat*, July 26, 1901.

Magazine Articles:

Author Unknown. "The Battle of Adobe Walls." *J. Marvin Hunter's Frontier Times Magazine*, April 1947.

Dalton, Frank. "The Aftermath." *True Magazine*, 1937/38, after the recovery of the Great Depression for The Kilgore News Herald, October 15, 1939.

McGrath, George. "Affidavit of John William Pierce, of Orrick, Missouri." *The National Police Gazette*, January 1952.

McGrath, George. "Interview with Jesse James just before his death." *The National Police Gazette*, January 1952.

McGrath, George. *The National Police Gazette*. August 1950.

Popper, Joe. "The Man Who Would Be Jesse." *Star Magazine within The Kansas City Star*. January 10, 1988.

The XIT Brand. X.I.T. Rodeo & Reunion Booklet. The Dalhart Publishing Co. August 1940. (author's personal collection).

Wood, Larry. "Western Lore." *Wild West Magazine*, June 2005.

Periodicals:

Donoghue, David. "Explorations of Albert Pike in Texas." *The Southwestern Historical Quarterly; Vol. 39, No. 2*, pp. 135-138. Texas State Historical Association. October 1935.

Hicks, Jimmy. "Some Letters Concerning the Knights of the Golden Circle in Texas 1860, 1861." *Southwestern Historical Quarterly*, No. 12. July 1961.

Trask, David S. "Episcopal Missionaries on the Santee and Yankton Reservations; Cross-Cultural Collaboration and President Grant's Peace Policy." *Great Plains Quarterly, Vol. 33, No. 2*. Spring 2013.

Victor, Frances Fuller. "The American Fur Trade in the Far West." *The Quarterly of the Oregon Historical Society 3, no. 3 (1902): 261.*

Websites: (Note – Some websites are no longer available at the time of the publishing of the book, but were active during the time of research from 2017-2024)

"(1776) The Deleted Passage Of The Declaration of Independence." *BLACKPAST*. 2009. Accessed 2022. https://www.blackpast.org/african-american-history/declaration-independence-and-debate-over-slavery/.

"1861 Confederate Half Dollar," https://coinsite.com/1861-confederate-half-dollar/.

"1861 Original Confederate Half Dollar PR40, Only Official Coin of the Confederacy."

"6th Texas Infantry Regiment." Accessed 2020. https://en.wikipedia.org.

Adams, John Quincy. Accessed 2022. https://secure.understandingprejudice.org/slavery/presinfo.php?president=6.

Alexander, Kathy, "Charles Jennison – Anti-Slavery Jayhawker," *Legends of Kansas*, Accessed 2023. https://legendsofkansas.com/charles-jennison/.

Alexander, Kathy. "Belle Starr – The Bandit Queen." *Legends of America*, 2022. https://www.legendsofamerica.com/we-bellestarr/.

Alexander, Kathy. "Benjamin Horrell – Texas Gunfighter." *Legends of America*, 2023. https://www.legendsofamerica.com/benjamin-horrell/.

Alexander, Kathy. "Fort Sidney." *Legends of America*, 2023. https://www.legendsofamerica.com/fort-sidney/.

Alexander, Kathy. "Old West Outlaw List" – "Sam Green." *Legends of America*, Accessed 2023. https://www.legendsofamerica.com/outlaw-list-g/.

Alexander, Kathy. "Pigeon's Ranch, New Mexico." *Legends of America*. Accessed 2023. https://www.legendsofamerica.com/piegeons-ranch/.

Alexander, Kathy. "The Lost Padre Mine, New Mexico." *Legends of America*. Accessed 2023. www.legendsofamerica.com/lost-padre-mine/

Alexander, Kathy. "Turley's Mill at Arroyo Hondo, New Mexico." *Legends of America*. 2023. Accessed 2022. www.legendsofamerica.com/turley-mill-new-mexico/.

Alonso, Alex. "John F. Kennedy's Visits to Victorio Peak Prior to His Death Still Resonate Today in New Mexico History." *Cision PRWeb*, Soledad Publishing Company, LLC. 2013. Accessed 2023. https://www.prweb.com/releases/john-f-kennedy/victorio-peak/prweb11361479.htm.

Anderson, H. Allen. "Arrington, George Washington." *Handbook of Texas Online.* Texas State Historical Association. Accessed 2023. https://www.tshaonline.org/handbook/entries/arrington-george-washington.

Anderson, H. Allen. "Big Die-Up," *Handbook of Texas Online.* Accessed 2024. https://www.tshaonline.org/handbook/entries/big-die-up.

Anderson, H. Allen. "Borger History" Borger, Texas, Accessed 2023. https://www.borgertx.gov/263/Borger-History.

Anderson, H. Allen. "XIT Ranch." *Handbook of Texas Online.* 1976. Updated 2020. Accessed 2024. https://www.tshaonline.org/handbook/entries/xit-ranch.

Anonymous, "Adobe Walls, Second Battle of," *Handbook of Texas Online. TSHA, Texas State Historical Association.* Published 1976 and updated 2020. Accessed 2023. https://www.tshaonline.org/handbook/entries/adobe-walls-second-battle-of.

Artists, Elmer Stewart and Anna Lee (Dillenbeck) Stacey, Collection of charcoal portraits taken from photographs. *The Kansas City Public Library.* Accessed 2023. https://kchistory.org.

Assmann, Cody. "All You Need to Know About the Goodnight-Loving Trail." *Frontier Life.* https://www.frontierlife.net.

Bamburg, Maxine. "Ardmore." *The Encyclopedia of Oklahoma History and Culture.* 2010. Accessed 2023. https://www.okhistory.org/publications/enc/entry?entry=AR008.

"Banks history, text, Ardmore Banking." Date Unknown. *The Gateway to Oklahoma History,* Crediting Ardmore Public Library. Accessed 2023. https://gateway.okhistory.org/ark:/67531/metadc1626268/.

Barr, Alwyn. "Fifteenth Texas Infantry." *Handbook of Texas Online.* Accessed 2023. https://www.tshaonline.org/handbook/entries/fifteenth-texas-infantry.

Baumier, Ellen. "Meriwether Lewis and a Forensic Mystery." Montana Moments. Montana Historical Society. 2013. Accessed 2022. https://ellenbaumler.blogspot.com/2013/10/Meriwether-lewis-and-forensic-mystery.html.

"Behind the Symbol: Historic Badges of the Texas Rangers." Accessed 2023. https://www.texasranger.org.

Bennion, Marilyn, and Joanne Linford, and Elna Nelson, daughters of Wayne and Elna. "Joseph Spaulding Works." Accessed 2024. www.familysearch.org.

Bible scriptures. https://www.biblegateway.com

Bizzack, Ph.D., John W. "How & Why Freemasonry Came to Kentucky: The Backstory." Reviewed by Michael Bronner, William O. Ware Lodge of Research. *William O. Ware Lodge of Research Book Review – July 2020.* Accessed 2022. https://williamowarelodgeofresearch.com/wp-content/uploads/2020/07/Bizzack-Review-How-and-Why-Freemasonry-Came-to-KY-July-2020-Book-Review.pdf

"Boer Wars." *New World Encyclopedia.* Accessed 2023. https://www.newworldencyclopedia.org/entry/Boer_Wars.

Book of Moses, Chapter 7: 45-47, (December 1830). *The Church of Jesus Christ of Latter-Day Saints,* 2022. https://www.churchofjesuschrist.org/study/scriptures/pgp/moses/7?lang=eng.

Bowden, Blake. "The Legend of Enoch." 2010. Accessed 2022. https://www.myfreemasonry.com/threads/the-legend-of-enoch.103984/#post-37912.

Brewer, Bob. Discussion on George Mitchell's book, "The Spider's Web." Accessed 2022. www.thehootowltree.com. (website is no longer active).

Britannica, T. Editors of Encyclopaedia. "Torreón." *Encyclopedia Britannica*, Accessed 2024. https://www.britannica.com/place/Torreon.

Brooks, Rebecca Beatrice. "The Funeral of Jesse James." Accessed 2020. https://civilwarsaga.com.

Brown, Kenny L. "Oklahoma Territory," *Encyclopedia of Oklahoma History and Culture*. 2010. Accessed 2023. https://www.okhistory.org/publications/enc/entry?entry=OK085.

Brown, Kenny L. "Oklahoma Territory." *The Encyclopedia of Oklahoma History and Culture*. 2010. Accessed 2023. https://www.okhistory.org/publications/enc/entry?entry=OK085.

Bryant, Jr., Keith L. "Atchison, Topeka and Santa Fe Railway System." Handbook of Texas Online. 1952. Accessed 2023. https://www.tshaonline.org/handbook/entries/atchison-topeka-and-santa-fe-railway-system.

Butler, Alan. "Washington DC's Chamber of Secrets." From the research of Christopher Knight and Alan Butler. Accessed 2022. www.washingtondcschamberofsecrets.com/absolute-proof.html.

Bushman, Richard Lyman. "Joseph Smith and Money Digging," Accessed 2022. https://rsc.byu.edu/sites/default/files/pub_content/pdf/Joseph_Smith_and_Money_Digging.pdf.

"Camp Colorado, Texas." *Texas Escapes*. Accessed 2023. www.texasescapes.com.

Carr, William R. "Col. Edmund D. Taylor and Conspiracy Theory" – "Lincoln/Taylor/Kennedy" – "The Greenback—Truth, Speculation, and Trivia," – "Money, Money, Money –Serious Business!" 2001. Accessed 2022. https://www.heritech.com/pridger/lincoln/lin-ken.htm

Cerise, Lucien. "A History of White Supremacism, Part 1: Freemasonry and the Confederacy." 2019. Accessed 2022. https://transnotitia.com/freemasonry-and-the-confederacy/.

"Chicago, Rock Island and Pacific Railway." *Encyclopedia of Arkansas*. Accessed 2024. https://encyclopediaofarkansas.net.

"Chickasaw Orpah Home and Manual Labor School." Accessed 2023. https://www.asylumprojects.org/index.php/Chickasaw_Orphan_Home_and_Manual_Labor_School.

"Cimarron." *Dictionary.com*. accessed 2022. https://www.dictionary.com.

Cole-Jett, Robin. "Epperson's Ferry in Bowie County, Texas." 2000-2024. www.redriverhistorian.com.

Cole-Jett, Robin. "Fort Sill, Still Active." September 17, 2023. *Red River Historian*. Accessed 2023. https://www.redriverhistorian.com.

Cole-Jett, Robin. "Trails blazed by Randolph B. Marcy and Black Beaver in the Red River Valley." *Red River Historian*, 2022. https://www.redriverhistorian.com/post/marcy-and-black-beaver-trails-red-river.

"Company Towns: 1880s to 1935." *VCU Libraries, Social Welfare History Project*. Housing, Labor, Programs. Accessed 2024. https://socialwelfare.library.vcu.edu/programs/housing/company-towns-1890s-to-1935/.

"Congress's Coinage Power," *Artl.S8.C5.1, The United States Constitution, Constitution Annotated – Analysis and Interpretation of the U.S. Constitution*. Accessed 2022, https://constitution.congress.gov.

Crabbe, Norman Williams. "The History and Symbolism of the Knights Templar Sword from the 11th to 20th Centuries." Accessed 2024. https://www.md-mrs.com.

Craddock, Van. "Say, Was That Billy the Kid in Gladewater?" August 2015, Accessed 2023. https://sfasu.edu/heritagecenter/9642.

"Cultural Resources CCC History Project – The CCC A Brief History." Accessed 2023. https://npshistory.com.

Cutrer, Thomas. "Anderson, William (Bloody Bill) T. (ca. 1839-1864)." *Handbook of Texas Online, TSHA, The Texas State Historical Association.* 1952, updated: 2020. Accessed 2023. https://tshaonline.org/handbook/entries/anderson-william-t.

Dalton, Rodney G. "An Interview Given by Ben Dalton at Coffeyville After the Raid." *Special Correspondence of the Globe Democrat.* Accessed 2023. https://www.daltondatabank.org.

"Daniel Baker College Brownwood, Texas 1888-1953." Accessed 2023. https://www.lostcolleges.com/daniel-baker-college.

Darcy, R. "The Oklahoma Territorial Legislature: 1890-1905." *Oklahoma State University.* Accessed 2023. https://docslib.org/doc/3939504/the-oklahoma-territorial-legislature-1890-1905.

"Declaration of Independence: A Transcription." *America's Founding Documents. National Archives.* https://www.archives.gov/founding-docs/declaration-transcript.

"Doaksville." *Oklahoma Historical Society.* Accessed 2023. www.okhistory.org/sites/ftdoaksville

"Dona Ana County, New Mexico Mines." Accessed 2023. (https://westernmininghistory.com/new-mexico/dona-ana/

Dude Ranchers Association. "Dude Ranchers Association Records, 1926-1971." *Archives and Special Collections, Maureen and Mike Mansfield Library, The University of Montana-Missoula.* Accessed 2024. https://archiveswest.orbiscascade.org.

"El Dorado." https://www.merriam-webster.com.

"Elfego Baca." https://www.newmexicomagazine.org.

"Elias Rector (1802-1878)." *Encyclopedia of Arkansas.* Accessed 2023. https://encylopediaofarkansas.net.

"Erin Springs." https://okgenweb.net/~okgarvin/towns/erinspringstown.html.

Etcheson, Nicole. "James Lane's Revenge." *The New York Times Archives, Opinionator.* October 26, 2011. Accessed 2023. https://archive.nytimes.com/opinionator.blogs.nytimes.com.

Everett, Dianna. "Indian Meridian (and Indian Base Line)." *The Encyclopedia of Oklahoma History and Culture.* 2010. Accessed 2023. https://www.okhistory.org/publications/enc/entry?entry=IN012.

"Exceptionally Rare Indian Used Custer Battlefield 1874 Sharps Rifle." January 20, 2017. *Old West Events.* Accessed 2023. https://www.oldwestevents.com/highlights/tag/Little+Bighorn.

"Executive Order – 11110 President John F Kennedy and The Federal Reserve." Accessed 2022. https://www.scribd.com/document/212260271/Executive-Order-11110-President-John-F-Kenndy-And-The-Federal-Reserve.

Federer, Bill. "The Bank War: Jackson v. Biddle." *American Minute.* Accessed 2022. https://myemail.constantcontact.com/THE-BANK-WAR---Jackson-v-Biddle.html.

Federer, Bill. "The Bank War: Jackson v. Biddle." *American Minute,* Accessed 2022. https://myemail.constantcontact.com/THE-BANK-WAR---Jackson-v-Biddle.html.

Federer, Bill. "The Bank War-Great Evils To Our Country....from such a concentration of power in the hands of a few men" – Pres. Andrew Jackson. n.d. https://myemail.constantcontact.com/The-bank-war--great-evils-to-our-country---from-such-a-concentration-of-power-in-the-hands-of-a-few-men/.

Feldberg, Michael. "Judah Benjamin (1811-1884)." Accessed 2022. https://www.jewishvirtuallibrary.org/judah-benjamin.

"Fort Abercrombie State Historic Site – History." *State Historical Society of North Dakota*, Accessed 2024. https://www.history.nd.gov/historicsites/abercrombie/abercrombiehistory.html.
"Fort Sidney, Nebraska." Accessed 2023. https://history.nebraska.gov.

"Fort Sill." *Cowley County Historical Society Museum*, Winfield, Cowley County, Kansas. 2023. www.cchsm.com/resources/misc/wortman_cc/fort_sill.html.

"Francis Marion (Tuck) Hill." *Collin County, Texas History*. Accessed 2023. https:www.collincountyhistory.com/hill-francis.html.

Garfield, James A. "James A. Garfield Quotes." AZQuotes.com, Wind and Fly LTD, Accessed 2022. https://www.azquotes.com/author/5343-James_A_Garfield.

Gates, Josh. "Josh Gates Goes Hunting For Jesse James' Buried Treasure." *Expedition Unknown*. Rush NZ, 2022. Accessed 2023. https://www.youtube.com

"General Orders, 2 May 1778." *Founders Online*, National Archives. https://founders.archives.gov/documents/Washington/03-15-02-0016. [Original source: *The Papers of George Washington, Revolutionary War Series*, vo. 15, *May-June 1778*, ed. Edward G. Lengel. Charlottesville: University of Virginia Press, 2006, p. 13.]

"General Orders, 5 May 1778," *Founders Online*, National Archives, https://founders.archives.gov/documents/Washington/03-15-02-0039. [Original source: *The Papers of George Washington, Revolutionary War Series*, vo. 15, *May-June 1778*, ed. Edward G. Lengel. Charlottesville: University of Virginia Press, 2006, pp. 38-41.]

"George W. Arrington." *Texas Ranger Dispatch Magazine*. 2017. Accessed 2020. https://www.ppolinks.com/texasranger/BIO-George-W-Arrington.pdf

"George Washington "Cap" Arrington." *Panhandle Masonic Cowboy Hall of Fame Association*. Accessed 2023. https://panhandlemasoniccowboyhalloffameassociation.com.

"Gold." Accessed 2022. https://www.symbols.com/symbol/gold.

"Gourgas Family Papers, circa 1834-2000;" Vault A45, Gourgas Unit 1. Accessed 2022. https://concordlibrary.org/special-collections

Grady Gay, Beatrice. "Camp Colorado." *TSHA, Texas State Historical Association*, Published 1952, updated 2019. Accessed 2023. https://www.tshaonline.org/handbook/entries/camp-colorado.

"Grand Commander Albert Pike, 33°." *Scottish Rite History*. Accessed 2023. https://www.srkc.org/history/famous/pike/.

Grant, Ulysses S. "U.S. Grant, Memoir on the Mexican War" (1885). *America – A Narrative Story*. W.W.Norton and Company: Studyspace. Accessed 2022. https://www.wwnorton.com.

Gray, Warren. "Guns and Bravery: Is this What Really Happened at the Little Bighorn?" 2019. Accessed 2023. https://gunpowdermagazine.com.

Greene, Michelle. "Go Wide: How Far Can Horses Jump Horizontally?" *Horse Rookie*, Accessed 2023. https://horserookie.com/how-far-horses-jump-horizontally/.

Hall, Manly P. *The initiates of the flame*, p. 59-60. (Los Angeles, Calif., 1922). The Library of Congress. Internet Archive. Accessed 2022. https://archive.org/details/initiatesofflame00hall/mode/2up.

Hall, Manly P. *Lost Keys of Masonry, The Legend of Hiram Abiff*, p. 76. (Hall Publishing Company, 1923), Internet Archive, Accessed 2022. https://archive.org/details/The.Lost.Keys.Of.Masonry.Manly.P.Hall.1923/mode/2up.

Hall, Sharon. "Ghost Town Wednesday: Navajoe, Oklahoma." 2014. Accessed 2024. https://digging-history.com.

Harper Jr., Cecil. "Epperson Ferry." *Handbook of Texas Online*, accessed May 29, 2020. https://www.tshalonline.org/handbook/entries/eppersons-ferry.

Hart, Brian. "Osceola, TX." *Handbook of Texas Online*. 1952. Updated 1995. Accessed 2023. https://www.tshalonline.org/handbook/entries/osceola-tx.

Hedglen, Thomas L. "Meridian." *The Encyclopedia of Oklahoma History and Culture*, 2010. Accessed 2023. https://www.okhistory.org/publications/enc/entry?entry=ME015.

Hendrickson, Jr., Kenneth E. "Brazos River." *Handbook of Texas Online. Published by the Texas State Historical Association.* 2019. Accessed 2022. https://www.tshaonline.org/handbook/entries/brazos-river.

"Henry County History," www.henrycountytn.org.

Heritage Auctions. Accessed 2022. https://coins.ha.com.

Hicks, Hillarie M. "I Never Was a Mason:" James Madison and Freemasonry." *Montpelier's Digital Doorway*.2019. Accessed 2022. https://digitaldoorway.montpelier.org/2019/03/05/james-madison-and-freemasonry/.

Hilton, Mark. "Daube's Store," www.hmdb.org/m.asp?m=142482.

"History of HPU Presidents," *Howard Payne University*, 2024. https://www.hputx.edu/our-story/history/history-of-hpu-presidents/.

"History of Lexington Lodge No. 1," Accessed 2023. https://lexingtonlodge1.org/lexington-lodge-1/.

"History of Newton County – Fugitive Faces." *Newton County, Arkansas Chamber of Commerce.* Accessed 2023. https://www.newtoncountychamber.com/history.

History.com Editors. "Gunfighter Clay Allison killed." *History.* 2009. Accessed 2023. https://www.history.com/this-day-in-history/gunfighter-clay-allison-killed.

http://Santeesiouxnation.net

https://en.wikipedia.org.

https://freemasonrywatch.org/the.masonic.roots.of.joseph.smith.and.mormonism/html

https://knightofthegoldencircle.wordpress.com

https://knights-of-the-golden-circle.blogspot.com.

https://libquotes.com

https://nmahgp.genealogyvillage.com/Grace%20Censuses/mo1870countymain.html

https://sites.rootsweb.com/-okcaddo/caddates.htm

https://thefederalistpapers.org

https://www.slideshare.net/uniquelee/checkerboard-floors-and-masonic-symbolism-in-movies-and-music

"Investigations: Still Digging." *Time*. 1962. Accessed 2022. https://time.com/archive/6871446/investigations-still-digging/.

Jackson, Andrew. "Andrew Jackson famous quotes." *inspiringquotes.us*, Accessed 2022. https://www.inspiringquotes.us/author/2318-andrew-jackson.

Jackson, Andrew. "Andrew Jackson Quotes," *AZQuotes.com*, Wind and Fly LTD, 2024. https://www.azquotes.com/author/19724-Andrew_Jackson.

Jackson, Andrew. "Andrew Jackson's Farewell Adress – 1837," *National Center for Public Policy Research*, 2001. Accessed 2022. https://nationalcenter.org/ncppr/2001/11/03/andrew-jacksons-farewell-address-1837/.

Jackson, Effie S. "An Interview With Red Orrington Lucas, Territorial Deputy United States Marshal, 1882-1902," Dec. 29, 1937. Interview #12571. Oklahoma and Indian Territory, Indian and Pioneer Historical Collection, 1937. *OU University Libraries, Islandora Repository/Indian-Pioneer Papers.* https://repository.ou.edu/islandora.

"Jacob "Big Jake" Yoes." Accessed 2023. https://sites.rootsweb.com.

Jefferson, Thomas. "Extract from Thomas Jefferson's Notes on the State of Virginia," *Th Jefferson-Monticello-Jefferson Quotes & Family Letters*, 2024. https://tjrs.monticello.org/letter/2355.

Jefferson, Thomas. "Thomas Jefferson famous quotes," *inspiringquotes.us*. Accessed 2022. https://www.inspiringquotes.us/author/5016-thomas-jefferson.

Jefferson, Thomas. "Thomas Jefferson Quotes," Accessed 2022. https://thefederalistpapers.org.

Jefferson, Thomas. Thomas Jefferson to Albert Gallatin, December 13, 1803. *Founders Online*. https://founders.archives.gov/documents/Jefferson/01-42-02-0100.

"Jefferson's Religious Beliefs." *Th. Jefferson Monticello*, Accessed 2022, https://monticello.org.

"Jesse & Frank James." *Paso Robles History Museum*. Accessed 2024. http://www.pasorobleshistorymuseum.org/jess.

"Jewish Pioneers of Ardmore, Ada, and Lehigh in South Central, Oklahoma," Ardmore – Accessed 2023. https://www.jmaw.org/jewish-oklahoma/.

"Joe Wood." www.photojournalismhalloffame.org/joe-wood.

"John Thomas Tatum Sr." *Fisher Funeral Home*. Accessed 2023. https: www.fisherfh.net.

"Joseph Smith copied Freemasonry." *LDS Facts*. https://ldsfacts.org/joseph-smith/joseph-smith-copied-freemasonry/.

"Joseph Wood (1914-1996)." Accessed 2023. https://files.shsmo.org/manuscripts/saint-louis/S0819.pdf.

Kabatebate, Stewart. "Alice Bailey 10 Point Plan to Destroy Christianity." *Inspired Walk*. https://www.inspiredwalk.com/6297/alice-baileys-10-point-plan-to-destroy-christianity.

Kleiner, Diana J. "Red River." *Handbook of Texas Online*, Accessed 2023. https://www.tshaonline.org/handbook/entries/red-river.

Kuzmarov, Jeremy. "Did Richard Nixon Secretly Steal 36.5 Tons of Gold Bullion from U.S. Army Base While He Was Telling America, "I Am Not A Crook?" November 3, 2022. Accessed 2023. https://www.covertactionmagazine.com.

Leon C. Metz. "Garrett, Patrick Floyd Jarvis (1850-1908)." 1952, updated 2019. *Handbook of Texas Online*. Texas State Historical Association. Accessed 2023. https://www.tshaonline.org/handbook/entries/garrett-patrick-floyd-jarvis.

"Lewis & Clark Expedition," *National Archives.* Accessed 2022, https://www.archives.gov/education/lessons/lewis-clark.

"Lieutenant Colonel George A. Custer (1839-1876)." Washita Battlefield-National Historic Site Oklahoma. *National Park Service.* Accessed 2023. https://www. nps.gov.

Lincoln, Abraham. "Abraham Lincoln Quotes," *AZQuotes.com*, Wind and Fly LTD. Accessed 2022. https://www.azquotes.com/author/8880-Abraham_Lincoln.

"Loans & Bonds – Brief History of World War Two Advertising Campaigns War Loans and Bonds." *Duke University Libraries.* Accessed 2023. https://blogs.library.duke.edu/digital-collections/adaccess/guide/wwii/bonds-loans/.

Lomax, John Nova. "When Belle Starr Married Outlaw Jim Reed, Her Legend as 'the Female Jesse James' Began," *Texas Highways.* 2021. Accessed 2023. https://texashighways.com.

Longley, Jay and Colin Eby. "Knights of the Golden Circle." 2022. https://knightsofthegoldencircle.webs.com. (No longer active as of 2024).

"Lost Dutchman Gold & Glenn Magill." *The Arizona Report.* Accessed 2023. https://arizonareport.com/lost-dutchman-gold-mine-glenn-magill/.

"Lucien Maxwell/The Maxwell Land Grant." *New Mexico Nomad.* Accessed 2023. https://newmexiconomad.com

"Lucifer vs. Satan, What's the Difference?" Accessed 2023. https://thisvsthat.io/lucifer-vs-satan.

Magill, Worshipful Brother Brian H. "Freemasonry In Tennessee: The First 100 Years." Accessed 2022. https://www.irish-freemasonry.org.uk/TENNESSEE.htm

"Major Elias Rector." http://wc.rootsweb.ancestry.com/cgi-bin/igm.cgi?op=GET&db=kingharry&id=I17801.

Manly P. Hall. *Lectures On Ancient Philosophy*, p 433. (Jeremy P. Tarcher/Penguin, a member of Penguin Group (USA) inc., 1929. Internet Archive. Accessed 2022. https://archive.org/details/ManlyP.HallLecturesOnAncientPhilosophy.

Manoah Richard Cheatham, "Early Coleman County, Texas Settler and Texas Ranger." Accessed 2023. https://www.txgenwebcounties.org/coleman/colemancounty/family-history/cheatham,m-r.html.

Mapp, Trooper John. "The Civil War Continues. The Buffalo Soldiers and Texas Rangers." *The New Buffalo Soldiers, Your History; Number 5: Texas Rangers.* Accessed 2023, https://abuffalosoldier.com/yh5rangers.htm#footnote5.

"Masonic Temple." Accessed 2023. https://christian-restoration.com/fmasonry/temple.htm

"Mayors of Wichita Falls." Accessed 2024, https://www.wichitafallstx.gov/DocumentCenter/View/19744/Mayors-of-Wichita-Falls-1889-2023.

McAtee, W. Peter. "Masonry in New Mexico," https://www.knightstemplar.org.

McCarthy, Senator Joseph (Excerpt from a 1956 speech, "George Washington's Surrender"), *Judaized Christianity: Front for New World Order – Sen. McCarth*, by Yvonne Nachtigal, 2018. https://christianobserver.net/judaized-christianity-front-for-new-world-order-sen-mccarth/.

"McClain County, Oklahoma History." *Oklahoma Genealogy Trails.* Accessed 2023. https://genealogytrails.com/oka/mcclain/towns.html.

McCormick, Mrs. E.D. "Early History of Dresden." *The Navarro County Scroll*, 1956. 2023. https://txnavarr.genealogyvillage.com/towns/dresden/early_history_of_dresden.htm.

McNamara, Robert. "Zebulon Pike's Mysterious Western Expeditions." *Thought Co.* 2019. Accessed 2022. https://www.thoughtco.com/zebulon-pike-led-two-expeditions-1773817.

Member of the Order. "An Authentic Exposition of the "K.G.C." "Knights of the Golden Circle;"or A History of Secession From 1834 to 1861;" 1861. Publisher C.O. Perrine. *Internet Archive.* https://archive.org.

"Meramec Caverns." Accessed 2023. https://www.americascave.com.

"Meridian." Accessed 2022. https://www.merriam-webster.com.

Millet, Robert L. "What Latter-day Saints Believe About Jesus Christ," 2001. Accessed 2022. https://newsroom.churchofjesuschrist.org/article/what-mormons-believe-about-jesus-christ.

Morton, Ella. "Gold, God, and Geometry: Inside the Lavish Grand Lodges of the Freemasons." 2014. Accessed 2022. https://slate.com/human-interest/2014/01/inside-the-lavish-grand-lodge-of-the-freemasons.html

Mullen, Paul. "Who Was Josiah S. Doak's Brother?" September 27, 2005. *Genealogy.com.* Accessed 2023. https://www.genealogy.com/forum/surnames/topics/doak/953/

Multiple authors and citations. "Capt. William Tucker, of Kiccowtan." Accessed 2024. www.geni.com/people/Capt-William-Tucker-of-Kiccowtan/6000000003853772881.

Multiple authors and citations. "Dr. John Woodson, of Flowerdew Hundred." Accessed 2024. www.geni.com/people/Dr-John-Woodson-of-Flowerdew-Hundred/6000000006788800910.

"National Bank Act of 1863." 2019 Accessed 2022. https://www.encyclopedia.com/history/encyclopedias-almanacs-transcripts-and-maps/national-bank-act-1863.

"New Orleans in the Civil War, A Southern City in Union Grasp." September 7, 2022. *American Battlefield Trust.* Accessed 2023. https://www.battlefields.org.

Newman, Darley. "Steeldusts on the Chisholm Trail." *True West Magazine*, 2011. Accessed 2024. https://truewestmagazine.com/article/steeldusts-on-the-chisholm-trail/.

"Ocate Creek Crossing." *Santa Fe Trail Historic Sites.* www.historic-trails.unm.edu/sites/ocate-creek-crossing-in-mora-county.html.

Okamura, Ryoko. "California Road." *Encyclopedia of Oklahoma History and Culture.* May 04, 2015. www.okhistory.org.

"Oklahoma Masonic History." 2023. https://okmasonichistory.glogspot.com/2022/09/three-grand-lodges-one-state-how.html.

Oliver, Liz. "This Missouri Funeral Home Has A Museum You Have to See To Believe." 2018. Accessed 2024. https://www.onlyinyourstate.com/missouri/mo-funeral-museum-st-joseph/.

Otto von Bismarck, "Otto von Bismarck Quotes," *AZQuotes.com*, Wind and Fly LTD, Accessed 2022. https://www.azquotes.com/quote/615228

Ouzts, Clay. "Georgia Guidestones." *New Georgia Encyclopedia.* Accessed 2022. https://www.georgiaencyclopedia.org/articles/history-archaeology/georgia-guidestones/.

"Parthenon." https://www.merriam-webster.com.

"Pearl of Great Price." Accessed 2022. https://www.churchofjesuschrist.org/study/manual/gospel-topics/pearl-of-great-price?lang=eng.

Pernier, John to Thomas Jefferson, 10 February 1810. *Founders Online – National Archives.* https://founder.archive.gov/documents/Jefferson/03-02-02.0171.

Perry, Suzanne. "Gregg County." *Handbook of Texas Online.* 1952. Accessed 2023. https://tshaonline.org/handbook/entries/gregg-county.

Petersen, Paul R. "Bloody Bill Anderson – Lies and Sensationalism," *The Hughes News,* October 2013. https://hughescamp.org.

Petersen, Paul R. "The True Account of William "Bloody Bill" Anderson." *Legends of America.* Accessed 2022. https://www.legendsofamerica.com/we-bloodybill/.

Phippen, J. Weston. "Kill Every Buffalo You Can! Every Buffalo Dead Is an Indian Gone." *The Atlantic.* 2023. https://www.theatlantic.com/national/archive/2016/05/the-buffalo-killers/482349.

Pickwick, Texas." *Texas Escapes.* Accessed 2023. www.texasescapes.com/TexasTowns/Pickwick-Texas.htm.

Pike, Albert. "Narrative of a Journey in the Prairie." from *Publication of The Arkansas Historical Association*, Edited by John Hugh Reynolds, Secretary, Vol. 4, Conway, Arkansas, 1917. (submitted by Dena Whitesell). 2007. https://genealogytrails.com/ark/historybook3.html.

Pike, Albert. "Taos." *All Poetry.* Accessed 2022. https://allpoetry.com/poem/8588561-Taos-by-Albert-Pike.

Pike, Albert. *Prose Sketches and Poems, Written in the Western Country.* Containing: "Narrative of a Journey in the Prairie" and "Narrative of a Second Journey in the Prairie." (Boston: Light & Horton, 1834). Internet Archive. Accessed 2022. https://archive.org/details/prosesketchespoe00pike/mode/2up?q=Americans.

"Pike's Expedition." Encyclopedia.com." Accessed 2022. https://www.encyclopedia.com/history/encyclopedias-almanacs-transcripts-and-maps/pikes-expedition.

Pilote, Alain. "Chapter 49-The History of Banking Control in the United States." *Sept.-Oct. 1985 issue of the Vers Demain Journal.* Accessed 2022. https://famguardian.org/Publications/InThisAgeOfPlenty/plenty49.htm.

Pinkerton, Gary L. "Trammel's Trace, The First Road to Texas From the North." accessed May 29, 2020. https://trammelstrace.com.

Professional Coin Grading Services, PCGS, a division of Collectors Universe, Inc. https://www.pcgs.com.

Quotes from various notable people. https://www.inspiringquotes.us.

Richie, Jonathan. "The Truth About Thomas Jefferson" – https://wallbuilders.com.

Rodenberger, Lou. "Maltby, William Jeff." *Handbook of Texas Online.* Accessed 2023. https://www.tshaonline.org/handbook.entries/maltby-william-jeff.

Rothschild Brothers to Messrs. Ikleheimer, Morton and Vandergould (New York), June 25, 1863. In *Col. Edmund D. Taylor and Conspiracy Theory, by William R. Carr.* 2011. Accessed 2022. https://www.heritech.com/pridger/lincoln/lin-ken.htm.

Rothschild, Mayer Amschel. "Mayer Amschel Rothschild famous quotes." *inspiringquotes.us.* Accessed 2022. https://www.inspiringquotes.us/author/3057-mayer-amschel-rothschild.

"Sacred Geometry," Accessed 2022. www.ancient-wisdom.com/sacredgeometry.htm.

Samuel Dutton Hinman, 1839-1890." Accessed 2023. https://history.nebraska.gov.

"Scholars Challenge Jefferson-Hemings Allegations." *Science Insights, News and Commentary from The National Association of Scholars,* Volume 6, Issue 3, September 2001. https://www.tjheritage.org/scholars-challenge-jeffersonhemings-allegations/.

"Scottish Rite Northern Jurisdiction Sovereign Grand Commander." Accessed 2022. https://www.geni.com/projects/Scottish-Rite-Northern=Jurisdiction-Sovereign-Grand-Commander/37136.

Seal, Corene and Etta Petree. "Taloga." *The Encyclopedia of Oklahoma History and Culture.* Accessed 2023. www.okhistory.org/publications/enc/entry?entry=TA009.

Serna, Louis. Accessed 2023. https:// www.louisserna.com.

Shirk, George H. "First Post Offices Within the Boundaries of Oklahoma." https://gateway.okhistory.org.

Shive, William. "Coggin Brothers," *Handbook of Texas Online. TSHA, Texas State Historical Association,* 1994. updated 2020. accessed 2023. https://www.tshaonline.org/handbook/entries/coggin-brothers.

Skaggs, Jimmy M. "Western Trail." *Handbook of Texas Online.* 1976. Accessed 2023. https://www.tshaonline.org/handbook/entries/western-trail.

Smith, Wilber. "The Amigo of 'Billy the Kid', "The Man Who Fought Side by Side With Lincoln County's Outlaw Character Tells About the Days of 'Judge Colt's Rule." *New Mexico Magazine*, April 1933, highlighted on the Roswell Daily Record website; Accessed 2023. https://rdnews.com.

Soellner, Alan. "Frisco Shootout "Legend of Elfego Baca." Accessed 2023. https://www.westernleatherholster.com/6666-2/.

Soodalter, Ron. "The 1861 Jayhawker Raid in Osceola" *Missouri Life*. Accessed 2023. https://missourilife.com.

Soodalter, Ron. "The Man Who Did Too Little." *Oklahoma Today Magazine*. 2020-Accessed 2024. https://oklahomatoday.com

"Southern Ute Indian Chronology." Accessed 2022. www.southernute-nsn.gov/history/chronology/.

"St. Louis World's Fair." Accessed 2023. https://www.encyclopedia.com/history/culture-magazines/st-louis-worlds-fair.

Starling, Susanne. "Scyene, TX." *Handbook of Texas Online.* 1952. Updated 2019. Accessed 2023. https://www.tshaonline.org/handbook/entries/scyene-tx.

Story on the burial of Bloody Bill Anderson in Richmond, Ray County, Missouri was previously found on https://raycountyhistory.webs.com in 2023. The site no longer exists as of 2024.

Sweeten-Shults, Lana. "Here Lies City's History." 2011. Accessed 2023. https://archive.timesrecordnews.com.

Swift, Roy L. "Chihuahua Expedition." *Handbook of Texas Online.* 1952. Accessed 2023. www.tshaonline.org/handbook/entries/chihuahua-expedition.

Sykes, Horace. *Ancient Religious Traditions and Symbols In Freemasonry*, p. 9-10. Internet Archive. Accessed 2022. https://archive.org/details/Ancient_Religious_Traditions_And_Symbols_-_H_Sykes.

"Texas Ranger Campsite near Crosbyton, Crosby County, Texas." *The Historical Marker Database.* Accessed 2023. https://www.hmdb.org.

"The 1861 Jayhawker raid in Osceola." *Missouri Life*, Accessed 2023. https://missourilife.com/the-1861-jayhawker-raid-in-osceola/.

"The Editors of Encyclopaedia Britannica. "Freemasonry." *Britannica,* Accessed 2022. https://britannica.com/topic/Freemasonry.

"The Election Case of William A. Clark of Montana (1900)," *United States Senate*, Accessed 2023, https://www.senate.gov/about/origins-foundations/electing-appointing-senators/contested-senate-elections/089.William_Clark.

"The Grand Architect of the Universe from a Masonic Perspective." Accessed 2022. https://freemasonscommunity.life/the-grand-architect-of-the-universe-from-a-masonic-perspective/.

"The Original Thirteenth Article of Amendment To The Constitution For the United States." Accessed 2022. https://ia804500.us.archive.org/9/items/pdfy-diSTAtsPggMorBFy/The%20Original%20Thirteenth%20Amendment.

"The Scottish Rite in Ohio." *HMdb.org, The Historical Marker Database.* Accessed 2022. https://www.hmdb.org/m.asp?m=1045.

"The Terrifying Collapse of the Plains American Indians." *History Dose.* Accessed 2023. https://www. youtube.com/watch?v=2qxvePKBjP4.

Thomas Jefferson Papers, 1606-1827. *Library of Congress.* Accessed 2022. https://www.loc.gov/collections/thomas-jefferson-papers/about-this-collection/.

"Titles of Nobility Amendment." Accessed 2022. https://simple.m.wikipedia.org.

Towers, Michael, *Oklahombres.* "Law Enforcement Officers Resident to Early Purcell." *McClain County Oklahoma Genealogical & Historical Society News*, August 2007. https://sites.rootsweb.com/~okmchgs/lawmen.htm.

Townsley, Bill. "The Three Spider Rocks." Accessed 2022. https://texaslostmines.com/spider_rock1.html.

Trevis, Michael. "Buffalo Bill Cody." In-depth series exploring the forts of Comancheria. *Fort Tours.* Accessed 2023. https: www.forttours.com.

Trevis, Michael. "Marcus L. Dalton, James Redfield and James McAster." *Fort Tours.* Accessed 2023. https://www.fortours.com/pages/dalton.asp.

"Two Wolves," *Virtues for Life, The Heart of Everyday Living*, Accessed 2024. https://www.virtuesforlife.com/two-wolves/.

Victor, Frances Fuller. "The American Fur Trade in the Far West." *The Quarterly of the Oregon Historical Society 3, no. 3 (1902): 261.* Accessed 2022. http://www.jstor.org/stable/20609534.

Visitors guide to Fort McKavett, state historic site." Accessed 2023. https:// www.thc.texas.gov/.

VOLUBRJOTR. "I Killed The Bank ~ President Andrew Jackson." *POLITICAL VEL CRAFT – Veil of Politics*, 2019. Accessed 2022. https://politicalvelcraft.org/2013/07/24/i-killed-the-bank-president-andrew-jackson/.

Waggoner Carr." *The Texas Politics Project – Texas Speakers of the House.* Accessed 2023. https://texaspolitics.utexas.edu.

"Washington DC's Chamber of Secrets." Accessed 2023. www.washingtondcschamberofsecrets.com/absolute-proof.html

Washington, George to Reverend G. W. Snyder, September 25, 1798. *George Washington Papers, Series 2, Letterbooks 1754 to 1799: Letterbook 21,-Feb. 10, 1799.* – February 10, 1799, 1797.

Manuscript/Mixed Material. Accessed 2022. https://www.loc.gov/resources/mgw2.021/?=Illuminati&sp=182&st=text.

Wasser, Alan, Chairman. "LBJ's Space Race: What We Didn't Know Then." *The Space Settlement Institute.* June 26, 2005. Accessed 2024. www.spacesettlementinstitute.org.

Watkins, Donald V. "The Rothschilds: Controlling The World's Money Supply For More Than Two Centuries." *Accessed* 2019. https://www.donaldwatkins.com/post/the-rothschilds-controlling-the-world-s-money-supply-for-more-than-two-centuries.

Websites produced by Jay Longley of Brownwood that were used in the book with permission from Jay Longley in 2022 but are no longer available regarding Bloody Bill Anderson and the Knights of the Golden Circle. https://bloodybillanderson.webs.com and https://knightsofthegoldencircle.webs.com.

Weems, Mason Locke. *The Life of George Washington: With Curious Anecdotes, Equally Honorable to Himself and Exemplary to his Young Countrymen.* Philadelphia: Lippincott, 1800. Internet Archive edition. Assessed 2022. https://archive.org/details/lifeofgeorgewashweem.

Weiser, Kathy. "Fort Abraham Lincoln, North Dakota." *Legends of America,* 2020. Accessed 2023. https://www.legendsofamerica.com/nd-fortabrahamlincoln/.

Weiser, Kathy. "Jerome, Arizona – Copper Queen on the Hill." *Legends of America.* 2022. Accessed 2024. https://www.legendsofamerica.com.

Weiser, Kathy. "Ocate, New Mexico – On the Santa Fe Trail." *Legends of America.* 2021. Accessed 2022. www.legendsofamerica.com/ocate-new-mexico/.

Weiser-Alexander, Kathy. "Jesse James Timeline." *Legends of America,* 2021. Accessed 2021. www.legendsofamerica.com/we-jessejamestimeline/.

Weiser-Alexander, Kathy. "Victorio Peak, New Mexico Mystery Treasure." *Legends of America.* Accessed 2023. www.legendsofamerica.com/victorio-peak-treasure/

"What Is Freemasonry," *The Grand Lodge of Ohio.* Accessed 2022, https://www.freemason.com/join/what-is-freemasonry.

Whisonant, Robert C. "Geology and History Of Confederate Saltpeter Cave Operations In Western Virginia." November 2001. *Virginia Minerals.* Published by the Division of Mineral Resources, Department of Mines, Minerals and Energy, Richmond, Virginia. Commonwealth of Virginia. https://energy.virginia.gov/commercedocs/VAMIN_VOL47_NO04.pdf.

Whitton, Betty. "Orr." https://ghosttowns.com/ste/ok/orr.html.

"Who Was Jim Dan Hill?" Accessed 2024. https://library.uwsuper.edu/aboutthelibrary/jdh.

"Who Was Murder Victim Capt. John Sheets and Why was he Shot?" *Daviess County in Northwest Missouri.* 2022. https://daviesscountyhistoricalsociety.com/1869/03/24/who-was-capt-john-sheets.

Wikipedia contributors, "5th Cavalry Regiment," *Wikipedia, The Free Encyclopedia,* Accessed 2023, https://en.wikipedia.org.

Wikipedia contributors, "Charles R. Jennison." *Wikipedia, The Free Encyclopedia.* Accessed 2023. https://en.wikipedia.org.

Wikipedia contributors, "George Armstrong Custer," *Wikipedia, The Free Encyclopedia.* Accessed 2023. https://en.wikipedia.org.

Wikipedia contributors, "Guthrie, Oklahoma," *Wikipedia, The Free Encyclopedia*, Accessed 2023, https://en.wikipedia.org.

Wikipedia contributors, "Judy Canova," *Wikipedia, The Free Encyclopedia*, Accessed 2023, https://en.wikipedia.org.

Wikipedia contributors. 'Battle of the Washita River.' *Wikipedia, The Free Encyclopedia*. 2023. https://www.en.wikipedia.org.

Wikipedia contributors. "George Coe (Lincoln County War)." *Wikipedia, The Free Encyclopedia*, Accessed 2023. https://en.wikipedia.org.

Wikipedia contributors. "6th Texas Cavalry Regiment." *Wikipedia, The Free Encyclopedia*. Accessed 2023. https://en.wikipedia.org.

Wikipedia contributors. "Aaron Burr." *Wikipedia, The Free Encyclopedia*. Accessed 2022. https://en.wikipedia.org.

Wikipedia contributors. "Adam Forepaugh." *Wikipedia, The Free Encyclopedia*, Accessed 2023. https://en.wikipedia.org.

Wikipedia contributors. "Adelbert Ames." *Wikipedia, The Free Encyclopedia*, Accessed 2023. https://en.wikipedia.org.

Wikipedia contributors. "Albert Pike." *Wikipedia, The Free Encyclopedia*. Accessed 2022. https://en.wikipedia.org.

Wikipedia contributors. "Alexander Hamilton." *Wikipedia, The Free Encyclopedia*. Accessed 2022. https://en.wikipedia.org.

Wikipedia contributors. "Andrew Ellicott." *Wikipedia, The Free Encyclopedia*. Accessed 2022. https://en.wikipedia.org.

Wikipedia contributors. "Andrew Jackson." *Wikipedia, The Free Encyclopedia*. Accessed 2022. https://en.wikipedia.org.

Wikipedia contributors. "Bank War." *Wikipedia, The Free Encyclopedia*. Accessed 2022. https://en.wikipedia.org.

Wikipedia contributors. "Battle of Little Bighorn." *Wikipedia, The Free Encyclopedia*. Accessed 2023. https://en.wikipedia.org.

Wikipedia contributors. "Benjamin Butler." *Wikipedia, The Free Encyclopedia*, Accessed 2023. https://en.wikipedia.org.

Wikipedia contributors. "Billie Sol Estes." *Wikipedia, The Free Encyclopedia*, Accessed 2023. https://en.wikipedia.org.

Wikipedia contributors. "Buffalo Bill." *Wikipedia, The Free Encyclopedia*. Accessed 2022. https://en.wikipedia.org.

Wikipedia contributors. "Buffalo Gap, Texas." *Wikipedia, The Free Encyclopedia, Accessed 2023*. https://en.wikipedia.org.

Wikipedia contributors. "California Road." *Wikipedia, The Free Encyclopedia*, Accessed 2023. https://en.wikipedia.org.

Wikipedia contributors. "Canyon de Chelly National Monument." *Wikipedia, The Free Encyclopedia*. Accessed 2022. https://en.wikipedia.org.

Wikipedia contributors. "Charles Bent." *Wikipedia, The Free Encyclopedia*. Accessed 2022. https://en.wikipedia.org.

Wikipedia contributors. "Charles H. Beaubien." *Wikipedia, The Free Encyclopedia*. Accessed 2022. https://en.wikipedia.org.

Wikipedia contributors. "Chris Madsen." *Wikipedia, The Free Encyclopedia*, Accessed 2023. https://en.wikipedia.org.

Wikipedia contributors. "Chris Madsen." *Wikipedia, The Free Encyclopedia*, Accessed 2023. https://en.wikipedia.org

Wikipedia contributors. "Clay Allison." *Wikipedia, The Free Encyclopedia*, Accessed 2023. https://en.wikipedia.org.

Wikipedia contributors. "Clifton House Site." *Wikipedia, The Free Encyclopedia*, Accessed 2023. https://en.wikipedia.org.

Wikipedia contributors. "Colfax County War." *Wikipedia, The Free Encyclopedia*, Accessed 2023. https://en.wikipedia.org.

Wikipedia contributors. "Confiscation Act of 1861." *Wikipedia, The Free Encyclopedia*. Accessed 2022. https://en.wikipedia.org.

Wikipedia contributors. "Cyrus Harris." *Wikipedia, The Free Encyclopedia*. Accessed 2022. https://www.en.wikipedia.org.

Wikipedia contributors. "Daniel Baker College." *Wikipedia, The Free Encyclopedia*, Accessed 2023. https://en.wikipedia.org

Wikipedia contributors. "Daniel Baker College." *Wikipedia, The Free Encyclopedia*. Accessed 2023. https://en.wikipedia.org.

Wikipedia contributors. "District of Columbia Organic Act of 1871." *Wikipedia, The Free Encyclopedia*. Accessed 2022. https://en.wikipedia.org.

Wikipedia contributors. "Divination." *Wikipedia, The Free Encyclopedia*. Accessed 2022. https://en.wikipedia.org.

Wikipedia contributors. "Evett Dumas Nix." *Wikipedia, The Free Encyclopedia*. Accessed 2023. https://en.wikipedia.org.

Wikipedia contributors. "First Battle of Mesilla." *Wikipedia, The Free Encyclopedia*, Accessed 2023. https://en.wikipedia.org.

Wikipedia contributors. "Fort Concho." *Wikipedia, The Free Encyclopedia*. Accessed 2023. https://en.wikipedia.org.

Wikipedia contributors. "Fort McKavett State Historic Site." *Wikipedia, The Free Encyclopedia, Accessed 2023*. https://en.wikipedia.org.

Wikipedia contributors. "Fort Sumner." *Wikipedia, The Free Encyclopedia*. Accessed 2022. https://en.wikipedia.org.

Wikipedia contributors. "Fort Worth and Rio Grande Railway." *Wikipedia, The Free Encyclopedia*, Accessed 2023. https://en.wikipedia.org.

Wikipedia contributors. "General Order No. 28." *Wikipedia, The Free Encyclopedia*, Accessed 2023. https://en.wikipedia.org.

Wikipedia contributors. "George Washington." *Wikipedia, The Free Encyclopedia*. Accessed 2022. https://en.wikipedia.org.

Wikipedia contributors. "Gladewater, Texas." *Wikipedia, The Free Encyclopedia*. Accessed 2023. https://en.wikipedia.org.

Wikipedia contributors. "Harold Preece." *Wikipedia, The Free Encyclopedia*, Accessed 2023. https://en.wikipedia.org.

Wikipedia contributors. "Hernan Cortes." *Wikipedia, The Free Encyclopedia*. Accessed 2022. https://en.wikipedia.org.

Wikipedia contributors. "Hexagram." *Wikipedia, The Free Encyclopedia*. Accessed 2022. https://en.wikipedia.org.

Wikipedia contributors. "Horrell Brothers." *Wikipedia, The Free Encyclopedia*, Accessed 2023. https://en.wikipedia.org.

Wikipedia contributors. "Horus." *Wikipedia, The Free Encyclopedia*. Accessed 2022. https://en.wikipedia.org.

Wikipedia contributors. "Hugh Hammond Bennett." *Wikipedia, The Free Encyclopedia*, Accessed 2023. https://en.wikipedia.org

Wikipedia contributors. "Isis." *Wikipedia, The Free Encyclopedia*. Accessed 2022. https://en.wikipedia.org.

Wikipedia contributors. "J. J. McAlester." *Wikipedia, The Free Encyclopedia*, Accessed 2023. https://en.wikipedia.org.

Wikipedia contributors. "James Madison." *Wikipedia, The Free Encyclopedia*. Accessed 2022. https://en.wikipedia.org.

Wikipedia contributors. "James K. Polk." *Wikipedia, The Free Encyclopedia*. Accessed 2022. https://en.wikipedia.org.

Wikipedia contributors. "James Monroe." *Wikipedia, The Free Encyclopedia*. Accessed 2022. https://en.wikipedia.org.

Wikipedia contributors. "James Wilkinson." *Wikipedia, The Free Encyclopedia*. Accessed 2022. https://en.wikipedia.org.

Wikipedia contributors. "James-Younger Gang." *Wikipedia, The Free Encyclopedia, Accessed* 2023. https://en.wikipedia.org.

Wikipedia contributors. "Jay Gould." *Wikipedia, The Free Encyclopedia*. Accessed 2022. https://en.wikipedia.org.

Wikipedia contributors. "Jesse Woodson James." *Wikipedia, The Free Encyclopedia*. Accessed 2020. https://www.en.wikipedia.org.

Wikipedia contributors. "John B. Jones." *Wikipedia, The Free Encyclopedia*, Accessed 2023. https://en.wikipedia.org

Wikipedia contributors. "John C. Calhoun." *Wikipedia, The Free Encyclopedia*. Accessed 2022. https://www.en.wikipedia.org.

Wikipedia contributors. "John F. Kennedy." *Wikipedia, The Free Encyclopedia*. Accessed 2022. https://en.wikipedia.org.

Wikipedia contributors. "John A. Quitman." *Wikipedia, The Free Encyclopedia*. Accessed 2022. https://en.wikipedia.org.

Wikipedia contributors. "John Sherman." *Wikipedia, The Free Encyclopedia*. Accessed 2022. https://en.wikipedia.org.

Wikipedia contributors. "John Tyler." *Wikipedia, The Free Encyclopedia*. Accessed 2022. https://en.wikipedia.org.

Wikipedia contributors. "Kearney, Missouri." *Wikipedia, The Free Encyclopedia*. Accessed 2020. https://en.wikipedia.org.

Wikipedia contributors. "Kit Carson." *Wikipedia, The Free Encyclopedia*. Accessed 2022. https://en.wikipedia.org.

Wikipedia contributors. "Lewis and Clark Expedition." *Wikipedia, The Free Encyclopedia*. Accessed 2022. https://en.wikipedia.org.

Wikipedia contributors. "Lexington, Missouri." *Wikipedia, The Free Encyclopedia*. Accessed 2023. https://en.wikipedia.org.

Wikipedia contributors. "Long Walk of the Navajo." *Wikipedia, The Free Encyclopedia*. Accessed 2022. https://en.wikipedia.org.

Wikipedia contributors. "Lucien Maxwell." *Wikipedia, The Free Encyclopedia*, Accessed 2023. https://en.wikipedia.org.

Wikipedia contributors. "Mayer Amschel Rothschild." *Wikipedia, The Free Encyclopedia*. Accessed 2022. https://en.wikipedia.org.

Wikipedia contributors. "Meriwether Lewis." *Wikipedia, The Free Encyclopedia*. Accessed 2022. https://en.wikipedia.org.

Wikipedia contributors. "Mexican-American War." *Wikipedia, The Free Encyclopedia*. Accessed 2022. https://en.wikipedia.org.

Wikipedia contributors. "Mexican Revolution." *Wikipedia, The Free Encyclopedia*, Accessed 2023. https://en.wikipedia.org

Wikipedia contributors. "Missouri-Kansas-Texas Railroad." *Wikipedia, The Free Encyclopedia*. Accessed 2023. https://en.wikipedia.org.

Wikipedia contributors. "Montezuma/Moctezuma." *Wikipedia, The Free Encyclopedia*. Accessed 2022. https://en.wikipedia.org.

Wikipedia contributors. "Nathan Bedford Forrest." *Wikipedia, The Free Encyclopedia*. Accessed 2023. https://en.wikipedia.org.

Wikipedia contributors. "Nicholas Biddle." *Wikipedia, The Free Encyclopedia*. Accessed 2022. https://en.wikipedia.org.

Wikipedia contributors. "Ojo Caliente, New Mexico." *Wikipedia, The Free Encyclopedia*. Accessed 2022. https://www.en.wikipedia.org.

Wikipedia contributors. "Osage Nation." *Wikipedia, The Free Encyclopedia*, Accessed 2023. https://en.wikipedia.org.

Wikipedia contributors. "Pancho Villa." *Wikipedia, The Free Encyclopedia*, Accessed 2023. https://en.wikipedia.org.

Wikipedia contributors. "Porfirio Diaz." *Wikipedia, The Free Encyclopedia*. Accessed 2023. https://en.wikipedia.org.

Wikipedia contributors. "Randolph B. Marcy." *Wikipedia, The Free Encyclopedia*. Accessed 2022. https://en.wikipedia.org.

Wikipedia contributors. "Religious views of George Washington." *Wikipedia, The Free Encyclopedia*. Accessed 2022. https://en.wikipedia.org.

Wikipedia contributors. "Robert B. Anderson (Texas politician)." *Wikipedia, The Free Encyclopedia*, Accessed 2023. https://en.wikipedia.org

Wikipedia contributors. "Roy Daugherty." *Wikipedia, The Free Encyclopedia*, Accessed 2023. https://en.wikipedia.org.

Wikipedia contributors. "Sam Houston." *Wikipedia, The Free Encyclopedia*. Accessed 2020. https://en.wikipedia.org.

Wikipedia contributors. "Second Battle of Adobe Walls." *Wikipedia, The Free Encyclopedia*. Accessed 2023. https://en.wikipedia.org.

Wikipedia contributors. "Seer Stone (Latter Day Saints)." *Wikipedia, The Free Encyclopedia*. Accessed 2022. https://en.wikipedia.org.

Wikipedia contributors. "Silver City, New Mexico." *Wikipedia, The Free Encyclopedia*, Accessed 2023. https://en.wikipedia.org.

Wikipedia contributors. "Stephen W. Kearny." *Wikipedia, The Free Encyclopedia*. Accessed 2022. https://en.wikipedia.org.

Wikipedia contributors. "Sterling Price." *Wikipedia, The Free Encyclopedia*. Accessed 2022. https://en.wikipedia.org.

Wikipedia contributors. "Susie Peters." *Wikipedia, The Free Encyclopedia*. Accessed 2020. https://www.en.wikipedia.org.

Wikipedia contributors. "Taos Revolt." *Wikipedia, The Free Encyclopedia*. Accessed 2022. https://en.wikipedia.org.

Wikipedia contributors. "Thomas Jefferson." *Wikipedia, The Free Encyclopedia*. Accessed 2022. https://en.wikipedia.org.

Wikipedia contributors. "Thomas Theodore Crittenden." *Wikipedia, The Free Encyclopedia*. 2023. https://en.wikipedia.org.

Wikipedia contributors. "Turley Mill and Distillery Site." *Wikipedia, The Free Encyclopedia*. Accessed 2022. https://en.wikipedia.org.

Wikipedia contributors. "United States Capitol cornerstone laying." *Wikipedia, The Free Encyclopedia*. Accessed 2022. https://en.wikipedia.org.

Wikipedia contributors. "United States Declaration of Independence." *Wikipedia, The Free Encyclopedia*. Accessed 2022. https://www.en.wikipedia.org.

Wikipedia contributors. "Ute People." *Wikipedia, The Free Encyclopedia*. Accessed 2022. https://en.wikipedia.org.

Wikipedia contributors. "Wild Bill Hickok." *Wikipedia, The Free Encyclopedia*. Accessed 2023. https://en.wikipedia.org.

Wikipedia contributors. "William Clark." *Wikipedia, The Free Encyclopedia*. Accessed 2022. https://en.wikipedia.org.

Wikipedia contributors. "William Henry Harrison." *Wikipedia, The Free Encyclopedia*. Accessed 2022. https://en.wikipedia.org.

Wikipedia contributors. "Woodrow Wilson." *Wikipedia, The Free Encyclopedia*. Accessed 2022. https://en.wikipedia.org.

Wikipedia contributors. "World's Columbian Exposition." *Wikipedia, The Free Encyclopedia*, Accessed 2023. https://en.wikipedia.

Wikipedia contributors. "XIT Ranch." *Wikipedia, The Free Encyclopedia*, Accessed 2023. https://en.wikipedia.org.

Wikipedia contributors. "Zebulon Pike." *Wikipedia, The Free Encyclopedia*. Accessed 2022. https://en.wikipedia.org.

William Tucker (Jamestown immigrant)." 2024. https://en.wikipedia.org.

Williams, R.H. (Robert Hamilton). *With the border ruffian: memories of the Far West, 1852-1868*, p. 3-4. Lincoln: University of Nebraska Press, 1982. Internet Archive. 2022. https://archive.org/details/withborderruffi01willgoog.

Wilson, Linda D. "Fraternal Orders," *The Encyclopedia of Oklahoma History and Culture*. Accessed 2023. https://www.okhistory.org/publications/enc/entry?entry=FR007.

Young, J. "Jose Chavez y Chavez"– "Mob Constable." Accessed 2024. https://palsofbillythekidhistoricalsociety.com

General Websites:

Ancestry.com

Biblegateway.com

Chroniclingamerica.loc.gov

Findagrave.com

Historical Marker Database. hmdb.org

Legends of America.com

Merrium-Webster.com

Newspapers.com

Okhistory.org – Oklahoma Historical Society

Texasescapes.com

Tshaonline.org - *Handbook of Texas Online.*

Wikipedia.org

Archived Documents:

Ancestry.com. *Fort Smith, Arkansas, U. S., Criminal Case Files, 1866-1900* for William Means, Crime: Counterfeit, Jacket Number 134. National Archives – Southwest Region. March 1876.

Ancestry.com. Fort Smith, Arkansas, U. S., Criminal Case Files, *1866-1900* for John Means, Crime: Larceny, Jacket Number 134. National Archives – Southwest Region. February 27, 1889.

Anderson, Gerald and Mrs. Sandra Boulden. "Robert B. Anderson: Papers, 1933-89." Dwight Eisenhower Library, Abilene, Kansas, 2004. National Archives. Accessed 2014 & 2024. https://www.eisenhowerlibrary.gov/sites/default/files/finding-aids/pdf/anderson-robert-papers.pdf.

"B.F. Johnson." *Texas Rangers Hall of Fame and Museum*, Research Center -The Armstrong Center. Waco, Texas.

"Coggin" – *Biographies of Concho County, Texas*. 2023. https:// www.genealogytrails.com.

Colton, J. H. Texas, map, 1855; New York. (https://texashistory.unt.edu/ark"/67531/metapth2437/: accessed August 22, 2024), *University of North Texas Libraries, The Portal to Texas History*, https://texashistory.unt.edu; crediting UNT Libraries Special Collections.

Confederate soldier's interview by General Julius Franklin Howell, Company "K," 24th Virginia Cavalry.

Examination of Wesley A. Rash for the Jackson County, Alabama, Pension Board, completed by E.R. Smith, M.D. and S. H. McMohan, J.P. *"Alabama, Texas and Virginia, U.S. Confederate Pensions, 1884-1958."* https://www.ancestry.com.

Find a Grave, database and images (https://www.findagrave.com/memorial/80241079/john_allison-shirley: accessed 2023. Memorial page for John Allison "Bud" Shirley Jr. (1842-20 Jun 1863), Find a Grave Memorial ID 80241079, citing Non-cemetery Burial, Jefferson County, Missouri, USA; Burial Details Unknown; Maintained by Lanie (contributor 47381115).

Find a Grave, database and images (https://www.findagrave.com/memorial/80245150/edwin_benton-shirley: accessed 2023. Memorial page for Edwin Benton "Eddie" Shirley (1850-27 Sep 1866), Find a Grave Memorial ID 80245150, Burial Details Unknown; Maintained by Lanie (contributor 47381115).

Find a Grave, database and images (https://www.findagrave.com/memorial/80246745/manfield-shirley: accessed 2023. Memorial page for Mansfield Shirley (1852-1867). Find a Grave Memorial ID 80246745, citing Greenwood Cemetery, Dallas, Dallas County, Texas, USA; Maintained by Lanie (contributor 47381115).

Find a Grave, database and images (https://www.findagrave.com/memorial/80248879/cravens-shirley: accessed 2023. Memorial page for Cravens "John Alva" Shirley (1858-unknown), Find a Grave Memorial ID 80248879, Burial Details Unknown; Maintained by Lanie (contributor 47381115).

Find a grave, database and images (https://www.findagrave.com/memorial/6562080/frank_marion-hill: accessed 2023, memorial page for Capt. Frank Marion "Tuck" Hill (20 Mar 1843-27 May 1920), Find a Grave Memorial ID 6562080, citing Pecan Grove Cemetery, McKinney, Collin County, Texas, USA; Maintained by Victor E. Everhart, PhD (contributor 47774451).

Find a Grave, database and images (https://www.findagrave.com/memorial/9973/john_w-sheets: accessed 2023, memorial page for CPT John W. Sheets (1818-7 Dec 1869, Find a Grave Memorial ID 9973, citing Lile Cemetery, Gallatin, Daviess County, Missouri, USA; Maintained by Jim Nelson (contributor 47275092).

Find a Grave, database and images (https://www.findagrave.com/memorial/39105851/henry_h-sackett: accessed 2023, memorial page for Henry H. Sackett (23 Feb 1851-19 Dec 1928), Find a Grave Memorial ID 39105851, citing Coleman City Cemetery, Coleman, Coleman County, Texas, USA; Maintained by Ralph Terry (contributor 47372532).

Find a Grave, database and images (https://www.findagrave.com/memorial/14524161/hewitt_preston-webb: accessed 2023). Memorial page for Hewitt Preston "Press" Webb (6 July 1836-31 Jan 1899), Find a Grave Memorial ID 14524161, citing Salem Cemetery, Independence, Jackson County, Missouri, USA; Maintained by J.C. Clark (contributor 47094715).

Find a Grave, database and images (https://www.findagrave.com/memorial/8456672/waggoner-carr: accessed 2023, memorial page for Waggoner Carr (1 Oct 1918-25 Feb 2004), Find a Grave Memorial ID 8456672, citing Texas State Cemetery, Austin, Travis County, Texas, USA; Maintained by Find a Grave.

Find a Grave, database and images (https://www.findagrave.com/memorial/35426917/jesse_ballard_james: accessed 2023, memorial page for Jesse Ballard James (1803-1861), Find a Grave Memorial ID 35426917, citing James Cemetery, Tecumseh, Ozark County, Missouri, USA; Maintained by John Carroll (contributor 46801961).

Find a Grave, database and images (https://www.findagrave.com/memorial/209621103/drury_woodson-james: accessed 2023, memorial page for Drury Woodson James (14 Nov 1826-1 Jul 1910), Find a Grave Memorial ID 209621103; Burial Details Unknown; Maintained by Butterfly Rose (contributor 47011600).

Find a Grave, database and images (https://www.findagrave.com/memorial/44310520/ozark_jack-berlin: Accessed 2023, memorial page for Ozark Jack Berlin (1867-1954), Find a Grave Memorial ID 44310520, citing Rockfield Cemetery, Veedersburg, Fountain County, Indiana, USA; Maintained by Lesa Epperson (contributor 46576986).

Find a Grave, database and images (https:www.findagrave.com/memorial/101107973/louis_john-hull: accessed 2023, memorial page for Louis John Lull (Jun 1847-20 Mar 1874), Find a Grave Memorial ID 101107973, citing Hewittville Cemetery, Pomfret, Windsor County, Vermont, USA; Maintained by David Edsall (contributor 46906546).

Find a Grave, database and images (https:www.findagrave.com/memorial/10137/Edward_capehart-o'kelley: accessed 2024, memorial page for Edward Capehart O'Kelley (c.1 Oct 1857-13 Jan 1904),Find a Grave Memorial ID 10137, citing Post Oak Cemetery, Patton, Bollinger County, Missouri, USA; maintained by Find a Grave.

Find a Grave, database and images (https:www.findagrave.com/memorial/68280553/billie_sol-estes: accessed 2023, memorial page for Billie Sol Estes (10 Jan 1925-14 May 2013), Find a Grave Memorial ID 68280553, citing Granbury Cemetery, Granbury, Hood County, Texas, USA, Maintained by CO GRAVE DIGGER (contributor 47056557).

Find a Grave, database and images (https:www.findagrave.com/memorial/6835783/john Wilson: accessed 2024, memorial page for John McHenry Wilson (3 Nov 1832-27 Feb 1912), Find a Grave Memorial ID 6835783, citing Frost Cemetery, Frost, Navarro County, Texas, USA, Maintained by Patricia Knowles Spencer (contributor 49488606).

Find a Grave, database and images (https:www.findagrave.com/memorial/18910182/robert_bernerd-anderson: accessed 2022, memorial page for Robert Bernerd Anderson (4 Jun 1910-14 Aug 1989), Find a Grave Memorial ID 18910182, citing Rosehill Cemetery, Cleburne, Johnson County, Texas, USA, Maintained by Find a Grave.

"Frank Dalton," *Texas State Library and Archives Commission*; Austin, Texas; Confederate Pension Applications, 1899-1975; Collection # CPA16526; Roll # 2538, Roll Description: Pension File Nos. 04385 to 52015, Application Years 1915 to 1947. Alabama, Texas and Virginia, U.S. Confederate Pensions, 1884-1958, Accessed 2023. https://www.ancestry.com.

"Frontier Battalion" List of Companies and their officers. Accessed 2023. https://www.texasranger.org.

Galik, Pete. "The Holland Family."

Gamble, Mrs. L. L. to the Confederate Pension Division, Pension Board, March 10, 1947. *Texas State Library and Archives Commission and Alabama Department of Archives and History*. Confederate Pension file – Alabama, Texas and Virginia, U.S. Confederate Pensions, 1884-1958, 2023. https://www. ancestry.com.

Harold Preece to Mr. J. H. Taylor, State Comptroller's Department, December 20, 1947. Alabama, Texas and Virginia, U.S., Confederate Pensions, 1884-1958. *Texas State Library and Archives Commission and Alabama Department of Archives and History.* https://www.ancestry.com.

Hicks, Zuleika B. to Confederate Pension Division, Pension Board, February 16, 1948. *Texas State Library and Archives Commission and Alabama Department of Archives and History.* Confederate Pension file – Alabama, Texas and Virginia, U.S. Confederate Pensions, 1884-1958, 2023. https://www. ancestry.com.

JCHS journal (Jackson County Historical Society, Jackson County, Missouri) in June 1976.

Jefferson, Thomas. *The Writings of Thomas Jefferson: Being His Autobiography, Correspondence, Reports, Messages, Addresses, and other Writings, Official and Private,* (Taylor & Maury, 1853-1854).

John F. Kennedy, Address "The President and the Press," Before the American Newspaper Publishers Association, New York City. April 27, 1961. *The American Presidency Project,* Accessed 2022. https://www.presidency.ucsb.edu.

Kemble, W. (William) "Texas and part of Mexico & the United States showing the route of the first Santa Fe expedition," map, 1844?; New York. (https://texashistory.unt.edu/ark:/67531/metapth192792/:accessed August 22, 2024), *University of North Texas Libraries, The Portal to Texas History,* https://texashistory.unt.edu; crediting University of Texas at Arlington Library.

"Knox E. Greer in History of Rhea County, Tennessee." compiled by Bettye J. Broyles. *Rhea County Historical and Genealogical Society,* 1991.

L. H. Tackett's affidavit from Claremore, Oklahoma, signed on August 31, 1908. He was the ex-husband of Mary Plina Norris. "Cherokee By Blood," *Records of Eastern Cherokee Ancestry in the U.S. Court of Claims 1906-1910, Vol. 3;* Applications 4201 to 7250, Compiled by Jerry Wright Jordan.

"Lieut. James Monroe "Jim" Anderson," (1842-1871) *Find a Grave,* database and images, Maintained by Gary & Nancy Glenn Clampitt (contributor 47464411), 2023, https://www.findagrave.com/memorial/65718679/james_monroe-anderson.

"Map of Marcy's Exploration to Locate the Texas Indian Reservations," map, Date Unknown; (https://texashistory.unt.edu/ark:/67531/metapth493540/: accessed August 22, 2024). *University of North Texas Libraries, The Portal to Texas History,* https://texashistory.unt.edu; crediting Hardin-Simmons University Library.

Marcy, Randolph Barnes, 1812-1887. "Topographical map of the road from Fort Smith Arks. To Santa Fe, N.M. and from Donna Anna N.M. to Fort Smith," map, 1850. [Washington D.C.] (https://texashistory.unt.edu/ark:/67531/metapth190605/: accessed August 22, 2024, *University of North Texas Libraries, The Portal to Texas History,* https://texashistory.unt.edu; crediting University of Texas at Arlington Library.

"Matthew Hardcastle came in the "Jacob" in 1624." Ancestry.com. *Wills and Administrations of Elizabeth City County, Virginia 1688-1800* [database on-line]. Provo, UT, USA: Ancestry.com Operations, Inc. 2006.

McCarthy, Harry. The Confederate Marching Song, *Bonnie Blue Flag,* 1861.

Original data: Chapman, Blanche Adams. *Wills and Administrations of Elizabeth City County, Virginia 1688-1800.* Baltimore, MD, USA: Genealogical Publishing Co., 2000.

"Ponil, Colfax County, New Mexico Genealogy," https://www.familysearch.org.

"President Dwight D. Eisenhower's Farewell Address (1961)." *Milestone Documents – National Archives.* Accessed 2022. https://www.archives.gov/milestone-documents/president-dwight-d-eisenhowers-farewell-address.

"Rev. Robert Sallee James Biography." (Broderbund WFT Vol. 15, Ed.1, Tree #1589) and (Broderbund WFT Vol. 5, Ed. 1 Tree #2180)

"Robert B. Anderson, Dwight D. Eisenhower Administration May 3, 1954-August 4, 1995." *Historical Office of the Secretary of Defense*. Accessed 2024. https://history.defense.gov/DOD-History/Deputy-Secretaries-of-Defense/Article-View/Article/585246/.

"Samuel and David Daube," *Ancestry.com*. Military Intelligence, U.S. Subject Index to Correspondence and Case Files of the immigration and Naturalization Service, 1903-1959, August 12, 1941. Ref. 56,078-721.

"Territory and military department of New Mexico." *Library of Congress, Geography and Map Division – United States Army*. Corps of Topographical Engineers, Cartographer, and William H. Dougal. [Washington, D.C.: War Departt, 1959] Map. https://www.loc.gov/item/2015591072/.

The "Bill Blevins family story" in Helen Hoffsommer Stout's personal collection.

The "R.K. Stout story" by Helen Hoffsommer Stout.

"The American Citizen's Manual of Reference: Being a Comprehensive Historical, Statistical, Topographical, and Political View of the United States of North America and of the Several States and Territories." published by W. Hobart Hadley, 1840.

The Hardcastle, Hays, Ryan, Swain, Whatley, Epperson, and Black family history.

The Wilcoxson and Stout family history compiled by Ruth Geraldine (Smith) Wilcoxson, Maxine (Wilcoxson) Parker, Helen Hoffsommer Stout, and Rosanne (Wilcoxson) Priddy.

To G. W. Snyder from George Washington, September 25, 1798, Founders Online, 2022, https://founders.archives.gov.

Travis, DeWitt to the Confederate Pension Division, Pension Board, March 10, 1947. *Texas State Library and Archives Commission and Alabama Department of Archives and History*. Confederate Pension file – Alabama, Texas and Virginia, U.S. Confederate Pensions, 1884-1958, 2023. https://www. ancestry.com.

United States Army. Corps of Topographical Engineers, Cartographer, and William H. Dougal. *Territory and military department of New Mexico*. [Washington, D.C.: War Depart, 1959] Map. https://www.loc.gov/item/2015591072/.

"William Hubert Key," *Texas State Library and Archives Commission*; Austin, Texas; Confederate Pension Applications, 1899-1975; Collection # CPA16526; Roll # 2277, Roll Description: Pension File Nos. 01578 to 35510, Application Years 1909 to 1918. Alabama, Texas and Virginia, U.S. Confederate Pensions, 1884-1958, Accessed 2023. https://www.ancestry.com.

Woodson II, Charles. "The Woodson Genealogy."

Younger Family Genealogy on the official website for Frank and Jesse James Ancestry.

Letters:

Clack, J.B. to Professor Washington Swisher Rector, October 1, 1872.

Videos:

"Albert Gonzalez – The 1847 Revolt: The Beginning of Modern Taos." *UNM-Taos Digital Media Services*. 2016. https://www.youtube.com.

"Alonso, Alex. "Gold, Lies & Videotape." *Discovery Channel* aired in 2023. https://www.youtube.com.

"America Unearthed: Montezuma's Gold Stashed Away in Utah." *The History Channel*, 2024. https://www.youtube.com.

Brad Meltzer's Decoded: Jefferson's Secret Presidential Codes. 2010. https://www.youtube.com

Carter, Terry. "Still alive to talk about treasure hunting with Crazy Jake in the Superstitions." 2023. Accessed 2023. https://www.youtube.com.

Clifford, Jeff. "That Fabulous Summer: The 1904 St. Louis World's Fair (1962)"-Vintage Documentary. Accessed 2023. https://www.youtube.com.

Edwards, Daniel A. "Billy the Kid: The Silver City Photo" with Emilio Estevez and original music by Tim Montana. *Alias Billy The Kid/Asocial Media, LLC*. 2023. https://www.youtube.com.

Epperson, Ralph. "Jesse James Lived to be 103: Part 1-4." https://www.youtube.com, 2018.

"Garcia, Emmett "Shkeme." Storyteller from the Santa Ana Pueblo of New Mexico. "Indigenous Peoples' Day: Pueblo Revolt Story/Web Extra." *New Mexico PBS*, hosted by Antonia Gonzales, 2019. https://www.youtube.com.

"Get Ready to Be Mind-Blown by This Interview with Battlefield Archaeologist Dr. Douglas Scott." 2019. Accessed 2023. https://www.youtube.com.

"Gold, Lies & Videotape." *Prime Video*.

Grangaard, Wendell. "The History and the Guns Used at the Little Big Horn Battle." 2017. Accessed 2023. https://www.youtube.com.

Hall, Brett. "Brushy Bill Roberts in His Own Words: The Lincoln County War and Debunking The Saga of Billy the Kid." 2022. https://www.youtube.com.

Hall, Brett. "Melton F. Hailey Interview with Dr. Jannay Valdez on Billy the Kid/Brushy Bill" on https://www.youtube.com.

Hall, Brett. "William Tunstill Interview With Ola Everhard," Friend of Brushy Bill Roberts/Billy The Kid conducted on March 6, 1956. 2019.

Hardcastle, Bud and Kenny Brown. "Interview with Aubrey Everhard," April 3, 1990. (Courtesy of Bud Hardcastle)

"History of Ft. Sill, Oklahoma." *Historically Speaking*. Episode 4, Season 1. 2023. https://www.youtube.com.

"In Search of History-Quantrlll's Raiders." (*History Channel Documentary*), https://www.youtube.com.

"Interview with Ex. Train Robber – Al Jennings," British Movietone, 2015. https://www.youtube.com.

"Jesse James Hideout." *Strange RV Tours*. Accessed 2023. https://www.youtube.com.

"Jonathan breaks down the lies about Thomas Jefferson." *Wallbuilders*, 2020. https://youtube.com.

"Montford Johnson: An Original Brand," 2022. on Prime Video.

"Murray, Dr. Arnold. "Update On Victoria Peak." *Shepherd's Student*. 2023. Accessed 2023. https://youtube.com.

"New Evidence of Montezuma's Golden Treasure, Cities of the Underworld." *The History Channel*, 2021. https://www.youtube.com.

"Podcast #568: The Untold Story Behind the Famous Robbers Cave Experiment, interview with Gina Perry/The Art of Manliness." Accessed 2023. https://www.youtube.com.

"Robber's Cave Experiment – Realistic Conflict Theory." *Practical Psychology*. 2021. Accessed 2024. https://www.youtube.com.

Stack, Robert. *Unsolved Mysteries*. Season 1, Episode 20. 2019. https://www.youtube.com.

Sullivan IV, Robert W. "Freemasonry – Royal Arch of Enoch, Cinema Symbolism." The Electric Pyramid, hosted by Michael Parker Media, aired on 6/26/14. https://www.youtube.com.

"The Greatest Treasure in American History! Gold lies and videotapes." *Discovery*. https://www.youtube.com

Tunstill, Dr. William. "Interview with Ola Everhard," March 6, 1986. (courtesy of Dr. William Tunstill)

"William Clark Quantrill." *Reeves Museum*. Dover, Ohio, April 2, 2020. youtube.com.

Wolter, Scott. "America Unearthed: Lincoln's Secret Assassins Exposed (S2, E12). https://www.youtube.com.

Wolter, Scott. "Did the Knights Templar Secretly Discover and Found The USA?" *The Cosmic Summit*. 2023. https://www.youtube.com.

Personal Interviews conducted by Rosanne Priddy:

Betty Lou Kilgore

Grace Hopkins

Jarret Bowers

Jay Longley

Johnny Means

Karen Ford

Ralph Epperson

Zach Harp, nephew of Bud

Numerous visits to Oklahoma to interview Bud and also our visits to Texas for interviews.

Over 150 audio tapes of Bud and author's phone conversations to discuss Jesse and Bud's research.

Notes

[1] "Duel to the Death. John Swain Mortally Wounded-Kills Garl Vincent," *The Purcell Register*, January 4, 1895.

[2] "The Dalton Gang. They Hold Up the Santa Fe Train in Oklahoma Territory," *Austin Weekly Statesman*, June 9, 1892.

[3] Daniel A. Edwards, *Billy the Kid: An Autobiography* (Creative Texts Publishers, LLC, 2014-2021), p. 70.

[4] JNO. H. Bass, P.C., letter to the editor, *Our Brother in Red,* February 21, 1895.

[5] Sally Stonum, *Susan Peters 1873-1965*, typed article given to Bud Hardcastle by the author in Hardcastle's personal collection.

[6] Letter from Frank Dalton to Howk, September 12, 1942, part of Bud Hardcastle's personal collection.

[7] Reggie Anne Walker-Wyatt, *Chasing Rivers, Trains and Jesse James,* 2000.

[8] Del Schrader, *Jesse James Was One of His Names,* (Santa Anita Press, 1975), Retrieved from Internet Archive, PDF format, 63, https://archive.org/details/JesseJamesWasOneOfHisNamesDelSchrader.

[9] Jesse Lee James, *Jesse James and the Lost Cause*, (Pageant Press, Inc., 1961), p. 41.

[10] "Claim Badman Jesse James Living in Oklahoma Town*," Newspaper* and date unknown, part of Bud Harcastle's personal collection.

[11] "Henchman." *Merriam-Webster Dictionary*, https://www.merriam-webster.com.

[12] "Missouri State Death Certificate," digital image s.v. "David Baxter" (1834-1925), Ancestry.com

[13] *The American Barbed Wire Journal*, Volume IX, Number 6, written June 1975.

[14] "Orvus Howks, Miss Redd are Wed Saturday," *Jacksonville, Journal Courier*, May 01, 1932.

[15] Census, military, and genealogy records in ancestry.com.

[16] "Are the History Books Wrong About His Death? Jesse James More Than A Legend Here," *The Granbury Tablet,* April 26, 1984.

[17] "Mrs. Elsie N. Howk Granted Divorce," *Great Falls Tribune*, June 9, 1950.

[18] Bud Hardcastle, *The Hoax That Let Jesse James Live*, (Creative Texts Publishers, LLC., 2021), p. 171.

[19] Edwards, *Billy the Kid, p.* 124.

[20] Orvus Lee Howk to Mrs. Clovis Herring on August 24, 1982.

[21] James (Howk), *Jesse James and the Lost Cause*, p. 12 and Schrader, *Jesse James Was One of His Names,* p.165 & 206.

[22] "Henry County History," www.henrycountytn.org.

[23] *Some Turn of the Century Henry County, Tennessee Obituaries* (1898-1913)

²⁴ Hardcastle, *The Hoax*, p. 57.

²⁵ Ibid.

²⁶ Dr. William Tunstill, "Interview with Ola Everhard," March 6, 1986.

²⁷Bud Hardcastle and Kenny Brown "Interview with Aubrey Everhard," April 3, 1990.

²⁸Rebecca Beatrice Brooks, *"The Funeral of Jesse James,"* 2020, https://www.civilwarsaga.com.

²⁹ Rodney G. Dalton, researched, compiled and edited from World Wide Web resources, "An interview Given by Ben Dalton at Coffeyville After the Raid," *Special Correspondence of the Globe Democrat*; daltondatabank.org.

³⁰ Harry E. Chrisman, *Fifty Years on the Owl Hoot Trail, Jim Herron*, (Publisher, 1969), p. 106.

³¹ "Police Gazette files of 1882 produced conclusive evidence that the famous Western outlaw was never killed", by George McGrath, April 1950.

³² Melinda E. Cohenour, Story on the Dalton family, Ancestry.com, 2009.

³³ "Mother of 'James Boys' is Dead," *The Choctaw Herald*, February 16, 1911.

³⁴"The Last Chapter is Written for a Fighting Frontiersman," *The Kansas City Star*, July 10, 1929.

³⁵ "William Clark Quantrill," *Reeves Museum*, Dover, Ohio, April 2, 2020, youtube.com.

³⁶ Frank Dalton, "Quantrell…In the Civil War, Reminiscences of Civil War Days," First Edition, Privately Published, May 20, 1935.

³⁷ Hardcastle, *The Hoax*, p.1.

³⁸ Ibid., p. 5.

³⁹ Lindsey Whitten, "Centenarian Tells Tale of Historic Ruse," *The Lawton Constitution*, May 19, 1948.

⁴⁰ Hardcastle, *The Hoax, p. 5-6*.

⁴¹ Paul R. Petersen, "The True Account of William "Bloody Bill" Anderson," 2022, https://www.legendsofamerica.com/we-bloodybill/.

⁴² Richard S. Brownlee, *Grey Ghosts of the Confederacy: Guerrilla Warfare in the West, 1861-1865*, (LSU Press, 1983), p. 138.

⁴³ Paul R. Petersen, "Bloody Bill Anderson – Lies and Sensationalism," *The Hughes News,* October 2013, https://hughescamp.org.

⁴⁴ Hardcastle, *The Hoax*, p. 69.

⁴⁵ Cole Younger, The Story of Cole Younger, by Himself," (The Henneberry Company, 1903), p. 4.

⁴⁶ "In Search of History -Quantrlll's Raiders" (*History Channel Documentary*), youtube.com.

[47] Randolph H. McKim, D.D. discusses the cause of the Civil War, *The Photographic History of the Civil War in Ten Volumes: Francis Trevelyan Miller, Editor in Chief, Robert Sampson Lanier, Managing Editor*, (Review of Reviews Co., 1911).

[48] Frank Dalton, "Men of Quantrill," *The Crittenden Memoirs*, complied by H. H. Crittenden, G. P. Putnam's Son

[49] W. Todd Groce, *Mountain Rebels: East Tennessee Confederates and the Civil War, 1860-1870*, (Univ. Tennessee Press, 1999).

[50] "Shall Not Stay Here," *Brownlow's Knoxville Whig*, January 9, 1864.

[51] Jonathan Williams, *Legions of Satan, 1781.*

[52] Bill Federer, "The Bank War: Jackson v. Biddle," *American Minute, 2022*, https://myemail.constantcontact.com/THE-BANK-WAR---Jackson-v-Biddle.html

[53] Mayer Amschel Rothschild, "Mayer Amschel Rothschild famous quotes," *inspiringquotes.us*, 2024, https://www.inspiringquotes.us/author/3057-mayer-amschel-rothschild.

[54] Thomas Jefferson to Albert Gallatin on December 13, 1803, *Founders Online*, https://founders.archives.gov/documents/Jefferson/01-42-02-0100.

[55] Thomas Jefferson, "Thomas Jefferson Quotes," 2022, https://thefederalistpapers.org.

[56] VOLUBRJOTR, "I Killed The Bank ~ President Andrew Jackson," *POLITICAL VEL CRAFT – Veil of Politics*, 2019, https://politicalvelcraft.org/2013/07/24/i-killed-the-bank-president-andrew-jackson/.

[57] Federer, "The Bank War."

[58] Andrew Jackson, "Andrew Jackson Quotes," *AZQuotes*.com, Wind and Fly LTD, 2024. https://www.azquotes.com/author/19724-Andrew_Jackson.

[59] Bill Federer, "The Bank War-Great Evils To Our Country….from such a concentration of power in the hands of a few men" – Pres. Andrew Jackson, n.d., https://myemail.constantcontact.com/The-bank-war--great-evils-to-our-country---from-such-a-concentration-of-power-in-the-hands-of-a-few-men/.

[60] Andrew Jackson, "Andrew Jackson's Farewell Adress – 1837," *National Center for Public Policy Research*, 2001, https://nationalcenter.org/ncppr/2001/11/03/andrew-jacksons-farewell-address-1837/.

[61] Abraham Lincoln, "Abraham Lincoln Quotes", 2022, https://www.azquotes.com/author/8880-Abraham_Lincoln.

[62] Otto von Bismarck, "Otto von Bismarck Quotes," 2022. https://www.azquotes.com/quote/615228

[63] Rutherford, Judge Joseph Franklin Rutherford, "Vindication," (Watch Tower Bible and Tract Society and the International Bible Students Association, 1931).

[64] "Congress's Coinage Power," *Artl.S8.C5.1, The United States Constitution, Constitution Annotated – Analysis and Interpretation of the U.S. Constitution*, 2022, https://constitution.congress.gov.

[65] Lord Goschen, spokesman of the Financiers, who wrote the article in the London Times, 1865, "Chapter 49-The History of Banking Control in the United States," by Alain Pilote, Sept.-Oct. 1985 issue of the *Vers Demain Journal*. https://famguardian.org/Publications/InThisAgeOfPlenty/plenty49.htm.

66 "National Bank Act of 1863," 2019, https://www.encyclopedia.com/history/encyclopedias-almanacs-transcripts-and-maps/national-bank-act-1863.

67 Rothschild Brothers to Messrs. Ikleheimer, Morton and Vandergould (New York), June 25, 1863, in *Col. Edmund D. Taylor and Conspiracy Theory, by William R. Carr.* 2011. https://www.heritech.com/pridger/lincoln/lin-ken.htm.

68 "John Sherman," 2022, https://en.wikipedia.org.

69 Ibid.

70 James A. Garfield, "James A. Garfield Quotes," 2022, https://www.azquotes.com/author/5343-James_A_Garfield.

71 Senator Joseph McCarthy (Excerpt from a 1956 speech, "George Washington's Surrender"), *Judaized Christianity: Front for New World Order – Sen. McCarth*, by Yvonne Nachtigal, 2018, https://christianobserver.net/judaized-christianity-front-for-new-world-order-sen-mccarth/

72 "What Is Freemasonry," The Grand Lodge of Ohio, 2022, https://www.freemason.com/join/what-is-freemasonry).

73 The Editors of Encyclopaedia Britannica, "Freemasonry," *Britannica*, 2022, https://britannica.com/topic/Freemasonry.

74 Mason Locke Weems, *The Life of George Washington: With Curious Anecdotes, Equally Honorable to Himself and Exemplary to his Young Countrymen* (Philadelphia: Lippincott, 1800), Internet Archive edition, https://archive.org/details/lifeofgeorgewashweem.

75 "Religious views of George Washington," 2022, https://en.wikipedia.org.

76 "General Orders, 2 May 1778," *Founders Online*, National Archives, https://founders.archives.gov/documents/Washington/03-15-02-0016. [Original source: *The Papers of George Washington, Revolutionary War Series*, vo. 15, *May-June 1778*, ed. Edward G. Lengel. Charlottesville: University of Virginia Press, 2006, p. 13.]

77 "General Orders, 5 May 1778," *Founders Online*, National Archives, https://founders.archives.gov/documents/Washington/03-15-02-0039. [Original source: *The Papers of George Washington, Revolutionary War Series*, vo. 15, *May-June 1778*, ed. Edward G. Lengel. Charlottesville: University of Virginia Press, 2006, pp. 38-41.]

78 George Washington Parke Curtis, "The Man Who Could Not Be Killed," *Recollections and Private Memoirs of Washington*, Philadelphia, J.W. Bradley, 1859.

79 William Jackson Johnstone, *George Washington, the Christian*, (Kessinger Publishing, 2007).

80 "George Washington," 2022, https://en.wikipedia.org.

81 Thomas Jefferson, "Thomas Jefferson famous quotes," *inspiringquotes.us.* 2022. https://www.inspiringquotes.us/author/5016-thomas-jefferson.

82 Jon Meacham, *American Gospel: God, the Founding Fathers, and the Making of a Nation, (Random House Trade Paperbacks; Annotated edition, 2007).

[83] Thomas Jefferson, "Extract from Thomas Jefferson's Notes on the State of Virginia," *Th Jefferson-Monticello-Jefferson Quotes & Family Letters*, 2024. https://tjrs.monticello.org/letter/2355.

[84] Francis Fox, *Sweet Land of Liberty: The Ordeal of the American Revolution in Northampton*, 1925.

[85] Thomas Jefferson, *The Writings of Thomas Jefferson: Being His Autobiography, Correspondence, Reports, Messages, Addresses, and other Writings, Official and Private*, (Taylor & Maury, 1853-1854).

[86] "Scholars Challenge Jefferson-Hemings Allegations," *Science Insights, News and Commentary from The National Association of Scholars*, Volume 6, Issue 3, September 2001, https://www.tjheritage.org/scholars-challenge-jeffersonhemings-allegations/.

[87] John Robison, "Proofs of a Conspiracy," 1798.

[88] "To G. W. Snyder from George Washington, September 25, 1798, Founders Online, 2022, https://founders.archives.gov.

[89] "United States Declaration of Independence," 2022, https://en.m.wikipedia.com.

[90] "Jefferson's Religious Beliefs," Th. Jefferson Monticello, 2022, https://monticello.org.

[91] Clay Ouzts, "Georgia Guidestones," *New Georgia Encyclopedia*, 2022, https://www.georgiaencyclopedia.org/articles/history-archaeology/georgia-guidestones/.

[92] Hilarie M. Hicks, MA, "I Never Was a Mason: James Madison and Freemasonry," *James Madison's Montpelier, https://montpelier.org.*

[93] "Titles of Nobility Amendment," 2022, https://simple.m.wikipedia.org.

[94] Ibid.

[95] Emmett "Shkeme" Garcia, Storyteller from the Santa Ana Pueblo of New Mexico. "Indigenous Peoples' Day: Pueblo Revolt Story/Web Extra." *New Mexico PBS*, hosted by Antonia Gonzales, 2019. youtube.com.

[96] Edward P. Dozier, "Rio Grande Pueblos," Edward H. Spicer, ed., *Perspectives in American Indian Culture Change*, 1961.

[97] Hiram Martin Chittenden, *The American fur trade of the far west: a history of the pioneer trading posts and early fur companies of the Missouri Valley and the Rocky Mountains and of the overland commerce with Santa Fe*, Volume II & III, 1902.

[98] Ibid.

[99] Albert Pike, "Narrative of a Journey in the Prairie," from *Publication of The Arkansas Historical Association*, Edited by John Hugh Reynolds, Secretary, Vol. 4, Conway, Arkansas, 1917. (submitted by Dena Whitesell). 2007. https://genealogytrails.com/ark/historybook3.html.

[100] Ibid.

[101] *Territory and military department of New Mexico.* Library of Congress, Geography and Map Division – United States Army. Corps of Topographical Engineers, Cartographer, and William H. Dougal. [Washington, D.C.: War Departt, 1959] Map. https://www.loc.gov/item/2015591072/.

[102] Pike, "Narrative of a Journey in the Prairie."

[103] Ibid.

[104] Ibid.

[105] Ibid.

[106] Ibid.

[107] Albert Pike, *Prose Sketches and Poems, Written in the Western Country*, (Boston: Light & Horton, 1834), p. 170. 2022, Internet Archive, https://archive.org/details/prosesketchespoe00pike/mode/2up?q=Americans.

[108] Ibid.

[109] W. (William) Kemble, Texas and part of Mexico & the United States showing the route of the first Santa Fe expedition, map, 1844?; New York. (https://texashistory.unt.edu/ark:/67531/metapth192792/: accessed August 22, 2024). University of North Texas Libraries, The Portal to Texas History, https://texashistory.unt.edu: crediting University of Texas at Arlington Library.

[110] "Digging for Lost Treasure of Aztecs in Taylor County, North of Abilene," *Fort Worth Star-Telegram* – Fort Worth, Texas, November 17, 1907.

[111] Steve Wilson, "Two Maps May Hold Key To "Spider Rock" Gold," *Wichita Falls Times*, Wichita Falls, Texas, October 13, 1963.

[112] Frances Fuller Victor, "The American Fur Trade in the Far West," *The Quarterly of the Oregon Historical Society 3, no. 3 (1902): 261*. 2022, http://www.jstor.org/stable/20609534.

[113] J. H. Colton, Texas, map, 1855; New York. (https://texashistory.unt.edu/ark"/67531/metapth2437/: accessed August 22, 2024), *University of North Texas Libraries, The Portal to Texas History*, https://texashistory.unt.edu; crediting UNT Libraries Special Collections.

[114] Schrader, *Jesse James was One of His Names*, p. 192.
[115] Geoffrey Plant, "Plaza construction closures to extend into 2025," *Taos News*, June 22,2023.

[116] Randolph Barnes Marcy, 1812-1887. Topographical map of the road from Fort Smith Arks. To Santa Fe, N.M. and from Donna Anna N.M. to Fort Smith, map 1850 [Washington D.C.] (https://texashistory.unt.edu/ark:/67531/metapth190605/: accessed Auguts 22, 2024, University of North Texas Libraries, The Portal to Texas History, https://texashistory.unt.edu; crediting University of Texas at Arlington Library.

[117] Robin Cole-Jett, "Trails blazed by Randolph B. Marcy and Black Beaver in the Red River Valley," *Red River Historian, 2022, https://www.redriverhistorian.com/post/marcy-and-black-beaver-trails-red-river.*

[118] Map of Marcy's Exploration to Locate the Texas Indian Reservations, map, Date Unknown; (https://texashistory.unt.edu/ark:/67531/metapth493540/: accessed August 22, 2024), University of North Texas Libraries, The Portal to Texas History, https://texashistory.unt.edu; crediting Hardin-Simmons University Library.

[119] Ulysses S. Grant, "U.S. Grant, Memoir on the Mexican War" (1885), *America – A Narrative Story*, W.W.Norton and Company: Studyspace, 2022, https://www.wwnorton.com.

[120] Book of Moses, Chapter 7: 45-47, (December 1830), *The Church of Jesus Christ of Latter-Day Saints*, 2022, https://www.churchofjesuschrist.org/study/scriptures/pgp/moses/7?lang=eng.

[121] Albert Pike, *Morals and Dogma*, p. 13-14. (The Council, 1871), Internet Archive, 2022. https://archive.org/details/MoralsAndDogmaAlbertPikeTheCouncil1871.

[122] Robert L. Millet, "What Latter-day Saints Believe About Jesus Christ," 2001. Retrieved in 2022. https://newsroom.churchofjesuschrist.org/article/what-mormons-believe-about-jesus-christ.

[123] "Seer stone (Latter Day Saints)," 2022. https://en.wikipedia.org.

[124] "Divination," 2022. https://en.wikipedia.org.

[125] Richard Lyman Bushman, "Joseph Smith and Money Digging," 2022. https://rsc.byu.edu/sites/default/files/pub_content/pdf/Joseph_Smith_and_Money_Digging.pdf.

[126] Manly P. Hall, *Lectures On Ancient Philosophy*, p 433. (New York: Jeremy P. Tarcher/Penguin, a member of Penguin Group (USA) inc., 1929), Internet Archive, 2022, https://archive.org/details/ManlyP.HallLecturesOnAncientPhilosophy1929.

[127] Manly P. Hall, *The initiates of the flame*, p. 59-60. (Los Angeles, Calif., 1922), The Library of Congress. Internet Archive, 2022, https://archive.org/details/initiatesofflame00hall/mode/2up.

[128] "United States Capitol cornerstone laying," 2022, https://en.wikipedia.org.

[129] Horace Sykes, *Ancient Religious Traditions and Symbols In Freemasonry*, p. 9-10 , Internet Archive, 2022, https://archive.org/details/Ancient_Religious_Traditions_And_Symbols_-_H_Sykes.

[130] Archibald E. Roberts, *Emerging Struggle for State Sovereignty*, (Betsy Ross Press, 1979).

[131] "Lucifer vs. Satan, What's the Difference," 2023, https://thisvsthat.io/lucifer-vs-satan.

[132] Manly P. Hall, *Lost Keys of Masonry, The Legend of Hiram Abiff*, p. 76. (Hall Publishing Company, 1923), Internet Archive, 2022. https://archive.org/details/The.Lost.Keys.Of.Masonry.Manly.P.Hall.1923/mode/2up.

[133] Stewart Kabatebate, "Alice Bailey 10 Point Plan to Destroy Christianity," *Inspired Walk*, https://www.inspiredwalk.com/6297/alice-baileys-10-point-plan-to-destroy-christianity.

[134] R.H. (Robert Hamilton) Williams, *With the border ruffian: memories of the Far West, 1852-1868*, p. 3-4, (Lincoln: University of Nebraska Press, 1982), Internet Archive, 2022. https://archive.org/details/withborderruffi01willgoog.

[135] Jay Longley and Colin Eby. "Knights of the Golden Circle. 2022. https://knightsofthegoldencircle.webs.com. (No longer active as of 2024).

[136] John Quincy Adams, https://secure.understandingprejudice.org/slavery/presinfo.php?president=6.

[137] "John C. Calhoun." 2022. https://en.wikipedia.org.

[138] William Head Coleman, "Historical Sketch Book and Guide to New Orleans and Environs," 1885.

[139] Harry Quinn, "96-Year-Old Frank Dalton Recalls Moving Missouri Capital to Marshall," *The Marshall News Messenger,* Marshall, Texas, August 13, 1944.

[140] "The Golden Circle and the Pacific Republic," *Daily National Democrat*, Marysville, California, February 13, 1861.

[141] "The Knights of the Golden Circle," *The Randolph Citizen*, Huntsville, Missouri, April 20, 1860.

[142] Geo. Bickley, K.G.C., President American Legion, letter to the Kentucky Legislature, *Daily Missouri Republican*, June 4, 1861.

[143] "Mysterious Revelations, From the Louisville Journal. The Order of the Knights of the Golden Circle," *The Wyandot Pioneer,* Upper Sandusky, Ohio, August 23, 1861 – Chronicling America: Historic American Newspaper, Lib. Of Congress. 2022, https://chroniclingamerica.loc.gov.

[144] "Knights of the Golden Circle-Frederick Court Before U.S. Commissioner White – Examination of Witnesses," *Daily Ohio Stateman*, Columbus, Ohio, October 18, 1861.

[145] "Astounding Developments before the United States Grand Jury; A Secret Society of Traitors in Indiana. In the District Court of the United States, for the district of Indiana, May Term, 1862." *Daily Missouri Republican*, St. Louis, Missouri, August 6, 1862.

[146] "Genesis Chapter 1st," *The St. Joseph Herald*, St. Joseph, Missouri, January 15, 1863.

[147] "Gold," 2022. https://www.symbols.com/symbol/gold.

[148] Frank Dalton, "Outlawry in Missouri," *The Crittenden Memoirs*, 1936, p. 367.

[149] Mack Robertson, "Ex-Member of Dalton Gang Talks of Wide Experiences Here," *The Kilgore Daily News*, Kilgore, Texas, October 13, 1939.

[150] H.D. Quigg, "Latest, 'Real' Jesse James Declares $2 million in Loot Cached Away in Mountains of Oklahoma", *The Austin Statesman*, Austin, Texas, January 10, 1950.

[151] "Jay Gould," 2022, https://. en.wikipedia.org.

[152] "The Sheets Murderers," *Gallatin Democrat* – date unknown, c.1869-1870, in Bud Hardcastle's personal collection.

[153] Byron Buzbee, "Last of Quantrell's Raiders, Now Living in Corpus Christi, Plans to Enter the Movies," *Corpus Christi Times,* Corpus Christi, Texas, June 30, 1939.

[154] "Frank James. His Trial Begins at Gallatin. Large Crowd in Attendance – Much Interest Felt." The Lexington Intelligencer, Lexington, Missouri, August 25, 1883, 2023, https://chroniclingamerica.loc.gov.

[155] Hardcastle, *The Hoax*, p. 14.

[156] James (Howk), *Jesse James and the Lost Cause,* p. 47.

[157] Schrader, *Jesse James Was One of His Names*, p. 160.

[158] J.A. Rogers, *Ku Klux Spirit,* Lushena Books, *2021.*

[159] Jack Hurst, *Nathan Bedford Forrest: A Biography* (Vintage Civil War Library), Vintage, Reprint edition, 2011.

[160] "Nathan Bedford Forrest," 2023, https://en.wikipedia.org.

161 Frank Dalton, "John Younger," Crittenden Memoirs, 1936.

162 "Man Passes on Memories of Frank, Jesse James," *Wichita Falls Times*, Wichita Falls, Texas, Dec. 19, 1982.

163 "Many Wichitans Recall Frank James Noted Bandit," *Wichita Weekly Times*, Wichita Falls, Texas, February 26, 1915.

164 Hardcastle, *The Hoax*, p, 18.

165 Ibid, p. 108.

166 Garland R. Farmer, "Frank Dalton Finds Peace." *Houston Chronicle Magazine*, March 28, 1948.

167 Kathy Alexander, "Belle Starr – The Bandit Queen," *Legends of America*, 2022, https://www.legendsofamerica.com/we-bellestarr/.

168 "Texas Horseback Wedding of the Long Ago. The Principals Were Cole Younger and Belle Starr, According to Mike Harrington of Fort Smith," St. Louis Globe-Democrat, March 15, 1903.

169 "Cravens "John Alva" Shirley," *Find a Grave*, 2023, https://www,findagrave.com/memorial/80248879/cravens-shirley.

170 Phillip W. Steele, *Starr Tracks: Belle and Pearl Starr*, Pelican Publishing Co., 1989
171 Hardcastle, *The Hoax*, p. 91.

172 Kathy Weiser-Alexander, "Jesse James Timeline," *Legends of America*, 2021 – www.legendsofamerica.com/we-jessejamestimeline/.

173 "Hite Family," Roots web by Patricia. Date unknown.

174 Hardcastle, The *Hoax*, p. 19.

175 Ibid, p. 19-20.

176 Schrader, *Jesse James Was One of His Names*, p. 153.

177 Bill Caldwell, "Belle Starr Was Her Own Woman," *The Joplin Globe*, Feb. 29, 2020.

178 "Kerry's Confession, Details of the Otterville Train Robbery, The James Boys and the Youngers in the Lead*," The Western Spirit,* August 18, 1876.

179 "The Train Robbers, A Pair of them Arrested in Cherokee County, Kansas." *The Atchison Daily Champion*, August 8, 1876.

180 "The Late Express Robbery, Bacon Montgomery's Account of It , Together with His Views, Based on a Variety of Evidence." *Columbus Courier*, September 7, 1876.

181 "The Younger Brothers," *The Bismarck Tribune*, Bismarck, North Dakota, April 28, 1893.

182 Interview with Sam Campbell by Bud Hardcastle, relating the story of Tilden Cramp.

183 Hardcastle, *The Hoax*, p. 18-19.

¹⁸⁴ Kathryn "Katie" E. (Vann) Brown from Porter, Oklahoma interviewed by Samuel G. Campbell from Fayetteville, Arkansas, January 23, 1950.

¹⁸⁵ "Younger's Bend," *Tulsa Weekly Democrat,* July 26, 1901.

¹⁸⁶ Bennett (Bennie) Patty (Mrs. William Tipton Patty) of Porum, Oklahoma, interviewed by Samuel G. Campbell from Fayetteville, Arkansas, November 25, 1949.

¹⁸⁷ Col. Charles W. Mooney, "Doctor In Belle Starr Country," The Century Press, Oklahoma City, Oklahoma; 1975.

¹⁸⁸ Ibid., p. 214-215.

¹⁸⁹ Ibid., p. 280-281.

¹⁹⁰ Frank Dalton, as told to Garland Farmer. "Belle Starr Was Noted Outlaw of Early West," *St. Joseph New Press*, Jan. 21, 1940.

¹⁹¹ "Fort Abercrombie State Historic Site – History," *State Historical Society of North Dakota*, 2024, https://www.history.nd.gov/historicsites/abercrombie/abercrombiehistory.html.

¹⁹² "Battle of the Washita River," 2023," https://www.en.wikipedia.

¹⁹³ J. Weston Phippen, "Kill Every Buffalo You Can! Every Buffalo Dead Is an Indian Gone," *The Atlantic*, 2020. https://www.theatlantic.com/national/archive/2016/05/the-buffalo-killers/482349.

¹⁹⁴ Kathy Weiser, "Fort Abraham Lincoln, North Dakota," *Legends of America*, 2020 https://www.legendsofamerica.com/nd-fortabrahamlincoln/

¹⁹⁵ Anita Lindsay, *From Pioneers to Progress,"* 1957, p. 4-5.

¹⁹⁶ "Fort Sill," *Cowley County Historical Society Museum*, Winfield, Cowley County, Kansas. 2023. www.cchsm.com/resources/misc/wortman_cc/fort_sill.html.

¹⁹⁷ Ibid.

¹⁹⁸ "Wild Bill Hickok," https://en.wikipedia.org.

¹⁹⁹ "Buffalo Bill," https,://en.wikipedia.org.

²⁰⁰ "Cherokee By Blood," *Records of Eastern Cherokee Ancestry in the U.S. Court of Claims 1906-1910, Vol. 3;* Applications 4201 to 7250, Compiled by Jerry Wright Jordan.

²⁰¹ "Federal Link Found in Bombing," *The Daily Oklahoman*, September 14, 1992.

²⁰² Steve Wilson, *Oklahoma Treasures and Treasure Tales,* 1989.

²⁰³ "To Be Avoided. Detectives and Desperadoes. The James Boys and Pinkerton's Detectives – Both Factions Are Daring, Desperate And Lawless," *The Indiana State Sentinel*, May 13,1875.

²⁰⁴ Wikipedia contributors, "Battle of the Little Bighorn," *Wikipedia, The Free Encyclopedia*, 2023, https://www.en.wikipedia.org.

²⁰⁵ Ibid.

[206] "Exceptionally Rare Indian Used Custer Battlefield 1874 Sharps Rifle," January 20, 2017, *Old West Events,* 2023, https://www.oldwestevents.com/highlights/tag/Little+Bighorn.

[207] Wikipedia contributors, "5th Cavalry Regiment," *Wikipedia, The Free Encyclopedia,* 2023, https://en.wikipedia.org.

[208] "The Terrifying Collapse of the Plains American Indians," *History Dose,* https://www.youtube.com/watch?v=2qxvePKBjP4.

[209] James (Howk), *Jesse James and the Lost Cause,* p. 134.

[210] Ibid, p. 131.

[211] Hardcastle, *The Hoax,* p. 21.

[212] Wikipedia contributors, "James-Younger Gang," *Wikipedia, The Free Encyclopedia,* 2023, https://en.wikipedia.org.

[213] Ibid.

[214] Wikipedia contributors, "General Order No. 28," *Wikipedia, The Free Encyclopedia,* 2023, https://en.wikipedia.org.

[215] Wikipedia contributors, "Benjamin Butler," *Wikipedia, The Free Encyclopedia,* 2023, https://en.wikipedia.org.

[216] Michelle Greene, "Go Wide: How Far Can Horses Jump Horizontally?" *Horse Rookie,* 2023, https://horserookie.com/how-far-horses-jump-horizontally/

[217] "Tommy Jake Chrestman," *El Paso Times,* May 13,1986.

[218] Kay L. Johnston to Bud Hardcastle, Date Unknown.

[219] Jess DeHaven, "Psychic views ability to 'see' as way to help," – Psychic predictions, *St. Joseph News-Press,* Nov 3, 1995.

[220] Alonzo Weston, "Research team takes paranormal seriously," *St. Joseph News-Press,* October 26, 2003.

[221] Buzbee, "Last of Quantrell's Raiders", *Corpus Christi Times,* June 30, 1939.

[222] "Versatile Vet," *Tyler Morning Telegraph,* January 22, 1948.

[223] Hardcastle, *The Hoax,* p. 12.

[224] Kathy Alexander, "Fort Sidney," *Legends of America,* 2023, https://www.legendsofamerica.com/fort-sidney/

[225] "M'Alester's Cattle Nearly Cost Life," *The Daily Oklahoman,* Jan. 11, 1920.

[226] Hardcastle, *The Hoax,* p. 11.

[227] Ibid., p. 219.

[228] Ibid., p. 112.

[229] Buzbee, "Last of Quantrell's Raiders", *Corpus Christi Times,* June 30, 1939.

[230] "Needle Guns," *The Galveston Daily News*, June 12, 1874.

[231] "Camp Colorado, Texas," *Texas Escapes*, www.texasescapes.com.

[232] Edgar Rye, *The Quirt and the Spur*, Vanishing Shadows of the Texas Frontier, 1909, p. 320.

[233] Ibid.

[234] "Masterson's Death Brings Recollections," *Amarillo Daily News*, November 21, 1921.

[235] "A Necessity," *The Snyder Signal*, Sept. 05, 1919.

[236] "Monument to Mark U.S. Fort, Shaft to Be Erected At Camp Colorado in Coleman County," *Abilene Reporter-News*, July 9, 1936.

[237] Beatrice Grady Gay, "Camp Colorado," *Handbook of Texas Online. TSHA, Texas State Historical Association*, Published 1952, updated 2019. Accessed 2023. https://www.tshaonline.org/handbook/entries/camp-colorado.

[238] Wikipedia contributors, "6th Texas Cavalry Regiment," *Wikipedia, The Free Encyclopedia*, 2023, https://en.wikipedia.org.

[239] J. Frank Dobie, "Indian Tales Lured Fortune Hunters On-Dobie Tells," *The Austin American*, September 17, 1931.

[240] Intercepted Letter from Jesse J., *The Kansas City Times*, April 3, 1882.

[241] Major William Redwood Price to AAG February 5, 1874, Letters Received, Department of New Mexico, courtesy National Archives. From *The Horrell Wars: Feuding in Texas and New Mexico* by David Johnson, 2014.

[242] Rick Miller, *Texas Ranger John B. Jones and the Frontier Battalion, 1874-1881*, 2012.

[243] Trooper John Mapp, "The Civil War Continues. The Buffalo Soldiers and Texas Rangers," *The New Buffalo Soldiers, Your History; Number 5: Texas Rangers*, accessed 2023, https://abuffalosoldier.com/yh5rangers.htm#footnote5.

[244] "Coleman Pioneer Recalls Concho As An Army Post." *The San Angelo Weekly Standard*, February 9, 1940.

[245] Miller, *Texas Ranger John B. Jones*, p. 172.

[246] Ibid., p. 173.

[247] Ibid., p. 181.

[248] Mrs. E.D. McCormick, "Early History of Dresden," *The Navarro County Scroll*, 1956. 2023. https://txnavarr.genealogyvillage.com/towns/dresden/early_history_of_dresden.htm.

249 "Waco. News of the Day Gathered by a Statesman Reporter," *Austin American-Statesman*, April 8 & 10, 1883.

250 James B. Gillett, *Six years with the Texas Rangers, 1875 to 1881,* 1925. Internet Archive. https://archive.org/details/sixyearswithtex00gill. p. 69.

251 Ibid. p. 10.

252 Jesse James, Letter to the editor of *The Clipper-Herald, Hannibal, Missouri.* The letter was postmarked in Brownwood, Texas. From the Pen of Jesse James. "Brownwood, The Hardest Town in Texas," November 7, 1879. *The St. Joseph Weekly Gazette*, November 20, 1879.

253 Ed Brice, "Booth," *Fort Worth Star-Telegram*, March 6, 1984.

254 "Texas News via Kansas," *The Galveston Daily News*, October 23, 1869.

255 James (Howk), *Jesse James and the Lost Cause*, p. 134-135.

256 "Texas Ku Klux Member Speaks," Dallas Newspaper, 1944.

257 James (Howk), *Jesse James and the Lost Cause*, p. 138.

258 Schrader, *Jesse James was one of His Names*, p. 191.

259 Wikipedia contributors, "Lucien Maxwell," *Wikipedia, The Free Encyclopedia*, 2023, https://en.wikipedia.org.

260 Stephen Zimmer, *For Good Or Bad: People of the Cimarron Country,*"1999, p. 62.

261 Ibid., p. 75.

262 James (Howk), *Jesse James and the Lost Cause*, p. 14.

263 "Lex Johnston named head of Dallas bank," *Brownwood Bulletin*, Nov. 29, 1977.

264 Les Johnston, "Pioneer had outlaw past," Brownwood Bulletin, January 02, 1977.

265 William Shive, "Coggin Brothers," *Handbook of Texas Online*, 1994, updated 2020, accessed 2023, https://www.tshaonline.org/handbook/entries/coggin-brothers.

266 Hardcastle, *The Hoax,* p. 44.

267 Wikipedia contributors, "Daniel Baker College," *Wikipedia, The Free Encyclopedia*, 2023, https://en.wikipedia.org.

268 "Henry Ford Rose From Unknown Youth To Outstanding Leader," *Brownwood Bulletin*, April 8, 1956.

269 Hardcastle, *The Hoax*, p. 68-69.

270 "James Russell Davis, 109, Civil War Veteran, Dies," *Evening Star*, March 14, 1950.

271 "Civil War Vet Dies at Age of 109 After Amazing Life Story," *The Ada Weekly News*, March 16, 1950.

272 "108- year-Old Man Renews License To Drive Own Car," *The Tennessean*, June 16, 1949.

273 "Jesse James' Son Will Fight for His Name," *Austin-American Statesman*, January 1950.

274 "109-Year Oldster Can Recall Days of Indian Wars," *Nashville Banner*, Oct. 1, 1949.

275 Hardcastle, The *Hoax*, p. 12.

276 "The 1861 Jayhawker raid in Osceola," *Missouri Life*, 2023. https://missourilife.com/the-1861-jayhawker-raid-in-osceola/.

277 "Bill" Anderson, The Guerilla, Still Alive, Texas Paper Says," *The Missourian*, May 22, 1924.

278 James (Howk), *Jesse James and the Lost Cause*, p. 136.

279 "History of HPU Presidents," *Howard Payne University*, 2024. https://www.hputx.edu/our-story/history/history-of-hpu-presidents/.

280 Hardcastle, The Hoax, p. 108-109.

281 Wikipedia contributors, "Baphomet," *Wikipedia, The Free Encyclopedia*, 2023, https://en.wikipedia.org.

282 Edwards, *Billy The Kid*, introduction XXII.

283 Hardcastle, *The Hoax*, p. 179.

284 Edwards, *Billy The Kid*, p. 4.

285 Mitch Graves' conversation with Bud Hardcastle, June, 2000.

286 Hardcastle, *The Hoax*, p. 138.

287 Edwards, *Billy The Kid*, p. 7.

288 Lee A. Silva, "Elfego Baca: Forgotten Fighter For Law and Order," *America – The Men and Their Guns That Made Her Great*, edited by Craig Boddington, 1981, p. 97.

289 Wikipedia contributors, "Silver City, New Mexico," *Wikipedia, The Free Encyclopedia*, 2023, https://en.wikipedia.org.

290 Silva, "Elfego Baca," p. 98.

291 Ibid. p. 95.

292 Schrader, *Jesse James was One of His Names*, p. 192.

293 "Denies Garrett Shot, Killed Billy The Kid," *El Paso Times*, November 10, 1937.

294 "Ex-Bad Man Scoffs At Idea Billy The Kid Is Alive," *The Paris News*, June 23, 1938.

295 Harry E. Chrisman, *Lost Trails of the Cimarron*, 1961, p. 182.

296 Mary Standifer, "Concho County," *Handbook of Texas Online*, 1952, updated 2020, accessed 2023, https://www.tshaonline.org/handbook/entries/concho-county. -And- Julia Cauble Smith, "Concho River,"

Handbook of Texas Online, 1952, updated 2020, accessed 2023, https://www.tshaonline.org/handbook/entries/concho-river.

[297] Wikipedia contributors, "Fort Griffin," *Wikipedia, The Free Encyclopedia*, 2023, https://en.wikipedia.org.

[298] Edwards, *Billy the Kid*, intro. p. xxiv.

[299] Frank M. King, *Wranglin' the Past*, 1946, p. 155.

[300] Ibid.

[301] Robert M. Utley, *Billy the Kid, A Short and Violent Life*, 1989, Photo section, #18. "John Simpson Chisum" cited (Special Collections, University of Arizona Library).

[302] Edwards, *Billy The Kid*, p. 27.

[303] Utley, *Billy The Kid, A Short and Violet Life*, p.108.

[304] Ibid.

[305] Ibid., p. 109.

[306] Elmo Scott Watson, "He Dined With Jesse James and Billy the Kid!" *Okeene Record*, March 6, 1930.

[307] "Who Can Tell?" *Galena Miner*, November 9, 1879.

[308] "Jesse James," *Chariton Courier*, November 8, 1879.

[309] "Jesse James Heard From. A Remarkable Letter." *The Ouachita Telegraph*. Monroe, Louisianna. December 12, 1879.

[310] "Louis John Lull," Find A Grave.com.

[311] "The Quiet, But Mysterious Boarder Was Jesse James," *St. Louis Post-Dispatch*, June 30, 1902.

[312] "Callaway Farmer, Host to Jesse James, Is Now 88 and Retired," *The Mexico Ledger*, Mexico, Missouri, May 21, 1948.

[313] Wikipedia contributors, "Thomas Theodore Crittenden," *Wikipedia, The Free Encyclopedia*, 2023, https://en.wikipedia.org.

[314] Hon. F. C. Farr, "Thomas Theodore Crittenden," *Distinguished American Lawyers: with their struggles and triumphs in the forum by Henry W. Scott. Charles L. Webster & Company, 1891.*

[315] Hardcastle, *The Hoax*, p. 32.

[316] Jay Donald, *Outlaws of the Border: a complete and authentic history of the lives of Frank and Jesse James, the Younger brothers, and their robber companions, including Quantrell and his noted guerrillas,"1882, p. 442.*

[317] William R. Denslow, *$10,000 Famous Freemasons*, Macoy Publishing & Masonic Supply Co., Inc. 1957.

[318] Video of William Tunstill and Ola Everhard on March 6, 1956. In Bud's personal collection.

[319] "Four Who Searched for Jesse James' Hidden Treasure in Ohio Stop Here," *Joplin Globe*, March 18, 1949.

[320] Dickson Terry, "Still Insists He's Jesse James," *The Everyday Magazine, St. Louis Post-Dispatch*, November 27, 1949.

[321] "Sheriff Timberlake Dead," *The Kansas City Times*, February 21, 1891.

[322] "Another Thomason Is To Be Sheriff of Clay County," *The Kansas City Star*, August 18, 1940.

[323] Hardcastle, The Hoax, p. 34.

[324] Ibid., p. 33.

[325] Rev. Dr. Flack to Dr. M. Munford, *The Kansas City Times*, April 12, 1882.

[326] "Jesse James Funeral," *Henry County Democrat*, April 13, 1882.

[327] Ibid.

[328] Hardcastle, *The Hoax*, p. 36.

[329] "A James Boy's story." *Atchison Daily Patriot*, April 7, 1882.

[330] "Ex-Sheriff Dead," *The Chillicothe Constitution-Tribune*, February 22, 1891.

[331] Schrader, *Jesse James was One of His Names*, p. 16.

[332] "Who Carved This Brick?" *St. Joseph News-Press*, July 12, 1967.

[333] "Services Monday for shooting victim," *St. Joseph News Press*, November 11, 1979.

[334] Dr. W. D. Chesney, "Who Lies Buried in Jesse Grave?" Date Unknown, in Bud Hardcastle's personal collection.

[335] "Bob Ford Again," *Austin American-Statesman*, September 25, 1884.

[336] "Bob Ford and Dick Liddle Have got Orders to Go," *El Paso Times*, September 27, 1884.

[337] "Board of Pardons," The Democrat-Herald, Date Unknown.

[338] "Bob Ford Killed," *St. Louis Globe-Democrat*, June 9, 1892

[339] "Edward Capehart O'Kelley," *Find a Grave, 2024.*

[340] Ex-Sheriff Dead," *The Chillicothe Constitution-Tribune*, February 22, 1891.

[341] "T.T. Crittenden, Ex-Governor of Missouri, Dies," *St. Louis Post-Dispatch*, May 29, 1909.

[342] Hardcastle, *The Hoax*, p. 177.

[343] Ibid.

[344] Robertus Love, Title unidentifiable, *St. Louis Post-Dispatch*, June 30, 1902.

[345] "Affidavits Submitted To Verify Outlaw's Claim," *Lawton News-Review*, May 20, 1948.

[346] "Booming Bowie," *Fort Worth Daily Gazette*, May 12, 1884.

[347] "Robert B. Anderson: Papers, 1933-89, Dwight Eisenhower Library, Abilene, Kansas, 2004.

[348] Betty Whitton, "Orr," https://ghosttowns.com/ste/ok/orr.html.

[349] Jack Hartsfield, "Outlaw's Kin Says Death Faked" and "James' Death Faked, Kin Says," Lubbock Avalanche, Sept. 1983)

[350] "Lee McMurtry, In Last Sleep, Fought with Quantrill and Jess James. Dies Here." *Wichita Daily Times*. Wichita Falls, Texas, June 23, 1908.

[351] Sheriff "Lee" Boon McMurtry, *Fort Worth Star Telegram*, July 5, 1908.

[352] "Where lies Jesse James? Some say in Granbury, where he died in 1951," *Dallas Times Herald*, Nov. 13, 1983.

[353] "James I. McDaniel." *The Oklahoma State Capital,* July 13, 1900.

[354] Linda D. Wilson. "Fraternal Orders." *The Encyclopedia of Oklahoma History and Culture*. 2010. Accessed 2023. https://www.okhistory.org/publications/enc/entry?entry=FR007.

[355] Wikipedia contributors, "Guthrie, Oklahoma," *Wikipedia, The Free Encyclopedia*, 2023, https://en.wikipedia.org.

[356] R. Darcy, "The Oklahoma Territorial Legislature: 1890-1905." *Oklahoma State University*. Accessed 2023. https://docslib.org/doc/3939504/the-oklahoma-territorial-legislature-1890-1905.

[357] Wikipedia contributors, "World's Columbian Exposition," *Wikipedia, The Free Encyclopedia*, Accessed 2023, https://en.wikipedia.

[358] George McGrath, *The National Police Gazette.* August 1950.

[359] Thomas L. Hedglen, "Meridian," *The Encyclopedia of Oklahoma History and Culture*, 2010. Accessed 2023. https://www.okhistory.org/publications/enc/entry?entry=ME015.

[360] Schrader, *Jesse James Was One of His Names*, p. 90.

[361] Ibid., p. 90-91.

[362] Ibid., p. 179.

[363] James (Howk), *Jesse James and the Lost Cause, p. 129.*

[364] Effie S. Jackson, "An Interview With Red Orrington Lucas, Territorial Deputy United States Marshal, 1882-1902," Interview #12571, Oklahoma and Indian Territory, Indian and Pioneer Historical Collection, 1937. *OU University Libraries, Islandora Repository/Indian-Pioneer Papers*, Dec. 29, 1937. p. 13. https://repository.ou.edu/islandora.

[365] Ibid. p. 15-16.

366 Lulu Anthis Pritchett, "Fred Raymond Anthis Family," Logan County Historical Society book.

367 "Old Document Reveals More About Life of Jesse James," *Garvin County Advocate*, Pauls Valley, Oklahoma, January 30 ? - Affidavit of Orrington Red Lucas, Franklin County, Missouri; July 6, 1950.

368 "Four Who Searched for Jesse James' Hidden Treasure in Ohio Stops Here," *Joplin Globe*, March 18, 1949.

369 Robert Byers, 'Not Shot by Ford, Jesse James Died in 1950, Says Old Friend," *Denver Post*, Nov. 18, 1954.

370 "116-Year-Old Negro to Get Doctor Study," *Seminole Producer*, Nov. 1, 1954.

371 Hardcastle, *The Hoax*, p. 47.

372 Dan R. Conway, "Calamity Jane – Unique Character of Old Frontier," *The Bozeman Courier*, Oct 08, 1926.

373 "Jewish Pioneers of Ardmore, Ada, and Lehigh in South Central, Oklahoma," Ardmore – Accessed 2023. https://www.jmaw.org/jewish-oklahoma.

374 Mark Hilton, "Daube's Store," www.hmdb.org/m.asp?m=142482.

375 "Samuel and David Daube," *Ancestry.com*. Military Intelligence, U.S. Subject Index to Correspondence and Case Files of the immigration and Naturalization Service, 1903-1959, August 12, 1941. Ref. 56,078-721.

376 "Temple to Be Opened Southern Oklahoma Citizens Cordially Invited to Attend," *The Daily Ardmoreite*, October 19, 1930.

377 Kathy Alexander, "Old West Outlaw List" – "Sam Green," *Legends of America*, 2023. https://www.legendsofamerica.com/outlaw-list-g/.

378 The story of Sam Green killing Sheriff Bullard, *Woodward Bulletin* – July 4, 1902.

379 "Got Their Man," The Daily Oklahoman, May 26, 1906.

380 "Murder!" *The Cheyene Sunbeam*, July 4, 1902.

381 "A Tussle With Casey's Gang," *The Norman Transcript*, August 14, 1902.

382 "After a Long Chase, Sam Green, an Alleged Murderer, is Taken in British Columbia," *The Guthrie Daily Leader*, May 25, 1906.

383 "Got Their Man," The Daily Oklahoman, May 26, 1906.

384 "Double Killing of Officers An Early Sensation," *Elk City Daily News*, August 29, 1935.

385 A.W. Neville: Backward Glances, "Frank Dalton Lives One Hundred Years," *The Paris News*, March 9, 1948.

386 Schrader, "Jesse James Was One of His Names." P. 162.

387 Hardcastle, *The Hoax*, p. 63.

[388] "Boer Wars," *New World Encyclopedia*, https://www.newworldencyclopedia.org/entry/Boer_Wars.

[389] Edwards, "Billy The Kid," p. 94.

[390] Ibid.

[391] Ibid., p. 95.

[392] Schrader, *Jesse James Was One of His Names*, p. 129.

[393] Ibid., p. 130.

[394] Wikipedia contributors, "Porfirio Diaz," *Wikipedia, The Free Encyclopedia*, Accessed 2023, https://en.wikipedia.org.

[395] James (Howk), *Jesse James and the Lost Cause*, p. 182.

[396] Edwards, *Billy The Kid*, p. 103.

[397] Ibid., p. 134.

[398] "James Boys' Mother Dead." *The Washington Post*, February 11, 1911.

[399] Edwards, *Billy The Kid*, p. 103.

[400] Schrader, *Jesse James was One of His Names*, p. 129.

[401] Neville, "Frank Dalton Lives One Hundred Years."

[402] Hardcastle, *The Hoax*, p. 80-81.

[403] Ibid., p. 80.

[404] "Loans & Bonds – Brief History of World War Two Advertising Campaigns War Loans and Bonds," *Duke University Libraries*, https://blogs.library.duke.edu/digital-collections/adaccess/guide/wwii/bonds-loans/.

[405] "Chihuahua, Treasure House of Mexico, Largest State Rich in All Resources; Development Fast," *El Paso Herald,* June 17, 1922.

[406] Schrader, *Jesse James was One of His Names*, p. 68.

[407] Ibid., p. 82.

[408] Ibid.

[409] Ibid., p. 195.

[410] Ibid., p. 132.

[411] Leon C. Metz, "Garrett, Patrick Floyd Jarvis (1850-1908)," 1952, updated 2019. *Handbook of Texas Online.* Texas State Historical Association. Accessed 2023. https://www.tshaonline.org/handbook/entries/garrett-patrick-floyd-jarvis.

[412] James (Howk), *Jesse James and the Lost Cause*, p. 129.

[413] Don Hedgpeth, *They Rode Good Horses: The First Fifty Years of the American Quarter Horse Association*, 1990.

[414] Wikipedia contributors, "Oklahoma Panhandle," *Wikipedia, The Free Encyclopedia*, Accessed 2023, https://en.wikipedia.org.

[415] H. Allen Anderson, "Arrington, George Washington," *Handbook of Texas Online*, Texas State Historical Association. Accessed 2023, https://www.tshaonline.org/handbook/entries/arrington-george-washington.

[416] Harrison Trow sells 8,640 acres to Sandy Murchison, *Fort Worth Record-Telegram*, March 27, 1920.

[417] "College Given Land Valued At $16,000," Fort Worth Star-Telegram, Dec. 15, 1925.

[418] Schrader, *Jesse James Was One of His Names*, p. 191.

[419] "Death's Door, It is Suddenly Opened for Daniel H. Askew by an Unknown Hand," *The Kansas City Times*, April 14, 1875.

[420] "Company Towns: 1880s to 1935" *VCU Libraries, Social Welfare History Project*. Housing, Labor, Programs, Accessed 2024. https://socialwelfare.library.vcu.edu/programs/housing/company-towns-1890s-to-1935/.

[421] "Buckskin Joe" Returns; City Seems Like Dream," *The Daily Oklahoman*, January 2, 1915.

[422] "Buckskin Joe." A Partner of Captain Payne, the Noted Oklahoma Boomer, and His Great Scheme," *Fort Worth Daily Gazette*, April 1, 1887.

[423] "Navajoe Established," *The Mangum Daily Star*, October 13, 1937.

[424] Argus Dickerson, "Greer County," *The Gould Democrat*, January 28, 1932.

[425] Argus Dickerson, "Greer County," *The Gould Democrat*, January 21, 1932.

[426] Marilyn Bennion, Joanne Linford, and Elna Nelson, daughters of Wayne and Elna, "Joseph Spaulding Works." Accessed 2024. www.familysearch.org.

[427] "Death of Bob James Ends Life Of Pioneer," *Oklahoma Democrat*, August 14, 1913.

[428] "Navajo Picturesque," *Mangum Daily Star*, Nov. 16, 1932.

[429] Schrader, *Jesse James Was One of His Names*, p. 191.

[430] Ibid.

[431] "New Officers Elected For Commandery," *The Altus Times,* December 19, 1912.

[432] H. Allen Anderson, "Big Die-Up," *Handbook of Texas Online*, Accessed 2024, https://www.tshaonline.org/handbook/entries/big-die-up.

[433] Ruth Geraldine (Smith) Wilcoxson and Rosanne Priddy. *The Would-Be Pioneers*, 2011.

[434] "A.M. James, 75, Rites in Dalhart," *The Amarillo Globe-Times*, March 4, 1958.

⁴³⁵ Darley Newman, "Steeldusts on the Chisholm Trail," *True West Magazine*, 2011. Accessed 2024. https://truewestmagazine.com/article/steeldusts-on-the-chisholm-trail/.

⁴³⁶ James (Howk), *Jesse James and the Lost Cause*, p. 39.

⁴³⁷ Schrader, *Jesse James was One of His Names*, p. 28.

⁴³⁸ Robertus Love, A story told by Captain James Daniel Koger (1845-1926), "The Rise and Fall of Jesse James," *Tulsa World*, August 28, 1925.

⁴³⁹ Hardcastle, *The Hoax*, p.24.

⁴⁴⁰ Ibid., p. 25.

⁴⁴¹ Ibid., p. 66.

⁴⁴² "John Thomas Tatum Sr.," *Fisher Funeral Home*- https: www.fisherfh.net.

⁴⁴³ James (Howk), *Jesse James and the Lost Cause*, p. 161.

⁴⁴⁴ Whitten, "Centenarian Tells Tale of Historic Ruse."

⁴⁴⁵ W. D. Van Blarcom, "Best Pistol Shot Visits City," *Fort Worth Star-Telegram*, February 14, 1930.

⁴⁴⁶ "Bob Goss Takes Position With Texas Rangers," *The Kilgore Herald*, November 22, 1936.

⁴⁴⁷ "The Cole Younger-Frank James Wild West Shows," *The Stroud Star*, September 18, 1903.

⁴⁴⁸ Hardcastle, *The Hoax*, p. 15-16.

⁴⁴⁹ "Where lies Jesse James? Some say in Granbury, where he died in 1951," *Dallas Times Herald*, Nov. 13, 1983.

⁴⁵⁰ "The Great Louisiana Purchase Exposition," St. Joseph News-Press, April 29, 1904.

⁴⁵¹ Hon. Murat Halstead, *Pictorial History of the Louisiana Purchase and the World's Fair At St. Louis*, 1904, p. 203-204.

⁴⁵² "Many Detectives Arrive," *The St. Louis Republic*, April 26, 1904.

⁴⁵³ "Days of Wooly Wild West," *The St. Louis Republic*, July 31, 1904.

⁴⁵⁴ "Wild West Show At World's Fair," *The St. Louis Republic*, November 12, 1904.

⁴⁵⁵ Whitten, "Centenarian Tells Tale of Historic Ruse."

⁴⁵⁶ "Pythians Elect St. Louis Officer," *St. Louis Globe-Democrat*, August 17, 1904.

⁴⁵⁷ "Hundreds Amuse the St. Louis Public" – *The St. Louis Republic*, September 08, 1904.

⁴⁵⁸ "Anderson Items," *Pineville Herald*, October 14, 1904.

⁴⁵⁹ "Jesse James lived 'til he was 103, says JP who believes he met him," *The Marshall News Messenger*," February 19, 1982.

460 Himself (Frank James), "The Only True History of the Life of Frank James," Part Two of *This was Frank James by* Columbus Vaughn, Sarah Snow, and Lester Snow, 1969, pg. 133.

461 James (Howk), *Jesse James and the Lost Cause*, p. 63-64.

462 Himself (Frank James), "The Only True History of the Life of Frank James.

463 "What Happened To Jesse James?" Interview with Alvin Seamster, *News Gazette*. Date Unknown. In Bud Hardcastle's personal collection.

464 Sarah Snow, Columbus Vaughn, and Lester Snow. *This was Frank James*. 1969, p. 35.

465 Ibid., p. 44.

466 Jeff Dezort, "Joe Vaughn (Frank James) Research is Outlined by 'Grandson' Columbus Vaughn," *The Times*, July 2, 1979. (In Bud Hardcastle's personal collection).

467 Ibid.

468 *Folktales* booklet, titled "Outlaw Stories," in Bud Hardcastle's personal collection.

469 "Many Wichitans Recall Frank James Noted Bandit," *Wichita Weekly Times*, February 26, 1915.

470 Snow, Vaughn, Snow, *This was Frank James*. p. 38.

471 Ibid., p. 39.

472 Ibid.

473 Dezort, "Joe Vaughn (Frank James)."

474 Schrader, *Jesse James Was One of His Names*, p. 72.

475 James (Howk), *Jesse James and the Lost Cause*, p. 18-19.

476 "More Proof That Dalton Is 'Jesse," The Guthrie Daily Leader, July 7, 1948 (from Bud Hardcastle's collection)

477 "History of Lexington Lodge No. 1," Accessed 2023. https://lexingtonlodge1.org/lexington-lodge-1/.

478 Hardcastle, *The Hoax*, p. 8.

479 James (Howk), *Jesse James and the Lost Cause*, p. 102.

480 Himself (Frank James), *The Only True History of the Life of Frank James*, p. 176.

481 Ibid., p. 96.

482 Wikipedia contributors, "Lexington, Missouri," *Wikipedia, The Free Encyclopedia*, Accessed 2023, https://en.wikipedia.org.

483 "Bowers Mill Has Been in Existence Sixty-five Years," Carthage Evening Press, July 09, 1903.

484 "Another Pioneer Passed Away," *Jasper County Democrat*. April 13, 1909.

[485] Frank Dalton, "Outlawry in Missouri," *Crittenden Memoirs*, p. 370-371.

[486] Wikipedia contributors, "Charles R. Jennison," *Wikipedia, The Free Encyclopedia*, Accessed 2023, https://en.wikipedia.org.

[487] Kathy Alexander, "Charles Jennison – Anti-Slavery Jayhawker," *Legends of Kansas*, Accessed 2023. https://legendsofkansas.com/charles-jennison/.

[488] Himself (Frank James), *The Only True History of the Life of Frank James*. p. 97.

[489] Ibid., p. 165.

[490] Ibid., p. 107.

[491] "Hamp Williams, 70, Dies; Was Arkansas Leader," Chattanooga Daily Times, May 17, 1931.

[492] "Hot Springs Banker To Be Buried Monday," *The Commercial Appeal*, May 17, 1931.

[493] Himself (Frank James), *The Only True History of the Life of Frank James*, p. 175.

[494] "History of Newton County – Fugitive Faces," Newton County, Arkansas Chamber of Commerce, Accessed 2023. https://www.newtoncountychamber.com/history.

[495] Snow, Vaughn, Snow, *This was Frank James*. p. 40.

[496] Ibid., p. 33.

[497] Jesse James Benton, *Cow by the Tail*, 1943, p. 28-29.

[498] "Bob James Dies at the Age of 82 Years," Obituary of Robert "Bob" James (1877-1959), *The Lathrop Optimist*, November 26, 1959.

[499] Himself (Frank James), *The Only True History of the Life of Frank James*, p. 177.

[500] Buzzbee, "Last of Quantrell's Raiders, Now living in Corpus Christi".

[501] Hardcastle, *The Hoax*, p. 95.

[502] Frank Dalton, "My adventures with Jesse James," *Crittenden Memoirs, p.* 362.

[503] "Garland R. Farmer Dies In Henderson," *The Kilgore News Herald*, July 19, 1956.

[504] Garland R. Farmer, "Frank Dalton or Jesse James, This Old Fellow Knows A Lot," *The Kilgore News-Herald*, March 19, 1950.

[505] Garland R. Farmer, "A Dalton Tells The Story of Quantrell," *The Whitewright Sun*, August 7, 1941.

[506] Brian Hart, "Osceola, TX," *Handbook of Texas Online*, 1952. Updated 1995. Accessed 2023. https://www.tshaonline.org/handbook/entries/osceola-tx.

[507] Correspondence with Frank Dalton and Dick Worsham, *The Journal of Tyler, Texas*, 1932. (In Bud Hardcastle's personal collection)

[508] "Another Member Of Quantrell's Band Is Found," *Mexico Weekly Ledger*, March 31, 1932.

[509] "Fought Under Black Flag of Quantrill; Is Visiting in Cameron," *The Cameron Herald*, October 28, 1943.

[510] "'Jesse James' to End, Man Takes Outlaw's Name to Grave," *The Independent,* Long Beach, California; August 17, 1951.

[511] Darcy, "The Oklahoma Territorial Legislature: 1890-1905.

[512] James (Howk), *Jesse James and the Lost Cause*, p. 143.

[513] "The Election Case of William A. Clark of Montana (1900)," United States Senate, Accessed 2023, https://www.senate.gov/about/origins-foundations/electing-appointing-senators/contested-senate-elections/089.William_Clark.

[514] Wikipedia contributors, "William A. Clark," *Wikipedia, The Free Encyclopedia*, Accessed 2023, https://en.wikipedia.org.

[515] Ralph Epperson, "Jesse James Lived to be 103: Part 1-4." YouTube.com, 2018.

[516] Wikipedia contributors, "Judy Canova," *Wikipedia, The Free Encyclopedia*, Accessed 2023, https://en.wikipedia.org.

[517] Hardcastle, *The Hoax*, p. 130-131.

[518] Ibid., p. 68.

[519] *Find a Grave*, database and images (https://www.findagrave.com/memorial/44310520/ozark_jack-berlin: Accessed 2023, memorial page for Ozark Jack Berlin (1867-1954), Find a Gave Memorial ID 44310520, citing Rockfield Cemetery, Veedersburg, Fountain County, Indiana, USA; Maintained by Lesa Epperson (contributor 46576986).

[520] "Interview with Ex. Train Robber – Al Jennings," British Movietone, 2015. https://www.youtube.com.

[521] Story on Cole Younger, *State Journal*, Mulhall, Oklahoma, July 24, 1903. (Bud Hardcastle's personal collection).

[522] "Fought Under Black Flag of Quantrill; Is Visiting in Cameron," *The Cameron Herald*, October 28, 1943.

[523] Wikipedia contributors, "Gladewater, Texas," *Wikipedia, The Free Encyclopedia*, Accessed 2023, https://en.wikipedia.org.

[524] "Rangers Ride At Well Fire," *The Amarillo Globe Times*, May 1, 1931.

[525] H. Allen Anderson, "Borger History" *Borger, Texas, Accessed 2023. https://www.*borgertx.gov/263/Borger-History.

[526] "Tom Hickman Dies at 75," *The Marshall News Messenger*, January 29, 1962.

[527] Anderson, "Borger History."

[528] "Ex-Ranger Hickman Dies In Gainesville," *San Angelo Standard-Times*, Jan 29, 1962.

[529] "100 Per Cent Curb in E. Texas, Vast Field Is Inactive; Jobs Secure," *Fort Worth Star Telegram*, August 19, 1931.

[530] Hardcastle, *The Hoax*, p. 101.

[531] A. W. Neville, "Bunch and Dalton See 'Jesse James'," *The Paris News*, March 25, 1948.

[532] Byers, "Not Shot by Ford, Jesse James Died in 1950, Says Old Friend."

[533] Travis, DeWitt to the Confederate Pension Division, Pension Board, March 10, 1947. *Texas State Library and Archives Commission and Alabama Department of Archives and History*. Confederate Pension file – Alabama, Texas and Virginia, U.S. Confederate Pensions, 1884-1958, 2023. https://www.ancestry.com.

[534] Quigg, "Latest, 'Real' Jesse James Declares $2 million in Loot Cached Away in Mountains of Oklahoma."

[535] "Longview Man's Rites Conducted," *The Kilgore News Herald*, November 14, 1960.

[536] "Ex-Confederate Soldier Dies at Ripe Old Age," *Tishomingo Leader and the Mannsville Herald*, April 3, 1914.

[537] Hardcastle, *The Hoax*, p. 107.

[538] Ibid., p. 107-108.

[539] William Hubert Key, *Texas State Library and Archives Commission*; Austin, Texas; Confederate Pension Applications, 1899-1975; Collection # CPA16526; Roll # 2277, Roll Description: Pension File Nos. 01578 to 35510, Application Years 1909 to 1918. Alabama, Texas and Virginia, U.S. Confederate Pensions, 1884-1958, Accessed 2023. https://www.ancestry.com.

[540] Hardcastle, *The Hoax*, p. 107-108.

[541] "George Kenneth Ford," *Longview News-Journal*, February 22, 1998.

[542] J.H. Taylor, Clerk to Mr. Harold Preece with the attached affidavit of Solomon Bedford Strickland. Confederate Pension Division Comptroller's Department. *Texas State Archives*. December 11, 1947.

[543] "Death Claims Indian, 108," Austin American-Statesman, August 14, 1947.

[544] "Adventurer Civil War Guerilla Dies at 108," *El Paso Herald-Post*, August 15, 1947.

[545] "Thousands of Heirs Interested In Rich Conroe Field Acreage," *Amarillo Daily News*, February 18, 1941.

[546] Harold Preece to Mr. J. H. Taylor, State Comptroller's Department, December 20, 1947.

[547] Wikipedia contributors. "Harold Preece." *Wikipedia, The Free Encyclopedia*, Accessed 2023. https://en.wikipedia.org.

[548] Hardcastle, *The Hoax*, p. 110.

[549] James (Howk), *Jesse James and the Lost Cause*, p. 163-164.

[550] "Versatile Vet," *Tyler Morning Telegraph*, January 22, 1948.

551 Zuleika B. Hicks to Confederate Pension Division, Pension Board, February 16, 1948. *Alabama, Texas and Virginia, U.S. Confederate Pensions, 1884-1958,* https://www.ancestry.com.

552 Neville, "Frank Dalton Lives One Hundred Years."

553 Thad Ricks, 'Jesse James' Twist To Dalton's Stories Greeted by Smiles Here," *The Kilgore News Herald*, May 23, 1948.

554 James (Howk), Jesse James and the Lost Cause, p. 46.

555 "Hoots Accompany Affidavits as Paper Claims Jesse James Is Still with Us," *Austin-American Statesman*, May 20, 1948.

556 Hardcastle, *The Hoax*, p. 110.

557 "Major Shelton Dies in Austin," *Times Record News*, December 29, 1952.

558 Hardcastle, *The Hoax*, p. 111.

559 Paula Dittrick, "Cousin Claims Jesse James died in 1951 at age 103," *Sunday Advocate*, Baton Rouge, La., Nov. 20, 1983.

560 Hardcastle, *The Hoax*, p. 190.

561 "1861 Confederate Half Dollar," https://coinsite.com/1861-confederate-half-dollar/.

562 Hardcastle, *The Hoax*, p. 113.

563 Lindsey Whitten, "Centenarian Tells Tale of Historic Ruse," *Lawton Constitution*, May 19, 1948.

564 "The Story Behind The James Story – News Vigil Is Long," *The Lawton Constitution*, May 19, 1948.

565 Hardcastle, *The Hoax*, p. 16.

566 Ibid.

567 "Detective John W. Shevlin To Be Chief At Hot Springs," *The St. Louis Republic*, September 27, 1903.

568 "Secret Societies. Knights of Pythias," *The St. Louis Republic*, August 6, 1900.

569 "Detective Chief Named as Guard," *Newport Daily Independent*, February 10, 1905.

570 Whitten, "Centenarian Tells Tale of Historic Ruse."

571 James H. Scott, "Odessan Looks Over New Jesse James Is Convinced He's the Real McCoy," *The Odessa American*, June 9, 1948.

572 "'Phooey' Says Nephew of Famed Bandit," *Springfield Leader and Press*, May 20, 1948.

573 "Personal Appearance Slated For Saturday On Courthouse Lawn; Invitation Given Public," *Lawton Constitution*, May 20, 1948.

574 "Oklahoma Ex-Outlaw Identifies Texan As Jesse James," *The Ottawa Journal*, July 5, 1948.

[575] "Jesse James Fled to Kemptville Great-Granddaughter Declares," *The Ottawa Journal*, July 6, 1948.

[576] Hardcastle, *The Hoax*, p. 117.

[577] Keough, "James' Identity 'Known' Secret."

[578] Schrader, *Jesse James was One of his Names*, p. 200.

[579] Hardcastle, *The Hoax*, p. 118.

[580] No title – Marriage of Mr. R. Earl Highley to Miss Helen Thirlwell, *The Humboldt Union*, Humboldt, Kansas, September 6, 1923.

[581] Hardcastle, *The Hoax*, p. 120-121.

[582] Ibid., p. 119.

[583] Ibid., p. 120.

[584] Ibid., p. 121.

[585] Ibid., p. 123.

[586] Ibid., p. 133.

[587] "James' Treasure Hunt Continues," *The Wewoka Times-Democrat*, March 14, 1949.

[588] "Just A Joke To "Jesse," *The Kansas City Times*, March 14, 1949.

[589] Hardcastle, *The Hoax*, p. 142-143.

[590] Jack Hartsfield, "James' Death Faked, Kin Says," *Lubbock Avalanche*. Sept. 1983.

[591] "Joe Wood, 82; Photographer For 27 Years At Globe-Democrat," *St. Louis Post-Dispatch*, December 5, 1996.

[592] Joe Popper, "The Man Who Would Be Jesse," Star Magazine within *The Kansas City Star*, January 10, 1988.

[593] "Doggerel," *Tampa Bay Times*, June 17, 1949.

[594] Terry, "Still Insists He's Jesse James."

[595] Ibid.

[596] "James R. Davis Is Dead At 109," *The Jackson Sun*, March 14, 1950.

[597] "Jesse James" Case Witness Dies of Heart Attack," The Wheaton Journal, March 16, 1950.

[598] "Is Jesse James Dead or Alive? Nashville Citizen to Testify," Newspaper unknown, March 1950.

[599] "108-Year-Old Man Renews License to Drive Own Car," *The Tennessean*, June 16, 1949.

⁶⁰⁰ "Andrew J. Berlin, 86, Well Known County Man, Succumbs In Hospital," Newspaper in Indiana, 1954, *Find a Grave*, database and images for Ozark Jack Berline (1867-1954).

⁶⁰¹ Wikipedia contributors. "Adam Forepaugh." *Wikipedia, The Free Encyclopedia*, Accessed 2023. https://en.wikipedia.org.

⁶⁰²*Find a Grave*, database and images (https://www.findagrave.com/memorial/14524161/hewitt_preston-webb: accessed 2023). Memorial page for Hewitt Preston "Press" Webb (6 July 1836-31 Jan 1899), Find a Grave Memorial ID 14524161, citing Salem Cemetery, Independence, Jackson County, Missouri, USA; Maintained by J.C. Clark (contributor 47094715).

⁶⁰³ "Ozark Jack Berlin Saved Truck Driver Not Jack Glosser," *Lawrence Country News*, September 27, 1934.

⁶⁰⁴ "Is Jesse James Alive? Lansing Pastor Thinks He Is," *Lansing State Journal*, August 1, 1949.

⁶⁰⁵ Hardcastle, *The Hoax*, p. 160-161.

⁶⁰⁶ Robert C. Ruark, "Jesse James, Alive of Dead," *Buffalo Courier Express*, July 8, 1949.

⁶⁰⁷ Hardcastle, *The Hoax*, p. 241.

⁶⁰⁸ Carl W. Breihan to the Confederate Pension Fund Division, April 4, 1950. *Texas State Library and Archives Commission and Alabama Department of Archives and History*. Confederate Pension file – Alabama, Texas and Virginia, U.S. Confederate Pensions, 1884-1958, 2023. https://www. ancestry.com.

⁶⁰⁹ Carl W. Breihan to Chamber of Commerce, Austin, Texas, April 18, 1950. *Texas State Library and Archives Commission and Alabama Department of Archives and History*. Confederate Pension file – Alabama, Texas and Virginia, U.S. Confederate Pensions, 1884-1958, 2023. https://www. ancestry.com.

⁶¹⁰ Carl W. Breihan to Comptroller of Public Accounts, June 5, 1950. *Texas State Library and Archives Commission and Alabama Department of Archives and History*. Confederate Pension file – Alabama, Texas and Virginia, U.S. Confederate Pensions, 1884-1958, 2023. https://www. ancestry.com.

⁶¹¹ Wikipedia contributors. "Hal Boyle." *Wikipedia, The Free Encyclopedia*, Accessed 2023. https://en.wikipedia.org.

⁶¹² Wikipedia contributors. "Dorothy Kilgallen." *Wikipedia, The Free Encyclopedia*, Accessed 2023. https://en.wikipedia.org.

⁶¹³ Wikipedia contributors. "Eleanor Roosevelt." *Wikipedia, The Free Encyclopedia*, Accessed 2023. https://en.wikipedia.org.

⁶¹⁴ Wikipedia contributors. "Bob Considine." *Wikipedia, The Free Encyclopedia*, Accessed 2023. https://en.wikipedia.org.

⁶¹⁵ The Norman Transcript" in an article titled, "James Story True?" dated January 15, 1950.

⁶¹⁶ Glen R. Cooper, "'Jesse James Is Alive,' Decatur Woman Claims Kin of Outlaw James," *The Decatur Daily Review*, May 11, 1950.

⁶¹⁷ "Redding," The Decatur Daily Review, October 7, 1975.

⁶¹⁸ "Oldster Loses Attempt To Claim Name of Notorious Desperado," *Tyler Morning Telegraph*, March 11, 1950.

[619] "Judge Denies Plea of 'Real Jesse James,' Blisters Gang as 'Black Spot on Missouri,'" *St. Louis Post-Dispatch*, March 11, 1950.

[620] Ibid.

[621] F. A. Behymer, "Judge Who Threw Out Jesse James Case," *St. Louis Post-Dispatch*, March 23, 1950.

[622] "Joe Wood, 82; Was Photographer At Globe-Democrat." *St. Louis Post-Dispatch*, Dec. 5, 1996.

[623] Hardcastle, *The Hoax*, p. 159-160.

[624] Ibid., p. 157.

[625] Ibid., p. 179.

[626] Ibid., p. 182.

[627] "J. Frank Dalton, Who Said He Was Jesse James, Dies," *Fort Worth Star-Telegram*, August 16, 1951.

[628] Bill Hanna, "Grave Debate," *Fort Worth Star Telegram*, March 14, 2000.

[629] "Had Photo Made On Hundredth Birthday," *The Progressive Age*, November 28, 1929.

[630] Examination of Wesley A. Rash for the Jackson County, Alabama, Pension Board, completed by E.R. Smith, M.D. and S. H. McMohan, J.P. "*Alabama, Texas and Virginia, U.S. Confederate Pensions*, 1884-1958.". https://www.ancestry.com.

[631] Robert C. Whisonant, "Geology and History Of Confederate Saltpeter Cave Operations In Western Virginia," November 2001. https://energy.virginia.gov/commercedocs/VAMIN_VOL47_NO04.pdf.

[632] "Sam Rash Died Sunday At His Home Here," *The Hood County Tablet*, January 7, 1943.

[633] Wikipedia contributors. "Fort Worth and Rio Grande Railway." *Wikipedia, The Free Encyclopedia*, Accessed 2023. https://en.wikipedia.org.

[634] Newspaper clipping on Sam Rash working for Jesse. *The Granbury Tablet*. May 24, 1984. (In Bud Hardcastle's personal collection).

[635] Hardcastle, *The Hoax*, p. 183-184.

[636] "33 'Bullet' Scars Found on Body of 'Jesse James,'" *Fort Worth Star Telegram*, August 18, 1951.

[637] Hardcastle, *The Hoax*, p. 189.

[638] Joseph L. Rosenberg of Rosenberg & Rosenberg in Decatur, Illinois to Estes Funeral Home. Nov. 2, 1953. (In Bud Hardcastle's personal collection).

[639] "Services Are Held For Former Slave," *Lubbock Avalanche-Journal*, January 22, 1956.

[640] "Versatile Vet," *Tyler Morning Telegraph*, January 22, 1948.

[641] "His Bones are Dust," *The Kansas City Journal*, June 30, 1902.

[642] "Judge wants better reasons for Jesse James' exhumation," *Hood County News*, Sept. 25, 1996.

643 Ibid.

644 "Jesse James' grandsons threaten to move body," *Hood County News*, September 28, 1996.

645 Leland Debusk, "Jesse James, Researchers hope for exhumation this month," *Hood County News*, May 4, 1996.

646 "For County Judge, Retired Prison Head To Run," *Hood County News*, Nov. 19, 1997.

647 "Is it really Jesse? Judge grants order to exhume reputed outlaw's bones." *Hood County News*, February 19, 2000.

648 "Exhumation of 'outlaw's' grave on hold," *Hood County News*, April 1, 2000.

649 Bill Hanna, "Rift delays Granbury exhumation," *Fort Worth Star-Telegram*, April 4, 2000.
650 Penny Owen, "Search for outlaw turns grave, 2nd casket found at burial site," *The Daily Oklahoman*, May 31, 2000.

651 "Waggoner Carr to Be Guest At Dinner of Historical Unit," *Fort Worth Star-Telegram*, April 6, 1965.

652 Bill Hanna, "Dalton Search Finds Wrong Body," *Fort Worth Star Telegram*, July 1, 2000.

653 James E. Starrs, Professor of Law, and Forensic Sciences, George Washington University in Washington D.C., to the editor of The *Washington Times*, May 31, 2000.

654 Dr. David Glassman to Mr. Robert A. Jackson, July 9, 2000. (Bud's personal collection).

655 "Cimarron," *Dictionary.com*, accessed 2022. https://www.dictionary.com.

656 Schrader, *Jesse James Was One of His Names*, p. 192.

657 Ibid.

658 "Ponil, Colfax County, New Mexico Genealogy," https://www.familysearch.org.

659 Louis Serna, Accessed 2023. https:// www.louisserna.com.

660 James (Howk), *Jesse James and the Lost Cause*, p. 47.

661 Schrader, *Jesse James was One of His Names*, p. 44.

662 James (Howk), *Jesse James and the Lost Cause*, p. 51.

663 "Chiropodist Moves to Santa Fe," *The Santa Fe New Mexican*, October 27, 1934.

664 Jeremy Kuzmarov, "Did Richard Nixon Secretly Steal 36.5 Tons of Gold Bullion from U.S. Army Base While He Was Telling America, "I Am Not A Crook?", November 3, 2022. Accessed 2023. https://www.covertactionmagazine.com.

665 Hardcastle, *The Hoax*, p. 172.

666 Ibid.

667 "Theodore Earle Studley," *New York Tribune*, May 1, 1908.

668 "Legends of Jesse James Live On in Minds of Many," The Daily Oklahoman, January 31, 1993.

669 Lindsey Whitten, "Kettle Bearing James Gang Names Displayed by Cityans" The Lawton Constitution, February 29, 1948.

670 Lindsey Whitten, "Lawton Trio Believe End of Trail is Near In 16-Year Search for Fabulous Treasure in Expansive Wichitas." *The Lawton Constitution Newspaper*, February 29, 1948.

671 "1882 Magazine Tells Of James Gang Exploits," Lawton News-Review, May 20, 1948.

672 Ibid.

673 Ibid.

674 "Legends of Jesse James Live On in Minds of Many," The Daily Oklahoman, January 31, 1993.

675 Josh Gates, "Josh Gates Goes Hunting For Jesse James' Buried Treasure," *Expedition Unknown*, Rush NZ, 2022. Accessed 2023. https://www.youtube.com.

676 "Funeral Services for John P. Vaughan," *The Lawton Constitution*, April 24, 1924.

677 "Cultural Resources CCC History Project – The CCC A Brief History," Accessed 2023. https://npshistory.com.

678 Schrader, *Jesse James Was One of His Names*, p. 190.

679 Frank E. Palmore, "Gold At Rock Crossing". (In Bud Hardcastle's personal collection).

680 Steve Wilson, "Two Maps May Hold Key To "Spider Rock" Gold," *Wichita Falls Times*, Oct 13, 1963.

681 Schrader, *Jesse James was One of His Names*, p. 190-193.

682 "Parthenon," https://www.merriam-webster.com.

683 Schrader, *Jesse James Was One of His Names*, p. 191.

684 Quigg, "Latest, 'Real' Jesse James Declares $2 million in Loot Cached Away in Mountains of Oklahoma."

685 Tamie Ross, "Jesse James Remains Mysterious," *The Daily Oklahoma*, September 6, 1995.

686 "A Sensitive Set, The Governor's Instructions," *Kansas City Times*, April 6, 1882.

687 "Missouri's First Negro School," *Muldrow Press*, July 15, 1912; now *the Vian Press*.

688 Schrader, *Jesse James Was One of His Names*, p 28.

689 "A James Boy's Story," *Atchison Daily Patriot*, April 7, 1882.

690 Robertus Love, "The Rise and Fall of Jesse James." *St. Louis Post Dispatch*, July 23, 1925.

691 "Another Thomason Is To Be Sheriff of Clay County," *The Kansas City Star*, August 18, 1940.

[692] Hardcastle, *The Hoax*, p. 205.

[693] "Arkansan Pal of Jesse James Dies. Aged Chiropodist Once Fitted Boots for Outlaw." *The Star-Journal*, March 22, 1929.

[694] Andrew Jackson's Farewell Adress – 1837, *National Center for Public Policy Research*, 2001, Accessed 2022. https://nationalcenter.org/ncppr/2001/11/03/andrew-jacksons-farewell-address-1837/.

[695] "Judge R. E. Thomason, Public Servant, Dies," *El Paso Times*, November 9, 1973.

[696] Wikipedia contributors. "Billie Sol Estes." *Wikipedia, The Free Encyclopedia*, Accessed 2023. https://en.wikipedia.org.

[697] "Robert B. Anderson, Dwight D. Eisenhower Administration May 3, 1954- August 4, 1995," Historical Office of the Secretary of Defense, https://history.defense.gov/DOD-History/Deputy-Secretaries-of-Defense/Article-View/Article/585246/.

[698] George Smith, "Former Navy secretary Anderson dies at 79," *Fort Worth Star-Telegram*, August 16, 1989.

[699] "President Dwight D. Eisenhower's Farewell Address (1961)," *Milestone Documents – National Archives*, Accessed 2022. https://www.archives.gov/milestone-documents/president-dwight-d-eisenhowers-farewell-address.

[700] John F. Kennedy, Address "The President and the Press," Before the American Newspaper Publishers Association, New York City. April 27, 1961. *The American Presidency Project*, Accessed 2022. https://www.presidency.ucsb.edu.

[701] Robert B. Anderson, *A Nation Needs to Pray*, with a preface by Dwight D. Eisenhower, Publisher – Nelson, 1963.

[702] Alan Wasser, Chairman, "LBJ's Space Race: What We Didn't Know Then," *The Space Settlement Institute*, June 26, 2005. Accessed 2024. www.spacesettlementinstitute.org.

[703] Robert B. Anderson, "A Statement by Robert B. (Bob) Anderson concerning the character of Lyndon B. Johnson and his qualifications as President of the United States," *Wichita Falls Times*, October 25, 1964.

[704] Jim Shaw, *The Deadly Deception*, 1988.

[705] "Two Wolves," *Virtues for Life, The Heart of Everyday Living*, Accessed 2024, https://www.virtuesforlife.com/two-wolves/

www.ingramcontent.com/pod-product-compliance
Lightning Source LLC
Chambersburg PA
CBHW080632170426
43209CB00008B/1550